# WINES
## of the
# WORLD

*Edited by*

André L. Simon

❦

*With contributions by*

H. WARNER ALLEN
H. ARNTZ
S. F. HALLGARTEN
ANTHONY HOGG
JOHN N. HUTCHISON
GEORGE RAINBIRD
CYRIL RAY
ANDRÉ L. SIMON

❦

# WINES
## of the
# WORLD

McGRAW-HILL PUBLISHING COMPANY LIMITED

LONDON     NEW YORK · TORONTO · SYDNEY

This book was designed and produced by
George Rainbird Ltd,
Marble Arch House, 44 Edgware Road, London w.2,
for McGraw-Hill Book Company, Inc.,
1221 Avenue of the Americas, New York, 10020

© George Rainbird Ltd, 1962, 1963, 1966, 1967, 1971, 1972
Photographs by Percy Hennell, Kenneth Swain,
George Rainbird and Ekhart van Houten
Maps by June Brown
Endpapers photographed by Derrick E. Witty
Index by Irene Clephane
Library of Congress Catalog Card Number: 67–14853
ISBN 07–057408–1

The color plates of the sections on
Italy and Spain were printed in the Netherlands by
L. van Leer and Company N.V., Daventer
The other color plates were printed by
Impact Litho (Tolworth) Ltd, England
The text and maps were printed by
Clarke Doble & Brendon Ltd, Plymouth, England

Fifth printing, revised, 1972

PRINTED IN GREAT BRITAIN AND THE NETHERLANDS
AND BOUND IN GREAT BRITAIN

# Contents

# THE WINES OF SPAIN

*by* George Rainbird · *page* 489

# OTHER VINELANDS
# OF THE WEST

*by* Anthony Hogg · *page* 565

# THE WINES OF
# AUSTRALIA AND
# NEW ZEALAND

*by* André L. Simon · *page* 603

# THE WINES OF
# SOUTH AFRICA

*by* André L. Simon · *page* 645

# THE WINES OF
# THE AMERICAS

*by* John N. Hutchison · *page* 661

# Colour Plates

7

# Maps

# Acknowledgements

Grateful thanks are extended to the many individuals and firms who have helped the authors in the preparation of their various sections of this book:

**ITALY** – Dott. Enzo Malgeri, Commercial Minister at the Italian Embassy in London; Dott. A. Giaroli, of the London office of the Istituto Nazionale per il Commercio Estero, and Dottori Silvio Barocas, Domenico di Paolo, Mario Rizzotti and Cesare Fristelli, of the Rome office; Mr Douglas Whybrow, sometime of British United Air Ferries; Dott. Arrigo Musiani, Secretary-General of the Enoteca Italica Permanente, Siena; Mr Gerald Asher, of the London firm of Asher Storey and Company; and Mr R. M. Scott, of the London firm of Aug. Hellmers and Sons, Ltd. I am indebted to the Baron Bettino Ricasoli of our own time, who carries on so devotedly the tradition established by his distinguished ancestor, Cavour's successor; to my fellow newspaperman, the Marchese de'Frescobaldi – 'Dino' – and to his brother Piero; and to the Marchese di Antinori and his brother Piero. Among my guides and hosts in various parts of Italy were Dott. Nino Anesi, of the Assessorato Regionale Industria e Commercio della Regione Trentino–Alto Adige, Trento; Dott. Guglielmo Anzilotti, Director of the Consorzio per la Difesa del Vino Tipico del Chianti; Signor Dante Carelli of the Camera di Commercio, Potenza, and his sister, Signorina Ada Carelli, of the Ente Turismo there; Signor Carlo Balzi, of the Chianti house of Ruffino; Dott. Arturo Bersano, of Nizza Monferrato; Signor Gaetano and Signor Guglielmo Bertani of the Verona firm of that name; Dott. Andrea Masala, of the Department of the Regional Government of Sardinia in Cagliari; Dott. Luigi Ruffino, Secretary-General of the Camera di Commercio, Pavia; Dott. Vittorio Pasqualini, of the Camera di Commercio, Bolzano, Dott. Richard von Mackowitz, of the Ufficio Estero of the Camera di Commercio, Bolzano, and Dott. Ludwig Kofler, Director of the Consorzio delle Cantine Sociale of Bolzano; Dott. Claudio Poncibo, of the Consorzio per la Difesa d'Asti Spumante; and Signor Antonio Mollo, of Reggio Calabria. Signorina Rita Ghezzi, of Siena, helped my lame Italian over many a stile; and Esme, Countess of Carlisle, who knows and loves Italy at least as well and as much as I do, and the Italian language a great deal better, has helped to tidy up some of my worst mistakes.

C.R.

**PORTUGAL** – Thanks are due to the following English and Portuguese friends for the help and encouragement they gave Percy Hennell in the production of the colour photographs: Mr R. M. Cobb and Mr John Smithes (Cockburn Smithes Ltd, Portugal), Mr C. C. Gordon (Cockburn Smithes & Co. Ltd, London), Mr G. F. Robertson (Crofts of London), Snr Fernando Guedes and Snr Roberto Guedes (Sociedade Comercial dos Vinhos de Mesa de Portugal Ltdª), Snr Saores Franco (José Maria da Fonseca Succs. Ltdª, Lisbon and Azeitão), Mr J. V. Baker and Mr G. E. Gooch (Evans, Marshall & Co. Ltd, London), Mr Noel Cossart (Cossart, Gordon & Co Ltdª, Madeira), Snr Mario Barbeito de Vasconselos (Vinhos Barbeito, Madeira) and Snr Rui de Brito e Cunha (Real Companhia Vinicola do Norte de Portugal).

H.W.A.

**SPAIN** – First, I wish to give my grateful thanks to the Dirección General de Expansión Comercial of the Ministerio de Comercio in Madrid, and particularly to its Sub-Director, Señor Don Miguel Angel Santamaría; and, in London, my thanks with equal gratitude to the Commercial Office of the Spanish Embassy, and in particular to Señor Don Manuel Quintero and Señor Don Gabriel Ferran.

Representatives of the Spanish wine trade in England have all been most helpful, including and in particular Señor Don Alejandro Cassinello of La Riva, and Mr L. W. Steer, who is the Chairman of the Rioja Wine Shippers Association.

I am further indebted to: Sr Don Antonio Alarcón, Alarcón Hermanos, S.A., Córdoba; Sr Don Francisco Rodríguez Alvárez, Secretario General, Sindicato Nacional de la Vid, Madrid; Sr Don Alvaro de Alvear, Alvear, S.A., Montilla, Córdoba; Sr Don Juan Amigó, Amigó Hermanos y Cía, Reus, Tarragona; Sr Don P. Ankersmit, Scholtz Hermanos, S.A., Málaga; Sr Don Joaquán Arteaga, Bodegas Bilbainas, Valdepeñas, Ciudad Real; Sr Don José María Vidal Barraquer, Estación de Viticultura y Enología, Villafranca del Panadés, Barcelona; Sr Don José Antonio López Cascante, José López Bertrám y Cía, Tarragona; Cooperativa Alella Vinícola, Alella, Barcelona; Sr Don Marcelo Frias, Bodegas Riojanas, S.A., Cenicero, Logroño; Sr Don Cruz García Lafuente, Bodegas Las Veras, S.A., Fuenmayor, Logroño; Sr Don Gerardo Sánchez Gómez, Bodegas Morenito, Valdepeñas, Ciudad Real; Sr Don Pedro López de Heredia, R. López de Heredia, Viña Tondonia, S.A., Haro, Logroño; Sr Don Antonio Larrea, Consejo Regulador de la Denominación de Origin Reoka, Logroño; Bodegas Marqués de Murrieta, Ygay, Logroño; Bodegas Palacio, S.A., Laguardia, Alava; Sr Don José María Raventós, Codorníu, San Sadurní de Noya, Barcelona; Sr Don Angel Santiago, Bodegas Rioja Santiago, S.A., Haro, Logroño; Sr Don Manuel Tapias, Bodegas Tapias S.A., Tarragona; Sr Don Miguel Torres, Villafranca del Panadés, Barcelona; Sr Don Juan de Ugarte, Bodegas Bilbainas, S.A., Haro, Logroño; I should like to pay tribute also to my interpreter, secretary, and co-driver, Caroline Price, and to Yorke Crompton, for editing this section of the book.

G.M.R.

## OTHER VINELANDS OF THE WEST

**OTHER VINELANDS OF THE WEST** – I record my thanks for much basic information supplied by the shippers in London, to Colonel Ian Ramsay, a former military attaché in Yugoslavia, to my friend Ian Cox for his report from Malta, to my correspondent in Istanbul who prefers to remain anonymous and to my wife, who first insisted that the writing of these chapters would be more useful and less destructive than swinging a golf club on her carpet and then gathered the material together.

A.S.H.

The publisher would like to thank the directors of Christopher & Co. Ltd, London, for granting facilities in their cellars for photographing the endpapers.

# Introduction

WINE is as old as the thirst of man, not the physical thirst which man can so easily slake with water, as his horse and his dog do, but the heaven-sent thirst for what will still our fears – that our mind be at peace; and stir our sense and sensibility – that we shall not ignore nor abuse God's good gifts – wine not the least of them.

Wine is the suitably fermented juice of the grape, the fruit of the vine, a tree which is older, more universal and more fruitful than all others. Long before the earth had become habitable, before any form of animal life had appeared on land or in the waters, there were wild vines groping clumsily in search of support on the ground or clinging to the branches of shrubs and trees. At Brjamslak, in Iceland, at Sézanne, in the Marne Valley, in Silesia, the Rhineland and other places, fossils have been found which modern palaeontology ascribes to the earlier stages of our globe's formation: they bear distinct impressions of different types of wild vines, making it abundantly clear that there were at the beginning, as there are now, different members of the great *Ampeladicea* family, and the noblest of them all were those of the genus *Vitis*.

All members of the genus *Vitis* have in common the distinction of being grape-bearing, although they do not all bear wine-making grapes. There are ten known different species of Asiatic *Vitis*, and sixteen known American species; all of them bear grapes from which some kind of wine can be made. There is but one known European species, the *Vitis vinifera*, and it is the one and only one from which all the better wines of the world are made.

Today, the European *Vitis vinifera* flourishes in the temperate zones of all civilized countries of both the North and South hemispheres. The Portuguese introduced it in Brazil, and the Spaniards in the Argentine, Chile, Peru and Mexico, in the sixteenth century; the Dutch brought the *Vitis vinifera* to the Cape of Good Hope in the seventeenth century; and the British brought it to Australia and New Zealand in the late eighteenth century and early nineteenth. Strange to say, the survival of the *Vitis vinifera* is due to its having been grafted upon the phylloxera-resisting American *Vitis labrusca*.

According to Pickett's *Origines Européennes*, viticulture and the art of making wine were introduced by the Aryans in India, Egypt and Persia. In Egypt there is no lack of documentary evidence that grapes were grown and that wine was made at a very early date: Delchevalerie, in his *Illustration horticole*, depicts the scenes of grapes being picked and pressed which formed part of the pictorial embellishments of the tomb of Phtah-Hotep, who lived in Memphis some 4,000 years before Christ. In his *Chronological History of Plants*, Pickering has given reproductions of similar glyptic illustrations, which he ascribes to the Third Egyptian Dynasty: he also adds that there are a number of other and more detailed illustrations of the growing of grapes and the making of wine belonging to the Fourth, Seventh and Eighth Dynasties.

Some sixty years ago, when the laws of Hammurabi, who was King of Babylon in about 1790 B.C., were discovered and deciphered, some of the regulations dealing with the sale of wine were found to be surprisingly similar, in conception at any rate, to those now in force in Britain. The taverner was not actually made to 'fill in forms', but if he overcharged, sold bad wine for good, or allowed riotous conduct on his premises, and was convicted, penalties were not fines or prison but the loss of a limb or of life.

In the West, Phoenicians, Greeks and Romans in turn did realize that they had no better ally than the grape to bring about a measure of civilization among the barbarians. There is no more striking example of this than the way the Romans fought their way right across Gaul and along the valleys of the Rhineland and of the Danube. Their ever-lengthening lines of communications, mostly along the rivers, would never have been safe so long as the thickly wooded river hills were alive with hostile natives, so they gave some of their own wine to those natives, and promised them trees that would give them the same wine year after year for ever: all they had to do was to cut down or burn the trees on the lower slopes of the riverside hills, and plant the vine in their place. Which they did. Presently, the people of the plains acquired as great a liking for wine as the people of the hills, so that they also planted vineyards and the time came when there was too much wine. The problem of over-production is not new, but Domitian, two thousand years ago, settled it in a way that neither the French Government nor the South African Government can adopt when, facing, as they do, the same problem today; Domitian just ordered all transalpine vineyards to be destroyed.

'Bacchus loves the hills,' so said Horace in Latin verse, and it is true, but it is not the whole truth: it does not mean that the higher the vineyard, the better the wine will be; altitude *per se* is not so important, and if many wines from hillside vineyards are particularly fine wines it is because their parent grape grew in poor soil, rich, however, in minerals only. Vines, of course, will bring forth a greater abundance of fruit when planted in the fertile soil of plains, but the wine made from such grapes will never be comparable in quality to the wine made in much smaller quantities from the best species of grapes grown in soil that is poor in fertility but rich in the mineral salts responsible for the 'bouquet' and 'breed' of all fine wines. There are many vineyards, happily, other than hillside vineyards, where the soil is very poor – sand, lime or gravel chiefly – in lowlands such as the Médoc, and they produce some of the greatest wines of the world, finer wines than those of the Visp Valley in Switzerland or of the Alto Adige in Northern Italy.

There are not so many vineyards in Europe now as there were a hundred years ago, but there are many more in both North and South America, as well as in Australia and South Africa, so that, on balance, the acreage is greater today than it has probably ever been.

The vine did grow and produced grapes that ripened in the open, but only when climatic conditions happened to be favourable, in many parts of Europe, in Normandy, Belgium, Holland, North Germany, and in England, where there are still a few vineyards, the two better-known being in Hampshire. Nowadays, the high price of land and the cost of fertilizers, as well as the shortage and high cost of labour, are such that all northern vineyards are an expensive hobby and not an economic proposition. There is another serious danger which is threatening the existence of vineyards, even in places long famous for the excellence of their wines: it is the ceaselessly rising tide of brick and mortar, the ever-growing demand for more homes and factories: Haut-Brion and Pape Clément, near Bordeaux, have been reached and by-passed, but the fate of some 'suburban' vineyards near San Francisco and Adelaide is very precarious.

Quite a number of small vineyards, in France and maybe elsewhere in Europe, have been given up when means of transport improved so much that it became possible to get supplies of mass-produced beverage wines, when wanted, at a cost so low that it was no longer worth while to give to one's own vineyard all the time and trouble it demanded.

During the first decade of the present century the vineyards of France and Italy produced a yearly average of 2,333 million gallons of wine, about half the total production of all the world's vineyards. Today there are fewer vineyards in France and more in Italy than before the First World War, and Italy, therefore, produces approximately fifty per cent more wine than does France. There are in Italy considerable quantities of common wines for the common thirst of the common man, and there are also very large quantities of the same type of wine made and drunk in France. There are also, both in Italy and in France, quite a number of good wines, wines with an individuality of their own, nice wines which may be bought at fairly reasonable prices. There never can be too many good wines, any more than there can ever be too many good people in the world, and it is certainly highly regrettable that there are not more great wines and great men. Great wines are not made by great men, but from the grapes of species of *Vitis vinifera* vines best suited to the soils and climate of a comparatively few vineyards which happen to be in France and in Germany. There are no red wines produced anywhere in the world with the balance, body, bouquet and 'breed' of the great red wines of Bordeaux and Burgundy, the still white wines of the Rhineland and the sparkling wine of Champagne. The outstanding excellence of the really great wines nowhere else to be had except from France and Germany is responsible for their very high cost which places them outside the reach of all but the wealthy, and it is most unfortunate that the people who have greater wealth do not necessarily possess a sensitive palate, a gift which one gets or does not get at birth; it cannot be bought over the counter.

Two world wars have, naturally, been responsible for many changes in the distribution and development of the vineyards of the world: some ceased to exist and others came into being. In Europe, Austria lost a great deal of wine-producing territory, mostly to the newly created state of Yugoslavia, but largely also to northern Italy: its pre-1914 average production of 140 million gallons dropped to 18 million in 1947, but it has risen again to near 50 million gallons, whereas Yugoslavia now produces some 155 million gallons and has built up quite a sizeable export trade; Czechoslovakia also now produces over 16 million gallons of wine. There have certainly been great efforts made in most countries behind the Iron Curtain to produce more wine, beginning with Russia, now placed fourth on the list in Europe after Italy, France and Spain, with a production of some 542 million gallons instead of 57 million before the First World War. The rise in the wine production of Bulgaria from 43 million gallons pre-1914 to 104 million gallons average 1968/69 is the most remarkable of all, but both Hungary and Rumania are also well up. On the other hand, Serbia, with a 12·5 million gallons pre-1914 production has ceased to exist as a state.

Spain has made steady progress and retained her place as the third greatest wine-producing country in Europe: her wine production rose from 379 million gallons pre-1914 to 415 million gallons in 1947, and 553·9 million gallons average 1968/69. Of course, sherry has held all the time pride of place as the most profitable export wine of Spain, but the acreage of the vineyards which produce table wines is much greater: it has increased appreciably during the past twelve or fifteen years owing to greatly improved methods of wine-making adopted since the last war and responsible for a rapidly

growing demand for Spanish table wines: land and labour are cheaper now than anywhere else in Europe, and none of the other European wine-producing countries can
compete with Spain as regards prices, Portugal excepted.

Although the name of Port has been protected by law in Great Britain longer than
the name of any other wine, the demand for Port is no longer as great as it was once, in
spite of which the production of wine in Portugal has risen from the pre-1914 average
to 181·9 million gallons in 1968/69. This is due to the remarkable improvement brought
about in the making of table wines, for which an important export trade has been built.
These wines, mostly the Vinho verde of the Minho and the wines, red, white and
rosé, of the Central Dão, cost more than similar table wines from Spain, being marketed
in bottles the shape and labels of which are more artistic and more attractive.

Of all European countries, Germany has made the most spectacular recovery.
From 56 million gallons average in the pre-1914 years, the production of the vineyards
of Germany fell to 22 million gallons in 1947, that is after the vineyards and people of
Alsace had returned to France. Since the end of the last war, however, the Germans
have been busy planting new vineyards, so much so that the average 1968/69 production
of wine reached 130·8 million gallons. Unfortunately, by far the greatest increase of
vineyards took place in Baden and Württemberg, and in other parts of the country,
but not in the Rhinegau or Mittel Mosel, where the great wines of Germany come
from.

In Switzerland, where there are very few sites suitable for the planting of vineyards
besides the existing ones, the production of wine has been fairly constant since the
beginning of the present century, round about 16 million gallons of wine, with ups and
downs due to the climatic conditions from year to year.

In North America the outstanding feature of the past sixty years has been the blight
of prohibition, which not only put an end to the production of fine quality wines but
also robbed a whole generation of any chance to appreciate and enjoy wine. Since
repeal, in 1933, much has been done and is still being done to plant more vineyards and
to make better wine in California, where the average 1968/69 production of wine
reached 150·5 million gallons. A menace to the vineyards of the San Francisco coastal
belt, which did not exist in pre-prohibition days but is now only too real, is the
encroachment of urban housing development. Since repeal, much more interest than
ever before has been taken in viticulture in New York, Ohio and other Eastern States.

In South America the Argentine Republic has made considerable progress in the
acreage of her vineyards and their wine production. From an average of 26·7 million
gallons, pre-1914, the Argentine vineyards production rose to 179·5 million gallons in
1947, and then leapt up to 394·2 million gallons in 1968/69. Argentina is now the fifth
largest wine producer in the world, after France, Italy, the U.S.S.R. and Spain. Chile
comes second as regards quantity, but well away first as regards the quality of her wines:
the latest available statistics gave 89 million gallons as Chile's production. Third place in
the South American continent belongs to Brazil, with 37 million gallons, fourth place
to Uruguay, with 18·4 million gallons, and fifth place to Peru, with 5·5 million gallons.

In North Africa, France has now lost the most remarkable winefields of Algeria: in
about one hundred years their pre-1914 average was 180·6 million gallons, and in
1947, in spite of World War II and the local civil strife, Algeria produced 198·9
million gallons of wine, most of it of the ordinaire but much of it from fair to fine in

quality. What may happen to the vineyards of Algeria under Moslem rule is, to say the least, uncertain.

In Tunisia and Morocco, east and west of Algeria, the people have become independent, but they have retained close ties with France, maybe more from interest than pure love, and their wine production has not suffered. In Tunisia the production was 19·8 million gallons in 1947, and it had risen to 22·0 million gallons in 1968/69. In Morocco the increase during the past fifteen years was even more remarkable, from 7·3 million gallons in 1947, it rose to 15·5 millions in 1968/69.

In South Africa the progress of viticulture since the beginning of the century has been sensational, but the improvement in the quality of many South African wines, chiefly the sherries, has been even more remarkable. From the 4·2 million gallons production of the pre-1914 days of depression, the figures leapt to 55 million in 1947, and to 107·8 by 1968/69.

In Australia viticulture has been progressing at a more modest rate from 4·5 pre-1914 to 27·5 in 1947, and to 52·7 million gallons in 1968/69.

There are also vineyards and there is wine made in a number of other lands and islands, large and small: Greece, Turkey, Lebanon, Iran, the Nile Delta in Egypt, Palestine, Luxembourg, Cyprus, Malta, and others. There is now wine made in more places than ever before, most of it, of course, of the plainer sorts, but none as bad as the bad wines of the 'good old days'. Modern science and a greater number of better educated wine-makers leave no excuse for making as bad wines as were sometimes made by ignorant or unlucky growers. The bad wines of today are always drinkable. Unfortunately, economic conditions have been mainly responsible for great wines being fewer and not as great as great wines were made occasionally in the past. Maybe too much manure is used to ensure more and bigger grapes, which does handicap the chances of the wines being quite as great as they might have been. Maybe wine costs too much to be put away and given all the time it needs to grow as great as it might be. But let us be grateful that there is as much and as good wine as there is throughout the world, wines of many different types and styles, wines to suit every taste and occasion, wines which may be dear but are worth more than any money that we have to pay for them: joy and health are the gifts of wine, and they are priceless.

ANDRÉ L. SIMON

# The Wines of
# FRANCE

☘

## ANDRÉ L. SIMON

# CHAPTER ONE

# A Short History of Wine in France

THERE were vines growing wild and free in many parts of the land which we now know as France long before there were Frenchmen or anybody else to eat grapes or to make wine. Fossils which modern palaeontology ascribes to the early stages of the crust formation of the earth bear witness to it. When the Phoenicians laid the foundations of Marseilles in 600 B.C. they had no need to bring cuttings of their own Eastern vines: they had only to prune, train and tend the native vines in order to get better grapes and to make wine. Centuries later, when flourishing vineyards and olive groves attracted the unwelcome barbarians from the North and the East, Marseilles appealed to Rome for help, and presently the people of Marseilles had no longer any cause to fear the inroads of barbarians, for Rome took over their hinterland altogether and made it into a Roman Province, known to this day as Provence. What Rome wanted from Marseilles as well as from Carthage, across the Mediterranean, was food, chiefly wheat, and not wine. Italy, with the exception of the northern plains and the Po Valley, is a mountainous and poor country, but grapes will grow and wine can be made where the soil is too poor for grain, root crops or pastures. Rome was always on the look-out for granaries overseas and outlets for the surplus wine of Italian vineyards, which is why Domitian ordered the uprooting of all transalpine vineyards in A.D. 92, when a poor harvest had caused much distress in Italy. Domitian's Edict[1] was certainly aimed at the sunny lands of Provence, where grain would surely grow in place of vines, grain which was so badly wanted in Italy, when it could be shipped from Marseilles so easily. Whatever vines were growing at the time on the steep slopes of the Jura and Vosges mountains, or in the faraway valleys of the Rhine and Marne, were most likely left alone; whatever wine they brought forth never reached Italy. Recently, when Roman galleys sunk outside the port of Marseilles nearly two thousand years ago were freed from the sand and slime which had sealed them and their contents so long, it was found that their cargo consisted entirely of great amphorae of Italian wine, proof that the Provence vineyards had ceased to exist at the time.

On the other hand, when Caesar forged ahead and completed the conquest of Gaul the rivers were his easiest lines of communication across a land without any roads, and, for safety's sake, he cleared the river banks and the slopes of their valleys from forests in which the hostile population could hide and harass his advancing legions. His next move was to coax here and there the more amenable of the natives to plant a vineyard and to make wine, as the surest means of attaching them to the soil and making them his allies in its defence. And to this day there are still vineyards along the great rivers of France, Rhône, Loire, Saône, Marne and Seine, claiming a Roman origin, although

---

[1] It was rescinded nearly two hundred years later.

many of those very ancient vineyards have completely or almost disappeared. There are still, unknown to most Parisians, two 'token' vineyards left on two of the seven hills of Paris, at Montmartre and Mont Valérien.

Caesar had nothing to do with Bordeaux. It was Crassus, triumvir with Caesar and Pompey, in 60 B.C. who brought the *Pax Romana* to the Atlantic coast, but there were flourishing vineyards already there, and their owners were not molested. We know how prosperous the Bordeaux vinelands were during the Gallo-Roman era, roughly speaking from 50 B.C. to A.D. 400, from memoirs and poems of that age, none better known than those of Ausonius, the Bordeaux-born son of a Roman senator: he had a very brilliant career as a lawyer, consul and governor in Italy, at Trier and in Asia Minor; he retired, wrote verse and eventually died at his villa just outside the walls of the old city of Saint-Emilion, where stands today the famous Château Ausone.

With the successive waves of barbarians from the East who swamped the Gallo-Roman culture during the fifth century, viticulture must have suffered greatly, but it was saved by the Church. Clovis, who had captured Soissons in 486, and then Paris, was the first king of the Franks to be received into the Church by St Rémi, the Bishop of Reims. St Rémi, according to tradition, gave Clovis a flask of wine which he had blessed so effectively that the King could and did drink out of it whenever in need of refreshment without the flask having to be refilled. St Rémi's will, which can still be read, provides more reliable evidence of the prelate's appreciation of wine, and of the antiquity of the Champagne vineyards: there are in this will a number of bequests of vineyards, some of which had been planted by the Bishop, while others had been given to him, in various parts of the Marne valley.

No evidence has so far come to light that any vineyards were planted in the valley of the Marne above Epernay and the Montagne de Reims before A.D. 210, when the Emperor Probus officially cancelled Domitian's Edict prohibiting the planting of vineyards beyond the Alps. According to tradition, the Roman legions were encamped at the time in the plain of Châlons-sur-Marne, without any fighting or anything else to do, and they were given the job of clearing the forests that covered the Montagne de Reims and to break up the ground so that vines could be planted, where they have been thriving ever since.

Saint Eloi, Bishop of Noyon, and Saint Ouen, Bishop of Rouen, were the advisers, in the seventh century, of good King Dagobert, who created the Duchy of Aquitaine for his brother Caribert. In the eighth century Charlemagne, Emperor of the West, gave his wholehearted protection to the Church and much encouragement to viticulture. During his long reign (771–814) many vineyards were planted in Burgundy and the Rhineland which were among the most famous in the world for the excellence of their wines. It was also during the reign of Charlemagne that the Saracens, who had ruined many vineyards of Aquitaine, were driven out of France.

All through the Dark Ages – and after – when force was the only law and life was cheap, wine was made from the grapes of one vintage to be drunk within the ensuing twelve months, just as bread was made from the grain of one harvest to last until the next and no more. No wine can hope to be a great wine within a year, and no one bothers to make with particular care a wine that can never be great, which is why the only great wines of France of long ago were some of the wines made by the medieval religious Orders. They had the land, the money, the knowledge, the labour and, above all, the will to make the best possible wine to the greater glory of God, and to keep it safely until it had attained its optimum quality.

There is no more illustrious example of a monastic vineyard in France than the Clos de Vougeot, the largest as well as one of the finest of the vineyards of Burgundy. When some poor, uncultivated land in the valley of the little River Vouge was bequeathed to the nearby Abbey of Cîteaux, in 1110, some of the owners of small vineyards close by also gave them to the monks, who were able to buy, now and again, whenever the opportunity offered, more land or vineyards; eventually, in 1336, they were able to build a wall enclosing a splendid vineyard of some 125 acres, which remained their property until the French Revolution of 1789. Today this vineyard has been divided among a large number of small owners, but most of the wall still stands, and the great *celliers* and *pressoir* of the monks still bear witness to their industry and skill.

An event which had the most unexpected consequences as regards the wines of Bordeaux was the marriage of Eleanor of Aquitaine, only child of the last Duc d'Aquitaine, with Henri Plantagenet, Comte d'Anjou, in 1152. When Henri Plantagenet became King Henry II of England, in 1154, the people of all his own and his wife's possessions in France became subjects of the King of England, with the same duties, rights and privileges as his English-born subjects. This meant that during the next three hundred years the Bordeaux-born merchants could – and did – sell their wines in England as Englishmen, not foreigners. They had their own company in London, the Vintners' Company, one of the twelve great Livery Companies, the liverymen of which elected then, as they do now, the Lord Mayors of London. This is how Sir Henry Picard, when Master of the Vintners' Company, was Lord Mayor of London in 1335, and entertained at Vintners' Hall five kings, Edward III, King of England and Duc d'Aquitaine; King John of France, who had been taken prisoner at the battle of Poitiers and was at the time Edward's 'guest' at the Savoy; David, King of Scotland; Hugh IV, King of Cyprus; and Waldemar, King of Denmark.

In France, at the time, difficulties of transport made it practically impossible to send wine from one province to the next; besides tolls and taxes, there were highwaymen who made it far too risky to be attempted. The people of Paris drank wines from the vineyards of the Seine and the Marne chiefly; some wines from Orléans and the Yonne, but never from faraway Bordeaux. To be given what amounted to a monopoly of the sale of table wines in England was for the *vignerons* and merchants of the Gironde a wonderful chance; it made the fortune of many of them, and it also made them all desperately loyal to the English crown. In those days, when most of the water available was surface water and anything but safe to drink, everybody but the poorest in the land drank wine, and lots of it, at a penny per gallon, so that the demand in England for the wines of Bordeaux was very considerable indeed.

After the Battle of Castillon, in 1453, when Talbot, whose name lives to this day in the wine of Château Talbot, one of the *Crus Classés du Médoc*, was killed, Bordeaux was lost to the English crown, the people of Bordeaux ceased to have any claim to English citizenship and their trade in England suffered a serious setback. In spite of this, however, the wines of Bordeaux were still in greater demand in London than in Paris, until the eighteenth century, when the Duc de Richelieu, a son of the great Cardinal de Richelieu's nephew, was Gouverneur de Guyenne et Gascogne.

During the reign of Louis XIV (1643–1715) there had been very keen competition between the wines of Burgundy and Champagne to gain the King's favour. There was only very little sparkling wine made in Champagne at the time. Most Champagne wines were still, red, table wines, made from Pinot grapes and not unlike the lighter red wines of Burgundy. Sparkling champagne, however, was something new and much more costly than the still wine, two perfectly good reasons why a court physician would recommend it to his royal master, who probably wanted to drink this new wine anyhow. The Burgundians were, of course, very cross with Fagon, Louis XIV's physician, for letting the King drink a wine, the only merit of which was to be a *'vin de débauche'* – a fast-living wine, said they. The Champenois held a meeting at the Reims Ecole de Médecine on 5 May 1700, when they claimed that champagne was not only the pleasantest of all wines to drink but also the most wholesome; they supported this claim by producing a document proving that a native of Hautvillers, Pierre Piéton, who had never drunk any other wine but champagne, had lived to the ripe age of 118. The challenge was immediately taken up by the Burgundians, who produced a native of Beaune, Baron de Villebertin, who had never tasted any other wine except burgundy, and who had lived to be 120. They also claimed that the Pope and the King of Spain always drank burgundy. The Champenois might have claimed that good King Henri IV, a Basque by birth, whose lips had first tasted Jurançon wine at his christening, had been so fond of champagne when he had come to the throne and to Paris, that he called himself 'Roi de France et de Navarre et Sire d'Ay'. His first wife, Reine Margot, had apparently a thirst both rabelaisian and regal; in 1600, after their marriage had been annulled, she sent a messenger to the King with a written request for an exemption of taxes on 500 *tonneaux de vin pour sa bouche*. Henri refused and wrote across the preposterous demand: *c'est se déclarer ivrognesse en parchemin* – this is legally to proclaim herself a drunk.

It was during the reign of Henri IV (1589–1610) that Olivier de Serres was able, thanks to royal patronage and encouragement, to introduce improved methods of viticulture which were responsible for greater quantities of wine of better quality being produced in many parts of France, in the Médoc more especially. Olivier de Serres did much to reclaim large areas of unproductive marshland between the Gironde and the sea, and the prosperity of the Médoc at the time was due to him.

Up to the latter part of the seventeenth century, the Graves vineyards produced the Bordeaux wines which were the more popular in England and Scotland, but the Médoc took the lead from the beginning of the eighteenth century and never lost it. In 1723, for instance, two English wine-merchants were in Bordeaux for the vintage: Mr Bruneval who sold wine to the Prince of Wales, and Mr Bennett, who was the wine-merchant of the prime minister, Sir Robert Walpole. One of Bruneval's letters, dated 16 October 1723, from Bordeaux, may still be seen at Raynham Hall, in Norfolk, among the Townshend MSS., and in it Bruneval placed Lafite, Latour, Margaux and Pontac[1] in a class by themselves, but adds 'never in my life have I tasted the Château d'Issan as good as this vintage'.

By the middle of the eighteenth century the principal growths of the Médoc had

[1] The name of the owner of Château Haut-Brion. In London, during the seventeenth century, Pontac was considered the best red bordeaux. John Evelyn wrote on 13 July 1683 that he had met Monsieur Pontac, 'the son of the famous Bordeaux President who owns the excellent vineyards of Pontac and Haut-Brion, whence the best bordeaux wines come from'.

already been 'classed' or grouped, if not officially, as in 1855, at least effectively, by a scale of prices which was agreed to by the growers of the Médoc and the merchants of Bordeaux. These were the agreed rates for the wines of the 1750 vintage, per *tonneau*, of approximately 252 (U.S.) gallons or 210 (U.K.) imperial gallons.

| Premiers Crus: | 2,400 Livres[1] | Quatrièmes Crus: | 850 Livres |
|---|---|---|---|
| Deuxièmes Crus: | 2,100 Livres | Cinquièmes Crus: | 500 Livres |
| Troisièmes Crus: | 1,400 Livres | Vins ordinaires: | 160–300 Livres |

Louis XV was not a good king, but a gay one who made sparkling champagne fashionable at court, and somewhat disreputable to the bourgeois mind at the time, that is, during the latter part of the eighteenth century. Of far greater importance to the prosperity of the vineyards of France during the reign of Louis XV (1715–74) was the great stimulus given to the export of wine overseas, chiefly to Scandinavia and Russia, and French settlements and colonies in North America, Africa and India. This export trade benefited the *vignerons* and merchants of Bordeaux far more than those of Burgundy or Champagne, who had nothing like the same facilities of despatch and shipment. Strange to say, the *Intendants*, the forerunners of today's *Préfets*, of the Gironde, were not in the least helpful: on the contrary, they prohibited the planting of new vineyards on a number of occasions, when the vintage proved to be excellent, both as regards the quality and the exceptionally large quantity of wines made. In 1723 the *Intendant* Boucher went further and ordered that the vines of some Bordeaux vineyards be uprooted. Montesquieu gallantly and successfully opposed him. As a lawyer and the owner of a vineyard at Château de La Brède, where he was born, he protested against what he called an insufferable interference with the liberty of each man to put to whatever use he thought best whatever belonged to him. Ten years later, when another *Intendant*, Tourny, prohibited the planting of new vineyards and ordered the uprooting of some old ones, on the plea that there would soon be too much wine and not enough bread, Montesquieu once more protested and very sensibly remarked that the more wine there was, the greater and the more profitable would be the sale of wine, adding that there would not be any likelihood of bread shortage if the *Intendant* removed or relaxed the iniquitous taxes that kept out of Bordeaux the wheat which nearby provinces, such as Languedoc, would be only too ready to sell. In 1717 Bordeaux exported 7,000 *tonneaux* of wine to French settlements in Africa, and 37,000 *tonneaux* fifty years later. The average production of the Gironde during the reign of Louis XV was 200,000 *tonneaux*, of which 125,000 *tonneaux* were exported and 75,000 *tonneaux* consumed locally, the more important markets being:

from 2,000 to 6,000 *tonneaux* of the best red wines of the Médoc to England;

30,000 *tonneaux* of red and white wines, mostly white, to Holland and the Scandinavian countries;

30,000 *tonneaux* of the commoner red wines to the French colonies;

25,000 *tonneaux* of both red and white wines, mostly from the Graves de Bordeaux vineyards, to Paris and other parts of France.

---

[1] *Livres tournois*, not *Livres sterling*. There were 20 *sols* to the *livre*, and 12 *deniers* to the *sol*, up to the French Revolution of 1789, when the old currency collapsed and was eventually replaced by the metric system with the *Franc* of 100 *centimes* as the basic unit. The *Livre tournois* corresponded roughly, in value, to 50 cents or 3s 6d of U.S. and U.K. currencies in 1967.

The French Revolution and the wars of the Napoleonic period were not favourable to the making and maturing of fine wines. Napoleon is said to have been partial to Chambertin, but it is very doubtful whether he ever appreciated any of the fine wines of France; his chance of drinking any of them came when he was not so much too old as too much otherwise preoccupied. Except on rare ceremonious occasions, he bolted his food and wine, a very bad habit indeed, which killed him in the end.

Napoleon's fiscal reform was less spectacular but of far more solid worth than the glory which crowned so many of his victories, at the cost of half the male population of the country. For over a hundred years the value of the French franc was absolutely stable, and the prosperity which France enjoyed was due, to a very great extent, to the confidence which such stability encouraged both at home and abroad.

During the hundred years from Waterloo to the First World War more wealth was lavished upon the great vineyards of France than ever before. Some of the richest among the families of the old French nobility and some of the more famous among the international bankers, as well as large landowners and merchant-princes whose wealth dated from the Revolution or the Napoleonic wars, were, as their descendants are today, equally proud to own some of the finest vineyards of France, and they never spared any expense to make and mature wines of superlative quality.

There were, in all probability, more and finer wines made in France from 1830 to 1880 than had ever been made before from all the vineyards of the world. Wines were so good and there was so much of them during these years that they could be, or often had to be, kept; they were thus given a chance to show how great they could be.

And then came that greatest of all calamities, which killed outright most of the French vines in less than twenty years. Other insect pests that attack and devour the leaves and the fruit of the vine do much harm and give the *vignerons* much trouble, but they can be checked. Not so the *phylloxera vastatrix*, or vine louse; it hits the vine most unfairly, underground, below the belt, unseen, pinned to the roots of the vine and sucking its life-sap at source. There is but one sure method of fighting phylloxera with any chance of success: it is to flood the vineyard long enough to drown the bug, but not long enough to rot the roots of the vines. Unfortunately most vineyards responsible for wines of quality are hillside vineyards and cannot be flooded.

The *phylloxera vastatrix* was first reported in Europe at Kew, near London, the famous Botanical Gardens, in a parcel of American native vines sent over as specimens. How this diabolical little pest managed to get from Kew, by the Thames, to Bordeaux, Burgundy and Champagne, to every vineyard of Europe and Africa, and to the island vineyards of the Mediterranean and of the Atlantic, nobody has ever been able to explain, but it did. By the end of the seventies of the last century the vineyards of Bordeaux had been wiped out, and ten years later those of Burgundy and Champagne were dead or dying. Salvation came from the original home of phylloxera, the eastern states of North America, where native American species of vine had become, through centuries of co-habitation, nearly immune to phylloxera. Ever since, Cabernets, Pinots, Sauvignons and all the other species of French vines have been grafted upon American phylloxera-resisting root-stocks. To replant millions of acres with these new 'Franco-American' vines could be done only at a cost in hard cash and harder work which must have been staggering. But it was done, and the great vineyards of France still bring forth every year as great wines as ever before, whenever the sun is kind to them.

# CHAPTER TWO

# The Wines of Bordeaux

Bordeaux is, after Marseilles, the oldest port of France – it welcomed Crassus and his Roman legions in 56 B.C.

Bordeaux, built upon the left bank of the River Garonne, some 40 miles inland from the Atlantic, has never ceased to expand during the past two thousand years, mostly westwards, burying its own vineyards under a relentless tide of *chais*, shops and houses.

Bordeaux is the metropolis of the Gironde Département, the largest of the French Départements, some 104 miles long and 75 wide, with over 2,500 million acres of vineyards, forests, pastures, marshes and sandy dunes, and with a population of close on a million, a large number of them ever-thirsty souls.

The Gironde Département takes its name from the River Gironde, a great tidal waterway, as much as 7 miles wide at its widest, and some 37 miles long, from the Bay of Biscay to the Bec d'Ambès, where La Garonne, from the south, and La Dordogne, from the north, meet and become La Gironde.

There are vineyards in most parts of the Gironde Département, vineyards which are expected to bring forth every year 203,000 *tonneaux* of red bordeaux wine and 153,500 *tonneaux* of white bordeaux, 356,500 *tonneaux* in all, equal to 1,426,000 casks, or nearly 500,000,000 bottles of perfectly genuine bordeaux wine – great, good or not so good wines, according to the soil of the vineyards and the whim of the weather.

Granting, as we must, that the best wine is the wine that we like best, there is no denying the fact that the vineyards of Bordeaux produce wines of the highest quality in greater quantities and also greater variety than any of the other vineyards of France. Quality is the result of the happy partnership between soil, vines and climate, conditions which may be, and are, just as favourable elsewhere; quantity is a matter of acres, and the Gironde Département is the largest of all Départements; variety is due to differences in the nature of the soil and sub-soil of the vineyards as well as to differences in the species of the vines.

In the Gironde Département there is a very large number of different sorts of soil: silt and alluvial deposits have been brought down in the course of past centuries from the south by the Garonne, and from the east by the Dordogne; there are pockets, veins and streaks of clay, lime, sand, gravel, flint and all sorts of soils, either by themselves or mixed together in an almost infinite variety of proportion and location, upon higher or lower ground, facing the rising sun or the briny humidity from the Bay of Biscay.

Then there are the vines, and they are responsible, in the Gironde, for a greater measure of variety of both red and white wines than anywhere else. In Burgundy all the best red wines are made from Pinots noiriens and the best white wines from Pinots Chardonnay. In Alsace different wines are made from different species of grapes, Sylvaner, Riesling, Traminer, etc. In the Gironde, however, the red wines are made from three or four different species of grapes, Cabernet chiefly, Malbec, Merlot and Verdot; and most of the white wines from three different species of grapes, Semillon,

Plate 1. *Previous page* Château Pontet-Canet, Pauillac; a typical vineyard of the Médoc. Plate 2. The *Cabernet franc*, one of the grapes responsible for the individuality and excellence of red bordeaux wines.

Sauvignon and Muscadelle. Cabernet grapes for the red wines, and Semillon for the whites, are always used to a greater extent in the making of all the better wines, but the proportion may vary from as much as 95% to as little as 60% of the whole, and the choice of the other grapes used at the same time varies with almost every individual vineyard. This practice of making wine from different varieties of grapes is responsible for differences in 'bouquet' and 'body' of different wines; it is also responsible for their rate of maturing. A Mouton-Rothschild, for instance, made from 80 to 90% of Cabernet grapes will be 'hard', and it will not have the same charm and appeal as another Pauillac wine made in the same year and in the same way from 65% Cabernet and 35% other grapes, that is, when both will be five or six years old; but, ten years later, the first will be a distinctly finer wine, and after another twenty years it will probably be superb, a really great wine, while the other will be a poor, feeble, tottering old man.

Of all red table wines, the red wine of Bordeaux, which has been known in England by the name of *Claret* for quite a while – the past seven centuries – may be called the perfect wine; like the perfect wife, it looks nice and it is nice; natural, wholesome; ever helpful, yet not assertive; dependable always; gracious and gentle, but neither dumb, dull nor monotonous: a rare gift and a real joy.

The red wines of Bordeaux, more particularly the more *ordinaires* among them, are acceptable when quite young, when three or four years old, but not, like some Beaujolais red wines, for instance, when twelve or eighteen months old. On the other hand, there are no table wines in the world capable of standing the test of time as the wines of Bordeaux do. They certainly possess the 'gift of age'.

No white wine will ever age as gracefully as the red, but the great white wines of Sauternes will outlive all other French white wines. At sixty years of age, in 1929, Yquem 1869 was still a truly magnificent wine.

The gift of age, which the wines of Bordeaux have enjoyed to such a remarkable extent for so long, is due to the fact that they are made with sound grapes, ripe grapes, whole grapes, lots of them, and nothing else; they are made with greater care and leisure than art. The grapes are bruised, crushed and pressed as they are picked: their sweet juice ferments and becomes wine in its own sweet way; the new wine is left alone to grow slowly but surely into a grand wine. There is no sugar, no spirit, no sulphur, no lime, nothing added at any stage: the new wine is 'racked' from time to time, i.e. moved from one cask away from its cast-off 'lees' into a clean cask, and that is all the attention it needs until it is old enough to be bottled.

Today, the soil of the vineyards of the Gironde is the same as before: the grapes are also the same; it is true that since the phylloxera tragedy the old French vines have to be grafted upon American bug-resisting root-stock, but they have proved abundantly that claret is as good as it ever was. Château Latour 1899 and Château Margaux 1900, for instance, were still very great wines when I last tasted them, in 1954, and so was the 1899 Château Pontet-Canet which I was privileged to drink, in March 1956, at Pontet-Canet. What has changed so much is the demand. The faster our means of transport, the more time do we save, and yet the faster the tempo of life, the less leisure do we have. There are fewer and fewer wine-lovers who are prepared or able to lay down wine of a good vintage and forget about it for twenty years, as used to be a common practice not so very long ago. Everything is against it: the considerably higher 'starting price' of wine – that is, its original cost at the time of the vintage, is the first limiting factor: then

Plate 3. The red wines of France when young are rich and brilliant. Plate 4. *Overleaf*
As the wine grows older it darkens, as in this Château Lafite 1887.

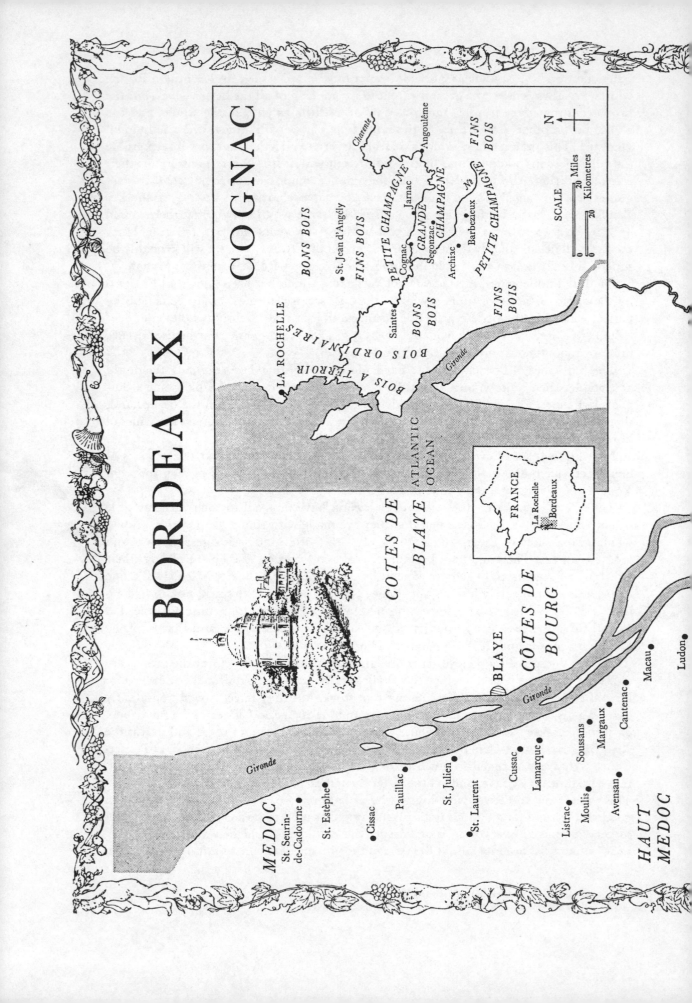

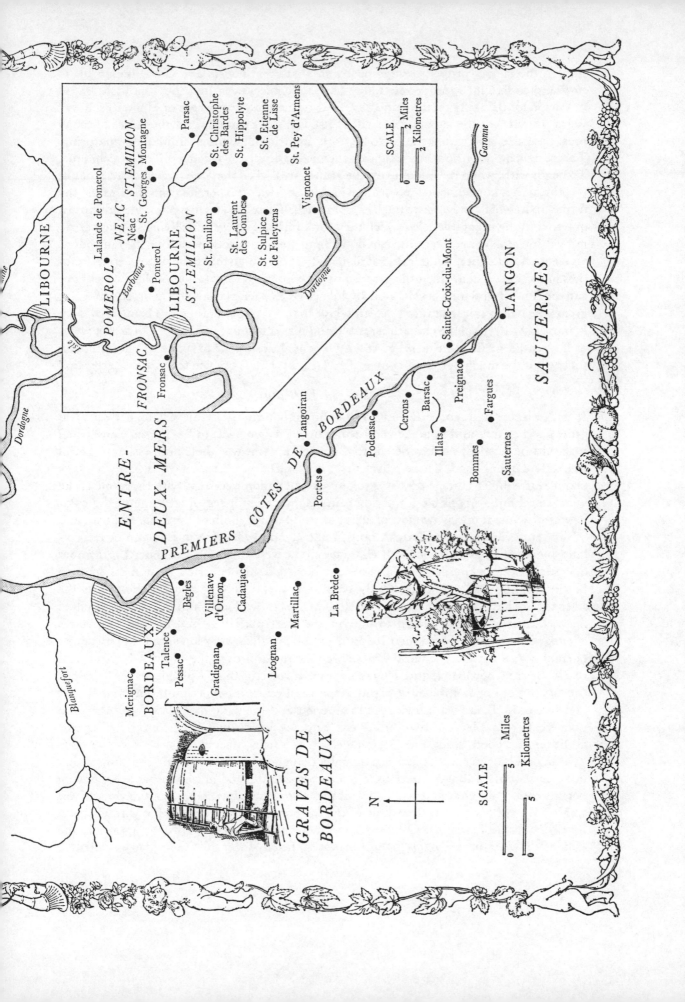

LIBOURNE

POMEROL

Lalande de Pomerol

NEAC
Néac

ST. EMILION
St. Georges Montagne

Parsac

St. Christophe
des Bardes

St. Hippolyte

St. Etienne
de Lisse

St. Pey d'Armens

FRONSAC

Pomerol

LIBOURNE
ST. EMILION

St. Emilion

St. Laurent
des Combes

St. Sulpice
de Faleyrens

Vignonet

Fronsac

Barbanne

Isle

Dordogne

Dordogne

SCALE

Miles
Kilometres

Garonne

LANGON

Sainte-Croix-du-Mont

SAUTERNES

ENTRE-

DEUX-MERS

PREMIERS

CÔTES

DE

BORDEAUX

Langoiran

Portets

Podensac

Cerons

Barsac

Illats

Preignac

Fargues

Bommes

Sauternes

Blanquefort

Merignac

BORDEAUX

Talence

Pessac

Gradignan

Villenave
d'Ornon

Cadaujac

Léognan

Martillac

La Brède

Bègles

GRAVES DE
BORDEAUX

N

SCALE

Miles
Kilometres

there is the lack of proper storage space now that great houses are all but impossible to staff and to live in. Most people today have no choice, even had they the wish, but to buy wine for drinking on the same day, or within a matter of weeks or of months, not of years. Inevitably the supply must adapt itself to the demand, and the wines of today must be made, and can be made, to be ready for drinking with a minimum of maturing. This can be done without any magic or chemicals, simply by using a different technique. To begin with, when the bunches of ripe grapes are picked they are now *égrappées*, that is, put through a kind of calender-drum which tears away the berries from the husks – the frame upon which they were attached from birth. These husks are separated and thrown out, so that the vegetable acids which they contain, like all vegetable living substances, do not get into the wine. The wine can do without them perfectly well, but they introduce an element of acidity, undesirable at first, and yet helpful to make the wine keep its freshness in old age. Then, when the grapes are pressed, the fermentation of their sweet juice can be slowed down or accelerated by longer or shorter periods in the open '*cuves*', or great vats, where all wines are born and have their fill of fresh air before being locked up in barrels, with much less breathing space and air. It is thus possible for Bordeaux wines to be 'ready' or fit to drink when still quite young, from four to six years old, although they would be much better, of course, if given another five or even ten years to 'grow up.'

## Château Bottling

It is the immediate concern and paramount responsibility of all Château owners to grow good grapes and to make good wine: how the wine was to be 'nursed', and when it should be bottled, used to be left to the merchants: it was their business, and a most important one indeed. There was a time, a hundred years or so ago, when a vintage claret was sold as vintage port was sold until much more recently, with the name of the wine-merchant responsible for the bottling. One can still see upon some of the catalogues of wine auctions two lots of claret offered for sale, both of the same Château and of the same vintage, one Château-bottled and the other bottled in England or in Scotland by some English or Scottish wine-merchant well known at the time. I remember one such sale when the English-bottling fetched a higher price than the Château-bottling of the same wine, evidently because it was a better wine. In those days the status of the family wine-merchant was that of the family doctor and the family solicitor: he was implicitly trusted, and to deserve the trust placed in him he had to give his clients wines which were to their liking; he also gave them very long credit. It was quite normal for a perfectly honest wine-merchant to 'improve' the claret which he had received from Bordeaux, and I have seen an invoice of the early thirties – of the last century – from one of the most highly respected Leith wine-merchants, for some 'Lafite Hermitaged'. There was no vintage mentioned and the wine may have been that of a poor year, or a blend of two indifferent vintages, which had been 'improved' by the addition of a good, stout, red Hermitage. There was no deception.

Château bottling was at first occasionally demanded by and accorded to a few rather fussy merchants who were anxious to offer a wine that could not be suspected of having been blended, or 'cut', as it was called at the time. It was in 1869, when the vintage was small but very good, that the whole of the wine made at Château Lafite was 'Château bottled' for the first time. Of course, the mere physical act of bottling a wine in the Château's *chais* or cellars is by no means sufficient to entitle the wine to call itself

'Château bottled': this is a privilege which the owner of the Château may grant or not, at his will. When he grants it the corks used at the bottling time are branded with the name of the Château and the year of the vintage; later on, when the bottles are 'dressed', the labels will bear the mention 'Mise en bouteille du Château' or 'Mis en bouteilles au Château'.

Until quite recent times the 'Château bottling' was not granted by all the Châteaux: there were some who never gave the 'Château bottling', while others granted it now and again, when they considered that the vintage was an exceptionally fine one. Lately, however, 'Château bottling' has become the rule instead of the exception. Some Châteaux, like Mouton-Rothschild, do their own bottling: they sell none of their wine in cask but bottled at the Château in half-bottles, bottles, magnums and larger bottles, which are numbered from 'one' upwards so that each can always be identified in whatever part of the world it may eventually stray before its cork be released and its contents deliver their glad message.

'Château bottling' still is what it has always been: a birth certificate, but it can no longer be regarded as necessarily a certificate of merit.

## The Gironde

There are vineyards in all parts of the Bordeaux country, and it is difficult to decide which might be the best way to visit them. Let us begin with the Gironde, the greatest of the three waterways of the Département that bears its name; we shall next turn to the Garonne and lastly to the Dordogne.

There are many vineyards along both banks of the Gironde, as well as in the islands, large and small, amidstream: they are responsible for about 33% of the total wine production of the Département, that is wine entitled to the proud name of Bordeaux, 40% of all the red wines and 25% of all the whites. The vineyards upon the left bank of the Gironde which produce most of the best red wines as well as a greater quantity than the vineyards of the Garonne and Dordogne are the vineyards of the Médoc, and they account for 22% of the total vinous production of the Département but only 1% of its white wines. The vineyards upon the right bank of the Gironde, those of Bourg and Blaye, as well as the vineyards of the Gironde islands, produce 18% of all the red wines and 24% of all the white wines, none of them, however, comparable in quality to the best wines of the Médoc.

### The Médoc

Médoc was originally the name given to all the country that stretches from the Garonne, above Bordeaux, and from the Gironde, westwards and northwards, as far as the Bay of Biscay. All along the Médoc seaboard, and for some miles inland, there are sand dunes, fir trees, heath and grass lands, lakes and marshes, but no vines. The vineyards of the Médoc have always been along its eastern fringe, some of them in Palus close to the Garonne or the Gironde, and the others, all the better ones, upon higher ground called Graves on account of the gravelly nature of the soil.

Both Palus and Graves vineyards of the Médoc are of alluvial origin, but not of the same age. The Palus are of comparatively recent formation, and they are rich in silt deposits: their vines bear more grapes than those planted in Graves vineyards, but their wines are not nearly so good: they never have the *finesse* or breed and charm of Graves-grown wines. The Graves vineyards of the Médoc are also of alluvial origin, but of much more remote antiquity; in the main they follow the courses of Garonne and Gironde, only the last few miles of the first but nearly the whole of the Gironde, upon a succession of ridges which vary both in height and width: more important still is the fact that the depth of this precious grit-cum-sand-cum-pebbles Graves soil also varies very much, from a few inches in some parts to as much as 10 feet in others.

It was only in the eighteenth century that the use of the name Médoc became restricted to the land lying north of the Jalle de Blanquefort (a *jalle* is a small stream), and westwards, to the Atlantic. It was also then that the name Graves ceased to be used for those wines of the Médoc made from grapes grown on Graves soil, and was reserved for those of the vineyards south of Blanquefort, on the left bank of the Garonne.

The Médoc, which now begins a little more than 5 miles north of Bordeaux, is divided into upper and lower, Haut-Médoc and Bas-Médoc. The first comprised twenty-nine Communes, the vineyards of which were, and still are, responsible for all the finer wines, and the second twenty-three Communes producing mostly *vins ordinaires*. During the Second World War the people of the geographically lower reaches of the Gironde objected to the name of Bas-Médoc and demanded that *Bas* be deleted, which was granted to them. So now plain Médoc officially means the northern or lower part of the old Médoc, while the southern part has retained its name of Haut-Médoc. All the greatest Médoc wines come from the Châteaux of the Haut-Médoc, most of them in the Communes of Margaux, Cantenac, Saint-Julien, Pauillac and Saint-Estèphe. There are, in the Haut-Médoc, about five hundred 'Châteaux' or estates, the vineyards of which are capable of producing 10,500 *tonneaux* of red wines or claret every year, wines of fair, fine and very good quality, besides about 15,500 *tonneaux* of commoner red wines, and only about 415 *tonneaux* of white wine.

Many attempts have been made to grade the wines of the Châteaux du Médoc, and the 'Classification' which still stands today after a hundred years was made in 1855, when four Châteaux were given first place (although the fourth, Château Haut-Brion, was included in spite of being in the Commune of Pessac in the Graves de Bordeaux district, not in Médoc); fifteen second, fourteen third, ten fourth and seventeen fifth. This Classification was drawn up at the request of the Bordeaux Chamber of Commerce by a number of Bordeaux brokers whose experience and integrity were universally acknowledged at the time. The Classification, over a hundred years old, was based on the prices paid by the merchants of Bordeaux for the wines of different vineyards during the best part of a century before 1855; it was considered safe enough to assume that the better the wine, the higher would be the price that the merchants would pay for it. Up to 1820 the practice of the Bordeaux trade had been to recognize four main grades of Médoc *crus*, paying for the second growths approximately a fourth less than the price paid for the first; for the third, one-fifth less than the price paid for the second; and for the fourth, one-fifth less than the price paid for the third. In 1824, when Wm. Franck published his *Traité sur les vins du Médoc*, he placed in a fifth class the *crus* which had been hitherto known in Bordeaux as '*Deuxièmes quatrièmes Crus*', and this division was adopted, in 1855, by the brokers for the official classification. Although the quality of all wines must necessarily depend in the first place upon the geological formation of the soil and sub-soil of each vineyard, which is why the 1855 Classification has stood the test of time so well, it must also be recognized that the care and skill of generations of *vignerons* may quite possibly make some difference for better or worse.

Today, for instance, most if not all claret lovers would unhesitatingly vote for moving up Château Mouton-Rothschild from the top of the second *crus* to the first. I, for one, and I am sure that I would not be alone, would like to move up Palmer and Calon-Ségur from third to second, Talbot and Beychevelle from fourth to third or second, Pontet-Canet and Cantemerle from fifth to third or, perhaps, second. But I would not hesitate to demote at least half a dozen other 'classed' growths and replace them by excellent *Bourgeois Supérieurs* more deserving to be '*classé*' among the fifth growths, Châteaux Meyney, Sénéjac, Lanessan and Le Boscq to begin with.

Next to the '*Crus Classés*', in point of the excellence of their wines, come four Estates of the Haut-Médoc, which are known as *Crus Exceptionnels*, and immediately after them there are some two hundred *Crus Bourgeois Supérieurs*, most of them capable of producing very good wines indeed, often better value than some of the 'classed' growths, which are dearer but not invariably better.

The *Crus Classés*, the *Crus Exceptionnels* and the *Crus Bourgeois Supérieurs* of the Haut-Médoc are responsible for all the finer red wines of the Médoc, but there are a great many more vineyards which produce a much greater quantity of wines, mostly wines which cannot compete with the rest in the matter of breed and charm, yet quite pleasant and acceptable table wines of the '*ordinaire*' and even '*grand ordinaire*' classes. There is also a number of gradings among them, the better ones being known as *Crus Bourgeois* and the others as *Crus Artisans*. There are also the *Vins de Palus*, from vineyards by the riverside or in the Gironde islands, and the *Vins de Terrefort*, from vineyards where clay takes the place of gravel.

Provided the weather happens to be all that it should be, that is when the sun shines and the rain comes at the right time and in due measure, the vineyards of the Haut-Médoc may be expected to produce the following quantities of wine in a year:

|  | *Tonneaux* |
|---|---|
| Crus Classés | 4,503 |
| Crus Exceptionnels & Crus Bourgeois Supérieurs | 6,019 |
| Crus Bourgeois et Crus Artisans | 12,821 |
| Vins de Palus et de Terrefort | 2,835 |
| Vins blancs | 415 |
|  | 26,593 |

## *Communes, or Parishes, of the Haut-Médoc and their Châteaux*

*(The complete 1855 classification of the wines of the Médoc will be found in Appendix 2, p. 158)*

Starting from Bordeaux, to visit the vineyards of the Haut-Médoc, we shall leave the city by the Barrière du Médoc, pass by the Bordeaux football ground and the race course and bear right, after 7 km., leaving the more direct road to the Pointe de Grave, the main road, for what is known as *La Route des Châteaux du Médoc*. After 9 km. we shall cross a small stream, La Jalle de Blanquefort, which divides at this point the Graves country from the Haut-Médoc. Proceeding in a n.n.w. general direction, with at first the last few miles of the Garonne, and then the whole length of the Gironde on our right, we shall pass through all the Communes of the Haut-Médoc before reaching and passing through those of the Bas-Médoc, now called Médoc *tout court*.

### BLANQUEFORT (10 km. n.n.w. Bordeaux)

About one-third of the Blanquefort red wines are Palus wines from riverside vineyards. Château Tujean, the only Estate of importance, is one of the *Crus Bourgeois*.

### LE TAILLAN (11 km. n.w. Bordeaux)

Château du Taillan is a modest *Cru Bourgeois*, but the Château itself is one of the finest of the Médoc; it is owned by, and is the residence of, Monsieur and Madame Jean Cruse. Its vineyards, the most important of the Commune, produced none but red wines until the early part of the present century, when white Semillon, Sauvignon and Muscadelle grapes were planted: ever since this Château's vines have produced on an average 50 *tonneaux* of red wine, sold as Château du Taillan, and 20 *tonneaux* of white wine, sold as Château Dame-Blanche.

### SAINT-MEDARD-EN-JALLES (13 km. n.w. Bordeaux)

One of the less important Communes of the Haut-Médoc: its *Crus Bourgeois* vineyards produce an average of 50 *tonneaux* of fair red wines, and its other vineyards about 150 *tonneaux* of quite *ordinaires* red wine.

### SAINT-AUBIN (15 km. n.w. Bordeaux)

About forty small *vignerons* make on an average from 1 to 6 *tonneaux* of red wine each every year. The only vineyard of any size is that of Château de Cujac.

### PAREMPUYRE (16 km. n. Bordeaux)

There are in this Commune two *Bourgeois Supérieurs*: one is the Château Ségur, operated by M. J. Grazioli for the Societé Agricole du Château Ségur; the other is Cru Ségur-Fillon, owned by M. J. Grazioli. These *Crus Bourgeois Supérieures* are responsible for some 40 *tonneaux* of good red wines, while the riverside Palus vineyards produce about twice as much *ordinaires* red wines.

### LUDON (16 km. n. Bordeaux)

In Ludon there is a *Troisième Cru Classé*, Château Grand-La Lagune, better known outside France as Château La Lagune, which produces an average of 200 *tonneaux* of excellent red wine. The prosperity of the Commune, however, rests mostly upon its riverside Palus vineyards which are responsible for an average of 600 *tonneaux* of more *ordinaires* but popular red wines. There are also eight *Crus Bourgeois Supérieurs* with an average aggregate production of 110 *tonneaux*. Also 200 *tonneaux* of less distinguished red wines from *Crus Bourgeois* and *Crus Artisans*.

### LE PIAN-MEDOC (17 km. n. Bordeaux)

This Commune, immediately west of both Parempuyre and Ludon, farther away from the river, has only one notable Estate, the Château Sénéjac, a *Cru Bourgeois Supérieur*, which produces some 60 *tonneaux* of a very elegant red wine. Other vineyards are responsible for a further 100 *tonneaux* of red and 10 *tonneaux* of white wines.

### MACAU (21 km. n. Bordeaux)

Macau is a very important Commune of the Haut-Médoc both quantitatively and qualitatively. Its pride is the Château Cantemerle, the home of that grand old man of

Plate 5. The *Merlot*, a grape grown in the Gironde, particularly suited to the soil of the Saint-Emilion and Pomerol districts.

the Gironde, M. Jean Dubos. Cantemerle was placed last of the fifth growths, in 1855, but the 100 *tonneaux* of red wine which it produces on an average usually fetch and deserve higher prices than most wines of the fourth and third growths. The 'second wine' of Cantemerle is sold under the registered name of *Royal Médoc*. There are no less than nine *Crus Bourgeois Supérieurs* in Macau, which are responsible for an average yield of 240 *tonneaux* of very fair red wine, besides Palus vineyards producing an average of 1,000 *tonneaux* of sound red wines and some *Crus Bourgeois*, *Artisans* and Terrefort producing 200 *tonneaux* of red wines. The three small white vineyards of Château Larrieu-Blanc, Priban and Maucamps, produce 5 *tonneaux* of white wines each.

ARSAC[1] (22 km. n.w. Bordeaux)

Arsac, immediately west of Macau, is a smaller Commune with one *Cinquième Cru Classé*, Château Du Tertre, with a yield of 100 *tonneaux* of good red wine; two *Crus Bourgeois Supérieurs* (Château d'Arsac, which produces 20 *tonneaux* of red and 10 *tonneaux* of white wines) and Château Monbrison with a yield of 40 *tonneaux* of red wine.

LABARDE[1] (24 km. n.n.w. Bordeaux)

Labarde lies east of Arsac, west and north of Macau and south of Cantenac. There are two *Cru Classés* in Labarde, a third Château Giscours (200 *tonneaux*), and a fifth Château Dauzac (100 *tonneaux*); their vineyards overflow into the adjoining Commune of Cantenac and their wines may be sold as Margaux wines. There are also in Labarde three *Crus Bourgeois Supérieurs*, of which the most important is Château Siran (100 *tonneaux*).

Château Dauzac was the property of one of the more important firms of Bordeaux merchants during the greater part of the nineteenth and the early part of the twentieth century, Messrs. Nathaniel Johnston & Cie: they not only made good wine but they made it one of the best-known clarets in the U.S.A. and the United Kingdom.

CANTENAC[1] (25 km. n. Bordeaux)

The vineyards of Cantenac and those of nearby Margaux produce some of the most delightful red wines of the Médoc and of the world. There are no less than seven *Crus Classés* in the Commune of Cantenac: one second, Château Brane-Cantenac (200 *tonneaux*); four thirds, Château Kirwan (60 *tonneaux*), d'Issan (80 *tonneaux*), Cantenac-Brown (70 *tonneaux*) and Palmer (120 *tonneaux*); and two fourths, Châteaux Le Prieuré-Lichine (75 *tonneaux*) and Pouget (20 *tonneaux*).

Château d'Issan is one of the finest examples of medieval architecture of the Gironde. The great building, which is surrounded by a very wide moat, and its vineyards were, most unfortunately, sadly neglected for some years until the end of the last war when the property was acquired by M. Emmanuel Cruse. The old castle has now been put into good repair and some of its best vineyards have been replanted. Formerly there were many acres of vines on lower land, on the Gironde side of the Château, which produced large quantities of inexpensive *Bourgeois* claret, sold as *Moulin d'Issan*: those acres are now under grass, and the farm of the Château d'Issan is one of the more important of the Médoc.

Château Palmer was known for a very long time as a popular wine under the name of *Château de Gasq*. It was acquired in or about 1820 by one of Louis XVIII's generals, named Palmer, who gave it his name. Château Palmer bears on its label the name of

[1] The *Crus Classés* of Arsac, Labarde and Cantenac have been given the *appellation contrôlée* 'Margaux'.

Margaux, not Cantenac, and other Châteaux of the Cantenac Commune do the same, when some of their vineyards, like those of Château Palmer, are partly in the Margaux Commune.

The vineyard of Château Le Prieuré, formerly known as Cantenac-Prieuré, was planted at the beginning of the seventeenth century by the Prior of Cantenac. The Château and its vines were acquired in 1952 by Alexis Lichine, since when Cantenac-Prieuré has been renamed Prieuré-Lichine.

Of the *Crus Bourgeois* of Cantenac, the most important is an exceptional Château Angludet (60 *tonneaux*), and the most unfortunate is Château Montbrun (40 *tonneaux*), owned by M. René Lebègue, which was destroyed by fire in 1954. There are also about 20 *tonneaux* of white wines made from Cantenac vineyards, 10 *tonneaux* are sold under the registered name *Château Montbrun Goutte d'Or* and 10 *tonneaux* as *Château Cantenac-Blanc*.

### MARGAUX (28 km. n.w. Bordeaux)

Margaux is one of the most universally known of all the Communes of the Haut-Médoc, and its many vineyards produce a considerable quantity of red wine, as well as a very little white wine. All the best red wines of Margaux possess a distinctive and very attractive bouquet that is quite impossible to describe in mere words; it is somewhat reminiscent of what might be wild violets-cum-amber perfume.

The pride of the Commune of Margaux is, of course, Château Margaux, *le roi du Médoc*, as it has been called, and one of the four *Premiers Crus*. It is certainly one of the show places of the Médoc; the Château itself is a very handsome mansion built in 1802 by the Marquis de la Colonille who pulled down what was left of the former Château de Lamothe, a *château fort* of the fifteenth century. It was bought in 1870 by the Comte Pillet-Will, whose heirs sold it in 1920, and during the fifty years of what may be called the Pillet-Will régime, the wine of Château Margaux was always as fine as that of the other three first growths and occasionally the best of them all. There was never a finer 1871, for instance, than the Château Margaux of that vintage. It was light, both in colour and texture, at sixty years old, when I last tasted it, but still possessing a delicate yet penetrating and typically 'Margaux' bouquet; it was sweet to the end; ethereal, fascinating, perfect. In 1888, not a great year in the Médoc, Château Margaux stood out lengths ahead of the 'field': it was not really great but it was delicious. Then there was the 1900 Château Margaux, which won first place by a very short head – all 1900s were so good! There have also been times, unfortunately, more particularly between the last two wars, when Château Margaux failed to live up to its very high standard of excellence, but its present owner, M. Pierre Ginestet, is determined never to allow that to happen again.

Château Margaux, as one approaches it along an avenue of fine trees, has great dignity and beauty, but the great *chai* of the Château, close to it, has even greater majesty as one enters it. The vineyards of Château Margaux produce on an average 180 *tonneaux* of first-class red wine, besides a smaller quantity of red wines sold as *Pavillon rouge de Château Margaux*.

There are four *Deuxièmes*, four *Troisièmes* and one *Quatrième Crus Classés* in the Commune of Margaux. The *Deuxièmes Crus* are: Château Rausan-Séglas (70 *tonneaux*); Château Rauzan-Gassies (60 *tonneaux*); Château Durfort (80 *tonneaux*); and Château Lascomes (200 *tonneaux*), owned by a syndicate of American financiers.

The *Troisièmes Crus Classés* are: Château Malescot-Saint-Exupéry (80 *tonneaux*) and Marquis d'Alesme-Becker (40 *tonneaux*); Château Ferrière (20 *tonneaux*); and Château Desmirail (30 *tonneaux*).

The *Quatrième Cru Classé* is Château Marquis de Terme (150 *tonneaux*).

There are five *Crus Bourgeois Supérieurs* in the Commune of Margaux; their average annual production is 150 *tonneaux* of very decent red wine. *Crus Bourgeois* and *Artisans* are responsible for a further quantity of 150 *tonneaux* of more *ordinaires* red wines, and the riverside Palus vineyards for some 200 *tonneaux* of commoner wines. There are also some 25 *tonneaux* of white wines made from the white grapes of Château Margaux; they are sold under the name of *Pavillon blanc de Château Margaux*.

From Margaux to Moulis, westwards, there are four Communes of little vinous importance:

## AVENSAN (29 km. n.w. Bordeaux)
Its best vineyard is that of Château Villegeorge (50 *tonneaux*), while five small *Crus Bourgeois Supérieurs* produce an average of 135 *tonneaux* of fair red wines; and *Bourgeois* and *Artisans* a further 300 *tonneaux* of commoner wines.

## CASTELNAU (28 km. n.w. Bordeaux)
Its vineyards are responsible for an average of 100 *tonneaux* of *ordinaires*, *Bourgeois* or *Artisans* wines.

## SOUSSANS (30 km. n.n.w. Bordeaux)
Its best vineyard is that of Château Bel-Air-Marquis d'Aligre (50 *tonneaux*), a *Cru Exceptionnel*. There are four *Crus Bourgèois Supérieurs* with an aggregate yield of 165 *tonneaux* of very fair red wines, much the largest of them being the Château La Tour de Mons (100 *tonneaux*), the property of Monsieur Dubos.

## ARCINS (33 km. n. Bordeaux)
There are no vineyards of particular excellence in this Commune, which produces about 250 *tonneaux* of *ordinaires* red wines from *Crus Bourgeois* and *Artisans*.

## MOULIS (33 km. n. Bordeaux)
This is an important Commune with no less than twenty-one *Crus Bourgeois Supérieurs*, producing an aggregate of over 700 *tonneaux* of sound, dependable, pleasant red wines. The best vineyard of Moulis is that of Château Chasse-Spleen (180 *tonneaux*), a *Cru Exceptionnel*.

## LISTRAC (34 km. n.w. Bordeaux)
This Commune is chiefly noted for the large quantity (1,000 *tonneaux*) of *ordinaires* but pleasing and dependable red wines, *Crus Bourgeois* and *Artisans*, sold as *Listrac* and also under the name of *Château Grand Listrac*. There is no such château, but it is the registered name under which the wines of the *Co-operative des Producteurs de Listrac* are sold.

There are, however, some better Listrac wines: they are those from the dozen *Crus Bourgeois Supérieurs* of the Commune – 625 *tonneaux* in all.

## LAMARQUE (36 km. n.w. Bordeaux)
Lamarque is one of the less important Communes of the Haut-Médoc. Its three *Crus Bourgeois Supérieurs* produce an average of 220 *tonneaux* of fair quality red wines, and its *Crus Bourgeois* and *Artisans* a further 350 *tonneaux* of *ordinaires* wines.

CUSSAC (33 km. n.n.w. Bordeaux)

This is also one of the minor Haut-Médoc Communes, with four *Crus Bourgeois Supérieurs*, producing an aggregate of 230 *tonneaux* of fair red wines, the wine of Château Lanessan (100 *tonneaux*) being probably the best and certainly the best known of the four. The *Crus Bourgeois* and *Crus Artisans* produce an average of 500 *tonneaux* of *ordinaires* wines.

SAINT-LAURENT (43 km. n.n.w. Bordeaux)

This Commune has three of the *Crus Classés*: Château La Tour-Carnet (80 *tonneaux*), a *Quatrième Cru*; Château Belgrave (120 *tonneaux*), a *Cinquième Cru*; and Château Camensac (100 *tonneaux*), also a *Cinquième Cru*.

The *Crus Bourgeois Supérieurs* of Saint-Laurent are four in number and produce an aggregate of 610 *tonneaux* of very fair red wines: the best known is Château Ballac (200 *tonneaux*). The *Crus Bourgeois* and *Artisans* produce 500 *tonneaux* of *ordinaires* red wines and 100 *tonneaux* of undistinguished white wines.

SAINT-JULIEN (44 km. n.n.w. Bordeaux)

Back again, nearer the Gironde, we come to one of the most universally known Communes of the Haut-Médoc, Saint-Julien-Beychevelle, better known as Saint-Julien. Its vineyards produce a very large quantity of red wines of superlative excellence, which possess a unique 'tenderness' or silkiness of body as well as a most attractive bouquet.

There are twelve *Crus Classés* in the Commune of Saint-Julien, including five of the most popular *Deuxièmes Crus*, the Châteaux Léoville-Las-Cases (200 *tonneaux*); Léoville-Poyferré (170 *tonneaux*); Léoville-Barton (100 *tonneaux*); Gruaud-Larose (200 *tonneaux*); and Ducru-Beaucaillou (200 *tonneaux*).

Château Gruaud-Larose is not one of the oldest Châteaux of the Médoc: it dates back merely to 1757. The daughter of the original Monsieur Gruaud married a Monsieur de Larose and the château became Gruaud-Larose until 1812, when it was sold to Baron Sarget, and was eventually divided among his heirs, which is why there were two Châteaux Gruaud-Larose during the best part of a century, one called Gruaud-Larose-Sarget and the other Gruaud-Larose-Faure. Recently, however, both parts of the original property were acquired by M. Desiré Cordier, since when there has been once more the one and only Château Gruaud-Larose.

The two *Troisièmes Crus* of Saint-Julien are Châteaux Lagrange (200 *tonneaux*) and Châteaux Langoa-Barton (100 *tonneaux*). The five *Quatrièmes Crus* of Saint-Julien are Château Saint-Pierre Bontemps (75 *tonneaux*) joined with Saint-Pierre Sevaistre, Branaire-Ducru (150 *tonneaux*), Talbot (300 *tonneaux*) and Beychevelle (150 *tonneaux*).

Château Talbot is one of the finest estates of the Médoc with, besides a splendid vineyard, a model farm and a famous stud. The Château itself is a modern and very handsome mansion which, according to tradition, stands on the site of the medieval castle which, five hundred years ago, was the home and headquarters of the brave and ill-fated Talbot who was killed at Castillon, near Libourne, in 1453.

The wine of Château Talbot has ranked among the best of the Médoc for many centuries, but its fame was never greater than during the eighteenth century, when the Château was owned by the Marquis d'Aux – which is why it is also called Talbot d'Aux.[1] It is now owned by M. Georges Cordier.

[1] The poet Biarnez reversed the order:

'Tout ce qu'un quatrième a de charme et de grâce
Résume d'Aux Talbot la gloire de sa classe.'

Château Beychevelle, the residence of M. Achille Fould, is a very charming house in a delightful setting. It stands on the site of the Château of the hereditary Grand Admirals of France whom ships had to salute by lowering their sails as they passed by on their way to or from Bordeaux. Beychevelle also had, until recent times, a port of its own on the Gironde, but it became silted up and its place was taken by the port of Pauillac, a little farther downstream. The Commune of Beychevelle lost much of its former importance when it lost its port, and it was eventually merged with its neighbour Saint-Julien, the full administrative name of which is Saint-Julien-Beychevelle.

There are, surprisingly enough, only two *Bourgeois Supérieurs* with an average aggregate production of 208 *tonneaux* of very fair red wine – Château du Glana (200 *tonneaux*) and Bontemps-Dubarry (8 *tonneaux*). The *Crus Bourgeois* and *Artisans* of the Commune produce some 250 *tonneaux* of the more *ordinaires* St Julien red wines. The only St Julien white wine is that of Château Sirène-Langrange (10 *tonneaux*).

## PAUILLAC (48 km. n.n.w. Bordeaux)

Pauillac is a more important village, almost a town, with nearly 6,000 inhabitants and a port which is second only to Bordeaux. Although its name has nothing like the world-wide popularity of St Julien and St Estèphe, the two Communes immediately to the south and to the north of Pauillac, it is the only Commune of the Haut-Médoc with two *Premiers Crus*, Lafite and Latour, besides the first of the *Deuxièmes Crus*, Château Mouton-Rothschild, which is today the peer of the *Premiers Crus*.

Château Lafite, or Lafite-Rothschild to give it its full name, is one of the oldest of the Châteaux du Médoc, and its wines have on numerous occasions been placed ahead of all others. Lafite 1864, for instance, was quite outstanding for fully half a century, and it outlived all the other great wines of that great vintage. As late as the early thirties, when it was very nearly seventy years old, Lafite 1864 was wonderful: it was still fresh, soft and sweet, and its exquisite bouquet made one pause and wonder whether there is any age limit to a really great claret. The Lafite 1869 was not so well known as the '64; there was very much less of it, but it was an astounding wine. We had a bottle of it given to us by Dr O. W. Loeb for our golden wedding, in October 1950, straight from the Château. We gave it a long rest and drank it in 1954: it was incredibly good! Not merely alive but lively; ruby red, not pink; fairly sweet still; very smooth, gentle and charming, its bouquet discreet but intensely clean, without any trace of 'dead leaves' not objectionable in very old wines, but a warning that the end is at hand!

Lafite 1870 also lasted almost 'for ever', but it was always somewhat hard. It had more power than grace, so unlike all other Lafites of that generation that one could not help identifying it at once. But I failed to do so, once. It was in 1932, at Wistler's Wood, when we were the guests of Gus Mayer. He gave us a bottle of Lafite 1870, not Château bottled, but bottled at Bordeaux by Nathaniel Johnston. It was perfect, so free from tannin, and so gracious, that I believed then and still believe now that it had been 'cut' or blended with the Lafite 1871, which was a honeyed wine.

After phylloxera and the replanting of the Lafite vineyards, there was no Château bottling granted from 1885 to 1905, in spite of the fact that Lafite 1895 was by far the best wine of the year. Lafite 1899 and 1900 were also two very good wines, although Latour, Margaux and Mouton were even better. In more recent years, Château Lafite 1924s and 1953s have been quite outstanding and voted the best of their vintage. The average yield of Lafite is 200 *tonneaux*.

Château Latour, with an average production of 250 *tonneaux*, is the other *Premier Cru Classé* of Pauillac. Its wines are extremely reliable, either the best or second best of the year, and never disappointing. The Latour 1878, 1899 and 1920 were distinctly finer wines than all others, but in my own experience, whenever any other *Premier* or *Deuxième Cru* is given first place, Latour is always very near the top.

Mouton was placed at the top of the *Deuxièmes Crus* in the 1855 Classification, but such care has been taken of its vineyards and of its wines that it would certainly be placed among the *Premiers Crus* today. The fact that ever since 1929 the wines of Château Mouton-Rothschild have always fetched in the open market the same price as, or a higher price than, the wines of the *Premiers Crus* of the same vintage is sufficient evidence of its excellence. Its average annual yield is 250 *tonneaux*.

There are, in Pauillac, two other *Deuxièmes Crus*, Châteaux Pichon-Longueville (100 *tonneaux*) and Pichon-Longueville-Comtesse de Lalande[1] (160 *tonneaux*). Also one *Quatrième Cru*, Château Duhart-Milon (140 *tonneaux*), and ten *Cinquièmes Crus*: Châteaux Pontet-Canet (400 *tonneaux*), the property and the summer residence of the Cruse family; Bateilley (200 *tonneaux*); Haut-Batailley (70 *tonneaux*); Grand-Puy-Ducasse (40 *tonneaux*); Grand-Puy-Lacoste (100 *tonneaux*); Lynch-Bages (200 *tonneaux*); Mouton Baron Philippe (so renamed in 1963) (150 *tonneaux*); Croizet-Bages (60 *tonneaux*); Pédesclaux (60 *tonneaux*); and Clerc-Milon-Mondon (50 *tonneaux*).

There are in the commune of Pauillac nineteen *Crus Bourgeois Supérieurs* with an aggregate production of 700 *tonneaux* of fine red wines. The *Crus Bourgeois* and *Artisans* are responsible for 1,000 *tonneaux* of more *ordinaires* wines, which are mostly sold under the name of *Grand Vin La Rose Pauillac, Haut-Médoc*, a name registered by the *Co-opérative de Propriétaires Viticulteurs de Pauillac*.

SAINT-SAUVEUR (6 km. w. Pauillac)
There are in this Commune three *Crus Bourgeois Supérieurs*. Châteaux Fontestau (60 *tonneaux*), Liversan (70 *tonneaux*) and Peyrabon (200 *tonneaux*); and on average of 300 *tonneaux* of more *ordinaires* red wines from *Crus Bourgeois* and *Artisans* which are mostly made, handled and sold by the *Co-opérative de Saint-Sauveur Haut-Médoc*.

CISSAC (55 km. n.n.w. Bordeaux)
The *Cave Co-opérative de Cissac-Haut-Médoc* handles the grapes of some 80 small *vignerons* of the Commune at the Château Cissac, the residence of M. and Mme Louis Vialard.

SAINT-ESTÉPHE (57 km. n.n.w. Bordeaux)
The Commune of Saint-Estèphe is one of the four most important wine-producing Communes of the Haut-Médoc. Its wines have a distinctive character of their own, rather more weight than those of Saint-Julien or Margaux, and an earthier bouquet.

There are in the Commune of Saint-Estèphe two *Deuxièmes Crus*, Châteaux Cos d'Estournel (200 *tonneaux*) and Montrose (240 *tonneaux*); one *Troisième Cru*, Château Calon-Ségur (200 *tonneaux*); one *Quatrième Cru*, Château Rochet (100 *tonneaux*) and one *Cinquième Cru*, Château Cos-Labory (40 *tonneaux*).

There are also no less than 30 *Crus Bourgeois Supérieurs*, the aggregate production of which averages 1,850 *tonneaux*. The *Cave Co-opérative de Saint-Estèphe* handles the grapes and wines of about 140 small *vignerons*, an average of some 560 *tonneaux* in all.

[1] This Château has been given the *appellation contrôlée* 'Saint-Julien'.

VERTHEUIL (56 km. n.n.w. Bordeaux)

The *Crus Bourgeois* and *Artisans* of this Commune produce 500 *tonneaux* of red wine. The only white wine of Vertheuil, Château Reysson, averages 10 *tonneaux*. *The Cave Co-opérative de Vertheuil* handles the grapes and wines of about 60 small *vignerons*.

SAINT-SEURIN-DE-CADOURNE (13 km. Pauillac)

The northernmost Commune of the Haut-Médoc, 13 km. from both Lesparre and Pauillac. Its *Crus Bourgeois* and *Artisans* produce 1,000 *tonneaux* of wine. The *Cave Co-opérative de Saint-Seurin-de-Cadourne* handles the grapes and wines of about 60 small *vignerons*; their wines are sold under the registered name of *La-Paroisse-Saint-Seurin-Haut-Médoc*.

## Médoc (*formerly called Bas-Médoc*)

Beyond Saint-Seurin-de-Cadourne, as one proceeds farther north and west, there are twenty-one other Communes between the lower course of the Gironde and the Bay of Biscay, with vineyards which are capable of producing 16,700 *tonneaux* of wine, mostly red wine, each year. None of the wines of the 'Médoc' vineyards is of outstanding excellence, and the only *appellation contrôlée* to which they are entitled is plain *Médoc*. There are wines of this part of the Bordeaux country, however, which are distinctly better than the rest, owing to the greater care given both to the growing of the grapes and the making of the wine. Such are the wines of the following Châteaux:

Du Castéra (Private Society): 150 *tonneaux* red and 125 *tonneaux* white wines.
Laujac (Cruse Fils Frères): 50 *tonneaux* red wine.
Livran (James Denman & Co.): 150 *tonneaux* red and 50 *tonneaux* white wines.
Loudenne (W. & A. Gilbey & Co.): 125 *tonneaux* red wine.

*Château Saint-Brice* and *Château Bégadan-Médoc* are registered labels used, the first for the wines of the *Cave Co-opérative de Saint-Yzans*, and the second for those of the *Cave Co-opérative de Bégadan*.

## Bourg and Blaye

Across the broad waters of the Gironde, facing the Médoc, the vineyards of Bourg and Blaye produce an average of 73,000 *tonneaux* of red and white wines, of which about 5,500 *tonneaux* are red wines of fair quality, the peers of the *Crus Bourgeois du Médoc*, while 31,000 *tonneaux* are more ordinary red wines, and 36,500 *tonneaux* are white wines, most acceptable wines, of course, but not remarkable. None but the better wines of both Bourg and Blaye vineyards are entitled to be sold either as *Côtes de Bourg* or *Premières Côtes de Blaye*, provided their strength is not inferior to 10·5° of alcohol.

In the Bourg district the more highly prized wines are those from Châteaux du Bosquet, Tayac, Falfas and Rousset. Another favourite is Château Mille Secousses, a showplace of some 250 acres, mostly alongside the right bank of the Gironde.

In the Blayais the more highly prized wines are those of Châteaux Charron and La Barre, in the parish of Saint-Martin; Château Bellevue, at Plassac; Châteaux Saugeron, Le Cone Taillasson and Cap-de-Haut, at Blaye; Château Les Alberts, at Mazion; Château Les Fours, at Fours; and Château La Tour-Gayet, at Saint-Androny.

To the east of Bourg and Blaye, the vineyards of the Cubzac district – or Cubzagais – produce an average of 5,000 *tonneaux* of red wines and 3,500 *tonneaux* of white wines every year, none better known than those of Château de Terrefort, the average yield of its vineyards being 300 *tonneaux* of red and 30 *tonneaux* of white wines. The red wines of the Cubzagais are entitled to the *appellation contrôlée* 'Bordeaux' when their strength is not less than 9·75° of alcohol, and 'Bordeaux Supérieur' when it reaches 10°. The white wines of the Cubzagais can claim to be 'Bordeaux Blanc' only when they reach 10·5° and 'Bordeaux Blanc Supérieur' with an 11·5° alcoholic strength.

## The Garonne

The Garonne is one of the great rivers of France, as every Frenchman knows, and the finest river in the world to all true *Bordelais*. The Garonne rises at the foot of the Maladetta, the highest of the mountains of the Pyrenees range, and it flows in a north-westerly direction through the Départements of the Haute-Garonne, Tarn-et-Garonne and Lot-et-Garonne, before entering the Département of La Gironde, which it crosses until it reaches Bordeaux, where it ceases to be a very ordinary river, in no way different from many other quite ordinary rivers. It develops greater width and depth, real majesty and grace, at the same time taking upon itself the very modern air and activity of a busy rendezvous of the merchant seamen of the world. Some 15 miles from Bordeaux, the Garonne meets the Dordogne, when the two become the Gironde.

During the whole of its course through the Département of the Gironde, with the exception of its passage through Bordeaux, the Garonne flows through vinelands, many of which produce some of the best and most famous of all red and white table wines, wines which may well be divided into three main sections: (1) Graves; (2) Sauternes and Barsac; (3) Cérons, Loupiac and Premières Côtes de Bordeaux.

### Graves

The vineyards of the district known as Les Graves or Graves de Bordeaux, on account of their gravelly soil or subsoil, are dotted along the left bank of the Garonne for some 12½ miles in length and 5 miles in width, from Blanquefort southwards.

The Graves vineyards produce a greater quantity of red wines, or claret, than white wines, in spite of the unshakable belief throughout the English-speaking world that a *Vin de Graves* invariably means a white wine. What is of much greater importance is the fact that a fair proportion of the red Graves wines, of which the average annual production is over 9,000 *tonneaux*, are wines of very high quality, some of them the peers of the finest red wines of the Médoc, whereas only a very small proportion of white Graves, of which the average annual production is below 6,000 *tonneaux*, has any claim to rank among the great table wines such as the best white wines of the Rhine or of Burgundy.

According to the ruling of the *appellations contrôlées* authorities, there are two qualities of *Vins de Graves*, depending upon their alcoholic strength: plain *Graves*, if their alcoholic strength is not less than 10° but under 12°; and *Graves Supérieures*, when their alcoholic strength reaches 12° or is higher than 12°. Besides their alcoholic strength, both *Graves* and *Graves Supérieures*, whether red or white, must be wines from grapes grown within the boundaries of one or the other of the only thirty-six Communes recognized as belonging to the *Graves de Bordeaux* district. A list of these Communes, given in alphabetical order for the sake of quicker reference, follows. Their geographical position will be seen on the map of Bordeaux on pages 30–31.

## Appellation d'Origine Contrôlée 'Graves'

### Crus classés by the Institut National des Appellations d'Origine

RED WINES

CADAUJAC: Château Bouscaut.
LÉOGNAN: Ch. Haut-Bailly, Ch. Carbonnieux, Dom. de Chevalier, Ch. Malartic-Lagravière, Ch. Olivier, Ch. de Fieuzal.
MARTILLAC: Ch. La Tour, Ch. Smith-Haut-Lafitte.
PESSAC: Ch. Haut-Brion, Ch. Pape Clément.
TALENCE: Ch. La Mission-Haut-Brion, Ch. La Tour-Haut-Brion.

WHITE WINES

CADAUJAC: Château Bouscaut.
LÉOGNAN: Ch. Carbonnieux, Ch. Chevalier, Ch. Olivier, Ch. Malartic-Lagravière.
TALENCE: Château La Ville-Haut-Brion.
VILLENAVE D'ORNON: Château Couhins.
MARTILLAC: Château La Tour.

## Communes of 'Les Graves'

| | Optimum output per annum in tonneaux | | | Optimum output per annum in tonneaux | |
|---|---|---|---|---|---|
| | RED WINE | WHITE WINE | | RED WINE | WHITE WINE |
| Arbanats | 250 | 300 | Mérignac | 70 | — |
| Aiguemorte-les-Graves | 250 | 50 | *Pessac | 350 | 8 |
| *Beautiran | 550 | 35 | Portets | 1,700 | 100 |
| *Bègles | 30 | — | Pujols-sur-Ciron | — | 650 |
| Budos | 100 | 200 | Roaillan | 50 | 250 |
| Cabanac-Villagrains | 25 | 100 | Saint-Médard d'Eyrans | 85 | 100 |
| *Cadaujac | 500 | 60 | Saint-Michel de Rieufret | 20 | 10 |
| Canejan | 50 | — | Saint-Morillon | 40 | 400 |
| Castres | 200 | 180 | Saint-Pardon | 40 | 30 |
| Cestas | 35 | — | Saint-Pierre de Mons (or St-Pey de Langon) | 150 | 500 |
| Eysines | 250 | — | | | |
| *Gradignan | 150 | 25 | Saint-Selve | 120 | 350 |
| Isle Saint-Georges | 1,350 | — | Saucats | 70 | 100 |
| La Brède | 250 | 250 | *Talence | 150 | 15 |
| Landiras | 150 | 450 | Toulenne | 100 | 200 |
| Langon | 200 | 450 | *Villenave d'Ornon | 600 | 15 |
| Léogeats | 50 | 50 | Virelade | 200 | 250 |
| *Léognan | 600 | 330 | | 9,185 | 5,728 |
| *Martillac | 350 | 70 | | | |
| Mazères | 100 | 200 | | | |

* indicates Communes producing the best Graves wines.

## (a) Red Wines

The wines of Graves have not been officially graded as the red wines of the Médoc and the white wines of Sauternes were 'classified' in 1855. The only red Graves which was included in the 1855 'Classification' was Château Haut-Brion, which was given a place among the *Premiers Crus Classés* of the Médoc, Lafite, Latour and Margaux.

The production of red wines of the Graves vineyards is much smaller than that of the vineyards of the Haut-Médoc, and the proportion of fine wines is also smaller, probably not more than 11% of the total, which represents roughly 1,000 *tonneaux* of red wines comparable in quality to those of the *Crus Classés*, *Crus Exceptionnels* and *Crus Bourgeois Supérieurs* of the Haut-Médoc.

No Château of the Médoc has a more illustrious lineage or a finer wine tradition than Château Haut-Brion. It was bought in 1837 by a Monsieur Larrieu, in whose family it remained until 1922. Under what may be called the Larrieu dynasty, the red wine of Haut-Brion was second to none and often the best of all. All who had, as I had, the privilege of enjoying the Haut-Brion 1864, 1865, 1868, 1874 and, above all, 1871 and 1875, and later 1893, 1899, 1900 and 1906, can never forget their exquisite delicacy and charm; there never was any better red table wine. Then came the tragedy of a change of ownership. M. André Gibert bought Haut-Brion in 1922, and the Haut-Brion 1923 was the last great Haut-Brion for twenty years! It was during this unhappy period that white grapes were planted at Haut-Brion and there has been ever since a white Haut-Brion, just one more white Graves wine, a wine that has no faults and no real appeal, neither sweet nor dry; quite good, of course, but not great.

Happily, Haut-Brion has now new masters, with both the resources and the will to make again wines really worthy of the proud name of Haut-Brion.

In the following list, first place has been given to the half-dozen Graves wines which I happen to like best, and then, in alphabetic order, the names of two dozen of the better-known Châteaux of the Graves de Bordeaux producing red wines, ranging from fair to very fine in quality:

| | *Optimum output per annum in tonneaux* | | *Optimum output per annum in tonneaux* |
|---|---|---|---|
| Château Haut-Brion, *Pessac* | 150 | Château La Garde, *Martillac* | 100 |
| Domaine de Chevalier, *Léognan* | 30 | Château La Louvière, *Léognan* | 85 |
| Château Haut-Bailly, *Léognan* | 60 | Château Larrivet-Haut-Brion, *Léognan* | 30 |
| Château La Mission-Haut-Brion, *Talence* | 80 | Château La Tour Haut-Brion, *Talence* | 18 |
| Château Pape Clément, *Pessac* | 100 | Château La Tour Martillac et Kress- | |
| Château Smith-Haut-Lafitte, *Martillac* | 200 | mann-La-Tour, *Martillac* | 40 |
| Château Baret, *Villenave d'Ornon* | 18 | Château Le Pape, *Léognan* | 15 |
| Château Bouscaut, *Cadaujac* | 100 | Château Malartic-Lagravière, *Léognan* | 50 |
| Château Carbonnieux, *Léognan* | 80 | Château Olivier, *Léognan* | 20 |
| Château-Neuf, *Léognan* | 20 | Château Poumey, *Gradignan* | 20 |
| Château de Hilde, *Bègles* | 70 | Château du Tuquèt, *Beautiran* | 75 |
| Château les Carmes-Haut-Brion, *Pessac* | 15 | Château Valoux, *Cadaujac* | 18 |
| Château Fieuzal, *Léognan* | 30 | | |

## (b) White Wines

The white wines of the Graves vineyards are of two sorts, the dry and the sweet; the dry wines being only fairly dry, never possessing the so clean finish of a genuine Chablis, for instance, and the sweet wines only fairly sweet, lighter of body, but not nearly so luscious as any of the fine Sauternes. Many of the white Graves are very pleasing wines indeed, but they are not endowed with any great character or outstanding personality which would make it possible even if it were fair to sell them at anything like the same prices as an Yquem or a Montrachet. The difference between good wines and great wines is that the first must of necessity be good value to be acceptable, whereas the great wines are so rare and so good that their cost does not matter so much, as there are always a few people who must have them, cost what they may. There are great wines among the red Graves, but not among the white, which belong, even the best of them, to the category of 'good' wines. All 'good' wines should be reasonably priced that they may be enjoyed by the many sensible people who, be they rich or not, expect to have their money's worth. This is why the majority of the white Graves are not sold under the name of the vineyard or the date or vintage of their birth, but under a registered trade mark and undated. They are mostly blends of white wines from different Graves vineyards, as well as of different years, the better wines of the better years bringing up the standard of quality of the wines of the less favoured vintages. The Bordeaux shippers responsible for such blends are thus able to offer white Graves of the same type and quality year after year, and at much the same price, irrespective of ups and downs – mostly ups – of market quotations.

There are, however, many dry white Graves which are sold under the names of their individual vineyards; they possess greater individuality and, when made in a good vintage year, they are superior to as well as dearer than the blends. Here is a list of some such white Graves, a small list selected on account of their greater popularity, sometimes the recognition of finer quality and sometimes also the reward of abler salesmanship.

| | *Optimum output per annum in tonneaux* | | *Optimum output per annum in tonneaux* |
|---|---|---|---|
| Château Baret, *Villenave d'Ornon* | 20 | Château Haut-Nouchet, *Martillac* | 10 |
| Château Bouscaut, *Cadaujac* | 20 | Château La Tour, *Léognan* | 10 |
| Château Cantebau-Couhins, *Villenave d'Ornon* | 10 | Château La Tour Martillac et Kressmann-La-Tour, *Martillac* | 15 |
| Château Carbonnieux, *Léognan* | 80 | Château Laville Haut-Brion, *Talence* | 22 |
| Château Chevalier, *Léognan* | 15 | Château Le Désert, *Léognan* | 10 |
| Château Couhins, *Villenave d'Ornon* | 30 | Château Le Pape, *Léognan* | 10 |
| Domaine de Grandmaison, *Léognan* | 5 | Château Malleprat, *Martillac* | 15 |
| Château de la Brède, *La Brède* | 16 | Château Olivier, *Léognan* | 100 |
| Château de Respide, *St Pierre de Mons* | 100 | Château Poumey, *Gradignan* | 10 |
| Château Ferran, *Martillac* | 10 | Château du Tuquet, *Beautiran* | 75 |
| Château Ferrande, *Castres* | 50 | Château de Virelade, *Virelade* | 10 |
| Château Fieuzal, *Léognan* | 15 | | |

## Sauternes and Barsac

*Sauternes* is the name given to one of the greatest white wines of the world by one of the smallest of the Communes or parishes of the Gironde Département, some 20 miles to the south of Bordeaux, four miles west of the Garonne, beyond Barsac and the little River Ciron.

Sauternes is a sweet white wine, different from and superior to other sweet white wines. It is made from white grapes grown in the vineyards of the Commune of Sauternes and from those of the four adjoining Communes of Bommes, Barsac, Preignac and Fargues. The excellence and characteristic features of the white wines known as Sauternes are due in the first place to the nature of the soil and subsoil of those five Communes, and in the second to the manner in which the grapes are picked at the vintage time, and pressed. When the Sauternes grapes are ripe they are not picked but allowed to 'rot', and although theirs may be a 'noble rot', *la pourriture noble*, it is none the less a form of rot which is brought about by a peculiar mould known as *botrytis cinerea*, a parasite which, like all parasites, lives at the expense of its host. Its fine rootlets pierce the tender golden skin of the ripe grapes, thirsting for the moisture within: the grapes lose their shape and colour, as their juice loses some of its water, hence the greater proportion of sugar to water which is responsible for the sweetness of the wine eventually. Besides this greater concentration of grape sugar, the intervention of the *botrytis cinerea* is responsible for quite minute yet most important changes in the constitution of the grape-juice, and it is to these changes that the wines of Sauternes owe, besides their sweetness, their characteristic individuality.

The *botrytis cinerea* settles upon the Sauternes grapes when they are ripe, but in so haphazard a fashion that, at the vintage time, there are in every bunch of grapes some 'sound' golden berries, which have so far been overlooked by the *botrytis*; others covered with a dust of spores, which have got a hold but are not yet at work; while some berries, those upon which the *botrytis* settled first and has got busy, are shrunk and shrivelled, brown and unappetizing. They are the best, the 'nobly rotted' berries, more rotten than noble to look at, but the only ones that the long, sharp-pointed scissors of the pickers will seek and cut off. During the next six or seven weeks, according to the weather, the same pickers will return to the same bunches in search of any more berries which may have become fit for the press. In the end, when fogs and frosts are threatening, all bunches are picked, whatever the condition may be of the few berries left on them, but the wine which is pressed from them is kept apart, it is very different from the *Tête de Cuvée*, that is the wine made from the pickings of chosen overripe grapes.

Barsac is one of the more important and one of the best-known Communes of the Gironde Département. It lies between the Garonne, to the east, and its tributary, the Ciron, to the south; with the Graves country both to the north and west. Its vineyards produce very large quantities of fairly sweet white wines, probably more than half of those that are sold as plain 'Sauternes', besides those sold as 'Barsac'. This is because Barsac has long been wedded to Sauternes, on the other side of the Ciron, but has not given up its own or maiden name; it is thus legally entitled to sell under either name the less distinguished of its wines. 'Haut-Barsac' is the name given to blends of white wines from those vineyards of the Barsac Commune which are farther away from the Garonne. Of course, all the finer wines of Barsac always bear the name of the Château or estate of their birth, and although they may look just the same as the anonymous blends, their bouquet, flavour, breed and appeal are altogether different.

In 1855, when the best wines of the Médoc were graded in five classes, the best white wines of the five Sauternes Communes were also graded in First and Second Growths, with Château d'Yquem in a class by itself ahead of the First Growths. The *Premiers* and the *Deuxièmes Crus Classés de Sauternes*, and their average production of white wines, are distributed among the five Communes of Sauternes, Bommes, Barsac, Preignac and Fargues as follows:

| | *Optimum output per annum in tonneaux* | | *Optimum output per annum in tonneaux* |
|---|---|---|---|
| SAUTERNES | | BARSAC (*contd.*) | |
| Château d'Yquem, *Premier Grand Cru* | 100 | Château Doisy-Védrines, *Deuxième Cru* | 80 |
| Château Guiraud, *Premier Cru* | 80 | Château Doisy-Daëne, *Deuxième Cru* | 20 |
| Château Filhot, *Deuxième Cru* | 50 | Château Doisy-Dubroca, *Deuxième Cru* | 50 |
| Château d'Arche, *Deuxième Cru* | 25 | Château Myrat, *Deuxième Cru* | 50 |
| Château Lamothe, *Deuxième Cru* | 25 | Château Broustet, *Deuxième Cru* | 30 |
| Château d'Arche-Lafaurie, *Deuxième Cru* | 35 | Château Caillou, *Deuxième Cru* | 50 |
| Château Lamothe-Bergey, *Deuxième Cru* | 20 | Château Suau, *Deuxième Cru* | 15 |
| Crus Bourgeois Supérieurs | 75 | Château Nairac, *Deuxième Cru* | 25 |
| Crus Bourgeois et Crus Artisans | 100 | Crus Bourgeois Supérieurs | 713 |
| | —— 510 | Crus Bourgeois et Crus Artisans | 350 |
| | | | —— 1,488 |
| BOMMES | | | |
| Château La Tour Blanche, *Premier Cru* | 90 | PREIGNAC | |
| Château Lafaurie-Peyraguey, *Premier Cru* | 60 | Château de Suduiraut, *Premier Cru* | 100 |
| Château de Rayne-Vigneau, *Premier Cru* | 100 | Château de Malle, *Deuxième Cru* | 40 |
| Château Rabaud, *Premier Cru* | 75 | Crus Bourgeois Supérieurs | 720 |
| Cru Haut-Peyraguey, *Premier Cru* | 30 | Crus Bourgeois et Crus Artisans | 250 |
| Crus Bourgeois Supérieurs | 80 | | —— 1,110 |
| Crus Bourgeois et Artisans Supérieurs | 15 | | |
| | —— 450 | FARGUES | |
| | | Château Rieussec, *Premier Cru* | 100 |
| BARSAC | | Château Romer, *Deuxième Cru* | 15 |
| Château Coutet, *Premier Cru* | 60 | Crus Bourgeois et Artisans | 150 |
| Château Climens, *Premier Cru* | 45 | | —— 265 |
| | | Total (*tonneaux*) | 3,783 |

Some 1½ miles to the east-north-east of Sauternes the Commune of Saint-Pierre-de-Mons, also known as Saint-Pey-de-Langon, half a mile to the east of Langon, on the left bank of the River Garonne, produces some quite ordinary red wines and about 500 *tonneaux* per annum of very fair white wines, some of them not unlike the white wines of Sauternes, although the only *appellation contrôlée* to which they are entitled is that of 'Graves Supérieures'. The best estate of this Commune is Château de Respide, with an average annual production of 100 *tonneaux* of good white wines.

## *Cérons, Loupiac and Premières Côtes de Bordeaux*

There are many other vineyards in the valley of the Garonne, above Bordeaux, which produce a fair quantity of red wines which are by no means remarkable, and a great deal more white wines of much greater merit.

On the left bank of the Garonne, 22 miles south of Bordeaux, immediately north of Barsac, there are three Communes which occupy a small plateau and are called Cérons,

Podensac and Illats. Their vineyards produce on an average 200 *tonneaux* of white wines, some of them fairly dry, more like the white Graves wines, and others distinctly sweet, more like those of nearby Barsac, and all of them are entitled to the *appellation contrôlée* 'Cérons'. Château de Cérons et Calvimont is one of the finest estates of this district.

On the right bank of the Garonne, 27 miles s.s.e. of Bordeaux, facing Langon and the Sauternes country beyond, the Commune of Sainte-Croix-du-Mont produces both red and white wines, but it is chiefly noted for the high quality of its rich white wines, the annual production of which reaches 1,500 *tonneaux*. The more renowned of the vineyards of Sainte-Croix-du-Mont are the Châteaux de Taste, Loubens, Lamarque, Lafue, La Mouleyre and Laurette.

Loupiac, immediately to the north of Sainte-Croix-du-Mont, facing Barsac on the other side of the Garonne, produces some 1,200 *tonneaux* of very fair white wines per annum, as well as a good deal of undistinguished red wines. None but the better white wines of Loupiac are entitled to the *appellation contrôlée* 'Loupiac'. The finest estate of Loupiac is Château de Ricaud, with an average annual production of 125 *tonneaux* of good white wines.

*Premières Côtes de Bordeaux* is an *appellation contrôlée* to which are entitled both the red and the white wines from the vineyards of 34 other Communes of the right bank of the Garonne, from Bordeaux to Verdelais, Saint-Maixant, Gabarnac and Saint-Germain-de-Grave, nearly 33 miles s.s.e. of Bordeaux. Their vineyards produce on an average 16,000 *tonneaux* of red wines and 17,000 *tonneaux* of white wines per annum.

## *The Dordogne*

The Dordogne is one of the fairest of the great rivers of France. It owes its name to two small rivers of the Mont Dore, La Dore and La Dogne, which meet and flow together in a westerly direction for some 300 miles, never for long out of sight of some vineyards, until they reach the Bec d'Ambès, where they join the Garonne and become the Gironde. During nearly half its course, the Dordogne meanders in a lazy fashion across the Gironde Département, with the many vineyards of Saint-Emilion and Pomerol to its right, and the even more numerous vineyards of the Entre-Deux-Mers to the left, that is mostly southwards.

The two more important cities on the Dordogne within the boundaries of the Gironde Département are Libourne and Castillon. Libourne, at the junction of the Dordogne and L'Isle, is, after Bordeaux, the most important wine mart of the Gironde Département. It was a flourishing town, called Caudate, during the Roman occupation, and it was rebuilt in 1286 by Edward I's *Seneschal*, Roger Leyburn, whose name it bears to this day. Castillon, a busy and pleasant little market town today, used to be one of the chief military outposts of Guyenne, and it was there that Talbot was defeated and killed in 1453.

Between the two rivers the Dordogne and the Isle, there is a cluster of vine-clad hills, and it is on top of one of these, the one that is nearest to Libourne, that the quaint old city of Saint-Emilion is perched. Its steep cobbled streets, its sun-tanned gabled houses and its ruined cloisters huddle around its very ancient and truly remarkable monolith church, hewn out of the living rock, over which was built some centuries later the great spire that is such a landmark for many miles.

## Saint-Emilion

The wines of Saint-Emilion are all red wines, deep, dark, true red, not blood-red, and without any trace of mauve or tawny twilight in their bright purple. The greatest wines of Saint-Emilion are the peers of the greatest Médoc and Graves clarets, but there are very few of them. The great majority of the wines of Saint-Emilion may not have the distinction or 'breed' of the great Médoc wines; they may lack something of the suave charm of the greatest red Graves wines; but they possess in an exceptional degree such obvious plain honest-to-God goodness that we immediately welcome them as friends that will never let us down or lay us low.

Besides the vineyards of the Commune of Saint-Emilion itself, those of five other Communes, immediately to the north, west, east and south of the quaint old city of Saint-Emilion, produce large quantities of red wines, which are entitled to the *appellation contrôlée* 'Saint-Emilion'. All the best wines, however, are known as '*Premiers Crus*', and they come from named vineyards of the Saint-Emilion Commune. Locally, as well as among the Bordeaux merchants, there is a distinction made between the wines from those vineyards which are closer to the city of Saint-Emilion, and the others which are half-way on the road to Pomerol: the first are called *Vins de Côtes*: they are upon higher and more stony ground; the others are called *Vins de Graves*: they are upon the lower, more gravelly and deeper soil.

We may well wonder why the 1855 Classification completely ignores the great wines of Saint-Emilion and Pomerol, the Ausone, Cheval Blanc and Petrus to name but three whose good vintages fetch in the open market prices just as high as, and often higher than, those paid for most classed growths of the Médoc. And it is likewise rather puzzling to find Haut-Brion among the First Growths but no other red Graves deemed worthy to be placed in any of the other four groups. The answer is that the red wines of Graves, Saint-Emilion and Pomerol were not enjoying, a hundred years ago, anything like the popularity which we consider to be their due today. There cannot be any doubt of this lack of appreciation, since the prices paid at the time for the wines of Graves and Saint-Emilion – there was no mention of Pomerol – are a mere fraction of the prices paid for those of the Médoc. I do not believe that there was ever anything like a corresponding difference in the quality of the wines themselves. If the wines of Graves and Saint-Emilion were in such poor demand during the first half of the last century that the Bordeaux brokers ignored them completely in 1855, and if those same wines are today enjoying a vogue far greater than they did only fifty years ago, I am inclined to blame fickle fashion. The soil of the vineyards and their grapes have been the same all the time, so that there cannot have been such an extraordinary change in the quality of the wines. They must have been grossly underrated in the past, and many of them are certainly overrated, or at any rate over-priced, today. Here is a list of the highest prices paid *de première main* before 1855 with prices given in francs per *tonneaux*:

|  | 1825 | 1830 | 1835 | 1840 | 1844 |
|---|---|---|---|---|---|
| *Premiers Crus* | 5,000 | 2,400 | 1,600 | 2,500 | 4,500 |
| *Deuxièmes Crus* | 4,200 | 2,000 | 1,200 | 1,100 | 2,800 |
| *Troisièmes Crus* | 2,400 | 1,400 | 1,000 | 850 | 2,400 |
| *Quatrièmes Crus* | 1,800 | 900 | 800 | 700 | 1,800 |
| *Cinquièmes Crus* | 1,100 | 700 | 600 | 550 | 1,300 |
| *Bourgeois Supérieurs* | 800 | 500 | 350 | 450 | 900 |

|                   | 1825  | 1830 | 1835 | 1840 | 1844 |
|-------------------|-------|------|------|------|------|
| Petits Bourgeois  | 600   | 400  | 280  | 280  | 600  |
| Bas-Médoc         | 450   | 550  | 200  | 180  | 350  |
| Graves            | 1,200 | 500  | 450  | 400  | 700  |
| Saint-Emilion     | 800   | 600  | 250  | 350  | 600  |
| Palus             | 550   | 400  | 180  | 230  | 300  |
| Côtes             | 380   | 350  | 150  | 180  | 260  |

(Wm. Franck: *Traité sur les Vins du Médoc*, 3rd ed.; Bordeaux, 1853.)

In the following pages the best growths of Saint-Emilion have been listed separately as *Vins de Côtes* and *Vins de Graves*. Two asterisks show those of the *Premiers Grand Crus Classés* and one marks those of the *Grandes Crus Classés*, according to the official Classification of the 16 June 1955, by the Institut National des Appellations d'Origine.

## Saint-Emilion – Vins de Côtes

| | Optimum output per annum in tonneaux | | Optimum output per annum in tonneaux |
|---|---|---|---|
| **PREMIER GRAND CRU** | | *Château Franc-Mayne | 30 |
| **Château Ausone | 25 | Château Franc-Pourret | 35 |
| | | Domaine du Grand-Faurie | 20 |
| **PREMIERS CRUS** | | *Château Grand-Mayne | 60 |
| *Clos de l'Angélus | 130 | *Château Grand-Pontet | 50 |
| Château Baleau | 80 | *Château Grandes Murailles | 10 |
| *Château Balestard-La-Tonnelle | 60 | *Château Guadet-Saint-Julien | 16 |
| Château Beau-Mazerat | 20 | Château Gueyrot | 41 |
| **Château Beauséjour (Duffau-Lagarosse) | 25 | Château Haut-Cadet | 25 |
| | | Château Haut-Pontet | 25 |
| **Château Beauséjour (Dr. Fagouet) | 40 | Château Haut-Simard | 30 |
| **Château Bélair | 40 | Château Haut-Trimoulet | 10 |
| *Château Bellevue | 30 | *Clos des Jacobins | 40 |
| *Château Bergat | 15 | *Château La Carte | 35 |
| Château Berliquet | 35 | *Château La Clotte | 16 |
| Château Bragard | 40 | Château La Clotte-Grand-Côte | 10 |
| *Château Cadet-Bon | 25 | *Château La Cluzière | 15 |
| Château Cadet-Peychez | 5 | *Château La Couspaude | 30 |
| *Château Cadet-Piola | 20 | Château La Fleur | 40 |
| **Château Canon | 75 | **Château La Gaffelière-Naudes | 100 |
| *Château Canon-La-Gaffelière | 100 | *Clos La Madeleine | 10 |
| Château Cantenac | 40 | Clos de la Magdeleine | 6 |
| *Château Cap-de-Mourlin | 75 | Château Laniote | 30 |
| Château Cardinal-Villemaurine | 40 | *Château Larmande | 45 |
| Château Cassevert | 20 | *Château Laroze | 100 |
| *Château Chapelle-Madeleine | 30 | Château l'Arrosée | 50 |
| Château Côte-Daugay-ex-Madeleine | 12 | *Château La Serre | 35 |
| *Château Coutet | 50 | Château La Tour-du-Guetteur | 3 |
| *Château Curé-Bon-La-Madeleine | 25 | Château La Tour-Saint-Emilion | 10 |
| *Château Faurie-de-Soutard | 50 | Château Le Couvent | 5 |
| *Château Fonplégade | 50 | *Château Le Prieuré-Saint-Emilion | 16 |
| **Clos Fourtet | 60 | Château l'Hermitage de Mazérat | 30 |

Plate 7. The *vignoble* at Aloxe-Corton in Burgundy, showing the gentle slopes of the Côte d'Or just north of Beaune.

| | Optimum output per annum in tonneaux | | Optimum output per annum in tonneaux |
|---|---|---|---|
| **Château Magdelaine | 20 | *Château Sansonnet | 35 |
| Château Magnan-La Gaffelière | 40 | Château Simard | 100 |
| Château Malineau | 20 | Clos Simard | 5 |
| Château Matras | 35 | *Château Soutard | 60 |
| *Château Mauvezin | 20 | Château Soutard-Cadet | 10 |
| *Château Moulin-du-Cadet | 20 | *Château Tertre-Daugay | 30 |
| Château Moulin-Saint-Georges | 55 | *Château Trimoulet | 60 |
| **Château Pavie | 150 | *Château Trois-Moulins | 15 |
| *Château Pavie-Decesse | 40 | *Château Troplong-Mondot | 125 |
| *Château Pavie-Macquin | 60 | **Château Trottevieille | 50 |
| *Château Pavillon-du-Cadet | 25 | Clos Valentin | 15 |
| *Château Petit-Faurie-de-Soutard | 80 | Château Vieux-Moulin-du-Cadet | 10 |
| *Château Saint-Georges-Côte-Pavie | 25 | *Château Villemaurine | 70 |
| *Clos Saint-Martin | 20 | | |

Average total production of the Premiers Crus de
Saint-Emilion (Côtes)                                    3,432
Average total production of the other vineyards of
Saint-Emilion (Côtes)                                    1,960
                                                         ————
                                                         5,392

## Saint-Emilion – Vins de Graves

PREMIER GRAND CRU

| | | | |
|---|---|---|---|
| *Château Cheval Blanc | 150 | *Château Jean-Faure | 80 |
| | | *Château La Dominique | 60 |
| PREMIERS CRUS | | *Château La Marzelle | 25 |
| **Château Chauvin | 60 | *Château La Tour-du-Pin-Figeac | |
| *Château Corbin | 100 | (Bèlivier) | 50 |
| *Château Corbin-Michotte | 50 | *Château La Tour-du-Pin-Figeac | |
| Château Cormey-Figeac | 45 | (Moueix) | 50 |
| *Château Croque-Michotte | 60 | *Château La Tour-Figeac | 80 |
| **Château Figeac | 100 | Château Monlabert | 50 |
| *Château Grand-Barrail-Lamarzelle- | | *Château Ripeau | 50 |
| Figeac | 120 | Château Vieux-Château-Chauvin | 20 |
| Château Grand-Corbin | 50 | *Château Yon-Figeac | 90 |
| *Château Grand-Corbin-Despagne | 100 | | |

Average total production of the Premiers Crus de
Saint-Emilion (Graves)                                   1,270
Average total production of the other vineyards of
Saint-Emilion (Graves)                                     726
                                                         ————
                                                         1,996

Plate 8. Wines of the Hospices de Beaune. The bottles show the traditional burgundy labels and the glasses are slightly curved-in.

## Communes entitled to sell their Wines with the Appellation 'Saint-Emilion'

| Communes | Tonneaux | Communes | Tonneaux |
|---|---|---|---|
| Saint-Christophe-des-Bardes | 1,550 | Saint-Sulpice-de-Faleyrens | 1,350 |
| Saint-Etienne-de-Lisse | 1,850 | Vignonet | 1,100 |
| Saint-Hippolyte | 1,100 | | |
| Saint-Laurent-des-Combes[1] | 700 | | 8,250 |
| Saint-Pey-d'Armens | 600 | | |

## Communes Producing Red Wines similar to those of Saint-Emilion

| | | |
|---|---|---|
| Saint-Georges: | *Appellation contrôlée* 'Saint-Georges-Saint-Emilion' | 1,100 |
| Montagne: | *Appellation contrôlée* 'Montagne-Saint-Emilion' | 3,200 |
| Lussac: | *Appellation contrôlée* 'Lussac-Saint-Emilion' | 2,550 |
| Puisseguin: | *Appellation contrôlée* 'Puisseguin-Saint-Emilion' | 2,750 |
| Parsac: | *Appellation contrôlée* 'Parsac-Saint-Emilion' | 500 |
| Libourne: | *Appellation contrôlée* 'Sables-de-Saint-Emilion' | 350 |
| | | 10,450 |

## Total Production of Saint-Emilion Wines

| Communes | Tonneaux |
|---|---|
| Commune de Saint-Emilion | 6,300 |
| Communes entitled to the *appellation* 'Saint-Emilion' | 8,250 |
| All other Communes | 10,450 |
| Grand Total | 25,000 |

## Pomerol

Immediately to the west of the Graves de Saint-Emilion, north-east of Libourne, the vineyards of Pomerol occupy a plateau of some 1,800 acres and produce some 1,500 *tonneaux* of very good red wines, the peers of the *Premiers Crus* of Saint-Emilion, practically the same in colour and body but possessing a very charming and characteristic bouquet of their own. Some of them are also somewhat softer and more gracious than their Saint-Emilion first cousins.

## Premiers Crus de Pomerol

| | Tonneaux | | Tonneaux |
|---|---|---|---|
| Château Beauregard | 65 | Château Gombaude-Guillet | 25 |
| Clos Beauregard | 50 | Château Grate-Cap | 30 |
| Château Bourgneuf | 50 | Château Guillot | 30 |
| Château Certan | 20 | Château Haut-Maillet | 17 |
| Château Certan-Marzelle | 20 | Château La Cabanne | 60 |
| Château Clinet | 30 | Château La Commanderie | 20 |
| Clos du Clocher | 20 | Château La Conseillante | 40 |
| Château Feytit-Clinet | 25 | Château La Croix | 50 |
| Château Gazin | 80 | Château La Croix-de-Gay | 20 |

[1] The finest Estate of this Commune, Château Larcis-Ducasse, has been given the *appellation contrôlée* 'Saint-Emilion Grand Cru Classé'.

|  | Tonneaux |  | Tonneaux |
|---|---|---|---|
| Château La Croix-Saint-Georges | 20 | Château Nénin | 100 |
| Château Lafleur | 16 | Château Petit-Village | 60 |
| Château La Fleur-Pétrus | 35 | Château Petrus | 25 |
| Château Lagrange | 20 | Château Plince | 40 |
| Château La Grave-Trignant-de-Boisset | 25 | Château Rouget | 80 |
| Clos de la Gravette | 10 | Clos du Roy | 15 |
| Château de La Nouvelle-Eglise | 10 | Château de Sales | 180 |
| Château La Pointe | 70 | Château Taillefer | 50 |
| Château Le Caillou | 30 | Clos des Templiers | 20 |
| Château Le Gay | 25 | Château Trotanoy | 30 |
| Clos l'Eglise | 25 | Vieux Château Certan | 50 |
| Domaine de l'Eglise | 20 | Château Vraye-Croix-de-Gay | 15 |
| Château l'Eglise-Clinet | 20 | | |
| Château l'Enclos | 40 | | 1,668 |
| Château l'Evangile | 45 | Other vineyards of the Commune of Pomerol | 815 |
| Château Moulinet | 40 | | |
| | | | 2,483 |

The Communes of Néac and Lalande-de-Pomerol, which adjoin the Commune of Pomerol, have a great many vineyards which produce on an average 2,200 *tonneaux* of very fair red wines, which are sold under the *appellations contrôlées* 'Néac' and 'Lalande-de-Pomerol'.

## The Fronsadais

The Fronsadais is the name given to the most extensive as well as the most picturesque of the Dordogne vinelands within the Département of the Gironde. It is named after its chief city, the little port of Fronsac, some two miles to the north-west of Libourne, facing south, and the River Dordogne, and with the valley of the River Isle as its eastern boundary.

The best wines of the Fronsadais are those of the many vineyards which crowd the slopes of the range of hills nearest to the Dordogne, and parallel to it, known as *Côtes de Canon-Fronsac*: none but the red wines of those vineyards are entitled to the *appellation contrôlée* 'Côtes de Fronsac', and all of them are within the boundaries of one or the other of the twin Communes of Fronsac and Saint-Hippolyte-de-Fronsac. Their total annual yield is not more than 1,200 *tonneaux*, 700 from Fronsac and 500 from Saint-Hippolyte vineyards.

Immediately behind this first range of hills, there are others which stand guard over them to the north and north-west, and their steeper slopes are also thickly planted in vines, partly in the same Communes of Fronsac and Saint-Hippolyte-de-Fronsac, but mostly on the territory of the four adjoining Communes of La Rivière, Saint-Germain-La Rivière, Saint-Aignan and Saillans. Their average annual yield is 3,500 *tonneaux* of very fair red wines which are entitled to the *appellation contrôlée* 'Côtes de Fronsac'. On the whole, the Côtes de Fronsac wines may not have the 'breed' or elegance which one associates with all the best wines of Saint-Emilion and Pomerol, but some of them, those of Château Rouet in particular, the most important as well as the finest estate of the Commune of Saint-Germain-La Rivière, are the peers of many better known, and also more expensive wines of other Dordogne vineyards.

The bulk of the wines of the Fronsadais, however, are plain *ordinaires* with no other claim than to the name of 'Bordeaux' or – the best of them – 'Bordeaux Supérieur'. They are produced by the vineyards of a number of Communes along a somewhat uneven plateau occupying the central and northern parts of the *Canton de Fronsac*. The names of those Communes and their average production per annum of both red and white wines, in *tonneaux*, are as follows:

| Communes | Red wines | White wines | Totals |
|---|---|---|---|
| Asques | 1,300 | — | 1,300 |
| Cadillac-en-Fronsadais | 500 | 300 | 800 |
| Galgon | 500 | 1,500 | 2,000 |
| Lalande-de-Fronsac | 300 | 500 | 800 |
| Lugon et L'Ile-du-Carney | 2,500 | 500 | 3,000 |
| Mouillac | 100 | 200 | 300 |
| Périssac | 200 | 800 | 1,000 |
| Saint-Genès-de-Fronsac | — | 1,200 | 1,200 |
| Saint-Romain-la-Virvée | 1,200 | — | 1,200 |
| Vérac | 300 | 600 | 900 |
| Villegouge | 800 | 600 | 1,400 |
|  | 7,700 | 6,200 | 13,900 |

The total wine production of the Fronsadais is about 22,000 *tonneaux* per annum, divided as follows:

|  | Tonneaux |
|---|---|
| *Côtes de Canon-Fronsac* (red wines) | 1,200 |
| *Côtes de Fronsac* (red wines) | 3,500 |
| *Bordeaux* and *Bordeaux Supérieurs* (red and white) | 13,900 |
| *Palus* wines from riverside vineyards of the Dordogne and the Isle | 3,300 |
|  | 21,900 |

Beyond the Fronsadais, but still within the Département of the Gironde, the Cantons of Guîtres and Coutras have a very large number of vineyards which are responsible for an annual production of some 21,000 *tonneaux* of *ordinaires* wines, 5,000 of red wine and 16,000 of white.

## Entre-Deux-Mers

The name Entre-Deux-Mers is given to the largest of the wine-producing areas of the Gironde Département, all the land that lies between the Rivers Garonne and Dordogne until they meet and become the Gironde. There are some 76,000 *tonneaux* of red and white wines produced every year by the vineyards of the Entre-Deux-Mers, mostly white wines and mostly ranging from '*très ordinaires*' to '*ordinaires*' and '*bons ordinaires*'. The white wines of the Entre-Deux-Mers vineyards are entitled to the *appellation contrôlée* 'Entre-Deux-Mers' or 'Bordeaux' when their alcoholic strength is not less than 10°, and they are entitled to the *appellation contrôlée* 'Bordeaux Supérieur' when their alcoholic strength is not less than 11·5°. Red wines are entitled to the *appellation contrôlée* 'Bordeaux' when their alcoholic strength is not inferior to 9·75°, and 'Bordeaux Supérieur' when it is 10° or over.

DÉPARTEMENTS DE LA GIRONDE

| | *Optimum output per annum in tonneaux* | | | |
|---|---|---|---|---|
| | Red wines | White wines | Totals | |
| GIRONDE | | | | |
| Médoc | 45,000 | 1,500 | 46,500 | |
| Bourgeais et Blayais | 36,500 | 36,500 | 73,000 | 119,500 |
| GARONNE | | | | |
| Graves de Bordeaux | 9,000 | 6,000 | 15,000 | |
| Sauternes, Barsac, Cérons et Sainte-Croix du-Mont | — | 6,500 | 6,500 | |
| Premières Côtes de Bordeaux | 16,000 | 17,000 | 33,000 | |
| Côtes de Bordeaux-Saint-Macaire | 3,500 | 5,500 | 9,000 | |
| Bazadais | 500 | 500 | 1,000 | 64,500 |
| DORDOGNE | | | | |
| Saint-Emilion | 25,000 | — | 25,000 | |
| Pomerol | 2,500 | — | 2,500 | |
| Néac & Lalande-de-Pomerol | 2,000 | — | 2,000 | |
| Fronsadais | 20,000 | 2,000 | 22,000 | |
| Cantons de Guîtres et Coutras | 5,000 | 16,000 | 21,000 | |
| Cubzagais | 5,000 | 3,500 | 8,500 | |
| Graves de Vaires | 3,000 | 1,000 | 4,000 | |
| Sainte-Foy-de-Bordeaux | 4,000 | 7,500 | 11,500 | 96,500 |
| ENTRE-DEUX-MERS | 26,000 | 50,000 | 76,000 | 76,000 |
| | 203,000 | 153,500 | 356,500 | 356,500 |

CHAPTER THREE

# The Wines of Burgundy

BURGUNDY is the name of one of the old Provinces of France which was cut up, at the time of the French Revolution, into three Départements: the Yonne, in the north; the Côte d'Or, in the centre; and the Saône-et-Loire, in the south.

Burgundy is also the name of the wine made from grapes grown in the vineyards of Burgundy, most of it red wine, but much of it white. Both the red and white wines of Burgundy are the only wines of France possessing such superlative excellence that they can and do challenge the wines of Bordeaux as the greatest table wines of the world.

In colour and alcoholic strength, most red wines of Burgundy, when unfortified or otherwise tampered with, are not unlike most red wines of Bordeaux, but they differ from them in bouquet, flavour, appeal and personality. They rarely possess quite the same light and delicate texture or body which is such an outstanding character of most fine clarets; they are as a rule more robust, more assertive, more immediately obvious, which is why there is a great number of people, more particularly among the young, who prefer burgundy to bordeaux. The difference between them is not one of 'quality' but of 'tone', just as the voice of a soprano differs from that of a contralto not necessarily in quality but inevitably in tone. We may prefer one to the other or we may, and I certainly do, love them both equally.

It is not quite the same, however, as regards the white wines of Burgundy. None of them is comparable to the fine luscious white wines of Sauternes, but most of them are wines of more distinctive and of finer quality than the other table wines of the Gironde, the Loire, the Rhône, the Rhine or anywhere else in France. There are, of course, many charming, light, white wines from other parts of France which are quite as good as the lighter white burgundies of the Yonne and Saône-et-Loire Départements, but do not possess the breed, body, bouquet and balance of the great white wines of the Côte d'Or.

The quality and the personality of the wines of Burgundy, be they red or white, are due primarily to the geological formation of their vineyards, that is to the nature of both soil and subsoil; this varies, of course, from place to place, but not from year to year. Wherever it happens to be best, usually upon the lower half of the hillsides, the wine will be best; wherever it is too poor or too cold, as it usually is on hilltops, the grapes will not ripen properly; and when it is too heavy and too rich, as it always is in plains and vales, the vines will give an abundance of grapes from which none but the commoner types of wine are made. The soil is a gift; it must be received gratefully and used as best we can, but it cannot be changed. Besides the soil of the vineyards, climatic conditions have also a great deal to do with the quality of the wine. Like the soil, rain and sunshine are gifts which we must accept as and when they come. Unlike the soil, however, climatic conditions are never quite the same from year to year, and they have the greatest share of responsibility in the differences of quality that exist between the wines made by the same man, from grapes grown in the same vineyard, in different years. Last, but by no means least, the quality and personality of the wines of Burgundy are due in a very large measure to the species of grapes from which they are made. This, of course, is entirely a matter of choice. Since grapes have been grown and wine has been made in Burgundy for over a thousand years, we can surely take it for granted that the grapes now being grown have been selected as best suited to both the soil and climate of Burgundy. All the great red and white wines of Burgundy are made from noble Pinot grapes. The red wines are made mostly from the *Pinot noir fin* or *Pinot noirien*; also, to a very much smaller extent, from two of its first cousins, the *Pinot Beurot* and the *Pinot Liebault*; all the best white wines are made almost exclusively from *Pinot Chardonnay*; also, in a very minor degree, from its first cousin, *Pinot blanc*.

But all burgundy wines are not great wines. There are many more good wines than great ones, particularly in the more southern vinelands of Burgundy, the Mâconnais and Beaujolais. Most of the plainer *ordinaires* red wines of Burgundy are made from *Gamay noir à jus blanc*, and a small quantity from both this black Gamay with the white juice and its poor relation, the *Gamay à jus coloré*. The *appellations contrôlées* authorities insist that the proportion of this commoner Gamay with red juice must not exceed 10% of the total vines in any one vineyard. As regards the more *ordinaires* white wines of Burgundy, there are but two species of grapes from which they are made; the one which is grown mostly is the *Aligoté*; the other is the *Gamay blanc*, also known as *Melon*.

In Burgundy a wine-producing village, parish or area is known as *finage*, and the site of any vineyard within the bounds or limits of each *finage* is known as *climat*. The best wines from the best *climats* of each *finage* are known as *Têtes de Cuvée*; the next best are called *Premières Cuvées*, and the next *Deuxièmes* and *Troisièmes Cuvées*, that is wines of the first, second and third class.

The making of red and white table wines in Burgundy rests on exactly the same basic principles as everywhere else. The grapes are picked when they are fully ripe, but not overripe; they are usually *égrappées*, that is, freed from their stalks in an *égrappoir*, a kind of rotating calender-barrel made for the purpose. The berries burst as they are torn from their stalks; their sweet juice runs and is collected as *vin de goutte* in wooden vats; then the deflated but still very moist grapes are pressed hard and they give up all the remaining juice that was in them, which is what they call the *vin de presse*. Both the *vin de goutte* and the *vin de presse*, either separately or after being mixed together, start fermenting in the open vats and cast off any dirt that may have come in with the grapes from the vineyards; a few days later, when their first bout of fermenting fever is over, the quieter newly born wines are lodged in casks, with the bung out or loose, so that any carbonic acid gas generated during the slower but still continuous process of fermentation may escape.

*Chaptalisation* is the addition of sugar to the grapes before they are pressed, in order to raise the sugar content of the new wine, hence also its alcoholic strength after fermentation; it is practised in Burgundy to a greater extent than in Bordeaux, because unsatisfactory vintages, when the grapes do not get all the sunshine and heat that they need, are more frequent in the Côte d'Or than in the Gironde. It is also due, however, to the fact that there is now a majority of wine drinkers, and more particularly throughout the English-speaking world, who have acquired somehow the conviction that a red burgundy is a wine more than half-way from Bordeaux to Oporto. Curiously enough, there was a time, during the nineteenth century, when one could see some white Chardonnay grapes growing in all the greatest red burgundy vineyards. The demand was at the time for 'elegant' burgundies, and it was considered that the blending of a little white Pinot wine with the red gave to the wine the lighter touch of 'elegance' that was demanded then.

The sugaring of wine in the making, or *chaptalisation*, is permitted by French law within certain limits, of course, but the mixing of burgundy with other wines, from the Midi, Algeria, Spain or anywhere else, can only be done at the cost of the loss of the name *Bourgogne*. The *appellations contrôlées* law, which is strictly applied in France, but has, of course, no claim to any jurisdiction outside France, does not allow any wine to be offered for sale under a geographical name other than that of its birthplace. Of course, it is only right, but at the same time it adds a great deal to the problems which many an honest Burgundy shipper must face, handicapped as no other is by the fact that the best vineyards of Burgundy are so small and so much divided among different owners; it makes it exceedingly difficult to secure adequate supplies of fine wines, more particularly those bearing popular names, which are in much greater demand than all others. This is why the practice of the Champagne shippers for the past hundred years has been adopted by most Burgundy shippers, and is rapidly spreading. That is, to ignore names of Communes and vineyards, and to make blends to be sold under merchants' names or trade marks, averaging quality and cost, and building up adequate supplies to meet the demand. Such blends are usually very good value, and some of them are also quite fine wines. The name and reputation of the shipper are, of course, all important.

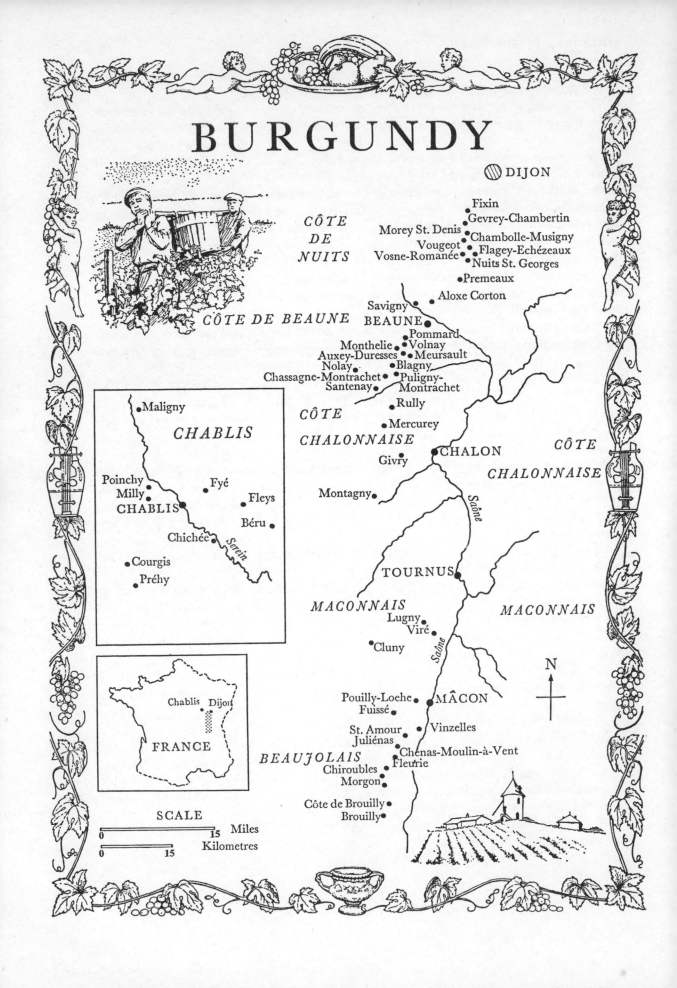

# BURGUNDY

DIJON

CÔTE DE NUITS

Fixin
Gevrey-Chambertin
Morey St. Denis
Chambolle-Musigny
Vougeot
Flagey-Echézeaux
Vosne-Romanée
Nuits St. Georges
Premeaux
Aloxe Corton

CÔTE DE BEAUNE

Savigny
BEAUNE
Pommard
Monthelie
Volnay
Auxey-Duresses
Meursault
Nolay
Blagny
Chassagne-Montrachet
Puligny-Montrachet
Santenay

Rully

CÔTE CHALONNAISE

Mercurey

CHALON

CÔTE CHALONNAISE

Givry

Montagny

Saône

CHABLIS

Maligny

Poinchy
Milly
CHABLIS
Fyé
Fleys
Béru
Chichée
Serein
Courgis
Préhy

TOURNUS

MACONNAIS

Lugny
Viré
Cluny

MACONNAIS

Saône

N

Chablis Dijon

FRANCE

Pouilly-Loche
Fuissé
MÂCON

St. Amour
Vinzelles
Juliénas
BEAUJOLAIS
Chénas-Moulin-à-Vent
Chiroubles
Fleurie
Morgon
Côte de Brouilly
Brouilly

SCALE
0        15  Miles
0        15  Kilometres

# Chablis

Chablis is a charming little town in the topmost corner of the Yonne Département, a little more than half-way between Paris (183 km. to the north) and Dijon (134 km. to the south).

Chablis has given its name to one of the most attractive dry white wines in the world, a wine that is pale gold in colour, free from sweetness and acidity alike, intensely 'clean' on the palate, light yet by no means weak, not assertive and not possessive but still less dull or flat. Chablis is the most universally welcome partner for fish, oysters and also for all sorts of white meat.

Unfortunately, the deserved popularity of Chablis is responsible for the fact that the demand all over the world is far greater than the supply of genuine Chablis, that is, the wine made from grapes grown upon the gentle slopes of a few hills in the valley of the small River Serein, within the bounds of the Commune of Chablis, and of a few other nearby Communes, from Pontigny, in the north, to Poilly-sur-Serein in the south; and from Viviers, near Tonnerre, in the east, to Chitry and Saint-Bris, near Auxerre, in the west. Even within this comparatively small area there are marked differences in the quality of the wines from various vineyards, and the authorities responsible for the *appellations contrôlées* have decreed that Chablis shall be sold, at any rate in France, under four different labels, according to the standard of excellence of the wines of four categories of Chablis vineyards, to be known as:

(1) *Chablis Grand Cru* or *Grands Chablis*; (2) *Chablis Premier Cru*; (3) *Chablis*; (4) *Petit Chablis* or *Bourgogne des Environs de Chablis*.

## (1) *Chablis Grand Cru or Grands Chablis*

A wine may not bear either of these names unless it complies with the following conditions:

(*a*) it must be made from Pinot grapes exclusively;
(*b*) and from the best of the named vineyards of the Communes of Chablis, Milly and Poinchy;
(*c*) its alcoholic strength must not be inferior to 11°;
(*d*) the vineyard which produced the grapes from which the wine was made must not yield more than 35 hectolitres (770 gallons) per hectare, or about 310 gallons per acre. This official limiting of the yield is the official recognition that quantity is never attained except at the expense of quality.

## (2) *Chablis Premier Cru*

To be allowed to use this name, followed by the name of an individual vineyard, a wine must comply with the following conditions:

(*a*) it must be made from Pinot grapes exclusively;
(*b*) and from any of the 'next best' vineyards of the same three Communes of Chablis, Milly and Poinchy;
(*c*) the alcoholic strength must not be inferior to 10·5°;
(*d*) the yield must not have exceeded 40 hectolitres of wine (880 gallons) per hectare, or about 360 gallons per acre.

## (3) *Chablis*

The conditions required for the use of the plain or unqualified name of Chablis are as follows:

(*a*) the wine must be made from Pinot grapes exclusively;

(*b*) and from the vineyards of any of the twenty *Communes chablisiennes*, or Communes of the Chablis district, i.e. Beines, Béru, Chablis, Chemilly-sur-Serein, Chichée, Courgis, Fleys, Fontenay, Fyé, La Chapelle, Ligny-le-Chatel, Lignorelles, Maligny, Milly, Poilly, Poinchy, Préhy, Rameau, Villy, Viviers;

(*c*) the alcoholic strength of the wine must not be inferior to 10°.

## (4) *Petit Chablis or Bourgogne des Environs de Chablis*

These names are given to the more *ordinaires* white wines of the Chablis district, and the only conditions attached to their use is that the wines that bear them will have:

(*a*) been made from any species of grapes other than *producteurs directs* – the ungrafted vine briars;

(*b*) that such grapes shall have been grown in any of the twenty *Communes chablisiennes*;

(*c*) that the alcoholic strength shall not be below 9·5°.

## *Chablis Vineyards*

The best Chablis vineyards, those which are responsible for the *Grands Chablis* or *Chablis Grand Cru*, are those which one sees as one leaves Chablis by the road leading to the north-east, upon the slopes of the hill rising from the right bank of the River Serein. The five best are Blanchots, Les Clos, Valmur, Grenouilles and Vaudésir. Then come Preuze and La Moutonne;[1] a little to the north, Vaulorent, Bougros and Fourchaume; also, to the south, Chapelot, Montée de Tonnerre and Mont de Milieu.

There are in the three favoured Communes of Chablis, Milly and Poinchy a number of less famous vineyards to the west and north-west of Chablis itself, responsible for many fair and fine wines which are not likely to reach the high standard of excellence of the wines from the vineyards upon the right bank of the River Serein, but they cost less and may be as good or better value. There are seventeen of these *Deuxièmes Crus*, as follows:

Beauroy, Beugnon, Butteaux, Châtin, Côte de Fontenay, Côte de Léchet, Les Forêts, Les Lys, Melinots, Montmain, Pied d'Aloup, Roncières, Séchet, Troëme, Vaillon, Vaucoupin and Vaupinent.

---

[1] La Moutonne is the name of a small vineyard of 128 *ares*, or about 3 and one-sixth acres, wedged between the Preuze and Vaudésir vineyards, but the name, which was registered as a trade mark, became widely known through judicious publicity. According to a ruling of the French Courts in 1951, however, the name of La Moutonne may no longer be used – in France – for any other white wine except that of the small La Moutonne vineyard.

# The Côte d'Or

The Côte d'Or is the name of a French Département, not one of the greatest, but one of the more illustrious in the annals of military history, piety and gastronomy. Dijon, its metropolis, was for centuries the capital city of the great warring Ducs de Bourgogne. It was also the birthplace of Saint Bernard, and the Abbey of Clairvaux is not far away. The vineyards of the Côte d'Or still bring forth, as they have done for over a thousand years, wines of superlative excellence to partner the fine fare from local farms, orchards and open country.

The Côte d'Or owes its name to the apparently inexhaustible gold mine of its vineyards, or so we are told by some authorities, but, according to others, it was so called on account of the 'cloth of gold' which it puts on in the autumn, when the woods of the hilltops and the vineyards of the hillsides are a riot of colour and a true 'slope of gold'. It is made up of a broken chain of vine-clad hills, of which there are two main groups, the Côte de Nuits, to the north, from below Dijon to below Nuits-Saint-Georges, with some 3,000 acres of first-class vineyards; and the Côte de Beaune, to the south, from above Beaune to below Santenay, with some 7,000 acres of first- and second-class vineyards. The whole length of both these groups of gentle hills is about 38 miles, and the background of both is high mountainous country known as *Arrières-Côtes* or *Hautes-Côtes*.

All the better vineyards of the Côte d'Or are planted upon the lower slopes of the hills, facing east, the rising sun and the sombre Vosges beyond; or south-east and south, facing the fir-clad Monts Jura not very far away and the snow-capped Alps in the distance. There are also vineyards upon the higher ground of the Hautes-Côtes, immediately behind the Côte itself, as well as in front of it in the great plain that stretches as far as the Saône, but they do not produce any wines comparable to those of the Pinot-planted vineyards of the Côte: their grapes are mostly Gamay, for the red wines, and Aligoté, for the whites; commoner, hardier and also more generous species of grapes than the noble Pinots.

The Pinot-planted hillside vineyards of the Côte d'Or cover barely 10,000 acres, and their vines do not give more than 27·5 gallons of wine per acre, on an average, which means a maximum production of 2,750,000 gallons of really fine red and white wines, or 1,375,000 dozens of fine burgundy, not a large quantity considering that, besides the local demand, there are so many wine lovers throughout the civilized world who would much like to drink genuine burgundy, if only they knew where to find it.

The figures given represent the approximate 'optimum' production of the more important vineyards in *queues*, the Burgundian term for two *pièces*, or 456 litres, very nearly equal to 100 gallons. It must be borne in mind that 'optimum' figures are very different from 'average' figures: they represent the maximum yield of wine not only obtainable but also permitted by the *appellations contrôlées* authorities of 275 gallons per acre. Unfortunately, there are frost-bitten springs and rain-soaked summers when the vineyards do not bring forth more than half, or even less, their 'optimum' or maximum.

## Fixin

Coming from Dijon, Fixin is the first village we reach where they make fine wine. There was a time when the wines of Chenôve, Marsannay-la-Côte and Couchey, three villages between Dijon and Fixin, enjoyed a fair measure of favour, but they have now fallen by the way. All Fixin wines are red, from fair to fine, with one great wine, the *Clos de la Perrière*.

| Tête de Cuvée | Queues (100 gallons) | Premières Cuvées (contd.) | Queues (100 gallons) | |
|---|---|---|---|---|
| Clos de la Perrière | 34 *queues* | All others | 56·25 | |
| *Premières Cuvées* | | | | 163 *queues* |
| Les Arvelets | 24 | *Deuxièmes Cuvées* | 31 | |
| Clos du Chapitre | 33 | *Troisièmes Cuvées* | 90 | |
| Aux Cheusots | 13 | | | 121 *queues* |
| Les Hervelets | 33 | | Grand Total | 318 *queues* |
| Les Meix-Bas | 3·75 | | | |

## Brochon

A Commune which is chiefly known locally for its inexpensive, *ordinaires* Gamay-grown red wines, but there are also about a hundred acres of Pinot-growing vineyards which are capable of producing 220 *queues* of red wine entitled to the *appellation contrôlée Vins fins de la Côte de Nuits*.

## Gevrey-Chambertin

Gevrey appears for the first time in the annals of Burgundy in A.D. 895, when the village was presented to the Abbey of Saint-Benigne, but it was only in 1847 that it hyphenated its name with that of its most famous vineyard, Chambertin (32 acres). Chambertin, as a vineyard, dates from the thirteenth century, but the *Clos de Bèze* (37 acres), which it adjoins, was planted in A.D. 630 by the monks of the Abbaye de Bèze. The wines of both vineyards are the only ones entitled to the illustrious name of Chambertin, Napoleon's favourite wine. Wines, however, made from grapes grown in the *Clos de Bèze* part of the vineyard may be, and are, often sold as *Chambertin-Clos de Bèze*. Seven of the *Premières Cuvées* of Gevrey-Chambertin may also add the name of Chambertin to their own.

| Têtes de Cuvée | Queues (100 gallons) | Premières Cuvées (contd.) | Queues (100 gallons) | |
|---|---|---|---|---|
| Chambertin and Clos de Bèze-Chambertin | 176 *queues* | Clos Saint-Jacques | 49 | |
| | | Etournelles | 14 | |
| *Premières Cuvées* | | Fouchère | 7 | |
| Chapelle-Chambertin | 56 | Varoilles | 42 | |
| Charmes-Chambertin | 88 | | | 568 *queues* |
| Griotte-Chambertin | 18 | *Deuxièmes Cuvées* | 162 | |
| Latricières-Chambertin | 49 | *Troisièmes Cuvées* | 556 | |
| Mazys-Chambertin | 61 | | | 718 *queues* |
| Mazoyères-Chambertin | 103 | | | |
| Ruchottes-Chambertin | 24 | | Grand Total | 1,462 *queues* |
| Cazetiers | 57 | | | |

There is no *Grand Chambertin* any more than *Petit Chambertin* in the Côte d'Or and a wine named *Grand Chambertin* in a wine-merchant's price-list or on an hotel wine-list may or may not be genuine and quite good, but it is wrongly described.

There are red burgundies as good as a good Chambertin, but none better. Unfortunately, the 70 acres of Chambertin-cum-Clos de Bèze vineyard belong to a number of people, all of whom have not got the same skill, means or pride, which is why two bottles of Chambertin may be equally genuine without being equally good, let alone great. It is also why it is of such importance, when buying burgundy, to find out whenever possible the name of the *vigneron* who made it or of the merchant who selected it. This does not apply to Chambertin alone, but to all the vineyards of Burgundy which are owned by a number of different proprietors.

Another remark which applies not only to Gevrey-Chambertin but to all the other Communes which have added to their original name that of their more famous vineyard, like Vosne-Romanée, Chambolle-Musigny, Nuits-Saint-Georges, etc., is that the first name is the one that really counts. A Gevrey-Chambertin is one of the plain or *ordinaires* wines of Gevrey without a drop of Chambertin in it; had it any claim to genteel birth, it would give the name of the vineyard of its birth, such as Latricières-Chambertin or Clos Saint-Jacques.

## Morey-Saint-Denis

Morey, the next village we come to as we leave Gevrey, is much older. It dates from the Gallo-Roman period, but it was only on the 19 January 1927 that Morey added to its name that of one of its smallest vineyards, the Clos Saint-Denis. Its two largest and more illustrious vineyards are the Clos de Tart and the Clos des Lambrays. Both owe their well-deserved reputation to the fact that they are the property each of a single owner. Clos de Tart belongs to M. Jean Mommessin and the Clos des Lambrays, formerly the property of M. Camille Rodier, now belongs to Madame Cosson. Both vineyards produce well-balanced, full-bodied red wines which deserve and reward long keeping, and single ownership means that one can be sure that all bottles bearing the same name and date are really the same wine. This cannot be said of the *Bonnes Mares* vineyard, a small part of which is on Morey soil, while much the greater part is in the adjoining Chambolle territory. *Bonnes Mares* can be, and should be, a softer and rather more gracious wine, but here again there are different owners, hence differences in the wines that bear and are entitled to bear the same name. In Morey-Saint-Denis they also make some small quantity of very pleasing white wine.

| | Queues (100 gallons) | | | Queues (100 gallons) | |
|---|---|---|---|---|---|
| *Têtes de Cuvée* | | | *Premières Cuvées* (contd.) | | |
| Bonnes Mares | 12 | | Froichots | 4·5 | |
| Clos de Tart | 49 | | Maison Brulée | 13 | |
| Clos des Lambrays | 61 | | Meix-Rentier | 8 | |
| Clos de la Roche | 32 | | Millandes | 30 | |
| Clos Saint-Denis | 15 | | Mochamps | 18 | |
| | — 169 *queues* | | Monts-Luisants | 22 | |
| | | | Morey | 22·5 | |
| *Premières Cuvées* | | | Ormes, Clos des | 31·5 | |
| Calouère | 9 | | Sorbet, Clos | 24 | |
| Chabiots | 15 | | | — 308 *queues* | |
| Chaffots | 9 | | | | |
| Charmes | 9 | | *Deuxièmes Cuvées* | 154 | |
| Charnières | 17 | | *Troisièmes Cuvées* | 106 | |
| Chenevery | 25 | | | — 260 | |
| Chéseaux | 18 | | | | |
| Côte Rôtie | 4 | | Grand Total | 737 *queues* | |
| Faconnières | 12 | | | | |
| Fremières | 16·5 | | | | |

## Chambolle-Musigny

Immediately south of Morey we come to Chambolle, once upon a time a Roman camp, and now one of the more prosperous communities of the Côte d'Or. It was in 1875 that Chambolle added to its name that of its most illustrious vineyard, Musigny. The two best vineyards of Chambolle-Musigny are *Bonnes Mares*, in the north, where it adjoins Morey-Saint-Denis, and *Musigny*, in the south, where it adjoins Flagey-Echézeaux. *Musigny* is one of the most exquisite of the great red table wines of the world, whether *Grand Musigny* or *Petit Musigny*. The Musigny vineyard is cut in two by a small country road, the larger half being locally known as Grand Musigny and the smaller half as Petit Musigny, but there is no difference whatever in the quality of the wine. Beyond the municipal boundary of Chambolle-Musigny, another vineyard, which is really the continuation of Musigny, but is in the adjoining Commune of Flagey-Echézeaux, is known as La Combe d'Orveau, but its wines are so good that they are allowed to be sold under the noble name of Musigny. There is a small quantity of white Musigny made in all good vintages: it is made of noble Chardonnay grapes and it is a fine wine, although it cannot ever claim to be as great a wine as the red. The Musigny vineyards are shared among a few proprietors, all of them anxious to make better wine than anybody else. The Comte de Vogüé owns the greatest share of the Musigny vineyards.

| Têtes de Cuvée | Queues (100 gallons) | | Premières Cuvées (contd.) | Queues (100 gallons) | |
|---|---|---|---|---|---|
| Les Musigny | 66 | | Gruenchers | 23 | |
| Les Bonnes Mares | 90 | | Haute-Doix | 14 | |
| | | 156 *queues* | Lavrottes | 8 | |
| | | | Noirots | 22 | |
| *Premières Cuvées* | | | Sentiers | 38 | |
| Amoureuses | 41 | | | | 342 *queues* |
| Baudes | 27 | | *Deuxièmes Cuvées* | 600 | |
| Charmes | 45 | | *Troisièmes Cuvées* | 216 | |
| Combe d'Orveau | 39 | | | | 816 |
| Cras | 32 | | | | |
| Derrière la Grange | 5 | | Grand Total | | 1,314 *queues* |
| Fuées | 48 | | | | |

## Vougeot

Vougeot is a modest little village: it owes its name to a small stream, the Vouge, which comes out of the hillside above Chambolle-Musigny and rushes down towards the plain through Gilly-les-Vougeot. The original village of Gilly, after adding to its own name that of its one vineyard, the finest of the Côte d'Or, *Clos Vougeot*, has now practically dropped the 'Gilly' altogether: it is now nearly always referred to as Vougeot, *tout court*.

The Clos Vougeot or *Clos de Vougeot*, as it was originally called and is still called today occasionally, was planted centuries ago by the monks of Cîteaux, and its 125 acres were surrounded by a high wall that enclosed it, hence its name of Clos. Much of the original wall still stands, but a number of entrances have been cut in it by some of the owners: there are fifty-four of them, of whom but two own a substantial share of the famous Clos. M. J. Morin has nearly 14 acres, and Madame Veuve Noëllat, nearly 6 acres. There are four other proprietors who own 5 acres, more or less; they are M. Louis Gros, Messrs

Champy Père et Fils, M. P. Misset and M. G. Grivot. The other forty-odd owners have a few vines only, but the little wine that they make is nevertheless genuine *Clos de Vougeot*. This makes it very difficult, however, to pass judgement upon the wines of so large a vineyard which has been broken up into so many small fractions. In the days of single monastic ownership there were three separate wines or *Cuvées* made each year. The best was the wine made from the grapes from the higher part of the vineyard, farthest from the road and close to the Château, where the monks had their wine-press and *cellier*; the second best wine was made from grapes half-way between the road and the *cellier*, and *cuverie*; and the third best was made from grapes from the lower part of the vineyard, those nearest the main road from Paris to Rome on its Dijon–Beaune lap.

There is a small country road which leads from the village to the Château, now the headquarters of the Confrérie des Chevaliers du Tastevin. At the Château end of this road there is a small vineyard of some 5 acres, 'la vigne blanche', which is entirely planted with white Chardonnay grapes. It is owned by L'Héritier-Guyot, who make the white wine known as *Clos Blanc de Vougeot*.

## Flagey-Echézeaux

Flagey, immediately south of Gilly-les-Vougeot, to the west of the Route Nationale, added the name of its most famous vineyard to its own in 1886. Its best vineyards produce red wines which are the peers of the very best, and one can hardly be surprised, since they enjoy the same kind of soil, altitude and aspect as the vineyards of Chambolle-Musigny, to the north, Vosne-Romanée, to the south, and the Clos Vougeot to the west.

| | *Queues* (100 gallons) | | | *Queues* (100 gallons) |
|---|---|---|---|---|
| *Têtes de Cuvée* | | | *Premières Cuveés* (contd.) | |
| Les Grands Echézeaux | 60 | | Quartiers de Nuits | 21 |
| Les Echézeaux du Dessus | 24 | | Rouges-du-Bas | 31 |
| | — 84 *queues* | | Saint-Denis, Clos | 14 |
| | | | Treux, Les | 38 |
| *Premières Cuvées* | | | | — 343 *queues* |
| Beaux-Monts-Bas | 42 | | *Deuxièmes Cuvées* | 50 |
| Champs-Traversins | 28 | | *Troisièmes Cuvées* | 77 |
| Cruots ou Vignes Blanches | 25 | | | — 127 *queues* |
| Loachausses | 29 | | | |
| En Orveau | 75 | | Grand Total | 554 *queues* |
| Poulaillères | 40 | | | |

Pinot-grape wines from unspecified Flagey-Echézeaux vineyards may be sold under the better known name of the nearby Commune of Vosne-Romanée.

## Vosne-Romanée

Vosne is a tight little island of stone houses in a sea of Pinots. Its vineyards stretch from those of Flagey-Echézeaux to the north to those of Nuits-Saint-Georges to the south, mostly between the village and the Route Nationale. The best vineyards of Vosne-Romanée, however, are all upon the other or west side of the village, upon the lower slopes of the Côte.

| *Têtes de Cuvée* | *Queues* (100 *gallons*) | *Premières Cuvées* (contd.) | *Queues* (100 *gallons*) |
|---|---|---|---|
| Romanée Conti | 11 | Malconsorts | 46 |
| La Romanée | 5·5 | Petits-Monts, Aux | 16 |
| La Tâche | 9·5 | Reignots, Aux | 13 |
| Les Richebourg | 33 | Romanée-Saint-Vivant | 73 |
| Les Varoilles[1] | 20 | Suchots | 101 |
| | —— 79 queues | | —— 353 *queues* |
| *Premières Cuvées* | | *Deuxièmes Cuvées* | 308 |
| | | *Troisièmes Cuvées* | 524 |
| Beaux-Monts | 19 | | —— 832 *queues* |
| Brulées, Aux | 30 | | |
| Gaudichots | 45 | | Grand Total 1,264 *queues* |
| Grande-Rue | 10 | | |

Romanée Conti is usually given first place among the Romanées, but there has been more than one occasion when I would have given the palm to La Tâche or to Richebourg, which is a Romanée under another name. There is no doubt that the Romanée-Richebourg wines are among the greatest of all red wines: they are the peers of Chambertin, Musigny and Clos Vougeot, with, of course, a personality entirely their own. Their bouquet has a spicy sweetness that is almost oriental, and there is in the texture of their body a caressing quality which is quite wonderful.

Romanée Conti and La Romanée are owned the first by M. de Vilaine and the second by Messrs Liger-Belair. M. de Vilaine is the chairman of the *Domaine de la Romanée Conti*, a syndicate who own, besides the Romanée Conti vineyard, the whole of La Tâche, and important parts of Richebourg and Grands-Echézeaux. Until the Second World War, the *Domaine de la Romanée Conti* managed to save many, if not most, of its old French vines, but the last of these had to be done away with soon after the end of the war. The Romanée Conti vineyard has now been replanted with French Pinots noiriens, grafted on bug-resisting American briars, and it is hoped that in due course these new vines will produce wines which may be worthy of the proud name that will be theirs.

## *Nuits-Saint-Georges*

Nuits-Saint-Georges is no village but a very much alive little town, with some 3,000 inhabitants, probably more than half of them members of well-to-do *vigneron* and wine-merchant families. Nuits-Saint-Georges is the principal market town and shopping centre of the Côte de Nuits, 13 miles south of Dijon and 10 miles north of Beaune. It was only in 1892 that Nuits added to its name that of its best vineyard, Saint-Georges. The reputation of the Saint-Georges vineyard dates back to A.D. 1023 when this vineyard was given to the Canons of Saint-Denis. The vineyards of Nuits-Saint-Georges and those of the adjoining Commune of Prémeaux, which has been granted the privilege of selling its wines under the name Nuits-Saint-Georges, are of much greater extent than those of the other Communes of the Côte de Nuits, and they produce more wine than any of them. All the red wines of Nuits-Saint-Georges are somewhat stout of body but by no means ungainly, the best of them, particularly the Saint-Georges and Vaucrains, are bigger than a Musigny or Richebourg of the same age, but by no means heavy:

[1] The wine of Les Varoilles is sold under the name of Richebourg.

Plate 9. The *Gamay*, shown in the *caque* or vintage basket-tray, makes the red wines of Burgundy and all the less expensive red burgundies.

they may not be as great as these, but they are certainly very good wines, always dependable, hence eminently satisfactory.

| Têtes de Cuvée | Queues (100 gallons) | Premières Cuvées (contd.) | Queues (100 gallons) |
|---|---|---|---|
| Le Saint Georges | 58 | Perrières et Clos des | |
| Boudots | 49 | Perrières | 23 |
| Cailles | 29 | Poulettes | 16 |
| Cras | 24 | Procès | 14 |
| Murgers | 37 | Richemonnes | 16 |
| Porrets | 54 | Roncières | 15 |
| Pruliers | 55 | Rue de Chaux | 24 |
| Thorey & Clos de Thorey | 48 | | —— 189 queues |
| Vaucrains | 42 | Deuxièmes Cuvées | 1,100 |
| | —— 396 queues | Troisièmes Cuvées | 440 |
| Premières Cuvées | | | —— 1,540 queues |
| Château Gris | 16 | | |
| Chaboeufs | 22 | Grand Total 2,125 queues | |
| Chaignots | 43 | | |

All the *climats* of Nuits-Saint-Georges are shared by different owners, except Les Porrets, the property of M. H. Gouges, and Château Gris, the property of Messrs Lupé-Cholet, an outstanding wine which well deserves a place among the *Têtes de Cuvée*.

## Prémeaux

This village dates back to the Roman occupation, but it does not appear to have ever hit the headlines in the course of the centuries. Its vineyards produce wines of the same character and excellence as those of Nuits-Saint-Georges, which they adjoin, their only particular distinction being that one of Prémeaux's *Premières Cuvées*, Clos Arlot, produces the only Nuits-Saint-Georges white wine.

| Têtes de Cuvée | Queues (100 gallons) | | Queues (100 gallons) |
|---|---|---|---|
| Didiers-Saint-Georges | 22 | Premières Cuvés | 220 |
| Clos des Forêts-Saint- | | Deuxièmes Cuvées | 177 |
| Georges | 39 | | —— 397 queues |
| Corvées | 60 | | |
| Corvées-Pagets | 18 | Grand Total 536 queues | |
| | —— 139 queues | | |

After Nuits-Saint-Georges and Prémeaux, the best vineyards of the Côte de Nuits come to an end. There are three small Communes, Prissey, Comblanchien and Corgoloin, which produce a small quantity of red wines and a much smaller quantity of white wines, none of them of outstanding merit, but some of them good enough to be entitled to the *appellation contrôlée* 'Vins fins de la Côte de Nuits'.

## Côte de Beaune : Aloxe-Corton

We then come to the Côte de Beaune, with the village of Aloxe which added to its name that of its best *climat*, Corton, in 1862. It nestles among its vineyards upon a steep hill of its own, the top of which is thickly wooded. There are some 500 acres of first-class

Plate 10. The *Aligoté*, the counterpart of the *Gamay*, used for making the less-expensive white burgundies.

vineyards within the administrative limits of the Aloxe-Corton Commune, mostly facing south or south-east and producing both red and white wines of very high quality. The best red wine of Aloxe-Corton is *Le Corton*, and many claim that it is the best red wine of the Côte de Beaune. The best white wine is made from Chardonnay grapes from the largest vineyard of Aloxe-Corton, called *Charlemagne* in memory of the great Emperor.

| | *Queues* (100 *gallons*) | | *Queues* (100 *gallons*) |
|---|---|---|---|
| *Têtes de Cuvée* | | *Premières Cuvée* (contd.) | |
| Le Corton | 88 | Les Grèves | 14 |
| En Charlemagne | 132 | Les Meix-Lallemant | 14 |
| Clos-du-Roi | 81 | Les Perrières | 5 |
| Les Chaumes | 29 | La Vigne-au-Saint | 83 |
| Les Renardes | 116 | Other *Premières Cuvées* | 18 |
| | —— 446 *queues* | | —— 299 *queues* |
| *Premières Cuvée* | | *Deuxièmes Cuvées* | 352 |
| | | *Troisièmes Cuvées* | 253 |
| Les Bressandes | 131 | | —— 605 *queues* |
| Les Chaumes-de-la-Voirosse | 24 | Grand Total 1,350 *queues* | |
| Les Fiètres | 10 | | |

There are two other villages, one below and the other above Aloxe-Corton, the best wines of which are entitled to be sold under the name of Corton. The first is Ladoix-Serrigny, which is cut in two by the Route Nationale 74 from Dijon to Beaune: its Pinot-planted vineyards cover about 75 acres, and the three best of them, locally known as Vergesses-Corton, Le Rognet-Corton and Clos des Corton-Faiveley, have an optimum production of 77 *queues* or 7,700 gallons of very good red wines, of the same standard of excellence as those of nearby Aloxe-Corton. The other village, to the n.n.w. of Aloxe-Corton, upon the other side of the same hill, is Pernand, which has added to its name that of its best vineyard, Les Vergelesses, and is now called Pernand-Vergelesses. Its only *Tête de Cuvée* is Ile des Vergelesses, with an optimum production of 66 *queues*, or 6,600 gallons, of fine quality wine. The best red and white wines of Pernand may be sold as *Corton* or *Aloxe-Corton* (the reds), and *Charlemagne* and *Corton-Charlemagne* (the whites).

## Savigny-les-Beaune

South of Pernand and north of Beaune, there are about 1,000 acres of vineyards: they are those of Savigny-les-Beaune, a straggling village clinging to both banks of the little River Rhoin, at the opening of the pretty Fontaine–Froide vale. The vineyards of Savigny stretch as far west as the Route Nationale 74, but those responsible for the best wines, all of them red wines, are the hillside vineyards both north, next to those of Pernand, and south, next to the Beaune vineyards.

| | *Queues* (100 *gallons*) | | *Queues* (100 *gallons*) |
|---|---|---|---|
| *Têtes de Cuvée* | | *Premières Cuvées* | 1,030 |
| Les Vergelesses | 131 | *Deuxièmes Cuvées* | 282 |
| Les Marconnets | 72 | *Troisièmes Cuvées* | 711 |
| Les Jarrons | 70 | | —— 2,023 *queues* |
| | —— 273 *queues* | | |
| | | Grand Total 2,296 *queues* | |

## Beaune

Beaune, about half-way between Dijon and Chalon-sur-Saône, is a very ancient walled city of the greatest possible interest. Whether it is actually the Bibracta of Caesar's *Commentaries* or not is for historians to settle, but there cannot be any doubt about its importance as the metropolis of the Burgundian vinelands, and the age-long fame of its own vineyards. Many were praised by name centuries before any other vineyards of France – the Clos de la Mousse, in 1220, when it was bequeathed to the Chapter of Notre-Dame de Beaune; Les Marconnets, in 1256; Les Cras, in 1303; Les Grèves, in 1343; Les Fèves, in 1483; and so on. Carthusians, Benedictines and the Knights of Malta were for centuries among the largest of the Beaune vineyard owners, but today their vineyards are shared by many different proprietors. *Les Grèves*, for instance, the largest of the *climats* or vineyards of Beaune, nearly 80 acres, upon the lower slopes of the Mont Battois, produces some of the best red wines of the Côte de Beaune, but by no means all of the same high standard: that which is made from the top corner of the vineyard, the property of the Carmelites of Beaune until 1789 and now owned by Messrs Bouchard Père et Fils, is of quite outstanding excellence. This particular corner of the Grèves vineyard was named by the Carmelites *La Vigne de l'Enfant Jésus*, and its wines have been sold under that name ever since: it was named after the arms of Beaune which represent the Blessed Virgin standing with the 'Enfant Jésus' upon her left arm, and in His right hand a vine branch with a bunch of grapes.

| Têtes de Cuvée | Queues (100 gallons) | Têtes de Cuvée (contd.) | Queues (100 gallons) |
|---|---|---|---|
| Clos-de-la-Mousse | 26 | Premières Cuvées | 2,222 |
| Clos-des-Mouches | 170 | Deuxièmes Cuvées | 562 |
| Les Bressandes | 143 | Troisièmes Cuvées | 440 |
| Les Champimonts | 128 | | ——— 3,224 queues |
| Les Cras | 39 | | |
| Les Fèves | 33 | | Grand Total 4,086 queues |
| Les Grèves | 245 | | |
| Les Marconnets | 78 | | |
| | ——— 862 queues | | |

In that part of the Clos des Mouches which belongs to M. Joseph Drouhin, Chardonnay grapes have been planted and a good white wine is made.

## Hospices de Beaune

In Beaune there are churches, quaint old houses, remains of the old city walls, great cellars and other tokens of the city's ancient fame as well of its civic and commercial activities today. But the pride of Beaune is Les Hospices de Beaune. There is nothing like it anywhere else in the world. Five hundred years of devoted service to relieve the sufferings of the poor is a fine record, but it may not be unique in the annals of charity. What is unique is the exquisite beauty of the Hôtel-Dieu which Nicolas Rolin built in 1443, and the fact that the ever rising cost of its upkeep has been met from the time of its founder's death until today by the wine made from the vineyards bequeathed to the Hospices, first of all by Nicolas Rolin and his widow, Guigone de Salins, and ever since by other benefactors. The vineyards belonging to the Hospices de Beaune are scattered all along the Côte de Beaune, from Aloxe-Corton to Meursault, and the Hospices wines

are sold every year by public auction on the third Sunday in November under the names
of 29 different *Cuvées*, most of them bearing names of benefactors, usually the names of
donors of the vineyards belonging to the Hospices.

## Hospices de Beaune

| Finage or Village | Cuvées | Finage or Village | Cuvées |
|---|---|---|---|
| | RED WINES | Volnay | Blondeau |
| Aloxe-Corton | Charlotte Dumay | Monthelie | Jacques Lebelin |
| | Dr Peste | | Henri Gélicot |
| Savigny-les-Beaune | Du Bay-Peste-Cyrot | Auxey-Duresses | Boillot |
| | Forneret | Meursault | Jehan de Massol |
| | Fouquerand | | Gauvain |
| Beaune | Nicolas Rolin | | |
| | Guigone de Salins | | WHITE WINES |
| | Dames hospitalières | Aloxe-Corton | François de Salins |
| | Estienne | Meursault | Albert Grivault |
| | Brunet | | de Bahèzre de Lanlay |
| | Hugues et Louis Bétault | | Baudot |
| | Rousseau-Deslandes | | Goureau |
| Pommard | Dames de la Charité | | Jehan Humblot |
| | Billardet | | Loppin |

In a good vintage year the Hospices de Beaune *Cuvées* may account for 500 casks.

## Pommard

Soon after leaving Beaune by the Route Nationale 74, a smaller country road branches
off on the right and leads to the large and prosperous village of Pommard, a name
second to none in point of world-wide popularity. The vineyards of Pommard were
mentioned by Courtépée in A.D. 1005, and today they cover nearly a thousand acres,
capable of producing, when both sun and rain have been kind, 2,640 *queues*, or 264,000
gallons, of fine, rather stout, red wines which require and reward long keeping. The vineyards of Pommard stretch without a break from those of Beaune in the north to those
of Volnay in the south.

| | Queues (100 gallons) | | Queues (100 gallons) | |
|---|---|---|---|---|
| *Têtes de Cuvée* | | *Premières Cuvées* (contd.) | | |
| Clos Blanc | 103 | Other *Premières Cuvées* | 838 | |
| Les Epenots | 45 | | —— 1,221 *queues* | |
| Les Rugiens-Bas | 33 | *Deuxièmes Cuvées* | 726 | |
| | —— 181 *queues* | *Troisièmes Cuvées* | 600 | |
| *Premières Cuvées* | | | —— 1,326 *queues* | |
| Clos de la Commaraine | 31 | | | |
| Les Petits Epenots | 154 | Grand Total | 2,728 *queues* | |
| Village de Pommard | 198 | | | |

## Volnay

Volnay, immediately to the south-west of Pommard, upon higher ground, is a smaller
village with only half the acreage of vineyards, but they produce a larger proportion of
really high-class wines than those of Pommard. Volnay's best wines are a little lighter

both in colour and body than most wines of Beaune and Pommard, but they possess great charm.

| Têtes de Cuvée | Queues (100 gallons) | Premières Cuvées (contd.) | Queues (100 gallons) | |
|---|---|---|---|---|
| Les Angles | 27 | Other *Premières Cuvées* | 580 | |
| Les Caillerets | 111 | | —— | 808 *queues* |
| Les Champans | 88 | *Deuxièmes Cuvées* | 202 | |
| Les Fremiets | 50 | *Troisièmes Cuvées* | 358 | |
| | —— 276 *queues* | | —— | 560 *queues* |
| *Premières Cuvées* | | | | |
| Clos-des-Chênes | 125 | | Grand Total | 1,644 *queues* |
| Village de Volnay | 103 | | | |

## Auxey-Duresses

Auxey is one of the smaller and oldest Communes of the Côte de Beaune, and it added the name of its best vineyard, *Duresses*, to its own only in July 1924. The village is perched upon a rocky spur on the left bank of the little Meursault river: this river separates the vineyards responsible for most red wines of the Côte de Beaune, from Savigny-les-Beaune to Monthelie, and those of a lower range of hills, from Meursault to Santenay, responsible for the finest white wines of the Côte d'Or.

Les Duresses, the only *Première Cuvée* of Auxey-Duresses, may yield up to 55 *queues*, or 5,500 gallons, of very good red wine, while the *Deuxièmes* and *Troisièmes Cuvées* may bring forth a total of 330 *queues* of very fair red wine. The other vineyards of this Commune yield some 440 *queues* of undistinguished wines, most of them red and some white.

## Monthelie

Monthelie, farther west and higher up than Auxey-Duresses, is perched upon the last tableland of the Côte de Beaune proper, overlooking the deep ravine which separates it from the Côte de Meursault. Although known by that name locally, the Côte de Meursault is more commonly included as part, the southern part, of the Côte de Beaune. Monthelie is a small village, and the whole of its small territory is given up to the growing of wine-making grapes: there are no pastures, no spinneys, no ploughed fields, in fact no wasted land. The total Pinot-planted vineyards of Monthelie cannot yield, even under the most favourable climatic conditions, much more than 660 *queues* of red wine: 55 of *Premières Cuvées*, 440 of *Deuxièmes Cuvées* and 165 of *Troisièmes Cuvées*.

## Meursault

Meursault is a little town with 1,500 inhabitants, its own Hôtel de Ville and Hospital, two hotels, the Chevreuil, which is very good, and the Centre, which is good, and a Château de Meursault, on its outskirts, the home of Comte and Comtesse de Moucheron. Meursault is the chief town of the *Côte des Blancs*, that part of the Côte d'Or which is responsible for the greatest quantity of white burgundies and wines of greater excellence than all others. It comprises the three Communes of Meursault, Chassagne and Puligny. Although Meursault is better known for its white wines of rare *finesse* and great charm, its vineyards produce some 660 *queues* of red wines as well as 1,100 *queues* of white wines. The vineyards of Meursault stretch without a break from those of Volnay in the north to those of Chassagne-Montrachet in the south. All the red wines of

Meursault are made from four vineyards in the north of the Commune, which adjoin those of Volnay. The best of these four vineyards, the only *Tête de Cuvée*, is called Santenots du Milieu (62 *queues*), and its wine has been known for the past 200 years as Volnay-Santenots. It is often regarded as a finer wine than any of the wines of Volnay. The other three vineyards are *Premières Cuvées*, known as Santenots de Dessus (23 *queues*), Santenots de Dessous (55 *queues*) and Les Pelures (46 *queues*): the wines of all three *climats* are entitled to the name of Volnay-Santenots. There are a further quantity of from 400 to 500 *queues* of more *ordinaires* red wines of Meursault which may be sold under their own name or as *Vins de la Côte de Beaune*.

As regards the white wines of Meursault, the finest *climat* of the Commune is Les Perrières, a *Tête de Cuvée* owned by Madame Grivault. Its optimum yield is 133 *queues* of a very delicate, fragrant and delicious white wine. Much the largest *climat* of Meursault is Les Charmes, a *Première Cuvée* with an optimum yield of 212 *queues* of a very nice white wine, all of it by no means always identical or even comparable in quality; this is due to the fact that there are 31 different people who own a larger or smaller share of Les Charmes. Another *Première Cuvée* of Meursault, Les Genevrières, with an optimum yield of 129 *queues*, is also divided among a number of different owners, but it is a great favourite and, as such, it is 'listed' by wine-merchants and hotels more frequently than any of the other Meursault *climats*, may be with the exception of Meursault Goutte d'Or. Goutte d'Or is the most popular *Deuxième Cuvée* of Meursault, with an optimum yield of 39 *queues;* this is a regrettably small quantity of wine, considering the world-wide demand for Meursault *Goutte d'Or*.

## Puligny and Chassagne

These two Communes are the home, or rather the source, of the greatest of all white wines of Burgundy, *Le Montrachet*, and both added its famous name to their own in 1879, when they became Puligny-Montrachet and Chassagne-Montrachet. *Rachet*, in Burgundian parlance, means bald, and *Mont-Rachet*, which was the original spelling still to be seen on old labels, meant the 'hill without a tree'.[1] The hill upon which the vines grow, which give us the famous Montrachet, is merely a mole-hill, and a little more than half the vineyard is on Puligny territory, the rest on Chassagne ground.

Le Montrachet is the name of this famous vineyard and of its grand white wine; *Grand Montrachet* is a fancy name given to the wine by some wine-merchants in their anxiety to make it clear that they are offering the one and only genuine *Montrachet*. Although under the most favourable conditions the Montrachet vineyard cannot produce more than 50 *queues* of white wine, its few acres are divided among eleven owners: there are but three of these who own a fairly substantial slice of the Montrachet *climat*. They are the Marquis de Laguiche, the Baron Thénard and Messrs Bouchard Père et Fils. The other eight proprietors share the remaining 7 acres among them.

Besides Le Montrachet, the only *Tête de Cuvée* of both Puligny and Chassagne, there are vineyards upon all the approaches to Le Montrachet which produce excellent white wines, *Premières Cuvées* in deference to Le Montrachet, but the peers, to say the least, of the *Têtes de Cuvée* of Meursault and Aloxe-Corton. The most important of the *Premières Cuvées* of Puligny and Chassagne is *Le Bâtard-Montrachet*, more than half of it on the

[1] This is why the correct pronunciation of Montrachet is *Monrachet*, without sounding the 't' of Mont, just as Montrouge is pronounced *Monrouge*.

Chassagne side of Le Montrachet and the rest on the Puligny side. The optimum yield of the Bâtard-Montrachet vines is 149 *queues* of one of the really great white wines of France, a wine which has elegance and breed as well as fullness of body and power. One of the best and more reliable Bâtards-Montrachet is that which bears the name of a small but knowledgeable and honest *vigneron*, Louis Poirier by name; his home and cellars are at Pommard, where he nurses and bottles with great care the few casks of Bâtard-Montrachet that he makes every year.

| | Queues (100 gallons) | | Queues (100 gallons) |
|---|---|---|---|
| *Tête de Cuvée* | | *Deuxièmes Cuvées* | |
| Montrachet | 50 | Les Pucelles | 43 |
| *Premières Cuvées* | | Les Referts | 102 |
| Bâtard-Montrachet | 149 | Les Sous-le-Puits | 29 |
| Blagny Blanc | 29 | | —— 174 *queues* |
| Champ-Canet | 30 | | |
| Chevalier-Montrachet | 41 | Grand Total | 537 *queues* |
| Les Combettes | 42 | | |
| Les Folatières | 22 | | |
| | —— 313 *queues* | | |

*Red Wines*: Although the fame of both Puligny and Chassagne rests on their white wines, both Communes produce also some red wines. The optimum yield of red wines of Puligny-Montrachet is 110 *queues*, of which about one-third is *Première Cuvée* (Le Cailleret), a third *Deuxième Cuvée* (Le Clavoillin) and a third *Troisième Cuvée* (Les Levrons and Les Charmes). Chassagne-Montrachet produces a great deal more, as well as some better, red wines than its twin Commune Puligny-Montrachet.

| | Queues (100 gallons) | | Queues (100 gallons) |
|---|---|---|---|
| *Têtes de Cuvée* | | *Deuxièmes Cuvées* | 577 |
| La Boudriotte | 119 | *Troisièmes Cuvées* | 594 |
| Le Clos Saint-Jean | 95 | | —— 1,171 *queues* |
| | —— 214 *queues* | | |
| *Premières Cuvée* | | Grand Total | 1,821 *queues* |
| Champain | 220 | | |
| La Maltroie[1] | 70 | | |
| Other *Premières Cuvées* | 146 | | |
| | —— 436 *queues* | | |

## Santenay

Santenay is the last of the Communes of the Côte d'Or at its southernmost limit. Some 600 acres of Santenay vineyards are planted with noble Pinots and produce a good deal of very nice red wines, the best of them being from Les Gravières, the only *climat* of Santenay to rank as a *Tête de Cuvée*; its optimum yield is 165 *queues*.

## Chalonnais, Mâconnais, Beaujolais

When it leaves Santenay, the Route Nationale 74 enters the Département of Saône-et-Loire and runs through two important towns, Chalon-sur-Saône and Mâcon, also on

[1] There is also a very fine white wine sold under the name of Château de La Maltroie: it has been given the *appellation contrôlée* 'Chassagne Montrachet'.

the Saône, to Villefranche, a distance of some 60 miles of vineyards which produce a very considerable quantity of wines, both red and white wines, but three times more reds than whites. The first section of these vineyards is called the Côte Chalonnaise. It consists of a range of hills which are the continuation of those of the Côte de Beaune, from Chagny near Santenay to Saint-Gengoux-le-National, nearly 20 miles farther south, and Saint-Léger-sur-Dheune about 6 miles to the east. The hills of the Côte Chalonnaise are really the foothills of the highlands of the Charollais: they face east-south-east and the Saône valley, with the forests of Chagny, Fontaine, Givry, Cluny and La Ferté between them and the Saône. At the northern end of the Côte Chalonnaise the vineyards of Cheilly-les-Maranges, Dezize-les-Maranges and Sampigny-les-Maranges actually belong, as to soil and subsoil and aspect, to the tail end of the Côte de Beaune, which is why they are entitled to the *appellation contrôlée* 'Côte de Beaune Villages'. Their best wines are the reds. A little farther south and east, that is on the way towards Chalon-sur-Saône, the wines of Chagny, Bouzeron, Rully and Montagny are either chiefly or entirely white wines, many of them quite good wines and usually good value as well, their price being appreciably below that of the Côte d'Or white wines. Then, some 5 miles south of Chalon-sur-Saône, Mercurey is sitting up atop a hill, completely surrounded by vineyards which stretch right and left to the Communes of Bourgneuf Val d'Or and Saint-Martin-sous-Montaigu. The wines made from the vineyards of all three Communes are red wines, and they are all sold under the name of *Mercurey*. They are the best red wines of the Côte Chalonnaise, challenged only for quality by the red wines of Givry, at the southernmost limit of the Côte Chalonnaise, and a short distance only from Mercurey.

We then come to the Côte Mâconnaise, which has much more *méridional* character, quite different from the Burgundian. It begins at or near Tournus, a quaint old medieval town on the River Saône, with flat-roofed houses as in Provence and Italy, where they have no fear of snow. The Côte Mâconnaise proper ends at Romanèche, where the Saône-et-Loire ends and where the Beaujolais begins, but the vineyards of both Mâconnais and Beaujolais are really one, an immense stretch of vines covering hundreds and hundreds of acres, as far as the eye can see, from the River Saône, in the east, to great tree-capped mountains in the west. The vineyards of the Mâconnais and Beaujolais produce more wine than all the other vineyards of Burgundy put together; their wines are mostly red and made from Gamay grapes. Until the latter part of the last century these wines were commonly known as *Vins de Mâcon*, but now the name of Beaujolais has acquired a measure of public favour so great as to be embarrassing: the demand for it in Paris alone is reckoned to be about twice as great as the supply of genuine Beaujolais.

The popularity of Beaujolais is due to a certain extent to the appeal of its pretty name, but chiefly to the fact that of all *ordinaire* red table wines it is the most acceptable within eighteen months, or even twelve, of its vintage, or birth: it has a soft, fruity quality that is very attractive, and its cost is or should be much less than that of red wines which have to be kept for five or more years before they are fit to drink.

Not only much but most of the red wines of the Mâconnais and Beaujolais are sold as *Beaujolais* or *Mâcon rouge*, but there are others, many other and better wines both red and white which are sold under the names of the vineyards of their birth. Of the reds, the best are the wines of Moulin-à-Vent, a name which covers a multitude of red wines made from the vineyards of Romanèche-Thorins, just in the Mâconnais, and those of the adjoining Commune of Chenas, just in the Beaujolais. Again, as a Moulin-à-Vent wine is a better and dearer wine, usually also an older one than a plain Beaujolais, there are a number of Moulin-à-Vent vineyards responsible for better wines than the rest, and these are sold with the name of their vineyard, such as *Clos de Rochegrès*, *Clos des Jacques*, *Clos du Carquelin*, etc. The Moulin-à-Vent *Château de Chenas* is the name given to the wines of the Cave Co-opérative of Chenas.

Among the other particularly good and justly popular red wines sold under the name of their native village, mention should be made of Brouilly and Côte de Brouilly, Chiroubles, Fleurie, Juliénas, Morgon, Romanèche-Thorins and Saint-Amour.

At Romanèche-Thorins the Hospices, like the Hospices de Beaune but on a smaller scale, bottle at the Hospices their wines, which are sold as *Moulin-à-Vent des Hospices de Romanèche-Thorins*, a blend always of dependable quality of Moulin-à-Vent wines.

As regards the white wines of the Mâconnais-Beaujolais, there are none better than those of Pouilly, Chaintré, Vergisson, Fuissé, Vinzelles and Loché, all of them on or near the great rock of Solutré, a short distance to the north-west of Romanèche-Thorins. Pouilly is not a Commune but a mere hamlet of the Commune of Solutré. Its white wine, however, is considered the best of the bunch, and its neighbours have tacked on its name to their own, Pouilly-Fuissé being used for the wines not only of Pouilly and Fuissé but also for those of Solutré, Vergisson and Chaintré, whereas the wines of Vinzelles and Loché are made by the *Cave Co-opérative* of each village and are sold as Pouilly-Vinzelles and Pouilly-Loché.

The white wines of Pouilly-Fuissé have become so popular that the demand has outgrown the supply. There are, of course, perfectly genuine Pouilly-Fuissé wines sold under that name and no other, but one can be quite sure not only of a genuine Pouilly-Fuissé wine but of one of the better ones if the label on the bottle also bears the name of a particular vineyard or Estate, such as Château de Fuissé, at Fuissé; Le Clos, at Pouilly; Le Mont Gacin, at Solutré; Les Charmes, at Vergisson; or Le Paradis, at Chaintré.

## La Confrérie des Chevaliers du Tastevin

The economic crisis of the early 1930s was world-wide. It may or it may not have been an inevitable consequence of the post-war boom, but it was certainly aggravated in Burgundy by the failure of three successive vintages, 1930, 1931 and 1932. The big firms, the 'Shippers', with great cellars full of 1928, 1929 and older excellent wines, for which the demand was not nearly as keen as it would have been under more normal, let alone prosperous circumstances, could well afford to wait for the return of good vintages. But the thousands of small vineyard owners, the great majority of the Burgundy *vignerons*, who had far too slender financial reserves to face a three years' failure, were in desperate straits. It was then that some of the more public-minded businessmen of Nuits-Saint-Georges decided to form an association of *vignerons* and merchants to devise the best means of attracting more visitors to Burgundy and of increasing the demand for the wines of Burgundy. This is how, in January, 1933, was formed the *Syndicat d'Initiative de Nuits-Saint-Georges*, the egg laid by Georges Faiveley and Camille Rodier, out of which was hatched, in 1934, the *Confrérie des Chevaliers du Tastevin*.

In Burgundy, as in Champagne, the beginning of October is usually vintage time, and the new wine generally 'falls bright', that is it has got over its first fermenting fever by the end of November: it can then be tasted and tested for the first time. This is why there was for a great many years a *Journée des Vins de Nuits* and a *Paulée de Meursault* during the last week in November, when *vignerons* and merchants met at Nuits-Saint-Georges, to taste the red wines of the Côte de Nuits, and at Meursault, to taste the white wines' of the Côte de Beaune, and not merely to taste wines but to talk about them as well as to eat and drink and make merry. It was also on the last Sunday in November that the new wines of the *Hospices de Beaune* were offered for sale by public auction. It is to the undying credit of the *Confrérie des Chevaliers du Tastevin* to have made of those three days a wonderful triptych with the *Hospices de Beaune* Sunday auction in the centre panel, the *Confrérie's* Saturday banquet on the left and the Monday *Paulée de Meursault* on the right, three festive days now known all the world over as *Les Trois Glorieuses*, three days devoted to the glory of the wines of Burgundy.

The banquet staged on the eve of the *Hospices* public auction by the *Confrérie des Chevaliers du Tastevin* is the culminating function of the annual *Chapitre*, when new *Chevaliers* are 'knighted' with great pomp and ceremony, choruses and trumpeting, scarlet robes and ermine facings, a most spectacular not to say theatrical setting which attracts crowds of people not only to the Château du Clos Vougeot, now the head-quarters of the *Confrérie*, but to the *Hospices de Beaune* auction the next day, and to Meursault, the day after. And all these people, *Chevaliers du Tastevin* or not, know much more about Burgundy than they ever did before; they and their friends also know and like the wines of Burgundy better than they ever did before. So much so that the Burgundy *vignerons* have now no difficulty in selling all the wine they make year by year.

The success achieved by the *Confrérie des Chevaliers du Tastevin* was so rapid and so complete that the wine-growers and wine-merchants of other districts were not slow in following so good an example, and it was not very long before there was a *Jurade de Saint-Emilion*, a *Commanderie du Bontemps du Médoc*, a *Confrérie des Sacavins d'Anjou*, *Chevaliers du Cep* and others.

CHAPTER FOUR

# *Champagne*

CHAMPAGNE is, today, the festive wine *par excellence*, the most lively and one of the most expensive of quality wines, a joy and a luxury. But it was not ever thus. During many centuries the wines of the great Champagne Province, stretching from Flanders in the north to Burgundy in the south, and from Lorraine in the east to the Ile de France in the west, were plain, still tables wines, mostly red. Whether better or not than the wines of Bordeaux and Burgundy is anybody's guess, but they can certainly claim, without fear of contradiction, to have been French much longer. It was only in the fifteenth century that the English lost Bordeaux and its wines, and it was only in the sixteenth century that the Emperor Charles V finally surrendered Burgundy to France.

# CHAMPAGNE

Reims

FRANCE

*Vesle*

REIMS

Villedommange

Sillery

*Ardre*

Villers-Allerand
Rilly
Ludes
Mailly
Verzenay
Verzy

*Vesle*

MONTAGNE DE REIMS

Trépail

Bouzy
Ambonnay

Cumières
Hautvillers
Dizy
Ay
Avenay
Mareuil

EPERNAY

*Marne*

Pierry
Chouilly

*Cubry*

Cramant

Avize

Oger

N

*Soude*

CÔTE DES BLANCS

Vertus

SCALE

Miles
0                    5
Kilometres
0              5

But it was in A.D. 496 that Saint Rémi, Bishop of Reims, received into the Church Clovis, first Christian King of the Franks, and all Kings of France have been crowned at Reims ever since.

That there was wine in Champagne in those early days is no mere speculation; there is ample documentary evidence of it, since we still possess Saint Rémi's own *Testament*, in which there are several Champagne vineyards mentioned among his legacies. Nor can there be any doubt about the excellence of the wines of Champagne of long ago, since they were praised by Urban II (Pope 1088–99) and 500 years later by Leo X (Pope 1513–21). The wines of Champagne had no other competitors in Paris except those of Orléans and Touraine until the seventeenth century, when both Bordeaux and Burgundy also sent in their wines. The wines of Burgundy were the more dangerous competitors of the two; they were of the same grape, the Pinot, and of the same type as the wines of Champagne, and they were very likely better wines, to judge from the still table wines of Champagne made today compared to the still table wines of Burgundy of the same vintages.

There is, therefore, every reason to assume that the *vignerons* of Champagne sought to produce a wine that would be, if not better than, at least different from any wine that had ever come out of Burgundy, and eventually Sparkling Champagne proved to be the right answer. This is where Dom Pérignon comes in.

Dom Pérignon was born at Sainte-Menehoulde in January, 1639. He renounced the world at the early age of nineteen and never regretted it. In 1668, when only in his thirtieth year, he was appointed to the post of Cellarer of the Benedictine Abbey of Hautvillers, near Epernay, in the Champagne country. During forty-seven consecutive years, until the day of his death, in September, 1715, Dom Pérignon was in charge of the cellars and of the finances of the Abbey. He had a remarkably keen palate and knew how to use it to good purpose. He had great experience in all matters pertaining to viticulture and wine-making; he was hardworking and shrewd; he made better wines than had ever been made before at Hautvillers; he also made some sparkling wine. He was a good man, he loved the poor. So much, and very little more, is tolerably certain.

Dom Pérignon has been hailed as the discoverer, inventor or creator of sparkling champagne. He has been described as the wizard who first put the bubbles into champagne.

This is mere romance. Dom Pérignon did not discover, invent or create sparkling champagne. He never claimed to have done so, nor did any of his contemporaries claim any such honour for him. He would certainly have greatly resented being hailed as the first to have 'put bubbles into champagne', when neither he nor anybody else ever put bubbles into champagne. The bubbles of sparkling champagne are the same as the bubbles of bottled beer: they are tiny drops of liquid disturbed, chased and whipped by escaping carbon dioxide or carbonic acid gas. This carbon dioxide is an inevitable by-product of a most natural phenomenon known as fermentation.

Champagne is a cold-blooded northerner. It begins fermenting cheerfully enough, but thinks better of it and settles down to a long sleep during the winter months. In the following spring or early summer it wakes up and takes up its half-finished job where it had left it. There is still some of the original grape-juice sugar left to be fermented, and after their long winter rest the saccharomycetes will now get busy again and supply the necessary zymase. In fact, to make sure that they will have plenty to do, a little more sugar is added to the wine, which is then bottled and corked securely down.

Exactly the same thing goes on within the bottle as in the cask, but with this difference, that the carbonic acid gas can no longer lose itself in the air; it remains in solution in the wine, a most amenable prisoner so long as there is no hope of escape. But once that gate of its prison, the cork, has gone, it rushes out of the wine with joy, carrying along in its haste thousands of dewdrops of wine; these are the champagne 'bubbles'.

Dom Pérignon did not create sparkling champagne, but he did a great deal for its fame. He made better wines than had been made in Champagne before, both still and sparkling. The excellence of Dom Pérignon's wines was due to the art with which he blended the grapes from various vineyards. It was due also to the fact that the Abbey of Hautvillers owned more vineyards and received by way of tithes a greater variety of grapes than any private vineyard owner.

Situated as they are so close to the northern latitude beyond which grapes will grow but will hardly ever fully ripen, the vineyards of Champagne are not blessed, nor were they blessed in the seventeenth century, with their full quota of sunshine year after year. They only enjoy a really fine summer now and again, and they produce then, but only then, grapes which give wonderful wine, wine truly deserving to be enjoyed and remembered as a vintage wine. Such years are the exception; other years, poorer years, years of acid, sun-starved wine, are the rule.

Just as reservoirs and irrigation have banished the spectre of famine in many subtropical countries, so judicious blending has brought fame and riches to the old province of Champagne. By saving wines of the better years and by finding out which blends of various vineyards will harmonize and give the best results, a very much higher level of average excellence has been reached and stocks of wines of fairly uniform quality have been built which have enabled the champagne shippers to dispense for years and years to a suffering humanity that most exhilarating from of relaxation known throughout the civilized world as sparkling champagne.

Dom Pérignon was the first to show the way; he was not the first to make sparkling wine nor to use corks, but he was the first to show the people of Champagne what was the best use they could make of their wines. It is not only the wine-growers and wine-shippers of Champagne who owe Dom Pérignon a deep debt of gratitude but all who appreciate the charm of sparkling champagne, all those to whom champagne has brought at some time that which is worth more than gold and silver: health and joy.

If there is one man who deserves to share with Dom Pérignon the gratitude of all true champagne lovers it is François, the man who first showed how sparkling champagne could be made with any degree of scientific precision and by so doing placed the whole of the champagne trade upon a sound commercial basis. He did this by inventing the *densimètre*, the all-important instrument which measures with precision the amount of sugar in the must at the time of bottling. Before the *densimètre*, it was left to the uncertain taste of man; too much sugar, the bottles burst; too little sugar, flat wine. The *densimètre* removed the element of uncertainty.

From the days of Dom Pérignon to those of François, that is roughly 150 years, from 1690 to 1840, the vogue of sparkling champagne had many ups and downs – mostly downs. There were all through that period a large class of connoisseurs who made no secret of their dislike of the 'green' sparkling wines of Epernay, and who definitely preferred the still wines of the Montagne de Reims. Still champagne had a far greater number of admirers, in France, than the sparkling variety, which seems to have been synonymous with 'new' champagne. In England the Dry Sillery and other still or barely creaming wines of Reims also had many supporters. Thus, in a letter written, in 1788, to Mr Moët, at Epernay, by Messrs Carbonnell, Moody & Walker, London wine-merchants, they asked for twenty dozen of champagne to be shipped to them in two hampers of ten dozen each, adding that 'the wine must be of good quality, not too charged with liqueur, but of excellent taste and not at all sparkling'.

Before François, there was no scientific means of ascertaining the quantity of unfermented sugar in the wine, and the most costly mistakes were made. According to Jullien, the proportion of bottles which burst in champagne cellars, and were consequently a total loss, varied from 15 to 40% in 1816. In 1833 the loss in Mr Moët's cellars, at Epernay, was 35%, and in 1834 25%. In 1842, according to the Académie de Reims, the loss due to 'casse en caves' was only 10%. Since François, others, and more particularly Maumené in 1858, Robinet in 1877 and Salleron in 1889, have brought the science of making sparkling wines to such perfection that the number of burst bottles in champagne cellars is now very small indeed.

When François's methods were generally adopted the champagne trade became much more profitable and less hazardous. Many new firms then came into existence and, in order to make their wines known to the public, offered them at low prices which had hitherto never been thought to be within the range of possibilities.

Thus it came to pass that the average sales of champagne rose from some thirteen million bottles per annum during the 'sixties to nineteen million during the 'seventies and over twenty-two million during the 'eighties and 'nineties.

The sales of champagne increased rapidly, but not nearly in the same proportion in all markets. In France, for instance, the sale of champagne remained practically stationary from 1861 – when a total of 6,904,914 bottles of champagne were exported to all parts of the world – to 1890 – when the total exports of champagne had risen to 21,699,108 bottles. During the same time the consumption of champagne in England rose from about three to over nine million bottles per annum, as the result of the introduction of dry champagne in England, while the sweet 'dessert' type of champagne remained the rule throughout France.

## The Making of Sparkling Champagne

It is now time to consider in what way the making of sparkling champagne differs from the methods for making a natural wine described in Chapter 12 on 'The Art of Wine Making'.

Sparkling champagne is a white wine made mostly from Pinot grapes that we call black, but they are not black; their juice is white and their skin is blue outside and red inside. To make a white wine from black grapes is not done by magic, but by care and skill. The colouring pigment of so-called black grapes is contained in the lining of their skin, so that grapes must be picked and brought to the press unbruised and without delay if their white juice is not to be dyed pink before they are pressed. In Champagne the grapes are picked with care as soon as they are ripe, but before being sent to the *pressoir* to be crushed they are first examined at the roadside nearest the vineyard of their birth by a team of women, mostly elderly ones who have had their full share of back-breaking grape-picking when they were younger: they sit in a row with a wide osier tray at knee height before them; the grapes gathered by the pickers are brought to the women at the roadside in baskets, which are tipped over on to the osier tray. The women quickly take up and look over bunch after bunch, removing expertly with a pair of long pointed scissors all defective berries, if and when there happen to be any, either unripe or mildewy, or otherwise undesirable for any cause whatsoever. All such 'rejects' are dropped in a refuse bin, while the bunches with none but sound and ripe grapes go into great osier baskets known as *caques*. These are then loaded on lorries and driven to the nearest *vendangeoir* of the person or firm who owns the vineyard or who has bought the grapes from the *vignerons*. At the *vendangeoir* the grapes are weighed in their *caques* and tipped out into the *pressoir* until there is enough for a pressing or 'charge', usually of 4,000 kilograms or nearly 4 tons. The bunches are kept whole, not *égrappées* nor *foulées* as in Burgundy or the Gironde, and the grapes remains whole when tipped in the *pressoir*. This consists of a square wooden floor with four adjustable open-work wooden rails which make a sort of cage in which the grapes are heaped. The *pressoir* has a heavy lid of oak boards which is lowered and raised at will by a screw, now driven, as a rule, by electricity, but until recently by muscle and sweat. When the lid is clamped on the heaped grapes in the *pressoir*, and slowly but relentlessly driven down, its crushing pressure bursts the grapes, and their sweet juice immediately runs off through the rails into a slightly sloping wide groove that leads it to a collecting 'station' without having been in contact for any time with the skins of the grapes; these are left behind in the cage of the press. The first flow pressed out of the grapes is either led or pumped into a vat which holds 450 gallons of this, the best grape juice or *Cuvée*. Greater pressure is then applied and more juice is squeezed out of the wet husks still in the cage of the *pressoir*, but it is neither as white nor as sweet nor as good as the *Cuvée*, and it is not mixed with it. Very soon after the *Cuvée* has been vatted, it begins to ferment in a rather boisterous manner, throwing off an ugly 'head' or scum, thus getting rid of any dirt or dust or anything else which is not wanted; some of which, the heavier stuff, falls to the bottom of the vat as lees. When the must, as this working grape-juice is called, returns to a more normal temperature, in 24 or 36 hours as a rule, all that is clear is drawn into 10 clean oak casks holding 44 gallons each, and these casks are sent at once by lorry to Reims, Epernay, Ay or wherever the persons or firms who own the wine-to-be have their cellars. All through the vintage, which may be long or short according to the more or less favourable weather conditions from year to year, lorries are busy day and night fetching casks to put the new wine in and delivering full ones at the *celliers* from all parts of the Champagne vineyards. During the next eight to ten weeks the must will be left alone to become new wine, most of the grape-sugar present in the must having become alcohol, which stays put, and carbonic acid gas, which loses itself in the air.

The new wines are then racked, that is transferred into new casks, leaving behind the sediment cast off during the process of fermentation. After being racked the new wines of different pressings or *marcs* of each vineyard or set of vineyards are 'assembled' or blended together, in order to obtain one standard wine from each place, irrespective of whether the wine was made at the beginning of the vintage or at the end, from grapes which might have been hardly fully ripe in the first instance and from what may be slightly overripe grapes in the second. The newly racked and 'assembled' wine is given another four or five weeks to rest and to proceed a little further with its slow fermentation, if it has a mind to do so. It is then racked another time, which serves the double purpose of separating it from any lees it may have cast off and to give it plenty of fresh air. Then comes the all-important business of making-up the *Cuvées*. The *Chef de Caves*, whose responsibility it is, must taste with the greatest keenness the wines of all the different vineyards or sets of vineyards, and he has to decide how much or how little of the wines of each different district he ought to blend together to secure the approximately right quantity and quality of each one of the different brands which his firm sells on different markets, in competition with other Champagne shippers. The *Chef de Caves* may also decide to add to his *Cuvées* more or less of older wines which have been kept in cask for that very purpose. When, after many tastings and much hesitation, his choice has been made, the chosen wines are mixed and blended together in great *foudres* or vats with an electrically actioned mechanical arm churning the wines thoroughly; after which they are tested for sugar, liqueured and bottled.

The style of each *Cuvée* depends entirely upon the skill and taste of the *Chef de Caves*, but the quality of the wine depends in the first place upon the quality of the grapes which, in Champagne as everywhere else, varies with the soil, sub-soil and aspect of different vineyards. No *Chef de Caves*, however skilled he may be in the art of blending, can possibly make a first-quality wine out of second-quality grapes. A champagne *Cuvée* made from different wines from none but the very best vineyards would not be an economic or commercial proposition, but the best *Cuvées* are always those in which there is a greater proportion of *Premiers Crus* grapes, a smaller proportion of *Deuxièmes Crus* and no *Troisièmes Crus* at all.

The quantity of '*liqueur de tirage*' which is added at bottling time to the *Cuvée de tirage* is such that the newly bottled wine will have just the right proportion of carbonic acid gas to make it as sparkling as it should be, no less and no more, after fermentation will have intervened. This *liqueur de tirage* is plain sugar candy melted in champagne wine. When the *Cuvée de tirage* is bottled its cork is held by a strong clamp which will keep it safely in the bottle at the '*prise de mousse*', that is, when fermentation does its job. As soon as bottled, the *Cuvée de tirage* is laid to rest in the deep, damp, cold, chalk cellars of Reims, Epernay and Ay, to be left alone for two or three years: long before that, the wine will have fermented out any of the sugar that was in it when it was bottled. It will be sparkling champagne right enough, but not fit to drink. During its bottle fermentation the wine throws off small but none the less objectionable pieces of tartaric acid, mucilage and other matters of either mineral or vegetable origin. This sediment lies quietly enough in the safely corked bottle, but it would foul the look and taste of the wine the moment glasses were filled. So it must be taken out of the wine somehow, and this is done most skilfully by the *remuage* and *dégorgement*. The *remuage* consists in giving each bottle, day after day, a twist sharp enough to make the sediment slide down towards the neck of the bottle, but not hard enough to make it rise into the wine. The process begins with the bottle in a horizontal position, but when completed the bottle stands vertically, neck downwards, and by that time the whole of the sediment has been gathered upon the inside face of the cork.

The next move is the removing of the cork with its wad of sediment, so that the wine is absolutely 'star bright' and will remain like it to the last drop. This must be done, and it is done, with practically no loss of wine and very little loss of the precious gas in it.

Plate 11. The vintage at Mareuil-sur-Ay in Champagne. The *Pinot noir* grapes have been picked and assembled under the eye of the *maître de vendange*.

The man who does it, *le dégorgeur*, is a skilled and valuable man indeed. He is the first of a team who deal with the bottle of sparkling champagne when the time has come to make it ready to leave the depths of the cellars and go into the world. Next to the *dégorgeur* comes the *doseur*, the man who adds to the bottle of wine more or less *Liqueur d'Expédition*, a very sticky mixture of sugar, still champagne wine and brandy: the wine to melt the sugar, the sugar to sweeten the wine and the brandy to stop the sugar fermenting. The object of this addition of *Liqueur d'Expédition* is to give to the wine just the degree of sweetness which is to the taste of the customer: it may be as little as $\frac{1}{2}\%$ if the wine is for people who like *Brut Champagne*, 1% for those who prefer *Extra Sec*, 3% for those who prefer *Sec* and 5% for the *Demi-Sec* connoisseurs. All such proportions are only approximate, since each Champagne shipper has his own technique in preparing the *Liqueur d'Expédition* and using it. When the *doseur* has done his job he passes on the bottle to the *boucheur*, who drives into the neck of the bottle a long and fat branded cork, which has to be forcibly squeezed to half its natural size for half its length to fit in the neck of the bottle. Next to the *boucheur* sits the *ficeleur*, who squashes down the half of the cork jutting out of the neck and makes it fast to the ring of the bottle neck with a three-branch or four-branch wire. The bottle of sparkling champagne is then ready; when the call comes, it is sent up from the cellars to the *cellier*, where it is washed, dressed up, packed up and sent off.

Champagne bottles are the most gaily decorated of all wines: body labels and shoulder *collerettes* are not peculiar to champagne, but the bright or dull 'foil', the sheet of gold, silver or coloured metal or paper which covers the cork and the whole of the neck of the bottle makes it looks festive, but its purpose in the beginning was purely utilitarian. Instead of the wire which now holds down the final cork, the *bouchon d'expédition*, string was originally used, and it was protected from damp and rats by a tightly fitting pewter cap with a dab of one colour or another over it to differentiate different wines. Gradually this protective pewter, growing more and more ornate and longer, became the champagne foil as we know it today.

## Vintage and Non-vintage Champagne

A vintage champagne is, or ought to be, the wine made from Pinot grapes grown in Champagne vineyards in one and the same year, the date of which it bears, printed on its labels and branded upon its corks. The vineyards of Champagne are very near the northern limit beyond which grapes will not mature in the open, and champagne grapes do not ripen fully unless there has been a particularly hot summer. There are, unfortunately, a number of years when the weather is not all that it should be, and the wines made in such years are likely to be somewhat tart and thin. Then it is that those wealthy Champagne shippers with immense reserves of wines of past good vintages bring forth the right quantity of soft and fat wine to blend with the others, and they often do produce in this manner very nice wines indeed which cannot be sold under the date of any one particular year, but they are none the less quite good wines, often better value than vintage wines.

Vintage wines possess, naturally, a greater degree of personality, and they age more graciously, especially when they are really self-wines – not assisted or 'bettered' by the addition of older wines. They also invariably cost more than non-vintage champagne;

Plate 12. The *Pinot vert doré* used for making champagne and the finest white Burgundies.

in the first place because they are, or ought to be, better wines, and in the second because there is a limited quantity of any vintage *Cuvée*; sooner or later the time must come when there will be no more; when that time approaches the scarcer and dearer the wines become.

## The Champagne District

The old Champagne Province was divided in 1790 into four Départements, Aisne and Haute-Marne in the north, Marne in the centre and Aube in the south. There are vineyards in all four Départements, but the fact that the roots of their vines are in champagne soil is not sufficient to give to the wine made from their grapes the right to the name of champagne. The soil, sub-soil and aspect of the vineyards must be such that the noble Pinots can thrive and produce a wine worthy to bear the honoured name of champagne. This is why the limits of the *région délimitée*, the only area allowed to call its wines champagne, have been drawn and fixed by law. This official *région délimitée* covers a total of, roughly speaking, 27,000 acres, of which 21,000 are in the Marne Département, 4,600 in the Aube and 1,400 in the Aisne. Obviously, although these 27,000 acres of vineyards are legally entitled to call their wines champagne, there are very great differences in the quality of their wines. We can, without any hesitation, discard, to begin with, the wines of the Aube and Aisne vineyards. They produce none but the cheaper qualities of champagne which are drunk either locally or in Paris night-clubs. All the better-quality champagne comes from the vineyards of the Marne Département, which does not mean, unfortunately, that all the vineyards of the Marne Département produce automatically very high quality wines.

There are in the Marne, as in the Côte d'Or and the Gironde, vineyards which are either very much better or just a little better than others. It depends chiefly upon the nature of soil and sub-soil, and also on the altitude and aspect of each vineyard. The climate is the same for all, although some may be more sheltered than others. In Champagne the weather is often bitter in winter, but the vines do not mind hard frost when dormant; spring is the most dangerous time of the year, as late frosts may do and often do incalculable damage.

Summers are often very hot, with occasional thunderstorms and hailstorms; autumn, vintage time, is often warm and sunny, which makes everybody very happy; a wet and cold vintage spells disaster. It was ever thus, or, at any rate, for the past 1,000 years; we can be fairly certain of the age-long uncertainty of the weather in Champagne, because records still exist of the prices paid at the vintage time from the tenth century to our own day, and they show that prices soared when spring frosts had brought about a shortage of wine, but slumped badly when there was a glut. In 1952, when a moderate quantity (7,354,000 gallons) of very fine wine was made, the best grapes were sold at 155 francs per kilogram, roughly equivalent to $5·60 or 40s. per gallon of wine. In 1953, when rather less (7,000,000 gallons) of a fair quality wine was made, the price rose to 160 francs per kilogram for the best grapes, or about $5·88 or 42s. per gallon of wine. In 1954 there was a greater quantity (8,344,000 gallons) of wine made, but of very poor quality, in spite of which the best grapes had to be paid for at the rate of 138 francs per kilogram, or about $4·76 or 34s. per gallon of wine. Happily, 1955 was a better year in every respect, and there were 10,351,000 gallons of wine made, and the quality of most of it was very good indeed; the best grapes were paid for at the rate of 141 francs per kilogram, which was roughly equivalent to 5·04 dollars or 36s. per gallon, that is 84 cents or 6s. per bottle of raw material, the rough wine which will require a hundred pairs of hands and at least six years to become the brilliant sparkling wine in a gaily dressed bottle that will be offered to us for sale – and at what price?

All the better vineyards of the Marne have been divided into many classes or categories, according to the quality of the wine which may be expected from their grapes: the best are in what is called the *Catégorie Grand Cru*, and the next three in *Première*, *Deuxième* and *Trosième Catégorie*. When vintage time is at hand the Champagne shippers and the growers, whose grapes the shippers are going to buy, meet and agree upon what shall be the right price to pay for the grapes of the *Catégorie Grand Cru* vineyards, and that settles the price of the grapes of the remaining categories; they are paid for according to an agreed descending scale, from 100 to 90% of the maximum price for *Première Cru* wines (the wines of this category rated at 100% are the *Grand Crus*); wines below 90% are of lesser quality. The margin allows for paying more or less according to quality, since all the wines of the same *Catégorie* are not likely to be identical. Some *vignerons* may have taken greater care, or they may have had better luck than others.

Nearly all the better growth vineyards are in the *Arrondissements* of Reims and Epernay, and a few only in the Canton of Vertus, of the *Arrondissement* of Châlons-sur-Marne. They cover the approaches to the Montagne de Reims and its lower slopes facing Reims and Châlons-sur-Marne; the hillside upon the right bank of the River Marne above and below Epernay; and the approaches and lower slopes of a range of gentle hills some distance to the left of the Merne, above Epernay, known as the Montagne d'Avize or Côte des Blancs.

## Montagne de Reims

The Montagne de Reims is a cliff of tertiary formation and in the shape of a flat iron with its sharp end pointing eastwards towards Châlons-sur-Marne; it rises sharply from the billowing plain crossed by the little River Vesle, on the north-east, and from the banks of the Marne, on the south-west. A great forest and wild-boar sanctuary covers the broad crest of the Montagne de Reims, but its sides and approaches are covered with closely planted vineyards on all sides. That part of the Montagne de Reims on the Vesle side, and farthest away from Châlons-sur-Marne, is known as *La Petite Montagne*, and its vineyards produce the less distinguished wines entitled to the name of champagne; the best of them, however, those of Sacy and Villedommange, are in good demand, being cheaper than most and considered to be very good value. Leaving *La Petite Montagne* for *La Montagne* and proceeding eastwards, we shall pass through the vineyards of Villers-Allerand, Rilly-la-Montagne, Chigney-les-Roses, Ludes, Mailly-Champagne, Verzenay, Verzy and Villers-Marmery, all of them hillside villages and vineyards, while we shall survey from our vantage point – none of greater beauty than the Moulin de Verzenay – a wonderful panorama of flourishing vineyards, including those of Sillery and Beaumont-sur-Vesle stretching to the Route Nationale from Reims to Châlons-sur-Marne.

All these 'Montagne' vineyards are practically back-to-back with the 'Marne' vineyards on the other side, but there are others at the eastern end, or turning-point of the Montagne, forming a sort of connecting link between the two: they are the vineyards of Trépail, Tauxières and Louvois, on the Châlons-sur-Marne side, and Bouzy and Ambonnay on the Marne side. We shall then turn our backs on Châlons-sur-Marne, and, facing Château-Thierry and Paris farther west, we shall pass through the riverside vineyards of Bisseuil, Mareuil-sur-Ay, Avenay and Ay, a little town as quaint as its name and well worth a visit. Beyond Ay, the vineyards of Dizy-Magenta and Cumières, and those of Champillon and Hautvillers much higher up, all produce very fine wines, but the same cannot fairly be said of the wines made from grapes grown farther west upon the right bank of the Marne, practically as far as Château-Thierry.

Some 80% of the grapes grown in all these vineyards are black Pinot grapes, with patches of white Pinot-Chardonnay grapes here and there, chiefly at Verzy. There are, in Champagne as in Burgundy, different kinds of *Pinots noirs*, the best, or at any rate the one which is grown to a greater extent than all others, is that which is known locally by the name of *plant doré*, of which there are three slightly different sorts, known as *Le Petit Plant doré*, *Le Gros Plant doré d'Ay* and *Le Vert doré*, which is also sometimes known as *Plant Jeanson* or *Plant d'Ay*. Other varieties are the *Plant Gris*, which has nothing to do with the *Pinot gris*, a white grape; it is also known as *Pinot de Trépail* and *Pinot de Vertus*. All these are 'noble' Pinots, but they have a poor relation, the *Pinot Meunier*, with more and heavier bunches of grapes but giving a commoner type of wine.

On the left bank of the Marne the better wines are those of Chouilly and Pierry, close to Epernay, to the right and left of the town, but the best wines are those of a range of gentle hills a little farther back from the river; they rise soon after one leaves Pierry and stretch as far as Vertus. This is the part of the *Champagne viticole* known as *La Côtes des Blancs*, or the hill of the white grapes, where the white Pinot–Chardonnay grapes are grown almost exclusively. It is also called *Blanc de Cramant* or *Pinot blanc Chardonnay*. The most important township of the Côte des Blancs is Avize, with Cramant on higher ground to its right, or west, Le Mesnil, Oger and Vertus to its left, or east. The other vineyards of La Côte des Blancs, those of Monthelon and Cuis, on the Pierry side of Cramant, and Grauves on the other side of the same hill, also produce white wines from white grapes, 'Blanc de Blancs', entitled to the name of champagne, but they are of distinctly plainer quality.

The immense stretches of vines give no idea of how small are most of the holdings of individual owners of the Champagne vineyards, but according to official statistics the vineyards of the Marne are divided among 11,298 proprietors:

| | |
|---|---|
| 4,300 . . . . . | own less than ½ acre each |
| 4,770 . . . . . | own more than ½ acre and less than 2½ acres |
| 2,080 . . . . . | own more than 2½ acres and less than 12 acres |
| 87 . . . . . | own more than 12 acres and less than 25 acres |
| 38 . . . . . | own more than 25 acres and less than 50 acres |
| 18 . . . . . | own more than 50 acres and less than 100 acres |
| 5 . . . . . | own more than 100 acres |
| 11,298 | |

The making and maturing of sparkling champagne is a skilled and costly business beyond the means of some ten thousand *vignerons*: they grow grapes and sell them to the wealthy concerns, or 'shippers', in whose cellars millions of bottles of sparkling champagne are prepared and matured to be sold eventually in all parts of the world.

CHAPTER FIVE

# *Côtes du Rhône*

T HE RHÔNE has no sooner risen from its icy cradle than its long run from Alpine snows to the blue waters of the Mediterranean starts among vines, those of the highest vineyards in Europe from Visp to Zermatt: their Heidenwein and Gletscher, or Glacier, wines are Rhône wines, but not *Côtes du Rhône* any more than the wines of Savoie and Bugey along the valley of the Rhône, from its entry into France until it joins the Saône at Lyons.

There are some very pleasant Savoie and Bugey wines, most welcoming and attractive when you call upon them, but poor travellers. Some of them, such as La Côte Grèle, once Brillat-Savarin's own vineyard at Valromey, and Montmélian, between Chambéry and Saint-Jean-de-Maurienne; the Coteaux de Crépy, south of the Lake of Geneva; Talloires, Thonon, Ayse and at a number of other places, the white wines enjoy a greater measure of popular favour than the red wines; there is also a sparkling white *Seyssel* and a sparkling *rosé Chautagne* in great demand locally, but none of these are Côtes du Rhône wines.

The greatest characteristics of the true Rhône wines are their essential stability and keeping quality. Bred from vines grown in inches of soil on stony, steep, terraced slopes, these wines have good colour and a distinctive bouquet: they will last for years without loss of either. A Rhône wine is often not bottled until five years old, and usually in burgundy-shaped bottles, sometimes with a conceit of thin silver wire netting round them, quite charming and infinitely useless.

The Côtes du Rhône wines are wines from grapes grown on either bank of the Rhône along the 125 miles of its run from Lyons to Avignon. The Côtes du Rhône wines vary greatly in style and quality, and they may be divided as follows:

1. Côte Rôtie        4. Saint-Péray
2. Condrieu          5. Châteauneuf-du-Pape
3. Hermitage         6. Tavel

### *Côte Rôtie*

Côte Rôtie is the northernmost of the Côtes du Rhône vineyards, and it produces the finest red Côtes du Rhône wine. The name is given to a range of hills, barely 2 miles in length, on the right bank of the Rhône, in the Commune of Ampuis-Côte-Rôtie, about 5 miles from Vienne on the opposite bank of the river. The *vignerons* of Ampuis claim that their vineyards date back to A.D. 600 and, if so, it is remarkable that the soil shows as yet no sign of being exhausted: on the contrary, it brings forth finer red wines than any of the other Rhône valley vineyards where the same black grape, the *Syrah*, locally known as *Sérine* or *Serène*, is cultivated.

A stony bluff that rises screen-like behind the little town of Ampuis-Côte-Rôtie is known as *Côte Brune*, and another immediately to the south of it is called *Côte Blonde*, on account of the greater proportion of lime in its soil. The terraced vineyards of both

# RHONE

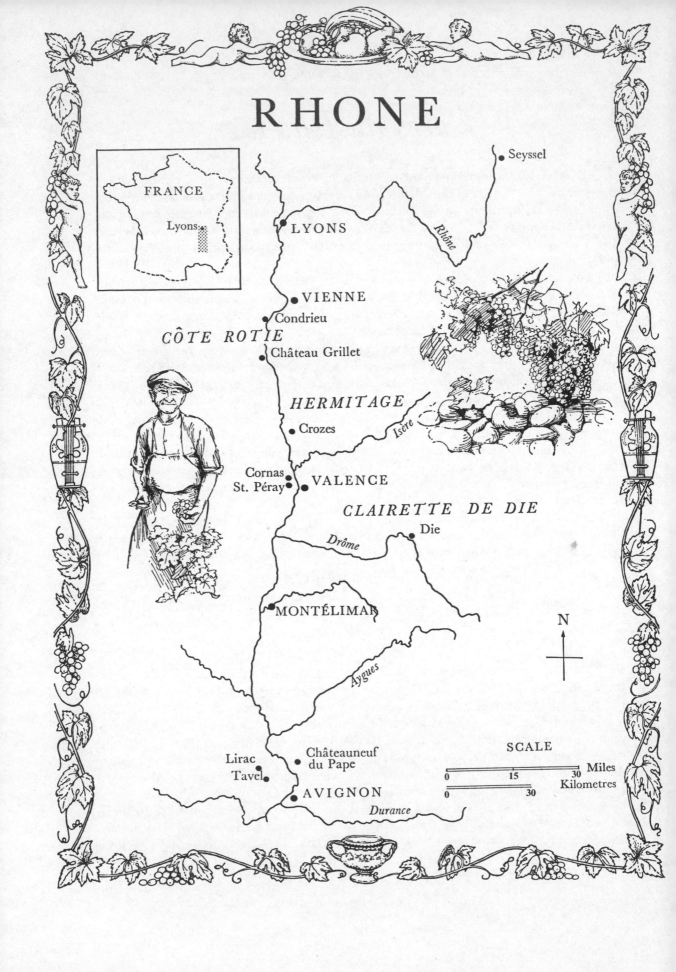

FRANCE

Lyons

Seyssel

LYONS

VIENNE

Condrieu

*CÔTE ROTIE*

Château Grillet

*HERMITAGE*

Crozes

*Isère*

*Rhône*

Cornas
St. Péray

VALENCE

*CLAIRETTE DE DIE*

Die

*Drôme*

MONTÉLIMAR

*Aygues*

N

Lirac
Tavel

Châteauneuf
du Pape

AVIGNON

*Durance*

SCALE

| 0 | 15 | 30 | Miles |
| 0 | | 30 | Kilometres |

the *Côte Brune* and *Côte Blonde* produce the finest of the red wines of the Rhône, those of the *Côte Brune* possessing rather greater breed and being regarded as the better of the two. To be entitled to the name of *Côte Rôtie*, the wines of both the *Côte Brune* and the *Côte Blonde* must have an alcoholic strength of at least 10°, and they must be made from at least 80% of *Syrah* or *Sérine* grapes.

## Condrieu

A little farther south, where the Département of the Rhône ends and the Département of the Loire begins, the vineyards of Condrieu are partly in the Commune of Condrieu (Rhône) and partly in the two adjoining Communes of Vérin and Saint-Michel-sous-Condrieu (Loire). The only grape grown is the *Voignier*, a white grape from which a golden wine of very fine quality is made, but, unfortunately, in very small quantities only. The few acres of Condrieu vineyards are shared among 17 different owners, and the finest vineyard of all, 2·47 acres only, known as Château Grillet, is the property of Monsieur Neyret-Cachet; the quality of its wine is superlative. It is one of the very best white wines of France. The alcoholic strength of the white wines of Condrieu and Château Grillet is never inferior to 11°.

## Hermitage

Rising sharply, pyramid-like, from a broad base to a height of a thousand feet, the Hermitage Hill towers over the sleepy little town of Tain-L'Hermitage sprawling along the left bank of the Rhône, opposite Tournon. The Hermitage Hill occupies a commanding position, yet there are no ruins of any fortress nor traces of ancient fortifications: there is, however, a small chapel built upon the site of the vineyard given, in 1225, to a returning Crusader knight turned hermit, Henri de Sterimberg.

These sloping friendly vineyards should be visited during the *vendange* when men with great tubs of grapes on their backs descend to the waiting carts with the agility of mountain goats, although it is not advisable to get in their way. The picture of grey stone, blue sky and the bright clothing of the *vendangeurs* is unique and unforgettable.

From Tain-L'Hermitage to St Christopher's Chapel, near the brow of the Hill, and a little distance beyond, there are 346 acres of vines cultivated in the folds of the Hill: they produce on an average 55,000 gallons of wine every year, about two-thirds of it red wine, from the black Syrah grape, and the rest white wine from Roussanne and/or Marsanne grapes. Both the red and white wines of Hermitage possess vinosity and breed, as well as an attractive bouquet faintly reminiscent of honeysuckle.

The vineyards of Crozes-L'Hermitage, close to those of the Hermitage Hill, towards the south-west, produce on an average 12,000 gallons of wine, mostly red, similar to the wines of Hermitage.

Upon the opposite side of the Rhône, in the Ardèche Département, beyond Tournon and immediately north of Saint-Péray, the vineyards of Cornas produce a fair amount of red wines similar in character to those of Hermitage but with more body and greater alcoholic strength, 11° instead of 10·5° (Cornas) and 10° (Hermitage).

## Saint-Péray

Saint-Péray is an old-world little town basking in the sun, on the right bank of the Rhône opposite Valence; it is hemmed in on all sides by vineyards which have produced during many centuries past red and white wines of high repute. Today, the red wines of Saint-Péray are consumed locally and anonymously, the *appellation contrôlée* 'Saint-Péray' being exclusively reserved for the white wines, still and sparkling. These white wines are made from Roussanne and/or Marsanne white grapes, but, owing to differences in the nature and depth of the soil, they produce much lighter wines at the Saint-Péray vineyards than they do upon the other side of the Rhône, up on the Hermitage Hill.

Ever since the year 1829, when some sparkling wine was made at the Château de Beauregard, near Saint-Péray, a good deal of the white wines of Saint-Péray are handled in the same manner as is champagne and rendered sparkling.

## Châteauneuf-du-Pape

When the Popes lived at Avignon some five centuries ago they probably had a summer residence built here, but it is likely that vines were cultivated long before. The name is romantic and has perhaps helped the wine, which it hardly needs, if for no other reason than its alcoholic strength, which is appreciably higher than that of most other French red wines.

The vineyards which produce the red, *rosé* and white wines of Châteauneuf-du-Pape stretch across what is probably the crater of a volcano extinct for many centuries. Their soil must be fertile, since it produces a great deal more grapes than all the other vineyards of the Côtes du Rhône put together, and yet it is entirely covered up by a relentless tide of shingle, pebbles and stones of various shapes, colours and sizes. Planted apparently haphazard, but may be according to some carefully thought-out plan, there are different varieties of grapes, all growing together, mostly the Syrah, Grenache, Clairette, Mourvèdre, Picpoul, Terret noir, Coudoise, Muscadin, Vaccarèse, Picardan, Cinsault and Gamay *noir à jus blanc*, for the red wines. The white grapes grown for the making of white wines are chiefly the Roussette, Marsanne, Bourboulenc, Carignan, Pinot *blanc de Bourgogne*, Voignier, Pascal *blanc* and Mauzac. The warmth and power which all good Châteauneuf-du-Pape wines possess in a greater measure than all other French tables wines is due to the fact that both red and white wines are made from about fourteen different species of grapes, as well as to the greater force of the summer sun than in either the Côte d'Or or the Gironde. The minimum alcohol strength of both the red and the white wines of Châteauneuf-du-Pape is 12·5°.

The best wines of Châteauneuf-du-Pape are those sold under the names of individual vineyards, estates or firms such as the Châteaux Fortia, de la Nerthe, Vaudieu, La Gardine, the Cru Saint-Patrice, the Clos de L'Oratoire des Papes, etc.

The white wine of Châteauneuf-du-Pape possesses a darker shade of gold than most white burgundy wines, often also more body, but its bouquet is usually very discreet.

## Tavel

Roquemaure, opposite Châteauneuf-du-Pape, was once a busy port from which Languedoc wines were shipped not only to Lyons and Paris but to England and Holland. Thus, in 1744, there were 12,000 hogsheads of wine loaded at Roquemaure, and there is every reason to believe that most of it came from the vineyards of Travel and Lirac, immediately to the west of Roquemaure, or those of Chusclan to the north, in the valley of La Cèze, a tributary of the Rhône.

Although there are late eighteenth and early nineteenth century 'Wine Labels' bearing the names of Roquemaure and Chusclan, none is known that bears the name of Tavel. Yet, today, the wines of Chusclan, Roquemaure and Lirac are all sold merely as *Côtes du Rhône*, whereas the wines of Tavel have their own *appellation contrôlée* in France, and they enjoy all over the world a greater measure of popularity than all other *vins rosés*. The soil of the Tavel vineyards is nought but sand, lime and loose flints: how vines can grow – nay, flourish – in such baked and barren ground must be seen to be believed, and yet their grapes yield a *vin rosé* that possesses both charm and a great deal more power than it is given credit for by unwary drinkers.

The *vignerons* of Tavel make their famous *rosé* in many ways, and some use as many as four or five different kinds of grapes. Two white grapes and two red is a common prescription in set and ordered proportions. Thus there is a great variation in Tavel wines which at their best are quite delicious and have more essential character than any other *rosés*. (See special note on *rosé* in glossary.)

CHAPTER SIX

# Loire

THE WINES of the Loire and its tributaries are made in one of the most beautiful parts of France, and one of the most interesting of the French vine-growing districts. Almost everywhere along the course of this long and gracious river from Blois to Saint-Nazaire the scenery is magnificent, a vast panorama of wooded and vine-clad hills, great châteaux and venerable cities. Lovely as are the vineyards of Burgundy, Alsace and the Rhône valley, those of the Loire have greater breadth and majesty. The same cannot be said, however, of the Loire wines, many of them quite charming, some of them very fine, but none of them great wines. Comparatively few of the Loire wines are sold under the name of the *vigneron* or his château, but mostly under the *appellation contrôlée* of the district, village and, sometimes, the vineyard responsible for the wine in the bottle. Bad vintages are the exception in the Loire Valley, so that less importance attaches to the date of different vintages than is the case for other French wines; many of the Loire wines are sold without any vintage date, and most of them are best when young.

The Loire is the greatest of the great rivers of France. It rises in the Cévennes highlands and flows from south to north as far as Orléans, where it turns sharply to the west, passing through Blois, Tours and Nantes before reaching the Atlantic opposite Saint-Nazaire, after a 625 miles' far-from-straight run. The Loire crosses twelve Départements with an aggregate of over 500,000 acres of vineyards, and those which produce the more popular Loire wines are the Nièvre, the Cher, the Indre-et-Loire, the Maine-et-Loire and the Loire Atlantique.

# The Upper Loire

## Nièvre

There are many vineyards all along the Loire before the river comes to Nevers, but none of them bring forth any wines of real merit until we come to those of the Nièvre Département. The vineyards of the Nièvre which produce the best and better known wines are those of Pouilly-sur-Loire, a busy little market town on the right bank of the Loire about half-way between La Charité-sur-Loire and Cosne. The wines of Pouilly-sur-Loire are mostly white wines, and there are two quite distinct sorts known, the first and much the better as *Blanc Fumé de Pouilly* or *Pouilly Fumé*, and the other, a much cheaper wine, which is simply called *Pouilly-sur-Loire*. The *Blanc Fumé de Pouilly* or *Pouilly Fumé* is a white wine which must not be below 11° in alcoholic strength, and must be made from Sauvignon grapes, grapes which are exactly the same as the Sauvignon of the Gironde, but they are better known in the Upper Loire by the name of *Blanc Fumé*. The plain *Pouilly-sur-Loire* wines, on the other hand, are made from Chasselas grapes, and their alcoholic strength may not be below 9·5°. They are not merely lighter wines, but they have not got the peculiarly attractive gunflint bouquet which the Sauvignon grapes, grown in these Upper Loire vineyards, impart to the *Blanc Fumé* wines. Both white wines, however, must come from the vineyards of Pouilly-sur-Loire or those of the adjoining Communes of Saint-Andelain, Tracy-sur-Loire, Saint-Martin, Saint-Laurent-sur-Nohain, Garchy and Mesves-sur-Loire. Of course, all the better wines add to *Pouilly Fumé* the name of their own Château or vineyard. There is but one Château in the district, Château du Nozet, but there are a number of particularly good vineyards, such as Les Loges, Les Côtes Rôties, Les Nues, Les Vourigny, Les Foletières and Les Chantalouettes.

## Cher

Upon the other bank of the Loire, in the Cher Département, almost opposite Pouilly-sur-Loire but a little farther north, the vineyards of the Sancerre district are more extensive and bring forth a great deal of very attractive white wines, produced also from Sauvignon grapes, wines which are very similar to the *Blanc Fumè de Pouilly*, but, as a rule, lighter than the best white wines of Pouilly-sur-Loire. To be entitled to the *appellation contrôlée* 'Sancerre', their alcoholic strength must not be below 10·5°. The only wine-producing Château of the Sancerre district is the Château de Sancerre, and the white wines of the Sancerrois which are reputed the best are those of Chavignol.

Some distance to the south-west of Sancerre, but still in the Cher Département, there are some very attractive, light white wines, with a distinctive bouquet of their own, made from the vineyards of Quincy, which overflow into the neighbouring Commune of Brinay. These vineyards, about 550 acres in all, occupy a fairly high tableland on the left of the River Cher. They are planted with Sauvignons, the noble white grape which, according to tradition, was first introduced to Quincy by the Cistercian Monks, in the fifteenth century, when the nearby Abbey of Beauvoir was built. To be entitled to be sold under the name of Quincy, the white wines of the Quincy vineyards must not be inferior to 10·5° in alcoholic strength.

# Touraine

## Indre-et-Loire

The Département of Indre-et-Loire corresponds to the greater part of what was, until 1790, the Province of Touraine. Its chief city is Tours, the capital of Touraine from Gallo-Roman times, and the vineyards which grace both banks of the Loire, as it twists and turns on its wayward way from east to west, across Touraine, produce a great deal of very nice wines, both white and red, still and sparkling.

*White Wines:* All the better white wines of Touraine are made from a white grape from Anjou called *Chenin blanc* in Anjou, but more commonly known as *Pinot de la Loire* in Touraine, although it has none of the characteristics of the Burgundian Pinots. Other white grapes grown in Touraine vineyards are the *Meslier du Gâtinais* and the *Sauvignon du Bordelais*; also the *Folle Blanche des Charentes*, to a very much smaller extent. The best and best known white wines of Touraine are the still and sparkling wines of Vouvray. The vineyards of Vouvray are perched on the top of some lime cliffs, which are honeycombed with the cellars and living-quarters of many *vignerons*, facing the right bank of the River Loire on one side and the valley of the little River Cissé on the other. They stretch from above Tours to Noizay, in two Communes west and two east of Vouvray, i.e. Sainte-Radegonde, Rochecorbon, Vouvray, Vernon and Noizay, on the Loire, as well as the two Communes of Chançay and Reugny, in the Cissé valley.

All Chenin blanc wines from any of those Communes are entitled to the use of the name of Vouvray when their alcoholic strength is not inferior to 11° for the still wines, or 9·5° for the sparkling varieties. The better wines of Vouvray bear the name of their native vineyard as well as that of Vouvray, such as Clos Moncontour, the wine of Château Moncontour; Clos Le Mont, owned by Messrs Ackerman Lawrance; Château Gaudrelle, owned by J. M. Monmousseau; Clos Paradis, owned by Ch. Vavasseur: all in the Commune of Vouvray. Also Clos de la Taisserie and Clos Chevrier, at Rochecorbon; Clos de la Halletière, at Sainte-Radegonde; Clos L'Hermineau and Château de l'Etoile, at Vernon-sur-Brenne.

Facing Vouvray, upon the left bank of the Loire, Montlouis, half-way between Amboise and Tours, is the centre of extensive vineyards; some of them, which face the Loire, are planted with Chenin blanc and produce white wines of the Vouvray type, but lighter in alcoholic strength, while the vineyards upon the other side of the hills, facing the Cher valley, are planted in Breton and Côt black grapes, and produce red wines.

Upstream from Montlouis, the vineyards of Saint-Martin-le-Beau and farther east those of Lussault, in the Amboise Canton, produce some very attractive but light white wines. Other vineyards of the Amboise Canton, more particularly those of Nazelles, on the right bank of the Loire, produce very nice but not great white wines.

South and south-west of Tours, the vineyards of the Indre valley produce some most acceptable Chenin blanc white wines, the best of them being those of Artannes, Azay-le-Rideau, Cheillé, Saché and Vallères, near the Loire; and those of Perrasson, Saint-Jean-Saint-Germain and Sepmes, a good deal farther up the Indre valley, beyond Loches.

The generally accepted practice in Touraine is to bottle white wines when about six months old and to let them age in bottles rather than in cask. To do this, however, the wine must be both bright and safe at the time of bottling; to be bright the wine has to be fined, and it may even be filtered as well; to be safe from any further fermentation, it may also be *bisulfité*, a chemical process that renders impossible any further yeast activity.

*Red Wines:* All the better red wines of Touraine are made from the *Cabernet franc* grape, which was brought to Touraine many years ago by one Abbé Breton, and ever since the Cabernet franc has been known in Touraine as Le Breton. The Malbec grape, another Bordelais grape, is also to be found in Touraine vineyards, more particularly those of the Cher valley, but its local name is Côt instead of Malbec. Other black grapes grown to a very much smaller extent here and there are the *Pinot noirien* of Burgundy, called *Plant Meunier* or *Plant noble*, the Grolleau and the Gamay.

All the better red wines of Touraine come from two main districts, one is Rabelais's own country, the *pays Véron*, Chinon and the Vienne valley on the left bank of the Loire; and the other the Bourgueil uplands, upon the right bank of the Loire.

## Chinon

There are red, *rosé* and white wines made from grapes grown upon both banks of the River Vienne on its last lap before joining the Loire at Candes. The best, however, are the red wines, which have a very attractive violet-scented bouquet and greater elegance than power: their alcoholic strength rarely exceeds 10°, and it must not be below 9·5° to be entitled to the *appellation contrôlée* 'Chinon'. Chinon itself and its vineyards are upon the right bank of the Vienne. The best growths are La Vauzelle, Rochette-Saint-Jean, Les Clozeaux, La Rochelle and Saint-Louans.

Downstream from Chinon, in the stretch of country between the right bank of the Vienne and the left bank of the Loire, known to Rabelais as *le pays Véron*, the best red wines are those from the vineyards of Beaumont-en-Véron: among their best growths, mention should be made of La Roche Honneur, Château de Danzay and Les Pouilles.

Upstream from Chinon, and upon the left bank of the Vienne, the best red wines are those from the vineyards of Ligré, and among their best growths are Saut-aux-Loups, La Noblaie, Les Roches-Saint-Paul and Le Vau Breton.

## Bourgueil

Bourgueil red and *rosé* wines have an obvious family likeness to those of Chinon across the Loire, but they are generally more masculine, that is of rather bigger frame and more assertive, even if not actually of greater alcoholic strength, although they often are a little stronger: their bouquet is more reminiscent of the raspberry than the violet. The red wines of Bourgueil cannot be fairly described as better than those of Chinon, but they are certainly better known, which is due to the fact that there is a great deal more red Bourgueil than there is red Chinon. The red wines entitled to the name of Bourgueil must not be below 9·5° in alcoholic strength, and they must be made from Breton (i.e. Cabernet franc) grapes from Bourgueil vineyards. The *appellations contrôlées* authorities recognize as 'Bourgueil' vineyards, besides those of Bourgueil itself and of the adjoining Commune of Saint-Nicolas-de-Bourgueil, all others upon a fairly high tableland rising from the right bank of the Loire, at the western limit of the Indre-et-Loire Département, and overflowing into the Maine-et-Loire Département, that is, from west to east, the

Communes of Benais, Restigné, La Chapelle-sur-Loire, Ingrandes and as far as Saint-Patrice. All the best red Bourgueil wines come from either the higher ground vineyards of all these Communes, known as *Côtes*, or those pockets of sandy gravel at lower levels known locally as *Graviers*. Some of the more popular of the *Côtes Bourgueils* are Le Clos de la Gardière and Le Clos de la Turellière, Saint-Nicolas-de-Bourgueil; Le Grand Clos and Le Clos des Perrières, Bourgueil; La Chevalerie and Les Brosses, Restigné. Among the best of the *Graviers* wines, mention should be made of the following: Le Clos du Fondis and Le Clos de la Chevalerie, Saint-Nicolas-de-Bourgueil; Le Clos de la Salpêtrerie and Le Clos de l'Abbaye, Bourgueil; Le Clos Jollinet and Le Clos de la Plâtrerie, Restigné.

The red wines of Touraine are made from black grapes picked when fully ripe, crushed or mangled and usually *égrappés* before being pressed in order to get most, if not all, of the red colouring matter from the inner lining of the grape skins. The must is left to ferment in an open vat for about 18 hours after it leaves the press; by then it should have got rid of all the dirt and dust that came in with the grapes, and it is drawn clear into the casks in which fermentation will be carried out to its completion at a progressively slower and slower rate. As a rule, the red wines of Touraine are ready for bottling two years from the date of the vintage, but they are generally bottled in their third year.

## Anjou

Anjou, the cradle of the Plantagenet dynasty, between Touraine in the east and Brittany in the west, ceased to be a Province in 1790, when most of it was included in the present Maine-et-Loire Département, with Angers as its chief city and the Loire as its main river, which divides it into two sections of about the same importance, north and south.

The vineyards of Anjou, which produce the greater quantity of wine, mostly white wines, both still and sparkling, are those of the southern half, or left bank of the Loire; those responsible for the best wines are the vineyards of Saumur and those of the Coteaux du Layon and Coteaux de l'Aubance, two of the many tributaries of the Loire. The northern half vineyards are responsible for a great deal of wine, but there is only a little of it of real merit, although many of these wines are charming.

### Saumur

Saumur is by far the most universally known of all Anjou wines: this is due to the commercial publicity responsible for the world-wide demand which sparkling Saumur has long enjoyed. Sparkling Saumur, either under its own or one of its many *noms de guerre*, is made, it is claimed, in exactly the same way as champagne, and this may well be true, but it is not champagne; it is sparkling Saumur, a good, clean, rather sweet sparkling wine considerably handicapped by having to pay the same heavy duty as champagne. No Loire or Anjou still wine would claim the peculiar attributes of the great wines of Burgundy or Bordeaux nor can its sparkling wines claim those of champagne. But much greater quantities of still wines than sparkling wines are made from the Saumur vineyards: some are red, and their alcoholic strength must not be below 10° to be entitled to bear the name of *Saumur*; more are white and others are *rosés*, the minimum alcoholic strength of the whites being 9·5° and that of the *rosé* 9°.

All the better white wines are made from the Chenin blanc grape, the original Plant d'Anjou which was adopted in nearby Touraine but renamed Pinot de la Loire. The more *ordinaires* white wines are made from commoner species of grapes, chiefly the Muscadet, also called Melon, and Gamay blanc, a Burgundian grape; or else the Folle blanche, Blanc Emery and Groslot blanc. All the best red wines are made from Breton, i.e. Cabernet franc, grapes, or Chenin rouge, which is also called Pineau d'Aunis; most of the *ordinaires* red wines are made from Gamay and *rosés* from Groslot grapes.

The vineyards of the Saumur hillsides are very extensive; they stretch from the left bank of the Loire, immediately west of the Touraine boundary southwards, to the boundaries of the Maine-et-Loire Département, covering the Communes of Bagneux, Bizay, Brézé, Brossay, Courchamps, Coutures, Cizay-la-Madeleine, Dampierre-sur Loire, Douces, Douée-la-Fontaine, Fontevrault-l'Abbaye, Meigne-sur-Doué, Saint-Cyr-en-Bourg, Rou-Marson, Montreuil-Bellay, Montsoreau, Parnay, Puy-Notre-Dame, Saint-Hilaire-Saint-Florent, Saumur, Soulanger, Souzay-Champigny, Turquant, Le Ulmes, Varrains, Le Vaudelnay.

### Coteaux du Layon

While the white sparkling wines are the best known wines of Anjou, the sweet white wines of the Coteaux du Layon are acknowledged to be wines of finer quality than any of the other white wines of the Loire Valley. They are made from Chenin blanc grapes, picked as late as possible, when fully ripe or overripe, from the vineyards of 28 Communes of the valley of the River Layon, one of the Loire's tributaries. The best vineyards are in the Communes of Thouarcé-Bonnezeaux, Faye, Rablay, Beaulieu, Saint-Aubin-de-Luigné and Rochefort-sur-Loire. Of all the different growths of these and other Layon Communes, none is more famous, and none deserves its fame more fully, than the Quarts de Chaume (Rochefort-sur-Loire). Other popular growths are the Clos de la Roche Gaudrie and Château de la Roche (Rablay); Château de Montbenault (Faye); La Guillaumerie (Rochefort-sur-Loire); La Saulaie and La Haie Longue, and Château Fresnaye (Saint-Aubin-de-Luigné); La Petite Croix and Château de Fesle (Thouarcé-Bonnezeaux).

## The Lower Loire

### Coteaux de la Loire

Upon the right bank of the Loire, at no great distance south-south-west of Angers, the vineyards of the Coteaux de la Loire produce much white wine of no great distinction, as well as a comparatively small quantity of very nice still white wines from the Coulée-de-Serrant and La Roche-aux-Moines, the two best vineyards of the Commune of Savennières. They are not so sweet as the wines of the Layon, across the Loire, but they have breed and charm, as well as a distinctive and attractive bouquet.

### Muscadet

Muscadet is the name of a white Burgundian grape which was renamed Muscadet when it was introduced into Brittany, where it has now practically ceased to be cultivated except in the Département of Loire-Atlantique, north of the Loire, round about Ancenis close to the border of Anjou; also south of the Loire, to the east and south-east of Nantes. *Muscadet* is also the name of the white wine made from the Muscadet grape, a light, fairly dry white wine, with little bouquet and a faint 'squeeze of lemon' sharpness which makes it most acceptable with oysters, *saucisson* and any vinegary hors d'œuvre.

Muscadet is not a wine to lay down. It is at its best, when young and lively, usually before it reaches its third year. As a wine it is too thin and hungry ever to be popular in England, where, however, it had many admirers during the eighteenth century, but in its distilled form. It used to be shipped from Nantes and called Nantz or Nancy Brandy, and there was quite a brisk demand for it, a demand which, particularly during the periods of war, was chiefly supplied by flourishing fraternities of smugglers.

CHAPTER SEVEN

# *Alsace*

ALSACE is that long tract of beautiful and fertile land that stretches from below Mulhouse, just north of Switzerland, to beyond Strasbourg, as far as the German Palatinate. It is protected from western gales by the high range of the Vosges mountains and, less effectively, from cold winds and worse from the east by the Rhine. Between the Rhine and the Vosges, the River Ill flows parallel to the Rhine for many miles before it joins it near Strasbourg. This river, the Elsus of the Romans and Elsass of the Germans, has given its name to Alsace, and it more or less divides the land lengthwise into plough and grass on its right, or Rhine side, and wine and timber on its left, or Vosges side. There are a number of small rivers twisting and bending, rushing and cascading down from the Vosges to join the Ill, and they have carved for themselves in the course of the centuries their way through the foothills of the great Vosges mountains wherever their waters found and eventually broke down lime and schist patches, more yielding than the all-pervading granite. Which is how and why there are so many and such beautiful little valleys in Alsace with vineyards thriving upon the lower half, from 75 to 300 feet, rarely higher than 600 feet, along the slopes of the hills, which are mostly thickly wooded higher up, and dominated at a short distance to the west by the 3,000-foot-high peaks of the Vosges.

The wines of Alsace were very little known, if at all, before the end of the First World War, and the end of the 77 years of the German occupation of Alsace. But long before this period, there were vineyards in Alsace and there were wines of Alsace drunk in Alsace and sent down the Rhine to the North Sea, Scandinavia and England. A thousand years, almost to the day, before that fatal war of 1870, Alsace was allotted to Louis the German by the Treaty of Mersen in 870, a decisive factor being that without Alsace, Louis would have been without wine. In 1300 there were 172 villages named as being responsible for the best wines of Alsace, but all through the Middle Ages and down to the end of the eighteenth century many of the Alsatian vineyards, and all the better ones, belonged either to the Church or to some great feudal lord. As late as 1790, when the French Revolution brought about the crash of the old order, the Rangen hill, near Thann, which had been famous for its wines for centuries, was still the property of the Cathedral of Strasbourg; the Clos in der Wanneri, near Guebwiller, belonged to Murbach Abbey; the best Bergheim vineyards to the Knights of St John; those of Sigolsheim hill to Ebersmunster Abbey; large vineyards at Alspach and Kaysersberg to the Counts of Alspach and Remiremont; and the best vineyards of Turckheim to the Abbey of Munster.

In Alsace, just as at Vougeot, Carbonnieux and Hautvillers, to name but three of the more famous Benedictine-blessed bacchic foundations, wine was made to the glory of God, as good as it could be made by men of good will. For many centuries labour was serf or near-slave labour, and money was not nearly as important as a good name, and what surer road to a good name is there than good wine? There were no hotels in those days, and no hospitals, other than the guest-houses for wandering scholars and hospitals for the sick built, staffed and run by the Church, which is why the Church had in Alsace perhaps more than elsewhere many vineyards, and as a rule the best.

After the French Revolution and the Napoleonic wars the big estates in Alsace were broken up, and the vineyards were sold to a very large number of peasant owners, whose great-grandchildren own the same vineyards, but divided again and again and now smaller than ever. Alsace itself was divided, like all French Provinces, into two smaller Départements, the Haut-Rhin and Bas-Rhin, Upper and Lower Rhine, the first with Mulhouse and Colmar as its two chief cities; the second with Strasbourg, the proud capital of old Alsace. Most of the best vineyards of Alsace are in the Haut-Rhin, from Thann, in the south, to Sigolsheim, in the north, and from the Vosges, in the west, to the Ill valley, in the east. Among the better known, pride of place must be given to Riquewihr and Ribeauvillé, two of the most picturesque and unspoilt villages, but Guebwiller, Eguisheim, Turckheim, Ammerschwihr, Hunawihr, Bergheim and others have very fine vineyards, even if most of them were less fortunate in the Second World War than Riquewihr.

The vineyards of the Bas-Rhin, from below Sélestat, in the south, to Haguenau beyond Strasbourg, in the north, are mostly in the plain and produce commoner types of wines for local consumption. There are, however, in the Bas-Rhin some hillside vineyards which produce excellent white wines, such as the vineyards of Mittelbergheim, Barr, Obernai and Kintzheim.

In the long and chequered history of Alsace the nineteenth century has an exceptionally black record. To start with, the quality of the wine was no longer what it had been for so long: all the smallholders who had for the first time wine of their own to drink and to sell were far too keen to make as much wine – and money – from their few acres of vines as they could, and they planted commoner grapes, pruned them 'long' instead of short, and gathered far bigger crops of grapes than ever before – but, of course, they made inferior wine. Then, after the Napoleonic wars, came the tariff war between France and the German States. There were so many better wines made in other parts of France at the time that there was little demand for Alsace wines; on the other hand, the German States taxed all French wines out of their territories as a reprisal for the taxation of German produce in France. Oïdium in the 1850s and phylloxera in the 1870s were scourges which all French vineyards suffered during the nineteenth century, but all the others were spared the German occupation which blighted the Alsatian

Plate 13. Early champagne bottles had a longer and narrower neck than those used today. The specially designed glasses display the unique colour and bouquet of the wine.

ALSACE                                                                                   113

vineyards from 1870 to 1918. The main purpose of the German authorities during that period was quite obviously to eradicate as much as possible everything that was French, in order to Germanize Alsace and its people; wine was unfortunately one of the first victims. Its identity was ruled out by the prohibition to offer it for sale under the name of Alsace wine; its quality was lowered by the permission to blend it with 49% of any kind of wine; its production was rendered unprofitable by the encouragement given to the manufacture of artificial wines and their sale at prices very much below that of the cheapest genuine Alsatian wines. Which explains why it was that nobody ever heard of any Alsatian wine until Alsace who restored to France by the Treaty of Versailles, 1919. Since then much has been done to bring back the better species of grapes in the Alsatian vineyards as the first condition for the making of good wine.

## The Vines

The vines which are cultivated in the vineyards of Alsace are mostly of the commoner sorts: Elbing, Burger, Knipperlé and Trollinger, which are responsible for nearly two-thirds of the vinous production of Alsace: the wines made from these species are sharp when young, and as they are mostly drunk within eighteen months of their vintage, they are sharp when drunk by the people of Alsace. They are not made for export and are suitable only for home consumption: pickled and fermented cabbage (*chou rouge et choucroûte*), as well as every part of the pig, roast, boiled, stewed, pickled or smoked, being the basic diet of the bulk of the Alsace people, a young and acid wine has a most beneficial splitting and moving quality.

All the better white wines of Alsace, roughly speaking a third of its total vinous production, are made from Sylvaner, Muscat, Pinot, Riesling, Traminer and Gewürztraminer grapes.

### Sylvaner

Sylvaner is a more popular grape in the Bas-Rhin vineyards than in those of the Haut-Rhin. The white wines made from Sylvaner grapes are light, elegant, pleasant and fresh when young, but they have little bouquet, and they do not repay keeping; it is the best value, as a rule, among the less expensive wines.

### Muscat

Muscat, of which there are three different varieties, is very different from the white muscat grapes grown in glasshouses. It has quite a highly developed bouquet which leads one to expect a wine with more body and of finer quality than most Alsatian Muscat wines possess: they usually lack breed or distinction and are somewhat earthy.

### Pinot

Pinot is another species of grape of which there are two distinct varieties: *Pinot blanc* and *Pinot gris*. The first is known also as *Weissklevener* or *Burgenberg*, and the second as *Rutlander* or *Tokay*. The white wines made from both these grapes have less bouquet than a Muscat-made wine, but more body and greater distinction.

Plate 14. The *Syrah*, at Tain l'Hermitage, a grape especially suitable for growing in the Rhône valley.

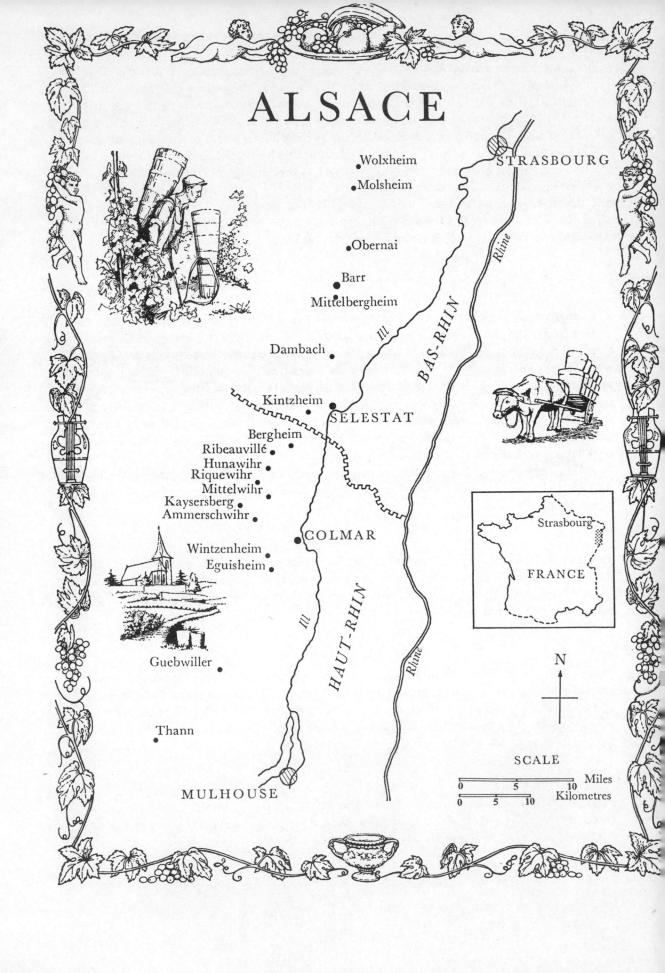

# ALSACE

Wolxheim

Molsheim

Obernai

Barr

Mittelbergheim

STRASBOURG

*Rhine*

BAS-RHIN

*Ill*

Dambach

Kintzheim

SELESTAT

Bergheim

Ribeauvillé

Hunawihr

Riquewihr

Mittelwihr

Kaysersberg

Ammerschwihr

Wintzenheim

Eguisheim

COLMAR

*Ill*

HAUT-RHIN

*Rhine*

Guebwiller

Thann

MULHOUSE

Strasbourg

FRANCE

N

SCALE

| 0 | | 5 | | 10 | Miles |
| 0 | 5 | | 10 | | Kilometres |

## Riesling

*Riesling* is a noble grape, one which is grown to a far greater extent than any other in the vineyards of Ribeauvillé, Riquewihr and Hunawihr, as well as in the choicest positions of all good vineyards. The Riesling is a late-maturing grape which makes it all the more important to give it a more sheltered place than hardier species. The white wines made from Riesling grapes possess both the bouquet and body which entitle them to a place in the front rank of the fine white table wines.

## Traminer and Gewürztraminer

*Traminer* and *Gewürztraminer* are two names for the same grape, a noble grape, smaller and rounder than the Riesling. The great advantage which the Traminer has over the Riesling is that its fruit sets and ripens earlier; this is important because when the weather happens to deteriorate in early autumn Rieslings are picked before they are quite ripe while Traminer, gathered at the same time, will be ripe and will give a better wine. If, on the other hand, the sun shines and the weather is all that one could wish it to be, Rieslings will be gathered fully ripe and their wine will be excellent, and the Traminer grapes may be left when they have come to the ripe stage to become over-ripe, through the *pourriture noble*, as happens at Yquem; the wine made from such *Trockenbeerenauslese*, or simply late gathered grapes, will produce a wonderful dessert wine, luscious and delicious, the peer of the great Sauternes and Palatinate dessert wines.

There are very few large estates in Alsace but a very large number of smallholders with just enough grapes to make from two to ten casks of wine, too little to go to the expense and trouble of marketing their wine. They sell it either to a Co-operative Society of their own or to one of the wine-merchants who have cellars at home to mature the wine and agents abroad to sell it. Either way, the wine which the grower sells is sold simply under the name of the grape from which it was made, Sylvaner, Riesling, Traminer and so on. The name of the actual grower does not matter any more than the name of his vineyard or village: all that the *Caves Co-opératives* or the wine shippers want to know is the *cépage* or grape variety so as to make their blends of Sylvaners, Rieslings or Traminers. These, when ready for sale, will be sold under the name of one of those grapes, with the name of the shipper added as well as his address. There are, however, a few of the more progressive shippers of Alsatian wines who do make wine from one species of grape, grown in one single vineyard, such as the Clos du Maquisard, shipped by Messrs Dopff and Irion, of the Château de Riquewihr. Students of both wine and architecture will find the village of Riquewihr of more than passing interest.

The tendency is for the Alsatian *vigneron* to spare no trouble to make better wines and to produce some of a finer type for export, comparable to the more delicate wines of the Moselle. It will, of course, take time, but the start has been made.

There are, according to official statistics, 440 wine-producing parishes in Alsace and 30,000 families of *vignerons*. The figures of wine-producing vary greatly: the highest on record being 1,678,400 hectolitres in 1875, and the lowest 121,469 hectolitres in 1917. 15,000,000 gallons would appear to be a fair average, two-thirds of it being consumed in Alsace and one-third being either sold in Paris or exported.

CHAPTER EIGHT

# Other French Wines

## Arbois

ARBOIS is an old and charming little town nestling in a bower of vines, half-way between Salins and Poligny, at the northern end of a long and narrow strip of vineyards facing south-west and with the beautiful fir-clad slopes of the Juras immediately behind them.

There are five different types of wines entitled to the *appellation contrôlée* 'Arbois':

(1) red and *rosé* table wines made from Poulsard and Trousseau grapes;
(2) white table wines, made from Chardonnay and Savagnin blanc grapes;
(3) *vin jaune*, made from Savagnin grapes exclusively, fermented according to a special technique and matured for not less than six years before being offered for sale;
(4) *vin de paille*, a white wine made from overripe Savagnin grapes, picked in November and even early December. It is fermented sherrywise so that it is quite dry, of high alcoholic strength, and it will keep and improve for a great many years;
(5) sparkling wines made according to the *méthode champenoise*.

There are other Jura wines and the best are those of L'Etoile. There are also finer *Vins jaunes* and *Vins de paille* than those of Arbois; they are those of Château-Chalon, the name not of a Castle but of a cluster of vineyards between Ménétru and Voiteur.

## Provence

Between Marseilles and Toulon, along the Mediterranean seaboard or southernmost part of Provence, there are many vineyards which produce much wine from middling to fine in quality.

Nearer Marseilles, the little fisherfolk village of Cassis has given its name to the wines from vineyards that crown the cliffs of the adjoining *Calanques*, those fiords of the Mediterranean. The vineyards of Cassis cover 675 acres, but there is not much more than a third of them planted with the shy-bearing old species of Provence grapes, which yield the only wines entitled to the *appellation contrôlée* 'Cassis'. Most Cassis wines, and all the better ones, are white wines.

Nearer Toulon, there are vineyards at La Gaude, Saint-Tropez, La Croix de Cavalaire, Cagnes and elsewhere which are responsible for red wines of fair quality, but the best known and best of them are those of Bandol, a small port where, they say, ships used to load, in days of long ago, wines for London, Rotterdam and Bremen. None but the wines from the vineyards of Bandol and a few nearby Communes are entitled to the *appellation contrôlée* 'Bandol'.

Near Nice the red, white and *rosé* wines of Bellet are the best known of the Alpes-Maritimes Département wines.

# Languedoc and Roussillon

Languedoc is the name given to an immense tract of land stretching roughly from the Rhône below Lyons to the Garonne above Toulouse, from east to west, and from the Forez in the north to the Mediterranean sea in the south. The Roussillon, a much smaller Province, is wedged between Languedoc and Spain, north and south, with the Comté de Foix to the west and the Mediterranean Sea to the east. That long stretch of Mediterranean seaboard from Marseilles to the Pyrenees and the Franco-Spanish frontier has been for centuries past, and still is, the home of the Muscat grape, and all the best dessert wines of France come from the coastal vineyards of Languedoc (Lunel and Frontignan) and Roussillon (Banyuls, Maury, Rivesaltes, Côte d'Agly and Côtes du Haut-Roussillon).

Both Lunel, some 15 miles north-east of Montpelier, and Frontignan, about 12 miles to the south-west of the same city, on the road to Sète, are in the Hérault Département. The only wines which are entitled to the *appellation contrôlée* 'Muscat de Lunel' are wines with an alcoholic strength not inferior to 15°, made exclusively from Muscat grapes from the vineyards of Lunel, Lunel-Viel and Vérorgues.

*Frontignan* is a slightly fortified wine with a minimum alcoholic strength of 15°, made exclusively from Muscat grapes from the vineyards of Frontignan and of the adjoining Commune of Vic-la-Gardiolle.

When we come to Rousillon we are in the land of the *vins doux naturels*, the unfortified sweet dessert wines with a minimum alcoholic strength of 14°, which is obtained through the slow and thorough fermentation of very sweet grapes, mostly Muscats.

From the Spanish frontier to Argelès-sur-Mer, there are four Communes along what is locally known as La Côte Vermeille, i.e. Cerbère, Banyuls, Port-Vendres and Collioure, which produce the sweet white, red and *rosés* wines entitled to the name of *Banyuls*. Banyuls is unsweetened as well as unfortified, but it is sweet and of higher alcoholic strength than any table wines simply because it is made from grapes so ripe and so rich that after reaching the optimum alcoholic strength through fermentation they still retain some unfermented sugar. This applies, of course, not only to the wines of Banyuls but to all the *vins doux naturels* of Roussillon.

Maury is a village farther away from the sea and higher up upon the foothills of the Pyrenees: it is surrounded by vineyards which, according to local tradition, were first planted in this district by some of Hannibal's soldiers turned *vignerons*! The *vins doux naturels* of Maury owe their characteristic bouquet to the *Grenache noir*, which is the local grape from which they are made.

Rivesaltes, nearer the sea, on the road from Narbonne (35 m. north) to Perpignan (5 m. south) was the birthplace of Maréchal Joffre. Its vineyards, and those of the nearby Communes entitled to sell their wines as *Rivesaltes* (Salses, Fitou, Leucate, Baixas, Pia, etc.), grow mostly Muscats but some Malvoisie grapes as well.

## Côte d'Agly

'Cote d'Agly' is also an *appellation contrôlée* for the *vins doux naturels* made from Muscat, Grenache and Malvoisie grapes from the vineyards of the Agly valley, between Rivesaltes, to the east, and Maury, to the west. The largest vineyard of the Agly valley is that of Château de Caladroy (250 acres). Tautavel, Estagel, Cases de Pène, Vingrau and Espoira-de-l'Agly are the five more important of the eleven Communes entitled to sell their wines under the name of Côte d'Agly, to which is usually added *Muscat, Grenache* or *Malvoisie*, according to the sort of grape from which the wine was made.

## Côtes du Haut-Roussillon

'Côtes de Haut-Roussillon' is an *appellation contrôlée* for the *vins doux naturels* made from Muscat, Grenache and Malvoisie grapes grown in the vineyards of the highlands immediately behind Banyuls, facing the sea from Perpignan to the Pyrenees and the Spanish frontier immediately to the south. The more important of the wine-producing Communes of the Haut-Roussillon are Argelès, Cabestany, Canet, Castelnou, Fourques, Laroque-des-Albères, Le Boulou, Llupia, Passa, Perpignan, Pollestres, Ponteilla, Saleilles, Sainte-Colombe, Saint-Jean-Zasseille, Saint-Jean-Pla-de-Cors, Saint-Genis-des-Fontaines, Saint-Nazaire, Sorède, Terrats, Thuir, Tordères, Tresserres, Trouillas, Villeneuve-de-la-Roho and Villemolaque.

## Gaillac

Besides the *vins doux naturels*, there are both still table wines and sparkling wines made in Roussillon, Languedoc and other vineyards of the south-west, chief among them the wines of Gaillac, Limous, Monbazillac, Bergerac, Montravel and Jurançon.

Gaillac, 14 miles from Albi and 35 miles from Toulouse, in the Tarn Département, is in Languedoc; it is built on the River Tarn and its vineyards produce a great deal of wines, both still and sparkling, the best of them being those from Mauzac grapes, grown upon granite on the left bank of the Tarn. They possess a distinctive and pleasing gunflint aftertaste which is completely lacking in the wines made from the same species of grapes grown on limestone upon the right bank of the Tarn.

## Limoux

Limoux, in the Aude Département, in Roussillon, some 15 miles from Carcassonne, is chiefly noted for its sparkling white wine, made according to the *champenoise méthode* and known as *Blanquette de Limoux*. It has plenty of gas in it, and it is fairly sweet.

# Monbazillac, Montravel

*Monbazillac* might be called the Sauternes of the Dordogne. It is made from Sauvignon and Muscadelle grapes, which are picked when they have reached the stage of *pourriture noble*; it is darker than most Sauternes, tinged with red, fuller of body, sweet, and its bouquet is rather more assertive, but it has not the same *finesse*.

The vineyards of Monbazillac and of the four Communes entitled to the *appellation contrôlée* 'Monbazillac' face the Dordogne, about as far south from Bergerac as the Sauternes vineyards are from Langon and the Garonne. Opposite, upon the right bank of the Dordogne, the vineyards of Bergerac and those of Montravel immediately to the west produce much white wine and a little red wine.

# Jurançon

Jurançon, just south of Pau, and the Communes entitled to the same *appellation contrôlée*, produce the finest white wine of Béarn and Bigorre, a full-strength wine of real distinction; it has a puzzling bouquet with a truffle-like quality which is unique. Jurançon is usually kept in cask for some years before being bottled, and it improves greatly with bottle-age. The grapes from which Jurançon is made are Béarn species – *Petit* and *Gros Manseng* and *Courbu*, which are not grown anywhere else.

## Other French Wines

There are not hundreds but thousands of other French wines, millions of gallons of *Vins du Midi* and other mostly homely or plain wines, which are wholesome and helpful, thirst-quenching and stimulating, but without any claim to 'breed', bouquet or distinction of any kind. There are also quite a number of very nice wines made in all parts of France, but in such small quantities that they are rarely, if ever, available to anybody other than the people who make them, and their own friends.

In my opinion, neither the mass-produced wines for the masses nor the totally uncommercial wines, however good they may be, deserve a place in this recording of the noble grapes and the great wines of France.

CHAPTER NINE

# *Brandy*

SPIRITS have been distilled from fermented liquids ever since man found out that there is less heat needed for alcohol than for water to reach boiling point; that is, when a liquid becomes a gas or vapour. This difference makes it possible to remove by the right degree of heat some or most of the alcohol present in fermented liquids. There are in all of them, besides alcohol, various by-products of fermentation, small quantities of which are distilled off with the alcohol. These by-products owe their importance to the fact that they are generally characteristic of the material subjected to fermentation, such as wine, sugar-cane, molasses, barley-mash, etc., and they give to brandy, rum, whisky and other spirits their individuality and appeal. But when spirits are distilled from potatoes, like vodka, or from cellulose, like some of the Swedish akvavit, their by-products are undesirable and they are removed by further distillation or 'rectification'.

Spirits therefore differ according to:

(1) the origin and nature of the fermented liquids from which they are distilled;
(2) the degree and manner of their distillation;
(3) whether or not rectified after distillation;
(4) if matured in casks, and for how long.

Brandy is the anglicized form of the Dutch *Brantewijn*, burnt wine, a more matter-of-fact name than the French *eau-de-vie*, water of life.

Brandy is a spirit distilled from wine, anywhere. It has been and it is distilled in most if not all lands where grapes grow and wine is made. There are wines, however, far more suitable than others for distillation, and there are very few indeed that have in their gift brandy of unchallenged excellence. There are, roughly speaking, ten casks of a new white table wine 'burnt' or distilled to secure one cask of brandy, a wasteful process unless the brandy obtained at such a cost be good enough to command a price at the very least ten times greater than that of the wine from which it was distilled.

The types, styles, qualities and prices of brandy differ greatly, owing chiefly to:

(*a*) the wines from which brandy is distilled;

(*b*) the manner of its distillation;

(*c*) the skill and the stocks of the blender;

(*d*) the casks in which the brandy is matured, the humidity of the cellar where it is kept and the length of time during which it is kept in cask.

## Cognac

Between Brittany and Gascony, south of the Loire and north of the Gironde, there is a much more modest river, but one that is just as famous in the annals of gastronomy, La Charente. On its leisurely roundabout way from up-country to the Atlantic, the Charente passes through three of the smaller former French Provinces, Angoumois, Aunis and Saintonge, corresponding roughly to the Upper (Angoulême), Middle (Cognac) and Lower (Saintonge) reaches of the river. These three small Provinces became, in 1790, two large Départements, La Charente and La Charente-Inférieure: the latter, however, after the fall of France in 1940, could not abide being 'Lower' or *Inférieure* any longer and changed its name to La Charente-Maritime. Cognac is the name that no brandy may be given other than the brandy distilled from wine made from grapes grown within the boundaries of those two Départements, as well as a very few and quite unimportant acres in two of the adjoining Départements.

Cognac, the town which has given its name to the finest brandy in the world, is 312 miles from Paris, 32 from Angoulême and 16 from Saintes. Built upon the right bank of the Charente some two thousand years ago, Cognac was a busy river port long before anybody had ever thought of distilling brandy, actively engaged for centuries in two branches of commerce concerned with salt and wine, both basic necessities of life. Salt came from Saintonge to Cognac, where it was stored and sent eventually by barge as far as Angoulême, and thence by road farther inland. Wine came from Aunis and Angoumois to Cognac to be stored and sold presently to overseas merchants, and then shipped by river and by sea from La Rochelle to England, Flanders, the Hanseatic cities and the Baltic ports. There is, however, no documentary evidence available today of the existence of any vineyards in the immediate vicinity of Cognac before the year 1031, when Robert Le Pieux gave to the Priory of Saint-Léger the undulating plain that slopes from the little hill where Merpins stands today – a modest village, but a fortified camp in the days of Caesar and the Roman occupation – at the junction of the little River Né and the Charente, down to the outskirts of Cognac, some three and a half miles away. The monks who cultivated the land planted a vineyard in that loop of the Charente which is to this day the very heart of La Grande Champagne. There is no lack of evidence of the activity of the wine trade of Cognac from the twelfth to the sixteenth centuries. Thus, in 1214 King John, whose wife was the daughter of the Count of Angoulême, commissioned the *Prud'hommes* or Elders of Cognac to buy Aunis wines for the royal cellars. There are many records not merely of the royal favour but of the popularity of the wines of Aunis in England, Lubeck, Flanders and Denmark, up to the sixteenth century when civil war utterly ruined viticulture and brought commerce to an end. Nowhere else in France was the fratricidal feud between Catholics and Protestants more bitter and disastrous, no pitched battle more bloody than the Battle of Jarnac, in 1569. When at long last, in 1598, the Edict of Nantes brought in some hope of greater tolerance and peace, houses had to be rebuilt and vineyards replanted. Whether different and unsuitable species of grapes were chosen at the time or whether the *vignerons* who had survived massacres and escaped being burnt at the stake had lost the art of making wine as good as their fathers made, we may never know, but what we do know is that the wines of Aunis, Saintonge and Angoumois practically ceased to be shipped during the seventeenth century. Available records leave no doubt as to the reason for this; there is nought but complaints about the bad quality of these wines, and more particularly about their unsuitability for shipment by sea. One cannot help thinking that the wines which were such bad travellers could not have been the same as those which had been shipped from La Rochelle for so long, to everybody's satisfaction, in former times. However, necessity being the mother of invention, the people of Cognac and thereabouts who could no longer sell their wines as wines were not long in discovering a new way of disposing of them under another form, as brandy.

The art of distillation was well known in France during the sixteenth century, when liqueurs and brandies were distilled and compounded by apothecaries and alchemists, and prescribed by doctors only. By the middle of the seventeenth century, however, liqueur compounding had become one of the privileges and accomplishments of the perfect housewife, while the distillation and sale of brandy had become a branch of the wine trade. It was then that the undoubted superiority of the brandy distilled from the wines of the Charente became known outside the Cognac country. Ever since, Charente white wines have had no particular merit as wines, but when distilled they are responsible for brandy of exceptional excellence.

Cognac brandy is distilled at the beginning of the year, during the winter months following the vintage, as soon as the new wine has finished fermenting and has 'fallen bright'. It is distilled from white wine, wine made from different varieties of white grapes, chiefly from a grape oddly named *Saint-Emilion*. It is very similar to, if not actually the same as, the Italian *Trebbiano* grape. All grapes from which white wine is made to be distilled into Cognac brandy must grow within the strictly defined boundaries of the Cognac area, roughly speaking the two Départements of Charente and Charente-Maritime. There are, of course, within those two Départements marked geological differences in the soil of their vineyards which means that different qualities of brandy are distilled from the wine of different vineyards. All the finest Cognac brandies are distilled from the wines of vineyards nearer to Cognac, in one or the other of three areas the soil of which is the richest in lime. The best of the three is known as *Grande Champagne*, the next best is called *Petite Champagne* and the third *Borderies*. Farther east, where the soil is quite different, vineyards have replaced forests, and those areas are still called *Bois – Fins Bois, Bons Bois, Bois éloignés*; the brandies distilled from the *Bois* areas have not got the finesse nor the breed of *Champagnes* and *Borderies* Cognacs, but they are nevertheless true Cognac brandies and brandies of good quality.

There are twenty-one Communes in the *Grande Champagne* area, all in the *Arrondissement* of Cognac, mostly between Cognac, Ségonzac and Châteauneuf. There are fifty-five Communes in the *Petite Champagne* area in the *Arrondissements* of Cognac, Jonzac, Barbezieux and Saintes. In the *Borderies* there are only eight Communes, and they are all in the Canton of Cognac.

Cognac brandy is always distilled in pot stills. A pot still is a copper pot with a broad rounded bottom and a long tapering neck to which is attached a copper spiral tube or worm condenser. The wine is put in the pot; it is slowly brought to boiling point and kept simmering; the wine rises from the pot in the form of vapours which are condensed into liquid form by the time they reach the condenser. The spirit collected from the first vapours to leave the pot is called the 'head': the last is the 'tail'; the head is too pungent, the tail not enough; both are drawn off and not mixed with the 'heart', that is the spirit distilled in between, which alone deserves to bear the name of Cognac.

There are in the true Cognac district over 4,000 *vignerons* who distil their own wine themselves, but very few of them have either the capital or the cellarage needed to keep the brandy they distil until it is fit to drink. The majority of the *vignerons* sell their newly distilled brandies to one or other of the great shipping houses possessing, besides the means of holding stocks of brandy, a world-wide distributing organization for its sale.

The Cognac shipper may and often does own some vineyards and distil his wine, but he also must buy newly distilled brandy from some of the 4,000 *vignerons* of the Charentes, in order to build up and keep up ample stocks or brandy of different ages, quality and price, from different vineyards and different vintages.

The more important and the more varied the shipper's stocks of brandy are, the easier it is for him to ensure the continuity of style of the different brandies which he sells under various marks or brands. This is important, because the consumer who calls for his favourite brand of brandy expects that it will be true to type, that it will look and taste 'the same as before'.

Good brandy must be given time to show how good it can be, and as it needs a fair amount of oxygen to bring forth the aldehydes and esters responsible for its delightful fragrance, it must be matured in casks. The casks must be perfectly sound and well seasoned; brandy would immediately acquire a fusty smell should a single stave be musty. A sound cask gives to the brandy matured in it a little colour; also a characteristic and softer 'finish'.

Brandy in cask will mature differently if kept in a dry or in a damp place; the drier the store or warehouse, the greater will be the evaporation, so that the brandy will lose more bulk and less strength. In a damp vault or cellar brandy will lose more strength and less bulk; it will hydrate itself or incorporate some of the hydrogen of the humid air, a better method than adding distilled water to it.

The finest brandies may gain by being kept as long as thirty or even forty years in cask, but most brandies are at their best long before, and there is no greater, nor any more popular fallacy, than to imagine that the older a brandy is the better it must be.

The climatic conditions prevailing in the Charentes are such that there are marked differences in the quality of the brandies distilled each year, in good and bad vintages. The brandies of all good vintages are very rarely sold as vintage brandy, as they are indispensable for making up the Cognac shippers' various blends.

There is, however, much Cognac brandy that is sold in bottles that bear a date, which most buyers take for granted to be the date of the vintage of the brandy in the bottle. But it is not always so. Sometimes it represents the age of the oldest brandy, a little of which was used in making the blend, but it may also bear no relation whatever to the age of the brandy in the bottle; it may be used merely for the sake of the selling value of an easily remembered date, such as 1066 or 1865; such dates may have been used merely as an indication that the brandy in the bottle is quite old enough to be enjoyed without waiting any longer. Napoleon brandies, upon the bottles of which are sometimes branded such dates as 1811 or 1815, are not for men of little faith. There *may* be such wonderful brandies, but *would* they be so wonderful?

There is some vintage Cognac brandy which it is sometimes possible to buy in England; it is that which was imported in cask immediately after it was distilled within about six months of the date of the vintage, lodged in bond on arrival and left alone until bottled years after. This is always a rare and often a very fine brandy, and it is to be sought after.

A liqueur brandy may be, quite exceptionally, a matured brandy of some particularly fine vintage, but as a rule, it is a blend of different brandies, all of respectable origin and may be some of illustrious pedigree, which have been matured for a number of years in casks.

It has long been the practice of many important Cognac shipping houses to give some indication of the age of their liqueur brandies by using the following initials:

V.S.O.      (very superior old), for brandies from 12 to 17 years old;
V.S.O.P.    (very superior old pale) for brandies from 18 to 25 years old;
V.V.S.O.P. (very, very superior old pale), for brandies from 25 to 40 years old.

Liqueur brandy need not be very old, but old enough nevertheless to be mellow and fragrant. It is the best of all liqueurs, to be sniffed and sipped at leisure after a good dinner: it also possesses the most valuable medicinal and therapeutic properties.

Liqueur brandy is called in France *Fine Champagne*, or *Fine Maison*, 'the brandy of the house', which is sometimes surprisingly good.

## *Armagnac*

Next to Cognac, Armagnac is the best brandy distilled in France. Of course, a good Armagnac is better than a poor Cognac, but in general the finest Armagnac is not so fine as the finest Cognac.

The Armagnac vineyards cover approximately 125,000 acres widely scattered in the Gers, Landes and Lot-et-Garonne Départements; they are divided into three districts known as Bas-Armagnac, Tenarèze and Haut-Armagnac, the first two being responsible for the finest brandies.

The Armagnac *vigneron* grows mostly *Picpoul* and *Jurançon* grapes, the first being similar to the Cognac *Folle Blanche*; he picks his grapes and makes his wine in October, and distils it in pot stills, as at Cognac, as soon as the fermentation is over; the new spirit is then lodged in casks made of locally grown black oak, which imparts to the brandy, when matured, quite a distinctive character.

There are in the Gers Département some vineyards which produce much better brandies than all others, and it is possible, even if not always easy, to buy the best Armagnac vintages direct from one or other of the owner-distillers or his agent.

# CHAPTER TEN

# Casks, Bottles and Glasses

## Casks

CASKS are the first homes of all wines, their nursery from birth to bottle. Most white wines rarely stay more than a few months in cask, whereas most red wines, and more particularly the better ones, may remain two or three years and even a good deal longer.

French wines are mostly 'lodged' in oaken casks, the shape and size of which vary according to different districts. The standard cask, whether called *fut*, *barrique* or *pièce*, never holds much more nor much less than 60 gallons (U.S.A.) or 50·5 gallons (U.K.), which means that it can be shifted about and stacked fairly easily by men who are both strong and skilled. Larger wine containers, whether made of oak or glass-lined cement, *foudres* and *cuves*, are not mobile.

At Bordeaux wine is sold at so much per *tonneau* or tun, which is not a cask, but the accepted trade unit equal to four *barriques* or hogsheads. The Bordeaux *barrique* is somewhat squat, fatter and shorter than the Burgundy *pièce* or hogshead. It holds 225 litres of wine, that is 59 gallons (U.S.A.) or 49·786 gallons (U.K.). There are two smaller casks in use in the Gironde, the half *barrique*, which is called a *feuillette* (112 litres) and the quarter *barrique*, which is called a *quartaut* (56 litres).

In Burgundy the accepted trade unit for the sale of wine is the *feuillette* in the Chablis district, and the *queue* everywhere else. There is no cask called a *queue*. The name means two *pièces* or hogsheads always sold in pairs. The standard hogshead of Burgundy is known as a *pièce*. In the Côte d'Or the standard cask is the *pièce de Beaune*, which holds 228 litres (60 gallons U.S.A. or 50·5 gallons U.K.); the *feuillette* and *quartaut* each holds 114 litres and 57 litres respectively. But in the Yonne white wine is sold by the *feuillette de Chablis*, which holds 172 litres of wine. In the Mâconnais and Beaujolais, at the southern end of Burgundy, the *pièce* holds from 215 to 216 litres, the *feuillette* half and the *quartaut* a quarter of the *pièce*. In the Côtes du Rhône the *pièce* holds 225 litres, in Champagne 216 litres, in Touraine 225 litres, in Anjou 220 litres, while in Alsace the cask commonly used is one that holds 116 litres of wine.

## Bottles

Bottles are a more permanent home than the cask for all the better French wines, still or sparkling, bordeaux, burgundy and champagne more particularly; their tenancy varies from three to seven, fourteen, twenty-one years and sometimes even much longer. For the majority of table wines, however, the bottle is merely a convenient container to bring to table a young wine, lately drawn from the cask; once in a bottle, the wine can be easily stored and kept at hand until wanted, whether for a few days or weeks, or for months and years as the case may be.

In France the standard bottle is the litre (33·81 fluid oz. U.S.A.). Most *ordinaires* wines and all the *très ordinaires* are sold in France in plain, white-glass and full-measure *litre*, *double-litre*, *demi-litre* or in a white-glass bottle called *Saint-Galmier*, being the bottle invariably used for the mineral water of that name. The better wines are mostly sold in slightly smaller bottles (*bouteilles*) or half-bottles (*demies* or *chopines*). Bottles vary slightly in both shape and size, and also in weight. The champagne bottle is much the heaviest of all, having to be made particularly strong to stand the carbonic gas pressure from within; its shoulders are sloping and its body bigger than that of the bordeaux bottle, which has more of a 'neck and shoulders'. The standard burgundy bottle looks very much like the champagne bottle, but it is a good deal lighter, in weight but not colour; there is a slightly smaller burgundy bottle called *Mâconnaise*. The Alsace bottles are without any shoulders, just long and thin, and green, very similar to the Moselle bottles. The Anjou bottles have long necks and thin bodies. The legal content of various bottles, in France, according to the Law of 1 January 1930, is as follows:

Litres: 100 centilitres
Saint-Galmier: 90 centilitres
Champagne, Burgundy and Rhône bottles: 80 centilitres
Bordeaux and Anjou bottles: 75 centilitres
Fillette d'Anjou and de Touraine: 35 centilitres
Alsace 'flute': 72 centilitres

*N.B. Post-1945 Burgundy and Rhône bottles contain 75 centilitres, the same as Bordeaux.*

The *Magnum* is a double and the *demie* is a half bottle, hence a *Magnum* of champagne holds 1·60 litres and a *Magnum* of claret 1·50 litres; a *demie* of champagne 40 centilitres and a *demie* of claret 37·5 centilitres.

Larger bottles are fancy bottles, the contents of which are approximately as follows:

| | | |
|---|---|---|
| Tregnum or tappit-hen | 3 bottles or 0·525 | gallons |
| Double Magnum | 4 bottles or 0·70 | gallons |
| Jeroboam (champagne) | 4 bottles or 0·70 | gallons |
| Rehoboam | 6 bottles or 1·05 | gallons |
| Methuselah (champagne) | 8 bottles or 1·40 | gallons |
| Impériale (claret) | 8–9 bottles | |

There are also larger bottles called Salmanazar, Balthazar and Nebuchadnezzar, which are supposed to hold 12, 16 and 20 bottles (2·10, 2·80, 3·50 gallons) respectively, but they are not really fit to use as wine bottles; they are monstrosities for show purposes, and anybody buying them would deserve to find the wine corked.

All the better quality French wines are now sold in bottles which are fully labelled, but the labelling of wine bottles, in France, is of fairly recent origin. Labels were first used for cordials and liqueurs, many of them home-made, at the beginning of the last century; then they were used for sparkling champagne and later on for all sorts of wines. Before labels came into general use bottles were 'dipped': when the cork had been driven in the neck of the bottle its outside face and a quarter of an inch or half an inch of the neck were dipped into some boiling sealing wax for just one moment; soon after, the wax which had stuck to cork and neck cooled off and became hard, protecting the cork from damp and insects. Wax of many different colours was used, black, yellow and various shades of red, blue and green, and the different wines in the cellar were identified by the colour of their wax-cap, duly recorded in the cellar book or bin book. There were wine-merchants who took a little more trouble and who had steel dies made to stamp on the wax, while still hot, their own name, or the name of the wine in the bottle or the date of its vintage.

There were also wine bottles made to the order of princes or wealthy merchants with their name, initials or arms embossed in the glass of the bottle, usually at the base of the neck, on the 'shoulder'. The best known of those French initialled wine and brandy bottles are stamped with the Napoleonic 'N'. Some are quite obviously older than the others; hand made, or mouth blown, never absolutely cylindrical, and they must be older than 1815, when the first Napoleon lost all interest in his cellar. The others are machine-made bottles, perfectly cylindrical, and were made from 1850 to 1870, the year when Napoleon III abdicated.

At large estates, like Château Lafite, for instance, some of the wine was sometimes bottled in the standard bordeaux bottle but with a 'button' stamped on the bottle's shoulder with the name 'Château Lafite' and the year of the wine's vintage, such as 1874. Neither name nor date could be washed or scraped off, which was all to the good, but as the bottle could not be used again for any other wine or vintage, its cost was excessively high. And so the paper label came, and it came to stay.

## Glasses

Wine glasses can make a very great deal of difference to our enjoyment of wine, which is why they must be chosen with great care. There is no worse mistake than to choose wine glasses as ornaments for the dining-room table, to 'look pretty', not giving as much as a thought to the wine which will fill them. There are some beautiful Salviati glasses with all the colours of the rainbow, and there are some very handsome cut-glass coloured glasses, not unlike old church stained glass, costly and admirable works of art, no doubt, but no good for wine. The first joy that a fine wine has to offer us is its clear, bright, cheerful and beautiful colour, so that the whiter the glass, the better it will be for the wine and for us.

Then there is the size of the wine glass. Wine is not tossed down like vodka at one gulp, nor is it swilled like foaming beer; wine is drunk without haste and with appreciation. There must not be too much nor too little in the glass. A glass that holds less than 3 fluid oz. is too small: the wine will be cramped in it. But a glass is too large which holds more than 5 fluid oz. A 4-oz. glass is about the best all-purpose size.

And lastly there is the shape of the glass. There are three French wines with glasses of their own, champagne, Alsace and Anjou, but quite a number of equally suitable glasses for bordeaux, burgundy and the rest. The original champagne glass was the *Flute*, which gives to the wine the maximum number of contacts, hence the greatest amount of *mousse* or bubbles; it was replaced some sixty-odd years ago by the *Coupe*, a flattish saucer on a pedestal, giving the wine the minimum amount of contacts, so that it kept its gas longer but looked rather flat. The *Coupe* was replaced by the *Tulipe*, a much more sensible shape, which the Champagne Syndicat has elongated and enlarged and made into a truly 'de luxe' glass.

Both the Alsace and Anjou glasses are tall glasses, but the shape of their bowl is quite distinctive.

## Brandy Glasses

The shape and size of brandy glasses depends very much upon the brandy and the occasion.

A tumbler is best for a three-year-old, or One Star brandy, served with a small bottle of cold soda-water, on a hot summer's day.

A *Ballon* or *Tulipe* wine glass of the finest and purest white material and holding half a pint is large enough for rotating a tot of brandy to coax its bouquet, and small enough to be cupped and warmed in the palm of the hand. It is the best glass for a liqueur brandy, and even after the whole of the brandy is gone, such a glass still holds delight for the connoisseur's sensitive and enquiring nose.

It is only when a *nouveau riche* must have 'the best' that there is any justification for bringing forth a footed aquarium, without water and goldfish, of course, and making it hot over a spirit-lamp, before pouring in it a few drops of a priceless centenarian brandy, which will lose most of its bouquet the moment it comes into contact with the heated glass.

The 'bar' and 'banquet' midget brandy glasses are a disgrace; they are much too mean to be acceptable at any time.


CHAPTER ELEVEN

# *The Care and Service of Wine*

WINE 'in the wood', or in casks, is young wine which needs the care of the expert to complete its fermentation and free itself from all undesirable matter, either vegetable or mineral, such as mucilage and tartar, before being bottled and sold to us to enjoy. As long as a wine is in cask it is in fairly free contact with the oxygen of the air, which is its friend at first, but may easily become its worst enemy after a time; this is why wine which is not drunk straight from the cask must be bottled. The amount of air which reaches the wine in a bottle through the cork – a porous substance, but only just – is infinitesimal but by no means negligible: it is probably responsible for the way in which bottled wines improve with age, 'probably' because the behaviour of bottled wines has as yet never been explained to the satisfaction of scientists.

What is quite certain, however, is that bottled wine must be given a decent home to live in until wanted. A cellar, or failing a cellar, a cupboard, bin or shelf which is to house bottled wine, must be as free as possible from variations of temperature. If we bear in mind that heat expands and that cold contracts, we shall easily realize that changes from heat to cold and cold to heat will 'tire' any wine in a bottle. Although we do not know very much about the 'ageing' process of wine, we do know that unless it be given complete rest and darkness, in a place free from draughts, vibrations and even noises, a cool place for choice, wine will go sick or flat or dumb. If one has no proper place to keep wine in one's home it is far better not to have more than just enough for day-to-day or week-to-week requirements: one's wine-merchant will always oblige, in town, and keep one's wines properly, delivering small quantities as and when wanted. Of course, if we live in the country we ought to have a cellar of our own, underground, facing north, away from the central-heating boiler; a cold, dark, dry, quiet, and clean cellar where wine may be left with every chance of improving. A dry cellar is more easily kept clean and free from mouldiness than a damp cellar, but a damp cellar is not necessarily a bad cellar; cork weevils do not like damp cellars.

Of course, every bottle of wine that is 'put down' in cellar or cellarette, in bin or on shelf, must be laid in a horizontal position so that the wine in the bottle be at all times in contact with the inside face of the cork.

When the time comes to 'pull a cork' the metal capsule on bottles of still wine must be cut below the ring of the bottle-neck, and not merely flush with the cork. The capsule is made of lead and is treated chemically to protect the cork: it stinks. The wine, as it is poured out, should not come into contact with the cut metal capsule, and the only way to make sure of this is to remove the capsule altogether, or to cut it below the ring, which is there to catch and divert any drops of wine. Once the capsule has been cut below the ring, the neck of the bottle should be thoroughly wiped. The cork should then be drawn and the inside lip of the bottle wiped with a clean cloth. Drive the corkscrew slowly right through the centre of the cork and draw the cork steadily without any jerks.

Generally speaking, clarets and ports of almost any age should be decanted, and so should all burgundies of more than ten years old. Any red wine will look better in a clear crystal decanter, especially if decanted with care. Decanting is a simple enough operation, particularly if a wicker cradle is used for the purpose of carrying the bottle from the bin to the table, and as a receptacle for holding the bottle firmly while the cork is drawn, and the mouth and neck of the bottle wiped clean. The wine should then be decanted by holding the bottle (not in the cradle) in the right hand over a lighted candle in a darkened room. The flame of the candle should be just below the shoulder of the bottle, and decanting should stop when the sediment, or crust, begins to run into the neck. The result should be a perfectly clear ruby liquid with all the sediment left in the bottle. Cradles used for serving at table are mainly used in restaurants for the flattery of customers who should know better. The constant ebb and flow of pouring will muddy the wine, except it be a Beaujolais or light burgundy, which can then be poured straight from the bottle without any chi-chi. When decanted, the cork can be allowed to lie across the mouth of the decanter, both as an indication of the contents and to impede the entrance of foreign bodies like midges, which are also wine-lovers.

Sometimes a cork breaks in the neck of the bottle, especially with very old wine, and here the wine cradle is very useful; it allows you to probe with your corkscrew, much as a dentist will deal with your teeth, once you are firmly placed in his chair. With experience most broken corks can be removed cleanly, but if all fails and pieces of cork reach the wine, decant the wine through a fine-mesh tea strainer or a wine strainer.

Corkscrews must *always* be of the 'cut' edge type, not of the 'round' wire type, and the great secret is to be sure to screw them well in.

*Very* old wine should not be decanted until just before serving, others from two to three hours before the meal. There is, however, no rule about this; some wines keep longer than others, but generally if a wine is more than, say, thirty years old there is a risk of fast fading once the bottle is opened.

Plate 15. The charming wines of Anjou, in an early bottle with its modern equiva‑
lent. The traditional glasses are not used elsewhere in France.

## Temperature

The temperature of the wine at the time of serving is of very great importance, but it is impossible to lay down any cast-iron rules. So much depends upon the wines themselves, the food served with them and climatic conditions.

One may, however, accept it as a general rule that all white wines are better served cold, and red wines at the temperature of the dining-room. But cold does not mean frozen. Wine that is too cold either numbs or burns the tongue and palate, so that it is quite impossible to appreciate any *finesse* or charm which the wine possessed originally. For the wine connoisseur no white wine should be colder than fifty degrees.

Red wines, and more particularly old red wines, are best *chambré*. This does not mean 'hotted-up', but brought gradually to the temperature of the dining-room – that of an average London or Paris dining-room, about sixty degrees. Never, for fear that it might be too cold, plunge a bottle of red wine in hot water or place it in front of a fire. It is much better to serve a red wine too cold than too warm. If it is too cold it can always be nursed in the palms of the hands; if it is too warm it is past all human help.

CHAPTER TWELVE

# The Art of Making Wine

WINE-MAKING is an art which the genius of man discovered at the dawn of the world's history; it has largely contributed to the well-being of mankind and to the growth of all arts ever since. The distinctive character of every wine is due principally to the species of grape from which it is made; to the geographical situation and to the geological formation of the vineyards where those grapes are grown; and to the more or less favourable weather conditions prevailing each year. But the striking differences which exist between various kinds of wines – either dark or light in colour; still or sparkling; sweet or dry – are due to the manner and degree in which they are fermented, and to the way they are treated during and after fermentation or, in other words, to different methods of vinification.

The art of wine-making comprises three principal stages: (1) the crushing of the ripe grapes to obtain their juice; (2) the fermenting of the must to obtain wine; and (3) the maturing of the wine either in cask or bottle, constantly and carefully watching it and attending to it, before it is ready for consumption.

While various processes of vinification obtain in different districts, there is one all-important factor in the art of wine-making which is common to all, viz. fermentation.

## Fermentation

Fermentation consists in a series of complex chemical changes, the most important of which causes the transformation of grape-sugar into ethyl alcohol and carbonic acid

ate 16. The best glasses for drinking brandy are the medium *ballon*, or the smaller
ass which can be held in the palm of one hand.

gas, a transformation which is rendered possible chiefly by the accelerating or catalystic action of the fermenting enzyme known as zymase. But grape-juice is not a mixture of water and grape-sugar with saccharomycetes in it. It is very complex, and there are in it other enzymes besides zymase. There are other chemical reactions taking place at the same time as those which are responsible for the presence of ethyl alcohol in wine, and these different reactions depend, in the first place, upon the chemical composition of the must, and the presence of certain enzymes – and, in the second place, upon external conditions existing at the time.

Climatic conditions are beyond the control of man. The soil of the vineyards may be improved to a certain extent by drainage and fertilizers, but its chief characteristics remain unaltered. Species of grapes may be judiciously selected and grafted. Grapes may be carefully picked and they may be pressed by different methods, but the last stage, the fermenting of grape-juice into wine, which is so important, may be controlled by man more than any of the other factors which are responsible for the making of wine.

Different processes of fermentation are suited to the different chemical composition of different musts, and their aim is to secure different types of wine.

On the whole, it may be said that the process of fermentation, which is an absolutely natural phenomenon, might be left to transform grape-juice into wine without any interference from man, except in the case of sparkling, fortified or other such wines. This is true, but like all truths, it is true only up to a point. Grass grows in the fields quite naturally, even in wet fields, but if no one attends to ditching and hedging moss may some day grow quite naturally where clover used to grow. Wine left too long to ferment upon its husks will draw colour from the skins if they be those of black grapes, but it will also draw from the pips, stalks or the small pedoncules more acidity and tannin and more of the unsuitable acids, which may prove objectionable later.

## Alcoholic Fermentation

Let us measure a gallon of grape-juice and weigh the quantity of grape-sugar it contains. Say that we find 32 oz. of grape-sugar present. Then let us look for our 32 oz. of sugar after the same grape-juice shall have finished fermenting. We shall not find any sugar, but in its place we shall find about 17 oz. of ethyl alcohol. What has happened? This. Each molecule of grape-sugar, representing 180 by weight, has been split up by fermentation into two molecules of ethyl alcohol (each 46 by weight) and two molecules of carbon dioxide (each 44 by weight). The carbon dioxide has lost itself in the air and the ethyl alcohol has remained in the wine – hence a gallon of wine will be lighter than a gallon of grape-juice, the difference being that of the weight of the escaped carbonic acid gas. At the same time 17 oz. of ethyl alcohol take up the same space as 32 oz. of grape-sugar, so that we shall have a gallon of wine in place of a gallon of grape-juice, the bulk of our wine being practically the same as the bulk of the grape-juice, although its weight will be slightly less.

We could, therefore, describe alcoholic fermentation by means of the following formula:

$$C_6H_{12}O_6 \quad = \quad 2C_2H_6O \quad + \quad 2CO_2$$
$$\text{(Grape-sugar)} \qquad \text{(Alcohol)} \qquad \text{(Carbon dioxide)}$$

Remembering that the atomic weight of carbon, hydrogen and oxygen are respectively $C = 12$, $H = 1$, $O = 16$, one molecule of grape-sugar, two of ethyl alcohol and two of carbon dioxide will represent:

<table>
<tr><td>(Grape-sugar)</td><td>(Alcohol)</td><td>(Carbon dioxide)</td></tr>
<tr><td>$C_6 = 12 \times 6 = 72$</td><td>$C_4 = 12 \times 4 = 48$</td><td>$C_2 = 12 \times 2 = 24$</td></tr>
<tr><td>$H_{12} = 1 \times 12 = 12$</td><td>$H_{12} = 1 \times 12 = 12$</td><td>$O_4 = 16 \times 4 = \underline{64}$</td></tr>
<tr><td>$O_6 = 16 \times 6 = \underline{96}$</td><td>$O_2 = 16 \times 2 = \underline{32}$</td><td>88</td></tr>
<tr><td>180</td><td>92</td><td></td></tr>
</table>

Alcoholic fermentation is therefore a molecular readjustment of the carbon, hydrogen and oxygen of grape-sugar. In theory, it seems simple – in practice it is complicated.

To begin with, grape-sugar is not a compact entity made up of six atoms of carbon, twelve of hydrogen and six of oxygen. On balance, there is that number of atoms to be found in one molecule of grape-sugar, but they are arranged in distinct groups:

<table>
<tr><td>Dextrose</td><td></td><td>Fructose</td></tr>
<tr><td>$CHO$</td><td></td><td>$CH_2OH$</td></tr>
<tr><td>$CHOH$</td><td></td><td>$CO$</td></tr>
<tr><td>$CHOH$</td><td>+</td><td>$CHOH$</td></tr>
<tr><td>$CHOH$</td><td></td><td>$CHOH$</td></tr>
<tr><td>$CHOH$</td><td></td><td>$CHOH$</td></tr>
<tr><td>$CH_2OH$</td><td></td><td>$CH_2OH$</td></tr>
</table>

There are 6 atoms of carbon, 12 of hydrogen and 6 of oxygen in their grouping; they are knit together in a strictly orderly manner, until the saccharomycetes give the signal, by a loud rap on the piano, for a wild game of musical chairs. Then all is confusion, order is destroyed, there is a rush, hot pursuit, until, all of a sudden, the music ceases and order reigns once more. Some have lost their seats, others have changed seats and have new neighbours. Of course, if there is no air in the room there cannot be any game. This is a very rough and unscientific simile, but it may serve to convey to the mind the main idea of alcoholic fermentation; it requires someone at the piano, i.e. an enzyme; it begins and ends with order, but the intervening period is very confused, and it is during this confusion that all sorts of things happen. There is a loss incurred in the process, and, above all, oxygen, i.e. fresh air, is wanted all the time.

Although zymase, the fermenting enzyme, is necessary to the process of alcoholic fermentation, it does not take any active part in the game which it sets going. Its chemical composition is such that it acts as a catalyst, that is to say a remover of hindrance or an accelerator of reactions. It does so without taking anything away or giving up any of its own substance.

## Temperature and Fermentation

A suitable temperature for the immediate growth of the saccharomycetes is of great importance, since their enzyme 'zymase' is indispensable to alcoholic fermentation. But wine is not merely grape-juice with its grape-sugar changed into alcohol and carbon dioxide: in grape-juice there are many other substances besides grape-sugar, and they cannot be expected to remain unaffected by the internal revolution which destroys the chemical structure of grape-sugar and rebuilds, with the same materials, ethyl alcohol and carbon dioxide. This revolution is the work of alcoholic fermentation, but other fermentations take place at the same time, other vegetable substances which were in grape-juice are altered, increased, reduced or may entirely disappear, in ways which differ according to the different enzymes and other catalysts present, as well as according to differences of temperature affecting not only the rate of molecular exchanges but also the degree of solubility of certain acids.

Temperature is an important factor in fermentation because of the influence it exercises upon the rate of molecular exchanges and upon the solubility of various acids. Grape-juice is so complex, it contains such a large number of various compounds, that any and every variation of temperature is liable to affect some chemical reaction upon which may depend, at a later date, some characteristic of the wine.

To sum up, let it suffice to say that the process known as fermentation is one which consists mainly in the splitting up of each molecule of grape-sugar present in grape-juice into two molecules of carbon dioxide. But let it be remembered: (1) that there are other fermentable substances in grape-juice besides grape-sugar; (2) that, besides zymase, there are other enzymes as well as other catalysts which render possible subsidiary fermentations which take place concurrently or subsequently, and are responsible for the presence, in wine, of compounds which did not exist in grape-juice.

## Wine

Grape-juice is a very complex aqueous solution. Besides water and grape-sugar, it contains acids and other substances, most of them in very small quantities, either of a vegetable or of a mineral origin.

Wine is a still more complex aqueous solution; besides water and ethyl alcohol, it contains glycerine, acids and many substances in minute quantities, some of which never were in grape-juice.

Water and ethyl alcohol form generally about 97% of the volume of wine, but the remaining 3% is made up of very small quantities of a large variety of substances, which vary and give to different wines the distinctive colour, taste and bouquet which are mainly responsible for the charm, or lack of charm, of individual wines.

These substances may be divided into two main groups, one to include all those which were originally present in grape-juice and the other all those which were not.

(1) *Substances, other than water, which are the same in grape-juice and wine*: Grape-sugar; saccharomycetes; some acids; cellulose; essential oils, mucilage, etc.

(2) *Substances other than ethyl alcohol present in wine, but not in grape-juice*: Glycerine; other acids; alcohols, other than ethyl alcohol; esters and aldehydes; sundry other substances.

### (1) *Substances, other than water, which are the same in grape-juice and wine*

#### (a) *Grape-sugar*

The proportion of grape-sugar which remains in wine after fermentation depends, in the first place, upon the proportion of grape-sugar present in the grape-juice and, in the second, upon the process or method of fermentation resorted to.

In the case of 'fortified' or 'sweet' wines, whether obtained like port, by the addition of brandy during fermentation, or, like Sauternes, from over-ripe grapes, the sweeter the grape-juice, the sweeter the wine. But, in the case of beverage wines such as claret, it is often the reverse.

### (b) Saccharomycetes

Although saccharomycetes are microscopic fungi, there are millions of them and they do not escape in air like carbon dioxide. They remain in suspension in the wine until the end of fermentation or until the proportion of alcohol is such that it arrests their growth. They are so fine and so light that they are neither swept down by finings nor do they fall to the bottom of the cask by their own weight; many are carried down into the lees by the microscopic crystals of cream of tartar to which they adhere, many more lose their identity altogether by reason of the chemical splitting up of their cells, and some remain in the wine for all time.

There is, of course, a very large variety of saccharomycetes and allied members of the vast tribe of yeasts, bacteria and moulds.

A form of yeast-fungi which is not unusual in wines is the *Mycoderma Vini*, or 'flowers of wine'. These micro-organisms multiply very rapidly at the surface of wine and remain on the surface in giant colonies, all holding together, and forming a film which can be so complete as to prevent the outside air having any access to the wine. There are quite a number of different species of film-forming microscopic fungi, all of which require much oxygen to grow and all of which grow with astonishing rapidity.

### (c) Acids

Generally speaking, the acids which disappear wholly or partly during fermentation are those which are soluble in water and not in alcohol, while acids which appear in much large proportions in wine than in grape-juice are those which are formed by the oxidation of ethyl alcohol. Let us take but one example of each glass, i.e. tartaric acid and acetic acid.

*Tartaric acid* is the principal acid in grape-juice. It forms a white crystalline salt which is potassium hydrogen tartrate, commonly known as cream of tartar. Cream of tartar is soluble in water but not in alcohol, and a good deal of the cream of tartar in solution in grape-juice becomes solidified in the shape of fine crystals in the presence of the alcohol of wine; in that form, it is heavier than wine, settles in the lees and is left behind when the wine is racked. Cream of tartar is also more soluble in a warm than in a cold aqueous solution, so that if the new wine be kept in a cold cellar the lower temperature and the alcohol present will help render a greater proportion of cream of tartar insoluble, thus depriving the wine, after racking, of much acidity present in the grape-juice.

An acid grape-juice does not necessarily ferment into an acid wine. Acidity in grape-juice is of great benefit because it assists the normal growth of yeasts and checks the development of bacteria, so that it is favourable to alcoholic fermentation. If as well as acidity there is a fair proportion of grape-sugar in the grape-juice this sugar will ferment and be replaced by a fair proportion of alcohol, which, in its turn, will cause the crystallization of a further proportion of cream of tartar, hitherto in solution. In other words, more sugar in the grape-juice means more alcohol in the wine and less cream of tartar. This is easy to prove in Burgundy where Pinot grape-juice and Gamay grape-juice from the same district may be compared: the first contains more acidity and more sugar than the second, but when both have become wine the first contains more alcohol and less acidity than the second.

*Acetic acid* in wine is due to the oxidation of ethyl alcohol, one atom of oxygen replacing two of hydrogen, thus:

$$\text{Ethyl alcohol} = CH_3CH_2OH \qquad\qquad \text{Acetic acid} = CH_3CO \cdot OH$$

The more alcohol there is in a wine and the less oxygen has access to it, the smaller will be the quantity of acetic acid formed. This replacement of two hydrogen atoms by one of oxygen is rendered possible by the presence of an enzyme secreted by the schitzomycetes, and they cannot grow without a free supply of oxygen from the air. Hence when 'flowers of wine' or other film-forming mycoderma cover the surface of wine and prevent all contact with the outside air no more acetic acid can be formed. On the other hand, wine of a low alcoholic strength kept in a fairly warm place and in contact with the air will soon become vinegar, almost the whole of its ethyl alcohol being changed into acetic acid. Of course, this should be avoided, and it can be avoided with a little care. At the same time normal and sound wine is seldom free from acetic acid when new and, with time, this acetic acid dissolves certain mineral salts in wine, forming acetates which are partly responsible for the flavour and bouquet of wine.

### (d) Cellulose

Cellulose is a danger in wine because it may fall a prey to certain bacteria which cause its decomposition into fatty acids and carbonic acid gas, the former being particularly objectionable. Decomposed or 'fermented' cellulose in red wine is the cause of an extremely light viscous sediment which it is almost impossible to keep out of the decanter and which spoils not only the look but the taste of the wine.

## (2) *Substances, other than ethyl alcohol, present in wine but not in grape-juice*

These substances are numerous and vary according to the chemical composition of the grape-juice, the enzymes or catalysts present, and the rate and mode of fermentation. They consist chiefly of glycerine and other alcohols, various acids, esters and aldehydes.

### (a) Glycerine

Most of the sugar in grape-juice is transformed by fermentation into ethyl alcohol and carbon dioxide, but not the whole of it. Pasteur's experiments, which more recent researches have completely confirmed, showed that alcoholic fermentation could not use up more than 95% of the sugar present in grape-juice in the proportion of about 48% ethyl alcohol and 47% carbon dioxide. The remaining 5% of sugar is used up in other ways; a small quantity being used by saccharomycetes themselves by way of food or means of cellular development; a small percentage being decomposed into minute quantities of various volatile acids and the greater proportion being used up in the production of glycerine.

### (b) Other Alcohols

Besides glycerine which, after and a long way behind ethyl alcohol, is the most important by-product of vinous fermentation, there are other alcohols in wine. Such are propyl and butyl alcohols, practically in all cases, and amyl alcohol sometimes. Although these and other alcohols are present in normal wines only in minute quantities, they have, like all alcohols, the property of forming esters with acids, and they play quite an important part, compared to their volume, in the formation of the bouquet or aroma of wine.

### (c) Acids

Some of the acidity in the grape-juice, particularly in the shape of cream of tartar, disappears during fermentation, but on the other hand there are some acids which were not in the grape-juice and which are normally present in the wine as by-products of fermentation.

First among these is succinic acid, which is the principal cause of the 'winey' flavour of wine, its 'saveur'; the proportion of succinic acid in a wine, according to Pasteur, is 0·61% of the grape-sugar in the must.

A very small quantity of grape-sugar is also transformed, during fermentation, into acetic acid, proprionic acid and traces of valerianic acid. These acids are present in very small quantities and they do not affect the taste of wine, but they are responsible to a certain extent for its bouquet; the esters, which give the wine its *bouquet*, being formed by alcohols at the expense of acids. Normal wine, that is, wine which is sound and suitably fermented, always contains a little acetic acid, but it is only a very little. When acetic acid is present in wine in a noticeable amount it is not the result of the decomposition of grape-sugar, but of the oxidation of ethyl alcohol; it is a sure sign that the wine is not absolutely sound, that it will soon be vinegar and no longer wine, if the progress of acetification is not promptly checked.

The variety of volatile and non-volatile acids in wine, which differ from those of the grape-juice, is very great, and Prior's researches have proved that the differences existing in the acids of different wines were due to the differences existing in the species of saccharomycetes and other micro-organisms present in the grape-juice or introduced in the wine at a later date. In every case, those acids are present only in minute quantities, sometimes there are only traces of each, but the importance of the part they play in the degree of excellence of a wine is out of all proportion to their volume.

### (d) Aldehydes

Aldehydes are always present in wine. They may be regarded as by-products of alcoholic fermentation and as an intermediary organic compound between alcohols and acids. They must eventually become either acids by the action of oxidizing agents, or else alcohols, by the intervention of reducing agents.

### (e) Esters

The ethyl formates, acetates, proprionates, butyrates, lactates and other such esters are due to reactions between alcohols and acetic acid, proprionic acid, butyric acid, lactic acid, etc. They are volatile and give to wines their distinctive aroma.

## Vintage Table

The ratings of the following table range from 'o', for a really very bad year, the wines of which are not likely ever to be offered for sale, to '1', a very poor year; '2', also a poor year but with a few exceptions; '3', a year which produced wines mostly from fair to middling in quality; '4' for an irregular year when both quite good and quite indifferent wines were made; '5', a fairly satisfactory year all round; '6', a good vintage which produced mostly fine wines – most of them, however, for early consumption; and '7', when the best vintage conditions obtained and when fine wines were made which should be long-lived and become great with age. It was prepared by the Wine and Food Society.

| Year | Bordeaux (Red) | Burgundy (Red) | Rhône | Champagne | Sauternes | Burgundy (White) | Loire | Alsace |
|---|---|---|---|---|---|---|---|---|
| 1935 | 2 | 4 | 3 | 3 | 2 | 5 | 4 | 5 |
| 1936 | 3 | 2 | 5 | 2 | 3 | 4 | 5 | 6 |
| 1937 | 5 | 5 | 6 | 5 | 7 | 7 | 7 | 6 |
| 1938 | 4 | 3 | 5 | 4 | 3 | 4 | 5 | 4 |
| 1939 | 2 | 2 | 3 | 2 | 2 | 2 | 4 | 3 |
| 1940 | 3 | 2 | 2 | 3 | 3 | 1 | 3 | 3 |
| 1941 | 1 | 1 | 3 | 4 | 0 | 1 | 6 | 2 |
| 1942 | 3 | 3 | 6 | 5 | 6 | 6 | 6 | 5 |
| 1943 | 5 | 5 | 6 | 5 | 6 | 6 | 7 | 5 |
| 1944 | 6 | 2 | 3 | 3 | 4 | 6 | 4 | 6 |
| 1945 | 6 | 7 | 6 | 6 | 7 | 6 | 7 | 6 |
| 1946 | 3 | 4 | 4 | 3 | 3 | 5 | 6 | 6 |
| 1947 | 7 | 7 | 7 | 6 | 7 | 7 | 6 | 6 |
| 1948 | 6 | 5 | 4 | 4 | 4 | 6 | 6 | 5 |
| 1949 | 7 | 7 | 6 | 5 | 5 | 6 | 5 | 7 |
| 1950 | 6 | 4 | 6 | 3 | 4 | 6 | 6 | 5 |
| 1951 | 3 | 3 | 4 | 2 | 6 | 6 | 4 | 6 |
| 1952 | 7 | 7 | 6 | 6 | 6 | 6 | 6 | 6 |
| 1953 | 7 | 7 | 6 | 6 | 7 | 7 | 6 | 7 |
| 1954 | 6 | 4 | 5 | 3 | 3 | 6 | 5 | 3 |
| 1955 | 6 | 5 | 7 | 7 | 7 | 6 | 7 | 5 |
| 1956 | 3 | 3 | 5 | 4 | 4 | 3 | 5 | 3 |
| 1957 | 5 | 5 | 4 | 3 | 5 | 5 | 6 | 5 |
| 1958 | 5 | 4 | 6 | 5 | 5 | 4 | 7 | 5 |
| 1959 | 7 | 6 | 6 | 7 | 7 | 7 | 7 | 7 |
| 1960 | 4 | 5 | 5 | 4 | 4 | 6 | 6 | 5 |
| 1961 | 6 | 7 | 5 | 7 | 5 | 6 | 6 | 5 |
| 1962 | 6 | 5 | 6 | 6 | 6 | 5 | 5 | 6 |
| 1963 | 4 | 4 | 5 | 4 | 2 | 5 | 5 | 6 |
| 1964 | 5 | 6 | 7 | 6 | 4 | 6 | 6 | 6 |
| 1965 | 6 | 4 | 4 | 5 | 6 | 3 | 4 | 5 |
| 1966 | 5 | 6 | 6 | 6 | 6 | 5 | 5 | 6 |

# APPENDIX TWO

## The Crus Classés du Médoc

| Châteaux | Communes | Production (tonneaux) |
|---|---|---|
| **Premiers Crus** | | |
| Lafite | Pauillac | 180 |
| Latour | Pauillac | 100 |
| Margaux | Margaux | 150 |
| Haut-Brion Graves[1] | Pessac | 100 |
| **Deuxièmes Crus** | | |
| Mouton-Rothschild | Pauillac | 95 |
| Rausan-Ségla | Margaux | 60 |
| Rauzan-Gassies | Margaux | 50 |
| Léoville-Las-Cases | Saint-Julien | 150 |
| Léoville-Poyferré | Saint-Julien | 120 |
| Léoville-Barton | Saint-Julien | 100 |
| Durfort-Vivens | Margaux | 30 |
| Lascombes | Margaux | 35 |
| Gruaud-Larose | Saint-Julien | 185 |
| Brane-Cantenac | Cantenac | 100 |
| Pichon-Longueville | Pauillac | 78 |
| Pichon-Longueville-Lalande | Pauillac | 100 |
| Ducru-Beaucaillou | Saint-Julien | 130 |
| Cos-d'Estournel | Saint-Estèphe | 50 |
| Montrose | Saint-Estèphe | 100 |
| **Troisièmes Crus** | | |
| Kirwan | Cantenac | 100 |
| Issan | Cantenac | 30 |
| Lagrange | Saint-Julien | 100 |
| Langoa | Saint-Julien | 75 |
| Giscours | Labarde | 20 |
| Malescot-St Exupéry | Margaux | 50 |
| Cantenac-Brown | Cantenac | 90 |
| Palmer | Cantenac | 100 |
| La Lagune | Ludon | 80 |

| Châteaux | Communes | Production (tonneaux) |
|---|---|---|
| Desmirail | Margaux | 30 |
| Calon-Ségur | Saint-Estèphe | 150 |
| Ferrière | Margaux | 20 |
| d'Alesme-Becker | Margaux | 20 |
| Boyd-Cantenac | Cantenac | 30 |
| **Quatrièmes Crus** | | |
| Saint-Pierre-Sevaistre | Saint-Julien | 40 |
| Saint-Pierre-Bontemps | Saint-Julien | 60 |
| Branaire-Ducru | Saint-Julien | 100 |
| Talbot | Saint-Julien | 140 |
| Duhart-Milon | Pauillac | 140 |
| Pouget | Cantenac | 30 |
| La Tour-Carnet | Saint-Laurent | 70 |
| Rochet | Saint-Estèphe | 60 |
| Beychevelle | Saint-Julien | 100 |
| Le Prieuré-Lichine | Cantenac | 30 |
| Marquis-de-Terme | Margaux | 75 |
| **Cinquièmes Crus** | | |
| Pontet-Canet | Pauillac | 200 |
| Batailley | Pauillac | 80 |
| Grand-Puy-Lacoste | Pauillac | 70 |
| Grand-Puy-Ducasse | Pauillac | 35 |
| Lynch-Bages | Pauillac | 100 |
| Dauzac | Labarde | 60 |
| Mouton Baron Philippe | Pauillac | 100 |
| Le Tertre | Arsac | 100 |
| Pédesclaux | Pauillac | 30 |
| Belgrave | Saint-Laurent | 150 |
| Camensac | Saint-Laurent | 70 |
| Cos-Labory | Saint-Estèphe | 45 |
| Clerc-Milon-Mondon | Pauillac | 35 |
| Croizet-Bages | Pauillac | 50 |
| Cantemerle | Macau | 100 |

## An Alphabetical List of Premiers Crus Bourgeois du Médoc

| Châteaux | Communes | Average Yield |
|---|---|---|
| Abbé-Gorsse-de-Gorsse | Margaux | 50 |
| Angludet | Cantenac | 100 |
| Anseillan, d' | Pauillac | 50 |
| Antonic | Moulis | 50 |
| Arche, d' | Ludon | 25 |
| Arsac, d' | Arsac | 20 |
| Avensan, d' | Avensan | 5 |
| Balogues-Haut-Bages | Pauillac | 100 |

| Châteaux | Communes | Average Yield |
|---|---|---|
| Barateau | Saint-Laurent | 25 |
| Beaumont | Cussac | 50 |
| Beauséjour | Saint-Estèphe | 60 |
| Beausite | Saint-Estèphe | 100 |
| Bégorce-Zédé, de la | Soussans | 18 |
| Bellegrave | Pauillac | 20 |
| Bellevue | Macau | 5 |
| Bellevue-Cordeillan-Bages | Pauillac | 15 |

[1] Although Château Haut-Brion is in the Commune of Pessac, in the Graves de Bordeaux district, it was included in this classification of Médoc.

| Châteaux | Communes | Average Yield | Châteaux | Communes | Average Yield |
|---|---|---|---|---|---|
| Bellevue-Saint-Lambert | Pauillac | 40 | Lamouroux, de | Margaux | 35 |
| Bibian-Darriet (Cru) | Listrac | 45 | Lancien-Brillette | Moulis | 20 |
| Biston-Briette | Moulis | 10 | Lanessan | Cussac | 75 |
| Bontemps-Dubarry | Saint-Julien | 20 | Larrieu-Terrefort-Graves | Macau | 5 |
| Boscq, Le | Saint-Estèphe | 50 | Lemoine-Lafon-Rochet | Ludon | 15 |
| Bouqueyran | Moulis | 30 | Lestage | Listrac | 125 |
| Cambon-La-Pelouse | Macau | 40 | Lestage-Darquier-Grand- | | |
| Canteloup | Saint-Estèphe | 80 | Poujeaux | Moulis | 30 |
| Capbern | Saint-Estèphe | 90 | Liversan | Saint-Sauveur | 100 |
| Caronne-Sainte-Gemme | Saint-Laurent | 80 | Ludon-Pomiès-Agassac | Ludon | 10 |
| Chesnay-Sainte- | | | Mac-Carthy | Saint-Estèphe | 30 |
| Gemme, La | Cussac | 15 | Mac-Carthy-Moula | Saint-Estèphe | 20 |
| Citran-Clauzel | Avensan | 80 | Malecot | Pauillac | 75 |
| Clarke | Listrac | 30 | Malescasse | Lamarque | 30 |
| Clauzet | Saint-Estèphe | 30 | Marbuzet, de | Saint-Estèphe | 50 |
| Closerie, La | Moulis | 25 | Martinens | Cantenac | 50 |
| Colombier-Monpelou, du | Pauillac | 100 | Maucaillou | Moulis | 20 |
| Conseillant | Labarde | 12 | Maucamps | Macau | 50 |
| Constant-Trois-Moulins | Macau | 10 | Mauvezin | Moulis | 20 |
| Corconac | Saint-Laurent | 15 | May (Clos de) | Macau | 10 |
| Couronne, La | Pauillac | 15 | Meyney | Saint-Estèphe | 150 |
| Coutelin-Merville (Cru) | Saint-Estèphe | 60 | Meyre-Estèbe | Avensan | 5 |
| Crock, Le | Saint-Estèphe | 125 | Meyre-Vieux-Clos | Avensan | 15 |
| Daubos-Haut-Bages | Pauillac | 10 | Monbrison | Arsac | 12 |
| Dubignon-Talbot | Margaux | 20 | Monpelou | Pauillac | 25 |
| Duplessis | Moulis | 100 | Montbrun | Cantenac | 25 |
| Duroc-Milon | Pauillac | 15 | Morère, La | Moulis | 20 |
| Dutruch-Grand-Poujeaux | Moulis | 50 | Morin | Saint-Estèphe | 50 |
| Egmont, d' | Ludon | 25 | Moulin-à-Vent | Moulis | 30 |
| Fatin | Saint-Estèphe | 60 | Moulin-Riche | Saint-Julien | 50 |
| Fellonneau | Macau | 40 | Moulis | Moulis | 20 |
| Fonbadet | Pauillac | 80 | Nexon-Lemoyne | Ludon | 10 |
| Fonpetite | Saint-Estèphe | 50 | Ormes-de-Pez, Les | Saint-Estèphe | 80 |
| Fonréaud | Listrac | 100 | Paloumey | Ludon | 20 |
| Fontesteau | Saint-Sauveur | 50 | Parempuyre, de (Cruse) | Parempuyre | 35 |
| Fourcas-Dupré | Listrac | 50 | Parempuyre, de | | |
| Fourcas-Hostein | Listrac | 50 | (Durand-Dassier) | Parempuyre | 20 |
| Fourcas-Laubaney | Listrac | 30 | Paveil-de-Luze | Soussans | 20 |
| Galan, du | Saint-Laurent | 25 | Peyrabon | Saint-Sauveur | 15 |
| Glana, du | Saint-Julien | 50 | Peyrelebade, de | Listrac | 20 |
| Grand-Duroc-Milon | Pauillac | 25 | Pez, de | Saint-Estèphe | 90 |
| Grand-Village-Capbern | Saint-Estèphe | 30 | Phélan-Ségur | Saint-Estèphe | 120 |
| Gressier-Grand-Poujeaux | Moulis | 40 | Pibran | Pauillac | 20 |
| Guitignan | Moulis | 25 | Picard | Saint-Estèphe | 60 |
| Gurgue, La | Margaux | 30 | Pierre-Bibian | Listrac | 30 |
| Haut-Bages-Averous | Pauillac | 40 | Pomeys | Moulis | 20 |
| Haut-Bages-Drouillet | Pauillac | 20 | Pomiès-Agassac | Ludon | 10 |
| Haut-Pauillac | Pauillac | 5 | Pomys | Saint-Estèphe | 25 |
| Haut-Senot | Soussans | 12 | Pontac-Lynch | Cantenac | 30 |
| Haye, La | Saint-Estèphe | 30 | Poujeaux-Castaing | Moulis | 65 |
| Houissant | Saint-Estèphe | 32 | Poujeaux-Marly | Moulis | 20 |
| Labégorce, de | Margaux | 40 | Priban | Macau | 30 |
| Ladouys | Saint-Estèphe | 20 | Ramage-de-Batisse (Cru) | Saint-Sauveur | 10 |
| Lafite-Canteloup | Ludon | 5 | Reverdi | Lamarque | 25 |
| Lafitte-Carcasset | Saint-Estèphe | 60 | Robert-Franquet | Moulis | 25 |
| Lafon | Listrac | 45 | Roche (Cru) | Saint-Estèphe | 40 |
| Lamarque, de | Lamarque | 20 | Romefort | Avensan | 30 |
| Lamothe de Bergeron | Cussac | 35 | Rose-Capbern, La | Saint-Estèphe | 20 |

| Châteaux | Communes | Average Yield | Châteaux | Communes | Average Yield |
|---|---|---|---|---|---|
| Rosemont | Labarde | 40 | Siran | Labarde | 100 |
| Saint-Estèphe | Saint-Estèphe | 35 | Testeron, du | Moulis | 25 |
| Saint-Estèphe (Clos) | Saint-Estèphe | 25 | Tour-de-Mons, La | Soussans | 125 |
| Saransot-Dupré | Listrac | 60 | Tour-Milon, La | Pauillac | 50 |
| Ségur | Parempuyre | 30 | Tour-Pibran, La | Pauillac | 25 |
| Ségur-Fillon (Cru) | Parempuyre | 25 | Trois-Moulins, des | Macau | 50 |
| Semeillan | Listrac | 40 | Tronquoy-Lalande | Saint-Estèphe | 60 |

## An alphabetical list of the 29 communes of the Haut-Médoc with their potential production of various grades of claret (red bordeaux)

Key: A. Wines of the Five Classes Growths (Crus Classés)
B. Wines of the Crus Bourgeois Supérieurs
C. Wines of the Crus Bourgeois and Crus Artisans
D. Wines of the Palus and Terrefort vineyards
E. Totals

| Communes | A | B | C | D | E |
|---|---|---|---|---|---|
| Arcins | — | — | 280 | — | 280 |
| Arsac | 100 | 32 | 150 | — | 282 |
| Avensan | — | 155 | 300 | — | 455 |
| Blanquefort | — | — | 133 | 300 | 433 |
| Cantenac | 510 | 205 | 200 | 325 | 1,240 |
| Castelnau | — | — | 100 | — | 100 |
| Cissac | — | — | 1,250 | — | 1,250 |
| Cussac | — | 175 | 500 | — | 675 |
| Labarde | 80 | 152 | 65 | — | 1,297 |
| Lamarque | — | 75 | 350 | — | 425 |
| Le Pian-Médoc | — | 85 | 50 | — | 135 |
| Le Taillan | — | — | 400 | — | 400 |
| Listrac | — | 615 | 1,000 | — | 1,615 |
| Ludon | 20 | 120 | 200 | 600 | 940 |
| Macau | 100 | 255 | 200 | 1,000 | 1,555 |
| Margaux | 140 | 175 | 150 | 210 | 1,675 |
| Moulis | — | 830 | 600 | — | 1,430 |
| Parempuyre | — | 110 | — | 150 | 260 |
| Pauillac | 1,058 | 728 | 1,000 | — | 2,786 |
| Saint-Aubin | — | — | 100 | — | 100 |
| Saint-Estèphe | 505 | 1,322 | 1,563 | — | 3,390 |
| Sainte-Hélène | — | — | 20 | — | 20 |
| Saint-Julien-Beychevelle | 1,300 | 120 | 250 | — | 1,670 |
| Saint-Laurent | 290 | 145 | 500 | — | 935 |
| Saint-Médard-en-Jalles | — | — | 200 | — | 200 |
| Saint-Sauveur | — | 115 | 250 | — | 365 |
| Saint-Seurin-de-Cadourne | — | — | 1,500 | — | 1,500 |
| Soussans | — | 205 | — | 250 | 455 |
| Vertheuil | — | — | 1,500 | — | 1,500 |
| | 4,103 | 5,619 | 12,811 | 2,835 | 25,368 |

These figures represent *tonneaux* of four *barriques*, roughly speaking 200 gallons or 100 dozen of wine to each *tonneau*.

# APPENDIX THREE

## *Champagne Shippers in 1862*

\* An asterisk indicates that either the firm is still trading today or that there is still champagne marketed under the brand of a defunct firm.

### Reims
Association Vinicole
  de la Champagne,
  L. Jaunay & Co
Bernard, F. & Co
\*Binet fils
Boden aîné
Burchard-Delbeck &
  Co
Châtelain, C., de
  Montigny & Co
Clicquot, E.
Clicquot, H.
Couvert, successor to
  E. Forest
Farre, Ch.
Fisse, Thirion & Co
\*Forest-Fourneaux,
  père et fils (now
  Taittinger)
Frissard, père et fils
Gibert, G.
Gigot, Alex
Gondelle, E.
\*Goulet, George & Co
Goulet, N. & H.
Grouselle fils
\*Heidsieck & Co
\*Heidsieck, Charles &
  Co
\*Irroy, Ernest
\*Krug & Co
\*Lanson, père et fils
Lelegard, A.
Loche, Ch.
Lossy (de) & Co
Manuel & Co
Minet, Jeune &
  Brown
Moreau, A., fils aîné
Morizet-Heut
Mumm, Jules & Co
\*Mumm, G. H. & Co
Ohaus, F.
\*Piper, H. & Co
\*Pommery, Veuve et fils
Rivart, C.
\*Roederer, L.
Roederer, Thésophile
  & Co

Ruinart, père et fils
Ruinart, Paul & Kurz
\*Saint-Marceaux, (de)
  & Co
Schoyer-Dorlodot
Soyez, Auguste, fils &
  Co
Sutaine (Veuve) Max
  & Co
Tassigny (de) o. et Co
Walther, J. H.
\*Werlé & Co.,
  successors to Veuve
  Clicquot-Ponsardin

### Epernay
\*Charles Abelé
Bremont Bardoux
Martin Boizel
\*Chanoine frères
Chaurey Jaune
Chausson frères
\*De Venoge & Co
A. Dutemple
Jules Fournier
St-Wallon de Lochet
  & Co
Veuve Locquard &
  Ch. Choque
L. I. Luquet & Co
Méchin Martin
\*Eugène Mercier
Meunier, frères
Moet & Chandon
\*Perrier Jouet & Co
\*Pétrot Bonnet & Co
Thiercelin Pissard
L. Plomb
\*Pol Roger & Co
Alfred Roger
J. Roussillon & Co
V. Sosthène Thomas
\*Wachter & Co

### Châlons-sur-Marne
Benjamin & Eugène
  Perrier
Bullot
Adolphe Collin
\*Dagonet et fils

Dailzon et Lesage
\*Freminet et fils
J. Goerg & Co
Eugène Grognot
\*Jacquesson et fils
\*Joseph Perrier, fils et
  Co
Lecat Lequed
Bertin Pithois
Rollett Soudant

### Canton d'Ay
Aubert & Fils
Alfred Aubert
Aubert & Brugnon
\*Ayala, Albrecht
Simon Bertault
Jaillot Besserat
Riché-Bin, Ed.
Bertault Blondeau
\*Bollinger-de-
  Villemont
Jules Camuset
\*Henri Couvreur
\*Deutz & Geldermann
\*Taverne Duminy
Folliet F. Duvernet
Parisot Foureaux
Robinet Gondrecourt
Moreau-Gustave
Renault Hazart
Gustave Janet
Billiet Lahave
\*Vve. Laurent-Perrier
Pinchon Lefèbure
Blancgard Louis
Le comte de Mareuil
Victor Padie
Bornot Phillipponat
Pottelain
Léon Pottelin
Brézol Robinet
Robinet de Fontenille
Guyard Robinet
Marignier Roulet
Gaspard Testulat
Vidal Tirode
Léon Vautrin
Vautrin Père et Fils
Walch & Co

### Mareuil-sur-Ay
Moignon Alise Fils &
  Co
Emile Batillet & Véry
\*Salmon Billecart
Bouche Fils & Co
Foucher Bruck & Co
Vve. Foucher, Olivier
  & Co
Pagin Francois
\*Saturnin Irroy
Pivin Labbey
Ch. Gaudon Malotet
Testulat Malotet
Hadot Mayeur
\*Alfred de Montebello
  & Co
Bruch Renault
A. Verrier
Hazart Verey

### Avize
A. Arnoult
Henri Aubert
Augé Colin
\*Charles de Cazenove
Desbordes père
Dinet, fils & Co
Perruchot Doerr
Ducognon
Ch. Francart & Co
Giesler & Co
Guizet
F. Jacoby
Jouron
Koch fils
Labouré jeune
Leon Le Brun
Lecureux &
  Lefournier
Lefournier jeune
Marchand Révelard
H. Moré
Grandjean Planckaert
A. Puisart
Lecler Révélard
August Soulés
Verron Varnier
Lafont Vincent
Bara Vix

# The Wines of
# NORTH
# AFRICA

❧

ANDRÉ L. SIMON

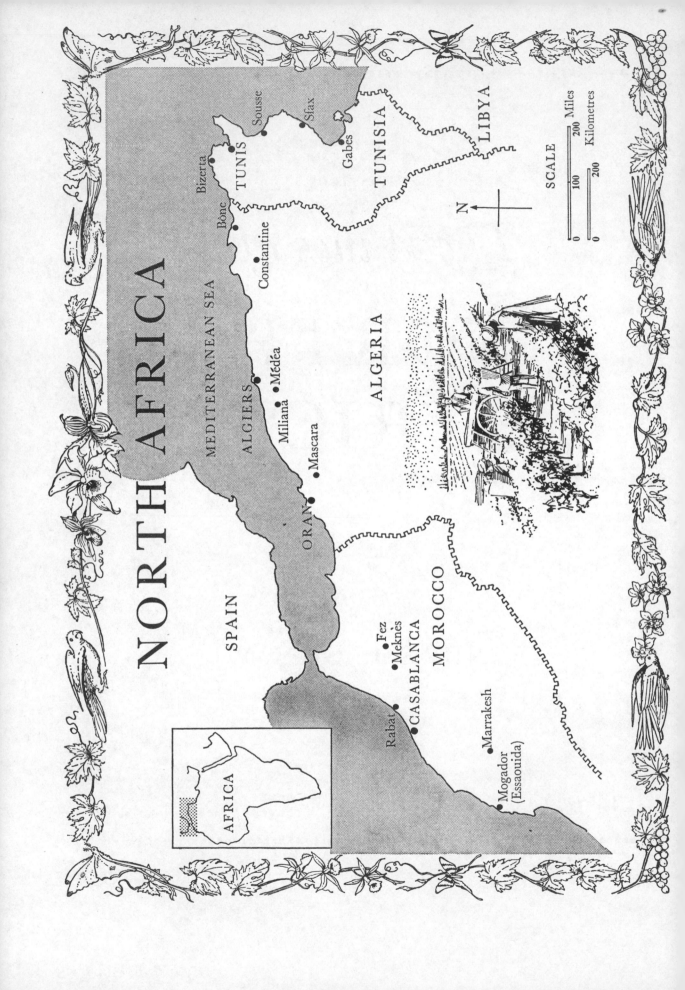

# NORTH AFRICA

MEDITERRANEAN SEA

SPAIN

Bizerta
Bone
TUNIS
Sousse
Sfax
Gabes
TUNISIA
LIBYA

Constantine

ALGIERS
Miliana • Médéa
Mascara
ORAN

ALGERIA

Fez
Meknès
CASABLANCA
Rabat
MOROCCO
Marrakesh
Mogador
(Essaouida)

AFRICA

SCALE

Miles
200
100
0

Kilometres
200
0

N

# North Africa

CLIMATIC conditions and soil fertility in many parts of the North African seaboard, and for some 80 miles of the hinterland from the Mediterranean, are quite suitable, sometimes even ideal, for viticulture. Italians have established vineyards in the Nile Delta, in Egypt, and between the two world wars, Mussolini was responsible for an ambitious planting of vines in Libya, chiefly at El Garscia, near Benghazi: they brought forth a quarter of a million gallons of wine, on an average, per annum from 1929 to 1933, and nearly a million and a half in 1938. Then came the war; 43,000 Italian men, women and children had to leave, never to return. They left 2,365 acres of vineyards, and 9,170 acres planted partly in vines, olive and other fruit trees, mixed vineyards–orchards so much in favour in Italy: all have now ceased to exist. Since January 1952 Libya has been an independent State, a Moslem State as dry as the nearby Sahara.

Although the whole of the North African countries are now under Moslem rule, there are still important vineyards and much wine being made in Algeria, Tunisia and Morocco.

## Algeria

Algiers was a nest of pirates, a constant menace and, only too often, a very real danger to all Mediterranean shipping during the past four hundred years: the Spanish tried to capture Algiers in the sixteenth century, the French Navy shelled Algiers in the seventeenth century and English ships did the same on various occasions since then, but all to no avail. In 1830, however, the French not only captured Algiers but, presently, they occupied, pacified and civilized the whole of the land west of Tunisia, east of Morocco and south of the sea as far as the Sahara and the Atlas mountains. French settlers came over at a slow but steady rate and, of course, most of them planted a vineyard. Land, in the early days, could be had for the asking, or at very little cost, and labour was very cheap indeed. The first vineyards were planted near Algiers, but it was not long before more suitable vineyard sites were planted in the Oran Département, west of Algiers, and there were soon as many acres of vines in the Oran area as in that of Algiers. Eventually, more than half the Algerian vineyards were in Oran territory, a little more than a quarter in that of Algiers and a little less than a quarter in that of Constantine. Here they were mostly in the fertile plains of the coastal area, where record crops of the commoner grapes brought forth record quantities of the commoner types of wine.

Fifty years after the conquest of Algiers, in 1880, there were 23,130 acres of vines in the Algiers Département, 25,350 acres in the Oran Département and 9,820 acres in the Constantine Département, 58,300 acres in all. The total output of wine of those vineyards in 1880 was 9,516,760 gallons: only two years before, in 1878, there had been only 44,000 acres, and their yield had been 7,440,840 gallons. As it happened, it was at that time that a great many vineyards of Metropolitan France were attacked, and many wholly destroyed, by the phylloxera, so that supplies of wine had fallen below the home demand in France, and consequently prices were constantly rising. Such a state of affairs proved to be, naturally, a great incentive for farmers and speculators to plant more and more vines in Algeria; this they did with wonderful enthusiasm, and they went on doing it for three score years and ten, that is, long after the vineyards of Metropolitan France had been replanted with phylloxera-resisting grafted vines; supplies of wine were in excess of the demand, and prices fell sharply.

The following figures give some idea of the trend of vineyard planting and wine production in Algiers during three-quarters of a century and two world wars:

|      | Acres   | Gallons     |
|------|---------|-------------|
| 1882 | 99,250  | 14,988,600  |
| 1906 | 409,750 | 163,416,000 |
| 1914 | 371,750 | 222,750,000 |
| 1930 | 678,250 | 298,364,000 |
| 1954 | 998,750 | 424,534,000 |
| 1957 | 952,500 | 336,270,000 |
| 1958 | 884,345 | 377,689,400 |

Then followed the long and costly civil war which ended four years later by the victory of overwhelming Moslem numbers. Most French residents, many of them Algerian born, some of them with parents and grandparents who were Algerian born, left Algeria for ever, and the 32,000 wineries which the French had built and equipped were taken by the Moslem administration and sold to the highest bidder, if any. The vineyards of Algeria still produced 409,211,000 gallons of wine in 1959, 348,717,600 gallons in 1960, 343,904,000 gallons in 1961 and 242,000,000 gallons in 1962. This downward trend continues, however, with a 1968/69 production of 192·2 million gallons.

Under French ownership and proper care the vineyards of Algeria produced both *ordinaire* and quality wines, red, white and *rosé*, mostly table wines, as well as some fortified and some sparkling wines. The *ordinaire* wines may not have much, if any, charm or appeal, but the reds had plenty of colour and stout body: their alcoholic strength varied from 11° to 13°, so that they were in great demand in France as blending wines, to give a welcome hand to many sun-starved wines from 8° to 10° alcoholic strength.

The figures of Algerian wines exported to France are really staggering, and one cannot help wondering what would happen to the wine trade in France if the vineyards of Algeria share the same fate as those of Libya. From 1920 to 1924 the annual shipments of Algerian wine to Metropolitan France were from 90 to 110 million gallons; from 1930 to 1937, from 240 to 275 million gallons; and approximately 250 million gallons on an average up to 1961. However, these figures are also rapidly declining.

Besides the *ordinaire* wines of Algeria, by no means the only wines, although it is only too commonly believed that all the wines of Algeria are of 'homely' quality, there were, during the French régime, many wines of very fair and some even of really fine quality made from vineyards in the first four of the six groups into which the Algerian vineyards were classified, as follows:

1. The best wines of the Mascara district; also part of the Tlemcen district, all wines with a minimum alcoholic strength of 12°.
2. Parts of the Mostaganem district, their minimum alcoholic strength: 11·5°.
3. Montagnac, Sebdon, Oran, Arzew, St Cloud and small sites of other districts; their minimum alcoholic strength: 11°.
4. The wines of Orléansville, Miliana, Medea, the alcoholic strength of which is not below 11°.

5 & 6. Two groups in which the more *ordinaire* wines of the Algiers and Constantine Départements are placed; their minimum alcoholic strength: 10°.

The pre-1961 average yield of V.D.Q.S. (*Vins de Qualité Supérieure*) or quality wines (gallons), and their location was as follows:

ORAN

| District | Average yield | Minimum strength |
|---|---|---|
| Coteaux de Mascara | 1,870,000 | 12° |
| Mascara (Plains S.E. Oran) | 1,980,000 | 12·5° |
| Coteaux de Tlemcen (S.E. Oran, near the Morocco frontier) | 660,000 | 12·5° |
| Monts de Tassalat | | 12·5° |
| Air-el-Hadjar | 66,000 | 12·5° |
| Mostaganem (E. Oran, near coast) | 990,000 | 12·5° |

ALGIERS

| | | |
|---|---|---|
| Medea (S. Algiers) | 1,980,000 | 12° |
| Haut-Dahra (W. Algiers) | 1,320,000 | 12° |
| Ain-bossem Bouira (S.E. Algiers) | 308,000 | 12° |
| Côtes de Zaccar (Miliana) (S.W. Algiers) | 396,000 | 12° |

According to the statistics of the French administration, the proportion of red quality wines was greater than that of *ordinaire* wines, but the reverse was the case for the white wines (gallons):

| | White wines | Red and Rosé | Total |
|---|---|---|---|
| *Ordinaire* wines | 8,536,946 | 120,019,878 | 128,556,824 |
| Quality wines | 6,189,832 | 213,970,944 | 220,160,776 |
| Total | 14,726,778 | 333,990,822 | 348,717,600 |

Most of the grapes grown in Algeria were, and presumably still are, the same as those grown in France for *ordinaire* and quality wines, such as Cinsault and Carignan for the cheaper reds and Cabernet and Pinot for the better kinds; Clairette, Ugni Blanc and Aligoté for the cheaper whites.

## Tunisia

There never was, and there never can be, any scope for viticulture in Tunisia comparable to that which exists in Algeria: the heat is too great and the rainfall too small, except along the Mediterranean seaboard. Up to 1880 the only grapes grown in Tunisia were grown by Italians in the Lower Tell, near the sea, east of Tunis, and they were table grapes. Wine-making grapes were then planted by French as well as Italian migrants at a time when so many French vineyards had been destroyed by the phylloxera, and there were tempting prices offered for the most ordinary table wines during a time of short supply. By 1910 there were some 40,000 acres of vines in Tunisia, but it was only after the First World War that there was an important increase in the number of European settlers and in the acreage of vineyards in Tunisia: the European settlers numbered 129,000 in 1901, 173,000 in 1926, 195,000 in 1931 and 213,000 in 1936, and the acreage of vineyards rose from 35,000 acres in 1901 to 70,000 in 1926, 110,000 in 1931, and 126,500 in 1933, the peak figure in the history of Tunisian viticulture. It so happened that the French Government of the day decided to settle in Tunisia quite a

number of war veterans and 'war victims', giving them plots of suitable land, and loans
for the purchase of vines and equipment to be repaid in twenty years, free of interest.
Between 1921 and 1932 seven *Caves co-opératives* were created by the French administration in Tunisia, at Sidi-Tabet, M'Rira, Chaouat, Mesratya, Schuiggui, Bordj-El-
Amri and Megrine; and during those same years five other *Caves co-opératives* were
established by the settlers at Kledia, Bejaoua-Manouba, Djeradou, El Mahrine and
Zribe. The *Distillerie co-opérative* of Djebel-Djelloud was also built at that time.

As was to be expected, such encouragement given to the planting of vineyards in
Tunisia resulted in very large quantities of wine being made, from ten to twenty-two
million gallons of wine, mostly plain wine of a high alcoholic strength, suitable for blending with some of the poorer and weaker French wines. What had not been expected,
however, was that the French administration decided that Tunisia was not to dump all
her cheap wines in France, and only allowed a comparatively small quota to be shipped
to France. This was a very unpleasant surprise for the 3,300 European wine farmers,
mostly French since 1948, when most Italian landowners had been bought out 'by
order': there were about a thousand non-orthodox native Moslems who owned small
vineyards, but their own consumption of wine, Koran or no Koran, was nil. Hence a
sharp fall in the acreage of Tunisian vineyards during the 'forties, but it proved to be a
temporary one, and the acreage increased again during the 'fifties, when shipments to
France were once more welcome: 28,300,000 gallons of Tunisian wine were shipped to
France in 1959, and practically the same quantity again in 1960.

Not all Tunisian wine was plain *ordinaire*: about 1% of the total wine production
was V.D.Q.S. wines with *appellations contrôlées* of their own, such as Muscat de Thibar,
Muscat de Rades and Muscat de Kelibir. There were also many tons of grapes the
juice of which never had a chance to become wine; chemically castrated at birth, it
remained 'grape juice' during its short, dull life.

QUANTITIES OF WINE PRODUCED IN TUNISIA AND QUANTITIES EXPORTED FROM
TUNISIA (GALLONS)

|      | Production | Exports    |
|------|------------|------------|
| 1923 | 17,188,600 |            |
| 1924 | 18,458,000 | 8,074,000  |
| 1925 | 20,217,000 | 12,469,600 |
| 1926 | 16,214,000 | 12,333,200 |
| 1927 | 13,596,000 | 3,040,800  |
| 1928 | 20,548,000 | 11,750,200 |
| 1929 | 23,034,000 | 9,477,600  |
| 1930 | 22,154,000 | 18,112,600 |
| 1931 | 15,554,000 | 17,147,800 |
| 1932 | 38,500,000 | 19,857,200 |
| 1933 | 30,822,000 | 13,255,000 |
| 1934 | 37,400,000 | 12,795,200 |
| 1935 | 37,136,000 | 19,298,400 |
| 1936 | 31,174,000 | 28,754,000 |
| 1937 | 31,988,000 | 21,153,000 |
| 1938 | 43,450,000 | 24,241,800 |
| 1939 | 28,600,000 | 21,808,600 |
| 1940 | 34,100,000 | 14,205,200 |
| 1941 | 23,100,000 | 14,205,200 |

|      | Production | Exports |
|------|------------|---------|
| 1942 | 27,500,000 | 6,003,600 |
| 1943 | 9,240,000  |         |
| 1944 | 9,548,000  |         |
| 1945 | 14,190,000 |         |
| 1946 | 12,060,200 | 1,168,200 |
| 1947 | 11,895,400 | 3,053,600 |
| 1948 | 16,588,000 | 3,113,000 |
| 1949 | 19,467,800 | 11,255,200 |
| 1950 | 17,045,600 | 6,877,200 |
| 1951 | 9,482,000  | 10,007,800 |
| 1952 | 14,687,200 | 7,913,400 |
| 1953 | 14,550,800 | 4,855,400 |
| 1954 | 23,177,000 | 10,161,800 |
| 1955 |            | 16,799,200 |
| 1956 | 27,951,000 | 17,424,100 |
| 1957 | 34,845,800 | 30,901,200 |
| 1961 | 31,621,898 |         |
| 1962 | 39,526,388 |         |
| 1963 | 43,670,000 |         |
| 1964 | 39,473,720 |         |
| 1969 | 22,000,000 |         |

## Morocco

In Morocco, on the whole, the population has both more intelligence and better physique than the native population in either Algeria or Tunisia. There had been native vineyards in Morocco long before Europeans planted theirs, and at a time when there were no vines anywhere else in North Africa. The grapes which the natives grew then and still grow today were never pressed, of course, but eaten as table grapes, the demand for which is today, and probably has always been, greater than the supply.

In 1907, when the French occupied Casablanca for the first time, there were only 25 acres planted in wine-making grapes, near Casablanca: they had been planted by three or four French pioneers who were followed by tide-waves of European migrants, immediately after the French occupation of Casablanca, so much so that there were 65,000 European settlers by 1911. Of course, they did not all plant vineyards, but quite a number of them did, and all of them drank wine, the cheapest Spanish table wines before they could drink even cheaper home-grown and home-made Moroccan wines.

By 1916 there were already 420 acres of wine-making vines planted in the Sebou–Oujda corridor-valley, 217 acres near Rabat and 75 acres near Meknes. After 1918 and the pacification of the whole country under General Lyautey the rush of migrants to Morocco all but flooded the land: the European population rose to 172,000 by 1931, and to 207,000 by 1936, and, as might have been expected, the acreage of the settlers' vineyards also grew apace, from 1,675 acres in 1919 to 5,000 acres in 1924, and 36,500 acres in 1934. The production of wine, obviously, also rose steeply, from 1,320,000 gallons in 1924 to 11,760,000 gallons in 1934.

Strange as it seems at first sight, there was, during the decade 1924–33, a great deal of wine imported, some from France, but a great deal more from Spain, and never a single

gallon exported from Morocco. Imports grew gradually less and less as the home production became greater and greater, and they ceased altogether in 1934. The consumption of wine *per capita* – and European *capita* alone – must have been higher than anywhere else in the world: this was due maybe partly to the hot and dry and thirsty climate
of Morocco, but chiefly to the fact that there never was any tax, licences or dues of
any kind to be paid by the makers and sellers of wine in Morocco. If we also remember that water in Morocco was than in even shorter supply than it is today, dearer and
far from safe to drink, one cannot blame the then European population for drinking
about a million gallons of wine per month.

The rapid rise in the planting of vineyards and the making of wine is clearly shown
by the following statistics:

|      | Acres  | Gallons    |
|------|--------|------------|
| 1924 | 5,000  | 1,320,000  |
| 1925 | 8,000  | 1,980,000  |
| 1926 | 10,250 | 2,750,000  |
| 1927 | 11,750 | 4,400,000  |
| 1928 | 15,500 | 4,180,000  |
| 1929 | 18,750 | 3,520,000  |
| 1930 | 19,250 | 4,400,000  |
| 1931 | 21,250 | 6,600,000  |
| 1932 | 22,750 | 8,580,000  |
| 1933 | 32,500 | 9,680,000  |
| 1934 | 36,500 | 11,760,000 |

Much of the rapid progress made during those ten years, in Morocco, both in viticulture and wine-making, was due to the establishment of Co-operative Wineries, with
the financial and moral support of the French administration. The two which were
responsible for better wines than all others were the *Caves co-opératives* of Beni-Snassen
and Aït-Souala, in the eastern part of Morocco; there were two in the Casablanca region, the Sahel and Fedala wineries; there was one at Meknes, one near Fez and one
in a suburb of Rabat, but it went into liquidation after a few years when the Rabat
vineyards were destroyed by the phylloxera and never replanted. At Meknes and Beni-
Snassen there was also a distillery with all the latest scientific equipment.

During the decade from 1935 to 1945 migrants continued to pour into Morocco, so
that there were in 1945, 570,000 European settlers – not counting, of course, European
visitors, but the planting of new vineyards did not grow quite as fast. It was rapid up to
1940, but the Second World War made it impossible to get tractors, bulldozers and
other agricultural equipment indispensable to bring new land into cultivation; it also
made it difficult if not altogether impossible to get in time and in sufficient quantities
all sorts of scientifically produced remedies to check various diseases to which grapes
are subject, some of them being now much more used than in days gone by in the making
of wine, its fining, filtering, etc. This explains the apparent discrepancies between the
figures of vineyard acreage and those of wine production. Back again to conditions that
existed at the beginning, the total production of wine in Morocco was not sufficient
to meet the local demand of the European population, and wine had to be imported.
Unfortunately, there was a war on at the time, and there were all manner of difficulties
in the way, some financial and exchange-control regulations, others due to the lack of
shipping. So, for the first time in the history of Morocco, wine for local consumption

was rationed, and the rationing of wine would have been much worse than it was had it not been possible to bring over from Algeria fairly large supplies of wine that saved the European population from being wholly dehydrated.

|       | *Acres*  | *Gallons*   |
|-------|----------|-------------|
| 1935  | 40,900   | 11,440,000  |
| 1936  | 44,500   | 5,830,000   |
| 1937  | 59,500   | 12,914,000  |
| 1938  | 63,750   | 17,180,800  |
| 1939  | 63,750   | 13,677,400  |
| 1940  | 61,500   | 11,600,600  |
| 1941  | 59,250   | 10,934,000  |
| 1942  | 57,250   | 11,255,200  |
| 1943  | 46,750   | 6,725,400   |
| 1944  | 43,750   | 11,994,400  |
| 1945  | 40,250   | 5,121,600   |

After the Second World War efforts were made to improve the conditions in existing vineyards and to replant others, and the best means to that end was the establishment new co-operative wineries at Marchand, Sidi-Slimene, Soul El Tieta and Rharb, Taza, Tifflet, Haut Rharb and Oujda. All expectations were fully realized, and the acreage of European vineyards in Morocco rose to 171,250 acres in 1957, a very remarkable figure considering that the lack of sufficient rainfall in most parts of Morocco is a very effective limiting factor as regards the planting of vineyards. The same applies to wineries: just as the vine must have some rain to grow and for the grapes to swell, so the wine-maker in the winery must have not gentle rain but lots of water to cool and wash the wine-press, the casks and tanks, his tools, etc., even if he can do with none himself.

|       | *Acres*   | *Gallons*   |
|-------|-----------|-------------|
| 1946  | 43,750    | 7,315,000   |
| 1947  | 50,500    | 9,165,200   |
| 1948  | 62,500    | 8,010,200   |
| 1949  | 64,750    | 10,971,400  |
| 1950  | 92,000    | 15,588,200  |
| 1951  | 82,500    | 22,457,600  |
| 1952  | 135,500   | 12,010,800  |
| 1953  | 140,750   | 25,768,600  |
| 1954  | 127,750   | 41,456,800  |
| 1955  | 136,250   | 42,119,000  |
| 1956  | 160,000   | 46,479,400  |
| 1957  | 171,250   | 40,040,000  |

Now that Morocco is independent there are not so many European settlers, but there are still some 148,200 acres of vineyards, and although the local consumption is much less than it was once upon a time, the co-operative wineries have succeeded in producing wine and wine products for which there is a demand overseas, and they have built up quite a good export trade for wine, *mistelles* and *mouts mutés* (sterilized grape juice), *jus de raisin* (deep-freeze grape juice), besides fresh table grapes much cheaper than any grown under glass, and dried raisins as well. Morocco is certainly one of the leaders in viticulture and oenology in North Africa.

FIGURES OF WINE IMPORTED INTO MOROCCO AND EXPORTED FROM MOROCCO
(GALLONS)

| Year | Imports | Exports |
|---|---|---|
| 1922 | 6,729,800 | |
| 1923 | 5,684,800 | |
| 1924 | 4,129,400 | |
| 1925 | 5,139,200 | |
| 1926 | 1,666,000 | |
| 1927 | 5,297,000 | |
| 1928 | 3,405,600 | |
| 1930 | 5,308,600 | |
| 1932 | 2,912,800 | |
| 1933 | 1,223,200 | |
| 1938 | | 2,774,000 |
| 1939 | | 3,790,600 |
| 1940 | | 2,239,600 |
| 1941 | | 1,962,400 |
| 1943 | 1,100,000 | |
| 1944 | 3,500,000 | |
| 1945 | 2,200,000 | |
| 1946 | 5,500,000 | 446,600 |
| 1947 | | 462,600 |
| 1948 | | 289,200 |
| 1950 | | 829,400 |
| 1951 | | 4,015,000 |
| 1952 | | 9,248,000 |
| 1953 | | 2,640,000 |
| 1954 | | 19,338,000 |
| 1956 | | 19,336,000 |
| 1957 | | 25,300,000 |

In 1963 a particularly favourable summer was responsible for a record production of 56,033,856 gallons, but the next year, in 1964, the total yield was 44,400,000 gallons. On the other hand, while the export of wine was also a record in 1963, with 34,389,630 gallons, it was handsomely beaten in 1964, when the exports rose to 42,688,294 gallons!

Unfortunately, in the years following these record growths the situation of Moroccan viticulture seems to have deteriorated and wine production is now more than halved, with a total of 15·5 million gallons in 1968/69.

# The Wines of
# ITALY

CYRIL RAY

# Introduction

ITALY is the greatest wine-producing country in the world. Not in the quality of her wines: few Italian wine-growers, save the most provincial and inexperienced, would claim for their products that they can vie with the greatest growths of France or Germany. (Though there are undoubtedly Italian wines, a few white and more red, that show far greater character and distinction than the coarse Midi reds, the sugared and blended – and sometimes even more dubiously concocted – wines labelled 'Niersteiner' and 'Liebfraumilch', that owe their place in the British market, and the prices they command, to the reputations earned by noble clarets and elegant hocks.) But, having been accustomed year after year to dispute the first place with France for volume of production in the years when Algeria's output was included with that of metropolitan France, Italy can now claim to grow more wine than any other country in the world,[1] and this although she is little more than half the size of France and, because of her mountains, with a smaller area, proportionately, suitable for agriculture; to export more wine to other countries; and to have a higher proportion of her population – almost twenty-five per cent – concerned with wine-growing and the wine trade.

Yet the wines of Italy are neither so well known nor so highly regarded in Britain as they deserve to be, and there are many reasons for this.

It is more than a century ago that Cyrus Redding observed that

> the wines of Italy are all made for home consumption. The interests of commerce, which lead to competition, have not yet interfered to improve them; [adding that] the petty sovereignties of Italy are a blight upon her manufactures no less than upon her civilisation. Many of these are shut up to themselves as regards their productions and cannot interchange with the neighbouring states without a great disadvantage, owing to pernicious duties . . .

It was twenty years after those words were written before the 'pernicious duties' finally disappeared; the effects lingered much longer; and the regionalism persists to this day, so that it is difficult for the English or the American visitor to Rome, say, or to Florence, to acquaint himself seriously with any Italian wines other than those of Rome or of Tuscany, to compare one with another and to take home with him an informed interest that would stimulate his wine merchant into enquiry and possibly into purchase.

A climate all too favourable for the production of common grapes with a high yield, combined with a lack of demand from neighbouring regions, let alone from the more discriminating markets abroad, naturally resulted in the peasants taking the easy way – of producing as much wine with as little effort as possible. Meanwhile, France and Germany were consolidating the position of their wines as the world's classics – the wines by which all others were, and are, judged. So that it is difficult now for such fine wines as Italy does produce to establish themselves abroad – for what British wine-lover,

---

[1] In the decade 1950–59 (according to the new, revised edition of Mr L. W. Marrison's Penguin Handbook, *Wines and Spirits*) Italy produced nearly twenty per cent more than France. Since then it has become more like thirty to thirty-five per cent more. Between them the two countries provide the world with half its wine.

brought up in a long claret-and-burgundy, port-and-sherry, tradition, is prepared to pay as much for an old Barolo, say, or Brunello, as a *château*-bottled claret or estate-bottled hock? The best Italian wines cost as much to produce; money must be tied up in them as they acquire the bottle-age necessary to the better Italian red wines; and Italian standards of living and of rates of pay are comparable, now at any rate, with those of the French countryside, and far higher than those of Chile, for instance, which is why Chilean reds of good *ordinaire* quality can come half-way round the world and still undercut similar wines from Europe. Nor does the Italian wine-grower enjoy the government backing that has enabled Yugoslavia to establish herself so firmly since the war as one of the most important single suppliers of white wines to this country.

Newly introduced wine laws, though, have encouraged the production of finer wines and ensured at the same time a greater measure of consistency than before in those of the middling sort, which make up the bulk of the wines that Italy sells abroad. Export figures have risen accordingly, with Germany and Switzerland by far the biggest customers – particularly for the red wines they lack themselves – and France taking more Asti Spumante than any other country. The United States, where a huge Italian population still thirsts for the wine of its fathers, ranks third, after Germany and Switzerland, among the importers of Italian wine. In the years immediately after this book first appeared (1966) Britain so increased her imports as to move above Austria and Belgium into fourth place, but this is so recent a development that Italian wines are still little known and understood here compared with those of France and Germany. This is doubly disadvantageous to the Italians, for this country is the home of wine scholarship, and still sets standards of taste and judgement for wine-drinkers every-where: Italy loses not only what we would pay for her finer wines but also what we would say and write about them.

Italians are individualists and find it hard to combine. There has been no concerted campaign by government, growers and shippers to familiarise Britain with the wines of Italy and to combat the ignorance and prejudices that undoubtedly still exist. Other-wise the light-bodied red wines of the Italian lakes might well have established them-selves as firmly on the British market as the *vinhos verdes* of Portugal. Italian restaura-teurs, ship-owners and airlines could also certainly do more to popularize their own country's wines among their foreign visitors – with eventual advantage to the tourist trade in general, in the way that travel in France increases interest in French wines among foreigners, and interest in French wines in turn sends foreigners to France. Italy has an enormous advantage here: it is quick and easy for British tourists to visit Italy, which they do in vast numbers; the language and the country are both reasonably familiar – much more so than Serbo-Croat and Yugoslavia; there is an immense good-will. It is a pity for both countries that we know as little as we do about her wines and that Italy does not try harder to teach us more.

In most parts of Italy the old methods of viticulture still obtain, just as Redding described them:

> Corn is sown between them [the vines], and other grain, or vegetables are grown. The vines are planted upon soils oftentimes the least congenial to their growth, as in the plain of Pisa. They are suffered to run up to any height, and in many places are never pruned

at all.[1] In the Roman States the vines producing every quality of wine grow together, without assortment of any kind. They are conducted from tree to tree, generally of the elm species, along the boundaries of enclosures, and even by the high roads, where they run up in wild luxuriance and waste their vitality, not in the fruit but in leaves and branches. Even where the vine is raised on trelliswork or on poles it is rarely pruned or trained.

The various Italian systems of land tenure and inheritance have not, in the past, made it easy for Italy to produce fine wines in the same way as those of the Médoc or the Rhine are produced. The great estates were too big, the peasant holdings too small, for any of them to be conducted as a Rothschild conducts Lafite, or a Prüm looks after the Wehlener-Sonnenuhr vineyards. But the noble families of Tuscany, for whom the Baron Bettino Ricasoli had set a pattern of dedicated large-scale wine-growing as long ago as the eighteen-sixties, produce serious wines on the scale in which serious wines are produced by the great firms of Champagne and, in the same way, by buying as well as growing their grapes, and by making wine in big wineries. They do not vary year by year, as the 1952 Lafite differs from the 1961, nor do they vary from vineyard to vineyard, as a Lafite will differ from a Latour, but we do not think any the less of Moët and Chandon or of Pol Roger for producing a non-vintage wine that remains pretty well constant year by year and wherever and whenever you buy it. Just as the great champagne houses produce, as well as the non-vintage wines, their fine vintage champagnes, so now do the big Chianti houses produce their '*riserva*' wines, or wines with an estate name, such as Brolio or Nipozzano.

A more recent development has been the growth of the co-operatives, particularly in the Oltrepo Pavese at one end of the country and in Sardinia at the other, making it possible to introduce modern methods of vinification that the small growers could never have been able to afford, and to reach a level of consistency all too little known hitherto in Italian wines. The same period – roughly since the nineteen-thirties but much more intensively since the war – has seen the growth of the *consorzi*, associations of growers and wine-makers dedicated to maintaining the standards and, in consequence, the reputation of the wines of their district. The growers of the 'Chianti classico' district set the pattern,[2] according to which each grower in the voluntary association has his output checked each year, both for quantity and quality: if the quality is right, if it has been made of the right grapes in the right district by the right method, then he gets *numbered* neck-labels to the number of bottles his yield will fill, and no more. There are now more than fifty such *consorzi* and, in the nature of things, some are better or more rigorous than others; many are new and still feeling their way; many exist in districts where the wine is nothing much to write home about, anyway, even when it is what it says it is, and guaranteed to be so. But the scheme works – I have seen inspectors of the Chianti classico and the Asti Spumante associations at work, and they were very impressive: I have no doubt at all that a bottle of either of these wines bearing the numbered neck-label of its association would be the real thing. The pity is that some

---

[1] In the South, in Sicily and Sardinia, in spite of recent improvements in methods of viticulture, many are still grown on the *albarello* ('little tree') principle, close to the ground, which means that they derive reflected heat from the soil in a part of the country where the wines are, in any case, coarsened by excessive sunshine. – C.R.

[2] *See* p. 219.

shippers in this country import wines that would never qualify for neck-labels at home in Italy, so that we, the consumers, knowing no better, condemn Chianti, say, or Valpolicella, in general, judging it by what is foisted on us under that name here.

I do not think that either France or Germany is stricter in its wine laws than this system at its best, and the new Italian wine law that has been coming into force in phases since the beginning of 1965 is based on the experience and advice of the *consorzi*, and with their co-operation.

Stricter legal standards do not mean that we now have to pay more in Italy for the highest categories of Italian wine – estate-bottled and, in effect, state-guaranteed. The best Italian wines have been estate-bottled and guaranteed by their growers' associations for the past generation. But it does mean that the British shipper – if he thinks it commercially worth while – is now able not only to buy the best Italian wines but also to assure his customers of their quality. And, of course, there will still, and always, be a market for the cheaper wines, 'stretched' or 'cut', with the coarser wines of the south, exactly as the cheapest French wines are – often, indeed, with the same Apulian or Sicilian or Sardinian wines, for much of the output of these heavy blending wines goes directly to France (and it ill becomes Frenchmen to disparage the wines of Italy, without which their own wine trade would be hard put to it to provide them with their *vins de consommation*, or their foreign customers with some of their 'French' wines).

Even before the new wine law came fully into effect, wine for export was checked for wholesomeness and alcoholic strength (quality is another matter: *chaptalisation* [sugaring] – permitted in France and Germany in certain circumstances and for certain wines – is forbidden in Italy in all circumstances, though not blending, which can, of course, be forbidden by a *consorzio*). Checking is by sample, and the responsibility of the Istituto Nazionale per il Commercio Estero, usually through local *consorzi* or regional centres of the Ministry of Agriculture. Clearly the officials can only check that the wine being exported is the wine that the foreign shipper has asked and is paying for – not what he is going to call it when he gets it home. Nor should Italian wines be judged abroad by the so-called 'commercial wine' bought by other countries, notably Germany (for making into German 'vermouth' and German brandy), which is not reckoned by the Italians to be fit for table wine – it is checked only for alcoholic content, and is permitted to be fortified – but may well be sold as such, or judged as such, when it gets to its destination.

Nor, for that matter, as I have said, should Italian wines of medium quality and medium price be judged by the standards set by the finest single-vineyard wines of France. With few exceptions, they are the equivalent of French district or village wines – of wine entitled only to be called Beaujolais, say, or at best of some such wine as is named simply 'St Julien'. And, because they are grown under more and stronger sunshine, they resemble the wines of the south or of the Rhône more than those of Burgundy or Bordeaux or the Loire. But the resemblances are not close: Italian wines are *different* – some of them, such as Lambrusco, very different – from anything grown in France, and they should be treated as such, judged by their own standards, not condemned for not being what they do not pretend to be. Nevertheless, they have character, and with the growing demand for wines in Britain, especially for wines of modest price, and with the growing number of British visitors to Italy, it is at least interesting, and possibly useful, for a people that knows so much about the wines of

France and Germany – more than most Frenchmen and Germans do – to know something about Italian wines in general, and how they differ in particular. Such, then, are
the reasons for offering to the English reader a book on Italian wines that I hope may
prove more comprehensive than any that has so far appeared in English, less indiscriminately eulogistic than those written by Italians.

My own interest in the wines of Italy dates back nearly thirty years, to the time when,
as the *Manchester Guardian*'s correspondent with Eighth Army, newly landed in Italy,
I quenched my thirst with the rough wine of the South, and then with the more
sophisticated wines (in both senses, sometimes, alas) of Naples, or celebrated our entry
into Rome with the sweet sparkle of Asti Spumante. For the last few months of the war,
and some months afterwards, a year in all, I lived in Rome, enlarging my experience
at such restaurants as Ranieri and Valadier and the Hostaria dell'Orso; imbibing
knowledge of Italian wines as I imbibed other forms of worldly wisdom, from old Carlo
Sforza (in the political wilderness at the time as the result of his quarrel with Churchill);
and spending week-ends with the Senni family at Grottaferrata, in the country of the
*castelli Romani* wines, where in those days the wine of that hospitable household was still
trodden, as I suppose few Italian table wines are trodden these days, though there
must be a few places in the South, as I know there are in Sicily, where the old practice
lingers on as it does in the Upper Douro.

Since those days I have visited Italy almost every year – in some years three or four
times – and have made notes of the wines I have drunk in every part of the peninsula,
from the Alps to Sicily, and from Sardinia to the Yugoslav frontier, completing my
researches in the course of five visits spread over the fifteen months before this book
was finished, renewing my acquaintance with those wines I had not tasted for years;
visiting those regions that I did not already know, so that I can now claim to have
visited, and to have tasted wine in, every region of Italy;[1] tasting such wines as were still
unfamiliar; and spending the last six weeks in Siena, filling the gaps in my experience
and completing this book, at its wine museum, the Enoteca Italica Permanente.

I have listed here every Italian wine the name of which I know to be in any way
officially or even generally recognized, taking as my check-lists the recent Italian works
mentioned in the bibliography, notably the *Nuova Enologia* and those by Luigi Veronelli
and Bruno Bruni. I have tasted virtually every wine named in this book, some in their
native regions, some at the Enoteca; some long ago, but most quite recently. For the
sake of completeness I have included those few that – because they are peculiar to some
remote locality to which I have not penetrated – I have not had the chance of tasting,
and a few that I suppose I must have tasted in my time, but have forgotten. I have
based my entries for them on what Bruni or Veronelli or the *Enologia* have to say about
them, though I have taken no single one of these as gospel – for a wine that is unknown
to me to have been included in this book it must have been mentioned in at least two
of these three recent Italian authorities.

The names of Italian species of vine will mean little to my readers, as indeed they do

[1] In Italy a 'region' is one of the historic divisions of the country: Piedmont, Lombardy, Tuscany, the
Veneto, are 'regions'. 'Province' – the word that I think one would have been more likely to use in this
sense in English – is applied to the districts administered by the main towns in each region. Thus, Siena
and Florence are not only cities but provinces within the region Tuscany. Potenza and Matera are the
two provinces in the region of the Basilicata.

to me, save when a species gives its name to a noted wine, as in the case of Moscato, say, or Aleatico. But wherever I have been able to discover the name of the grape from which a wine of another name is made I have included it here, so that students may know what family connections there are between various wines, and trace a resemblance or puzzle their heads over dissimilarities.

Finally, in most cases I have given the alcoholic strength of a wine: such figures are not regarded in England as being of major importance, but in Italy they are always given, and the price of common wine is based on them. As the figures exist, they are useful in showing relative strengths, and in assessing them the English reader will be helped by bearing in mind that claret is usually rather more than 10°, Sauternes rather more than 13°, Châteauneuf du Pape rather more than 12·5° (these are the minimum strengths for the wines to qualify for their *appellations contrôlées*); sherry about 20°; and that 14° is the point above which the British Customs and Excise exact almost twice as much duty as on 'light' (i.e. table) wines: an important point in considering Italian wines, for many are above this strength.

I have found a great deal of pleasure and interest, as well as the inevitably tedious donkey-work, in compiling and composing this reference book: I hope it will help those who consult it to find similar pleasure and interest in the wines of Italy. If so, and they feel grateful to me, they must feel grateful too, as I do, to the following who, among others, have helped to make the book possible:

Dott. Enzo Malgeri, Commercial Minister at the Italian Embassy in London; Dott. A. Giaroli, of the London office of the Istituto Nazionale per il Commercio Estero, and Dottori Silvio Barocas, Domenico di Paolo, Mario Rizzotti and Cesare Fristelli, of the Rome office; Mr Douglas Whybrow, sometime of British United Air Ferries, so courteously efficient in getting me and my car to Geneva; Dott. Arrigo Musiani, Secretary-General of the Enoteca Italica Permanente, Siena; Mr Gerald Asher, whose scholarly notes on the Italian wines he introduced to London some few years ago have been so useful; and Mr R. M. Scott, of the London firm of Aug. Hellmers & Sons Ltd, who first introduced me to the charming wines of the Alto Adige. I am indebted to the Baron Bettino Ricasoli of our own time, who carries on so devotedly the tradition established by his distinguished ancestor, Cavour's successor, and who has been my kindly host both at Brolio and in Florence; to my fellow newspaperman the Marchese de'Frescobaldi ('Dino') and to his brother Piero, who entertained me so handsomely at Nipozzano with a wine of the house of the year of my birth, before he died untimely in a car crash; and to the Marchese di Antinori and his brother Piero. Among my guides and hosts in various parts of Italy have been Dott. Nino Anesi, of the Assessorato Regionale Industria e Commercio della Regione Trentino-Alto Adige, Trento; Dott. Guglielmo Anzilotti, Director of the Consorzio per la Difesa del Vino Tipico del Chianti; Signor Dante Carelli of the Camera di Commercio, Potenza and his sister, Signorina Ada Carelli, of the Ente Turismo there; Signor Carlo Balzi, of the Chianti house of Ruffino; Dott. Arturo Bersano, of Nizza Monferrato; Signor Gaetano and Signor Guglielmo Bertani of the Verona firm of that name; Dott. Andrea Masala of the Department of the Regional Government of Sardinia in Cagliari; Dott. Luigi Ruffino, Secretary-General of the Camera di Commercio, Pavia; Dott. Vittorio Pasqualini of the Camera di Commercio, Bolzano; Dott. Richard von Mackowitz of the Ufficio Estero of the Camera di Commercio, Bolzano; and Dott. Ludwig Kofler,

Director of the Consorzio delle Cantine Sociale of Bolzano; Dott. Claudio Poncibo of the Consorzio per la Difesa d'Asti Spumante; and Signor Antonio Mollo of Reggio di Calabria. Signorina Rita Ghezzi of Siena helped my lame Italian over many a stile; and Esmé, Countess of Carlisle, who knows and loves Italy at least as well and as much as I do, and the Italian language a great deal better, has helped to tidy up some of my worst mistakes. But those that remain, along with errors of commission, errors of omission, and errors of judgement, are all my own.

CYRIL RAY

*Siena, Italy; Rolvenden, Kent.* 1964–5
*Hawkhurst, Kent.* 1970

CHAPTER ONE

# The Wines of the Past

THERE was wine in Italy before there was Rome. It is still a matter of scholarly debate whether the Bronze Age inhabitants of northern Italy made wine from the wild grape vine which is known (from the grape pips found where their lake dwellings used to be) to have flourished in their time, but it is as certain as can be that the Etruscans were making and drinking wine in the regions we know now as Tuscany and Lazio in the ninth and tenth centuries B.C. (The traditional date for the founding of Rome is 732 B.C.) It is generally agreed, except by Warner Allen, that the Etruscans, 'in the days of their glory' as the late Dr Charles Seltman put it, 'must have made fine drink after the manner of the Greeks and the inhabitants of Anatolia, whence this remarkable people had come to settle in Italy' (in about 800 B.C.). And William Younger also held that 'they would certainly have known about viticulture in the ninth century and . . . would certainly not have been content to lead a life without wine'. They even paid their devotions to a wine god of their own, Fufluns.

Warner Allen, in his *A History of Wine*, stated that 'the Etruscans seem never to have mastered the art of viticulture', but he seems to have been alone in his belief. It would be fairer to say that the Etruscans, though not by any means completely ignorant of viticulture, were amateurs at it – drinkers of immature wine from unpruned vines – compared with the Greeks who founded a colony at Cumae, on a promontory near what is now Naples, in about 750 B.C., bringing with them:

> a tried system of viticulture as well as cuttings of their vines and, equally valuable, the art of pottery, which made it possible for wine, favoured by a good year, well made from fine grapes and stored in an airtight earthenware receptacle, to ripen into something very different from the best wine then known in Italy.

Not long after, it is interesting to note, other Greeks, from Ionia, founded Marseilles, and the art and science of viticulture began to spread along the valleys of the Rhône and, perhaps, the Rhine.

The Greeks of Cumae conquered the Etruscans, and the Sabines conquered the Greeks. By that time, about 420 B.C., the region around Cumae – Campania – was already famous for its wines and Father Sabinus, the legendary founder of the Sabines, who had appropriated to themselves the culture of the conquered, eventually makes his appearance in Virgil as the Vine-Grower, with his pruning knife.

All the same, the Romans of the time seem to have imported their fine wines direct from Greece rather than to have drunk the wines grown in Campania from Greek vines in the Greek way, and to have gone on doing so well into the period when, with the conquest of Greece and the fall of Carthage, Rome became the mistress of the Mediterranean world.

Pliny, in his *Natural History*, writing in about A.D. 70, gives a curiously precise date – 154 B.C. – as the year in which Italy became the greatest wine-growing country in the world, producing about two-thirds of the eighty known varieties of fine wine. Even then Greek wines were competing with native growths on the Roman market, and still enjoyed such prestige that that great gourmet Lucullus, a couple of generations earlier than Pliny, distributing Greek wine to the Roman people on his return in triumph from his campaigns in the East, flattered himself on his own open-handedness, for he recalled that in his father's time it was only one cup of Greek wine apiece: guests at public banquets then had to continue with Italian wines. But by this time Falernian from Campania seems to have been prized as highly as the wines of Chios and Lesbos, and in his third consulship Caesar, in addition to Chian and Lesbian, offered not only the now famous Falernian of Campania but Mamertine from Sicily as well.

In his immense, and immensely learned, history of wine and of wine-drinking, William Younger listed eighteen wines as being regarded by the Romans of the golden age – the latter years of the Republic and the earliest of the Empire – as being the finest in the world. Three were Greek, and all three came from the farthest of the Greek islands – Cos, Chios and Lesbos. At one time the Greeks used to treat their wines with sea-water, as the Greeks of our own time treat theirs with resin, but the resinated wine that Rome knew, and that Martial inveighed against, came not from Greece but from northern Italy. Greece took to it later. Younger's belief, following Pliny, is that it was only as this sea-watering declined that the Chian, Lesbian and Coan wines became fashionable in Rome, but it is clear that even before they became fashionable they had been popular when very heavily salted, and enough Romans were fond of them for Cato, in his *De Agri Cultura*, to give more than one recipe for counterfeiting Coan wine, all of them involving the addition of brine or sea-water.

There are four Spanish wines, too, in Younger's list, but it is the eleven Italian wines that concern us here. One was Sicilian – the Mamertine already mentioned, from around Messina, which Julius Caesar made fashionable, and the remaining ten came from the mainland. Most famous of all was – and is, thanks to the frequency with which the classical writers referred to it – Falernian,[1] which came from the hills forming the boundary between Latium and Campania, near where Mondragone now stands. Like so many modern Italian wines with a single name, there were a dry and a sweet, a red and a white, but Warner Allen was sure that the great classic was the dry red Falernian, 'probably not unlike such a Rhône wine as Châteauneuf du Pape', but with

[1] *See* pp. 236 and 240.

a much more powerful bouquet (though Henderson thought that it must be like a sherry or madeira), and he quotes Martial, who 'wanted not merely to drink the kisses left in the loved one's cup but to kiss lips moist with old Falernian'. Again, like so many Italian red wines of our own time, Falernian seems to have had a remarkable capacity for ageing, probably in glass or earthenware jars, sealed with a sort of plaster of Paris; Petronius, in Nero's time, makes the *nouveau riche* Trimalchio serve his guests with the most expensive wine obtainable in Rome – Falernian, a hundred years old.

Similarly, Surrentine, from the Sorrentine peninsula, was said to need at least twenty-five years to lose its youthful asperity; it takes its place among Younger's preeminent eighteen wines largely, it seems, because of its reputation in classical times as a tonic, much prescribed by the physicians, though two Roman emperors in succession, Tiberius and Caligula, found it too thin for their tastes – Caligula, indeed, scorned it as *nobilis vappa*.[1]

Calenian, a lighter wine than Falernian, but from the same parts (near the present-day Calvi), is mentioned time and again in Horace – though Horace admits that he offers it to Maecenas only because he cannot afford Falernian; and so is the dry, full-flavoured Caecuban, which before the time of Augustus was tremendously fashionable, though it must have been a coarse, heavy and headachy wine (Henderson believed it to be a rough sweet wine), from vines trained up the poplars that grew in the marshes between Terracina and Formiae. As Warner Allen observed, vines grown in a marsh can never produce really fine wines, and Cyrus Redding goes farther in excluding 'soil infected by stagnant waters' as the only ground in which the vine will not grow. In any case, Caecuban ceased to be produced when Nero drove the Baiae–Ostia canal through its native swamps.

Setine must have been finer: it came from notably beautiful vineyards overlooking the Pontine marshes, and was thought by some of his courtiers to be Augustus's favourite wine, which meant, of course, that it became theirs. Others, though, claimed the distinction for the north Italian Rhaetic, which must have pleased Virgil, for it came from the hills above Verona, near his birthplace, Mantua, and he loved it dearly. With the Sicilian Mamertine, Rhaetic is the only Italian wine of the eighteen not from either Campania or Latium, and is the exception to the general opinion of the time that no wine worth drinking came from north of Rome. Opinion in modern times is all the other way, and Rhaetic came, in any case, from just about the same region as the Soave of our own time, and may perhaps have been a similar wine – we know it to have been light and delicate, a pleasant change for Augustus from the heavy wines of Latium and Campania, the admirers of which found it mawkish.

Of the remaining wines, Alban was the precursor of the present-day *castelli Romani* wines, coming from the Alban Hills: there were a sweet and a dry, both perhaps white. Massic came from the same area as Falernian and Calenian, which it resembled, and Fundanian was very similar to the heavy Caecuban; Statanian came from the fringe of the Falernian country and was lighter than most.

---

[1] Badly kept wine turns to vinegar, and the Latin word for vinegar that in its turn had become insipid was *vappa*. The emperor considered Surrentinum to be flavourless vinegar with ideas above its station. By extension the word *vappa* came to be used for a stupid good-for-nothing: it persists as *voppo* in Neapolitan slang, and entered the American vocabulary by way of immigrants from the South, becoming 'wop' in the process – all this according to the late Dr Charles Seltman in his *Wine and the Ancient World*.

'In ancient times', wrote Cyrus Redding a century ago, 'the Romans trained their high vines as they now do in Tuscany, along palisades, or from tree to tree.' In Tuscany this pattern is only now beginning to change[1] and far more vines than not in central and south-central Italy are still trained in this way, so that the twentieth-century holiday-maker, on his way to Florence and Siena, to Verona or Bologna, can see how Horace's Calenian or Virgil's Rhaetic was grown by the system known to the Romans as the *arbustum*.

A variation of this method was the *compluvium*, a rectangular trellis raised above the ground, forming a sort of arbour – still a 'high vine' system, and with the same advantage as the *arbustum* in that either under the trees or over the trellises the vines could be trained in such a way as to be shielded by foliage from too great a measure of sunshine.

Then as now, on the other hand, the vines of Southern Italy were trained low, by the system now known as *albarello*, perhaps brought in by the Greeks – an easier and cheaper method, for it obviates the expense of trees or of trellises, and much of the trouble of training, but produces coarse wines because of the reflection of heat from the soil, and in Roman times was said to encourage the depredations of foxes, rats and mice.

Cellaring must have been well understood by the Romans, even though they seem to have kept their wines above ground, in what the French would call *chais* rather than *caves*, but various writers, Henderson points out,

> . . . generally advise a northern aspect, and one not much exposed to the light, in order that it may not be liable to sudden vicissitudes of temperature; and they very properly inculcate the necessity of placing it at a distance from the furnaces, baths, cisterns, or springs of water, stables, dunghills, and every sort of moisture and effluvia likely to affect the wine.

The better wines were matured in a *fumarium*, and references in Latin authors to 'smoky' wines have suggested to some historians that the wine itself was smoked, and led to curious speculations as to what it could have tasted like. But it seems reasonable to suppose that the reference was not to a sort of kippered claret but simply to the process to which the wine had been subjected. Rather, it must be thought probable that Roman wines were subjected to heat, as Madeira is to this day, for the purpose both of mellowing and stabilizing it.

From Cato, who flourished around 200 B.C., to Columella, between two and three hundred years after – as it might be from Isaac Newton to our own time – a great number of Latin authors produced treatises on agricultural methods, and from them William Younger made tentative identification of some of the grapes of classical times with some of present-day Italy, notably the Aminean with the Greco Bianco and the Trebulan with the Trebbiano, both producing white wine.

Columella preferred the Aminean to the more prolific Nomentan for precisely the same reason that in Burgundy, for instance, the Pinot is a 'noble' grape and the more prolific Gamay is not. By this time (in the early years of the Empire, under Claudius or Nero), wine-growing on the sizeable estates of Latium and Campania was well informed and highly sophisticated, which is not to say that the greater part of Italian wine production did not come from smallholdings on which peasant farmers made

---

[1] *See* p. 216.

rough wines from common grapes by the simplest methods, and drank them young. But a wine-grower such as Columella himself took great trouble over his cuttings and graftings, picking each variety of grape individually, and laying it down that 'we judge to be best every kind of wine which can grow old without any treatment, nor should anything at all be mixed with it, which might dull its natural flavour. For that wine is immeasurably the best which needs only its own nature to give pleasure.'[1]

Macaulay wrote that

> This year the must shall foam
> Round the white feet of laughing girls
> Whose sires have marched to Rome.

But that was in the time of Tarquin, which is pre-history, and there is plenty of evidence that the finer wines of classical times were pressed, not trodden, before fermentation in great earthenware jars, and that the Romans knew a great deal about fining and racking, as well as having devised a sort of *chaptalisation*, making use of honey or of boiled must for thin wines lacking in natural grape-sugar. Boiled must was also used to produce fortified dessert wines, as is done with *vin cotto*;[2] some wines were preserved, or flavoured, or both, by the addition of herbs, spices or, as in Greece, resin; and there are unappetizing recipes in Cato, Virgil, Pliny and others for cheap wines, many of them made from a second pressing, as rations for farm workers. Pliny, indeed, writing in the first decades A.D., complained that even the nobility were fobbed off with coloured and adulterated wines.

No doubt there were genuine wines, carefully produced by wine-growers as dedicated to quality as Columella, but as William Younger has deduced from the cookery books of the time, those Romans who were not given to country dishes and the simple life, as Horace was (or, at any rate, as Horace sang), lusted after pungency and richness, their dishes spiced and peppered, and enjoyed wines to match. Spiced and aromatic wines, or the Roman version of *retsina*, would no doubt go well with such dishes as dormice fattened on chestnuts and cooked in a sauce made of the entrails of salted Spanish mackerel and pepper. And we know that there were wines made specially to be drunk as aperitifs or as dessert wines, by flavouring with honey, with violets, with roses or with pepper, as well as an absinthe (*absinthites*) made of wine and wormwood.

Most of the true, unadulterated wines such as Falernian were probably, as we have seen, big, full-flavoured heavy red wines – the light, dry Rhaetic, possibly white, was one of the few exceptions: perhaps the Romans drank it with the oysters they loved so much – and the Roman love for rich dishes would explain their popularity, though there are many references to their being drunk diluted with water or with snow. There were drinking parties and there were heavy drinkers, but the Romans generally, in the great days of the city, were an abstemious people, and to drink wine undiluted was to go it, rather. Catullus sang the promise of a drinking bout with a hard-drinking companion in his *Minister vetuli puer Falerni*:

> Bearer of old Falernian wine,
> Good boy, a stronger glass be mine.

[1] Warner Allen's translation.
[2] *See* pp. 212 and 265.

> Mistress of toasts (as drunk as she
> Not ev'n the drunken grape can be)
> Postumia will have it so.
> You, water, wine's destruction, go:
> Away with you to folk austere:
> The god of wine himself is here.

– which suggests that Falernian was usually offered diluted, and that this was a special occasion.

All the same, the great wines, even if destined for dilution, were handled with some connoisseurship, for they were usually decanted, strained either through linen or through metal wine-strainers that may perhaps have resembled those made by the great Georgian silversmiths.

They would need decanting, too, for the best and most highly prized of these big, heavy wines spent many years in cask (or, more likely, in earthenware jars, though wooden casks were not unknown), and in smaller glass or earthenware bottles, before being served. There are endless references in the classical authors, from Cato onwards, to the age of wines of the better sort – such lines as Horace's promise to Maecenas that a jar of mellowed wine had long been waiting for him, and Columella's assertion that almost all wine improved with age. Not that there were vintage years as such: as in Italy now it is how many years a wine has aged in cask and bottle that matters not in what year it was made.[1] True, most of the wine of Italy was for immediate consumption by the farmer who grew it and for his family – wine of the country that was drunk within the year. But even Horace's modest Sabine wine, which no doubt bore about the same relation to Falernian as a common Beaujolais would to a Romanée-Conti, or a Blayais to a first growth of the Médoc, and was by no means, it would seem, a 'big' wine, was ready to drink, wrote Horace, after from seven to fifteen years; the marsh-grown Caecuban took many years to mature; and we have already recorded the quarter of a century that was needed to smooth away the harshness of Surrentine. We cannot know now, for certain, what any of these wines tasted like, but it is clear, at any rate, that the best wines of classical Rome were grown, made, cellared and decanted as carefully as any first-growth claret that reaches the table of a twentieth-century connoisseur, and that although much of this skill and care and devotion were forgotten, along with much else, for centuries after the fall of Rome to the barbarians, much remained. It is not so much that the arts of living were all lost in the Dark and the Middle Ages as that a great deal went unrecorded: there is a link between the vineyards that Virgil knew in northern Italy and the Vernage, or Vernaccia,[2] that came to England from those parts in the fourteenth and fifteenth centuries; and Trubidiane, recorded as having been imported into London by 1373, is a corruption of

---

[1] Though the Romans usually knew a wine's year, and some were especially highly thought of. 'The ancients noted the years of celebrated growths, as that of the Opimian year, or the year of Rome, 632, when Opimius was consul. It was in high esteem a century afterwards. The Romans marked their amphorae, or wine vessels (containing seven gallons and a pint modern measure), with the consul's name, which indicated the year of the vintage. Many amphorae now exist with the legible mark of the vintage' (Redding). The Opimian year was 121 B.C., and it was the Opimian wine that Trimalchio offered his guests (see p. 26). But it was age rather than vintage that usually impressed.
[2] Not to be confused with the Sardinian Vernaccia.

Trebbiano, which has been at any rate tentatively identified with the Trebulan that was grown in Campania in Julius Caesar's time.

We know little of Italian viticultural techniques in the Middle Ages, but Italy always remained a wine-growing country: André Simon, in his *History of the Wine Trade in England*, recorded the capture by French pirates in 1472 of a Venetian carrack bound for England with more than four hundred casks of sweet wine on board. It may well be that this particular cargo was of wines from Greece or the Levant, for Venice enjoyed the carrying trade between those parts and the west and north of Europe, but that there were sweet Italian wines being carried to this country at the same time is shown by the monopoly granted to the port of Southampton by Henry IV for the importation of 'Malmseys, Muscadels, and all the sweet Levant, Greek or Italian wines, imported either by foreigners or by natives'. And in modern times, by the seventeenth century, 'Florence wine', white and red, meaning in fact the wine of Tuscany, is being constantly mentioned in English literature, from Lady Sandwich's present of two bottles to Pepys to take home for his wife to Salmon's complaint that although red and white Florence wines are both very good stomach wines, 'the red is something binding'. The same period sees mention of Lacrima Christi and of 'Leattica' – Aleatico – both to be found in the following pages among the familiar Italian wines of our own time.

The Florence wines were apparently exported in uncorked flasks, sealed with olive oil and packed in chests: they were very popular in England. A silver wine-label, or bottle ticket, inscribed 'Flore' is listed in Dr N. M. Penzer's book, where an offer in a *London Gazette* of 1707 is noted of 'A Parcel of extraordinary good Red Florence at 6s. a Gallon', and there is reference in a letter of Horace Walpole's to the British ambassador at the court of the Grand Duke of Tuscany, asking him to send Fox 'two chests of the best Florence wine every year'. A century earlier, according to Henderson, 'in the time of our own James I, to have drunk Verdea is mentioned among the boasts of a travelled gentleman'.[1]

It seems clear, though, that Italian wines were no longer as sturdy or as capable of ageing as in the days of the great Falernians. Warner Allen quotes Dean Swift's complaint, in 1711, of going to a tavern, after 'a scurvy dinner', to drink Florence 'at four-and-sixpence a flask; damned wine'. The same irascible cleric was given one of the chests that the Grand Duke of Tuscany had sent to Bolingbroke, which he 'liked mightily' at first, but which began to spoil within a fortnight, causing Swift to write to Stella: 'Do you know that I fear that my whole chest of Florence is turned sour, at least the first two were, and hardly drinkable? How plaguy unfortunate am I! And the Secretary's own is the best I ever tasted!'

There can be little doubt that Italian wines were made less carefully than in classical times and that, as William Younger wrote, there was no scientific viticulture between the fall of the Roman Empire and the agricultural innovations of the eighteenth century. Even then technical improvements came more slowly on the Continent, and especially in Italy, than in the England of the enclosures, of Coke of Holkham and 'Turnip' Townshend. Indeed, by Cyrus Redding's time, in the eighteen-fifties, Italian wine had gone completely out of favour in England, simply because, as Redding observed, 'Italian wines have stood still and remained without improvement, while

[1] *See* p. 249 for the Verdea of our own time.

those of France and Spain . . . have kept pace to a certain extent with agricultural improvement and the increasing foreign demand.'

After examining the difficulties that the wine-grower of a still disunited Italy found in the way of producing good wines for export ('trampled by the Austrian military tyranny, or by the feet of Church despots, destitute of adequate capital, and weighed down by a vexatious system of imposts, what has he to hope for by carrying towards perfection an art which can bring him no benefit?'), Redding went on:

> There are places, however, where very good wine is made and something like care bestowed upon its fabrication; but those exceptions are the result of the care of the proprietor for his own individual consumption. The curses of a foreign yoke and of domestic exaction blight the most active exertions and render that land, which is the gem of the earth in natural gifts, a waste, or a neglected and despoiled heritage to its inhabitants. The Italians would soon make good wine, if good wine would repay the making – if they might reap that reward due to industry and improvement, which common policy would not withhold in other countries. The peasantry generally are not an idle race.

Though Redding somewhat qualifies that final tribute in going on to give another of the reasons why Italy lagged so long behind France in producing wines worthy of her soil and her long tradition:

> A fine climate, to which the wine seems wedded, produces a large quantity of rich fruit with little trouble, and why should the peasant not enjoy, without extra care and labour, that which, on his bestowing care and labour, will yield him no additional benefit?

Even while Redding was revising his book, though, there were reforms on foot in the Chianti country.[1] He admitted himself that

> . . . in Tuscany, indeed, things have been at times somewhat better. [And went on] In particular districts in Italy it is by no means a rare thing to meet with good wine. The general neglect of a careful and just system of culture, and the want of that excitement that interest creates, have not prevented the capabilities of the Italian vineyards from being known. In certain instances much care is bestowed upon the vine. In spots among the Apennines the vines are carefully dressed, terrace fashion, and were they well pruned and the fruit taken in due maturity, and regularly assorted, which it rarely or never is, a vast deal of excellent wine might be made, without altering anything essential besides, in the present system of vine husbandry. There is good-bodied wine to be produced in Naples for twopence-half-penny English a bottle, and at Rome and Florence for fourpence.

The Austrian military tyranny, the temporal despotism of the Church, the imposts between petty principalities have all long disappeared, and now, with the new wine law, with the growers' associations, viticultural stations experimenting with French vines and German hybrids, and new co-operative wineries, another era is dawning for Italian wines, possibly as golden as in the days when Horace, over his glass of modest Sabine, knew that he was at the centre of the wine-growing world.

[1] Redding's classic work first appeared in 1833. The third edition, added to and revised, consulted for this present book, appeared in 1860.

# CHAPTER TWO

# Piedmont and the
# Val d'Aosta

As a wine-producing region Piedmont – with which I include, for convenience's sake, the autonomous French-speaking Val d'Aosta[1] – usually comes third for volume of output among the provinces of Italy: after Apulia, and often after the Veneto. But no province – not even Lombardy, with such red Valtelline wines as Sassella; not even the Veneto, with its charming lakeside wines and its Soave; not even Tuscany, with its old Chiantis – produces more distinguished or more varied *vini pregiati*, fine wines.

My Italian friends would not thank me if I suggested that this might be due partly to French influence, though there are western and northern fringes of the old kingdom of Savoy – Antico Piemonte – that are still French-speaking, and Italians from farther south or farther east have been known to speak tartly of Turin as 'the most Italian city of France'. Certainly Francis I was showing enough interest in Piedmontese wines in the sixteenth century to have them imported into France.

But more especially it is soil, long tradition and climate.

The vine has been established in Piedmont certainly since Roman times, and the more settled history of the kingdom in the past century or so, compared with those other parts of Italy still under Austrian or Papal or Bourbon rule, enabled the Royal family – notably King Charles Albert (reigned 1831–49) – to take a practical interest in establishing and improving cellars and vineyards, setting an example followed by Cavour (whose successor as prime minister of united Italy, Ricasoli, followed the same example in his turn, but in Tuscany).

The softly rounded hills that lie east and south of Turin, on either side of the Tanaro river, tributary of the Po – the Monferrati to the north and the Langhe to the south – are where the great Piedmontese wines come from. They are the gentlest of mothers of the noble Nebbiolo grape,[2] and lie in the same latitude as those slopes of the Rhône valley that grow Tavel and Hermitage and Châteauneuf du Pape, but are protected by the great sweep of the Alps from the winds that harry the French vineyards. It is a sunny, smiling countryside, not scorched and seared as are the vineyards of the south of Italy, the wines of which, like those of the sunbaked south of France, under too fierce a sun, are prolific and undistinguished.

Yet again the proximity of big, rich and stable markets must have encouraged not only intensive but painstaking production, and the maintenance of high standards: the Monferrat and the Langhe vineyards lie largely within a triangle of which the

---

[1] The Val d'Aosta ranks as a separate region, but its production of wine is far too small for it to be listed separately.
[2] The word is related to *nebbia*, mist, perhaps because it is gathered when the season of mists has begun.

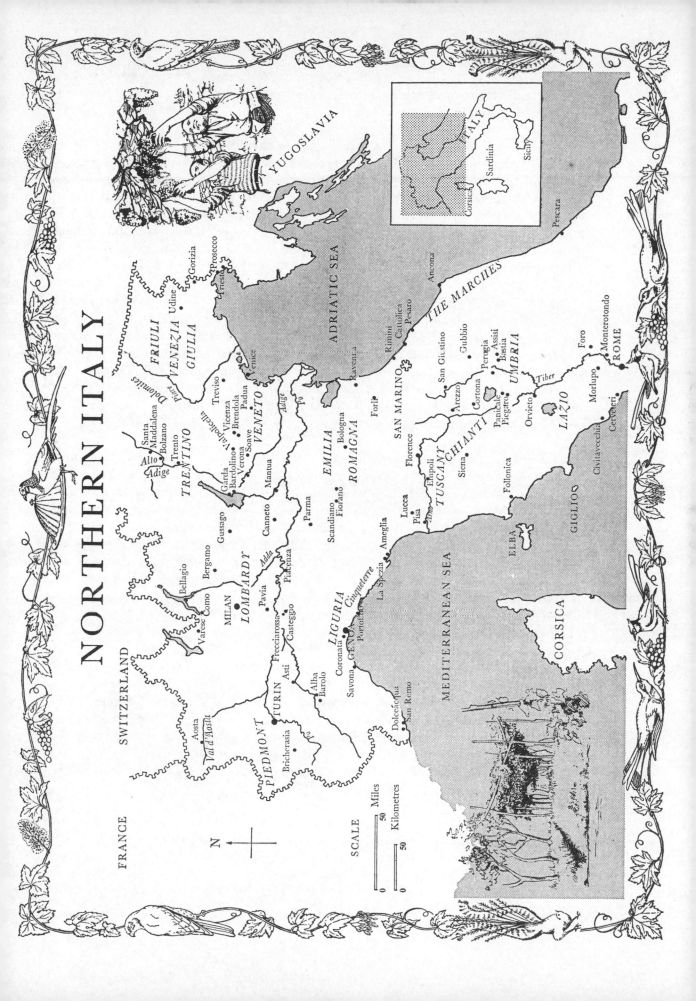

corners are the great cities of Turin, Milan and Genoa, none of them more than fifty
or sixty miles from the centre of the area, and the holiday coast of the Italian Riviera is
a shop-window as well as a market.

Given a more benign climate and more sunshine than the classic wine-growing areas
of France and, to an even greater degree, of Germany, Italy tends in the nature of
things to produce in general bigger and fuller red wines and the grapes from which
sweet, aromatic whites can be made without late gathering. This is not true of all Italian
wines, of course: there are dry whites and delicate reds, for climate is not the only
factor – there are methods of vinification, too, as well as soil and altitude. But it tends
to be true of Italian wines in general; and the wines of Piedmont, even though its
climate is more temperate than that of other wine-growing regions of Italy, are good
examples.

The red wines are usually big and full-bodied, similar in character to the French
Rhône wines, but requiring to be aged in cask for far longer, and improving notably
with greater bottle-age still. And although only ten per cent of the total wine production
of Piedmont is of white wine, that small proportion includes one of the great white wines
of the world – Asti Spumante, not only sparkling but sweet, and not only sweet but
sweet without (as in sweet champagne) added sugar, and without being made from
over-ripe and sun-dried grapes (as in Sauternes and the German *trockenbeerenauslesen*).
Asti is sweet simply out of the sweet nature of the Muscat grape it is made from.

France (except for Alsace) names its wines after the regions, sub-regions, communes,
villages or vineyards in which they are grown – no mention of Merlot or Cabernet in
labelling or demanding a Lafite, for instance, which, besides being a Lafite, no less,
is also entitled to be called by such lesser names as Pauillac, Médoc and Bordeaux.
Alsatian wines, on the other hand, are Rieslings or Sylvaners, Traminers or Gewürz-
traminers. But some Italian wines are one thing, some the other, which is confusing,
and particularly so in Piedmont, for of the familiar Piedmontese wines Barbera is a
grape, whereas Barbaresco is a village, after which a wine is named that is made not
from the Barbera but from the Nebbiolo, the noble grape that also produces Barolo –
which is confused in its turn with the Brolio of the Chianti country.

One can but speak generally in dealing with the names of Italian wines, for such
rules as there are differ from region to region, and are applied, without anything like
the sanctions that the French are able to apply in enforcing their laws of *appellation*,
by the various *consorzi*, or voluntary associations of growers and merchants, which
differ enormously in earnestness and vigour. Speaking generally, then, those Piedmontese wines that bear place names are protected as to the use of those names by
associations: when a wine made from the same grape is known only by the name of the
grape – Nebbiolo, for instance, instead of Barolo – it is grown outside the delimited
and protected region. It may be no worse a wine: it may (though this is unlikely) be
better; one cannot be sure.

Drive into Italy by way of the Great Saint Bernard, and the first vines you see are
Nebbiolo, trained into pergolas over trellises on terraced hillsides high up in the valley
of the Dora, in the autonomous French-speaking region of Val d'Aosta, against a

Plate 17. Roman wine glass, first century B.C.; Roman wine glass jugs, A.D. 200 an
first century A.D. (Moussaieff collection).
Plate 18. *Overleaf* Brolio estate, near Siena, Tuscany, seen from the castle of Brolio

background of snow-topped Alpine peaks and themselves a couple of thousand feet above sea-level. (Some, I am told, flourish at three thousand. Even in the Langhe, vines from which fine wines are made grow at over two thousand feet: fifteen hundred is common in Piedmont.) The Nebbiolo here produces red wines – Donnaz and Carema, after communes in the region – lighter in shade and in style than those made from the same grape, trained more in the French way, in the gentle hills – the Vercelli, the Monferrati and the Langhe – on either side of the upper reaches of the Po and its tributaries: wines such as Gattinara, Barolo, Barbaresco, and those known simply as Nebbiolo, or Nebbiolo Piemontese.

These, with Asti Spumante (made from the Moscato, which used to provide most of the white wine base for the vermouths of Turin, though more, nowadays, come from Apulia), are the noblest grapes and greatest wines of Piedmont. As will be seen, the Nebbiolo and the Moscato flourish, too, in Lombardy. Other Piedmontese grapes are the Barbera, the Grignolino, the Freisa, the Brachetto, the Cortese, the Dolcetto, the Bonarda and the Erbaluce, each of which has a place in the list of officially recognized Piedmontese wines that follows. Some French Pinot and some German (or Alto-Atesino) Riesling are also grown in the province, but only tentatively and in small amounts, and not producing wines named as yet in any official or semi-official list.

I do not regard vermouth, a manufactured, blended wine, as falling normally within the scope of this book, but it would be absurd to discuss the wines of Piedmont without any mention of it. Vermouth has been made in Turin since the late eighteenth century, the Moscato of the region proving itself an admirable base with which to blend extracts from the aromatic herbs of the neighbouring mountains. (It is significant that the centres of French vermouth manufacture, Marseilles and Chambéry, are also within reach of never-ending supplies of mountain herbs.) Turin is still the centre of the industry, with firms such as Martini, Cinzano, Carpano, Gancia and others earning immense amounts of foreign exchange for Italy.

Nowadays wines from the south are more widely used – Piedmont could hardly produce enough for the great vermouth houses of Turin – but the basic principles are the same, and Italian law lays it down that seventy per cent of anything called 'vermouth' must be pure natural wine (which does not mean that there are not other aperitifs under other names, which are made of alcohol, sugar and flavourings, without any wine at all).

The various brands of vermouth differ, but the main styles are *bianco* and *rosso*, both sweet; and another white vermouth, made after the French style, which is not called *bianco*, but 'dry'. The firm of Carpano makes a distinctively bitter variety called Punt è Mes (allegedly because it used to be served at a café near the Turin Stock Exchange, where, on one occasion, an excited broker went on shouting to the waiter the phrase 'point and a half', that he was hammering away at in the business deal he was trying to clinch) and Campari is another bitter aperitif not, strictly speaking, a vermouth, though used in the same way, and a particularly good aperitif with soda. Many wines of the region are quinined into an appetizing bitterness as aperitifs – Barolo Chinato is the best example.

The great vermouth houses have the resources and the facilities for making Asti Spumante and other sparkling wines.

Plate 19. Making *fiaschi* covers in the Tuscan countryside.

# The Wines of Piedmont and the Val d' Aosta

**Ara.** Dry *frizzante* red wine from Grignasco.

**Asti Spumante.** Almost the whole yield of the Moscato grape, which is widely grown in Piedmont, is made into a delicate, sweetish, aromatic sparkling wine, generally considered too sweet for the more sophisticated English tastes, but delicious with fruit or sweets after a meal, for a mid-morning drink or at parties. The finest quality is Asti Spumante, production of which is rigorously supervised and controlled by inspectors of the consortium of growers, which grants a neck-label showing San Secondo, patron saint of the town of Asti, mounted, in blue on a gold ground: Moscato d'Asti (*q.v.*) also carefully controlled, is less fine and sweeter.

One firm – Contratto – still makes a very little Asti by the *méthode champenoise* (involving secondary fermentation in bottle; *remuage* to settle the sediment on the cork; *dégorgement* of the sediment by quick freezing of the neck of the bottle; and subsequent liqueuring by filling the gap with sugar dissolved in champagne). But virtually all production of Asti, and all the production of Moscato Spumante – the centre of which is not in Asti itself but in the small neighbouring town of Canelli – is by the Charmat, or *cuve close*, method of fermentation in closed vats, and bottling under pressure. Not only is this method much cheaper (it is forbidden in France to any wine that is to be called champagne) but the makers claim that it preserves much better the fragrance of the Muscat grape, which suffers under the lengthy *méthode champenoise* – the *cuve close* method takes days as against months.

Indeed, many of the big houses – and Asti is largely produced by big houses and co-operatives – do in fact maintain the *méthode champenoise* for the production of *dry* sparkling wines made from the white Pinot grape, and sold under brand names. These wines are increasingly popular in Italy, as they are considerably cheaper than champagne, though about twice the price of sparkling Asti and Moscato. Typical examples are the Fontanafredda firm's Contessa Rosa; the Cinzano Principe di Piemonte; the Gancia Royal Cuvée; the Martini Riserva Montelera; the Contratto Bacco d'Oro, and many others.

Curiously enough, even though these very acceptable wines are made from French grapes in the French way, my experience of them is that they share with the sparkling Asti and Moscato the characteristics of having a much smaller, weaker and shorter-lived bubble than champagne.

**Barbaresco.** Red wine made, in small quantities, of the Nebbiolo grape in Barbaresco and neighbouring communes in the gently hilly country just to the east of the great white-truffle centre of Alba. A full-bodied, rich, fragrant wine, deep in colour and acquiring slight amber tinges with age, it matures more quickly, losing its harshness earlier, than its close relative Barolo (*q.v.*), made in the same way, of the same grape, only a few miles away. Protected by an association of growers of Barolo and Barbaresco, the approved wines bear a neck-label showing the tower of the ancient township of Barbaresco in gold on a blue ground. 12·5°–14°.

**Barbera d'Asti; Barbera di Cuneo; and Barbera with other district names.** Quite the commonest vine in Piedmont – twenty times as common as the aristocratic Nebbiolo – is the Barbera, producing red wines that vary widely in quality, many of them made in co-operatives. Harsh when young, Barbera mellows with age to about the quality of a modest Rhône wine, which it resembles in style. Mr Gerald Asher, a discriminating student of Italian wines, which he used to import into England, has observed that while the Barbera wines 'do not have the strength and nerve of Nebbiolo', they 'lack none of its colour, nor its robust earthy flavour'. The finest, grown chiefly round Asti, are accorded an association neck-label showing blue grapes superimposed on the old city's tall, part-Roman, part-medieval tower, in red, and allowed to be styled 'd'Asti'. Others are permitted to be styled Barbera Riserva or Barbera Extra and are also full-bodied and improve with bottle age, though they are usually sold after four years in wood and only six months in bottle. Wine that is styled Barbera, simply, is a common wine, often slightly *frizzante* and sweetish, like a subdued Portuguese *vinho verde*. 12°–15°.

**Barberati.** A name given to wine made in the Langhe of a mixture of Dolcetto and Barbera grapes.

**Barengo.** Very limited production of a straw-coloured dry wine made in the Novara region from the Greco Bianco grape. 12°–14°.

**Barolino.** A name given to wine made in the Langhe of a mixture of Dolcetto and Nebbiolo grapes.

**Barolo.** One of the great red wines of Italy – many experts consider it the greatest – made of the Nebbiolo grape in compact, smoothly hilly areas, strictly delimited by the two associations, around the commune of Barolo, near Alba. Deep red in colour, full and fragrant. (Writers in official publications claim to detect the mingled aroma of tar and violets.) It spends at least three years in cask before bottling, and ages as well and as long in bottle as a good claret[1] (longer than burgundy), taking on a similar tinge of orange-brown at the rim of the glass. Considered rather superior to its close relative, Barberesco, because of its greater capacity for ageing in bottle, it is usually very slightly the fuller and heavier. It carries a neck-label showing either a golden lion or a helmeted head, according to the particular district it comes from. 13°–15°.

**Bianco di Castel Tagliolo.** White wine made in Tagliolo Monferrato: the common sort made of Cortese grapes and sold as a café wine, but a finer variety, the Cortese mixed with Riesling and Sauvignon, is bottled, and is a pleasant, dry, straw-yellow table wine. 10°–13°.

**Blanc de Morgex.** Dry white wine, with a faint suggestion of herbs in scent and flavour, made from local varieties of grape in the highest vineyards of the Val d'Aosta, some as much as 3,000 feet above sea-level. 8°–10°.

**Boca d'Asti.** Dry, ruby-red table wine made from Vespolina, Spanna, Bonarda and Croatina grapes: drunk locally after a couple of years in bottle, and also exported to Switzerland. 12°–13°.

**Bonarda d'Asti.** Sparkling, semi-sweet, red wine made near Asti from a grape of the same name. Deep in colour, but light in alcohol (10°–11°) and refreshing, served cool. Rarely found outside its own region.

**Brachetto d'Asti.** Similar to Bonarda, but made from the Brachetto grape, lighter and much sweeter – a sort of cherry-red Moscato Spumante. Becoming rare. 12·5°–13·5°.

---

[1] Indeed – as will be observed, too, of the finest Tuscan wines – these full red Italian wines have an immense capacity for ageing in bottle. Paolo Monelli records having tasted a Barolo 1858 that had lost colour but of which the bouquet was 'still racy and generous'.

**Bricherasio.** See under Nebbiolo.

**Camarino.** Rare red wine, similar to Ghemme (*q.v.*), but credited with aphrodisiac qualities that it was difficult to put to the test in the cloistered quiet of the tasting-room. 12°–13°. There is a Camarino Rubino, said to be 'most gentle' – presumably for patients in not such dire need.

**Camiglione.** See under Nebbiolo.

**Canavesano; Campiglione.** Roughish red wines made near Turin of mixtures of Barbera, Freisa and Avarengo grapes; fairly common wines of no great merit. 10°–11°.

**Carema.** Red Nebbiolo, close kin to Barolo and Barbaresco, but lighter, perhaps because of the altitude at which it is grown – up to about 2,000 feet – in the valley of the Dora, around the village of Carema in the Val d'Aosta, where a grape festival is held every year at vintage time. Here the vines are trained into pergolas, as in the Alto-Adige. 12°–13°.

**Cari.** *Rosé*, semi-sweet wine from a grape of the same name. 9°–10°.

**Castel la Volta.** A charming, dryish white *frizzante* (sometimes *spumante*) wine, made in some years, not all, from what is really a table grape, with few pips. Comes from the neighbourhood of Santa Vittoria and Monticello.

**Castel Taglioli.** Similar to Cortese dell'Alto Monferrato (*q.v.*).

**Castello di Sommariva.** Dry, fragrant, delicate white wine from the Cortese grape. (See Cortese dell'Alto Monferrato.)

**Cesnola.** A local Nebbiolo, lighter than most, and drunk fairly young.

**Chiaretto di Cavaglia.** Sweetish, *rosé* wine, of no great distinction, from near Vicelli.

**Chiaretto del Viverone.** Light red, almost *rosé* wine, slightly *frizzante*, from same area as above.

**Cortese dell'Alto Monferrato.** Dry white wine, light and fragrant, made in the Monferrato hills from the Cortese grape: to be drunk young, and excellent with fish. (Some is used as a base for vermouth.) A sparkling version is sometimes to be met with: the semi-sweet is called Gavi (*q.v.*). 10°–12°.

**Dolcetto; Dolcetto d'Alba; Dolcetto delle Langhe; Dolcetto di Strevi; Dolcetto d'Ovada.** A red wine that is dry or dryish, despite its sweet-sounding name, which is that of the grape it is made from, one of the commonest in Piedmont (next only to Barbera and Freisa). Pleasant country wine, sometimes with a little sugar retained, by temperature control, to render it *amabile* – very slightly sweet, though not rich or luscious – and there is a sparkling version. Dolcetto d'Alba is the finest – a dry wine with a bitter tang; the others are commoner and cheaper. 10·5°–11·5°.

**Donnaz.** Another Val d'Aosta version of the Nebbiolo. See under Carema.

**Enfer.** Clear red, common wine of the Val d'Aosta.

**Fara.** A Gattinara (*q.v.*) of Fara, near Novara, but not of the highest quality.

**Freisa di Chieri; Freisa d'Asti.** The garnet-red wine made from the local Freisa grape is one of the commonest of the region: that made in the Chieri district near Turin is more highly regarded than that of Asti, though the latter has the protection of an association's neck-label (black grapes superimposed on a yellow tower of Asti). Dry, and all the smoother for a couple of years in bottle, when it offers a pleasant raspberry bouquet. There is also a sweet, sparkling version. 10°–12°.

**Frossasco.** See under Nebbiolo.

**Gattinara.** Made, like Barolo, from the Nebbiolo grape, in a very restricted region near the town of Gattinara (near Vercelli, in the low-lying Po Valley) and preferred by some experts to Barolo itself, as perhaps the greatest of all Italian red wines. (Indeed, it has acquired so much prestige for a wine produced in such small quantities, that reputable bottles are very hard to come by, as unscrupulous dealers have taken to blending it with inferior wine from the South.)[1] Tends to be lighter in colour than Barolo, a garnet rather than a ruby red, less strong and rather more elegant in style. In some bottles I have thought to detect a hint of the flavour of fennel – not unpleasing, but odd. Needs at least three years in bottle. 12°–13°.

**Gavi.** Semi-sweet version of the white Cortese (*q.v.*).

**Ghemme.** Similar to, but not as fine, as Gattinara (*q.v.*), being made with Bonarda and other grapes, as well as Nebbiolo. From commune of Ghemme, near Novara, where they also make a sweetish white wine consumed locally, called Greco di Ghemme; th e Greco di Sizzano is similar.

**Grignasco.** Similar to Ghemme (above).

**Grignolino d'Asti.** Red wine, from Grignolino grape, grown in the Alessandria–Asti area, lightish in colour and style, usually drunk young and cool, like Valpolicella and Bardolino, though Mr Gerald Asher, who describes it as 'fine in style and attractively perfumed', considers it can be 'drunk young with pleasure, and old with delight'. (There is also a sweet, sparkling version.) 11°–13°.

**Lessona.** Similar to Gattinara (*q.v.*) though not quite as fine, and also sometimes called Valdengo or Vigliano, according to its commune of origin.

**Masserano.** Similar to Gattinara (see above).

**Moscato d'Asti.** The commoner, cheaper, usually rather sweeter, but still quite respectable version of Asti Spumante (*q.v.*). About ninety per cent of the total production of the Moscato vines in the Asti area goes to making sparkling wine, but a very little still white wine is produced; a little goes to Turin as a basis for vermouth, as in the old days, though the great vermouth firms rely more and more on cheap wines from the South (notably Apulia); and a very little indeed is made from semi-dried grapes into a richly luscious dessert wine, the Passito di Moscato, now very rarely seen. According to the delimited region it comes from, Moscato d'Asti bears a neck-label showing the mounted San Secondo of Asti in red on a blue ground, or a helmeted head in blue on gold. 7°–10°.

**Moscato di Canelli; Moscato di Strevi.** A very small amount of dry but highly perfumed still Moscato is occasionally found in this region.

**Mottalciata.** Similar to Gattinara (*q.v.*) but not generally thought to be as fine.

**Nebbiolo.** The finest Nebbiolo wines are Barolo, Barbaresco, Gattinara and the others listed here as being similar to Gattinara. Minor but good examples are Camiglione, Bricherasio and Frossasco. Red wines from the same vines grown in other areas are not so fine and are styled simply Nebbiolo, or Nebbiolo Piemontese. But Nebbiolo is a sound, decent wine, and goes well with meat. There are sweet, semi-sweet (*amabile*) and sparkling versions. 12°–13° dry; 10°–11° sweet.

**Passito di Caluso.** In Italy *passito* wines are made from grapes that have been part dried in the sun after picking (cf. the French *vins de paille*), so that their sweetness and

---

[1] But now has a *consorzio* of growers, which presumably will be able to withhold labels from such wines.

flavour are concentrated, making rich, fragrant dessert wines. This particular example is made in very small quantities from the Erbaluce grape (and is sometimes known simply as Erbaluce, or sometimes Albaluce) in the high sub-alpine country south of Ivrea – a golden wine with a pronounced bouquet. A dry Erbaluce is sometimes found. 12°–16°.

**Passito di Moncrivello.** Dessert wine from Vercelli.

**Passito della Val d'Aosta.** Dessert wine from Moscato grapes produced near Chattillon and Aosta itself.

**Pellaverga and Quagliano.** Produced in small quantities from the Pellaverga grape in the mountains north of Cuneo: light, sweet red wines of only small importance. 9°–10°.

**Prunent.** Rare red wine from a grape of the same name; dry and rather sharp, grown near Trontano, not far from Novara.

**Ramiè.** Local name for a rather ordinary, lightish Barbera.

**San Marzano.** Red, slightly *frizzante* wine made of ninety per cent Barbera and ten per cent Nebbiolo, peculiar to the communes of San Marzano and Nizza Monferrato, near Asti. Bottled in the spring after picking and kept in bottles for two to three years before rebottling. Fresh, frothy and fragrant, and something of an oddity.

**Sizzano.** Similar to but less fine than Gattinara (*q.v.*). Other wines of the same sort usually made by mixing other grapes with the Nebbiolo, distinguished only by place names, are:

> Briona (or Caramino)
> Fara
> Grignasco
> Maggiora
> Ronco del Frate.

**Torretta di San Pietro.** Rich dessert wine found rarely, and in small quantities, in the Val d'Aosta.

**Vino della Serra.** Red and white wines from the Serra d'Ivrea – high country north of Ivrea. The white is made from Erbaluce grapes, dry but full (9·5°–11·5°), the red from Barbera, Freisa and others, including a little of the better-bred Nebbiolo, which gives it some finesse. 10°–12°.

Minor wines of Piedmont and the Val d'Aosta, usually found only in the localities where they are grown, include:

**Agliè.** The sweetish light red wine from near Turin.

**Candia Canavese.** A sweetish red wine, made from Barbera, Brachetto and Freisa grapes.

**Chambave (also Grand Cru de Chambave, or Moscato de Chambave).** A Val d'Aostan strong, sweetish white wine, made from Moscato grapes.

**Chiomonte.** A dryish red table wine.

**Malvasia di Nus.** Dessert wine. highly esteemed but rare, produced by one grower in Val d'Aosta.

**Malvasia Rosa.** Rather more common (in both senses) than the above; *frizzante* or *spumante*, and sweet. 10°–12°.

**Meana di Susa.** Red, sweetish, semi-sparkling wine.

**Mesolone.** Full-bodied red wine, with strong bouquet, made of seventy-five per cent Nebbiolo, twenty-five per cent Bonarda. 13°–14°.

**Montouvert.** The only place I know of outside Alsace and Germany where they sometimes make an *eiswein*[1] – otherwise the wine of this little place near Villeneuve is like that of Chambave (*q.v.*).

**Rosso Rubino del Viverone.** Full red wine made from a mixture of Barbera, Bonarda, Dolcetto and Freisa grapes.

CHAPTER THREE

# *Liguria*

LIGURIA, the narrow coastal strip that runs between mountain and sea, from the French frontier to La Spezia, with Genoa at its middle, is the smallest of the regions of Italy. Its production of wine is small, even in proportion to its size, for so much of the region is given up to olives and carnations;[2] so much of its manpower to fishing and to the tourist industry; though Genoa itself is, perhaps, the major centre of the Italian wine trade, both for home and for export, much of the wine of the south of Italy reaching it by sea.

Although the passing tourist may notice many vineyards as he drives – or waits in the traffic jams – along the coastal road, most of these are small plots only, cultivated to provide a family with its own simple table wine, not for sale. What commercial wine-growing there is in Liguria is concentrated mainly between and around Genoa and Savona, and near La Spezia. Few Ligurian wines are to be found far from where they are grown.

## *The Wines of Liguria*

**Arcola Bianco; Arcola Rosso.** Quite undistinguished table wines, red and white, produced between La Spezia and Lerici, and unlikely to be met with much farther afield.

**Ameglia.** Similar to Arcola (above).

**Barbarossa.** Rather pretty pink wine, made from a vine of the same name that is so called because of the long branches of red grapes that it bears, considered to be like

[1] Wine made from grapes that are fully ripe but have been frozen on the vine, so that the grape juice is highly concentrated, giving a wine of very high quality in very small quantities.
[2] Some wines, indeed, once well known, no longer exist, or not on any commercial scale, because the ground where once they grew has been given over to the more immediately profitable flower-growing: Piematone, once grown very near to Ventimiglia, springs to mind.

long red beards. This wine grows on the slopes above the stretch of holiday coast between Noli and Pietra Ligure, on either side of Finale Ligure. There is a sweet variety called Barbarossa Dolce: the drier Barbarossa is described by an Italian writer on wine as being 'full of *brio*' – just the thing for a carefree holiday region. 12°–14°.

**Busetto.** Very much a local white wine, dry and drunk young in the fish restaurants around Finale Ligure.

**Campochiesa Bianco.** A full-flavoured and heavily scented but dryish white wine, made chiefly from the Pigato grape, which has the unusual characteristic for a white wine (and a not very strong white wine at that) of not only lasting but even improving for very long periods in bottle – some writers say for twenty to twenty-five years, though I have no experience myself of a Campochiesa of so great an age. But it is, at any rate, the local custom in the region between Ceriale and Albenga (just to the west of the Barbarossa district, see above) and in the hills behind to lay down a demijohn on the birth of a son, with a view to drinking it at his wedding. 10°–11°.

**Campochiesa Rosso.** Not so fine a wine and neither so well known nor so plentiful as the white, nevertheless the red Campochiesa is also extremely fragrant, and ages well in bottle. Made from a mixture of many types of grape, including the white Pigato. 11°–12°.

**Casteldoria.** See under Dolceacqua.

**Chiaretto del Faro.** Just outside the Cinqueterre district (see below) on the Spezia side, they produce an interesting pink wine by adding to the *cépage* used in the white Cinqueterre wines a certain amount of red must from Sangiovese and Canaiolo grapes. Dry and delicate.

**Cinqueterre.** Quite the most famous of all the wines of Liguria comes from the five villages or 'lands' – *cinque terre* – of Corniglia, Biassa, Monterosso, Vernazza and Tiomaggiore, which lie between rocky cliffs (tunnelled by the railway) and the sea, between Cape Mesco and Cape Cavo, west of La Spezia. The villages are still difficult to get at for the visitor: the vineyards seem impossible – some can be reached only by boat, others from the cliffs above by ropes and ladders. But what is grown there is very fine wine indeed – or rather two fine wines: a Cinqueterre Bianco (14°), full-flavoured yet dry, almost salty, which I have drunk with pleasure as an aperitif, served cold, though the relative dryness depends on the year: most of it is drunk very young indeed, the year after the vintage. It is made from the Vernaccia grape which, when dried or semi-dried (*passito*), makes the much rarer sweet wine of the district. This is done by leaving the grapes spread out in the sun on the flat roofs of the village houses, pressing them when they are almost raisin-like and leaving the must to ferment on the skins for seven to fifteen days, producing a rich, luscious wine, deep gold in colour and extremely rare (only about one-tenth as much of it is made as of the dry Cinque-terre) and therefore, alas, much counterfeited commercially elsewhere. It is difficult to find the genuine sweet Cinqueterre anywhere but in the district itself, and especially at Monterosso (even the Enoteca at Siena does not have one), where it is known as Sciacchetra (16°) – the same word being applied to the local drunks, for it is powerful stuff, fit for heroes, even if some Italian gourmets do say that it is the only wine to drink with ice-cream. (There is also a wine here called Schiacchetrau – the extra letter at the end apparently indicating lower strength, though I cannot be sure, for the authorities differ.)

**Coronata.** Dry white wine, produced only in very modest quantities and consumed locally, made from the Vermentino, Bosco, Bianchetto and Rollo grapes, along a small stretch of coast just to the west of Genoa, from one of the villages of which it takes its name. It has a faintly lemony taste, which makes it an especially pleasant and suitable accompaniment to the local fish. 11°–12°.

**Cortese di Liguria.** Strongish and rather coarse white wine, found at various points along the coast, made from the grape of the same name, and suitable to drink with fish. 13·5°–14°.

**Dolceacqua (or Casteldoria, or Rossese di Val di Nervia).** After Cinqueterre, undoubtedly the best-known Ligurian wine, perhaps because of the mild jokes that can be made about a wine that is called 'sweet water'. It comes from the handsome hill country that lies behind Ventimiglia and Bordighera, almost on the French frontier, and is a deep ruby red, made from seventy per cent Rossese grapes and thirty per cent of three or four others. Dolceacqua is found in most of the restaurants of this holiday area, as well as in Monte Carlo, and goes well with the rich local dishes, especially if it has had four or five years in bottle, for it is a full, heavy, flavoury wine, with a rather sweetish under-taste (though it is by no means in itself a sweet wine) and a strongly aromatic bouquet. 12°–14°.

There is a tradition that Napoleon drank it in these parts in 1794, at one of the Doria palaces, and liked it so much that he used to have it sent to Paris. Hence, the claim on some labels that it was 'Preferito di Napoleone', though this is to say little for any wine: Napoleon was no judge, and used to water his Chambertin.

Note that other, neighbouring, districts make a wine from the same *cépage* that ought to be – and sometimes is – called Rossese, simply, but that Dolceacqua is considered the best, with the obvious result that a lot of it gets called Dolceacqua, anyway. A pale pink, very dry wine from the same grapes, taken earlier from the skins, is made at Ventimiglia and called Vino di Latte – certainly not because it is as mild as milk, for its alcoholic strength is 14°.

**Dolcetto Ligure.** Similar to the Dolcetto of Piedmont (*q.v.*), though the wine made here from the same grape usually shows a rather deeper colour, and is not quite as dry.

**Limassina or Lomassina.** The same wine as Busetto (*q.v.*).

**Marinasco.** Dry and semi-sweet white wines are made from the Trebbiano grape in the commune of this name near La Spezia, very similar in style to the white wines of Arcola (*q.v.*).

**Massarda.** Precisely similar to Busetto (*q.v.*).

**Mattaosso.** Precisely similar to Busetto (*q.v.*).

**Morasca Cinqueterre.** A dry white wine, not precisely from the Cinqueterre itself (*q.v.*), but from the area immediately adjacent, and neither as fine nor as rare as those that bear that name alone. 12°–13°.

**Moscatello.** A light, sweetish, semi-sparkling white wine, made from Moscatello grapes at the western end of the Ligurian coast, notably near the picturesque village of Taggia, in the Argentina valley behind San Remo. A mere 8° of alcohol, which makes it eminently suitable, served as cold as possible, for family picnics. Sometimes called Moscato di Ventimiglia.

**Pigato.** A sound, full-flavoured dry white wine, and also a sweeter semi-sparkling one, are made from the grape of this name near Alassio. The former is one of the most reliable of the white wines of the coast for drinking with fish meals (11°–14°) and the other is light and fresh, and only 8°.

**Polcevera.** White wines from near Genoa, some dry, some semi-dry, made from Vermentino, Bosco, Bianchetta and Rollo grapes, and often served in Genoese fish restaurants. 11°–12°.

**Portfiono.** Modest dry white wine, of which few would probably have heard had not so many heard of the self-conscious, picturesque and over-frequented little place it comes from. 11°.

**Riviera, Bianco della.** Much the same may be said of this wine as of the Portofino: it is found at Santa Margherita.

**Rossese.** See under Dolceacqua.

**Rubino di Canavisse.** A bright red wine from near Savona, dry with a sharply bitter finish.

**Sarticola.** In the valley of the Magra river, from which one can see the white Carrara marble quarries, they grow a sweet, semi-sparkling white wine and also a full-bodied red, both with this name, and both highly prized in and around La Spezia, though unlikely to be found elsewhere.

**Sciacchetra.** See under Cinqueterre, but note that there is also a less important and quite different wine of the same name, pink and dry, from near Imperia.

**Verici.** A dry and a sweet wine, both deep gold in colour: both made from Bosco, Bianchetta and Rollo grapes – the same *cépage* as the wine of Portofino (*q.v.*), producing much better wines – around the village of this name near Sestri Levante. The dry goes well with fish, the sweet as a dessert wine. 11°–12°.

**Vermentino; Vermentino di Pietra Ligure.** White wines from the grape of this name are made in the hills just behind the middle stretch of the Riviera coast, roughly between Savona and Imperia. All are dry, some are slightly sparkling. Among the best and most delicate are those that have been made from grapes more shaded by the foliage than others, and so less lusciously ripe: there is a faint suggestion of the Riesling in their fragrance. 10°–13°.

**Vernaccia di Corniglia.** Another name for the sweet Sciacchetra of the Cinqueterre (*q.v.*), often made from the Vernaccia grape, which is said to derive its name from Vernazza, one of the five villages of the Cinqueterre. (To make up the five Vernazza and Corniglia are counted separately, though I think that officially the one is a part of the other.) No connection with, or any resemblance to, the Vernaccia of Sardinia: it may well be that the vines are quite different.

**Vezzano.** Similar to Arcola (*q.v.*).

CHAPTER FOUR

# *Lombardy*

IN recent years there has been a decline in the production of the thin, foxy wines of the wide, flat Po valley, where rice matters more than the vine and where the *contadini* can now afford the better wines grown in the hillier parts of the province: the Valtelline, the Oltrepo Pavese and those western and southern shores of Lake Garda that lie within the boundaries of Lombardy.

In the Valtelline, between the Alps to the north and the mountains behind Bergamo to the south, the hills are terraced with vineyards, some as high as 2,500 feet above sea-level, though the best wines come from the lower terraces, facing south, along the right bank of the Adda. Here, and throughout the region generally, the noble Nebbiolo is the chief vine, as it is in Piedmont, though it is often known locally as the Chiavennasca, and some of the Lombard wines, unlike the fine wines of Piedmont, and in the same way as the commoner ones, mix the Nebbiolo with others – with the Rossola for the lower-quality wines from the mountain vineyards and with the Brugnola and, in some places, the Pignola, even for such distinguished wines as the Inferno.

At their best, then, such wines of the Valtelline as (in particular) the Sassella, the Grumello and the Inferno – all red wines, of course – are comparable with the great Piedmontese Nebbiolo wines, Barolo and Gattinara themselves. But for various reasons they are harder to come by, not so easily recognizable, and less consistent. For one thing, the custom prevails in the Valtelline of separating the bunches of grapes after the vintage into three qualities – the two better qualities making two grades of, as it were, *auslese* wines, that find their way more frequently into Switzerland, a notable market for the finer red wines of Northern Italy, than into the *trattorie* of Lombardy. Then again, the better wines are frequently sold under brand names, which tend to confuse the foreign visitor who is looking for the name of a grape or a region; and there is not the same measure of control over the quality of the Valtelline wines as is exercised by the Nebbiolo growers of Piedmont over Barolo and Barbaresco, nor by another of the three main wine-growing districts of Lombardy, the Oltrepo Pavese.

Nevertheless, a Sassella or a Grumello from a good grower, with five or six years of bottle-age, such as ought to be found at any of the good wine merchants or better restaurants of Milan or, nearer to their birthplace, in Sondrio or Bergamo,[1] is one of the fine red wines of Italy, and well worth the amateur's leisurely consideration.

Lighter red wines, and wines more rosy than red, are grown along the south-western shores of Lake Garda, between Brescia and Desenzano – wines very similar in character to those from the south-eastern shores, which lie in the Veneto – as well as one notable white wine, the Lugana.

But it is in the Oltrepo Pavese – the part of the administrative province of Pavia, that is to say, that lies over the Po (to the south) from the city of Pavia itself, in the hill

[1] Where the Ristorante Moro, starred in the Michelin for Italy, lists Grumello as one of the wines of the house.

country rising to the foothills of the Ligurian Apennines, that the greatest progress in the viticulture of Lombardy seems to have been made in recent years, and that the strictest control over quality seems to be exercised. Big co-operative wineries have established high standards for cheap table wines, while at the same time a small number of dedicated individual proprietors, as in Tuscany, are producing wines of high and – in Italy at least as important – consistent quality. In addition, there is a vigorous association, the Consorzio Volontario per la Difesa dei Vini Tipici e Pregiati dell' Oltrepo Pavese, sponsored by the Pavia Chamber of Commerce, that jealously watches standards of production, and grants numbered neck-labels (showing the end of a wine-butt, tapped and flowing) to the approved wines of the district. The Oltrepo wines in the following list are all entitled to the label.[1]

## The Wines of Lombardy

**Angera.** A fruity red wine with tawny highlights after it has aged in bottle, made from a mixture of Barbera, Bonarda and Nebbiolo grapes in the extreme north-west of Lombardy, rather outside any of the three main wine-growing areas, near Lake Varese, which lies between Maggiore and Como. Luigi Veronelli speaks highly of a variety known locally as Roccia Rossa.

**Barbacarlo.** Very like the Piedmontese Barbera (*q.v.*), though to some tastes not so firm, and sometimes to be found semi-sweet and semi-sparkling. This deep-red wine is made in the Oltrepo Pavese, and named after a commune there, from a mixture of Barbera, Ughetta, Croattina and Maradella grapes. 11°–13°.

**Barbera.** See under Piedmont. A fair amount of this red wine is made in the Oltrepo Pavese, one of the finer ones being Pezzalunga, clear in colour and fresh in scent and flavour. There is also a good Riserva Oltrepo Antico Piemonte which, in spite of its name, is made at Stradella, in Lombardy, between Piacenza and Pavia. 12·5°–13·5°.

**Bellagio.** The red wine of Bellagio, on Lake Como, is made from grapes the names of which are hearteningly familiar to all lovers of French wines – Malbec, Merlot, Cabernet and Pinot. Not that this wine reaches Bordeaux heights, but it has a certain finesse, and makes an agreeable and, at its best, even rather elegant light luncheon wine, very suitable for summer picnics in this beautiful lake district. Griantino and Tremezzino are pleasant red wines from this part, as is also a Chiaretto di Bellagio, a *rosé*, semi-sparkling wine made from the same *cépage*, which tends to be stronger alcoholically than the red; also a sparkling white Bellagio Spumante.

**Bonarda.** Made from the same Bonarda (or Croattina) grape as the Bonarda of Piedmont, but a still wine where the Piedmontese Bonarda is usually sparkling. A light red wine from the Oltrepo, to be drunk young, and not taken too seriously.

**Botticino.** A sweetish, brilliantly red wine from near Lake Garda, made from a mixture of grapes that includes the Barbera of Piedmont and the Sangiovese of Tuscany. Drunk young and, locally, cool. Sometimes found under the more general heading of Colline Rocciose.

**Buttafuoco.** A softish, fruity, mild red wine from near Pavia, made largely from

---

[1] More recently an association has been formed to protect the wines of Brescia.

Barbera, along with Bonarda (Croattina) and others. Dry but frothy and semi-sparkling (hence its name – it is said to crackle like *fuoco*, fire). 12°.

**Cabella.** A local variant, from between Pavia and Piacenza, of the Bonarda (*q.v.*) of the region, given rather greater distinction by an admixture of Barbera and Croattina, a smooth, velvety red wine, with a pronounced bouquet.

**Canneto Amaro and Canneto Dolce.** The 'bitter' (or dry) and the sweet, frothy red Canneto wines are made (in the Oltrepo) from exactly the same mixture of Croattina (mostly), Barbera and other grapes, the difference between them being due to vinification. These *frizzante*, frothy red wines are strange to English eyes and palates, but served cool, as they should be, they are both pretty and refreshing under a hot Italian sun. There is also a Canneto Gran Spumante.

**Casteggio.** A general name for a wide range of the white wines of the Oltrepo, most of them made from Cortese, Trebbiano and Malvasia grapes, though there are variants. Lightish yellow in colour, dry and refreshing. See also under Clastidio.

**Castelli di Calepio.** Undistinguished light red and white wines, drunk young, the whites often sweet and the reds *frizzante*, but offering a rather confusing inconsistency.

**Cellatica.** Precisely similar to the other Lake Garda red wine, Botticino (*q.v.*).

**Chiaretto di Cellatica.** Pink version of the above, very popular in Milan and Brescia.

**Chiaretto del Garda.** The distinction is not always clear in these parts between *chiaretto*, *rosato* and even *rosso*. The red wines of this Riviera Bresciana coast of Lake Garda are light in colour: the *rosés* deeper in shade than comparable French wines. All are drunk cool, like their very near relatives, the Bardolino and the Valpolicella of the opposite, Veronese, shore. Delightful light luncheon wines, all the more refreshing for the slightly bitter after-taste offered by some, made from Gropello, Schiava, Berzamino and Corva grapes, and drunk young.[1] Some are found under the name of Moniga del Garda, and there is a wide range of precisely or almost similar wines offered under such names as Retico, Manerba, San Felice and others, or, more simply and generally, as Vini della Riviera del Garda. The red wines of the Valtenesi region, just inland from the lakeside riviera and higher (and not to be confused with the Valtelline) are very similar. See also under (Vini delle) Colline Mantovane e del Garda.

**Chiaretto del Lago d'Iseo.** Very like the Chiaretto of Lake Garda.

**Clastidio Bianco; Clastidio Rosato; Clastidio Rosso; and Clastidium Gran Riserva.** Clastidium was the Latin name for the small town of Casteggio, centre of the wine-growing area of the Oltrepo Pavese. In three of these wines the old Roman name has been partly re-Italianized into Clastidio: it retains the old form for the Gran Riserva, a fine, sweet, golden dessert wine made from Pinot Nero and Pinot Grigio grapes and made '*in bianco*' – the must taken off the skins before it can take on their colour. 12·5°.

The white Clastidio is made from a mixture of the Italian and the Rhine Riesling (Riesling Renano), and although it never achieves the delicacy of a fine German or Alsatian wine, it is crisp and fresh. The red and the *rosato* are made from the Barbera, Croattina and Uva Rara grapes, the *rosato* being taken off the skins earlier. 11°–12°.

**Colli dei Frati.** Red wines from near Bergamo, made of Corva, Sangiovese and

---

[1] According to Mr Gerald Asher, a great deal of Chiaretto del Garda is now being made exclusively of Merlot.

Barbera grapes, fairly light and dry, and usually drunk young. Similar wines are called Giuramento, Pontido and Val San Martino.

**Colline Mantovane and Colline del Garda (Vini delle).** A wide range of red, white and *rosé* wines from the region that lies between the southern shores of Lake Garda and the city of Mantua, linking those vineyards that lie between the lake and Brescia (whence come the wines already referred to under Chiaretto del Garda) and the Bardolino–Valpolicella area, to be listed later in the section devoted to the wines of the Veneto. All three regions produce similar wines: clear, light or lightish red wines, to be drunk cool, like the whites and the pinks. Some of the best wines of this particular district are also referred to generally as '*vini del Serraglio*',[1] and other minor commune names to be noted include those of Monzambano, Cavriana, Volta and the battlefield of Solferino. In his *Dizionario del Gourmet* Felice Cùnsolo claims to detect in the reds of this region a slight taste of almonds, and in the whites (which, incidentally, tend to throw a deposit, unsightly but harmless) a scent of lemons.

**Colline Rocciose.** See under Botticino.

**Croattina.** Some of the red Oltrepo wines made from this grape are sold under that name alone, but those with any distinction have a more precise district, commune or brand name.

**Domasino.** Local white wine, rather light, made near Como from a mixture of Trebbiano, Cortese and other grapes.

**Doppo Secco.** See Montevecchia.

**Forzato di Valtellina.** Strong, sweet red dessert wine from the mountain country near Sondrio, almost at the Swiss frontier. Tirano is a centre of its production – an ancient town that suffered heavily in the massacre of the Valtelline Protestants of 1620 that inspired Milton's 'Avenge, O Lord, thy slaughter'd Saints . . . .'

**Fracia.** Red and white wines of the Valtelline. The *bianco* (12·5°–13°) is fuller-bodied than other white wines of the district; the *rosso* (12°–13°) is a fine wine, closely related, though inferior, to Sassella. (See Valtelline Red Wines.)

**Franciacorta.** A light red wine from the slopes to the south of Lake Ideo, made from Barbera, Berzamino, Sangiovese, along with certain white grapes, and similar to the other lakeside wines of Lombardy and the Veneto, though with perhaps a more marked bouquet than some. 10°–11°.

**Frecciarossa.** This is one of the relatively few examples in Italy of a widely recognized and widely accepted *appellation* pertaining to a single grower – and one with a much smaller property than the great Chianti families of Tuscany. The vineyards of the village of Frecciarossa, near Casteggio, in the Oltrepo Pavese, belong to the Odero family, having been bought and developed by the father of the present owner, Dott. Giorgio Odero, who has devoted himself for the past forty years to producing the finest possible wines, all estate-bottled, as carefully as by any *château*-proprietor of Bordeaux. (Indeed, Dott. Odero rather fancies the word '*château*', which is what he uses himself on his labels.)

There are four Frecciarossa wines: all have the name Frecciarossa as the most prominent word on the label, but each has its own brand name in addition. The dry white wine (brand name 'La Vigne Blanche') is made from equal quantities of Pinot Nero and Riesling Renano (the German Riesling), though the Pinot is the more noticeable

[1] There is no exotic significance: Serraglio is the name of a township in the district.

to nose and palate. It is a clear, dry wine (12°–12·5°) with a slightly bitter finish.[1] Luigi Veronelli, in his great book *Vini d'Italia*, recommends the white Frecciarossa especially as an accompaniment to oysters – not that these are encountered frequently in the Oltrepo Pavese. But then, Dott. Odero's wines are exported a great deal and can, I understand, be obtained in England through Messrs Giordano of Soho (the Frecciarossa vineyards can, in fact, boast two viceregal appointments: to Lord Linlithgow and Lord Willingdon, Viceroys of India, of all odd places to have found Italian wines).

The white demi-sec 'Sillery' (Dott. Odero named it after a friend's racehorse long before he realized that Sillery used to be the English name for a particular still champagne), is only lightly, not lusciously, sweet – rather like one of the more flowery Graves, or a good Entre deux Mers. It is made chiefly of Pinot Nero, with smaller amounts of Riesling Renano and Moscato, the proportions depending on the vintage. 12°–12·5°.

The *rosé* 'Saint George' is crisp, with a fine bouquet, made of Barbera, Croattina and Uva Rara grapes, '*vinificato in bianco*' – taken quickly off the skins. 12°–12·5°. The red 'Grand Cru' (the grower insists by his choice of brand names in French on challenging comparisons with fine French wines) is one of the best red wines of Italy, made of the same grapes as the *rosé*, four years in cask before bottling, and well repaying another four or five in bottle. 12°–13°. The high quality of this red Frecciarossa wine is a tribute especially to careful viticulture, vinification and bottling, for the grapes – Barbera and the others – are not considered so noble as the Nebbiolo that makes the fine wines both of Piedmont and of Lombardy (such as the Sassella) or as the Sangiovese of Tuscany. Yet I would place the wine itself in the same class.

**Giuramento.** See under Colli dei Frati.

**Gran Spumante di Canneto and Gran Spumante la Versa.** Sparkling wines, dry, semi-dry and sweet (*secco*, *semi-secco* and *abboccato*), made by the *méthode champenoise* from Pinot Nero and Pinot Grigio grapes, just as the Piedmontese makes of Asti Spumante also make their rather more expensive dry, champagne-type wines.

**Grumello.** See Valtelline red wines.

**Gussago.** Similar to Botticino (*q.v.*).

**Inferno.** See Valtelline red wines.

**Lacrima Vitis.** Strong, luscious, golden dessert wine made from the semi-dried grapes of a particular species of Moscato – the Moscato Fior d'Arancio, or orange-blossom Moscato – grown in the Santa Maria Versa district of the Oltrepo Pavese. Also found under the name of the grape, simply, and also as Gran Moscato.

**Lugana.** Undoubtedly the best white wine of the Garda district, and one of the best in the whole of Lombardy, Lugana is made from the Trebbiano (sometimes in these parts called the Torbiano) grape, and is aged in cask for as much as four years before bottling – very rare indeed with any white wine. It acquires, with this ageing in wood, a pale golden colour, and some connoisseurs find in it a taste of saffron, which I confess has so far eluded me. However that may be, it is a good wine to drink with fish, and makes a natural accompaniment to the fresh-water fish from the neighbouring lakes. 11°–13°.

**Mombrione.** See Montespinato.

[1] 'The dry white wine is of particular interest,' wrote Allan Sichel in *The Penguin Book of Wines*, 'being crisp, fragrant and refreshing.'

**Monteceresino.** Modest wines – a white, a *rosé* and a red – from the commune of the same name in the Oltrepo Pavese. The white is usually made from the Sauvignon and Italian Riesling grapes; the *rosé* and the red from Croattina and Uva Rara. The white and the *rosé*, 12°–13°; the red (which seems to be rather better of its kind than the others), 13°–13·5°.

**Montelio.** This is the name of a property near Codevilla, in the Oltrepo, specializing in wines of above average quality – red and white – usually sold under that name, but the reds also to be found under the name of Rosso di Costarsa, a prize-winner at the International Wine Fair at Ljubljana in recent years. The same grower makes a particularly good Merlot from the French grape and a Müller-Thurgau from the German hybrid, which is labelled 'Müller', simply. (It is a pleasant, well-balanced wine, but not as crisp nor as scented as German wines from the same grape). These two last wines are not entitled to the Oltrepo Pavese neck-label, as the vines are not yet accepted as being natural to the district, but the Riesling, the Cortese and the grower's other two reds are labelled. (Another grower's Rosso di Codevilla is recorded in Veronelli, along with a Roccasusella and a Rosso Montu, but they are not in the official lists.)

**Monte Napoleone.** Lightish, sweetish red wine, made from Barbera, Croattina and Uva Rara grapes in a village in the Oltrepo Pavese that used to be called Montebuono until the Corsican passed that way. 13°–13·5°.

**Montespinato.** The name given in the Cignognola Hills, in the Oltrepo Pavese, to the red wine made from the usual Barbera, Croattina and Uva Rara mixture. There is an *amabile* – semi-sweet – version. 13°–13·5°. The Mombrione of Casteggio is similar but perhaps rather finer. 12·5°.

**Montevecchio.** Dry red and white wines (sometimes called Rubicchio and Doppo Secco, respectively) grown in limited quantities in the lush Brianza district, south of Como. The white is especially well thought of, but neither is easily found outside the immediate district, where it is drunk by the rich Milanesi with villas there.

**Moscato.** The Moscato grape – many varieties of it, indeed – is grown all over Italy, and Lombardy produces sweet, scented Moscato dessert wines of varying quality under various local and brand names, among which the Moscato di Scanzo of the Valtelline, which is made from the Merera grape, and the Moscato of the Oltrepo Pavese, from the Moscato grape, are especially worth noting. The Moscato di Casteggio, also from the Oltrepo, has a singularly strong bouquet. See also under Lacrima Vitis and note, too, that a particularly rich Moscato Passito from Moscato grapes rendered even sweeter and more luscious by being semi-dried, is also to be found in the region.

A considerable quantity of a Moscato Spumante, similar and not inferior to that of Asti – some people find it lighter and better balanced – though not so well known, is produced at Casteggio, in the Oltrepo Pavese and, in the same district, co-operatives (*cantine sociale*) and private growers make a drier Gran Spumante from the Pinot grape by the *méthode champenoise*. The Santa Maria della Versa *brut* is one of the very best of all the dry Italian sparkling wines and one of the most expensive.

**Nebbiolo.** A sweet red Nebbiolo is recorded by both Luigi Veronelli and Felice Cùnsolo in their recent books as coming from Retorbido, but it does not occur in the official lists of the regional association of growers, nor have I met it. See also under Valtelline red wines.

**Perla Villa.** See Valtelline red wines.

**Pezzalunga.** See Barbera.

**Pinot dell'Oltrepo.** Good red wine is made from the French Pinot Noir in many parts of the Oltrepo, particularly around Pernice and Santa Maria della Versa, but most are named after an estate or are given a brand name by a co-operative.

**Pontida.** See under Colli dei Frati.

**Prosecco dell'Oltrepo.** In various parts, a light (10°) semi-sweet and semi-sparkling, refreshing wine, is made from a mixture of Riesling and Pinot grapes.

**Pusterla Bianca.** A rather bland, though dry, white wine grown near Brescia from the rare Invernenga grape, and not found much elsewhere. A pleasant accompaniment to light dishes. 10·5°–12·5°.

**Riesling.** The Italian and the German Riesling (Riesling Renano) are both grown fairly widely in the Oltrepo Pavese, sometimes for blending with other grapes, as in the excellent Frecciarossa (*q.v.*), sometimes used together – never separately in this region, to my knowledge – to produce a wine styled, simply Riesling, or with some special brand or place name, such as the Riesling Fiore, the Sanrocco Riesling and the Imperial Riesling of various growers and co-operatives in the area. Never so delicate nor so fragrant as the German or Alsatian Rieslings, but pleasant and refreshing wines: there is a Riesling *frizzante* made at Stradella.

**Rubicchio.** See Montevecchio.

**San Colombano.** 'Worth bottling in good years' is Felice Cùnsolo's comment in his *Dizionario del Gourmet* on this light, often *frizzante*, red wine – along with a white wine of the same name, even less distinguished – the only wine grown in the province of Milan itself.

**Sangue di Giuda.** Rather sweet, frothy red wine, made from Barbera, Croattina and Uva Rara grapes in the Oltrepo Pavese.

**Sassella.** See under Valtelline red wines. Sassella is the name of a variety of grape, but the wine is made largely of Nebbiolo, with only a small admixture of Sassella.

**Tre Valli.** A deep-red table wine made between Bergamo and the Lago d'Iseo, of a mixture of Barbera, Berzamino, Merlot and other grapes, including an interesting new Italian hybrid, the 'Incroci Terzi 1 and 2', which is a cross between Barbera and the French Cabernet. Not a fine wine but agreeable, with a pleasant bouquet. 10°–11·5°.

**Tocai del Garda.** A small amount of the Tocai grape is grown near San Martino and Pozzolengo, to the south of Lake Garda. This is a much sweeter wine than that made from the same grape – and deservedly better known – in Venezia Giulia (*q.v.*). 12°–14°.

**Val San Martino.** See under Colli dei Frati.

**Valtelline Red Wines.** The River Adda flows east to west into Lake Como, just inside the northern frontier of Italy, entering the lake at Còlico. Its steep northern bank, stretching either side of Sondrio, is terraced with vineyards, the vines trained over frames, benefiting from the southern aspect, the sunshine intensified – as it is in the Rheingau – by reflection from the surface of the water. Here are grown the great red wines of Lombardy: Sassella, Grumello and Inferno being the most highly esteemed, and usually in that order, with Perla Villa (sometimes called Villa, simply), Fracia and Valgella as rather less distinguished members of the family and Valtellina Rosso as the general name for the common wines of the district.

As in Piedmont, the Nebbiolo is a noble grape here (where it is also known as the Chiavennasca), but none of these wines is made exclusively of the Nebbiolo, as are the finest wines of Piedmont: eighty-five per cent is the usual proportion in Sassella, Grumello and Inferno, with the remaining fifteen per cent made up by Brugnola, Sassella, Pignola and Rossola Dura in varying degrees. The inferior wines of the region have less Nebbiolo.

There is little to choose between Sassella, Grumello and Inferno. None, to my mind, is quite so fine or quite so full in flavour as Barolo or Gattinara at its best (perhaps because they are grown higher above sea-level and farther north; perhaps because of the mixture of Nebbiolo with less distinguished grapes). But they are very good wines indeed, admirable accompaniments to roasts, grills and game, and they sometimes seem to have a more brilliant colour and a prettier nose than the Piedmontese wines, to make up for their shortcomings elsewhere. The Sassella is said to be rougher when young than the others, but with greater bottle-age (up to about six years) to show more breeding. The Grumello is said to be at its best after about four years in bottle (as is the lighter Fracia), and some people prefer it to the Sassella, as being rather softer. The Inferno usually has a greater proportion of the Brugnola grape than the others, and with it a nuttier after-taste.

None of these admirable wines is at all well known in England, nor indeed are they easily to be found in Italy outside their own region and in Liguria, but a considerable amount is exported to Switzerland, always a good market for the best Italian red wines, and a very close neighbour in this particular case.

**Vecchio Piemonte.** A Lombard wine, in spite of its name (and not to be confused with Vecchia Romagna, a brandy). This is a dry, but fruity, red wine from near Stradella. 12·5°.

In addition to the wines listed here by name there are many simple wines offered merely under regional names, such as 'Bianco Secco dell'Oltrepo', and the like, which may still bear the association's neck-label. There are also many wines, particularly in the Oltrepo, too many to list here, produced in smallish quantities, but each with its own name, whether that of a village, an owner, or the brand name of a co-operative. They can be identified in shops and restaurants, for they will always bear, in addition, the name of the type and the region, and usually of the grape, on the label.

CHAPTER FIVE

# *Trentino-Alto Adige*

UNLIKE the French-speaking region of the Val d'Aosta, which is administratively separate from Piedmont, and autonomous, the German-speaking Alto Adige – its inhabitants much more different in character and feeling from their Italian-speaking neighbours than are the Val d'Aostans – is combined with the Trentino to form a joint autonomous region that thus has an Italian-speaking majority.

Italy's sound strategic reasons for this, and the equally inevitable tensions and resentments (and international complications with Austria) are not our concern here, but they cannot be ignored by anyone visiting the superbly beautiful Alpine region that stretches from Merano south to Bolzano, for more than ninety per cent of the wine-growers here are German-speaking;[1] the wines have German names and are exported mainly to Germany, Switzerland and Austria (in that order of volume, Germany taking more than half of the total export), remaining virtually unknown to the rest of Italy. I have even been told by some, though others have denied it, that it is the unwillingness of the German-speaking growers of the Alto Adige (which in any case they prefer to call the South Tyrol) to collaborate with the Italian-speakers of the Trentino that prevents the formation of a growers' association for the whole province, to protect the names and maintain the standards of all the local wines, as the Trentino itself has recently done for its own.

Nevertheless, there is some measure of co-operation, for the Istituto Agrario Provinciale, at San Michele all'Adige, in the Italian-speaking part of the region, near Trento, a Government organization, controls the quality of all wines for export, and is a much respected adviser to both parts of the province. Nor would it be impossible for the Alto Adige to set up a *consorzio* of its own, like the Trentino's, as the Oltrepo Pavese district does within the province of Lombardy – there is certainly sufficient solidarity of feeling and community of interest among the growers.

The Trentino produces rather more wine than the Alto Adige – in the proportion, usually, of about a million hecto-litres a year to three-quarters of a million – but the Alto-Atesino wines are finer, more varied, and more valuable, and account for about ninety-seven per cent of the total wine exports of the whole province.

Throughout the province the vineyards are exceptionally trim and well cared-for, in marked contrast to some of the regions farther south. The vines, whatever their variety, and both in the Trentino and in the Alto-Adige, are trained to turn into pergolas at an angle of about 45 degrees or so to their long trunks. One of the most beautiful sights, even in Italy, is in the Alto Adige, where the climate is mild enough to grow oranges, though there is always snow to be seen on the mountains, to see the long lines of golden-leaved pergolas, in the autumn, just after the vintage, catching the sunlight, with the glittering snow-clad peaks of Alps and Dolomites in the distance.

As the two wine-growing regions of the district are so distinct, their wines shall be listed here separately.

## The Wines of Alto Adige

There are so many small growers and co-operatives in this tiny district that there are more than two hundred entries in the list of Alto-Atesino wines at the autonomous joint province's Ministry of Commerce (the Assessorato Regionale Industria e Commercio of Trentino–Alto Adige). Most of them, as in the Oltrepo Pavese, are family names, vineyard names, commune names and the brand names of co-operatives. All

[1] And even of the remaining few, some speak not Italian but Ladin.

that we can do here is to list those more general and descriptive names that derive from varieties of grape or from sizeable districts within the area, and those most likely to be met with, whether in Italy or abroad.

More than three-quarters of the production here is of red wine, more than half of which is exported, largely to Germany and Switzerland (and a smaller amount to Austria), both of which countries have a great thirst for red wines, especially those of Italy, and both of which are conveniently placed for commerce with the region and speak the same language. Mostly the whites stay at home, though a certain amount finds its way to England, where at least one firm makes something of a speciality of the Terlaner Rieslings.

Wine was grown in these parts in Roman times, and the Lex Domitiana of A.D. 90, by which the Emperor Domitian hoped to cure the results of over-production of wine in Italy by forbidding its production in the military provinces of the Rhine and the Danube (where the Romans had in fact introduced the vine) gave a great impetus to wine production in the Adige valley, whence it could be more easily transported to the thirsty legionaries than could those of Spain (whence so many of the legions came) or of the rest of Italy.

**Barzemino.** A garbled word for Marzemino (*q.v.*).

**Blauburgunder.** The German name for the black grape of Burgundy, the Pinot Noir (also labelled here as Pinot Nero or Borgogna Nero), which is grown widely throughout the whole of the province, Trentino as well as Alto Adige, but at its best in the vineyards around Caldaro, Bolzano and Terlano, where it produces a smooth, full red wine, more 'French' in style than the other red wines of the region and fairly consistent as to quality.

**Cabernet.** Grown in the Alto Adige as well as in the Trentino, and vies with the Blauburgunder as producing the finest red wine of the region. Ages well in bottle: a 1955 tasted at the end of 1964 was about the level of a really good minor *château* of the Médoc, and not so far advanced as some, which by then were showing past their best.

**Caldaro; Rosso di Caldaro; Lago di Caldaro; Caldaro Appiano.** It is under these names that these red wines are shown in all Italian works of reference, and to have four of them is in itself confusing enough: Lago di Caldaro usually indicates a rather higher quality than the simple Caldaro. What makes it all more confusing, though, is that more often than not the wines of the district are labelled Kalterer or Kalterersee, the German name for the lake, south of Bolzano, where they are grown, and in this case an *auslese* label is worth looking for. They are lightish wines, made from the Schiavone, Schiava and other grapes, popular locally and in Switzerland, and said to show some character after a year or so in cask, and a couple in bottle, but I have found the bouquet unpleasing, and the quality very variable. There is a newly created *consorzio* of growers to maintain the quality of Caldaro wines, and to issue labels.

**Caldaro di Collina.** From higher slopes above the lake than the wines mentioned above, and both stronger in flavour (though not in alcohol) and sharper. 10°–11°.

**Castel Rametz.** The name given around Merano to the Blauburgunder (*q.v.*).

**Colline Bolzano or Leitwein.** General term for the red wines, of varying quality, made from the Schiavone (or Frankenthal) and other grapes grown on the hillsides around Bolzano. Probably the best of these fairly common, but pleasant, wines are the

Santa Giustina and the Eppaner Justiner, which in spite of the similarity of name and district, seem to be made of different *cépages*. 11·5°. The Santa Maddalena of the district merits an entry of its own.

**Colline di Merano; Meranese di Collina; or Küchelberger.** Like the Bolzano wines, but from farther north, and also from Schiavone and Schiava grapes. 11°–12°.

**Gewürztraminer or Traminer Aromatico.** The people of the region claim that the Traminer of Germany and Alsace derives its name from the South Tyrolean village of Tramin, or Termeno, just south of Caldaro. Certainly the vine is well established here, though the Gewürztraminer of the region never seems to me to achieve the full fragrance of its Alsatian namesake, which I have heard Alto-Atesino growers criticize as being opulent to the point of vulgarity. In these parts it is a full, flavoury and moderately fragrant white wine, none the worse for a little bottle-age. 12·5°–13°.

**Girlaner Hugel.** The wine is red, mild and dryish and comes from Cornaiano, near Appiano. 12°.

**Guncina or Guntschna.** Soft red wine, made from Schiava grapes near Bolzano. Has a heavy bouquet and improves with bottle-age. 11·5°.

**Jungfrau.** From various parts of the Alto Adige, made from the Schiava grape – a very light, fresh, dry white wine of 11°, drunk in cafés between meals.

**Kreutzbichler.** The Bolzano name for the Blauburgunder (*q.v.*).

**Küchelberger.** See under Colline di Merano.

**Kurtatscher Leiten.** A red wine from Schiava and other grapes, very similar to those of Lake Caldaro (*q.v.*).

**Lagrein or Lagarina.** The Lagrein vine grows right up to the town boundaries of Bolzano and Gries. A very small amount is made fully red, and this is well worth looking for, but the *rosé* (Lagrein or Lagarina Rosato, or Lagreinkretzer), which is a very deep pink, is so popular, both at home and in Switzerland, for its freshness, charm and occasional slight prickle, that less and less of the red is being made. To English tastes it seems quite different from other *rosés*, and some have detected in it a slight and not unpleasing flavour of vanilla. 12°.

**Leitacher.** See under Santa Maddalena.

**Moscato Atesino.** A sweet, highly scented dessert wine (14°–15°), is made from Moscato grapes around Bolzano, Merano and elsewhere; and an unusual Moscato Rosa, made from a grape which was imported into the region thirty years or so ago from the Adriatic coast near Trieste, cherry red and smelling of roses, is grown in very small quantities at various parts of both the Alto Adige and the Trentino. A special taste, no doubt, but then I once knew a man, lower middle-class by origin, far from being a fop, and determinedly heterosexual, who ate rose-petal jam for breakfast.

**Moscato Giallo.** Similar to the above, but paler in colour, and weaker in alcohol. 13·5°.

**Müller-Thurgau.** This valuable German hybrid (Riesling × Sylvaner) is being gradually introduced into various parts of Northern Italy (see under Lombardy: Montelio) and is to be found in the Alto Adige as well as in the Trentino and the Oltrepo. Never, in my experience, as fragrant here as in Germany, but it makes a wine of obvious quality, and is always worth looking for.

**Riesling.** Although the whole region – both Alto Adige and Trentino – was under Austrian rule until 1918, and although the Alto Adige is still German both in language and in feeling, it must not be supposed, as I had long myself supposed, that the Riesling Renano – the Rhine Riesling – must have been here since time immemorial: it came to these parts from Germany no longer ago than the 1850s. (It would be interesting to know when the Riesling reached that other part of the old Habsburg Empire that is now Yugoslavia's province of Slovenia.)

It now produces in this region a charming, well-balanced wine, not perhaps so pretty as the young wines of Alsace and the Moselle, but without the underlying coarseness of so many Yugoslav Rieslings, and much to the taste of their admirers – most of them local or, at any rate, in Italy, for it is the red wines of the region that are exported, but British shippers import some very pleasant Terlaner Riesling from around the picturesque Alpine-valley village between Bolzano and Merano.

The Riesling Renano is grown in the Trentino, as well as in the Alto Adige, and there is also some Riesling Italico in the region, sometimes blended with the Renano, sometimes with other white grapes.

**Rülander, Pinot Grigio or Borgogna Grigio.** A white wine from this Pinot grape is made in most parts of the Alto Adige, but chiefly in the north. Often *frizzante*. 11°–13°.

**Santa Maddalena or S. Magdalena.** In every wine-growing region of the Northern Hemisphere there are wines that are grown on the northern bank of a river flowing east and west, or on the northern bank of a lake, deriving benefit not only from the southern exposure but also from the reflection of sunshine from the water.[1] In the Alto Adige, the Santa Maddalena, grown on the hills to the east of Bolzano, facing south across the Isarco river, is the finest of the red wines of the region, made largely from the various Schiava and Schiavone grapes, as are the commoner local wines, but with about ten per cent Lagrein, which gives it great finesse, as the sunshine gives greater body and character. Deeper in colour and fuller in flavour than the Caldaro wines, and showing its superiority in both body and bouquet, with a sort of bitter-almond back taste, after three or four years in bottle. 12°–14°. Leitacher is very similar, but with even less Lagrein, and grown on shadier slopes – it is both drier and less strong, and many people prefer it.

**Sylvaner.** Another import from Germany, which flourishes – as do the Rülander and the Traminer – in vineyards as much as 2,500 feet high in the Alpine valley that stretches up to Bressanone and the Austrian frontier. Makes a light, rather sharp, not particularly distinguished white wine, similar to the more modest Alsatians. 12°–13°.

**Terlaner.** There are both red and white Terlaner wines from the Alpine township already mentioned. The red is made from a mixture of Vernaccia, Merlot and Lagrein grapes, and should be drunk young. 10°–12°. There is also a Terlaner Merlot, with much more finesse, but not so widely known, nor perhaps so consistent, as the Merlot of the Trentino, farther south. Some of the whites are Rieslings (*q.v.*); some a mixture of Pinot Bianco and Riesling Italico, with quite a touch of style. 11°–13°.

**Termeno.** Dry, lightish red wine, to be drunk young, made from Schiava grapes in the hills around the village of Tramin (Termeno) – whence the Traminer of the Rhine is said to have come and to have derived its name – about half-way between

[1] In Italy itself, cf. the Valtelline red wines of Lombardy.

Bolzano and Trento, almost at the southern extremity of the German-speaking area. 10°–11°.

**Traminer.** Most of the Traminer of the district seems to have become Gewürz-traminer, or Traminer Aromatico, by the time the label is put on the bottle, but there is some of the more modest wine about, though the village from which the grape is said to derive its name (see above) goes in more for Schiava grapes and red wine.

**Veltliner.** A favourite wine of the region, but not known outside it, from the grape of the same name; dry, fresh and rather light, both in flavour and in alcohol (10°–12°). Much used as an accompaniment to the excellent local trout.

**Weissburgunder, or Pinot Bianco, or Borgogna Bianco.** Widely grown through-out the region, both for use as a white *ordinaire*, and also as a base (with other grapes, including the Pinot Nero) for a local sparkling wine – made by various co-operatives and private firms in the area, some by the *méthode champenoise*, some by the Charmat, or *cuve close*, method.

**Note:** Many wines of the Alto Adige with names other than those listed above are, in fact, the same or similar wines with brand, district or family names on their labels, as well as the type or the grape names. My tasting notes, for instance, include such wines as Schwanburg, Kolbenhof, Kettmeir and others, which it would be more confusing to list than it is to omit. The use of two languages, with German preferred, is an added complication.

## The Wines of the Trentino

There are fewer varieties of wine in the Italian-speaking Trentino than in the Alto Adige and, contrary to what one might expect, the Italian-speaking Trentinesi are readier to co-operate with each other, less individualistic than their German-speaking neighbours. At any rate, there is an association of the Trentino growers, one of the growers of the Isera district, and another of the co-operatives in the district, which issue between them labels for at least three of the outstanding wines of the region.

**Avio.** A *rosé* wine grown in the extreme south of the region, not far from Borghetto, just over the hills from Lake Garda, to the *chiaretti* of which it bears some resemblance. Rather bland for a pink wine; made from Teroldego, Merlot and Marzemino grapes, each of which, unblended, produces a rather more stylish wine than this. 12°–13°.

**Borgogna Bianco.** The same as the Weissburgunder (*q.v.*) of the Alto Adige.

**Cabernet.** Some is produced north of Trento: see under list of Alto Adige wines; a notable variety is the Castel S. Michele.

**Casteller.** *Rosé* wine grown in the immediate surroundings of Trento, and sometimes called Vino di Trento. Made from Schiava grapes, which give it its body, and Merlot and Lagrein, which give it delicacy. Marked bouquet, dry and – for a pink wine – rather full. 11°–12°. Some qualities are labelled Casteller Gran Rubino, and the Nova-line Casteller and Torre Franca are similar wines.

**Castelli Mezzocorona.** Soft, mild and rather fruity red wine (mostly Schiava with a large variety of others, separately and in blends – a Pinot Nero from here won a gold medal at Ljubljana in 1964) made in the valley of the Adige, north of Trento, at the limit of the Italian-speaking region, across the river from San Michele all'Adige, where the Istituto Agrario is. 12°–12·5°. Protected by the Trentino *consorzio*, approved bottles carry a neck-label showing one of the *castelli* of the district in its vineyard.

**Garda Trentino.** Red, white and *rosé* wines are grown at the northern end of Lake Garda, the whites from Nosiola, Trebbiano and Pinot Bianco grapes, the reds and the pinks (taken earlier from the skins) from Schiava, Merlot and Lambrusco. The whites range from dry to semi-sweet and some are *frizzante*: Perla del Garda is perhaps the best. The reds and pinks are all dry and the red and pink Val del Sarca are better than most. All about 10°–12°.

**Marzemino.** Red wine from the grape of that name, grown pretty well all over the southern part of the Trentino, but chiefly around Isera, south of Trento. It has the distinction of having been mentioned by the librettist of *Don Giovanni* as '*l'eccelente Marzemino*'. It is a biggish wine, that has suffered some loss of reputation since Mozart's time because of over-production, but a *consorzio* of Isera growers is now making serious efforts to rehabilitate it, and awards appropriate labels to approved wines. There is also a *rosé*. 11·5°–12°.

**Merlot.** The French Merlot grape produces a stronger, fuller red wine in the Trentino than in the Friuli, the Veneto and elsewhere in Italy; certainly ranks with Santa Maddalena (*q.v.* under Alto Adige) as one of the outstanding red wines of the region; and is in great demand from Germany and Switzerland. 12°–13°. One grower is said to produce a dessert Merlot.

**Moscato and Moscato Rosa.** See under the wines of Alto Adige. Both are produced in the Trento, where the San Vigilio is well thought of.

**Negrara.** Dry, full red wine made from the Negrara grape near S. Michele all'Adige.

**Nosiola.** Dry golden wine from the grape of the same name grown in the Val di Cembra, just north of Trento. Perhaps the most common white wine of the region after Vernaccia (*q.v.*). 10·5°.

**Novaline Bianco.** Rather full-flavoured white wine, made from a mixture of Pinot Bianco and Italian Riesling grapes, and a sounder table wine than its fancy bottle would suggest. 11·5°–12°.

**Novaline Casteller.** See under Casteller.

**Passito di Arco.** Rich, sweet dessert wine, made from dried grapes near Arco, the pretty little resort at the head of Lake Garda.

**Perla del Garda.** See under Garda Trentino.

**Riesling.** Grown in various parts of the Trentino: see under wines of the Alto Adige.

**San Zeno.** See under Vallagarina Rosso.

**Sorni Bianco.** Rather delicate white wine, made from Nosiola and the hybrid Müller-Thurgau (Riesling×Sylvaner) grapes in the San Michele all'Adige district, mainly for local consumption.

**Sorni Rosso.** Lightish red wine, with a pleasing bouquet, made chiefly from Schiava grapes, in the same region as the Sorni Bianco (*q.v.*), much of it exported to Switzerland. 11°–12°.

**Teroldego (or Teroldico) Rotaliano.** Protected by the Consorzio per la Difesa del Vino Classico Trentino, and accorded its neck-label, this big red wine, made from the grape of the same name in the beautiful vineyards on either side of the Noce river, north-east of Trento, is the backbone of the region's wine production. It is full-flavoured – even coarse – with a rather bitter, nutty back-taste, and various qualities are produced: to be drunk young, to be aged in bottle, and also for blending with other red wines, to give them body, as are the wines of the South of France. Some consider it the finest red wine of the area, when at its best, but the English amateur, his taste formed by French wines, will hardly rank it as high as the Merlot, the Cabernet or the Santa Maddalena, though it has an enjoyable robustness of character when aged in bottle. The local *consorzio* issues a numbered neck-label showing a gold crown and crossed keys on a red ground.

**Torre Franca.** See under Casteller.

**Val del Sarca.** See under Garda Trentino.

**Vallagarina Bianco.** White wine of the Isera region, made chiefly from Vernaccia grapes.

**Vallagarina Rosso.** Robust red wine (one Italian writer's description of it is *di buona stoffa*), made from a mixture of Schiavona, Marzemino and Merlot grapes, which combine to give it a deep colour with a slightly bitter – some of the locals describe it as being salty – taste, varying in quality, but worthy of attention: the San Zeno Rosso is well spoken of. 11·5°–12°.

**Valdadige.** The common red wine of the district, rather light and nutty, made from a mixture of Teroldego, Lambrusco, Schiava and Merlot grapes. 11°. A better grade, rather stronger (11·5°–12°), is exported, its quality controlled by the Istituto Agrario.

**Vernaccia Bianca, Vernaccia Trentina or Vernaccia di Aldeno.** A very light white wine, grown from the grape of the same name, fermented without its stalks, which makes it delicate for so common a wine. Often slightly *frizzante*. Made near Trento. 10°–10·5°.

**Vino Santo.** Often labelled, and always referred to, as Vin Santo – sometimes even as one word – a sweet dessert wine made in most parts of Italy. But those who like this kind of wine hold that the Vino Santo of the Trentino is outstanding, made from Nosiola, Trebbiano and Pinot grapes, dried on straw after the vintage and not pressed until as late as the following Easter. (Hence the term Vino Santo – made in Holy Week. Though I do not know what happens if Easter is unusually late or unusually early.) Aged in cask for four to six years, the Vino Santo from this region is a heavily scented, amber-coloured dessert wine, with more individuality than most and – considering its lusciousness – some delicacy.

**Note:** A certain amount of Negrara and Lambrusco grapes is grown in the Trentino, producing wines of moderate quality, and there is a sweet, sparkling Recioto del Trentino, so called from the word *recie*, a corruption of *orecchie* – 'ears' – only the 'ears' or outermost grapes of each bunch being gathered, these having had the most sunshine, and yielding most sweetness.

CHAPTER SIX

# *The Veneto*

IN output alone the Veneto would rank high among the wine-growing regions of Italy – in some years second only to Apulia. But it ranks high in quality, too, for the light red wines of Lake Garda, such as Valpolicella and Bardolino, and of the Valpantena, even if not so distinguished as the fine red wines of Piedmont, or as the best Chiantis, are wines of grace and charm; while Soave, from the hills between Vicenza and Verona, is unquestionably one of the finest white wines of Italy.

Geographically this is a varied region, stretching from the shores of Lake Garda to the lagoons of the Adriatic; from the foothills of the Lessini Mountains and of the Dolomites to the plains of the Po. It has always been a rich region, too – from Roman times, when Livy was born in Padua; through the golden age when Venice held the gorgeous East in fee; later, when Palladio built villas by the Brenta for those who had inherited the fortunes thus made; and now, when German and American and British and Swedish tourists pour money into the coffers of the hotels and the restaurants of Venice and of the lakeside resorts.

Tourism exacts its penalties: at the smartest hotel in Verona they offer you a 'Romeo and Juliet' cocktail (though no steak-house in Venice that I know of advertises a pound of flesh as the speciality of the house). But it can mean, too, as it does in the Veneto, that there is a sizeable enough local demand to encourage wine-growers to go in for good wines, carefully made. (To say nothing of the German, Swiss and Austrian markets for the red wines of Garda.)

I was once a member of the jury at a Venice Film Festival, and at a grand party given by the city for the jurymen I found myself at the splendid buffet cheek by jowl with a French diplomatist. He demolished his *langouste* as greedily as I did, but when he came to his glass of Soave he sniffed it suspiciously, tasted it dubiously, and then turned to me with 'You know, they call a lot of things *vino* in Italy that we should never call *vin* in France'. Politer to him than he was to his hosts, I forebore to say how much better this admirable, fresh, dry wine was than many a so-called Chablis or Pouilly-Fuissé that I had drunk, not only in English oyster-bars but in Paris restaurants that ought to have known better: the wines of the Veneto in general, and Soave in particular, are probably as consistent as any in Italy. (The growers can hardly be held responsible for what some of the Soho wine-merchants tell us is Valpolicella: I doubt if it was sold to them as that.) I have never had a Soave, it is true, to rank with a really distinguished white burgundy, but then I have never had one as nasty as some of the 'Chablis' I have had in my time.

## Wines of the Veneto

**Arcugnano.** Red and white wines of the Colli Berici (*q.v.*).

**Arzignano.** Dry red and white wines from near Vicenza. Light, unimportant table wines – the white is also known as Durello.

**Barbarano.** Red and white wines of the Colli Berici (*q.v.*).

**Bardolino.** Bright, fresh, clear red wine made from the Corvina and Negrara grape – for colour and body respectively, according to Mr Gerald Asher: with Molinara and Rondinella for brilliance and suppleness, all used together, as in Valpolicella and Valpantena (*qq.v.*). The Bardolino wines are grown on the eastern shores of Lake Garda, around the southward-looking bay on which Garda and the charming village of Bardolino stand, as far south as Lazise, opposite the slender outline of Sirmione, where the soil produces rather lighter wines than do the heavier clays of the Valpolicella villages farther inland. There are Italians who talk and write of Bardolino as being a wine worth ageing in bottle, as a wine to go with roast meats – Paolo Monelli claims that it is only with age that it loses a slight sweetness he finds in all the wines of this region – but my own preference is to drink it young (when it is often a little *frizzante*) and cool, which is the way that most of it seems to be drunk locally. I have had a great fondness for this charming and refreshing wine ever since I found that Max Beerbohm used to take a glass of it every day at his villa in Rapallo at what a lesser mortal would have referred to as his teatime, and my affection for it was increased when I visited the village of Bardolino itself a couple of years ago on the day the vintage was celebrated, to see the peasant wine-growers trooping happily in to sell their fresh, young wine at the tasting-booths – threepence for an eighth of a litre, which is quite a substantial glass – along with salami sandwiches and crisply-fried freshwater sardines straight from the waters of Garda. A young priest officiated at the microphone, waxing more and more eloquent as they went on filling his glass.

It is certainly one of the most charming wines of Italy – which does not mean that it is a great wine, but charm too has its place at the table. 9·5°–11·5°. Protected by the association of Veronese growers, and shares with Valpolicella and Soave a neck-label showing the Roman arena at Verona (though there was news recently of an association being set up purely of Bardolino growers).

**Breganze.** On the southern foothills of the high country between Lake Garda and the Piave, near the towns of Breganze and Thiene (where there are remarkable Veronese frescoes in a Colleoni castle), they grow red and white wines of some interest the whites (11°–12°) from a wide mixture of local grape varieties, dry and pleasantly fragrant, the reds from Negrara, and other local varieties, good light table wines not unlike the Lake Garda wines. 11°–12°.

**Brendola Bianco.** One of the wines of the Colli Berici (*q.v.*).

**Cabernet.** Grown here in the Veneto, as in the neighbouring provinces (see under the wines of the Alto Adige). Produces some very good red wines, notably in the hills around Vicenza (the Colli Vicentini), Breganze, Barbarano and San Dona di Piave. The Colfortin Rosso is especially highly thought of. 11°–13°. A Cabernet of the Valdobbiadene won a gold metal at the Ljubljana Exhibition in 1964.

**Cabernet-Merlot.** This classic combination, responsible for the great clarets, produces a lighter but moderately claret-like wine in a small region towards the mouth of the Piave, almost at the Venetian lagoon, between San Dona di Piave and Portogruaro, near the Lido di Iesolo. Sometimes to be found in Venice and Iesolo restaurants, but production is small. 10·5°.

**Cartizze.** A sparkling Prosecco (*q.v.*) from Valdobbiadene (*q.v.*).

**Colfortin Rosso.** See under Cabernet.

**Clinton.** An American vine, grown near Padua, producing a light red wine with a marked bouquet, very low in alcohol (8°–10°), much appreciated locally, but perhaps chiefly for its lightness.

**Colli di Asolo-Maser and Colli di Conegliano.** White wines made from Prosecco, Verdiso and other grapes on the hills on either side of the Piave river, where it leaves the high country for the plains that stretch to the Gulf of Venice. Asolo and Conegliano are both charming small towns, the latter very much and very obviously a wine centre. The wines are fresh and pleasing when young, but are said to maderize very quickly: the Conegliano wines are said to be finer than those of Asolo. 10°–11°.

**Colli Berici and Riviera Berici.** Just south of Vicenza are the Berici hills where, around 1870, a number of French vines were introduced, among them Sauvignon and the white Pinot, which are blended with Italian varieties, and give some pleasant full white wines, with a touch of sweetness but also a hint of bitter almonds. 10°–12°. The red wines from Merlot, Molinara, Negrara and Raboso Veronese grapes are sometimes a little astringent, but can be good table wines. An association of growers has just been set up.

**Colli Euganei.** White wines from the hills to the west of Padua, made from Garganega, Prosecco and other grapes, with a certain amount of Riesling, both German and Italian, which gives lightness and delicacy to quite an agreeable local wine for fish dishes. 10°–11°. There is a Moscato Spumante from this area, too, sometimes known as Moscato dei Colli Euganei, sometimes as Moscato d'Arquà (8° upwards) and there are said to be some local red wines, too, dry, with a flavour of raspberries, one of them called Rosso del Venda, but I have found it little in evidence.

**Colli di Valdobbiadene.** Two types of white wine: a still dry and a sweetish *frizzante* – sometimes fully *spumante*, even – made chiefly from Prosecco grapes in the Piave valley, not far from the famous battlefield of Vittorio Veneto. The dry (11°) is drunk, as a 'wine of the year', when it is light and fresh, with a hint of bitterness in the after-taste; the other, though no stronger alcoholically, is a dessert wine. Most of the *spumante* come from the small parish of Cartizze, in the Valdobbiadene, and take its name.

**Colli Vicentini Centrali.** Some authorities, and many of the locals, distinguish between the Colli Vicentini and the Colli Berici wines, but the distinction is slight geographically, and non-existent viticulturally. Here I have classed all the wines worth mention as being of the Colli Berici, as they are in most Italian works of reference.

**Colli Veronesi.** General name given to the wide range of wines grown north and north-west of Verona, including such well-known growths as Bardolino, Valpolicella and others. All such wines that are of any consequence are listed here under their more specific names.

**Colline Trevigiane.** Modest white wines, most of them from the Prosecco grape, grown along the lower reaches of the Piave.

**Colognola.** A red and a pink wine are made near Soave, more famous for its white, of the same mixture of grapes as the Colli Veronesi wines (*q.v.*), such as Valpolicella, to which both the red and the pink Colognola are quite similar, for most of the wines of this district are betwixt and between, if rather nearer red than pink.

**Costoza.** One of the Colli Berici wines (*q.v.*). The white Costoza used to be known as 'the ladies' wine' – for no special reason that I can discover: it is no more ladylike than any of the others. The red Costoza is rather better than most of these local wines, and seems to me sometimes to have something of a claret 'nose'.

**Durello.** See under Arzignano.

**Fara Vicentino.** A red wine very similar to those of Breganze (*q.v.*). 13°.

**Fonzarso or Fonzaso.** A red wine from near Bellino (where there is very little wine-growing), made from a mixture of grapes that includes Merlot, Barbera and a rare local variety called Nera Gentile di Fonzarso. It is full-bodied and dry. 10°–12°. There is also a dry white Fonzarso that is very hard to come by.

**Friularo.** Made south of Padua, inland from the picturesque fishing port of Chioggia, from a grape that owes its name to having been introduced in the seventeenth century from Friuli. A red wine, light in alcohol (10°) and rather sharp in taste. Unlike most other red wines of the region, it ages well, because of its acidity, and has many admirers. The Friularo from Bagnoli is especially highly thought of.

**Garganega di Gambellara and Gambellara Rosso.** White wine made of Garganega grapes in the hills south of Vicenza that face those of Berici across a small river valley. Of mainly local interest: one is told that at its best it bears some resemblance to Soave (*q.v.*). But this may be when finer wines are made locally by adding Sauvignon and Pinot Bianco to the Garganega grape (though they are not used in Soave). The same district produces a less important red wine, and also a Gambellara Passito, or *vin santo*, in very small quantities, a very good dessert wine.

**Malvasia di Nanto.** A light, sweet dessert wine from near Vicenza, the digestive properties of which, according to Cùnsolo, are so effective that people take it in order to *fare il rutesin* – to belch.

**Marzemino Trevigiano.** An unimportant light red wine, made from the grape of the same name, in the same area as the whites of the Colline Trevigiane (*q.v.*), usually semi-sweet to sweet.

**Merlot.** Red wine from this noble red grape is made pretty well all over these parts of Italy – the Merlot is said to be fifth in quantity of the vines grown in the three Venetos. The Merlot of the Veneto itself, the region we deal with here, is neither so strong nor so full in flavour as that of the Trentino (*q.v.*).

**Montegalda and Montelungo.** Rather flavoury, dry, light red wines produced for drinking young in the hills between Padua and Vicenza. 11°–12°.

**Orgiano Bianco.** One of the wines of the Colli Berici (*q.v.*).

**Prosecco.** This is one of the most widely grown vines of the North of Italy, from the Oltrepo to the Friuli. In the Veneto it is the main grape for the white wines of the various hill districts already listed here. In the Conegliano district, along the Piave, some of the wines are known by its name rather than that of the district. There are sweet and dry, still and sparkling, versions, and the sparkling Prosecco Spumante di Conegliano is really quite good. 11°. A Prosecco of the region won a gold medal at Ljubljana in 1964, and the Prosecco wines of both Conegliano and Valdobbiadene are protected and labelled by a local growers' association.

**Raboso.** This is the name of a local variety of grape, from which red wine is made pretty well all over the flatter middle part of the Veneto, and particularly between the Piave and Livenza rivers (when it is called the Raboso or Rosso – a finer version – or Rubino de Piave (*q.v.*), and around Padua, where it is called the Raboso Veronese).

These two main types differ a little in *cépage*, but both mix Merlot, Cabernet, the Italian
Riesling and some of the local Tocai (*q.v.* under Friuli-Venezia-Giulia) with the Raboso
grape. With the exception of the Rubino, the Piave wines, especially, are roughish – it
may be that the grape and the wine are so called because of this (*rabbioso* means furious,
angry or froward), or perhaps because of a tumultuous fermentation – and although
some people drink them young, like the wines of the Lakes, most Italian authorities
I have consulted claim that the Raboso del Piave wines become unexpectedly round
and mellow with bottle-age – some counsel putting them away for as much as ten
years. The Veronese Raboso is another matter, for this is certainly pleasanter young,
and therefore has less to gain by ageing: I have thought that this may be because it has
less of the Raboso grape in the *cépage*, and more of the lighter varieties. 10°–12°. There
are also sweet, semi-sparkling versions of the Veronese.

**Recioto Bianco or Recioto Soave.** Sweet white wine made from Garganega and
other grapes, largely around Soave, that have been specially picked (see below) and
allowed to become semi-dried. 13°–14°.

**Recioto.** Red wine made of much the same *cépage* as Bardolino, Valpolicella and
Valpantena, and from the same general area, as well as from the hills around Soave,
save that only the 'ears' of the bunches of grapes are gathered which have had more sun
and more ripening than the others.[1] A fuller, heavier wine is the result – not, to every
taste, as light or agreeable as the other red wines of the same districts. Indeed, I have
found the so-called Recioto Amarone, which is held to be the best of its kind, at once
harsh and flabby, although the wine I tasted had plenty of bottle-age. There is also a
Recioto Nobile, a sweetish red sparkler that soon loses its bubble in the glass but keeps
a sharp prickle – quite an amusing wine, if no more than that. 13°–14°.

**Rubino del Piave.** Dry red wine, from the same district as the Raboso (*q.v.*) but
better bred and better cared for; I find it delicate by Italian standards, but one writer
has described it as 'peppery' – perhaps he means tasting of sweet peppers. What I have
found myself is a hint of clove in the scent. 12°.

**Soave.** One of the best known and, deservedly, one of the most highly regarded of
the white wines of Italy, made largely of Garganega grapes, but with about twenty
per cent Trebbiano, in the immediate vicinity of the picturesque walled town of Soave,
at the southern edge of the hill country between Verona and Vicenza. Many Italian
white wines are fermented on the skins, to give body and staying power, but the
best Soave is made in the French way, which gives greater freshness and fragrance.
Sometimes likened by Italian enthusiasts to Chablis, but it is not so delicate as Chablis
at its best, though it is a firm, well-balanced wine, and less mawkish than Chablis at its
worst, with an agreeable hint of floweriness in its bouquet. Should be drunk fairly
young and very cool, when it goes extremely well with the fish-fries of neighbouring
Venice – it is to be found in every Venice restaurant (though in pretty varying qualities).
Protected, along with Bardolino and Valpolicella, by the local growers' association,
and acknowledged bottles carry the Veronese neck-label. 10°–11°.

**Sona-Custoza.** A light red wine, similar to Bardolino and Valpolicella (*qq.v.*) and
grown just south of their districts, in the area to the west of Verona. Always drunk
'*nell'annata*' – in its first year. 12°.

---

[1] Cf. 'Note' under Trentino-Alto Adige.

**Terrematte.** A Barbera (*q.v.* under Piedmont) grown at Montegalda, near Vicenza – rather more heady than its Piedmontese cousin, but a respectable table wine, produced only in very limited quantities.

**Tocai.** A little is grown at Lison, part of Portogruaro, near Venice, but see under Friuli-Venezia-Giulia.

**Torcolato.** Golden dessert wine made from semi-dried Garganega and Durella grapes, mostly in the vicinity of Breganze, north of Vicenza. 14°–16°.

**Ussolaro.** A sweet *vin santo* made at Brendola, near Vicenza, from Ussalara grapes – a wine fast disappearing and unknown to me.

**Val d'Alpone, Val di Illasi, Val Mezzane, Val Squaranto and Val Tramignia.** Red wines of the Colli Veronesi, not unlike those, better known, of Valpantena (*q.v.*).

**Valpantena.** Light red wine, very similar to Bardolino and Valpolicella (*qq.v.*), made of the same grapes, but in the valley that runs north from Verona rather to the east of the districts where the others come from. It is said by experts to be the merest shade drier and more austere than they, but I confess that I find it hard to detect the difference from Valpolicella. 11·5°–12·5°.

**Valpolicella.** The best known and the most popular abroad – in Germany, Britain and the United States – of all the wines of the region, and rightly so, for Valpolicella is a wine of considerable grace, with only a hint of underlying sweetness, suitable to drink with almost any dish, and for almost any climate. Ideally, though, it is a wine to drink cool, with light summery dishes: it is made of the same grapes as Bardolino and Valpantena (*qq.v.*), but grown in rather heavier soil, in hills away from the lakeside slopes where Bardolino is grown and – probably because of the soil – very slightly fuller in flavour and deeper in colour.[1] This slightly greater fullness may be the reason why some of the better Valpolicellas lend themselves to ageing in bottle – more, at any rate, than the other two wines of the district – though even then they are not the wines I would choose myself for laying down. 11°–12°. Protected and labelled by the local growers' association.

**Verdiso.** Dry white wine grown fairly widely around Treviso, from the grape of this name, to be drunk very cool and young. 9·5°–11°.

**Vespaiolo.** Light, sparkling, sweet but not too heavily luscious dessert wine grown near Breganze. 11·5°–12·5°.

CHAPTER SEVEN

# *Friuli-Venezia-Giulia*

THERE are Austro-Hungarian influences on the architecture and on the gastronomy of this north-eastern corner of Italy, and some of the vines nearest to Trieste grow

---

[1] According to Mr Gerald Asher it is the Corvina vine, particularly, that does well in the Valpolicella clay, and it is the Corvina that is the principal grape in both Valpolicella and Bardolino.

in Yugoslav soil. Yet the wines of this frontier region owe more to France than to Austria or to Yugoslavia – more than to Hungary, too, for the Tocai of the great plain of Friuli is not the Tokay of the great Hungarian plain. The Gamay, for instance, has been recently introduced, and does well, and the Cabernet of these parts makes a sound red wine.

There seems to be less parochial pride in the local wines here than in most of the other regions of Italy: many of the excellent fish restaurants of Trieste, for instance, are as likely to offer you a Soave from the Veneto, or a Verdicchio from the Marches, as they are a Tocai, which they profess themselves flattered to be asked for, yet often are unable to produce.

No other part of Italy is so modest about its own wines, but then this part of Italy – Trieste, at any rate – is like no other. The high-cheekboned, snub-nosed market women sitting behind their stalls under the Serbian Orthodox church by the quay, with the Church Cyrillic letters on its facade, may be chattering and chaffering in Italian, but they look like Slavs, and in the Café Danubio opposite I have heard a bearded priest who was speaking Italian and reading an Italian newspaper call for a *slivovitz* as his aperitif.

Trieste is in Italy now because the Triestini desired so intensely to be Italians, and yet at Miramare they put on every summer a *son et lumière* romanticization of the life and death of Maximilian and his Carlotta; where else in Italy will you find them sentimentalizing over a Habsburg, and in German? So perhaps it is fitting that the Hungarian goulash that has become acclimatized in Trieste as an Italian dish should be accompanied by a Merlot, or a Cabernet, and the iota Triestina, which is an aromatic sort of sauerkraut, with a Riesling Renano from almost on the Yugoslav frontier.

## The Wines of Friuli-Venezia-Giulia

**Borgogna Bianco, Borgogna Grigio and Borgogna Rosso.** Red and white wines made in various parts of Friuli from the Pinot Bianco, Pinot Grigio and Pinot Nero grapes (under which names the wines themselves are sometimes found).

The *bianco* is a fairly light wine, both in texture and in colour, usually dry. 10°–13°. Quite a lot is exported and there is a *spumante* version. The *grigio* is a more deeply coloured white wine, and is the same as the Rülander of the Alto Adige (*q.v.*). The *rosso* (the same as the Blauburgunder of the Alto Adige, just as the *bianco* is the Weissburgunder) is not so plentiful as the others. It is a reasonably smooth local table wine, perhaps a little more like French wines – like the commoner wines of Burgundy, say – than some Italian reds, but of no great distinction. 11°–12·5°.

The local growers' association of Friuli protects and issues numbered heraldic necklabels for various of these wines under the names of Pinot Bianco, Pinot Grigio, Pinot Nero; Bianco and Rosso dei Colli Friulani, dei Colli Goriziani and others.

**Cabernet.** The Cabernet of the region is produced from a mixture of Cabernet Franc and Cabernet Sauvignon, and is a full big wine – much more so, whenever I have been able to compare them, than the Cabernet of the Alto Adige – and certainly not to be drunk young, when it is harsh and astringent. Veronelli recommends not less than three years in bottle, and says that it is at its best after eight. That of Buttrio is said to be especially good. The wine is protected and labelled by the local growers' association. 12°–13°.

**Caneva or Bianco Misto di Caneva.** Simple, dry, white table wine from near Udine, to be drunk very young. 10°–11°.

**Collio or Collio Goriziano.** White wine made from a mixture of Tocai Friulano, German and Italian Rieslings, and a number of other varieties, grown chiefly in the hills that encircle Gorizia. Similar to Caneva (above), but with rather more style. It is drunk young – '*nell'annata*' – when it has a fresh taste and a flowery bouquet: some experts claim to detect a slight taste of nutmeg. 11°. The Borgogna Rosso (above) produced in this district is also sometimes referred to as Collio Rosso.

**Gamay.** Imported quite recently from France, the Gamay does very well in the gently hilly country north-east of Udine, producing a clear, brilliant red wine, with an underlying sweetness, especially when young, becoming rather more austere when older, with a faint strawberry taste, and a high alcoholic content, which means that it will 'travel' well and stand up to ageing, both in cask and in bottle.[1] There should be quite a future for this wine in Italy, where the climate and much of the country-side would seem to be suitable, and where many of the local red wines could well be improved upon. 13°–14°.

**Malvasia del Collio and Malvasia di Ronchi.** The first comes from near Gorizia, and the other (which is sometimes called Malvasia Bianca Friulana) from nearer the coast. The same wine, though – deep yellowish in colour, full in flavour, that goes well with the local richer dishes. 11·5°–12·5°. Protected and labelled by the local growers' association.

**Merlot.** Another French grape that is doing well in Friuli though it is not such a recent innovation as the Gamay, for it is grown quite widely throughout Northern Italy, and has been for half a century or so. The Merlot of this region is not so distinguished as that of the Trentino – perhaps not so elegant, either, as that of the Veneto – and is a notably lighter wine than the Gamay. 12°. Protected by the local growers' association, which issues a heraldic neck-label.

**Monfalcone.** Red and white wines of some quality are produced in this district very near Trieste, the whites including Sauvignon, Tocai and Malvasia; the reds Cabernet and Merlot.

**Piccolit or Picolit.** This golden dessert wine, made from the Piccolit or Picolit grape, semi-dried, was once the great pride of Friuli, but the vine is vulnerable to the disease of 'floral abortion', and many of the finest vineyards have been destroyed. Professor Giuseppe Dalmasso has been experimenting with crossing the Piccolit vine with the Tocai, Ribola, Verduzzo and others, and a certain amount of the wine is still produced from these immune hybrids, a certain amount from the small remnant of the original Piccolit stock. I do not share the view, expressed by some of its more perfervid Italian admirers, that Piccolit is a rival to Château d'Yquem, though it may reasonably be described as the Château d'Yquem of Italy, which is very much another matter. Certainly it has a finesse lacking in most of the other Italian dessert wines, and in

[1] There is more than one Gamay in France, but none is regarded as a 'noble' grape in Burgundy, though the Petit Gamay is considered as such in the Beaujolais.

Victorian times it was much admired at the Austrian, French and English courts. 12°–14°. Protected and labelled.

**Prosecco Triestino.** This is rather complicated. The Prosecco grape, which we have already come across in the Veneto, is named after the district of Trieste around the Miramare. But the Triestini call the grape not Prosecco but Glera, and the wine called Prosecco Triestino is named after the place and *not* the grape, which is not highly regarded in its native district. The wine is, in fact, made from a mixture of Malvasia, Sauvignon and Garganella, as well as Prosecco; is sometimes known as Malvasia Triestina (a particularly good one is said to come from San Dorligo); and is appreciated to the extent that the Malvasia and the Sauvignon fragrance come through. It is a lightish, sweetish white wine, served with fruit. 12°–14°.

**Raboso Rosato.** Made from Verduzzo grapes (and so sometimes called Verduzzo di Ramandolo), semi-dried, grown in the foothills of the high mountains north of Udine, near Tarcento – a highly aromatic golden dessert wine, sweet but not intensely so, usually semi-sparkling, and a pleasant accompaniment, well chilled, to fresh fruit. 12°–13°. Protected and labelled by the local growers' association.

**Refosco.** Light, dry – even rather sharp – red wine, with a pretty violet tinge, made from a vine called Refosco dal Peduncolo Rosso, the Refosco with a red stalk. Varies a good deal in style and quality: there is a lighter and a darker, and a sweet Refosco made from the same grape, semi-dried. 11°–13°. Protected and labelled.

**Ribolla Gialla.** A very light, sweetish white wine, made from the grape of the same name, grown in the low country south-east of Udine. 9°–10°. There is also a fuller, sweeter variety, reaching 15°, and a Ribolla Nera that resembles the Refosco (*q.v.*).

**Riesling.** A good deal of Riesling Italico, and rather less Riesling Renano, is grown throughout the region. The Renano is to be preferred, though the Italico has the benefit of the protection and labelling of the local association.

**Sauvignon.** This grape, of French importation, is grown extensively throughout Friuli, as in other parts of Northern Italy. Here it makes a white wine of some note, straw-yellow, with something of the Sauvignon fragrance we meet in the great Sauternes and the Loire wines, for instance, and an appetizingly bitter finish. (There are also semi-sweet versions.) Protected and labelled by the local association. 12°.

**Terrano or Terrano del Carso.** A vine common to Italy and Yugoslavia, for it is grown on both sides of the frontier north-east of Trieste, though in the Italian vineyards – I cannot speak of the Yugoslav – it is being replaced by other, presumably more prolific, varieties. So there is not a great deal to be found, and I doubt whether there is any outside Trieste. A pity, for it is a wine of some character: light red, with a flowery fragrance, but a clean and refreshing acidity, to be drunk young and cool, and very low in alcohol. 9°–9·5°.

**Tocai.** No connection at all with the Tokay of Hungary, though the Hungarians once tried in the Italian courts to obtain a ruling against the Italian use of the name. But it was established that this particular vine had been grown in Friuli, and known as such for centuries, the name deriving either from a Slav word meaning 'here' (there are, of course, many Slavs in the area, and there used to be more in Habsburg times), indicating that this was 'a wine of here' – a local wine – or perhaps from a village near Gorizia once called Tocai.

In any case, the Italian Tocai is very different from the Hungarian dessert wine –

it is a dry, yellowish white wine, with a rather bitter under-taste, highly regarded in these parts, and justifiably so, as an accompaniment to the excellent fish dishes of this part of the Adriatic coast. Protected and labelled. 12°–15°.

**Verduzzo.** Golden-yellow wine, semi-sweet and sweet. 9°–11°. That of Ramondolo (*q.v.*) is fuller and stronger. Both the simple Verduzzo and that of Ramandolo are protected and labelled.

CHAPTER EIGHT

# *Emilia-Romagna*

THIS region is to Italy what Burgundy is to France – this is where the noblest dishes and the most famous cooks come from: there are more good restaurants in and around Bologna and Modena than in and around any other Italian cities of comparable size, just as Dijon and Lyons have more than any other French cities. This is the belly of Italy.

The cuisine of the region, usually referred to as Bolognese, though Modena is as distinguished a gastronomic centre, is rich and hearty, and the Romagnoli are noted for their size and their appetites. Rossini came from these parts (he was born in Pesaro just over the regional border, in the Marches, but he made his home in Bologna for many years, and the Bolognesi regard him as a native son), and it is characteristic that a *garniture Rossini* involves truffles, *pâté de foie gras*, butter and Madeira. Italians from other regions criticize the *cucina Bolognesa* as being *ingrassamento*, fattening, but it is noticeable that they gladly patronize any restaurant in their own towns that offers Bolognese cooking, and strive to be able to afford a Bolognese cook. Usually Italians are so proud of their own regions that they affect to despise every other, yet even the great Sabatini Restaurant in Florence, a temple of Tuscan gastronomy (to take only one example), boasts of the fact that not only is its *pasta* made freshly every day in its own kitchens, but by a Bolognesa.

Yet the wines of Emilia-Romagna are not the robust, full-bodied wines one would expect in a region where the cooking and the eating are so wholehearted, in the way that the wines of Burgundy go with the hearty Burgundian dishes. At its best the white Albana, for instance, though it has its touch of sweetness, is far from being a big or a luscious wine, and most of the red wines of the region (the local Sangiovese is an exception) are on the lighter rather than the fuller side.

The red wine peculiar to Emilia-Romagna is peculiar indeed – Elizabeth David has written of it that 'the most interesting and original of Italian wines . . . Lambrusco, is that oddity, a dry sparkling red wine which sounds so dubious and is in fact perfectly delicious'. It sounds dubious only, of course, because we are not used to the idea that a dry red wine should sparkle. It is not at all dubious to the Bolognesi and, oddly enough, it seems to be Americans who react most vigorously against it: Schoonmaker has described it as being 'as nearly undrinkable as a well-known wine could be', and Samuel Chamberlain records having sent this sparkling red wine back at one of Bologna's most distinguished restaurants (and Bologna's distinguished restaurants are distinguished indeed), advising those of his readers who travel in these parts always to ask for a non-sparkling wine. Myself, I am with Elizabeth David and the Bolognesi in this matter, which is to be on the side of the angels.

## The Wines of Emilia Romagna

**Albana, or Albana di Romagna.** White wine produced throughout the region, from the grape of the same name, and especially around Forlì, and near the small town of Bertinoro,[1] between Forlì and Rimini. The road from Rimini to Bologna runs along the edge of the hills, and it is on the slopes just above the road that the vines flourish. This grape retains a certain amount of unfermentable sugar, so that Albana is, as Mr Charles Bode has put it, 'definitely on the sweet side of the vaguely defined borderland that separates the clearly sweet wines from the perfectly dry ones'. Yet it is light and fresh, far from being so sickly that one could not drink it with fish, though some Albana is rather sweeter than others, and there is also a fully sweet, luscious one for dessert. Much drunk along the holiday coast from Rimini to Ravenna.[2] It is protected by the *consorzio* of the growers of the Romagna, which issues a neck-label showing a stylized white cock and bunch of grapes on a red ground. 12°–13°.

**Alionza.** Local white wine, dry but full, notable only for the Bolognese phrase '*al gd'a in di'alionza*' – 'he's fond of his glass'.

**Barbera.** A certain amount is grown near Bologna (Barbera di Maggio, or di Bologna) and near Parma (Barnera Langhirano). See under Piedmont.

**Biancale di Rimini.** A sound white wine from the grape and the place of the name – the grape being a species of Trebbiano.

**Bosco Eliceo or Rosso del Bosco.** Dry, rather sharp, deep-red wine made along the Adriatic coast from a grape called Uva d'Oro (although it is, in fact, a black grape) perhaps because of its prolific yield. All the better for a little bottle-age, when it becomes a full, mellow wine that goes well with meat dishes. 11°–12°.

**Cagnina or Canina.** A full-flavoured, dry *rosé* wine grown in small amounts in the Ravenna, Ferrara and Faenza districts. 8°–9°.

**Castelfranco.** Takes its name from a district round Modena, where a mixture of Montu, Albana, Trebbiano Romagnolo and Pinot Bianco grapes, grown together in the same vineyards, produces a dry white wine with a pleasing fragrance. 10·5°–12·5°.

**Clinton.** A little red wine is grown here from this American importation. See under Lombardy.

**Corregio.** See Lancellotta.

**Fogarina.** One of the frothy, alcoholically light, red wines of the district, made from the grape of the same name, growing on the banks of the Po, north of Parma.

---

[1] The story goes that Bertinoro gets its name from a medieval princess's having been offered Albana here in a rough mug and exclaiming, 'It should be drunk in gold!' (*vorrei berti in oro* – Bertinoro).
[2] And it is the only white wine nominated as a speciality of the house by the three Bologna restaurants starred in the *Michelin Guide for Italy* – Pappagallo, Tre Vecchi and Cesarina.

Almost violet in colour and sometimes used to blend with the lighter wines of the district. To be drunk cool. 10°.

**Fortana.** Light-bodied red wine from various parts of the Parma district, from a grape of the same name that gives a half-sweet, half-dry, semi-sparkling or *frizzante* wine, with only about 9° of alcohol. A rather finer sub-species of the Fortana grape, sometimes called Fortanina, or Fortanella, gives a lighter-looking but rather stronger, sweeter wine that is the traditional partner of the *spalla* – shoulder of pork – of San Secondo. 10·5°.

**Gutturnio.** A clear, bright red wine, made from a mixture of seventy per cent Barbera, thirty per cent Bonarda grapes, in the district west and south of Piacenza, and intended to be drunk young, as a 'wine of the year' – '*nell' annata*'. Dryish, with an underlying hint of sweetness and usually – and very rightly – served cool. This is a particularly pleasing wine of its kind and class and is likely to appeal to those who like young Beaujolais and the Lake Garda wines. 11°.

**Lambrusco.** Quite the best known and most characteristic wine of the region – a dry red wine, with an evanescent sparkle, so that it pours out with a great deal of froth, which soon subsides, leaving not a bubble, as in champagne, but a pronounced prickle, as in the *vinho verde* of Portugal. This is strange to English eyes and palates, but Lambrusco is worth getting used to – it is fresh and clean and, as every writer on Italian wines observes, complementary to the rather rich dishes of the region. Every restaurant in Bologna offers it, and it is held to go especially well with the *zampone* – stuffed pig's foot – of Modena.

Lambrusco comes from the grape of the same name, grown throughout the region, and there are Lambruschi of Sorbara (which is to say, of Modena) – this is considered the best[1] – of Castelvetro; of Fiorano; of Fabrico; of Correggio (or of Reggio Emilia); of Parma; of Salamino; of S. Croce; of Maestri and of Montericco; and a Lambrusco Scorza Amara – 'the Lambrusco with a bitter skin', though I do not find it different from the others. I have also tasted a Lambrusco *amabile* – semi-sweet – but I found the sweetness less pleasing in a prickly red wine than I would have done in a white. Protected by the growers of the Romagna, the Lambrusco wines carry either the same label – a white cock and grapes – as Albana or, if made at one of the local co-operatives (those of Modena and Bologna having a *consorzio* of their own) with a label showing a man and a girl treading grapes – a method hardly surviving anywhere in Italy and certainly not at the co-operatives. The Lambrusco of Parma seems to have a *consorzio* to itself. 10°–12°.

**Lancellotta or Filtrato di Lancellotta.** Clear red wine with a particularly strong bouquet, made from the grape of the same name, which varies a great deal in strength and style. Usually sweet, with a prickle, and much admired in Switzerland, though I cannot class it with the best Lambrusco. One of the better known varieties of this wine is Correggio.

**Malvasia di Maiatico.** A sweet white wine made from the Malvasia grape with about fifteen per cent of Moscato, light for its type, and pleasant with fruit or between meals, served very cold. 9·5°–11°.

[1] Two restaurants in Modena – Fini and Oreste – are starred in the *Michelin Guide for Italy*. It is usua for starred restaurants to have the specialities of the house quoted in the *Guide*, and for at least two wines to be mentioned, but these restaurants each mention only the Lambrusco di Sorbara.

**Monterosso.** It is the *monte* that is *rosso* not the wine, which is white, from Belverdino, Santamaria and Trebbiano grapes, grown in the Piacenza area and meant to be drunk fresh, from the cask. Dry with a touch of sweetness, and very slightly *frizzante*. 10°–11°.

**Montuni or Montu.** A dry white wine, rather full and hard, from Castelfranco: Cùnsolo likes it better than I do.

**Moscato di Torre Chiara.** Here the proportions of the Malvasia di Maiatico are reversed – the eighty per cent or so of Moscato giving a richer, more luscious wine. 10°.

**Pomposa Bianco.** Dry white wine made from Trebbiano and Malvasia grapes, chiefly in the same area as the Bosco Eliceo (*q.v.*). 9·5°–11°.

**Rossissimi del Reggiano.** Extremely dark red wines from the same area as the Lancellotta – much used for mixing and for blending with white wines into cheap *rosé*.

**Sangiovese Romagnolo; Sangiovese (or Sangioveto) dell'Ravennate; Sangiovese di Forlì.** Red wine from the grape of Chianti and the great wines of Tuscany, widely grown throughout Emilia-Romagna. It has a great reputation, is protected by the local association, carrying the same label as the Albana (*q.v.*) and I must have been unlucky in never having met a really distinguished bottle – I have always found this a rather flabby, disappointing wine. But authorities whose opinions I must respect describe it as a full-bodied, serious red wine, well balanced and agreeable – both as a young wine, when it is said to have a fruity freshness, and when aged in bottle, after which its bouquet intensifies and the flavour mellows. Felice Cùnsolo describes it as being 'livelier than Lambrusco' (not that it is *frizzante*: he means in character), and with more personality than Chianti, and I am sure that he has far more experience of the wine than I have. 11°–13°.

**Sauvignon di Castel San Pietro.** Similar to the Sauvignon of Friuli (*q.v.*) and grown only in one very small area near Bologna. A firm, dry wine, with a quite individual scent and a flavour that some describe as 'tarry'. 11°–12°.

**Scandiano Bianco.** Both a still dry and a sweet sparkling white wine, each of very modest quality (though a local association has been formed to protect and label them), are made from local varieties of grape around Scandiano, near Reggio Emilia. 10°.

**Tocai Rosato.** Sweetish pink wine from the Tocai Rossa grape of Friuli (*q.v.*) grown near Piacenza.

**Trebbianino.** White wine, in a dry and a sweet version, made from Trebbiano and other grapes, near Piacenza. It is a 'little Trebbiano' by name, indicating that it does not ask to be taken too seriously. One of the Vini del Piacentino (*q.v.*). 12°.

**Trebbiano.** In various parts of the region the white Trebbiano grape produces both common wine, to be drunk young, and a finer quality, aged in bottle, which goes well with fish, being dry – even rather acid – but with style and character. There is a small production, too, of a sweeter, *frizzante* wine. Although we have met it in other regions, the Trebbiano is presumably a native of Emilia-Romagna, taking its name from the Valley of the Trebbia, which cuts into the hills south of Piacenza, towards Bobbio, and this is where some of the best wines come from. There are also a Trebbiano di Forlì and a Trebbiano Ravennate. The Trebbiano di Romagna is protected and labelled by the local *consorzio*. 10°–11°.

**Valtidone Bianco.** Dry white wine, sometimes *frizzante*, from Trebbiano, Malvasia and Ortrugo grapes grown in the hills south-west of Piacenza, above the Trebbia valley, mentioned above. Not widely known and not of any great distinction. 10°–11°.

**Vien Tosc Rosso.** Very light red wine grown rather high in the Apennines from a grape called Tosca, which may be closely related to the Sangiovese. Sharp and fresh and low in alcohol. 8°–10°.

**Vini del Piacentino.** Generic name given to some of the wines grown nearest to Piacenza Gutturnio; Monterosso; and Trebbianino (*qq.v.*).

**Note:** The tiny mountain republic of San Marino, a little enclave in Emilia-Romagna, also grows a Sangiovese, a dry Verdicchio (cf. that of the Castelli di Jesi, to which it is inferior) and a sweet, sparkling Moscato Spumante that is particularly low in alcohol (only about 6°) and strong in bubble – just the thing for child marriages.

CHAPTER NINE

# The Marches

THE hills of the Marches are more abrupt than those of Tuscany, the roads more winding, the cities smaller and less frequented by tourists. This is simple, peasant country, its cooking rough and savoury, and its wines the modest reds and whites that go with such a cuisine. With one exception – the Verdicchio of the Castelli di Jesi, a white wine that I am not alone in ranking with Soave as one of the best of all Italian white wines, though it is made to look at once more pretentious and more frivolous than it really is by the deplorably fancy bottles in which it is sold.

## The Wines of the Marches

**Bianchello.** Rather light, dry white wine, made from the Bianchello grape near Pesaro, where it goes well with the Adriatic fish, as an alternative to the much more widely publicized Verdicchio dei Castelli di Jesi. Low in alcohol (10°), which normally means that a wine does not 'travel' well, but quite a lot of this is exported satisfactorily to Switzerland. Sometimes called Bianchetto Pesarese; a better quality being called Bianchello del Metauro and protected and labelled by a local growers' association.

**Colli Ameni.** See Colli Piceni.

**Colli Maceratesi.** See Colli Piceni.

**Colli Piceni.** At the southern end of the region, between Ancona and Ascoli, the hills come close to the coast and grow a vast amount of rather modest red and white wine – variously referred to as Piceni dei Colli Ripani, or Piceno Bianco or Rosso. They are all sorts – dry and sweet, red and white, still and sparkling – and none is remarkable. Other names are Montereale and Colli Maceratesi, both red and white, and there are a red and a pink from the Colli Ameni, near Ancona. At Cignoli, near Macerata, they make a *spumante* of the same grapes (mostly Vernaccia and Sangiovese) that has something of a local reputation.

**Conero Rosso.** Dry red wine, sometimes called Montepulciano del Conero, after the grape it is made from, chiefly around Ancona, though it is widespread throughout the region. Rather fruity in taste and in scent – quite a pleasant modest local wine to drink in pleasant modest local restaurants. 11°–13°. A better quality of the same wine is more usually called Montepulciano Piceno.

**Cupramontana.** Produces one of the best of the Verdicchio wines, and also a *spumante*, consumed locally.

**Loro Piceno.** A village near Macerata which makes a particularly fine Verdicchio (*q.v.*). It also produces a sweet *vin cotto* (*q.v.*), very strong and rich. 20°.

**Montereale.** See Colli Piceni.

**Montesanto Rosso.** Sound, dry, red wine, made from a mixture of Sangiovese with the locally prolific Montepulciano – rather more Sangiovese than Montepulciano, which gives it, to my mind, a little more distinction than most of the red wines of the region. 12°. There is also a red wine made of the Sangiovese only and called Sangiovese Marchigiano, simply, very light in alcohol (10°), which at its best is delightful, drunk young. In good local restaurants, such as Cortigiano, in Urbino, it is served as a simple carafe wine – dry, but with the faintest underlying sweetness, and very refreshing.

**Verdicchio dei Castelli di Jesi.** This, of course, is the one really well-known wine of the Marches, widely sold on the holiday coast just to the north – from Cattolica to Rimini – and in Britain too. The desperately fancy bottles and labels should not be allowed to put one off: it is a good, sound white wine, made chiefly from the Verdicchio grape, in the valley of the Esino river, on which Jesi stands, and which runs into the Adriatic north of Ancona. All the writers on the subject, English and Italian, seem to agree that this is a 'delicate' wine, but that is not my experience, which is that it is full-flavoured, uncompromising in its hard austerity, with a bitter finish, though I understand that there is a *semi-secco* or *amabile* version, which has not come my way. The best Verdicchio is made like Chianti (*q.v.*), by the *governo* system of inducing a second fermentation. Fairly high in alcoholic strength (12°–15°), which is why it travels well – I have enjoyed very good bottles in London, notably at the Tiberio restaurant. Protected by a local growers' association, each approved bottle carried a neck-label showing a heraldic lion. One of the best comes from Cupramontana. There is also a local *rosato* wine, rather full and bland, made by growers of the Verdicchio, but not protected, and also a Verdicchio di Matelica and a Verdicchio dei Colli del Nevola, similar in style to the Jesi, but not quite so consistent.

**Vernaccia di Serrapetrona.** Sweetish sparkling red wine made from the Vernaccia Rossa grape, and interesting to those who are interested in sparkling sweet red wines. 11·5°–13°.

**Vin Cotto.** In many parts of Italy, but especially in the Marches and in the Abruzzi, the peasant growers make a *vin cotto* ('cooked wine') by reducing must over the fire to two-fifths of its original volume, and then bringing it up to its original volume with uncooked must. After fermentation it is aged for two years and over, producing a sweet, rich Malaga-like wine of about 20°.

**Vin Santo.** The Marches are famous for their *vin santo* (the final vowel of *vino* is dropped in conventional usage, as in *vin cotto*) – a sweet wine made from semi-dried grapes: some of the best comes from Urbino and Ripatransone.

Plate 20. (*Above*) Vineyards on the Bertani estate at Bardolino, Lago di Gar Veneto; (*below*) Workers in the vineyards on the Brolio estate, near Siena, Tuscan

# CHAPTER TEN

# *Tuscany*

IN the time of Cyrus Redding, whose *A History and Description of Modern Wines* was published in 1833, the wine of Chianti came 'principally from a creeping species of vine, *vite bassa*', and was little thought of. Luigi Barzini has told, in his endlessly fascinating book *The Italians* (Hamish Hamilton, 1964) how it was a point of husbandly honour that brought Baron Bettino Ricasoli (who succeeded Cavour in 1861 as Prime Minister of the newly united Italy) to create the Chianti we know today, and a vastly profitable industry: it was

> . . . the case of a jealous and moral gentleman, who disliked being cuckolded, but managed to avoid it without harsh words and bloodshed. He was . . . a religious man, dedicated to politics and serious studies in his favourite field, agriculture. He was by no means handsome. In fact, he was extremely cross-eyed, but had a tall and lean figure, and carried himself with a military and proud bearing.
>
> One night, when he had been married only a few months, Bettino, who had been nicknamed *Barone di Ferro*, or Iron Baron (such unbending characters are not necessarily admired in Italy, where *souplesse* is prized above all; the sobriquet has a derisive quality it would not have elsewhere), took his young wife Anna Bonaccorsi to a ball in Florence. There the poor lady was briefly and perfunctorily courted by a young man, who danced with her a few times. The husband immediately told her: 'We must leave, my dear'. He escorted her to their waiting carriage, sat down next to her, and told the coachman: 'To Brolio'. Brolio was the family seat, a lonely and gloomy castle, lost in barren and sterile hills, where none of the Ricasoli had lived for ages. The couple rode in silence through the snow, until dawn, he in his black evening clothes, she shivering in her ball dress. They lived in Brolio for practically the rest of their lives.
>
> To while away the time he reconstructed the manor, which now looks as if it had been dreamed up by Sir Walter Scott or designed as a background for *Il Trovatore*. He also experimented with planting different qualities of new vines and producing wines with improved processes. (One must have patience and a firm character for such pursuits. It takes approximately five years for a man to taste the first product of a new combination of grapes he has planted.) The Baron came across a pleasing mixture of black and white grapes, Sangiovese and Malvasia, and a way to make them ferment in two successive waves, which imparted a novel taste to the *cru*. The wine became popular, was copied by the vineyard owners of the region, the Chianti, and acquired, in the end, a world-wide fame. One of the best Chiantis is still the Ricasoli, of which the Brolio Castle is the choice and most expensive variety. Thus the Baron managed to preserve the sanctity of the family, his wife's name and his honour unblemished, to amass a fortune, and to enrich his neighbours, all at the same time.

Now there is a further revolution under way that is changing the very face of the Tuscan countryside, background to so many and such familiar paintings of the Italian Renaissance. More and more in the past few years, and now at an increasing pace, new vineyards are being made, planted with trim rows of vines, many of them trained low as in France, and wide enough apart for a tractor to pass between them, where once

Plate 21. Vineyards near Amalfi, Campania.

the share-cropping peasant grew olive trees, alternating with vines that had been allowed to grow nearly as tall, trained up stakes or living trees, with either straggling wheat, or a grazing cow, also in the same field.

That was under the old Tuscan system of *mezzadria*, or share-cropping, under which the peasant took half the crop, his landlord the other half. The peasant needed wine, oil and wheat, or meat or milk, from each field for his subsistence, rather than half the profits (and the heavy risks) from one crop only.

Now, under a series of land reforms, *mezzadria* is doomed: every political party, from the Communists to the Christian Democrats, is pledged to its abolition. Not that it would have survived anyway: *mezzadria* or no *mezzadria*, the Tuscan peasant nowadays would be off in any case to sell souvenirs in Florence, or to make mackintoshes at Empoli – for what girl, these days, within a bus ride of a town, will marry a man who tills the soil? (It is the same story everywhere: they told me in Germany that if it were not for the Spanish labour taking the place of the German countryman who has gone off to the oil refineries and the chemical plants, we would be hard put to it for many a famous hock.)

And so the landlord is having to rationalize his wine-growing, with properly planted vineyards, where a tractor can do the work of many men, uprooting olive trees to do so, for although the olive is a profitable crop, especially here in Tuscany, and needs little tending, the fruit has to be gathered later in the year, in November or December, when casual labour is more reluctant to work in the open than at vintage time, in September or October. On the whole the Tuscan landscape looks none the worse, for a well-tended vineyard is a comely thing. But it looks *different*, for one used not to notice the vines here, and now one misses the olives – although some intelligent landowners are keeping a few olive trees scattered about in the new vineyards at points where they will not obstruct the tractors, as much for the look of the thing as for the oil. As one of them said to me: 'There should always be grey as well as green in this countryside.'

As for the wine, Chianti should be all the better for it, for it is already being more carefully grown and made than it used to be, and the new vineyards will be easier to tend, to guard against pests and to irrigate. There is room here, too, for additional vineyards, as there is not in France. Which is all to the good, with demand rising all the time for sound wines at a reasonable price – a demand that Italy, the Chianti area of Tuscany particularly, ought to be able to meet.

I have listed separately the wines of the Tuscan archipelago, which consists not only of the islands of Elba and Giglio but also of the mainland promontory of Argentario (where stands the increasingly popular resort of Porto Ercole), the wines of which are closely related to those of the islands. There is a *consorzio* in Portoferraio, the capital of Elba, but virtually all the wines of the archipelago come from small independent proprietors, and until more modern methods are established, as they have been, for instance, in the new Sardinian co-operatives, they will continue to be inconsistent. But wine looms large in the Elban economy, and many of the local growths have some merit. There is a great deal of iron in the soil of the island (long famous for its mines – hence the capital's name), and there is much in the wine, which gives it tonic qualities as well as its characteristic tang. The wines from the east of the island are also rich in flavour and in sugar: those of the centre are noted for their deep and glowing colour;

and in the west it is white wines that predominate. On the smaller neighbouring island of Giglio table grapes are as important as wine-making.

The wines of the archipelago in general, and of Elba in particular, have their devoted admirers (I am fond of Elba myself, but I drink its wines with modified rapture): Paolo Monelli, author of *O.P., ossia Il Vero Bevitore*, upbraids Luigi Veronelli, author of *I Vini d'Italia*, for omitting from the seven hundred odd wines listed in his book an Aleatico of Porto Ercole; the Riminese dell'Elba; three local wines of Orbetello (which is by Porto Ercole); and a clear Elban wine that he had once described, he says, as 'more platinum than Jean Harlow'. Well, only one of these very local, very modest, wines is listed here, and Monelli's own list is only two-thirds the length of the one he complains about.

## The Wines of Tuscany

**Arbia.** Dry white wine grown on the banks of the Arbia river, in the open country noted for its sheep (and its *pecorino*, the sheep's milk cheese) that stretches almost to the very edge of the city of Siena; sometimes known as Val d'Arbia, sometimes Bianco Vergine della Val d'Arbia – 'virgin' because it is made by fermenting the must without stalks or skins. Light and delicate in consequence: not found very far from its native place, probably because its delicacy makes it not a good traveller. There is a similar Bianco di Montalbuccio from very near by. Cortona Bianco, Bianco di Santa Margherita and Val di Chiana are similar. 10°–11°.

**Artimino.** Another name for the Chianti di Montalbana Pistoiese (see under Chianti).

**Bianco di Montalbuccio.** See under Arbia.

**Bianco di Santa Margherita.** See under Arbia.

**Brolio.** See under Chianti.

**Brunello di Montalcino.** The vineyards of a small Tuscan hill-town, south of Siena, grow one of the great red wines of Italy, made from the Brunello grape only, a variety of the noble Sangiovese grape that goes into Chianti, but without the other Chianti grapes. The Brunello grape by itself gives a stronger, fuller and more fragrant wine than Chianti; this wine would be entitled by Italian law and the rules of the local association to style itself 'Chianti Colline Senesi', but sails proudly under its own colours and does not always carry even the growers' association label.

Brunello is so 'big' that it is aged in cask for five to six years before bottling, thus acquiring even more staying power, and is then kept in bottle for two years before being put on the market. I doubt whether it should be drunk for another ten years after that, for it enjoys – and deserves – a fantastic reputation for longevity: Luigi Veronelli gives it up to fifty years of bottle-age. Whether Brunello ranks with the finest burgundies, as so many Italian enthusiasts claim, I cannot say – it is different, and I think nothing is gained but confusion and hurt feelings in trying to compare unlikes. I have no doubt at all that this is a great wine, in its own immensely full way, and the 1955 I have in my own cellar I propose to leave for twenty years.

The one really important grower of Brunello is Signor Biondi-Santi, and hardly any of his wine leaves Italy, for it would be extremely expensive abroad and would suffer the competition of fine French wines that might well be cheaper. (I am told that a very little finds its way to Switzerland.)

Experts recommend decanting Brunello as much as twenty-four hours before serving. 13°.

**Candia.** Sweetish to sweet red and white wines from the extreme north-west of Tuscany, near the Carrara mountains.

**Capezzana Bianco.** Semi-sweet white wine, almost entirely from Trebbiano grapes, grown near Florence. 11·5°–12·5°.

**Carmignano, or Chianti di Montalbano.** See under Chianti.

**Castello di Meleto.** See under Chianti.

**Chianti.** As already explained, it was Baron Bettino Ricasoli who, rather more than a century ago, hit upon the particular mixture of Sangiovese and other grapes that gives Chianti its particular style and frangrance.[1] Whether it was he, too, as Luigi Barzini supposes, who devised the *governo all'uso toscano* – the deliberately contrived secondary fermentation that gives freshness and sometimes a slight prickle to the young wine – seems more doubtful: I fancy that this is a practice that had been established in Tuscany much earlier.

The *governo* system, to put it simply, is that after the first fermentation is over, at about the end of the year, between three and ten per cent of a rich must from dried grapes is added to the racked wine, and this, to quote Mr Gerald Asher's notes, 'uses up all residual sugar, and provokes an early malolactic fermentation to make the wine more supple' – a fermentation that lasts about another fifteen to twenty days. (Originally peculiar to Tuscany, this practice is now spreading to other Italian regions.) But it is most important to note that the *governo* system is for wines meant to be drunk young. The finest wines of the Chianti district are meant to be aged in bottle: they are not put into *fiaschi* and they are not made by the *governo* system.

Three things have combined to make Chianti the best known abroad of all Italian wines. It is grown in a big zone, so that there is a large amount of wine, of the same kind, entitled to the same name: other wines are produced in such small quantities that their names make no impact. Much of it has always been grown on big estates, many owned by old and noble families (the Ricasoli family itself being one of them), that could and can afford modern methods of viticulture, vinification and marketing. Thirdly, the wicker-covered *fiasco*, devised long ago as being easy and cheap to make, and at the same time ideally suited to wine made by the *governo* system (for it holds more wine offering less surface to the small amount of air contained than does an ordinary bottle, thus preserving the freshness and prickle of the young wine) caught the public imagination all over the world as being the picturesque symbol of Italy. Never mind that the wicker nowadays is often replaced by plastic, or that the finest wines of the region are bottled not in *fiaschi* but in claret bottles – by now Chianti is the archetype of Italian wine, and firmly established.

As will be explained later, there are two – or even three – types of Chianti: wine to be drunk very young, straight from the vat; wine to be drunk almost as young, as soon as bottled; and wine to be aged – and aged very considerably. The young wines are fresh and fruity, often with a slight prickle – not actually resembling young Beaujolais,

[1] The classic proportion is: 70 per cent Sangiovese, 20 per cent Black Canaiolo, 10 per cent Malvasia and Trebbiano, but there are many variations. The Frescobaldi house, for instance, uses only 60 per cent Sangiovese, as much as 15 per cent Trebbiano, and much less Malvasia.

but the same *sort* of wine as young Beaujolais, and to be enjoyed in the same way. The older wines are full-bodied and fragrant, sometimes with a distinction (such as in the Brunello I have already mentioned) not necessarily like that of a fine burgundy, but of the same order. It would be a pity if their reputation were to be spoiled by the amount of Chianti on the market that is indifferent because it was meant to be drunk young, and has not been. As will be seen, many growers bottle their finest Chianti under other, special, names.

It is well over forty years since the Consorzio per la Difesa del Vino Tipico del Chianti was founded, and in 1932 it persuaded the Italian Government to delimit the area to which the name *Chianti classico* could be applied – a region of about a couple of hundred square miles of the gently hilly Tuscan countryside, stretching from just south of Florence to just north of Siena, corresponding to the country of the fourteenth-century League of Chianti.

But so much precisely similar wine, made from precisely similar grapes, in precisely the same way, is made in precisely the same sort of country, immediately adjacent, that there were many growers who felt, with some justice, that they had a right to call their wine Chianti too – for how, under any other name, could it compete with a wine so well known at home and abroad? All the *Chianti classico* growers could say was that, well, such wines *might* be Chianti, but they were not *classico*. So the Government permitted wine made in the same way, in adjacent areas, to be called Chianti, but not *Chianti classico*.

So now there are the following wines of the district, all much of a muchness, all protected by growers' associations (not necessarily at daggers drawn, either: they often combine usefully), all with neck-labels. Some of these associations and labels are quite new.

**Chianti Classico.** Label shows black cockerel on gold ground. 12°–13°.

**Chianti Colli Aretini.** The neck-label shows a chimera. From the hills around Arezzo, to the east of the *zona classica*: harder and more acid than the others and not often aged – it is generally drunk within the year. 11°–13°.

**Chianti dei Colli Empolesi.** A newly formed group, its wines from around Empoli, the ancient hill-town twenty miles from Florence, on the road to Pisa. The wines are similar to those of the *zona classica*, though not, perhaps, so well balanced. One of them retains its own name of Dianella. The neck-label shows a bunch of grapes.

**Chianti delle Colline d'Elsa.** Another newly formed group, its wines coming from the Elsa valley, near Poggibonsi, and resembling the Senesi wines. The neck-label displays the Florentine lily in red on gold.

**Chianti Colli Fiorentini.** Also known as Chianti del Putto from the design of the neck-label, shared by the Chianti Rufina. Comes from the area immediately between Florence itself and the *zona classica*, the wine of which it closely resembles. 11·5°–13°.

**Chianti Colline Pisane.** The neck-label bears a centaur (it used to be the Leaning Tower). From the Pisan hills, and not highly regarded. 11°–12°.

**Chianti Colli Senesi.** From the district immediately to the south of the *zona classica*. The vines here are grown up living trees (maples and poplars, severely pollarded), and the wine they produce is not particularly consistent, though at its best it is true Chianti in style, but to be drunk young. The Association's neck-label shows Romulus and Remus and the she-wolf – badge of Siena as well as of Rome. 12°–13°.

**Chianti Montalbano Pistoiese.** The newly formed association has adopted a neck-label showing the towers of Montalbano. The district lies between Pistoia and Florence, and its wines are widely sold in Milan, Genoa and abroad, though they are not always consistent in quality.

**Chianti Rufina.** Sometimes rather fuller than other Chiantis (Nipozzano [*q.v.*], comes from this region). Some of the wines of the district that are meant to be drunk young are subject to two *governo* processes, instead of the usual one. Carries the *putto* neck-label, along with the Chianti dei Colli Fiorentini. 11·5°–14°.

As has already been explained, it is the wines meant to be drunk young that are put into *fiaschi* (so much for most of the Chianti we get in wicker-covered flasks in England, which has lost its freshness and has no right in a flask of this sort). The Chianti wines meant for ageing are made in a different way (without *governo*, that is) and are put into claret-shaped bottles. Many of the important houses use the word Chianti as only a secondary name for their finest wines, and anyone seeking the best wines of this area should look for:

**Brolio Riserva.** The best of the Ricasoli Chiantis, aged five years in wood before bottling. Mr Charles Bode recorded in 1956 having come across a 1923 Brolio at the Canelli Restaurant in Turin that 'was a sheer delight'.

**Castello di Meleto.** Also a Ricasoli wine and a cut above the ordinary Chianti, but not quite so full nor so fine as the Brolio. Along with the 1923 Brolio already mentioned, Mr Charles Bode found a 1937 Meleto, 'equally good, with a distinct shade of onion-skin' – but I doubt whether it would have lasted so well as the Brolio.

**Nippozzano.** The claret-shaped bottle in which the Frescobaldi firm put up its Nipozzano carries the *putto* neck-label of the Chianti dei Colli Fiorentini, to which it is entitled, but there is no mention of Chianti on the main label. Nipozzano is a fine, full wine, with the great power of ageing in bottle already observed in the Ricasoli wines and the Brunello di Montalcino: when I lunched at Nipozzano early in 1964 with the Marchese de' Frescobaldi and his brother Piero, and was asked what year I should like to drink, I remembered the great range of old wines I had seen in the cellar, and asked for the year of my birth, 1908. It was superb – full, soft, majestic, with no sign of fading in the glass. When I exclaimed that it would be a rare French wine indeed that could match such longevity, my hosts expressed gratification but no surprise – true, they said, they hadn't tasted the 1908 recently but they had had the 1912 the other day, and it had been excellent.

**Riserva Ducale.** The best Chianti of the house of Ruffino (a family name: these wines are entitled to the *putto* label of the Fiorentino Chiantis, and should not be confused with those of Rufina, a place-name).

**Stravecchio Melini.** The best Chianti of the Melini firm. It is interesting to note that although the Melini wines come from grapes grown in the *Chianti classico* area, they are made and bottled just outside it, and by the strict rules of the association they are not entitled to the *classico* neck-label. They refuse to carry the *putto* label to which the position of the cellars and bottling plant entitles them, on the grounds that this would misrepresent the contents of the bottle, and although they cannot carry the *classico* neck-label, they do describe the wine as Chianti classico on the house-label.

**Villa Antinori.** The best red wine of the Antinori house, in the *zona classica*. (This firm deserves well of the English visitor: Italian courses are held in the beautiful Antinori Palace in the heart of Florence, where there is also a ground-floor 'cantinetta', at which the Antinori wines can be tasted, very cheaply, by the glass, along with very good sandwiches and snacks.)

There is also a so-called 'white Chianti', sometimes known as Bianco delle Colline del Chianti, sometimes rather vaingloriously as Chablis di Montepaldi, produced in San Casciano Val di Pesa, near Florence, in the *zona classica*, made of the Trebbiano grape and others. It is dry and full-flavoured but hardly as distinguished among Italian white wines as the best Chianti among the reds. Among the so-called white Chiantis one might include Arbia, Lacrima d'Arno, Trebbiano Toscano and others listed here under their own names.

**Colle Salvetti.** Deep red wine made near Leghorn, from the usual Chianti combination of grapes, very similar in style to the Chiantis of the Colline Pisane (*q.v.*) though sometimes *frizzante*. 12°.

**Colline Lucchesi.** Modest red and white wines from the olive-growing hills near Lucca, between Florence and the sea. The white, mainly from Trebbiano and other grapes, is dry and light. 12°. The red is sometimes *frizzante*, but dry. 13°. More distinguished wines from this district are the Montecarlo, red and white (*q.v.*).

**Colline della Lunigiana Bianco.** Dry, semi-sweet and sweet white wines from near Massa-Carrara, in the north-western corner of Tuscany. Lightish (10°–12°) and undistinguished.

**Colline Sanminiatesi.** Red wines are grown near Empoli on the other side of the river from the district where the Empolese Chianti comes from, but made from the same grapes in the same way. They are not in the same class as the best Chiantis but their growers feel important enough to have formed an association to protect the 'Vino Toscano Colline Sanminiatesi', with a label of its own, showing an old Barbarossa tower of the district destroyed in the war. 11·5°–12·5°.

**Colline val di Nievole.** Dry white wine from near the smart spa of Montecatini: often *frizzante*. 11°–13°.

**Cortona.** Dry white wine grown at Cortona, between Arezzo and Lake Trasimene, from a mixture of local grapes. 10·5°–12·5°. See under Arbia.

**Dianella.** See under the Chianti dei Colli Empolesi.

**Follonica.** Local red and white wine from the mainland opposite Elba, the white tending to be sweet and the red sweetish. 12·5°.

**Lacrima d'Arno.** Fancy name given to the white wines from the upper Arno very like Arbia (*q.v.*).

**Malvasia Toscana.** Deep-amber dessert wine made in many parts of the region from semi-dried Malvasia grapes. 12°–14°.

**Maremma.** Similar to Follonica (*q.v.*).

**Montalbuccio.** Similar to Arbia (*q.v.*).

**Montecarlo.** Red and white wines of some interest from the hills around Lucca; there are two qualities of each – a *corrente* for local café use and a *nobile*. The 'noble' wines, both red and white, are full but dry (the red 13°, the white 12°–13°) and are, in effect, similar to German *auslese* wines, in that they are made of selected grapes – by the Chianti *governo* method, the white aged in cask for some three years, the red for as much as eight. To be found in the smart hotels and restaurants of Montecatini.

**Montepescali and Monteregio.** Both similar to Follonica (*q.v.*).

**Moscadello di Montalcino.** From the same hill-town as the fine Brunello (*q.v.*) comes a wine made from three parts of Moscatello grapes to one of Malvasia. This mixture gives a very light but sweet and fragrant wine, quite unlike any from other parts of Italy, though there are one or two similar Tuscan wines, in its combination of freshness and lusciousness. Drunk young and cold. 6°–8°. There is also a much heavier dessert wine, Moscadello Liquoroso, 15°–16°, and some confusion is being caused these days by a new tendency to call the heavy wine Moscadello, and to refer to the lighter wine, although this was the original Moscadello, as Moscadelletto – 'little Moscadello'.

**Moscato di Subbiano.** Similar to the Moscadello di Montalcino (see above) and made not far away, near Arezzo, though in small quantities, and not so consistent.

**Pitigliano.** Dry, but softish – flabby even – white wine, from near Grosseto, of Trebbiano grapes, and made in the same way as the Umbrian Orvieto (*q.v.*). Sometimes I have fancied to find a faint lemon flavour. 11°–13°.

**Pollera.** Sweet red wine grown in the hills behind La Spezia, all consumed locally.

**Pomino.** Good red and white wines from the same area as Nipozzano (*q.v.* under Chianti). The white is made on the skins, which gives it more body than many white wines of the region. 11°–12°.

**Rosatello Ruffino.** A *rosé* wine made by one of the big Chianti houses from Sangiovese grapes, and with some of the Chianti style and fragrance. 11°–12°.

**Scansano.** Red wine, made largely of Sangiovese, though in these parts – in the hills inland from Grosseto – this grape is known as the Morellino. Quite like some of the neighbouring Chiantis and worth looking for locally. 12°–13°.

**Trebbiano Toscano.** Similar to Arbia (*q.v.*).

**Ugolino Bianco.** Dry white wine, made fresh and prickly by applying the Chianti *governo* system to Trebbiano grapes (with a very small admixture of others, including the French Cabernet and Sauvignon). Comes from the coast on either side of Leghorn, and is drunk a great deal, usually very young – *nell' annata* – in the admirable local fish restaurants. Sometimes called Bianco del Littorale Livornese. 11°–12°.

**Val di Chiana.** A white 'virgin' wine very like that of Arbia (*q.v.*) but from the Chiana river valley. Sometimes known and labelled as Valchiana. 11°–12°.

**Val di Nievolo.** Red and white wines of the usual Tuscan grape varieties, of no especial merit, produced in the district around Montecatini.

**Val d'Elsa, Bianco della.** Rather better than average local dry white wine, made from the usual local white grapes, mainly Trebbiano, but with some finer additions – Traminer and Sémillon, for instance – in the better qualities. Comes from the same district as the red Chiantis of the Colline d'Elsa, and is unusual among Tuscan whites in being possibly as good of its kind as the reds. 11°–12°.

**Vecchienna.** Similar to Follonica (*q.v.*).

**Vernaccia di san Gimignano.** From the extremely picturesque (and extremely self-conscious) many-towered hill-town near Siena comes this white wine, made from the Vernaccia grape, treated in the same way as the 'virgin' wine of Arbia and the Val di Chiana, and protected and labelled by the association that looks after the Chianti of the Colli Senesi and the Vin Nobile di Montepulciano, and to which the Brunello di Montalcino is entitled to belong. An important dry white wine that improves with a couple of years in bottle. 11°–13°. There is said to be a sweet version, too, which has not come my way, but of which Luigi Veronelli, expressing one of his extremely infrequent subjective judgments, says flatly, 'I do not advise'.

**Vin Nobile di Montepulciano.** A fine red wine, made of more or less the same *cépage* as the various Chiantis, but with rather more white grapes and not by the *governo* system, for this is a wine intended to be aged in bottle, and not to be drunk young from a *fiasco*. Comes from a pleasant small hill-town near Siena, very near and very like Montalcino, and very similar to that town's fine Brunello, though it is not known to live to quite such an age – perhaps because it is not made of the Brunello (which is to say, the Sangiovese) grape only but has about twenty-five per cent of white grapes. But it is certainly a fine wine, especially after enough years in bottle (five upwards) for it to be showing its tawny tints, when it is big and flavoury, like a fine Hermitage, well balanced and smooth. Protected by the Senese association of growers, and carries the Senese she-wolf label. 12°–14°. There is also a sweet Montepulciano wine of small importance, and it should be noted that it is the *nobile* wine that is considered here, and that has its name protected – the local red wine called simply 'Montepulciano' is an ordinary common wine.

**Vin Santo.** Quite a lot of this sweet, rich dessert wine is made throughout Tuscany as, indeed, it is throughout Italy. (See under the wines of the Trentino-Alto Adige.) Here, as elsewhere, it varies a great deal in quality: the best are said to come from the *zona classica* of Chianti, from the Val di Pesa (just south of Florence) and – very good indeed but hard to find – from the Casentino hills to the east of Florence, along the curve of the Arno. Some is made by using one-third black and two-thirds white grapes, giving the partridge-eye colour from which it gets its name – Occhio di Pernice.

## Wines of the Islands of Elba and Giglio

**Aleatico di Portoferraio.** Dark, sweet, muscat-flavoured dessert wine, made in every part of Elba from the grape of the same name – a sort of dark Moscato – different in flavour and character, though not so much in scent, from the Moscato of the mainland and from Aleatico wines of other parts of Italy. Rich in iron, as is the soil it grows in, and said to be good, therefore, for invalids, especially those suffering from anaemia. 12°–15°.

**Ansonica.** Dry and semi-sweet white wines of only moderate importance and interest, grown on Giglio from the grape of the same name; also produced in the Argentario district of the mainland, and in a small part of Elba near Porto Azzurro. 13°–15°.

**Elba Spumante.** Dry and semi-sweet white sparkling wines are made on Elba from the local Procanico grape (a variety of Trebbiano) by the *cuve close* method – secondary fermentation in tanks, like Asti Spumante (*q.v.*). 'Not for the educated palate', says the Italian wine enclopaedia, and I agree: I suspect that many bottles find their way into the less reputable night-clubs of Europe, to be sold as champagne.

**Moscato dell'Elba.** Golden dessert wine, heavily scented, similar to Aleatico (*q.v.*) save in colour, and made from semi-dried Moscato grapes. 14°–15°. There is also a

Moscato Spumante, usually rather more carefully made, and better in quality, than the drier Elba Spumante (*q.v.*).

**Procanico.** White wine made on Elba from a local variety of the Trebbiano grape. At its best is quite the outstanding table wine of the island, red or white, and enthusiasts claim for it that it is of the same type and class as a Chablis (but there is Chablis and Chablis). Very good with the excellent local fish, and worth paying for the best quality. 12°–13°.

**Riminese.** A dry, full white wine made near Porto Ercole, on the mainland, from a grape said to have come originally from Rimini. Good with fish. 11°–13°.

**Roselba.** See Sangiovese, below.

**Sangiovese or Sangioveto.** The Elban red wine, made from the Sangiovese of the mainland and, at its best, not unlike the Tuscan Chiantis. That is when it is made of the Sangiovese grape only, but there is a lot of common red wine on the island with little claim to the name of Sangiovese, though it assumes it, and less to its fame. Sometimes known as Roselba. 13°.

CHAPTER ELEVEN

# *Umbria*

ITALY is so diverse a country, and the Italian people themselves each so individual, that it is difficult to say of any place or any person that he, or it, is typically or characteristically Italian. Yet there is something of the *essence* of Italy in Umbria, one of the smallest regions, lying half-way between hip and toe of the long peninsula, and the only one entirely surrounded, so to speak, by Italy, for all others have either a coastline or a foreign frontier.

The Umbrian landscape has changed little since it served as model for the background of so many religious paintings of the fifteenth century.

In his admirable book on the region Mr Michael Adams writes:

> Behind the cross, or over the shoulder of a Saint Sebastian transfixed with arrows, there opens out one of those Umbrian vistas, of meadows and cypress trees and hills swimming in the luminous distance, which appear so romantically improbable when you see them in captivity on the walls of some stuffy gallery, but which you recognise at every turn in the Umbria even of the twentieth century, so that you wonder at once how any artist could have captured so perfectly not merely the lineaments but the very essence and feeling of a landscape, and how the landscape could have preserved into our own day a beauty so pristine that the dew of the first day of creation seems to be still moist upon it.

One reason, alas, for that miraculous preservation is that although the system of *mezzadria* – share-cropping – is officially at an end, as we have seen in Tuscany, it is far from being so in practice. Much less so in Umbria than it is in more progressive, more prosperous Tuscany. Hence, indeed, the immensely heavy Communist vote in Umbria – some forty per cent as against just over twenty-five for Italy as a whole.

(And even in Tuscany, in Siena, as I wrote these very words, no longer ago than November 1964, I could look up from my desk and see a long procession of *contadini* from round about the town, dour-faced and sombrely dressed, in their go-to-town black trilbies and their thick stiff suits, winding its way into the Piazza Giacomo Matteotti, in front of the provincial Chamber of Commerce and Agriculture, carrying placards and banners demanding an end in practice, as well as in promise, to *mezzadria*; for payment in cash instead of in kind; and for the land to go to the people who work it.)

This is why there is no mention of the vine in that evocation by Michael Adams of the eternal Umbrian landscape; why Perugino did not paint it in his pictures; and why the twentieth-century visitor is nothing like so conscious of its presence here as he is in Piedmont, or Lombardy, or the Alto Adige, or in the newly organized and replanted great estates of the Chianti country: in most parts of Umbria, the vine still grows higglegy-piggledy with wheat and olive, and it is the olive trees that mark the land-scape.

So Umbrian wine production is fairly modest, and only one of its wines has more than a local reputation. That, indeed, is well and widely known, and I suspect that more Orvieto, so called, finds its way into those characteristic squat *fiaschi*, flatter than those of Chianti, than the slopes of the fantastic hilltop city ever grew. But there is now an association in being to protect its good name, and to award neck-labels to flasks of the authentic wine, made in the right place and of the right grape.

## Wines of Umbria

**Alte Valle del Tevere.** The country of the upper Tiber, north of Perugia, between Citta di Castello and Umbertide, produces a range of table wines, two-thirds of them red, one-third white (the reverse of what is the general Umbrian proportion), of modest quality, the reds chiefly made of the Sangiovese and Canaiolo of neighbouring Tuscany, and made in much the same way as Chianti; the whites of Trebbiano (the grape that makes it more famous neighbour, Orvieto), along with Pinot Bianco and a certain amount of Riesling, fairly recently introduced. Some of the white wines of this district are known as Tevere Bianco, and some by the name of the grape, Trebbiano. On the whole both red and white wines of the Alte Valle del Tevere are simple picnic wines and are not too heavy for summer-time luncheons. 12°–14°.

**Amelia.** This district near Terni produces modest dry red and white table wines, to be drunk young. 10°–12°. Finer varieties are the Oro di Lugnago and the Rubino di Lugnago (*qq.v.*).

**Bastia.** The local wine of Assisi. (Bastia is a little township only a couple of miles away.) White, from Verdicchio as well as Trebbiano grapes; dry and quite un-remarkable. 11°.

**Canaiolo.** See under Lazio.

**Castiglione Teverina.** A white wine from very near Orvieto, the wine of which it closely resembles.

**Colli Perugini, Bianco and Rosso; Colline del Trasimeno, Bianco and Rosso.** The hills around Perugia, and those around Lake Trasimene, grow a fair amount of common table wines. Those of any interest are listed here under their more specific names: those sold under generic names are the commonest.

**Fontesegale, Bianco di and Rosso di.** Among the rather better-quality wines of the Alte Valle del Tevere (*q.v.*). The red is said to improve with bottle-age. 12°.

**Montecastelli, Bianco and Rosso.** Also better-quality wines of the Alte Valle del Tevere.

**Nebbiolo.** A small amount of red wine, from the noble grape that makes the fine wines of Piedmont, is made near Gubbio, in the north-eastern corner of the region, and is quite good, though I have never known a bottle of the Umbrian Nebbiolo even to approach the majesty of a great Barolo, or the elegance of a Gattinara. 10°–11°.

**Oro di Lugnago.** Dry white table wine from near Terni, made of Trebbiano and Malvasia Toscana grapes. (See under Amelia.) 10°–12°.

**Orvieto.** The cathedral city of Orvieto heaves itself out of the Umbrian countryside on a great rocky bluff: 'A strange dark mass like the bulk of an aircraft-carrier out at sea', as Mr Michael Adams has described it. 'The rock on which it stands is a volcanic deposit, left by some freakish cataclysm in the childhood of the world, a base of yellowish tufa whose almost vertical walls rise six hundred feet out of the plain.' This great cliff is riddled with caves, in which for centuries past the wine of Orvieto has fermented and matured – a wine already famous in the fifteenth century (and certainly long before), for it is recorded that when Pinturicchio was working on his frescoes in Orvieto Cathedral he had a special clause in his contract stipulating that he should be supplied with as much wine as he wanted of the grapes of Trebbiano, from which Orvieto is made to this day.[1]

This was the Orvieto *abboccato* or *amabile* – semi-sweet; the Orvieto *secco*, though now perhaps more commercially important, is a relatively recent innovation. The *abboccato* is made by allowing the grapes to begin to rot *after* they have been picked (not on the vine, as with Sauternes, and the German *trockenbeerenauslesen*), developing what the Italians call *muffa nobile*, which means exactly the same as the French *pourriture noble* and the German *edelfäule*. This while the grapes lie in open casks in the tufa caves, before pressing. The curious thing is that this produces quite a light, delicate, only semi-sweet wine, nothing like so luscious or so cloying as the French and German wines already mentioned – not too sweet, indeed, to be drunk cool with one of the richer fish or chicken dishes, especially as a good example of the Orvieto *abboccato* will show quite a clean, fresh back-taste.

Both the dry and the semi-sweet Orvieto white wines are made of about sixty per cent Trebbiano grapes (sometimes here called Procanico, as on Elba), with twenty per cent Verdello, fifteen per cent Malvasia and five per cent of the small, sweet, scented Grechetto. Both wines are also kept for two years in cask before bottling. The dry Orvieto should be well balanced, with a pleasant flowery bouquet, and a slightly bitter after-taste; sometimes it can seem rather flat and lifeless, but at its best it is among the most delightful white wines of Italy. Both wines are bottled in the characteristic Orvieto *fiasco*, called *pulcianelle*, squatter and bigger-bellied than that of Chianti,[2]

[1] It was not unusual in those days for a painter's contract to include payment in food and wine as well as in cash: Signorelli, working on his 'Last Judgement' in the cathedral at about the same time as Pinturicchio, was paid two measures of wine and two quintals of grain a month, as well as his fee and his lodging. It is Pinturicchio's stipulation that the wine should be of Trebbiano that is so interesting
[2] But of smaller capacity: it holds three-quarters of a litre to the *fiasco*'s litre. There is a two-litre Orvieto *fiasco* called a *toscanello*.

and both are protected by the local Consorzio per la Difesa del Vino Tipico di Orvieto, which grants a numbered neck-label. Orvieto *secco*, 12°–14°; Orvieto *abboccato*, 11°–13°.

There is also a small amount of red Orvieto produced, made largely of Sangiovese grapes, like Chianti, and said to be kept for seven years in cask before bottling. Perhaps the best red Orvieto is, but I have never found one that is as distinguished in its own class as the white Orvieto is among the Italian whites. And there is an Orvieto Vino Santo; sweet, rich and luscious after five years in wood, of a deep topaz colour.

**Panicale.** Another of the red wines of the upper Tiber, usually drunk young, and consumed locally. 10°–12°.

**Piegaro.** Dry red wine, similar to Scacciadiavoli (*q.v.*).

**Rubino di Lugnago.** Dry red table wine, made from Sangiovese, Barbera and Pinot Nero grapes, rather better of its kind than the other wines of its district, around Terni. 11°–12°.

**Sacrantino.** A curious strong, sweet and heavily scented red wine grown in a very small area in the hilly district south of Assisi, near the villages of Montefalco, Giano Umbro and Gualdo Cattaneo – a sort of red Vino Santo, and hence perhaps its name, a diminutive of Sacro. There is an *amabile* (semi-sweet) and a *dolce* (sweet). 13°–15°.

**Sangiustino.** Another of the dry white wines of the upper Tiber, but from higher up the river than most, near the small town of San Giustino, north of Citta di Castello, with rather more flavour and fragrance than many others of the region, perhaps because both Malvasia and Riesling grapes are used, as well as the predominant Trebbiano. 9°–11°.

**Scacciadiavoli.** A full red wine, made from a mixture of Sangiovese and Barbera, with the Barbera predominant, and grown in the hill country south of Assisi. Strong (13°–14°) and heavy, with a great deal of tannic astringency when young. The name means 'drive the devil out', and it is interesting that it should come from the same region as the Sacrantino, and so near a city dedicated to two saints – St Francis and St Clare.

**Tiferno.** Modest red wine from the upper Tiber, often *frizzante* and drunk young. 11°.

**Trebbiano Spoletino.** From the grape that makes the white upper Tiber wines and the Orvieto, but grown in the Terni area, in the south of the region, and said to be fuller than these others, and especially fragrant. 13°.

**Vernaccia di Cannara.** Sweet, deep-red wine made from a variety of Barbera, dried in the sun after picking, and with fermentation arrested.

**Vin Santo.** Like most parts of Italy, Umbria makes a sweet dessert *vino* or *vin santo*. This Vin Santo d'Umbria is one of the best, golden and heavily scented: the Greco di Todi, so called from the name of the grape and the district in which it is grown, has an especially high reputation.

CHAPTER TWELVE

# *Lazio*

ONLY a hundred years ago the Campagna stretched right into Rome itself and, as Mr Bernard Wall has recorded, vines grew around St John Lateran. Even now the countryside presses close in on Rome, so that the hill-towns of only a dozen miles or so away, such as Frascati and Grottaferrata, are still separated from the capital by wheat-fields and vineyards, cypresses and chestnut groves.

As the Roman businessman is not a commuter, but lives in a block of flats in the smart suburb of Parioli, or in part of a more or less modernized *palazzo* in the heart of the city, the little towns themselves have kept their character, as places where country-folk live, and where the neighbouring farmers bring their fruit and their wine to market. Romans go there for the day, but not to live, and in a mere Sunday afternoon's drive can see the vineyards from which came the Frascati they drank for lunch or, on a rather longer excursion, taking a whole day off to bathe in Lake Bolsena, sixty miles away, those that yielded the Est! Est!! Est!!! of Montefiascone that they mean to have for dinner.

For there are two main areas of wine-growing in Lazio – the *castelli Romani*, or country of the Roman castles, in the Alban hills, and the area around Lake Bolsena, which would seem to be geographically part of the Orvieto district in Umbria, with which indeed it has close affinities. All three areas are volcanic: Orvieto, as we have seen, stands on a great bluff of tufa, and the lakes of the Alban hills, Nemi and Albano, are ancient craters, as is Bolsena. The wines do have a cousinly resemblance, deriving no doubt from the fact that they are all grown in volcanic soil, but the Est! Est!! Est!!! is more like the other wines of Lazio, the *castelli* wines, than it is like Orvieto, although Orvieto is so much nearer, for both groups of Lazio wines are made from a similar mixture of grapes.

## *The Wines of Lazio*

**Aleatico di Genzano.** A wine from the district of the Castelli Romani (*q.v.*) though not classed as such, for the *castelli* wines are primarily light table wines, and this is a sweet dessert wine made from the Aleatico grape, served cold with fruit. 12°–15°.

**Aleatico di Viterbo.** Made from the same grape as the Aleatico di Genzano, but from the other wine-growing area of the region, near Lake Bolsena, and much fuller and more luscious. 14°–16°. Note that other Aleatico wines of this particular district have begun to be labelled 'di Pitigliano' and 'di Montefiascone'.

**Aleatico di Terracina.** An Aleatico from the southern-facing coast between Terracina and Gaeta, more closely resembling the Viterbo than the Genzano. 14°–15°. An interesting variant here is the Aleatico Secco, a dry but extremely full and strong (16°–18°) wine made from the same grape, semi-dried, and more fully fermented out, and capable of immense ageing in bottle – up to twenty years or so.

**Anagni, Bianco and Rosso.** Local wines from the Frosinone area, the white

228

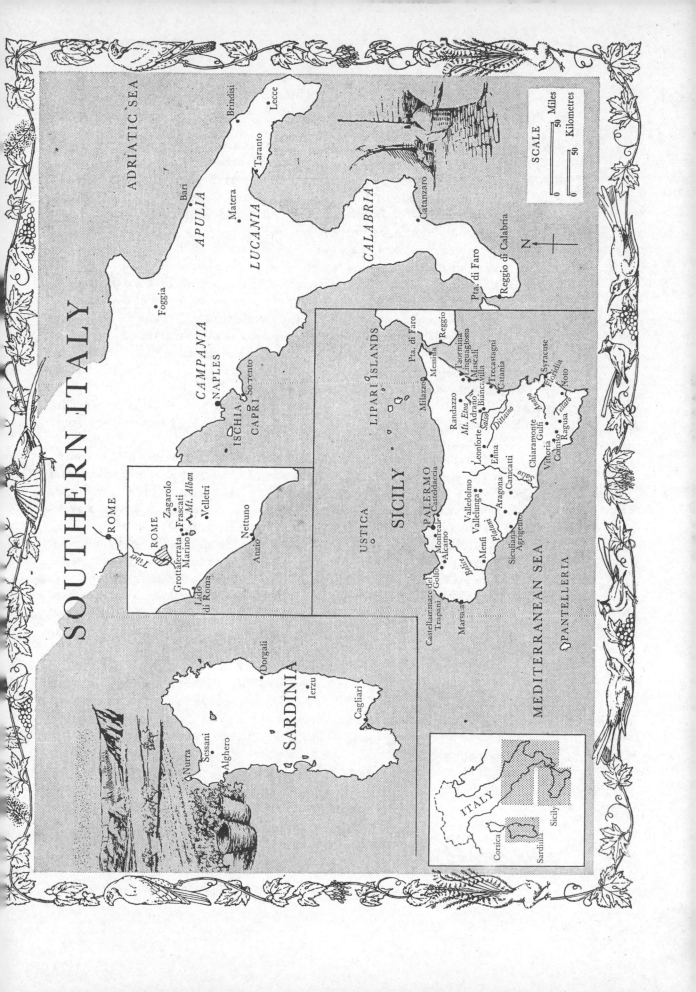

# SOUTHERN ITALY

ADRIATIC SEA

Brindisi
Lecce
Bari
Taranto
APULIA
Matera
LUCANIA
CAMPANIA
Foggia
CALABRIA
Catanzaro
NAPLES
Sorrento
Pta. di Faro
ISCHIA
CAPRI
Reggio di Calabria

ROME
ROME
Zagarolo
Grottaferrata  Frascati
Marino  Mt. Alban
Velletri
Tiber
Nettuno
Anzio
Lido di Roma

USTICA

LIPARI ISLANDS
Pta. di Faro
Milazzo
Messina
Reggio
Taormina
Linguaglossa
Mascali
Trecastagni
Randazzo
Mt. Etna  Biancavilla
Adrano
Catania
Leonforte  Salso
Dittaino
Syracuse
SICILY
PALERMO
Chiaramonte  Floridia
Castelladaccia
Arabo  Neto
Monreale  Valledolmo
Enna  Vittoria  Noto
Alcamo  Vallelunga
Gulfi
Aragona  Comiso  Ragusa
Tellaro
Canicatti
Castellammarc del  Golfo
Trapani  Siculiana
Salso
Belice
Menfi  Platani
Agrigento
Marsala

MEDITERRANEAN SEA

PANTELLERIA

SARDINIA
Dorgali
Ierzu
Cagliari
Sessani
Nurra
Alghero

SCALE
Miles
50
Kilometres
50
0
0

N

ITALY
Corsica
Sardinia  Sicily

(10·5°–12·5°) made from Romanesco, Bello Velletrano, Agostinella and Malvasia di Candia grapes, straw-yellow to gold in colour, usually dry, but sometimes slightly *abboccato* and sometimes, too, slightly harsh; the red (11°–13°) from Cesanese Commune and other grapes, and of very modest quality.

**Aprilia, Bianco, Rosso and Rosato.** The flat country between the hills of the Castelli Romani and the sea at Anzio was a battleground after the Anzio landings. Now it is wine-growing country, its marshes drained, producing white, red and pink wines. The white (11°–13°) from Trebbiano, Malvasia di Candia and Bellone grapes, trained along horizontal wires, from post to post, is a modest dry wine; the red (12°–13°), from Sangiovese, Merlot, Montepulciano and Ciliegiolo grapes, has rather more character, as local wines go. The *rosato* (12°–13°) is made from the same grapes as the red, taken earlier off the skins, and is rather full for a pink wine.

**Barbera di Anagni.** In the hill country rather to the east of the Castelli Romani, north of Frosinone, they grow a certain amount of Barbera grapes (see under Tuscany) from which they make a generous, full-bodied red table wine only to be found locally, but worth asking for in those parts, for big red wines are rare in this region. 13°–13·5°.

**Canaiolo.** Soft, light, sweet red wine from the grape of the same name, semi-dried, grown on the southern shores of Lake Bolsena, and pleasant to drink with fruit, or between meals. A similar wine is grown in Umbria, near Trevi.

**Capena.** One of the wines grown in the Colli Teverini. See under Monterotondo.

**Castelli Romani.** The district was delimited by law as long ago as 1933 – only wines produced in an area of about fifty square miles, in the Alban hills south-east of Rome, can be described as *vini dei castelli Romani*, though many of these wines, of course, give themselves a more specific name, of village or commune, or a co-operative brand name. Chiefly they are white, and there are dry, semi-sweet and sweet versions, of which perhaps the sweet and semi-sweet are the most plentiful, though there is a growing demand for the dry. For the sweeter wines the grapes are gathered late, when they are semi-dried on the vine, and may even be subject to the *muffa nobile* – the 'noble rot' that gives the great French sweet wines their character, though these Roman wines are far less luscious. These semi-dried grapes are described as *infavata*, which seems not to be a dictionary word but which I take to mean of the colour of cooked dried beans. The late gathering means that the weather is cold by the time fermentation is taking place: fermentation is slow, therefore, especially as the musts are *ingrottate* in the deep, cold caves that riddle the soft volcanic rock of the Alban hills.

The white wines are made from Bellone, Malvasia di Candia, Malvasia Gentile, Buonvino and – a recent importation into this area – the Trebbiano Toscano, and reach an alcoholic strength of 11°–14°. The dry *castelli* whites are firm, fresh wines, with plenty of body – quite enough, for instance, for them to be drunk with, and not be overwhelmed by, the savoury *pasta* dishes of Rome, such as *spaghetti carbonara* or *spaghetti matriciana*, or with the baby lamb, baby kid or sucking-pig that the Romans love so much. The semi-sweet (*abboccato*) wines are good of their kind, though it is not so easy to find suitable dishes to enjoy them with – it might be interesting to try them with a first course of *prosciutto e melone* or *prosciutto e fichi*: raw smoked ham with melon or figs, according to season. The really sweet (*dolce*) *castelli* wines are delicious with these fruits, or with peaches or pears after dinner.

Certain red wines, such as the sweet, dark Aleatico (*q.v.*) and the dry red Cesanese

Plate 22. (*Above*) Umbrian food and wine and (*below*) vineyards near Orvieto, Umbria.

(*q.v.*) are grown in the Castelli Romani district, but are not regarded, or referred to, as *castelli* wines, a name normally reserved for the light white wines of the district.

Outstanding among the *vini dei castelli Romani* are:

CANNELLINO. The sweet wine of Frascati (*q.v.*).

COLLI ALBANI, BIANCO DEI. This is a narrower designation than Castelli Romani, and applies to the wines of the district in the Alban hills, more particularly around Albano Laziale, Arriccia and Castelgandolfo (where the Pope has his summer palace), all to the west of Lake Albano. The wine tends to be rather lighter than other wines of the district, perhaps because it is made mainly from Trebbiano and Malvasia, without some of the other grapes used in other communes, and I would choose it to go with fish in preference to others, when opportunity offered: there is also, as usual, a sweet version, and there is a less important red wine – Rosso dei Colli Albani – made in the same parts.

COLLI LANUVI, OR LANUVIO, BIANCO DEI. Similar white wines to the above, dry, semi-sweet and sweet, from the more southerly parts of the *castelli* area, some from near Genzano, between Lakes Albano and Nemi, but mostly from around Lanuvio, whence they derive their name, south of Lake Nemi. There is also a Rosso dei Colli Lanuvi.

COLONNA. A white wine like the others, though rather deeper in colour than most and lighter in alcohol, from the north-easternmost part of the Castelli Romani district, towards Palestrina.

CORI. The red and white wines of Cori, in the group of hills (the Lepini) to the south of the Castelli Romani, are very like the *castelli* wines, but tend to be stronger and drier.

FRASCATI. The most famous name among the *castelli* wines, partly because of the virtue of the wine itself, partly because of the charm of the country town, so near to Rome yet with so much character of its own and with such enchanting villas and gardens and sweeping views over the Campagna. (Once, too, it gave its name to a notable London restaurant, now no longer with us, but well known to Victorian and Edwardian diners-out – a further help towards making the word familiar.)

A fragrant wine, dry, semi-sweet and sweet, the dry rather firmer – more masculine, as it were – in flavour than some other dry *castelli* wines, such as those of the Colli Albani. A good bottle of Frascati has a delightfully clear, golden colour, so much so that one writer swears that a lover of Frascati should be able to recognize his wine without tasting it – just by looking. Higher in alcoholic strength than most *castelli* wines and suitable, therefore, for ageing in bottle.

The *consorzio* for the protection of Frascati was set up in 1949: there is a neck-label for authentic wines, which must come from a district limited to Frascati, Grottaferrata, Monteporzio Catone (where Cato came from) and a small outlying part of the city of Rome itself. The sweet Frascati is usually known as Cannellino and regarded as the finest of all *castelli* wines, much drunk by the glass in Roman wine shops, mid-morning or mid-afternoon. A very small amount of red Frascati is produced and is of no consequence.

GROTTAFERRATA. One of the Frascati wines (above) and usually sold under that name.

GROTTAFERRATA, MALVASIA DI. It is a long time since I tasted this wine. Only

Plate 23. Orvieto, Umbria.

one Italian book on the wines of Italy lists it, and that only because the name has been made copyright: I never come across it these days in any Roman or Castelli Romani restaurant – not even in Grottaferrata itself. But a very small amount of this delightfully delicate dry white wine *is*, I am assured, still made, from Malvasia grapes, around the small town, and is to be enjoyed by fortunate guests in private houses: it is made on too small a scale, and with too much care, to be a commercial proposition.

MARINO. Along the northern shores of Lake Albino, on terraces facing south across the waters of the lake, a higher proportion of Malvasia grapes is grown than is usual in the area, and the local white wine, though dry (there is less sweet wine made here than in other parts of the Castelli) is rather fuller and more spicily fragrant. In the little town of Marino itself the priest leads a procession of thanksgiving to church at vintage time, and the fountain in the middle of the town plays wine for the day instead of water. There are said to be a Marino Rosato and a sparkling Spumante di Marino, both dry and semi-sweet. The red Marino, produced only in very small quantities, is really a Cesanese (*q.v.*).

MONTECOMPATRI. From the lower northern slopes of the Alban hills, along the road to Palestrina – one of the lighter and drier *castelli* wines. 11·5°.

VELLETRI. Very similar to Montecompatri (above) – if anything, even lighter, in alcohol (11°), flavour, scent and colour, so that it sometimes seems insipid: it would certainly seem so if tasted against a good Frascati. This is perhaps the only corner of the Castelli Romani where the red wine (see under Cesanese) has greater character than the white.

**Castelbracciano.** Sweet, golden wine from the shores of Lake Bracciano, a favourite week-end picnicking place for Romans. It is said to be exported, though I have never come across any save on its native shores – not even in Rome.

**Castel san Giorgio, Bianco and Rosso.** See under Maccarese.

**Castiglione in Teverina.** One of the few examples in Italy of a delimited zone stretching from one region into another. Castiglione is in Lazio, but hard by Orvieto, which is in Umbria, and its white wines are entitled to the appellation Orvieto (*q.v.* under Umbria).

**Castrense, Bianco and Rosso.** The caves that give their name to the township of Grotte di Castro are just on the north-west of Lake Bolsena, diagonally across from Montefiascone, where Est! Est!! Est!!! comes from. Around Castro they grow both red and white wines, the white from Greco, Romanesco and Malvasia grapes, both dry and semi-sweet, sometimes *frizzante*, and the red, of which rather more is produced, from Sangiovese (about sixty per cent), Canaiolo and Aleatico. Both are very light (9°–11°), and the red is said to resemble one of the lighter Chiantis.

**Cecubo.** The name is that of a wine that Cicero drank and Horace sang; but, as Cùnsolo observes, the soil may be the same, but are the vines? This is a very pale red, almost *rosé*, wine made from a variety of local grapes, with a very strong fragrance, dry but soft and fairly full. It comes from near the coast, on either side of, and behind, Gaeta. 13°–14°. A local sweet red wine, made from semi-dried grapes, is fancifully known as Sorriso d'Italia.

**Cerveteri, Bianco, Rosso and Rosato.** Modest local table wines, red, white and *rosé*, from the coast on either side of Civitavecchia. 11°–13°.

**Cervicione.** See under Nettuno Bianco.

**Cesanese.** This local grape gives its name to most of the red wines of the region, including those of the Castelli Romani. The typical Cesanese wine, whether described as Cesanese, simply, or dei Castelli Romani, d'Affile, d'Olevano, del Piglio, or di S. Vito, is a very deep red in colour, with a pronounced bouquet. There is a dry and a sweet Cesanese and both are often *frizzante*; that of Piglio tends to be fuller and stronger than the others (13°–14° as against 11°–13°).

**Colli Cimini.** Modest red and white wines, typical of the region – Sangiovese, Montepulciano and Canaiolo grapes for the reds; Trebbiano, Malvasia and others for the whites, along with a local grape called Sylvoz: 10°–12° for the whites, 12°–14° for the reds. Both reds and whites may be either dry or semi-sweet. More distinguished among them are the Vignanello, both red and white, and Ronciglione, white only.

**Colli Etruschi, or Etruria, Bianco and Rosso.** Wines precisely similar to the reds and whites of Castrense (*q.v.*), from the same grapes, and with the same character, but from the country of the ancient Etruscans, around Vetralla and Viterbo.

**Est! Est!! Est!!!** The story is all too often told, yet this list of Italian wines would be incomplete were it not told here yet again. In 1110 Bishop Johann Fugger was on his way from Augsburg to Rome for the coronation of the Emperor Henry V. A devoted amateur of wine, the Bishop sent his major-domo, Martin, a day's journey ahead, with orders to write in chalk on the door of any inn where the wine was good the word 'Est!'. History does not relate how many inns on the long journey to Rome were so marked – only that in Montefiascone, the small hilltop town looking out over Lake Bolsena, sixty miles or so north of Rome, the wine was so good that major-domo Martin, beside himself in his enthusiasm, wrote 'Est! Est!! Est!!!' on the door of the inn.

The good Bishop got no farther. His retinue went on to Rome but he and Martin stayed in Montefiascone, tasting and tippling, until the Bishop tasted and tippled himself into his tomb,[1] still to be seen in the church of S. Flaviano, with Martin's inscription (*Defuk* being the Italian form of *di Fugger*):

> *Est. Est. Propter Nimium*
> *Est Hic Jo. Defuk Dominus*
> *Meus Mortus Est*
> ('On account of too much Est Est *Est*
> my master Johannes di Fugger died here.')

Not, however, before the Bishop had devised in his will that the town of Montefiascone should be his heir, on condition that every year, on the anniversary of his death, a barrel of the local wine should be poured over his grave. The custom obtained until the Cardinal Barberigo, Bishop of Montefiascone, ruled that instead of being spilled and wasted, the wine should go to the local seminary for the benefit of the young priests – where, as far as I know, it is enjoyed to this day.

A modest English footnote to the familiar story is that only a few years ago the wife of the then British ambassador to Rome, at a tasting of fine Italian wines, marked a particularly fine Barolo on her list with the words 'Best! Best!! Best!!!'

What about the wine itself? It is a light white wine, which can be dry (10°–12°) or

---

[1] Perhaps the first to justify the old Italian saying '*Bere come un Tedesco*' – to drink like a German: i.e. heavily.

semi-sweet (9°–10°) and sometimes slightly *frizzante*, made of Trebbiano, Rosetta and Malvasia Toscana grapes – a mixture more like that of the *castelli Romani* wines than the much nearer Orvieto; though Est! Est!! Est!!! is sold in the flattish Orvieto *fiasco*.

The dry version is, indeed, quite like one of the lighter *castelli* wines – more like a Colli Albani than a Frascati. It is much drunk with the eels from Lake Bolsena, over which the picturesque but rather self-conscious little town enjoys splendid views, and I have drunk it with great pleasure as an accompaniment to a herb-flavoured roast chicken at the modest Dante restaurant, where they have an excellent carafe Est! Est!! Est!!!. The sweeter version is very light and fragrant, and goes pleasantly with fruit. Both dry and sweet versions have always been highly popular wines in Rome, and the dialect poet Belli, who flourished in the time of Dickens, wrote of the local wines:

> *E bono bianco, è bono rosso e nero;*
> *de Genzano, d'Orvieto e Vignanello;*
> *ma l'este-este è un paradiso vero!*

The same little town gives its name to a good *vin santo* (*q.v.* under Trentino-Alto Adige).

**Falernum or Falerno.** Disputes with a better-known wine of Capua (see under Campania) the dignity of descent from Horace's Falernian: made from Falanghina grapes, a dry white wine with a bitter finish, from around the bay of Gaeta. 12°–13°.

**Fiorano Bianco.** A white wine made in small quantiities from Malvasia di Candia grapes grown in vineyards about ten miles from Rome, along the old Appian Way. Veronelli speaks highly of its delicate flinty taste and advises it as an accompaniment to oysters, but it is hard to come by. 12°.

**Maccarese, Bianco, Rosso and Rosato.** From the area of drained marshland just along the coast from the Roman playgrounds between Fregene and Lido di Roma– one flies over the vineyards as one comes into or takes off from the new Leonardo da Vinci airport at Fiumicino. The white wine is made from the usual Trebbiano and Malvasia grapes, grown along horizontal wires, and is dry and light (10·5°–12°). The red and *rosé* are from Cesanese and other grapes and are also dry, light table wines (11°–12·5°). A better and rather fuller and stronger variety of each colour is the Castel San Giorgio. There is also a sweet, dessert Moscato di Maccarese.

**Malvasia di Grottaferrata.** See under Grottaferrata.

**Mentana.** One of the Colli Teverini wines: see under Monterotondo.

**Monte Giove.** A rather better than average local dry red wine, made from Cesanese grapes, grown in vineyards between Terracina and Monte Circeo, west of Gaeta, facing south over the sea, and on the edge of the Circeo National Park. Usually drunk young, locally, but worth asking at local restaurants for any with a few years of bottle-age, when the wine acquires a pleasing softness of taste and a slightly flowery scent, some say of violets. 12°–14°.

**Monteluci Rosso.** A dry red wine, made chiefly from Olivella grapes, near Ponte-corvo, within sight of Cassino. It is usually made after the stalks have been removed, so that the wine is lighter in texture and colour than some of the more run-of-the-mill local wines. Very small production. 13°–14°.

**Monterotondo, Mentana, Morlupo, Capena.** Wines, red and white, from com-munes of these names in the Colli Teverini – the low hills on either side of the Tiber north of Rome. The usual grapes of the district – Trebbiano and Malvasia for the whites: Sangiovese and others for the reds. More whites than reds, more sweetish than not, and none particularly remarkable. 11°–13°.

**Morlupo.** See above.

**Moscato di Maccarese, Moscato di Terracina, Moscato di Viterbo.** Sweet, rich, golden dessert wines made from Moscato grapes in the same district as the Maccarese table wines (*q.v.*) (14°–15°); on the coast west of Gaeta, and much lighter (10°–12°); and on the shores of Lake Bolsena respectively.

**Nettuno Bianco.** A dry white table wine made from the same grapes as the *castelli* wines, but around Anzio and Nettuno. 12°–13°. Some of the better quality is called Cervicione, becoming better known in recent years and much appreciated in Rome.

**Olivella.** This is a grape grown in the Pontecorvo district, usually in the Tuscany fashion – trained up living trees that have been heavily pollarded. It makes a light red table wine, not much known outside the immediate district. 11·5°–13°.

**Ottonese.** Local dry white wine made only from Buonvino grapes, in the steep hills around Palestrina. Drunk young, and all consumed locally, but rather highly spoken of by those who know it. 11°–12°.

**Palestrina Bianco.** Another local wine, from the same district as the above, but made of the same grapes as the *castelli Romani* wines, and with more body and less grace than the Ottonese.

**Romagnano or Romanesco.** Dry white wine made from Trebbiano and Malvasia grapes near Anagni, north of Frosinone. Listed only by Veronelli, who recommends it as a wine to go with fish. 12°–12·5°.

**Ronciglione.** One of the white wines of the Colli Cimini (*q.v.*).

**Sabina.** This is the country, in the Tiber valley north of Rome, where the Sabine women came from; a certain amount of local white wine is grown there, to be found under the name of such villages as Cantalupo in Sabina, Fara in Sabina and Montopoli in Sabina, and listed only in Veronelli.

**Sanmichele, Rosso and Bianco.** An experimental viticultural station near Cassino produces limited quantities of red wines from the French Cabernet, Pinot and Syrah grapes (some from Syrah alone); and whites from the Sémillon. Very good wines indeed, and of great interest to the future of Italian wine-growing, but not often met with.

**Setino.** This is the name of a wine that Caesar Augustus used to drink, and there is said to be some grown near Sezze, from which it takes its name, near Latina. I have never met it.

**Sorriso d'Italia.** See under Cecubo.

**Torre Ercolana.** A rather full, dry red wine, grown in the hills north-west of Frosinone. 13°–13·5°.

**Vignanello.** Red and white wines of the Colli Cimini (*q.v.*).

**Vin Santo di Montefiascone.** Rich dessert wine from the same district as Est! Est!! Est!!! (*q.v.*).

**Zagarolo, Bianco and Rosso.** From the hills around Palestrina – the white, usually semi-sweet, from Bellone grapes (here called Uva Pane – bread-grape) as well as the usual *castelli* grapes, and the red from Cesanese and Buonvino Rosso. Both red and white. 11°–12°. Not much is produced, and it is sold on the Rome market usually rather more cheaply than the *castelli* wines, though I suspect that much of it reaches the consumer by way of carafes in small Roman restaurants under the nobler name.

# CHAPTER THIRTEEN

# Campania

THIS is the region that is dominated by Naples, a mixture of luxurious holiday resorts – Capri and Ischia; Ravello, Amalfi and Positano – and the grinding poverty of the narrow streets off the Via Roma, on the bare slopes of the Apennines, and in the fertile but overcrowded plains of volcanic soil.

Wine was grown in these parts in Roman times and, indeed, probably earlier still, for this was part of Magna Graecia, as the temples at Paestum bear witness, built by the Sybarites, Greek colonists whose wealth and luxurious tastes have given a word to the English language that may reasonably be applied to many of those who come holiday-making here, if not to the locals. There are few wines in the region that it would be unreasonably sybaritic to indulge in: much of the wine of Campania goes north for blending, and what remains is proper enough for holiday hotels, seldom more distinguished.

## The Wines of Campania

**Acinato or Alcinato.** A *vino cotto* made in the Avellino area by cooking a must made of poor quality grapes in the oven, or over the fire, with more grape juice added. Quite nasty.

**Aglianichello.** Sweetish red wine, made from Aglianico and other grapes, chiefly near Pozzuoli, on the promontory jutting out towards the islands of Procida and Ischia. Pleasant enough in the little holiday resort restaurants of the district. 12°.

**Aglianico.** A grape that is widely grown in Southern Italy and that we shall meet again in the Basilicata: it seems to do particularly well in volcanic soil. It makes a good, robust red table wine, not unlike the Barbera of Piedmont (*q.v.*), sometimes rather astringent when young, which suggests that it might become a quite good wine with bottle-age, which it rarely gets much of. In Campania it is grown a great deal around Salerno and inland towards the north, taking in Avelino and Benevento. The name is said to be a corruption of the word *ellenico*, and to indicate that the vine is a descendant of those introduced by the Greeks. 12°–13°. Some is sold as Avellino, from its place of origin: it tends to be lighter than the others, whereas Taurasi, which comes from the hills north-east of Avellino, is bigger altogether, and more of it than others is chosen to age in bottle.

**Alburno.** See Calore degli Alburni.

**Asprinio or Asprino.** This wine, which sounds like something in a chemist's shop, is a sharp, *frizzante* white wine, made from the grape of the same name, drunk young and cold, especially in Naples in the summer. It is a mere 8°–10°, and all authorities agree on its diuretic qualities.

**Avellino.** One of the Aglianico wines (*q.v.*).

**Barano.** One of the lighter white wines of Ischia (*q.v.*).

**Biancolella.** One of the lighter white wines of Ischia (*q.v.*).

**Boscoreale.** See under the wines of Vesuvio.

**Buonopane.** One of the white wines of Ischia (*q.v.*).

**Calitto.** One of the wines of Ischia (*q.v.*).

**Calore degli Alburni.** Dry, full red wine made from Aglianico, Strepparossa and Sangiovese grapes in the hills behind Salerno, with rather more breeding than the common Aglianico, and a particularly pleasing nose. 14°. Also called Alburno and Gelbison.

**Campi Flegrei, Bianco, Rosso and Rosato.** The white is made from Falanghina Verace, Falanghina Falsa, Soricella (or Cavalla), Biancolella and Forastera grapes, and is light, dry and rather sharp. 10°–12°. The red and the *rosé* are made from Aglianico, Piede di Palumbo, Tintore and other grapes, are sometimes sweetish, and used for blending as well as for local consumption. 11°–13°. Sometimes known as Procida or Monte di Procida, which is the district it comes from.

**Capri, Bianco, Rosso and Rosato.** 'As famous as the island', writes one enthusiastic Italian of the white Capri wine,[1] but there is more Capri wine on sale than could ever be grown on Capri: much comes from the nearby mainland and from Ischia and Procida. (Wine made from the same grapes – Greco and Fiano – on the Sorrentine peninsula, which is geologically identical with Capri, and on the neighbouring islands, is entitled to the name by Italian wine law, and quite reasonably so.) There are small peculiarities about the vinification – the must ferments on a paste made of some, only, of the skins. It is pale and dry, with a sort of burned after-taste, and a fresh bouquet. The red and *rosé* wines of Capri and the neighbouring islands and peninsula are not so highly thought of: they are made from Aglianico, Tintore (or Guarnaccia) and Olivella grapes, and make reasonably good table wines. 11°–14°.

**Casamicciola.** One of the white wines of Ischia (*q.v.*).

**Castellabate, Rosso and Rosato.** Blending wines, red and *rosé*, from around Salerno, also used locally as common table wines: Moio della Civitella is one of the better ones. There is also a rich, dessert Liquoroso di Castellabate.

**Cilento Alto and Cilento Basso.** Just such wines as those of Castellabate (see above). It is said that they are much exported to give bouquet to some of the commoner wines of France and, of all unlikely places, Brazil.

**Colli del Sannio, Bianco, Rosso and Rosato.** Local red, white and *rosé* wines from around Benevento, in the mountainous middle of the region: the whites from Coda di Volpe, Greco and Trebbiano Toscano grapes, the reds and *rosés* from Aglianico, Piedirosso and Montonico rosso. All 11°–13°, and all rather sharp. There are also San Giorgio red, white and *rosé* wines, from a mountain town north of Benevento, in the same district and made from the same grapes, that have a touch more character about

---

[1] Even the sober La Nuova Enologia describes it as 'one of the best wines in the world', which really is stretching it a bit. It is not bad.

them: they seem to have had more ageing in wood before bottling than the others, and then longer in bottle.

**Colli Sorrentini.** Much of the wine grown on the Sorrentine peninsula qualifies, as we have seen, as Capri wine. But there are some local wines here, of modest pretensions, made of other grapes, and sold either under this general name or as: Colli Stabbiesi, Gragnano, Lettere and Corbara. They include reds and dry whites, some of the red being semi-sweet. 11°–13°.

**Conca.** A purplish red wine, rather sharp in flavour, made from a wide mixture of grapes, including Sangiovese, grown near Caserta, and frequently met with in the restaurants, where it will do the enquiring visitor no harm: indeed, it goes well with the richer dishes. 13°.

**Corbara.** One of the wines of the Colli Sorrentini (q.v.).

**Epomeo.** One of the wines of Ischia (q.v.).

**Falerno, Bianco and Rosso.** From the coastal plain north of Naples, named after Falernum, the capital of the Volsci,[1] and claims descent from the Falernian of classical times. The white wine, made these days from Falanghina grapes, is dry but full in flavour, the must being fermented on some of the dried skins, as with the Capri wines. 12°–13°. There is rather more red Falerno than white, made largely from Aglianico grapes, and similar to the wines described under that name. 12°–13°. There is also a sweet red Falerno that I have not come across, and some of the Falerno wines are sold under the name of Mondragone.

**Fiaiano.** One of the white wines of Ischia (q.v.).

**Fiano.** A light, frequently *frizzante* white wine, made from the grape of the same name, near Avellino. 11°–12°. There is also a pleasing Fiano Spumante, and a sweeter, non-sparkling version, for dessert drinking. Production is said to be declining.

**Fontana-Serrara.** One of the *bianchi superiori* of Ischia (q.v.).

**Forastera.** One of the wines of Ischia (q.v.).

**Foria di Salerno.** See under Irno Rosso.

**Forio d'Ischia.** One of the white wines of Ischia (q.v.).

**Furore (or Gran Furore) Divina Costiera.** Three wines enjoy this resounding title – an amber-white, rather strong in flavour; a lighter white, more delicate and often *frizzante*; and a rich, flavoury red. They come from, and are largely consumed in, the Amalfi peninsula (made from the grapes that hang so prettily from the pergolas around Amalfi and Positano), and are pleasant enough table wines. 12°–13°.

**Gelbison.** Another name for Calore degli Alburni (q.v.).

**Giovi Rosso.** From the immediate surroundings of Salerno – one of the better red table wines of the district, made from a mixture of Sangiovese with the local Aglianico and other grapes. 11°–13°.

**Gragnano.** One of the wines of the Colli Sorrentini (q.v.) – better than average, so that many mediocre wines of the district sail under its flag.

**Greco di Tufo.** *Tufo* means volcanic rock, but is also the name of a village between Benevento and Avellino, in the middle of the hilly district from which these dry and

---

[1] Not that Falernum was near here, but much closer to Rome: there is a Falerno grown in Lazio (q.v.) not so well known but with perhaps a better claim to the name.

semi-sweet white wines come. Made from a grape called Greco di Vesuvio – very strongly scented, often *frizzante*, with a strong under-taste. 12°–13°.

**Irno, Bianco and Rosso.** Light wines from the valley of the Irno, which runs into the sea at Salerno, the white made from a variety of grapes including Sanginella, after which it is sometimes named (11°–13°); the red from the usual mixture of Aglianico, Sangiovese and others (11°–14°). Among the better Irno reds are Foria di Salerno and Monte Iulio (which is said to have been a favourite of King Bomba's).

**Ischia, Bianco, Bianco Superiore and Rosso.** As we have seen, wines made on Ischia from the same grapes as those of Capri are entitled to the appellation 'Capri'. But Ischia has wines of its own, too, made of different grapes – the whites from Biancolella and Fontana – and they seem to me to have more individuality than those of Capri, even if they are not quite so publicized. There is a very light and delicate white, only 8°–10°, with a very pretty scent, to be drunk young, usually sold simply as Ischia Bianco; the Bianco superiore has more Biancolella grape to it, a little Forastera, and less of the others, and has more body and flavour (11°–13°). The reds are not quite so distinctive, but are pleasant enough local wines, made chiefly from Guarnaccia and Piede di Palumbo grapes, and drunk young (11°–13·5°). Among the reds the Calitto and the Epomeo are perhaps a cut above the others, and there is a dry, rather harsh Tintone, made from the grape of that name. Some of the whites are made of one type of grape only, and are sold as Biancolella or Forastera, as the case may be, and there are many other local names.

**Lacco Ameno.** One of the white wines of Ischia (see above).

**Lacrima Christi.** Like Liebfraumilch, this is a wine that owes its fame to its name – as memorable and as evocative and a good deal easier for the Englishman to pronounce. Alas, there is no association as yet to protect the name Lacrima Christi, and it will be some time before the new Italian wine law – in the absence of any association's rules to base itself upon, as it can with Chianti, for instance, or Barolo – will be able to delimit its zone of origin, or the grapes it must be made from. And so a good deal of so-called Lacrima Christi is simply the cheaper white wine of Vesuvio (*q.v.*).

Meanwhile, it is a matter of seeking out a reliable shipper or restaurant, for there is good Lacrima Christi to be had – the true Lacrima Christi being a white wine made from Coda di Volpe, Greco di Torre and Biancolella grapes in the district to the seaward side of Vesuvius, and also some of the eastern slopes: dry, delicate, with a hint of sweetness, like a German wine, or a dry white Bordeaux, but with a flowery fragrance peculiar to itself, and hard to define – of elder flowers and broom, suggests Bruno Bruni. It is a good wine to drink in the excellent fish restaurants of Naples, but is rather headier than it seems, certainly more so than many an apparently comparable Rhine or Moselle wine. 12°–13°.

The sweet Lacrima Christi Liquoroso is made of the same grapes semi-dried and comes from a rather wider area: the red and the *rosé* Lacrima Christi are not really true Lacrima Christi at all but simply local *vins ordinaires* exploiting a famous name. They are often quite sound table wines, made of Aglianico, Piede di Palumbo, Soricella, Palombina and other grapes, but not really any more distinguished, or worth more money, than other modest red and pink wines of the area. They should really be called Vesuvio Rosso (*q.v.*) or Vesuvio Rosato.

**Lettere.** One of the wines of the Colli Sorrentini (*q.v.*).

**Liquoroso di Castellabate.** See under Castellabate.

**Moio della Civitella.** See under Castellabate.

**Mondragone.** One of the Falerno wines (*q.v.*).

**Monte di Procida.** Another name for Campi Flegrei (*q.v.*).

**Monte Iulio.** One of the light red wines from the valley of the Irno (*q.v.*).

**Moscato di Baselice.** A dessert Muscat wine rather lighter than those of other areas from near Benevento. There is also a less important Moscato di Ravello.

**Pannarano and Partenio.** Stout red mixing wines, not unusually heavy in alcohol as such wines go (11°–13°) but very hard, and showing a great deal of tannin, made from a mixture of grapes in which Aglianico predominates. They come from the Avellino-Benevento area, where they are also served as cheap table wines.

**Pellagrello, Bianco, Rosso and Rosato.** Rather pleasing light local table wines from near Caserta, where the white-wine grape Coda di Volpe Bianca is known as Pellagrello Bianco, and where a black grape, called simply Pellagrello, seems to be peculiar to the district. All three wines are faintly sweetish – the *rosato* perhaps the freshest and pleasantest of the three. 11°–13°.

**Piedimonte.** One of the light white wines – alcoholically quite the lightest (7°–8°) – of Ischia (*q.v.*).

**Procida, Bianco and Rosso.** Other names for the red and white wines of Campi Flegrei (*q.v.*).

**Ravello, Bianco, Rosso and Rosato.** From the Sorrentine peninsula, west of Salerno, and much the same as the wines described under Colli Sorrentini: pleasant enough light wines (11°–13°), with the *rosé* as a rule rather sweeter than the others, though there is also a quite sweet white, *frizzante*, that makes an agreeable dessert wine, and also a local Moscato. These wines are also known as Vini di Salerno.

**Sanginella.** The name of the grape from which the white Irno wines (*q.v.*) are made, and by which they are sometimes known.

**San Giorgio.** A full-flavoured white wine, a deepish gold in colour, with rather an acid under-taste, rather like the Greco di Tufo from near by, but with an even more noticeable fullness of flavour, especially at the finish. Made from Coda di Volpe and Fiano grapes as well as the Greco. 12°.

**Sangiovese.** A certain amount of rather strong (14°), full red wine is made from the noble grape of Chianti in the Avellino area, but it has nothing like the charm or character of the better Tuscan wines. It is produced only in small quantities, probably more or less experimentally, and is hardly worth the trouble it takes to find.

**Sele.** Sometimes referred to as Alto Sele and Basso Sele, though there seems to be no discernable difference – red wines made from Aglianico and other grapes in the valley of the Sele river around Eboli (the last town, and pretty depressing it is, before the really deep South begins: 'Christ Stopped at Eboli'). Mostly used for mixing and sometimes called, when drunk locally as a table wine, Vino di Valva. 12°–13°.

**Solopaca, Bianco, Rosso and Rosato.** Wines from around Benevento – the dry whites made from Trebbiano and Malvasia, as well as the local Greco, which gives them more charm and fragrance than the Greco alone would afford (12°); the reds and *rosés* from the usual mixture of Aglianico and others, sometimes a little sharp, and drunk locally young and cool. 11°–13°.

**Sorrento.** The red, white and *rosé* wines of Sorrento are the same as those described under Capri and under Colli Sorrentini, but they sometimes put on airs and call themselves Sorriso di Sorrento, which does nobody any harm, and lends a typical Neapolitan touch to many a *diner à deux* under an arbour, with a fiddler playing '*Torna a Sorrento*' over the lady's veal cutlet.

**Sorriso d'Ischia.** There is also a sweet, rich dessert wine from Ischia, with a laugh on its label, and nothing very serious in the bottle.

**Taurasi.** One of the Aglianico wines (*q.v.*).

**Terzigno.** One of the wines of Vesuvio (*q.v.*).

**Tintone.** See under Ischia.

**Torre Gaia, Bianco, Rosso and Rosato.** Precisely similar to the wines of Solopaca (*q.v.*).

**Tramonti.** A sweetish, local red wine, rather big in flavour and bouquet, made in the hills north of Amalfi, from Tintore, Strepparossa and Coda di Volpe grapes. 10°–12°.

**Valva, Vini di.** Another name for the wines of Sele (*q.v.*).

**Vesuvio, Bianco and Rosso.** Pretty commonplace wines, red and white, from the slopes of the volcano: if they have anything about them at all (and sometimes when they haven't) they call themselves Lacrima Christi. Under their own colours, the white should be very light but with a rather burnt under-taste. 9°–12°. There is very little of it, for reasons that are all too obvious. The red is dry and sometimes *frizzante*. 10°–11°. Boscoreale and Terzigno are among the better reds.

**Vitulano, Bianco and Rosso.** Mixing-wines from the wild country around Benevento, but when the red gets a chance of ageing it shows a certain touch of quality, thanks probably to the Sangiovese and Barbera grapes that are mixed with the predominant Aglianico. If frothy when poured out, it is young. 11°–13°.

CHAPTER FOURTEEN

# The Abruzzi and Molise

THIS is the mountainous middle of Italy, culminating in the Gran Sasso d'Italia, ten thousand feet or so above sea-level – a rugged region in which bears roam nowadays in the National Park and in which it was not unknown during the Second World War for Indians of the Eighth Army on night patrol to die of exposure. The mountains crowd close to the sea, leaving only a narrow coastal plain, where much of the viticulture is for table grapes, though some wines are made for export to the north for blending or for making into some of the cheaper *spumanti*. A few better wines are produced, however, notably as a result of the importation of nobler grapes from Tuscany, at about the beginning of the century, in an attempt at improvement.

## The Wines of Abruzzi and Molise

**Abruzzo Bianco or Trebbiano.** The white wine of the province, from the grape that it is sometimes named after, often rather sharp, but with a pleasant nose, and quite a good companion to the fish dishes of the coastal towns, sometimes with a slight prickle, and with a clean, fresh finish. 11°–13°.

**Abruzzo Rosso or Montepulciano.** A light red, almost *rosé*, wine, made from the Montepulciano grape, sometimes mixed with Sangiovese, produced throughout the region. It is said to resemble the reds of the Castelli Romani, which will not commend it to everyone, and cannot really be regarded as anything more important than a local *vin ordinaire*, not to be taken too seriously. Sometimes *frizzante*. One of the better ones is Giulianova. 12°–14°.

**Cerasuolo.** Light red, or *rosé*, wine, very similar to the Abruzzo Rosso (above), from the middle of the region, near the bigger towns of Pescara, Chieti and L'Aquila, and not at the northern or southern extremities. Like the Abruzzo, it is made from the Montepulciano grape, sometimes mixed with Sangiovese, and is taken early off the skins. Sometimes slightly sweet (*amabile*), sometimes sharpish. Usually seems to be drunk cool, like the light red wines of the Italian lakes or a French *rosé*. 11°–13°.

**Giulianova Bianco.** A light white wine, made from Trebbiano grapes – to all intents and purposes the same as the Abruzzo Bianco, but the name is applied only to the wines of the coast north of Pescara.

**Giulianova Rosso.** See under Abruzzo Rosso – it is the same wine, but from the coast north of Pescara.

**Marsicano, Rosso and Rosato.** Red and pink wines made of Montepulciano, Sangiovese, Ciliegiolo and other grapes in the district of Aquila – lighter in colour and in alcohol than Montepulciano, and fresh to the taste when drunk young, as becomes them. 10°–12°.

**Moscato del Pescarese.** A sweet Moscato wine from near the coast, not so good as others.

**Peligno Bianco.** Perhaps the best, and best known, of the Abruzzo Bianco wines (*q.v.*). From Pratola Peligna, near Aquila.

**Torre de' Passeri.** A village in the district from which come both Cerasuolo and the Abruzzo Rosso or Montepulciano, which are therefore sometimes known as Rossi di Torre de' Passeri.

# Apulia, the Basilicata and Calabria

MORE wine is grown in Apulia than in any other region of Italy – in an average year as much as in Piedmont and Lombardy put together, or as in Tuscany and the Veneto combined. It is the great economic staple of the region. But there are no Apulian wines in the same class as any of the fine wines of these four regions: the strong sunshine, in addition to, in some parts, the heavy soil, produces strong, coarse wines, the reds used for blending and the whites as a base for vermouth. Sweet unfermented grape juice for soft drinks (and for export to countries that make wine of sorts from it) is also produced. No great body of tourists from abroad, or of holiday-makers from the northern cities, reaches this region to demand good wine in the hotels and the restaurants, and there is little in the way of a well-to-do local middle class, so that there is little inducement to the grower to plant nobler vines or to produce wines that will tie up capital while they age.

The same is true of the Basilicata, though production here is as low as it is high in Apulia, for this is a bare, wild countryside of mountains and high moorland, handsome but unprofitable (Potenza, the biggest town, the size of Leamington Spa, is 2,500 feet up, surrounded by higher country still and bitterly cold in winter). Only here and there are vineyards to be seen, the straggling vines supported on tripods of cane, from the feathery clumps that grow alongside: most of such vineyards are around the foot and on the lower slopes of the extinct volcano Vulture – yet another of the Italian volcanoes, dead and alive, in the soil of which vines thrive.

Good wines could be produced in these three southernmost regions of Italy – Calabria, the toe of the peninsula, is the third – if more money were forthcoming to provide better care for the vines, modern machinery in the wineries, and up-to-date methods of marketing. As it is, their wines are unknown in other parts of Italy, except as blending wines, let alone abroad, and they are not all that highly thought of on their home ground. This part of Italy is nearer to Africa than it is to Switzerland, and not only geographically: there is an African look about the towns, and about much of the countryside and many of the people. So, too, the wines, which are not unlike those of Algeria and of the vineyards in Libya which were, in fact, planted and cared for by people who came from these very regions in Mussolini's time. In Calabria, particularly, the wines are all the coarser for the vines being trained close to the ground, absorbing additional heat from the soil.

## The Wines of Apulia

**Aleatico.** The rich, dark red, sweet dessert wine found in many parts of Italy, and made from the grape of the same name, is probably more frequent in Apulia than elsewhere, and is made here by taking the must off the skins of semi-dried grapes rather quickly (the colour is fairly fully taken up, but this may explain why the Apulian Aleatico has pale orange tints to it that seem to be lacking in others), and then arresting fermentation by the addition of spirits, which is not done in every part of Italy, and is probably the reason for its being stronger than most. 14°–17°. As it is grown so widely throughout the region, it has many local names – that of Brindisi is said to be the finest.

**Asprinio.** See under Capo di Leuca.

**Avertrana.** A variety of Manduria (*q.v.*).

**Barbera Leccese.** The Barbera grape of the north is grown in limited quantities around the little baroque city of Lecce, where it makes a much bigger, stronger red wine (15°–16°) than it does in Piedmont, and with nothing like the distinction, but interesting to meet down here in the heel of Italy, where they drink it young and – rather surprisingly – cooled.

**Barletta.** A coarse, red, mixing wine from the east coast, made chiefly from Troia grapes.

**Borraccio.** See under Capo di Leuca.

**Brindisino or Brindisi.** One of the wines of Salento (*q.v.*).

**Capo di Leuca.** Wines are grown widely in the very bottom of the heel of Italy from a wide mixture of local grapes. The Parasini is a pale red, dry and *frizzante*, and is said to have a tarry taste; the Borraccio is paler still, and more delicate; the Asprinio is white, semi-sweet, *frizzante*, and rather like a Moscato to the nose. (All about 14°–16°.)

**Carasino.** See under Tarantino.

**Casarino.** One of the wines of Salento (*q.v.*).

**Castel Acquaro.** One of the wines of Salento (*q.v.*).

**Castel del Monte, Bianco, Rosso and Rosato.** From between Barletta and Bari, but inland, where the Bombino Bianco grape produces a fresh white wine with, usually, a pronounced prickle, and rather light (11°–12°) for the region and where red and *rosé* wines of only moderate interest are made from local varieties of grape. Rather better wines, more carefully made, come from the local co-operative, and are marketed under the name Rivera.

**Castellana and Conversano.** Two townships in the hills above Monopoli, which is on the east coast, south of Bari, where some white, red and *rosé* wines are grown. One Italian writer, having described them as being of 'distinct quality', winds up by saying that the red and the pink 'can aspire to the honour of being bottled' – which indicates what they are: very modest local wines indeed, usually drunk young, *nell' annata*, and from the cask, and also used for mixing with their betters. The red is probably the best of the three.

**Cerasuolo delle Murge.** A cherry-red wine from near Bari, the best quality coming from around the small town of Bitonto, made from a black grape called Primativo (*q.v.*) and a variety of white grapes, drunk young and all consumed locally. 12°–14°.

**Cinque Rose.** See under Salento.

**Colatamburo.** A dry white wine from near Bari, pale with a marked bouquet and rather strong. 14°.

**Conversano.** See under Castellana, above.

**Copertina.** One of the wines of Salento (*q.v.*).

**Galatina.** One of the wines of Salento (*q.v.*).

**Gallipoli.** One of the wines of Salento (*q.v.*).

**Grottaglie.** One of the Tarantino wines (*q.v.*).

**Lacrima di Gallipoli.** A dry *rosé* wine from the Gallipoli peninsula – inside the heel, so to speak, of Italy – and also to be found around Lecce. It has a fine nose, and I seem to see in it the nearest Apulian approach to what one describes as 'elegance' in French wines. Sometimes known as Lacrima del Salento. 14°.

**Lacrima di Corato.** Similar to the above but from near Bari.

**Lecce, Rosato di.** See under Salento.

**Locorotondo, Bianco di.** An almost colourless white wine, made in enormous quantities around Bari, from Verdea, Alessano and Buonvino grapes, in varying proportions, with the skins and pips removed, to produce a neutral base for vermouth, for which it is largely used. Veronelli says that it deserves a better fate, as he has drunk a good bottle of it with the local fish – being luckier than me. It is true, though, that rather better qualities than the wine exported to the Turin vermouth factories are to be met with locally under various names, such as those of the grapes (Verdea di Albarello), or of local communes (Martina Franca and San Carlo).

**Malvasia di Brindisi, or di Puglia.** Dry (or semi-sweet) and sweet wines made from Malvasia grapes, the dry and semi-sweet being pleasant table wines, though not so fine as the Malvasias of Friuli and elsewhere; the sweet made from semi-dried grapes, and a very ordinary dessert wine. 12°–14°.

**Manduria.** This – if the Italian wine-writers are to be believed – is one of the most curious wines of Italy, perhaps of the whole wine-growing world. It is made of the Primitivo grape, in the flat country east of Taranto, and when young – as usually consumed – it is a frothy, naturally semi-sparkling red wine (18°) with a heavy bouquet, very rich in flavour and much used for mixing. This is the only form in which I have come across it, but many authorities maintain that in two years it becomes like Aleatico, in four like Barolo, and in seven like Marsala. But very little is produced; I have never seen it outside its own immediate district; and opportunity for research into this phenomenon is limited. Meanwhile, I suspend my disbelief.

**Martina Franca.** See under Locorotondo.

**Massafra.** One of the Tarantino wines (*q.v.*).

**Melisano.** One of the wines of Salento (*q.v.*).

**Mesagne.** One of the wines of Salento (*q.v.*).

**Moscato di Puglia.** One of the strongest (15°–17°) of the rich, sweet dessert wines found pretty well all over Italy, though not so fine as some – certainly not in the same class as that of Siracusa, which has both more depth and greater subtlety of flavour. But a good, smooth after-dinner wine – among the better examples being the Moscato del Salento and the Moscato di Trani. The latter is produced in very small quantities, and is probably the better, especially the particular Moscato di Trani produced at the experimental station at Barletta. There is also a Moscato d'Amburgo, which I do not know.

**Nero del Brindisino.** See under Salento.

**Ostuni Bianco.** A very uninteresting dry white wine from where the hills begin, north of Brindisi, made of Impigno, Francavidda, Verdea, Fiano and other grapes. 11·5°–13°.

**Ottavianella.** The name of a grape from which a pink wine is made in the same district as the Ostuni Bianco. 12°–13°.

**Parasini.** A red wine of Capo di Leuca (*q.v.*).

**Passito di Novoli.** A very strong, amber-coloured *passito* dessert wine, from Novoli near Lecce.

**Primativo or Primitivo.** The latter is the proper Italian form; Primativo is the way that the Pugliesi spell and pronounce the word, which in these parts means not 'primitive' but *primaticcio* – early. For here is another of the wine curiosities of the region: the grapes and bunches of grapes that receive the most sun ripen and are gathered in August – the earliest vintage in Europe, and in good time for the young wine to be sent to fortify the weaker wines of the north, of the same vintage. Then comes the second vintage – of the grapes that had been shaded by foliage, and these give a fine red wine that ages as well as a good Tuscan or Piedmontese wine: I have heard tell of fifty-five-year-old bottles of Primativo. So this second wine is of some importance, big and full-flavoured, and well worth looking out for in the Taranto area: Primativo di Manduria, Primativo del Tarantino and Primativo di Gioia del Colle are names it goes under.

**Primofiore.** One of the wines of the Salento (*q.v.*).

**Rivera.** See under Castel del Monte.

**Salento or Salentino, Rosso and Rosato.** An enormous range of red and *rosé* wines are grown all over the flattish country of the heel of Italy, in the triangle formed by Taranto, Brindisi and the southernmost cape, Capo S. Maria di Leuca. Among the grapes are Negro Amaro, Malvasia Nera, Malvasia Bianca and others, including the Primativo mentioned above. They are mostly wines for export to the north or abroad as mixers and strengtheners, and have no especial character or distinction – not even much consistency, with strengths ranging from 12° to 15°, colours from the palest pink to the deepest red, tastes from dry to semi-sweet, and quality from fairly good to downright nasty. Such examples as are offered locally as tables wines do tend to be better than those shipped elsewhere as fortifiers: they include some dozen that are included in this list, all with references to this entry: the best is possibly the red Castel Acquaro, from Mesagne, near Brindisi, a single-establishment wine that is produced in small quantities and given a chance to age in bottle, which I have found rather more refined than one may normally hope for in these parts.

The pink wine is sometimes known as Rosato di Lecce, and there is a *consorzio* to protect the Rosato del Salento. There are also a Vecchio Bianco and a Vecchio Rosso di Salento, both strong, sweet dessert wines (16°–18°), not to be compared with such other dessert wines of the region as the Aleatico and the Moscato.

**San Carlo.** See under Locorotondo.

**San Pietro Vernotico.** One of the wines of Salento (*q.v.*).

**San Severo.** A rather coarse white wine produced in considerable quantities in the Foggia plain. It is said once to have been an Austrian favourite, but it has dwindled now into being exported chiefly as a base for vermouth. It is made from Bombino Bianco and other grapes, and some of the better qualities are kept as table wines, among which I have heard the white Torre Giulia and the white Torre Quarto well spoken of. 11·5°–13°.

**Santo Stefano.** A very much smaller quantity of sharpish, dry red wine (12°–13°)

comes from the same region as the white San Severo, made from Montepulciano, Lagrima, Alicante, Uva di Troia and other grapes, and not exported, but consumed locally. As with the whites, the Torre Giulia and Torre Quarto labels indicate a touch of quality, but I cannot recommend the dessert Torre Quarto, fortified, and the fermentation arrested, by the addition of neutral spirits, and very strong.

**Sava.** A variety of Manduria (q.v.).

**Squinzano.** One of the wines of Salento (q.v.).

**Tarantino.** Strong, coarse, red wines for blending and for even less dignified industrial purposes are made from Primativo grapes around Taranto. Those retained for local consumption may be drunk with mild enjoyment by hardened travellers.

**Torre Giulia and Torre Quarto, Bianchi and Rossi.** For the reds see under Santo Stefano, and for the whites under San Severo.

**Trani.** This is the name by which the Milanesi – the length of Italy away – describe the Apulian wines, such as the rough open wines they drink in their wine-bars: hence the Milanese slang word 'tranatt' for a hardened drinker.

**Troia.** The name of a common grape, so called after the village of Troia, near Foggia, and from which a strong mixing wine is made.

**Verdea or Verdeca.** See under Locorotondo: sometimes frizzante.

**Vecchio Salento, Bianco and Rosso.** See under Salento.

**Zagarese.** A strong, sweet, Malaga-like, or Marsala-like, dessert wine (15°–18°) made from the grape of the same name in the Bari–Brindisi–Lecce area. Very plentiful before the phylloxera, but since then a lot of the vineyards that once produced it have gone over to strong blending wines for export, and Zagarese is now hard to find outside the little farms that grow it for their own table: an old bottle is worth tasting.

## The Wines of the Basilicata

**Aglianico del Vulture.** Around and on the lower slopes of the extinct volcano, Vulture, there grows the Aglianico grape, recording in its very name – a form of ellenico – that this was once part of Magna Graecia. The dry Aglianico del Vulture, with a few years of bottle-age, is one of the best red wines of Southern Italy – so much less well off than the North for good table wines. My impression is that it is capable of considerable improvement in bottle over many years, like such wines of the North as Barolo and Brunello, but I have been unable to find any Aglianico old enough to prove my theory. At its best it is full, rounded and well balanced, and goes well with the richer meat dishes of the region. 12°–14°. There is also a sparkling Aglianico Mussante.

**Aglianico di Matera.** A very similar wine to the above, made from the same grape, grown in the vicinity of Matera, much nearer the coast, and sometimes called Val Bradano Rosso, from the valley of the river near which Matera stands. 12°–14°.

**Asprinio or Asprino.** This medicinal-sounding wine is so called not because of any analgesic qualities (though it is said to be diuretic) but after the grape of the same name, which makes a dry but frizzante white wine, grown in the Potenza area, and said to be good with oysters. Light in alcohol but stout enough to travel, for a lot is sold to Naples, where the locals drink it between meals as an aperitif or café drink.

**Malvasia, Malvasia di Vulture.** Naturally sparkling, sweet golden wine from the Malvasia grape, which is grown widely throughout the region: the best is said to be that of Rapolla, near Melfi. Enthusiasts claim to detect in it the scent of almond blossom. 10°–12°.

**Moscato.** Another sweet sparkling wine, deservedly less well known than those of the North, but pleasant enough, drunk cool, here in the sun-baked deep South of Italy, especially as it is fairly light in alcohol. 10°–12°.

## The Wines of Calabria

**Arghilla Rosato.** A strong, rich and rough *rosé* wine made from Malvasia and Alicante grapes in a district of the name at the very edge of the town of Reggio di Calabria. It is listed in none of the reference books, but I have found it much in evidence in the local wine-bars and restaurants. 14°–17°.

**Attafi Greco, Attafi Rosso and Attafi Mantonico.** The name of Attafi is mysterious to me, as it seems to be the name neither of a place nor of a grape. These wines come from near Reggio di Calabria: the red is a strong (14°) table wine made from Alicante and other grapes, coarse and heavy. The other two are rich, sweet dessert wines, made from the Greco and Mantonico grapes respectively. 18°.

**Balbino.** A strong white wine, in both dry and sweet versions, though the sweet is much more frequent and better known, made from a grape of the same name in the mountainous Altomonte district, near Cosenza. It is sometimes known as Balbino d'Altomonte. 15°–16°.

**Cafaro.** A red wine, fairly light for this part of Italy (12°–15°), made from Magliocco, Greco Rosso, Greco Bianco, Montonico and other grapes in the district of Cafari, which is part of the small town of Nicotera on the Gulf of Gioia. Dry or semi-sweet, some is kept by local families to acquire age in bottle, but a good deal finds its way north to cut and stretch lighter wines. The same wine grown in the next commune takes that commune's name, Limbadi.

**Cerasolo (or Cerasuolo) di Scilla, di Palmi.** As the name denotes, a cherry-red wine from Scilla, on the Strait of Messina (the Scylla of Scylla and Charybdis) and also from a little farther north, near Palmi. Other well-known names are Favagreca, Ieracare and Paci. Made from a wide mixture of grape varieties, rather sweet and fairly light. 12°–14°.

**Cirò.** North of Crotone, on the ball, so to speak, of the Italian foot are Ciro and Melissa, around which grapes have been grown, and wine made, since the time of the ancient Greeks. (The *cremissa* given to athletes returning victorious from the Olympic Games is said to have come from here.) Now the district produces a big, robust red wine, from Gaglioppo and Piedilungo grapes, drunk locally as a table wine, and also sold to the North. A local variety is known as Collina di Crotone. There is a *rosé* (Cirò Rosa) and a sweet red wine. 13°–15°. The white Cirò is made from the Greco Bianco grape, grown *ad alberello* – 'as a little tree', close to the ground, that is – and is one of the best table wines of the region, with a marked bouquet and a full, flowery but dry taste. 12°–13·5°.

**Collina di Crotone.** See under Cirò above.

**Coticchietto.** See under Greco Rosso.

**Donna Camilla.** A dry, rather sharp, fragrant red wine (there is also a *rosé*) from near Gioia, on the west coast. 12°–13°.

**Donnici.** A dry, red table wine, made from Montonico grapes, in the hilly country around Costenza. Deep red in colour, with orange tints, and rather full in flavour. 12°–14°.

**Favagreca.** One of the Vini di Scilla: see under Cerasolo.

**Frascineto.** Precisely similar to, and from the same grape and district as, Lacrima di Castrovillari (*q.v.*).

**Gioia, Bianco, Rosso and Rosato.** The district wines from the shores of the Gulf of Gioia, north of Reggio, where they are the commonest table wines. The white is made from Malvasia grapes only, and is dry, almost bitter. 13°. The red is very coarse and common, from a mixture of local grapes, and the *rosato* very pale indeed, almost amber in colour, and alcoholically the strongest. Better varieties have a neck-label awarded by a consortium set up by the provincial government, but even these are not remarkable.

**Greco di Gerace.** A really distinguished dessert wine, made in the hills around Gerace, just inland from Locri, on the east coast of the toe of Italy. The grape, Greco di Gerace, is not to be confused with the white and red Greco grapes (see below). Little of the real stuff – a deep amber in colour, rich in flavour, and smelling deliciously of orange blossom, 16°–17° – reaches the market,[1] though it is much in demand: the local small farmers grow a few modest rows of the Greco di Gerace between those of the more common grapes used for table wines, and keep the wine they make from it to celebrate births, baptisms, wedding and, no doubt, funerals.

**Greco Rosso, Greco Rosso di Pontegrande or Coticchietto.** A cherry-red wine, from the mountainous district near Catanzaro, made from Greco Nero, Greco Bianco, Nerollone and Nerello grapes. Harsh when young but seldom found with any bottle-age. Sometimes called Coticchietto, after a small commune in the district that has the reputation of producing better wine than its neighbours – enquiring outsiders find it hard to discern the distinction. 13°.

**Ieracare.** One of the Vini di Scilla: see under Cerasolo.

**Lacrima di Castrovillari.** Dry red wine from the Lagrima grape, grown in the Cosenza district, said to be worth keeping in bottle for a year or so. 14°.

**Lametino.** A dry white wine with a full, rather Madeira-ish taste.

**Limbaldi Rosso.** A precisely similar wine to Cafaro (*q.v.*).

**Magliocco or Magliocco di Calabria.** A big red wine, from the Magliocco, Marsigliana and other grapes, grown widely around the region, and especially near Nicastro (after which it is sometimes called Nicastro Rosso. It is also known as Sambiase, and there are local varieties known as San Sidero and Rossano). Extremely deep in colour and high in alcoholic strength (14°); a great deal is sent north for blending.

**Malvasia di Catanzaro.** A strong, sweet wine made from the white Malvasia grape, grown in rows between those of commoner vines, in the plains of Cirò and Sambiase and on the hills around Catanzaro. 16°.

**Mirto.** A strong (16°–17°) red wine with amber tints, aged locally in bottle for as much as fifteen years – when it is still coarse.

**Montonico.** Another strong, sweet dessert wine, from the grape of the same name,

---

[1] Though there is a commercial brand of some repute: Greco Rizziconi.

grown in much the same areas as the Greco di Gerace, which it closely resembles, and under which name I suspect it is sometimes sold. 16°.

**Moscato.** As elsewhere, a good deal of sweet dessert wine is made in Calabria from the Moscato grape: according to locality, it is known here as Moscato di Cosenza, di Frascineto, di Reggio Calabria and di Saracena – this last variety being said to differ slightly from the others, as being made from a slightly different *cépage* which gives a little less sweetness and more character. 15°–16°.

**Nicastro Bianco.** Semi-sweet and fragrant white wine, made from Malvasia, Greco Bianco and other grapes around Nicastro (better known for its red Magliocco) on the hills facing the Gulf of St Eufemia, or Nicastro. Probably the lightest table wine of the region. 11°.

**Paci.** One of the Vini di Scilla: see under Cerasolo.

**Palizzi and Pellaro.** Full red wines, made from Nerello grapes in the very tip of the toe of Italy, and largely sent north for blending. 13°–16°. Drinking it locally I have found the Pellaro very sharp and bitter under a superficial sweetness.

**Pollino.** More general name for the robust red wines of which Lacrima di Castrovillari (*q.v.*) is an example.

**Provilaro.** A dry white wine, of some delicacy as Calabrian white wines go, from south of Cosenza. 13°.

**Rogliano Rosso.** Another name for Savuto (*q.v.*).

**Rossano.** See under Magliocco.

**Rubino.** A common red wine of Reggio di Calabria, very strong and very deep in colour. 14°–15°.

**Sambiase.** See under Magliocco.

**San Sidero.** See under Magliocco.

**Savuto.** From the same area as Provilaro, but red, made from Magliocco (known here as Arvino), Greco Nero and Greco Bianco grapes. A full-bodied, hearty wine, sometimes rather frothy when poured, but not as a rule *frizzante*. 13°. Was well knwon enough before the phylloxera, which struck here in 1870, to have been exported to the United States (no doubt because of the number of immigrants there from this poverty-stricken part of Italy), but now little known outside its own area.

**Scilla, Vini di.** See under Cerasolo.

**Sila, Rosso della.** Red table wine from the district of the same name, near Cosenza.

**Trasfigurato di Seminara.** Veronelli records a curious wine from Seminara, near Reggio, which is smoked in jars. I have never come acrosss it and cannot imagine what it must taste like.

**Verbicaro, Rosso di.** A dry, big red wine from near Cosenza. 14°.

# CHAPTER SIXTEEN

# Sicily

As poor as the southern region of the mainland, and even more over-populated, Sicily presents a more luxurious face to the visitor than does Calabria, with its forbidding mountains and thick forests, the Basilicata with its bleak moorlands, or Apulia's drab villages, in the mountains or by the shore. What is not mountain in Sicily is taken up by vineyards and orchards and olive groves, dates and figs and pomegranates, especially in the country around Marsala, at the flat western end of the island, and in the Conca d'Oro or 'golden shell' of rich countryside around Palermo.

The Greeks were in Sicily nearly three thousand years ago – in the eighth century B.C. – and it is certain that wine was being grown there at that time. According to Critias, the Athenian tyrant who was writing some four centuries later, Sicily was already then legendary as birthplace of the art of good living, and the Sicilian Greeks as the inventors of kottabos, the game of tossing the last drops of wine in a glass with a flick of the wrist into a vase across the room. Archestratus, a Sicilian Greek, who wrote a book on gastronomy in epic hexameters, was, according to Mr Warner Allen, the Brillat-Savarin of Aristotle's time.

Nowadays Sicily is neither so distinguished as to set the style in eating and drinking, nor so carefree as to play games with heeltaps. The vivid chapter on 'The Vine Harvest' in Gavin Maxwell's *The Ten Pains of Death* reflects something of the bitterness of the Sicilian peasant who sees the shops selling wine at ten times the price he was paid for it by the big wholesale dealers who, with the large-scale cultivators, now have a grip on the Sicilian wine trade. Most of the wines of Sicily are made in big commercial wineries, and those peasants who have any land at all, or the use of any (all too many are both landless and jobless, hiring themselves out to the big growers at vintage time), move their modest vineyards every twenty years or so and sell either the grapes or the wine they have made from them to the big firms.

Eventually, no doubt, the spread of co-operatives will do something to provide a better life for the peasant grower, as well as raise the standards of quality of Sicilian wines, most of which, at present, are coarse and heavy, used largely for blending, although the dessert wines of the island, of course, have a special place among the wines of Italy; there are, in fact, some few pleasant enough table wines to be found in the island, but they do not get exported even to the mainland, let alone abroad.

## The Wines of Sicily

**Adrano.** A red wine from the foot of Etna, very similar to Biancavilla (*q.v.*).

**Akracas Bianco.** The un-Italian name derives from the old Greek name for Agrigento, on the south coast, around which they grow Catarratto Lucido, Insolia and other grapes, which make a dry white wine, much used on the mainland for blending but here as a table wine, which takes on something of a Marsala flavour when it has any bottle-age – or so the locals say, though to many palates it will seem simply to have become maderised. 12°–15°.

**A.L.A.** The initials stand for Antico Liquor Vino Amarascato, a curiosity of the island, which one would be inclined to omit from a book about wines as being a liqueur, save that all the reference books include it, where they exclude such other after-dinner digestives as Strega, Sambuco, and the like. This oddity is said – like so much else Sicilian – to date from Graeco-Roman times, and is made by allowing sweet, semi-dried black grapes to ferment in casks made of cherry-wood, the scent and flavour of which are imparted to the resultant heavy sweet wine, which is drunk in these parts both as an aperitif and as a liqueur. 19°.

**Albanello di Siracusa.** From the grape and the district of the same names. There is a dry and a sweet Albanello: the dry I have found to be full and flavoury – more suitable as an aperitif than as a table wine; it has a bitter and appetizing finish. Some experts detect a flavour as of Marsala about it, especially as it is aged in wood for eight or ten years, and reaches a strength of 17°–18°. Veronelli does not recommend the sweet Albanello, made of semi-dried grapes, though other Italian experts regard it as the more important of the two.

**Alcamo.** A dry white wine from Alcamo and the district around the Gulf of Castella-mare, made from Catarratto Lucido, Grecanico, Damaschino and other local grapes. Soft and lacking in acidity; a great deal of it is used as a basis for vermouth, both locally and on the mainland. 12°–15°. A local variety is sometimes known as Segesta Bianco, from the Roman city near by, and there is a new *consorzio* of growers, who aim to improve quality and award labels.

**Ambrato di Comiso.** Heavy, dry white wine, reaching as much as 18°, deep amber in colour, made from Catarratto, Calabrese, Damaschino and other grapes in the south-east of the island, near Ragusa. In deference to changing tastes, the growers are now trying to produce a wine lighter both in taste and alcoholic strength, though soil and sun are against them.

**Aragona-Canicatti.** A dry, full, fairly strong, cherry-red wine, with pretty tawny lights in it, made around Agrigento, by taking the must off the skins fairly early, as for a *rosé*, but then adding a concentration of sweet must to give more body and alcoholic strength. Drunk as an aperitif, it is said to resemble Marsala – but so is every strong aperitif wine in Sicily. 13°.

**Barcellona.** See under Capo Rosso.

**Bazia.** A red wine from the north-east of the island: see under Capo Rosso.

**Belice Bianco.** A dry, heavy wine, made from Catarratto Comune, Catarratot Lucido and other grapes in the south of the island, some used as a basis for Marsala, some sold as table wines. A new growers' association is beginning to watch quality. 11°–15°.

**Biancavilla.** A full, deep-red wine, with a powerful bouquet and a bitter after-taste, deriving a great deal of its character from the volcanic soil at the foot of Etna, where it comes from. Adrano and Ragalna are similar wines, though not quite so well known. (Adrano and Biancavilla are twin townships, south-west of Etna, and Ragalna is a smaller village near by.) Made from Nerello, Montellato, Spagnolo and Vernaccia

Rossa grapes. 12°–14°. A good, sound table wine that is said to acquire greater distinction with bottle-age.

**Bianchi Carta.** Strong, dry white wines (17°–18°) grown from a wide variety of common local grapes around Castellamare del Golfo, west of Palermo, in the north-west corner of the island, and exported for blending, though a lighter local wine of much the same breed, and no particular merit, is drunk as a table wine and known as Bianco di Castellamare.

**Bosco dell'Etna.** A red wine from those slopes of Etna that descend towards Catania: see under Etna.

**Capo Bianco, Capo Rosso.** Wines from the north-east corner of Sicily, opposite the Lipari Islands. The white is made from Catarratto Bianco, Chasselas Doré and Panse Precoce grapes, light, dry and fairly delicate as Sicilian wines go (12°–12·5°) and to be drunk young and very cool, when it goes well with the local shellfish. The red is lightish in shade, often between a red and a *rosé*, made from Nerello Cappuccio, Mascalese, Nero d'Avola, Nocera and, in some cases, some Sangiovese and Barbera grapes, but stronger and fuller than its colour would suggest. One of the better local red wines of the island but rather astringent when very young, as it is too often served. 13°–15°. Very similar wines from the same district are Milazzo, both white and red (the red sometimes known as Barcellona) – the red tends to be stronger and coarser (13°–17°) than the Capo Rosso – and Furnari and Bazia, which are not quite so rough, and sometimes fuller in colour.

**Cerasuolo.** Wines with this name – which means cherry-red – come from Vittoria, Isola and Floridia, in the south-east corner of the island. They get their colour from a mixture of black and white grapes, chiefly Frappato (hence the alternative name of Frappato di Vittoria), Calabrese, Grossonero and Albanello, fermented very quickly. These are generous, full-bodied wines that mature quickly, with a herby, fruity scent, and go well with rich dishes. The Vittoria is probably the finest of the group (13°–14°); the Floridia the heaviest and headiest (15°–17°) and better used for blending.

**Ciclopi, Bianco, Rosso and Rosato.** See under Etna.

**Corvo di Casteldaccia, Bianco and Rosso.** From near Palermo, the white made from Catarratto and Insolia grapes, dry, rather pale, and with not a great deal of character, but the red, to my mind, one of the best in the island (not so like a claret as the locals would wish to think, and often say, but more like one of the red wines of the Loire), made from Perricone and Catanese grapes, clear, light and dry, and credited by some writers with all sorts of medicinal qualities. It needs a couple of years in bottle. White, 12°–14°. Red, 13°–14·5°. One of the whites is also called Corvo Colomba Platino, which means platinum-blonde dove-raven, a phrase much harder to swallow than the wine. (The name Corvo comes from a complicated local legend involving a hermit, a noisy raven, the big stick the locals gave the hermit to beat the bird away with, and the vine that sprang from the stick.)

**Eloro, Bianco, Rosso and Rosato.** Eloro was the old name for the river Tellaro, which flows through the plain of Noto to the sea at the south-east corner of Sicily: hence the name of these rather coarse red, white and *rosé* wines – the whites made from Grillo, Catarratto and Albanello grapes (13°–14·5°), the reds and the *rosés* from Calabrese, Nerello d'Avola and Nerello Mascalese (13°–15°).

**Etna, Bianco and Rosso.** The lower and some of the middle slopes of Etna are covered with vineyards, producing red and white wines of moderate quality and with various names. Generally speaking the whites are made from Carricante, Catarratto Comune, Catarratto Lucido, Minnella and Insolia grapes, and are dry and a little *frizzante*. They are much more plentiful than the reds. 12°–13·5°. The reds are made from Nerello Mascalese and Nocera grapes, and are rather astringent and light-bodied. 12°–14°. The wines from the middle slopes (Etnei di Mezza Montagna), grown at a height of about two thousand feet, tend to be finer than the others – such district names as Linguaglossa and Sant'Alfio are worth looking for – but in general the reds are for export as mixing wines, or even as 'industrial wines', in which latter case they go abroad (notably to Germany) to be made into brandies and vermouths, and it is permitted, as they will not bear Italian names of origin, to add neutral alcohol to them. (Indeed, the Germans require so high a strength as to make this necessary.) Among the individual Etna wines are Ciclopi, Ragabo, Biancavilla, Ragalna (these four being among the better reds), Sparviero, Trecastagni, Villagrande, Mascali, Randazzo and Solichiata.

**Etna Madera.** A sort of poor man's Marsala, from the coast east of Etna, fortified with alcohol. 16°–17°.

**Faro.** One of Sicily's better red wines, made from Nerello Cappuccio, Nerello Mascalese, Nocera and other grapes, near Messina: said to have been imported a great deal by the French at the height of the phylloxera crisis and still exported to the United States and elsewhere. Matured two years in cask before bottling, it is dry and rather pale in colour: I have always found it flat and disappointing at the finish, but quite an acceptable table wine. 13°–14°.

**Fontana Murato, Bianco, Rosso and Cerasuolo.** See under Valledolmo.

**Francofonte.** A heavy red mixing wine, the only claim to distinction of which is that it is quaffed by Turiddu in *Cavalleria Rusticana*.

**Frappato di Vittoria.** One of the main Sicilian Cerasuolo wines (*q.v.*).

**Furnari (or Bazia).** See under Capo.

**Garitta.** See under Maniaci.

**Goccia d'Oro.** See under Moscato.

**Lacrima d'Aretusa.** Sweet wine from Moscatellone and Zibibbo grapes, grown in various districts around Syracuse.

**Leonforte, Bianco and Rosso.** The white (12°–14·5°), made from Catarratto, Minella and Carricante grapes, is dry and rich in flavour; the red, from Nerello Mascalese, and Nocera rather more coarse (13°–15°). They come from the mountainous middle of the island, between Leonforte and Enna.

**Malvasia di Lipari, Malvasia di Milazzo.** Quite one of the best – perhaps the best – of the sweet golden dessert Malvasia wines found all over Italy is that called 'di Lipari', though in fact most of it comes from the other islands in the little Aeolian group: Stromboli and Salina. It is rich and luscious, much prettier to the nose than one would think from the enthusiastic Cùnsolo, who describes its scent as being 'a marvellous mixture of broom, fennel and liquorice'.

Not perhaps quite so fine, but well above the national average, is the Malvasia di Malazzo, from the Sicilian promontory that juts out towards the Aeolian Islands. Both the Lipari and the Milazzo come from a Malvasia grape that is said to differ slightly from the mainland variety, pressed when semi-dried, and the fermentation arrested by the addition of spirits. The maturing and bottling (after three years in cask) takes place in Messina and Naples, where production is now commercialized. 14°–16°.

**Mamertino.** Named after the Mamertini, a tribe that inhabited the north-eastern corner of Sicily some centuries before Christ, this was a wine known to the Romans and referred to by Martial, Pliny and others. Made from Catarratto, Insolia and Pedro Ximenes, the grape of Southern Spain that adds sweetness to dessert sherries, there are both dryish and very sweet types, but most of it is drunk on the spot, semi-sweet, by the people who grow it. 15°–17°.

**Maniaci and Garitta.** Red wines from the shores of Lake Garitta, not so coarse and heavy as many local Sicilian wines. 13°–14°.

**Marsala.** This rich fabrication is Sicily's most famous wine, for which the British may well take some credit, for it was John Woodhouse, a Liverpool merchant, who, visiting Sicily about 1760, realized that the wines of the extreme western end of the island, grown in the dry, iron-bearing soil, under the blazing sun, between Trapani and Marsala, had strong affinities with the basic wines from which port, sherry and madeira were made, and set up, with his sons, the Marsala firm of Woodhouse, soon to be joined in rivalry with such others as Inghams and Whittakers. The name of Marsala was soon well known because Nelson victualled his fleet here, and had dealings with Woodhouse (though it was probably ordinary table wine that he took aboard for his men), and although it is rather out of fashion in England nowadays as an aperitif or a dessert wine, in Regency and Victorian times it rivalled Madeira. The world was again reminded of its name in 1860, when Garibaldi landed with his Thousand at Marsala, with British men-o'-war offshore to protect what by this time were substantial British interests, though there is no historical foundation for the pleasing legend that a bombardment by Bourbon ships was stopped because of representations that British property – the Woodhouse and Ingham factories – was being, or was in danger of being, damaged.[1]

Like sherry and port, Marsala is a fortified wine, and it bears some resemblance to Madeira in that one, at any rate, of its constituent parts is cooked, or heated. Marsala is made by adding to the dry – even harsh – fragrant white wine of the district,[2] in the proportion of six parts to every hundred, a mixture of one-quarter wine brandy and three-quarters of a much sweeter wine of the area made from semi-dried grapes. Then a third component is added, also six parts to every hundred of the original 'straight wine – a young, unfermented grape juice that has been slowly heated until it has become thick, sweet and caramelly in colour, texture and flavour.

The mixture rests in cask for anything from four months to five years, taking on a deep-brown colour, with the original dry white wine giving a dry under-taste to the general sweetness – a sweetness that slowly diminishes with age. (Many of the finer Marsalas are made on the same *solera* system as sherry, so that a date such as 1840, or 1870, indicates only the oldest wine in the blend. But age is to be prized in a Marsala.)

By laws of 1931 and 1950 the zone in which Marsala is produced has been strictly delimited, and the grades of wine have been defined as follows:

---

[1] There is a detailed account of how the British ships came to be present, and the part they played, in G. M. Trevelyan's *Garibaldi and The Thousand* (London, 1909), Chapter XIII.
[2] Made from Grillo, Catarratto, Insolia and Damaschino grapes and reaching a strength of 14°–16°.

**Marsala Fine** (sometimes labelled 'I.P.' or 'Italia Particolare') must be aged at least four months, and reach 17° of alcohol and 5° of sugar;

**Marsala Superiore** (sometimes labelled 'L.P.', 'S.O.M. – for 'Superior Old Marsala' or 'G.D.' – for 'Garibaldi Dolce', in honour of the landing of the Thousand) must be aged at least two years and have 18° alcohol and – if a sweet Marsala, for there are drier types – 10° sugar;

**Marsala Vergine.** This is the original wine, without the additions, but aged, often by the *solera* system. Must be at least five years old and reach 18° alcohol; and

**Marsala Speciale.** These are the special types, such as Marsala Uovo, Marsala Crema and Marsala Mandorla – thickened, sweetened and flavoured: 18° alcohol and 10° sugar.

Marsala is not to everyone's taste – it is not to mine – but it is an important dessert wine, with one particular virtue: it does not deteriorate after the bottle has been opened, so that one can be sure in any Italian café or restaurant of having a glass of Marsala in decent condition. Blended with egg yolks, it makes one of the best of all after-dinner sweets, *zabaglione*, the bottled commercial version of which, *Marsala Uovo* (or *all'Uovo*) tastes simply like toffee and is nothing like so nice, though I have no doubt that it is wholesome.

Virtually all the production of Marsala is in the hands of big companies, both those with the English names already mentioned and other, Italian, foundations, of which Florio is probably the most distinguished, as its wines seem to be the most highly thought of. The leading firms are now joined in a Consorzio per la Tutela del Vino Marsala, and all bottles of the real thing should bear a numbered neck-label showing the outline of the island of Sicily in red.

**Mascali.** See under Etna.

**Menfi.** Very little of this dry white wine is consumed as a table wine: most is used in the making of Marsala, as the district from which it comes, on the south-western coast of the island, lies just within the delimited Marsala area.

**Mezza Montagna dell'Etna** (**Vino di**). See under Etna.

**Mila, Bianco di.** An extremely light, rather acid, white wine, a rare thing in these parts (9°–10°), from the Etna district, without a great deal of interest, and used to lighten some of the coarser Sicilian wines.

**Milazzo, Bianco and Rosso.** See under Capo.

**Monreale.** Both Marsala (*q.v.*) and Partinico Bianco (*q.v.*) are produced here, and sometimes take the name – also a very strong but pale white table wine.

**Moscato.** Good sweet wines are made in various parts of Sicily, as elsewhere, from the Moscato grape, semi-dried, that of Siracusa being the finest – and the most difficult to find. Others are from Chiaramonte, Comiso, Note, Pantelleria, Segesta, Vittoria and Zucco. (This last is also known as Goccia d'Oro.) The Moscato of Pantellerie, which is protected by a *consorzio*, is made not from the true Moscato but from a variant called Zibibbo, which is said to have been brought to the island by the Arabs, the word meaning 'raisin' or dried grape.

**Naccarella.** Another golden dessert wine, also – like the finest Moscato – from Syracuse, made from a small local grape that is allowed to be attacked on the vine by the 'noble rot' that makes the great Sauternes. 18°.

**Ombra.** A cherry-red dry wine, made on the outskirts of Catania from Nerello, Mascalese, Carricante and Vesparo grapes, fairly light in flavour and texture, unlike the Cerasuolo wines (*q.v.*) in that it is taken earlier off the skins and is meant to be drunk young. 12·5°–13·5°.

**Pachino Rosso.** A heavy red wine made from Calabrese and Negro d'Avola grapes in the Syracuse district, and meant largely for export as a blending wine, though some small growers age it for family use by a sort of *solera* system, called here the *botte madre* or 'mother-cask' system, by which is produced what is claimed to be a very fine table wine, though it has never come my way. 14°–17°.

**Partinico Bianco.** Made from local varieties of grape between Trapani and Palermo around the Gulf of Castellamare, and included among the 'virgin' Marsalas. Also drunk in its own right, chilled, as an excellent dry aperitif or, young, as a table wine. 16°.

**Passito di Linguaglossa, Passito di Misilmeri, Passolato di Trapani.** Sweet golden wines made from semi-dried (*passito*) grapes in the various districts named. See under Piedmont.

**Piana di Catania, Vini della.** Mixing wines made very harsh and strong, in the Catanian plain, by keeping the must on the skins for at least twenty-four hours – a method known locally as *scrudazzato*.

**Piana di Mascali, Vini della.** Wines somewhat similar to the above but more frequently used locally as table wines, from the narrow strip between Etna and the sea, north of Catania.

**Pollio.** Another name for the Moscato di Siracusa (*q.v.*).

**Porto Casteldaccia.** They say now that the little town of Casteldaccia (the Corvo wine of which we have already listed: see above) once had a port, and that this sweet dessert wine owes its name not to any deliberate attempt to imitate the wine of Oporto but because wines destined for Genoa used to lie in cask on the quay of the *porto*, acquiring flavour and character under the Sicilian sun. Personally, I doubt this tale, for there is also a so-called 'Sherry Stravecchi odi Casteldaccia': this is a town the wines of which aim to please by adopting the names of their betters.

**Ragabò.** One of the wines of Etna (*q.v.*).

**Ragalna.** Red and white wines of Etna (*q.v.*).

**Randazzò.** One of the wines of Etna (*q.v.*).

**Ribollito di Marsala.** Called 're-boiled' because fermented with the stalks. A dry red wine, very full and big, with a taste like that of a young Manduria (*q.v.* under Apulia). 12°–14°.

**San Salvador.** A deep red, dry wine, made from Catarratto and Morello grapes near Catania, and aged in wood for three years before bottling, to produce a sound, full-bodied table wine of some modest distinction and, according to Veronelli, considerable therapeutic properties. But the same seems to be said in Sicily of any drinkable red wine. 13°–14°.

**Scoglitti.** A heavy red mixing wine from near Vittoria, once distinguished above its present apparent merits as having been imported by the Bordelais at the time of the phylloxera.

**Segesta Bianco.** A variety of Alcamo (*q.v.*).

**Sherry Stravecchio di Casteldaccia.** See under Porto di Casteldaccia.

**Sicilia Liquoroso.** General name for the rich sugary wines produced pretty well all over the island as a basis for dessert wines, aperitifs of various kinds, and for blending, both in Sicily and on the mainland.

**Siculiana.** Made from Calabrese, Nerello, Insolia and Catarratto grapes in the coastal area west of Agrigento, on the south coast. A red wine, lightish in colour, but big enough in body to be used on the mainland as a mixing wine, though Sicilians like it as a table wine. 14°.

**Solichiata.** One of the wines of Etna (*q.v.*).

**Sparviero.** One of the wines of Etna (*q.v.*).

**Taormina.** Not all the wines offered as 'local' in the smart hotels and tourists' restaurants of Taormina come from around the fancy little town itself – many are the cheapest Etna wines. But there *is* produced, on the nearest Etna slopes, a very good dry, fragrant white wine, from Catarratto, Grillo, Insolia, Minella Bianca, Damaschina and Carricante grapes, admirable with fish, to the amount of only about 50,000 bottles a year – nothing like enough for the total number of visitors, and nothing like so many as claim the name. 12°–12·5°.

**Terreforti, Rosso delle.** A powerful red wine, made in the Catanian plain, drunk young locally as a table wine and also exported for blending. 14°–16°.

**Tintone or Tintore.** A similar wine to the above, not so strong, but of a particularly intense red, which is also useful in blending or, as they say, 'as a corrective'.

**Trecastagni.** See under Etna: the wine is drunk in vast quantities on every 10th of May, the day of the local Saint Alfio.

**Val d'Anapo, Rosso (or Rubino) and Bianco (or Ambra).** From the Anapo valley, inland from Syracuse. The white is made from Catarratto and Insolia grapes, and is deep gold in colour and quite uncompromisingly dry. 12°–13°. The red, very clear in colour and also very dry and light, is made from the same grapes, along with Nero d'Avola and Calabrese. 12°–13°. Sometimes served rather too young, when they have a rather astringent finish, but with a mere year or two in bottle are among the pleasantest of the island's table wines.

**Val di Lupo, Bianco, Rosso and Rosato.** From the same area as Leonforte (*q.v.*), but wines of a greater delicacy, for the white, which is dry and elegant, has Trebbiano, Malvasia Toscana and Pinot Grigio grapes in its *cépage*, as well as those of Leonforte; the red and the *rosé* also have Sangiovese, the red Val di Lupo being particularly soft, though dry, and an admirable table wine. 11·5°–12°.

**Valledolmo and Vallelunga.** Two names for the same wines, white and red, the Valledolmo from near Palermo, the other from the middle of the island, but both made from the same grapes – the white from Catarratto and Insolia grapes, producing a dry, rather full, golden wine of 12°–13°; the red from Perricone and other grapes, not particularly full for a Sicilian red but rather light and dry. 12°–13°. Fontana Murata is another name for very similar red and white wines.

**Villagrande, Bianco and Rosso.** Among the wines of Etna (*q.v.*).

**Vittoria.** Another name for Scoglitti (*q.v.*).

**Zucco.** Another name for Corvo di Casteldaccia (*q.v.*).

# CHAPTER SEVENTEEN

# *Sardinia*

'NOT a bit like Italy.' The theme recurs throughout D. H. Lawrence's peevish yet frequently perceptive *Sea and Sardinia*: Cagliari, the capital, is 'strange and rather wonderful, not a bit like Italy'; the countryside 'is very different from Italian landscapes . . . much wider, much more ordinary, not up-and-down at all, but running away into the distance. Unremarkable ridges of moor-like hills running away, perhaps to a bunch of dramatic peaks on the south-west. This gives a sense of space, which is so lacking in Italy . . . like liberty itself, after the peaky confinement of Sicily.'

As with the critics and the countryside, so with the people and the wines. The people, as Mr Alan Ross has observed,[1] displaying 'none of the superficial gaiety of the Italians, none of their malleability or lightness of heart. They are courteous, generous, but essentially reserved.' And the wines are strangely individual: dry wines drunk as dessert wines, sweet wines drunk as aperitifs and tables wines 'powerful of impact and dark in colour', in Mr Iain Crawford's summing-up:[2] the whites almost *rosé*, and reds that truly deserve to be called, as they are, *vini neri*, black wines. Many of them are stronger than the 14° that the British Customs and Excise decrees as the upper limit of alcoholic strength for table wines: were they to be imported, they would pay as high a duty as port or sherry. Mention of sherry reminds one of the strangest Sardinian wine of all, Vernaccia, uncannily like a sherry, though made without any of the elaborate processes that a true sherry demands – an unfortified aperitif wine that may well have a great future as Sardinia develops.

The island is changing fast – faster, perhaps, than any other part of Italy. A post-war Italo-American campaign, backed by the Rockefeller Foundation, cleared the island of malarial mosquitoes, and this made it possible to open the island to tourists. Already there are night clubs and an airport, and new hotels and millionaires' beaches in the north-east corner of the island, providing new markets for the island's wines, and new inducements to make them more carefully and market them more skilfully.

All the more so because with the stricter application of the new Italian wine laws there will be at any rate a slightly diminished demand from the mainland for strong, coarse Sardinian wines of high alcoholic strength as 'cutting' wines: such wines will have to be taught their manners (ageing can mellow wine as it mellows men) so as to be able to enter the more sophisticated society brought to Sardinia by the tourist trade.

It is all the easier for this to happen because of the amazing growth of the co-operative system in Sardinia in the past few years. Much of the money that both the central government in Rome and the regional government in Cagliari have put into Sardinian agriculture has wisely been spent on new co-operative wineries with new equipment – about eighty per cent of the island's wine now comes from co-operatives, and the extra money they earn for the growers may well, as the next stage, go towards replan-

[1] In his *South to Sardinia* (London, 1960).
[2] In 'Giustamente Alcoolico', article in *Wine* magazine, March–April 1964.

ning the older vineyards and replanting them with newer and perhaps better-bred vines.

# Wines of Sardinia

**Anghelu Ruju.** The curious name is that of one of Sardinia's strange prehistoric townships, near Alghero, in the north-west of the island, near which a strong, sweet, red dessert wine is made in small quantities from the Cannonau grape, dried in the sun for a week after picking, and with stalks removed. Not so much like port as the local people fondly imagine but somewhere between a ruby port and an Aleatico in style – with a little of the distinction of the port, and less of the fragrance of the Aleatico. 19°.

**Arbaia.** A rather finer variety of Gallura (*q.v.*).

**Barbera Sarda.** The Barbera grape of Piedmont was introduced into Sardinia in the last century and is grown fairly widely in the south of the island, around Cagliari, where it makes a good red table wine, though rather coarser than those of Northern Italy – perhaps because of the greater heat and stronger sunshine, the heat intensified by the Sardinian method of growing vines *ad alberello*, close to the ground, from which the heat is reflected onto the vines. 13°–15°.

**Campidano di Cagliari.** A simple local red table wine, from the Campidano plain, which stretches north-north-west from Cagliari, made from Cannonau, Bovali, Girò and Monica grapes, light in colour and drunk young. The name is fairly general and some of the wines are called Sandalyon, Parteollese and Marmilla: the Sandalyon, in my experience, being very pale, with tawny tints, dry but with an underlying blandness – a pleasant table wine. 12°–14°.

**Castelsardo.** Similar to the red wine of Sorso (*q.v.*).

**Cannonau.** The Cannonau grape is widely grown throughout the island, and dry, sweet and semi-sweet red and *rosé* wines are made from it. (Note that the so-called Cannonau Bianco di Jerzu, or Ogliastra Bianco, is in fact a *rosé* wine.) The sweeter varieties make pleasant light dessert wines (about 15°–16°); the dry Cannonau is fairly commonplace, though I have drunk in the mountains a 1958 Perla Rubia, which is one of the 'white' Cannonaus of Jerzu, a pale pink with orange tints, that was a table wine of considerable character, but strong (16°) for midday drinking. (It fortunately lacked what the enthusiastic Cùnsolo found to praise in the dry Cannonau: 'a scent of roses; a taste of bitter almonds; and an under-taste of chocolate'.)

**Capo Ferrato.** One of the outward and visible signs of the rehabilitation of Sardinia, partly due to the regional government, partly to money from Rome, is the sweep of newly planted vineyards in many parts of the island. Near Capo Ferrato, in the south-eastern corner, are those of the *Ente di Trasformazione Fondiaria Agraria della Sardegna* (ETFAS), where they grow a good strong red table wine, largely from Cannonau grapes, dry but mellow, heavy enough to accompany the local game. 15°–17°.

**Capo Giglio.** One of the wines of the Nurra (*q.v.*).

**Dorato di Sorso.** An almost orange-coloured wine made from Cannonau grapes grown near Sorso, the great wine-growing centre near Sassari; light but strong, bitter-sweet, and drunk as an aperitif or a dessert wine. 16° and over.

**Dorgali, Rosso and Rosato.** Dry red and *rosé* wines from near Dorgali, in the middle of the east coast, from Cannonau and other grapes, and said to be perhaps the strongest table wines of Italy (the *rosé* not quite so strong). Authorities differ as to their alcoholic strength: I have seen it put as low as 14·5°, which makes nonsense of the boast, but as high as 19°. Certainly not fine wines.

**Embarcador.** An attempt to fabricate a sort of port, by mixing various wines or musts – some, I am told, from Portugal itself – at Alghero. Not to be recommended. 20°–22°.

**Fior di Romangia.** A dry, deep-pink table wine that I have drunk in Cagliari, but that is not recorded in any of the reference books. (Cf. Lagosta.)

**Gallura.** A dry red table wine, with a bitter finish, made from a mixture of Cannonau and other grapes in the Sassari area; rather light for a Sardinian wine, and more advisable, therefore, than most for midday meals in high summer. 11°–13°.

**Girò.** A very pretty, topaz-coloured lightish dessert wine made from the Girò grape, similar to Monica and Nasco (*qq.v.*). 16°–17°.

**Ierzu or Jerzu.** See under Cannonau.

**I Piani.** Among the better red wines of the Nurra (*q.v.*).

**Lagosta.** A dry – even tart – white table wine from Alghero, made from a mixture of grapes that includes Vermentino. Possibly a brand name, as it is not recorded in the reference books.

**Logudoro.** Wines very similar to the Gallura wines (*q.v.*) but rather lighter and sweeter, from south of Sassari and the Lago del Coghinas. 11°–13°.

**Malvasia di Bosa; Malvasia di Cagliari.** Made from Malvasia grapes in various parts of the island but chiefly in the two named: an aperitif or dessert wine, according to individual fancy – it smells sweeter than its taste, which is almost that of a medium sherry, an amontillado or an oloroso, not luscious, but not wholly dry. The bouquet is pleasantly flowery. The Malvasia of Bosa has the more intense colour of the two named here, and a rather fuller flavour. 17°.

**Mamuntanas.** One of the better red wines of the Nurra (*q.v.*).

**Mandrolisai.** A good red table wine, from one of the newly established co-operatives in the very middle of the island, in the district from which it take its name. Made from Cannonau grapes and the recently introduced Dolcetto of Piedmont (not, as is sometimes stated, Nebbiolo), it is clear, brilliant red, with a pleasant bouquet, and a firm dry finish. 12°–13°.

**Maristella.** One of the better white wines of the Nurra (*q.v.*).

**Marmilla.** One of the wines of Campidano (*q.v.*).

**Mògoro, Bianco, Rosso and Rosato.** All are dry – even rather acid – table wines, from the north-western end of the Campidano, almost at the middle of the west coast: the whites (11°–13°) from Nuragus, Vernaccia and other grapes; the others from Cagnulari, Monica and Greco Nero. 12°–14°. The same wines are sometimes called Terralba, according to which end of the district they come from.

**Monica.** A sweet dessert wine made from the Monica grape, similar to Girò but much redder: not unlike the Spanish Malaga. 15°–18°.

**Moscato or Moscato Sardo.** Sweet dessert wines are made in various parts of the island from the Moscatello grape – that of Gallura (or Tempio) being perhaps the richest and finest. There is also a Moscato Spumante. The Moscato of Campidano has a pleasant musky scent. 15°–16°.

**Nasco.** Another of the island's lightish golden dessert wines, of the same type as the

Monica and the Girò but made from the Nasco grape. It has a quite charming orange-blossom bouquet, and the faintly bitter under-taste to the sweetness makes it perhaps the most interesting of its type. 15°–17°.

**Ninfeo.** A white dessert wine, sweeter, stronger and more scented than the other Nurra wines.

**Nuraghe Majore.** One of the better white wines of the Nurra (*q.v.*).

**Nuragus.** This is the name of what is economically the most important grape of Sardinia (opinions differ as to whether there is any etymological connection with the *Nuraghi*, the island's curious little stone houses). It is grown pretty well everywhere, but especially in the Campidano, and makes a simple, almost neutral, dry white wine much used not only as the local carafe wine – it goes pleasantly enough with fish – but to export for blending with the mainland wines, and as a basis for vermouth and sparkling wines. 11°–14°.

**Nuoro.** Virtually the same wine as the red Dorgali (*q.v.*).

**Nurra, Bianco and Rosso.** The north-western horn of the island is called the Nurra, a great wine-growing area. The whites are made from Vermentino, Torbato and the recently introduced Tocai Friulano grapes, and are dry with a fruity smell and a full flavour – used locally as common table wines drunk young, and for export. 12°–14°. The reds are rather heavier and of no great distinction (13°–14°), though there are some finer varieties sold under more specific names: I Piani, Mamuntanas and S. Maria la Palma. The better whites include Nuraghe Maggiore, Maristella and Capo Giglio.

**Ogliastra Bianco.** See under Cannonau.

**Ogliastra Rosso and Rosato.** Only slightly more deeply coloured versions of the above.

**Oliena.** A big, full-flavoured, almost bitter, red wine from the middle-east of the island, made from Cannonau, Monica and other grapes, which one Italian wine writer says has a tarry after-taste, and another says tastes of bitter chocolate. D'Annunzio praised it highly: it is, in fact, a good robust wine, to be drunk with rich dishes, and at dinner rather than at luncheon, preferably in the place where, like Jorrocks, one not only dines but sleeps – it reaches a strength of 18°. There is also a sweeter, dessert version, with the lusciousness of the Monica (*q.v.*) coming through.

**Parteollese.** One of the red wines of the Campidano (*q.v.*): there is also a *rosato*.

**Perla Rubia.** A particularly fine example of the Cannonau wines (*q.v.*).

**Sandalyon.** One of the wines from the Campidano (*q.v.*).

**Sangiovese Sardo, or di Arborea.** An acclimatization vineyard in Arborea, by the reclaimed marshland and salt-pans of Terralba, has had considerable success for the past thirty years or so with the noble Sangiovese of Chianti, producing an admirable red table wine not unworthy of its parentage. It is surprising that this grape has not been planted more extensively in Sardinia, but it may well be that it is not so prolific and not, therefore, so profitable, as the local varieties. Also, it will be a long time before a Sardinian Sangiovese can command the same price on the mainland or abroad as that of Tuscany. But it is worth seeking out when visiting Sardinia – a sound red table wine, with more than just a hint of the Chianti fragrance and flavour, but rather stronger and fuller, as one would expect from a sunnier, hotter climate. 13°–14°.

**Santa Maria la Palma.** One of the better red wines of the Nurra (*q.v.*).

**Sardinian Gold.** One of the brand names, now protected, of a Vernaccia (*q.v.*) from one of the island's most important co-operatives.

**Sardus Pater.** A deep red, strong (16°) and very fragrant dry table wine, made chiefly from Caregnano grapes, in the little island of Sant'Antioco, just off the south-west of Sardinia. There is also a less strong *rosato*.

**Semidano.** A dry white wine from the Campidano area, made from local grapes, but rather like a drier version of the Malvasia of the district.

**Sorso, Rosso di.** The district north of Sassari grows a variety of red wines from a mixture of grapes – wines that vary according to whether the Cannonau or the Cagnulari predominates, the one making a pleasant local table wine, the other, stronger and darker, being exported for blending. The wine of Castelsardo, hard by, is said to be more delicate and of better quality. 13°–14°.

**Sorso, Dorato di.** See under Dorato di Sorso.

**Terralba.** The same wines as those of Mògoro (*q.v.*).

**Torbato di Alghero.** This local variety of grape, grown only around Alghero, produces three types of wine:

**Torbato Secco.** A dry aperitif, though some drink it as a table wine. 14°.

**Torbato Extra.** A medium-sweet aperitif or dessert wine. 15°.

**Torbato Passito.** Made from the semi-dried grape, and very sweet. 18°.

Without being *like* sherry these wines can be regarded as similar in style to sherry, and as corresponding to a very light fino or manzanilla; a sweetish amontillado or oloroso; and a cream or golden sherry, respectively. If one does not expect too much of them they are very agreeable, and show an individual character.

**Torrevecchia.** One of the few wines to come from salty, marshy country – that of Marceddi at Faro di Capo Frasca, which juts into the sea near Terralba. It is made from a wide variety of grapes, including some Barbera and Sangiovese, as well as local varieties, and is a heavily scented, full, dry red wine, sometimes frothy and *frizzante*. 12°–14°.

**Trebbiano Sardo or Trebbiano di Arborea.** Another of the mainland grapes being successfully acclimatized at Arborea, like the Sangiovese (*q.v.*). It makes a light, fresh table wine: see under Emilia-Romagna and elsewhere.

**Vermentino, or Vermentino di Gallura.** An amber-coloured white wine, so dry and with such a bitter finish that it makes an admirable sherry-type aperitif like Vernaccia (see below), though it is also drunk locally as a table wine. From the Vermentino grape, grown chiefly in the Gallura district, in the extreme north of the island. 14°. There is also a Vermentino Spumante, semi-sweet, known usually simply as Gallura Spumante.

**Vernaccia.** A curiosity of the island and by far its best-known wine – a very dry, appetizingly bitter aperitif, made from the Vernaccia grape, with something of the style and character of a natural, unfortified sherry. The Sardinians drink it after, as well as before, meals: there are Vernaccia wines described as being di Nuoro, di Siniscola and di Oristano – the branded Sardinian Gold (*q.v.*) from near Oristano.

**Vin Cotto.** A certain amount is made in Sardinia: see under Marches.

# NOTE to
# THE WINES OF GERMANY

A revised German Wine Law was introduced in 1972.
Some of the information in this section
has been affected under these new regulations.

The chief effect is that all German wines must in future be classified
in three main categories: Tischwein (table wine),
Qualitätswein (wine of quality) and Qualitätswein mit Prädikat
(wine of special quality). The designation Naturwein is now
abolished. Existing sites are to be grouped into larger areas
(Bereich). There are strict rules about the amount of sugaring
permitted (none in the Qualitätswein mit Prädikat) and about
the degree of blending (progressively less in the better
quality wines). Basically the information on the label will
provide a very accurate indication of the nature of the wine
inside the bottle.

# The Wines of
# GERMANY

ANDRÉ L. SIMON
*and*
S. F. HALLGARTEN

*with a chapter on Sekt by*
H. ARNTZ

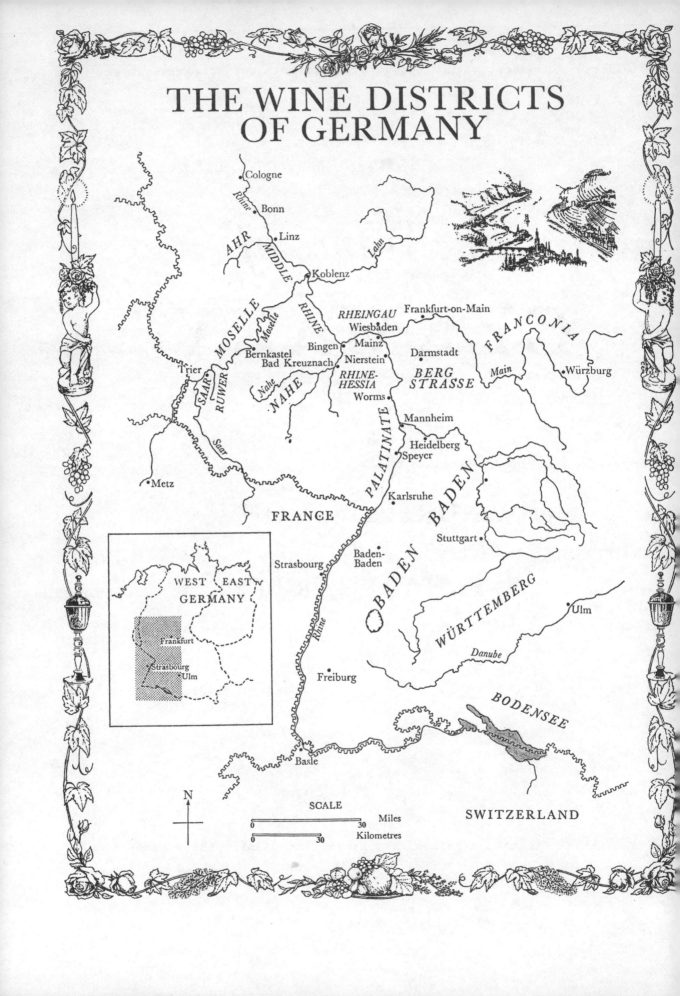

# THE WINE DISTRICTS
# OF GERMANY

Cologne

Bonn

Linz

Koblenz

AHR

MIDDLE

RHINE

Lahn

RHEINGAU — Frankfurt-on-Main

Wiesbaden

MOSELLE

Bernkastel

Bingen — Mainz

Bad Kreuznach — Nierstein

Trier

SAAR — RUWER

NAHE

Nahe

RHINE-
HESSIA

Worms

Darmstadt

FRANCONIA

BERG
STRASSE

Main — Würzburg

Mannheim

Heidelberg
Speyer

PALATINATE

Metz

FRANCE

Karlsruhe

BADEN

BADEN

Stuttgart

WEST   EAST
GERMANY

Frankfurt

Strasbourg
·Ulm

Strasbourg

Baden-
Baden

WÜRTTEMBERG

Ulm

Danube

Rhine

Freiburg

BODENSEE

Basle

N

SWITZERLAND

SCALE

0                    30   Miles
0                    30   Kilometres

CHAPTER ONE

# A Short History of German Wine

THERE has been wine in the Rhineland for nearly two thousand years; that is, ever since the Romans settled there and had it sent to them from Italy. It was not long, however, before they taught the natives how to grow grapes and make wine. Long before Romulus and Remus were born there had been vines growing wild and un-attended not only in the Rhineland but in many parts of Germany, their wayward tendrils clinging where they climbed from bush to tree. But the first wine to be drunk on the banks of the Rhine and Moselle must have been Italian commissariat wine that came with the Roman legions. The planting of new vineyards in Gaul, Spain and North Africa was not encouraged, and on several occasions it was prohibited altogether by Rome, because there was wine in plenty in Italy but often a grievous shortage of corn and other cereals. It must have been obvious from the first, however, that the steep wooded hills of the Rhine and Moselle could never be cornlands, whereas those of their slopes which faced south, south-east and south-west offered excellent sites for vineyards; all that was needed was muscle and sweat – of which there was no shortage, we can well imagine, where Rome ruled.

Trier or Trèves, on the Moselle, claims to be the oldest city in western Europe, built by a Prince Trebets who is believed to have come all the way from India many years before Rome was founded. It is by no means certain that it was so, but we do know that Augusta Treverorum, as the Romans called this city of the Trevii, their capital beyond the Alps, was second only to Rome for the number and beauty of its temples, palaces and baths. Roman emperors often resided there, and there must have been a great deal of social activity and many festive occasions, resulting in a large wine consumption. It is quite possible that better wines were imported from Italy or Gaul, by or for patricians and officials, but it is certain that in all parts of the land under Roman rule not only the army but also the civilian population who had adopted the Roman way of life must have been drinking home-grown wine in plenty.

Remains of Roman drinking cups and vessels have been found in great quantities in many parts of the Rhineland, proving beyond doubt that wine was in common use during the first century of the Christian era. This could not have happened had there not been vineyards at hand.

The best possible evidence that vineyards flourished on the hills of the Moselle at the beginning of the fourth century is to be found in the writings of Ausonius, a Roman proconsul who was born near Bordeaux and held an important post at Trier for some years. The hillside vineyards of the Moselle immediately bring back to his mind those of the Côte Pavie as seen from the terrace of Château Ausone, and he exclaims: 'O patria, insignem Baccho . . .' (Oh, my native land, dedicated to Bacchus . . .) There follows a heroic poem in praise of the wine-bearing hills of the Moselle, the echo of which may still be heard today along the banks of the same river, but in another tongue: 'O Mosella! Du hast ja so viel Wein!'

There are numerous records of early vineyards in many parts of the Rhineland. Such was the vineyard which the monks of Haslach, near Strasbourg, planted in A.D. 613. Others were being cultivated in A.D. 628 and A.D. 638 in the Ladenburg district and the lower Neckar valley at the time when, in A.D. 634, Dagobert confirmed the then Archbishop of Trier in all grants of vineyards in the valleys of the Rhine, Moselle and Loire. In A.D. 644 the Monastery of Wissemburg owned vineyards at Lautenbach, Grunnesbrunnen and 15 other places.

At the beginning of the ninth century we find in the household regulations of Charlemagne many instructions and remarks concerning wine and vineyards in Germany. It is during this century that appear the earliest records of such renowned vineyards as those of Rüdesheim, Geisenheim, Kreuznach, Eisenach and a great many more, while Nierstein wines are mentioned at the close of the tenth century.

Although we may give the Romans credit for being the first to bring to the Rhineland the right type of wine-making vines, and to teach the natives how to make wine, we also have ample evidence that Germany, and not only the Rhineland, owes a far greater debt of gratitude to the Church. The early missionaries who brought Christianity to the heathen populations of Central Europe were not merely preachers of the Gospel but priests of a church for which the Eucharist was then, as it is today, the all-important sacrifice of atonement. Without both bread and wine there could be no Mass. Hence the records of vineyards planted in Saxony and as far north as the Baltic, as soon as those missionaries were able to build a church or monastery.

Strange as it seems to us, there were German wines from northern vineyards which enjoyed a very fair reputation for a long time.

In the Rhineland, where climatic conditions and the nature of the soil were much more favourable, viticulture became at an early date one of the more important branches of agriculture, one which has retained not only its economic interest but its human appeal to this day, in spite of adverse conditions from time to time. Charlemagne was so generous in his gifts of land, including some vineyards which are among the most famous to this day, that he laid the foundation of the extraordinary power, temporal as well as spiritual, which a wealthy Church enjoyed in Germany from the tenth to the sixteenth century. The archbishops of Mainz, Trier, Cologne, Augsburg and other cities became very powerful sovereign princes, as did also the abbots of Fulda, Gall and other famous abbeys. The Archbishop of Mainz owned the whole of the Rheingau, including Hochheim, when in A.D. 983 the emperor gave him Bingen as well.

A number of emperors of the Holy Roman Empire and some German princes followed the example set by Charlemagne, and gave land to the Church, or built abbeys and churches which they endowed by the gift of vineyards. It was also a common practice during the Middle Ages for gifts of money and land to be bequeathed to the church of one's parish or to the bishop of one's diocese. As ecclesiastical property was never sold or confiscated in those days, the Church in Germany became the owner of a very considerable proportion of the Rhineland vineyards.

The medieval archbishops owned so many vineyards and so much land that they could well afford to be generous. Thus, in the eleventh century one of them gave to the Benedictines of the St Alban's Priory the Mons Episcopi, the Bishop's Hill, above Winkel, where they planted a vineyard and renamed the hill St John's Hill or Johannisberg; they must have made good wine until the sixteenth century, when the hill was taken back from them by the Archbishop of Mainz; later, in 1716, it became the property of the Prince Abbot of Fulda. Not far away, the Cistercian monks of Eberbach cleared the forest of Steinberg in the twelfth century, and planted a vineyard which they surrounded by a wall, just as at Clos Vougeot; they went on making good wine there for some seven hundred years, until Napoleon turned them out.

In the Moselle valley it was very much the same story. The Benedictines of St Maximin Abbey of Trier owned vineyards at a very early date at Detzem, Leiwen and Longuich, so much so that in A.D. 783 – evidently a good vintage year – they cellared 900 Fuder or 3,000 double aums of wine. Another Benedictine Abbey, St Eucharius, owned vineyards in the eleventh century at Bernkastel/Cues, on the Moselle, and Trittenheim in the Saar valley. In 1136 Archbishop Albero of Trier presented the Cistercians with land at Himmerode, near Wittlich, and they later acquired many vineyards in the valley of the Moselle, the famous Tiergarten at Trier, as well as at Casel and Eitelsbach on the Ruwer, where the Karthäuserhofberg still bears witness to their earlier ownership.

There are many other such names today which provide ample evidence of the great influence which ecclesiastical communities and religious orders enjoyed throughout the Rhineland vinelands in former times. We shall refer to them when we take our journey through the wine districts.

It is likely that the wine made from grapes grown in the better vineyards belonging to church, abbey or college, and under the direct supervision of their owners, was of much better quality than the wines made by tenants who, besides rent and various 'dues', had to pay a tenth, or *dîme* or *Zehnt*, to the Church. This *Zehnt*, which had passed from the Old Testament to the New, was the ordained share of the poor; it was paid to the Church, not for church needs but to be given to the poor. The Church was at that time solely responsible for the care of the poor, the sick and the aged, and for the safety of students, pilgrims and others who journeyed from university to university or from shrine to shrine. Wayfarers in those times carried no money, a wise precaution when travelling through lands infested by highwaymen and marauding barons: they knew that they could always be sure of a free meal and a roof over their heads at any of the numerous monasteries on their route.

If further proof were needed of the prosperity of viticulture in the Rhineland at an early date it would be found in the importance of the sales of German wines in northern lands, the cities of the Baltic, Flanders and particularly England. There are recorded sales of wine in England, for instance, during the reign of Otto the Great in Germany (936–973) and that of Ethelred (978–1016) in England.

William of Malmesbury, the Benedictine historian who wrote in the twelfth century, remarks that 'the noble city of London, rich in wealth of its citizens, is filled with these goods of merchants from every land, and especially from Germany'. German merchants were clearly given special trading privileges in England and the right to have a *Hanse* or guildhall of their own, not only in London but in Boston, Lynn and other cities at a very early date, for these privileges were not first granted but only confirmed by

William the Conqueror and by the Plantagenets after him. In London the German traders' headquarters, known as the Steelyard, was an important house even before 1260, when it was enlarged by the purchase of the adjoining house and garden.

Henry II of England, a Frenchman by birth and parentage, owned far more vineyards from Angers to Bordeaux than his cousin, the King of France, but he was none the less anxious not to let this fact interfere with the commercial relations between England and Germany. In 1157 he wrote to the Emperor Frederick: 'Let there be between ourselves and our subjects an indivisible unity of friendship and peace, and safe trade of merchandise.' Henry followed this declaration by extensive privileges granted particularly to the merchants of Cologne. They were to be safeguarded as his own men; their merchandise, their possessions and their house in London were to be protected, and no one could impose new exactions on them. Later, they obtained a further concession allowing them to sell their wines on the same terms as French wines. Again, when King Richard I returned from captivity he passed through Cologne and was most lavish in his grants to the traders there; they were to pay two shillings yearly for their guildhall in London, to be free of all tolls and customs in the City, and to be at liberty to buy and sell at fairs throughout the land. This charter was subsequently confirmed by King John and Henry III.

Henry II also regularly purchased Ruwer and Moselle wines for his household, and so did his two sons when in due course they became King Richard and King John. In 1174 Henry II purchased some Moselle wines at 2d per gallon plus cost of transport. In 1213 some 358 casks of wine were bought for King John; most of it came from Bordeaux and other French districts, but there were three casks 'de Saxonia', the only mention in royal accounts of any Saxon wine. In 1243, 22 tuns of St John and Moselle wines were bought for the king in London at the rate of 1½d per gallon; a further quantity was purchased at Sandwich in 1246 for 1¾d per gallon.

When in 1453 Henry VI lost the last of the great Plantagenet vineyards in France the wines of Bordeaux and La Rochelle lost their English citizenship and became taxable on a par with other 'aliens' like Rhenish. Their higher cost in England was responsible for an increased demand for the wines of the Rhine and Moselle. Unfortunately, politics interfered with economics then as they have done on many occasions since. In 1493 Henry VII, being angry at the protection given by the Dowager Duchess of Burgundy to Perkin Warbeck, banished all Flemings out of England and prohibited all trade with the Netherlands. This brought to an end all imports of Rhenish wine until 1496, when matters were mended by the *Intercursus Magnus* or Great Treaty, which gave rise to prolonged public rejoicings.

In 1520 the merchants of the Steelyard, having been asked to pay for a licence if they were to sell Rhenish wine in London, protested that Edward IV had renewed their ancient privileges and that the Royal Grant had been confirmed by an Act of Parliament. In 1547 Parliament granted Edward VI an additional tonnage due of 12d per aum of Rhenish wine.

In December 1550 Lord Rutland, riding from Eagle, his Lincolnshire manor, to London, stayed overnight at an inn at Stamford. The account which was presented to him the next morning included '4 pottells and 1 quart of *Raynsche wyne*' for which he was charged 4s 6d, as well as '2 pottells and one pint of Claret', costing 1s 6d, apples and oranges 6d, 'fire in the Chamber where the gentlemen supped 3s 4d', and – hottest of all – 'fyer in the kechen 2s'. This account is of particular interest as evidence that Rhenish was being sold in the country at inns and was not imported solely for members of the royal household and nobility.

Most, if not all, of the wines which reached England from the Rhineland during the Middle Ages were bought either in London or in east coast ports and cities such as King's Lynn, Canterbury, Orwell, Durham and Deal, where they were brought by merchants from Lübeck, Bremen, Dordrecht, Bruges and Antwerp. A tavern close by the Steelyard was known as the Rhenish or the German tavern, where none but German wines were sold.

Ever since 1369 the sale of German wines had been prohibited in taverns where Gascon or Bordeaux wine was sold. The Vintners' Company, one of the 12 Great Livery Companies of the City, still flourishing today, was then called the Merchant Vintners of Gascony, and had the right of 'search' within the boundaries of the City of London. This meant that their officials could, and did, visit all London taverns where Gascony wine was sold – and roughly 80% of the wine then coming to England came from Bordeaux – and had the right to condemn and destroy any wine which they considered faked or unsound. It was therefore much safer, even if the sale of it had been legal, for Rhenish wine not to be found in the same cellar as Gascon wine by the Vintners' searchers.

Every year the maximum prices at which bread and wine were allowed to be sold were published by the newly elected Lord Mayor, either in November or early in December. This was known as the Assize of Bread and the Assize of Wine. The first time the retail price of Rhenish wine was fixed by the Assize of Wine was in 1420: 4d per gallon was then its maximum price in London. There is every reason to believe, however, that the price of German wines in London during the Middle Ages was what they would fetch in the market.

In 1515, 1517 and 1530, three years when supplies of Rhenish wine must have been adequate, its selling price was recorded in the Assize of those years as 10d per gallon. In 1539 it was raised to 1s per gallon. Records of prices paid for Rhenish wine in different parts of the country show remarkably few changes in the course of a hundred years, from the mid-fifteenth century to the mid-sixteenth, but there was a sharp rise during the second half of the sixteenth century.

In two of the Guildhall Letter Books we are given the figures of stocks of wine in some of the London taverns on the same day in five consecutive years. They show that there was not much Rhenish wine in stock but that the taverns were never without it. There is a good deal of evidence to show that during the fifteenth century a great deal of attention was paid in the Rhineland to all matters pertaining to viticulture and the art of making better wines. To sell wine, more particularly to sell the wine made from one's own grapes, was regarded in an entirely different light from any branch of commerce, and membership of the various Wine Guilds was a privilege which many members of the Rhineland aristocracy eagerly sought.

During the sixteenth century, according to Andrea Bacci, the reputation which the wines of the Rhineland enjoyed in many markets, and more especially in England and Scotland, was much greater than it had ever been before. Bacci gives a list of names, some of them impossible to identify today, of German wines which were popular in 1596. Stuttgart, Heidelberg and Cologne appear to have been three of the more important centres of the German wine trade, and Bacci praises the wine of Franconia, from the Main valley, and those of the hillsides in Württemberg and Baden.

It is surprising to find Bavaria, which we associate with beer, praised solely for its wines, and it comes as a shock to find that, in November 1543, John Grousby 'gentleman', and William Wurden, merchant of the Steelyard, were granted a special licence to export 800 tuns of English beer on condition that they imported 800 tuns of Rhenish wine. Three other conditions were stipulated in the licence granted to them:

1. The wine must be of the finest quality, 'such as the Emperor and the Duke of Cleves and other persons of high rank did drink'.
2. The price must not be above 30s per gallon.
3. 400 aums of 36 gallons each must be imported for the king's use before Christmas 1543; more of the same wine to bring the total to 400 tuns must be imported before Easter 1544; the balance of 400 tuns must be imported by midsummer 1544.

Such a large quantity as 800 tuns of Rhenish wine would have been unusual at any time, but it was exceptional at a time when religious feuds in Germany between Catholics and Protestants greatly added to difficulties of wine supply and transport. What is of particular interest in this contract is the stipulation that the wine must be of the 'finest quality' and such as 'persons of high rank did drink'. This is a reminder that then, as now, there was a good deal of sharp, acid wine made from grapes of indifferent summers which had found it difficult to ripen, while there never was enough of the really fine wine of good vintages.

It was ever thus, and it cannot be otherwise, for the vineyards of the Rhineland happen to be at the northern limit beyond which grapes cannot reach full maturity except in years with particularly fine summers. At a much later date it was not exceptional for the owner of a cask of fine wine to refuse to sell it unless the buyer agreed to buy a like quantity of a cheaper and poorer wine. The gap between the wines of good and of bad vintages still exists, but it is not quite so great today, thanks to Gall and Chaptal, who taught us that sugar added to the reluctantly fermenting juice of imperfectly ripe grapes will mend matters to a certain – alcoholic – extent. We can well imagine how difficult it must have been in those days to buy wines of the highest quality and such as persons of 'high rank' were privileged to enjoy. It is not much easier to do so today.

It is very likely that the majority of German wines sold in England were the wines which William Turner, who was at the time one of the doctors of Queen Elizabeth I, had in mind when he wrote about the 'small and subtil' Rhenish. In his little book, the first book on wine written and published in English, William Turner defended Rhenish wines against those in the medical profession who claimed that such wines were not safe for people suffering from bladder or kidney troubles: a claim which we know, as William Turner also knew 400 years ago, to be utterly baseless. Here is the whole title of his book: 'A new Boke of the natures and properties of all wines that are commonly used here in England, with a confutation of an error of some men, that holds that Rhenish and other small white wines ought not to be drunken of them that either have, or are in danger of the Stone, the reume, and divers other diseases, made by William Turner, Doctor of Phisicke' (*London, Seres, 1568*).

A hundred years later another English medical authority, William Salmon, also shared Dr Turner's faith in Rhenish wine, only more so. He wrote in his *Compleat*

*English Physician* (1693 edition, p. 926): 'It [Rhenish] is a good nephritic and vehemently diuretick, opening all obstructions of urinary parts, and bringing away stones, sands and gravel, and other tartarous matter from the reins, uretera and bladder; it strengthens the stomack admirably, causes a good appetite and a good digestion, and opens obstructions of the lungs.'

All German wines, whether they came from the Rhine, the Palatinate, the Neckar or the Main, were uniformly known in England as Rhenish wine. This is clear from all the references to the wines of Germany in contemporary records and documents of the sixteenth century and of the greater part of the seventeenth century. Shakespeare, for instance, invariably uses 'Rhenish' for German wine.

Although records of sales of Rhenish wine in England during the seventeenth century are comparatively few, they suffice to show that there was a demand for this wine at all times, and that it was obtainable in some if not all the London taverns. Rhenish wine was served not only at Charles II's royal table but also at Cromwell's more frugal board. If the quantities of Rhenish wine that reached England appear very modest, and they certainly do, we must not suppose that the wine was in short supply: it was not. It is on record, for instance, that in 1631, when the troops of Gustavus Adolphus of Sweden occupied the Rheingau, they demanded an 'indemnity' of 46,000 Thaler, a very large amount of money at the time; merchants of Frankfurt found the cash which saved the land from the scorched-earth treatment, but the real saviours of the homelands were the wine-growers of the Rheingau who promised to give to the Frankfurt bankers 1,650 Fuder of wine – a very large quantity (360,000 gallons United Kingdom or 470,000 gallons U.S.A.) – before March 1634; and they delivered the wine on time.

It was only during the second half of the seventeenth century that two Rhineland place-names replaced the popular generic name of Rhenish: they were Bacharach and Hochheim. The second was soon anglicized into 'hock', the name which has generally been used for all Rhine wine to this day, wherever English is spoken. There were, of course, vineyards in those days, as there are now, both at Bacharach and Hochheim, but there is no reason to believe that the quality of the wines they produced was responsible for their greater popularity overseas. The truth is that all the wines of Franconia sent down the Main to Frankfurt were shipped from Hochheim down the Rhine to Antwerp and other ports, and thence to London, Ipswich, Lynn and other east-coast ports. Bacharach – named after Bacchus – was the last port of call for the fairly large boats which were unable to negotiate the Bingen 'Hole'. There was no other means of sending any of the wines of the Pfalz or Palatinate and those of Rheinhessen to Bonn, Cologne and the North Sea except from Bacharach by the Rhine.

It was therefore not so much the excellence of what little wine was made from the vineyards of Bacharach that was responsible for the great reputation the name acquired during the seventeenth and eighteenth centuries as Bacharach's privileged position as a port on the Rhine. In the fourteenth century Nuremberg had to send the king every year a fee of a Fuder of wine, and it had to be Bacharach wine. In the fifteenth century Pope Pius II also claimed a Fuder of Bacharach wine every year, and he declared that in his opinion it was the best German wine. There were many people in England who agreed with the Pope, on this count at least, even after the Reformation. In 1634 Howell wrote: 'The prime wines of Germany grow about the Rhine, specially in the Pfalz and Lower Palatinate, about Bacharach.'

In a very old German song Bacharach is given first place among the best wines of Rhine and Main:

Zu Bacharach am Rheim,
Zu Klingenberg am Main,
Zu Würzburg am Stein,
Sind die besten Wein.

Shirley, in his comedy *The Lady of Pleasure* (Act v, sc. 1) alludes to the German Wine House by the Steelyard where what he calls 'Deal wine', German wine landed at Deal from Holland, and Bacharach wine were sold.

On 8 September 1681 Charles Bertie wrote from London to his niece, the Duchess of Rutland: 'I am glad your hogshead of Bacharach is arrived. Very little pure Rhenish is drunk in England. I will try to help you to another hogshead of Moselle or Pincair. I have written for a foudre of Hochheim.'

In Oldham's *Paraphrases from Horace*, published in 1681, wealthy merchants count among their more costly wines 'Their Aums of Hock, of Bachrag and Moselle'. In this instance, 'Hock' stood for Hochheim, but from that time to our own 'Hock' has been used in England as a generic term for all Rhine wines in place of 'Rhenish'.

At a time when wines were mostly drunk young, Hock appears to have stood the test of time better than other wines, and 'old Hock' was practically the only old wine to be offered by merchants or sung by poets. Thus in Gay's poem *Wine* (1708) the waiter asks some guests as they enter the tavern what they will be pleased to order:

Name, Sirs, the wine that most invites your
taste, Champagne or Burgundy or Florence pure,
or Hock antique, or Lisbon new or old,
Bordeaux, or neat French wine, or Alicant.

Bickerstaffe, in *Lionel and Clarissa*, also refers to old hock:

COLONEL OLDBOY: Well, but, zounds! Jenkins, you must not go till you drink something. Let you and I have a bottle of hock.
JENKINS: Not for the world, Colonel! I never touch anything strong in the morning.
COLONEL OLDBOY: Never touch anything strong! Why, one bottle won't hurt you, man, this is old and as mild as milk.

The appeal of old Hock must have been handed from one generation to another, since we find it, as young as ever, in Meredith's *The Egoist* (Chapter 20) when Dr Middleton, the wine-loving divine, delivers the following judgment upon an 'aged and a great wine' in Sir Willoughby Patterne's cellar:

Hocks, too, have compassed age. I have tasted senior Hocks. Their flavour is a brook of many voices; they have depth also.

In 1831, at the Vauxhall Royal Gardens in London, both Moselle and old Hock were listed, the first at 6s per bottle, which was also the price charged for a bottle of port, sherry, Lisbon, or Bacellas, and old Hock, which cost 12s per bottle, the same as a bottle of Hermitage, champagne, burgundy or Arrack.

In 1878 Sir Walter Trevelyan, Bt, died, and the cellar of wine which he had inherited from his father in 1846, at Wallington, was sold. Among the contents of this famous cellar there were four magnums of Hock, which the cellar book faithfully recorded as having been there since before 1777! Old Hock, indeed! Old, of course, but far, far older Hock was uncorked on 7 July 1961 in London, in the offices of Messrs Ehrmanns, the Grafton Street wine-merchants. The two oldest wines were not only pre-phylloxera but pre-Shakespeare – Steinwein of 1540; the two youngest were two 1857 Rüdesheimer, and there was also a Johannisberger of 1822. All these venerable bottles came from the royal cellars of Ludwig II, the 'mad' king of Bavaria, and they had been purchased by Ferdinand Bazuch Ehrmann in 1887, when the contents of the royal Bavarian cellars were sold by public auction, a year after the king's death.

The 1857 and 1822 were opened first. They were dead; not vinegar, but just dumb wet rags. Not so the 1540! Of course it was old, and very old, but not dead: there was a vinous quality reminiscent of some antique Madeira, and the wine was clear up to the last fifth of the bottles. It certainly bore out the centuries-old tradition that there never was in Germany a wine comparable to the wine that was made in 1540, a year unique in the annals of German viticulture. The warm weather started on 22 February and the flowering of the grapes began on 5 April. By August the grapes were more like raisins: then came the rain, and the swollen grapes, which were picked in October, gave a wine of outstanding excellence which appeared to defy decay for centuries.

Rhenish, then Hochheim and Bacharach, Hock and old Hock were for a very long time the only names by which the wines of the Rhineland were known in England. The names of grape and vineyard responsible for the wine in the bottle were not recorded on label or invoice before the nineteenth century. The names of important wine-producing villages, more particularly of the Rheingau and Palatinate, frequently appear on eighteenth-century German bottles, but, curiously, their wines were exported anonymously. Strange as it may seem, it was the French Revolution which brought about a change so complete that it may rightly be called revolutionary in the viticulture and the wine trade of the Rhineland. The French Revolution was responsible for the situation in which Napoleon came to power, and Napoleon was responsible for the Treaty of Lunéville of 1801, which secularized all religious orders, causing some of the largest and best vineyards of the Rhineland to be split up among a very large number of small holders; these could hope to make a living only if they could sell at a fairly high price the limited quantities of wine they were able to make whenever the sun smiled upon them and their grapes. They not only took far greater care to make better wine than their fathers, who had farmed the same vineyards for some noble lord, some arch-bishop or abbot, but they gave to their vineyards individual names by which their individual wines were to be known and to become famous, as so many of them have remained to this day.

However, the practice of giving to all quality wines the name of their native village, with the name of their individual site added, did not really become general in the Rhineland before 1830. It was in that year that the provincial authorities decreed that the names of all vineyards, together with the names of their owners, of the nearest village or township, and of their own site should be recorded in an official land register. Mention was also to be made in this register of the nature of the soil of each vineyard, and of the species of the vines planted therein; the standard of quality of the wine and its chief characteristics were also to be recorded. This land register led to some kind of unofficial classification of the chief growths of the Rhineland, but its original purpose had been to provide a guide for the collector of taxes: the better the soil, the better the wine and the better its selling value: so, the better also the land tax it was to pay.

The first immediate result of the land register was to increase the demand for the better 'registered' wines and to render very much more difficult the sale of the commoner types of wine, the price of which, in Germany, fell from 250 to 10 or 20 thaler per hectolitre or 22 gallons; many wine-growers failed to sell their wines at any price. Conditions became so desperate in some of the vinelands that for a few pfennigs a toper would be given the key of the cellar and allowed to drink as much wine as he could carry, and land might be sold at one to two pfennigs per square yard. It was then that quite a number of Rhineland families left Germany for Australia, the Argentine, Brazil and North America.

In 1834 came the German Customs Union, which did away with all the fiscal barriers between the different German states. It was immediately responsible for a considerably greater demand, in all parts of Germany, for the better wines of the Rhineland – Riesling wines from named vineyards – while the commoner, anonymous wines made from any kind of grape, anywhere and anyhow, were not wanted. It proved to be a lesson which led all the growers who could raise credit to replant their vineyards with Rieslings and give greater care to the making of the wines. They were particularly fortunate in having an unprecedented run of fine vintages in 1857, 1858 and 1859; for when in 1860 Mr Gladstone reduced the duty on all table wines to 1s per gallon they were in a position to take advantage of the opportunity to sell a far greater quantity of Hocks and Moselles in England than ever before. Good German wines could then be bought in England at such low prices that they were for the first time within the reach of practically everybody in the land, except the really poor.

As was to be expected, the demand for Hocks and Moselles now grew year by year, much faster than the supply. And it was in 1871 that Bismarck robbed France of Alsace and parts of Lorraine; the vineyards of Alsace produced a great deal of wine which the shippers of German wines found most useful.

Ever since the first big drive to export Hocks and Moselles in the 1860s, most German wines, the great names excepted, were sold at exceptionally low prices in overseas markets by shippers who paid the growers famine prices. Then in 1874 the *phylloxera vastatrix* was first reported in the Palatinate, and although its progress was not as rapid and catastrophic as in the Médoc, it steadily spread and destroyed vineyard after vineyard. The phylloxera was the worst scourge of all, because this accursed vine louse cannot be seen: it sticks to the roots of the vines and sucks their life sap.

Other enemies of the vine attacked it above ground and cost the unfortunate wine-growers a considerable amount of extra work and expenditure merely to save at least some proportion of the year's grapes. The oidium, mildew and black rot are crypto-gamic diseases which attacked the leaves and the fruit of the vine, while a number of insect pests – the *Cochylis* the worst of all – did their best to rob the *vignerons* of any hope of a bumper crop of fine grapes, even in the all too few years when there had been no late spring frosts and when the sun had done its best during the summer and autumn!

To make matters worse, it was at this time that the German banks decided that it was in their own and in the country's best interests to give all possible financial backing to industry and no longer to viticulture.

Much as one may – and must – regret it, one cannot be greatly surprised that quite a number of those unfortunate wine-growers resorted to means, not illegal at the time, of producing more and cheaper wine. The commonest offence was over-chaptalisation, the adding of some water and a great deal of sugar to the grapes that were being pressed, in order to raise both the quantity and eventual alcoholic strength of the wine.

It was to put an end to such malpractices that the German Wine Law of 1909 was enacted and strictly enforced. It was the beginning of a long struggle, which has lasted more than 50 years and is still going on, to protect the public from misrepresentation and to protect honest growers and merchants from unfair competition.

During the last decade of the nineteenth century and the first 14 years of the twentieth the wine trade of Germany enjoyed its highest measure of prosperity. Hocks and Moselles were exported to all civilized lands throughout the world, and they were awarded many honours at a number of international exhibitions. On the wine lists of the luxury hotels and restaurants of Europe and America there were more German wines listed – dearer as well as cheaper – than white wines from all other vinelands.

Then came the First World War, which all but halted the export trade of Hocks and Moselles for nearly five years. When resumption became possible in 1919 German wine shippers could no longer get cheap wines from Alsace, and the world economic crisis, which the appalling cost in lives and treasure of the war had rendered inevitable, meant that the demand for the better and highly priced wines of the Rhineland was non-existent in, for instance, Russia and much smaller in the United Kingdom, the U.S.A., and elsewhere.

Nature did its best to come to the help of the Rhineland *vignerons* and the German wine trade by giving them two very fine vintages in 1920 and 1921, when wines of quite exceptional quality were made in fairly large quantity. There was a satisfactory quantity of wine made in the Rhineland during the 20 years of truce between the two wars, and the German wine trade regained a large share of its pre-1914 prosperity. But the Second World War not only halted its export trade once again but impoverished the whole world to such an extent that new methods had to be found to reduce the cost of production.

Science has by now made such progress in all departments of viticulture and oenology that vines are now grown which give more grapes than ever before, and – *mirabile dictu* – vines also that beat the frost! As to wine, it can now be made to look, smell and taste well every year, sun or no sun – though the better wines, of course, still depend on the sun shining as it should. Science has also beaten present economic difficulties by making it possible to enjoy really good wine when it is months old instead of years old.

There has been a great deal of good quality wine made in the Rhineland since the end of the Second World War, some wines of superlative excellence which command superlative prices and many more which are quite reasonable in price and of very fair quality.

In 1958, for the first since 1913, the exports of German wine reached the 2 million gallons figure, the United Kingdom and the U.S.A. being responsible for over 50% of the total, as the following figures show:

|      | U.K.      | U.S.A.    | Others    | Total     |
|------|-----------|-----------|-----------|-----------|
| 1960 | 953,062   | 717,112   | 1,195,238 | 2,865,412 |
| 1961 | 997,185   | 972,203   | 1,194,130 | 3,163,518 |
| 1962 | 851,588   | 865,543   | 1,205,751 | 2,922,882 |
| 1963 | 978,652   | 964,478   | 1,224,152 | 2,167,282 |
| 1964 | 1,109,480 | 1,113,221 | 1,431,112 | 3,653,813 |
| 1965 | 1,203,352 | 1,166,309 | 1,660,720 | 4,030,381 |

# From Vine to Bottle

THE MOST picturesque process in the manufacture of wine is the gathering of the grapes. Many a traveller has been attracted to a particular locality in the hope of watching activities during the harvest season in the vineyards. Few, however, suspect how much the quantity and the quality of any vintage depend on the proper selection of the date on which the fruit is to be gathered. Yet this date is vitally important, a fact that has been recognized by wine growers from time immemorial. In feudal times it was the seigneurs who set the date and kept a strict eye on the peasant to see that no one entered the vineyard without special permission, particularly when the grapes were nearly ripe. This was not only to guard against pilfering but in order to ensure delivery of a flawless harvest of fruit and grape-juice (must), for no berry was allowed to be severed from the vine before it was fully ripe. Even when the grape harvest was in full swing, the vineyard might be entered only at specified times, the object of this precaution being to prevent a neighbouring grower from trespassing and taking one's fruit.

Based on a by-law of the German Wine Law, the Government of Rheinland Pfalz (Rhineland Palatinate) issued a decree on 12 August 1965 to settle harvesting, and it has been laid down that in each wine-growing community a special committee has to be formed consisting of the mayor of the village as chairman, a member of the local council connected with viticulture, the three most important growers of the village, three further members owning small vineyards, a representative of the local co-operative and a representative of the local wine-growers' association. This representative body must decide the beginning of the harvest for each kind of grape, and it has been laid down that the beginning of harvesting must be fixed *for the time of the maturity of the grapes*. (But, as it happened, the time of maturity never came for the grapes in 1965.)

Some further points may be made on the contents of this by-law. The picking of the grapes *before* the general harvesting starts (*vorlese* or *vorauslese*) can be permitted if the grapes have suffered from a natural catastrophe, and there is a danger that the grapes would be spoilt if the sick or rotten grapes were not gathered in advance of the general harvest. This by-law is interesting because of the new control for quality wines, namely: Spätlese can be made only after the end of the general harvesting, taking into consideration the kind of grape and the geographical situation of the vineyard. In order to make control of denomination of quality easier, the growers who want to produce Spätlese, Auslese, Beerenauslese, Trockenbeerenauslese and Ice Wine (the first time that the denomination Ice Wine appears in any law) have to inform the local council in advance and make statements about the grapes, the size of the vineyard and the name of the vineyard. These documents are kept by the council and can be checked at any time by the wine controllers.

Should a grower have forgotten to give this information and apply beforehand, he can apply for permission to use the above-mentioned denominations. The decision lies with the local committee after the grower has given an affidavit about the correctness of his statement.

Plate 24. *Riesling grape*

This new control will prevent the misuse of quality denominations, and the phoney Spätlese wines with 56 g/l alcohol, must, and will, disappear.

The Commission makes daily observations and then orders the ringing of local church bells to denote the beginning and ending of picking time. At the sound of this early bell whole families – men, women and children – stream forth to the vineyards, vine-cutters in their hands. There is work for all and plenty to spare.

The picking of the grapes is of necessity preceded by considerable preliminary preparation in the pressing houses and cellars. The cellar-master and vineyard owner have to work in close co-operation to see that no mistakes occur which might impair the good quality of the future wine. The necessary tools must be clean; the scissors handed to the pickers have to be sharp to ensure a clean separation of each bunch from the vine and so that no grapes fall to the ground. The casks, too, have to be prepared for the reception of the must; and so on. Undoubtedly there is a great deal of work to be done.

In ancient days there were progressive methods of picking the grapes. The Greeks, and later the Romans, held the same views on the picking and selection of the grapes. They knew that different kinds of grape ripened at different times; they knew also how to get the best out of the grapes by letting them remain on the vine until they were over-ripe and then making special collections of dry berries. Strangely enough, in Germany this technique was not used until the eighteenth century. The revival, according to legend, was due to chance. The Bishop of Fulda, owner of vineyards in the Rheingau, is said to have delayed sending his permission to begin grape-harvesting until too late; in other words, until the fruit had become over-ripe. To everybody's amazement, the resulting vintage was superb.

From the moment the must reaches the cellar the vintner has but one aim – to give it the finest treatment so that the wine comes to the drinker in the best possible condition.

We must not forget that tastes have changed. Whereas 50 years ago Rhine and Moselle wines were served in tinted cut glasses, today the glasses are colourless. The wine drinker wants to enjoy the beautiful colour of the wine and to be able to judge its age from the development of that colour. From the moment the wine goes into bottle ready to be sent out to the consumer, therefore, it must be star-bright. And, as the wine-grower says, it must have the capacity to withstand a journey either to the north pole or to the equator.

Furthermore, it must be sound, it must be digestible and, above all, it must be enjoyable. To attain this goal the grower has to observe the wine in all its stages, and if he finds any fault he has to try to eradicate it exactly as one eradicates a fault in a naughty child. After long years of experiments scientists have put at the disposal of the wine-grower many means of reaching this aim. The grower, moreover, knows full well that prevention is better than cure, and does his utmost to clear the must of any impurities before fermentation ever begins. Growers who can afford it accomplish this by means of centrifuging the must, but the same result can also be reached by cheaper means. If the grapes taken off the vines contain many rotten or diseased berries, or are very dirty, it is necessary first to remove the sludge from the must. The freshly pressed must is allowed to stand for some time – perhaps twenty-four hours. This allows all solid and flocculent sediments, stemming either from the actual flesh of the grapes or from foreign bodies such as fungi or ordinary dirt, to settle and leave a completely clean liquid above, entirely free from flocculence.

The grape-must delivered by the wine-press is treated to such an extent that the incidence of fermentation is delayed by several days. The must is then left to itself in as cool a room as possible, and all bad and wild ferments which effect a quick fermentation – and a quick fermentation is likely to impair the quality of the future wine – are killed. After a day or two the clarified must is separated from the flocculence by draining it off (racking). It is then transferred to a warmer fermentation cellar where it is left to ferment, sometimes with the addition of biologically pure yeast, which is normally taken from the lees of some high-class wine. There is no doubt that this treatment of the must effects a slow fermentation, and, even more important, a fermentation which can be controlled. The fermentation can be controlled more easily if it takes place in hermetically sealed vats, or in the pressure tanks which abound in the Rhineland today.

Now that we have seen the must supply deposited in its vat, there to await fermentation and gradual transformation into a wine fit for the bottle, it is time to consider more closely some particular aspects of wine-making.

What, for example, is this 'must' we have been discussing? Clear must is an aqueous solution of various substances, the most important quantitatively being sugar and acids. The average content of sugar is from 14 to 22%. An unseasonal crop of unripe berries can bring this down to 6 or 7%, while a crop of 'sleepy' grapes will yield a sugar content of 35% or more. Selected 1921 and 1959 vintages show as much as 52%, and those of 1949 43%.

The sugar content is not uniform, but is composed, on the one hand, of grape-sugar (dextrose, glucose) and on the other, of fruit-sugar (levulose, fructose). Fully matured grapes contain about equal quantities of the two kinds of sugar; unripe grapes have a preponderance of grape-sugar, while over-ripe and 'sleepy' grapes have more fructose.

The more noteworthy acids found in must are tartaric acid, malic acid and tannic acid. Tartaric acid, absent in almost all other fruits, is characteristic of the grape. Its quantity increases until the fruit begins to ripen, and then remains practically static until full maturity is reached.

It is, however, malic acid, a frequent phenomenon in all fruits, that fills the leading role of all wine acids. It is almost always present and increases rapidly in quantity up to the moment when the fruit begins to ripen; then it decreases, but even in the ripe grape does not entirely disappear.

The amount of tannic acid in must depends on the way the mash is treated. The longer the mash is allowed to stand, the more tannic acid is present in the must and, eventually, in the wine itself. If the mash is put through the wine-presses immediately, the resulting wine is poor in tannic acid; whereas if the mash is allowed to stand and ferment (as with red wines) the tannic acid content is high.

Besides sugars and acids, grape-juice contains traces of numerous other substances, all of which have their part to play in determining the development and the quality of the wine. Among these are the nitrogenous compounds – albumen, peptones, amides, ammonium salts and nitrates – which provide the ferment with its nitrogen, and the mineral components from which the ferment derives the bases needed for its development, namely, potassium, phosphoric acid and calcium.

Of inestimable value to the wine are the substances which give it its bouquet, or peculiar aromatic odour. In the must the only recognizable aroma is that of the primitive grape-bouquet, the chemical origin of which is still unknown. Its nature is decisive for the value of the wine, and in certain kinds of grapes, such as Muscats, Gewürz-traminer (spicy Traminer) and Riesling, the primitive bouquet has a particularly strong influence on the wine's final character.

Finally, the must contains colouring matter. Both white and red must will invariably absorb decomposition particles from the chlorophyll in the grape-skin and stalks, and it is these latter which give Hock its characteristic colour.

When grape juice is transformed into wine by fermentation the most noteworthy chemical development is the change of the sugar content into roughly equal quantities of alcohol and carbon dioxide. The alcohol content of any wine is somewhat less than half the sugar content of the must.

The flesh of red grapes is white, and if red grapes are pressed immediately and treated like white grapes the resulting wine is white, or perhaps a wine with just a slight tinge of rose colour. It is the skin of the red grape which contains the colouring particles. In order to extract the colour from the grape skins, fermentation must take place before the grapes are pressed.

During the last few years great progress has been made in methods of fermenting red grapes. For centuries the process took place in upright, open casks. When the mash was put into these casks fermentation started at once; the ensuing escape of carbonic acid would lift the grape-skin above the level of the liquid, with the result that the 'hat' was in the open, not being covered by the wine, or must, and it was the task of the wine-grower to be ready at any moment to push the 'hat' back into the liquid. If the 'hat' were left in the open there would be a risk of acetic acid bacteria infection, which produces acetic acid by oxidation of the alcohol that was produced during the fermentation. Furthermore, if the 'hat' were outside the liquid the wine would not acquire its characteristic colour and, even worse, such colour as had already been produced might well be destroyed. All in all, it was extremely important to prevent the 'hat' from leaving the liquid, and many were the devices invented for the purpose.

Today the fermentation of red wine often takes place in hermetically sealed enamel or glass-lined pressure tanks. These tanks are kept at a constant temperature of approximately 22° Centigrade, and fermentation is terminated within three to four days. It is no longer necessary to stand by and watch the 'hat' emerging from the must; the carbonic acid resulting from the fermentation is collected at the top of the pressure tank and the formation of a 'hat' is avoided by the simple manipulation of a switch. The mash is put on the press, and further vinification and treatment of the red wine takes place in wooden casks. This results in milder, rounder and perhaps more velvety wines.

Unfavourable climatic conditions in many German wine-growing districts often prevent a (varying) proportion of the grapes from reaching full maturity. In most years, therefore, many German wine-growers are unfortunately compelled to take steps to improve a large part of their crop. This improvement is effected by adding sugar or sugar solution to the deficient must. Unripe grapes produce a wine which not only keeps badly, falling an easy prey to acidification and other diseases, but also one which is unpalatable, since, when alcohol and acid are blended in the wrong proportions, a lack of 'body' is the inevitable outcome. Yet the effect of the climate in these districts is not entirely a bad one, since it is the climate that is largely responsible for the variety in type, the flavour and other individual characteristics of the resulting wines.

The German Wine Law lays down that sugar or sugar dissolved in pure water may be added to grape-must or wines derived from home-grown grapes, provided that this is done for the sole purpose of supplementing the natural sugar or counteracting natural excess acidity – and only enough to reproduce the same sugar content as that of a wine made in a good year from exactly similar grapes. Moreover, this proceeding is legal only if the defects are due to natural causes. It is not permissible where the premature gathering of the grape is deliberate and unjustifiable. It is therefore wrong to suspect all German wines of being doctored simply because in certain specified conditions it is permissible to add extraneous sugar. It is not only in Germany that such measures are allowed. Other countries too, even those with more favourable climatic conditions than Germany, make similar concessions to their growers. French growers, for example, are permitted to add sugar or sugar-water to their wines, though if they do add sugar-water they lose the right to market their products with the title *appellation controlée*. Tarragona wines are usually sweetened with grape juice, while the sweet taste of port wine is preserved only by interrupting fermentation by means of the addition of brandy.

Wine control in Germany is efficiently organized. Trading is supervised from the moment the wine reaches the presses until it is sold for consumption. Wine Controllers with expert knowledge are appointed for each of the German regions. They have wide powers and can, at their own discretion, visit growers and merchants, check their books, correspondence, price lists, etc. (there are detailed provisions for obligatory book-keeping), and taste the wine in storage. Should the Controller find anything amiss, or become suspicious of any of the products, he can impound samples for chemical analysis. If the analysis shows grounds for objection the owner will then be prosecuted and the wines may be confiscated, or their sale permitted for the manufacture of vinegar only.

Soon after the must has been deposited in the vats, the vital process of fermentation starts. Yeasts act on the fermentable sugars and generate not only alcohol and carbon dioxide but also glycerine, succinic acid, volatile acids, higher alcohols and various esters (bouquet compounds).

Fermentation is a gradual process. By the time it ceases, the sugar has been broken down, and the expiring yeast precipitated to the bottom of the cask. Not very long ago people liked to see the fermentation finished in a very short time, and spoke of a very 'stormy' fermentation – *Sturmische Gärung*. The aim of the grower was to have the fermentation concluded as quickly as possible, and in a fermentation-cellar one always found a coke-oven for increasing the temperature of the cellar in order to speed up fermentation. Today the coke-ovens have disappeared and the young must is laid down in very cold, or at least cool, cellars, so that fermentation goes forward very slowly. This has the great advantage that the fermentation may come to a standstill and leave some unfermented sugar in the wine. If the grower succeeds in balancing this remaining sugar content against the acid content he will produce a very harmonious wine which is both mild and round – in any case not harsh and hard. These wines, bottled later through a sterilizing filter, keep this remnant of sugar and produce a sweeter type of German wine than was known 40 or 50 years ago.

The so-called cold fermentation has great advantages. Most important of all, the alcohol content of the wines is increased; in a stormy fermentation the aroma material and the carbonic acid – the natural contents – of the wine are torn out of the cask.

During January the young wine can generally be separated from the sediment by racking, i.e. draining off into another cask. This racking is repeated two or three times (second racking approximately six weeks, third racking approximately four months, after the first racking) and is usually supplemented by a mechanical clearing of the young wine by 'fining', or filtering in an asbestos filter which retains all the sediments and impurities. Success or failure of the resulting wine may depend on the proper and well-timed application of these measures and on selecting the moment for bottling.

Another important factor in determining the quality of the wine is the manner in which it is stored. For many centuries both theory and practice followed the principle of allowing wines to ferment in wooden vats and of storing them in the same way, the idea being that wines must 'breathe' and that only porous wood would allow them to do so. These techniques have undergone a great deal of modification in recent years. Immense progress has been made, and experiments are still continuing. For example, it has been found that the carbon dioxide that develops in the hermetically sealed tank is the best medium for regulating fermentation. If it can then be preserved in the wine itself the result is a mild and pleasant drink which is just perceptibly sweet. Wines which are bottled with a relatively high natural carbon dioxide content are less likely to suffer from a slight sediment of sugar particles than others which are poor in carbon dioxide content. Their flavour is also more aromatic. Another advance of knowledge was made when it was found that, in the case of 'little' wines, not more than a residual sweetness can be achieved by controlled fermentation. It was further observed that in small vintages no more aroma and bouquet can be obtained by tank fermentation than by fermentation in the cask. Lovely as the transient stronger fermentation bouquets may be, they remain a characteristic of young, unfinished wines. If small, ordinary wines with residual sugar are fermented by prolonged, controlled fermentation methods the final result is only slightly better than that obtained by fermenting in a normal wooden cask. In the case of medium vintages tank fermentation automatically produces an improvement. In the case of good-class wines, i.e. with musts above 90 and 95 Öchsle, controlled fermentation in the tank may well produce very much better results than those obtainable by cask methods.

The great economic advantage of the tank is that it has an inert surface, is always ready for use and can be charged in turn with all kinds of wine, whereas the wooden cask needs a lot of attention and may occasionally have an adverse influence on the wine. A tank has the further advantage that finished wines can be stored in it for years and still retain their freshness without appreciably ageing, whereas wines can be stored in wooden casks for a short time only, and in consequence are often bottled prematurely.

All this does not mean, however, that in future growers will dispense with their wooden casks. There is no doubt that good wines do acquire an individual regional character through being stored in the wood after fermentation in tanks, and it is unlikely that the old methods will ever be entirely superseded.

In the tank the wine undergoes some degree of chemical change. Tank wine has invariably 2–3 g./litre alcohol more than cask wine, the must weight being equal. On the other hand, the contents of extract and glycerine are sometimes lower. Tank wines require more sulphur than cask wines and take a longer time seasoning. Where it is possible also to control fermentation in the cask by clarifying the must and keeping the temperature in the cellar low, the same advantages in respect of taste can be obtained as with the tank. The great expectations the trade had in connection with tank fermentation a few years ago have, in part, been realized, but in other cases, more especially in small vintages, not to the extent hoped for. Most suitable for tank fermentation are good, harmonious vintages.

When fermentation is over and the wine has been drawn off from the lees – first racking – growers and wine-merchants start its treatment for bottling. In former days this process was left to nature; that is, the wine was left in cask until it became impervious to air and had lost every vestige of cloudiness. This usually entailed a succession of rackings and often operated to the detriment of the consumer, the wine having lost its freshness by the time it was finally bottled.

Old wine in our sense has become known only since the middle of the eighteenth century. Until that time no means had been discovered of preserving wine from deterioration. For a long time wine was drunk very young as must, in all stages of fermentation (*Federweisser*, see p. 296) – but only for one year after the harvest. Longer than that it would not keep, and its quality suffered from many apparently incurable diseases. It was not until the use of sulphur was introduced into vinification that it became possible to bring wine to the stage where it could be stored or bottled without turning acid or being affected by other diseases.

Sulphurization as a method of treating wine has long been known, but opinion of its suitability and usefulness has differed through the centuries. In 1465 a councillor in the town of Cologne was deprived both of his position and of his licence as a wine trader on the grounds that he had used sulphur in vinification; and at the end of the last century some eminent authorities declared that a high content of sulphur would be dangerous to health.

Today the sulphurization of wines is regulated by law, a very necessary precaution in the interests both of viticulture and of the ultimate consumer. The wine law does not define exactly how much sulphur may be used, but just as (it will be recalled) the addition of sugar is permitted only within certain natural limits, so the use of sulphur is confined to the absolute necessities of good cellarage. Sulphurization is needed to keep the wines sound and prevent the formation of organisms which might cause decomposition. The quantity which is absolutely necessary depends upon the type of wine: rich wines need more sulphur to mature than do ordinary wines. But German food chemists have agreed that it is essential for the quality of the wine that a maximum should be set for the use of sulphur. With regard to ordinary wines the limit should stand at 200 milligrammes per litre, to include no more than 50 milligrammes of the free (sulphurous) acid.

It may be interesting to show the limits of sulphurization fixed by various countries (in milligrammes per litre): Germany, 200; Spain, 450; France, 450; Portugal, 350; Italy, 200; South Africa, 200 for dry wine, 357 for sweet wine; England, 450.

The last stage of development concerns the storage of the finished wine. Here the cellarman's main purpose is to keep the wine both fresh and young and also, if possible, to improve its quality.

The wine drinker of today asks for wines which are star-bright. The first aim of the wine-grower is therefore to stabilize the wine. In order to do this, he may utilize refrigeration, heat, separation by centrifuge, filtration or sterilization.

Fifty years ago it would have been considered a crime to filter wine when bottling. Racking and fining were the only means used to make the wine ready for bottling.

Growers had plenty of time and money, and the chemical and physical proceedings during the maturation of the wine were not well known as they are today. When the first filter appeared on the market, everybody said the filtration would 'dem Wein den Rock ausziehen' – in other words, would take the cream from the milk (literally, 'tear the coat off the wine').

'Airing' of the wine was, in olden times, the most important means of stabilization. All German wines, with the possible exception of Moselles, were exposed to air as much as possible during the first racking, because the cellarmaster knew that wines which had been aired would become ready for bottling more quickly. But the immediate result of the airing was that the wine became cloudy when the albumen and other materials contained in the wine were deposited. The disadvantages of airing were indeed manifold. A wine treated in this way was likely to lose its freshness, age quickly and take on a murky-brown colour; from a chemical point of view, the sulphurous acid – previously a free compound in the wine – would become oxidized into fixed sulphur, and the eventual formation of sulphuric acid would render the wine dull and old. Today, airing of wine takes place only in exceptional cases (if the wine is faulty, if it has a taste of mould, etc.), since scientists have at last evolved a method of fining which avoids these hazards.

The current methods of fining are founded on important and thorough scientific experiments, so that it is now possible to stabilize wine accurately and achieve the exact state required. No damage is done to the wine – on the contrary, those particles which are taken away during the fining and stabilization are those which tend to undermine the fine and noble bouquet and aroma material which is so important in the judgment of a good wine. By quick work it is possible to save all the fine parts of a wine.

Today, with the help of scientists, the treatment of wine is carried out in such a way that bottling of the small, average wines is effected before the summer. Such wines will thus not be left in cask during the summer when the cellar is likely to be warmer. They are put into bottle young and fresh so that they can have all the development in bottle which they previously had in cask. Formerly the influence of the air made them lose both bouquet and aroma, whereas lying in bottle they escape this influence.

We know that bacteria may be eliminated by filtering. Obviously the filter used for this purpose cannot be one of the ordinary asbestos filters used for clearing the wine of impurities, but must be specially constructed. Sterilization filters are made on the model of the cellar-presses which were formerly in common use in wine cellars. The minute pores of the filter sheets will not allow even the smallest microscopic particles to penetrate, which means that they are capable of excluding not only dirt but also bacteria and fermenting fungi. This method makes it possible to sterilize liquids without heating them – i.e. by a 'cold' process. The replacement of pasteurizing apparatus (until recently still employed for sterilizing wines) by these filters represents an immense improvement. The pasteurization of wine meant heating it to 167° Fahrenheit, the temperature at which all undesirable bacteria and fermenting fungi may be considered to be rendered harmless; the filter achieves the same object at normal cellar temperature, thus removing the risk of change in the character of the wine which is inevitable whenever heat is applied. Sterilization filters may also be used for the bottling of wines which, though perfectly healthy and fully matured, still contain a quantity of unfermented sugar. The use of the filter eliminates the risk that such wines will later become clouded with lees or turn acid.

The development of the wine will not be hampered by the use of sterilization filters. It is true that they destroy any ferments which have been left in the wine, but, after all, no ferment should remain in the wine once it has finally been bottled. In the making of port, the growers use brandy to stop the fermentation and kill any remaining ferments; for table wines, sterilization filters serve the same purpose.

It was actually the sterilization filter which made it possible for the German grower to keep his wines sweet – very often too sweet in comparison with the alcohol content.

In 1958 a new law[1] introduced yet another innovation. For many years opinions had differed regarding the treatment of German wines, and many complaints had been made to the effect that the new vinification would kill the character of German wines. This was a reference to the so-called *süssgehaltene* wines – those wines in which fermentation had been interrupted artificially by sterilization, filtration or refrigeration, and where a high percentage of sugar was left unfermented. Under the new law this treatment must not result in a wine which contains more than 25% sugar in an unfermented state in relation to the actual alcohol present in the wine (weight) at the time when the wine is being marketed, i.e. either offered *en carafe* or bottled for sale. The law, of course, recognizes that in some vintages certain wines, especially of the Auslese, Beerenauslese and Trockenbeerenauslese classes, may contain so much original sugar that it is impossible to gain a full fermentation. Such wines have a great amount of unfermented sugar.

Bottling through a sterilizing filter prevents a secondary fermentation in bottle, but before the bottler can take this step he must know that the wine is stable in other ways and that no turbidity is to be feared. Chemical processes are going on in the wine all the time, processes which create turbidity. If he can get rid of the causes the bottler can bottle the wine young and fresh. One of the causes is the presence of metals – such as iron, copper and zinc – or of albumen, tannic acid and tartaric acid, which prevent the wine from remaining bright. Iron is the main cause of chemical turbidity.

Most of the copper is precipitated during fermentation, probably as cuprous sulphate or phosphate, or possibly through combination with yeast-gum. The copper traces that remain can be eliminated by what is known as 'blue-fining'. So, incidentally, can any zinc particle (found in wine only when zinc-coated apparatus has been used), as well as the traces of iron always present in natural wines. In combination, as iron phosphates, iron traces frequently produce a whitish-grey turbidity in the wine which shows an obstinate tendency to recur even when temporarily removed by filtration. A fining with potassium ferrocyanide, a non-poisonous compound, is the remedy. When it is added to the wine the latter takes a dark blue colour: hence the term 'blue-fining'.

The use of potassium ferrocyanide was legalized as far back as 1923 because other clarifying media merely remove the solid substances which make the wine cloudy; to deal with the heavy metal salts dissolved in the wine, it is necessary first to turn them into solids. The action of potassium ferrocyanide on the metal salts does that, and the precipitated solids are then easily removable.

Experiments had been undertaken to precipitate the iron content of wine in the form of ferrous tannin by the addition of oxygen, but it turned out that wines thus treated with oxygen took on a very dark colour and were apt to age very quickly. This method was therefore abandoned in favour of blue-fining.

In all German establishments wine is bottled through asbestos filters. Wines which

[1] By-law of 17 January 1958.

still contain a small proportion of unfermented sugar are, however, always bottled through sterilizing filters. The grower takes special precautions when bottling these classes of wine; not only the filter but also the corks and the bottles are sterilized.

After bottling, the wine is stored in special wine-cellars; it is now on the way to maturity. Whereas some wines take only a short time to mature, others need years, sometimes decades – especially the fine Riesling and Tarminer wines, which obtain their full finesse only after years of storage.

CHAPTER THREE

# Naming the Wines

QUALITY in wine cannot be won except at the expense of quantity. Small-bearing but noble species of grapes, be they Rieslings or Pinots, grown on poor soil, on Moselle slate or Champagne lime, will yield a poor crop in terms of gallons per acre. They will, however, be wines of quality, the kind of wines which possess body and bouquet and breeding in perfect harmony. This is true of all the vine-lands and wines of the world, but what is absolutely unique in the history of wine is the degree of individuality which, after a century of untiring efforts towards perfection, the better wines of Germany have managed to attain.

The wine made from the first pickings of grapes will eventually be offered for sale by the vintner, after vinification and bottling, with its birth certificate printed on a label which provides the following information:

1. The name of the village or town where it was grown – Zeltingen, Piesport, Geisen-heim, Rüdesheim, Forst, Deidesheim, Nierstein, Oppenheim, etc.
2. The name of the particular vineyard within the administrative bounds of the said town or village – Schlossberg, Kirchenstück, etc.
3. The name of the grape from which the wine was made – Riesling, Sylvaner, Scheurebe, etc.
4. The date of the vintage when the wine was made.

A bottle bearing all such credentials indicates that it contains a good wine. But it is not necessarily the best; there are a number of rungs to climb before getting to the top.

The German wine-grower has developed various special harvesting procedures to enhance the excellence of his wine. Names, e.g. Spätlese, Auslese, Beerenauslese, Trockenbeerenauslese, on the labels imply such special procedures. What do they mean? First, according to the German Wine Law a wine with *any* of the labels described must be a wine to which no sugar has been added, a 100% natural wine.

## Spätlese

The grapes which are used for making a *Spätlese* must have been harvested only after the general picking of the grapes and must have been in a state of full ripeness. In other words, the Spätlese label shows that the wine is natural and the grapes have been gathered with special care. The small grower who depends upon the harvest for his livelihood for the next year will not wait longer than he has to for gathering his crop; and as soon as the Commission has given its licence he will pick his grapes regardless of their degree of maturity, for the Commission presumably knows that they contain sufficient sugar to produce wine. But a Spätlese must contain grapes in full-ripe condition only; the state of full ripeness is recognized by the highest possible content of sugar and the lowest possible content of acidity. When the grape starts the ripening process, i.e. when it goes soft and yellow and its skin becomes so thin that the inner part of the grape is visible, the sugar content and the content of acidity are approximately 21–31 promille; but with the progressive ripening of the grape the content of sugar increases and the content of acidity decreases.

Grapes also contain a proportion of malic acid. The riper the grape, the lower the content of malic acid. The characteristic acidity of the grape – tartaric acid – should outweigh the malic acidity when the grapes are fully ripe.

It is only during the ripening process that the aroma materials – the etheric oils – are formed in the grape. Only at this stage is the actual bouquet developed which will later play such a great part as the distinguishing mark of each individual wine (Riesling, Muscatel, Traminer, etc.).

When the grower leaves his wines until after the general picking of the grapes, and is harvesting only the grapes of one single vineyard, then we have a Spätlese wine.

## Auslese

The *Auslese* constitutes another method of increasing the quality of the wine. Again the Auslese grapes must be fully ripe, but the procedure is somewhat different. There are in fact three procedures which may be resorted to in order to produce an Auslese.

The most refined method is to gather all bad, sick, rotting or otherwise damaged grapes and leave the remainder hanging on the vines. The grower then has the choice either of gathering his good grapes immediately or of leaving them on the vines with the opportunity of ripening still further. The process can be repeated again, but this time it is not the damaged but the over-ripe grapes which are selected. This procedure may be repeated as often as the grower wishes until he is satisfied that all the grapes have been gathered. Clearly, this procedure is exceptionally expensive, since it involves an enormous amount of labour; yet there is no doubt that it is by this method that the finest Auslese wines are produced.

A more usual procedure is as follows. Again, all the bad grapes are gathered at one special picking. The grape-picker is then provided with either a container divided into two or three compartments or one large container with two small sickle-shaped buckets attached. The picker will then separate the berries according to their degree of ripeness and place them in the correct container or compartments – Auslese, Beerenauslese and Trockenbeerenauslese.

The third method is for the picker to put all the grapes into a single container, leaving out only the diseased and damaged grapes. The real sorting process then takes place at a spot just outside the vineyard. The grapes are spread out on a large trestle table and the experts separate the berries into their various grades. This method has the advantage that the standards adopted are more or less uniform and not those of the individual picker.

### Beerenauslese and Trockenbeerenauslese

The *Beerenauslese* is made by selecting for separate pressing only over-ripe or 'sleepy' grapes. The *Trockenbeerenauslese* is much the same, only more so; as its name implies, it consists in the selection of 'sleepy' berries which have been semi-dried by the sun to an almost raisin-like consistency.

'Sleepiness' in grapes is caused by the fungus known as *Botrytis cinerea*, which is apt to attack the fruit in a mild and sunny autumn. Its action is beneficial and greatly improves the quality of the grape. Depending for its existence on large quantities of acid, it destroys the grape-skin by means of its mycelial filaments, causing the water in the berry to evaporate in the dry, sunny, autumn air; the fruit pulp thus grows more concentrated, with a relatively high sugar content, until the berry is finally sun-dried into a natural raisin. The dehydration process may result in the evaporation of as much as three-quarters of the water content, bringing the harvest down to a mere quarter of its normal amount.

When gathering the grapes, the harvesters collect these rarer, raisin-like berries in special sickle-shaped containers hung in the punnets into which they throw the rest of the fruit. A foreman in charge of every eight to ten women keeps careful watch to see that no ordinary grapes are mistaken for the genuine sleepy berries and wrongly placed in the special containers. By this process it takes anything up to 20 workers a full two weeks to gather enough fruit from a vineyard of 3 hectares (nearly $7\frac{1}{2}$ acres), and the net result may be no more than 300 litres of must.

The highly concentrated must from the over-ripe berries dried upon the vine is so rich in sugar that it may fairly be described as syrupy. This makes its fermentation and after-fermentation a difficult task which can be entrusted only to an expert with long experience and specialized knowledge. Once it has been accomplished, however, the result is a dream of perfection. The finesse, the delicate aroma, the rare bouquet and the noble quality are indescribable. Honey-sweet richness tempered by the clean, pure, finely acidulated flavour of the grapes makes this wine the connoisseur's joy. Not easily obtainable, it is, of course, correspondingly high-priced. The greatest wines of this class are probably the highest-priced in the world.

The partial dehydration of over-ripe grapes which turns them into raisins is an ancient process. It is mentioned in the Old Testament, and Homer speaks both of allowing the grapes to hang on the vines till they are over-ripe and partially dried and of the process by which they are dried (after picking) by being exposed to the sun on hurdles or beds of straw.

'Edelbeerenauslese' is synonymous with Beerenauslese. The term 'Edelbeerenauslese' is used when the honey-like bouquet produced by the noble rottenness is very 'visible'. A 'Goldbeerenauslese' is an Auslese (not a Beerenauslese) of fully-ripe golden grapes (as a Beerenauslese is made of sleepy grapes, i.e. grapes attacked by the fungus *Botrytis cinerea*, which have passed the golden stage).

After the wines have been classified by degree further categories of selection may be shown on the wine labels. Thus a wine may be described as *Kabinett*, or *Cabinet*.

## Kabinett (Cabinet)

What is a *Kabinett* wine? The German Wine Law gives no answer to this question. *Kabinett-Wein* is mentioned in only one by-law, Article 5, where it is merely defined as a term which may be applied to natural wines only. The expression has yet to be given a judicial definition.

Without doubt, the name Kabinett originated in the Rheingau under the administration of the dukes of Nassau, who in Napoleon's time obtained control of many important vineyards. Ducal administrators stored a few casks of their best wines in small cellars (hence the name), and it is said that the top-class wines of the Steinberg vineyard were the first wines to receive this additional designation. At that time the label of a Kabinett wine bore the signature of the cellarmaster or of two officials of the domain, and this can still be seen in facsimile. Later on, some estates, now confined to the Rheingau, named their best wines in this way, so that in time Kabinett became a special guarantee that the wine was natural.

The name Kabinett, wherever it is found, is the personal guarantee of the wine-grower that he considers the wine under this label to be of specially high quality. One important point is that Kabinett wines need not be estate-bottled.

While the wine-grower who owns, say, a dozen or so acres of Montrachet will equalize his whole crop and therefore make only one single wine, his opposite number in the Rhineland, with the same acreage of less, may make five different wines, each of a different degree of sweetness and excellence. He is, indeed, a perfectionist! So much so, in fact, that he goes still one step further, or one rung higher: the wine of each grade or quality is not averaged down or blended, as at Château d'Yquem, but the wine of each cask is kept separate to be bottled and sold under its own number – Fass No., or Fuder No., clearly stated on the wine label.

No wonder the label on a bottle of German wine is of such importance! It gives the whole history of the wine within the bottle – its place and date of birth, its grape, whether it has been produced from specially selected or over-ripe grapes, whether it is an *Original-Abfüllung, Kellerabfüllung* or *Schlossabzug*. All these last expressions mean that the wine has been *château-* or cellar-bottled by the grower. If the wine is not bottled by the grower the label carried the word *Creszenz, Gewächs* or *Wachstum* ('the growth of') followed by the name of the grower who, or the concern which, owns the vineyard. All the above expressions contain the guarantee according to German law that the wine is natural.

These, then, are the best wines of Germany. Many of them are indeed great wines, and for that reason perhaps they are the exception rather than the rule, just as great men are the exception rather than the rule.

When the label simply bears the expression *natur* or *naturrein*, it means that the wine is natural, genuine, made from the fermented grape-juice without any added sugar. But absence of these descriptions does not necessarily denote that the wine is sweetened. Sugar is a carbohydrate which will ferment and raise the alcoholic strength of the new wine. Sugar addition will not add anything to the bouquet or charm, but will provide a drinkable wine. Among this category of 'improved' wines we must also mention the wines which are sold under popular names such as Moselblümchen or Liebfraumilch but which may be blends of different vineyards or different vintages; the names are invented names and do not exist geographically.

All this adds up to one important conclusion: the importance of the guarantee of quality which rests on the reputations of wine-growers and merchants.

There are not many vineyards in the Rhineland and Moselle owned by one single proprietor: most of them are shared by two, three or more growers, all of whom have an equal right to sell their wine under the same vineyard name. Yet it is quite certain that while the names will be the same, the wines will be different. This is inevitable, since it is unlikely that any two wine-growers could be found with identical views on the use of fertilizers, the time of day to pick the grapes, the most effective methods of mashing, the handling of the fermentation, and finally the nurturing and storage of the newly made wines. Even if their views were identical on such matters, they would be unlikely to have the same financial and natural facilities available; and it would prove impossible for them to produce exactly similar wines.

## Eiswein (Ice Wine)

An interesting phenomenon met only in German wines is the so-called ice wine. In a report dating from 1869 there is evidence that a grower in Traben–Trarbach had produced 'ice wine' as early as 1842. Finding that his grapes had become frozen, he nevertheless continued with picking and pressing, more or less as a desperation measure, and was astonished and delighted to discover that he had produced a most beautiful wine which contained not the slightest taste of frost.

In the year 1890 the ripe berries on the vines of certain vineyards were frozen by an 'ice rain', that is, by rain falling at a temperature below freezing point. Despite all prophecies to the contrary, the wine proved to be exquisite. The water in the berries had turned to ice, leaving the remaining grape-juice more concentrated and proportionately richer in sugar content. The wines made from this thick syrup were so sweet and fine as to be comparable with outstanding Auslesen.

It is, of course, essential that the grapes be gathered and pressed immediately, while the ice remains frozen within the body of the grape. The so-called grape-cake consists of a large lump of ice, and the resulting wine is really the extract of the grape. Moreover, the grapes should already be over-ripe when first affected by the frost. In a year when the grapes have not achieved the maximum degree of ripeness an extract may still be made by the ice-wine process, but the absence of the necessary aroma materials inevitably results in a lack of true finesse.

Ice wine has seldom been made. Over the last hundred years it is known to have been produced in only eleven vintages: 1875, 1880, 1890, 1902, 1908, 1912, 1949, 1950, 1961, 1962 and 1965. (Attempts to make ice wine in 1954 and 1956 met with little success.) Most of these vintages produced only small quantities – two casks in 1949, for instance, and one in 1950. Large quantities were made in 1961 for the first time in the history of German viticulture, and in 1962 production increased. In those two years the cold weather came unusually early.

In order to make real ice wines, the weather during the late harvesting must be exceptionally dry, so that the grapes remain healthy before they are attacked by frost. When the frost comes, they must also be so ripe that the wine retains no disagreeable frosty taste – caused by the green stalks of unripe grapes, therefore many of the 1965 ice wines do not deserve this name.

The vinification of ice wines is discussed in Appendix 3.

### St Nikolaus Wine

A special Spätlese is the *St Nikolaus Wine*.

In Germany one celebrates St Nikolaus's Day (the English Santa Claus is a corruption of the saint's name): on his name-day, 6 December, he visits the children to ask if they have been good during the past year, and to hear their wishes for Christmas. In some vintages, if the weather is favourable, the grower waits to gather his grapes until St Nikolaus's Day; he may lose the whole harvest, but if he succeeds, the grapes may be more concentrated, and the wine may be a fuller, fruitier wine than the wines gathered earlier. In any case, St Nikolaus wines have some sentimental value. In 1961 this risk was taken by quite a number of wine-growers in Rhinehessia and the Nahe. St Nikolaus wines do not attain the concentration of ice wines; the ice wines in the Moselle district reached 146°, and those of the Nahe 115°, but the Nikolaus wine only between 95° and 100°. These wines, however, reflect the risk the grower has taken; he is proud of his venture, and wine lovers value it.

It seldom happens that the grapes remain in the vineyards until the beginning of January, but it has happened that grapes were gathered on 6 January, Twelfth Night. These 'Three Kings' wines are always a curiosity, available in very small quantities only and actually considered museum-pieces. This shows what *can* be done in the moderate climate of the German wine-growing districts! Wine made from grapes gathered on New Year's Eve (St Sylvester's Day) is called Sylvester wine.

Incidentally, the Nahe in 1920 produced 12–14 Half-Stücks of St Nikolaus wines, which were considered the best wines of this century, and which kept better than the 1921 of the same district.

### Federweisser

When the must is deposited in the fermentation cask and fermentation has proceeded for a short while, leaving behind a remnant of sugar, the must takes on a milky colour and contains plenty of carbonic acid. This 'new' wine is called *Federweisser* and the local inhabitants – especially in the Palatinate district – like drinking the must in this state of fermentation. They drink it to the accompaniment of brown bread and the new season's walnuts or chestnuts. The wine remains in this condition, of course, for only a very short time, and it could never be exported, or even bottled, in this state. It has to be drawn from the cask and drunk on the spot.

### Maiwein (May Wine)

May wine is actually one of the many *Bowle*, or Hock cups. The mixing of cups, an old German custom, is the characteristic form of German conviviality. The name *Bowle* is taken from the vessel – the bowl – in which these drinks are mixed. The wines used are usually the most ordinary light table wines. Whereas most cups are based on fruits, such as strawberries, peaches and pineapple, May wine is based on the fragrant woodruff (*Waldmeister*), the herbal plant growing wild in many German woods. The woodruff is put into a mixing vessel, and wine is added and sugared according to taste.

May wine is bottled commercially in small quantities, using woodruff essence, but May wine remains essentially the thirst-quenching drink for May or June.

### *Jungferwein (Virgin Wine)*

*Jungferwein* is the first wine produced from a newly planted vineyard. After a vineyard has been left uncultivated for some years the new wine – which is produced three or four years after replanting the vineyard – is considered especially good and elegant, as the vine has been able to get all the nourishment from ground which has been unproductive for so many years. Generally speaking, the *Jungferwein* has no staying power, but when drunk young it shows an especially fine bouquet and flavour.

CHAPTER FOUR

# *The Vineyards of Germany and their Grapes*

VIRTUALLY all the vineyards of Germany have always been, and still are, in the south-west; roughly speaking, in the basin of the Rhine. All the best vineyards, that is to say the vineyards responsible for the best German wines, are those which grace both banks of the Rhine from Frankfurt, where the Main flows into the Rhine, to Bingen, at the junction of the Nahe; those of the Palatinate; those of the Moselle, Saar and Ruwer valleys from Trier to Koblenz; those of the Main valley from Hochheim to Würzburg and beyond; and those of the Nahe and other tributaries of the Rhine.

There are no longer any important vineyards in Silesia, Saxony or other northern and north-eastern parts of Germany. Vines could still be coaxed to grow here, as they were in former times, but they would not pay, and never did pay, a worthwhile dividend.

During the last decade of the nineteenth century the total acreage of the German vineyards was about 300,000 acres. By the end of the Second World War they hardly covered half that area. There were several reasons for this sensational reduction. First in importance was the return of Alsace to France in 1919, which removed at one stroke some 93,000 acres from the viticultural map of Germany. The phylloxera pest may be given second place, since it destroyed many more vineyards than the growers could or would replant with the right grapes; for the law of the land henceforth prohibited the planting of hybrids, hardy and free-bearing grapes, the kind of grapes from which only the common wines could be made. Another adverse factor was the growing attraction of the industrial centres, which offered the younger generation higher wages and brighter social amenities than their native villages could provide. This was not a trend peculiar to Germany, but the German vineyards suffered more than most because of their steep gradients, on which it was impossible to replace man-power by tractors and other mechanical devices.

However, the higher prices paid for grapes and wines since 1949 have encouraged the replanting of many more vineyards. Unfortunately these have not always been in sites suitable for the production of quality wines – hence, in 1959, yet another new law, limiting the range of districts where new vineyards could be planted.

The progress made by the replanting of Rhineland vineyards since 1949 is borne out by the following figures (in acres):

| 1949 | 128,718 | 1956 | 149,238 | 1961 | 165,662 |
|------|---------|------|---------|------|---------|
| 1951 | 131,362 | 1957 | 146,858 | 1962 | 167,843 |
| 1952 | 133,398 | 1958 | 147,840 | 1963 | 170,885 |
| 1953 | 136,215 | 1959 | 152,488 | 1964 | 171,557 |
| 1954 | 145,355 | 1960 | 160,450 | 1965 | 172,040 |
| 1955 | 149,902 |      |         |      |         |

The 1960 total acreage was divided as follows:

| Palatinate | 38,660 | Rheingau | 6,292 |
|------------|--------|----------|-------|
| Rhinehessia | 36,300 | Franconia | 5,900 |
| Baden–Württemberg | 32,205 | Middle Rhine | 4,042 |
| Moselle, Saar, Ruwer | 21,043 | Ahr | 1,283 |
| Nahe | 7,410 | All others | 7,315 |

Although the acreage of the German vineyards is appreciably less than it was in pre-war times, the production of German wines has not decreased in anything like the same proportion; far from it. Thanks to the use of more effective fertilizers and other scientific methods of cultivation, an acre of vines now produces nearly three times as much wine as it did 50 years ago under similar weather conditions. Progress in viticulture and the promotion of quality wines has, moreover, been effectively aided by viticultural associations like the Deutsche Weinbauverein. The viticultural colleges founded in all wine districts help in the education of the wine-grower.

Since we are not so ambitious as to try to deal with all the wines of Germany, but only with the great ones, we do not propose to give more than a few courtesy lines to the vineyards of the Ahr, the Middle Rhine, the Bergstrasse and the Bodensee. We shall deal mostly, if not solely, with the vineyards responsible for the finest wines of Germany, many of which are the peers of the great white wines of the world – some of them the greatest of all. But first a word about the grapes which produce these wines.

## The Grapes

Whatever the care and skill of the grower, it is the nature of the soil and the local climatic conditions that are responsible for the proportion of quality wine which may be made from any vineyard. The geological formation of the vineyard's soil must necessarily be accepted for what it is, although manure and fertilizers can certainly help a great deal. But there is nothing that can be done about the climate. Rain and sunshine come as and when they choose – not to mention late spring frosts, hailstorms and other unpredictable freaks of the weather.

There is, however, one factor man is free to choose as he thinks best: the right kind of grape to grow, the grape that is most likely to flourish and yield the best wine. In Germany, as it happens, there is virtual unanimity as to the most suitable grape for quality wines: it is the *Riesling*. The Riesling is to the Sylvaner what the Pinot is to the

Plate 26. Schloss Vollrads, in the **Rheinga**

Gamay. It is a truly noble grape, responsible for the outstanding excellence and inimitable distinctiveness of all the finer German wines.

The Riesling is practically the only grape grown in all the named sites of the Rheingau, Moselle, Saar and Ruwer vineyards. Other parts of the Rhineland grow a greater or lesser proportion of other grapes, mostly Sylvaner grapes but also some Elbling, Traminer and Gutedel for white wines and Portuguese and Pinot for red wines. But although the greatest of all fine German wines have always been made from Riesling grapes, it must not be forgotten that Rieslings must be given the soil, the aspect and the other conditions which happen to suit them best. They cannot be grown anywhere and everywhere. In the sandstone of the Mittelhaardt of the Palatinate, for instance, the Traminer (or Gewürztraminer) – also a noble grape – is more suitable than the Riesling. The Traminer is also grown in the better vineyards of Baden, where they usually know it by the name of Klevner.

The Riesling grape has, however, the grave faults of bearing fewer bunches and of being more susceptible to frost than other species. Hence the many attempts which have been made to cross the Riesling with the hardier Sylvaner. The *Sylvaner* grape is grown to a greater extent than any other species, including the Riesling. It enjoys this privileged position because it matures earlier than the Riesling and because its vines thrive in the richer soil of plains and plateaux, yielding a greater quantity of grapes from which a high grade of wine can be made. Such wine is made in some parts of Rhinehessia, the Palatinate, the Nahe valley, Franconia and Württemberg.

One of the most successful of the attempts to cross the Riesling with the Sylvaner resulted in the grape known as the *Müller-Thurgau*, which not only bears more fruit than the Riesling but ripens two or three weeks earlier. From an economic point of view both Sylvaner and Müller-Thurgau grapes commend themselves to wine-growers and wine-merchants. They produce many more grapes per acre than the Riesling and the Traminer, and their wines are ready to drink in a matter of months, sometimes weeks, rather than years. Sylvaner-made wines are fresh and pleasing, but of course they do not possess anything like the body or bouquet of Riesling-made wines, let alone their 'breeding'.

So far the most successful of the many attempts at crossing Sylvaner and Riesling with the object of producing a quality wine is Herr Scheu's *Scheurebe*, a grape utterly unlike the Müller-Thurgau. Its good points are that it bears more fruit and ripens 10–14 days earlier than the Riesling; it also has a much greater volume of bouquet. It grows best in the Palatinate, although many sites in the Rheingau and Rhinehessia have been planted with the grape. The Scheurebe thrives on poor rather than rich soil.

Further new crossings are: the *Morio-Muscat*, a cross between Sylvaner and Pinot blanc; the *Siegerrebe*, a cross between Riesling and Traminer, also grown by Herr Scheu, producing mild wines with a fine Traminer flavour; the *Rieslaner* (formerly Mainriesling since this name has been considered misleading), a crossing of Rhine-Riesling and Franconian Sylvaner which ripens a fortnight before the Riesling grape and, on good or even average sites, produces a really fine wine with all the characteristics of the original Riesling.

There are quite a number of other grapes grown for the making of the commoner sorts of table wine. Such is the *Elbling*, also called *Räuschling* and *Kleinberger*; these are cultivated in various places, but never in large quantities. Wine of indifferent quality is also made, in small quantities only, from the *Chasselas*, a table grape which is very sweet

ate 27. (*Above*) Leinsweiler, in the Palatinate. (*Below*) Kiedrich, in the Rheingau.

because of its lack of acidity; it is known in Germany as the *Gutedel*. The *Auxerrois* and *Ruländer* are white grapes from France grown in some vineyards of the Upper Moselle, the Saar, Baden and Franconia for the making of good white wines. Their chief asset is that the grapes ripen earlier than either Riesling or Sylvaner.

The latest and most remarkable species of grape introduced in Germany is the *Würzburg Perle* which can stand an unheard-of degree of cold – minus 35° Centigrade during the winter and minus 6° in the spring when the sap is actually rising. This remarkable *Weinperle* produces an abundant crop of grapes, and the wine made from them is soft and flowery. It also matures early. It was introduced by Dr Breider, who may have more surprises in store for the viticultural experts of the future.

All these and a few other grapes are grown for the production of white wines. But there are also black grapes, which the Germans rightly call blue, grown for the production of red wines.

## *The Wines of the Moselle — Saar — Ruwer*

It must have been in Olympus, long ago, that a marriage was arranged between pretty Moselle and handsome Rhine. Both flow for many miles in the same northerly direction, but not within speaking distance, the Moselle west and the Rhine east of the Vosges mountains. For a long time the Moselle is a reluctant bride, twisting and curling fretfully in a most feminine and capricious manner, but when she leaves Lorraine at Thionville and enters Luxembourg she turns resolutely towards the east as if her mind were at last made up to surrender. Yet even then the Moselle does not appear to be in any great hurry as she meanders softly through the rich meadows and gentle hills of Luxembourg and its old-world cities, Remich, Wormeldange and Grevenmacher. The Moselle leaves Luxembourg at Wasserbillig, passes through imperial Trier 7 miles farther on, and then seems to become timorous of the approaching meeting with her groom. The last lap of her course, until she slips finally into his bed at Koblenz, is made up of miles of hair-pin turns and loops, often rushing due south-west back almost to the point she has just left.

Whenever there are hills, plenty of air and sunshine, grapes will grow and give us wine, which may be fair or fine according to the weather each year. If anybody has any doubts, however, regarding the relative importance of sun and soil for the making of fine wine, the Moselle is there to show that the soil holds first place. The Moselle vineyards, during the river's long run through France, get their full share of sunshine and are protected by the Vosges mountains from those blasting east winds which the vines hate as much as we do. But the soil is not right. It brings forth grapes in plenty, but the wine made from them is just plain wine; it is refreshing, it is sharp and wholesome, splitting fats, removing stains and stimulating the bladder – but not the brain. There is nothing to be done about it. It is not the soil, and never can be, to give us fine wine.

Then the Moselle enters Germany, and it is on her way from Trier to Koblenz that her vineyards bring forth truly remarkable white wines, wines possessing an enchanting perfume, slender of body yet by no means thin, wholly admirable. The Riesling grape is, of course, responsible for a great deal but not for everything: it cannot possibly give us anywhere else any wine comparable in charm to the finer Moselle, Saar and Ruwer wines. These are made from Riesling grapes grown fairly high up the steep hillsides of those favoured rivers, and the slate which is the peculiar geological formation of those hills is of the utmost importance and value.

During the first 7 miles of her course in Germany, from Wasserbillig to Trier, the Moselle passes through a number of vineyards which yield a fair amount of useful but quite undistinguished wines; yet the Saar, the largest German tributary of the Moselle, which it enters about 3 miles above Trier, is able to boast vineyards whose wines are as fine as the finest wines of the Moselle proper. This does not mean, unfortunately, that all Saar wines are wonderful: they are not. Riesling and soil will not show how good their wines can be unless the sun shines long enough and at the right time: the upper Saar valley has the blast furnaces of heavy industry to keep it warm day and night, but the lower Saar valley is a very cold corridor where grapes find it difficult to ripen every year. When the sun does oblige, however, the superlative excellence of the Saar wines richly rewards the obstinate optimism of the wine-growers who refuse to be beaten by the weather.

As one comes down the Saar towards the Moselle the first vineyards of any note are those of SERRIG, a village straight out of Grimm's fairy tales, sheltering at the foot of a line of wooded bluffs with a chapel on the cliff's edge, the König Johann Berg, where they laid the bones of the blind King of Bohemia who was killed at Crécy in 1346. The remains of King John were transferred, in 1947, to the Cathedral of Luxembourg, where they have been given the place of honour of a national memorial.

The best vineyards of Serrig are as follows. (Names in SMALL CAPITALS, here and below, are those sites or vineyards reputed to produce the best wines.)

| | | |
|---|---|---|
| Antoniusberg | Saarstein | Wingertsheck |
| Hindenburglay | Schloss Saarfelser | Würzburger Helenenberg |
| Kupp | VOGELSANG | Würzburger Marienberg |

SAARBURG is only a small town, but it is the most important of the lower course of the Saar; it has only a few vineyards of its own, and none of great merit, but it has incorporated the vineyards of Niederleuken near by, the best of them being:

| | | |
|---|---|---|
| Antoniusbrunnen | Layenkaul | Rausch |
| Klosterberg | MÜHLENBERG | Schlossberg |

OCKFEN's vineyards do produce some quite outstanding wines – if and when the sun is kind! Most of them were planted by the Abbey of St Martin, Trier, which owned the site from 1037 to 1803.

| | | |
|---|---|---|
| BOCKSTEIN | Heppenstein | St Irminer |
| Geisberg | Herrenberg | |

AYL is a small village, on the left bank of the Saar, with a beautiful fanlike stretch of vineyards facing south, most of them still ecclesiastical property, the property of the Bischof Konvikt and Bischof Priesterseminar of Trier.

| | | |
|---|---|---|
| Euchariusberg | KUPP | Scheidterberg |
| Herrenberg | Neuberg | Silberberg |
| Junkerberg | HERRENBERG | Sommerberg |
| KAPELLENBERG | | |

KONZ is a modest village, so modest that it does not give its name to the wines made from its vineyards; most of them are sold as *Oberemmeler* and some as *Falkenstein*, the only Konz vineyard of any importance, which is owned by the Friedrich Wilhelm Gymnasium.

OBEREMMEL is not actually in the Saar valley but in a tributary valley close by, adjoining Wiltingen.

| | | |
|---|---|---|
| Agritiusberg | Hütte | Raul |
| Altenberg | Karlsberg | Rosenberg |
| Eltzberg | Lauterberg | SCHARZBERG |

WILTINGEN is on the right bank of the Saar, and its vineyards produce both more and better wines than any of the other Saar vineyards. The pride of Wiltingen are the wines of the *Scharzhof* and *Scharzberg*. The *Scharzhof* itself is a fine old mansion, the home of the Egon Müller family for many years, and its vineyard is divided into three strips which belong to Egon Müller, Apollinar Joseph Koch and Trier Cathedral: the first two sell their wine as *Scharzhofberger*, without any mention of Wiltingen; the Trier Cathedral sell theirs as *Dom Scharzhofberger*. The *Scharzberg* vineyard adjoins the Scharzhofberg and overflows into the adjacent territory of Oberemmel, but Scharzberg wine, one of the truly great wines of the world, is sold as Scharzberger without any mention of either Wiltingen or Oberemmel.

| | | |
|---|---|---|
| Braune Kupp | Johannisberg | Rosenberg |
| Braunfels | Klosterberg | SCHARZBERG |
| Dohr | Kupp | SCHARZHOFBERG |
| Gottesfuss | Neuberg | Schlangengraben |

The following are proprietors of Scharzhofberg:

| | |
|---|---|
| Egon Müller (largest owner) | v. Volxem |
| Hohe Domkirche (second largest owner) | Rautenstrauch |
| Vereinigte Hospitien | Kesselstadt |
| Apollinaris Koch | v. Hovel |

According to a local saying, a vintage is a good vintage when there are 1,400 Fuder of wine made from Wiltingen vineyards, that is, as many Fuder as there are inhabitants.

KANZEM or CANZEM is an important village built on the west or left bank of the Saar, facing north, but its vineyards are up on a slope of the hill, facing south, on the other side of the river.

| | | |
|---|---|---|
| Altenberg | Kelterberg | Unterberg |
| Berg | Ritterpfad | Wolfsberg |
| Hörecker | SONNENBERG | |

WAWERN is a small village below Kanzem and on the same left bank of the Saar, and its vineyards adjoin those of Kanzem, but there are not so many of them.

| | | |
|---|---|---|
| Goldberg | Jesuitengarten | Ritterpfad |
| Herrenberg | | |

FILZEN is the last village of the Saar valley before the Moselle: its vineyards are not important, and their wine is not of any merit, unless of an exceptionally hot vintage.

| | | |
|---|---|---|
| Neuberg | Urbelt | VOGELBERG |
| Pulchen | | |

TRIER is a most interesting city from an antiquarian, an ecclesiastical or an artistic point of view, but it has also been for centuries past and still is the heart of the vineyards of the Moselle, Saar and Ruwer. Its own vineyards are almost negligible, barely 50 acres of Riesling-planted slopes:

Herrenberg       Klosterberg       Neuberg

Its municipal cellars, however, can, and often do, house 30,000 Fuder, or over 6½ million gallons of Moselle, Saar and Ruwer wines. In the past the Archbishops of Trier were among the greatest owners of vineyards as well as most generous in their gifts of vineyard sites to religious orders; to this day the Trier Cathedral Chapter, and several episcopal colleges and hospitals, could not meet ever-rising costs if they did not have an assured revenue from the sale of some of the finest white wines of the Moselle, Saar and Ruwer wines of their own vineyards. Trier is also today, as it has been since medieval times, noted for those famous annual public auctions at which great quantities of newly made wines, and some of the older wines as well, are sold. It is also the seat of the provincial *Weinbaulehranstalt* (viticultural college), a seat of wine lore and learning, responsible for the high standard of the quality of the Moselle, Saar and Ruwer wines.

Here, too, are the headquarters of the five famous ecclesiastical, charitable, educational and state organizations. A list of the widely distributed vineyards owned by them:

*Bischöfliches Priesterseminar*

| | | |
|---|---|---|
| Ayler Kupp | Kanzemer Altenberg | Ürziger Würzgarten |
| Dhronhofberger | Kaseler Nies'gen | Wiltinger Kupp |
| Erdener Treppchen | Trittenheimer Apotheker | |

*Hohe Domkirche*

| | |
|---|---|
| Dom Avelsbacher Herrenberg | Dom Scharzhofberger |

*Vereinigte Hospitien*

| | | |
|---|---|---|
| Braunfels | Saarfelser Vogelsang | Wiltinger Hölle |
| Kanzemer Kellerberg | Scharzhofberger | Wiltinger Kupp |
| Piesporter Goldtröpfchen | Serriger Schloss | |

*Friedrich Wilhelm Gymnasium*

| | | |
|---|---|---|
| Bernkasteler Rosenberg | Jesuitenhofberg | Ockfener Geisberg |
| Dhroner Hofberg | Mehringer Treppchen & | Trittenheimer Altarchen |
| Falkensteiner Hofberg | Zellerberg | Zeltinger Sonnenuhr |
| Graacher Abtsberg | Neumagener Rosengärtchen | |

*State Domain*

| | | |
|---|---|---|
| Avelsbacher Hammerstein | Ockfener Bockstein | Serriger Heiligenborn |
| Avelsbacher Kupp | Ockfener Heppenstein | Serriger Höppslei |
| Avelsbacher Rotlei | Ockfener Oberherrenberg | Serriger Vogelsang |
| Avelsbacher Thielslei | Herriger Hindenburglei | Serriger Wingertsheck |
| Avelsbacher Vogelgesang | | |

There are practically no fine wines made from the vineyards of the Moselle between the Saar and the Ruwer above and below Trier. One exception should be made, however, for the vineyards and wines of AVELSBACH, close to Trier. Its best vineyards are owned by the Trier Cathedral and the Rheinland-Pfalz State; the first sold as Dom-Avelsbacher with the site name added. The State sells the wine of its HAMMERSTEIN vineyard, which owes its existence, if not its excellence, to convict hard labour.

A little more than 2 miles downstream from Trier, the Moselle welcomes yet another tributary from the east, the Ruwer, a brook rather than a river, its clear waters babbling and tinkling as they flow faster than do the trains on the ancient narrow-gauge railway which follows its course. As one leaves the village of Ruwer, where the two rivers meet, one sees from the road a broad curving slope of serried vines, like a segment of an enormous amphitheatre facing the sun. They are the vines of EITELSBACH, on the right bank of the Ruwer. The Karthaus Hof was originally a Dominican property, but it was owned by the Carthusians from the fourteenth century until 1802, when Napoleon gave it to the Rautenstrauch family, who have owned it ever since; it is now under the direction of the present Rautenstrauch's son-in-law, Herr von Tyrell. Whenever the sun obliges (as in 1959), he makes wines of quite outstanding excellence sold under the name of *Eitelsbacher Karthäuserhofberg*. Other vineyards of Eitelsbach are:

| | | |
|---|---|---|
| Dominikanerberg | Kehrnagel | Paulinsberg |
| Hitzlay | Kohlenberg | Sonnenberg |
| Katharinenberg | Lorenzberg | Steininger |
| Käulen | Nieschen or Nies'gen | Taubenberg |

MERTESDORF-GRÜNHAUS is the village which faces Eitelsbach on the opposite bank of the river. Grünhaus is the residence of the von Schubert family who own the narrow tree-crested slope on which is grown the famous Maximin-Grünhauser.

| | | |
|---|---|---|
| ABTSBERG | Johannisberg | Spielberg |
| BRUDERBERG | Lorenzberg | Treppchen |
| Harrenberg | | |

KASEL or CASEL, a little higher up the valley, is the largest of the wine-producing villages of the Ruwer, and its vineyards are also the most important: they produce some very fine wines, although not the peers of the Karthäuserhofberger or Maximin-Grünhauser. One of its vineyards – KATHARINENBERG – is the property of the City of Trier for its School of Viticulture and Wine-Making. Other Kasel vineyards are:

| | | |
|---|---|---|
| Dominikanberg | Kohlenberg | Paulinsberg |
| HITZLAY | Lorenzberg | Steininger |
| Käulgen | NIESCHEN or NIES'GEN | Taubenberg |
| KEHRNAGEL | | |

WALDRACH, at the back of Kasel, has one vineyard of note, Waldracher Doktor.

Coming now to the vineyards of the Moselle proper, travelling from the Ruwer to the Rhine, we find a considerable number on both banks of the river. They produce each year a great deal of wine, some of quite outstanding excellence, some of very fair quality and some, of course, in the plain or *ordinaire* category. The many twists and loops of the Moselle are due to the number of hills which throw their spurs in the way of the river at all sorts of different angles, forcing it to alter its course all the time, but also providing a much greater number of suitable sites for vineyards facing the sun and protected from cold winds. All the finest Moselle wines come from vineyards of the Middle Moselle, from Leiwen to Enkirch, but there are some very pleasant wines made, in good sunny years, from the vineyards of the other territories above Leiwen and below Enkirch. Here is a list of wine-producing villages, and their vineyards, as one journeys downstream from the Ruwer to the Rhine.

## LONGUICH (*longus vicus*—the long village)

| | | |
|---|---|---|
| Herrenberg | Kirchberg | Maximiner-Herrenberg |

## MEHRING

| | | |
|---|---|---|
| Goldkupp | Hüxlay | Plattenberg |
| Heidenkupp | Kuckuckslay | ZELLERBERG |

## DETZEM (*decima lapis*—ten miles mark)

| | |
|---|---|
| Königsberg | Maximiner-Klosterlay |

## THÖRNICH

| | | |
|---|---|---|
| ENGASS | RITSCH | Schiess-Lay |
| Ley | | |

## KLÜSSERATH

| | | |
|---|---|---|
| BRUDERSCHAFT | Königsberg | St Michel |

## LEIWEN

| | | |
|---|---|---|
| Klostergarten | LAURENZIUS LAY | Ohligsberg |

Before reaching Trittenheim, the Moselle meanders through the rich fields, orchards and gardens of half a dozen villages, some of them near the river, and others a short distance away. Of course, there are vineyards also, but their wines are practically all consumed locally, possibly because wine-growers hate to let them go, but more likely because they do not attract or retain the attention of merchants.

TRITTENHEIM owes its name to Trithemius, a saintly fourteenth-century Abbot of Spanheim, who was renowned for his learning. It is built upon a rock on the left bank of the Moselle, opposite to Leiwen, its slopes covered with vineyards and crowned by a small chapel dedicated to St Lawrence, hence the LAURENZIUS LAY vineyard of Leiwen and LAURENZIUSBERG of Trittenheim.

The better vineyards of Trittenheim are:

| | | |
|---|---|---|
| ALTÄRCHEN | LAURENZIUSBERG | Sonnteilen |
| APOTHEKE | Neuberg | Vogelsang |
| Clemensberg | Olk | Weierbach |
| Falkenberg | Sonnenberg | |

NEUMAGEN (*Novigamus*). A little way down the Moselle, on the opposite bank, Neumagen, one of the oldest villages of the Moselle, stands upon the high ground which rises where the little River Dhron flows into the Moselle. Its vineyards do not produce any wines of remarkable quality, and Neumagen is chiefly noted for the interesting Roman remains which have been unearthed there.

| | | |
|---|---|---|
| ENGELGRUBE | Lasenberg | Pichter |
| Hengelberg | LAUDAMUSBERG | Rosengärtchen |
| Kirchenstück | Pfaffenberg | Thierlay |

DHRON lies behind Neumagen along a little tributary valley.

| | | |
|---|---|---|
| Grosswingert | Kandel | ROTERD |
| Hengelberg | Pichter | Sangerei |
| HOFBERG | | |

PIESPORT is said to derive its name from *Pepini Portus* (the Gate of Pepin), Pepin the Short (died A.D. 768), the first king of the Carolingian dynasty (A.D. 752) – although it is difficult to imagine that Piesport ever had any military value. It consists of a

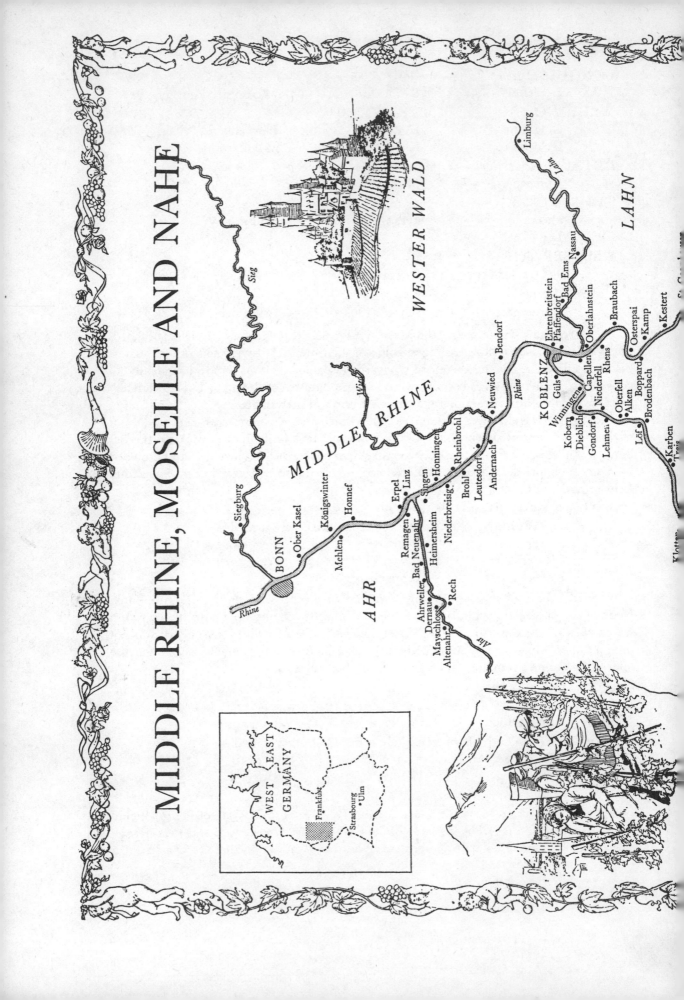

# MIDDLE RHINE, MOSELLE AND NAHE

WESTER WALD

LAHN

Limburg

Lahn

Sieg

MIDDLE RHINE

Nassau
Bad Ems
Ehrenbreitstein
Pfaffendorf
Oberlahnstein
Braubach
Osterspai
Kamp
Kestert

KOBLENZ
Güls
Winningen
Koberg
Diebich
Gondorf
Niederfell
Lehmen
Oberfell
Alken
Löf
Brodenbach
Boppard

Capellen
Rhens

Karben
Treis

Siegburg
Bendorf
Neuwied
Rhine
Ober Kasel
Königswinter
Honnef
Wied

BONN
Mehlen
Erpel
Linz
Singen
Rheinbrohl
Honningen
Brohl
Leutesdorf
Andernach

Remagen
Bad Neuenahr
Heimersheim
Niederbreisig

AHR

Ahrweiler
Dermau
Rech
Mayschloss
Altenahr

Ahr

Rhine

WEST
GERMANY
EAST
Frankfurt

Strasbourg
Ulm

Klotten

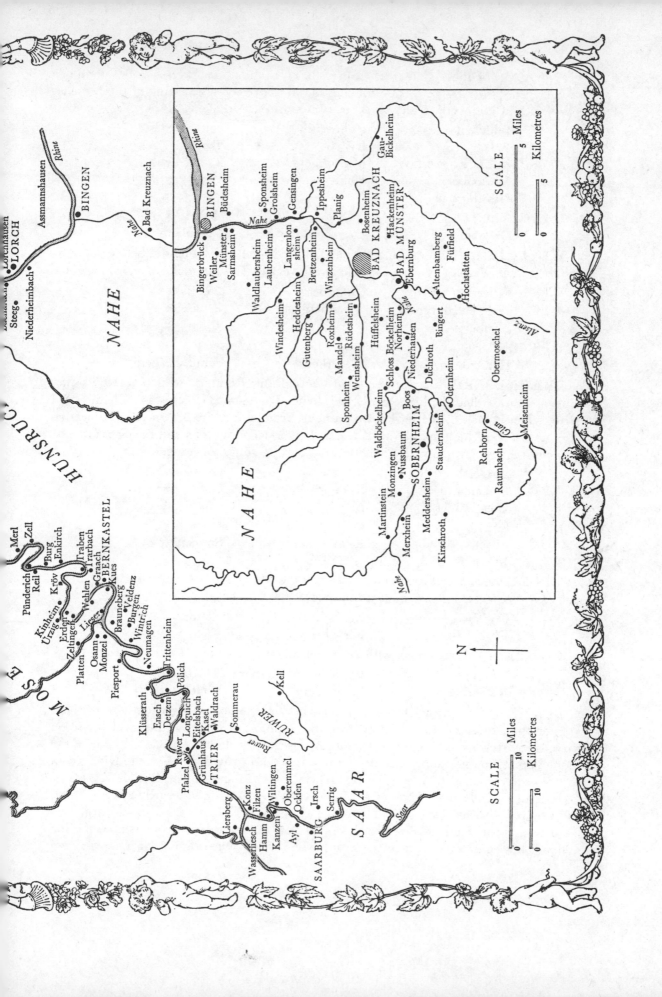

RHINE

Assmannshausen
Lorennausen
LORCH
Steeg
Niederheimbach

Bingen

Bad Kreuznach

Nahe

NAHE

HUNSRÜCK

Merl
Zell
Pünderich
Reil
Burg
Enkirch
Kröv
Traben
Trarbach
Graach
BERNKASTEL
Kinheim
Urzig
Erden
Platten
Zeltingen
Wehlen
Kues
Veldenz
Brauneberg
Burgen
Osann
Wintrich
Monzel
Neumagen
Piesport
Trittenheim
Klüsserath
Ensch
Longuich
Pölich
Detzem
Kasel
Eitelsbach
Waldrach
Pfalzel
Grünhaus
Ruwer
Sommerau
TRIER
RUWER
Kell

MOSEL

Liersberg
Konz
Filzen
Wiltingen
Obermennel
Wasserliesch
Hamm
Kanzem
Ockfen
Irsch
Ayl
Serrig
SAARBURG

SAAR

Saar

SCALE
Miles
10
0
Kilometres
10
0

N

BINGEN

Rhine
Rhine

Bingerbrück
Weiler
Büdesheim
Münster
Sponsheim
Grolsheim
Sarmsheim
Gensingen
Nahe
Ippesheim
Planig
Gau-
Bickelheim
Waldlaubersheim
Langenlon
sheim
Laubenheim
Bretzenheim
Heddesheim
Winzenheim
Bosenheim
Hackenheim
Windesheim
Gutenberg
Roxheim
Rüdesheim
Hüffelsheim
BAD KREUZNACH
BAD MÜNSTER
Mandel
Norheim
Ebernburg
Altenbamberg
Fürfeld
Sponheim
Weinsheim
Schloss Böckelheim
Niederhausen
Duchroth
Bingert
Hochstätten
Waldböckelheim
Boos
Odernheim
Alsenz
Nahe
Martinstein
Monzingen
SOBERNHEIM
Staudernheim
Obermoschel
Nussbaum
Meddersheim
Merxheim
Rehborn
Raumbach
Glan
Meisenheim
Kirschroth

N A H E

Nahe

SCALE
Miles
5
0
Kilometres
5
0

straggling row of houses squeezed between the river and a mountain with tier upon tier
of vineyards rising in great curves facing south, above the north bank of the Moselle.
The wines of Piesport are among the very best of the Moselle.

| | | |
|---|---|---|
| Bildchen | Hohlweid | Schubertslay |
| Falkenberg | Lay | Taubengarten |
| GOLDTRÖPFCHEN | Michelsberg | Treppchen |
| Gräfenberg | Pichter | Weer |
| Güntherslay | | |

**MINHEIM**

| | | |
|---|---|---|
| Grauberg | Lay | Rosenberg |

WINTRICH, a village round the bend of the Moselle, sits unafraid below the butt-
ressed terrace walls of its vineyards along the very face of the rock.

| | | |
|---|---|---|
| Geierslay | Ohligsberg | SIMONSBERG |
| Grosser Herrgott | Rosenberg | Sonnseite |
| Neuberg | | |

**KESTEN**

| | | |
|---|---|---|
| Herrenberg | Niederberg | Paulinshofberg |

BRAUNEBERG is a former settlement of the Romans, who planted its first
vineyard and called the hill *Dulcis Mons*, hence Dusemond, which was its name until
1920, when it took the better-known name of Brauneberg, the Brown Hill. It owes its
fame to the very high quality of its wines. It is a steep and lofty hill facing south-east
and completely covered with vines – all of them Rieslings, of course.

| | | |
|---|---|---|
| Bürgerslay | JUFFER | Obersberg |
| Falkenberg | Kammer | Sonnenuhr |
| Hasenläufer | Lay | |

**MÜLHEIM**

| | | |
|---|---|---|
| Bitsch | Kloster | Sonnenlay |
| Johannisberg | | |

VELDENZ is about 2 miles to the east of the Moselle in the valley of the Veldenz,
one of the Moselle's many small tributaries.

| | | |
|---|---|---|
| Carlsberg | Geisberg | Neuberg |
| Elisenberg | Kirchberg | |

LIESER is a small village with an important stretch of fine vineyards behind it.

| | | |
|---|---|---|
| Kirchberg | Paulsberg-Niederberg | Rosenberg |
| Niederberg | Pfaffenberg | Schlossberg |

BERNKASTEL is the chief city of the Middle Moselle, not a great city in size, but
greater than most in fame. Viewed from the topmost of the vineyards which rise on
three sides from its old houses with roofs of variegated colours, Bernkastel is one of the
most picturesque and attractive little towns imaginable, with the Moselle lying like a
silver girdle around it. Across the bridge, on the left bank of the river, is KUES or
CUES, also with vineyards all around. By far the best known vineyard of Bernkastel is
the DOKTOR, owned by Dr H. Thanish, Deinhard of Koblenz, and Lauerburg. Unfortunately, the fame of Bernkastel Doktor has grown to such an extent that the
demand has completely outrun the supply. The heirs of the original Dr Thanish have

met the difficulty by offering their Doktor wine under the label *Doktor und Graben*, GRABEN being the vineyard next to the *Doktor*. Messrs Lauerberg sell their wine under the label of *Bernkasteler Doktor und Bratenhöfchen*, and Deinhard, the third part-owners, sell part of theirs as *Doktor und Badstube*. There are a number of other good vineyards of both Bernkastel and Kues, on the right and left banks of the Moselle, such as:

## BERNKASTEL

| | | |
|---|---|---|
| BADSTUBE (includes Eich, Theurenkauf, Olk, Lay and Kirchgrabe) | BRATENHÖFCHEN (includes Held, Rosenberg, Pfalzgraben) | DOKTOR JOHANNISBRÜNNCHEN Schlossberg SCHWANEN |

## KUES

| | | |
|---|---|---|
| Kardinalsberg | Rosenberg | Weissenstein |

GRAACH. The Moselle changes its course from east to west as it leaves Bernkastel for Graach and Wehlen, which is why the vineyards of those two famous growths are on the right bank of the river. The Weingut *Josephshof* wines of Graach are sold under the name of the Estate *Josephshöfer* without the name of Graach or site names. Sites:

| | | |
|---|---|---|
| Abtsberg | HIMMELREICH | Münzlay |
| Bistum | Hömberg | Petrus |
| DOMPROBST | Kirchlay | Rosenberg |
| Goldwingert | Lilienpfad | Stablay |
| Heiligenhaus | Münich | Tirlei |

WEHLEN can pride itself on having the finest vineyard of the Moselle in its SONNENUHR (which takes its name from the sun-dial fixed in the heart of this steep, sundrenched, hillside vineyard). The greatest owner of Wehlen vineyards is Zach. Bergweiler-Prüm, who for some years has refused to use the cream of his vineyards for *Beeren-* or *Trockenbeerenauslesen*; but his *Spätlesen* and *Auslesenweine* are most refined and distinguished wines.

| | | |
|---|---|---|
| Abtei | LAY | Rosenberg |
| Feinter | Münzlay | SONNENUHR |
| Klosterlay | NONNENBERG | Wertspitz |

ZELTINGEN is a small town of no great interest in itself but with a wonderful expanse of vineyards, nearly 500 unbroken acres of Rieslings, rising sharply behind it: they produce a very large quantity of wine, some of which is excellent, the peer of the best wines of Wehlen or Bernkastel, while a good deal of plain Zeltinger is *plain*.

| | | |
|---|---|---|
| Bickert | Kirchlay | Sonnenuhr |
| HIMMELREICH | Rotlay | Stefanslay |
| Hirzlay | SCHLOSSBERG | Steinmauer |
| Kirchenpfad | Schwarzlay | Welbersberg |

ERDEN is a small village perched on a narrow ledge above the right bank of the Moselle. Its vineyards, at the rear, climb a cliff as nearly perpendicularly as any wine can possibly grow.

| | | |
|---|---|---|
| Buslay | Herzlay | Rotkirch |
| Filiusberg | Hötlay | Schönberg |
| Franklay | Kaufmannsberg | TREPPCHEN |
| Herrnberg | Prälat | |

ÜRZIG is a more important village than nearby Erden, and its vineyards rise steeply behind it at a safe distance from the flood waters of the Moselle, which find their way occasionally into the cellars, and even into the living-rooms, of its old stone houses.

| | | |
|---|---|---|
| KRANKLAY | Schwarzlay | WÜRZGARTEN |
| Lay | | |

From Ürzig the Moselle changes its course once more from west to east, and leaves behind it those vineyards which are responsible for all truly great Moselle wines. The next villages are:

### KINHEIM

| | | |
|---|---|---|
| Eulenberg | Löwenberg | Rosenberg |
| Hubertusberg | Peterberg | |

### KRÖV or CRÖV

| | | |
|---|---|---|
| Halsbach | Niederberg | Petersberg |
| Heislay | Paradies | STEFFENSBERG |

The most popular wine of Kröv, in Germany, is that which is sold under the label *Nacktarsch*, showing a bare-bottomed boy.

### WOLF

| | | |
|---|---|---|
| Goldgrube | Herrenberg | Sonnenlay |

TRABEN-TRARBACH are little twin towns, Traben on the left and Trarbach on the opposite bank of the Moselle. The vineyards of Trarbach are on the lower slopes of the Grafenburg and produce better wines than those of Traben.

### TRARBACH

| | | |
|---|---|---|
| Burgberg | Hühnerberg | Ungsberg |
| Halsberg | SCHLOSSBERG | |

### TRABEN

| | | |
|---|---|---|
| Backhaus | KRÄUTERHAUS | Steinbacher |
| Bergpächter | Rickelsberg | WÜRZGARTEN |
| Geispfad | | |

ENKIRCH, the next village, is most picturesque and its vineyards produce some pleasant wines, although it is at the limit of the Middle Moselle, beyond which few wines possess real merit except in unusually hot years.

| | | |
|---|---|---|
| Edelberg | Hinterberg | STEFFENSBERG |
| Herrenberg | Monteneubel | Weinkammer |

### REIL

| | |
|---|---|
| Heissen Stein | Görlay |

From here to Koblenz, where the Moselle meets the Rhine, the only places with vineyards responsible for some fair white wines are as follows:

### PÜNDERICH

| | | |
|---|---|---|
| Farlay | Marienburg | Rosenberg |
| Goldlay | Peterslay | Staaden |

### ZELL

| | | |
|---|---|---|
| Burglay | Nossberg | Schwarze Katz |
| Domherrn | | |

The Schwarze Katz (Black Cat) has, like the Kröver Nacktarsch, achieved great popularity in Germany.

### COCHEM

| | | |
|---|---|---|
| Langenberg | Pinnerberg | Schlossberg |

### POMMERN

| | | |
|---|---|---|
| Goldberg | Kapellenberg | Rosenberg |
| Greismund | | |

### KOBERN

| | | |
|---|---|---|
| Fahrberg | Uhlen | Weissenberg |

### WINNINGEN

| | | |
|---|---|---|
| Hamm | Röttgen | Uhlen |
| Rosenberg | | |

The vineyards of the Moselle, Saar and Ruwer cover some 20,000 acres, but fully two-thirds produce none but the commoner sort of table wine, refreshing and pleasant enough and above all cheap enough to be within the means of all but the really poor. The vineyards responsible for the great white wines of the Moselle, Saar and Ruwer, whose superlative excellence commands superlative prices, total only about 6,200 acres.

Before leaving the Moselle, just a few words about *Moselblümchen*. *Moselblümchen* – the flower of the Moselles – how many promises does it contain to the occasional wine drinker! But in reality, generally speaking, *Moselblümchen* is the cheapest of all Moselles listed; it is a fancy name for a Moselle wine not entitled legally to a geographical name, or it comes from an unknown place, usually from the Upper Moselle.

The wine drinker who is looking for value should always remember that all expenses – from the gathering of the grapes to the bottling, for packing, dispatch and freight, not to forget the duty – are in most countries much the same for *all* table wines. A wine which costs only a fraction more represents therefore a much greater quality.

## The Wines of the Rheingau

When the Rhine decides to turn its back on its native Switzerland at Basle it keeps a remarkably straight course to the north until the River Main joins it opposite Mainz. From there to Bingen, where it is joined by another river, the Nahe, the Rhine is forced to change it course from north to west by the massive barrier of the Taunus mountains. The Rheingau is the name given to the strip of land which lies between the right bank of the Rhine and the Taunus foothills and extends a few miles both north and east. Its vineyards are by no means as extensive as those of Rheinhessen, on the opposite bank of the Rhine, from Mainz to Bingen, but they are responsible for a greater proportion of fine wines, as well as for some which may rightly claim to be among the greatest of the great white wines of the world. The great white wines of the Rheingau possess an intensity of bouquet which can be almost overpowering, a fullness of body which is entirely free from coarseness and, above all, an aristocratic distinction or 'breeding' which is impossible to describe but as admirable as it is rare. Of course, not all Rheingau wines are aristocrats; they are not all Riesling and hillside wines, but it may be said that of the 5,500 acres of Rheingau vineyards, fully one-third produce really great wines – an exceptionally high proportion; one-third produce quite good wines; and one-third produce commoner beverage wines which are consumed locally and never exported.

Going downstream from the Main to the Nahe, the vineyards of the Rheingau are:

HOCHHEIM. The vineyards of this old city, some 3 miles upstream on the River Main before it joins the Rhine, are quite remarkable in one respect: they are the only vineyards of the Rheingau planted on what is practically flat ground. Yet their wines are not only good wines but the best of them possess the distinctive personality of the best Rheingau wines. This is evidently why Hochheim has always been included in the Rheingau, although it is over 10 miles from the Taunus foothills and the Rheingau proper.

Hochheim and its vineyards were sold by the Chapter of Cologne Cathedral in 1273 to the Chapter of Mainz Cathedral, which owned the best vineyards of Hochheim until 1803. Today the two best vineyards of Hochheim still bear their original ecclesiastical names, Domdechaney (cathedral deanery) and Kirchenstück (church piece), the first being much better known than the second. The greater share of the Domdechaney vineyard is owned by the *Domdechant Wernersches Weingut*, but the State Domains, the city of Frankfurt-on-Main and Graf von Schönborn also own parts of it. Another of the fine ecclesiastical vineyards near Hochheim's old church is named Hölle. Hölle is derived from the Old German *Halda* or *Helda*, which meant the slope of a hill: it stands for 'hillside' and not 'hell', as it is sometimes wrongly translated. It belonged to the Carmelites until 1803, when the city of Frankfurt-on-Main finally acquired it. To this day, Hochheimer Hölle is the municipal tipple at Frankfurt's famous *Ratskeller*.

Just a word about the estate known as the 'Queen Victoria Vineyard' (Königin-Viktoria-Berg). This vineyard was christened after Queen Victoria. In 1850 she paid a visit to the vineyard which produced her favourite wine, as a result of which permission was asked of the Royal Court to give the 'Lage' the new name. It displays a monument to her within its own precincts, and on 5 December 1950 the town of Hochheim celebrated the centenary of the Lage 'Königin-Viktoria-Berg'.

Other Hochheim vineyards:

| | | |
|---|---|---|
| Bein | Kohlkaut | Stein Kreuz |
| Bettelmann | Neuberg | Stiehlweg |
| Daubhaus | Raber | Wandkaut |
| Domdechaney | Rauchloch | Weid |
| Gehitz | Sommerheil | Weisserd |
| Hölle | Stein | Wiener |
| Kirschenstück | | |

WALLUF. When we reach the little Rhine harbour of Nieder-Walluf we set foot on old Rheingau territory and, turning our back on the river, soon come to the vineyards of Ober-Walluf, in a narrow valley leading to Martinsthal. Although there is still a lower and an upper village, the *Nieder* and *Ober* are no longer used and the name of Walluf applies to both.

| | | |
|---|---|---|
| Bildstock | Oberberg | Steinritz |
| Gottesacker | Röderweg | Unterberg |
| Langenstück | Sonnenberg | Walkenberg |
| Mittelberg | | |

MARTINSTHAL is the new name of a very old village which grew tired of being called *Neudorf* – New Village: its vineyards on the foothills of the Taunus mountains produce some very fair wines, although none of outstanding merit.

| | | |
|---|---|---|
| Geisberg | Oberrödchen | Steinberg |
| Heiligenstock | Pfaffenberg | Wildsau |
| Langenberg | Sand | |

KIEDRICH, like Martinsthal and Rauenthal (see below), lies back in the hills above Eltville, and its vineyards are mostly in a sheltered valley dominated by the Scharfenstein, the ruins of a medieval castle. Their wines are superior to those of Martinsthal, most of them being the peers of the second-best wines of nearby Rauenthal. The famous church, known as 'the house of Our Good Lady', contains many gifts from Sir John Sutton, Bt, of Norwood Park, who loved the 'wine village' of Kiedrich and its church. It contains the oldest German organ (1630) and a second one with pipes of the fourteenth century. It was the reason why Sir John Sutton came to Kiedrich in 1857, and became a Maecenas who donated no less than 240,000 guilders.

| | | |
|---|---|---|
| Berg | Heiligenstock | Turmberg |
| Brück | Klosterberg | Wasserros |
| Dippenerd | Langenberg | Weihersberg |
| Gräfenberg | Sandgrube | |

RAUENTHAL is a small village, and its vineyards produce less wine per acre than any other vineyards in the Rheingau, which in all likelihood is why the wines of Rauenthal are certainly among the best, and known as such in overseas markets.

| | | |
|---|---|---|
| BAIKEN | Herberg | Pfaffenberg |
| Burggraben | Hilbitz | Siebenmorgen |
| Ehr | Hünnerberg | Steinmächer |
| Eisweg | Kesselring | Wagenkehr |
| Gehrn | Langenstück | Wieshell |
| Geierstein | Maasborn | Wülfen |
| Grossenstück | Nonnenberg | |

ELTVILLE. Returning to the Rhine we come to Eltville, no longer the important city it once was, but still the largest of the Rheingau towns. Here are the headquarters or administrative offices of the former Prussian domains, now and since 1945 the Hessian domain. They originally formed the bulk of the Duke of Nassau's vineyards, and even today they remain the largest stretch of vineyards under one ownership in the Rheingau, the domain being predominant particularly in the following vineyards:

| | | |
|---|---|---|
| Albus | Hühnerfeld | Rheinberg |
| Alte Back | Kalbpflicht | Sandgrube |
| Bunken | Klümbchen (sole | Schlossberg |
| Freienborn | property of | Setzling |
| Grauer Stein | Schloss Eltz) | Sonnenberg |
| Grimmen | Langenstück | Steinmächer |
| Hahn | Mönchhanach | Taubenberg |
| Hanach | Posten | Weidenborn |

ERBACH. Only about half a mile downstream from Eltville, we come to Erbach, the most famous vineyard of which, MARCOBRUNN, is a narrow strip of vines alongside river, road and rail as far as the next village of Hattenheim; which is why the vineyard is called Marcobrunn, the 'boundary fountain' – *Marke* being in Old German a boundary. The best wines of Erbach are among the greatest of all Rheingauers, that is to say, the greatest white wines of the world. Although St Mark happens to be the patron saint of Erbach's parish church, his name has nothing to do with Marcobrunn. Six proprietors own the Marcobrunn vineyard: Baron von Simmern, Hessian Domain, Prince of Prussia, Baron von Ötinger, Graf Schönborn and Kohlhaas.

| | | |
|---|---|---|
| Brühl | Kalig | Seelgass |
| Gemark | Langenwingert | Siegelsberg |
| Herrnberg | Michelmark | Steinchen |
| Hinterkirch | Pellet | Steinmorgen |
| Hohenrain | Rheinhell | Wormlock |
| Honigberg | | |

HATTENHEIM, which is close to Erbach, is a much more important as well as a more picturesque village, almost a little town, with green meadows sloping gently to the Rhine in front of its old houses and high mountains behind them, with vines, of course, everywhere, on both low and high ground. The low-level vineyards are practically the continuation of the Marcobrunn vineyard of Erbach, from the 'boundary fountain' westwards to the first houses of Hattenheim. However, good as the wines of the low level of Hattenheim may be – and they are quite good – their fame is eclipsed by that of the *Steinberger*, the wine of a wonderful vineyard of 62 acres which was originally planted and walled in by the Cistercian monks, and is now owned by the Hessian State. Steinberg is just about a mile from Hattenheim and so is Kloster Eberbach close by: this is an ancient monastery wonderfully well preserved, and housing a remarkable collection of old wine-presses; its great hall is used for wine auctions and its cellars are a most fitting home for the Steinberg wines to lie and mature in peace. The great advantage of undivided ownership of a large vineyard is the consistently dependable quality of all its wines: there is no such dependability, for instance, in the wines of Clos Vougeot. There are, however, quite a number of different Steinbergers of one and the same vintage, because the wines which are made each day are never blended with those of the day before or the day after, as is done at the great Sauternes *châteaux*. The less remarkable wines of Steinberg are labelled plainly *Steinberger*, and the better ones *Steinberger Kabinett*, with the addition of Spätlese, Auslese, Beerenauslese or Trockenbeerenauslese, and with the number of the individual cask in which the wine was reared.

Among the other fine vineyards of Hattenheim, the following deserve notice:

| | | |
|---|---|---|
| Aliment | Gasserweg | Pfaffenberg |
| Bergweg | Geirsberg | Pflänzer |
| Bitz | Hassel | Rothenberg |
| Boden | Hinterhausen | Schützenhäuschen |
| Boxberg | Kilb | Stabel |
| Deutelsberg | Klosterberg | Weiher |
| Dillmetz | Mannberg | Willborn |
| Engelmannsberg | NUSSBRUNNEN | Wisselbrunnen |

HALLGARTEN is one of the upland villages of the Rheingau: it is sheltered from the east by the *Hallgartener Zange* (Hallgarten Pincers), and its vineyards are close to the Steinberg, immediately to the west: they produce wines of superlative excellence.

# RHEINGAU AND RHINEHESSIA

*RHEINGAU*

Lorchhausen
Lorch

Rauenthal          Frauenstein
Kloster Eberbach   Kiedrich   Martinsthal
Hallgarten                    Oberwalluf          WEISBADEN
                             Niederwalluf   Schierstein
Johannisberg       Huttenheim   Eltville
           Schloss Ostrich   Erbach
Assmannshausen  Johannisberg          Budenheim
           Geisenheim   Winkel   Heidenfahrt
Rüdesheim                                         Hochheim

BINGEN                                 MAINZ        Main
        Gau-Algesheim  Nieder Ingelheim
        Büdesheim      Ober Ingelheim

                                       Laubenheim
        Sponsheim          *RHINEHESSIA*
                                       Bodenheim
Grolsheim                              Gau-Bischofsheim
Gensingen                              Nackenheim

        Ippesheim
        Planig                         Nierstein
        Bosenheim
BAD                                    Oppenhelm
KREUZNACH
        Hackenheim   Gaubickelheim     Dienheim

                                       Guntersblum

                Wörrstadt              Alsheim

        Albig      Odernheim           Mettenheim
                                       Bechtheim
        Alzey                  Westhofen

                                       Osthofen
                Dalsheim

                        Pfeddersheim        WORMS

WEST   EAST
   GERMANY
  Koln
  •Mainz

 •Strasbourg

N

SCALE
0 ——————— 5  Miles
0 ——————— 5  Kilometres

| Biegels | Hitz | Reuscherberg |
|---|---|---|
| Deutelsberg | Jungfer | Rosengarten |
| Egersberg | Kirchenacker | Sandgrub |
| Frühenberg | Mehrhölzchen | Schönhell |
| Geiersberg | Neufeld | Würzgarten |

Hallgarten has four co-operatives: the English, the Boers, the Germans and the Boxers. The first was established at the time of the Boer War, and was composed of the wealthier growers. They were dubbed 'the English' by the poorer growers, who were excluded – and whose co-operative, in turn, became 'the Boers'. 'The Germans' were a third group of growers, excluded from the first two, who formed their own co-operative shortly afterwards. The names have since come to be used officially. The Boxers, formed a few years ago, took their 'period' name from the Chinese Boxer Rebellion.

Close together below and west of Hallgarten there are three other wine-producing villages: Östrich, Mittelheim and Winkel.

ÖSTRICH'S vineyards slope gently in a semicircle from the vineyards of Hallgarten down to the Rhine.

| Aliment | Klosterberg | Pflänzen |
|---|---|---|
| Deez | Klostergarten | Räuscherberg |
| Doosberg | LENCHEN | Rheingarten |
| Eiserberg | MAGDALENENGARTEN | Rosengarten |
| Hölle | Mühlberg | St Gottesthal |
| Kellerberg | Pfaffenpfad | St Nikolaus |
| Kerbesberg | | |

MITTELHEIM'S vineyards produce wines of fair to fine quality.

| EDELMANN | Magdalenenacker | St Nikolaus |
|---|---|---|
| Goldsberg | Neuberg | Schlehdorn |
| Gottestal | Oberberg | Stein |
| Honigberg | Rheingarten | |

WINKEL adjoins Mittelheim, but its vineyards produce some very remarkable wines, none finer nor more famous than the great wines of SCHLOSS VOLLRADS, the property of the noble Matuschka-Greiffenclau family. Its 81 acres of vines are the largest privately owned vineyard of the Rheingau. The estate-bottled wines of Schloss Vollrads are today, in good vintages, among the best of the Rheingau schloss wines, and they are sold under five capsules of different colours (according to their individual standard of excellence), as follows. The colours in brackets are subdivisions of the five grades, each in ascending order of quality.

Schloss Vollrads, green capsule (green, green-silver)

Schloss Vollrads Schlossabzug, red capsule (red, red-silver, red-gold), Hallgarten Selection, silver-red

Schloss Vollrads Kabinett, blue capsule (dark blue, light blue, blue-silver, blue-gold) Hallgarten Selection, gold-blue

Schloss Vollrads Auslese, pink capsule (pink, pink-gold, pink-white)

Schloss Vollrads Beerenauslese, white capsule (Trockenbeerenauslese: white-gold plus neck label showing the tower of Schloss Vollrads)

All the above wines, bottled on the estate of the Schloss Vollrads, bear, in addition to the name, the statement: *Originalablfülg Graf Matuschka-Greiffenclau'sche Kellerei und Gutsverwaltung* ('Genuine produce of the cellars and estate of Count Matuschka-Greiffen-clau'). It is noteworthy that the Auslese and higher qualities are not called *Kabinett* wines. This variety of qualities is, of course, produced in excellent vintages only. In some vintages no other than the ordinary Schloss Vollrads or *Schlossabzug* are pro-duced. Wine which does not come up to standard, and has to be improved, is sold without the right to the use of its name of origin and goes to Sekt-manufacturers.

Among the other fine vineyards of Winkel are the following:

| | | |
|---|---|---|
| Ansbach | Gutenberg | Kläuserberg |
| Bienengarten | HASENSPRUNG | Kreuzberg |
| DACHSBERG | Honigberg | Oberberg |
| Eckeberg | Jesuitengarten | Plankener |
| Ensing | Klaus | Steinchen |

A short distance westwards, one is bound to stop and admire from the river road the most spectacular vineyard in all Germany, JOHANNISBERG, an immense sym-metrical, really beautiful amphitheatre of vines, crowned by the Schloss. From this point there is no sign of the little village of Johannisberg, which hides behind the Schloss. There never could be a more ideal site for a vineyard, but, contrary to popular belief, there is no evidence that Charlemagne was responsible for its first vines. It is known, however, that Archbishop Ruthard of Mainz (1088 to 1109) gave the site to the Bene-dictines; they built a monastery and planted the first vineyard on the hill which was called at the time Bischofsberg. Napoleon gave it to his Maréchal Kellerman, but at the Congress of Vienna in 1815 it was given to the Emperor of Austria, who in turn pre-sented it to the Fürst von Metternich of the day, whose descendants still own it today, but the Habsburgs have still reserved the right of a tenth of the crop.

In most years there are three different *cuvées* made at Schloss Johannisberg. Here is the classification of the 1959 vintage: the first *cuvée* is of the wines of ordinary quality and is bottled at the estate with a red seal; the second *cuvée* is of better quality wines and bottled at the estate with a green seal; the third *cuvée* is made up of Spätlese wines and bottled with a pink seal. In good vintages, when it is possible to make Auslese, Beerenauslese and Trockenbeerenauslese wines, these are not made into *cuvées*, but each is kept separately and bottled individually at the estate, also with a pink seal.

In each category of the Schloss Johannisberg wines there are some which are selected to be bottled as Kabinett wines: the ordinary wines are bottled with either a white or an orange seal, the Spätlesen and Auslesen with a blue seal, the Beerenauslesen and Trockenbeerenauslesen with a gold seal. Unfortunately, Schloss Johannisberg, despite its position on such a favoured site, was unlucky in 1959 and did not produce a Beeren-auslese or Trockenbeerenauslese wine; but the memory of great wines produced there in 1943, 1945 and 1949 lingers on.

All other wines of Johannisberg are sold either as 'Johannisberger and site name' or as 'Dorf Johannisberger'.

The other vineyards of Johannisberg are as follows:

| | | |
|---|---|---|
| Erntebringer | Hölle | Klaus |
| Goldatzel | Kahlenberg | Kläuserberg |
| Hansenberg | Kerzenstück | Kochsberg |

| | | |
|---|---|---|
| Mittelhölle | Steinacker | Unterhölle |
| Nonnenhölle | Steinhölle | Vogelsang |
| Schwarzenstein | Sterzelpfad | Weiher |

GEISENHEIM is next: an old town by the Rhine famous for its viticultural training college and its extensive vineyards stretching almost from those of Johannisberg in the east to those of Rüdesheim to the north and west, a distance of nearly 2 miles.

A memorial to Longfellow, in the form of a fountain of Nassau marble, stands on the Bishop Blum Platz, at the foot of the Rheingau 'Dom' (cathedral) whose bells inspired Longfellow to write the closing stanzas of his *Golden Legend*. Laid into the walls are plaques on which is inscribed the verse referring to the Geisenheim Bells.

> What bells are those that ring so slow,
> So mellow, musical, and low?
> They are the bells of Geisenheim,
> That with their melancholy chime
> Ring out the curfew of the sun.

The vineyards of Geisenheim produce a great deal of wine from fair to fine (on occasion very fine), and none better than the wines from the vineyards owned by the school of viticulture:

| | | |
|---|---|---|
| Altbaum | Kapallengarten | Marienberg |
| Backenacker | Katzenloch | Mäuerchen |
| Decker | Kilsberg | Monchpfad |
| Fegfeuer | Kirchgrube | Morschberg |
| Fuchsberg | Kläuserweg | Rosengarten |
| Hinkelstein | Kosakenberg | Rothenberg |
| Hoher Decker | Kreuzweg | Schlossgarten |
| Hoher Rech | Lickerstein | Steinacker |

RÜDESHEIM, opposite Bingen, with its wine museum in the Brömserburg, is the westernmost town of the viticultural Rheingau proper, its houses strung in a long line by the Rhine, and its many vineyards occupying terraces cut into the face of the steep mountainside – the Berg – high past the ruins of the Ehrenfels Castle. The wines of Rüdesheim, more particularly those of the Berg vineyards, are among the best of the Rheingau wines.

Rüdesheim, too, is something of a pleasure resort with many good hotels and pensions along the Rhine. The Rhenish wine taverns flourish along the world-famous *Drosselgasse*, an excellent venue for tasting all Rheingau wines to the sound of music and feasting, although it is not recommended for contemplation.

| | | | |
|---|---|---|---|
| Berg Bronnen | Berg Mühlstein | Berg Stumpfenort | Häuserweg |
| Berg Burgweg | Berg Pares | Berg Zinnengiesser | Hinterhaus |
| Berg Dickerstein | Berg Platz | Berg Zollhaus | Kiesel |
| Berg Engerweg | Berg Rammstein | Bienengarten | Linngrub |
| Berg Hellpfad | Berg Roseneck | Bischofsberg | Mühlstein |
| Berg Katerloch | Berg Rottland | Dickerstein | Wilgert |
| Berg Kronest | Berg Schlossberg | Engerweg | Wüst |
| Berg Lay | Berg Stoll | Hasenläufer | |

The following are among the most noteworthy wine-growers in the Rheingau:

Verwaltung der Staatsweingüter im Rheingau, Eltville.
Gräfl. Eltz'sche Gutsverwaltung, Eltville.
Graf von Schönbron-Wiesentheid'sches Domänen-Weingut, Hattenheim.
Weingut Dr R. Weil, Kiedrich.
Graf Matuschka-Greiffenclau'sche Kellerei- und Güterverwaltung 'Schloss Vollrads', Winkel.
A. von Brentano'sche Gutsverwaltung, Winkel.
Fürst von Metternich, Winneburg'sches Domäne-Rentamt 'Schloss Johannisberg', Johannisberg.
Staatl. Lehr- und Forschungsanstalt für Wein-, Obst- und Gartenbau, Geisenheim.
Domdechant Werner'sches Weingut, Hochheim.
Geh.-Rat Aschrottsche Gutsverwaltung, Hochheim.

The first three growers own vineyards in a number of communities, viz.:

*State-owned Domains*

| | |
|---|---|
| Hattenheim: | Engelmannsberg, Steinberger |
| Erbach: | Marcobrunn |
| Kiedrich: | Grafenberg |
| Rauenthal: | Baiken, Gehrn, Grossenstück, Langenstück, Pfaffenberg, Steinhaufen, Wieshell |
| Hochheim: | Domdechaney, Kirchenstück |
| Rüdesheim: | Bischofsberg, Hinterhaus, Klosterkiesel, Berg Roseneck, Berg Rottland, Schlossberg, Wilgert |
| Assmannshausen: | Höllenberg (red hock) |

*Graf Eltz' sche Gutsverwaltung*

| | |
|---|---|
| Eltville: | Klümbchen, Langenstück, Mönchhanach, Sonnenberg |
| Kiedrich: | Sandgrub |
| Rauenthal: | Baiken, Burggraben, Gehrn, Herberg, Siebenmorgen, Wieshell |

*Graf von Schönborn-Wiesentheid' sches Domänen Weingut*

| | |
|---|---|
| Hochheim: | Stein, Kirchenstück, Domedechaney |
| Johannisberg: | Klauser Garten, Klauser Berg |
| Geisenheim: | Rothenberg |
| Hattenheim: | Wisselbrunnen, Hassel, Pfaffenberg |
| Rüdesheim: | Berg Bronnen, Roseneck |

## The Wines of Rhinehessia

Although there are in Rhinehessia some 30,000 acres of vineyards to the Rheingau's 5,000, and over 150 wine-producing localities to the Rheingau's 25, the average quality of its wines is not comparable to that of the Rheingau wines. This is due to the richer soil of Rhinehessia and to the fact that not more than 10% of the Rhinehessia vineyards are planted with Riesling grapes. Rhinehessia, in shape, is a rectangle some 30 miles in length and 20 miles in width, clearly marked on the north and east by the bend of the Rhine, from Mainz to Bingen, on the west by the Nahe and on the south by the Pfalz.

Rhinehessia is divided into a number of wine-producing administrative areas (*Kreise*, or districts): Mainz, Oppenheim, Worms, Bingen and Alzey are the five most important.

## MAINZ

Mainz is the least important of the five districts from a wine-producing point of view, but it is the first city of the *Land* of Rhineland-Palatinate and, incidentally, the birth-place of Gutenberg, traditionally the father of printing.

In Mainz is situated the head office of the Rhinehessian Domain – the greatest vineyard owner in Rhinehessia with vineyards in the following villages:

| | | |
|---|---|---|
| Bingen | Nackenheim | Oppenheim |
| Bodenheim | Nierstein | |

There are 15 localities in the Mainz district with vineyards, but none of them produces any wine of real merit, unless one is willing to make an exception for LAUBEN-HEIM (Edelmann, Hitz, Kalkofen, Johannisberg, Klosterberg, Neuberg) and GAU-BISCHOFSHEIM (Gickelsberg, Glockenberg, Herrnberg, Kellerberg, Kreuzwingert, Pfaffenweg, Pflänzer).

## OPPENHEIM

Oppenheim is by far the most important *Kreis* of Rhinehessia. There are in the Oppenheim *Kreis* no fewer than 43 wine-producing localities, including Nierstein, the vineyards of which produce more and far better wines then the vineyards of any of the other 42 localities, though four of these situated on the 'Rheinfront' are responsible for some fine quality wines: Bodenheim, Dienheim, Nackenheim and Oppenheim. Here is a list of the best vineyards of these five Rhinehessian localities:

### BODENHEIM

| | | |
|---|---|---|
| Bock | Hoch | Mönchpfad |
| Braun | Kahlenberg | Neuberg |
| Burgweg | Kapelle | Bettberg |
| Ebersberg | Leidhecke | Silberberg |
| Heitersbrünnchen | Leistenberg | WESTRUM |

### NACKENHEIM

| | | |
|---|---|---|
| Engelsberg | Kapelle | Rotenberg |
| Fenchelberg | Kirchberg | Sommerwinn |
| Fritzenhölle | Rheinhahl | Spitzenberg |

### NIERSTEIN

REHBACH This name comprises the following site names as registered in the Land Register:

Floss, Hinkelstein, Obere Rehbach, Untere Rehbach, Rehbacher Steig, Sommerseite

Spiegelberg comprising:

Bettzüge, Böllengewann, Diebsweg, Domtal, Findling, Flossgewann, Geisenberg, Grasweg, Hessbaum, Kindswiese, Klauer, Klostergewann, Loch, Lörzweilerweg, Mittelgewann, Mommenheimer Weg, Nackenheimer Loch, Nassgewann, Ohrenberg, Ohrenbrunnen, Ohrenfloss, Pulver, Hoher Rechen, Über der Rehbacher Steig, Vorderer Rolländer, Hinterer Rolländer, Hintere Schmitt, Leimen Schmitt, Steinrutsch, Warte

Fockenberg comprising:

> Brudersberg, Fockenberg, Fritzenhölle, Ober der Fläschenhahl, Vorderer Rosenberg, Hinterer Rosenberg, Schappenberg, Schmitt, Kleiner Schmitt, Stumpfenloch, Weisenberg.

HIPPING comprising:

> Eselspfad, Fläschenhahl, Fuchsloch, Unterer Hipping, Oberer Hipping, Hinterer Hipping, Kehr, Pfütze, Sommerbirnbaum, Tal.

ST KILIANSBERG comprising:

> Bergkirche, Dorf, Oberer Granzberg, Unterer Granzberg, Kiliansweg, Kiliansäcker, Kreuz, Langgewann, Mockenberg, Reisenberg.

AUFLANGEN comprising:

> Unterer Auflangen, Oberer Auflangen, Hinter den Häuser, Löhgasse, Pfuhlweg, Rohr, Hinter Saal, Ober der grossen Steig.

Ölberg comprising:

> Ölberg, Oberer Ölberg, Schiessmauer, Schlangenberg, Steig, Streng, Warte.

HEILIGENBAUM comprising:

> Bruch, Entenpfuhl, Heiligenbaum, Kelterbaum, Orbel, Riedmühle, Schwabsburger Weg, Stall.

Bildstock comprising:

> Bildstock, Bleiche, Brückchen, Daubhaus, Fäulingstrunnen, Heugasse, Hörsterweg, Läusbrunnen, Mittel, Muhl, Die Neunmorgen, Oberdorf, Ostergärten, Ried, Riedmühle, Rossberg, Säuloch.

Paterberg comprising:

> Brückchen, Brudersberg, Dalheimer Brunnen, Ober dem Dalheimer Brunne, Burgrechen, Burgweg, Dauzklauer, Essigkaut, Fahrt, Galgenberg, Galgenhohl, Gemarkrech, Die Glöck, Hasaenwörth, Heuwiese, Hölle, Hummertal, Ober dem Hummertal, Hummertaler Hohl, Kanal, Ketzenrechen, Monzenberg, Die dreizehn Morgen, Auf den sechszehn Morgen, Oppenheimer Strasse, Ottenberger Gewann, Ober dem langen Rech, Scheinbügel, Sas Taubennest, Taubhaus, Wiesengewann, Die zehn Morgen.

'Gutes Domtel' is the generic name for all Nierstein sites.

## OPPENHEIM (seat of a viticultural college)

| | | |
|---|---|---|
| Daubhaus | Kreuz | SACKTRÄGER |
| Goldberg | Krötenbrunnen | Schlossberg |
| Herrenberg | Kugel | STEIG |
| Herrenweiher | REISEKAHR | Zuckerberg |
| Kehrweg | Saar | |

## DIENHEIM

| | | |
|---|---|---|
| Goldberg | Krötenbrunnen | Silzbrunnen |
| Guldenmorgen | Rosswiese | Tafelstein |

And here are the better-known wine-producing villages (with vineyards shown in brackets) of the Oppenheim *Kreis*:

| | |
|---|---|
| Armsheim | Bechtolsheim |

Biebelnheim
Dalheim
Dexheim (Doktor, Hölle, Königsberg)
Dolgesheim
Eichloch
Eimsheim
Ensheim
Friesenheim
Gabsheim
Gau-Bickelheim (Frongewann, Gans, Goldberg, Hollerstrauch, Kapelle, Kaus, Ober-intersteig, Saukopf)
Gau-Weinheim
Guntersblum (Authental, Bornpfad, Dreissigmorgen, Eiserne Hand, Enggass, Gänsweide, Haseweg, Himmelthal, Kachelberg, Kehl, Kellerweg, Kreuz, Neuweg, Neubaum, Oppenheimerweg, Rost, Sonneberg, Spiegel, Steig, Steinberg, Vogelsrech, Vogelsgärten, Wohnweg)
Hahnheim
Hillesheim
Köngernheim a.d. Selz
Lörzweiler

Ludwigshöhe (Appenthal, Geierscheiss, Honigpfad, Modern, Rheinpfad)
Mommenheim
Nieder-Saulheim
Ober-Saulheim
Partenheim
Schimsheim
Schornsheim
Schwabsburg (Birkenauer, Ebersberg, Federberg, Heileck, Domtal, Kirschplatte, Kupferbrunnen, Neuberg, Schlossberg, Schnappenberg, Tafelstein)
Selzen
Spiesheim
Sulzheim
Udenheim
Undenheim
Vendersheim
Wald-Ulversheim
Wallertheim
Weinolsheim
Wintersheim
Wörrstadt
Wolfsheim

## WORMS

Worms (Katterloch, Liebfrauenstift, Luginsland, Maria Münster) is famous in wine history above all for its *Liebfrauenkirche* (the Church of Our Lady) and its *Liebfrauenstiftswein*, the wine from the Liebfrauenstift vineyard which adjoins the church. Here originated the name 'Liebfraumilch', a term whose meaning is explained by Dr E. G. Zitzen in *Der Wein in der Wort- und Wirtschaftsgeschichte* (Bonn, 1952):

*Liebfraumilch* is not a geographical denomination, but a fancy name applicable to all Rhine wines of good quality and pleasant character. The name originated from the vineyards round the Liebfrauenkirche in Worms – the vineyard of the Monks of the Liebfrauenstift. In former days the name of the wine was not Liebfraumilch, but Liebfrauenminch. The word 'Minch' is developed from 'Münch' which later on became 'Mönch'. Minchgärten, Minchwege, Minchgassen and Minchpfade, which were formerly in Worms and in other Rhenish wine-villages, were all situated within the walls of old cloisters and belonged to the gardens of the monks. In other words, the term Liebfraumilch arises out of the natural development of the language, and the 'milk' in this name has nothing whatsoever to do with the nourishing beverage which we all enjoy in one way or another, and which was not in the minds of the originators of the name Liebfraumilch. It is certainly wrong to translate Liebfraumilch, as it has been translated, as 'Milk of Our Lady'. In other words, when I say that the name Liebfraumilch originated in Worms, I want to emphasize that the name is the result of shifting of consonants of the spoken word, a phenomenon common to the development of all languages.

Plate 28. Sonnenuhr vineyard, at Wehlen, the best site of the Moselle. Plate 2:
(*Following page*) Baden vineyards near Neuweier, in the Black Forest.

The name Liebfraumilch is now given to a considerable quantity of German white wines of very different standards of quality; it may come from any part of the Rhine wine districts – Rhenish Palatinate, Rhinehessia, Rheingau, Nahe, Middle Rhine – or may be a blend of wines from one of these or even all the districts, and may contain wines of the hinterland only or of the finest vineyards. Under the name Liebfraumilch may be hidden a number of sins; hence the importance of the name of a shipper of repute, or of its registered brand, appearing on the Liebfraumilch labels.

Here, in alphabetical order, are the localities within the administrative boundaries of Worms which have vineyards of their own producing pleasant white table wines which, in good vintages, attain an astonishingly high quality:

Abeheim
Alsheim mit Hangenwahl-
    heim (Fischerpfad,
    Friedrichsberg, Früh-
    messe, Goldberg,
    Ohligstück, Rheinblick,
    Römerberg, Rosenberg,
    Sommerhäuschen,
    Sonnenberg)
Bechtheim (GEYERSBERG,
    Rosengarten, Hasen-
    sprung, Löwenberg,
    Pilgerpfad, Wölm und
    Stein)
Bermersheim
Dalsheim (Bürgel, Heck,
    Hubacker, Sauloch,
    Wachenheimer-Weg,
    Wingertstädten,
    Zellerweg)

Dittelsheim
Dorn-Dürkheim
Eppelsheim
Frettenheim
Gimbsheim
Gundersheim
Gundheim
Hangen-Weisheim
Heppenheim a.d. Wiese
Herrnsheim
Hessloch
Hohen-Sülzen
Horchheim
Ibersheim
Kriegsheim
Leiselheim
Mettenheim (Goldberg,
    Hellborn, Kandelberg,
    MICHELSBERG, Mittel-
    berg, SCHLOSSBERG)

Mölsheim
Monsheim
Monzernheim
Nieder-Flörsheim
Osthofen (Goldberg,
    Hasenbiss, Köhm,
    Lerchelsberg, Leckz-
    apfen, Liebenberg,
    Neuberg, Schnapp,
    Wölm)
Pfeddersheim
Wachenheim
Westhofen (Dautensatz,
    Erkelnest, Gries,
    Hackgraben, Prob,
    Schenk, Stassbühl)
Worms a. Rh.

## BINGEN

Bingen, on the left bank of the Rhine, facing Rüdesheim across the river, is at the mouth of the River Nahe but officially in Rhinehessia. It has now absorbed and hyphenated with its own name its two nearest neighbours, Bingen-Büdesheim (Nahe) and Bingen-Kempten. Behind Bingen and running eastwards rises the Rochusberg with vineyards practically everywhere, those of Scharlachberg, or Scarlet Hill, a name they owe to the reddish colour of the soil at its western end. The best wines of Bingen are those of the Scharlachberg.

Here are some of the other vineyards of Bingen, with a list of the other 22 wine-growing localities within its administrative *Kreis*.

### BINGEN

EISELBERG
Mainzerweg
Ohligberg

Rochusberg
Rosengarten

Schlossberg
Schwätzerchen

Plate 30. *Sylvaner* grapes.

*Bingen Kreis*

Appenheim
Aspisheim
Bingen-Kempten (Berg, Lies,
    Pfarrgarten)
Bubenheim
Dietersheim
Dromersheim
Elsheim
Engelstadt
Gau-Algesheim
Gaulsheim
Gensingen

Grolsheim
Gross-Winternheim
Horrweiler
Jugenheim
Nieder-Hilbersheim
Nieder-Ingelheim
    (famous for red wines)
Ober-Ingelheim
Ockenheim
Schwabenheim
Sponheim
Wackernheim

## ALZEY

Alzey has within its district no less than 40 wine-producing localities, all of them farther away from both the Rhine and the Nahe, and they produce vast quantities of wine, both red and white, none of which is deserving of the connoisseur's attention:

Albig
Alzey
Badenheim
Bermersheim
Biebelsheim
Bornheim
Bosenheim
Dautenheim
Eckelsheim
Erbes-Büdesheim
Flonheim
Framersheim
Frei-Laubersheim
Fürfeld
Gau-Heppenheim
Gau-Odernheim
Gimbsheim
Hackenheim
Heimersheim
Ippesheim

Lonsheim
Neu-Bamberg
Offenheim
Pfaffen-Schwabenheim
Planig
Pleitersheim
St Johann
Siefersheim
Sprendlingen
Stein-Bockenheim
Tiefenthal
Uffhofen
Vollheim
Wahlheim
Weinheim bei Alzey
Welgesheim
Wendelsheim
Wöllstein
Wonsheim
Zotzenheim

The most important growers of quality wines in Rhinehessia, next to the Domains, are: Franz Karl Schmitt, Nierstein; Anton Balbach Erben, Nierstein; Weingut Baron Heyl. z. Herrnsheim, Nierstein; Weingut Reinhold Senfter, Nierstein; Gunderloch-Lange'sche Weingutsverwaltung, Nackenheim; Weingut Gunderloch-Usinger, Nackenheim; Weingut Oberst Schultz-Werner, Gaubischofsheim b. Mainz; Obersteutnant Leibrecht'sche Weingutsverwaltung, Bodenheim am Rhein; Weingut Kommerzienrat P. A. Ohler, Bingen am Rhein; Weingut 'Villa Sachsen', Commerzienrat Curt Berger Ergen, Bingen am Rhein.

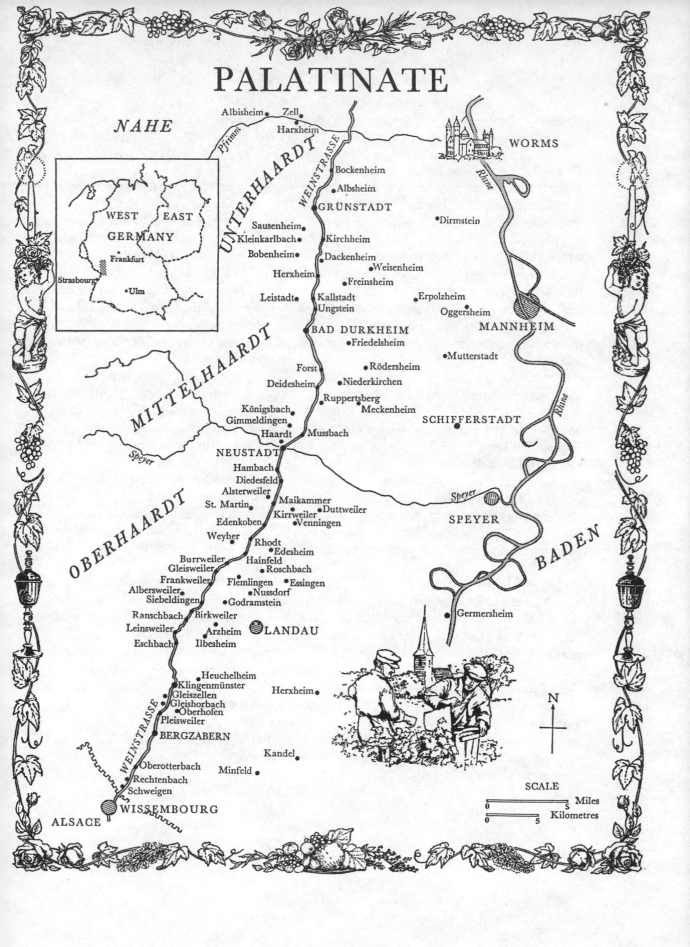

# PALATINATE

NAHE

WORMS

WEST GERMANY
EAST GERMANY
Frankfurt
Strasbourg
Ulm

UNTERHAARDT

WEINSTRASSE

Albisheim    Zell
Harxheim

Bockenheim
Albsheim
GRÜNSTADT

Dirmstein

Sausenheim
Kleinkarlbach    Kirchheim
Bobenheim    Dackenheim
Weisenheim
Herxheim    Freinsheim
Leistadt    Kallstadt    Erpolzheim
Ungstein    Oggersheim
MANNHEIM

MITTELHAARDT

BAD DÜRKHEIM
Friedelsheim
Forst    Rödersheim
Deidesheim    Niederkirchen
Ruppertsberg
Königsbach    Meckenheim
Gimmeldingen    SCHIFFERSTADT
Haardt    Mussbach
Speyer
NEUSTADT
Hambach
Diedesfeld
Alsterweiler    Speyer
St. Martin    Maikammer    SPEYER
Edenkoben    Kirrweiler    Duttweiler
Weyher    Venningen
Rhodt
Edesheim
Burrweiler    Hainfeld
Gleisweiler    Roschbach
Frankweiler    Flemlingen    Essingen
Albersweiler    Nussdorf
Siebeldingen    Godramstein
Ranschbach    Birkweiler
Leinsweiler    Arzheim    LANDAU
Eschbach    Ilbesheim

OBERHAARDT

BADEN

Mutterstadt

Germersheim

Heuchelheim
Klingenmünster    Herxheim
Gleiszellen
Gleishorbach
Oberhofen
Pleisweiler
BERGZABERN
Kandel
Oberotterbach    Minfeld
Rechtenbach
Schweigen
WISSEMBOURG
ALSACE

WEINSTRASSE

Pfrimm

Rhine

N

SCALE
0    5    Miles
0    5    Kilometres

# The Wines of the Palatinate (Rheinpfalz)

The Bavarian Pfalz was the name given in 1816, at the time of the reshuffling of the kingdoms, duchies and principalities of Europe when Napoleon's reign had come to an end, to the major part of the lands long held by the Pfalzgrave or Pfalzgräf north of Alsace, east of Lorraine, south and west of Hessia. The outstanding features of the Palatinate are its wonderfully mild climate, the fertility of its soil and the range of the Haardt mountains, a northern extension of the Vosges. The Haardt mountains protect the great Palatinate plain from icy winds from the north as well as from rain and snow from the west: their lower slopes are covered with vineyards which have also invaded the plain: acre upon acre of undulating land 600–700 feet above the level of the Rhine, which flows some 10 miles to the east.

The vineyards of the Palatinate cover an area seven times as great as that of the Rheingau. They produce more wine per acre than any of the other German vineyards, but a smaller quantity of fine quality wine than either the Rheingau, Rhinehessia or Moselle vineyards. The fine quality wines of the Palatinate, however, are of quite remarkable excellence, the peers of the greatest white wines of the Rheingau or of the world.

The Palatinate is divided into three unequal parts, known as Oberhaardt, Mittelhaardt and Unterhaardt. The Oberhaardt or Upper Haardt is the largest; it stretches from the French frontier in the south to Neustadt in the north. The Mittelhaardt or Middle Haardt stretches from Neustadt to Herxheim along the *Weinstrasse* or Wine Road. The Unterhaardt or Lower Haardt is the smallest of the three; it stretches from Herxheim to Zell in Hessia.

There are in the Upper Haardt over a hundred wine-producing localities, the more important of them being Maikammer (1,500 acres), Edenkoben (1,100 acres), Hambach (825 acres), Diedesfeld (700 acres), Kirrweiler (650 acres), Edesheim (600 acres), St Martin (600 acres), Hainfeld (480 acres), Godramstein (450 acres), Bürrweiler (450 acres) and Ilbesheim (400 acres). The Upper Haardt produces more wine, both red and white, than all the rest of the Palatinate vineyards.

The Middle Haardt vineyards produce all the greatest Palatinate wines. There are some 40 different wine-producing localities, the largest being Bad Dürkheim (2,200 acres), Mussbach (1,100 acres), Wachenheim (1,000 acres), Deidesheim (1,000 acres), Ruppertsberg (800 acres), Neustadt (760 acres), Ungstein (700 acres), Kallstadt (600 acres), Freinsheim (575 acres), Ellerstadt (550 acres), Weisenheim a. Sand (530 acres), Forst (530 acres), Herxheim (400 acres), Gimmeldingen (400 acres), Weisenheim a. Berg (400 acres) and Haardt (375 acres).

The Middle Haardt is about 18 miles in length, and the four villages whose vineyards produce the greatest wines of all – Ruppertsberg, Deidesheim, Forst and Wachenheim – are in the very centre; one other, Königsbach, south of Ruppertsberg, and three more, Bad Dürkheim, Ungstein and Kallstadt, north of Wachenheim, are responsible for the next best wines of the Palatinate.

The best vineyards of the principal localities are as follows:

KÖNIGSBACH

| Bender | Jesuitengarten | Mückenhaus |
|--------|----------------|------------|
| IDIG | Ölberg | |

## RUPPERTSBERG

| | | |
|---|---|---|
| Goldschmitt | LINSENBUSCH | Reiferpfad |
| Hoheburg | Mandelacker | Spiess |
| Kreuz | NUSSBIEN | Weinbüchel |

## DEIDESHEIM

| | | |
|---|---|---|
| Geheu | KIESELBERG | Mühle |
| Grain | Klostergarten | Petershöhle |
| Grainhübel | Kränzler | RENNPFAD |
| Hahnenböhl | Langenböhl | St Michelsberg |
| Herrgottsacker | Langenmorgen | Sonneneck |
| Hofstück | Leinhöhle | Weinbach |
| Hohenmorgen | Linsenbusch | |
| Kalkofen | Maushöhle | |

'Paradiesgarten' is the generic name for all Deidesheim wines.

## FORST

| | | |
|---|---|---|
| Alser | JESUITENGARTEN | Langkammert |
| Altenburg | KIRCHENSTÜCK | LINSENSTÜCK |
| Elster | Kranich or Granich | MUSENHANG |
| Fleckinger | Langenacker | Pechstein |
| Freundstück | Langenböhl | UNGEHEUER |
| Gerling | Langenmorgen | |

## WACHENHEIM

| | | |
|---|---|---|
| Altenburg | Goldbächel | Luginsland |
| Bächel | Goldberg | Rechbächel |
| Böhlig | Königswingert | Schenkenböhl |
| Gerümpel | Mandelgarten | Schlossberg |

What were formerly some 70 sites have recently been combined to form these 12.

## BAD DÜRKHEIM

| | | |
|---|---|---|
| Feuerberg | Hochbenn | MICHELSBERG |
| Forst | Hochmess | Schenkenböhl |
| Fuchsmantel | Klosterberg | SPIELBERG |

## UNGSTEIN

| | | |
|---|---|---|
| Herrenberg | Michelsberg | Vogelsang |
| Honigsäckel | Spielberg | |

## KALLSTADT

| | | |
|---|---|---|
| Annaberg | Kreuz | SAUMAGEN |
| Horn | Kronenberg | Steinacker |
| Kobnert | Nill | |

## FREINSHEIM

| | | |
|---|---|---|
| Goldberg | Musikantenbuckel | Oschelskopf |
| Gottesacker | | |

## FRIEDELSHEIM

| | | |
|---|---|---|
| Feuerberg | Letten | Rosengarten |
| Forster Neuberg | Neuberg | Schlossgarten |
| Gerümpel | Neumorgen | Tiergarten |

GIMMELDINGEN

| | | |
|---|---|---|
| Bienengarten | Hofstück | Meerspinne |
| Fürstenweg | Kirchenstück | |

HAARDT

| | | |
|---|---|---|
| Herrenletten | Mandelring | Ritter |
| Herzog | Paradies | Schlossberg |
| Kirchpfad | | |

MUSSBACH

| | | |
|---|---|---|
| Bischofsweg | Johannismorgen | Spiegel |
| Eselhaut | Kurfürst | |

HERXHEIM

| | | |
|---|---|---|
| Berg | Himmelreich | Mahlstein |
| Blume | HONIGACKER | Sommerseite |
| Felsenberg | Kirchenstück | Steinberg |
| Goldberg | | |

NEUSTADT

| | | |
|---|---|---|
| Erkenbrect | Hag | Ritterberg |
| Grain | Klosterberg | Rosengarten |
| Guckins Land | Mandelgewann | Vogelsang |

NIEDERKIRCHEN

| | | |
|---|---|---|
| Kirchgarten | Martenweg | Rittershöhe u.a. |
| Klostergarten | | |

The proportion of Riesling grapes (which are responsible for quality wines) to commoner grapes (from which the more ordinary beverage wines, both red and white, are made) varies very much, as these approximate figures show:

| | | | |
|---|---|---|---|
| Forst | 70% | Wachenheim | 24% |
| Deidesheim | 62% | Ruppertsberg | 23% |
| Königsbach | 31% | Ungstein | 18% |

All Palatinate wines made from Riesling grapes in a good year possess a family likeness, in body, bouquet and breeding, and a richness of flavour which is quite distinctive. There are, however, appreciable differences of bouquet and taste among them, and also of sweetness, of course, according to whether the wine is an Auslese, a Beerenauslese or a Trockenbeerenauslese, the last named being the most remarkable of all natural sweet white wines in the world. Most good judges agree that of all the finest Palatinate wines those of Forst deserve the first place. One cannot, however, agree with such a categoric statement. It very much depends upon the vintage.

In the Lower Haardt there are some 50 wine-producing localities, but only a very small proportion of their wines, even in good vintages, have attracted wine lovers outside their native Palatinate. Many of them, however, are quite fair beverage wines which are not merely acceptable but very enjoyable upon a hot summer's evening.

An alphabetical list of the wine-producing localities of the Unterhaardt:

| | | |
|---|---|---|
| Affenberg (Fuchsloch, | Albisheim a.d. Pfrimm | Bennhausen |
| Hochgewann, Himmelsreich, | Albsheim a.d. Eis | Bissersheim |
| Jesuitenhofgarten) | Asselheim | Bolanden |

| | | |
|---|---|---|
| Bubenheim | Kerzenheim | Mörsfeld |
| Colgenstein-Heidesheim | Kindenheim | Mühlheim a.d. Eis |
| Einselthum | Kirchheim a.d. Eck | Niefernheim |
| Eisenberg-Stauf | Kirchheimbolanden | Obersülzen |
| Gauersheim | Kleinbockenheim | Obrigheim |
| Gerolsheim | (Burggarten, Dom, | Orbis |
| Grossniedesheim | Gretenbrunnen, | Ottersheim |
| Grünstadt | Kieselberg) | Quirnheim |
| Harxheim | Kleinniedesheim | Ridzheim |
| Hessheim | Laumersheim | Rittersheim |
| Heuchelheim | Mauchenheim | Rüssingen |
| Immelsheim | Mertesheim | Sausenheim |
| Jakobsweiler | | |

A further part of the Palatinate north of the Unterhaardt is the *Zellertal* with the village Zell and its sites, which include Philippsbrunnen and Schwarzer Herrgott.

The most important wine-growers of the Palatinate are von Buhl, Bürklin-Wolf and Bassermann-Jordan.

## The Wines of the Nahe

The valleys of the River Nahe and its tributaries, from the valley of the Alsenz which branches off from the Nahe into the northern tip of the Palatinate, down to Bad Kreuznach (the geographical, historical and commercial centre of the Nahe), must be reckoned among the most picturesque and beautiful vinelands of the world. From Bad Kreuznach down to Bingen, where it joins the Rhine, the Nahe flows mostly through rich meadows and agricultural land, dotted with vineyards and orchards wherever there is a clump of houses or a village. The area of the Nahe vineyards is about a thousand acres more than that of the Rheingau, and the average yield of Nahe wines is about 1,500 hectolitres more than that of the Rheingau. Unfortunately, if we turn from quantity to quality, the Nahe vineyards do not produce more than one-third of the proportion of quality wines produced by the Rheingau vineyards. But they do produce a fair number of quality wines of superlative excellence which deserve the attention of the more fastidious among wine lovers.

The Nahe district is easily subdivided into 11 viticultural regions. The most important communities and sites are as follows:

*Left bank of the Nahe up to Bad Kreuznach*

| | |
|---|---|
| Martinstein | Burgwingert |
| Monzingen | Auf der Lay, Auf der Fels, Rosenbaum, Kronenberg, FRÜHLINGSPLÄTZCHEN |
| Waldböckelheim | Königsfels, Mühlberg, Welschberg |
| Schloss Böckelheim | KUPFERGRUBE, Felsenberg, Mühlberg |
| Niederhausen | Steinberg, Hermannshöhle, Rossel, Rosenheck, Steier, HERMANNSBERG |
| Hüffelsheim | Gutenhöll, Brauneberg, Hipprich |
| Norheim | Kafels, Hinterfels, Dellchen |
| Bad Münster am Stein | Kirschheck, Oberberg, Schmalberg, Rotenfels, Höll, Felseneck |

| | |
|---|---|
| Bad Kreuznach | Kauzenberg, Kronenberg, Hinkelstein, Forst, Narrenkappe, BRÜCKES, Steinweg, Kahlemberg, Galgenberg, Kehrenberg, Monau |

*Ellerbachtal*

| | |
|---|---|
| Weinsheim | Kellerberg, Frohnberg, Schafskopf |
| Mandel | Kranzwingert, Schlossberg, Dellchen, Rosengarten |
| Rüdesheim | Rosengarten, Wiesberg |

*Grafenbachtal*

| | |
|---|---|
| Dalberg | Schlossberg, Wingertsberg |
| Hergenfeld | Mayen, Herrschaftsacker, Münchrech |
| Wallhausen | Johannisberg, Pastorenberg, Hahnenbach, Rebsgrund |
| Braunweiler | Weingarten, Heide |
| Sommerloch | Steinrossel, Lett, Neuberg, Kaul |
| St Katharinen | Berg, Heide, Steinig |
| Gutenberg | Schlossberg, Stein, Heide, Fels, Vogelgesang |
| Roxheim | Birkenberg, Mühlenberg, Hüttenberg, Neuenberg, Bangert |

*Valley of the Nahe up to the estuary of the Guldenbach*

| | |
|---|---|
| Winzenheim | Rosenheck, Honigberg, Metzler |
| Bretzenheim | Manik, Kronenberg, Vogelgesang |

*Guldenbachtal*

| | |
|---|---|
| Schöneberg | Schäfersley, Eichenreis, Hölle |
| Schweppenheim | Steyerberg, Hölle, Homberg, Hardt |
| Windesheim | Hölle, Hüttenberg, Sonnenmorgen, Hinkelstein, Rosenberg, Römerberg |
| Waldhilbersheim | Rödern, Apostelgraben, Butterberg, Kilb |
| Heddesheim | Kilb, Hipperich, Geisemann, Bemerich, Honigberg, Goldloch, Höll, Huttenberg, Scharlachberg, Rosenburg, Rörnerberg, Sonnenmorgen |
| Waldlaubersheim | Domberg, Rosenberg, Wingertsberg |
| Genheim | Genheimer Berg |

*Valley of the Nahe upwards to the mouth of the Rhine*

| | |
|---|---|
| Langenlonsheim | Rotenberg, Borngraben, RIETH, Grems, Sonnenborn, Löhr |
| Laubenheim | Karthäuser, Hörnchen, Löhr, Remicher, Vogelgesang |
| Dorsheim | Burgberg, Goldloch, Pittermännchen, Honigberg |
| Rümmelsheim | Honigberg, Hölle, Hirschhorn, Rotenberg |
| Sarmsheim | Mühlberg |
| Münster bei Bingerbrück | Pittersberg, Kapellenberg, Mönchberg, Dautenpflänzer |
| Weiler | Rechte Mühe, In der Lay, Hungerborn |
| Bingerbrück | Elisenhöhe, Mühe, Hörnchen |

*Valley of the Nahe upwards to the mouth of the Glan*

| | |
|---|---|
| Becherbach | Rotenberg |
| Krebsweiler | Delberg |
| Meckenbach | Weidentell |
| Merxheim | Vor der Burg, Aresberg, Hinterberg |
| Kirschroth | Sand, Nauenberg |

| | |
|---|---|
| Meddersheim | Altenberg, Scherendell, Eisendell |
| Staudernheim | Hohrech, Grube, Kauzenberg |

*Valley of the Glan*

| | |
|---|---|
| Offenbach | Hinterberg, Kellenbach, Freifrauenloch |
| Medard | Rattenfels, Götzennell |
| Meisenheim | Altenberg, Heimbach |
| Raumbach | Raumberg, Allenberg |
| Lauterecken | Schäfersberg, Oberberg |
| Odenbach | Bornberg, Leckberg |
| Callbach | Fastenberg, Im Mai, Delbchen |
| Rehborn | Raumberg, Eschbach, Hahn |
| Odernheim | Klosterberg, Sonnenberg |

*Valley of the Nahe up to the mouth of the Alsenz*

| | |
|---|---|
| Duchroth Oberhausen | Vogelschlag, Kaisergrund |
| Ebernburg | Schlossberg, Weidenberg, Erzgrube, Zennerrech |

*Valley of the Alsenz*

| | |
|---|---|
| Hochstätten | Häuserweg, Glückerberg |
| Feil-Bingert | Kahlenberg, Hochstätterberg |
| Altenbamberg | Rothenberg, Schlossberg, Treuenfels |

*Valley of the Nahe right bank up to where the Nahe meets the Rhine*

| | |
|---|---|
| Hackenheim | Galgenberg, Heide |
| Bosenheim | Bosenberg, Honigberg |
| Planig | Frenzenberg, Rieth |
| Ippesheim | Steiler, Baumann |
| Gensingen | Nühlenberg, Kirchberg |
| Grolsheim | Nauenberg |
| Dietersheim | Pfingstweide |
| Bingen-Büdesheim | SCHARLACHBERG, Steinkautweg, Rosengarten, Rochusberg, Kieselberg |
| Bingen (adjoining the Rhinehessian district) | Eisel |

The best of these are definitely the wines grown on the left bank up to and including Bad Kreuznach, and among them first place is taken by Schloss Böckelheim – which is, surprisingly, the name of a village. Here is the seat of the State Domain. The volcanic and slate soils produce wines of elegance, flavour and breeding.

The vineyards of the State Domain were carved out of the hillsides, terraced and planted by convict labour only some 70 years ago. This may be the latest of the Nahe vineyards, but the first were planted some 2,000 years ago, and the considerable quantity of Roman remains from excavations in and near Bad Kreuznach leaves no doubt about the early settlement of the valley by the Romans.

The 7,500 acres of the Nahe are planted mostly with Sylvaner and only to a small extent with Riesling grapes. In their character the wines of the Nahe are considered first cousins of the Rhine and the Moselle wines. Wines of the Upper Nahe (between Martinstein and Boos) remind one of the Saar wines, wines of the Glan valley and of some Palatinate wines. They range from the simple luncheon wine of Rüdesheim

(Rosengarten) in the Ellerbachtal to kings of wine such as the 1945 Schloss Böckelheimer Kupfergrube Trockenbeerenauslese or the 1959 Kreuznacher Brückes Trockenbeeren-auslese. Of the 1953 Nahe wines it was said: 'They are real beauties. They have the charm of a good Moselle, the aroma of a Rheingau and the fruit of a Rhinehessian wine.' The 1959 vintages even surpass the '53s!

A list of some proprietors owning vineyards in various villages:

| | |
|---|---|
| Weingut August Anheuser | Kreuznach, Schloss Böckelheim, Niederhausen |
| Paul Anheuser | Kreuznach, Schloss Böckelheim, Monzingen, Nieder-hausen, Norheim |
| Landesweinbaulehranstalt | Kreuznach, Norheim, Niederhausen |
| State Domain | Schloss Böckelheim, Niederhausen, Münster am Stein |

## The Wines of Franconia (Franken)

Franconia was once an independent duchy within the Holy Roman Empire, but it has long since been dismembered. Parts of the former duchy are now in Bavaria, Württemberg, Baden and Hessia. Happily, the vineyards of Franconia have survived all political upheavals and administrative partitions. They still flourish along nearly the whole of the many curves of the River Main from east of Frankfurt to Bamberg, producing a great variety of wines, most of which possess a very distinctive character.

The great majority of the wines of Franconia are plain beverage wines made from Sylvaner, some red, others white; but there are a number of white Franconian wines which are truly fine wines, possessing body, breeding and a fine bouquet that are all their own. The fine white wines of Franconia are well balanced wines, and this rare quality gives them a better chance to withstand the changes of temperature and the usually rough handling which so many wines resent on long journeys by land and sea. This is why the wines of Franconia were so popular in England from an early date and why the demand for them has been steadily growing since the Second World War, in both the British Isles and the U.S.A.

Of the three administrative divisions of Franconia – Lower, Middle and Upper – some 95% of the vineyards are in Lower Franconia, in Bavaria, and the best of the Franconian wines are those from the vineyards of Würzburg, Randersacker, Iphofen, Escherndorf and Hörstein.

The vine is no newcomer to Franconia: it was first planted near Würzburg in the eighth century, when St Kilian first brought the Gospel and the grape to the heathen populations of the Upper Main valleys. Today some 520 acres of vineyards are within the administrative bounds of Würzburg, which is more than any other locality possesses in Franconia. What is of greater importance is that the vineyards of Würzburg are responsible for some of the finest white wines of Franconia, including especially the wines from the Stein vineyard, the only ones legally entitled to the name of *Steinweine*. This vineyard and the *Leisten* vineyards were planted, according to tradition, by order of Charlemagne; since then, they have been enlarged and improved without any doubt by successive princes and bishops of Würzburg. They now belong mostly to the Bavarian State, the Würzburg Municipality and two Würzburg hospitals (Bürgerspital and Juliusspital). We may be quite sure that they are tended with as much care and love as ever before, as well as with a greater measure of scientific knowledge.

Experts have called the Würzburger Stein the most beautiful site in all Germany. There are parts or strips of the original Stein vineyard which have been given different names for the sake of differentiation and identification, such as:

| | | |
|---|---|---|
| Steinmantel | Löwenstein | Ständerbühl |
| Jesuitenstein | Harfe | Schalksberg |

Strips of the site Leiste are called Innere Leiste, Felsenleiste and Aussere Leiste.

There are 160 villages in Franconia, the vineyards of which produce honest wine, for the honest thirst of the local people who have no wish and no chance to compete in the world's markets.

The State *Hofkellerei* is the largest owner of vineyards in Franconia: nearly 250 acres, which originally belonged to the Prince-Bishops of Würzburg, then to the Duchy of Würzburg, before being transferred to the Bavarian Crown in 1816. Here is a list of the vineyards now the property of the *Hofkellerei* or State Domain:

## WÜRZBURG

| | | |
|---|---|---|
| Innere Leiste | Löwenstein | Stein-Schalksberg |
| Jesuitenstein | Neuberg | |

## RANDERSACKER

| | | |
|---|---|---|
| Hohenbuch | Marsberg | Spielberg |
| Lämmerberg | Pfülben | Teufelskeller |

## HÖRSTEIN

| | | |
|---|---|---|
| Abtsberg | Reuschberg | Schwalbenwinkel |
| Langenberg | | |

## GROSSHEUBACH

Bischofsberg

Bürgerspital owns vineyards in Würzburg, Randersacker and Himmelstadt, and the Juliusspital in Würzburg, Randersacker, Escherndorf, Astheim, Dettelbach, Iphofen, Rödelsee and Bürgstadt.

The Franconian wines have a traditional bottle of their own, the *Bocksbeutel*, which is entirely different from all other wine-bottles: it is flat-sided instead of cylindrical.

The origin of it is obscure. Possibly a glass-blower may once have turned out the strange shape, either accidentally or intentionally, or maybe the Low German *Bockesbeutel* (a bag in which prayer-books or other volumes were transported) had something to do with the original invention, and its name. It must be remembered, too, that there is a grape called *Bocksbeutel*, possibly a reference to its shape. Dr Kittel ascribes the origin of the name directly to the baglike shape (*Beutel*) of one of the internal organs of a goat's anatomy (*Bock*), which the characteristic Franconian flask resembles. This interpretation is far fetched. If we remember that Rabelais in *Gargantua and Pantagruel* speaks quite often of bottles called *bréviaires*, in other words of bottles similar to a *Bocksbeutel*, we can accept the solution of the puzzle as *Bockesbeutel*.

Franconia has a monopoly of its use, with the proviso that three co-operative societies in Baden are allowed to bottle an average of 30% of their yearly crop in *Bocksbeuteln* and, in specially full vintages such as 1959, up to 50% (*Mauer Weine*).

Do not let us make the mistake of thinking that all Franconian wines are identical, or even similar. It is true that most wine merchants list just one wine from this large and important district, the *Steinwein*. But the Franconian wines bear on their label their birth certificate, just as do the wines of all other German wine districts. And if we really care, and take the trouble to make the wine journey through the many villages and vineyards, we shall find a wealth of difference in quality and character. And of course it is here that we find the *Rieslaner* (formerly Mainriesling) and the *Perle* – two new vine crossings which will have a great influence on the viticulture of Franconia.

In our wine journey we shall travel through five distinctive districts. Beginning at Frankfurt, our first stop will be in the district Alzenau: Hörstein, whose wines remind us of the Rheingau wines.

Moving along the U-formation in the Untermain district:

| | |
|---|---|
| Erlenbach | Homburg |
| Grossheubach | Klingenberg |
| Grossostheim | |

We then turn aside to visit the Franconian valley of the Saale with:

| | |
|---|---|
| Hammelburg | Sulztal |
| Langendorf | Schloss Saaleck |
| Ramsthal | Wirmsthal |

In the triangle of the Main (*Maindreieck*) we come to the heart of Franconian viticulture:

Abtswind
Buchbrunn
Castell
Dettelbach
Eibelstadt
Erlabrunn
Escherndorf (Lump, Eulengrube, Hengstberg, Kirchberg, Fürstenberg)
Frickenhausen
Grosslangheim
Iphofen (Julius-Echter-Berg, Kronsberg, Kalb, Burgweg, Pfaffensteig)
Kitzingen
Köhler
Mainstockheim
Marktbreit
Nordheim
Obereisenheim
Randersacker (Pfülben, Hohenbuch, Teufelskeller, Spielberg, Marsberg, Sonnenstuhl, Altenberg, Häslein, Lämmerberg)

Retzbach
Rödelsee
Sommerach
Sommerhausen
Stetten
Sulzfeld
Thüngersheim (Johannisberg, Freiberg, Neuberg, Scharlach, Ravensburg)
Veitshöchheim (with its viticultural college, now also under the administration of the Hofkellerei: Fachtel Wölflein, Neuberg)
Volkach
Wiesenbronn
Würzburg (in addition to the above-mentioned Stein and Leiste: Rossberg, Pfaffenberg, Schlossberg, Klinge, Gutental, Stephanspfad, Albertsleite and, last but not least, the Neuberg with its wines rich in bouquet and aroma)
Würzburg Heidingsfeld

We end our journey in the Obermain district:

| | |
|---|---|
| Mainberg | Schweinfurt |

## Other German Wines

All the better wines of Germany, the only wines for which there is a demand in the British Isles, the U.S.A. and other countries outside Germany, are the wines of the Moselle, Saar and Ruwer, the Rheingau, Rhinehessia and the Nahe, the Rhein-Pfalz or Palatinate, and Franconia. There are, however, a considerable number of other wines made in Germany which enjoy a high degree of local popularity; these come from the vineyards of other parts of Germany, from the Middle Rhine and the Ahr Valley in the north to Lake Constance, or Bodensee, in the extreme south.

## Middle Rhine (Mittelrhein)

The Middle Rhine may be considered, in theory, the stretch of the Rhine valley from Bonn in the north to Bingen in the south, with Koblenz approximately in the centre. In practice, however, with the exception of some vineyards on the right bank of the river at Königswinter, south of Bonn, and at Linz, opposite the Ahr valley, all the worthwhile wines of the Middle Rhine come from vineyards south of Koblenz. The best are those of Caub on the right bank of the Rhine and of Boppard, Oberwesel, Bacharach and Steeg, and Oberdiebach on the opposite bank.

The finest vineyard of BOPPARD is HAMM, which runs along the river on the lower slopes of the Altenberg. CAUB's best vineyards are known as Backofen, Blüchertal and Pfalzgrafenstein. The principal wine-growing centres and the best-known vineyards are the following:

**OBERWESEL**
| | |
|---|---|
| Ölsberg | Rheinhell |

**BACHARACH**
| | |
|---|---|
| Posten | Wolfshöhle |

**STEEG**
| | | |
|---|---|---|
| Flur | St Jost | Unkel |
| Mühlberg | | |

**OBERDIEBACH**
Fürstenberg

On the right bank of the Rhine, LORCH and ASSMANNSHAUSEN, farther up the river, although part of the Rheingau officially, produce wines more in keeping with the style and quality of the Middle Rhine wines. Assmannshausen is chiefly noted for its red wines; made from the Pinot noir or Spätburgunder, they are considered to be the best red wines of Germany.

## Bergstrasse

Bergstrasse is a stretch of land upon the right bank of the Rhine, part of which is in the northern tip of Baden, but most of which is in Hessia. It is a particularly fertile and sheltered piece of country, chiefly famous for its orchards, but it also has its vineyards, mostly in two *Kreise*:

**BENSHEIM**
| | | |
|---|---|---|
| Geiersberg | Kalkgasse | Streichling |

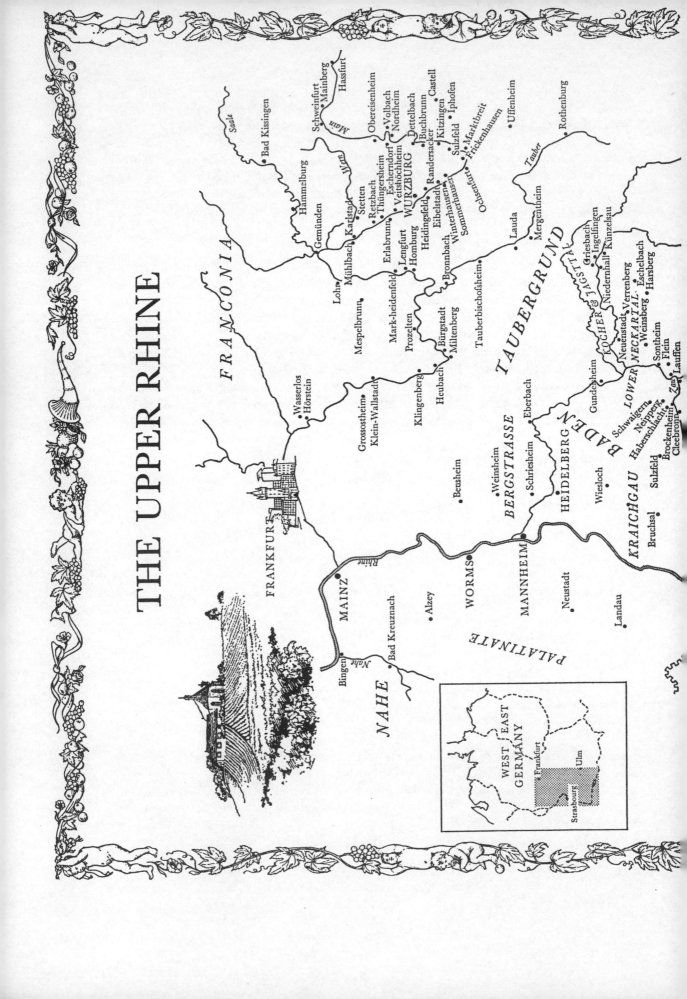

# THE UPPER RHINE

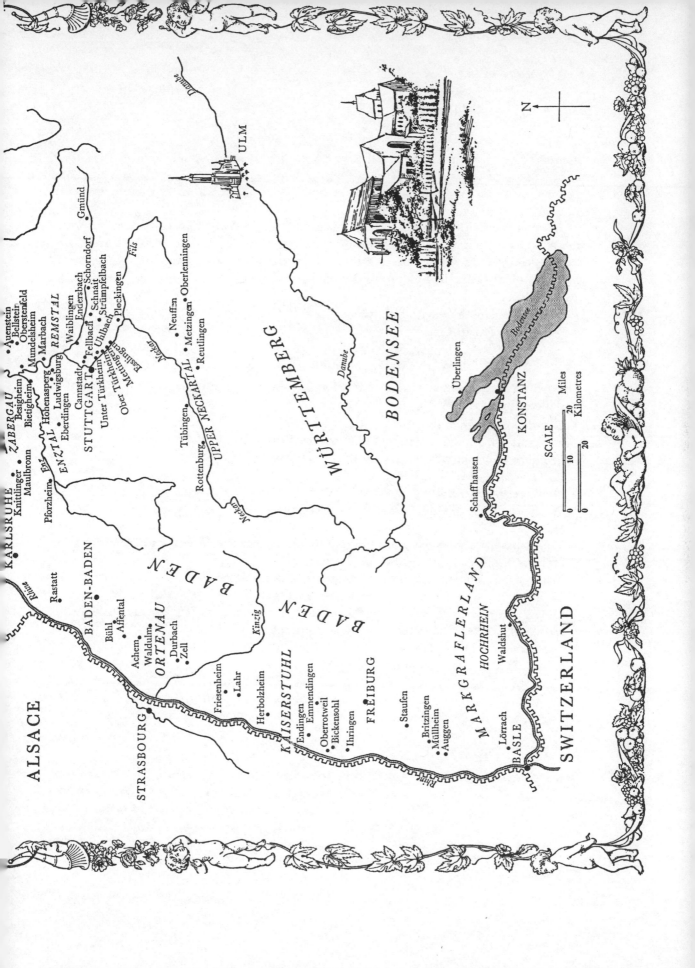

HEPPENHEIM

Mausnest            Steinkopf            Stemmler
Schlossberger

## Württemberg–Baden

For many years Württemberg and Baden were independent states, then in 1871 they became federal states of the German Empire. Until 1918 Württemberg was a kingdom and Baden a duchy. From then on they became republics within Germany, and that status continued until 1953.

In 1953 the two were amalgamated into the state of Württemberg-Baden, but from the viticultural point of view we still have to treat them as separate districts. In Württemberg-Baden are 72,100 viticultural holdings with a vineyard area of 17,654 hectares, which is approximately 6·5% of the whole agricultural area of the state. This is made up as follows:

| | |
|---|---|
| North Württemberg | 9,785 |
| North Baden | 2,025 |
| South Baden | 5,669 |
| South Württemberg including Hohenzollern | 175 |

The whole is distributed among 845 wine-growing communities. Important growers in Baden-Württemberg:

Staatliches Weinbauinstitut Freiburg i. BR.
Weingut Dr H. Mackenstein, Schlossruine, Burkheim am Kaiserstuhl
Freiherr v. Neveu'sche Gutsverwaltung, Durbach
H. Germann, Müllheim, Baden
Heiliggeist-Spitalstiftung, Freiburg im Breisgau
Weingut Bühler Söhne, Freiburg im Breisgau
Weingut Dr Heger, Ihringen/Kaiserstuhl
Weinbauversuchsgut des Landkreises Offenburg, Schloss Ortenberg, Baden
Staatsweingut Meersburg, Schloss Neuweier
Frhrl. v.u.z. Franckenstein'sches Rentamt, Offenburg, Baden
Weingut Fritz Blankenhorn, Schliengen/Markgräflerland
Gräflich von Berckheim'sche Schlosskellerei, Weinheim an der Bergstrasse
Fürstlich Löwesntein-Wertheim-Rosenberg'sches Weingut, Kreuzwertheim am Main
Württ. Hofkammer-Kellerei, Stuttgart
Von Stapf'sches Weingut, Erlenbach, Kreis Heilbronn
Weingut Graf Adelmann, Kleinbottwar (Kreis Ludwigsburg)
Fürstl. Hohenlohe-Waldenburg'sches Weingut, Waldenburg, Kreis Ohringen
Weingut H. Vetter

## WÜRTTEMBERG

Generally speaking, the Neckar with its tributaries is the main centre of Württemberg viticulture. But the vineyards start only at the Upper Neckar near Rottenburg. In the valley of the Albtrauf we find a very little viticulture in towns, e.g. Reutlingen, which has the highest-situated vineyards of Württemberg – nearly 1,800 feet above the sea. But where the Neckar turns to the west, viticulture is the main occupation of the inhabitants, for here there are many places reached by the southern sun. In this middle part of the Neckar we find Stuttgart and to the east of Stuttgart is the beautiful Rems valley, with well-known sites such as Stettener Brotwasser, Schnaiter Halde. The greatest wine district is the lower valley of the Neckar, with 3,600 hectares of vineyards. Still part of this district, on the left side of the river, are the Enztal, the Zabertal and the Leintal; on the right side of the river, the Murrtal, the Bottwartal, the Schozachtal, the Weinsbergertal, the Kochertal and Jagsttal. It is in the Bottwartal and Schozachtal that the *Schillerweine* are produced.

In addition to the vineyards along the Neckar, there are vineyards along the Tauber and in the Vorbachtal in the north-east of Württemberg which belong to Württemberg. Part of the vineyards of the Bodensee (Lake Constance) district also belong to Württemberg.

It is noteworthy that in the eight wine-growing districts of Württemberg a large part of the vineyards is devoted to the growing of red wine, which in 1953 came to 28% of the whole German harvest of red wine grapes. Besides the red and white wine there is a considerable production of *rosé* or *Schillerwein*, the red and the white grapes being planted in mixed lots in the vineyards and gathered and treated together. Today the State discourages the growing of mixed grapes in the same ground, and the quantity of *Schillerwein* is getting smaller every year. It can be said that many wine drinkers in Württemberg, and indeed many visitors to Württemberg, regret very much that these *Schillerweine* are becoming scarce, and the local demand is such that, good and even fine as some of them are, Württemberg wines are never available for export. But it was not ever thus, and the 'Neckarine' wines were obtainable in the Hanseatic cities and in Scandinavia during the late Middle Ages. Most Württemberg wines come from the very large number of very small vineyards which grace both banks of the Neckar valley. There are few, very few, large vineyards; the great majority belong to farmers, artisans and even labourers and other wage-earners who have just enough spare time to devote to their few vines. Some of them make only just enough wine for their own home consumption, while others, those who make the better quality wines, sell them through the local co-operative society.

The best of the Neckar wines are those of the Lower Neckar above and below Heilbronn, more particularly by Weinsberg, the seat of the viticultural institute. The upper valley of the Neckar, south of Stuttgart, may not bring forth quite so much good wine, but Stuttgart itself is the chief market for all the wines of Württemberg. It is also the seat of the Wine Growers' Co-operative Central Organization with its extensive cellars.

The most important wine-growing communities of Württemberg are:

*Neckar Valley*

| | |
|---|---|
| Beilstein | Grossbottwar |
| Besigheim | Heilbronn |
| Bönnigheim | Hessigheim |
| Eberstadt | Kleinbottwar |
| Erlenbach | Lauffen a. N. |
| Esslingen | Lehrensteinsfeld |
| Fellbach | Löwenstein mit Reisach und Rittelhof |
| Flein | Mundelsheim a. N. |

Oberstenfeld m. Weingut Lichtenberg          Stuttgart-Untertürkheim
Stuttgart-Bad Cannstatt                      Stuttgart-Wangen
Stuttgart-Obertürkheim                       Walheim
Stuttgart-Rohracker                          Weinsberg
Stuttgart-Rotenberg                          Willsbach
Stuttgart-Uhlbach

*Remstal*

Beutelsbach                    Schnait
Endersbach                     Stetten
Grossheppach                   Strümpfelbach
Grunbach i. R.

*Enztal*

Hofrheim                       Rosswag

*Zabergau*

Brackenheim (red)              Nordheim
Cleebronn                      Schwaigern (red)
Dürrenzimmern (red)

*Kochertal and Jagsttal*

Criesbach                      Verrenberg
Ingelfingen

*Württemberg Taubergrund*

Bad Mergentheim                Weikersheim
Markelsheim

## BADEN

This is the country which faces Alsace and stretches from the Swiss frontier to the Bergstrasse and Hessia, and beyond Mannheim all along the right bank of the Rhine, with Württemberg and Bavaria north and east. There are many vineyards, more now than up to 1939, in all parts of Baden, and they produce a considerable quantity of red, white and *rosé* wines which vary greatly in style and flavour according to the district.

Over the last few years Baden wines have become better known. Better weather conditions in 1955, 1956 and 1957 helped to produce better and riper wines than in most other districts. The Baden wine-growers have founded many local wine co-operatives, so that the small-holders can rely on the skill and experience of the co-operatives' managers. Some 80% of Baden wines are stored and treated in 110 co-operatives' cellars.

Here we must also refer to the Baden *Weissherbst*. Whereas in Württemberg *rosé* wine is produced by the pressing and fermentation of mixed red and white grapes, in Baden the blue burgundy grape is treated like a white wine grape. The grapes are not fermented on the skins, but are treated as in white wines: very small particles of colour thus come into the wine, giving it a touch of rose.

Like the Palatinate wine districts, Baden, too, has its well-marked *Weinstrasse*, or Wine Road; it is a district which is well worth visiting. It leads from Baden-Baden via Neuweier, Lauf, Oberkirch, Oppenau, Hundseck and Richtental back to Baden-Baden.

The chief wine-producing districts of Baden from east to west and south to north are the following:

*Bodensee*: that is, those vineyards upon the north shore of Lake Constance, facing south. Most of them are in Baden, but not all, since both Württemberg and Bavaria have a foot in the lake, so to speak. The white wines made from these lake-side vineyards are known locally as *Seeweine*, and are pleasant, refreshing wines but no more; the best of them come from the vineyards of Meersburg and Hagnau and are made from Pinot gris (or Ruländer) grapes.

*Breisgau* lies farthest west, where the Rhine reaches Basle and swings sharply to the north; at this point there is a 30-mile-long stretch of deep, dark soil (on the foothills of the fir-clad slopes of the Black Forest) in which the Gutedel (or Chasselas) grapes thrive, bearing quantities of fruit from which much plain but pleasant wine is made. This stretch of land, which is almost completely covered with vineyards and orchards from Basle to Freiburg, has the following communities:

| | | |
|---|---|---|
| Friesenheim | Kenzingen | Schmieheim |
| GLOTTERTAL | Köndringen | Wagenstsadt |
| Herbolzheim | Malterdingen | |

The next district, the *Markgrafschaft*, counts among its more important wine-producing villages:

| | |
|---|---|
| Auggen (Kirchbuck, Schäf, Letten) | Kirchhofen |
| Britzingen | Laufen |
| Ebringen (Sommerberg, Klämmle) | Müllheim |
| Efringen-Kirchen (Katzenrain, Hardberg, Weingarten) | Pfaffenweiler |
| | Rheinweiler |
| Ehrenstetten (Öhlberg, Kirchberg) | Schallstadt-Wolfenweiler |
| Haltingen (Lette, Stiege, Rohrbrunnen) | Schliengen |
| Istein | Sulzburg |

*Kaiserstuhl.* North-west of Freiburg a jumble of volcanic rocks is known as the Kaiserstuhl, and there are many vineyards upon its lower slopes, mostly Ruländer or Pinot gris. They yield wines with more body and a higher alcoholic strength than other Baden wines. The best-known wine-producing districts of the Kaiserstuhl are the following:

| | |
|---|---|
| Achkarren (Schlossberg, Rittersprung) | Königschaffhausen (Scherchbuck, Halve) |
| Bahlingen | Oberbergen (Winzburg, Limburg) |
| Bickensohl (Steinfelsen, Eichberg) | Oberrotweil (Henkenberg, Eichberg) |
| Bischoffingen (Enselberg) | Sasbach |
| Burkheim (Burgberg, Käsleberg, Feuerberg) | Merdingen (Tüniberg) |
| Eichstetten | Rimsingen (Tüniberg) |
| Endingen | Tiengen (Tüniberg) |
| Ihringen (Winklerberg, Fohrenberg, Abtsweingarten) | Wasenweiler (Kreuzhalden, Steig, Eichen) |

Following the Rhine downstream one comes to the region of Baden known as *Ortenau*, of which Offenburg is the principal township.

The vineyards of Ortenau are blessed with the poorest soil in Baden, and they accordingly produce the best wine – wine which is mostly made from Riesling and, to a lesser extent, from Traminer grapes. The local name for Riesling is *Klingelberger* and the Traminer is called *Clevner*.

The most important wine-producing villages of Ortenau are as follows:

| | | |
|---|---|---|
| Altschweier | NEUWEIER | Tiergarten |
| AFFENTAL | Oberkirch | Varnhalt |
| Durbach | Rammersweier | Waldulm |
| Fessenbach | Steinbach | Zell |
| Kappelrodeck | | |

Affental, Eisental, Altschweier and Neuweier are known for their red wines. Affental, on account of a monastery which was situated in the valley (*thal*), was originally called Ave Thal, i.e. 'Ave-Maria-Thal'. In this part of the country 'v' is pronounced as 'f', so that people called the village Affental. But 'Affe' in German means a monkey. As a result of all this manipulation of the language, and in order to distinguish their wine, the growers used, and still use, a bottle on which a monkey is embossed.

We come next to the *Kraichgau* with the following villages:

| | |
|---|---|
| Bruchsal | Rauenberg |
| Dietlingen | Sulzfeld |
| Ellmendingen | Unteröwisheim |
| Landshausen | |

Passing the Neckar river, we reach Heidelberg and the Bergstrasse. The following are the villages of the Bergstrasse district belonging politically to Baden:

| | |
|---|---|
| Heidelberg-Handschusheim | Sulzbach |
| Heidelberg-Rohrbach | Wiesloch |
| Schriesheim | |

A further 40 villages of Baden are situated in the *Taubergrund* and the *Maintal*, including Wertheim with its famous Kallmuth district which adjoins the Franconian wineland, dealt with above.

The Neckar flows through Baden to reach the Rhine at Mannheim, but nearly the whole of its course is through the vineyards of Württemberg.

## Germany's Red Wines

The proportion of red wine produced in Germany is larger than most people imagine. Red wines are in fact grown in all districts except those of the Moselle, Saar and Ruwer.

In the production of red wines Germany uses many species of grapes. In the forefront, of course, stands the Pinot noir (Spätburgunder), but in addition to this there are the Limberger, Trollinger (originating in Tyrol), Müller Vine (Schwarz Riesling) and the Samtrot – a newly developed grape from the child of the Schwarz Riesling. The best known red wines are:

### THE AHR DISTRICT

The German red wine region *par excellence* is the Ahr Valley, which is also the most northerly wine region in the world. The wine produced there is called Ahr burgundy.

The Ahr, a little river having its source in the Eiffel mountains, is very little known for its wine. It is better known for its waters. In the middle of this district lies the spa, Bad Neuenahr, with its world-famous 'Apollinarisbrunnen', from which the world drinks. But its viticulture is as old as that of the Moselle, though the area of vineyards under cultivation has been reduced over the last few decades.

Its fame has long been based on its red wines, though the growing of red grapes was started only about 300 years ago. Formerly the red grapes were used to make a *rosé* wine known as *Ahrbleichert*.

For a long time when Germany did not import foreign wines on account of lack of currency, the Ahr products had almost a clear field and reigned supreme; but as soon as foreign wines came on the market again, the Ahr wines lost a lot of their popularity.

Moreover, the cultivation of red wine on the Ahr is waning for other reasons. The growers are of the opinion that the vineyards on the Ahr are 'burgundy-weary', an opinion based on the discovery that in many places new cuttings lack vigour in their development, while other species – when planted in vineyards earlier devoted to burgundy wines – bear good fruit. Just as a farmer rotates his crops, so the vine-grower must from time to time change the species of vines in his vineyards. As a result of these considerations, the growers on the Ahr have begun to plant grapes which produce white wines. At the present red and white wines are being grown in about equal proportions.

Wine-growing communities:

| | |
|---|---|
| Altenahr | Dernau (Lantershofen, Herznersheim) |
| Rech | Ahrweiler (Daubhaus) |
| Walporzheim (Honigberg) | Bad Neuenahr |
| Mayschloss | Bodendorf |

## THE FRANCONIAN DISTRICT

Franconia's red wines grow in the Untermain district, especially on the hot southern slope of the Spessart mountains or in the sandy soil of the Erv valley. In the eighteenth century this part of the country, between Hassloch and Klienberg, was the centre of a flourishing viticulture, but today for the most part we find in its place just a few trees and bushes. The terraces, however, are still there to remind us of the lost viticulture. And on the old site of the Hasslocher Stockmeister a new vineyard with blue Pinot grapes has been planted by the viticultural College of veitshöchheim. On the sites of some old vineyards we find American vines which form the root base for the grafting of new vines, now a necessary precaution in the fight against the phylloxera, these American roots being sent from here to all German districts. In BÜRGSTADT, a site belonging to the Würzburger Juliusspital, the vineyards are planted with the early ripening burgundy grapes. Adjoining Bürgstadt is MILTENBERG, known as the pearl of the Main; its wines are spicy and strong. Its vineyards are:

| | | |
|---|---|---|
| Helferich | Mainhölle | Steingrube |

Last but not least we have to mention GROSSHEUBACH with its Bischofsberg and its Engelberg.

'Und nicht vergessen Sie vom Main der Klingenberger Rote' ('One must not forget the "Red" from Klingenberg on the Main') which is considered a speciality among the German red wines.

## OTHER DISTRICTS

### Rhinehessia

Early and late burgundy grapes are planted at Ingelheimer (Hundsweg, Langenberg, Hirschtal, Bein, Höllenweg, Steinacker, Sonnenberg), and the wines are round, velvety, with a good spicy flavour and bouquet.

### Palatinate

One-fifth of the wines produced in the Palatinate are red wines, but to a large extent come from the Portuguese grape, which gives only a very light wine – mostly used *en carafe*. However, some full-bodied wines from the Pinot grape are made.

> Dürkheimer Feuerberg   Forster Neuberg   Kallstadt
> Herxheim (according to a document in the Speyer Museum dated 1597, the 'Red Traminer' from Rhodt in the Oberhaardt was at that time considered to be the best wine 'growing on the long chain of hills from Basle to Cologne')

### Baden-Württemberg

Baden and Württemberg produce more red wine than white wine. The proportion of red to white is approximately 60 to 40%, and Baden and Württemberg each have a speciality produced from red grapes. Baden has its *Weissherbst*, and Württemberg its *Schillerwein*.

*Weissherbst* is the wine produced from red grapes by vinification of the red grape in the same fashion as with white grapes: in other words, they are pressed immediately after the gathering and the must is separated from the skins and pips immediately after pressing. The result is a white wine tinged sometimes with grey or pink. This wine can be full-bodied and harmonious – even some Spätlesen are made – but generally speaking, these wines, without the tannic acid of the red wine, are no more than ordinary table wines.

Württemberg has its *Schillerwein*, the name given to a wine pressed from a mixture of red and white grapes. The name has nothing to do with the poet Schiller, but is derived from the red-white (merging into pink) radiance or 'shimmer' of the wine. (The German verb for 'shimmer' is *schillern*.)

This species of wine was developed mainly during the worst crisis ever suffered by German viticulture – after the Thirty Years War. During that period the many devastated vineyards were hastily replanted with any kind of vine likely to afford a good crop, regardless of whether it was a red-wine or a white-wine grape.

Even nowadays the Swabians are very fond of their '*Schiller*', but its production has been drastically reduced. In Württemberg as elsewhere there is a very strong tendency – wholly admirable from the viticulture point of view – to keep grape-strains and their wines pure by selective planting, selective harvesting and selective wine-production. This tendency will no doubt lead to a still greater improvement in the quality of German wines.

The best known red wines of Baden are Oberrotweiler Kirchberg and Affenthaler Klosterreberg. Brackenheim and Schwaigern are the best known red-wine communities of Württemberg.

### Rheingau

In very fine vintages the State Domain produces the so-called *Rot-Weiss* (red-white) wine, but only in the grade of *Edelbeerenauslese*. This is a wine resulting from a very special kind of Beerenauslese made from the late burgundy grape. The grape-gatherers of Assmannshausen – in good vintages – have a sickle-shaped enamel container hanging from their punnets; into these containers they put the selected sleepy berries, some of which have already shrunk and dried out to a raisin-like consistency. Oddly enough, the chief purpose of this is not so much the production of a truly fine Beerenauslese as the protection of the bulk of the wine, since in these raisin-berries the beautiful blue dye in the grape-skin has been destroyed by a fungus (*Botrytis cinerea*), and the use of these otherwise valuable berries in the manufacture of the red wine would be detrimental to its natural ruby-red colour. Now whereas, in preparing red wines, the grape mash is allowed to ferment in order that the grape-juice (colourless even in blue-skinned berries) may be enabled to absorb the blue dye from the skins, these sleepy raisin-berries are pressed immediately. The resulting coloured, rather sticky, grape-juice is then fermented on the lines of the normal white-wine process. If these raisin-berries were to be fermented with the rest in the mash the must and eventually the wine would take on an unpleasant mouldy taste. As it is, they produce a white wine, pressed from the noblest red-wine grapes; the juice having absorbed a certain amount of the skin-dye, the wine has a yellowish, brownish or reddish tinge according to its quality.

As mentioned previously, these wines are produced in the finest red vintages only and are really of exceptional quality – as was proved by the 1934, 1938 and the 1950 vintages.

Assmannshauser Höllenberg is the best known red wine of the Rheingau.

The export of red wine in 1958 amounted to less than 4,000, in 1959 to less than 8,000 dozen bottles. Japan was the biggest buyer, followed by the U.S.A.

To end this chapter we must frankly confess that we cannot feel enthusiastic about German red wines. In most vintages German vineyards produce red wines with insufficient ruby-red colour, and the vintner must make use of the concession of the wine law to use 25% of foreign *Deckwein*, that is, imported dark-coloured red wine to give more colour to the native wine.

CHAPTER FIVE

# *Brandy*

THE GERMAN Wine Law contains, in paragraph 18 under the heading *Weinbrand-Weinbrandverschnitt-Cognac*, the following definition: '*Trinkbranntwein*: Wine whose alcohol has been won exclusively from wine, and which has been distilled according to the method of Cognac, can be called *Weinbrand* (Brandy).'

The word *Weinbrand* means nothing else but 'burnt wine'. *Weinbrand* for German grape brandy is synonymous with the word *Branntwein*. The alcohol contained in wine is known as the *Weingeist*, whereas the alcohol resulting from the fermentation of other fruits is called *alkohol* or spirit.

Aristotle knew that there were combustible materials in wine, but he did not understand how to separate the alcohol from the watery substances of the wine. Distillation of brandy was discovered in Europe in the eleventh or twelfth century. We know too that the Chinese had discovered the secrets of distillation by the thirteenth century at the latest. Li Chi-tschin, in his encyclopaedia of the sixteenth century, reports that the Chinese knew about distillation of Araki (or, in Chinese, *Alaki*) from rice-wine in 1260–1360, in the time of the Mongolian dynasty.

Brandy was much enjoyed by sick people, but by others too; one of the characteristics of brandy praised in literature is that it strengthens the memory and gladdens the heart. The classical country for this distillation is, of course, France.

The great wine district of Charente is famous, not for the vinification of table wines, but for distillation. In the centre of this district is Cognac, which produces the most noble brandy of all. St-Emilion, Colombard and other white grapes are cultivated there; the soil and climate are excellent for their growth and ripening.

Almost as famous is the district of Armagnac, part of Gascony in the south of France. Other districts are not so important, but the wines from Béziers, Sète, Marseilles, Montpellier and Narbonne are used for distillation. According to French law, however, the wines coming from those districts cannot be used for the distillation of Cognac because, according to both French and German law, 'Cognac' is a pure geographical denomination and must not be used for wines of any other district. Brandies from other districts are sold as *alcool de vin*.

The beginning of German wine distillation, the manufacture of *Weinbrand*, was caused by the bad economic conditions in which some Rhenish wine-growers found themselves in the middle of the nineteenth century when many of the small and mediocre wines were not saleable at all. The first German to use the Cognac method for distilling these low-quality wines was an apothecary, P. Dahlem of Trier, and he was quite successful with his products. He showed them at various exhibitions, including Paris 1866 and Metz 1868, and he won prizes. It is unnecessary to say that his factory had to overcome many difficulties, especially as the Germans continued to prefer imported brandy. When the State introduced protective measures on imported brandies this helped the new industry to establish itself, and German brandy was even exported to England and the U.S.A.

Although Germany is quite famous for distilleries, let it be said immediately that it does not produce any wines which could be useful for distillation – or, rather, that although Germany produces wines which could be used for distillation, and might produce some good brandies, generally speaking for economic reasons this is not done. The German distilleries, if they use German wine at all, tend to use those wines which have been confiscated by the Government as being concoctions that are not allowed to be sold as wine. If, for instance, the grower adds too much sugar to the wine in a bad vintage this wine must not be sold; it is confiscated and sold to distilleries for the preparation of brandy. The same thing happens if the sulphur content is too high, or if he offers or sells his wine under a misleading denomination.

The wines which are used for distillation in Germany come from all over the world. Quite a good proportion still comes from the Charente – from the original Cognac district – but it is usually mixed with wine from other parts of the world – Italy, Greece, Spain, Bulgaria, Hungary, Yugoslavia or from any wine-producing country which has wines for distillation to offer. The reason for this is, of course, quite clear: German wines are too expensive, even more expensive than the Charente wines which are grown for brandy in the district in which Cognac is made.

This method alone allows German distilleries to compete with French Cognac – at least in Germany, for the German distiller buys wine which may be useful for his brandies wherever he finds it. In Germany, as in all countries, fiscal laws have a great influence on the brandy trade for good or evil.

Plate 31. (*Above*) Bad Kreuznach, in the Nahe. (*Below*) The Kafels vineyard Norheim, in the Nahe.

The German distiller imports the wines at exactly the strength he needs, and in order to achieve this the foreign wines are imported not as natural wines but as fortified wines. This is done by adding brandy distilled in the district of the imported wine. In Germany the duty is levied per 100 kg. of a basic wine up to 23% alcoholic strength, so by importing the wines in this state not only duty but freight is saved.

To give an idea of German brandy distillation, here are some total import figures, expressed in terms of hectolitres, of basic wine for conversion into brandy:

| 1936 | 91,150 | 1938 | 270,588 | 1949 | 631,179 |

These figures have continued to increase.

From 5 litres of the imported 23% wine, 1 litre of distillate is produced. As a rule, the German distiller has agreements with his suppliers that the wines he imports should be prepared in the same way as the wines he imports from the Charente. This ensures that the basic wines are at least similar in their method of vinification, although, on account of the different soil and climate, they can never be considered identical in quality with the wines of the Charente.

After the ending of fermentation the wines do not undergo a racking from the lees, but are distilled together with the lees after the principal secondary fermentation is over. In a normal wine the yeast content is approximately 5 promille, and wines are imported into Germany from the various countries of origin after the first fermentation, still mixed with the yeast produced by the fermentation.

The first *Branntwein* was made in the same way as it is made today – by distillation, that is, by steaming and condensation. Nothing has changed in this method in all the centuries. More often than not, corn, potatoes and other cereals, rather than wine, were used for the basic product. For a long time *Branntwein* distillation was lost altogether – after all, spirit made from potatoes and cereals was much cheaper than brandy made from wine, especially from German wine, which contains very little alcohol; but the brandy of today is different from the brandy made centuries ago.

Cognac distillers learnt to use a second distillation after the first (the *brouilles*). In this way they gained the heart of the brandy. It is also true that newly distilled brandy gains in quality by storage in special oak casks made from trees in the French Limousin and Angoumois district.

German brandy is made in exactly the same way as Cognac, and the qualities obtainable vary enormously; none are equal to the finest Cognac, although some good German brandies can be bought.

Germany has also found export outlets for her brandies. In 1957, 73,000 litres were exported to the U.S.A., Belgium and Switzerland, which were the leading customers. In subsequent years the figure has increased.

### German Exports of Brandy

|      | Hectolitres | Value in 1,000 DM | Average price |      | Hectolitres | Value in 1,000 DM | Average price |
|------|-------------|-------------------|---------------|------|-------------|-------------------|---------------|
| 1952 | 371         | 0·266             | 716·99        | 1959 | 3,091       | 2·066             | 668·40        |
| 1953 | 464         | 0·317             | 683·19        | 1960 | 3,780       | 2·313             | 611·91        |
| 1954 | 815         | 0·559             | 685·89        | 1961 | 3,082       | 1·881             | 610·32        |
| 1955 | 1,059       | 0·710             | 670·45        | 1962 | 4,000       | 2·284             | 571·00        |
| 1956 | 1,456       | 0·918             | 630·50        | 1963 | 4,369       | 2·516             | 575·88        |
| 1957 | 2,405       | 1·522             | 632·85        | 1964 | 9,007       | 2·664             | 295·77        |
| 1958 | 2,239       | 1·440             | 643·15        | 1965 | 10,594      | 3·089             | 291·60        |

Plate 32. *Edelfäule* – noble-rotting grapes for making Trockenbeerenauslesen.

# CHAPTER SIX

# Casks, Glasses and Bottles

## Casks

OAK WAS unchallenged for many centuries as the best home a German wine could possibly wish for, and the coopers of the Rhineland were unexcelled for the size as well as the artistic decorations of their vats and casks. White wines were kept in enormous tuns, none more famous than the Great Tun of Heidelberg, 31 feet by 21 feet, holding 150 Fuders, or 600 hogsheads, of wine: it was built in 1663 to replace an earlier one holding 132 Fuders.

The pride of Bremen has long been the *Rosenwein*, the wine kept in a great tun known as the *Rosentun* on account of a bronze bas-relief of roses at its head. This great tun was originally laid down in 1624 and filled with 12 vats of the finest wine of that vintage, six from Johannisberg and six from Hochheim. In the next cellar there are 12 other great butts, each of them named after one of the 12 Apostles, and filled only a few years after the *Rosentun*. There are yet other casks, mere hogsheads, in another nearby cellar – they might be called the 'Disciples' – filled with younger wines. As and when any of the *Rosenwein* is drawn off to gladden the heart of V.I.P.s and alleviate their infirmities, a like quantity is drawn from one of the 'Apostles' to keep 'Rosen' full to the bung, and the same quantity of a younger vintage is drawn from one of the 'Disciples' to fill up the 'Apostle'. Whether the Jerez vintners copied Bremen or not is immaterial, but the 'Solera' system of Bremen is older than that of Jerez.

Many German towns, large and small, were proud of the capacity and carvings of the great tuns in their municipal cellars, even more than of the wine which they held – inevitably blends of wines of a number of successive vintages. Tübingen, Grüningen and Königstein, for instance, could never compete with Bremen in size or wealth, but they all boasted a larger municipal great tun than that of Bremen.

Great tuns were never removed from their original cellars, less cumbrous containers being used to deliver wine sold within the land or shipped overseas. German wines were sold retail mostly by the Stübchen in Germany, and in England by the gallon, which was the measure nearest to the Stübchen: Rhenish was usually sold wholesale in Germany by the aum (aam, ohm, awne or ahm), known in England as a 'piece' or a 'butt', of about 40 gallons; and occasionally by the *fat* or *vat* (called a tun in England), and holding about 5 aums. It is, however, quite impossible ever to be certain of the actual contents of old German wine measures and containers: so many of them had the same name but not at all the same size. Here is a list of some of those still used today, giving the capacity of each in litres.

| *Rheingau* | | | | | |
|---|---|---|---|---|---|
| Stück | 1,200 | Logel | 50 | Mass | 2 |
| Halbstück | 600 | Eicher | 10–12 | Schoppen | $\frac{1}{2}$ |
| *Rhinehessia* | | | | | |
| Stück | 1,200 | Ohm | 150 | Schoppen | $\frac{1}{2}$ |
| Halbstück | 600 | | | | |

*Bavaria (Donau)*

| | | | | | |
|---|---|---|---|---|---|
| Eimer | 60 | Mass | 1 | Schoppen | ¼ |

*Bavaria (Lake Constance)*

| | | | | | |
|---|---|---|---|---|---|
| Fuder | 1,220 | 15 Bayr. Mass | 16 | 1 Butte | 50 |
| Eimer | 68 | | | | |

*Palatinate*

| | | | | | |
|---|---|---|---|---|---|
| Stück | 1,200 | Ohm | 150 | Eicher (Stütz) | 10 |
| Fuder | 1,000 | Logel | 40 | Schoppen | ½ |
| Halbstück | 600 | | | | |

*Franconia*

| | | | | | |
|---|---|---|---|---|---|
| Stück | 1,200 | Ohm | 150 | Eicher | 10 |
| (formerly | 1,124) | Eimer | 75 | Schoppen | ¼ |
| Fuder | 900 | Butte | 40 | Mass | 1–1.17 |
| Halbstück | 600 | Beerbutte | 180 | | |
| (formerly | 562) | | | | |

*Moselle, Saar and Ruwer*

| | | | | | |
|---|---|---|---|---|---|
| Fuder | 960 | Ohm | 160 | Kessel (Eicher type) | 6–7 |
| Zulast | 480 | Bürde (Hotte type) | 40 | Schoppen | ½ |

*Baden*

| | | | | | |
|---|---|---|---|---|---|
| Fuder | 1,500 | Ohm | 150 | Mass | 1½ |

*Nahe*

| | | | | | |
|---|---|---|---|---|---|
| Stück | 1,200 | Eimer | 160 | Viertel | 8 |
| Fuder | 1,000 | Schoppen | ½ | Remies'chen | ¼ |
| Halbstück | 600 | Mass | 1 | | |

*Wurttemberg*

| | | | | | |
|---|---|---|---|---|---|
| Eimer | 300 | Schoppen rund | ½ | Eiche (of wine casks) | |
| Imi | 18¾ | Stütze | 10–15 | approx. | 150 |
| Mass | 1,875 | | | | |

## Jars or Jugs

Oak was not the only home given to German wines in olden days. They were also kept and sent to distant markets in capacious pot-bellied stoneware jars or jugs which were first made in the early years of the sixteenth century in the Rhineland, and copied in England during the second half of the seventeenth century. The very large number of these jugs which still exist today is sufficient proof in the first place that they must have been made in very considerable quantities, and in the second that there was quite a brisk demand for German wine in the Netherlands, the Baltic ports and in England, where such 'Greybeards', as they are commonly known, are by no means rare even today. Their name was due to the bearded head or mask stamped in relief upon their short necks. There are also either floral or armorial decorations which occasionally occur on the brown or grey salt glaze of their rotund bodies.

In England the more popular (and quite unjustified) name for the Greybeard jugs has been 'Bellarmine', upon the assumption that the bearded mask on the neck was the caricature of the Jesuit Cardinal Bellarmine, a widely known writer and Catholic theologian who was highly unpopular in Protestant countries. Strange to say, as late as 1849 one William Chaffers read a paper before the British Archaeological Association in which he claimed that he was justified in 'christening anew' the Greybeards with the name of Cardinal Bellarmine, which had been one of the names given to them during the previous 200 years. That Chaffers was entirely wrong is beyond argument, since it is known that Greybeards were made in the Rhineland before Bellarmine was born in 1542, and one of them may be seen in the Tower of London dated 1560, when the future cardinal was but 18, presumably beardless, and certainly quite unknown.

Ben Jonson, who had a lot to say about Greybeards, does not mention Bellarmine's name or any other. Cartwright, however, gives the jugs two different names in his play *The Ordinary* in 1634: 'Like a larger jug, which some men call a Bellarmine, but we a conscience.' In the same play, however, the author refers to the same greybeard jug, mentioning that the mask is said to represent Eglon, King of Moab, 'a very fat man' (*Judges III*, 17). Dr Plot, in his *Natural History of Oxfordshire* (1676), says that Greybeard jugs were called 'D'Alva Bottles' on the assumption that the head was the caricature of the Duke of Alva, Spanish Governor of the Netherlands.

Evelyn, in *Numismata* (1697), also mentions the Duke of Alva 'of whom there are a thousand pictures not on medals only but on every Jugg-Pot . . .'

Why the pottery workers of the Rhine should have ever bothered to stamp upon the neck of their stoneware jugs the head of a Jesuit Cardinal (before he was even born), or of a Spanish Governor of the Low Countries (who meant nothing to them), or of a King of Moab out of Holy Writ (of which they had never heard), does not appear to make sense. Nor did any of those people whose names have been given to the Greybeards ever have any connection whatever with wine or vineyards. Our own suggestion is that the bearded head on the Greybeards was, as near as they could make it, the representation of Father Rhine, an invariably bearded figure in all the old statues and portraits. It seems to us only natural that potters who worked exclusively for Rhine vintners would have chosen the head of Father Rhine for jugs used solely for Rhine wines to be sent to distant markets. It was as good as a pictorial 'made in Germany' device, or rather 'made on the Rhine'.

Besides the bearded head of Father Rhine upon the neck, the smooth and spacious rotundity of the Greybeards gave artists a chance to display their skill in stamping floral and foliate decorations, or else some heraldic or armorial design, chiefly the arms of the German and Dutch towns where the demand for Rhine wine was greatest. Of all the heraldic designs upon Rhineland Greybeards, the arms of Queen Elizabeth I puzzled antiquarians quite a lot, until the mould of those English Arms was found on a kiln site, at Rären, in the Rhineland, where evidently Greybeards were made to the order of merchants trading in Rhine wine in England.

All Greybeards to be found on the Continent were most likely made in Germany or the Low Countries, but in England it is not at all easy to tell Rhineland-made from English-made Greybeards. Charles I granted a patent, in 1626, to Thomas Rons and Abraham Cullen, whose first kiln was probably in the City of London: their Greybeards are difficult to tell from the Rhineland models unless, as often happens, arms, crests or initials give some indication of the tavern or cookshop owners to whom the Greybeards were originally sold. *The Times* of Saturday, 19 July 1958 published an article 'Antiques and Pictures' which gave interesting information about Greybeards, some of which has been incorporated in this chapter.

## Wine Glasses

Venice and Murano hold a very important place in the history of modern glass on two major counts, the first being the artistic merit of the glasses due to their creative genius, and the second, perhaps the more important of the two, being the lead which their craftsmen gave to the glass-makers of France, England, Germany and the Netherlands. Their influence, however, was less noticeable in Germany than anywhere else, and the *Römer*, the most typical Rhineland glass, may claim a closer association with the early Romans than the Venetians. Its very name is said by some to be due to the tradition of its early Roman ancestry.

What is perhaps the most remarkable feature of the *Römer* is that in a world of ever-shifting fashions the popularity of this glass has not been affected by changing habits and taste. Unlike those beautiful English eighteenth-century ale, wine and cordial glasses, which are now in museums and the cabinets of private collectors, the *Römer* is still in common use after some three hundred years. There cannot be more positive evidence that the *Römer*, besides the appeal of its pleasing appearance, which is merely a matter of taste, is also admirably suited for the purpose for which it was originally made, that of drinking and enjoying wine – a matter of taste also, no doubt, but less liable to changes of mood.

The Romans imported wine when they occupied the Rhineland, and taught the natives how to grow grapes in the open and how to make wine; they also taught them how to make vessels of glass, and, like viticulture, glass-making has flourished in Western Germany ever since. Proofs of the fame which the Rhineland glass-makers enjoyed abroad are not lacking; there is, for instance, the recorded dispatch to Jarrow, in Northumbria, by Cuthbert, Bishop of Mainz, of a glass-maker from his diocese in response to an appeal from Benedict, Bishop of Wearmouth. Albert Hartshorne, in his monumental work on English and other glasses (*Old English Glasses*, London, 1897), remarks that the glass drinking vessels found in the tombs of Merovingian and Frankish kings on the Continent were made from late Roman models with small bases or feet and devices so distinctive and so constant as to point to a common source of supply, presumably Cologne or Trier, and within the sixth and seventh centuries.

According to Francis Buckley (*European Glass*, London, 1926), glass-making was carried on in the Rhineland continuously from the days of the Roman occupation to our own. There are still in existence glasses of the Merovingian and Carolingian periods which prove that the custom of drinking wine from glass vessels was widespread in the Rhineland long after the Romans had left. Those early German glasses were small, rather thick and ornamented with 'stringing', and with applied little lumps or bosses, technically known as 'prunts' and called *Nuppen* by the Germans. These *Nuppen* or 'prunts', which were in all probability inspired by the projecting bosses of earlier Roman drinking cups, are the most distinctive form of ornamentation of the Rhineland wine-glasses, the most typical of which was the *Römer*, a tall, cylindral green glass, without a lid, studded all along its sides with *Nuppen*, its green colourings being classified as moss green, apple green, yellow green, olive green and sea green: it had a glass ring at the base, but no foot. Presently this ring or base was replaced by a narrow spun foot while the top or mouth of the glass was widened to a bowl and eventually the height of the foot was raised until the beautiful seventeenth-century *Römer* reached its most perfect proportions with the bowl about 4 inches, the stem 3 inches and the foot 1 inch high. During the seventeenth and eighteenth centuries the bowl, which is, of course, the most important part of the glass, remained practically the same, but the foot rose steadily, always at the expense of the stem until at the end of the eighteenth century the stem had practically disappeared and there was only room between foot and bowl for an almost invariably quilled neckband and three or four stamped *Nuppen* or 'prunts' set horizontally. As the foot rose it also broadened out, giving to the glass perfect stability on table or shelf. *Römer* have been for the past 300 years the most typically German as well as the most suitable glasses for the service and enjoyment of wine; their bowl is now often made white, which does not add to their visual attractiveness but enables the drinker to enjoy the beautiful colour of the wine in the glass.

The nineteenth-century Hock glass, which may be called the rival of the *Römer*, is not lacking in grace and artistic charm, but it does not 'sit' as the *Römer* does on the table nor does it fit so well in the hand. It has a flat foot and a long rod of a stem, at the end of which the bowl opens out like a flower on its stem: there is, of course, no room for any *Nuppen* or other ornamentations. Sometimes the stem and bowl are both of cut glass, white or coloured, and there is no denying that the finest of these modern Hock glasses can add to the beauty of a well-laid dinner-table; they are always taller than all other wine-glasses, which is an added attraction, but they are distinctly top-heavy, whereas one can grasp and hold a *Römer* of wine with much greater assurance and satisfaction.

'All the ancient varieties of the Rhine-land glasses have been reproduced at Ehren-feld, near Cologne, not with the natural artistic irregularities inseparable from the old examples, but with the frigid accuracy associated with modern science. Fanciful names such as "Dagobert-Römer", "Wieland-Humpen", "Weinbecher-Clodwig", "Gambri-nus-Pokal", etc. have been given to these productions, apparently for identification for purposes of trade.' (Albert Hartshorne, *op. cit.*)

*Römers* and Hock glasses are Rhineland glasses for Rhenish and Moselle wines, but there are other German wine-glasses, chiefly from Silesia and Bavaria, which ought not to be overlooked. The mountains which divide Bavaria in the south and Silesia in the north from Bohemia were covered with dense forests which provided glass-makers with an almost inexhaustible source of fuel, while suitable quartz, sand and other minerals were available in many locations. Hence the importance of the glass-making industry, more particularly in the valleys and on the north and south slopes of the Riesengebirge. Herr von Czihak (in *Schlesische Gläser*, Breslau [Wroclaw], 1891) showed that there was one glass-works in Silesia in the fourteenth century and at least three in the fifteenth and sixteenth, which were increased to seven in the seventeenth century. At the present day there are 56 glass-works in six principal centres, a wonderful testimony to the merits of the local materials. Most of the forests, unfortunately, have literally gone up in smoke, but there is coal in plenty.

The glass-makers of Silesia became famous chiefly for cut glass and for coloured, engraved and enamelled glasses, as did the glass-makers of Bohemia. Ruby glass was brought to perfection about 1679 by Johann Kunckel, a distinguished Silesian chemist, while in the service of Frederick William, Elector of Brandenburg, at his glass-works on the Isle of Peacocks at Potsdam. In Bavaria glass-makers appear to have devoted more attention to the making of mirrors than of drinking glasses.

By far the most spectacular, as well as the most distinctive, drinking glasses from Silesia, Bavaria and Saxony were large, tall, cylindrical glasses, plain or decorated, with or without a lid, which are usually known as *Humpen* or 'brimmers'. They are chiefly used on ceremonial occasions, for pledging honoured guests; in France such glasses are called *verres de parade*. Small and plain glasses must have been made for daily use which met the fate of all domestic glasses and crockery, but some of the great *Humpen* survived, owing to the greater care taken of them as valuable specimens of the glass-maker's art. Some of these *Humpen* are beautifully decorated, the most striking of them all being the *Reichs-* or *Adlergläser* (empire or eagle glasses). They vary very little in shape, being usually plain cylinders with low bases and rims ornamented with gildings of various colours. One one side of the glass the Imperial double-eagle is enamelled with its wings spread, each head crowned and nimbed; or else the imperial orb of sovereignty in place of the eagle. Round the rim of the glass is usually inscribed, with certain variations, 'Das heilige Römische Reich mit sampt seinen Gliedern' ('the Holy Roman Empire, with all its subjects'). The date is generally at the back of the glass, the earliest recorded being 1547; but they continued to be made until about 1725, together with other large enamelled glasses.

The *Kurfürsten* and the *Apostel Humpen* are also highly decorative and very large glasses, the first displaying the Emperor surrounded by the seven Electors mounted on white horses; the second with caricatures rather than portraits of the Apostles, each one with his own emblem.

The *Pass-glas* is a cylindrical glass from 8 to 9 inches high, tapering from $3\frac{3}{4}$ to $2\frac{1}{2}$ inches in diameter at the top to 3 or $1\frac{3}{4}$ inches immediately above the base. It is decorated by a stringing which sometimes encircles the glass spirally, and in other specimens forms a number of rings more or less equidistant one from the other, the intervening space being occasionally marked with numerals.

## Bottles

Wine tastes much better out of a glass than when drunk from a cup, even a cup made of solid gold or silver, let alone pewter or pottery, which is why there were wine-glasses long before wine-bottles were made of glass. It was only about 200 years ago that wine-bottles were first used, as we use them today, as a home for wine to await our pleasure. Earlier glass wine-bottles were merely decanters, containers which were filled in the cellar below, then brought to the table to be passed from hand to hand among the guests, or for their glasses to be filled and refilled by serving men. Old wine, in the past, was aged in wood. Bottle ageing became a possibility only in comparatively modern times, that is to say after the cork bark first came to be used for making stoppers some 300 years ago, and especially after the invention, 50 or 60 years later, of the cork-screw, which allowed a cork to be driven hard into the neck of the bottle with the certainty of getting it out again when the wine was wanted. It was then, and then only, that cylindrical wine bottles were made which could be binned away horizontally without any fear of the wine's oozing out when left alone for months or years to mellow and mature slowly. During the many centuries when there were wines but no cork-screws, most bottles were made of leather, wood, pewter or pottery, which were not so easily cracked or smashed as when made of glass. Sir Kenelm Digby has been credited with the introduction of the first wine-bottles made of glass to England, in 1632, only nine years after the grant by James I to Sir Robert Mansell of letters patent to make objects of glass. Be that as it may, there is no lack of evidence to show that glass wine-bottles, at first with a long funnel-like neck and a fat globular body, were replaced fairly quickly during the latter part of the seventeenth century by the Fulham stoneware jugs, made in imitation of the Rhineland Greybeards, and the Lambeth Delft bottles, those charming and much smaller jugs of glazed pottery. Many of those Delft bottles are dated, very few of them after 1653, the latest date of all being 1672; it is most likely that by then they had been replaced by wine-bottles made of dark green glass, used exclusively as decanters.

But not all wine-bottles were made in pre-corkscrew days to stand squarely, or rather roundly, upon the table after having been filled from the cask. People did not spend the whole of their lives by their own fireside. Many travelled a great deal on foot or on horseback, on business or pleasure, and also from shrine to shrine, on pilgrimage. Princes and bishops travelled in great style, with armed escorts and loaded wagons, but everybody else travelled with very little baggage: it was so much safer. There was one piece of personal equipment, however, which was carried by all; it was a *costrel* or pilgrim's bottle. Circular or pear-shaped, it was flat, with a small spout and a couple of rings or lugs for a rope which was flung over the shoulder and held the *costrel* at one's side, or *costó*. These pilgrim's bottles were made in all kinds of materials before being made of glass, but in size they hardly varied at all, holding just about a quart of wine, a moderate quantity which appears to have been accepted as a fair draught for a thirsty man for the best part of 2,000 years. There is, indeed, very little difference in size and shape between the wine flasks of Egypt's twenty-sixth Dynasty (656–525 B.C.) and the pilgrim's bottles of the Middle Ages.

We have so far failed to find out how and why the old *costrel* or pilgrim's bottle happened to be chosen, as it obviously was, as the pattern of the *Bocksbeutel*, the glass wine-bottle used to this day for the white wines of Franconia, and for a few wines of a small district of Baden (*Mauer Weine*). The present Hock and Moselle bottles, the first made of red-brown glass and the other of blue-green glass, are quite modern, not much more than a hundred years old. At the beginning of the last century bottles of various shapes – but never *Bocksbeuteln* – were used for bottling Hocks and Moselles; many of them were very similar to the present-day burgundy bottle, which gradually became slimmer as well as taller.

Whatever their style and size, all German bottles are exceedingly well dressed. There are no wine labels comparable in artistic merit to some of the finest German wine labels. But even more valuable is the completeness of the information they give – the names of village and vineyard where the wine comes from; the date of the vintage of its birth; the name of the grape from which it was made and when it was picked; the name and titles, if any, of the owner of the vineyard or of the merchant who bottled the wine. No other country's wines carry such a concise yet complete birth certificate, usually displayed with both skill and taste.

# CHAPTER SEVEN

# *Sekt*

SEKT has a peculiarity as the name of a drink. Champagne refers to the area with which this drink is inextricably linked, both historically and legally. Sparkling wine (*Schaumwein*) indicates the particular characteristic of the wine. Sekt, on the other hand, is a name which originally referred to a drink of a quite different style: Spanish still wine.

Wine that is not sweet is described as 'dry' in all Latin languages: French *vin sec*, Spanish *vino seco*. In the Middle Ages large quantities of Spanish wine were exported to England and with the wine went the name: dry Spanish wine was known in the sixteenth century as *wyn seake, wyne seck*. The word 'wine' soon disappeared, and by Shakespeare's time the drink was called sack. Of course, sack and the Spanish *vino seco* had only the name in common, for the English liked their wine sweet. They therefore added sugar, honey and spices, and sack came to denote sweet Spanish wine.

The word reached Germany in the seventeenth century (1647: *seck*) and always meant still, sweet Spanish wine, but thanks to a tavern jest it sparkled. The actor Ludwig Devrient used to drink champagne every evening in an old Berlin tavern and would cry, like the thirsty Falstaff, 'Give me a cup of sack!' He ought, like Falstaff, to have been served sherry, but as he only drank champagne no one listened to what he said. So, in Berlin one could say Sekt (as the word had meanwhile become) when one wanted sparkling wine. For decades this was only so in Berlin, then the new meaning slowly spread.

Since then the two words Sekt and Schaumwein have been synonymous in the German language. In the draft of the new German Wine Law, however, a distinction is provided for: Sekt will be reserved for the home product provided it fulfils certain standards of quality. All other sparkling wines will be called Schaumweine.

For a hundred years the French could claim the glory of making the only sparkling wines. But 1780 we hear of experiments in Baden and by 1792 in Mainz, but the lasting foundations were only laid in 1825 in Württemberg and Silesia, and a few years later on the Rhine and the Main, in Saxony and Franconia.

In 1823 Georg Christian Kessler returned home from the champagne house of Veuve Clicquot in Reims. He founded, in Esslingen on the Neckar in 1826, a Sektkellerei whose products soon won the highest distinctions. Only native grapes were used, and through high-quality standards the local viticulture was spurred to special achievements. After a few years the glassworks found out how to blow sparkling wine bottles which could withstand a pressure of up to seven atmospheres.

From 1824 Carl Samuel Häusler, a well-known fruit-wine maker, undertook research in Silesia into making sparkling wine from Grünberg grapes. However, more and more wine of foreign origin was used, since the area planted with the Grünberg vine – as much appreciated as dreaded for its legendary acidity – diminished each year.

The first lasting foundations of the Rhine Sektkellereien were laid in 1832, when Ignatz Schweickardt left France after the July Revolution of 1830 and returned to

363

Hochheim am Main to make use of the knowledge he had acquired in Reims. As he used native wines, he could depend on their being the finest in Germany, distinguished both by their vigour and their delicacy. By 1800 the English (and soon, too, the Americans) were so familiar with the wines of Hochheim, which they had come to know from drinking them at the spas in Hessen, that they used the word 'Hock' to describe all German wines except Moselles. The export of still hock was followed by that of the sparkling wine in the first years of its production, through the chance which took Schweickardt's partner Carl Burgeff to London in 1841. A decade later half the production was being exported to the British Isles.

In 1837 it was suggested to Philipp August Müller, a childhood friend of Carl Burgeff, that he should undertake practical research at his large vineyard property in Eltville. This was so successful that the first sparkling Eltville wine popped its cork at carnival time in 1838. This was the cell from which developed the house of Matheus Müller, known the world over as MM. Today 15 million bottles of Sekt mature in its three-storey cellars.

In 1850, while Burgeff's exports to England increased yearly, the firm of Kessler opened up new markets in Poland and Russia for their sparklings from Clevner and Riesling grapes. In 1897 Germany produced 6 million bottles of Sekt (of which one million came from Burgeff) and one million bottles were imported from France. Ten years later imports were only one-tenth of home production.

It is amusing to read how German Sekt in its first years achieved success after success abroad, while at home it had to struggle for recognition. The saying that one can only be famous in Germany if one is a foreigner was at least true of champagne. It enjoyed a legendary reputation, and for many years the Germans could not imagine that their own product was its peer. Certainly, many German Sekt firms were partly to blame as they decorated their products with French labels – which also enabled them to ask a higher price. It is to the lasting credit of the Verband Deutscher Sektkellereien that they relentlessly suppressed the imitations of foreign products and thus enabled Sekt to be judged on its own merit.

Champagne has remained as a model of lightness, while Sekt, especially when made from the Riesling grape with its powerful bouquet and flavour, can be said to be a sparkling wine which equals champagne in value but with which it cannot be compared.

From the beginning white grapes have been more used in Germany than in France, though in the early days black grapes played a much larger part than today. White Sekt was mostly made from the juice of black grapes, for which the name Klarett was borrowed quite early. The possibility of producing red Sekt from black grapes was exploited though Rotsekt has always remained a speciality and its character lacks the typical Sekt style. Connoisseurs, however, value it for its high sugar and tannin content. Red Sekt from the State Domain at Assmannshausen, for example, or Geiling's Bourgogne Mousseux are numbered among the highest quality wines.

The German export trade mainly used district names such as Sparkling Hock, Sparkling Moselle, Sparkling Franconia and variants such as Sparkling Moselle Muscatelle. Later Sekt was named after the best-known types of blend: Sparkling Johannisberger, Sparkling Bernkasteler, Sparkling Brauneberger, etc. In the second half of the nineteenth century the German Sektkellereien began to manufacture special brands from unblended wines of particularly good years or sites (or both). The origin of such

Lagensekte or the vintage of Jahrgangsekte inspired every confidence, since the wine employed had to comply with the Wine Law. The first Riesling Sekt brands appeared shortly after 1900.

The description Rieslingsekt has become so widely adopted that it might appear to be the only vine which produces typical German Sekt. This is not at all the case; indeed, it would be an impoverishment thus to limit the diversity of German production. Sekt can be made of any grapes provided they are suitable. There are not merely regional differences but the wishes of the consumers as so varied. Here the German Sektkellereien have differed basically from the champagne houses: they are not geographically limited in the choice of their wines. This fact, sometimes considered a weakness of Sekt, is actually its particular strength, since it permits the blending of the most diverse characteristics without addition to the basic wines. There are firms which use exclusively German wines or which do so for some types. A random selection of Sekte which bear site names follows: Kessler Eilfinger Berg, Kupferberg Weiss-Gold Freiherr von Schorlemer Serriger Herrenberg, Kurpfalz Original Ockfener Bockstein, MM Hohe Domkirche, Schloss Vaux Assmannshaüser Höllenberg, Schultz-Grünlack Reichsgraf von Kesselstatt, Söhnlein Fürst Metternich, Schloss Johannisberg.

Other Sekte come exclusively from French wines and embody the true champagne styles, as is often indicated by the name: Deutz & Geldermann Cuvée la meilleure, Geiling Bourgogne Mousseux, Henkell Royal, Hoehl Corps Diplomatique, Henkell Brut.

Both types, however, represent only a small percentage of Sekt production, though it would be easy to concentrate on German or French basic wines. But the taste of the public, which, though not impossible to influence, is nevertheless the decisive factor for a luxury industry, expects German Sekt to be neither too close to the German nor the French types but to be a blend of both or more wines.

Blending, as it is meant here, was not discovered by the Germans, but is one of the oldest French processes associated with champagne. In Champagne it is concerned with wines (for example, white and red) from geographically close neighbourhoods and of different varieties and vintages. In Germany the gigantic blending vats are filled with wines of various vintages and sometimes from widely separated districts which add together their characteristics in the second fermentation.

In the second half of the nineteenth century Sekt firms grew up in almost all the well-known spots in the Rhine and Moselle valleys and in the Palatinate, mostly based on wine merchants' businesses. In 1902 the Rhine firms made up 37% of the then 225 Kellereien; in 1952 they represented 71% of the total, by then reduced to 86 firms, and their share of total production was over 88%. Since 1903 production had never dropped below 10 million bottles, of which a large proportion was exported – in 1912 and 1913 together, 2·8 million bottles. After the First World War the damage to the export market weighed heavily on the Sekt industry. In 1920 and 1921 barely 1·1 million bottles were exported. In 1913, 850,000 bottles went to the United Kingdom, in 1921, 46,000 bottles.

At home two good years (1927 and 1928) were followed by the world wide economic slump. The climax was reached in 1931 with a production of only 4,360,000 bottles. After the removal of the tax on sparkling wine with effect from 1 December 1933 the market climbed to 19·2 million bottles in four years. But two years later the Second World War broke out, which catastrophically cut the market.

An additional burden was the effect of the currency revaluation in 1948 on the wartime surtax of 3 Marks per bottle. On 1 November 1952, when nearly all Sektkellereien were showing losses, the surcharge was at last replaced by a sparkling wine tax of DM 1 per bottle. Then the fetters fell away: turnover rose from 7·5 million bottles in 1951 to 64·5 million in 1961, and almost doubled again by 1965. But the State has again reached out, and as the budget showed a deficit the tax was increased to DM 1·50 on 1 January 1966. The reaction followed, and turnover went down by 20%, while in previous years it had increased by between 10 and 20%.

There are 125 Sektkellereien in the Federal Republic of Germany. Their number rose in 1952 with the tax change. Before the war there were only half as many firms, but the centre of gravity remains the same: on the Middle Rhine from Speyer to Koblenz, along the Moselle, around Stuttgart and Würzberg.

The removal of the wartime surcharge unleashed a boom which even the wildest dreamer of economic miracles would never have predicted. The miserable 7·3 million bottles in 1952 (all in bottles of 75 cl.) are confronted by 120 million in 1964. No one knows how the 50% increase of the sparkling wine tax from 1 January 1966 will operate in the long run.

Sekt production, unlike some sectors of the economy, is well spread out. In 1964, 45 firms produced up to 100,000 bottles, 52 produced between 100,000 and 1 million, and 28 produced more than 1 million.

DM 500 million flowed into the Sektkellereien in 1965, and this figure is even more striking when compared with the proceeds of viticulture. It is about two-thirds of the total for German viticulture after an above-average vintage.

While the sales of German Sekt rose steeply in 1965 and reached 140 million bottles, Champagne produced 70 million. The essential difference here is that Champagne exports a large part of its production, for example 15·5 million bottles in 1961, while the export of Sekt barely reached 1·5 million. The Germans not only drank around 138 million bottles of Sekt (140 million less 1·5 million exported) but they also imported another 3 million bottles, of which about 2·5 million were champagne.

In 1964 Germany already took first place among the sparkling-wine producers of the world. French production in 1966 should total between 110 and 115 million bottles, Russian production 55 to 60 million, Italian 45 to 50 million (all calculated in 75-cl. bottles).

Those who made Sekt in Germany in the first half of the nineteenth century bottled native wine and called the product, as appropriate, Sparkling Hochheimer, Sparkling Neckarwein and so on. The preparation of Sekt, however, calls for a selected and uniform grape and a ripe harvest which must be very carefully picked. The unripe as well as the overripe grapes must be removed, and the must – particularly *Klarett*, the white juice of black grapes – is pressed and vatted according to strict procedures. Any addition, any influence on the fermentation is forbidden. We take this for granted today, but at one time it meant a revolution in many German wine-growing areas as fine and inferior varieties were cultivated, picked and fermented together. The development of the Sektkellereien in the first half of the last century also marked permanent progress in the care and improvement of German wine. This is also evident geographically: nearly all the Sekt firms originated in the midst of wine-growing areas.

It is true that the taste of the consumer demanded a light Sekt of which the basic wine was not generally produced in Germany. Until the First World War this was no problem, since after 1871 Alsace-Lorraine formed part of the German state and the *Klarett* wines produced there from the Pinot noir grape proved to be ideal basic wines for Sekt. After 1919 the requirements had to be met further afield.

However, the Sektkellereien did not decline as buyers of German wines. They turned more and more to manufacturing Sekt from white wines and obtained great success, particularly with the noblest of white wine grapes, the Riesling. Sekt produced from this vine is distinguished by its fruit and its fine bouquet. As Rieslingsekt is generally dry and any faults would be more noticeable than in a sweet wine, its production calls for a particularly careful selection of grapes, and expert handling.

Since 1952 the authorities have given tax rebates to Sekt firms which use more than three-quarters basic German wine in order to guarantee a market for a definite part of their crop to those dependent on wine-growing.

On average, the Sekt firms take 5–6% of the German wine harvest, and at first sight this may appear little enough. It is, however, a special demand, and therefore of particular importance to certain wine-growing areas. The wines needed are just those that the wine trade can most expect to have difficulty in selling, since, as well as lightness and elegance, they show a high degree of acidity. The wines of the Saar and Upper Moselle, where often 60–70% of the vintage is sold for Sekt manufacture, are a well-known example. For the many small wine-growers of these areas the demand from the Sektkellereien is a question of existence, whereas the better-known areas are protected in the market by their fine-quality growths.

Germany has economic centres both for production of raw materials and for manufacturing industries. The Moselle, Palatinate, Rhinehessia and Rheingau are dominated by viticulture. Wine-growing is not one among many alternative forms of cultivation, since the steep slopes will only support the vine, whose long roots permit its survival. If vines were to disappear from the slopes only brushwood and occasional fruit trees would prosper. For the vine, however, this situation is not merely tolerable, but the climatic conditions are actually ideal. The variations in temperature cause the vine to struggle and produce a balance of sugar, acidity and perfume which will never be found where sun and a favourable climate are settled. Herein lies, however, the enormous risk to the wine-growers, quite often the weather produces grapes with sufficient acidity and bouquet but not enough sugar.

Apart from the furtherance of tradition, the maintenance of viticulture lies at the heart of the political economy which sees it in its entirety year by year balancing quantity and deficiencies in the harvest. It falls almost automatically to the Sekt industry to intervene in years when wines are made which are low in sugar but high in acidity. Through the second fermentation a substantial reduction of acidity takes place. Were the Sekt firms not represented in the framework of the whole wine industry, these wines would have to be heavily sugared (*verbessert*) or blended in order to make them saleable, and this would detract from their character. Economically, the Sekt firms thus act as a balance or a regulator, even a necessary complement to the wine industry. Their intervention makes it possible to bridge deficits which otherwise – unless substantial parts of wine-growing were to be sacrificed – could only be covered by state subsidies.

There are years when the German wines do not meet the requirements of the Sekt producers, since a high degree of ripeness has reduced the acidity and the high alcohol content has changed elegance and lightness into body and heaviness. In such years the wine-trade is not displeased when the Sektkellereien withdraw from the market, as they can easily sell such wines – 1959 was typical. The Sekt firms are then forced to make nearly all their purchases abroad, since the Sekt lover expects to be offered each year not only the same quality but also the same flavour and characteristics of his chosen brand. This is no less true of brands which in general are not made from German wine and for which the Sekt firms happily have at their disposal the most suitable wines of the world for their *cuvées*.

The purchases of the Sekt manufacturers – one year more from Germany, another year more from abroad – thus have nothing to do with a variation between nationalistic and cosmopolitan outlook. The producers of good branded Sekt have never refused the wine-growers when their help was needed (for example, in the exceptionally large 1960 vintage), and they have not been deterred by higher prices from buying German wines in preference to equally suitable foreign wines. The official bodies have always gratefully recognized that, on average, in each year since the Second World War the value of the share of wines from the German wine districts employed in Sekt production was far above 50% of total purchases. On the other hand, the Sekt firms can only honour their duty to their customers if they buy their special needs, which German production cannot meet, wherever the most suitable grapes grow.

German sparkling wine need not be fermented in bottle. It can start its life in a tank or, after fermentation, can be disgorged into a tank and bottled ready for sale.

Why should Sekt, whose second fermentation takes place in a tank, be inferior to one fermented in bottle? On the contrary, say the microbiologists: the larger surface area and the more vigorous mixing of the ingredients by electric agitators are the guarantee of better quality. The French regulation which defines the product as *vin mousseux produit en cuve close* and thereby stamps it as inferior is, in the opinion of the experts, an anachronism which technical developments have long since left behind.

In 1926 the German Sekt firms still made 97% of their Sekt by the *méthode champenoise*. Since then, new filtration processes have been developed which are superior to disgorging by hand, and glass-lined or double-jacketed tanks have been built whose contents can be warmed or cooled as needed. The wine is no longer at the mercy of chance and the laws of nature, which are part of wine, as is style, breed, sugar and yeast. Man can now intervene in the second fermentation, accelerate or retard processes, raise the alcoholic content by repeated additions of sugar and control the exact taste. Sekt has become an industrial product; the best technician will produce the best Sekt.

Fortunately, that is not true. Even Sekt made by the tank method cannot be better than the wine from which it is made. This explains the fact that in Germany too the tank method is restricted to the more ordinary Sekt. The possibility of control allows one to forego the costly years of maturing. Tank-fermented Sekt can be produced in a few weeks, and it is therefore markedly cheaper than that fermented in bottle. It is therefore not worth while fermenting expensive wines, and thus the wheel comes full circle: in the general view of the experts there is no difference between Sekt made by the *méthode champenoise* or by the *cuve close*, provided they are both made with the same care and from the same wine. However, since a comparable price cannot be obtained for tank-produced Sekt, the best wines are reserved for fermentation in bottle.

Second fermentation in bottle means, above all, long storage. With the completion of the alcoholic fermentation, the microbiological changes are not yet ended. On the contrary, many substances which have been absorbed by the yeast during fermentation are reassimilated by the wine after the death of the yeast and during the long storing. In this process nitrogen and certain vitamins play an important role, which contributes intrinsically to the improvement of the flavour and dietetic qualities of Sekt. Thus a minimum storage of five months is regarded as necessary, and it is regarded as of great importance that the newly produced Sekt should remain in contact with the yeasts as long as possible. The French wine law prescribes twelve months for champagne, and the writer is not aware of any firm in which German quality Sekt has been kept for a shorter time; it is frequently a matter of eighteen months to three years.

But are the bottles disgorged by hand? The fascination of this process lay in the fact that Sekt was an individual that had remained unchanged in the same habitation from the first day of fermentation until it was poured into the Sekt glass. As long as production amounted to 100,000 or even 1 million bottles, this traditional process, by which each bottle was handled 165 times before the wine could sparkle in the glass – remained unchallenged, even from the economic point of view. But it became ever more difficult to find the labour to disgorge each one of millions of bottles, and there were even scientists who expressed doubts that disgorging by hand was as safe as filter equipment.

Here too it was technological progress which made a new process possible. The second fermentation of the Sekt takes place in the usual way in the bottle. The bottles, however, no longer undergo *remuage*, but when the Sekt has matured they are emptied under pressure into a tank. This already contains the *dosage* which is traditionally added to each bottle of Sekt or champagne in order to reach a certain degree of sweetness. The Sekt is then run through a filter apparatus and returned to the bottles, which have meanwhile been cleaned. In this way it is rid of all lees and any other possible impurities.

The writer believes in tradition both for Sekt and for the market; he knows equally that the public will always weigh this against results and that the oldest and the youngest Sektkellereien have almost equal chances in the biggest competition they have ever faced among themselves and with Champagne: the Common Market.

# APPENDIX ONE

## Wine-Producing Communities

| Community | District | Area (hectares) | Red | White | Community | District | Area (hectares) | Red | White |
|---|---|---|---|---|---|---|---|---|---|
| Abenheim | Rhinehessia | 73·3 | R | W | Bad Kreuznach | Nahe | 373 | | W |
| Abstatt | Württemberg | 71 | R | W | Bad Krozingen | Baden | 13 | | W |
| Abtswind | Franconia | 42·8 | | W | Bad Mergentheim | Württemberg | 3 | | W |
| Achkarren | Baden | 76 | R | W | Bad Münster am Stein | Nahe | 18 | | W |
| Affaltrach | Württemberg | 33 | R | W | Bad Neuenahr | Ahr | 29 | R | W |
| Affental | Baden | 60 | R | | Bad Salzig | Middle Rhine | 2 | | W |
| Ahrweiler | Ahr | 230 | R | W | Bad Wimpfen | Baden | 1·6 | R | W |
| Albersweiler | Palatinate | 144 | R | W | Bahlingen | Baden | 135 | | W |
| Albig | Rhinehessia | 110 | R | W | Ballrechten | Baden | 75 | | W |
| Albisheim | Palatinate | 24 | R | W | Bamlach | Baden | 20 | | W |
| Albsheim | Palatinate | 29 | R | W | Battenberg | Palatinate | 25 | R | W |
| Alf | Moselle | 69 | | W | Bausendorf | Moselle | 9 | | W |
| Alken | Moselle | 33 | | W | Bayerfeld–Steckweiler | Nahe | 35 | | |
| Allensbach | Lake Constance | 5·6 | | W | Bechenheim | Rhinehessia | 6 | | W |
| Allmersbach | Württemberg | 100 | R | W | Becherbach | Palatinate | 5·5 | | W |
| Alsenz | Palatinate | 43 | R | W | Bechtheim | Rhinehessia | 192·5 | R | W |
| Alsenz/Nahe | Nahe | 70 | | W | Bechtolsheim | Rhinehessia | 44·8 | R | W |
| Alsheim | Rhinehessia | 306 | R | W | Beckstein | Franconia | 31 | | W |
| Altdorf | Palatinate | 43 | R | W | Beilstein/ Untermosel | Moselle | 16 | | W |
| Altenahr | Ahr | 70 | R | W | Beilstein/ Württemberg | Württemberg | 102 | R | W |
| Altenbamberg | Palatinate | 36 | | W | Bekond | Moselle | 39 | | W |
| Altenburg | Weissenfels | 6·5 | R | W | Bellheim | Palatinate | 12 | R | W |
| Altschweier | Baden | 23 | R | W | Bellingen | Baden | 32 | | W |
| Alzey | Rhinehessia | 105 | R | W | Benningen | Württemberg | 16 | R | |
| Andel | Moselle | 13 | | W | Bensheim | Rhinehessia | 70 | | W |
| Appenheim | Rhinehessia | 58 | R | W | Berghaupten | Baden | 3·5 | R | W |
| Appenhofen | Palatinate | 54 | R | W | Berghausen | Palatinate | 12 | | W |
| Archshofen | Württemberg | 7 | | W | Bergzabern | Palatinate | 75 | R | W |
| Armsheim | Rhinehessia | 85 | R | W | Berlichingen | Württemberg | 5 | | W |
| Arnstein | Lower Franconia | 1·17 | R | W | Bermatingen | Bodensee | 7 | | W |
| Arzheim | Palatinate | 152 | R | W | Bermersheim | Rhinehessia | 23 | R | W |
| Asperg | Württemberg | 25 | R | W | Bermersheim/ Worms | Rhinehessia | 31·7 | R | W |
| Aspisheim | Rhinehessia | 152 | | W | Bernkastel–Kues | Moselle | 180 | | W |
| Asselheim | Palatinate | 85 | R | W | Besigheim | Württemberg | 92 | R | W |
| Assmannshausen | Rheingau | 75 | R | W | Beuren | Württemberg | 15 | | W |
| Astheim | Franken | 15·8 | | W | Beutelsbach | Württemberg | 85 | R | W |
| Au | Baden | 4·5 | | W | Bickensohl | Baden | 45 | R | W |
| Auen | Nahe | 17 | | W | Biebelhausen | Saar | 10 | | W |
| Auenstein | Württemberg | 90 | R | W | Biebelnheim | Rhinehessia | 40·3 | R | W |
| Auggen | Baden | 140 | | W | Biebelsheim | Rhinehessia | 42·6 | R | W |
| Aulhausen | Rheingau | 10 | | W | Bieringen | Württemberg | 12 | R | W |
| Avelsbach | Moselle | 200 | | W | Bietigheim | Württemberg | 27 | R | W |
| Ayl | Saar | 61 | | W | Billigheim | Palatinate | 30 | R | W |
| Bacharach | Middle Rhine | 89 | | W | Bingen | Rhinehessia | 247·2 | R | W |
| Bachem | Ahr | 40 | | W | | | | | |
| Bachenau | Württemberg | 4·5 | R | W | | | | | |
| Bad Dürkheim | Palatinate | 800 | | W | | | | | |
| Badenheim | Rhinehessia | 34·7 | R | W | | | | | |
| Badenweiler | Baden | 12 | | W | | | | | |
| Bad Kösen | Saale | 6·5 | R | W | | | | | |

Plate 33. (*Above*) Castle Ehrenfels, in the Rheingau, between Rüdesheim and Assmannshausen. (*Below*) Nierstein vineyards on the Rhine front, in Rhinehes[sia]

| Community | District | Area (hectares) | Wine produced Red | White | Community | District | Area (hectares) | Wine produced Red | White |
|---|---|---|:---:|:---:|---|---|---|:---:|:---:|
| Bingen–Büdesheim | Nahe | 114 | R | W | Burg | Moselle | 80 | | W |
| Bingen Kempten | Rhinehessia | 70 | R | W | Bürg | Württemberg | 1·7 | R | W |
| Bingerbrück | Nahe | 33 | | W | Burgen/ Bernkastel | Moselle | 45 | | W |
| Binsfeld | Franconia | 2 | | W | Burgen/St Goar | Moselle | 26 | | W |
| Birkweiler | Palatinate | 145 | R | W | Burg-scheidungen | Saale | 3 | R | W |
| Bischheim | Palatinate | 6 | | W | Burgsponheim | Nahe | 32 | | W |
| Bischoffingen | Baden | 75 | R | W | Burkheim | Baden | 55 | R | W |
| Bissersheim | Palatinate | 78 | R | W | Burrweiler | Palatinate | 200 | R | W |
| Blansingen | Baden | 24 | | W | Callbach | Palatinate | 20 | | W |
| Bobenheim | Palatinate | 66 | R | W | Carden | Moselle | 16·5 | | W |
| Böbingen | Palatinate | 18 | | W | Casbach | Middle Rhine | 4 | R | W |
| Böchingen | Palatinate | 107 | R | W | Castell | Franconia | 17·1 | R | W |
| Bockenau | Nahe | 35 | | W | Castel–Staadt | Saar | 10 | | W |
| Bodendorf | Ahr | 5 | R | W | Cleebronn | Württemberg | 130 | R | W |
| Bodenheim | Rhinehessia | 275 | R | W | Cleversulzbach | Württemberg | 78 | R | W |
| Bohlingen | Lake Constance | 5·1 | | W | Cochem | Moselle | 90 | | W |
| Bolanden | Palatinate | 6 | | W | Colgenstein–Heidesheim | Palatinate | 12 | R | W |
| Bollschweil | Baden | 15 | | W | Cölln | Nahe | 8 | | W |
| Bombach | Baden | 10 | R | W | Creglingen | Württemberg | 5 | R | W |
| Bönningheim | Württemberg | 200 | R | W | Criesbach | Württemberg Kocher-Jagsttal | 30 | R | W |
| Boos | Nahe | 13·5 | | W | Dakenheim | Palatinate | 81 | R | W |
| Boppard | Middle Rhine | 106·5 | | W | Dahenfeld | Württemberg | 23 | R | W |
| Bornheim | Palatinate | 16·7 | R | W | Daimbach | Franconia | 3 | | W |
| Bornheim | Rhinehessia | 48 | | W | Dalberg | Nahe | 21 | | W |
| Bornich | Middle Rhine | 55 | | W | Dalheim | Rhinehessia | 112 | R | W |
| Bosenheim | Rhinehessia | 62 | R | W | Dalsheim | Rhinehessia | 180 | R | W |
| Bottenau | Baden | 25 | R | W | Dammheim | Palatinate | 39 | R | W |
| Böttigheim | Franconia | 3·6 | R | W | Damscheid | Middle Rhine | 22 | | W |
| Bötzingen | Baden | 77·1 | R | W | Dattenberg | Middle Rhine | 16 | R | W |
| Brackenheim | Württemberg | 60·6 | R | W | Dattingen | Baden | 28 | | W |
| Braubach | Middle Rhine | 28·2 | | W | Dautenheim | Rhinehessia | 25·5 | R | W |
| Brauneberg | Middle Rhine | 54 | | W | Deidesheim | Palatinate | 400 | R | W |
| Braunweiler | Nahe | 45 | | W | Dellhofen | Middle Rhine | 23 | | W |
| Breisach | Baden | 14·5 | R | W | Derdingen | Franconia | 77 | R | W |
| Breitscheid | Middle Rhine | 20 | | W | Dernau | Ahr | 150 | R | W |
| Bremm | Moselle | 105 | | W | Dertingen | Franconia | 32 | | W |
| Bretzenheim | Nahe | 105 | R | W | Desloch | Nahe | 10 | | W |
| Breunigsweiler | Württemberg | 8·5 | R | W | Dettelbach | Franconia | 16·62 | | W |
| Brey | Middle Rhine | 6 | | W | Dettingen | Württemberg | 7 | | W |
| Briedel | Moselle | 115 | | W | Detzem | Moselle | 65 | | W |
| Briedern | Moselle | 55 | | W | Deubach | Württemberg | 52 | | W |
| Britzingen | Baden | 65 | | W | Dexheim | Rhinehessia | 77·7 | R | W |
| Brodenbach | Moselle | 13 | | W | Dhron | Moselle | 80 | | W |
| Bruchsal | Baden | 58 | R | W | Diebach | Franconia | 5 | | W |
| Bruttig | Moselle | 86 | | W | Dieblich | Moselle | 11 | | W |
| Bubenheim | Rhinehessia | 2 | R | W | Diedesfeld | Palatinate | 330 | R | W |
| Buchbrunn | Franconia | 20 | | W | Diedesheim | Neckar | 4·2 | R | W |
| Buchholz | Baden | 11 | R | W | Diefenbach | Württemberg | 23 | R | W |
| Budenheim | Rhinehessia | 2 | | W | Dielkirchen | Nahe | 56·7 | | W |
| Bühl-Kappel-windeck | Baden | 15 | R | W | Dienheim | Rhinehessia | 3 | R | W |
| Bühlertal | Baden | 34·5 | R | W | Dierbach | Palatinate | 14 | R | W |
| Buggingen | Baden | 50 | | W | Diersburg | Baden | 24 | R | W |
| Bullay | Moselle | 39 | | W | | | | | |
| Bullenheim | Franconia | 26·5 | | W | | | | | |

ate 34. (*Above*) Kaub, in the Middle Rhine. (*Below*) The Lorelei Rock.

| Community | District | Area (hectares) | Red | White | Community | District | Area (hectares) | Red | White |
|---|---|---|---|---|---|---|---|---|---|
| Diesbar | Saxony | 3·6 | | W | Ellmendingen | Baden | 90 | | W |
| Dietersheim | Rhinehessia | 10 | R | W | Elpersheim | Württemberg | 12 | R | W |
| Dietlingen | Baden | 90 | R | W | Elsenz | Baden | 11 | | W |
| Dilmar | Moselle | 3·83 | | W | Elsheim | Rhinehessia | 102·8 | R | W |
| Dingolshausen | Franconia | 6·5 | | W | Eltville | Rheingau | 165·5 | | W |
| Dintersheim | Rhinehessia | 5 | | W | Endersbach | Remsthal, Württemberg | 49 | R | W |
| Dirmstein | Palatinate | 200 | R | W | | | | | |
| Dittelsheim | Rhinehessia | 149 | R | W | Endingen | Baden | 178 | R | W |
| Dittwar | Franconia | 5 | | W | Engehöll | Middle Rhine | 100 | | W |
| Dolgesheim | Rhinehessia | 41·9 | R | W | Engelstadt | Rhinehessia | 49 | R | W |
| Dörnbach | Nahe | 3 | R | W | Engental | Franconia | 6 | | W |
| Dorn– | | | | | Enkirch | Moselle | 184 | | W |
| Dürkheim | Rhinehessia | 66·6 | R | W | Ensch | Saar–Ruwer | 50 | | W |
| Dörrenbach | Palatinate | 110 | R | W | Ensheim | Rhinehessia | 100 | R | W |
| Dörscheid | Middle Rhine | 17 | R | W | Enzberg | Württemberg | 6·8 | R | W |
| Dorsheim | Nahe | 75 | R | W | Eppelsheim | Rhinehessia | 18 | R | W |
| Dörzbach | Württemberg | 12 | R | W | Erbach | Rheingau | 160 | | W |
| Dossenheim | Baden | 22 | R | W | Erbes– | | | | |
| Dottingen | Baden | 25 | | W | Büdesheim | Rhinehessia | 23·8 | | W |
| Dromersheim | Rhinehessia | 140 | R | W | Erden | Moselle | 65 | | W |
| Duchroth | Palatinate | 112 | | W | Erlabrunn | Franconia | 36·9 | | W |
| Dudenhofen | Palatinate | 105 | | W | Erlenbach | Franconia | | | |
| Durbach | Baden | 170 | R | W | | (Marktheiden- | | | |
| Dürrenzimmern | Württemberg | 70 | R | W | | feld) | 18·8 | | W |
| Duttweiler | Palatinate | 101 | R | W | Erlenbach | Franconia | | | |
| Ebelsbach | Franconia | 1·7 | | W | | (Obernburg) | 3·4 | R | W |
| Ebernburg | Nahe | 65 | R | W | Erlenbach | Württemberg | 275 | R | W |
| Ebersheim | Rhinehessia | 72 | R | W | Erligheim | Württemberg | 42 | R | |
| Eberstadt | Württemberg | 113 | R | W | Ernsbach | Württemberg | 8 | R | W |
| Ebringen | Baden | 110 | | W | Ernst | Moselle | 130 | | W |
| Eckelsheim | Rhinehessia | 62 | | W | Erpel | Middle Rhine | 5·5 | R | W |
| Eckenroth | Nahe | 10 | | W | Erpolzheim | Palatinate | 96 | R | W |
| Edenkoben | Palatinate | 450 | | W | Ersingen | Baden | 50·5 | | W |
| Edesheim | Palatinate | 315 | R | W | Eschbach | Baden | 17 | | W |
| Ediger | Moselle | 108 | | W | Eschbach | Palatinate | 100 | | W |
| Efringen– | | | | | Eschelbach | Württemberg | 34 | R | W |
| Kirchen | Baden | 40 | | W | Eschenau | Württemberg | 47 | R | W |
| Ehrenbreitstein | Middle Rhine | 15 | | W | Escherndorf | Franconia | 78·1 | | W |
| Ehrenstetten | Baden | 70 | R | W | Esselborn | Rhinehessia | 1·8 | | W |
| Eibelstadt | Franconia | 41·5 | R | W | Essenheim | Rhinehessia | 74 | R | W |
| Eibensbach | Württemberg | 18 | R | W | Essingen | Palatinate | 138 | R | W |
| Eichelberg | Baden | 20 | | W | Esslingen | Württemberg | 100 | R | W |
| Eichelberg | Württemberg | 39 | R | W | Ettenheim | Baden | 20 | R | W |
| Eichenbühl | Franconia | 1·9 | R | W | Eussenheim | Franconia | 6 | | W |
| Eichstetten | Baden | 100 | R | W | Fachbach | Middle Rhine | 9 | | W |
| Eimeldingen | Baden | 15·8 | | W | Fahr | Franconia | 25·4 | | W |
| Eimsheim | Rhinehessia | 51·2 | R | W | Fankel | Moselle | 52 | | W |
| Einselthum | Palatinate | 32·5 | R | W | Fastrau | Saar–Ruwer | 26 | | W |
| Eisental | Baden | 70 | R | W | Feil–Bingert | Nahe | 73 | | W |
| Eisingen | Baden | 34 | R | W | Feldberg | Baden | 22 | | W |
| Eitelsbach | Saar–Ruwer | 22 | | W | Fell | Saar–Ruwer | 55 | | W |
| Elfershausen | Franconia | 20 | | W | Fellbach | Württemberg | 178 | R | W |
| Ellenz– | | | | | Fellerich | Saar | 22 | | W |
| Poltersdorf | Moselle | 110 | | W | Fessenbach | Baden | 26 | R | W |
| Eller | Moselle | 65 | | W | Feuerthal | Franconia | 5 | | W |
| Ellerstadt | Palatinate | 130 | R | W | Filzen | Moselle | 56 | | W |
| Ellhofen | Württemberg | 25 | R | W | Filzen | Saar | 25 | | W |

| Community | District | Area (hectares) | Red | White |
|---|---|---|---|---|
| Fischingen | Baden | 46 | | W |
| Flein | Württemberg | 150 | R | W |
| Flemlingen | Palatinate | 107 | | W |
| Flomborn | Rhinehessia | 25 | R | W |
| Flonheim | Rhinehessia | 122 | R | W |
| Flörsheim | Rheingau | 3 | | W |
| Föhrental | Baden | 3·8 | R | W |
| Forchtenberg | Württemberg | 20 | R | W |
| Forst | Palatinate | 206 | R | W |
| Framersheim | Rhinehessia | 17 | R | W |
| Frankfurt-am-Main–Seckbach | Rheingau | 1·5 | | W |
| Frankweiler | Palatinate | 147 | R | W |
| Franzenheim | Saar | 13 | | W |
| Frauenzimmern | Württemberg | 21·6 | R | W |
| Freckenfeld | Palatinate | 10·5 | R | W |
| Freiburg/Breisgau | Baden | 84 | R | W |
| Freilaubersheim | Rhinehessia | 40 | | W |
| Freimersheim | Palatinate | 40 | R | W |
| Freinsheim | Palatinate | 245 | R | W |
| Freisbach | Palatinate | 4·7 | | W |
| Frettenheim | Rhinehessia | 17 | R | W |
| Freudenstein | Württemberg | 25 | R | W |
| Freyburg | Saale | 30 | R | W |
| Frickenhausen | Franconia | 49·8 | R | W |
| Friedelsheim | Palatinate | 150 | R | W |
| Friesenheim | Baden | 3·4 | | W |
| Friesenheim | Rhinehessia | 33·4 | R | W |
| Fuchsstadt | Franconia | 4 | | W |
| Fürfeld | Rhinehessia | 30 | | W |
| Fussgönheim | Palatinate | 14·5 | R | W |
| Gabsheim | Rhinehessia | 26 | | W |
| Gaienhofen | Lake Constance | 3 | R | W |
| Gau-Algesheim | Rhinehessia | 150 | R | W |
| Gau-Bickelheim | Rhinehessia | 100 | R | W |
| Gau-Bischofsheim | Rhinehessia | 60 | R | W |
| Gau-Grehweiler | Palatinate | 4·6 | | W |
| Gau-Heppenheim | Rhinehessia | 48 | | W |
| Gaulsheim | Rhinehessia | 4 | R | W |
| Gau-Odernheim | Rhinehessia | 110 | R | W |
| Gau-Weinheim | Rhinehessia | 65 | R | W |
| Geddelsbach | Württemberg | 30 | R | W |
| Geinsheim | Palatinate | 32·5 | R | W |
| Geisenheim | Rheingau | 81·3 | | W |
| Gellmersbach | Württemberg | 40 | R | W |
| Gemmrigheim | Württemberg | 41 | R | W |
| Gengenbach | Baden | 7 | R | W |
| Genheim | Nahe | 16 | | W |
| Gensingen | Rhinehessia | 41·4 | R | W |
| Gerbach | Palatinate | 6 | R | W |
| Gerbrunn | Franconia | 6 | | W |
| Gerlachsheim | Franconia | 9 | | W |
| Gerlingen | Württemberg | 10 | R | |

| Community | District | Area (hectares) | Red | White |
|---|---|---|---|---|
| Gerolsheim | Palatinate | 53 | R | W |
| Gerolzhofen | Franconia | 11·11 | | W |
| Gimbsheim | Rhinehessia | 32·8 | R | W |
| Gimmeldingen | Palatinate | 160 | R | W |
| Gleisweiler | Palatinate | 84 | R | W |
| Gleiszellen–Gleishorbach | Palatinate | 58 | R | W |
| Gochsen | Württemberg | 3·8 | R | W |
| Göcklingen | Palatinate | 150 | R | W |
| Godramstein | Palatinate | 220 | R | W |
| Golgenstein–Heidesheim | Palatinate | 7·8 | R | W |
| Golk | Saxony | 3·7 | R | W |
| Gönnheim | Palatinate | 112 | R | W |
| Goseck | Saale | 2 | | |
| Gossmannsdorf | Franconia | 11 | R | W |
| Gottenheim | Baden | 29 | R | W |
| Graach | Moselle | 134 | | W |
| Gräfenhausen | Palatinate | 14·5 | R | W |
| Gräfenhausen | Württemberg | 14·5 | R | |
| Grantschen | Württemberg | 50 | R | W |
| Grenzach | Baden | 17·5 | R | W |
| Grewenich | Moselle | 4 | | W |
| Grolsheim | Rhinehessia | 40 | R | W |
| Gronau | Hessische Bergstrasse | 4·9 | | W |
| Gronau | Württemberg | 10 | R | W |
| Grossbockenheim | Palatinate | 135 | R | W |
| Grossbottwar | Württemberg | 130 | R | W |
| Grossfischlingen | Palatinate | 36 | R | W |
| Grossgartach | Württemberg | 59 | R | W |
| Grossheppach | Württemberg | 61 | R | W |
| Grossheubach | Franconia | 29·9 | R | W |
| Grosskarlbach | Palatinate | 112 | R | W |
| Grosslangheim | Franconia | 35·4 | | W |
| Grossneidesheim | Palatinate | 25 | R | W |
| Grossostheim | Franconia | 16 | R | W |
| Gross-Sachsen | Badische Bergstrasse | 6 | R | W |
| Gross-Umstadt | Hessische Bergstrasse | 20 | | W |
| Grosswallstadt | Franconia | 5 | R | W |
| Gross-Winternheim | Rhinehessia | 95·3 | R | W |
| Grunbach | Württemberg | 53 | R | W |
| Grunnern | Baden | 26 | | W |
| Grünstadt | Palatinate | 36 | R | W |
| Güglingen | Württemberg | 40·50 | R | W |
| Güls | Moselle | 24 | | W |
| Gumbsheim | Rhinehessia | 50 | R | W |
| Gündelbach | Württemberg | 35 | R | W |
| Gundelfingen | Baden | 3·6 | | W |
| Gundelsheim | Württemberg | 42 | R | W |
| Gundersheim | Rhinehessia | 112 | R | W |
| Gundheim | Rhinehessia | 75 | R | W |
| Guntersblum | Rhinehessia | 250 | R | W |

| Community | District | Area (hectares) | Red | White | Community | District | Area (hectares) | Red | White |
|---|---|---|---|---|---|---|---|---|---|
| Güntersleben | Franconia | 5·4 | R | W | Herxheim am Berg | Palatinate | 156 | | W |
| Gutenberg | Nahe | 110 | | W | Hessheim | Palatinate | 9 | | W |
| Haagen | Baden | 2·8 | | W | Hessigheim | Württemberg | 112 | R | W |
| Haardt | Palatinate | 150 | R | W | Hessloch | Rhinehessia | 109·6 | R | W |
| Haberschlacht | Württemberg | 38 | R | W | Hetzerath | Moselle | 6 | | W |
| Hackenheim | Rhinehessia | 91·9 | R | W | Heuchelheim/ Bergzabern | Palatinate | 78 | R | W |
| Häfnerhaslach | Württemberg | 17 | R | W | Heuchelheim/ Frankenthal | Palatinate | 23 | R | W |
| Hagnau | Lake Constance | 48 | R | W | Heuholz | Württemberg | 42 | R | W |
| Hahnheim | Rhinehessia | 65 | R | W | Heuweiler | Baden | 4 | R | W |
| Hainfeld | Palatinate | 203 | R | W | Hillesheim | Rhinehessia | 68 | R | W |
| Hallgarten | Rheingau | 250 | | W | Hilsbach | Baden | 14 | R | W |
| Haltingen | Baden | 26 | | W | Himmelstadt | Franconia | 12 | | W |
| Hambach | Hessische Bergstrasse | 16 | | W | Hirzenach | Middle Rhine | 18 | | W |
| Hambach | Palatinate | 356 | R | W | Höchberg | Franconia | 1·2 | R | W |
| Hammelburg | Franconia | 43·2 | | W | Hochheim | Rheingau | 205 | R | W |
| Hammerstein | Middle Rhine | 42 | R | W | Hochstätten | Nahe | 40 | | W |
| Hangen– Weisheim | Rhinehessia | 25 | R | W | Hockweiler | Moselle | 4 | | W |
| Hanweiler | Württemberg | 15 | R | W | Hof unter Lembach | Württemberg | 30 | R | W |
| Hargesheim | Nahe | 43 | | W | Hoheim | Franconia | 2 | | W |
| Harsberg | Württemberg | 42 | R | W | Hohen–Sülzen | Rhinehessia | 80 | R | W |
| Harxheim | Palatinate | 37 | R | W | Hohenfeld | Franconia | 4·4 | | W |
| Harxheim | Rhinehessia | 60 | R | W | Hohenhaslach | Württemberg | 130 | R | |
| Haslach | Baden | 8·3 | | W | Hohenstein | Württemberg | 25 | R | W |
| Hattenheim | Rheingau | 200 | R | W | Homburg | Franconia | 17·7 | | W |
| Hatzenport | Moselle | 46 | | W | Honnef | Middle Rhine | 8·9 | R | W |
| Hechtsheim | Rhinehessia | 23 | R | W | Hönningen | Middle Rhine | 14 | R | W |
| Hecklingen | Baden | 30 | | W | Höpfigheim | Württemberg | 35 | R | W |
| Heddesheim | Nahe | 224 | R | W | Horkheim | Württemberg | 17 | R | W |
| Heidelberg– Handschusheim | Baden | 9·8 | R | W | Horn | Lake Constance | 3·9 | R | W |
| Heidelberg– Rohrbach | Baden | 39 | R | W | Horrheim | Württemberg | 100 | R | W |
| Heidelsheim | Baden | 15 | R | W | Horrweiler | Rhinehessia | 80·8 | R | W |
| Heidesheim | Rhinehessia | 16·4 | R | W | Hörstein | Franconia | 25 | R | W |
| Heilbronn | Württemberg | 441 | R | W | Hösslinsülz | Württemberg | 40 | R | W |
| Heiligenstein | Palatinate | 18·6 | | W | Hüffelsheim | Nahe | 27 | | W |
| Heiligenzell | Baden | 3 | R | W | Hügelheim | Baden | 34 | | W |
| Heimbach | Baden | 7 | | W | Hugsweier | Baden | 8·5 | R | W |
| Heimersheim | Ahr | 70 | R | W | Hüllenberg | Middle Rhine | 9 | | W |
| Heimersheim | Rhinehessia | 55·5 | R | W | Humprechtsau | Franconia | 3 | | W |
| Heinsheim | Baden | 6 | | W | Hupperath | Moselle | 4·5 | | W |
| Helfant | Moselle | 20 | | W | Hüttenheim | Franconia | 22·3 | | W |
| Hemsbach | Badische Bergstrasse | 16 | R | W | Ibersheim | Rhinehessia | 17 | | W |
| Heppenheim | Hessische Bergstrasse | 48 | R | W | Ickelheim | Franconia | 3·5 | | W |
| Heppenheim | Rhinehessia | 37·5 | R | W | Iffigheim | Franconia | 1 | | W |
| Herbolzheim | Baden | 40 | R | W | Igel | Moselle | 9 | | W |
| Hergenfeld | Nahe | 20 | | W | Ihringen | Baden | 300 | | W |
| Hergolshausen | Franconia | 3 | | W | Ilbesheim | Palatinate | 177 | R | W |
| Herten | Baden | 5·2 | R | W | Illingen | Württemberg | 20 | R | W |
| Hertingen | Baden | 14 | | W | Ilsfeld | Württemberg | 30·5 | R | W |
| Hertmanns- weiler | Württemberg | 4·5 | R | W | Immenstaad | Baden | 4·5 | | W |
| | | | | | Impfingen | Franconia | 1·25 | | W |
| | | | | | Impflingen | Palatinate | 48 | R | W |
| | | | | | Ingelfingen | Württemberg | 50 | R | W |
| | | | | | Ingelheim | Rhinehessia | 365 | R | W |

| Community | District | Area (hectares) | Wine produced Red | Wine produced White | Community | District | Area (hectares) | Wine produced Red | Wine produced White |
|---|---|---|---|---|---|---|---|---|---|
| Ingenheim | Palatinate | 48·1 | R | W | Klein–Umstadt | Hessische | | | |
| Ingolstadt | Franconia | 3·6 | | W | | Bergstrasse | 6·7 | | W |
| Insheim | Palatinate | 29 | R | W | Kleinbocken- | | | | |
| Iphofen | Franconia | 124 | | W | heim | Palatinate | 125 | R | W |
| Ippesheim | Franconia | 21·5 | | W | Kleinbottwar | Württemberg | 37 | R | W |
| Ippesheim | Rhinehessia | 16·5 | R | W | Kleingartach | Württemberg | 54 | R | W |
| Irsch–Saarburg | Moselle | 66 | | W | Kleinheppach | Württemberg | 38 | R | W |
| Irsch–Trier | Moselle | 12 | | W | Kleinkarlbach | Palatinate | 100 | R | W |
| Istein | Baden | 22 | | W | Kleinkems | Baden | 11 | | W |
| Jagsthausen | Württemberg | 7·5 | R | W | Kleinniedes- | | | | |
| Jechtingen | Baden | 35 | R | W | heim | Palatinate | 28 | R | W |
| Jeckenbach | Nahe | 4·5 | | W | Kleinochsenfurt | Franconia | 9·3 | | W |
| Johannisberg | Rheingau | 132·5 | R | W | Kleinwallstadt | Franconia | 7 | | W |
| Jugenheim | Rhinehessia | 118 | R | W | Klein– | | | | |
| Kaimt | Moselle | 42 | | W | Winternheim | Rhinehessia | 11·2 | R | W |
| Kalkofen | Nahe | 6 | | W | Klepsau | Baden | 7·8 | | W |
| Kallstadt | Palatinate | 320 | R | W | Klingen | Palatinate | 46 | R | W |
| Kamp | Middle Rhine | 25 | R | W | Klingenberg am | | | | |
| Kanzem | Moselle | 60 | | W | Main | Franconia | 15·3 | R | W |
| Kappelrodeck | Baden | 65 | R | W | Klingenberg | Württemberg | 8·5 | R | W |
| Kappishäusern | Württemberg | 5 | | W | Klingenmünster | Palatinate | 79 | R | W |
| Kapsweyer | Palatinate | 9 | R | W | Klotten | Moselle | 85 | | W |
| Karlstadt | Franconia | 15·1 | | W | Klüsserath | Moselle | 160 | | W |
| Karweiler | Ahr | 12 | R | W | Knittelsheim | Palatinate | 8 | R | W |
| Kasbach | Middle Rhine | 11 | R | W | Knittlingen | Württemberg | 40 | R | W |
| Kasel | Moselle | 71 | | W | Knöringen | Palatinate | 78 | | W |
| Kattenes | Moselle | 11 | | W | Kobern | Moselle | 40 | | W |
| Katzenbach | Palatinate | 14 | | W | Koblenz | Middle Rhine | 29 | | W |
| Kaub | Middle Rhine | 95 | | W | Kocherstetten | Württemberg | 1·1 | | W |
| Kenn | Moselle | 23 | | W | Kohlberg | Württemberg | 5·6 | | W |
| Kenzingen | Baden | 25 | R | W | Köhler | Franconia | 19·9 | | W |
| Kerzenheim | Palatinate | 2 | | W | Köllig | Moselle | 24 | | W |
| Kesselfeld | Württemberg | 10 | R | W | Kommlingen | Moselle | 40 | | W |
| Kesten | Moselle | 60 | | W | Köndringen | Baden | 25 | | W |
| Kestert | Middle Rhine | 13 | | W | Könen | Moselle | 20 | | W |
| Kettenheim | Rhinehessia | 19 | | W | Köngernheim | Rhinehessia | 29·3 | | W |
| Kiechlins- | | | | | Königheim | Franconia | 14 | | W |
| bergen | Baden | 40 | R | W | Königsbach | Palatinate | 135 | R | W |
| Kiedrich | Rheingau | 113 | R | W | Königschaff- | | | | |
| Kindenheim | Palatinate | 100 | R | W | hausen | Baden | 45 | R | W |
| Kinheim | Moselle | 102 | | W | Königshofen | Baden | 21 | R | W |
| Kippenhausen | Lake Constance | 3·5 | | W | Königshofen | Franconia | 12 | | W |
| Kippenheim | Baden | 30 | R | W | Königswinter | Middle Rhine | 20 | R | W |
| Kippenheim- | | | | | Konstanz | Lake Constance | 9·2 | R | W |
| weiler | Baden | 3 | | W | Konz–Karthaus | Moselle | 65 | | W |
| Kirchberg a.d. | | | | | Korb– | | | | |
| Murr | Württemberg | 4·5 | R | W | Steinreinach | Württemberg | 90 | R | W |
| Kirchheim a.d. | | | | | Kövenich | Moselle | 21 | | W |
| Eck | Palatinate | 105 | R | W | Köwerich | Moselle | 26 | | W |
| Kirchheim a.d. | | | | | Krassolzheim | Franconia | 4 | | W |
| Neckar | Württemberg | 60 | R | W | Krautsostheim | Franconia | 2 | | W |
| Kirchheim- | | | | | Krebsweiler | Nahe | 4 | | W |
| bolanden | Palatinate | 17 | R | W | Kressbronn | Lake Constance | 11 | R | W |
| Kirchhofen | Baden | 100 | | W | Krettnach | Moselle | 63 | | W |
| Kirrweiler | Palatinate | 400 | R | W | Kreuzberg | Ahr | 6 | R | W |
| Kirschroth | Nahe | 24 | | W | Kreuzweiler | Moselle | 5·6 | | W |
| Kitzingen | Franconia | 23 | | W | Kreuzwertheim | Franconia | 1·5 | | W |

378

APPENDIX ONE

| Community | District | Area (hectares) | Red | White |
|---|---|---|---|---|
| Kriegsheim | Rhinehessia | 38·4 | R | W |
| Kröv | Moselle | 200 | | W |
| Krutweiler | Moselle | 9 | | W |
| Künzelsau | Württemberg | 3 | | W |
| Lachen–Speyerdorf | Palatinate | 80 | R | W |
| Lahr | Baden | 20 | R | W |
| Laibach | Württemberg | 1 | | W |
| Lambsheim | Palatinate | 31 | R | W |
| Landau | Palatinate | 36 | R | W |
| Landshausen | Baden | 11 | | W |
| Langen-beutingen | Württemberg | 10·5 | R | W |
| Langenbrücken | Baden | 21 | | W |
| Langenlonsheim | Nahe | 250 | | W |
| Langscheid | Middle Rhine | 11 | | W |
| Langsur | Moselle | 14 | | W |
| Laubenheim | Nahe | 130 | R | W |
| Laubenheim | Rhinehessia | 150 | R | W |
| Lauda | Franconia | 9·5 | R | W |
| Laudenbach | Badische Bergstrasse | 13 | R | W |
| Laudenbach | Franconia | 2·64 | R | W |
| Laudenbach | Württemberg | 43 | R | W |
| Lauf | Baden | 3·5 | | W |
| Laufen | Baden | 75 | | W |
| Lauffen | Württemberg | 226 | R | W |
| Laumersheim | Palatinate | 70 | R | W |
| Lautenbach | Baden | 11 | R | W |
| Lauterecken | Palatinate | 10 | R | W |
| Lay | Moselle | 21 | | W |
| Lehmen | Moselle | 33 | | W |
| Lehrensteinsfeld | Württemberg | 102 | R | W |
| Leimen | Badische Bergstrasse | 35·7 | R | W |
| Leinsweiler | Palatinate | 82 | R | W |
| Leiselheim | Baden | 20 | | W |
| Leistadt | Palatinate | 190 | R | W |
| Leiwen | Moselle | 226 | | W |
| Lengfurt | Franconia | 7 | R | W |
| Leonbronn | Württemberg | 4·5 | R | W |
| Lettweiler | Palatinate | 29 | | W |
| Leutershausen | Badische Bergstrasse | 12 | R | W |
| Leutesdorf | Middle Rhine | 115 | R | W |
| Liel | Baden | 43 | | W |
| Lienzingen | Württemberg | 7·5 | R | W |
| Liersberg | Moselle | 17 | | W |
| Lieser | Moselle | 110 | | W |
| Lindelbach | Franconia | 1·7 | | W |
| Linz | Middle Rhine | 6 | R | W |
| Lipburg | Baden | 5 | | W |
| Lippoldsweiler | Württemberg | 3 | R | W |
| Löchgau | Württemberg | 35 | R | W |
| Löf | Moselle | 12 | | W |
| Löffelstelzen | Württemberg | 7 | R | W |
| Lohnweiler | Palatinate | 4 | | W |
| Longen | Moselle | 7 | | W |
| Longuich | Moselle | 44 | | W |
| Longuich–Kirch | Moselle | 28·7 | | W |
| Lonsheim | Rhinehessia | 48·3 | R | W |
| Lorch | Rheingau | 235 | R | W |
| Lorchhausen | Rheingau | 68 | R | W |
| Lörrach | Baden | 12 | | W |
| Lörzweiler | Rhinehessia | 81 | R | W |
| Lösnich | Moselle | 36 | | W |
| Löwenstein mit Reizach und Rittelhof | Württemberg | 130 | R | W |
| Ludwigsberg | Württemberg | 17 | R | W |
| Ludwigshöhe | Rhinehessia | 51·3 | | W |
| Lützelsachsen | Badische Bergstrasse | 4 | R | W |
| Machtilshausen | Franconia | 12 | | W |
| Mahlberg | Baden | 14 | R | W |
| Maienfels | Württemberg | 15 | | W |
| Maikammer | Palatinate | 645 | R | W |
| Mailheim | Franconia | 7 | R | W |
| Mainberg | Franconia | 15·9 | | W |
| Mainstockheim | Franconia | 36·3 | | W |
| Mainz | Rhinehessia | 1·4 | | W |
| Mainz–Kostheim | Rheingau | 89 | R | W |
| Mainz–Weisenau | Rhinehessia | 6·8 | R | W |
| Malsch | Badische Bergstrasse | 50 | R | W |
| Malschenberg | Baden | 33 | R | W |
| Malterdingen | Baden | 50 | | W |
| Mandel | Nahe | 100 | | W |
| Mannweiler | Nahe | 15·3 | | W |
| Manubach | Middle Rhine | 65 | | W |
| Mappach | Baden | 7 | | W |
| Marbach | Franconia | 6 | | W |
| Marbach | Württemberg | 10 | R | W |
| Maring–Noviand | Moselle | 113 | | W |
| Markdorf | Lake Constance | 5·7 | R | W |
| Markelsheim | Württemberg | 85 | | W |
| Markgröningen | Württemberg | 46 | R | W |
| Markt–Einersheim | Franconia | 16·5 | | W |
| Marktbreit | Franconia | 19·3 | | W |
| Marksteft | Franconia | 4·6 | R | W |
| Martinstein | Nahe | 4 | | W |
| Martinsthal | Rheingau | 53 | | W |
| Massenheim | Rheingau | 7·4 | | W |
| Mauchen | Baden | 34 | R | W |
| Mauchenheim | Palatinate | 30 | R | W |
| Maulbronn | Württemberg | 22·2 | R | W |
| Mayschoss | Ahr | 116 | R | W |
| Mechtersheim | Palatinate | 16·8 | R | W |
| Meckenheim | Palatinate | 90 | R | W |
| Medard | Nahe | 5 | R | W |

| Community | District | Area (hectares) | Red | White | Community | District | Area (hectares) | Red | White |
|---|---|---|---|---|---|---|---|---|---|
| Meddersheim | Nahe | 70 | | W | Murr | Württemberg | 12 | R | W |
| Meersburg | Lake Constance | 46 | R | W | Mussbach | Palatinate | 382 | R | W |
| Mehring | Moselle | 114 | | W | Nack | Rhinehessia | 8 | | W |
| Meimsheim | Württemberg | 36 | R | W | Nackenheim | Rhinehessia | 70 | R | W |
| Meisenheim | Nahe | 34 | | W | Nassau | Lahn | 20 | R | W |
| Meissen | Saxony | 27 | R | W | Neckarmühl- | Badisches | | | |
| Merbitz | Saxony | 1 | R | W | bach | Neckargebiet | 4·3 | R | W |
| Merdingen | Baden | 80 | R | W | Neckarsulm | Württemberg | 131 | R | W |
| Merl | Moselle | 135 | | W | Neckar- | | | | |
| Mertesdorf | Moselle | 53 | | W | weihingen | Württemberg | 11 | R | W |
| Mertesheim | Palatinate | 10 | R | W | Neckarzimmern | Badisches | | | |
| Merxheim | Nahe | 35 | | W | | Neckargebiet | 9 | R | W |
| Merzhausen | Baden | 5·5 | | W | Neef | Moselle | 90 | | W |
| Merzweiler | Nahe | 1·5 | | W | Nehren | Moselle | 7·5 | | W |
| Mesenich | Moselle | 61 | | W | Neipperg | Württemberg | 72 | R | W |
| Mesenich– | | | | | Nennig | Moselle | 36 | | W |
| Untermosel | Moselle | 19 | | W | Nenzenheim | Franconia | 13 | | W |
| Mettenheim | Rhinehessia | 122·6 | R | W | Nerzweiler | Palatinate | 2 | R | W |
| Metzdorf | Moselle | 8 | | W | Nesselried | Baden | 16 | R | W |
| Metzingen | Württemberg | 30 | R | W | Neu–Bamberg | Rhinehessia | 28 | | W |
| Michelbach | Franconia | 15 | | W | Neuershausen | Baden | 4·4 | R | W |
| Michelbach | Württemberg | 9 | R | W | Neuffen | Württemberg | 27 | | W |
| Michelfeld | Baden | 7·4 | R | W | Neuhausen | Württemberg | 36 | R | W |
| Miltenberg | Franconia | 3·6 | | W | Neuleiningen | Palatinate | 47 | R | W |
| Minheim | Moselle | 71 | | W | Neumagen | Moselle | 105 | | W |
| Mittelheim | Rheingau | 120 | | W | Neusatz | Baden | 7 | R | W |
| Möckmühl | Württemberg | 11·6 | R | W | Neuses | Franconia | 28·6 | R | W |
| Möglingen | Württemberg | 2·5 | R | W | Neusetz | Franconia | 4·5 | | W |
| Mölsheim | Rhinehessia | 64 | R | W | Neustadt an der | | | | |
| Mommenheim | Rhinehessia | 92·2 | R | W | Weinstrasse | Palatinate | 207 | R | W |
| Monsheim | Rhinehessia | 46·5 | R | W | Neustadt | Württemberg | 16 | R | W |
| Monzernheim | Rhinehessia | 84 | R | W | Neuweier | Baden | 140 | R | W |
| Monzingen | Nahe | 125 | | W | Niebelsbach | Württemberg | 8·5 | R | |
| Morsbach | Württemberg | 1·4 | | W | Niederberg | Middle Rhine | 15 | | W |
| Morschheim | Palatinate | 7 | | W | Niederbrechen | Lahn | 1·1 | R | W |
| Mörsfeld | Palatinate | 5 | | W | Niederburg | Middle Rhine | 24·1 | | W |
| Mörstadt | Rhinehessia | 18·2 | R | W | Niederdollen- | | | | |
| Mörzheim | Palatinate | 117 | R | W | dorf | Middle Rhine | 10 | R | W |
| Moselkern | Moselle | 42 | | W | Niedereisenbach | Nahe | 8·1 | | W |
| Müden | Moselle | 66 | | W | Niederemmel | Moselle | 105 | R | W |
| Mühlacker | Württemberg | 4 | R | W | Niederfell | Moselle | 20 | | W |
| Mühlbach | Baden | 20 | R | W | Nieder– | | | | |
| Mühlhausen | Baden | 38 | R | W | Flörsheim | Rhinehessia | 145 | R | W |
| Mühlheim an | | | | | Niederhausen | Nahe | 118 | R | W |
| der Eis | Palatinate | 38 | R | W | Niederhausen | Palatinate | 23 | | W |
| Mülheim | Moselle | 52 | | W | Niederheimbach | Middle Rhine | 30 | | W |
| Müllheim | Baden | 125 | | W | Nieder– | | | | |
| Münchweier | Baden | 8 | | W | Hilbersheim | Rhinehessia | 32·6 | R | W |
| Mundelsheim | Württemberg | 135 | R | W | Niederhochstadt | Palatinate | 68 | R | W |
| Mundingen | Baden | 6·3 | R | W | Niederhofen | Württemberg | 3·5 | R | W |
| Münster | Württemberg | 8·5 | R | W | Niederhorbach | Palatinate | 45 | R | W |
| Münsterappel | Palatinate | 14 | | W | Niederkirchen | Palatinate | 160 | R | W |
| Münster bei | | | | | Niederlustadt | Palatinate | 4·5 | | W |
| Bingerbrück | Nahe | 210 | R | W | Niedermennig | Moselle | 45 | | W |
| Münster– | | | | | Niedermoschel | Palatinate | 26 | | W |
| Sarmsheim | Nahe | 210 | R | W | Niederhall | Württemberg | 24 | R | W |
| Munzingen | Baden | 96 | R | W | Nieder-Olm | Rhinehessia | 37·8 | R | W |

| Community | District | Area (hectares) | Red | White |
|---|---|---|---|---|
| Niederrimbach | Württemberg | 3·4 | R | W |
| Niederrimsingen | Baden | 16 | R | W |
| Nieder–Saulheim | Rhinehessia | 160 | R | W |
| Nieder-schopfheim | Baden | 19·4 | | W |
| Niederstetten | Württemberg | 50 | R | W |
| Niederwalluf | Rheingau | 35 | R | W |
| Nieder–Wiesen | Rhinehessia | 1 | R | W |
| Niefernheim | Palatinate | 38·5 | R | W |
| Nierstein | Rhinehessia | 600 | | W |
| Nittel | Moselle | 170 | | W |
| Nochern | Middle Rhine | 22 | | W |
| Nonnenhorn | Lake Constance | 6·8 | | W |
| Nordhausen | Württemberg | 324 | R | W |
| Nordheim | Franconia | 129 | | W |
| Nordheim | Württemberg | 150 | R | W |
| Nordweil | Baden | 30 | R | W |
| Norheim | Nahe | 56 | | W |
| Nussbaum | Nahe | 13·5 | | W |
| Nussdorf | Palatinate | 208 | R | W |
| Oberachern | Baden | 10 | R | W |
| Oberbillig | Moselle | 66 | | W |
| Oberderdingen | Württemberg | 90 | R | W |
| Oberdiebach mit Winzberg und Rheindie-bach | Middle Rhine | 110 | R | W |
| Oberdollendorf | Middle Rhine | 12·5 | R | W |
| Oberdürrbach | Franconia | 1·1 | R | W |
| Obereggenen | Baden | 176 | | W |
| Obereisenheim | Franconia | 30·9 | | W |
| Oberemmel | Moselle | 120 | | W |
| Oberfell | Moselle | 30 | | W |
| Ober–Flörsheim | Rhinehessia | 27·6 | R | W |
| Oberglottertal | Baden | 2 | R | W |
| Obergriesheim | Württemberg | 4 | R | W |
| Obergrombach | Baden | 30 | R | W |
| Oberhausen | Palatinate | 23·5 | R | W |
| Oberheimbach | Middle Rhine | 95 | R | W |
| Oberhochstadt | Palatinate | 35 | R | W |
| Oberkirch | Baden | 36 | R | W |
| Oberlahnstein | Middle Rhine | 25 | | W |
| Oberlauda | Franconia | 4·8 | | W |
| Oberleinach | Franconia | 18·5 | | W |
| Oberlustadt | Palatinate | 13 | R | W |
| Obermoschel | Palatinate | 37 | | W |
| Obernbreit | Franconia | 4 | | W |
| Oberndorf | Palatinate | 22 | | W |
| Obernhof | Lahn | 10 | R | W |
| Ober–Olm | Rhinehessia | 30 | R | W |
| Oberrotterbach | Palatinate | 56 | | W |
| Oberrotweil | Baden | 100 | R | W |
| Obersasbach | Baden | 6 | R | W |
| Ober–Saulheim | Rhinehessia | 45·7 | R | W |
| Oberschopfheim | Baden | 42 | | W |
| Oberschüpf | Franconia | 5·7 | R | W |
| Ober-schwarzach | Franconia | 10 | | W |
| Oberspay | Middle Rhine | 100 | | W |
| Oberstenfeld mit Weingut Lichtenberg | Württemberg | 100 | R | W |
| Oberstetten | Württemberg | 12 | R | W |
| Oberstreit | Nahe | 7 | | W |
| Obersülzen | Palatinate | 17 | R | W |
| Obervolkach | Franconia | 12·3 | | W |
| Oberwalluf | Rheingau | 15 | R | W |
| Oberweier | Baden | 7 | R | W |
| Oberweiler im Tal | Palatinate | 2 | R | W |
| Oberwesel | Middle Rhine | 110 | R | W |
| Obrigheim | Palatinate | 31 | R | W |
| Ochsenbach | Württemberg | 38 | R | W |
| Ochsenfurt | Franconia | 1·8 | | W |
| Ockenfels | Middle Rhine | 4 | R | W |
| Ockenheim | Rhinehessia | 150 | R | W |
| Ockfen | Moselle | 90 | | W |
| Odenbach | Palatinate | 6 | R | W |
| Odernheim | Nahe | 70 | | W |
| Ödheim | Württemberg | 43 | R | W |
| Offenau | Württemberg | 4 | R | W |
| Offenbach–Glan | Nahe | 30 | | W |
| Offenbach am Queich | Palatinate | 17 | R | W |
| Offenheim | Rhinehessia | 19·6 | R | W |
| Offstein | Rhinehessia | 26·2 | R | W |
| Ohlsbach | Baden | 7 | R | W |
| Öhningen | Lake Constance | 7 | R | W |
| Ölbronn | Württemberg | 10 | R | W |
| Olnhausen | Württemberg | 2·5 | R | W |
| Onsdorf | Moselle | 18 | | W |
| Oppenheim | Rhinehessia | 282·2 | | W |
| Ortenberg | Baden | 70 | R | W |
| Osann | Moselle | 100 | | W |
| Osthofen | Rhinehessia | 208 | R | W |
| Östrich | Rheingau | 271 | | W |
| Östringen | Baden | 40 | R | W |
| Ötisheim | Württemberg | 32 | R | W |
| Ötlingen | Baden | 14 | | W |
| Ottersheim | Palatinate | 17 | R | W |
| Owen | Württemberg | 4·5 | | W |
| Palzem | Moselle | 31 | | W |
| Partenheim | Rhinehessia | 81 | R | W |
| Patersberg | Middle Rhine | 12 | R | W |
| Pellingen | Moselle | 25 | | W |
| Perl | Moselle | 16 | | W |
| Perl–Oberhof Sehndorf | Moselle | 53 | | W |
| Perscheid | Middle Rhine | 23 | | W |
| Pfaffenhausen | Franconia | 2 | | W |
| Pfaffenhofen | Württemberg | 53 | R | W |

| Community | District | Area (hectares) | Red | White | Community | District | Area (hectares) | Red | White |
|---|---|---|---|---|---|---|---|---|---|
| Pfaffen–Schwabenheim | Rhinehessia | 72·7 | R | W | Riet | Württemberg | 5 | R | W |
| | | | | | Rietenau | Württemberg | 5 | R | W |
| Pfaffenweiler | Baden | 87 | | W | Ringelbach | Baden | 7·5 | R | W |
| Pfeddersheim | Rhinehessia | 60 | R | W | Riol | Moselle | 16 | | W |
| Pfedelbach | Württemberg | 11·30 | R | W | Rivenich | Moselle | 40 | | W |
| Pferdsfeld | Nahe | 2 | | W | Riveris | Moselle | 6 | | W |
| Pfullingen | Württemberg | 1·2 | R | W | Rockenhausen | Palatinate | 28 | | W |
| Piesport | Moselle | 62 | | W | Rödelsee | Franconia | 47·5 | | W |
| Planig | Rhinehessia | 75 | R | W | Röllfeld | Franconia | 1·9 | R | W |
| Platten | Moselle | 23 | | W | Rommelshausen | Württemberg | 12 | R | W |
| Pleidesheim | Württemberg | 4 | R | W | Rommersheim | Rhinehessia | 24·5 | R | W |
| Pleisweiler–Oberhofen | Palatinate | 71 | R | W | Roschbach | Palatinate | 97·5 | | W |
| Pleitersheim | Rhinehessia | 15 | | W | Rosswag | Württemberg | 35 | R | W |
| Pluwig | Moselle | 3·5 | | W | Rotenberg | Baden | 22 | R | W |
| Pölich | Moselle | 54 | | W | Röttingen | Franconia | 10 | | W |
| Pommern | Moselle | 75 | | W | Roxheim | Nahe | 84 | | W |
| Poppenweiler | Württemberg | 85 | R | W | Rück | Franconia | 5 | | W |
| Prappach | Franconia | 3 | | W | Rüdesheim–Eibingen | Rheingau | 89 | | W |
| Proschwitz | Saxony | 5 | R | W | Rüdesheim–Nahe | Nahe | 25 | | W |
| Pünderich | Moselle | 84 | | W | Rüdesheim–Rheingau | Rheingau | 271 | | W |
| Radebeul | Saxony | 9·5 | | W | Rüdisbronn | Franconia | 3·2 | | W |
| Ralingen | Moselle | 6 | | W | Rümmelsheim | Nahe | 95 | R | W |
| Rammersweier | Baden | 24 | R | W | Ruppertsberg | Palatinate | 174 | | W |
| Ramsthal | Franconia | 24 | | W | Ruwer | Moselle | 18 | | W |
| Ramsweiler | Palatinate | 2·5 | R | W | Saarburg mit Beurig und Niederleuken | Moselle | 92 | | W |
| Randersacker | Franconia | 158·7 | R | W | Sachsenflur | Franconia | 3·2 | | W |
| Ranschbach | Palatinate | 97 | R | W | St Goar | Middle Rhine | 12 | | W |
| Rappach | Württemberg | 11·5 | R | W | St Goarhausen | Middle Rhine | 24·4 | | W |
| Rauenberg | Baden | 120 | R | W | St Johann | Rhinehessia | 85 | R | W |
| Rauenthal | Rheingau | 86 | | W | St Katharinen | Nahe | 17 | | W |
| Raumbach | Nahe | 30 | | W | St Martin | Palatinate | 292 | R | W |
| Rech | Ahr | 68 | R | W | Sasbach | Baden | 19 | R | W |
| Rechtenbach | Palatinate | 70 | R | W | Sasbachwalden | Baden | 17·8 | R | W |
| Rehborn | Palatinate | 26 | | W | Sausenheim | Palatinate | 132 | R | W |
| Rehlingen | Moselle | 38 | | W | Schallbach | Baden | 3·1 | | W |
| Reichenau | Lake Constance | 10 | R | W | Schallstadt | Baden | 42 | | W |
| Reichenbach | Baden | 7 | R | W | Schelingen | Baden | 6·5 | R | W |
| Reichholzheim | Franconia | 4 | | W | Scheppach | Württemberg | 10 | R | W |
| Reil | Moselle | 170 | | W | Scherzingen | Baden | 24 | | W |
| Remagen | Middle Rhine | 3 | R | W | Schimsheim | Rhinehessia | 31 | R | W |
| Remlingen | Franconia | 2·2 | | W | Schlatt | Baden | 5 | | W |
| Repperndorf | Franconia | 10 | | W | Schleich | Moselle | 18 | | W |
| Rettigheim | Badische Bergstrasse | 12·5 | | W | Schliengen | Baden | 50 | | W |
| Retzbach | Franconia | 7·5 | | W | Schloss Böckelheim | Nahe | 60 | | W |
| Retzstadt | Franconia | 23·3 | R | W | Schloss Saaleck | Franconia | 25 | | W |
| Reusch | Franconia | 2 | | W | Schluchten | Württemberg | 16·5 | R | W |
| Reutlingen | Württemberg | 10 | R | W | Schmidhausen | Württemberg | 30 | R | W |
| Rheinbreitbach | Middle Rhine | 1·8 | R | W | Schmieheim | Baden | 5·3 | R | W |
| Rheinbrohl | Middle Rhine | 33 | R | W | Schmittweiler | Palatinate | 4 | | W |
| Rhens | Middle Rhine | 24 | | W | Schnait | Württemberg | 130 | R | W |
| Rhodt unter Rietburg | Palatinate | 270 | R | W | Schoden | Moselle | 50 | | W |
| Riedlingen | Baden | 6·5 | | W | | | | | |
| Rielingshausen | Württemberg | 10 | R | W | | | | | |

| Community | District | Area (hectares) | Red | White |
|---|---|---|---|---|
| Schöneberg | Nahe | 20 | | W |
| Schonungen | Franconia | 4·8 | | W |
| Schorndorf | Württemberg | 8 | R | W |
| Schornsheim | Rhinehessia | 44·4 | | W |
| Schozach | Württemberg | 23 | R | W |
| Schriesheim | Badische Bergstrasse | 7 | | W |
| Schuttern | Baden | 3 | | W |
| Schützingen | Württemberg | 16·8 | R | W |
| Schwabbach | Württemberg | 18 | | W |
| Schwabenheim | Rhinehessia | 125 | R | W |
| Schwabsburg | Rhinehessia | 98 | R | W |
| Schwaigern | Württemberg | 90 | R | W |
| Schwegenheim | Palatinate | 15 | R | W |
| Schweich | Moselle | 65 | | W |
| Schweigen | Palatinate | 28 | R | W |
| Schweigern | Franconia | 28 | | W |
| Schweighofen | Palatinate | 8 | | W |
| Schweinfurt | Franconia | 8·5 | R | W |
| Schweppenheim | Nahe | 57 | | W |
| Seefelden | Baden | 45 | | W |
| Segnitz | Franconia | 16 | | W |
| Sehndorf | Moselle | 2·5 | | W |
| Seinsheim | Franconia | 23 | | W |
| Selzen | Rhinehessia | 105·2 | | W |
| Senheim | Moselle | 75 | | W |
| Serrig | Moselle | 100 | | W |
| Sexau | Baden | 5 | R | W |
| Sickershausen | Franconia | 8 | | W |
| Siebeldingen | Palatinate | 145 | R | W |
| Siebeneich | Württemberg | 20 | R | W |
| Siefersheim | Rhinehessia | 50 | R | W |
| Siglingen | Württemberg | 18 | R | W |
| Simmern | Nahe | 1·5 | | W |
| Sinzheim | Baden | 65 | R | W |
| Sitters | Palatinate | 3 | | W |
| Sobernheim | Nahe | 25 | | W |
| Sölden | Baden | 5·5 | | W |
| Söllingen | Baden | 4 | | W |
| Sommerach | Franconia | 69·6 | | W |
| Sommerau | Moselle | 5 | | W |
| Sommerhausen | Franconia | 18·9 | | W |
| Sommerloch | Nahe | 40 | | W |
| Sörgenloch | Rhinehessia | 15 | R | W |
| Sörnewitz | Saxony | 30 | R | W |
| Spielberg | Württemberg | 13 | R | W |
| Spiesheim | Rhinehessia | 90 | R | W |
| Sponheim | Nahe | 40 | | W |
| Sprendlingen | Rhinehessia | 150 | R | W |
| Stadecken | Rhinehessia | 75 | R | W |
| Stadelhofen | Baden | 7 | R | W |
| Stammheim | Franconia | 15·5 | | W |
| Staudernheim | Nahe | 12 | | W |
| Staufen | Baden | 45 | R | W |
| Steeg | Middle Rhine | 85 | R | W |
| Stein am Kocher | Badisches Neckargebiet | 7 | | W |
| Steinbach | Baden | 65 | R | W |
| Steinbach | Württemberg | 4 | R | W |
| Stein-Bockenheim | Rhinehessia | 23·8 | | W |
| Steinheim a.d. Murr | Württemberg | 14 | R | W |
| Steinweiler | Palatinate | 16·5 | R | W |
| Sternenfels | Württemberg | 25 | R | W |
| Stetten | Franconia | 21 | | W |
| Stetten | Württemberg | 90 | R | W |
| Stockheim | Württemberg | 57 | R | W |
| Stromberg | Nahe | 3 | | W |
| Strümpfelbach | Württemberg | 70 | R | W |
| Stuttgart | Württemberg | 332·5 | R | W |
| Sulz | Baden | 10·5 | R | W |
| Sülzbach | Württemberg | 23·5 | R | W |
| Sulzburg | Baden | 3 | | W |
| Sulzfeld | Baden | 40 | R | W |
| Sulzfeld | Franconia | 65 | | W |
| Sulzheim | Rhinehessia | 62 | R | W |
| Sulztal | Franconia | 9·1 | R | W |
| Tairnbach | Badische Bergstrasse | 12 | R | W |
| Talheim | Württemberg | 80 | R | W |
| Tamm | Württemberg | 15 | R | W |
| Tannenkirch | Baden | 20 | | W |
| Tarforst | Moselle | 15 | | W |
| Tauberbischofsheim | Franconia | 5·6 | | W |
| Tauberrettersheim | Franconia | 15·2 | | W |
| Tauberzell | Franconia | 2·3 | | W |
| Tawern | Moselle | 13 | | W |
| Temmels | Moselle | 46 | | W |
| Theilheim | Franconia | 2 | | W |
| Thörnich | Moselle | 35 | | W |
| Thüngen | Franconia | 1·3 | | W |
| Thüngersheim | Franconia | 97·4 | R | W |
| Tiefenbach | Baden | 48 | R | W |
| Tiefenthal | Rhinehessia | 6 | R | W |
| Tiengen | Baden | 15 | | W |
| Tiergarten | Baden | 30 | R | W |
| Traben-Trarbach | Moselle | 180 | | W |
| Traisen | Nahe | 34 | | W |
| Trechtingshausen | Middle Rhine | 38 | | W |
| Treis | Moselle | 83 | | W |
| Trier | Moselle | 130 | | W |
| Trimberg | Franconia | 10 | | W |
| Trittenheim | Moselle | 137 | | W |
| Tübingen | Württemberg | 3 | R | W |
| Tutschfelden | Baden | 35 | | W |
| Überlingen | Lake Constance | 6 | R | W |
| Ubstadt | Baden | 19 | | W |
| Udenheim | Rhinehessia | 90 | | W |
| Uffhofen | Rhinehessia | 53 | R | W |

| Community | District | Area (hectares) | Red | White | Community | District | Area (hectares) | Red | White |
|---|---|---|---|---|---|---|---|---|---|
| Ulm | Baden | 10 | R | W | Wasserliesch–Reinig | Moselle | 22 | | W |
| Ülversheim | Rhinehessia | 98·5 | | W | Wawern | Moselle | 29 | | W |
| Undenheim | Rhinehessia | 30 | | W | Wehlen | Moselle | 104 | | W |
| Ungstein | Palatinate | 269 | R | W | Wehr | Moselle | 18 | | W |
| Unkel | Middle Rhine | 26 | R | W | Weigenheim | Franconia | 9 | | W |
| Unkenbach | Palatinate | 13·5 | | W | Weikersheim | Württemberg | 18 | R | W |
| Unterdürrbach | Franconia | 10·9 | R | W | Weil am Rhein | Baden | 28 | R | W |
| Untereisenheim | Franconia | 27·2 | | W | Weiler | Lake Constance | 2·7 | R | W |
| Untereisesheim | Württemberg | 2·7 | R | W | Weiler bei Bingerbrück | Nahe | 26 | R | W |
| Unterglottertal | Baden | 13 | R | W | Weiler bei Monzingen | Nahe | 62 | | W |
| Untergriesheim | Württemberg | 1·5 | R | W | Weiler a.d. Zaber | Württemberg | 14 | R | W |
| Unter-grombach | Baden | 18 | R | W | Weilheim a.d. Teck | Württemberg | 5·5 | | W |
| Unterheimbach | Württemberg | 35 | R | W | Weinähr | Lahn | 10·5 | R | W |
| Unterjesingen | Württemberg | 20 | R | W | Weingarten | Palatinate | 20 | R | W |
| Unterleinach | Franconia | 19 | | W | Weinheim | Badische Bergstrasse | 10·3 | R | W |
| Unteröwisheim | Baden | 25 | R | W | Weinheim | Rhinehessia | 100 | | W |
| Unterriexingen | Württemberg | 10 | R | W | Weinolsheim | Rhinehessia | 65 | R | W |
| Untersteinbach | Württemberg | 4 | R | W | Weinsberg | Württemberg | 158 | R | W |
| Ürzig | Moselle | 50 | | W | Weinsheim | Nahe | 50 | | W |
| Vailhingen/Enz | Württemberg | 13 | R | W | Weisenheim am Berg | Palatinate | 183 | R | W |
| Vallendar | Middle Rhine | 8 | | W | Weisenheim am Sand | Palatinate | 313 | R | W |
| Valwig | Moselle | 77 | | W | Weissbach | Württemberg | 9 | | W |
| Varnhalt | Baden | 70 | | W | Welgesheim | Rhinehessia | 50 | R | W |
| Veitshöchheim | Franconia | 46·1 | R | W | Wellen | Moselle | 22 | | W |
| Veldenz | Moselle | 42 | | W | Wellmich | Middle Rhine | 17 | | W |
| Vendersheim | Rhinehessia | 58 | R | W | Welmlingen | Baden | 12 | | W |
| Venningen | Palatinate | 100 | R | W | Wendelsheim | Württemberg | 4 | R | W |
| Verrenberg | Württemberg | 25·4 | R | W | Werbach | Baden | 15 | | W |
| Vögisheim | Baden | 26 | | W | Werlau | Middle Rhine | 20 | | W |
| Volkach | Franconia | 34·6 | | W | Westheim | Franconia | 5 | | W |
| Vollmersweiler | Palatinate | 6 | | W | Westheim | Palatinate | 2 | | W |
| Volxheim | Rhinehessia | 90 | R | W | Westhofen | Rhinehessia | 300 | R | W |
| Vorbach-zimmern | Württemberg | 41 | R | W | Westum | Ahr | 10·2 | R | W |
| Wachenheim | Palatinate | 350 | R | W | Wettelbrunnen | Baden | 20 | | W |
| Wachenheim | Rhinehessia | 60 | R | W | Weyher | Palatinate | 137 | R | W |
| Wackernheim | Rhinehessia | 16 | R | W | Wicker | Rheingau | 27 | | W |
| Wagenstadt | Baden | 34 | R | W | Widdern | Württemberg | 40 | R | W |
| Wahlheim | Rhinehessia | 19·3 | | W | Wiesbaden | Rheingau | 4·5 | | W |
| Waldböckelheim | Nahe | 91 | | W | Wiesbaden–Dotzheim | Rheingau | 2 | | W |
| Waldenburg | Württemberg | 8·5 | R | W | Wiesbaden–Frauenstein | Rheingau | 35 | R | W |
| Waldhilbersheim | Nahe | 102·5 | R | W | Wiesbaden–Schierstein | Rheingau | 20 | | W |
| Waldlaubersheim | Nahe | 47 | | W | Wiesenbronn | Franconia | 42·6 | | W |
| Waldrach | Moselle | 74 | | W | Wiesloch | Badische Bergstrasse | 105·5 | R | W |
| Waldulm | Baden | 45 | R | W | Wies–Oppenheim | Rhinehessia | 19 | R | W |
| Wallburg | Baden | 2·2 | R | W | | | | | |
| Wallertheim | Rhinehessia | 88 | R | W | | | | | |
| Wallhausen | Nahe | 250 | | W | | | | | |
| Walporzheim | Ahr | 85 | R | W | | | | | |
| Walsheim | Palatinate | 146 | R | W | | | | | |
| Waltershofen | Baden | 11·5 | | W | | | | | |
| Wasenweiler | Baden | 60 | R | W | | | | | |

| Community | District | Area (hectares) | Wine produced Red | White |
|---|---|---|---|---|
| Willsbach | Württemberg | 74 | R | W |
| Wiltingen | Moselle | 168 | | W |
| Wincheringen | Moselle | 87 | | W |
| Windesheim | Nahe | 139 | R | W |
| Windischenbach | Württemberg | 21 | R | W |
| Winkel | Rheingau | 217 | R | W |
| Winnenden | Württemberg | 26 | R | W |
| Winningen | Moselle | 212 | | W |
| Winterbach | Württemberg | 1·1 | R | W |
| Winterborn | Palatinate | 7·5 | R | W |
| Winterhausen | Franconia | 14 | | W |
| Wintersheim | Rhinehessia | 6·8 | R | W |
| Wintersweiler | Baden | 17 | | W |
| Wintrich | Moselle | 100 | | W |
| Winzenheim | Nahe | 45 | R | W |
| Wipfeld | Franconia | 18 | | W |
| Wirmsthal | Franconia | 10 | | W |
| Wittlich | Moselle | 50 | | W |
| Wolf | Moselle | 43 | | W |
| Wolfenweiler | Baden | 70 | | W |
| Wolfsheim | Rhinehessia | 70 | R | W |
| Wolfstein | Palatinate | 5·2 | R | W |
| Wollbach | Baden | 13 | | W |
| Wollmesheim | Palatinate | 95 | R | W |
| Wöllstein | Rhinehessia | 80·9 | R | W |
| Wonsheim | Rhinehessia | 30·5 | R | W |
| Worms | Rhinehessia | 26 | R | W |

| Community | District | Area (hectares) | Wine produced Red | White |
|---|---|---|---|---|
| Worms–Herrnsheim | Rhinehessia | 39 | R | W |
| Worms–Horchheim | Rhinehessia | 21 | R | W |
| Worms–Leiselheim | Rhinehessia | 24 | R | W |
| Worms–Weinsheim | Rhinehessia | 5·8 | R | W |
| Wörrstadt | Rhinehessia | 75 | R | W |
| Wöschbach | Baden | 3 | | W |
| Würzburg | Franconia | 300 | R | W |
| Zaberfeld | Württemberg | 21 | R | W |
| Zaisersweiher | Württemberg | 15 | R | W |
| Zeil | Franconia | 4 | | W |
| Zell | Franconia | 10 | | W |
| Zell | Moselle | 212 | | W |
| Zell | Palatinate | 69 | R | W |
| Zell–Weierbach | Baden | 70 | R | W |
| Zeltingen–Rachtig | Moselle | 224 | | W |
| Zeutern | Baden | 25 | | W |
| Ziegelanger | Franconia | 9·5 | | W |
| Zornheim | Rhinehessia | 125 | R | W |
| Zotzenheim | Rhinehessia | 44·7 | R | W |
| Zunsweier | Baden | 27·6 | R | W |
| Zwingenberg | Hessische Bergstrasse | 10·1 | R | W |

# APPENDIX TWO

## Production of Wine

### 1938–65

| Year | Area under viticulture (hectares) | Crop Hectolitres per hectare | Total (hectolitres) | Year | Area under viticulture (hectares) | Crop Hectolitres per hectare | Total (hectolitres) |
|---|---|---|---|---|---|---|---|
| 1938 | 73,000 | 33·4 | 2,438,000 | 1959 | 60,995 | 70·5 | 4,302,000 |
| 1949 | 51,487 | 26·5 | 1,363,000 | 1960 | 64,180 | 115·8 | 7,433,000 |
| 1951 | 52,521 | 59·3 | 3,112,000 | 1961 | 66,265 | 53·9 | 3,574,000 |
| 1952 | 53,359 | 50·8 | 2,713,000 | 1962 | 67,137 | 59·5 | 3,993,000 |
| 1953 | 54,486 | 45·1 | 2,456,000 | 1963 | 68,354 | 88·3 | 6,034,147 |
| 1954 | 58,142 | 52·6 | 3,098,000 | 1964 | 68,123 | 104·7 | 7,185,349 |
| 1955 | 59,961 | 40·1 | 2,405,000 | 1965 | 68,816 | 73·2 | 5,035,000 |
| 1956 | 59,695 | 15·6 | 929,000 | | | | |
| 1957 | 58,743 | 38·5 | 2,264,000 | Average | | | |
| 1958 | 59,136 | 81·1 | 4,796,000 | 1959–64 | 65,927 | 82·1 | 5,409,634 |

# APPENDIX THREE

## *Vinification of Ice Wines*

The juice of a grape with 75° Öchsle will freeze at −3° to −4° Centigrade. The freezing process in the grape is as follows.

First of all, pure water contained in the grape is formed into ice crystals, with the result that the concentration of the extracts and the sugar, but also those of the fruit, and acidities, are made stronger. The result is that the Öchsle degree of the resulting must increases. It is noteworthy that the formation and concentration of the tartaric acid does not increase in the same proportion as the sugar concentration, because, as a result of the frost, the tartaric acid is precipitated in ice crystals, and therefore the tartaric acid content decreases. The greater the degree of frost, the more ice crystals are formed and the more concentrated the extract becomes. This process can go so far that, at the end, even the extract which remains can freeze. In other words, the frost can be so strong that, instead of a must rich in extract, it can turn the other way, and a too thin must can result.

One should try to make ice wine only at 5° Centigrade of frost, because when the grapes are gathered and brought into the pressing house the temperature of the must may increase sufficiently to prevent the making of ice wine altogether. In 1961 the temperature was −6·6° to −9° Centigrade when the grapes were gathered. The resulting grape-juice had a sugar content of approximately 25° Öchsle higher than the original. In 1962 the frost was so strong that some of the Öchsle degrees were doubled, so that the 1962 Spätlese ice wines have actually the fullness of Feine Auslese and Beerenauslese wines. It is interesting in this connection that, during the ice-wine days in November 1962 the frost was strong during the night, but very sunny weather prevailed during the day-time; if the grapes were not gathered before ten o'clock in the morning the temperature rose so much that it was impossible to make an ice wine, as the grapes started thawing long before they reached the pressing house.

It is, of course, difficult to bring must at this temperature to fermentation, and in 1962 it was necessary to use cultivated yeast, which was added to 5% of the ice wines, which had been brought to a moderate temperature, in order to start the fermentation, which usually lasted no less than 50 days.

The average original acid content of those observed was 15·8 promille, which, during fermentation, decreased to 13 promille, as tartaric acid was precipitated in cold casks.

*Famous Ice Wines*

1949 Wehlener Sonnenuhr Feinste Auslese 'Eiswein'
1949 Avelsbacher Thielslei 'Eiswein'
1950 Schloss Johannisberger Spätlese 'Eiswein'
1961 Kreuznacher Krötenpfuhl Riesling Feinste Spätlese 'Eiswein'
1961 Kreuznacher St Martin Riesling Feinste Spätlese 'Eiswein'
1961 Winkeler Hasensprung Riesling Auslese 'Eiswein'
1961 Serriger Saarsteiner Schlossberg Riesling Spätlese 'Eiswein'
1961 Trierer Kreuzberg Riesling 'Eiswein' Spätlese
1961 Serriger Schloss Saarfels Vogelsang Riesling Cabinet 'Eiswein'
1961 Ürziger Würzgarten Riesling Spätlese 'Eiswein'
1961 Deutschherrenköpfchen Riesling 'Eiswein' Spätlese
1961 Scharzhofberger Riesling Feine Auslese 'Eiswein'
1961 Berncasteler Badstube Spätlese 'Eiswein' Kabinett

1961 Scharzhofberger Riesling Feinste Auslese 'Eiswein'
1961 Eitelsbacher Karthäuserhofberg Riesling Feinste Auslese 'Eiswein'
1961 Berncasteler Badstube und Pfalzgraben Spätlese 'Eiswein' Kabinett
1961 Wehlener Sonnenuhr 'Eiswein' Auslese
1961 Wehlener-Zeltinger Sonnenuhr 'Eiswein' Auslese
1961 Scharzberger Riesling 'Eiswein' Spätlese
1961 Serriger Vogelsang Riesling 'Eiswein'
1961 Oberemmeler Scharzberg 'Eiswein' Edelwein
1962 Kreuznacher Narrenkappe Riesling Feinste Spätlese 'Nikolaus-Eiswein'
1962 Kaseler Nies'chen Feinste Spätlese 'Eiswein'
1962 Niersteiner Kehr Sylvester-Eiswein
1962 Kreuznacher Narrenkappe Riesling Hochfeine Spätlese 'Eiswein' Edelgewächs
1962 Bodenheimer St Alban Riesling 'Eiswein'
1962 Niersteiner Glöck Riesling St Barbara 'Eiswein'
1965 ice wines were in most cases a failure (grapes under 75° were just not ripe, the final
     concentrated must contained too much malic acid and too little unfermented sugar).
     Exceptions are:
     von Simmern 1965 Marcobrunner 'Eiswein'
     von Eltz Eltviller Tonnenberg 'Eiswein'
     Egon Müller Scharzhofberger Cabinet 'Eiswein' Edelwein (cask 33)
1966 produced a range of ice wines; the most outstanding are:
     Scherf's Waldracher Krone 'Eiswein' – the swan song of a 75 year old vineyard
     Eitelsbacher Karthäuserhofberg Kronenberg 'Eiswein' (cask 53)
     Serriger Vogelsang 'Eiswein' (cask 104)
     Scharzhofberger 'Eiswein' Edelwein (Egon Müller) (cask 25)
     Trierer Tiergarten unterm Kreuz Spätlese 'Eiswein' Edelwein
     Waldracher Krone Scherf's Mühle Auslese 'Eiswein' Edelwein

# The Wines of
# PORTUGAL

❧

## H. WARNER ALLEN

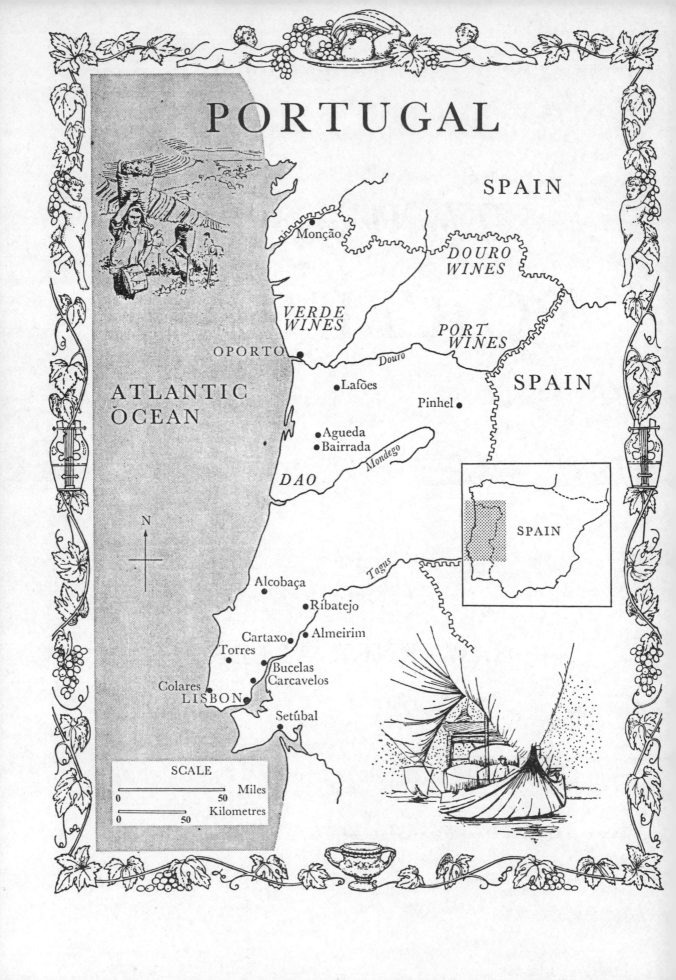

# PORTUGAL

SPAIN

Monção

*DOURO WINES*

*VERDE WINES*

*PORT WINES*

OPORTO

SPAIN

*Douro*

ATLANTIC OCEAN

Lafões

Pinhel

Agueda
Bairrada

*Mondego*

*DAO*

N

SPAIN

*Tagus*

Alcobaça

Ribatejo

Cartaxo

Almeirim

Torres

Bucelas
Carcavelos

Colares

LISBON

Setúbal

SCALE

0          50    Miles

0          50    Kilometres

# The Wine Wealth of Portugal

PORTUGAL, allowance being made for its size, produces a greater variety of wines than any other country in the world and is unique among wine-growing lands in its self-sufficiency. According to André Simon's *Concise Encyclopaedia of Gastronomy*, it imports only one gallon of wine for every thousand gallons it exports. Its shape, a long narrow stip of land, running three hundred miles due north and south with an average breadth of scarcely over a hundred miles, imposes a great diversity of climates. Its northern frontier lies well to the south of all French vineyards, and every Portuguese vine is subject to the dominion of the southern sun, which bestows on the wine pressed from its grapes an alcoholic strength and a fullness of body which more northern vineyards envy. Against this tendency to coarseness, an exceptional geographical environment, which makes for subtlety and delicacy of flavour, holds its own and has been reinforced by the intervention of a fuller scientific knowledge of the principles of fermentation.

Throughout Portugal the supremacy of the sun wrestles with two opponents, the ozone of the Atlantic and the more rarefied atmosphere of high mountains. The country is tightly enclosed on the west by the barrier of the ocean and on the east by the wall of mountains of the Spanish frontier. Not one Portuguese vineyard is entirely out of reach of this double influence, and the vine is as susceptible to atmospheric conditions as to the imponderable stimuli of the constituents of the soil in which it grows. Obdurate granite predominates as the basis of Portuguese vineyard soil, giving its wines a kinship with those of the Rhône, and its unyielding firmness of character brings most Portuguese wines into Virgil's category of *firmissima vina*, wines of thews and sinews, which can stand up against time and rough handling.

To these mainland wines, bearing the national stamp which distinguishes the people of one nation from that of another, must be added wines which, both in their growing and making, stand apart in a class of their own, unique beyond the possibility of plausible imitation: the wines of Madeira. They were the great dessert wines of the New World just when port became the Englishman's wine, and their renown, limited only by the area of their little island, would never have faded but for the ruthlessness of nature, which twice, once with oidium, then with phylloxera, wiped out its vineyards. Experience leagued with science has now restored the vineyards of Madeira, an island regarded by the Portuguese as an integral part of the homeland, and its wines are resuming the high place they held in wine-lovers' estimation.

In these conditions it is not surprising that there is no type of wine which is not grown in Portugal: wines to be drunk between or just before meals, wines to be drunk with or after them, all hall-marked with the national stamp. The British workman has to drink tea for what he calls his 'elevenses'. The French workman drinks a glass of country wine *pour tuer le ver*; the Portuguese, using a similar metaphor, a *mata-bicho*, to help him through the morning.

More is asked of the wine drunk immediately before a meal, since it is intended to stimulate appetite and prepare the palate. Of the appetizers Portugal offers, dry Carcavelos is an exceptional wine, too rare to leave its home; Sercial Madeira claims to rank in the eyes of the connoisseur as an acceptable rival of dry sherry; dry white port has made its bow since the last war as a pre-prandial drink. Dry white port now takes its place beside sherry in the Oporto Factory House, and it goes best before a meal accompanied by Portuguese table wines, looking forward to the final valediction of its red brother. Even the lightest tawny port is too self-assertive to play the *apéritif*, and vintage port quite impossible. If the French often drink the great Portuguese after-dinner wine before a meal – a fashion to be compared with what I hope is now the passing craze for drinking Scotch whisky at the same unsuitable moment – it emphasizes the remarkable expansion of Portuguese wines during recent years into countries where they were unknown. 'What's in a name?' In spite of Shakespeare a great deal. The 'Porto' which the French once drank was an insipid, synthetic imitation, compounded in the Midi expressly as an *apéritif*, with nothing in common with the Douro wine except the name. When I lived in Paris there was only one wine-shop where one could be sure that an order for a glass of port would be answered by a glass of true Douro wine: Sandeman's Bodega in the rue des Pyramides, that morsel of Britain in France which was so English that Huysmans's hero in *À Rebours* felt that a couple of glasses drunk there had so transported him to the England of Dickens that he was excused from the inconvenience of a Channel crossing. The ill wind of war has blown at least one good. International agreements between wine-growing countries have protected the birthright of wines to the name of their birthplace and 'Porto' has been given in other countries than Britain its proper significance as wine shipped over the bar of Oporto. Doubtless time will assign to it everywhere its proper position in the procession of wines. A similar story is to be told of 'Madère', that equally fraudulent product of the Midi, which in days gone by Parisian ladies drank for their afternoon *goûter*. It was conceivably pardonable in *sauce madère*, but who could say more than that its suppression by the 'five-o'clock' fashion of tea marked an advance in civilization?

At the turn of the eighteenth and nineteenth centuries dessert wines, wines fortified with brandy to be drunk at the end of a meal, established Portugal in the front rank of countries famous for really great wines. Almost simultaneously port in Britain, Madeira in America, attained such a reputation as no wines had enjoyed since the fall of the Roman Empire, and, as the reader will learn, the discovery of the cylindrical port bottle and its value for the maturing of fine wine marks a cardinal date in the history of the fermented juice of the grape. During the last century and a half the history of port has passed through many vicissitudes, though the Douro wine has been spared the knock-out blows suffered by Madeira. Its inherent excellence has in Britain always triumphed over trade difficulties and fashion. The exigencies of the Second World War and consequent austerity struck a heavy blow at the port trade; its cumulating recovery in the British Isles and the extension of its markets to countries where port was little known bear witness both to the vitality of the wine and the efficiency of the organization which controls its growth, making and export, the Instituto do Vinho do Porto.

Madeira, the only fortified wine which has ever challenged the supremacy of port as a dessert wine, has had to pass through a long period of darkness owing to the plagues of nature, but it has risen phoenix-like from its ashes. From those ashes – the wonderful wines grown before the plagues descended, with such foresight stored and treasured – the wines of the new vineyards have been able to absorb into the blends of the solera system the magic touch which only old age can give, a virtue concentrated by time into an essence which with little more than a few drops pervades a whole blend. The system by which wines of different vintages and characters were blended into a wine of constant quality through many decades, the solera, was introduced into Spanish Jerez at some early unknown date and found its way into Madeira at the end of the eighteenth century, flourishing alongside the vintage wines, which had no admixture of wine of other years.

Under the heading of dessert wines, a word should be said of the great Moscatel wine, the Moscatel of Setúbal, which is an incomparable expression of the delicious flavour of the Muscat grape. Unfortunately it is a wine that must always be rare.

In the last two decades a new factor has affected the world status of the wines of Portugal, the emergence of natural table wines challenging in their own right their better known competitors in quality and price. It can, I think, be fairly said that before 1950 Portuguese table wines were practically unknown outside their own country and dominions. The political campaign after 1688 to force British wine-drinkers to drink the table wines of our ally Portugal, although as then made they were quite unequal to the competition, instead of the Gascon wines to which they had been accustomed for centuries, led surprisingly enough to the discovery of port, but that discovery for the time being extinguished the market for Portuguese natural wines in Britain. Not till recently was science able to control the fermentation of the Douro wines to make them palatable as table wines. Its arrest by the action of wine spirit turned them into port. After the Peninsular War there was a certain demand for some of the Lisbon wines which Wellington's veterans had drunk on campaign, but it did not survive competition. Today between 140 and 150 varieties of Portuguese table wines, red, white and pink (rosé) are being imported into Britain, and their export is spreading out all over the world.

This new chapter in the history of Portuguese wine coincides with a new chapter in the history of Portugal, which opens with the assumption of power by the son of a modest wine-grower in the Dão, Antonio de Oliveira Salazar, whose name will go down to history with those of the most famous rulers of this little country, a world power long before Britannia even thought of ruling the seas. He has waged a battle against poverty in a country with few natural resources and from the very first directed his efforts at developing Portugal's chief potential source of wealth, the wine export trade. I remember how the Oporto Shippers welcomed his coming into power. It is no exaggeration to say that at that time the only stable institution in the country was the Port Wine Export Trade. As soon as Dr Salazar became Premier in 1932 he established a carefully designed organization, with the Instituto do Vinho do Porto at its head, to protect the growers, favour and control the exporters, and guarantee the quality of port throughout the world.

Years of patience and perseverance had to pass before a similar system could be established to include all the wines of the country which did not enjoy the traditional advantages of port and Madeira. The Portuguese are a conservative nation. Slowly with the respect for tradition, local custom and prejudice which inspires Dr Salazar's policy, the Junta Nacional do Vinho, the National Wine Commission, with its Guild of Exporters, has been absorbing in its organization all the wine-districts of Portugal. Once the great bulk of the vast output of the Portuguese vineyards, other than port and Madeira, was destined so far as export was concerned to the fate of a mass-production blend, which thanks to the consistency of the Portuguese climate was available to relieve scarcity in wine-drinking countries with less trustworthy vintages. It played an important part in the French Army *pinard* of the First World War, and since then has often come to the rescue when the wines of France, even reinforced by those of Algeria, have failed to quench the thirst of that country for ordinary beverage wine.

The wines of Portugal can compete in price and quality with those of any other country, but it is no reservoir of very cheap, very ordinary wines, the treasure of the unscrupulous wine-faker, who can congratulate himself that Greece has had no Salazar to restore Greek wines to their classic fame. In modern Portugal state support and direction, with the encouragement of co-operation among the growers, has put at the disposal of the peasant small holders all the advantages which the progress of science can offer, without obscuring the vital reservation that wine is one thing under scientific analysis and quite another thing, far more important, to nose and palate, which are only concerned with the sensations which it produces. Today almost every Portuguese wine district worthy of the privilege has within its boundaries the material means of making the best of each local wine in accordance with up-to-date methods of vinification, and everywhere that wine is subject to the severe criticism of men who have spent all their lives in making wine from the grapes of those vineyards. Official encouragement is given to quality, to the production of each local wine at its very best, by what I take to be a leaf from the French system of *appellations contrôlées*, by the award of the title *designação de origem*, the exclusive right of local representation which the nobleman once arrogated to himself in his title.

The Portuguese classify their wines as *vinhos verdes* and *vinhos maduros*. The green wines might well return in England to the term of *eager*, since though they may be red, white or pink, they are never green. They are light and acidulous, to be drunk young, and *eager* really expresses better than green their zest and youthful lightness, for the green of the greenhorn is scarcely complimentary. Their home lies between the Minho and the Douro, the extreme north of Portugal, though wines of the same character, often illustrating a transitional phase, are to be found here and there south of the port river.

In the north the vine has to compete almost on equal terms with other crops, but in the far larger area south of the Douro the vineyards which yield the *vinhos maduros*, big, serious, full-bodied wines, the best of them by their nature capable of maturing to a fine old age, predominate with far less competition. The national system, as it was bound to do, mainly favours the production of excellent cheap table wines to be drunk young, but due attention is being bestowed by estate bottling, *garrafeira*, to vintage wines worthy of growing to a noble old age, thus promising to confer on Portuguese table wine the prestige given by vintage port to the dessert wine of the Douro.

Most Portuguese wine districts produce wines of all colours, red, white and *rosé*. Some, like Colares, outstanding for its exceptional history and quality, depend on red wine for their reputation. The white wine of Bucelas looks back to the vogue it had a hundred years ago as a wine specially adapted to the fish course. Of late there has been a rage for *rosé* wines. I have never been able to understand why English-speaking peoples do not call them pink. As Morton Shand points out in his *Book of French Wines*, these wines with rare exceptions are very much the same wherever they are grown owing to their 'almost standardized uniformity of taste'. Their redeeming virtue is 'their welcoming freshness'. 'Incomplete, unbalanced and immature' he calls them, liable to 'give rise to the aggressive thirst which accompanies a "mouth" or wakefulness at night'. There is no accounting for the fashionable craze for pink wines, but those anxious to be in the swim will acquire merit if they prefer the *rosé* wines of Portugal to all others. The process of fermentation which tones down the natural red or gold of a wine to a Laodicean shade of pink has something of the same effect on the distinctive flavour of the grape and that satisfying fullness of taste which is called body. The grapes of the Portuguese vineyards as a rule possess a depth of national flavour of their own and a persistent vinosity which counteract the tendency towards faintness of character and taste of the *vins rosés* without dulling their freshness. Some of them, the very popular Mateus and the Faisca of Setúbal, for example, add to these attractions the agreeable prickle of a slight secondary fermentation, present in many *vinhos verdes*, once so prized in a young Moselle or Vouvray, which makes them a very refreshing summer drink.

CHAPTER ONE

# The Wines of Portugal

## Fortified Wines

PORT, a wine shipped over the bar of Oporto, is grown in the Douro mountains some 50 miles upstream from Oporto within the boundaries of a legally defined area.

For port, fermentation is arrested by the action of wine spirit in order to retain in the wine the desired amount of grape sugar. The wine is made in the vineyard country and transferred to mature in the Wine Lodges of Vila Nova de Gaia, the transpontine suburb of Oporto.

VINTAGE PORT is declared by the shipping firms in a year when they consider that they have at their disposal wine of outstanding quality. They set aside a small fraction of these wines to be bottled, unblended with the wine of any other year. As a rule vintage port is a blend of the wine of several vineyards, but very occasionally it is the produce of a single *quinta*, as in the case of Offley's Boa Vista, Da Silva's Noval and, long ago, Taylor's Roeda. Bottling in Britain, whenever possible in close proximity to the place in which the wine would be drunk, was the secular rule, until the last war, when the shipping problem enforced bottling in Oporto. It was not without precedent, since some of the Oporto residents had regularly bottled the wines which had appealed to them. British port-lovers may still argue as to the nice distinctions between wine bottled in Britain and wine bottled in Oporto, just as they are not of the same mind as to whether vintage port should be bottled in its second or third year, but the admission of bottling in Oporto has helped to extend to the whole world the pleasures of vintage port, once the exclusive privilege of the British Isles.

Since vintage port should deposit its sediment in a crust clinging to the side of the bottle (the whitewash splash warning 'This side up with care') it needs careful handling both in the cellar and in the operation of decanting. If the obstinate cork of an old wine shows signs of crumbling round the corkscrew the neck of the bottle can be neatly removed with the aid of special tongs. These are heated red-hot to grip the neck of the bottle just below the flange until their glow dies down. Cold water is applied with a feather at the same place and the top of the neck will come away clean.

CRUSTED PORT, otherwise port of vintage character, if a step lower in rank, belongs to the aristocracy, since it also owes its maturity to the bottle. It must be called a happy afterthought, since it is a blend of fine wines of several years which have spent longer in the wood than true vintage port before they reach the bottle. Since wine ages far more quickly in the wood than in the bottle, their youth has been speeded up, and in the bottle they reach maturity more speedily than vintage port, after seven or eight years throwing a crust worthy of their name.

WOOD PORT. Glass and wood divide the fortified wine of the Douro into two distinct categories. The crusted port just discussed owes its maturity to the tutelage of the glass bottle, but wood port spends its whole life in the wood, the bottle being no more to it than transport from cask to wine-glass. On this wood port the prosperity of the port wine trade ultimately depends, for the fraction of wine which in the best of years receives the accolade of vintage port is very small.

As port matures in the wood, its colour changes, and it is on colour that the description of its types is based. Its colour moves naturally along the spectrum from the purple of extreme youth, in which blue blends with red, to pure red, which gives it the name of ruby, and from red to orange, where red blends with yellow to become tawny. Fashion inclines rather to tawny than ruby, and a ruby wine may be given a tawny hue by a mixture with white port without gaining or losing quality; but the real tawny which has gradually shed its red after many years is a wine that can hold up its head in the company of vintage port. The steady natural shift over the spectrum of wood port is subject to the irregularity caused by the periodical transfusion of younger wine.

White port differs from red port only by being pressed from white grapes instead of black. Those who are convinced that port at its best should be red may argue that the flavour of wine pressed from the black grape is not identical with that pressed from the white grape, but they have against them the makers of champagne who use grapes of both colours. Once, as a very sweet wine with fermentation checked very early, it was popular in Russia, where only extreme sweetness could compete with the alcoholic kick of vodka, but today it comes forward in quite a different guise, a wine with fermentation stopped so late that it makes an excellent dry *apéritif*.

MADEIRA is a wine unique in its origin, making and character. Madeira is the only wine which has ever seriously challenged the supremacy of port as the greatest of dessert wines. Just when port was establishing itself as the Englishman's wine *par excellence*, Madeira was making a triumphant entry into America to deserve the title of the Wine of the New World. The shipping magnates of Boston, Charleston, New York and Philadelphia vied with one another in their quest for the very best of the island wine, which grew more and more wonderful the longer its sea voyage, and George Washington is said to have honoured it by making it his favourite wine. The lonely little island, 'the Pearl of the Atlantic', with a climate favouring almost every crop, nearly despaired of the vine during the nineteenth century, when two plagues, oidium and phylloxera, destroyed its vineyards in quick succession. But they have been restored and replanted, and Madeira is resuming its due place among the great wines of the world. Its unequalled longevity, its unique quality which reconciles an ingratiating richness with a tonic austerity, derive not only from its soil and climate but from a special system of maturing, the 'stoving' of its wines in hot cellars.

Four varieties of vine have survived the catastrophe of the plagues, and they give their names to the four types of Madeira wine produced today, Sercial, Verdelho, Bual (Portuguese Boal) and Malmsey. Sercial, the palest wine, the driest of Madeiras, is at its best as an appetizer with the nuttiness of a fine *amontillado* and an austere depth of flavour which is the characteristic of all Madeiras and which gives them the versatility of sherry, a first rate drink at any time. Verdelho, a golden wine, is rather less austere, softer and rounder, a pleasant wine for every occasion, best of all, perhaps, between meals with a slice of the homonymous plain cake, devised as its accompaniment. Bual is essentially a dessert wine conspicuous for that strange pungent softness which is Madeira's peculiar charm. 'Its chief attraction', writes André Simon, 'is its perfect balance, the harmony between bouquet, fruit and body.' Finally, Malmsey the magnificent, which in the glory of old age can claim to be the very finest wine in the world. 'Luscious,' writes Croft-Cooke in his *Madeira*, 'fruity, heavily fragrant, round, aromatic, grand, full.' Malmsey deserves all these epithets, and to them I would add the virtue that it never cloys.

## The Table Wines and Districts of Portugal

The Portuguese have adopted a system similar to that of the French *appellations d'origine*, which gives approved wines a legal geographical status and accords them the right of *designação de origem*, the exclusive property of a name which guarantees their authenticity and corresponding quality. This classification is far from being complete, and many wines of high quality are still on the waiting list.

The main table wine districts may be grouped as follows under the headings of *vinhos verdes*, the light wines of the north, and the *vinhos maduros*, more serious wines and more fully-bodied.

*Vinhos verdes*: Monção, Basto, Braga. Also Lima, Amarante and Penafiel. Lafões, south of the official green wine region, yields wines of a similar character.

*Vinhos maduros*: The Douro, Dão, Colares and Bucelas.

Other regions which have not yet made their mark:

Pinhel, *vin rosé* with agreeable bouquet.

Agueda, transition type between light *vinhos verdes* from grapes grown high and fuller *vinhos maduros* from vines pruned low farther south.

Bairrada, good beverage wines and sparkling wines.

Alcobaça, good beverage wines (Obidos noted for white wine).

Ribatejo, good beverage wines (Almeirim and Cartaxo).

Torres Vedras, good beverage wines.

Setúbal with Periquita, excellent red wine and other table wines.

Lagõa, in Algarve, the extreme south, where a wine long ago popular in Flanders as Fuseta or Tavira wine is being revived.

CHAPTER TWO

# The Historical Glory of Vintage Port

PORTUGAL plays in the history of wine as important a part as Hamlet in Shakespeare's tragedy. Without Hamlet no tragedy, without Portugal no great vintage wines. Every wine lover discussing with his friends some fine old vintage wine from no matter where should remember that he owes the highest pleasure taste and smell can give to little Portugal which, strangely seconded by the little non-wine-growing country Britain, rescued from 'the dark backward and abysm of time', from the almost impenetrable curtain of a millennium and a half, a secret lost since the fall of the Roman Empire. In the British Isles this debt is recognized by the honoured tradition that the royal toast should always be drunk in port. The Hanoverians drank port, the wine of our ally; the Jacobites drank French wine, the wine of the enemy. Wherever fine wine is drunk by those who love it, each glass should carry with it the memory of such a debt to those who discovered vintage port as that acknowledged by the scholars of an ancient foundation of learning to their benefactor and founder. There are many connoisseurs, lovers of fine wine, in lands where the tradition of our royal toast does not prevail, and on them I would urge the raising of a glass, a silent toast of gratitude to Portugal, when they are drinking and discussing with their friends perhaps a great French or German wine, as the source and origin of all the pleasure they are experiencing.

Great vintage wines disappeared from the world after the fall of the Roman Empire, and fifteen centuries had to elapse before wine lovers were to enjoy again wine in its highest perfection. Not till the last years of the eighteenth century did the Portuguese growers, in alliance with the British shippers settled in Portugal, recover the long lost secret and show the world that fine wine could be matured in glass to just such a glorious old age as it had attained in the classical air-tight earthenware. How so simple a solution had evaded human intelligence for so long may seem a mystery, but it had to be thought of, and it was first thought of in Portugal. It is the old story of the egg of Columbus. He had to think of the possibility of the New World, just as he had to think of a simple expedient, unthought of by his detractors, before he could make an egg stand on one end in stable equilibrium. It is a great achievement to recover such a lost secret and be responsible for the birth throughout the world of a new Golden Age of Wine, a Renaissance of the classical ages, when wine, recognized as the hall-mark of civilization throughout the civilized world, could mature to the perfection of its full potentialities.

Plate 35. The Visitors' book at the Factory House, Oporto. The names are those of Captain Freemantle and the Earl of March, A.D.Cs. to the Marquis of Wellington; and the glass that was used by Queen Elizabeth II in 1957.

How was it that this revelation came from Portugal, a narrow strip of land between mountains and ocean, a land of the boundless Atlantic, not the Mediterranean, isolated from the Greek settlers who had brought the wine grape to Italy? How was it that the collaboration of Portuguese wine-growers with the people of an island, who had always loved wine but never been able to grow any worth mention, can have found the answer to a riddle which had so long defeated the rest of the world?

To my mind it belittles rather than glorifies the Portuguese achievement in these latter days to seek for its origin in some imaginary ascendency attained in viticulture in the classical days when Rome called Portugal Lusitania. Local patriotism, which provides the spectacles through which a wine country views its native wine, has suggested that Marcus Terentius Varro, the greatest scholar of his age, who fought on Pompey's side in the Iberian Peninsula in 49 B.C., sang the praises of the Lisbon wines, but my researches into his agricultural treatise *De Re Rustica*, the most likely source for such a reference, and into his other surviving works have failed to discover any authority for the statement. As for Lisbon, Olisipo, he seems to have said nothing about its wine, but he reports an 'incredible' though 'true' sensation from the hills above the Tagus. There mares are fertilized by the wind, like the hens which lay wind eggs, and give birth to foals, which never live more than three years. Lusitania is given credit for a sow of Gargantuan proportions, and Varro warns his reader against buying a farm in Hispania anywhere near the Lusitanian border, however good the land, for fear of brigands.

The late learned Dr Seltman, in his *Wine in the Ancient World*, makes no reference to Varro, but he writes: 'In the Hellenistic and Roman Republican age the famous wine from Lusitania – perhaps from the regions of Oporto – was astonishingly cheap, since ten gallons were sold for the equivalent of tenpence.' Since writing my *History of Wine*, in which I queried this statement, I have unearthed the authority on which it is based, five words in the 34th book of Polybius's *Universal History* (*c.* 150 B.C.). 'Wine one drachma the metretes' finds a place in a long list of foodstuffs and other commodities which impressed that much-travelled historian with the cheapness of living in Lusitania and its wonderful fertility. Wine was extremely cheap in Portugal, as it is today, but there is no reason to suppose that any of it was exported, for nowhere else is it mentioned in classical writers – not even in the exhaustive catalogue of classical wines we owe to the connoisseurs of Athenacus's *Banquet*.

From the end of the fourteenth to the middle of the seventeenth century a Portuguese dessert wine or two, one from the Algarve, the extreme south where wine-growing is now being revived, the other possibly from Setúbal, competed with the host of sweet wines from the Levant, but they left no enduring mark in the history of wine, precursors though they were of port. In those days no wine left Portugal with a claim to that title, since no wine of account was grown in the valley of the Douro until the century of the discovery which with vintage port opened a new epoch in that history. It was paradoxical that the wines of the Alto Douro made their indelible mark on history, not through their excellence, but through their natural shortcomings. The correction of their faults culminated in the resurrection of the great vintage wines forgotten since the classic days of Greece and Rome. Surely final accomplishment is the more glorious and praiseworthy when national genius overcomes all historical and physical disadvantages.

The Lusitanians were accepted by Augustus, that wise ruler, as an exceedingly

tough and original people when he established Lusitania as a separate province apart
from the great and prosperous province of Hispania, which had submitted far more
readily to the Roman lordship. History is the proof that the genius of the Lusitanians
and their Portuguese descendants was essentially the adventurous spirit of the pioneer.
Just as they led Europe in the exploration of the New World, so they took the lead in
the recovery of the lost secret of fine vintage wines. Doubtless it was only a minor mani-
festation of the Portuguese genius that the wine-growers of the Douro, stimulated by
the wine-drinkers of our distant island, should have introduced into the chronicle of
wine a reawakening from the slumber of many centuries, but it was in its humble way
an achievement parallel to the Renaissance in Medieval Europe of the classical tradition. For these reasons I deprecate the idea that Portugal should seek in its Roman
conquerors the source of its accomplishment. The Lusitanian spirit of enquiry and
experiment worked the miracle, not any lessons learnt from Rome.

The history of wine is almost as curious as that of human nature. I do not know
whether botanists have ever discovered a plant hardier and more capable of adapting
itself to conditions of soil and climate within the limits of its habitat than the vine. Mankind does not flourish on mountain peaks or at the poles, and the range of the vine is
even more restricted, but within that range its varieties almost challenge in number the
varieties of humanity. It absorbs from the sun and the soil a multiplicity of qualities
which give to its wine a distinctive character unique and never duplicated on the face
of the earth. Botanists have lately told us of a common weed gifted with the Midas gift
of seizing from the soil infinitesimal specks of gold so effectively that burnt in tons it
yields fine gold of great value, but all the gold in the world, including the flakes which
float in Danziger Goldwasser, has never given the senses such pleasure as the produce
of the vine. No one has ever been able to answer Omar Khayyam's doubt:

> *I often wonder what the Vintners buy*
> *One half so precious as the Stuff they sell.*

Within the limits imposed by climate, the vine flourishes best as far as concerns its wine
in soil of a grudging austerity which rebuffs other crops, and history shows how futile
it is to try to increase food supply by grubbing up vineyards and growing corn. Through
its deeply penetrating roots its grapes draw up and developed their special qualities.
No laws or treaties should be needed to safeguard for a wine the birthright of its home
name, which tradition has associated with its distinctive characteristics. A man's
nationality need not depend on his birthplace, but the nature of a wine depends on the
place in which it is born. Unhappily human greed is blind to reason and honesty and
often even to its own interest. The theft of the place names of famous wines to provide
false colours for wines which cannot possibly reproduce the qualities that made those
wines famous cannot be condoned. It is bad for the public whom it is intended to de-
ceive, bad for shippers and merchants, since the passing-off of paste for diamonds can
only prejudice their trade, bad for the grower, since he is encouraged to imitate a
model he cannot copy instead of concentrating on the development of the good qualities
inherent in the soil and climate of his native region. The protection of treaty rights, the
fruits of an alliance which has lasted six centuries, the oldest alliance in history, as well
as its distinctive character, have spared port the degradation of its name suffered by so
many other famous wines, and this privilege is a small return for the benefits conferred

on all wines by the emergence of vintage port. It is as impossible to make port from grapes outside the area prescribed and sanctioned by law, long years of experience and custom, as, to use a proverbial phrase, to make a silken purse out of a sow's ear; or as the Portuguese put it, *nunca de rabo de porco bom virote*, no good arrow from pig's tail.

The part played by nature is essential, but for the making of a good wine the hand of man is also needed. Wine can be made from the grapes of the wild vine, a wishy-washy beverage turning to vinegar if not promptly drunk. Such in Homer was the local wine of the Cyclops Polyphemus. In his island they neither tilled nor sowed nor pruned, but took what the gods gave them. Evidently Polyphemus did not think much of his wine, for he washed down with ewe's milk his first cannibal meal on two of Odysseus's comrades. The wine that the civilized Odysseus gave him was something very different, a wine pressed from the cultivated grape, aged as a wine should be, a Thracian wine from Ismarus, the birthplace of the wine god, and then as honoured by the wine-lover as the vineyards of the Upper Douro today. With that wine as different from the wines of the Cyclopes as cheese from chalk the man of many wiles made the one-eyed monster blind to the world, first metaphorically, then literally.

The story is particularly interesting, because it shows that Homer, some two and a half millennia ago, knew much more about wine than Brillat-Savarin, the French prince of gourmets, who died in 1826 just too early to profit in his country by the Portuguese discovery. If he had lived in Portugal or Britain he might have known vintage port, but the first vintage claret known in this island, where old vintage wines are more generally prized than across the channel, the 1815 vintage, cannot then have attained its zenith. Brillat-Savarin, poor·man, died believing that the palate found its highest joy in sweet liqueurs. The comet of 1811 did not give its name to port as it did to claret. Port had to wait for its comet year till 1854.

Symbolic statues of the wine god were regularly armed with the pruning knife, the implement which to the wine-grower is what the alphabet is to a child. The natural luxuriance of the vine has to be mercilessly disciplined if it is to yield wine worthy of the name. The pruning knife belongs to pre-history. In Homer it is taken for granted, the unpruned vine belonging to primitive barbarism. In the dim distant past of Italy, Numa Pompilius, the legendary second king of Rome, both king and priest, prompted perhaps by his wise Egeria, recognized its value when he ordained that only wine pressed from the grapes of the pruned vine might be offered to the gods. The priesthood has always been the guardian angel of wine.

Yet the loving chastisement of the plant to make it yield, not big clusters of fleshy watery fruit, but small, rather acid, grapes to be transmuted by fermentation into the wine that makes glad the heart of man, is not in itself enough to draw from the grape the revelation of the wine god's full glory. The fermented grape juice can only fulfil its highest purpose in a complete seclusion from the outer world which allows the slow alchemy of time to work its miracle. Wine may run through the seven ages allotted to man by Shakespeare, but they are reckoned by another and more slowly moving standard of time.

# CHAPTER THREE

# The Early Precursors
# of Port

COMING events are said to cast their shadows before. When their shadow stretches over centuries it is not surprising that it should be distinctly shadowy and indistinct. At least four centuries before port became the Englishman's wine, Portuguese wines found their way into the outer world through the outlet of Britain, but the records of their entry are scanty and have to be pieced together from many sources. The Portuguese wine-growers profited at an early date from the secular friendship between England and Portugal, which may be said to have begun in 1147, when Anglo-Norman crusaders played an important part in the recovery of Lisbon from the Moors. After its surrender, a Norman Englishman, Gilbert of Hastings, was consecrated Bishop of Lisbon; as envoy of the Portuguese king, Afonso I, he led missions to both England and France. Trading relations were established, the Portuguese shipping wax, leather, salt and oil in exchange for our woollens and cloths. They continued, in accordance with agreements of which the terms have not survived, for the next century and a half, when they were confirmed and extended by the signing of a Treaty in London on 20 October 1353, the earliest Anglo-Portuguese Treaty of which the text has been preserved.

Soon after the signature of this treaty we first hear of the importation of Portuguese wine. The treaty contained a clause which granted to Portuguese fishermen the right to fish off the English coast, and there is reason to believe that they introduced into these islands their native wine for the first time in small quantities. Probably they smuggled it in and bartered it, but if it passed through the customs it would have had to pay the tunnage duty of two shillings a tun imposed on imported wine in 1347. Wool was the main source of our trading wealth, but fishermen and fish played such an important part in the history of our relations with Portugal and the discovery of vintage port that no historian of Portuguese wines can ignore them. In 1479 the Portuguese, who had been fishing in British waters for over a century, established fisheries on the banks of Newfoundland. They were always adventurous sailors, and their empire was founded on sea power. It was a long time before our own marine drew level with theirs, and as late as 1578 there were fifty Portuguese craft fishing on the Banks as against thirty British. They found a market for their catch not only in Spain and the Levant but in the British Isles. They landed it not only for immediate sale in Britain but for salting and curing for their home market.

The British had long excelled in their skill in the dull but useful process of salting and curing fish. In 1230 Henry III sold for twenty marks the monopoly licence of curing fish, and it was one of the monopolies abolished in Elizabeth I's reign. It must be one of the oldest British specialities. When the Protectorate introduced in 1656 a tax on salt, the salt required for the curing of herrings, cod, ling, pilchards and other fish was exempted from it. I believe we still have something like a monopoly of bloaters, kippers and finnan haddock. Salted fish has always been a staple diet in poor countries, and cod cured in Britain sold in Portugal for a halfpenny more the pound than the home-cured variety, a consideration in so cheap a commodity. The exchange of salted fish, *bacalhau*, for the wines of the Douro was in days to come a prime encouragement to our shippers in the long and weary task of adapting those wines to the English palate. *Bacalhau* is still to Portugal what beef was to Old England, and the Portuguese have learnt to convert this lenten fare into a far more palatable dish than any other people, though possibly an exception should be made for the *brandade de morue* of Provence.

In 1375 the English Crown lost the duchy of Aquitaine, which since the marriage of Henry III and Eleanor of Provence in 1236 had kept England provided with wine which Englishmen could call native. Its supply dried up and there was an immediate increase in the import of wines specially made for export from the Levant and Spain, sweet wines which were to be called Sacks from *saca*, a Spanish term for export. There has been much dispute about the derivation and meaning of the word Sack so widely used in England in the sixteenth centry, but there can be really no doubt that it had nothing in the world to do with *seco*, *dry*, for it was applied to sweet wines of every kind. Dessert wines were always described as Sacks, whatever part of the world they came from, because they were wines specially made for export, and as long as Spanish was a familiar language in this country, their derivation from *saca* was taken for granted.

A wine of this type from Portugal made its appearance, if not in Britain, on the Continent, long before the Portuguese fishermen were entitled to fish in British waters. A metrical romance with the title of *The Squire of Low Degree*, attributed to the reign of Edward II, the first years of the fourteenth century, tells of all the wonderful rich wines with which the king of Hungary proposes to regale his daughter; among them is Algarde, which seems to be Algarve, and 'pottes of Osey'. In 1381 its name received in England the sanction of official recognition as Osey, variously spelt Oseye and Osaye, in an ordinance imposing on it the retail price of sixpence a gallon, the same as that of Gascon, Rhenish and Spanish wine. It might seem that Osey, since it was to be sold at the same price as the natural wines of Gascony, was like them an unsweetened natural wine, but the Spanish wines were unquestionably sweet. It has often been stated that these and the Levant wines were sweetened with honey, but it is far more probable that the bulk of them owed their sweetness to grape juice boiled down to syrup, a sweetener in common use in Greece and Rome and still used in Jerez. Other flavourings such as spices with the zest which the palate demanded, in an age in which delicacy of taste was unknown, no doubt often contributed to their sophistication, and in Spain their alcoholic strength was fortified at a very early date by the addition of brandy after fermentation had taken place.

The customs levied a uniform tunnage duty on all wines, whether sweet or not, until 1453, when a distinction was drawn between the beverage wines and the dessert wines from the Iberian Peninsula and the Levant, the former paying a duty of three shillings a tun, the latter twice as much. This customs discrimination between beverage and dessert wines had come to stay. It was based on a simple formula: all wines imported from the Peninsula and the Levant had to pay a higher luxury duty. This geographical basis of taxation proved a serious handicap to the Portuguese shippers when, as the reader will learn, in the eighteenth century they first tried to popularize Portuguese wine in Britain. It was not until accurate scientific tests of alcoholic degree were available that duties could be based, not on the place of origin, but on alcoholic strength. As soon as the twofold duty was imposed the Osey wines were classed in the dessert category.

In the fifteenth century Lisbon was the great centre of oriental trade, and our Merchant Adventurers were attracted there by the special privileges accorded them by 'our oldest ally'. In 1500 King Manoel I of Portugal styled himself 'Lord of the Conquest, Navigation and Commerce of India, Ethiopia, Arabia and Persia' and that same year the discovery of Brazil by the great Portuguese explorer, Pedro Cabral, added the glory of the New World to his title. Our merchants had been sending home the luxuries of the gorgeous east, such as spices and sugar, a rare and expensive luxury until the New World entered into the market. All the trade of the Portuguese Empire had to pass through Lisbon, and now our merchants had at their disposal the produce of the New World as well as that of the east. It was not long before sugar began to come in from Brazil far more generously than from the east, and Lisbon sugar became a trade term.

It was a wonderful moment. Our traders could exchange their homely woollens and salted cod for strange exotic novelties which dwarfed in magic all the classical dreams of the golden fleece and the apples of the hesperides. All our speculations about space flight must pale before that inrush of concrete wonders from a New World. The daring of those pioneers who braved the ocean in their tiny ships did bring back something tangible from their wrestle with death. The space traveller, if ever he reaches moon or planet and returns, promises a harvest of abstract mathematical equations, and one may doubt if humanity would not have got on better without those which find their consummation in universal destruction. Smoking statistics suggest that mankind does regard the nepenthe of tobacco as a boon in defiance of all medical denunciations, and the generous bounty of the sugar cane, replacing the grudging bee, so long almost the sole purveyor of sweetness, must have come as a gift from the gods. Small wonder that our merchants relied mainly on the trade of rarities from the east and the New World and treated wine as a makeweight in their cargoes rather than as one of their most valuable commodities. Osey had to compete in England with dessert wines of a reputation established before it had appeared on the market. It could not command such high prices as the Malmseys from Crete, the Rumneys from Spain and the rest, as it had done to begin with. In 1504 Archbishop Warham's accounts show that for his enthronement feast a butt of Malmsey cost him £4 and a pipe of Osey £3. It is perhaps interesting to note that Osey from Portugal is already being sold in casks called pipes just as port is today, while the casks of the other dessert wines are recorded as butts.

We hear very little of Osey after Robert Cecil, quoted by Harrison in his *Description of England* (1577), includes it in the list of dessert wines partly responsible for the enormously increased consumption of the wine in the island. 'England', he wrote, 'now consumes four times as much wine as formerly', the French wines being 'ordinary drinks' and the dessert wines 'of great strength and value'. Just before the end of the sixteenth century another mysterious Portuguese wine appears in English literature. As the reader will learn, I am inclined to hazard a guess that Osey came from the Setúbal district, and perhaps the mystery of philology may one day explain how Setúbal could become Osey in a foreign language. This second wine Charneco, a name immortal as long as Shakespeare is read, set me off on a wild-goose chase in quest of its origin. How often does the study of wine remind its student that a little learning is a dangerous thing! When my good friend Tony Mendes enriched my jejune Portuguese vocabulary with the word *charneca* as Portuguese for *barren land*, I lordily dismissed Henderson's theory that Shakespeare's Charneco must have come from one of two villages of that name near Lisbon, one on the coast between Carcavelos and Colares, the other a league and a half above the capital. I suggested audaciously that Charneco might have come from any vineyard on *charneca*, that sterile soil in which the vine gives of its best. No one I consulted had ever heard of a village named Charneco near Lisbon. My beautiful argument is reduced to nonsense by the discovery that one of the legally recognized districts of Bucelas is named Charneca, and since names of wines change almost as slowly as those of the stars, everything points to Charneco being a Bucelas wine.

An interesting point about Charneco distinguishes it from all the other dessert wines except Spanish sack. It claims age as a merit. A play, *Wit without Money*, dating from just before 1600, describes 'old Charneco' and 'Anchoves' as the mark of a first-rate hostelry; and an establishment which did not provide them was to be avoided. Falstaff took anchovies with his Sack, presumably to stimulate thirst, and they are still a favourite relish in Portugal; indeed, they found an important place, as will be said, in a tasting of Bucelas in its home which I attended.

Charneco attained its abiding place in English literature in Shakespeare's *Henry VI*, Part II, Act II, Scene iii, printed in 1594, where in distinctly grim comic relief Horner the Armourer and Peter, his apprentice, have to fight a duel, a parody of that incumbent on knights of pedigree, that the master might purge himself of the charge of talking treason brought against him by Peter. The terrified youth, convinced that he has not a chance against a professional armourer who must have learnt so much about fence already', wisely leaves his apprentice supporters to do all the drinking to his victory. Horner makes the mistake of mixing his drinks, and when his friends were cheering him with them, sandwiched a cup of Charneco between a cup of sack and a pot of double beer. With one mighty blow the sober Peter finishes off the pot-valiant Horner, no doubt much to the glee of the apprentices in the audience.

Only twice again do we meet with Charneco. In the *Discovery of a London Monster called the Black Dog of Newgate* (1612) it keeps company with Sherris-Sack as 'a quick-spirited liquor', that wine which made Falstaff's spirit so quick. Some years later Charneco is coupled in Dekker's *Honest Whore* with a bottle of 'Peter-sameen' or 'peter see-me', that extraordinary transmogrification of the name of the wine from the luscious Pedro Ximenez grape, which is so prized by the sweet tooth of the ladies of Andalusia and which still sweetens the best rich sherries.

Charneco disappears from the stage and with it Osey. Neither Charneco nor Osey is mentioned in the Great Statute of Customs, drawn up after the Restoration in 1660, and in 1664 Charles Davenant, the economist, states with the authority of a Commissioner of Excise that 'the import of wine from Italy and Portugal is not worthy of mention, being limited, if any, to presents from abroad, and therefore not entered in the customs house books'. There was a complete lull before a veritable and quite unprecedented storm of Portuguese wine swept into Britain.

# CHAPTER FOUR

# The Open Door
# for Portuguese Wines

THERE were two factors mainly responsible for that brewing storm, the parlous predicament of our merchants in Portugal and the international situation. The Brazilian trade was dwindling fast in face of the competition of the New World produce imported direct into the British Isles. Much of their prosperity had been wrapped up in the sugar trade, that erstwhile rarity and oriental luxury gradually being transformed into an universal necessity, so precious that Bacon, in his *New Atlantis*, dedicated a statue to the discoverer of sugar in Solomon's temple. Lisbon sugar from Brazil had become supreme in the London market. In the third decade of the seventeenth century English colonists settled in Barbados. They planted the sugar cane, and by the middle of the century the island had begun to export sugar. It under sold the Lisbon sugar and, reinforced by Jamaica, drove it out of the market. Other produce suffered the same fate. Our merchants in the trade with Portugal could not survive unless they could find some other counter of exchange. Portugal was a fertile but poor country with few commodities tempting for export. There was one commodity it had in abundance, cheap wine, and they began to take seriously the possibility of finding in wine the life-belt they were looking for. Osey and Charneco had had no great success in their competition with the Spanish and Levant Sacks, dessert wines. Might it be better policy to pit the natural Portuguese wines against the French beverage wines against which a tariff war was being sporadically waged? They had not really pushed Osey and Charneco, and it was only occasionally, if ever, that politics favoured them in the customs. The case was very different with France. Under the Commonwealth the import of French wines had been prohibited from 1648 to 1656 as a retaliatory measure, and in 1667 Colbert unwillingly declared a tariff war against England which was to last for many generations.

The international situation was playing into the hands of our traders in Portugal. With Charles II on the throne, playing fast and loose with Louis XIV, the English attitude towards France might seem politically ambivalent, but everything pointed to that policy of war to the knife, which threw off all disguise after the Revolution of 1688.

In view of the international situation, with the marriage of William of Orange and Mary foreshadowing the Revolution which was destined to establish port as the Englishman's wine, it is surprising how modest were the demands of the Portuguese merchants, no more than the thin edge of the wedge. Since the tariff war with France began in 1667, the policy of striking at that vital target of the French economy, the wine industry, was gaining strength. There had been no great increase of the importation of wine into England since the days of Elizabeth I, when its annual average was estimated at between 20,000 and 30,000 tuns. In 1672, before the customs really got to work on retaliation, 20,000 tuns of French wine were shipped into this country, but by 1675 the thumbscrew of the tariff had squeezed the quantity down to 7,500 tuns. In the four years 1675 to 1685, French imports remained at about this average, 31,141 tuns in all. There was a big gap for Portuguese wines to fill, but all the wines our traders could scrape together amounted to a total of 478 tuns, rising from 20 tuns in 1675 to 199 tuns in 1678, the merest drop in the ocean. But that last consignment, though small was of historic importance, since it marked the first entry of the wines that were to become port.

There were in the earlier seventeenth century two main wine regions in Portugal, in the south the extensive area round Lisbon, in the extreme north on the Spanish border the Minho district with Monção as its wine centre and Viana do Castelo as its port. The Lisbon wines had a home market and an overseas trade in Brazil, and the merchants looked elsewhere in their rather dilatory plans to find another source for cheap wine in large quantities. In their desire to undersell the French wines they overlooked the importance of quality. At first the Minho region seemed to offer the most promising prospect. Though it was a corn-growing province, vines grew there abundantly and there was a considerable yield of cheap wine. British traders settled at Viana do Castelo, many of them super-cargoes who planted themselves there as at Lisbon, seeking fortune abroad rather than returning home. After Cromwell had in 1656 appointed a Consul General at Lisbon, later in the century vice-Consuls were appointed at both Viana and Oporto. The Viana traders are said to have had their representatives at Monção in the wine country, but their trade does not seem to have been active for a good many years.

Occasional orders for the Navy must have come to them as a godsend. The Navy Commissioners were exempt from the duty which handicapped Portuguese wines, and from time to time they ordered Minho wines from Viana as 'beverage for the sailors'. Prizes doubtless kept officers well provided with French wines. Sellers quotes from the State of Papers of 1662:

*Consul Maynard to the Navy Commissioners: Has sent his bills for beverage wines for the Navy. Asks an order to dispose of the remaining wines which are spoiling.*

A hundred years later, in 1762, when Britain was fitting out a fleet for the successful West India Expedition, every ship was supplied with port wine, and exports increased from 18,000 to 27,000 pipes; the fillip given to the trade lasted for many years.

The Minho wines were no doubt cheap, but they were singularly ill-suited for distant export. Probably if wine had been the principal industry in the Minho there would have been more pruning of the vines, but the Minho district was a corn-growing region and vineyards only a secondary consideration. The vines were allowed to grow haphazard up trees and trellises, bearing their fruit high above the ground, to make a light acidulous wine from grapes less ripe than those grown low enough to profit by the refracted heat of the sun-baked soil; this wine made a delightful summer drink, more *spritzig* than a young Moselle, and with such a tendency to sparkle as to be quite unsuited for shipment in the wood. Even today, when these wines are made with far more care, they have to be shipped in bottle with wired-down cork. *Vinhos verdes*, green wines, the Portuguese call them. In their earlier days they were known in English as *eager* wines, a word which gives just the right twist to the French *aigre* from which it is derived to express their pleasant acidulous freshness, when they are young and sound. Many of them must have been little better than vinegar by the time they reached the British wine-drinker's glass.

The failure of these wines to stand the voyage and their habit of turning to vinegar before they could be sold were evidently ascribed by some shippers to faulty casks. As late as 1704 some optimists were still hoping that the Minho wines might play their part in replacing the French wines, though the Douro vineyards were approaching full production, since English coopers were sent to the Minho to improve the native cooperage. In a letter from Thomas Woodmass, the son of a Kettering wine-merchant who was serving his apprenticeship in wine at Viana, under the date of 23 January 1704, we find the pregnant sentence: 'Ye English cupers are a drunken lot, but ye natives now know how to make casks.' After they had done their work at Viana the coopers went on to Oporto. Eight months later he wrote: 'The cupers are here and at work.'

I suspect that John Croft, in his famous *Treatise on the Wines of Portugal* (1788), lumped these wines together with those grown over the Spanish frontier under the name of Ribadavia wines, of which he says that before the introduction of port some 2,000 to 3,000 pipes annually reached this country. The customs figures suggest that they cannot have come in in such quantity before 1682. 'They were', he writes, 'a thin sort of wine; the Red not unlike what is called or termed in Portugal Palhete – straw-coloured – or Methuen Wine, from one Mr Paul Methuen, who was the first that mixed the red and white grapes together, and you may suppose a liquor nearly the same as Red and White Port being mixed. When the demand for this sort of wine became greater than its produce, especially in a scanty vintage, it put some English Super-Cargoes, who resided there and at Viana near Oporto, at that time, on teaching the Portuguese to cultivate the vineyards on the heights or mountains bordering on the River Douro.'

Paul Methuen, son of John Methuen, Chancellor of Ireland and afterwards Ambassador to Portugal, signed on 16 May 1703 during the War of the Spanish Succession the treaty which guaranteed to Portugal naval protection and an expeditionary force of 12,000 men, if she was attacked by Spain or France. The more famous treaty guaranteeing Portuguese wines a tariff preference over French wines was signed by John Methuen at the end of the same year. Paul Methuen evidently had interests in the wine trade, but it seems highly unlikely that he was primarily responsible for the mixed pressing of red and white grapes. There was nothing new in this, and we hear perpetual complaints of the higgledy-piggledy way the Portuguese grew and pressed their grapes without concern for colour, and they grew louder and louder as public opinion in England kept calling for darker wine. Croft may well be right that the demand for wine of the deepest colour was not unconnected with the scarcity of Florence wine, which was very deep-coloured and had considerable popularity here a generation or so after Davenant had registered it as non-existent. In 1711 Swift grumbled at the Florence he drank in a scurvy alehouse: 'four and sixpence a flask: damned wine'. The Grand Duke of Tuscany used to send chests of his wine to important personages, and in the same year Swift 'liked mightily' the Florence he had sent that year to Henry St John, created in the following year Viscount Bolingbroke. St John gave him a case, but within a fortnight it began to spoil and he wrote to Stella: 'Do you know that my whole chest of Florence is turned sour, at least the first two were, and hardly drinkable? How plaguy unfortunate am I! And the Secretary's own is the best I ever tasted!' We hear of Florence being sold in 'betties', which stood for the Italian *boccette*, a pet name for the *fiasco*. The flasks were imported with no better seal than olive oil in their necks, and if as Simon says they had no corks at all they must have lost a good deal of their contents in the journey, however carefully they were kept upright. The Italian casks of chestnut wood were so porous that ullage in transit was disastrous.

It is clear that our Portuguese merchants soon after the middle of the century had had thoughts of developing as a wine area, a practically virgin area, the Douro valley with all the facilities of Oporto at the river's mouth, but they went very slowly to work. Probably they clung to their Lisbon sugar and other Brazilian produce until it was completely driven out of the market. The Minho wine offered a more tempting proposition, for there were plenty of vines there, but the development of the Douro valley demanded vineyard plantation on a large and expensive scale. There was an industrious and poverty-stricken peasantry there, and they made wine of a kind for their own consumption, but the heights of the Alto Douro, the destined home of the great port vineyards, were waste and barren. In 1681, when the ruthless prohibition of the import of French wines was at its height and they had disappeared from the English market, the development of the valley was in its infancy. Sellers quotes from a document published in 1791 by the Lisbon Royal Academy of Sciences on the trade and agriculture of the Alto Douro from 1681 to 1756:

'In the year 1681, viticulture was not on such an extensive scale as now, as the English taste was for sweet wines the farmers *were obliged* to rear vines in appropriate situations, viz., on the banks of the streams more exposed to the sun, and these were of very limited area. In those days the large Quintas of today were unknown; the *lagares* (presses) did not contain more than 3 to 5 pipes . . . the remainder of the land was uncultivated and only after the lapse of some years was the gorse that covered the hills cut down and burnt on the spot. Attempts were then made to grow rye, but with little success.'

It was asking too much of human reason to suppose that vines would flourish where even rye would not grow. Our merchants when they began to encourage the planting of vineyards in the Upper Douro had very little idea of the conditions which bring the stubborn vine to its best, and the peasants were naturally inclined to choose sites where richer soil promised quantity rather than quality. W. H. G. Kingston, once a popular writer of boys' books, came of a port-shipping family and served an apprenticeship with the family firm at Oporto. In the forties of the last century he wrote a series of *Lusitanian Sketches* and more or less confirms the account of early viticulture in the Douro given above. He says that at first the vines were planted in the red clayey soil of the undulating ground and hills 50 miles from Oporto. In his time the wine they grew was considered a thin, light-coloured wine without body or strength, unfit for export. Its colour was probably due to a mixture of white grapes, and it did no doubt seem thin and light when compared with the fully fledged port which was then available. The real trouble with the Douro wines, their basic defect which it took nearly a century to overcome and that with a quite unforeseen result, arose from their too violent fermentation. The Douro grapes, exceptionally rich in sugar, if left to themselves to ferment in a hot climate fermented right out and converted every trace of sugar into alcohol to make a harsh, coarse, strong wine, with no flavour but only alcoholic strength to recommend it.

The first step towards quality called for the abandonment of the rich clayey soil, and Kingston registers that first step in the following words. 'It was at last discovered that the most advantageous situations for the growth of the vine were on the steep sides of the rocky mountains, exposed to the full force of the sun's rays: and it is truly surprising to see the spots brought under cultivation – now the most valuable in the country – which had previously, since the formation of the world, remained in sterile grandeur. Terraces, a few feet wide, have been cut in the sides of lofty mountains, rising one above another from the water's edge to near the summit. Walls four to five feet high are built to keep in the soil, which is composed of the chips of the clayey slate or limestone broken from the rock, the debris of which contributes much to retain the necessary moisture.' He does not exaggerate the really formidable task which our merchants undertook when they set out to turn the Alto Douro into a land of vines.

In 1657 Thomas Maynard, our Consul General at Lisbon, considered that trading activity justified the appointment of his brother Walter as Vice-Consul at Oporto, but it is not till 1678 that there is any official record of wine being shipped from that port. There are two stories about the individuals who took the first practical steps to set in motion a real activity in the Douro wine trade. One of them is obviously apocryphal, but at least it agrees with the other in crediting traders from the Minho, doubtless disappointed with the wines they had been trying to ship from Viana, with the initiative in opening the Douro region. The date confirms the account given by Ernest Cockburn of the first shipping to England of the Douro wines. A Liverpool wine-merchant had sent his two sons to Viana 'to learn the wine business'. In 1678 on a holiday excursion they visited Lamego on the fringe of the Upper Douro and were entertained at a monastery, where they tasted a wine new to them from Pinhão, which is in its depths. They were so struck by its excellence that they purchased all of it they could get and shipped it through Oporto to England after adding a little brandy to help it withstand the rigours of the voyage. 'This', writes Cockburn, 'may no doubt be claimed as the original importation of *"Port Wine"* . . . as the wine in question came from the Douro.' The light brandying of the natural Douro wine for the journey was, of course, a very different matter from using brandy for the checking of fermentation, a process which was first tried some forty years later and eventually led to the production of the dessert wine, port.

In 1678 204 tuns were shipped from Oporto, and in all 199 tuns of Portuguese wine passed through the English customs. No wine from any other source can have been exported. Did the young pioneers with youthful enthusiasm ship to their father's firm all of the 204 tuns which left Oporto to lose five tuns between Portugal and the customs? Perhaps they had friends who followed their example. How the wine was received at Liverpool we are not told. That year 7,000 tuns of French wine were imported, and demand for wine greatly exceeded supply. A new kind of wine had plenty of opportunity.

John Croft tells another story of the first shipping of Douro wines, and though his Mr Bearsley cannot really claim priority, his account has an interest of its own and confirms Cockburn's suggestion that the Douro wine industry was really set in motion by merchants from the Minho. 'A Mr Peter Bearsley, an Englishman, who resided at Viana, was the first who went to Oporto in the view and for the purpose of speculating in the Port wines; and on the road to the Wine country at an inn he met with an Elder tree, whose juice he expressed and found it had the effect of heightening and improving its colour.' Cockburn's young men must have considerably anticipated Peter Bearsley, since he was the son of Job Bearsley, who only came to Viana in 1692 and was the founder of the famous firm Taylor, Fladgate and Yeatman. That encounter of his with the elder tree was distinctly unfortunate, since elder-berries, *baga* in Portuguese, were to be a skeleton in the port cupboard for many years. Croft agrees that the initiative came to the Douro from Viana.

In 1679 the Portuguese shippers were given their first great opportunity, but they were slow to grasp it. In that year an absolute prohibition was imposed on the entry of French wines. The prayer put forward two years before by the Commercial Agent at Oporto was far more than granted. During seven years only four tuns of French wine found their way through the customs, and for three years Portugal did practically nothing to relieve the drought of the English wine-drinker. In 1679 and 1680 a thousand tuns of Portuguese wine were shipped and in 1681 1,700 tuns. Very little of this wine had a claim to the title of port, if port is taken as a wine shipped over the bar of Oporto, for the wines so shipped dropped from 805 tuns in 1679 to 353 in 1680 and 71 in 1681. In 1682 the shippers pulled themselves together, and their exports of wine showed a re-markable leap from 1,718 tuns to 13,860, but still they were not exporting port in any quantity, for the Oporto contribution to the total amounted to no more than 350 tuns. They must have been buying wine indiscriminately wherever they could find it, how-ever indifferent it might be, and the total was swelled by the shipping of French wine to Portugal to be reshipped more or less blended with the native wines to dodge the ban. For the next four years it remained at about the same level, with 1683 a peak year with nearly 17,000 tuns, the Douro contributing a mere 1,400 tuns to the four years' total of 55,000 tuns of nominal Portuguese wine. The camouflage of French wines as Portuguese as far as the customs were concerned must have seriously prejudiced the customs revenue and persisted with more advantage to the rich than to the average wine-drinker as such devices for cheating the tax gatherer always do. About 1706 we learn from J. H. Plumb's *Sir Robert Walpole* that that statesman along with some minor Government officials was smuggling into England French wines 'disguised as Port so that they only paid the lower duty'.

In 1686 the ban on French wines was lifted, and for the next four years Portuguese imports fell to an average annual level of less than 500 tuns against the French average of over 13,000 tuns. It must have struck the shippers that their wine business was most precariously speculative, but the international situation still promised well, and they did not relax their efforts in the Douro. With William and Mary on the throne, pros-pects were even brighter, and in 1689 the ban on French wines was reimposed, and henceforward Portuguese and French imports see-sawed up and down with occasional peace breaking the continuity of war, the Portuguese steadily gaining predominance.

In 1690 the Douro vineyards began to pull their weight. 865 tuns exported in 1682 rose to 2,494 tuns in that year and over 6,000 tuns in 1692 and 1693. Wines with a geographic right to the name of port, natural wines very different from those known to us today under that name, flowed into London, and the name of port entered into com-mon parlance. As has been said, practically no Douro wine was included in the emer-gency shipments of the previous decade, but many Lisbon white wines helped to swell the total. It was with the epithet of red that the first ports were sold. They did not meet with an enthusiastic reception among wine-drinkers accustomed to the light wines of France. Since all the French wines had to be drunk young from the wood, their stock was very quickly exhausted, and many a wine-drinker found himself faced with the dilemma of port or nothing. The situation was one with which we became only too familiar in the 1940s. The claret-lover found his favourite wine as elusive as the wild

goose, when he set out on his quest with perhaps a hint or two from some knowing-one
who professed secret information that he probably did not possess.

Redding rightly fixes 'the durable commencement of the Oporto trade' at this period,
though it still had ups and downs to face. Absolute prohibition of a commodity has the
drawback of depriving the exchequer of a source of revenue. There might be more
profit in admitting a trickle of French wine through a customs gate preferentially
straitened, and in 1693 the ban was eased. Practically all the Portuguese wine reaching
England was now shipped from Oporto. French competition had its effect, exports falling from 6,500 tuns in 1693 to an average of 4,500 tuns during the next four years.
French wines were first penalized with an extra duty of £8 a tun, and in 1697 the im-
position of a duty of £30 a tun on wines from the enemy country administered the *coup
de grâce*. French wine had to pay 4s. 0½d. the gallon, Portuguese only 1s. 8d. Today we
pay on all natural wine treble that duty, not without grumbling but without complete
abstention, and the preference of 2s. 0d. a gallon on Commonwealth wines has not
driven the wines of France out of the market. In 1697 a miserable two tuns of French
wine came into the country so far as the customs were concerned, and during the next
hundred years French imports only three times exceeded 2,000 tuns, a tenth of what were
once imported.

Croft asserts that 'the general use of Port Wine in Great Britain' dates from the
Methuen Treaty of 1703. The Duoro wines, as we have said, began to come into Britain
in significant quantities in the last decade of the seventeenth century, but their reception
hardly suggests that they could be described as in 'general use', bought as they were
under compulsion. Statistics suggest that the Methuen Treaty did encourage the
Portuguese wine trade, for after it exports do show a generally ascending if rather zigzag
curve, but undoubtedly Croft should have dated his 'general use' very much later, if it
implies that port had become the Englishman's wine. Simon argues in his *Bottlescrew
Days* that the effects of the Methuen Treaty were negligible, but he is a trifle unfair
when he chooses a comparison between the years 1699 and 1730 to demonstrate its in-
effectiveness. 1699 with 8,703 tuns was a peak year for the Portuguese exports, while
1730 with 8,279 tuns was an exceptionally low level. In 1728 they exceeded 18,000 tuns,
in 1729 14,000 tuns and during the decade after 1730 they only once fell below 11,000
tuns. A great deal more port was exported after the Methuen Treaty than before.

The Methuen Treaty may not have led to the general use of port wine in Britain as
Croft supposed, but I think Simon underestimates its long-term effects. It did really
lead to the day which he has so vividly painted when 'matured bottled wines were made
possible, wines which could be sipped at leisure, which could be talked about and enjoyed over the mahogany with the dessert, while reminiscences flowed and candles
burnt brightly into the night'. It gave growers and shippers a promise of security in the
British market without which they might well have despaired of success and abandoned
that long expensive series of experiments which culminated so gloriously.

# CHAPTER FIVE

# The Quest of the Lost Secret

Extract from the Anglo-Portuguese Commercial Treaty of 1703:

### Article I

*His Sacred Royal Majesty of Portugal promises, both in his own name and that of his successors, to admit for ever hereafter into Portugal the woollen cloths and the rest of the woollen manufactures of the Britons, as was accustomed till they were prohibited by the Laws: nevertheless upon this condition;*

### Article II

*That is to say, that her Sacred Royal Majesty of Great Britain shall in her own name and that of her Successors, be obliged for ever hereafter to admit the wines of the growth of Portugal into Britain; so that at no time, whether there shall be Peace or War between the Kingdoms of Britain and France, anything more shall be demanded for these wines, by the name of Custom or Duty, or by whatsoever other title, directly or indirectly, whether they shall be imported into Great Britain in pipes or hogsheads or other casks, than what shall be demanded from the like quantity or measure of French wine, deducting or abating a third part of the Custom or Duty: but if at any time this deduction or abatement of Customs, which is to be made as aforesaid, shall in any manner be attempted and prejudiced, it shall be just and lawful for his Sacred Royal Majesty of Portugal again to prohibit the woollen cloths, and the rest of the British woollen manufacturers.*

### Article III

*The Most Excellent Lords the Plenipotentiaries promise, and take upon themselves, that their above-named Masters shall ratify this Treaty, and that within the space of 2 months the Ratifications shall be exchanged . . .*
*Given at Lisbon, 27th December, 1703, Signed John Methuen, Marquis de Alegrete.*

THE TREATY certainly conferred on the wines of Portugal advantages far exceeding those of which the shippers had dared to dream twenty-three years before. Then they had only pleaded to be spared the heavier sweet wine duty and as natural wines given equality of treatment with the natural wines of France. But in the interval they had been enjoying far more favoured conditions. There had often been a total prohibition of the entry of French wines, and after 1697 they had had to pay less than half the duty. All the Treaty guaranteed was a preference of one-third.

Its value to the growers and shippers was a long-term guarantee of security with such a tradition of permanence as no other international agreements could offer in a world in which international relations were in a state of perpetual flux. The history of Anglo-Portuguese friendship was already so long, the interests of the two countries had apart from inevitable minor changes in policy so long been identical, that treaty promises, so often pie-crust, possessed a claim to enduring validity to an extraordinary extent. The unexampled nature of this continuity inspired the eloquence of the Prime Minister, when on 12 October 1943 in the House of Lords, the bombed House of Commons being in ruins, he announced the agreement which permitted the use of the Azores as a war base. In Volume V of *The Second World War* he reports how he opened his speech with the following statement: 'I have an announcement to make to the House arising out of the Treaty signed between this country and Portugal in the year 1373 between

His Majesty King Edward III and King Ferdinand and Queen Eleanor of Portugal.'
'I spoke', he adds characteristically, 'in a level voice, and made a pause to allow the
House to take in the date, 1373. As this soaked in there was something like a gasp. I do
not suppose any such continuity of relations between two Powers has ever been, or
will ever be, set forth in the ordinary day-to-day work of British diplomacy.' Actually
the alliance had its birth in 1151, when a crusading English expedition took part in the
conquest of Libson from the Moors, though the text of its conditions has not survived.
The treaty of 1353 was a Commercial Treaty.

'This treaty', Mr Churchill went on, 'was reinforced in various form by treaties of
1386, 1643, 1654, 1660, 1661, 1703 and 1815 and in a secret declaration of 1899. In
more modern times the validity of the Old Treaties was recognized in the Treaties of
Arbitration concluded with Portugal in 1904 and 1914. Article I of the treaty of 1373
runs as follows: "In the first place we settle and covenant that there shall be from this
day forward . . . true, faithful, constant, mutual, and perpetual friendships, unions,
alliances, and deeds of sincere affection, and that as true and faithful friends we shall
henceforth, reciprocally, be friends to friends and enemies to enemies, and shall assist,
maintain, and uphold each other mutually, by sea and by land, against all men that
may live or die." '

Never has there been a comparable continuity in international relations, and the
shippers and growers were justified in their confidence that that continuity would be
reflected in the treatment of their wines.  But for that assurance they could scarcely
have had the courage and patience to persevere for the better part of a century in a
campaign which for so long met with little but failure, even though their future depended on its success. The Methuen Treaty attained its supreme fulfilment in the discovery of vintage port, which opened a new epoch in the history of wine, but its virtue
was not exhausted. The Anglo-Portuguese Commercial Agreements of 1914 and 1916
set an example to the world by giving to port a treaty guarantee that its name should
not be taken in vain. Such a guarantee should be the natural inviolable right of the
place name of every wine, since local conditions are the essence of its being, but it is
a right which unenlightened lack of scruple has so generally ignored.  Shamelessly the
names of famous wines have been stolen to provide false colours for upstart wines that
cannot possibly reproduce the qualities which made them famous. Port with Madeira,
lately happily linked with champagne, stood alone and apart in our islands legally
protected from the degradation of their names. On 18 September 1916 a notice was
issued from the London Custom House announcing that any wine to which the description port or Madeira was falsely applied, whether or not the description was accompanied by a geographical indication of the actual country of production of the wine,
would be liable to seizure.

After this glance at the long-term benefits of the Methuen Treaty, the signature of
which should mark a red-letter day in the calendar of every wine-lover, we must return
to the years of disappointment and failure which were its immediate sequel.

When it was concluded the Douro wines, which alone could provide the quantity to
fill the gap in the English market left by the disappearance of French wines, had a long
way to go before they could establish themselves as worthy of a premier position. I am
afraid that there is no doubt that our merchants in Portugal were too greedy, though
they could plead extenuating circumstance. Their prosperity had faded away with the

loss of the New World trade, and they were deeply involved in the extension of wine-growing in the Douro valley. With French wine out of the field and gin still only a menace, they gambled on recouping themselves through the cheapness and not the quality of the wines they imported. They aimed at recovering their money by buying as cheaply as possible, and the growers were in their hands. It was a short-sighted policy to think that English wine-drinkers, deprived of their habitual beverage, would accept wine of any kind. Yet they bought their wines at £2 or £3 a pipe of 115 gallons, say from ¾d. to 1d. a bottle – a price which offered the peasant growers no alternative but to squeeze out of their grapes the maximum quantity of wine without consideration of its quality in the hope of keeping body and soul together. If the shippers could have sold their wines they would have done very well. In 1710 red and white Oporto wine was on sale at 5s. a gallon, eight or nine times the price paid the grower, and Lisbon wine was quoted at only 6d. a gallon more, but in 1712 we find a pipe of Oporto wine sold for less than half the price of a pipe of Lisbon wine, and in 1713 Oporto wine was sold at from £24 10s. to £27 10s. as against £32 10s. for Lisbon wine the pipe.

André Simon gives these figures in *Bottlescrew Days* and dwells on the indifferent quality of the Douro wines. The wine-merchants, deprived of their French stand-by, clamoured for more wine, but there were endless complaints about the wines shipped from Portugal. With the cheapest of labour, the extension of the vine country in the Douro Valley, the planting of vineyards on the steepest slopes and the gathering of the vintage in a mountainous country without communications had been a most expensive speculation, and the whole scheme was threatened with disaster, since a great part of the once wine-drinking public was turning to spirits.

The fight must have seemed won when the Methuen Treaty guaranteed that for many years to come the French wines would have to struggle in the London market against their challengers from Portugal, handicapped with one hand tied behind their back by penal duties and occasionally with both hands immobilized by prohibition. Yet from the very policy which gave the Portuguese wines their privileged superiority there was to spring a new and far more insidious opponent, home-distilled spirits under the leadership of gin. There was nothing to be feared from the competition of British 'wines' concocted in a country where no wine grapes grew, but the alembic could work anywhere on almost anything.

Distillation of alcohol entered Western Europe through Spain, where it was introduced by the Moors, paradoxically enough, since the Prophet had forbidden it even in the form of wine. At first *aqua vitae*, the water of life, was distilled from 'the blackest of wine', and fallacious common sense suggested that the magic essence of wine which in the steam of the still was separated from subsidiary constituents would naturally snuggle down into the lees. Only experience by the process of trial and error could discover that the finest alcohol was best distilled from thin wines of low alcoholic degree throwing no sediment, and that nothing good could be steamed out of the impurities of which wine purged itself. The Continent gained that experience a long time before it reached Britain, where for centuries crude spirits were distilled from wine lees, to be used almost entirely as medical prescriptions. The French, with their abundance of wine, learnt relatively soon to make the best brandy in the world, and the Dutch, whose reputation as heavy drinkers equalled that of the Germans, took to brandy and other spirituous liquors most kindly.

With the Restoration, brandy, *brandewijn*, burnt wine, found its first statutory recognition in the Navigation Act, and French brandy, now a spirit worthy of the name of wine spirit with more than mere alcohol to recommend it, flowed into Britain in excellent company with French wine, both doomed to the same fate after the Revolution of 1688. In 1677, two years before the ban on French wines, the tariff war imposed prohibition on French brandy. It was soon relaxed, with very heavy duties to take its place and occasionally reimposed. French brandy and French wines were then submitted to a régime which made them the perquisites of the smuggler. Up went their price and down their quality. They became luxuries for the rich, though some of the landed gentry of moderate means in the middle of the eighteenth century still clung to their brandy and, even though they had resigned themselves to the deprivation of French wines and drank port and Canary Sack, insisted on their brandy being French.

At the very moment that the Portuguese shippers, encouraged by the Methuen Treaty, were entering seriously on their campaign, Queen Anne's Ministers swept away the safeguard of the Distillers' Company, which with its monopoly had exercised a certain control over the distilling of potable spirits in England, and passed a Bill 'for incouraging the consumption of malted corn and the better preventing the running of French and Foreign Brandy'. Distillation was open to all, and distillers were free to distil anything they pleased and in any way they liked. A liquor dirt-cheap, named at its birth Geneva, not from the town but from the corruption of the French *genièvre*, the juniper berry, to which it owed its first flavour, and contracted in the eighteenth century to 'gin', a name which disguised something very different from the wholesome purified spirit now drunk so widely, offered to the poorest the escape of alcoholic stupor at a heavy price. An orgy of drunkenness swept over Britain such as had never been known before: in the days of ale, beer and wine it had been a sober island.

There could be no question of Portuguese wine competing with this poison in price or strength, but from the first importance of high alcoholic degree was forced upon growers and shippers. Their wine had to be strong if it was to have a chance in a land where so much raw spirit was being drunk, and the fortification of the Douro wines, the addition of brandy after fermentation, appeared as the most obvious and hopeful expedient. But that was not enough.

It soon became clear that bankruptcy could be warded off only by the discovery of means which would give the Douro wines something more than strength, something that would appeal to the English palate. For once the Portuguese had to take a leaf out of the Spanish book, in which the word Sack, Export, had been writ large for centuries. Perhaps they would prefer to say that they followed the example of the wine countries of the Levant, which had so long been making their dessert wines specially for export. Also they had the precedents of Osey and Charneco to encourage them, if the tradition had not been entirely forgotten. It is recorded that the idea that Douro wines would have to be expressly treated for export to the English market began to take shape in 1715, and in the darkness which shrouded the mystery of fermentation, various expedients, doomed to failure, over which it is best to draw a veil, were tried.

There were two hidden keys to the solution of the port problem, and one of them was brandy. The first step towards that employment of brandy, which at long last after endless years of violent controversy has come to be accepted by the world not only as beneficial but essential to the making of that supreme dessert wine, port, is foreshadowed in a Portuguese handbook on viniculture published in 1720. It was not till Pasteur, a hundred years ago, solved once and for all the mystery of fermentation that the function of the brandy could be understood, and as late as 1926 Morton Shand inveighed against its use with biblical vituperation when he denounced port in general. When he advocated the export of the unfortified Douro wine as it was made in those days he made it clear that he had never drunk *consumo* in its home; one might compare the translation into port of that unattractive beverage, as it was then, to the transformation of a chrysalis into a butterfly.

At the end of the eighteenth century common sense and experiment, later confirmed by Pasteur, arrived definitely at the basic cause of the reluctance of the British public to drink the natural wines of the Douro. In the paradoxical way wine has, the Douro wines largely owed their lack of sweetness to the extreme sweetness of their natural grape juice. Fermented in a hot climate with no means of refrigeration, they fermented furiously right out, until every trace of their natural sugar had been converted into alcohol, leaving them coarse, harsh, heavy wines with no attraction beyond their alcoholic effect – and that could not compete with that of the cheap, crude spirits flooding the market. Something had to be done to check fermentation in time to retain some of the natural sugar in the finished wine, and the addition of brandy at the right time fulfilled that purpose.

The history of port has been bedevilled by dogmatic prejudice. Fortification shocked to the core the purists of the school of Bacchus, who held any interference with the natural course of fermentation as sacrilege in the inmost temple of the wine god. The precisian connoisseur shudders at the thought of any alien intrusion into the masterpiece which nature so often produces best with the minimum of human intervention and is not to be reconciled by the argument that the spirit is itself distilled from wine. Indeed, the sins of brandy can be very grave, as primitive port was to show. The purist is often not at all comfortable about sherry, though he may shut his eyes to a little brandy after fermentation. Sherry is so attractive, on such good terms with itself that it seems born not made, the only perfect *apéritif*. If he is a writer he may be inclined to suggest that it would be even nicer if only it had no brandy in it. Redding regards the addition of two bottles of brandy to the butt of sherry as an absurd custom. Personally I doubt if sherry would have been able to fight the cocktail without a little brandy as its ally. It may be a confession of a blunted palate that I have found Château Châlon a trifle flat. At any rate, the fortification of sherry is condoned as a venial sin.

It is the brandy in port, the checking of fermentation, which used to be denounced as mortal sin. I have known connoisseurs who, yielding to the temptation of cracking a bottle of vintage port, showed symptoms of guilt such as afflicts those who find themselves breaking a good resolution of lenten abstinence, but I am thankful to say that this feeling did not generally prevent them from enjoying their after-dinner wine.

Great claret might be called a masterpiece of nature, great port a masterpiece of man, but without man there would be no claret and without nature no port. As a claret-lover I do sympathize with the idea that wine is a gift of God to be guarded as far as possible from unnecessary mortal interference, but I equally claim to be a port-lover. The proof of the wine is in the drinking, not in theories as to how it should be made. There are wines which are only at their best when the less man and science have to do with them, the better. There are other wines which can attain the fulfilment of their potentialities only with the aid of human skill, and port has proved that one of the greatest wines in the world comes under this category. It has demonstrated that a judicious checking of fermentation may be a benediction, not a mortal sin. A catholic taste in wine should be the basis of connoisseurship.

After this brief survey of some of the difficulties which dogged for so long the development of port it is time to return to the state of the English market at the time of the Methuen Treaty. The wine drought had been aggravated by the falling off of the imports of Spanish wine owing to the international situation. In 1703, for the first recorded time and probably the first time in history, the Portuguese exported more wine to this country than the Spaniards, indeed 9,000 tuns against 1,500. Their exports remained at about this figure until 1715, when they began to increase; the wines were beginning to be made specially for export and could boast more and more alcoholic degree as the dose of brandy was increased. The annual volume of imports attained 14,000 tuns four times during the next decade, but there can be little doubt that most of it was of very indifferent quality and only sold under protest. It paid a negligible duty of £7 5s. 3d. the tun as against the duty of £55 5s. levied on French wine, but even that preference could not make it popular, and the complaints of both the trade and the consumers were endless. Smuggling was encouraged. In 1726 there was a terrible slump, imports of port fell to 7,700 tuns, as against 14,500 the previous year. Again more Spanish wine was admitted, a thousand tuns more than Portuguese.

The shippers were faced with a desperate moment. There is something in all branches of the wine trade which makes for individualism. Wine is only itself when it is a living thing, and its life demands contact with living personalities in those who deal with it, not machines. Personalities in the aggregate cease to be human beings and become statisticians' convenient mathematical machines. Great wine can only be smothered by vast impersonal corporations, doomed to rely on the mass production which reduces the best to the level of the mediocre, for the individuality of the grower and his vineyard should be the soul of the commodity in which these corporations deal. History shows that those who are intimately concerned with the protean individuality of wine will condescend to co-operation only under the most serious compulsion, and in 1726 that pressure must have been irresistible.

In 1727 the Oporto merchants combined to form an Association with the dual purpose of tackling seriously the problem of the making of wines for export and keeping down the price of their basic material at the cost of the peasant growers. It would be a misrepresentation of human nature, a shutting of the eyes to that original sin which whatever its origin is one of its ineradicable elements, to ascribe the spirit of our Merchant Adventurers to motives of humanitarian altruism. They were out of their country to make money, not improve the lot of those whose goods they bought, and far more likely to starve than pamper the Portuguese goose to which they looked for their golden eggs, since that species was deprived of a delectable liver. The adaptation of their wines to the English taste was a long-term difficult operation, but a ring to keep down their prices was of easier accomplishment.

Co-operation seems to have had an immediate effect on the export trade, since exports doubled in 1727 and nearly trebled in 1728 with 18,000 tuns, a total not equalled until sixty years later when vintage port was in the offing, but they soon began to decline, and in 1730 once again more Spanish wine than Portuguese entered this coun-

THE QUEST OF THE LOST SECRET

try. That year port described as good was sold at 2s. the bottle both red and white, Canary was a third dearer and French wine double. Redding, writing in the middle of the nineteenth century as an out-and-out excommunicator of brandy in the port bottle to whom the Methuen Treaty was anathema maranatha, believed that in the first half of the eighteenth century the Oporto wines brought in in their natural state, if they lacked the delicacy of the highest French wines, were everything else that could be desired, stomachic, mellow, of good strength and colour. It was only the wicked Methuen Treaty which encouraged the growers to sophisticate their wines with brandy and other far more deleterious liquids. To prove his point he refers to the occasion when he believes he drank port wine for the first time in his life, a few years before 1833, the date of the first edition of his book. He was dining with a Portuguese diplomat, and a better wine he never tasted. He attributed its excellence to the fact that it was not an export wine prepared for the English market, but he spoils his argument by adding that it had been shipped from Lisbon. He would surely have been rather less enthusiastic if his diplomatic friend had given him Douro wine as *consumo in puris naturalibus*.

There may have been some better wines made in some of the quintas, but there was certainly not enough to begin to supply the demand. The Lisbon as well as the Minho wines, handicapped though they were by the sweet wine duty, had long had a limited public, but only the new Douro vineyards could possibly cope with the situation. It must be remembered that neither shippers nor growers nor indeed the British vintners, who tried their hands at making their wines more palatable, had the remotest idea of their eventual goal. The obvious easy way was to make their wine sufficiently alcholic to compete with the spirits which were entrenching themselves in the English market, and since the idea was abroad that the deeper the purple of the wine, the more effective its alcohol, they did not hesitate to use the inexhaustible crop of wild elder-berries to deepen it. In point of fact, they were making neither a table nor a dessert wine, and were exporting an unamalgamated mixture of wine and brandy, a compound which could not possibly appeal to even an uncultured palate, exceedingly unwholesome, with a headache and gout in every bottle. It was impossible for them to guess that if only the fortified wine could be given time, its warring constituents would be reconciled into the finest of dessert wines.

After 1728 the exports of port declined, though they jumped in some years, when the level of Spanish imports fell nearly to the level of the French. The shippers fell out and accused one another of malpractices. Things were not improved when in 1745 an additional duty of £4 the tun was imposed on Portuguese wine. A perpetual war was waged with the growers, who really had not enough to live on and did succeed in so far forcing up prices that in 1750 they were getting from £14 10s. to £21 7s. the pipe. In 1755 the vintage was abundant and the wine promised well. The shippers forgot their discords in a determination to bring the peasants to their knees and reduce the price of their wines to the old level, agreeing not to pay more than £3 a pipe. It is not surprising that the situation in the Douro valley became so threatening that the Portuguese Government was impelled to step in and save the wretched growers from utter destitution. The measures taken, like all Governement interference, opened the door to many abuses, and vested interests naturally subjected them to a furious attack which lasted for many years, but I feel sure that without them port never would have become the Englishman's wine. Their history has nearly always been written by those whose

422                                                        THE WINES OF PORTUGAL

sympathy is less with the native growers than with the merchants who bought their wines. I must confess to a prejudice in favour of those who grow wine and, perhaps I should add, drink it, as opposed to those who only sell it, with the reservation that the history of wine owes much to the influence and palate of those vintners who in their secret hearts are not convinced that they can actually buy anything more precious than the stuff they sell.

There was really every reason for the formation of the Douro Wine Company on 18 September 1756 under Royal Charter and the patronage of the famous Marquis de Pombal and other prominent wine-growers with absolute control over the Douro Wine Trade. The shippers, not the peasant growers, were brought to their knees. They had to buy their wines on the terms dictated by the monopoly, terms which infringed many of the legal privileges they had enjoyed under the most-favoured-nation treatment accorded to the oldest ally, and it is not surprising that with their wine trade anything but prosperous they were furious. It cannot be gainsaid that the general principles of the Douro Wine Company as stated in their programme were highly praiseworthy, and could have been of real value to the trade, if only they had been put into practice with scrupulous observance of their purpose. Even Redding, who burdens its shoulders with all the bad wine which came into the country from the Douro for many years to come, admits in a footnote that some of its regulations were good and useful. Unhappily not all of those who directed it accepted its provisions as binding on themselves. The Marquis de Pombal was generally accused of passing wine grown in vineyards outside the defined area into the Douro valley to be exported as port, and it is pretty certain that it was not his best wine. Yet I think it is only fair to say that the greater part of the blame heaped on the Company belonged, indeed, to the factor which for so long prevented the transformation of the Douro wines into wines acceptable in the English market, in other words the inevitable ignorance of the principle of fermentation.

The Company began by marking out the boundaries of the area in which wine with the port character could be grown. In this measure the Portuguese, as so often, anticipated by many years the rest of the world in recognizing the dependence of the vine on local conditions nowhere else reproduced and giving official significance to the place name of a wine. How well I remember the political squabbles when the French Prime Minister, M. Monis, separated the sheep from the goats, if wines may be qualified by such terms, first in Bordeaux, later in Champagne, by what then seemed the magic word delimitation – a cantrip which had been operative in Portugal for over a century and a half. The Company at any rate professed the policy of converting Oporto from the dumping ground of the cheapest Portuguese wines on which the shipper could lay hands into the centre of a local export wine industry. The immediate result was an increase of the value of a vineyard within the prescribed area and the price of the wine it grew. The goose at last had the chance of having enough to eat to keep it alive.

A second ordinance was based on a principle sanctioned by age-long experience. If a wine country intends to keep up its export trade the standard of its exports must be maintained at a high level, and the rule does not apply only to wine. Even in these days I have heard of the purchaser of a new motor car who found under one of the seat cushions 'not fit for export'. As long ago as 1482 the Governor of Jerez, founding the town which today is known as Chipiona, prescribed that all wines intended for export must be made in Jerez fashion and might be pressed only from three specified grapes, doubtless grapes of quality rather than quantity. With a similar end in view the Company appointed tasters to classify the Douro wines as either fit for export or fit only for the less fastidious taste of home consumers.

No wine-lover could raise objection to the decree that no elder-berries were to sneak into the grape juice to deepen the colour of the wine and that all elder trees in the wine region were to be uprooted. The Greeks rated the goat as enemy number one of the vine – they were spared the deadly louse phylloxera – and, since a stray goat in a vineyard was a disaster, made it pay for its sacrilege by sacrificing it to Dionysus, with the curious compensation that *tragos*, the he-goat, lent its name to tragedy from the celebrations which took place at its sacrifice in the great Dionysiac festivals. In Portugal the elder was a less deadly, if more subtle, foe of the wine god. It seems to be a practically inextirpable plant with a range of habitat far exceeding that of the wine grape. Who has not drunk here elder-berry wine of a fine deep colour, though a quite exceptional palate would be needed to distinguish its taste from other so-called wines homemade from such bases as the parsnip or cowslip. From my experience I should say that it was as hopeless to outlaw it legally as to prohibit the growth of weeds by law. Its flower, naturally pleasantly sweet in the open air, but cloying in concentration, has served in other countries, not Portugal, as a meretricious imitation of the muscat grape flavour. The elder-berries, in Portuguese *baga*, have plenty of colour, but such taste as they have definitely dulls all those delicate flavours which are the birthright of the vine. The cheek raddled with rouge is a poor imitation of the flushing damask cheek of youth. Admittedly its wonderful colour is one of the joys of wine, whether it be gold or amethyst or purple mingled with gold, hues which the painter's palette can only imperfectly reproduce, but colour, with its appeal to the eye, though it may have a high selling value, as the artificial colours of liqueurs prove, weighs very light in the scales against the appeals to nose and palate of bouquet and flavour. It is important only as the outward and visible sign of health and quality. In an article in the *Wine Magazine* André Simon has commented on the extraordinary craze which insists that white wines must be *paper white* without a trace of colour, demanding some artificial bleaching process, and has banished from champagne the variety of hue which once distinguished various vintages, to say nothing of insisting that burgundy must be darker red than claret. The craze prevailing in the eighteenth century which insisted on the deepest of purples for the Douro wines may well have been connected with a desire to emulate the dark natural colour of the Florence wines which, as has been said, once well thought of, had lost their market probably through their importation in uncorked *fiaschi*.

Simon, in his *Bottlescrew Days*, gives an excellent summary of the principal objects of the Douro Wine Company. – 'The better to support with the reputation of the wines the culture of the vineyards and, at the same time, to benefit the commerce which is carried on in this commodity, establishing for it a regular price, from which may result a competent convenience to those who cultivate it, and a respective gain to those who trade in it, avoiding, on the one hand, the excessive prices which render the consumption impossible and therefore ruinous to the commodity; and on the other hand, avoiding its decline so much that the wine growers cannot afford to support the annual expense of its culture.'

There can be no better proof of the drastic action needed at the time of the formation of the Company than the correspondence exchanged by the English merchants of

Oporto with their factors in the Douro wine region. The merchants' letter of complaint shows how blind they were to the future fate held in store for the Douro wines. 'The grower', they wrote, 'at the time of the vintage, is in the habit of checking the fermentation of the wines too soon by putting brandy into them whilst fermenting – a practice which must be considered as *diabolical*, for after this the wines will not remain quiet, but are continually tending to ferment and to become ropy or acid.' It seems extremely unlikely that brandy was guilty of these crimes. Later the Company expressed its own very different point of view not without exaggeration. They asserted that all wines needed brandy to quiet, cleanse and preserve them, and added that when brandy and wine had been incorporated by mature age it nearly doubled the flavour.

The Merchants' letter called forth from their factors in the hills among the vineyards a magnificent reply which must surely have been inspired by copious potations. 'The English merchants knew', they wrote, 'that the first-rate wine of the Factory had become excellent; but they wished it to exceed the limits which nature had assigned to it, and that when it was drunk, it should feel like liquid fire in the stomach; that it should burn like inflamed gunpowder; that it should have the tint of ink; that it should be like the sugar of Brazil in sweetness, and like the spices of India in aromatic flavour. They began by recommending, by way of secret, that it was proper to dash it with brandy in the fermentation to give it strength; and with elder-berries or the rind of the ripe grape to give it colour; and as the persons who used the prescription found the wine increase in price, and the English merchants still complaining of a want of strength, colour and maturity in the article supplied, the recipe was propagated till the wines became a mere confusion of mixtures.'

The desperate situation which led to the formation of the Company could not be immediately remedied by its formation, and in the following year there were riots and bloodshed in Oporto and the Douro valley. Simon tells us that a score of sympathizers with the English shippers were shot, and though he does not say so, it sounds as if our merchants had reacted against what was evidently a breach of the Treaty privileges by encouraging or at least countenancing a protest of violence. They can scarcely have had any genuine supporters among the wine-growers to whom the Company promised protection. The Company survived and the shippers resorted to the slow-grinding mills of diplomacy. They addressed a petition to William Pitt, then Secretary of State, and pleaded for Free Trade in face of a State export monopoly in terms which would have brought tears to Cobden's eyes. 'The engrossing of the wines into one hand cannot impose quality or price, or keep the wines better or purer; but must make it worse or more adulterated than a free trade would do, for such would make every Merchant *emulous* for his own interests to improve them and keep them pure.' Such arguments addressed to such an inveterate drinker of the primitive forerunner of what was to be the Englishman's wine as the Great Commoner should surely have been more effective than the statement of legal and Treaty grievances which followed them.

They claimed, unquestionably with justice, that the law which established the monopoly of the Company violated all their commercial rights guaranteed by the Treaty of 1654, which promised to them free and uninterrupted commerce throughout Portugal. Unhappily for them their appeal to a port-loving statesman was as muted by international conditions as if in 1940 the shippers of champagne had complained of unfair treatment to a Prime Minister credited with a taste for their wine scarcely less than his

Plate 38. The Douro vintage.

taste for cigars. Simon has set out in the book so often quoted the singularly unproductive results of the diplomatic exchanges which followed, and so we pass to 1775, another decisive date, when the great vintage had both quality and quantity.

Time had worn down the deadlock between the Company and the shippers to the friction of ill-adjusted cogs. Having lost hope of remedy of their legally just grievances, a majority of the merchants had come to terms with the monopoly and others had invested in its shares. One of its functions was the purchase of wines when supply exceeded demand, and considerable stocks had been accumulated before the very abundant vintage of 1775. Simon's researches have shown that in 1776 the Company embarked on a campaign on a large scale to compete with the independent merchants and sell its wines direct in this country. With all its privileges it was in a very strong position and planned to secure the support of at least one wine-merchant in every important town in England. A letter from the Company's Chief Agent, dated 24 June 1776, quotes prices for the wines of the five vintages from 1771 to 1775. The independent shipping firms, however, managed to hold their own, and Simon considers that they actually profited by the publicity given to port through the Company's enterprise in sending free samples to the nobility and gentry as well as to the trade. But it was not till 1787 and 1788 that the imports of Portuguese wine increased and, often exceeding 20,000 tuns, established its premier position in the English market, and by then a completely new factor, the solution of the port problem, had entered into the statistics.

CHAPTER SIX

# The Recovery of the Lost Secret

THE NINETEENTH century, which dawned with England not for the only time alone against a world in arms, was to see the Pax Romana reborn in the Pax Britannica. In the history of wine it marks the rebirth of that Golden Age of great vintage wines, which had ended so abruptly, apparently for ever, with the fall of Rome. Britain, that land where Tacitus said neither vine nor olive would grow, shared with wine-growing Portugal the honour of this renaissance. Vintage port, though still in its swaddling clothes, was growing up to challenge the memory of the wine which the Greeks called Saprias, or of the Falernian of great age which the great physician Galen approved for his Emperor Marcus Aurelius from the imperial cellars, such wines as the world had not known for a millennium and a half. Wine was being raised from the level of a pleasant merry-making beverage, to be forgotten as soon as swallowed, to the rank of a joint masterpiece of nature and human art, which appealed to nose and palate as painting and music appealed to eye and ear. The patience and enterprise of the Oporto shippers and growers was coaxing the stubborn Douro wines, at least the best of them, into that gracious charm which only the alchemy of time can give, and the beneficence of their efforts spread far afield beyond the boundaries of Portugal, involving all other wine-growing countries in a debt which they have been slow to acknowledge.

Plate 39. Black port grapes, *Tinta Cão*, with the schistous rock in which the Douro vines grow.

## The Factory House

The ancients out of the fullness of their grateful hearts raised temples to the glory of the wine god, and Christianity paid its tribute in its acceptance of wine as a sacramental symbol. The Hellenic city states might sponsor with the approval of their wine-loving citizens pious testimonials to the mystic power of Dionysus, but the British wine-lover may glow with complacent surprise at the thought that the Parliament of this non-wine-growing country took the initiative in founding that enduring monument to the advent of vintage port, the finest palace of wine in Europe, the Factory House of Oporto. It stands as a splendid memorial to that combination of Portuguese enterprise and British common sense which made port the Englishman's wine and restored the golden age of vintage wines. Above its portal the architect might well have engraved the prophecy which so nearly made Virgil a Christian, REDEUNT SATURNIA REGNA, the golden age returns.

Traditional friendship and the Brazilian trade had favoured the establishment of Factories, groups of resident traders, in Portuguese ports, and their importance in contributing to the national economy was fully recognized by the home authorities. Legislation was passed which empowered or rather required them to finance themselves by levying a small duty, payable on consular clearance, on all goods imported into Portugal from Britain. From this fund they paid the salaries of consuls and chaplains – the presence of a Protestant chaplain in a Roman Catholic country often led to disputes with the Portuguese authorities – and defrayed such other expenses as the community should incur. The official standing accorded to these Factories is illustrated by the instructions given to the fleet stationed off the Portuguese coast in 1741, when the War of the Austrian Succession had broken out. In April of that year the members of the British Factory at Oporto were informed that: 'The Admiralty had instructed the commanders of His Majesty's ships stationed on this coast to obey the directions of this Factory and to be entirely at their disposal.' It seems probable that these instructions were qualified by a private order of discrimination between members of the Factory, many of whom had strong Jacobite leanings, in accordance with their politics, to judge from a consular dispatch to the Secretary of State, the Duke of Newcastle: 'The Factory is mightily pleased with this unexpected Power given them, which they look upon as an unprecedented favour; I wish they may use it with discretion and that it may be means to suppress the Malignity which reigns in most of the members towards the present Administration.'

The Oporto Factory House owes its existence to the special legislation of the 'Contribution Fund Act', which established for the disposal of the Factory an additional tax levied on goods travelling in the opposite direction; that is, a levy on all exports from Portugal to Britain. This fund was devoted to the building and installation of the Factory House. John Croft tells us that the exchange at this time stood at about four milreis (1,000 reis) to the pound sterling and the contributions levied were fixed at 300 reis on the pipe of wine, 400 reis on the pipe of oil, 100 reis on the bag of wool, 60 reis on the box of fruit, 25 reis on the quintal of cork wood and 60 reis on the barrel of tartar. Wine must have been the principal contributor to the building fund, and as at this time an annual average of about 25,000 pipes was being exported from Oporto, the levy should have amounted to between £3,500 and £4,000 per annum. The Factory House took four years to build. The local material, Portuguese granite, and local labour were exceedingly cheap and, allowing for the income from sources other than from wine, something like £20,000 must have been available for the building, furnishing and general embellishment of a palace really worthy of the merchant princes who built it.

It stood on Crown property in the street that was to be known as the Rua Nova dos Ingleses, though a characteristic urge of patriotic pride, rather like that which requires in Oporto that in the town shoes must be worn by the women who, barefooted, balance so beautifully on their heads enormous loads, has renamed it the Rua Infante Dom Enrique. In this street the British traders had long conducted their word-of-mouth business. Secretaries and computers are superfluous when a bargain is struck with a nod between principals. In 1727 the merchants leased three houses in this street, forming a corner block, for club and residential purposes with a rent of 2,311 reis. With a view to something far finer, with the Contribution Fund in view, they decided to pull these houses down and build on the site. Demolition began in 1785 and the new building was completed in 1790, the work being superintended by the Vice-Consul John Whitehead. History does not relate how it was that in 1805 the original lease had disappeared and the granting of a new lease set a whole army of officials very busy compiling documents faithfully reproduced by Sellers. The Appraisers who surveyed and valued 'the newly erected Palace', the Stone Mason, the Master Carpenter and the Carpenter attached to the Record Office of the Crown Lands in Oporto and the appraiser appointed by the British Consul were of a merciful disposition. Unimpressed by the splendour of the Factory House, they determined on their sacred oath that the new building justified an increase of the original rent by 689 reis, say 6s. Their tidy minds were satisfied by the conversion of the rent into the round figure of 3,000 reis, and one can only hope that that tidiness was uninfluenced by an unofficial generosity.

The Italian merchant princes built themselves in Genoa and Venice palaces of architectural splendour with a wealth of adornment; their cup would have been full if the renaissance had recovered, along with the glory of classical art, the wines which had inspired the classics. The British Merchant Princes of Oporto, with the rich spirit of port to enrich and gild any palace they might build, were content with the severe austerity of an unadorned granite exterior, a magnificent model of Georgian architecture, dependent for its effect on admirable proportions and quietly contrasting with the Portuguese love of the ornate. I hope that the many Scottish shippers whose ancestors made their contribution to the Factory House will forgive me if I suggest that, seen from without, it is as faithful a monument of the John Bull tradition as that inspirer of confidence, the Victorian gold sovereign, used to be. Solid and trustworthy with no attempt at showiness, it is the concrete symbol of the value which, one hopes, is still attached by the Portuguese and others to the word of an Englishman.

The Englishman's wine in the interior engenders a rich and rosy glow stolen from the southern sun, and the spiritual essence of the greatest port pervades with its richness the interior of the Factory House. The exit from a blazing sun into the cool of the vestibule preludes the plunge into the gracious past, into an atmosphere redolent with the bouquet of fine wine. Severe simplicity had designed the columned vestibule with arched interspaces just of the size to shelter a sedan chair and, like a time machine, to carry back the visitor to the days when the uniforms of the victorious Iron Duke's officers coloured its whiteness. In one recess there still nestles a dainty survivor of that means of transport, the only vehicle for a lady up and down the street precipices of Oporto, which no horse can negotiate and which still test to the utmost the patient, almost irresistible plodding pull of the great oxen. Graceful little lamps on long rods were used to light the bearers and now serve, enslaved to electricity, to illuminate the great staircase.

Was Mr Consul Whitehead thinking of Mahomet's coffin when he approved the design for that monumental staircase? Ponderous slabs of granite invisibly let into the wall appear to have no means of support other than that supernatural force which held Mahomet's tomb suspended between earth and heaven. I remember Jennings, Sandeman's manager, told me with a twinkle in his eye that he never felt quite comfortable on that version of Jacob's ladder. Surely some day the force of gravitation must have its way and bring back to earth those ponderous slabs.

When I first went to Portugal forty years ago revolutions were far more common than general elections here, and it was a reassuring thought that the massive walls of the Factory House could defy the assault of any mob. *Les Portugais sont toujours gais*, said Alphonse Allais, and in these latter days my enjoyment of the Factory House as an outward and visible sign of the inner grace of vintage port was the more unalloyed, because the national gaiety had beneath it such a lining of material prosperity as it had never before possessed; things had changed.

The Factory House, with its palatial ballroom and magnificent chandeliers, its fine library and above all those rooms consecrated to the contemplation of the wine to which it owes its existence, should be a place of pilgrimage for every wine-lover. I hope that my impression of it may not be unduly prejudiced by memories associated with it on my first visit. For me it has a background of the garden of Sandeman's palace, Campo Alegre, with its great camellia hedges in full bloom, its sanctuary for singing birds worthy of Dante's Earthly Paradise and a view over Vila Nova de Gaia with its Lodges brimming with wine and brandy piled one above the other on the steep slope – a peaceful scene which might become a nightmare if ever fire set wine and brandy in conflagration to pour down to the river in a torrent of flame.

As a novice I went to the Factory House, eager to learn all I could about the Englishman's wine, and found myself in a circle of masters of the art of wine-making as eager to teach as I to learn. The environment of the Factory House dining-room, in which I studied with palate the wine and with the ear the circumstances which made it, was in itself a lecture. There was no need to indulge the foible of dressing up in obsolete picturesque costume, which in some wine-growing countries has been adopted for wine festivals to link the present with the past, for the tradition was alive around us in the imperishable solidity of granite and the beauty of furnishings more enduring than even the finest wine. The spirit of the Hellenic symposium was there, and the searcher after knowledge found around him a band of sages with a zeal to answer questions which Socrates did not share, however keen he was to ask them. With such long suffering was my curiosity suffered that the circulation of the port decanters, appointed by tradition to time by its arrest, normally at three o'clock, the end of luncheon, by a miracle contrary to that of Joshua was prolonged in its course for an extra two hours – then, I was assured, the longest luncheon on record in the history of the Factory and one certainly more worthy of the name than that meal which, by lumping luncheon and supper together in spite of an interval of several hours, Brillat-Savarin termed *le plus long repas* he had made in his life and described as a *bonbon* for his readers.

At that time the port trade was recovering from the repercussion of the First World

War thirst, which had drunk too deeply into the reserves that are its life blood, and was facing a new menace which was the main cause of my first visit. A conspiracy was on foot under the guise of imperial solidarity to prostitute the good name of port, its geographical birthright, by legalizing its application to any wine which liked to steal it. I like to think that my articles in the *Morning Post* after my visit, later published in pamphlet form, were not without influence in the defeat of that plot. The Factory House had known far sadder times, months of trial still remembered. The world from the English point of view looked very black, when on 22 July 1808 Sir Arthur Wellesley, having sailed from the Expeditionary Force at Coruña, landed at Oporto, and was able to prepare for the future, his eagle eye registering all the tactical possibilities of the town cascading down to the great river spanned by a bridge of boats. His appearance must have been greeted by the Oporto shippers as a divine visitation. They had been through a very bad time. From October 1807 to June 1808 the whole of Portugal had been occupied by the French, and they had been driven to such expedients as the nominal transference of their stocks of wine and other property to Portuguese citizens to avoid confiscation. To judge from the customs figures, they had succeeded, more by crook than by hook, in maintaining their shipments to Britain. The world had not yet been cursed with the efficiency of total warfare. The General enjoyed the lavish hospitality with which wine-lovers are wont to entertain far less welcome guests and marked his approval of the wine by ordering some port for himself. A draft on his bankers Messrs Greenwood and Cox for £35, payable to the firm which later became Taylor, Fladgate and Yeatman, has survived.

During his short visit – he sailed from Oporto on 25 July – business was only just returning to normal, for the town had been free of the French for little more than a month, Oporto having been evacuated as a result of the revolution which had broken out throughout Portugal in June. The presence of the British general must have brought home to the shippers the advantage of the command of the sea, which had made their trade possible against all obstacles, but Oporto had not seen the last of the French. In January 1809 the invading army was back again. In the occupied town the shippers did their best to keep in the background. The Factory House, Sellers tells us, was turned into a hostelry with an eating house for all English travellers, and there was a public coffee room at the entrance, free admission being granted to English captains and clerks to read the public papers in a special room. Presumably English captains could read their newspapers in Oporto only when the French were not in possession.

On 12 May Wellesley came to the relief of Oporto, and by the brilliant passage of the Douro sent Marshal Soult, who had relied too confidently on his destruction of the bridge of boats, into headlong defeat. It seems almost a pity that the Marshal had not chosen the Factory House as his headquarters; perhaps its severe unpretentious beauty gave precedence to the more showy Palace of the Carrancas. It would have added just one more feather to its many-plumed hat if the victorious general and his staff had eaten there the dinner prepared for the defeated Marshal instead of in the palace. In 1810 Wellesley, facing Masséna in the lines of Torres Vedras, did not lose contact with the shippers of Oporto, and there can have been no shortage of the best port in his mess.

As the French menace was rolled back, his staff still kept in touch. Plate 35 of the Visitors Book of the Factory House depicts history over very nearly a century and a half. The entries of two of Wellington's A.D.C.s, Captain Freemantle and the Earl of

March, were signed on 23 December 1813, when the decisive victory of Vittoria had relieved the Iberian Peninsula of every fear and opened the gate of France to invasion. The glass in which Queen Elizabeth II drank in 1957 in that palace of wine the very cream of tawny port commemorated the celebration of that unbroken alliance, which has for centuries found expression in the Englishman's wine, the wine of the royal toast, that toast which she alone in all her dominions cannot drink (see Plate 35).

Everywhere the Second World War and subsequent doubtful peace have muffled the joys of hospitality, and port has been among the worst sufferers, but it is bravely and surely struggling back to the former glory which is its right. In the Factory House the frequency of the gatherings has been curtailed, and luncheon has become a weekly institution, but it has even gained in its magnificent exposition of the art of good living. One of the beautiful rooms which used to lie idle specially offers a preface to the meal, recognizing the advent of the *apéritif*. Before, there was sherry drunk, it seemed to me a little shamefacedly, as an admission that Oporto was not entirely independent of Jerez. There is still sherry, but its supremacy is challenged by dry white port, which goes so well before a Portuguese table wine and has the virtue of demanding that the meal should end with the richness of its red or tawny brother. Once the feast began and ended in the dining-room, which can seat a party of forty; the table wine was vinho verde, white or red, and the Douro *consumo* appeared only as a curiosity to enable the stranger to appreciate the miracle of its transformation into port. Now the Douro wine takes pride of place, with its shortcomings eliminated by scientific vinification, though vinho verde is still available. The port decanters and dessert call for a move to another room, but the Factory House goes one better and rules out the problem of the moment when tobacco can be admitted by having a third room for liqueurs and cigars.

The history of the Factory House has had its internal ups and downs, and the question of its proprietorship has raised bitter controversy. From the time of its foundation to the French occupation it served as a kind of royal exchange for all British traders. When business was resumed after the evacuation and merchants who had left the town returned a British Association was formed which claimed the Factory House as its property, since its members had paid the contributions which formed its building fund. In 1810 a treaty signed in Rio de Janeiro, well out of the way of the French, confirmed the privileges mutually granted to their citizens by Britain and Portugal, and a number of new firms set themselves up in Oporto. These newcomers, still subject to the Contribution Fund Act, found themselves excluded from the Factory House, as they had contributed nothing to the building fund. They embarked on a campaign to obtain admission on the ground that the Factory House was intended to be the common property of all British merchants in Oporto. They became known as Memorialists, since they kept sending memorials to the home government, demanding the redressal of their grievance but the repeal of the Contribution Fund Act in 1825 seriously weakened their case. In 1834 the controversy came to an end with the defeat of the Memorialists and an agreement that the fabric of the Factory House and its contents were the property of its original members, though the site was still the property of the Portuguese Crown. In 1851 those members purchased the freehold of the property, which became vested in the firms listed as its members on 16 June 1851, thirteen of them. After that date any firm retiring sacrificed its share in a valuable non-commercial asset, and any new firms which might be elected were granted a share in that property.

# CHAPTER SEVEN

# The First Vintage Ports

SOON after the turn of the century vintage port had proved itself a supreme dessert wine of a quality worthy of the commendations bestowed by the ancients on their finest wines. Between 1772 and 1815, only one vintage – that of 1775, with what was at the time the remarkably high export yield of nearly 56,000 pipes – was awarded the highest commendation of 'very fine', with 1806 and 1815 as runners-up with the mark 'very good'. The cylindrical bottle was available for the great 1775 vintage, and it seems a fair guess that best Douro wine of 1775 profited by it to become the first great vintage port in history. But the possibilities of the bottle were still a matter of speculation, and only experience could show how it could be best used. At what stage in the wine's life should it be immured in its glass home to age? And how long could it be expected to improve to its prime in this environment? Pipes of 1775 port will have been bottled after their arrival, but of how long they were kept in the wood before bottling, of how long they lived, no record remains.

The first vintage of which a record survives, throwing light on the answers to these questions, is that of 1797, and its history when closely inspected is both odd and interesting. Previously I was content to follow other writers on port and quote George Sandeman, the founder of the famous shipping firm, assuring Viscount Wellington, when dining with him in the lines of Torres Vedras, that the 1797 vintage was the finest port year within his experience. It was a moral certainty that he would have seen that the mess of the Commander-in-Chief and his staff was well provided with his finest wine, and not only for the occasions when he was a guest, all the more perhaps because two years before the great man had favoured another shipper. Since young Mr Sandeman did not come to Oporto until 1790, the 1775 vintage may well have been outside his cognizance. I should have been content to leave it at that, if I had not been startled by a chance glance at the official list giving the quality and yield of the Oporto vintages from 1722 to 1822, quoted in Henderson's *History of Ancient and Modern Wines*. After 1775 no vintage received even the alpha minus mark of 'good' until that of 1796, which with a yield of 68,000 pipes was so described. But 1797, George Sandeman's greatest year, was damned as 'very bad, tawny', the worst year there had been since 1777. Tawniness was then anything but a virtue in port: the demand was all for wines of the darkest purple; black-strap was the order of the day. In a young wine tawniness was damnation.

At first I could only imagine that someone had blundered in recording the date of the vintage of which George Sandeman thought so much. Perhaps he really spoke of the 1796 vintage. But an examination of the basic authority for the story made this explanation highly improbable, for it did not begin and end with the wine in Portugal, but followed its history in Britain. Sellers put me on the track of the original authority, *Recollections of Old Country Life* (1893), by John Kersey Fowler, Quartermaster of the Bucks Volunteers, and what it has to say, when quoted in full, speaks for itself.

John Kersey Fowler was a typical country gentleman of the Victorian era, with interests ranging from politics, cattle breeding and volunteering to gastronomy, epitaphs and the classics (he quotes in the Greek a eulogy of his favourite flower, the rose). Moreover, he was a port-lover. 'My own opinion is', he writes, 'that there is no wine so grand and truly great as a fine vintage port, bottled young – say after three or four years in the wood – and drunk from twelve to fifteen years afterwards.' His judgment on wine was evidently highly thought of, and it is inconceivable that there can be any mistake as to the date of the vintage of the wine of which he tells the following story.

'The Bucks Volunteers, of which regiment I was Quartermaster, were encamped in Claydon Park, the residence of my revered friend Sir Harry Verney. He asked me to go over his stock of wine in the vaults under the mansion, as there were certain bins of wine rather deficient in character, and some were undrinkable from their great age. He came down into the cellars with me and I carefully sampled the contents. I discovered a bin of wine which completely baffled my judgment. Sir Harry said that none of the family would drink it, as it had become decayed. I minutely examined it; it was in curious old-fashioned bottles, was of a really beautiful colour, light ruby, *not tawny*, and I pronounced it perfectly sound because there was no acetous fermentation. There was, however, scarcely any rich flavour, and at last I discovered at the bottom of some of the bottles large flakes of crust, which I found had slipped off the sides and were then floating in the wine, but they did not discolour or foul it; on again tasting it I felt sure that it was Port, evidently of great age. Sir Harry then fetched an old wine-book of his father's and the mystery was solved. His father, General Calvert (Sir Harry having taken the name of Verney on succeeding to the Claydon property), was Quartermaster-general to the Duke of Wellington throughout the Peninsular War. When the British army was safely encamped and protected on the masterly lines constructed by the great Duke at Torres Vedras, on or about 1809, Mr Sandeman, the head of the great wine house at Oporto, was a frequent guest at the Duke's dinner-table, and the conversation once turned upon fine and noted vintages. Mr Sandeman said he thought that the vintage of 1797 was the finest Port wine ever known, and that vintage was as much talked of then as the 1834, '47, or '51 vintages are talked of now. General Calvert, as a great favour, requested him to send two pipes of this celebrated wine to England. Mr Sandeman did so, and the general made a present of one to the Duke of York, at that time commander-in-chief of the army; and the other he had bottled for himself, and this was the remains of that very wine. Sir Harry wished to get rid of it, and I agreed to exchange as many dozens of the finest 1873, which I had lately shipped from Martinez and Gassiot, as there were dozens of the 1797. He was well pleased with the bargain, and I found that there were nineteen dozens of it. When I got it home into my vaults, I drew out six dozen from each of two pipes of 1873, and blended the same amount of the last century wine, and bottled it in 1876, and in three years' time it turned out some of the finest wine I ever tasted. I sold six dozen of the original Port to Messrs Spiers and Pond . . . at a moderate price, and the following Christmas, at the dinner of the Farmers' Club, at the Criterion, I observed in the special wine list, "Duke of York's Port", vintage 1797, price £2 per bottle. I heard that at this well-known establishment this wine was often called for, and that it is much appreciated . . . I have one or two bottles in my present cellars, and hope to live long enough to open one at the hundredth anniversary of the vintage . . . This when I tasted it was therefore eighty years old, and shows how well a really grand wine will keep sound.'

It is interesting that our author should italicize the words *not tawny* almost as though he was aware of the adverse judgment pronounced officially on the 1797 vintage, but he obviously was not. If he had been, he could not have introduced into his account something that could not possibly have been contained in Sir Harry's old cellar-book, the statement that in its day the 1797 vintage was as much talked of as the most famous of its successors at the time it was consulted. It was not till the autumn of 1810 that Wellington fell back on the lines of Torres, so the Sandeman 1797 sent to General Calvert must have had thirteen or fourteen years in the wood before it was bottled. Its longevity is the more remarkable. He was writing in 1893, so that he may well have drunk his Duke of York's Port when it was a hundred years old.

Mr Sandeman's palate and knowledge of port must be taken as above reproach. How, then, can we account for a judgment which must surely have been seriously weighed before it was pronounced in the august presence of the future Iron Duke? It seems an almost impossible coincidence, but I am driven to find the explanation of Sandeman 1797 in Sandeman 1911. I can think of no other solution of the mystery. The time had not yet come when the shippers met formally to compare notes on the wines of the year and, later, each individual firm decided on the basis of its individual interests whether it would be justified in shipping some fraction of its wines expressly as vintage port. The wine merchant then decided what wine he would bottle and how long he would keep it.

In our days as a rule there is a majority consensus of opinion about the shipping of vintage wines, though even in 1927 agreement was not quite universal. In the best of years there is variety in the quality and character of the wines from various vineyards used by various firms, and it is not only in the best of years, generally speaking, that wines of the highest quality are shipped. In 1911 only two firms shipped vintage wines, though there was the incentive of a Coronation year. I do not think any great quantity of Martinez was shipped. I only tasted it once and found it quite an excellent wine, though it could not compare with the Sandeman, which I should rank as one of the most beautiful wines of the century. Mr R. Croft-Cooke cannot have come across it, since in his book on *Port*, he omits 1911 from his roll of twentieth-century vintage ports, though he includes 1954 with its single shipper. It was light in colour and matured early into an exquisitely harmonious bouquet and flavour, and its beauty, so delicate for port, faded very slowly. At the age of forty its hue in my opinion was none the worse for being tawny; it was perfectly sound without a trace of spiritiness and still delightfully delicate.

The story of this wine seems to me to throw light on the confidence with which Mr Sandeman extolled the merits of its precursor, Sandeman 1797, for he was surely upholding the virtues of a wine for which he was responsible. The instinct of the weather-wise in my friend Hubert Jennings smuggled through the contrariness of nature a wine which, even if it claims no place among the heavyweights of vintage port, has given me and many others untold enjoyment. Does not Ernest Cockburn say that it will long be remembered as a first-class specimen of all that is best in vintage port? Only the other day a discriminating wine-lover told me ruefully that he had bought at auction a parcel of magnums of Sandeman 1911 and, listening to the advice of an all-too-knowledgeable friend who assured him that no port worth drinking was made in 1911, resold them all with the exception of two, before he had tasted the wine. As soon as he tried one of the remaining magnums he realized how ghastly was the mistake he had made.

In 1924, on my first admission into the magic circle of the wines of the Alto Douro, as the guest of that most perfect of hosts, Hubert Jennings, I was first introduced to this wine, a most promising youth, not yet of age, but already attractive. It provided background music to the story of its birth told with gusto by its creator. In 1911 Jennings was making his first vintage in full control as Sandeman's Manager in Oporto, and the first vintage means as much to the Manager of a great shipping firm as virginity to a maiden. The vintage opened gloriously with the grapes in fine condition and perfect sunny weather. Suddenly the weather broke and every shipper had to make up his mind whether the downpour could be treated as a passing phase, as a benediction to swell the grapes and increase the harvest, or whether it would keep on and ruin the whole vintage. A considerable quantity of fine wine had been already made, but if the sun drove away the rain even finer wine might be made, and prices would drop with the increased yield. Jennings was a man who could take a momentous decision with his seriousness masked by his love of fun and caustic wit. I am sure that he made up his mind as to the line he was going to follow without a sign of hesitation or worry. The others played for safety, hoping for the best and gambling on the chance of a return of the fine weather. Undue optimism was never one of Jennings's faults. For him the bad weather had come to stay. Without more ado, he bought up every fine wine on which he could lay hands, and there was plenty of first-class wine available. He was right, and the others were wrong. So he inaugurated his managership by shipping a Coronation vintage with only one rival, a wine that was to outlive him, though it came to its prime before he died, a wine that was to be long remembered.

It is my conviction that Jennings all unknowingly did exactly what the founder of his firm had done a hundred and fourteen years ago with the vintage of 1797. George Sandeman was a most enterprising and ambitious young Scotsman. He left his native Perth for London, determined to make his fortune. In May 1790 he wrote to his sister saying that he would not return home until he had done so and amassed a sum on which he could retire from business. This end he expected to achieve in nine years, unless 'some fortunate circumstance should reduce the time to five or six years'. At the end of that year he invested £300 borrowed from his father in a City wine vault, transacting his business after the custom of his time at Tom's Coffee House in Birchin Lane, Cornhill, but he promptly extended his activities abroad to the sources from which the wine he sold came. Determined to make the most of the opportunity given by our hostility with France to the wines of Portugal and Spain, he travelled extensively in the Iberian Peninsula and established his firm in Oporto. At that time the shippers usually shirked the difficult journey to the vineyards of the Upper Douro and left it to factors there to buy from the growers wines sent down by river. A man of Sandeman's initiative, who in London wanted to visit the regions from which the wines he sold came, was not likely to be content with such a system. He must have wanted to choose the wines and buy them on the spot where they were grown and made, relying on his own judgment, and I can see no way of accounting for Sandeman 1797 other than the hypothesis that he was in a position to buy up all the best wines made at the beginning of a vintage which suffered the same fate as that of 1911.

# CHAPTER EIGHT

# *Great Vintage Ports*

WITH the vintage of 1878, both in Portugal and France, the last note of the swan song of the great pre-phylloxera wines died away. In both countries the golden 'sixties and 'seventies passed, leaving a memory of supreme excellence, marking a peak, to which all future wines, if indeed phylloxera had not dealt a death blow to greatness, would have to aspire as to an ideal. Some of the native vines in ever-diminishing force still struggled on. In 1881, the year of my birth, a certain amount of good port was made. It promised well, but proved disappointing, and despondency descended on the shippers, many of whom were persuaded that vintage port was doomed.

Yet Portugal in general and the Douro in particular were more favoured than other wine lands in the death struggle against the all-destroying transatlantic louse. Events have shown that it is far less at home in Portugal than in any other country. Today Portugal boasts a considerably more extensive area of vineyards in which the native ungrafted vines still defy the pest than any to be found elsewhere. The insect cannot crawl down to the vine roots which are its prey through the depths of shifting grains of sea sand in the Colares vineyards, and I do not think that any grower outside Portugal has dared to emulate Senhor Luis Porto's courageous and successful experiment of openly defying the enemy with his plantation of native vines at Quinta Noval.

Moreover, port shares with sherry the advantage that man plays a more important part in its making than in that of natural wines. It would seem to follow that in these wines the malignity of nature as exhibited in phylloxera and other pests should be nullified more effectively by human effort. Sherry indeed claims that phylloxera has done it no harm at all, rather the contrary. Mr Jeffs, in his *Sherry*, says that in the general opinion of the shippers the wines of the grafted vines are rather better. If grafting has made a change in the character of vintage port, producing wines lighter, less full bodied and quicker to mature, many of the vintages which have come into being since phylloxera was reduced to abeyance can hold up their heads unashamed in the company of their famous classic predecessors.

Faced with the peril which was sweeping through Europe, the Douro growers began by experimenting with the chemical and other palliatives recommended by despair, but they showed greater wisdom than the French in a greater readiness to adopt the drastic remedy for established phylloxera, which has so far alone proved effective, the grafting of the native vine on the American stock, which has become inured through centuries to the assaults on its roots of its native louse. Cockburn dates 1884 as the turning-point in the battle. That year a small quantity of really fine vintage port was made from the grapes of the surviving vines. It matured better than the 1881s and was re-regarded by many port-lovers as the last of the pre-phylloxera vintages. More important historically was the fact that in 1884 the grafted vine had been generally accepted as the only means of staying the plague.

In 1887 there was a general demand in the British trade for a Jubilee Port to commemorate the fiftieth year of Queen Victoria's reign and the shippers did their best to live up to the occasion, but as a rule the wines shipped lacked stamina and were not up to vintage rank. There were some exceptions. Nicholas Block described Offley Forrester's *Boa Vista* 1887 as a unique specimen of this 'rather exploited vintage', far surpassing any other specimen in his experience. The *Boa Vista* of that year has never come my way, but the Smith Woodhouse remains a very pleasant recollection, and I am flattered to find my judgment confirmed by Saintsbury, who observes that he never drank a better 1887.

The port-lover may well consider himself lucky, if he compares the list of post-phylloxera vintages really worth remembering with the dreary sequence of indifferent vintages which saddened the claret-lover throughout the beginning of the twentieth century after the closing scene of 1899 and 1900, when two following years prophesied falsely that claret had risen from its grave. In the Douro there was 1890, a little light and dry perhaps, but good enough for Saintsbury to hand it down to fame as one of the best three vintage ports he ever had in his cellar.

With 1896 and 1897 vintage port returned to its classic days when round the candle-lit mahogany argument waxed hot as to the merits and demerits of one vintage and another, of one shipper and another. Those within the sacred inner circle of port con-noisseurs found abundant material for discussion and disagreement in weighing the pros and cons of two beautiful wines. As for the 1896 vintage Ian Campbell tells us how the old school of merchants – as Emerson says, all men are conservative after dinner – complained at first that it was wine and water, 'nothing like the manly vintages of old times', but it developed so well that all complaints died away and Campbell doubts whether we have ever had a vintage so majestic and manly since. Cockburn, Taylor and Ferreira of this year he judged superlatively fine and well able to hold their own with the giants of the past. The success of the 1896 wines was certainly a surprise – it is as safe to prophesy about wine as about the English weather – for they had had many difficulties to contend with, but they were generally shipped and were so well received that little welcome was left for the following vintage, which though inferior in yield gave wines at least equal, many said superior, to those of 1896. It has always puzzled me that patrio-tism did not inspire the trade, even though it was well stocked with the 1896 Vintage, to agitate for a second Jubilee Port. I have no reason to suppose that people thought a second Jubilee too much of a good thing: on the contrary, if my memory serves, it was celebrated with even more enthusiastic jubilation. As to the first Jubilee, perhaps my recollections are not very trustworthy, as, imprisoned with scarlet fever, I only heard and read about it, apart from a few rockets which soared over Portsdown Hill and the beams of searchlights from Portsmouth Harbour seen from a bedroom window. Of the second Jubilee I can speak with authority, for I watched from a London balcony the great procession headed by the most magnificent and gigantic Guards officer I have ever seen, the more impressive because he was an old boy of my school. If I had been a bit older I should certainly have clamoured for the general shipping of a Jubilee Port to commemorate the great event. I wish I could drink the old Queen's health in 1897 port today. As it was, only about ten shippers shipped 1897 as a vintage and narrowed the occasions when connoisseurs could argue the nice point whether the one or the other was the better. Most of those who were able to compare the two wines seem to agree that 1897 was the better wine, the shippers' palm being awarded to Graham and Sandeman. It was even rumoured that the best of the 1896s had some 1897 wine in them.

Of 1900, Cockburn 1900 in particular, I have treasured recollections, and as a vintage I definitely preferred it to the 1904. But Cockburn 1900 is associated in my mind with an election at Banbury some time in the twenties, and evening relaxation, after work for the *Morning Post* was done. The landlord of the inn which was the Conservative Headquarters – I think its name was The White Horse – was one of those jolly country hosts, now become so rare, proud of his cellar and always ready after dinner to devote a bottle of his best wine for the drinking of a toast to the right cause. My first night there, on the strength of the politics of my paper, he summoned me to his snuggery along with various Conservative supporters to drink that toast in his Cockburn 1900. I raised my glass with due reverence and by preaching abstention from smoking in its honour, I went so much up in his estimation that he reserved the 1900 for us two and sent down for a bottle of 1904 for those who had come in smoking or had lit up cigarettes. That summons was repeated every night that I was there.

## Modern Port Vintages

1917 – 'good colour, body and richness . . . soft, full and very "raisiny" ' (Cockburn).

1920 – elegant, very attractive wines.

1922 – rather delicate, but some outstanding.

1924 – a fine year, if with a touch of 'greenness'.

1927 – a great year, still splendid and in the century unsurpassed.

1931 – famous for a single wine, Da Silva's Quinta Noval, a giant of extraordinary body and vinosity, presumably partly due to grapes from Senhor Porto's plantation of ungrafted vines. It has not yet come of age.

1935 – better, wines which have turned out well and are much sought after.

1942 – bottled in Oporto, rather light, but of fine quality.

1945 – also bottled in Oporto, of remarkable quality. Croft 1945, not yet at its best, is a beautiful example of the first vintage year which challenges 1927.

1947 wines ripening rapidly with plenty of fruit and vinosity. Cockburn 1947 promises soon to attain that aristocratic excellence which long ago delighted me in Cockburn 1900.

1950 – a delicate wine of quality, growing up very quickly and valuable to fill the gap between 1947 and 1955.

1955 – wines to be laid down with the half-dozen Vintage Ports of 1958 for the end of the coming decade.

1960 – a great year comparable to 1945.

1963 – year of big production, some very fine wines, probably rather better than the 1960s and may develop like the 1935s.

1966 – good wine.

1967 – good wine.

### PORT WINE TRADE ASSOCIATION OF LONDON

*List of Members*

Brown, Gore & Welsh Ltd, Corn Exchange Chambers, Seething Lane, EC3

Cockburn Smithes & Co Ltd, Ingersoll House, 9 Kingsway, WC2

Croft & Co Ltd, 1 York Gate, Regents Park, NW1

Dent & Reuss Ltd, 22 Queen Street, Mayfair, W1

Evans Marshall & Co Ltd, 6 Idol Lane, EC3
Percy Fox & Co Ltd, 24/25 Whitechapel High Street, E1
Gonzalez Byass (U.K.) Ltd, 91 Park Street, W1
Grierson, Oldham & Adams Ltd, 25 Haymarket, SW1
Hunt Roope & Co Ltd, 23 Wormwood Street, EC2
Jarvis Halliday & Co, 102 Bicester Road, Aylesbury, Bucks
Geo. Jones & Co (London), 24/26 Great Suffolk Street, Blackfriars, SE1
Jules Duval & Beaufoys, Great West Road, Corner Syon Lane, Isleworth, Middx
C. N. Kopke & Co Ltd, 58 Southwark Bridge Road, SE1
Mackenzie & Co Ltd, 20 Eastcheap, EC3
Martinez Gassiot & Co (Sales) Ltd, 9 Kingsway, WC2
Morgan Bros (London) Ltd, Walbrook House, 23/29 Walbrook, EC4
J. R. Parkington & Co Ltd, 161 New Bond Street, W1
Reid, Rye & Campbell, Dashwood House, Old Broad Street, EC2
W. & T. Restell, 9 Union Court, Old Broad Street, EC2
Rutherford, Osborne & Perkin Ltd, 28 Monument Street, EC3
Geo. G. Sandeman Sons & Co Ltd, 20 St Swithin's Lane, EC4
Sereno & Co, 20 St Swithin's Lane, EC4
Silva & Cozens (London) Ltd, 3 St Dunstans Lane, EC3
Stowells of Chelsea, Britten Street, Chelsea, SW1
J. Turner & Co (Wines) Ltd, 57/60 Minories, EC3
Williams & Humbert Ltd, Sherry House, 39 Crutched Friars EC3
Wilson & Valdespino Ltd, 110 Cannon Street, EC4
Edward Young & Co Ltd, 5 Lloyds Avenue, EC3

## MEMBERS OF THE GREMIO DOS EXPORTADORES DE VINHO DO PORTO

### (Guild of Exporters of Port Wine)

A. A. Calem & Filho Ltda
A. P. Santos & Ca Ltda
Adolfo de Oliveira & Ca
Adriano Romos Pinto-Vinhos (S.A.R.L.)
Alberto De Castro Lanca Ltda
Alcino Correia Ribeiro
Amandio Silva & Filhos Ltda
Antonio José da Silva-Vinhos (S.A.R.L.)
Barros, Almeida & Ca
Butler, Nephew & Co
C. N. Kopke & Ca Ltda
C. da Silva-Vinhos (S.A.R.L.)
Campbell & Menzies
Cockburn Smithes & Ca Ltda
Companhia Agricola e Commercial dos Vinhos do Porto (S.A.R.L.)
Companhia Geral da Agricultura das Vinhas do Alto Douro (S.A.R.L.)
Croft & Ca Ltda
Delaforce Sons & Ca Ltda
Diez Hermanos Ltda

Feuerheerd Bros. & Ca Ltda
Gilberts & Ca Ltda
G. & J. Graham & Ca or W. & J. Graham & Co
Gonzalez, Byass & Ca
Grierson, Oldham & Adams Ltd
Guimaraens-Vinhos Ltda
H. & C. J. Feist Vinhos Ltda
H. & C. Newman
Hunt Roope & Ca Ltda
Hutcheson & Ca Ltda
J. Carvalho Macedo, Ltda
J. H. Andresen, Sucrs. Ltda
J. Serra & Sons Ltd
J. T. Pinto Vasconcellos Ltda
J. W. Burmester & Ca Ltda
MC. da Costa Oliveira Ltda
Mackenzie & Ca Ltda
Maison Manuel Misa
Manuel D. Pocas Junior Ltda
Manuel R. d'Assumpaco & Filhos Ltda

Martinez Gassiot & Co Ltd
Mìguel de Sousa Guedes & Irmao, Ltdᵃ
Morgan Brothers Ltdᵃ
Niepoort & Cᵃ
Offley Forrester Ltdᵃ
Pinto Pereira Ltdᵃ
Quarles Harris & Cᵃ Ltdᵃ
Real Companhia Vinicola do Norte de Portugal (S.A.R.L.)
Richard Hooper & Sons (Portugal) Ltdᵃ
Robertson Bros. & Cᵃ Ltdᵃ
Rodrigues Pinho & Cᵃ
Rozes Ltdᵃ
Sandeman & Cᵃ
Serafim Cabral Ltdᵃ
Silva & Cozens Ltd
Smith Woodhouse & Cᵃ Ltdᵃ
Soares Gomes, Filhos & Cᵃ Ltdᵃ

Sociedade Agricola e Commercial dos Vinhos Messias (S.A.R.L.)
Sociedade dos Vinhos do Alto Corgo Ltdᵃ
Sociedade dos Vinhos Antonio Ferreira Meneres, Sucr. Ltdᵃ
Sociedade dos Vinhos Borges & Irmao (S.A.R.L.)
Sociedade dos Vinhos F. Nogueira
Sociedade dos Vinhos do Porto Constantino (S.A.R.L.)
Sociedade dos Vinhos do Porto Serra Ltdᵃ
Taylor, Fladgate & Yeatman-Vinhos (S.A.R.L.)
The Douro Wine Shippers & Growers Association Ltdᵃ
Vieira de Sousa & Cᵃ
Warre & Cᵃ Ltdᵃ
Wiese & Krohn, Sucrs.

## INSTITUTO DO VINHO DO PORTO

Director General: Engenheiro João de Brito e Cunha
Directors: Engenheiro Américo Padrosa Pires de Lima
Engenheiro Alberto Ferreira da Silva
Secretary General: Dr José Ribeiro Pereira

## GREMIO DOS EXPORTADORES DO VINHO DO PORTO

President: Armando Augusto Fernandes e Silva
Directors: Ian Douglas Fullerton Symington
José Artur Lello Sá Fernandez

Alternate Directors: José António Ramos Pinto Rosas
Robin Allan Noel Reid
Dr Fernando Luiz Van-Zeller

Secretary General: Horácio Ferreira de Oliveira

## CASA DO DOURO

President: Engenheiro Orlando Augusto Ferreira Gonçalves
Vice President: Dr Amandio Rebello Figueiredo

# CHAPTER NINE

# The Emergence of Wood Port

By 1815 what we now know as vintage port had established itself in this country as a great wine, as is shown by the enduring renown of Waterloo Port, though it had not entered into a definite category of its own, definitely distinguished from the humbler members of its clan. It had proved that the pick of the wines of the Alto Douro in a fine year, duly treated with brandy during fermentation and matured for years in bottle, could claim its place in the highest aristocracy of wine and had fulfilled its historic mission by imparting to all wine lands the secret of great vintage wines lost since the fall of the Roman Empire. Waterloo Claret bears witness to its triumph. But this achievement, so important in the history of wine, was far from solving the problem with which the Oporto shippers had been struggling for over a century.

No wine industry can hope to flourish on the exclusive production of rare fine wines, only available in exceptionally good vintages and necessarily beyond the pocket of the average wine-lover except as an occasional treat. Such wines with capital locked in them for years cannot be cheap. The trade must draw its life blood from an abundance of sound palatable wines, excellent accompaniments to a meal, before it, with it or after it, retailed at a reasonable price. Great wines give to wines of their clan of less degree an invaluable prestige, but they must emerge from humbler wines certain of general popular approval which maintain, year in, year out, the upkeep of the vine-yards and all those who live by their produce. More than fifty years had to pass before those fortified wines of the Upper Douro, which for many reasons could not aspire to the rare splendour of vintage port, had overcome the obstacles to general popular approval set by the handicap of too easy admission into a practically open market, the limitations of nature and ignorance of the basic principle of fermentation.

As has been said, the Portuguese wine came into our market to take the place of the French table wines, but, even without competition, the English palate quite rightly rebelled against the coarseness and harshness of the Douro natural wines, so different from the lightness and natural sweetness of the Gascon wines. In those early days there can have been no doubt that something had to be done to correct the shortcomings of nature, if the Douro wines were in any way to fulfil the function assigned to them. At the turn of the century British merchants continually complained that the wines shipped to them were quite unreliable and very difficult to sell, and their complaints forced on shippers and growers a host of expedients, nearly all undesirable, but one at least necessary: brandy, the scapegoat of everything that was wrong in port. The triumph of the aristocracy of port naturally shed something of its glamour on those ordinary wines which could have no pretensions to its qualities, and I suspect that the glorious wines of the past, so rare and far between, were largely responsible for the perpetually reiterated grumblings that abominable sophistications had been introduced, that port

442

Plate 40. *Rabigato*, a white port grape

was not what it once had been and was steadily growing worse. Living evidence of the heights to which port could rise survived in the select fine wines which had matured in the security of the bottle to a glorious old age, and no one remembered those ordinary wines which had been drunk so reluctantly, since nothing else was available. In consequence, we are confronted with the extraordinary spectacle of port-lovers praising to the skies a purely imaginary natural Douro wine rather as philosophers once celebrated the nobility of the savage, completely blind to its original reception by the cultured palate. How those of them who had visited Oporto and had had an opportunity of drinking *consumo* can have maintained this attitude is beyond my comprehension.

Experiments in wine doctoring and protests against their results gathered force through the first half of the nineteenth century, and grumbling about port attained its maximum of violence round about 1850. British writers, blind to the difficulties which growers and shippers had so long been facing, indulged in a kind of commination service, cursing alike conditions, expedients and people held responsible for corrupting the beautiful virginity of *consumo*. They cursed the Oporto Wine Company in an orchestral *tutti*, and it was certainly guilty of enough corruption and inefficiency to deserve their objurgations. They cursed the elder-berry and *geropiga* and other expedients which no honest wine-drinker could approve with a justified vigour, but bell, book and candle were reserved for that angel in disguise, brandy, which they took for the devil.

Ferocious, too, were the denunciations of the Methuen Treaty, which was accused among other crimes of depriving the Douro growers of that healthy competition which would have set them to work reforming their viticulture and wine-making methods. In the Alto Douro the vines grow in circumstances utterly different from those which condition the wines of Bordeaux and Burgundy, yet again and again it is suggested that all would be well if only the Portuguese had learnt to grow their vines and to make their wine exactly as the French did. When a Briton approves of a system in one place and in one set of conditions nothing will persuade him that it will not be equally satisfactory everywhere else, or open his eyes to flat contradictions of his conviction. How we applaud the transport of our political institutions to people utterly unsuited to them and are blind to the sorry figure they cut in exile. If we had had a wine-growing system of our own we should have insisted that the Portuguese could only hope for salvation by adopting it, but, as it was, we had made up our minds that what was sauce for the French was sauce for the Portuguese, and the critics of port could not rid themselves of an obsession to advise the Portuguese to imitate the French.

First they should reduce to a minimum the number of varieties of vine they cultivated. At the time the number grown, which included inferior varieties, was excessive. Time has decreased their number, but experience has shown that about twenty varieties are required for the making of port. The whole system of wine-growing in the Douro is based on a delicate adjustment of the various qualities of different grapes. Then an idea prevailed that the quintas might reproduce the châteaux of the Bordelais, turning out natural wines, which one day might compete with the famous growths of the Médoc. Port would no longer be a blended wine from divers wines of divers vineyards. How surprised those critics would have been if they had been able to guess that blending raised to the level of a fine art would prove the salvation of the port trade and make port one of the most trustworthy of wines. Above all, the demon brandy was to be exorcised from the port bottle, unless it was a mere suspicion to fortify the wine for its sea journey.

THE WINES OF PORTUGAL

All this advice was very well meant, but a wine tradition has to grow out of soil and climate; its growth is nearly as slow as a political tradition. In point of fact the advice was completely meaningless, since it did not touch the crux of the problem. No one had any suggestion as to how the Douro grapes fermenting in their climate were to be saved from the bitter end to which they came if left to themselves.

Henderson, the historian, writing in 1824, considers that in the matter of port it might be held presumptuous to condemn where many approve, but for him port is on the downward grade with the exception of the 1820 wines, later a famous year, which were naturally so good that they had been more lightly brandied. His judgment on the past was based on having tasted 'once or twice, but certainly not oftener', wines which seemed to be free from any admixture of brandy. He is exceptional in favouring the addition of brandy during fermentation, if any was to be added, though he did not know that it checked the process; he thought that wine and brandy would amalgamate more easily.

Ten years later a Bristol wine-merchant, F. C. Husenbeth, strikes rather a different note in a little book evidently written with an eye to his wealthy customers. He lays down the principle that a natural wine should possess all we ought to look for in wine, but he bows to the habit which has made highly brandied wines palatable in this country and admits that this warmer sort of wine would remain our standard wine. Perhaps not without a thought to his calling, he even registers a recent improvement in the quality of port. 'It has no longer that astringent harshness which it formerly possessed in so high a degree that to many it could only be offered medicinally, but could never be taken by them with that pleasure with which they now use it in its improved state.' It has become 'not only more palatable to the real connoisseur of wine, but also more wholesome'. He realizes that control over the initial fermentation is essential to the making of palatable port, but he does not seem aware that brandy was the only available agent of control.

In 1851 the third edition of Cyrus Redding's *History of Modern Wines* summed up everything bad that could be said to the disadvantage of port in that period. His first edition appeared in 1833, and this last edition presumably expresses his mature opinions. It is hard to say whether the Methuen Treaty, the Oporto Wine Company or brandy is the Iago of the tragedy of port, as seen by Redding. Their combined villainies have resulted in five-eighths of the port brought into England being so coarse and such a medley of heterogeneous vine produce, brandy and other matters that it invites adulteration to make it drinkable. He shudders at the introduction of brandy into the fermenting must, for it is then in the most delicate state of transition, and the least interference is destructive to its quality. Redding was, I think, the first to give prominence to the Satanic figure of *geropiga*. *Geropiga* is today a perfectly innocent very sweet port used in small quantities for sweetening a blend exactly as *dulce apagado* is used for sweetening sherry, fermentation being stopped much earlier than for other wines. Redding's *geropiga* was something very different, and he says that very little port escaped from its evil touch. It consisted of 56 lb of dried elder-berries, 60 lb of coarse brown sugar and treacle, 78 gallons of unfermented grape juice and 39 gallons of the strongest brandy. The worst of this abomination was that it could be exported and used to turn wines which had never known the sun of Portugal into imitation port.

As Cockburn says, the port trade just before the middle of the eighteenth century went through a very bad period when speculation prevailed over honest trading and much harm was done to the reputation of port in England. In 1831 a brilliant young man, Joseph James Forrester, afterwards Baron Forrester, came to Oporto to join his uncle's firm, to be styled Offley Forrester, and in 1843 with an anonyomus pamphlet he presented himself as purist champion denouncing quite rightly every form of adulteration of the wine, but unfortunately classing brandy as an adulterant. How a man of his gifts and understanding can have persuaded himself that the Douro *consumo*, which was certainly no better in his time than it was when I first tasted it at the Factory House in 1924, could hope for a place in the London market, I can only dismiss as a psychological curiosity. It detracts from the debt which port unquestionably owes him, since his hot-headed campaign affirmed the truth that nothing should enter port that was not the product of the vine. If only he had not forgotten that brandy is the spirit of wine!

The one blind spot in Forrester's eyes is the more curious, because there is evidence that the true doctrine of port was still alive in Oporto. I have already quoted the writer W. H. G. Kingston, whose *Peter the Whaler* was a friend of my childhood. His apprenticeship in the making of port must have been far shorter than the lifetime spent by Forrester in its service, but in his *Lusitanian Sketches* published two years after Forrester's first anonymous pamphlet, he describes the critical moment in the making of the wine just as I saw it in action when I was with Jennings at the vintage. The drawing off of the fermenting must on the brandy which arrests the process is 'a very critical moment'. 'Then the rich and generous qualities of the grapes are to be retained, or lost, never to be restored. From the rich nature of the Douro grape, the fermentation once begun will not stop of its own accord . . . till it has caused it to become a bitter liquid, almost, if not entirely undrinkable. . . . To retain therefore those much prized qualities, it is absolutely necessary to add brandy at the very critical moment, so critical to decide, before that stage which produces bitterness commences.'

Kingston joins the hate chorus against the Oporto Wine Company, denouncing it as 'an abominable monopoly' of benefit only to its officials, who made their fortune out of it, but writing just at the time when the port trade was in its greatest difficulties – in 1842 exports to Britain had fallen below a half of the annual average – he is optimistic in outlook and gives detailed advice to the English consumer as to how he should purchase his wine. Ideas were still vague as to when the wine was at its best. 'The shortest time', he writes, 'Port wine, to give it fair play, ought to be kept in bottle is two years; four improve it more, and in six it reaches perfection.' Barham writing a year or two later in *Ingoldsby Legends* suggested a far longer stay in the bottle. Kingston recognizes three classes of port. First there is old tawny port grown old in cask with five or six years in bottle as particularly attractive, though the wine will show a certain 'softness', and he doubts whether any fine tawny port improves after about three years in bottle. Kingston's second class is ruby port, bottled younger, but kept afterwards as long as or longer than the other. Here we have an approximation to crusted port.

These two sorts of wine he recommends for summer consumption, but for the fogs and cold of the English winter he is in favour of a rich, generous rosy wine such as that of the famed vintage of 1834, which at the time when he wrote had reached with about six years in bottle what he regarded as its prime, a wine to drink after a hard day's shooting or hunting. Thanks to his family connection, he drank 'every day at dinner of the vintage 1786, still perfectly sound and vinous'. It had been refreshed with later vintages and had had constant attention paid to it, or it would not have lived so long. An invaluable wine he calls it. The principle on which this wine lived to a fine old age forms the basis on which the highly complex and delicate system which has made port one of those wines that can be bought and drunk with absolute confidence in their character and quality. The chaos of the mid-eighteenth century has given place to a system founded on experience, masterly tasting and expert foresight in strict accordance with the genius of the wine.

The emergence of wood port lacks the historical importance of the first experiments which adapted the bottle to its new purpose, since it merely developed the principle responsible for Old Rhenish and Old Sack, the prolongation of a wine's life by the transfusion of younger wines, but it carried its application to an amazing degree of perfection in the face of exceptional difficulties.

CHAPTER TEN

# The Making of
# the Wine

SINCE wood port is the life blood of the industry, a discussion of its making may serve some good purpose. Its home is in the beautiful Douro mountains, where Herculean labour constructed those terraced vineyards on the sheer hill slopes and still preserves them against the hostility of nature, which too often with rain and frost sweeps away vines and soil and the unmortared stones of the supporting walls. With a touch of imagination, one will be able to transmute the scene into another of its phases, its autumn glory after the vintage, when the landscape is ablaze with every shade of colour from scarlet to gold, flashing with an almost metallic sheen, for each of the many vines which are the parents of port dyes the rich foliage of its decline with its own shade of brilliant colour. The ordered lines of the terraces seem to sketch out a vast multicoloured heraldic design, its regularity only broken here and there by the white splash of a vineyard farm, or rugged masses of naked rock too sheer for the vine, and in the background olive plantations and a horizon broken by a rare cork oak or eucalyptus.

It would have been so much simpler to plant the vine in the easier richer soil down by the river, but there no good wine can be grown, and it is poor consolation that only thin wine of low degree can be grown above the middle slopes. Often the builder of a vineyard terrace can only overcome the adamant resistance of the granite, which from the quarries provides props for the vines grown along wire, by resort to explosives; perhaps this necessity accounts for the familiarity amounting to affection with which the

Portuguese in these parts regard dynamite. No festival is complete without fusillades of rockets carrying aloft one or two sticks of dynamite, which when all goes well produce artificial thunder high above the earth. Enthusiasm is not damped by occasional premature or delayed explosions and the resulting casualties. Dynamite is a tradition of long standing, and I treasure the picture Mr Tovey, that highly respectable and be-whiskered Victorian wine-merchant, has bequeathed us of himself in 1872 utterly flummoxed by the claps of thunder rumbling from a cloudless sky at blazing noontide and most disagreeably impressed by the shock of a rocket stick piercing the armour of his umbrella. Perhaps my enjoyment of such merrymaking has been impaired by war memories. Yet I wish Mr Hennell had been able to photograph the 'sound' atmosphere of this happy people. It would have to be a noisy one and include not only dynamite rockets but the ear-splitting roar of massed sheepskin drums, from which my ears have never fully recovered since an Amarante festival.

There is a Douro proverb that the wine-grower should carry in one hand his basket and in the other his pruning knife; he should start pruning his vines as soon as the fruit is picked. They are pruned very low, not higher than 3 feet 6 inches, so that the grapes may take full adavntage of the heat radiated from the sun-baked soil. The wooden props which raised the vintage clusters above the dust have to be stacked for the next year. A hole is dug round the grafted vine and any roots sprouting from the native graft above the American stock are removed, for they would be easy victims to the phylloxera. Into these holes the fallen vine-leaves are swept as the perfect fertilizer. Wine is as susceptible to the imponderables of its origin as a child according to modern psychology, and consequently in all wine lands the problem of a fertilizer is a very delicate one. The fertilizer is generally advertised as increasing quantity; with wine it is almost a general rule that quantity is an enemy of quality. A prejudice against farm manure still persists in many regions, and I should like to have seen the face of the cellar-master of Château Mouton when our friend Mr Tovey asked him whether there was any truth in a yarn that he had heard in the Reform Club that it owed its name to its use of sheep dung. In the Douro a crop of lupins dug in between the vine can claim the classic authority of Cato and Columella, and more store is set by the aeration of the soil through the digging of pits in which branches of furze are buried. Of digging, weeding and spraying in the vineyard there is no end.

Perpetual toil accompanies the flowering and fruiting of the vine. Unceasing war has to be waged against the inroads of insect pests, and the weather remains as supreme arbiter over success or failure. The picture of the Tinta Cão (Plate 39) grape gives a good idea of the ripeness of one of the black grapes from which good port is pressed and shows incidentally the shaly soil through which the Douro vine has to drive its penetrating roots. Plate 40 shows the white grape *Rabigato*; I leave it to the reader's ingenuity to guess why it is sometimes known as the *rabo de ovelha*, or sheep's tail. Far fewer varieties of grape are grown for white port than for red, and it may not be out of place to say here a few words about what Saintsbury unkindly called a mere albino. Many white wines are made from black grapes. In Champagne, for instance, the black Pinot plays almost a leading part. But white port is pressed from white grapes treated exactly as the black grapes for red port. I do not quite understand why a recent writer on port should accuse of 'appalling snobbishness' those who share Ernest Cockburn's opinion as to the relative merits of the two wines. 'There will no doubt', Cockburn writes, 'be a limited number of consumers (mostly ladies and teetotallers) who will prefer it to Red Port Wine, but it should be remembered that "the first duty of Port Wine is to be red" and that Red Port Wine is intrinsically much more attractive than White Port in this climate. I have heard it said that those who favour White Port wines as against Red could hardly be regarded as connoisseurs of wine, and I for one should certainly share this view.' The reference to teetotallers pleasantly recalls their long-enduring happy illusion (perhaps it still endures in places) that port was non-alcoholic and that its comfortable warming of the cockles of the heart was no breach of the blue ribbon pledge.

In the distant past white port, with its fermentation checked very early and therefore very sweet, found its chief market in Russia, until it was closed by a prohibitive duty, but since Cockburn wrote, white port has assumed a new guise. In the humbler role of an *apéritif*, dry white port with most of its sugar converted into alcohol looks exceedingly tempting in the glass and deserves its increasing popularity in a world where too often wine with the meal is regarded as a rare treat and its place is taken by some such horrid and unwholesome beverage as iced water. Before a wineless meal it has the virtue of clamouring for its red brother with dessert. If it is followed by a sturdy Portuguese table wine the vinosity of the latter will stand up against its self-assertion, but it is altogether too big and opinionated to usher in the lighter table wines.

We now pass to the vintage, and here the reader's imagination must supply animation to the scene for the vintage is agog with rapid movement. It has something in it of a ritual dance, for all its figures are prescribed by a prehistoric tradition. The vintagers have danced their way to the vineyards, often from distant mountain villages, for dancing is food and drink to the Portuguese. Indefatigably on the vintage pilgrimage they tramp from village to village, and wherever they stop for refreshment they relax their muscles and put fatigue to flight by dancing as if their lives depended on it. As fresh as paint after many miles of foot-slogging, the women swarm among the vines, stooping to gather the low-grown clusters with knives or long narrow scissors, and as they pick they never stop chattering and munching pounds and pounds of grapes. From each cluster any defective berries are removed, before it is laid in a small basket, from which it is eventually transferred to the great vintage baskets which hold 130 lb of fruit. When the baskets are full the women help to hoist them into position high up on the men's backs. They are balanced on a small leather support which hangs between the shoulder blades and is suspended from a broad leather band which crosses the forehead rather as the Pharisees bound their phylacteries on their brows. By this arrangement the whole weight of the load is thrown upon the forehead and neck muscles, leaving the hands free.

It is as natural for the Portuguese to carry things in this way as according to Gilbert it used to be for an English child to be born either a little Liberal or a little Conservative. On some of those sands near the river the author once watched some little children playing the game of the vintage: tiny tots were trying to balance big stones on their head and shoulders with a rag across the forehead, just as their big brothers balanced their baskets in the vintage. Throughout Portugal, where mechanical transport is still very far from having superseded the human beast of burden, head and neck always take the strain of a heavy burden. The Portuguese live very near to those Straits of Gibraltar where, according to the ancients, Hercules raised his Pillars to warn mortals that they should not venture through them to the hazards of the ocean, with Atlas in the background holding up on head, bowed neck and shoulders, the burden of the earth and the

THE MAKING OF THE WINE

heavens; we know so little of the Lusitanians that the learned will have little ground to scoff at the hypothesis that they found in the giant Atlas upholding the universe a model to be imitated. Even the Douro oxen (Plate 41) have adopted the national system. On my very first day in the Douro I was both startled and ashamed when the smiling little maid who met me on the road outside the Val do Mendiz swung my heavy kit bag on her head as if it was a feather, and with a hand for each of my other two bags trotted like a goat down the rough breakneck path which was then the only approach to the house. I never wearied of admiring from the window of the Sandeman's Lodges the superb carriage of the walking caryatids who, with a heavy piece of office furniture or a vast washing basket on their heads, went their way as easily as if their load was weightless. Physiologists tell me that this perfection of posture can only be fully attained with bare feet. I wish the Oporto Town Council had consulted them before passing a by-law on the ground that Oporto was too grand a town to tolerate unshod feet on its pavements, imposing a fine on those unshod within its precincts. So the caryatids topped their load with a pair of slippers within which they hid their shapely feet, provided they remembered, when they crossed the bridge which links Vila Nova de Gaia with Oporto.

In the Douro vineyards the men vintagers might well challenge the professional gymnast. With nearly ten stone on their heads, the wise ones bare-footed, they hop, skip and jump down from the terraces with walls which may be ten or fifteen feet high with extraordinary agility, and in the descent they have nothing but a few stones protruding precariously from the wall to receive their feet. In the hot Douro climate haste spurs on the vintage. Very ripe grapes are only too ready to start a precocious and most undesirable fermentation. Taking at a fast jog trot every obstacle, they put to shame, in their race with fine wine as its purpose, the barren efforts of those professional runners whose glory is expressed by fractions of seconds on a stop watch. They have borne through blazing heat their heavy burden, perhaps for a mile or more, when they approach the *adegas* with the wine press. At once they quicken their pace and, to show that they are not downhearted and have plenty of breath left, let loose a pack of blood-curdling yells – wolf howls they call them with childlike complacency at their own indefatigable ferocity. At journey's end they shoot their grapes into the *lagar*, the great stone tank of the wine press, through a side window, and trot back again for another load.

Human ingenuity has never devised a machine for the pressing of the wine grape which can compare with the human foot. Its sole will never break the pips and release their astringency into the must, and the method of its application by the leg rising and falling quickens the must with just that aeration which is needed. Prejudice against the foot, the pride of Du Maurier's Trilby, so beautiful when unconfined and undeformed in lands where shoes stifle the feet no more often than gloves the hands, belongs to a morbidly sophisticated civilization, an absurdity from which one hopes it will recover as it has from the equally absurd notion that there is something so inherently improper about a leg that the leg of a table should be swathed and hidden. A healthier generation saw only poetry in Macaulay's picture of the vats of Luna with the must foaming 'round the white feet of laughing girls'.

It will be a sad day for port if ever the machine smothers the ritual treading dance. It reminds me of T. S. Eliot's symbolic country dance in *East Coker*, though a strange gallimaufry of instruments is added to 'the music of the weak pipe and the little drum'.

'The association of man and woman . . . Rustically solemn or in rustic laughter . . . Lifting heavy feet . . . lifted in country mirth . . . feet rising and feet falling.' Feet must be raised so high for the quickening air to penetrate to the depths of the must. The first figure, the opening square dance called the *corte*, the dancers in a double row with arms linked, must be as orderly as drill and continue until every single grape in the great mass has been trodden. In this fashion, Agathias, a poet of the Anthology, tells us that the grapes were trodden fifteen hundred years ago. 'Arm in arm we weave the Bacchic rhythm.' And he tells us how the must as it ferments grows warmer and warmer round the legs of the treaders just as it does in the *lagar*, but the ancient vintager had an encouragement denied to the Portuguese. There were wooden cups floating on the must with which he could scoop up the fermenting grape juice to refresh his labours, not that I should have thought it a very wholesome or stimulating beverage. In Portugal the dancers when they grow weary and thirsty raise a wild wolf cry, and wine and cigarettes are promptly served. When the head man, master of the ceremonies, is sure that the *corte* has done its work he gives the word, arms are unlinked and couples begin to dance furiously as their fancy dictates, but they must still step high. The band grows wilder and wilder, until at the end of four hours of this violent exercise the first gang is relieved by a second lot of treaders.

Fermentation is allowed to go on unchecked for from two to four days, great care being taken to break up and submerge the *manta*, the solid mass of skins, pips and stalks, which keeps rising to the surface. The Manager of the Oporto shipping firm on whose judgment the future wine depends has decided on the wines most suitable for his purpose, buying as far as possible from farmers with whom he has already dealt. He is guided to some extent by his experience of the past wines grown by a given farmer in a given vineyard, though wines are never constant. The critical moment has now arrived when he must choose the exact instant when fermentation shall be arrested by running off the wine on the brandy in the *tonels*, the large casks in which it will live until the spring. Outlying farms have to be visited, some still only approached by a narrow ox track, and every day fermenting musts will be brought to his vintage headquarters for his inspection and tasting. Their rich purple, deeper and more imperial than all the dyes of Tyre and Sidon, spreads itself out in a thin film over the raised centre of a white china saucer and its intensity appears to penetrate and stain the smooth glazed surface. If time did not mellow that colour to the ruby and the tawny, appreciated by those who know, the wicked elder-berry would never have dared intrude. If the sweetness of the finished wine was the only matter at stake the scientific evidence of the saccharometer which registers the sugar content in terms of the specific gravity of the must might pronounce final judgment on the moment when fermentation should be arrested and spare the conscientious port maker, who looks for imponderables that only his palate can discern, many a grimace and the pangs of bitter astringency as he spits out the sample, for the new wines are nasty and, even unswallowed, leave an unpleasant memory.

After they have been confirmed by the brandy in the state chosen for them by the shipper, the new wines are left in their native hills to find themselves and with the cold of winter shake off any inclination to a secondary fermentation, if such should remain. Then in the spring they enter on the first stage of their long journey to the distant wineglass. In the past they depended for their transport on the river for the voyage to the

Lodges at Oporto and on oxen to take them to and from the river, and both these means of transport still survive under the shadow of approaching doom. The wine-boats, *barcos rebelos*, craft, high-prowed, high-pooped, with square sail and long sweeps, that would not look out of place in those Ostia mosaics which show the freighters of the Roman Empire, once had the monopoly of carrying upstream, after the autumn rains had swelled the river, the brandy needed after the vintage, and in the spring down-stream the young wines. It is no child's play to navigate the rapids and shoals and treacherous currents of the Douro. The steersman perched high on the poop with his long steering paddle exercises tremendous leverage, and he needs it. The *barco rebelo*, with its sail set, wind and tide favouring, makes a brave show, as with its cargo of brandy it threads its way through the busy harbour up river.

Their crews are a class apart, chattering and singing and piously devout with even more than the usual Portuguese gaiety and religious sense, but it is to be feared that their days are numbered. No prophet warned them of the ominous future. A warning might have kept them on their best behaviour in the days of their unchallenged useful-ness, but, alas!, they sometimes presumed on their monopoly. Thirsty with the exertions of their dangerous calling, they are charged with succumbing to the temptation of knocking the bung out of a wine-cask, drinking deep and replenishing its contents with what Lovelace would have termed 'allaying Douro'. The Greek galley slaves who played the same trick with Coan wine and sea-water had at least the consolation for any punish-ment they received, when their offence was discovered, that the Coans were so pleased with the mixture that they ever afterwards salted their wines deliberately – a process not so strange as it might seem, since it was legally forbidden in France in 1891. Douro-ed port met with no such approval, and the tricks of the boatmen served as an excuse for their desertion, when a maundering and very leisurely railway nosed its way up the valley. Some firms refused to be tempted to a breach with tradition, and it is to be hoped that in gratitude the boatmen mended their ways.

Whether river or rail is chosen for transport, brandy and wine have to be conveyed to boat or train and from them to the Lodges. Here in spite of the menace of the internal-combustion engine oxen still play their solemn part. The motor car made its first appearance in the Douro vintage in 1913, and its introduction was viewed by many shippers with terrible misgivings. It was feared that the Douro peasants would see in this expensive newfangled means of transport a symbol of unlimited wealth and put up the price of their wines accordingly. Nowadays lorries compete with the oxen, but happily there are still farms making good wines which only oxen can reach. The Portu-guese oxen deserve a special chapter to themselves, great gentle beasts, patient with the excellent strength of the giant never tyrannously abused. Varieties have been bred specially adapted to special environments.

When I first went to Oporto with its headlong precipitous streets there were trams which as they plunged madly up and down reminded me of adventures in the *teleferica*, the transporter cable, in the Italian Alps in the First World War. There were a few motor cars which could take the gradients with more or less confidence, but the oxen with their high carved yokes were to Oporto what the gondola is to Venice. It was a joy to know that the long sticks which steered and controlled their slow progress, were un-equipped with the sharp points of a goad, because the value of oxen skins vanishes if the leather is riddled with the goad pinpricks which never close.

In Oporto the oxen used to indulge in a panoply of spreading horns. In the north, in the country of the 'green' wines, 'eager' wines, they have complied with the human demand for a greater restriction of those horns, which are to an ox what St Paul said her hair was to a woman, its glory. In the rolling country of the Minho, naturally corn-land rather than vine-land, it might seem that they could safely indulge in extravagance, but whereas in the steep-terraced Douro oxen can only ply on the tracks between the vine-yards and there is no place for them among the low-grown vines, in the Minho the vines are grown high above the ground, often in rows and on trellises, and there is room for them to work in the narrow interspaces between the vines; they have conveniently grown horns so modest and well-disposed that there is no danger of their being entangled with the stocks and shoots and bines.

I trust my Lusitanian friends will forgive me, if I address to them Virgil's apostrophe to those who live by the soil – *O fortunatos nimium, sua si bona norint*, Blest beyond all bliss, did they but know their happiness. Dr Salazar has been guiding his countrymen slowly and surely to select from what we call progress what is best and eschew its worst. May they remain true to this doctrine. May they continue to cling to their wine-boats and oxen as a much needed protest against the blasphemy that speed, profit and gadgets are the final end of life.

In these days of broadcast noise, sometimes pleasing and often not, the memory of the port vintage comes as an oasis of peace with a music of its own, where the music of the ox-cart accompanies the rhythmic rub-a-dub of distant drums.

Wine-boats, oxen, railway, lorries, all serve to convey to the skilled artist who works in port wine the replenishment of his raw material, necessary to the continuity of his art, which he manipulates as the painter his colours or the poet his words. The new wines, still needing like children careful nursing, first assembled in lots according to the distinctive qualities ascribed by experience to their various vineyards, are housed in the great Wine Lodges of Vila Nova de Gaia, the transpontine suburb of Oporto. The Lodges, so called from the Portuguese *loja*, a single-storey ground-floor building as distinguished from the *armazem*, a warehouse of several storeys, spread over acres of ground with slightly differing levels in a rambling plan which tells how with the lapse of time more and more ground has been taken in.

Unfortunately nothing can reproduce the faint, fresh, all-pervading fragrance of wine which delights the nose and the impression of an endlessness not unlike that of the great mosque at Córdoba, affecting the visitor with a feeling of complacent admiration similar to that engendered by a glass or two of the very wine for which they exist, as he wanders down the avenues between triple tiers of the wine Lodge pipes, varied occasionally by a single row of brandy casks. On entrance, a dim religious light relieves the eyes after the blazing sunshine outside. There reigns an atmosphere of calm and silence, scarcely broken by the cellarmen pattering about in their rope-soled shoes, a hush such as befits port, that wine of philosophic contemplation. It is almost intensified by the light hammer raps administered with woodpecker-like regularity to a pipe dwarfed by the gigantic blending vat beneath which it lies. Such vats may have a capacity of 10,000 gallons and almost emulate the fabulous dimensions of the German tuns. Dark wine is gushing from a tap near its base, and surely must soon overflow in a flood to waste from the cask into which it is running unchecked. But those taps on the head of the pipe over which the cellarman is leaning tell his expert ear of the exact level of the wine within as it rises, and at the precise moment the cask is full to the bung his hand darts out. The tap is turned and not a drop is lost. Sherry is a wine that can sleep with open windows, its home in the butt bathed with the outside air, but port must sleep in a closed room, leaving not the smallest place in its chamber to receive the air, to it not unlike a tonic compounded of poison only to be taken in prescribed doses at prescribed intervals. The ullaged cask is the enemy of port. Due reverence is demanded by the sanctum sanctorum, guarded by an iron grill and locked gate, the treasure-house of the ancient wines, the mother-stocks born perhaps a century and a half ago, so precious in a blend that their drops must almost be counted and so magic in their operation that the inexperienced blender is tempted to start his work with them instead of reserving them for the final touch.

In a fine vintage year the shipping of a vintage port is a relatively straightforward matter. A fraction, say 10%, of the very finest wines is set aside, chosen and blended with attention to the special style with which the name of the shipping firm is associated. In the Lodges wines rid themselves of their first wild oats of youth and in two, perhaps three years, are shipped to England to-spend the rest of their lives in the bottle. A fine vintage wine is to a shipping firm what a scoop is to a newspaper, but no newspaper can live by scoops alone; its circulation depends on the excellence of its daily presentation of the news, and that is what wood port is to the port trade. But for the impossibility of his being admitted into the Exporters' Guild, a very rich man might descend on Oporto in a fine year and buy up enough experience and skill and good wine to ship a vintage port in his own name, but his ambition would be utterly defeated if he tried to compete in the field of wood port, unless he bought up an old-established firm lock, stock and barrel.

Port from its birth is a harmony in which more or less conflicting elements have been reconciled. The farmer in his vineyard grows grapes of several varieties, which correct one another's shortcomings and bring out one another's virtues. Then there is the brandy which only long companionship can reconcile with the wine. What the farmer has done with his grapes has to be repeated by the port artist, the blender, on a far more complicated scale. He has to harmonize scores, often hundreds, of wines in different keys, and what is more, with no recorder to make those harmonies automatically reproducible, to repeat them accurately whenever called upon.

The heart of every port shipping firm beats in the tasting room, the artist's studio. It must be a spacious *atelier*, light, airy and above all peaceful, where neither disturbance nor distraction can interfere with the concentrated attention of eye, nose and palate on delicate shades of colour, bouquet and flavour. It is easier for a writer to discuss the art of blending in terms of the poet than in those of the painter. The port poet has continually to relearn the arts of writing and spelling. The new wines might be compared to the pothooks and hangers that help to form letters as they are fitted into the standard blends, as different from one another as A from Z, which form his alphabet. With the aid of this alphabet, each standard being kept as constant in character and outline as possible, he has to spell out the poetry of wine. In one respect he differs fundamentally from the poet in words. Only occasionally does he aim at creating something new and original. It is his main object to reproduce exactly those blends of his standards on whose names and sale the reputation of his firm is based and justify the confidence of his customers that they will be supplied with exactly what they ordered.

As I stood in the Sandemans' silent sunlit tasting room with its tranquil outlook on an ancient roof where smart yellow wagtails were bobbing up and down, the tasters very professional in their white coats and surrounded by rack on rack of sample bottles, thousands of them, since they stand for all the accumulated reserves, the new wines, the standards, blends in various stages and every shipment of finished port dispatched during recent years, it occurred to me that their task seemed scarcely less difficult than that of Psyche when angry Venus ordered her to sort into their kinds a great heap of mixed tiny seeds. The kindly ants came to Psyche's rescue, but the taster has only his memories of colour, scent and flavour, his experience, and trial and error as judged by eye, nose and palate to help him pick out from an embarrassment of choice the wines he needs and in a most promiscuous marriage wed them together in the required union.

The tawny is not a vintage wine, but Mr Croft-Cooke is mistaken in saying that vintage tawny is a contradiction in terms. Vintage tawny port is very rare, but it can exist. Nicholas Block delighted in a Dow 1863 specially shipped for him in 1896, which had been untouched in the wood except for replenishment with the identical wine. I expressed somewhere in print my envious regret that I had never shared my friend Nick Block's experience and that a vintage tawny had never come my way. My complaint came to the eyes of that great and generous port artist, Senhor Luiz de Vasconcellos Porto, and when he gave me lunch at the Portuguese Club while I was in Oporto he drew on his precious store of Quinta Noval 1880, a wine refreshed by no other vintage but its own, to set my desire at rest. It raised to supreme heights that combination of delicacy and strength which marks the peculiar charm of all sound tawny port that owes its colour to age, and it remains in my memory as one of the finest wines it has every been my privilege to taste. The story of such a long friendship between two countries could not but be chequered with family wrangles and disputes, which arouse more heated emotion than quarrels with a stranger, and perhaps I have laid too much stress on the clash between the home Government's interests, and its not always scrupulous policy of protecting them, and those of the British exporting merchants, since it had at least the triumphant upshot of establishing port as the Englishman's wine. It is pleasant to conclude with a review of the system which, evolving from violently contradictory points of view, has so successfully reconciled these opposing interests, with the result that the buyer of a bottle of port is buying a wine with such guarantees of quality and genuine identity as no other wine in the world can boast.

In 1932 when wine-growing countries everywhere were confronted with a crisis of over-production, the Portuguese Government introduced a carefully considered organization to counter the world financial chaos by measures to ensure that the port wine trade, one of its most important industries, should face the situation with that best of weapons, the guaranteed high quality of its wine. Three bodies were set up to control and regulate the growing, the making and the export of port wine, the *Instituto do Vinho de Porto*, the Port Wine Institute, the senior body, which works with the *Gremio dos Exportadores do Vinho do Porto*, the Port Wine Shippers Guild, in charge of exports, and the *Casa do Douro*, the Douro House, which superintends farms and vineyards.

The Institute has powers of inspection of all Lodges in Vila Nova de Gaia, and grants its Certificates of Origin, which licence exportation, only after its tasters have approved the wine to be exported, thus ensuring that none but wines worthy of the good name of port wine shall ever leave the country. These tasters are men of experience and skill, who have the assistance of an up-to-date laboratory in the Institute itself. In addition, the shipper is subject to strict laws governing the quantity he may ship in any one year, and this has the effect of ensuring that wines are properly matured before exportation.

All these methods of control are frequently under review for the betterment of port wine, and while it is only natural that criticism should at times be heard, they certainly achieve two of their ends, the production of none but wines of high quality for sale as port wine and the protection of the consumer in every country.

*Tantae molis erat* – not indeed such a Herculean labour as that to which Virgil ascribed the foundation of Rome, but years and years of patience and experiment were needed to raise port to its glory as a supreme dessert wine. That period of probation passed, Britain almost monopolized the privilege of drinking it, though its emergence benefited every wine-growing country in the world by its broadcasting of the lost secret of maturing great vintage wines. Not till the beginning of this century did the wine begin to travel to any great extent into other lands, first to Scandinavia with Sandeman's in the lead. Thence later its popularity has been spreading far and wide, and in other wine-growing countries is triumphantly holding its own as in France. In Britain it has long been honoured in Universities and other centres of learning as the wine of philosophy and contemplation, a precious stimulus of good fellowship and conversation. Its kindly influence has spread through every class, and the manual worker finds a glass of port as encouraging and helpful as the obliging lady who chars, and on whom we are so dependent, her port and lemon.

Today thanks to more than a quarter of a century of the stability of the Salazar régime and the enterprise of the Oporto Shippers, port is embarking on a worldwide campaign, no longer a lonely knight with his pilgrim companion Madeira crippled by the evil fairies of oidium and phylloxera. With Madeira at his side, port sallies forth at the head of a whole army of natural table wines, once too shy to risk themselves abroad, and to drink good luck to the whole host the reader can scarcely do better than repeat the order Tennyson gave to the plump head-waiter of the Cock to bring him the wine which served as Pegasus to his Muse:

> *Go and fetch a pint of Port*
> *But let it not be such as that*
> *You set before chance-comers,*
> *But such whose father-grape grew fat*
> *On Lusitanian summers.*

CHAPTER ELEVEN

# *Immortal Madeira*

MADEIRA is the only wine that ever challenged the claim of port to be the Englishman's wine. That challenge might well have been more serious – since at its best Madeira has no superior, some say no equal, among the great dessert wines of the world – if nature and geography had not loaded the dice against it. When it first made its mark in these islands it had already entered a claim to a very different title, that of being the wine of the New World, a claim it owed to Charles II. An island only about a third larger than the Isle of Man, though with five times the population, could scarcely be expected to yield a sufficient quantity of wine to justify the double claim, since, as has been said, no wine industry can live on the exclusive production of rare and expensive wines of high quality. According to Voltaire, *Dieu est toujours pour les gros bataillons*, and in the case of Madeira, Nature, the deity's deputy, descended on the little island with the Assyrian ruthlessness of the wolf on the fold.

In the van came *Oidium tuckeri*, a fungoid disease, giving credit to the English botanist who identified it for his discovery of ill. The Madeira pipe with its 92 gallons is a good deal smaller than the port pipe of 115 gallons, and in 1851 the wine yield of the island was estimated at 30,000 pipes. In 1852 oidium swept over the vineyards with annihilating effect, and for that year and eight more there was not a drop of wine for the thirteen resident English shipping firms to export. Only three of them survived. In 1860 a London firm which had been dealing in Madeira wines since the previous century informed its customers that Madeira could no longer be numbered among wine-growing countries.

Happily for the peasants, with their wonderful climate and soil they had sugar cane, maize and other crops. But their faith in the vine was shaken. It was only the influence and encouragement of those English merchants who refused to be defeated, and still clung to the island, that persuaded them to replant their vineyards with an eye to anything more ambitious than the provision of their own tables with that necessity, a beverage wine. In this campaign the lead was taken by Thomas Leacock, a name still associated with the finest Madeira, who fought the battle in the vineyards and attacked the pest scientifically. He was so far victorious that in 1873 the vineyards had struggled back to about a third of their previous yield, when the second blow fell. Phylloxera, with the fell efficiency of the locust, obliterated the vines, replanted and restored with so much toil, even more completely than oidium. Nothing daunted, Leacock tackled the new foe, and when he died in 1883 there were signs that his courage had not been in vain and that in years to come Madeira might again take its honoured place in the aristocracy of wine.

Yet a terrible blow had been struck against the fair name of Madeira, and many held that the great wines which had for a generation or so raised Madeira above port were dead beyond hope of resurrection. So we find as late as 1920 Saintsbury apologizing in his *Notes on a Cellar-Book* for devoting a mere post-script to 'so famous, and at its best so exquisite, a liquor as Madeira' on the ground that 'the very best Madeira is,

458

and always has been since the pre-oidium wines were exhausted, mainly a memory'. Their memory in fact was being reborn in twentieth-century wines. It was still an uphill struggle, but the battle was not lost, and ten years before he wrote a vintage Madeira was grown, Verdelho 1910, which when it was fifty years old ranked with the great wines of the past and promises to be a glorious centenarian. Another English merchant, Charles Blandy, had seconded Leacock's efforts to rescue Madeira from the dragon, and he was so confident of the eventual rescue that he took the future as his province. Leacock, the inheritor of fine vineyards, fought among the vines with all available insecticides. In 1877 Vizetelly found him with oidium mastered by sulphuring, struggling to check phylloxera, then at its worst, with a kind of varnish applied to the principal roots of the vine.

'What Leacock did for the viticulture of Madeira', writes Simon, 'Charles Blandy did for the wine trade of the island.' Despondency bred despair and panic among the majority of the shippers. Before they left the sinking ship they were ready to stave off bankruptcy by flooding the market with their stocks of old wines. Blandy had the courage not to sell, but to buy, and proceeded to build up a great stock of the finest wines grown in happier days. As long as they existed, the renown of fine Madeira was more than a memory and they were there to provide a wonderful basis, ready to be refreshed and stretched by younger wines, as soon as the island again produced wines of quality, and to give to a Solera that wonderful depth of tone which only very old and very great wine can give. He did not live to reap the fruit of his courage. He was dead in 1877, when Vizetelly visited his Armazems at Funchal and his firm held the largest stock of Madeira held by any shipping firm in Funchal, 5,000 pipes, then valued at from £35 to £250 each. Blandy, Leacock and Cossart Gordon, the latter two having been members of the original Factory which in the eighteenth century had almost a monopoly of the island wine trade, were the three shipping firms which refused to be routed by oidium and phylloxera, and between them they held such a store of fine wine as was needed to uphold the prestige of Madeira for many years to come.

The history of the 'Pearl of the Atlantic', called Madeira (wood) by its discoverer, we are told by a Portuguese historian, on account of the vast and thick forest with which it was covered, begins in 1419. In that year João Gonçalves, known as Zarco the blue-eyed, sailed boldly out into the unexplored expanse of the Atlantic, an adventure into the unknown as daring as that of any space explorer today, found land and disembarked at the Camara de Lobos, which I take to mean the House of Seals, as such an island is no place for wolves. As a reward for the success of his venture, he was appointed Captain General of the desert island, which he at once proceeded to colonize. Determined to make the name he had given the island meaningless by reducing all its overgrowth to ashes, he set fire to the forest; it was seven years before fire had completed its work. Zarco has been highly praised for his ruthless onslaught on nature, but I cannot help wondering whether he was not too drastic. Rain and irrigation have since his day been a problem in Madeira, and the connection between trees and rainfall is, I believe, extablished. Again, were there no trees like the Portuguese oak which would have served as well as casks for the beverage wines that were the first produce of its vineyards? Early in its history pipe staves from America are among its principal imports.

Be that as it may, Zarco planted vines, sugar-cane, maize and other crops, which flourished. The ashes of the forest may have served it to increase the fertility of the soil, and the rocky nature of the island provided in places such austere soil as the vine demands for the development of its highest virtue. It is, like the Douro, largely a land of terraced vineyards. Of all dessert wines the Malmsey of Candia has the greatest and longest historical reputation, and Prince Henry the Navigator added to his exploits in seafaring the brilliant idea of transplanting to the newly discovered island the famous Malvasia or Malmsey vine from Crete. By 1455 the Madeira vineyards were flourishing. In that year Alvise da Mosto, a Venetian traveller, visited the island and reported that it was growing remarkably good wines, considering how recently the vines had been planted. It grew enough to provide for the needs of all its inhabitants, and a considerable surplus was shipped abroad. He specially mentions the Malvasia vines brought by Prince Henry from Candia, *quali riuscirono molto bene*, which have been most successful. The vines, he tells us, produced almost more fruit than leaves, and he is full of admiration for the enormous clusters, two, three – even, he ventures to say, four palms in length – *la più bella cosa del mondo da vedere*, the most beautiful thing in the world to see.

Already in the fifteenth century the Malmsey of Madeira had begun to compete with the world-famous Malmsey of Crete, but not on a very large scale. Madeira was certainly not responsible for the legend of Clarence and the butt of Malmsey. Francis I seems to have had Madeira Malmsey in his cellar, and in England the earliest reference to the island's wine appears in Part I of Shakespeare's *King Henry the Fourth*, when Falstaff is accused of having sold his soul for a cup of Madeira and a cold capon's leg. The play is dated about 1597, so that at this date Madeira wine of some kind was evidently imported, though Spanish Sack still ruled the roost.

In 1654 Cromwell enforced on Portugal the granting of special privileges to British merchants in Madeira, and in 1663 Charles II excepted Madeira from the prohibition on the export of European produce to British possessions overseas except from a British port and in a British ship. The wines of Madeira could be shipped direct from the island to any of the King's Dominions, which otherwise had to depend on wines that had passed through a British harbour. Madeira's opportunity had come and offered tempting prospects to the British merchant. Simon, in his *Madeira*, which unfortunately devoted only 45 pages to the wine in the cellar as against over 100 pages allotted to Elizabeth Craig for the wine in the kitchen, tells the story of William Bolton, a pioneer in the history of Madeira. In 1676 he sailed with a shipload of merchants from London bound for the New World. When the ship touched at Madeira he decided to settle in the island with the intention of trading both with his friends in the home land and his ship-mates in America. Into Madeira he imported goods of every description from many countries and exported some sugar, but mainly wine with a little brandy. Some of the brandy he expected 'to arrive at the goodness of the French'. In 1660 the first Parliament of the Restoration had granted the King tonnage on 'wines commonly called sweet', and in enumerating these wines, a distinction was drawn between 'Maderaes' and Malmseys and other Sacks. Bolton found some market for wine in England and Ireland, but the bulk of his trade was with the West Indies and America, where there was an ever-increasing demand for the Madeira wines. Then, Funchal was a port of call and there was a perpetual demand for wine from passing ships, both merchantmen and ships of war.

The fame of port, except perhaps in Russia, was built on red wine. The fame of Madeira rests on its golden wines called by contrast white, though in the island's

Plate 42. A Douro boat (*barco rebelo*) under sa

earliest days its vineyards produced far more red wine than white, a beverage wine to be drunk very young. If the Douro had been able to grow in quantity such natural wines more or less adapted to fill the yawning gap left by the banished French wines it is likely that the world would have been robbed of the pleasure of port. A small quantity of Malvasia wine was made, and there was a market for it on both sides of the Atlantic always demanding more than there was. These Malmsey grapes made a rich sweet natural wine very much to the taste of our forebears and capable of holding its own against the fortified Spanish Sack. Congreve may well have been thinking of Bolton's Malmsey when he wrote *The Old Bachelor*, acted in 1693. The timid and silly would-be rake Sir Joseph Wittol has dined with his braggart hanger-on Captain Bluffe and the pair have gone to St James's Park bent on amorous adventure. 'Nay, gad, I'll pick up!' says Sir Joseph, 'I'm resolved to make a night of it. Adslidikins! bully, we'll wallow in wine and women! Why this same Madeira wine has made me as light as a grasshopper.' 'Tearers', as he calls them, two masked ladies, make their appearance, and when with Bluffe's support he prepares to accost them he exclaims, 'Egad, t'other glass of Madeira, and I durst have attacked them in my own proper person without your help'.

On the other side of the ocean Madeira went from strength to strength, and in 1699 the Earl of Belmont wrote from America to Lord Somers: 'There is a white Madeira, which is called the Jesuits' wine and, I think, equals any of the Spanish Mountain wines (Malaga) so much liked of late. These Jesuits there so engross it that it is a hard matter to get any.'

The Jesuits, who never forgot the divine commandment that the harmlessness of doves should be accompanied with the wisdom of serpents, once owned the finest Malmsey vineyard in the island at Camara de Lobos, just as in Portugal their order owned some of the finest Douro vineyards, which they managed so well, as Croft tells us, that in England there was a great and fashionable demand for Priest Port. It was not the fault of the Jesuits, but the fault of nature, that the wine was so scarce. Bolton in his letters is always lamenting the scarcity of Malmsey, and in 1794 all the Malmsey made in the island did not exceed 100 pipes.

Though the natural Madeira wines were not handicapped by the shortcomings of the natural Douro wines, which caused so much trouble to the Oporto shippers, and though its Malmsey could compete with the historic Malmsey of Crete, it was not till port was establishing itself as a vintage wine that Madeira took its place among the great vintage wines of the world. It was presumably the experiments made in Oporto which led the Madeirans to test the effect of a dose of brandy on their wines, though their use of spirit was more akin to that prevailing in Jerez. They had no need to check fermentation, but by the addition of a little brandy after fermentation in relatively small quantities they gave their best wine a marvellous constitution, which revelled in its long sea voyage across the ocean to such an extent that it was all the better for an extended itinerary taking in India or China in a round trip, and in addition a longevity beyond compare.

Madeira is the only great wine pressed from grapes grown high above the ground. The island of Madeira lies so far south of Europe that the direct rays of the sun with no added refraction from the sun-baked soil working day and night, ripen the grapes to their full potentiality. A Portuguese writer compares the precipitous island with its terraced, trellised vineyards to a pile of vast honeycombs to which human bees bring their store of labour and perseverance, reaping the reward of their patient toil when the vintage comes in grapes and wine. In the gathering of the harvest there is none of the back-breaking stooping suffered by the vintagers in other wine-lands, as they bow low in reverence to the wine god over his gift of purple or amber clusters. The Madeira pickers, sheltered from the semi-tropical sun by the vine leaves overhead, strain upwards in graceful attitude to gather the hanging clusters, stooping only to pack them tenderly in the great baskets which bear them to the wine-press.

The grapes are trodden in a press near the vineyard with the bare-foot, high-step dancing to the strains of a guitar or other rural music, which belongs to the age-old ritual of the vintage, though the fair sex takes no part in treading. There are many vintage songs both in Portugal and Madeira, and I venture to quote and translate into doggerel a rustic ditty which seems to me instinct with the half-serious, half-joking spirit in which those who live by the vine regard the mystery of fermentation, quite unaffected by Pasteur's unravelling organisms:

| | |
|---|---|
| *Nasce a uva na ramada* | *The grape is born on the gadding vine,* |
| *Para ser mártir um dia;* | *Doomed to martyrdom thereafter:* |
| *Mas depois de torturada,* | *Torture of treading crowns it wine,* |
| *É Vida, Graça, Alegria.* | *Canonized Saint of Life and Laughter.* |

But after the torture of treading and before the change to martyr's status, the newly pressed grape juice, the *mosto*, must be hurried down to the Lodges in Funchal before it ferments. Once roads, negotiable even by oxen, were very rare in the island, and where they existed the must was taken down the steep gradients by ox-drawn sledges. In the northern vineyards, where no fine wine is grown, the must is left to ferment on the spot and used to be brought round to Funchal, where there was neither mole nor pier, in small boats. Vizetelly gives a pleasant view of the scene of its landing. The boats anchored at some short distance from the shore. The casks were slung overboard, and man after man of the crew stripped, crossed himself religiously and plunged into the sea, to place his hands on a cask and swim behind it, until it reached the breakers, whence it was hauled up the steep beach. Mr Croft-Cooke tells us that the same picturesquely primitive method survives for loading the must into the boats which take it to Funchal in the neighbouring little island of Porto Santo, where Zarco first landed and whence he sighted Madeira hanging like a cloud in the west. The casks are rolled down to the shore and pushed by a swimmer to the boat to be hauled aboard.

In the southern Madeira vineyards, when rough and stony tracks were almost the only means of communication, the must was transported from the vineyard press to the Lodges in the true Portuguese manner on human head and shoulders in that traditional wine receptacle, the goat-skin, the *borracho*. Whatever effect the goat-skin may have on fermented grape juice stored in it for any length of time, the must runs no risk of any hircine taint from its brief sojourn in the skin, and fermentation absolves far more grievous sins. The hide of the goat, turned inside out and filled through the neck, is fitted round the neck of its carrier, the *borracheiro*, bulging over the shoulders and steadied with the forehead strap used by the Douro vintagers. Mr Croft-Cooke compares its appearance *in situ* to that of a fat pig carried on a man's shoulder, its legs to the fore. Once the *borracheiro* had to jog-trot over rough and smooth for several miles to a single journey, but now he plies to and fro from the *lagar* to a collecting point on the road accessible to lorries, for the return journey inflating his skin to prevent it from cracking, and only the old hand knows whether modern transport has saved him much fatigue.

In the Lodges the must ferments in ullaged casks with no more than a vine leaf to cover the bung hole, until it has become *vinho claro*, and before it can claim its martyr's crown it has to pass through what might be called a purgatory of fire, with a memory perhaps of Martial's *Accipit aetatem quisquis ab igne cadus*. Long ago the Romans discovered that wines aged more quickly in heated storage and that some wines were the better for the treatment, if it was skilfully administered. They kept their wines for varying periods, before they were removed to a cold cellar, in *fumaria*, usually attics into which both the heat and the smoke from the furnaces, responsible for the central heating of their villas, penetrated. They regarded the visible smoke as opposed to the invisible temperature as the operative agent in the maturing of wine, just as they credited it with the seasoning of wood stored in similar attics. Though smoke could not find its way into the sealed jar, it would encrust the exterior, and a blackened well-smoked amphora was treated with the same reverence as a dusty cobwebbed bottle in a later age.

There is no evidence that the Madeira shippers were aware that they were taking a leaf out of the book of the ancients when they began to 'stove' their wines, but it is more than likely that in those days some of them knew their classics. At any rate, experience had proved that Madeira was wonderfully improved by long sea voyages, in which it suffered such a merciless shaking as is prescribed on the label of the medicine bottle, and sweltered in the tropics in the suffocating atmosphere of a sailing-ship's hold. The freight of the wine carried as ballast might be small, but globe-trotting in a wind-jammer, even if it meant no more than the trip to the West Indies, was a very lengthy course of education for a wine, still more so when it was the grand tour to the east. A system which could artificially produce the benefits of a long voyage offered many obvious advantages. There seems to have been no attempt in the island to reproduce the pitching and rolling motion as effective in amalgamating wine and brandy and other liquids as in upsetting the stomach. Madeira, more lightly brandied than port, needed less drastic measures, and it thrived in the wood. It may have been thought that the buffeting of a direct voyage across the Atlantic would be all that was needed, if it had been already mellowed by such heat as it would experience in voyages through the tropics.

There were one or two Madeira lovers in this country who did try the experiment of artificially applying to the finished wine the rock and roll treatment of the ocean, and apparently not without some success. An editor of *The Times*, it is said, made use of two cylinders forming part of his printing press, which rose and fell alternately. On the top of each he perched a cask of Madeira, the one on the eastern cylinder, the other on the western, the one representing the East Indies, the other the West Indies. In those days wine-lovers argued about their favourite wines with theological heat, and there was much argument about the respective merits of the Madeira which owed its sea legs to a visit to the West Indies and that which had made the longer voyage. Common sense plumps for the latter. Simon regards it as quite certain that the best wines were 'those which had had the benefit of the long sea trip from Madeira to India or China via the Cape of Good Hope and back'. 'The constant motion of the sailing ships,' he adds, 'the heat of the tropics, crossed twice, the greater access of oxygen to the wine, all helped to mature it, gently stimulating its retarded fermentation.' But the palate is rarely governed by the laws of logic and common sense, and the question was hotly argued. The Editor found a lot of malicious enjoyment in setting the warring champions of one Madeira and the other disputing whether his West Indian did not compare favourably with his East Indian.

Mr Tovey, too, tried a similar experiment. From the beam of a steam engine in a temperature of between 90 and 100 degrees Fahrenheit he suspended a quarter cask of Madeira, 'where it oscillated for three or four months, and it acquired all the softness and character of wine that had been shipped to and from the East Indies'. Unfortunately this treatment proved more expensive than that in operation in Madeira, where some 10 or 15% of the wine is lost by evaporation. The merchant himself, the engineer and interested visitors felt it incumbent on them to follow the development of the wine with such close attention of nose and palate that when the quarter cask was removed from its slings it was found to have lost nearly half its contents. 'Not an experiment to be repeated!' thought that wary wine-merchant and wise businessman, Mr Tovey.

The Madeira *estufas*, heated cellars, in which the *vinho claro* undergoes the ordeal of heat, were introduced in the first years of the nineteenth century, more with an eye to America than to this country, for here Madeira was only just beginning to be taken seriously. The series of heated chambers at different temperatures which enable each shipper to make his wine exactly after his fancy and tradition would have delighted the heart of Columella; temperature suitable for each individual wine can be maintained for just the time which experience has shown to be most beneficial. The *vinho claro* leaves the *estufas* as *vinho estufado* to be racked with no painful suggestion of torture and fortified with the wine spirit, becoming *vinho generoso*, ready for the blender.

I do not think that there has ever been a satisfactory explanation of the hardiness of Madeira and the way it thrives to a Methuselah old age with unrationed oxygen and unsheltered from the innumerable enemies of wine in the atmosphere. Pasteur, experimenting with the wine of his native Arbois, the home of Château Châlon, incidentally explained the debt owed by sherry to the protective shield of the 'flower', but though some wines grown in the north of the island are said by Vizetelly to 'flower' like sherry, it is no more encouraged in Madeira than *mycoderma vini* in other wine-lands. Simon put forward the suggestion that the trouble taken with the young wines of Madeira is responsible for the fact that they will stand more rough usage and live longer than any other wine. I cannot think that this is a sufficient explanation. Surely a great deal of trouble is taken over young wines in every self-respecting wine country. Certain wines, Madeira, sherry, Château Châlon, all seem gifted with a congenital talent for living long and resisting disease. With sherry and Château Châlon, the 'flower' does for a time set up a barrier against intrusion from without, but after it has disappeared the quality of resistance and longevity such as no other wines possess persists, and why that should be remains an unsolved mystery.

The Americans were the first to profit by the magnificent new wines. Not for nothing had Christopher Columbus lived in Madeira. The very finest were shipped direct by the wealthy shipowners of Boston, Charleston, New York and Philadelphia for their own use. Each family boasted Madeiras of its own, styled by the family name, or perhaps by the name of the ship from which the wine had landed and possibly also the date. They could see to it that their wine should have all the advantages of long seafaring, which worked such miracles upon the fortified wine. Simon mentions eighteen families of Charleston, New York and Philadelphia which named their Madeiras as if they had been grown in their own vineyards. From *Old Madeiras*, by F. G. Griswold, he quotes the story of a pipe which had journeyed via Canton. It was placed in a cradle in which it could be easily rocked in an office corridor and every clerk passing it was instructed to give it a push, so that the wine might still believe that it was being rocked in the soothing cradle of the deep and be agitated into an even more complete union with itself. That author's father had a store of old Madeiras named after his ships. In those days Madeira across the ocean was never bottled. There was a superstition that cork injured the delicate flavour of the wine. The news of the discovery that the corked bottle could work magic had not crossed the Atlantic, and Madeira could not yet rise to the full stature which bottle age was to give it. As things were, the wine when considered ripe was transferred to large demijohns such as the Portuguese peasant still uses for his wine and kept in an attic to clarify and mellow. Then it was siphoned and filtered into decanters and left to settle. A certain Mr Habisham of Savannah, a Madeira enthusiast, was responsible for saddling a very light and pale Madeira with the not very encouraging name of Rainwater, treated by some fining method which it was claimed affected neither its bouquet nor flavour, but its merits were disputed.

The battle between Madeira and sherry, ascribed in Britain to the Prince Regent's palate, crossed the Atlantic, and in 1833 we find Washington Irving ordering from Duff Gordon and Co. of Puerto de Santa Maria two half butts of the VERY BEST Brown Sherry, and expressing the hope that a great revolution was taking place among wine-drinkers in New York, whence he wrote, and that sherry was completely superseding Madeira. He must have had rather an odd digestion, since he adds that it was a change peculiarly favourable to his stomach; I have always found both wines equally digestible. It does not appear that his propaganda in Boston met with much success, though no doubt the sherry supplied him by the famous sherry shipping firm was of the highest order and must have pleased the friends among whom he distributed it.

The vogue of Madeira in Britain begins with the recognition of the independence of the American colonies in 1783 and the return of soldiers, officials and others of this country. They brought with them a taste for Madeira, which diverted more of the island's wine-trade to these islands, and introduced into current conversation the names of wines called after the grapes from which they had been pressed, previously unknown. In 1785 Madeira had for the first time, with 1,200 pipes, a place of its own in the customs' returns. In addition to Malmsey, there began to appear on wine labels Sercial, Boal, Verdelho. The fashion was launched by the Prince Regent, and for a time he drank no other wine. I rather doubt if H.R.H. would in 1795 have justified his preference by an appeal to Dr John Wright's *Essay on Wine*, published in that year and quoted by Simon in that connection, though his salad days were drawing to an end at the age of thirty-three. 'Madeira, when good, though too potent for common use, is one of the most useful and best for elderly persons in gouty habits, when the functions of life have begun to fail'. For a time Madeira swept port off the board. Its triumph was complete when that leader of fashion, Beau Brummell, asked whether the King of the Dandies approved of port, replied in a puzzled tone: 'Port? Port? What, the hot intoxicating liquor so much drunk by the lower orders?' But port had its revenge in 1815, when he fled from his creditors, and his wines were put up for sale at Christies. The main lot consisted of 10 dozen of Capital Old Port, knocked down at 80s. the dozen. Perhaps when he quarrelled with his patron he quarrelled with Madeira.

The decline in the vogue of Madeira in England has often been ascribed to the fickleness of the Prince Regent's palate, its off with the old love of Madeira and its on with a new love of sherry, but as a matter of fact it was only after his death that Madeira really lost its hold in Britain. His passion for sherry indeed seems to date from a time when Madeira had still a number of years of glory before it. Quartermaster Fowler, to whom we owe the history of Sandeman 1797, credits Mr John Kaye, some time proprietor of the Albion Tavern in Aldersgate and in 1853 High Sheriff of Buckinghamshire, with the following account of the Prince's conversion to sherry. During the war, about 1810, a British privateer captured a French merchantman, bound for Le Havre from Cadiz. In her cargo were two butts of remarkably fine brown sherry of the highest quality, specially shipped for the Emperor Napoleon. They were presented to the princely arbiter of elegances, who had one butt bottled for his own cellar and had another bottled at the Albion to be reserved for himself and his guests. The Albion was at that time recognized as by far the best restaurant in London, and according to Fowler it was the only public place of entertainment which the Prince honoured with his presence.

The excellence of that sherry goes a long way to excuse His Royal Highness's desertion of Madeira. Fowler tells us that several dozens of this 'superb wine' had been left at the Albion after the death of George IV, and the High Sheriff, proud of his reputation as a great restaurateur, and planning to startle the county with such a banquet as it had never before seen, an assize dinner in which the famous Greenwich whitebait made their first appearance in Buckinghamshire, decided to crown the feast with the Royal Sherry. 'Delicious it was', says Fowler, 'after forty years in bottle.' Later a few bottles of this wine found their way into his cellar, and he bears witness that it had never been his lot to drink anything finer than this glorious brown sherry.

On this side of the Atlantic the vogue of Madeira has undergone many vicissitudes, and so far as Britain is concerned the fluctuations of fashion in the days of its glory may be roughly traced in the import statistics. In France, as has been said, neither port nor Madeira ever established themselves; they had too many native competitors. In 1801 that diplomatic gourmet Talleyrand introduced the fashion of a glass of Madeira with the soup in high society, and then no doubt the wine really came from the island vineyards. A hundred years later in Paris a glass of *madère* meant a horrid concoction compounded in a wine factory in the Midi with not a drop of Madeira wine in its composition – an abomination which the law has now happily suppressed.

In Britain the statistics show that fashion first approved the wine between 1788 and 1793, just the time when the naughty, handsome Prince Charming had some claim to be the First Gentleman in Europe. Then between 1794 and 1800 its popularity declined. Was it then that H.R.H. was faithless to his first love and took to sherry? Did he take to sherry before he had the excuse of the Napoleon wine? Did he return to Madeira with the new century? In any case, there was a sudden doubling of the imports in 1801 to nearly 3,600 pipes, and in 1808 and 1809 they reached a level of 6,000 pipes, a figure roughly maintained until 1827, when a slow and steady decline reached the nadir of oidium in 1853. There were other more powerful forces at work than a royal palate.

These hostile influences were still in the future in 1820, when literature gives us glimpses of Madeira in the height of its glory. That year Byron, in his skit on the fashionable ladies' Blue-Stocking Clubs, *The Blues*, tells us that at luncheon after a lecture at Lady Bluebottle's Lady Bluemont took a glass of Madeira with the chicken, and Madeira was evidently an attraction of Lady Bluebottle's parties, since we hear of

> *Blues, dandies, and dowagers, and second-hand scribes.*
> *All flocking to moisten their exquisite throttles*
> *With a glass of Madeira at Lady Bluebottle's.*

Borrow, in *Lavengro* (published 1851), gives us a period sketch of Madeira in the English country. He had to visit a magistrate on business, and after a sixteen miles tramp was asked if he would like a glass of wine. He was very young and said he would like a glass of Madeira, a wine he had never tasted.

'The magistrate gave a violent slap on his knee: "I like your taste," said he. "I am fond of a glass of Madeira myself and can give you such a one as you will not drink every day . . . you shall have a glass of Madeira, and the best I have." '

The justice of the peace went off to his cellar, leaving Borrow to continue his meditation on Pilate's question, which had occupied him on his walk, and he was just asking himself, 'What is truth?', when after a quarter of an hour the magistrate returned with a servant and a tray and provided an answer. 'Here it is,' he said. 'Here's the true thing, or I am no judge, far less a justice. It has been thirty years in my cellar last Christmas.' Borrow approved this answer to his philosophical problem, and the scene closes with the justice of the peace singing of his readiness to live to a hundred given 'the haunch of a buck to eat and to drink Madeira old' and sundry other conditions of earthly bliss.

In 1824 Madeira was suffering a temporary set-back so far as the reputation of its wines was concerned, attributed by Henderson to its popularity, which had led to the importation of many of the inferior island wines. The demand was such that wine of low quality was shipped on the long eastern voyage, purchased on speculation, and nothing can give to wine the fulfilment of potentialities lacking in its youth. Husenbeth says that in 1834 the Madeira planters had been greatly injured by an imitation made in the south of France, a strong and fiery wine pressed from a grape with the Madeira flavour, brought to Britain by circuitous shipments and very cheap. Madeira, like all other wines of repute, suffered much from the base flattery of imitation at the hands of the wine-factories of Hamburg and the Midi, but it has been fortunate that upstart wine-growing countries have never stolen its good name. We never hear of American or Commonwealth Madeira.

It is impossible to write of Madeira without writing about Thomas Love Peacock, that novelist of the original and quaint self-pleasing fancy, whose novels *Crochet Castle* (1831) and *Gryll Grange* (1860) should be the bedside books of every gourmet and wine-lover. Erudition tempered by a pretty wit, cynicism mellowed by a generous sense of humour, uncompromising realism corrected by a zest for all the good things of life, combine to glorify the art of good living, in which he gives a prominent role to Madeira. He seems to have lived and died in happy ignorance of the troubles with which one of his favourite wines had to wrestle. It is very strange that in *The Egoist* Meredith's Dr Middleton in his famous lucubrations on 'the light of the antique' in wine, on the glory of old age in port, Hermitage, Hock and burgundy, has not a word to say of Madeira, that wine of unrivalled longevity. In 1849 Meredith made an unhappy match with

Peacock's daughter; his father-in-law had a great influence on his work, and he must surely have drunk with him Madeira more senatorial than any port likely to have come his way, before the matrimonial troubles which inspired him to write the sonnets of *Modern Love*.

Peacock immortalized himself in two characters of 'purple cheer', rosy men 'right plump to see', under the thinnest of veils. His *alter ego*, Dr Folliott, he amiably described as 'a gentleman endowed with a tolerable stock of learning, an interminable swallow and an indefatigable pair of lungs', a description which applied equally well to Dr Opimian, named after the vintage of 121 B.C., the greatest of historic vintages. In *Crochet Castle* Dr Folliott lays down the principle that the *verre de santé*, the glass of wine after the soup, the first drink of dinner with in those days no appetizer to precede it, should be Madeira. He could not fancy Hock until he had laid a substratum of Madeira – and a solid substratum it had to be, as he followed it up cheerfully with Hock, champagne, Graves, Sauternes, Hermitage and claret. In *Gryll Grange* the spate of Dr Opimian's conversation is checked only by the offer of a glass of old Madeira which his host believed was really what it professed to be. This assurance, which called from Dr Opimian the suggestion that the proof lay in the wine with the tag *in vino veritas*, is the only sign that Peacock had any idea of the difficulties, which had already culminated in the oidium disaster, that Madeira had to face. He was then seventy-six and perhaps reckoned that he had enough Madeira in his cellar to last his time.

It was Dr Opimian who sang the praise of Madeira in terms borrowed from an Italian song addressed to a Tuscan wine. 'It is the true potable gold, which straightway banishes every ill without remedy. It is Helen's Nepenthe, which makes the world joyful, for ever free and immune from dark and gloomy thoughts.' Another character in the same novel shows the wine working its magic. A young man, living in a tower and blest with seven chaste and beautiful virgins to pour his wine and make him music, as well as a staff of servants to do the rough work, falls in love with the Lady of Gryll Grange and can find nothing but Madeira to stifle the pangs of his heart. Lonely and love-lorn, he gulps down a bottle of Madeira as if it had been so much water. In the heat of his passion Madeira became almost 'his eating and his drinking solely', a phrase borrowed from Beaumont and Fletcher's *Scornful Lady*. All ends happily with Dr Opimian celebrating nine weddings in which the lover's seven Hebes are included, and the ceremonies wound up after a terrific breakfast with a fusillade of champagne corks, all discharged simultaneously as 'a peal of Bacchic ordnance'.

During this period, though Henderson says that in his time the only Malmsey brought into Britain was Madeira, we hear of Madeira only as Madeira *tout court*, unqualified by the names of the grapes which have so great an effect on its character. The exported wine, unless it was the rare and precious Malmsey, was like port, a blended wine with no specific grape to name it, but in the island, as the ancient wines yet to be discussed prove, the individual qualities of the various grapes were prized and developed in wines called by their names. In 1901, on his accession, King Edward VII, who was always short of money, put up for auction 5,000 dozen of Madeiras and sherries which had accumulated in the Buckingham Palace cellars since the days of George IV. Why he did not start with the herds of white elephants, stabled in the Palace, let loose on Queen Victoria as tribute to her two Jubilees by her loving and faithful dominions, re- mains a mystery to the writer, who was in their day one of her loyal subjects. They would have brought in more money than they were worth, while the wines, though they sold well according to the prices of the day, were worth far more than anything money could buy. In explaining the royal whim, a journalist insisted that His Majesty was merely getting rid of obsolete wines and boldly asserted that there was no palate in the country which could distinguish between Madeira and sherry – a gross mis-statement, since I was very much alive then and I doubt if there was one of my friends with such an insensitive palate. Simon praises the King for having given his people and all the wine-lovers of the world the chance of drinking those marvellous wines, but it is a question whether that sale was a good advertisement for Madeira, with its suggestion that the wine was numbered among the 'has-beens'.

It was not until after the First World War that Madeira began to resume its sway in Britain, and perhaps it was as well, since recovery from the diseases of oidium and phylloxera demanded a long convalescence. Now Madeira is itself again. For all wine-lovers its recovery marks a red-letter date. For those who believe that wine can claim to be for the senses of taste and smell such a medium as colour and line for that of sight and music for hearing, Madeira, in its humble way, represents an instance of that philosophical ideal, the reconciliation of the opposites, in its reconciliation of sweet and dry. Like the bitterness of love, the out-of-this-world richness of ancient Malmsey is saved from cloying by an underlying austerity, and the austerity of Sercial is tempered with a deep undertone of richness. It may be that the light acidulous freshness of the *vinhos verdes* of the Minho, grown high above the ground under a less blazing sun, is sublimated into something rich and rare in wines pressed from grapes also grown high on trellises in a semi-tropical climate.

Today the student of wine has a wide choice of moderately priced wines to make him familiar with the basic taste of Madeira. There are four main types associated with the four noble vines which are now principally cultivated in the island: Malvasia or Malmsey with its very grudging yield and at its best supreme, Bual (in Portuguese Boal) less rich and more prolific, still a dessert wine, Verdelho with something of the maid-of-all-work virtue of sherry, equally at home with the soup *à la Talleyrand*, particularly turtle soup, Stilton cheese or a slice of cake, and Sercial the austere with a farewell on the palate as cleansing as sea air.

## MADEIRA WINE SHIPPERS OF LONDON

| | |
|---|---|
| Cock Russell & Spedding Ltd | 16 Devonshire Row, EC2 |
| Coverdale & Co Ltd | 7/8 Idol Lane, EC3 |
| Davis Hammond & Barton Ltd | 44/46 Leadenhall Street, EC3 |
| Deinhard & Co Ltd | 9 Idol Lane, EC3 |
| Evans Marshall & Co Ltd | 6 Idol Lane, EC3 |
| Feuerheerd Wearne & Co Ltd | 5 Lloyds Avenue, EC3 |
| Charles Kinloch & Co Ltd | Queensbury Road, Wembley |
| C. N. Kopke & Co Ltd | 58 Southwark Bridge Road, SE1 |
| MacIntosh, Pelengat & Walford Ltd | 12 Hobart Place, SW1 |
| Rutherford Osborne & Perkins Ltd | 28 Monument Street, EC3 |
| Southard & Co Ltd | 56 Palace Road, East Molesey |
| C. H. Tapp & Co Ltd | 3/4 Lincoln's Inn Fields, WC2 |
| L. R. Voigt | 25 Great Tower Street, EC3 |

# CHAPTER TWELVE

# Setúbal, Colares and Bucelas

PORT and Madeira reign in acknowledged royalty as the kings of dessert wines. Before passing to the wines of lower degree, which are as essential to the emergence of great wines as ordinary people to that of men of genius, consideration is due to another fine dessert wine, which though less in the public eye can claim a place beside them as a modest queenly sister, the Moscatel of Setúbal. The wine god has chosen Portugal as his earthly paradise. Most wine-growing regions are either monotonously dull like the Bordelais or can be adequately described in prose such as the Burgundy slopes of gold and the smiling vineyards of the Loire, and if poetry is needed for those of the homely Moselle it is satisfactorily supplied by the rather pedestrian Ausonius. None of them can compare in their setting with the beauty of that of most of the Lusitanian wine-lands, which cries out for such superlatives as only a poet can make tolerable.

One of the lovelist homes of noble vines lies just south of the estuary of the Tagus, where a gathering of softly outlined hills which we should call mountains embraces a bay that has at its heart the little land-locked port of Setúbal. It is said that Byron at twenty-one in the first years of his indiscretion, after venturing forth on the Lisbon packet for the east, had not time to cross the Tagus and add to his picture of Cintra another word picture of the little County of the Three Castles, where the wine-lover drinks in with his eye nature in her fairest aspect and where through his mouth his palate perceives reflected in its wine the sweetness of its sun-blest beauty. The castle of Saint Philip above Setúbal itself commands a breath-taking view over land and sea, though there are so many viewpoints in the hills which call for a gasp. The castle of Sesimbra, wedding into harmony the nearby ocean and the mountains, marks a victory of the wine god, since its capture from the Moors in 1165 restored to the region of Setúbal the wine which Mahomet forbade. The castle of Palmela belongs to the aristocracy both of birth and wine. Its *grand seigneur*, the Duke of Palmela, Portuguese ambassador in London, true to a tradition dating back to Rome to which Portuguese diplomats have been exceptionally faithful, oiled the wheels of diplomacy with his Moscatel, such wine as (to change the metaphor) would pour oil on the troubled waters of a Summit Meeting.

Wines often take their names from the ports from which they are shipped with a more inclusive label than that of the locality in which they are grown, and the wines known as Moscatel of Setúbal are best represented by those grown in the wine centre of Azeitão some few miles to the west and those of Palmela to the north. There was a time when the facilities of the port were a bone of contention between the various districts, but the last traces of such a rivalry were obliterated by the union through marriage of the ducal family of Palmela with the descendants of José Maria da Fonseca of Azeitão, who in the mid nineteenth century was made Knight of the Tower and Sword in recognition of his services on behalf of the wines of Setúbal both at home and abroad.

I fear that the legend which connects Setúbal with Tubal, Noah's grandson, does exaggerate its antiquity a trifle, but it is certainly one of the oldest wine-growing regions in Portugal. Though there is no historical evidence available, I hazard a guess that it was from this region that Osey, whatever the derivation of its name, found its way abroad, even before the Moors had been driven from Granada, for I know of no other wine district where, before the Spanish Sacks had emerged, a natural wine could compete in richness and sweetness with the more sophisticated Sacks of the Levant. If any wine can claim to be the lineal descendant of the *vitis apiana*, commemorated by both Pliny and Columella, it is the Moscatel of Setúbal. The *vitis apiana*, the bees' vine, owes its name to those insects' passion for its grapes. Another branch of the same family may account for the Spanish Pedro Ximenez grape which, laid out on mats in the sun to sweeten its intense natural sweetness, gathers round the piles the music of the lazy murmuring of innumerable bees, but the Moscatel has a more exquisite flavour and a wider-ranging fragrance, which its growers grudge to the marauding swarms. In 1759 the Town Council of Azeitão passed a by-law to keep the winged robbers at a distance, forbidding all bee-hives within a distance of a quarter of a league from the vineyards.

There are two varieties of the Moscatel grape, both of which give to their wines an intense, and yet fresh and delicate, flavour and bouquet as enchanting as the taste of the hot-house-grown muscatelle grape, the Moscatel do Setúbal, white, and the Moscatel Roxo, black. The former, the most widely cultivated, grows in large clusters with berries large for a wine grape, thick-skinned and luscious, passing in colour with the season from the green of the vine leaves to yellow-gold and yellow-amber. The black variety has smaller clusters and smaller berries, ripens earlier and yields wines with a special character of their own for which they are prized.

In the ripening of the grapes the scorching summer sun is tempered at night by Atlantic breezes softened by the shelter of the hills, and their sweetness owes nothing to the noble mould of Sauternes. The vintage lasts from some day in the first fortnight in September to the end of October. The fruit freed from its stalks is pressed as quickly as possible, but the berries are so fleshy and the juice so viscous that they offer little resistance to pressure, and the operation generally takes about 24 hours. Fermentation is checked with brandy as soon as the desired balance of sugar and alcohol has been reached. There follows a treatment which to the best of my knowledge has no parallel elsewhere and to which the wine owes the exceptional freshness of its bouquet and aroma, the scent and sweetness of fresh ripe fruit. A quantity of fresh moscatel grape skins is added to the wine and left to macerate in it until the spring racking, thus intensifying the fragrance to some extent overlaid by fermentation and the added spirit.

Senhor José Maria da Fonseca invited me to visit his cellars at Azietão with their treasures of ancient wine.

I accompanied Senhor de Fonseca to Azeitão into the atmosphere of secular peace and assured tradition, which reigns in those temples of the wine god, the cellars where his treasures are stored. Everywhere these temples have their own special incense. Every wine sheds round its home the aura of its natural scent, and the perfume of Moscatel intensifies for me that pursuit of sweetness and light – even in the dusk of the cellar where its gold has to be imagined – which Matthew Arnold said was the pursuit of perfection. Guards of honour under royal inspection lack the dignity of files of ancient forest oaks, but the line of huge secular vats has not lost the stateliness of the great trees from which their staves were hewn, and impress the visitor with his own insignificance.

'These ancient casks', said Senhor da Fonseca, as I saluted them, 'make fine Moscatel of themselves. They are so impregnated with its essence that they work miracles on the wines they receive.'

My host, with a glance at these heirlooms as expressive of family tradition as a gallery of portraits, struck in a casual remark the note which always re-echoes for those who look to wine for the aesthetic pleasure given to the sense of taste, given by art to the other senses. 'A wine-grower', he said smiling, 'must be a poet and I compose my poems in Moscatel.' There followed in the shady courtyard a cavalcade of the poems composed by our host and his forebears, which I found more grateful to my nose and palate than many modern metrical and musical compositions. The first wine was very young. Its bouquet was almost overwhelming though as fresh as lavender just picked in the garden, thanks, I felt sure, to those fresh grape skins which added their scent to the fermented must, but wine and spirit were still unreconciled. As the wine aged, its colour deepened. There were wines of 1950, 1945, 1940, 1920, 1910, 1900 and a Methuselah, probably centenarian, dating from the foundation of the firm. Morton Shand describes the colour of Moscatel as ruddy amber, but I should say that it begins with the colour of what Peacock called 'potable gold' and grows dark quite quickly, until in its old age it is as dark as the darkest sherry. The bouquet of the young wine with a scent quite in place in a lady's boudoir, though so much more refreshing than artificial perfumery, was tempered by time into something more ethereal and had to be tasted, that is savoured within the closed chamber of the mouth, before it could be fully enjoyed.

I found perfection in the 1920 vintage, in which the vinous quality of the Moscatel grape had absorbed the added alcohol and released in its full sweetness the charm of its perfume. To a student of wine the oldest Moscatel was of exceptional interest. It explained a puzzling phrase of Pliny's, comparing the famous Opiminian wine in extreme old age to *mee asperum*, rough honey, the adjective being applied to tastes which were the opposite of smooth on the palate, sea-water, garlic, pepper, vinegar. In it the saccharinity which the Romans mainly connected with honey was so concentrated that the palate could scarcely register it as sweet and was numbed as in a centenarian vintage sherry by the opposite concentration of dry austerity in which it can only grasp an impression of steel and salt.

For some reason a snobbish superiority has become attached to a preference for dry wines, but as André Simon says: 'Most people love sweet wines, although very few care to say so.' The place for a sweet wine is with the sweets, and no wine is more perfectly at home with them than the Moscatel of Setúbal with its sunny fragrance. The Portuguese charmingly call sweet wine *adamado*, lady-like, from *dama*, a lady, and with it a foreign ear may catch a hint of *amor*. In Britain, where barbarous fashion not so long ago exiled the ladies from the dinner table while the men drank their port, better manners now prevail, and some ladies would find an added pleasure in their relief from exile if the decanter of post-prandial port was reinforced by a decanter of post-prandial Moscatel.

When phylloxera descended on Setúbal the Moscatel vine growing in the richer soil of the district could only be saved by grafting it on immune American stocks, and it was fortunate to find congenial stocks in the riparias. Even more fortunate was the Periquita, which yields the red table wines of Setúbal. I first made the acquaintance of Periquita on the voyage to Lisbon and picked it out with a Colares of the Visconde de Salreu as the best of the Portuguese wines on the ship's list. It has something of that silkiness of texture which marks a good burgundy, with a stout body, pleasant finish and agreeable bouquet. The Periquita of Setúbal and the Ramisco of Colares stand practically alone among the vines of the world, for their grapes are grown in defiance of phylloxera on their original ungrafted stocks just as they have been for centuries. The unique privilege will be more fully discussed with the more famous Colares wine. Here it is sufficient to say that Periquita, driven out from some vineyards where the soil did not offer adequate resistance to the invading insect, was able to flourish in others more sandy, where the shifting grains of sand defeat its efforts to climb down to the rootlets which are its prey. Today there is not a wine district in the world which can boast such a triumph over the plague that once obliterated the vineyards of the western world as Setúbal and Colares.

## The Lusitanian Hall-mark

Before passing to the vast wine-growing regions north of the Tagus, a word should be said of Algarve, the extreme south of Portugal, where the Salazar régime is encouraging viticulture. At Lagõa in this province a wine once popular in Flanders under the name of Fuseta or Tavira is being revived. This scheme of revival is still in its infancy, but it has a good historic tradition to work on, for Algarve, as has been said, entered very early into the history of wine and is mentioned as a companion of Osey long before the Moors were driven out of Granada. The Algarve wines so far to the south may well prove to be in a class of their own, but dealing with the Portuguese wines as a whole, it is, I think, possible to detect in nearly all of them a national stamp, a Lusitanian hall-mark, which distinguishes them from the wines of all other countries, just as national characteristics distinguish the Portuguese nation. Mr Croft-Cooke was at once far from and near to the truth when he wrote in the preface to his *Madeira*: 'It is not the vine that matters, but the place in which it is grown, the soil in which its roots spread and the air it breathes.' No one who writes about Sercial, Verdelho, Bual and Malmsey can really think that the vine does not matter, but it is almost impossible to exaggerate the importance of the influence of geography, soil and climate on the nature of the wine it yields.

The unique shape and situation of Portugal give to its wines a common basic character comparable to the individual tang of its language, and the port-lover might almost interpret the history of its shaping as the fateful prelude to the birth of his favourite wine, just as, according to Virgil, the fate of Troy was preordained for the foundation of Rome. He might well ascribe to the wine god a part in the establishment of its boundaries. The Roman Province of Lusitania had as its northern frontier the Douro, 60 miles south of its present frontier, the Minho, but what it lost in length it gained in breadth, spreading eastward to include Salamanca and Àvila in a bulge in which the wine god had little or no interest. Submerged for centuries by Vizigoths and Moors, it rose again in the twelfth century, as Portugal, a tiny independent kingdom between the Minho and the Tagus, narrowed by the absorption in Spain of the non-wine-growing territory on the east and lengthened by the addition of the vine and corn land between the Douro and the Minho, the home of the *vinhos verdes*.

In this long narrow strip of land with a length almost three times its breadth between the mountains and the ocean, no vineyard can be out of reach of the mountain air and the ozone of the Atlantic. In nearly all Portuguese wines I seem to detect a special touch of the mountain and the sea, a clean refreshing zest – it tempers the sweetness of the Moscatel – which corrects the strength and tendency to coarseness inseparable from southern sun and is varied by the subtle influence of varying soils ranging from the schist of the Alto Douro to the sea sand of Colares – and always in the background a hint of granite. The wines of the Lisbon region owe more to the ocean than the mountains, and the close proximity of their vineyards to the Atlantic, with its buffeting gales and breezes and tonic ozone, gives them a common hall-mark, though their variety is very great. According to John Croft, writing in 1788, four or five thousand tuns of wine were at the end of that century being shipped each year from Lisbon to Britain 'all promiscuously called Carcavelos', because the wines from the Carcavelos vineyards of the Marquis de Pombal, whose seat was at Oeiras on the edge of the vineyards, were richer and stronger than the common sort of Lisbon wines, and so commanded a higher price. In those days the wines sold as Carcavelos were natural wines grown north of the Tagus, but since then Carcavelos has taken a leaf out of the book of port and has taken its place among the four fortified Portuguese dessert wines styled *generosos*.

Carcavelos lies near Estoril at the point where the estuary of the Tagus opens into the Atlantic. Its vineyards are not very extensive, and I fear they are exposed, as are the vineyards round Château Haut-Brion to the extension of Bordeaux, to the encroachment of the growing suburbs of Lisbon. The demand for building on that lovely coast of the sun steadily increases. Its wine, which in its drier form may serve as an *apéritif*, is at its best when time has given its sweetness that curious twist of originality, characteristic of nearly everything Portuguese. Shand describes it well: 'a dryish-tasting fortified wine, topaz-coloured, with a peculiar almond flavour that is not usually appreciated at the first glass'. I do not think I can do better than repeat what I first wrote about it in my *Good Wine from Portugal*: The first impression of luscious sweetness which it gives is promptly saved from excess by a curious nutty flavour, vaguely reminiscent of Amontillado, but quite distinct as the quintessence of that flavour which is the hall-mark of Portuguese wines. At the first taste this special tang is rather disquieting, but the taste is soon acquired and grows on one, as Shand implies, with succeeding glasses.

Beyond Estoril, through scenery continually more ravishing, lies Cintra, Byron's 'glorious Eden . . . in variegated maze of mouth and glen'. Just beyond it on the range's outlying spurs, the vineyards of Colares stand four-square facing the furious Atlantic blasts. The contrast between the approach to the home of Portugal's greatest table wine, so voluptuous with views which Byron held more dazzling than Dante's dream of Paradise, and the stern wind-swept sandy waste where only the vine can flourish, invites a poet's pen, but Byron unhappily was too worried about the Convention of Cintra to visit Colares. Yet I cannot resist quoting Childe Harolde's vision of Cintra.

> *The horrid crags, by toppling convents crown'd,*
> *The cork-trees hoar that clothe the shaggy steep,*
> *The mountain-moss by scorching skies imbrown'd,*
> *The sunken glen, whose sunless shrubs must weep,*
> *The tender azure of the unruffled deep,*
> *The orange tints that gild the greenest bough,*
> *The torrents that from cliff to valley leap,*
> *The vine on high, the willow-branch below,*
> *Mix'd in one mighty scene, with varied beauty glow.*

It is a shock to pass from such a scene to an area of barren sand, chequered by a laby-rinth of small palisaded and walled resistance points, for so they seem to one who re-members the First World War, the work of such digging and toil as with the aid of high explosives created the fantastic landscapes of trench warfare. A touch of nightmare in the huge and rugged bear-shaped rock which gives its name to the *pousada* beneath it, where I lunched before my first visit to the Colares vineyards, fittingly prepared an entry to a strange land, but there was nothing nightmare-ish in the admirable cuisine of its restaurant. How Apicius would have doted over the *ameijoas*, cockle-like clams served hot, the fish called *cherne* unknown to me elsewhere, and the melting-in-the-mouth veal for which the region is famous! I wonder if he would have had a palate sensitive enough to appreciate the two bottles of Colares, Visconde de Salreu, 1950 and 1947, full-bodied, silky wines made unique by their kinship with the ocean, Shakespeare's magic 'sea-change into something rich and strange', compared by a fanciful young lady to the far-away look in a sailor's eyes – perhaps it gave Zarco his nickname.

Thus fortified, I entered that world of sea sand in which those wines had grown. The grapes had been gathered and the leaves had fallen, leaving the twisted vine stems to crawl over such sand as children love to dig in, each vineyard a little rectangular plot, separated from its neighbours by high bamboo palisades facing the sea, intersected by waist-high fences and loose stone walls built up from large blocks dug up from deep down in the sand, which seem to be conglomerations of sand grains. This honeycomb of defences is cunningly designed to keep at bay the enemy, the merciless Atlantic blast, which, when defeated in frontal attacks, swirls round, caught in the encircling moun-tains, in all directions in quest of a weak point.

Against its direct assault, the creeping vines are defended by 'master' palisades con-structed of tall elastic bamboos bound into a wind-proof shelter with osiers from those Cintra willow trees which Byron observed. These resilient parapets share the nature of the reeds, the only plants which could grow on the shore of Dante's Purgatory, since they alone yielded to the ocean's waves and winds, and they are so skilfully woven that they can defy the direct violence of an Atlantic gale. They are raised parallel to the coast-line and are intersected at right angles by the lower defences, fences and walls, which defeat the less violent, if more insidious, flank assaults of circling blasts, and are known as 'traverses'.

Even the stubborn vine could not live in these dunes, unless the barren sand, left there by the receding Atlantic in some forgotten past, had beneath it at a depth varying from 3 to 30 feet a solid substratum, a bed of clay. The humidity of the ocean keeps the vineyards well freshened with rain and mist, but the moisture seeps down through the unabsorbent sand to be held in the substratum, and there the roots of the vine must find their nourishment. There can be no easy straightforward planting of young vines on the surface soil. The farmer planting a new vineyard must begin by digging down to the clay, opening a hole of a depth often twice his height below the original level with the unstable sand he has excavated piling up in a shifting wall around it. The slightest carelessness in the building up of that crumbling heap and it will collapse and bury the man digging many feet below. The rescue of a man being smothered by innumerable tiny grains of sand reduces the rescue of a man drowning in water to mere child's play, and when these divers in the sand have reached a dangerous depth they work with a basket over their heads as a helmet to save them from suffocation, if a down-rush of sand buries them, and give the rest of the gang time to extricate them still breathing.

The vine is a cruel master. Every true wine-grower thinks it mortal sin to leave fallow the smallest patch of land on which wine might be grown, and there are still some areas in these dunes unsounded by Bacchus. Sometimes in some hitherto virgin spot the clay bed lies so deep that it is too dangerous to dig down to it, and hours of work far more onerous than ploughing the sand end in its proverbial disappointment.

A new vineyard is planted by gangs of three men. One digs down through the sand, throwing back the sand to a man behind him, who passes it back to the third, who with the special Colares tool, a big hoe-like mattock, tries to give solidity to the ever-threatening wall as it rises. The excavation may be either circular and funnel-shaped with a circumference of several yards and tapering down as it descends or a broad oblong parallelogram. If the shape of the vineyard is to be circular, at the bottom of the hole some thirty vine plants, each slender stem ten to fifteen feet tall, are set eight or nine inches deep in the clay in such a pattern that as they grow, they will slope outwards from the centre and eventually cover with their off-shoots the whole of the sand above them. In the oblong excavation, which is more usual, a row of young vines held upright by bamboos is planted in its centre to seek the upper air direct. The steep sandy banks which form its sides are each of them fringed with another row of plants, leaning against them and so growing outwards away from the central row.

As soon as the infant plants are held in the mothering clay, the sand from above is worked round them until their heads emerge just sufficiently to bud and extend their lateral shoots. As they grow, the level of the sand round them is raised. Each year they are layered to strike out new roots, but they are never separated from the mother root on which their life depends. That vital root does not increase in size, though the layers above it put forth much bigger ineffectual roots. In five years a family of thirty vines rooted far below in the clay will have a hundred dependent plants spreading over the soil above, and in six years a hectare, two and a half acres, will be covered with four thousand fruit-bearing plants drawing their life from sixteen hundred roots deep down in the clay. As the vines grow upwards, the level of the sand is made to keep pace with their growth. As one trudges along the narrow tracks between fences and walls with shoes filling with sand, the eye wanders over the unearthly landscape, a patchwork labyrinth of little vineyards, all at different levels and separated into wind-proof compartments. Where workmen have been plying their mattocks among the vines, they raise little mounds of sand, recalling the first efforts of a child with a wooden spade to build a sand castle, though there is more method in their form and order.

As soon as the vines have been planted, their heads showing above the sand, there must be no delay in enclosing them within their wind-proof fortresses, for the rage of the Atlantic winds trapped in the intricacies of the lofty hills knows no truce. The twirling sails of the little squat pepper-pot windmills perched on every bare hill-top betray their ubiquitous presence and every little white house snuggles down under a massive shield of stone-pines.

The vines are heavily pruned and trained to hug the sand. I know of only one parallel to these crawling vines, the vines of Lesbos, grown in this lowly fashion from time immemorial, before they were described, probably in the third century A.D., in the famous Greek romance, *Daphnis and Chloe*. 'The vine in Lesbos grows low, neither upgrowing nor trained up trees, but spreading its branches over the soil and creeping like ivy. The veriest baby with hands released from its swaddling clothes could reach the fruit.'

Usually a vine patch gives the impression of carrying a multitude of independent vine stocks, since layering has given the off-shoots independent establishments, though they depend for their living on the mother root far below. Sometimes, however, the vine has been left to sprawl across the sand at its own sweet will, none of its shoots being pegged into the sand, and it is easy to trace its origin to a single stock sinking down to the clay. I have seen a gnarled and twisted trunk of an enormous vine, which for a hundred years has been crawling like a gigantic boa constrictor over its enclosure, with some of the countless clusters it bears each year, just raised above the sand by one of the little bamboo vine-props called *pontões*, fitted at the beginning of the summer when the clusters are forming. The props save the grapes from being burnt and scorched by contact with the sun-baked sand. Fine red wines can never be made from grapes with skins cooked and scorched by excessive heat, as the 1921 vintage proved in France. On its little props, generally about a foot long, the fruit ripens as it should, and when the vintage comes, round about 8 September the grapes are gathered as they ripen. No rotten berries must find their way into the must. It takes all a man's strength to raise a fraction of the length of the vine from the ground.

It is not surprising that in these extraordinary conditions there is only one vine which can flourish, the Ramisco, and true to the principle that the vine is at its best only when it has to struggle for existence against fearful odds, it is capable of yielding a really great wine; it is unquestionably the premier table wine of Portugal, and if only there had been more of it its fame would be worldwide. It has a unique place in wine history. The sand which imposes such labour and skill on its growers is impervious to the deadly phylloxera. Just below Colares, the Cabo da Roca, the extreme western point of Europe, stands in the forefront of the Old World, and the vineyards behind it, still unconquered, can boast themselves the tiny heroic remnant which never surrendered to the invading plague from the New World, when its innumerable insect hosts swept over and laid low every Old World vineyard. Nowhere else in the world is a wine of high degree grown ungrafted from the actual vines to which it owes its pre-phylloxera renown, still drawing their nourishment through their natural root channel. The admirer of *Vathek*, that one work of sombre and terrifying genius from the pen of the eccentric and all too wealthy misanthrope, William Beckford, haunted throughout his life by the fantastic beauty of Cintra, where he had lived in state in a villa in 1797, can today drink a vintage Colares with full confidence that he is enjoying a wine identical in origin with one of those 'admirable wines, the tribute of every part of the Portuguese Dominions', which gave Beckford so much pleasure when he dined and talked with the Archbishop-Confessor to the Queen in the Archiepiscopal Palace.

Of the 4,500 acres under vine in the Colares district, about 300 may be dismissed since they are on the *chão rijo*, the *terra firma*, as opposed to the *chão areia*, the sand of the dunes. Their wine is of interest only because it gives the peasants the thews and patience without which the true Colares could not exist. It is in place in the wickered demijohns, the nice large jars which provide the many members of a Portuguese family from grandfather to baby with that daily generous allowance of wine that plays such a part in the national gaiety and happiness. The true Colares is retailed only in the bottle, symbol of the victory of vintage port.

Colares with its punning arms of *tres colares*, three necklaces, is a land of small holdings. Its vineyards are distributed between some 600 growers, the great majority making under 10 pipes of wine and well under a hundred making over 15 pipes in a normal year. Its average annual yield amounts to only 2,000 pipes, less than half the 115-gallon pipe to the acre. It has always been a scarce wine, and in the past its name was continually taken in vain to its prejudice, though it is now fully protected by law. In the days of primitive port the little that reached Britain was often robbed of its individuality by being sold as Colares port. In the 'sixties of the last century Tovey drank and enjoyed it so much in his Lisbon hotel that he wanted to buy some for his customers, but in the Lisbon export warehouses he met with nothing but wines 'made up for Brazil where strength and coarseness appear to be preferred to purity'. The estranging ocean exercises a strange effect on those who settle beyond it, since everywhere they develop a thirst for drinks of the highest alcoholic strength artificially induced. That failing in the United States bids fair to convert with the wand of that evil fairy, the sugar cane, Beaujolais into a heavy wine, contradicting its natural genius, and in Portugal, where sugar is forbidden, the temptation to ginger up their natural wine with the brandy available from a multitude of stills, excused in port as its good fairy, did much harm to those Lisbon wines, which might otherwise have found a valuable market in Britain.

Tovey found the Colares he was looking for at the branch office which Sandeman's had at that time established in Lisbon to trade in the local wines. He was assured that the wines he had been shown by the shippers in the Brazil trade had almost certainly no right to the name of Colares at all, and that even in Portugal its scarcity was regularly corrected by blending with the ordinary wines of Torres. Shand very rightly says that to call Colares the Portuguese claret is doing it a grave injustice, for, though it has a very pleasant and individual flavour of its own, it no more resembles claret than claret does burgundy. Unfortunately he adds: 'This is a very clean, round, sweet-tasting wine that gives one a very fair idea of what natural port would taste like.' He would never have written that even if he had tasted the natural Douro wine as it is made today. Grown relatively far from the ocean in the High Douro, these excellent wines from a mountain home are as different from Atlantic Colares as claret from burgundy.

The Portuguese wine industry, both viticulture and commerce, is now admirably centralized by the Junta Nacional do Vinho, and I would urge on that body the importance of treating Colares as a very special jewel in the wine crown of Portugal, a fragile pearl, which in the modern world might so easily lose its lustre and indeed perish. With a multitude of small peasant growers modern methods of vinification demand a central concentration of their grapes for transformation into wine, which flattens out many interesting vineyard peculiarities, but in Colares they should go hand in hand with a memory of the traditional procedure which enabled the Visconde de Salreu to produce vintage wines worthy of taking their place at the side of world-famous vintage port. Everything should be done to encourage the production of such wines which can be made only from picked Ramisco grapes in a fine year, and Portugal is fortunate in that good vintages are rather the rule than the exception. Even so, such wines must be rare, and their quality should command a high price. The prestige of such expensive wines is a precious national asset. Considering the unique nature and history of the Colares vineyards, the growers still receive a far from adequate pecuniary reward for their Herculean labours.

## The Arinto Wines of Bucelas

Farther inland between Cintra and the Tagus, far more sheltered from the ocean, lies Bucelas, the home of white wines and, as has been said, very probably that of Shakespeare's Charneco. In the early years of the nineteenth century Wellington, full of praise for the military qualities of his Portuguese allies, returned to Britain with his veterans, and they all shared a taste for the Portuguese wines which they brought home with them. We could not expect to hear much of Colares, but the white wine of Bucelas became the most popular of Portuguese table wines. 'A delicious, mellow, golden-coloured wine,' Shand calls it, and if only it had maintained its standard its vogue would have lasted. It was within reach of the humble pocket. It is one of the three wines contributed to the merriment of a festive occasion by the male boarders of Mrs Tibbs's Boarding House, no place for expensive wines, in Dickens's *Sketches by Boz* (1836). A few years later, Thomas Hood, in a comic rhyme on a public dinner very unlike a mayoral banquet, pilloried among the wines served

> *Bucelas made handy*
> *By Cape and bad brandy.*

No blame on Portugal, but a lurid light on the horrid proceedings of some early Victorian vintners!

Tovey was as disappointed with the Bucelas he tasted in the export cellars as he had been with the Colares, 'a coarse, potent wine of deep colour'. Very different was his attitude towards the Bucelas he tasted at Sandeman's. Evidently he gave an order, for he rather coyly admits that he anticipates a considerable demand for his Bucelas. He accepts the identification of the Bucelas Arinto, a vine of undoubted breed and distinction, with the German Riesling – vines vary so much in different environments that all such identifications should be taken with a grain of salt – but he wisely adds that though Bucelas is somewhat of the style of Hock, no one would take it for a Rhenish growth. There is none of the Lusitanian whiff of the ocean in the Rhine wines. Good Bucelas is still today exactly as he described it. 'It is light in colour and of an agreeable flavour. As a dinner wine, especially with fish, it will supply the requirements of those who want more strength and character in their wine than is found in light Hocks and cheap Sauternes.'

We could do with a great deal more Bucelas, and perhaps if those who could supply that demand devoted to their wine a little more of the attention they give to the incomparable olive oil, the foundation of their prosperity, vine and olive in close fellowship would flourish together as they did in classical days. Bucelas is most up-to-date in its wine-making methods; the German filter is used, which makes wines brighter and sweeter when they are young, though their precocity forbids their growing up out of their salad days – a handicap that does not affect wines which are not required to age. I feel sure that Tovey would have given a big order for Bucelas if he had been in my place a hundred years after he bought wine from the Sandeman's in Lisbon, when Senhor Camilo Alves, the *grand seigneur* of Bucelas, did me the honour of inviting me to taste in his ancient cellars his finest wines. A magnificent ancient candelabrum shed its gentle rays, enhancing the dim light of the vaults in readiness for the traditional test of 'candle-brightness', over a table spread with snacks to cleanse and stimulate the palate. I must confess that I was as surprised to see fillets of anchovy among them as I had been when

I watched a German wine-grower tasting delicate Moselles between puffs of a fat cigar. Actually I found that the predominating salt of the anchovies did so cleanse the palate between glasses that their pungent fishy taste was absorbed in the distinctive flavour of the wines. Perhaps this acceptance was favoured by a flash of memory recalling *Charnico and anchoves*, which marked the good hostelry according to the play of three hundred and fifty years before, and I should have been even more easily persuaded that Bucelas and anchovies went well together if I had known then, as I know now, that in all probability Charneco came from the very vineyards which had yielded the wines I was tasting.

CHAPTER THIRTEEN

# *From the Tagus to the Minho*

SPACE forbids more than a brief glance at the vast region of luxuriant vineyards which supplies Lisbon with that abundance of table wine regarded by its inhabitants as a primal necessity. What is true of the coastal province of Estremadura is true of Ribatejo behind it and the whole rich valley of the Tagus. A Portuguese rhyme runs something like this:

> The sun sweeps on his course and shines,
> But o'er Estremadura lazes,
> Wooing the enamoured vines,
> To quench the fiery thirst he raises.

Dessert wines are made in Estremadura, but the whole region is a land of wines *pour la soif*. The vine grows rampant in the rich alluvial soil, competing with the fruits and crops of an earthly paradise. It bears the stamp of a land of exuberant plenty. In an industrial age Portugal may count as a poor country, but nature has been very kind to it. I had no difficulty in believing my guide when he assured me that the overlapping tasselled tips of the conical caps such as our ancestors wore at night, worn by the husky peasant and dangling by their ears, were weighted down with a good wad of paper money; the peasant uses his cap as his purse.

Moving northwards up Portugal from Colares and Bucelas, we find four well-marked wine-bearing regions, each with a multiplicity of local growths: Torres, Ribatejo with Cartaxo on the right and Almeirim on the left bank of the Tagus, the former for red wines, the latter for white, and Alcobaça, separated from the Tagus basin by a range of hills. On the coast Torres, famous in Britain for the lines of Torres Vedras against which the might of France broke in vain, the largest wine-producing district in Portugal, yields big heartening red wines, which must have provided Wellington's army with a *pinard* far better than that which the French said won the First World War. Once they were conveyed to the capital in goatskins on mule-back. Farther inland Cartaxo is linked with Almeirim by the first bridge across the Tagus from the sea. Cartaxo prides itself on the 'esperas de toiro', the bloodless contests of cunning and strength between man and bull, an arduous sport in which as in Provence youth loves to show its courage and agility and win the sweetheart's smile, and ascribes that courage and agility to the virtue of its wine. Wineshops in the working-class quarters of Lisbon attract custom by promising genuine Cartaxo rather as in the same quarters in Lyons no restaurant can hope for custom which cannot offer the true unsophisticated young Beaujolais.

Great wines are not to be expected in a land of such fertility, and I was most pleasantly surprised by the quality of a wine, the pride of a local grower, I drank in Santarem, the bridge-head on the right bank of the river. It was as full-bodied as some of the Rhône wines, but it was conspicuous for an exceptional delicacy of bouquet and flavour. Perhaps it owed something of that delicacy to the conditions enforced on growers in the Tagus valley by the river floods. Their vines have to be pruned very high to surmount the level of the flooded river, and so the ripening of their grapes depends on the direct rays of the sun and not on refraction from the soil. On the left bank of the river the strong white wines of Almeirim match well with the local goat's milk cheese.

A rocky ridge separates Alcobaça from the Tagus valley, and beyond the little fortressed town of Obidos, noted for its white wines, the wines both red and white grow lighter and more aromatic. A pious cleric, no doubt a native, blessed them as 'the key that needs no turning to unlock the heart and set thought free'. The white wines reminded me of that other 'potable gold', Orvieto. In the Italian town long draughts of its pale golden seductive wine mellow the drab spirit of our sunless north into an intoxicated sympathy with the riot of sunshine gold and brilliant colours of mosaic and marble which make the facade of the Duomo a fantastic vision, 'a wilderness of beauties' as a connoisseur has said. So the golden wine of Alcobaça offers the perfect introduction to that terrific blossoming in granite and marble, the Convent of the Battle, the Convent of Batalha, the battle of Aljubarrota, in which the Portuguese against fearful odds defeated the hosts of Spain and laid the foundation of a world-wide empire, an enduring and splendid monument of national pride and national piety.

Travelling north, one comes to Coimbra with its great University, the brain of Portugal, on the banks of the River Mondego, which runs into the sea at Figueira do Foz, a little port which once had a lively wine trade with Britain, presumably exporting wines from the Dão, though they never carried that name. Near the coast Bairrada is chiefly remarkable for its sparkling wines, all the more remarkable that like the other Portuguese wines of this kind they do not pretend they are champagne. The Portuguese sparkling wines stand out in the category of *vins mousseux* of so many nationalities by virtue of a rich vinosity, a real wine flavour, which qualifies them beyond all others to rescue champagne from death in champagne cocktails. The Barraida wines are said to be at their best in company with the local delicacy of sucking pig roasted on the spit and basted with salt, garlic and wine.

The Mondego and its tributary the Dão, which joins it nearer the sea, water the midland region of the Dão, which, isolated in its mountain fastness, might well be called the Shangri-La of wine countries. The vine has been cultivated there for untold centuries, but its wines were quite unknown to the outside world until the twentieth century. Those that were not drunk locally found their way by precipitous tracks to the valley of the Douro and the coast, where they were unscrupulously deprived of their individuality, blended with inferior wines and sold under names not their own. In its way the Dão is a vine country almost as unique as the sand dunes of Colares, and its wines bid fair to compete with the Colares wines for the title of premier Portuguese table wine.

Its capital, Vizeu, a charming summer resort, is reached from the coast by a modern road, with 250 spirals, if I can trust the comments of my driver, as we near-skidded round the ice-bound bends, in a distance for a crow of a flight of forty miles. In a wild mountain glen with a torrent diving down between sheer bare rocks, pine-clad slopes and enormous boulders, where there would seem to be no place for the works of man, tiny terraced vineyards are squeezed between precipitous fir forest and barren rock on the edge of deep ravines. Here the vine has to struggle for its life, wringing nourishment from the granite crumbled under the influence of frost, rain and man-power.

The planting of a new vineyard demands the opening of a trench about three feet deep. While the spade can work in the crumbled rock, where the rock crops up to the surface it must be attacked with batteries of crowbars, sledge hammers and often enough explosives. The rockier the soil, the better the wine. At the bottom of the trench pine branches and ling are buried to enrich the soil. The principal vines, grafted on American stocks, are the Tourigo do Dão and the Tinta Pinheira with black grapes and the white Arinto of Bucelas. Just as Côte Rôtie is said to be at its best when it blends the wine from the slopes known as the Côte Blonde with that from the Côte Brune, so the typical Dão combines wine grown in the Mondego valley with that of the Dão valley, each of them possessing its own natural particular quality, which sets off the beauty of the other.

These wines, grown at between 1,500 and 2,000 feet above the sea, ferment naturally at a lower temperature and more slowly than the Douro wines did, retaining their grape sugar and developing a fragrant bouquet. The white wines are full-bodied and dry, and make excellent luncheon wines. A considerable percentage of the Arinto grapes is pressed along with the black grapes to give the wine a brilliant ruby colour. The red wines seem to me full of possibilities. Dare I suggest that Dr Salazar, who was born at Santa Comba Dão, should encourage a special effort on their behalf? It needs so little to establish their reputation throughout the world almost on the level of port. Their sudden unheralded appearance on the English market won them such popularity, and they are so nice to drink when they are young, that there may be a temptation to let the Dão region prosper on the sale of ordinary table wines without sufficient attention to their potentialities as fine vintage wines. They are by nature fragrant, sweet and velvety, sliding down the gullet most comfortably. Their satiny smooth texture, which makes them a notable exception to Seneca's rule that a wine must be *asperum et durum* in its youth if it is to age well, I can ascribe only to the exceptional percentage of natural glycerine detected in them by chemical analysis. They certainly age well. The vintage red Dãos I have tasted – I remember one of 1942 particularly – have persuaded me that a special effort to make the very best of a good vintage, the choice of the best grapes and the expensive exercise of the patience needed to allow the wine to reach its prime would be rewarded by the promotion of vintage Dão to an honoured place among the fine vintage wines of the world without interfering with the routine production of cheap and excellent table wines.

Agueda, which lies between Dão and the ocean, deserves a word of mention, as its wines mark a transition stage between the full-bodied wines of the south, called *generosos*, and the light acidulous wines of the extreme north, the *vinhos verdes*, though with the Douro on the north it is an enclave completely surrounded by vine-lands growing *vinhos generosos*. Farther north Oporto has added to the supreme glory of port, of which we have spoken at length, the subsidiary honour of shipping excellent table wines.

Brandy is no longer the only available control of fermentation. How happy would the shippers have been a century ago if they had been able to meet the demand in the British market for natural wines to replace the French with such wines as have now begun to sell in it so well, but their shades can console themselves with the thought that in that case there would probably have been no port.

With the memory of *consumo*, the natural wine which is the basis of port, as it was before science intervened, still unforgotten, I was offered at a restaurant a natural Douro wine, a vintage wine at that, Reserva da Ferreirinha 1941, and truly the chrysalis had turned into a butterfly. Pleasant in bouquet, light and smooth on the palate, it had aged with the grace of Hermitage. The *generous* Portuguese wines are more akin to the Rhône wines than to any other growths, though they are unmistakably distinguished by that basic flavour which I have connected with Atlantic and mountains. Today the progress of fermentation can be regulated throughout its course by the use of a cement vat hermetically sealed from the outer air, in which the exit of carbonic acid gas and the entry of air can be controlled. The process is based on the principle that the Douro must in boisterous fermentation exhales furiously the gas generated by its conversion into wine, and its escape carries with it most of those subtle imponderable constituents which are the joy of nose and palate. The admission of oxygen into the bulk of the fermenting liquid has always been regarded as the tonic of fermentation; nowadays it can be administered in doses and the carbonic acid gas held in it until the precious volatile elements have settled down and been absorbed.

The wine god in modern scientific trappings may cut a sorry figure as unhappily he does in many countries without a wine tradition but the spirit of a glorious past broods with beneficence over Portugal. Learning that admirable table wines were a scientific transformation of the *consumo* which was so very ordinary, my first thought on my last visit to Oporto sent me to Senhor F. van Zeller-Guedes, responsible for Campo Grande, to ask him to show me how the metamorphosis was worked. He introduced me to one of his vintage wines, Reserva Tinto 1944, which proved how a Douro wine could age to high quality with an attractive bouquet, a delicious flavour and a finish almost as velvety as that of the vintage Dão. Then he drove me out to his historic estate, the Quinta da Avelada, where I found an example of the revolution which, clinging to all that is best in the past and taking from progress what is best and most easily assimilated, has been going on all over Portugal since Dr Salazar came to power. Into this world of history, the modern installations, worked the miracle of converting *consumo* into Campo Grande.

The Douro wine country marks the northern boundary of the generous wines and the northern extremity of Portugal between Douro and Minho, the country of very different wines, in a sense their opposite, the *vinhos verdes*, the *green wines*, the *eager wines*. As has been said, after Osey and Charneco they were the first Portuguese wines to reach Britain, exported through Viana do Castelo, and British shippers had their establishments at Moncão on the Minho, a centre of the wine industry and famous for its salmon. It was the failure of these wines to stand the sea voyage which directed the attention of the Viana shippers to the Douro, and so they can claim a share in the discovery of port.

Throughout the eager wine region the vine is probably more in evidence than in any other country, because with the paradox inseparable from wine the region has always been a land of corn rather than of wine. Left to itself, the vine will climb and spread itself with an ubiquitous luxuriance. As a side issue, it is treasured for its beauty as a creeper, its shade and its fresh fruit – yet even so, it can provide a most refreshing and thirst-quenching wine. Everywhere in the smiling land between the Minho and the Douro there are vines with their branches, foliage and tendrils climbing up trees and over walls, roofing verandas and porches, and encouraged to play at will over trellises.

Great wines are not grown in such conditions. Just alcoholic enough to make the drinker gay, with a pleasant flavour calling for no effort of palate discrimination, in fact an ideal summer beverage, they have a delightful little prickle, a titillating sparkle, so prettily called by the Italians *frizzante*, which the Portuguese wine chemists assure us is owing, not to a secondary fermentation such as makes champagne sparkle, but to the presence of natural 'malolactic' acid. They have the charm of unsophisticated Vouvray, today so rare, which maybe has its touch of sparkle too from that mysterious constituent. The eager wines are handicapped abroad by their nature, so that they have to be exported in bottle with corks secured with string, a device which the early Viana shippers were unable to explore, and consequently cost more than the other Portuguese table wines, but the popularity they have earned proves how delightful they are to drink.

Portugal produces a great variety of *vins rosés*, which to my mind might just as well be called pink wines. Pink wines are very much the same all over the world, with the one exception of Tavel, which has no equal. They can be very pleasant to drink, but most of them differ very little in flavour. Their virtue is their cheapness. The Portuguese pink wines, however, can boast an exceptional virtue, the national quality of vinosity, the 'wininess', as Thackeray called it, which is so often lacking in this type of wine.

The immense variety of types of Portuguese wines, each with its local character, would provide material for a far longer study than this. Of all European wine countries, Portugal can face the future with the greatest confidence, for a vista of great possibilities still to be achieved lies open before it. The achievement of port has become a matter of history, and the Instituto do Vinho do Porto need only direct its main efforts to the maintenance of the high standard set by long experience. Portuguese table wines have entered world markets only during the last two decades, and the welcome they have earned is the best proof of their merit. Their success must be ascribed to the efficiency of the national organization, which could hardly have worked so well if it had not been able to profit by the experience gained in the Douro. The Junta Nacional do Vinho, the National Wine Commission, corresponding to the Instituto of Oporto, centralizes and co-ordinates the manifold activities of viticulture and wine-making. It works in collaboration with the Guild of the Export Trade, which watches over the standard of export wines and their foreign markets, conferring on each wine the hall-mark of its name and status, and protecting the consumer. The system has already done wonders in the popularization of ordinary Portuguese table wines, and I hope its directors will not ignore what might seen to be a side issue, since it offers little immediate pecuniary profit. Their vineyards can yield fine wines of a quality which, given age, approach the status of vintage port, and they should be better known abroad. Wines of the vintages of the beginning of the 1940 decade that I have tasted, made, I suspect, more for the delectation of the grower than for the market, were worthy to attract the attention of any connoisseur, and the excellence of such wines, if they were more readily available abroad, would be as valuable to the Portuguese wine industry as many advertisements.

# The Wines of
# SPAIN

❦

## GEORGE RAINBIRD

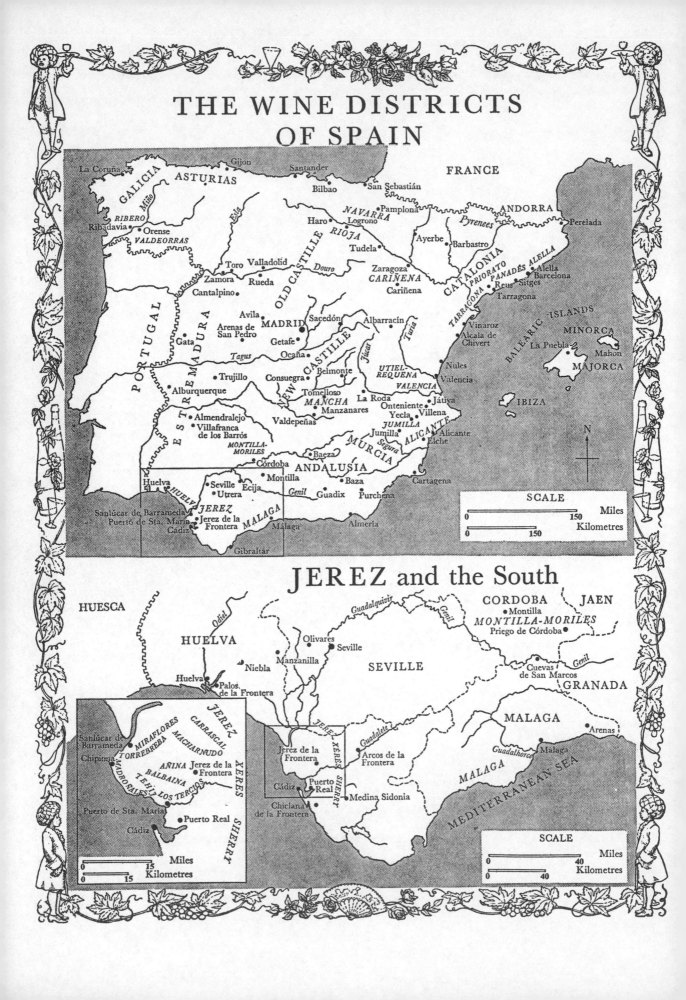

# THE WINE DISTRICTS
## OF SPAIN

FRANCE

La Coruña  Gijon  Santander  ANDORRA
GALICIA  ASTURIAS  Bilbao  San Sebastián
*Miño*  NAVARRA  Pamplona  Perelada
*RIBERO*  Haro  Logrono  *Pyrenees*
Ribadavia  Orense  Tudela  Ayerbe  Barbastro  CATALONIA
*VALDEORRAS*  RIOJA  Zaragoza  PRIORATO  PANADÉS ALELLA
Toro  Valladolid  *Douro*  CARIÑENA  Alella  Barcelona
Zamora  Rueda  Cariñena  TARRAGONA  Reus  Sitges
Cantalpino  OLD CASTILLE  Tarragona

Avila  Sacedón  Albarracín  Vinaroz  BALEARIC ISLANDS  MINORCA
Arenas de  MADRID  Alcala de  La Puebla  Mahon
San Pedro  Getafe  *Turia*  Chivert  MAJORCA
Gata  *Tagus*  Ocaña  *Jucar*  Nules
PORTUGAL  Trujillo  Consuegra  Belmonte  UTIEL-  Valencia  N
ESTREMADURA  NEW CASTILLE  REQUENA  IBIZA
Alburquerque  Tomelloso  VALENCIA
Almendralejo  *MANCHA*  La Roda  Onteniente  Játiva
Villafranca  Valdepeñas  Manzanares  Yecla  Villena
de los Barrós  JUMILLA  Alicante
*MONTILLA-*  Baeza  Jumilla  ALICANTE  Elche
*MORILES*  Córdoba  *Segura*  MURCIA
Huelva  Montilla  ANDALUSIA  Baza  Cartagena
*HUELVA*  Seville  Ecija  *Genil*  Guadix  Purchena
Sanlúcar de Barrameda  Utrera  Guadix
Puerto de Sta. Maria  *JEREZ*  Jerez de la  SCALE
Cádiz  Frontera  Málaga  0  150  Miles
*MALAGA*  Almeria  0  150  Kilometres
Gibraltar

# JEREZ and the South

HUESCA  *Odiel*  *Guadalquivir*  *Genil*  CORDOBA  JAEN
Montilla
HUELVA  *MONTILLA-MORILES*
Olivares  Priego de Córdoba
Niebla  Manzanilla  Seville
Huelva  SEVILLE  Cuevas
Palos  de San Marcos  *Genil*
de la Frontera  GRANADA

Sanlúcar de  *JEREZ*  MALAGA
Barrameda  MIRAFLORES  CARRASCAL  Arenas
Chipiona  TORREBREBA  MACHARNUDO  JEREZ-  *Guadalhorce*  Málaga
*MADRORALES*  AÑINA  Jerez de la  Jerez de la  XERES  Arcos de la
BALBAINA  Frontera  Frontera  Frontera  MALAGA
*TEH*  LOS TERCIOS  Cádiz  Puerto  MEDITERRANEAN SEA
Puerto de Sta. Maria  SHERRY  Real
Cádiz  Puerto Real  Medina Sidonia
15  Miles  Chiclana
0  15  Kilometres  de la Frontera

SCALE
0  40  Miles
0  40  Kilometres

# Introduction

I FIRST visited Spain in 1950 with my wife, and I drove a small car down through France, entering Spain at Irún. We crossed to Burgos, and went on to Galicia and through Portugal to Seville and Jerez, and then up the Mediterranean coast, and back to England by way of Perpignan and Narbonne. We had not much money, and for economic reasons we started a habit that has persisted ever since: that of picnicking in the middle of the day. We would go to a bodega in a small town and buy a litre of the local wine, and we would shop in the market for fruit, cheese, bread, and whatever cold meat we wanted. Thereafter we chose our picnic place with a full view of some of the best scenery in the world, and enjoyed ourselves marvellously. I commend this plan.

The wine, I may add, in those days cost the equivalent of sixpence (or seven cents) a litre, and it isn't much more now. In the evenings we would drink with our dinner one of the two 'Marqueses' (Riscal or Murrieta), or perhaps a Palacio or Paternina or Santiago, usually one of the better wines of the Rioja. Thus on that trip I came to know Spanish wines at least reasonably well, and I have had a very considerable interest in them ever since.

I have been back to Spain on and off in the intervening fifteen years, and I have always drunk the common wines with appreciation and mostly with pleasure, and the better wines with considerable pleasure: hence this study. I have never found *bad* Spanish wine, which is more than can be said for the wines of some other countries; and, in making the fairly intense researches necessary for a study of this sort, my opinion was confirmed that the 'faking' of wine is virtually unknown in Spain. Spanish wines from the cheapest to the best are made simply and with integrity, without fuss and, sometimes, in rather a slap-happy way. This, I think, may well be one of the main reasons why the wines of France and the wines of Spain will never really compare. Your Spaniard is essentially a practical wine-maker, who believes in his wine and produces it in quantity for consumption mainly by his fellow Spaniards. He does not bring to his wine-making the philosophy and the dedication of the Frenchman, to whom the pleasures of the table are really a form of religion, and not a bad one at that. No, he will make his wine honestly, and more or less with care according to the tradition of his particular part of the country, and he will firmly believe that he makes the best wine in all Spain. This I found to be absolutely true throughout that pleasant land. In no place more so than in some of the largest co-operatives, where perhaps five or six million litres of wine are made in a year, and where last year's wine will be brought up from every vat for one to taste and admire. Indeed, one has very little difficulty in doing so.

One of the problems of writing this study is to give a reasonable description of a wine so that the reader will get some idea of what to expect. This I have found to be all but impossible, because I do not like wine jargon, and I try to avoid it; on the other hand, Spanish wine has suffered considerably by calling itself Sauternes or Chablis or Claret or what have you, which it most certainly is not. And yet what do you do? How can you convey to the reader the taste of wine unless you use a form of comparison that he is likely to know? Therefore I have found comparisons of this sort unavoidable, although

491

I have used them only sparingly. But I cannot too much emphasize that Spanish wine is Spanish wine, and French wine is French wine, and never the twain shall meet when they are both *in puris naturalibus*. Spanish wine will never achieve the greatness of the great French *châteaux* or *domaines*, for this is a matter of soil and climate more than anything else; but fine and good wines are made everywhere in Spain, and they have their own distinctive character, which I hope this book will encourage the reader to cultivate.

The wines of Spain are ridiculously cheap for what they are. The best wines of the Rioja are comparatively inexpensive, and the cheap wines of Valdepeñas and the Levante and Catalonia are very cheap indeed. It is not their fault that there is a swingeing tax on them of four or five times the actual cost of the wine, or that bottles cost a shilling (14 cents) each, and therefore they can never do the same service for England that they do for Spain, where every Spaniard can have his litre a day and afford it in whatever station of life. And does, usually, although I am told that the drinking of *mosto*, the unfermented grape-juice, is very much on the increase.

In the course of my researches, I visited all the important wine districts in Spain and at one time or another tasted all, or nearly all, the wines described in this book. When I was not able to visit a district, the Sindicato Nacional de la Vid in Madrid were kind enough to arrange for bottles to be sent to me.

The production of wine in Spain in 1969, for instance, was from something over 1,616,000 hectares (1 hectare is about 2½ acres) of vines cultivated. This represents about 10% of the total area of land cultivated in Spain, and it produces 25,177,000 hectolitres of good wine per year, as against 49,800,000 in France and 71,470,000 in Italy. The average Spaniard drinks less than the Frenchman or Italian and, I imagine, eats less too. He is a grave and sober person and sometimes eats extremely well, but always with moderation, and the same applies to his drinking habits. The cultivation of vines and the making of wines are of tremendous importance to the economy of Spain. It takes third place after cereals and olives.

Finally, let me exhort you to do your own research on the wines of Spain, preferably in their country of origin, because then you will certainly continue to buy the wines when you return home. If you do go to Spain, search out one of the little bodegas found everywhere from the smallest town upwards, where you will find anything up to 24 barrels of wine on tap, mostly local wine, but also wines from other parts of Spain, brandies and anises, usually with some little bits and pieces to eat on the counter; and where a glass of local wine, or of Valdepeñas, is sold for two pesetas, or about threepence in 1965 – say four cents. Sometimes you can pay as much as fourpence for a better one. Even more, perhaps; but not much more. These bodegas exist throughout Spain, and, if you are in Madrid you should visit the narrow streets behind the Puerta del Sol, where the standard price for a glass of *blanco* or *tinto* (not a very large glass, mark you) is two pesetas. And, if you do, buy a plate of *gambas a la plancha*, which are simply luscious prawns put on to a hot plate before your eyes and served with tiny paper napkins. Tear off the head and tail of the prawn, shuck it, put it in your mouth, throw the remnants on the floor and drink your white wine. It all sounds rather crude, but it is marvellous. Then, having visited half a dozen of these little bodegas and bars, you can go happily along to the Jockey or the Botín and have delicious sucking pig and an even more delicious bottle of fine Rioja, if you are feeling extravagant. In any case, it will not break you. But (and such is the lesson of this study) somewhere on the wine list you will find a wine – good, fine, or perhaps common – that will just suit you in whatever mood or state of affluence. You can't do that everywhere.

CHAPTER ONE

# A Short History of Spanish Wine

And God said, Let the earth bring forth grass, the herb yielding seed, and the fruit tree yielding fruit after his kind, whose seed is in itself, upon the earth; and it was so.                                      Genesis i, 11

ON THE third day of Creation, God put plants upon the earth in preparation for the creation of mankind, and undoubtedly, in His wisdom, He made the grape among the first of living plants. I strongly suspect the olive was a good second, for the fruits of these two important plants provide sustenance to mankind both physical and spiritual, to a proportion altogether greater than that of any other plant life, with the possible exception of corn. The grape and the olive have much in common; they thrive in hot climates and on very poor soil, and thus provide fruit, and from the fruit drink, in places where both are otherwise hard to find. The grape, when eaten fresh from the vine, is food; its juice, when pressed, makes a delicious drink, and when it is fermented it provides in wine a food and drink combined, which, in moderation, can do nothing but improve the lot of man. The olive provides food and, when pressed, oil. If mankind had nothing but these it would at least not starve, and certainly not die of thirst.

Spain, by reason of its climate and poorish soil, has been amply provided with both vine and olive, and the history of wine-making in Spain goes back to prehistory. There are many legends about the discovery of wine as apart from grape-juice, but its origin, like that of the wheel, is unknown. We know that wine was used and appreciated in the most ancient days of Egypt; indeed, sealed wine jars have been found in Pharaonic tombs in the Valley of the Kings with a dusty viscous kind of mess in them, which is all that remains of the 2000 B.C. vintage of the local Cru Cléopâtre or Clos de Ptolemis. Although the early Iberian civilizations were not comparable with the Egyptian, no doubt wine was made throughout the length and breadth of Spain in the earliest days.

Edward Hyams, in his book *Dionysus*, published in 1965, says he thinks that the first vineyards were planted in Spain before 500 B.C. I am not at all sure of his authority, and I see no reason myself why the vine should not have been cultivated long before then. Certainly the Phoenicians, who were the first settlers in Spain and who were knowledgeable about wines, could well have improved methods of viniculture. There were Greek settlements too in Spain, and no doubt there would be exhanges of ideas between all settlers and the local farmers, who have always taken some pride in making good wine. I never knew a *vigneron* yet who did not make the best wine of his country – and to blazes with all the great *châteaux* of France! William Younger, in his *Gods, Men and Wine*, gives the result of many years' patient research into the history of wine generally, including the wines of Spain, and he lists the chief ancient wine-producing areas of Spain as follows: Baetica, Valdepeñas, Barcelona and Gerona, Valencia, Tarragona, the Balearic Islands, south-west Andalusia. What we can never know is whether, for instance, the wine that was exported from Gades (modern Cádiz) and Baetica, now Andalusia, was anything like the sherry from Jerez near by. I would say that it very probably was, because the character of the wine is very distinctive and is partly the result of the soil, although dozens of new grapes have been introduced over the centuries. Certainly sherry as we know it now did not really start to emerge until the end of the eighteenth century.

In Roman days (that is, from the first century B.C. onwards) wine was a major export from Spain to Rome, and it might well have been part of the tribute. In Rome today *Vinum Digatanum* may be read on amphoras of 31 B.C.: this would be the wine of Gades and would be the forerunner of the present sherry. We also know that in the province of Baetica it was the custom to ferment and keep the wine in great Ali Baba earthenware jars called *orcae*, in which the wine of Montilla and Moriles is still kept. In the heyday of the Roman Empire it was estimated that by the second century A.D. something like 20,000,000 amphoras of Spanish wine had been shipped into the city of Rome. The evidence of this is largely in that extraordinary artificial hill, just behind the British cemetery in Rome, called Monte Testaccio. This is the place to which I recommend that every visitor to Rome should go, even if he is there only for a couple of days. Monte Testaccio is in fact a small but substantial hill, composed simply of broken amphoras from the nearby docks on the Tiber, which was at that time navigable, and to which the ships from the Roman world brought in their tribute of oil, grain, wine and so on. Everything in those days was carried in amphoras, with their pointed bases for standing in the earth: grain, oil and wine. The amphoras, being of clay, were also fragile, and one imagines that the casualties on a rough voyage across the Mediterranean were enormous. Consequently, when the ship docked the broken amphoras were carted off to what is now Monte Testaccio, and, during a thousand years or so, it became an enormous monument to the losses of ship-owners and the profits of manufacturers of amphoras. It was the custom in this period to stamp a seal on the shoulder of the amphora, usually just the initials of the owner or purveyor, and sometimes also the place of origin; and from the proportion of these shards that can be traced to Roman Spain we can today discover something of the extent of the wine business. Anybody can potter about Monte Testaccio if he has the energy to climb it where it stands like an enormous slag-heap – and the shards are everywhere under the sparse grass that grows on it. Some of the seals come to light with a little poking. They are very interesting and are worthy of a collection.

After the time of the Romans the wine continued to flourish, no doubt. And then in the eighth century came the Moors, Koran in hand, preaching the pussyfoot fanaticism of Mohammed. But there is plenty of evidence that the rule of abstinence was honoured more in the breach than the observance. Quite a substantial literature, dating back to the Moorish occupation, proves that the grape was held in high esteem. Grape-juice was consumed in quantity, and fermented grape-juice, alas! also in considerable quantity. Some of the Spanish wines of this period, like the Zebbibi of Seville, had a considerable reputation, and so did the wines of Málaga, both (we note) sweet and luscious. Efforts were certainly made to extirpate the vines, but, for the purposes of this particular exercise, the Faithful became the Unfaithful, and the Faithful envied them. All sorts of dodges were employed to get round these very uncomfortable tenets of the Koran. In Córdoba it is recorded that an arrested drunk was brought before the Chief Kadi for sentence; but he, wise man, employed a special official who, upon being asked to certify that the accused's breath smelt strongly of wine, would always say that, certainly, the man's breath smelt, but whether of grape-juice or wine it was impossible to tell. Whereupon the judge dismissed the case smartly and saved his soul from the sin of hypocrisy.

Eventually the Moors departed. People enjoyed their wine in peace; the cultivation of the grape improved, and wine was exported to France and England and, with the discovery of the New World, extensively to Mexico and Central America, where it was in demand for sacramental use in the Mass. William Younger gives a list of wines grown in and exported from medieval Spain as follows:

| | |
|---|---|
| Alicante | From Alicante. |
| Caprick | From Spain or Portugal. |
| Espaigne | White wine. |
| Garnarde | Probably from Granada, in the fourteenth century. |
| Lepe | Probably from ancient Illipula (modern Niebla), between Seville and Huelva; it could also be a general term for wine coming from, or through, Seville. |
| Málaga | Málaga wine. |
| Ordiales | From Castro Urdiales, Province of Santander. |
| Osey | From Spain and Portugal. |
| Ryvere | From the River Ebro – possibly modern Rioja; from Logroño and nearby parts, but more probably Zaragoza and Tarragona. It was also called a wine 'of the river'. |
| Tente | From Spain certainly. |
| Torrentyne | From the River Ebro (see Ryvere above). |
| Xéres | From Jerez de la Frontera. |

Of these wines, Málaga is probably the best-known today. Tente has long gone out, although it survived into the nineteenth century. The Lepe was much loved of Chaucer, who mentions it on several occasions, but especially in:

> Now kepe yow fro the whyte and fro the rede,
> And namely fro the whyte wine of Lepe,
> That is to selle in Fish-strete or in Chepe.
> This wyn of Spayne crepeth subtilly
> In othere wynes, growing faste by,
> Of which ther ryseth swich fumositee,
> That whan a man hath dronken draughtes three,
> And weneth that he be at hoom in Chepe,
> He is in Spayne, right at the toune of Lepe,
> Nat at the Rochel, ne at Burdeux toun.

Lepe indeed may well have some affinity with the sherry of today. From that time onwards the wine of Spain became fairly well noted and quoted throughout the literature of Spain. It is recorded that in 1237 Ordiales was bought for Henry III of England, while in 1358 good Spanish wine cost sixpence (seven cents) a gallon in England; but this might well have been expensive. The history of sack, which was the wine of Shakespeare's day, I shall deal with in the next chapter. I shall give a certain amount of historical information there and in later chapters, as being more suitable places for it than this general introduction.

Comparatively modern authors have dealt with Spanish wine, continuing in the tradition of Cervantes. To conclude this brief introduction, I must add that I could not but be delighted to find that the pigskins of wine so horribly slashed and gored by Don Quixote are still largely in use in La Mancha. Traditions and customs die hard in conservative Spain. May this one, with its roots deep in history, never die.

CHAPTER TWO

# Sherry

SHERRIS, Scheris, Xérès, or Jerez – whatever you may call it, it ends up as sherry. And this incomparable wine is probably the greatest jewel in the crown of Spanish wines. As its name denotes, it comes from that part of western Andalusia of which Jerez de la Frontera is the principal town, but the *denominación de origen* areas also include Sanlúcar de Barrameda, famous for its *manzanillas*, and Puerto de Santa María, and stretches as far as Chiclana in the south and up to the Guadalquivir river in the north. Not so long ago, the district was very much larger, and places like Niebla and Manzanilla (from which no *manzanilla* comes now) could and did export their wine as sherry; but this has all been stopped, with some considerable hardship, I am told, to the inhabitants.

Sherry wines are made in the surrounding country and taken to the great bodegas in Jerez, Puerto de Santa María and Sanlúcar de Barrameda for blending into that glorious wine we all know as sherry. For sherry is not a complete wine; it is in fact a blend of wines that have some affinity, and it is normally a fortified wine, by which is meant that grape-brandy is added at some stage in the fermenting process. Consequently, we must examine at considerable length the whole process of making sherry wine, so that we may understand its peculiar and especially good qualities, which have made it renowned throughout the world, and which distinguish Jerez from parts of Spain that produce by the same process a wine that is not the true sherry wine.

The wines of Jerez appear in the most ancient chronicles of the times of the Phoenicians and the Romans. So do they also in most of the other parts of Spain, especially on the Mediterranean coast. It was not until 1635 or thereabouts that the wine became known as sherry; before that it appeared chiefly in the Elizabethan form of sack or sherris sack. Shakespeare is simply full of it, and every schoolboy knows that it was Falstaff's favourite tipple by a long way. Throughout *Henry IV*, Parts 1 and 2, Falstaff needs no encouragement to launch forth into praise of sack, of which he drinks aplenty and all the time. 'O monstrous! but one half-pennyworth of bread to this intolerable deal of sack!' exclaims Prince Hal, examining Falstaff's enormous bill for a party at the Boar's Head Tavern with a few gallons of sack and a very small amount of bread.

Sack in those days was drunk by the pint and normally in tankards drawn straight from the barrel, but it need not necessarily have come from Jerez or even Spain, for a great deal of a similar type of wine was imported from the Canaries; there seems, however, to be little doubt that the very great popularity of sack led eventually – in Victorian days, when many of them were founded – to the prosperity of the great Anglo-Spanish houses. In one of these John Ruskin's father was a partner. Its success enabled him to provide his son with a more than liberal education, and thus made possible his writings, which in their turn made a tremendous impression for good on Victorian life and letters.

Just exactly what the sack of those great and hard-drinking days was like we shall never know, because although sherries (I suppose by reason of their being fortified) do last to a very great age, they won't last for centuries. There are, however, soleras in Jerez that are authenticated well back into the middle of the eighteenth century. Whether or not the famous Williams & Humbert 'Dry Sack' has any affinity with Falstaff's sack is purely a matter of conjecture. I imagine, for instance, that the sherry of today might well be stronger than it was then, and yet undoubtedly any wine made by the solera system and using the grapes and the methods of Jerez will be of very high alcoholic content.

The vineyards that supply the wines made into sherry lie adjacent rather than close to the three principal towns, and, as has been pointed out by Rupert Croft-Cooke in his excellent book on sherry, the vineyards are not apparent from the road or the railway. There are two major areas between Jerez de la Frontera and the Guadalquivir river. One comprises the districts of Carrascal and, more importantly, Macharnudo; and the other, farther west, Miraflores and Balbaina. South of Jerez de la Frontera, Puerto de Santa María and the River Guadalete are those vineyards near Puerto Real, San Fernando and Chiclana; and other patches lie farther inland.

There are three kinds of soil, some of them almost together in quite a small area, and the chief of these soils is called *albariza*, a fine chalky soil with which one soon becomes smothered when walking round the vineyards in Macharnudo. It is undoubtedly this remarkable soil that makes this remarkable wine, just as the rather heavier chalky soil of Champagne makes champagne, and the pebbly sand of the Médoc makes the greatest claret in the world. The *albarizas* are the best soils; though they produce the fewest grapes per vine, they are essential for the making of *finos*, which are the basis of most Jerez wines and the most important. After the vines grown on the *albarizas* are those grown on the *barros*, which are much less chalky soils but are more prolific. After the *barros* come the *arenas* – sandy types of soil, producing far more grapes to the vine than either the *barros* or the *albarizas*; but all play their part, and we must appreciate their importance against the background of the solera system by which they are blended.

After the soil, we have the sun. In this respect, the region round Jerez de la Frontera is probably one of the most favoured in Spain. The rainfall is light, and only in an exceptional year will there be more than eighty to a hundred days in which rain will fall. I remember when I was there some years ago, in mid-October, the few showers that descended were the first since the previous April; the grapes had been gathered, and this was considered absolutely right for the making of good wine. The rain will, however, be quite heavy for nearly a month or two; then the sun will begin to shine un-interruptedly again in the very early spring. This climatic condition has been taken care of in the system of vine-planting, whereby a plot a metre or so square is excavated to a very great depth indeed, and the chalky soil is pulverized, mixed with humus and heaped round the stump of the vine to form a kind of porous bed, into which the winter rains seep and maintain some degree of moisture during the long summer when the vines will flower and the grapes form and eventually ripen. This method is adopted throughout Spain; but, so far as I know, the depth of the excavation is usually not more than a metre, whereas in the Jerez district some $2\frac{1}{2}$–3 metres may be dug before planting the vine. So much for soil and sun.

Next we have the grapes. According to Rupert Croft-Cooke, there are records that numerous types of grapes, including some black ones, were used until a hundred years or more ago; but this has now changed, and the two principal grapes used in Jerez, besides the common Canacazo and Mollar varieties, are the Palomino, which is used for the *finos* and the *amontillados*, and the Pedro Ximénez or P.X. grape used largely for the *olorosos* and the dessert wine of the same name. The Palomino is essentially a grape of the sherry district and is eminently suitable to *albariza* soil, which makes *finos*, while the Pedro Ximénez grapes are grown in some quantity more or less all over Spain, especially where sweet wines are made.

Normally in the Jerez district the vintage will begin around 9 September and go on until the end of the month or possibly early October, both according to the season and to the grapes, because some grapes are gathered much earlier than others. The grapes are cut, not with the scissors or little shears used elsewhere, but with sharp knives. I don't know why this should be, and I doubt whether the vintagers of Jerez do either, but it is the traditional instrument for the job, and so it goes on from year to year.

The bodegas in which the wines are made will invariably be found near the middle of the vineyard, and they are usually composed of a long whitewashed tiled building, with a covered courtyard in which stands the platform where the treading of the grapes is done, while outside there is a pretty big expanse, a kind of terrace or apron, upon which the picker will unload his grapes on to large, circular hempen mats, where they are left to dry for a day or so in the strong Andalusian sunlight. At this stage the grapes are 'plastered' by a small quantity of gypsum that is sprinkled on them, although I believe this part of the operation is not always carried out. Certainly the enemies of sherries in the past have made great play with the 'plastering' of sherry wine, but the gypsum additive is so small as to have no particular significance so far as the essential quality of the wine is concerned. At night the grapes are covered with another mat to stop the dew from damping them, and to ensure that they are quite dry when they go into the *lagar* or wine-press.

The *lagares* are wooden troughs 12 feet square with sides, as far as I can remember, about 2 feet high, and with a slightly sloping floor and holes through which the pressed *mosto* or must pours after the treading. The men who tread the grapes are called *pisa-dores*, and they are splendidly tough specimens clad in bathing trunks and singlets wearing otherwise only their berets and iron-shod shoes called *zapatos*. They have wooden shovels, and they marshal the grapes, brought in on mats, into great heaps in the *lagar*. When they have arranged them to their satisfaction they start their one–two rhythmic tread, systematically working through the grapes and treading them with their *zapatos*. It takes a little time for the juice to start running, but gradually the stream increases as the treading becomes more intense. This operation is necessarily lengthy, but it is none the less thorough and goes on for hours at a time. The iron studs in the *zapatos* are arranged with enough space between them to ensure that, when the treading takes place, the pips and stalks and skins will not be bruised, to affect the must with an addition of tannin contained in those parts of the grape. Sometimes the treading of the grapes is accompanied – I suppose to alleviate boredom – by a traditional treading-song, which is nothing if not Andalusian, punctuated by the double mark-time of the treaders. They do not sing this all the while, but, since they may be treading grapes for four or more hours at a time with intervals for changing the grapes, they certainly need the Spanish equivalent of the Song of the Volga Boatmen.

After the *pisadores* have extracted all the juice they possibly can from the grapes the resulting mess of pips, skins, and the rest is shovelled first of all into hand-presses for a second pressing, which produces a certain amount, and then into mechanical presses for yet a third pressing, which produces a little more; this, however, is not added to the original must, but kept either for distillation or for making an inferior quality of wine. The grape-juice from the first and second pressings is put straight into butts, and is left in the sun to start its fermentation before being removed to the bodegas, possibly some miles away, in Jerez, Puerto de Santa María or Sanlúcar de Barrameda. The scene along the roads at vintage time is remarkable, with the heavy tumbrils, drawn by teams of long-horned oxen, hauling the great butts of wine, which have started the fermentation that will one day make them into some of the greatest wine in the world.

At this stage something must be said about the sherry butt and its importance to the wine contained in it. Air and oxygenization are more essential in sherry than in almost any other wine, mainly for the development of the yeast and organisms contained in the 'flower' and so on. Consequently, the butt in which the wine is matured needs to have a certain porous quality, even though, obviously, the vessel must be watertight. Therefore all the bodegas have a very important cooperage department, making as many of their own butts and casks as they can, though they usually have to buy some. This is becoming increasingly difficult through the shortage of the right kind of oak, but I expect the sherry trade will cope with it, although costs are rising all the time. So, for that matter, is the price of sherry. I suppose I could take two or three pages to describe the technical intricacies of making a good sherry butt; suffice it to say that they are necessarily of the best possible construction, and have built into them those qualities that have been designed over a few hundred years as being ideal first of all for the maturing and then the transport of the wine.

In some parts of Spain the new butt is matured by filling it with sea-water for three weeks or so; but I never heard that this was done in Jerez, where the normal practice is to fill it with *mosto* until it is thoroughly soaked.

The great bodegas of Jerez, most of which were built or expanded in the prosperity of the nineteenth century, and which I shall discuss in detail later, are really tremendous: great cathedral-like naves with butts five or six deep, each containing more than a hundred gallons, in rows two or three hundred yards long. These, however, are the soleras, and the new wine that has just come from the *lagares* is left until it has finished its first tumultuous fermentation and gone through most of its second; that is to say in two or three months.

During this time is formed that unique but essential element of the true sherry *fino*, the 'flower'. The 'flower' forms at the end of the secondary fermentation. It is a kind of scum composed of yeasts and ferments on the top of the wine, and it stays there and increases during its whole period in butt before the final blending; you see it in the form of tiny specks of matter in the maturing wine. It is difficult to describe, but it is everywhere present even when the wine is fortified, always provided too much alcohol is not added, because the alcohol kills the 'flower', and people generally consider that it is the 'flower' that gives the true *fino* its essential character and quality.

It is at this stage – that is to say, when the first and secondary fermentations have finished and the wine has become clear – that the head of the bodega will classify it according to its quality, and will mark the butt by a series of strokes and cross-strokes; in accordance with the marking, it will be allocated to the solera most suited to the wine. The classification will be explained later, when *finos* are discussed.

The wine has now been allocated and classified according to the taster's judgment, and it will be put into new butts that have been fumigated with sulphur, and that will have in them the degree of alcohol considered necessary to bring the wine up to the required standard of vinosity and to stop further fermentation. It should be noted that this wine-alcohol, which I suppose could be termed brandy, is used only sparingly in the *fino* wines. This is called fortification. At least two of the Jerez bodegas do not fortify their wines at all for the domestic market, and do it for the English market only to enable the wines to travel. The resulting *finos* are extremely delicate and fine, and while it might be a degree or so below standard in alcoholic strength, it is certainly a delicious wine. The odd thing about it is that I find this practice of making unfortified sherry universally denied throughout Spain; yet I know it to exist, and I personally like the natural wine very much indeed.

The grapes have been pressed; the wine has been made and has been allocated to a solera, and will take its place as a member of the choir in one of the great cathedrals of Jerez. For that really is what a solera is.

The time has come to discuss in detail the solera system upon which these great wines are made, and this is simply a matter of superb blending of young and old wines. No matter which types of wine are bought from Jerez de la Frontera, Puerto de Santa María or Sanlúcar de Barrameda, they one and all have been made by the solera system, and it is these great soleras that constitute the wealth of the whole district. It would be almost impossible now for a new bodega to start making sherry unless its owners had been able to buy an existing solera. I must explain this mystery.

Sherry is essentially a blended wine. The blending is both vertical and horizontal, by which I mean that old wine is blended with new wine, and new wines are blended with other new wines of a similar but not always of an identical character. The solera starts with a few butts, sometimes of a given year, and, as years go on, more butts are added to the solera; so, to produce a standard-quality wine (such as – shall we say? – the 'Tío Pepe' of González Byass or the 'Macharnudo Fino' of La Riva, the first selling in enormous and the second in substantial quantities), the solera would necessarily be of many, many hundred butts. A certain quantity of wine, possibly a third or a half, is taken from the oldest butts, and these are filled with wine from the next oldest, and so on, right down the enormous row. Thus the oldest and best elements in the wine are always present in proportion to the quality of the wine required.

The matching of wine before entry into a solera is yet another thing again; and here the sherry-taster reigns supreme with his cane, called a *venencia*, which is a metre-long piece of whalebone with a silver cup at one end and a hook at the other to save it from falling into the butt. The taster will thrust the *venencia* into the bung-hole at the top of the barrel, through the 'flower' that has already formed, then bring a sample up in the tiny cup from the middle of the butt, and pour it into his *copita* or tasting-glass at arm's length without spilling a single drop. Obviously, in the case of a very popular sherry, selling in enormous quantities, the wine will not be terribly old, neither is it desirable that it should be so, though it would normally not be less than about three years old. On the other hand, most of the older bodegas have what corresponds to the 'paradise' of the brandy-shippers of Cognac, and also have a little private solera of only two or three butts, which are broached maybe once a year, and which are known to have been started anything up to a couple of hundred years ago. These wines, I need hardly say, are not sold, but are kept for state occasions and opened only rarely, tapped lightly and refreshed from wine nearly as old.

The truly remarkable wine that I had the pleasure and privilege of tasting from the La Riva private cellar goes back to 1770. It is very dark and absolutely dry, and there is a crust so fine as to be no more than a misting in the bottle, which, even taking the greatest possible care, I find extremely hard to decant without disturbing, and I have to use a filter paper when, rarely, I open one of my few remaining half-bottles.

Again, as with Cognac, the very old soleras are normally used only for blending and to give tremendous character to younger wines. The oldest soleras are *amontillados*, *olorosos* or Pedro Ximénez. *Finos* cease to be *finos* after a few generations and become with age true *amontillados*, which can be very dry and a little nutty and are delicious. The *olorosos*, which are made as a rule from the Pedro Ximénez grapes, are sweet (but this I will discuss later on), while a true solera of 'Uncle Peter', or Pedro Ximénez, has the consistency of lubricating oil and a cloying sweetness that I find quite impossible although there are some who like it.

Thus the wine of Jerez de la Frontera and district has been famous for centuries, but when exactly the present system of wine-making known as the solera system was introduced we do not know for certain; it is, however, generally agreed as having been in the eighteenth century. At one time, no doubt, the wine was just a natural wine of the country (the local *vino de mesa*, as it were), and this might well have been in Shakespeare's day. Possibly the grapes were left to become overripe and fermented, and were then pressed; the wine would be clarified and shipped. Somewhere along the line the solera system was perfected, probably in the last half of the eighteenth century, but exactly when is not known by any of the sherry experts with whom I have discussed the problem.

So we have the vast bodegas and the enormous soleras of these three towns. When the time has come, the sherry is racked from the solera, usually from the lower tier of the *fino* solera, and put into a standard butt of 108 gallons (the solera butt is somewhat larger) and shipped off to England or wherever its final destination may be, to delight connoisseurs all over the world. For domestic use and South American countries, the sherry is usually sold in bottles. And very bright some of them are, completely encased in gold or silver foil, or with lovely gold silk netting and large red tassels. The wine therein is usually rather on the sweet side for our taste.

## *Types of Sherry Wine*

There are three basic types of sherry, with various subdivisions up and down throughout. These types are essentially the *fino*, the *oloroso* and a third type that I classify as a Pedro Ximénez, which in a way is a form of *oloroso*, but is, I feel, so individual as to make a class by itself. An easy distinction is that the *fino*, with its sub-classification of *amontillado* and *manzanilla*, is essentially dry and usually pale; the *olorosos* are dark and rather sweet, and of course Pedro Ximénez is very sweet indeed. There are great wines in each of these classes, and most of the big shippers make sherry in them all.

The true *fino* is very, very pale, with a hint of gold. Before it is finally bottled the specks of the *flor* or 'flower' are present in it. It is always dry, and for the domestic market it is sometimes unfortified. It may be drunk, as it is in its best qualities, as an *apéritif* before lunch or dinner; in its more common varieties it is served purely as a drinking wine, especially in the bars. If you order *vino tinto* in a bar anywhere in Spain you get just that, the *corriente* or common red wine of the district, or possibly you get Valdepeñas. If, however, you order *vino blanco* you will in all probability get a cheap *fino* sherry, and there won't be any difference in the cost. These *corrientes finos* are excellent wines, with very little acidity and no roughness, and I have drunk them with a great deal of pleasure, whereas I could not possibly drink the better sherries as I did the *corriente* sherry in Spain. If you want a simple white wine you must always be very careful to ask for a *vino blanco de mesa*. *Finos* are usually rated at between 15° and 16° of alcohol, and they have a further technical subdivision, which may be called 'palmas', and are simply *finos* from Jerez or Puerto de Santa María of good quality. With the exception of the La Riva 'Tres Palmas', I do not know of any other brand that uses the technical division as a brand name: this is mostly used within the bodega to denote the quality before marketing under the bodega's own special *marque*, and it can be one *palma*, two *palmas*, three *palmas* or four *palmas*. If you see sherry marked *cuatro palmas* you should buy it because it is about the best there is.

*Manzanilla* wine comes from Sanlúcar de Barrameda at the mouth of the Guadalquivir river, a small port where some of the ships stand in before going up to Seville; alternatively, if they are too large they may take off their cargoes from Andalusia. There is also a fishing village attached, on rather good sands, and I remember eating at a restaurant actually on those sands a most delightful fish meal, in which course after course of splendid fish was served Chinese fashion, to the complement of jugs of new, young *manzanilla* of excellent genus, browny-gold and with the faintly nutty taste that makes it an altogether excellent and exceptional *fino*. Just exactly why *manzanilla* should have this distinctive quality, I have never quite discovered, because the grapes are the same and the soil is much the same. I suppose it must be bred into it in the local formula for vinification. Long may it reign!

The oldest *finos* become *amontillados*, but *amontillados* need not be old. To make up the *amontillado* soleras, the grapes for this type of wine are gathered a few days earlier, and they remain therefore somewhat dry. *Fino*, being left in butt for a long time, automatically becomes *amontillado* and develops its own very special and distinctive flavour, while retaining its extreme dry qualities; it is from *finos* that have grown old naturally in butts that the *amontillado* soleras have been made up over a few generations. Some *amontillados* grow to a very great age, and I should think they will keep for ever. In

Córdoba, which is where the bodegas of Montilla and Moriles are situated, they will tell you that *amontillado* really comes from their district; hence the name Montilla forms part of the word *amontillado*. This is hotly, if not bitterly, contested in Jerez, where people deny that the Córdobans could possibly make such good wine as *amontillado*. My advice is that the reader should go to a little trouble and try the Córdoba variety as well as the Jerez; he might get a pleasant surprise. But I am all for *amontillado* as a clean, dry, altogether satisfactory wine, whether it comes from Jerez or Montilla.

*Olorosos* are wines that are made mainly from the Palomino grapes, but with a proportion of Pedro Ximénez grapes; fermentation is stopped, while the wines are still quite sweet, by the addition of alcohol. There is an internal qualitative classification of these wines, as there is in the case of *finos*, but, instead of specifying different qualities of *palmas*, the makers use the word *cortado*, and the wine is classified for bodega purposes as anything between one and four *cortados*. Again, the only firm I know that markets an *oloroso* under the *cortado* label is La Riva; the wine is called 'Tres Cortados', which is the equivalent in *oloroso* to the 'Tres Palmas' in *fino*, but it is not so sweet as some *olorosos* and is excellent with game soup. *Olorosos* are not necessarily all sweet wines, although most of them are, mainly because the public expect them to be. A great many of the old East India sherries were *olorosos*, and the reason for their name is that people thought the sea voyage of some months helped to age the sherry and give it a special quality; consequently, the great butts of *oloroso* were sometimes sent to the East Indies and back via London, and the wines received a better price. It was possibly a better wine.

I had a very small bin of such wine some years ago, and I used to bring it out at eleven o'clock on Christmas morning, which seemed to be the right occasion, together with a mince-pie. It was an extremely rich but by no means sickly sherry, which was looked forward to by the whole family until, alas! the last bottle was consumed a few Christmases ago. I am looking for some more to take its place now, but the fashion of sending sherry to the East Indies has long gone out, and I haven't heard of it for many years. If you should come across it you can be sure you will have a very old and probably very good sherry.

The last class, and it could possibly be a subdivision of the *olorosos*, is the sherry made entirely from the Pedro Ximénez grape, and with its fermentation stopped long before the sugar has been broken down into alcohol, thus retaining its almost sickly sweetness. I am no lover of Pedro Ximénez (or P.X., as it is called), because I don't like wines that cloy, and P.X. certainly does. There is no question about its quality, but I have never yet found a peach sweet enough to eat with it, and it will kill the taste of its own grape.

The famous Bristol *marques* of sherry – that is, the 'Milk', which may come from Harvey's, Avery's or any Bristol shipper, and the 'Cream', which I believe can be sold under that name only by Harvey's – are all of the rich *oloroso* dessert type of wine. As might be expected, they constitute the best of these wines. Vast quantities are shipped all over the world from Puerto de Santa María, which is the port of Jerez, and they have done more for sherry and for Bristol than almost any other kind of wine.

Any other forms of sherry can be considered as *marques* of the particular bodega rather than the type of wine. 'Tío Pepe', for instance, is simply a *fino* with its own particular character; 'Dry Sack', which is not terribly dry, is an *amontillado*, and 'Walnut Brown' is an *oloroso*. Each of these famous names has been blended by the shipper from his own soleras to suit his market and in the best ways he knows how.

Hence the great names and the great sherries have spread, from Jerez to Puerto de Santa María and Sanlúcar de Barrameda, through the length and breadth of the civilized world.

The alcoholic content of sherry varies a great deal, but as a general guide we can take something like the following:

*Finos*          From 15° to 16°.
*Amontillados*   From 16° to 18°, rising at times, according to age and vinification, to 20°, and very exceptionally even to 24°.
*Olorosos*       Starting at about 18°–20° and rising sometimes to 24°.
Pedro Ximénez    Rarely less than between 20° and 24°, and, in the case of a very old solera, rising perhaps even higher.

## The Great Sherry Bodegas

I do not know how many bodegas there are in Jerez – indeed, large and small, there must be hundreds; but the greatest of them, and those that are responsible for nearly all the exports, particularly to England, while having their roots in Spain, have considerable British interests, both financial and commercial. The more insular Spaniard has not allowed the infusion of British blood in the same way as port shippers have done in Oporto; at least, not nearly to the same extent. It is true the great firm of Williams & Humbert is British in origin, but this is an exception rather than the rule; and, while (as in the case of Domecq, through the redoubtable Ruskin senior) a few firms have British connections, the firms are essentially Spanish, keeping their commercial contacts with collaborators in London through the agency system, which, in the case of sherry, has always worked extremely well and amicably.

Jerez de la Frontera is a large town of, I suppose, about 100,000 inhabitants; I also suppose it could be one of the most prosperous towns in Spain outside Madrid. Its well-ordered streets, its squares and gardens, its ancient honey-coloured churches and buildings, together with the *palacios* of what Mr Croft-Cooke calls the sherry barons, make it an altogether pleasant place. The principal hotel, under the sign of Los Cisnes, is extremely comfortable and, naturally enough, it displays some hundreds of different sherries collected from every bodega in town, and some outside it. There is also a formidable list of Spanish wines, especially from the Rioja.

The heat in Andalusia is something quite remarkable, and the town shuts down between midday and four o'clock in the afternoon, after which hour things start coming to life again. Nothing moves at any speed, least of all the rumbling tumbrils of sherry, still often hauled by long-horned oxen, but inside the white walls of these great bodegas, with their row upon mighty row of maturing sherry, little seems to happen at any time. Inside a bodega, indeed, there is usually a court-yard, perhaps there are two or more courtyards, often with orange trees, and many are filled with bougainvillea and other lovely exotic flowers; at least one shipper is reputed to grow jasmine in his bodega, hoping that something of its delicate scent will work itself into the wine. I should like to think this was possible.

The larger bodegas, especially the exporting ones, have two things in common: a tremendous sense of hospitality and a carefully contrived bar at which the welcome visitor will be asked to 'look' at the wine of the bodega after being shown over the

Plate 46. These vineyards at Montserrat, near Barcelona, were planted when th Roman viaduct was built; Plate 47. (*Following page*). The glorious Rioja: a vine yard near Haro.

establishment. Very little formality is needed for a visit of this sort, although a letter of introduction from a local wine-merchant is by no means a bad thing to have. Moreover, in the case of the great bodegas, language does not present any particular problem. This is unusual, because the essential language in Spain is Spanish, and, elsewhere in the bodegas of Spain, even in the very large ones, to find anybody speaking English is the exception rather than the rule.

The particular *marques* of the great bodegas are a matter entirely for the bodegas themselves and originate in their own soleras. Many of these brands started long, long ago; each indicates a particular character of sherry, one that the proprietor at the time thought best suited to his trade and to public demand. All the wine produced must come under the three general classifications already discussed, but some of the deviations are extremely interesting, especially those blended for the South American market.

Those best known in England must be mentioned: firms like the giant González Byass y Cía, whose world-famous 'Tío Pepe' (Tío Pcpc is reputed to have been the founder of the firm) is known wherever sherry is drunk. Sandeman Brothers are as well known for their sherries as for their ports; and Williams & Humbert, whose name speaks of the British foundation of an Anglo-Spanish firm, have their 'Dry Sack' and 'Walnut Brown' sherries, which are also as famous as they are excellent. Another Jerez giant, Pedro Domecq, comes in here with 'La Ina' *fino* and, of course, a list of Spanish brandies, of which more in the appropriate chapter. Osborne of Puerto de Santa María was founded in 1772, and markets the famous 'El Cid' sherry and many others. The house of Terry, also in Puerto de Santa María, markets the sherry of that name and also the formidable Puerto de Santa María brandy. In Puerto de Santa María the Duff Gordon Company was really founded by Sir James Duff, the British Consul in Cádiz at the end of the eighteenth century, although his family no longer control the Spanish side of the business. The firm of M. Ant. de la Riva has the longest history in Jerez; although it may have existed earlier, since 1776 it has been passed down from father to son, and the family is happy in the ownership of some of the oldest soleras in the town. It is not a big concern as compared with the Jerez giants, but it certainly has excellent wine; its *fino* 'Tres Palmas' is a perfect example of this type of wine. They also market an excellent *manzanilla* called 'M.Z.A. La Riva', and some superb *olorosos*, among them 'Guadalupe Amontillado' (from the vineyards of that district), which is an excellent wine of its type when drunk with a really strong soup.

In Sanlúcar de Barrameda, the home of *manzanilla*, the firm of Antonio Barbadillo, S.A., is among the best, but González Byass have also a very large bodega, in which they have soleras of this special and altogether charming wine. Most of the Jerez bodegas have somewhat smaller installations here, but there are also many local firms.

## Sherry in England

I suggest that, if you asked which was the best known sherry throughout the world the answer would be 'Bristol Cream', which is the *marque* so well established by Harvey's. This company was built up in Bristol at the end of the eighteenth century by a long line of sea-captains and ship-owners, most of whom no doubt brought back as cargo the wines of Spain, and especially sherry. Now Harvey's dominate the trade with this *oloroso* dessert wine, which they have made very much their own; but the Bristol Milk,

Plate 48. A Macharnudo vineyard, near Jerez.

which is more of a generic term for certain *oloroso* wines, can be bought elsewhere. Avery's of Bristol, for example, also have an excellent Bristol Milk; so do one or two other Bristol firms. Unlike the other firms, however, Harvey's maintain their own bodegas both in Jerez and Montilla.

Something should certainly be said here about the sherry imported directly from Jerez by reputable wine-merchants throughout the length and breadth of the land, and marketed under their own particular trade-names. It would be impossible to supply a complete list, because, in every town where there are cultured and intelligent people you will nearly always find a cultured and intelligent wine-merchant who has, over the years, had his own particular mark of sherry blended for him in Jerez, and has imported it in bulk and bottled it himself, selling it under his own name. It is easy to come by one or two examples of this, such as the 'Elizabeta' of Avery's of Bristol, which is an extremely good *fino* from Jerez, and the equal of many of the *grandes marques* marketed under the Spanish label; Findlater, Mackie, Todd are famous for their 'Dry Fly', and Grants of St James's also have a wide range. I cannot therefore do more than recommend that you buy from your local wine-merchant a bottle of his own brand, and match it with the larger ones. Your personal taste will decide the issue.

There are hundreds of good sherries coming from Jerez, and I recommend that people ask for them through their local wine-merchants and find out for themselves.

CHAPTER THREE

# The Wines of Montilla and Moriles

THE WINES of Montilla and Moriles – they are practically the same thing – deserve to be a great deal better known outside Spain, and especially in England, than they are, although it is possible that they have often been drunk by people who have never heard the name or known whence they came. Roses by any other name would smell as sweet.

I have always known these wines as the sherries of Córdoba, for Córdoba is the commercial centre of the area where some of the bodegas are situated, and it is the distributing centre for the whole district. The wines not only have an affinity with the true sherry of Jerez but are almost identical with it. Montilla can be, and is, blended to match all the standard grades of sherry, and, while there is a basic difference in the method of making, as we shall see, the result is so similar as to be almost indistinguishable to the lay palate. There is one big difference in that all the wines of Montilla and Moriles have no addition whatever of alcohol, even for export, in contradistinction to Jerez wines, which although sometimes entirely pure for the domestic market, are otherwise nearly always fortified by the addition of grape alcohol to bring them up to the required standard of alcoholic content and to stabilize their keeping and travelling

qualities. True Montilla seems to need no help in this respect, and I have in my own
cellar the remnants of a small bin that I bought in the Ashburnham House sale some
years ago, after it had lain in that cellar since 1875. All of it, so far, has been perfectly
sound, very slightly *maderisé*, bone-dry and quite delicious.

Córdoba has, as is well known, a long history under Phoenician, Roman, Moorish
and Spanish rulers. Its wine was well known in Rome, where it was served to the Caesars,
and Munda – the name of the present Montilla – was a thriving Roman town; there is
even evidence that an amphora, bearing the seal of Munda, and undoubtedly containing Montilla of that day, has been excavated recently in Italy. This need not be surprising, as none of the wines of Italy approximate in any way to the special qualities of
the Andalusian wine, and the Caesars, who were always on the look-out for special kinds
of food and drink to break the monotony of their table, would certainly go to the trouble
of shipping in a few amphoras to impress their friends. Whether or not the viniculture
suffered under the Moors is problematical, for, while the Koran lays down that there
was a devil in every berry of the grape, evidence exists that these particular devils were
not despised, especially in Córdoba, for many Arab writers have extolled the virtue of
wine in general and of Montilla in particular.

The area in which Montilla wine is made reaches far north of Córdoba, but in practice these northern vineyards, 50 miles from Córdoba itself, do not produce the characteristic wines of the region. The true Montilla and Moriles wines come from grapes
grown in and around the villages of Montilla, Aguilar, Cabra, Puente Genil and Lucena.
Moriles itself is a tiny village, but it gives its name to an administrative region. Montilla,
on the other hand, is a thriving town of about 25,000 people, in which can be found
upwards of a hundred bodegas, although only about 15 are of a substantial size.
Whether they be large or small, however, the wine is made to a system corresponding
almost exactly with the making of the wine and the blending processes of the Jerez
system. Thus, as in Jerez, the great value of the wine derives from its having been produced by established and often very ancient soleras, which are quite irreplaceable and
without which fine wines cannot be made. This has already been explained in the
chapter on Jerez.

Unlike Jerez, however, this wine is one in which virtually only a single type of grape
is used, the Pedro Ximénez, which accounts for more than 90% of the wine; a very small
amount of Lairén and Moscatel grapes is also used. In Jerez the Pedro Ximénez grape
is associated nearly always with the richer and sweeter *oloroso* soleras and with the Pedro
Ximénez wine. Rarely, if ever, is it used for the *finos* and *amontillados*, but in Montilla the
grape is used universally, and the finest wines are completely dry, because fermentation
is allowed to go its full course and the grapes are not sun-dried after picking; the sugar
in the grape is transmuted into alcohol and does not retain its sweetness.

The best wines of Montilla and Moriles come from the Sierra de Montilla, and the
Moriles Alto. The grapes are grown on arid, chalky, intensely white soil which, while
giving a small yield, certainly produces the finest wines. Some care and skill are applied
in the blending of the two wines in the great bodegas, and it is said that the wines of
Moriles can be likened to a strong, handsome man and the wines from the Sierra de
Montilla to a very beautiful girl; the resulting combination is all that might be expected
of such a union. In point of fact, the Moriles wines are fractionally sharper (to say that
they are bitter would be to put it too strongly), but both wines have very considerable

character. There is a tiny glint of green in the gold of the wine; it is not always present in sherry, and I found it very attractive.

The vines are planted, more or less as in Jerez, by digging out a cubic metre of soil, pulverizing it and mixing it well with humus before replacing it; the vine is then planted in the centre, thus making a kind of pocket, which will assimilate the winter rains and retain a degree of moisture during the long, hard and intensely hot summer, for it is said that Córdoba is the hottest corner of Spain. The vines are pruned down to four or six shoots, and the vintage is somewhat earlier than in most parts of Spain. I saw the last grapes from the 1965 harvest unloaded at the press-house on 22 September, at which time the vintage had not begun in some bodegas in Valdepeñas, 150 miles to the north, and was still a month away in other parts of Spain.

The Bodegas Alvear in Montilla have two fine modern bodegas, and in one everything was over; the place had been swept clean and all the presses and the crushing machinery had been washed up for another year. In the other, some seven or eight kilometres into Moriles Alto, the last load was being delivered with the customary cheerful bustle. The smell of fermenting grapes hung heavily on both bodegas.

After crushing and the removal of the stalks, the grapes are pumped into chambers above the modern hydraulic presses, and the juice is allowed to run into collecting sumps, while the stalks, skins and pips are consigned to the presses that at once operate a second pressing. The must is pumped from the sumps into *tinajas* – that is, fermenting-pots (in the big bodegas they are made from cement, but in most of the small ones the old clay pots are still used); and there they lie in symmetrical and attractive rows. They each hold between 6,000 and 7,000 litres of must, and in a large bodega, e.g. Alvear, there are sometimes more than a hundred pots. The pots are left without lids at this stage while fermentation is developing, and every stage can be seen and examined, from the newly poured must to the wine that has achieved its first boisterous fermentation. This is extremely interesting to watch, the liquid apparently boiling, with bubbles breaking and the whole liquid appearing to seethe. It also looks extremely unpleasant, rather like water from the River Thames; and yet in a few weeks it will clear and the wine become like crystal.

The wine is left in the fermenting-pots for two months after fermentation stops. The first fermentation takes between fifteen days and a month, and then follows the secondary fermentation, without disturbing the wine, while it clarifies completely. It is then piped off into butts, for removal to the bodegas so that it can be blended and take its place in the appropriate solera. It is in this process that the vinification differs from that of Jerez, where, up to now, the must is fermented in the butt and not in pots or vats; but I am told that more than one of the great Jerez bodegas are changing over to the pot system. Certainly it would be difficult to find a better wine than that made in Montilla by the pot system, and indeed it is said that the old clay pots do contribute to the quality of the wine; but this may come under the heading of old wives' tales. The modern cement vats appear to produce wine of equal quality. As in Jerez, the wine develops in the oak butts and produces the yeasts that form the 'flower', which appears in the spring and autumn. This we have discussed in the last chapter.

Montilla can be, and often is, sold a year old, and this is the common wine of the country, the *vino corriente de Montilla*, although in no way to be confused with a *vino de mesa* (which it is not). Most of the wine, however, is sent to its appropriate solera, where it goes through the usual process, emerging as a *fino*, an *amontillado* or an *oloroso*. Before bottling, the special wines are clarified with beaten white of egg, and in some bodegas the vintagers are said to add a pinch of earth brought from Lebrija in Seville, which is supposed to have a special property for clarifying wine very quickly. I cannot find the truth of this; it may be a local ritual. Or maybe it doesn't happen at all. But I like the idea of it.

In the large and small bodegas of Córdoba and Montilla the whole business of making up the soleras, blending and finally bottling and distribution is carried on. I saw two of these. One was comparatively small; it belonged to Señor Antonio Alarcón, who is justly proud of the excellent wine he produces in most grades. He is especially proud of an *oloroso* that comes from a hundred-year-old solera. It would indeed be difficult to fault. After dinner I was taken over his bodega and through the Arabian Nights streets of old Córdoba. We tasted wines until nearly two in the morning – which was about the latest I had ever looked at wine with a critical eye. However, dinner had been light and late, so I thoroughly enjoyed the selection of wines from *finos* to *olorosos*, which were all excellent of their type.

The next day in Córdoba I visited a very large bodega belonging to Señor Carbonell. When his family bought it a hundred years ago it was the oldest bodega in Córdoba, and it had some correspondingly interesting soleras. Those great bodega naves, with hundreds of butts in treble rows, are indeed a sight; they always amaze me, despite the many occasions on which I have seen them. From a barrel somewhere in the middle of the solera, using the same method as in Jerez, were taken samples, first, of a *fino* that I judged to be at about its best; next, of a twenty-year-old *fino*, now of course an *amontillado*, that was a pale golden brown and, I was delighted to see, still retained that green glint which I have come to look for. This was followed by a collection of four soleras from the four oldest butts in the bodega. Five years were assumed to have passed between each two, and the youngest was about a hundred years old. They were naturally very dark, and I couldn't find any green; but then there is very little green in any of us at that great age. They varied in taste, but all were uniformly dry and very good indeed.

After making the acquaintance of these very old gentlemen, I was given a glass of the Pedro Ximénez that every bodega apparently likes to trot out at the very end to ruin the taste of those that have gone before. They are always superb of their kind, as this was. But, without being ungracious, I cannot help wishing bodegas wouldn't do it.

I should mention that this one has the happy idea of complimenting visitors by asking them to write in chalk on the end of a butt of wine in one of the soleras, instead of in the more customary visitors' book. You see the usual appropriate remarks – with the usual inanities too, I fear – in every language under the sun.

Montilla and Moriles wines are grouped officially into four classes.

| | |
|---|---|
| *Finos* | These have an alcoholic content of not less than 16°–16½° after fermentation, with an acidity of less than 0·60. |
| *Finos viejos* | Corresponding to the Jerez *amontillado*, these have a degree of alcohol from 17° to 17½°. Again the acidity is less than 0·60. |
| *Olorosos* | In Montilla these are called strong-scented wines, which indeed they are, of 18° or 19° alcohol and with a volatile acidity of less than 0·70. |
| *Olorosos viejos* | These come from the oldest bodegas and go as high as 19°–21° alcohol, with a volatile acidity of not more than 0·70. |

Some of the large bodegas in Córdoba distil their own brandy, which I found rather sweeter than the Jerez brandies; I am told that there is a lively export trade with Italy, as they have become popular through the predilection for them of the American Armed Forces in Spain, who have now spread this rather apocryphal gospel abroad. They also make a highly interesting punch or *ponche*, a mixture of brandy and fermented fruit juices, called 'Seductor' – and it might well be used as one. It is presented in what appears to be a solid silver bottle; actually it is a glass bottle completely covered in silver paper, with a nice little red tassel at the top, and it is reputed to have a considerable vogue in South American countries. I tasted it, but I cannot for the moment think of an appropriate way of describing in detail this potent and interesting concoction.

CHAPTER FOUR

# The Wines of the Rioja

THE RIOJA, like all Gaul, is divided into three parts – and, like Gaul, it produces excellent wines. The Rioja district is partly in the provinces of Burgos, Alava and Navarre, and comprises the whole of Logroño. It starts a few miles to the east of Miranda de Ebro on the main San Sebastián to Burgos road, and it stretches as far as Alfaro about 80 miles to the west. Vines are grown and wine is made all over this wonderfully beautiful land of gentle hills, many capped with castles, villages and churches, and surrounded by the mountains of the Sierra de Cantabria in the north, which your local grower will tell you is the great protector of the Rioja vines, giving them shelter from the bleak winds of winter. This land, through which the Ebro flows from beginning to end, is in my opinion one of the most beautiful vine-growing areas in the world; even without its superlative wines it would be well worth a visit for any tourist with an eye for scenery. I am writing this as I sit on the balcony of my room in the Conde de Haro Hotel at Haro, overlooking this altogether wonderful landscape, with the poplar-lined Ebro quietly flowing a hundred yards or so below, and with patches of vines growing everywhere within sight until they reach the higher slopes of the sierra.

Wines have been made in the Rioja, as in most places in Spain, from time immemorial, but there is a particular history attached to these particularly good wines, mainly because of their special excellence and the fact that they have been much sought after by the kings and grandees of Spain, who would obviously go to some trouble to provide themselves with the best wine, even though transport might be difficult. This region is roughly at the meeting-place of Aragon, Navarre and Castile; it was therefore easily accessible for those kingdoms and provided indeed their *vino corriente*. Just exactly what happened to the vineyards under the Moors is not recorded; but, as elsewhere in Spain, there are records that the Prophet was disobeyed in his tenet that proscribes wine for the Faithful, so we must suppose that wine went on being made here in Rioja. Certainly in the sixteenth and seventeenth centuries the wines had become world famous, but long before that Sancho III, the Great, king of Navarre 1000–1035, founded a monastery in the Rioja, and its vineyards were specially mentioned in the deeds.

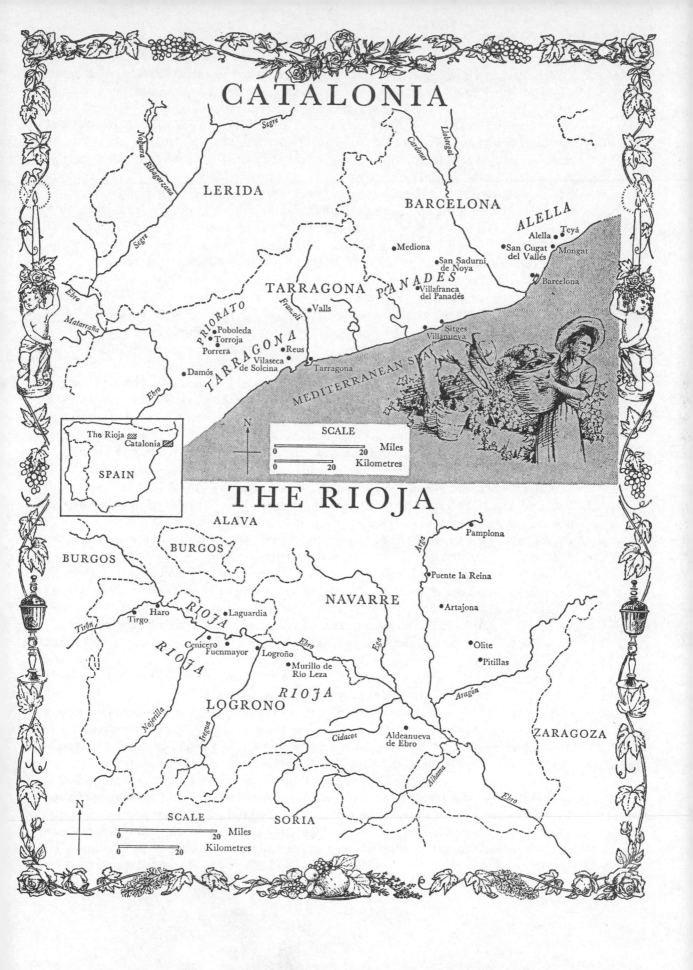

# CATALONIA

NOGUERA RIBAGORZANA

Segre

Cardoner

Llobregat

LERIDA

BARCELONA

ALELLA

Segre

Mediona

Alella · Teyá
San Cugat · · Mongat
del Vallés

TARRAGONA

PANADES

San Sadurni
de Noya

Barcelona

Ebro

Villafranca
del Panadés

PRIORATO

Fran-oli

Valls

TARRAGONA

Matarraña

Poboleda
Torroja
Porrera

Reus

Sitges
Villanueva

Vilaseca
de Solcina

Tarragona

Damós

MEDITERRANEAN SEA

Ebro

**SPAIN** inset: The Rioja ▨ · Catalonia ▨

### SCALE
Miles 0 — 20
Kilometres 0 — 20

N ↑

# THE RIOJA

ALAVA

BURGOS

Arga

Pamplona

BURGOS

NAVARRE

Puente la Reina

Haro

RIOJA

Laguardia

Artajona

Tirón

Tirgo

RIOJA

Ega

Cenicero
Fuenmayor

Logroño

Ebro

Olite

Pitillas

Murillo de
Río Leza

Najerilla

RIOJA

Aragón

LOGRONO

ZARAGOZA

Iregua

Cidacos

Aldeanueva
de Ebro

Alhama

Ebro

N ↑

### SCALE
Miles 0 — 20
Kilometres 0 — 20

SORIA

It is interesting that even in the sixteenth century the imitation of wine, or the steal-ing of the good name to put on an inferior wine (a practice that is certainly not in disuse today), was pretty well established, and the Riojans in 1560 adopted what must have been one of the first trade-marks ever made, so that they could mark their casks and institute their own *denominacion de origen*. They designed an odd kind of anagram and the first trade association of wine-growers in Spain was founded thereby. In 1635 the authorities in Logroño made an order against any kind of cart traffic on certain streets, as the rumbling shook the must in the cellars below and harmed the ageing of the wines (but I think there must be something more to it than this; it hardly sounds possible) while in 1655 the Vicar-General of the Diocese is reported to have excommuni-cated the Municipal Council for harvesting their wines without observing the rules that had been laid down to regulate the vintage. This again sounds apocryphal.

Rioja is to Spain more or less what the Bordeaux vineyards are to France; it produces wine by the same methods, and with sometimes nearly as much care. It is a distinctive wine on its own merit and makes no claim to be otherwise, but it owes much of its technique and know-how to the French *vignerons*. When the phylloxera scourge hit France in the late nineteenth century and partly wiped out its vineyards many of the French *vignerons* came to the Rioja, which is reasonably near, and bought or rented vineyards and made wine that they blended with what they could find of their own, to maintain their trade, although those years were very bad indeed for them. With them they brought French techniques which, when added to the centuries-old Spanish methods, improved the wine a great deal. These methods are now the traditional methods of wine-making in the Rioja area, and certainly the vine is cultivated and the wine made with some care, and indeed with love.

Later, when the French vineyards had been replanted after the phylloxera with immune American vine-stocks, the phylloxera crossed the Pyrenees, probably with one of the French *vignerons* whose business Rioja had saved. At the same time it appeared in the south of Spain through Gibraltar, which no doubt the Spanish put down to one of the little tricks of perfidious Albion. The scourge came up from the south and down from the north, wiping out numerous areas of vines in the same way as it had in France, al-though, for some reason or other, part of the Valdepeñas area was spared, and there are still pre-phylloxera vines growing there. These were years, I am told, of tremendous hardship throughout the vineyards of Spain; but eventually the phylloxera-immune stocks were imported and planted, and the wine is better than ever. Although it is often claimed in France that the pre-phylloxera wine was better, few of my generation and those younger will ever know the truth. Certain it is, however, that the fine wines made today are of superb quality, as they are indeed in the Rioja.

Having already said much in praise of the wines of Spain (and I hope to say a good deal more before this study is finished), I doubt whether Spain will ever produce really *great* wine. Good wine certainly, fine wine often in the Rioja and in one or two pockets of viniculture; but the great wines of France are bred on soils such as Spain does not possess, and made by techniques that are foreign to the Spanish nature, and in a climate very different from that which exists only a comparatively few miles away across the Pyrenees. The great wines of France are uniformly produced from grapes (usually of a single variety) grown in pockets of gravelly, stony soil, where they are gathered and made into wine under the direction of a single *vigneron* and marketed by him under his

THE WINES OF THE RIOJA

own name and that of his *château*. They may be produced, as most of them are, by a time-honoured process of fermentation, ageing and racking and ageing in cask, and sold as the completely authentic wine of a certain very limited area and of a given year, bottled at exactly the right time in the place where it was made. Thus, if the wines are kept properly and the year is a good one, they will be brought to the table in as perfect a condition as they possibly can be, given their age. They may be drunk too young or too old, but the wine at least started its life with a good birth certificate.

Nothing comparable to this exists in Spain. The wine is universally made, usually in the bodega of the shipper, but from grapes bought from great numbers of little growers, and sometimes from wine bought from a co-operative, or made by a small grower, and blended to form a standard type of wine. In the Rioja, for instance, the vines are grown by small farmers, with an average of between 2 and 5 hectares of land, who tend to grow the kind of grape they like best. Thus, while certain strains of grape are popular and certainly go well with similar grapes, there is no consistency; the art is in the blending rather than the cultivation of a specific grape made in a given year and sold. I have been talking, of course, about the fine wines of Bordeaux and the Côte d'Or, for most of the ordinary wines in France are made on much the same principle as the Spanish.

There is, however, one big difference: throughout Spain *chaptalisation*, or the addition of sugar to the wine in fermentation, is unknown, while, although not practised (much) in Bordeaux, it is greatly practised in other parts of France. In Spain a certain amount of *mistela*, or unfermented must, which is very sweet, is kept for blending some types of wine. Again, a certain proportion of the old wines in the Rioja area are kept as a reserve for blending, and this is why you find the words ' 'Reserva' or 'Gran Reserva' on standard wine labels, which simply means that these comparatively old, matured wines are used for blending table wines in a very modified way, as they are used universally in the sherry country of Jerez.

The climate of the Rioja is fairly stable and is altogether suitable for viniculture. The winters, although cold, are seldom terribly severe, and the rains are usually consistent in the rainy season; the summers are very hot, but rain falls occasionally, and this makes for excellent wine. Sometimes there is a disastrous year, like 1959, when it rained all the time, and the grapes arrived mildewed at the bodegas, and most of the wine went for vinegar. Indeed, it was worth very little more.

The soil varies according to the three parts of the Rioja, but it is chalky in its general formation and not particularly rich. This, again, makes for good wine. The three parts of the Rioja are the Rioja Alta, which is to the west and is centred on Haro – here are produced fine wines of a not very high alcoholic content, never more than 14°, and usually about 12°; the Rioja Baja, where the bodegas are centred on Logroño and the villages around it, which produce again a fine wine but of a higher alcoholic strength, without quite the breeding of the Rioja Alta; and the third, much smaller district, which is contained in the two pockets to the north of the River Ebro near Haro and is called the Rioja Alavesa – this produces a slight variation in the wine which is different from the others in that it has a certain smoothness; this I found very attractive.

Generally speaking, the Riojan tradition is to make wines by the Bordeaux method: that is to say, the wine is fermented in great oak vats, where it undergoes its first tumultuous fermentation in about 10–12 days, after which it is either racked off into storage-vats, also mostly of oak, or passed directly into the barrel, where it undergoes its second fermentation, to be racked by moving the wine from one cask to another three times in the first year. It is then clarified and put into the ageing barrels, being racked perhaps once a year; after two or three years it is ready for bottling or being sold in bulk. After bottling it is binned for six months or so, or as long as it is required before selling.

The great bodegas of Haro – where there are no fewer than 12 large bodegas that export wines, besides many smaller ones – are indeed imposing, with endless great buildings containing literally thousands of hogsheads of wine in five-tiered rows. Ageing of the wine is considered of great importance in the Rioja; even the white wines are sometimes kept for four or five years before being bottled, and many of them for much longer. Most of the bodegas show with great pride this *reserva* wine, and many of them, too, have their private cellars of bottled wines, which they do not sell but produce for the interested visitor. And very good they are.

I think it is necessary to say something about the years that are printed on the labels, which are not always strictly accurate. It is perfectly true that there are casks of very, very old wine in the Rioja of a given year, and I have myself seen and tasted wines of 1904, 1910 and later that are indeed authentic of those years. On the other hand, we must remember that a modified solera system operates with table wines, and it may mean only that the wine has been made with a proportion of the old wine from that year added. Then again, it may sometimes happen that one bodega has had a big success with a wine of a certain year, such as 'Gran Reserva 1928', and this has tended to establish itself as a *marque* rather than a mere matter of fact. The 'Gran Reserva 1928' I was given to taste was actually about 15 years old, and probably all the better for it, but the bodega-owner thought it the most natural thing in the world to keep his *marque*. Furthermore, the year in which the wine has been made is not by any means of so much significance as it is in France, because the climate is very much more consistent, and the wines of one year, with certain exceptions like 1959, do not vary a great deal. What is important is the age of the wine, because the Rioja wines do age tremendously well, both in cask and in bottle, and there is a very big difference between a young wine, three or four years old, and the older wines in which the great bodegas take such pride.

Apart from the wines in the Rioja that are made by the great bodegas, some of them world-famous names, wine is also made in village co-operatives, which produce a *corriente* wine of superb quality for what it is, and by a diminishing number of small growers who may buy the grapes of their neighbours but who make the wine themselves, usually to sell to the big bodegas, or sometimes to their own private trade customers, always in Spain. The wine may be made, in the case of the big bodegas, and certainly of the two co-operatives that I have seen, by the most modern methods and in very large quantities indeed; and, while there is nothing in Rioja to match the stainless-steel splendour of Château Latour, some of the bodegas have very good and efficient systems of tile-lined cement vats and similar modern fittings. The small bodega has none of this, and I am rather glad to say that many of the larger bodegas still retain their faith in the oak vats. All, however, age their wine in cask, with the exception of the co-operatives, where the wine must be sold and cleared within two years of being made.

I stayed for some days in the Rioja and visited many of the bodegas, large and small. These I shall describe – for, as in France, the wine varied from one to another. I have tasted excellent wine, indeed very excellent wine, from those bodegas that keep the traditional system of cobwebby oak vats and barrels, and I have had excellent wine from more modern installations. I do not think it would be fair to make a distinction on this point; after all, it can well be argued that, if super-modern methods can be used in Château Latour, which is generally agreed to have produced the best wine of the Médoc recently, certainly there can be nothing against it.

Most of the bodegas produce two qualities of wine: the first and best I suppose we can term the export quality, although far more of it is sold in Spain than elsewhere, and it is to be found universally throughout Spain on the wine list of every good restaurant and hotel. They also make for their national consumption wine that is usually sold in bulk, and again it is of very good quality, but I have the impression that most of the *corriente* wines of the Rioja came from the co-operatives. The wines, whether they are sold in England or in Spanish restaurants, are cheap; and this is true throughout Spain, although unfortunately the big hotels and restaurants will not serve the *corriente* wines – especially the enormous number of large hotels that have sprung up all along the Mediterranean coast. While I suppose that most holiday-makers are prepared to spend a bit more for their wine when they are abroad, I for one deplore the fact that you cannot have an occasional good *corriente*, which in Spain is usually very drinkable indeed, especially if it comes from Rioja, and very much cheaper.

The large bodegas nearly all produce a range of about three *tintos*, which are classed rather by age than by anything else, starting with a wine of four years old, and another one of perhaps six years, and a *reserva*, which may be ten or fifteen years old. It is the *tintos* of the Rioja that are its chief glory. Then again, they will produce a dry white and a *semiseco* and a somewhat sweeter white wine and, of course, the inevitable *rosado* to take care of the growing market for this now popular wine, so delicious on a hot summer day when it is served really cold. This constitutes the main difference between the French and Spanish types of wine-production; in Spain most districts make wine of several types, whereas, in France, Médoc wines come from Médoc, Graves from Graves, wines of Burgundy from the Côte d'Or and the Beaujolais (some of them) from Beaujolais. It is possible and, I think, very probable that a good many of the French wines from all these districts have some Spanish blood in their veins, and indeed they are none the worse for it, since in the Rioja as in most other districts of Spain, the wine is perfectly honest, both in its essential character and its alcoholic strength, which qualities make it very suitable for blending – and I can think of some wines from outside Spain that could be improved by an infusion of good Spanish wine.

In all the great bodegas in Haro that I had the pleasure of visiting I found a wide variety of wine; where popular demand from England and elsewhere had not tended to alter the basic style of the wine they were universally good. Most of the bodegas have their special pride and joy in the wines that they, no doubt rightly, consider they make better than anybody else, as (for instance) Bodegas 'Rioja' Santiago, who make their wine, and market it in square bottles, under the *marque* 'Yago'. This method of bottling, which they have been using for 15 years, makes for easy storage (obviously square bottles are much easier to bin than round ones, and they also save a great deal of space); it is, I am told, being adopted by the German wine trade, and I was able to give this very unpalatable piece of information to Señor Don Angel Santiago, who had clapped a patent on his form of bottling – he was, to say the least of it, disconcerted to know that it was no longer all his own. I suspect that he went off to consult his lawyers, but I doubt whether he will have much luck, because every kind of bottle has been made at some time or other in the long history of wine-making. The bottle is quite attractive, rather like a square hock bottle, tapering off into an ordinary round neck, but of course it has nothing whatever to do with the wine inside. Señor Santiago makes his wine from grapes from the Rioja Alta and also the Rioja Alavesa. He makes the wine in his bodega at Labastida, a village about 7 kilometres from Haro.

In passing, I should mention that the word *bodega* is the same whether the wine is made there or merely stored, blended and bottled there, in contradistinction to the French *pressoir* for the place where the grapes are pressed and fermented and the *chais* where the wine is stored and aged. In Spain the bodega where the wine is made is called a *bodega de elaboracion*; the Spanish equivalent of *chais* is *bodega de crianza*. Señor Santiago's *bodega de elaboracion* was then being scoured out ready for the vintage that was due to begin in about a fortnight.

The wines of which Don Angel is most proud are his old red wines called 'Rioja Santiago', of which he has really enormous stocks, and he is especially proud of a genuine 1949, which is a very good wine indeed, but with, I think, rather a dry after-taste; this may have been due, in the bottle that was opened for me, to a little too much tannin, but the wine has great character. His white wines, which are well aged and never sold until after four years, are pale golden and are perfectly fresh and lively. He was kind enough to open for me a bottle of white wine; the label was printed with the mystic number 1908. But this, with the best will in the world, I cannot take too seriously. The wine, although very mellow and quite delicious, showed no trace of age at all, except for a suspicion of woodiness, which might perhaps be due to the sulphur with which all the white-wine casks are prepared, as they are everywhere else. His great pride, however, is a wonderful bin of 1904 red wine, which is never sold – and I don't blame him. It was a great privilege to drink it, and an even greater privilege to be given a bottle to take away. This wine is truly remarkable, and, had I been given it in a decanter without any knowledge of its origin, I should have been hard pressed to say whence it came. It was perhaps the finest of the Spanish wines that I have drunk.

The Bodegas Bilbainas are the biggest in the Rioja, and, in the absence of the present managing director, I was shown round by the previous head of the firm, who has now retired after 51 years in Haro and Valdepeñas, where they have another large bodega. This bodega in Haro is truly enormous, and it was a great pleasure and relief when, having been shown with justifiable pride every operation, from the making of casks and the hammering together of the wooden boxes in which the wine is exported, backwards to the actual making of the wine, I found myself seated in the office of Señor Don Santiago de Ugarte with a bottle of his best sparkling wine opened for the occasion.

This bodega is the only one in the Rioja to make sparkling wine by the *méthode champenoise*. The owners are quite justifiably proud in this division of the business; although relatively small, it compares favourably with some of the *cavas* in Panadés and certainly with any of the bodegas that make Spanish sparkling wines by other methods. The quality is exceptionally good, and while (in common with all other Spanish sparkling wine) it is not comparable in actual taste with true champagne, it is an excellent wine. It has generally a softer taste, but it is well made, and the *brut* is very dry indeed, with a liqueur addition of less than 1%. The Bodegas Bilbainas have some vineyards of their own adjoining the bodega, and their grapes, the Gasnacha Blanca (which are comparatively small, white grapes, not over-sweet), are considered to be especially suitable for the making of sparkling wine; the producers reckon to have them out of the way before the normal Riojan vintage starts. Three great presses work on them. The first fermentation is carried out in oak vats, and the wine is transferred immediately into the cask for the secondary fermentation, after which it is clarified, blended and bottled with its temporary corks. It then starts on its long period of ageing in a horizontal position, before the penultimate stage of being put in racks at an angle of 45 degrees, with its daily shake-up; and so after six months into the upside-down vertical position before being finished. The sparkling wine is usually sold in about five to seven years.

Owing to the complexity of the export market, this bodega makes a great many wines, both red and white – about ten *tintos* and eight *blancos* in qualities and prices to suit most demands throughout the world. I tasted a good many of them; the best seemed to be the 'Viña Pomal', which is an excellent *tinto* of some age, and the 'Cepa de Oro', which is a pale gold, and the 'Viña Paceta'. It also makes a sweet white wine called 'Brillante'. This is certainly brilliant to look at, and it is much beloved by the tourist trade, but in my opinion it appears to have lost character to sweetness. It is difficult to describe this truly enormous bodega. Like Topsy, it 'just growed', and now every nook and cranny is filled with wine – wine in tanks, wine in barrels, wine in bottles. Vast quantities of wine can be seen, most of it growing deliciously older every day.

At the medium-sized bodega of R. López de Heredia, Viña Tondonia, S.A., oak is considered to be the only material in which wine should be contained, apart from bottles. Here again the great presses were being made ready, and everything was being cleaned and furbished, but all the fermenting-vats – and some of them were huge, containing 40,000–50,000 litres – were of oak; the whole process of first and second fermentation is carried out in the casks. Señor Don Pedro López de Heredia is an enthusiast and a great believer in wood; his wines have all the character you would expect from their being carefully made and long matured. The house of Tondonia, founded in 1877, makes four white wines, five reds and a *rosado*. The white wines, which vary from a *semidulce* wine called 'Viña Zaconia' to a very dry wine called 'Viña Tondonia', are excellent. 'Viña Tondonia' *blanco* is bottled from the wood after six years; it has a good nose, is splendidly golden and is quite delicious. The red wines are all excellent, strong, full-bodied wines with a good nose, and they vary from the 'Rioja Clarete Fino', which is bottled after three years in wood, to the 'Viña Tondonia' *tinto*, which has had six years in barrel and is a wonderful dark red and quite exceptional.

The pride and joy of this bodega is the private cellar, which contains a hundred or more bins of the wines that have been made over the last fifty years or so. The wine of every year is not present, and when I asked if they had any wine of my year (which is 1905) they regretted very much that they could offer me only 1904 or 1906. This great private cellar is most impressive. In its centre is a round table, made from the bottom of an immense fermenting-vat and standing on barrels, at which you sit and taste the wine. I was given a dry white wine of 1938, which certainly had lost none of its body and was not appreciably darker than the four- or six-year-old wines of the same breed that I also tasted. Moreover, I was given a 'Viña Tondonia' 1934, which was brilliant in colour and had a lovely nose and a great deal of character; if I had to choose between a Bordeaux of 1934, which is considered by some to be a good year, and this particular wine, I would choose the Rioja. This splendid and altogether remarkable cellar of very fine wines is dubbed colloquially the *cementerio* (cemetery) – and not inappropriately, since paradise is usually entered that way. Behind oak doors are wines from the foundation of the bodega in 1877; but the head of the firm was away, and he had very wisely taken the key with him.

It was in the process of being interred, or rather pickled, in the cemetery that I discovered the origin of the slender silver or gold chicken wire with which the best Spanish wine is always enmeshed. I have often wondered about this because, while pretty, it seemed to perform no useful function whatever; but, upon mentioning this fact, I was told that it was in the first place a very sensible idea. The best wines, as in other parts of the world, were imitated by unscrupulous wine-merchants who were not above forging a label or two; and so, to ensure the integrity of the wine in the bottle, a few of the best shippers encased their bottles in this charming wire and sealed it off at the bottom with the private seal of their own bodega. This they thought would make their wine less vulnerable to imitation. In consequence, everybody else started to do exactly the same thing; the seals are no longer used, but the wire remains as an embellishment and as a kind of outward and visible sign that the wine within has an inward and spiritual grace that requires protection.

Some very good wines are made at the Compañia Vinicola del Norte de España, again a large bodega. It is the second largest in Haro, and I have long known it for the good wine that is marketed under the name of C.V.N.E. The wines are made by comparatively modern methods (the ageing in wood is taken for granted in the Rioja for all fine wines) from grapes of both the Rioja Alavesa and the Rioja Alta, and they have a smoothness that I found excellent; in fact, the best of them are very fine wines indeed. Their *blanco-seco* is called 'Monopole'; it is dry, fragrant and comparable with the wines grown in countries farther north. But I suppose their chief pride is in their three main types of red wine: the 'Corona', which is their younger wine (that is, about four years old); the 'Imperial Gran Reserva', which bears the date 1949; and the 'Viña Real Oro'. This last wine is extremely smooth – a completely natural, clean wine with none of the dry after-taste that is typical of most Riojan wines. I found it very, very good indeed. It is not surprising that on the wine list of the local restaurant in Haro this particular wine is by far the most expensive, although the list, naturally enough, includes all the best *marques* of Rioja. It is extremely expensive by Spanish standards, and very cheap for its quality by any other; but I can well understand that it should fetch, as it deserves to fetch, a good price.

The restaurant I have mentioned, called 'El Terete', is worth a note because, among those I know, it is the only one that you enter through a butcher's shop. You go upstairs to tables and benches of pine scrubbed to an immaculate white; the food there is first class by any international standards. You order from the menu, and the waiters pop down and cut the meat off the joint in the shop downstairs. In passing, besides their baby lamb, I can recommend their *alubias* – a delicious bean soup, made from butter beans, the only trouble being that one eats too much of it to enjoy the baby lamb to follow.

The fine wines of the bodega Federico Paternina are well known all over the world. Natually they have a very big export trade, and the stacks of wooden cases ready for shipment can be seen to be going to the uttermost corners of the earth. The bodega's best known wine is the *tinto* 'Banda Azul' which, I suppose, would be about four years old and is uniformly good; but it has another wine called 'Viña Bial' – an excellent wine of about 10 years – and also a real giant of a wine, 'Gran Reserva', some bottles having a label calling it 1928, though I don't think I could vouch for the validity of this age, and I must say that my hosts seemed rather surprised that they should be asked to do so. On the other hand, the wine itself has the dignity of a wine of great age, and I have no doubt at all that there is in it some very old wine somewhere along the line. It can certainly be recommended as a big wine with lots of character and with not too much dryness in the after-taste. Federico Paternina also make some excellent white wines, although their 'Monte Haro' is *dulce* – too *dulce* for me. They have a good *blanco seco* that is a very good example of a fine white Rioja wine, and another wine rejoicing in the name of 'Rinsol', which is a good deal better than the name sounds.

My mentor in some of these expeditions was Señor Don Antonio Larrea, the local official representative of the Consejo Regulador de la Denominación de Origen Rioja (the Spanish equivalent of the French *appellation controlée* authority), who was unprejudiced in his views. I also found him uniformly courteous and interested in all that I was trying to do and say. Under his guidance I visited one of the largest co-operatives in the Rioja, at San Vicente de la Sonsierra, an altogether charming village perhaps 14 kilometres from Haro, with the tiled houses rising on the little hill crowned by a castle and a church in the best Spanish tradition.

The vintage had not yet begun, but this quite vast factory – and I am aware that this is an unkind word to use for a place that makes nearly 5,000,000 litres of good wine a year – is really the last word in a *bodega de elaboración* for the mass-production of *corriente* wine. It is a perfectly straightforward operation; the grapes are brought in by the farmers, the machinery for removing the stalks and so on is absolutely modern, there are four great presses for the second pressing, and the *mosto* is pumped into row upon row of fermenting-vats in three tiers. The bodega is built on the side of the hill, so that each storey of vats has its own entrance. After the first fermentation of 10–12 days the wine is pumped into the second range of storage-vats, and it is ready to drink in the year following. Most of it is sold in the second year; indeed, it all has to be cleared by then because the vats are needed. I was told that there is never any difficulty in selling the output from this extremely well run co-operative, and I was given the wine to taste directly from four of the storage tanks. There was a slight variation; this might well be expected, because they use more than one kind of grape, but, considering that this wine is sold in the wine-shops at about eight to ten pesetas a litre, it was quite excellent, clean and a rich ruby colour, but not too dark and with quite a good nose. If I never had anything else but this *vino corriente* to drink for the rest of my life I should come to no harm at all. When I consider the *ordinaires* that I have had to put up with at one time or another in various places around the world I find myself full of admiration for these very honest, decent wines.

On a morning in very early October I slipped out on to my balcony at the Hotel Conde de Haro, to find the valley of the Ebro below me shrouded in mist, with the low hills, topped by their castles, villages and churches, rising out of a white sea like islands, and with the vineyards draping the slopes and the mountains behind in the early morning sun. It was indescribably beautiful, like an old Japanese print. Soon the mists disappeared, and my courteous guide arrived to take me to see a bodega or two that he thought would be of special interest.

First of all we visited the Bodegas Riojanas in Cenicero (which means 'ash-tray'), where they appear to be not unreasonably proud of the wine they make, which is exported in really enormous quantities to almost every part of the world except England. This Señor Marcelo Frias regretted; but, as he sold without difficulty all of his excellent wine, he did not consider it a major problem. The wines in his bodega seemed to be universally good. A mixture of the grapes from the Rioja Alta and the Rioja Alavesa is used, and the wines are made, as far as the *tintos* are concerned, from the Garnacha, Tempranillo and Granciano varieties, and from the Malvasía and Viura for the *blancos*. Señor Frias has considerable vineyards of his own, and he also buys other carefully selected grapes from local farmers. His wines are made entirely in wood (he will not have anything in stainless steel or cement near the place), and they undergo the first fermentation in vats holding 20,000–40,000 litres. They receive their secondary fermentation in wood, and then they go through the process of being racked three times in the first year, twice in the second and once in the third; after which some are sold, and the others are kept for sale later and possibly put into a *reserva*.

The most important wines of the Bodegas Riojanas are the 'Monte Real' and the 'Viña Albina' as regards *tintos*; I was given both the six-year-old wines, and a bottle was opened of the 'Viña Albina 1942 Reserva'. The 'Viña Albina' is the drier of the two, but both wines are full-bodied and a dark ruby in colour. All these wines were first class, especially the 1942, which I was assured belonged honestly to that year – and I believe it. This bodega makes several white wines, but the most attractive I found to be the *marque* called 'Medieval', which is sold at about three years old and is a very pale wine for a Rioja, very dry, with a good nose, and altogether acceptable and comparable with white wines anywhere, other than the classic vintages.

Courteous farewells were made, and we were on our way to Elciego a few kilometres away; but the barriers over the level-crossing were down, and my mentor groaned, 'Why are the barriers always down at Cenicero? I have never yet known them to be up.'

There was a goods train in the siding in Cenicero station, with steam up and facing our way. After a quarter of an hour or so a whistling was heard a long way down the line, and the Bilbao–Logroño express came in sight along the single track, stopping a couple of hundred yards from the goods train and whistling for a signal. Nothing happened for some time, while the two engines whistled at each other intermittently, each obviously trying to stare the other out. Meanwhile the barriers remained resolutely down, and we could see an argument proceeding on the station platform a little distance away. More whistles – and no hope that the two engines were any nearer an agreement than the United Nations. So I did the only sensible thing. I descended from the car and, gathering some grapes from the adjoining vineyard of Bodegas Riojanas, spent an agreeable quarter of an hour watching or rather listening to the two trains arguing the toss and waiting for the barrier to go up. After which I decided I would take a constitutional along the road and leave the car to pick me up, which it did another quarter of an hour and one kilometre later. I gather that the express triumphed, even though the goods train had received reinforcements from somewhere else in the form of another train – and so I spent three-quarters of an hour in the middle of a lovely country.

Just outside the ancient little walled town of Laguardia are the Bodegas Palacio. Here they make a great deal of excellent quality wine and more *mosto*, which is not one of my favourite drinks. Nevertheless, it has apparently an increasing trade, both domestic and for export. The grapes are crushed and the must extracted in exactly the same way as for wine, but fermentation is stopped by refrigeration, and the resulting grape-juice is filtered and sold as a delicious, natural sweet drink in vast quantities – millions of litres from the Bodegas Palacio alone.

The wine made here is all from the grapes of the Rioja Alvesa, and entirely from their own vineyards and those of their employees who have a few vines of their own; and this is very unusual. These grapes are exclusively used for the making of wine, while the brought-in grapes are made into *mosto*. The company owns something like a hundred hectares of vines, which – under the new system of cultivation, using tractors instead of mules – maintain much fewer vines per hectare than they used to do. In the old days, 2,500 to 3,000 vines to the hectare was quite usual, and now it is between 1,500 and 2,000. These vines will produce 2–3 kilos of grapes in an average year, and 23 kilos of grapes will make one quintale or 16 litres of wine, so if you are good at arithmetic you can work out how much wine this very well run company of bodegas can make.

Here delicious *entremeses* were spread out on a table in the shade, and a bottle of 30-year-old wine and other wines laid out for tasting. The *marques* of which they feel particularly proud are, as regards white wines, 'Regio', which is sweet and contains Moscatel grapes, though not too many (I found the wine very clean and attractive and by no means cloying to the palate), and 'Semillon', which has nothing to do with the grape of that name and is an extremely dry white wine, by all means to be recommended. The red wines are the 'Glorioso' – a clean, light wine with a faint, rather fragrant nose and a light colour; and their 'Reserva Especial', which is the same wine only older. Both the white and the red wines are of about 12° to 12½° alcohol. I was given to drink two wines from the private cellar, a *vino blanco seco*, of the same quality as the 'Semillon', that was 30 years old, and had been 25 years in bottle. This wine was very little darker than the three-year-old wine I had just tasted; it was dry and full-bodied, with a faintly *maderisé* nose, and a first-class wine, but how I longed for that little touch of magic one finds in a Montrachet of good lineage! But it was not there. And yet I am continually surprised at the great age to which these white wines of the Rioja live. To match this beautiful white wine, an equally old bottle (exact age unknown) of the 'Reserva Especial' was produced. In this case there was little of the dry after-taste, and the wine was darker, absolutely clean, and old beyond question, but with no sign of decay or deterioration.

A few hundred yards up the road from the Bodegas Palacio, you leave the car and enter this old walled hill town, once a favourite resort of the medieval kings of Navarre, and now, with Venice, one of the few places remaining on this earth where the motor-car is not allowed to enter. The vines encircle the hill and come up to the walls; inside, the only sound, apart from the cheerful chattering of children, is the rumbling of the wine-casks as they are trundled through the narrow, balconied streets and through one of the six main gates of the town to the waiting *camiones*. One can walk right round the walls, and the view from almost any part, and especially from the little bandstand to the north, is absolutely marvellous. Everywhere the vineyards spread over the low hill, but never more than a hectare or so before the vines are intermixed with other crops.

The kings of Navarre maintained a castle here, and, although all that remains is a twelfth-century tower, which is now being restored, there are many of the large houses or small palaces where their court used to live. Laguardia is entirely devoted to wine; it reminds me of that other walled town of about the same size, Riquewihr in Alsace, where the whole town is occupied in wine-making; but you can drive around Rique-wihr, and it has lost much of its charm thereby, wonderful though it is. In Laguardia none of this happens. As you walk through the narrow streets, you can see, about 6 inches from the bottom of every house, or at least every other one, a little hole in the wall; it is through this little hole that the wine is pumped up from the vats in the bodegas, where they were cut in the solid rock under the town, into the casks before being trundled out through the gates to the waiting trucks.

I entered one of these bodegas under a house, passing first through a medieval iron-studded door into a small patio with patterned cobbles, very redolent of the mule that undoubtedly quartered there at night, and then deep down into the bodega itself. There, in two long narrow cellars, I counted 12 enormous barrel-shaped vats, each holding 5,000 litres. These huge vats are of such a size that they could quite obviously not be brought in through the door and down the steep stairs; they must have been brought in stave by stave and hoop by hoop and coopered in the actual bodega. Once in position they will make wine for a few hundred years. But even here, in this little bodega in Laguardia, the owner has his private *cementerio* at the end of the cellar, where he keeps half a dozen or so bottles of the wine of each year; they go back quite a long way, and I expect they are kept for the great occasions – births, marriages and deaths.

Here the general practice is to tread the grapes as they have been trodden for the last thousand years or more; and, while I was unfortunate in that the vintage had not yet started, the vats were ready and the *comportas* had been washed and everything was being prepared for the harvest. These dim bodegas, with their wealth of good wine, have to be seen to be believed. I am told that the whole hill is honeycombed with them, and certainly, in this little town, where there is no danger of being run down by a car or having one's nerves shattered by the roar of an unsilenced motor-scooter, I can conceive that some remains of tranquillity in life may be preserved here for a little time yet.

The wine of Laguardia – well, it is not a 'Marqués de Riscal', but it is damned good, and I wish I had a barrel of it on its way to me now. It is usually sold quite young; that is, within two years of its being made. It usually goes to Bilbao, whence the brokers and wine-merchants come out and buy. It has a delicious, fresh, young virility that reminds one of that rarity, an honest Beaujolais when drunk at the *chais*. It also has much the same integrity and touch of sharpness. Whether it would travel or not I do not know, but I shall contrive to find out.

Apart from the delicious wine of Laguardia, the town itself is interesting architecturally, with two very splendid medieval and Renaissance churches like small cathedrals; the town itself is unspoilt, essentially lived in, and a small edition of Ávila or Aigues Mortes, with a bursting prosperity of its own within its medieval walls and houses – and, don't forget, no motor-cars.

I lunched in Logroño, where Franco Espagnol produces 'Viña Sole', a good wine, dry and sharp. After that I visited the village of Fuenmayor in the Rioja Alta, and received a welcome at Bodegas Las Veras from Señor Cruz Carcia Lafuente, who is 83 years old and the shepherd of his flock. He is called the shepherd because he started his working life as a shepherd-boy at the age of 11. So far as I can see, he now owns a large part of the Rioja, and he certainly controls one of the three large bodegas in Fuenmayor. During this time he has fathered a flock of 14 children; he is a firm believer in the beneficial effect of Riojan wines.

We were shown wines of the three large bodegas in the area, Bodegas Las Veras, Bodegas del Romeral and Bodegas Entrena; and, while the wines varied slightly, they were all of a good quality and made from grapes of all the three districts of the Rioja, but mostly from the Rioja Alavesa and the Rioja Baja, these latter because of their high alcoholic content. The first fermentation takes place in cement vats, and the must is moved after 10 or 12 days to similar vats for the secondary fermentation, and then put into wood for the second year and for a further two or three years, after which it is either sold, mostly in barrel, or bottled. Bodegas Las Veras is a very big concern indeed, dispatching between 100,000 and 120,000 litres every day and keeping something like 20,000,000 litres of wine in stock, maturing in the vast bodegas. Belgium and Switzerland are its chief markets, and more wine is exported than is sold domestically – which is rather a rare condition. I was given to drink two kinds of 'Reserva Especial', one white and one red, and both bearing the date 1956 on the label, which I assume to be a *reserva* date; but both wines were of excellent Rioja quality. I was also given a five-year-old 'Viña Tera', which is a comparatively cheap wine; however, I found it smooth to the palate and with a minimum of tannin. A long day finished in the Rioja, and it was dark when I said good-bye to the shepherd before returning to Logroño.

The two best known wines of the Rioja are without doubt the 'Marqueses' made by the two bodegas, one of which is owned by the Marqués de Riscal and the other by the Marqués de Murrieta. These bodegas, although quite a long way away from each other (Riscal is in the Rioja Alavesa, and Murrieta is at Ygay, a few kilometres from Logroño, roughly where the three Riojas meet), have certain methods in common that are unique in Spain. In these two bodegas, and also, incidentally, in that of López de Heredia, you find something approaching *château*-bottling.

The wines of both these great bodegas are made partly from their own grapes, but also largely from carefully selected grapes brought in and made into wine at the bodega. The grapes are carefully pressed; they are fermented in oak vats, and they receive their secondary fermentation in barrels, where they are racked three times in the first year, and so on. Now, there is a difference, for they are not necessarily bottled at the same time; and, although in the case of Riscal the cork is branded with the name of the bodega and the date, and the wine is always of that date, at Murrieta the corks are not so branded, but the date is printed on the label, and it is a true date (the year, however, as I have remarked before, is not so important). Riscal makes, for all practical purposes, only two red wines and markets them in two qualities, at six years old and older. The bodega produces a very tiny amount of white wine, rather as Château Margaux does in the Médoc. Murrieta makes three red and three white wines, but I must emphasize that the wine that is made in these two world famous bodegas approximates most to the great wine-making *châteaux* of Bordeaux and the Côte d'Or. As to which is the better wine of the two, in the absence of any great difference in the years – well, who shall say whether Ahmed's beard or Mahmound's was the longer? No doubt they have their ideas, but I found it hard to choose.

The bodega of the Marqués de Riscal at Elciego is interesting in that it is divided by the main road; not a very big main road, admittedly, but still a road. The Marqués de Riscal claims by some ancient law to have the right of way between one side of his bodega and the other, so that the barrels can be trundled across in safety – and woe betide an unfortunate motorist who hits a man trundling a barrel to the hurt of the man or the loss of the barrel. I gather that this right of way has not yet been contested, and to make sure of the matter there is an aged pensioner on duty who controls the proceedings. The bodegas themselves are very much like so many middle-sized French Bordeaux *châteaux*, but (and I mean no bad reflection when I say this) they are not so highly finished. The *chais* in France is usually a spacious affair, with polished barrels inside for fermentation; not so in the usual Spanish bodega, including Riscal. The barrels in it hold excellent wine, but superficially there are plenty of cobwebs – though I'm sure the wine is not a whit the worse for this. At the back of the bodega there is a private cellar of the wines of Marqués de Riscal, where, as in Mouton Rothschild and Latour in Bordeaux, wines have been kept from every vintage since, I believe, 1862. This is very impressive, and I imagine most of them are still drinkable, for the lasting qualities of these Rioja wines are extraordinary. I was given to taste the 'Marqués de Riscal' 1961, which was excellent, and a bottle of 1946 was decanted from the private cellar. This was all one could expect of a twenty-year-old wine, rich red, and having thrown an absolute minimum of crust that hardly clouded the last inch of the bottle.

I should like to have met the Marqués of Riscal to discuss his wines, but, although he was in, he was not receiving. Nevertheless, one of his men showed me around, and after all I came to look at the wine.

The bodega of the Marqués de Murrieta at Ygay is also rather like a French *château*, but the atmosphere is different from that of Riscal, with an extremely friendly welcome from the resident director who showed me around the *bodega de elaboración* with considerable pride. I could form no opinion as to which of the two marquises produced the more wine; but, of course, Murrieta makes some excellent white wines, and most of the wine, but not quite all, is made from his own grapes. The *tinto* grapes are the Tempranillo and the Mazuela, with very little Graciano and as little as possible Garnacha; the white wine is mostly made from the Viura grape, with a little Malvasía. Wine is not kept in bottle here, and, although it is shipped as the wine of a certain year, it is kept in wood until it is required. In addition to the red and white, they make a little *rosado* too. The red wines, which I think are the chief glory of this vineyard, come in three classes: 'Marqués de Murrieta' *tinto*; 'Marqués de Murrieta Reserva Especial', which is a much older wine; and the 'Castillo Ygay', which is the *marque* for the Marqués de Murrieta's very old wine. I was given to taste the 1942 'Castillo Ygay', both *blanco* and *tinto*; they were both quite excellent, and I leave it at that merely because I have run out of superlatives. I can only suggest that you should call and taste for yourself, and I am sure you will get the same friendly reception that I did.

Obviously it was impossible for me to visit all the great bodegas of the large Rioja area, and I feel an apology is due to those whom I have been unable to report on. I have, however, tasted wines from many of these bodegas, and they are all uniformly good; some are excellent.

# CHAPTER FIVE

# The Wines of La Mancha and Valdepeñas

THE WINE-growing district of La Mancha is situated in four provinces – Toledo, Albacete, Cuenca and Ciudad Real; Valdepeñas is in this last province. La Mancha, which is to Spanish wine-growing largely what the Midi is to France, supplies most of Spain with the sound, cheap wine sold in its wine-shops, straight from the barrel at about eight pesetas a litre, as you bring your own bottle; this corresponds roughly to sevenpence or eight cents for an average English bottle of about one and a third pints. Thus, this excellent wine is brought within the reach of all, for the benefit of mankind in general, and in particular of those people lucky enough to live in Spain.

The annual output of La Mancha is 800,000,000 litres, and 75% of it or more is sold on the domestic market. The name La Mancha is derived from the Moorish *marzo*, which means 'dry land'; and this plain is very suitable for the cultivation of vines because the strong summer sun favours the ripening of the grapes. La Mancha wines, in common with other wines in Spain and especially the Rioja, gained considerably from the phylloxera scourge that all but wiped out French vineyards in the last two or three decades of the nineteenth century. To keep the trade going, the French imported vast quantities of wine from Spain, and especially from La Mancha, where the wine was suitable for blending with the native French wines, and was perfectly honest, clean wine to boot. With the end of phylloxera and the importation of immune stocks from America, this trade tended to drop; but by that time the Spanish wine-merchants of Valdepeñas had learnt a thing or two and had created and developed markets of their own. They, in turn, were treated to a dose of phylloxera, but Valdepeñas suffered least of all, and there are still pre-phylloxera vine-stocks growing there.

Good sound wine is made throughout the whole area of La Mancha, and it is made in the overall average quality of the wine, except that certain areas specialize in quantity rather than quality, and the rougher wines are distilled into alcohol and are not sold for table consumption. The best wine – although you might have some difficulty in persuading the vintners of Toledo, Albacete and Cuenca about this – is centred in the town of Valdepeñas, which boasts 30,000 inhabitants and around 400 bodegas large, small and medium. In Spain, Valdepeñas is synonymous with wine, and, like Jerez, the whole town is born, is married and dies with the smell of the grape in its nostrils. Bodegas or at least a bodega can be found in every street, and through the heavy double doors, with the graceful wrought-iron lunettes over them, can be seen the cool, whitewashed courtyard and sometimes great *atrojes*, which are the cages into which the crushed grapes are poured, and in which they are pressed under their own weight before the juice starts its journey to one of the dozens of clay *tinajas*.

La Mancha is the ancient world of Don Quixote, and there is still a substantial – but, alas! declining – trade in those wines that are contained in *pellejos*, or wine-skins made from a single skin of the pig and still in the same form. The wine can be kept for long periods in these skins, and the connoisseurs of the wine-shops in Madrid prefer it that way. The *pellejos* hold between 100 and 125 litres of wine. And very odd they look.

Valdepeñas produces no great or even fine wines, and does not try to compete with the Rioja, for instance, where great pride is taken in its ageing and some care in its making. Your bodega-owner in Valdepeñas is slightly contemptuous of the whole proceeding; to him wine must be well made, from sound grapes, sold quickly and drunk fresh. Valdepeñas can be ready to drink, clear and bright, in three or four months, but this is unusual. Normally the wine is sold from its original fermenting clay *tinaja* round about the spring following the vintage. It is simply pumped out of the *tinaja*, filtered (sometimes) and then poured straight into either a *bocoy* (barrel of 800 litres) or a *barrica* (hogshead of 225 litres). Sometimes it is bottled into a *garrafa* of 16 litres, which is a wicker-covered glass jar; it also comes in a small size of 4 litres only. Thus the wine travels in vast quantities to Madrid and Spain generally and in small quantities abroad. We can best examine the process from the beginning.

The vineyards of La Mancha start around the mountains of Toledo in the north of the district where they adorn the mountains; and they cover the landscape in the centre of the plains around Ciudad Real, Manzanares and Valdepeñas, where the country is flat, with occasional low hills. The otherwise rather dull landscape is made much more attractive by these vineyards, which get larger as Valdepeñas is approached, until, in the town itself, the vineyards reach to its very walls on every side. The soil is correspondingly rich, although it varies somewhat and is of a lovely chestnut colour. It is ploughed and levelled, and each vine is planted in its own square of 80 centimetres and cultivated to a depth of 45 centimetres, thus making a pocket of loose soil that will retain the moisture. The soil and the vines demand a good deal of rain, which is usual in this part of Spain during the winter, and the size of the grape will depend largely upon the rainfall.

A total of 1,500 vines is thus planted in a hectare, and each vine should, in an average year, produce about 3 kilos of sound grapes. There are four main types of grapes grown, two white and two black. The white grapes, making the *vino de mesa blanco*, are the Airen, the principal grape grown in the Valdepeñas district, and the Vidoncha, which is more prolific and produces a large quantity of wine of an indifferent quality; this is often sold for distillation into alcohol. The black grapes, which make the *tintos*, are the Cencibel, in the Valdepeñas district, and the Garnacha, in other districts.

The vintage begins about the end of September, and, as I write this on 21 September, the first load of white grapes is just coming into the Bodegas Morenito under the keen eye of its owner, Señor Don Gerardo Sánchez. After being weighed, they are fed into the machine that removes the stalks; the crushed grapes are pumped up into the *atrojes*, which will contain, when full, 28,000 kilos of crushed grapes, and will soon be spurting the grape-juice through their slatted sides. After as much juice as possible has been squeezed out of the grapes by the colossal weight of those above them, the remainder of the husks will be put into wine-presses for a second and mechanical pressing, after which the dehydrated husks, which are dry indeed by the time they have had their second pressing, are consigned to an enormous pit; thence they are carried away for distillation into some form of alcohol. In Valdepeñas, and in Spain generally, the bodega-owner will not make his own *marc* or *eau-de-vie* as in France – and no great loss at that, for some of the liquid razor-blades distilled by the French peasant do not make the kind of liquid with which one should insult one's stomach.

The grape-juice is then pumped into the *tinaja* awaiting it. These *tinajas* stand in long, cool rows often below ground level. They are shaped like great Ali Baba jars, and they may contain anything from 3,000 to 12,000 litres. They are truly great works of potters' art, and, while they are being replaced to some extent by cement and glass-lined vats, they are still in general use and are likely to remain so, for most of the Valdepeñans consider, and I think probably rightly, that the best wine is made in the clay vessels. The *tinaja*, so much a feature of the wine of La Mancha, is built, rather than turned, by a man inside it, until it reaches shoulder height, when the top is put on and the whole 'welded' together, after which the potter climbs out of the hole in the top. Many of these splendid pots are of considerable age; some have passed their three score years and ten. When, by reason of their great strength, they achieve four score years or more, they tend to break suddenly (usually during the night, I am told), and if they happen to be full of wine, as they sometimes are, it makes a bad day for the owner of the bodega, who is welcomed on his arrival by a place swimming with wine; he has to buy a new *tinaja*, which in these days costs something like 7,000 or 8,000 pesetas. The wine, by the way, is scooped up off the floor with maledictions and sent to a distillery – at any rate, it isn't wasted. When the new *tinaja* arrives, it is erected in the place of the old one, and the bung-holes are then drilled out in the right position, and it is ready for immediate action.

Here the wine goes through its first boisterous fermentation, which can last as long as a month or more. It is not moved to storage-vats for its second fermentation, but is left in the *tinaja*; the sludge sinks to the bottom, and within a few weeks the wine becomes perfectly bright and clear. It is interesting to walk along the gallery at the top of these huge pots. Their mouths are covered by what appear to be conical straw hats. When one of these is removed you can see the wine lapping the brim. It is crystal clear and very drinkable.

Valdepeñas *tinto* has none of the dark colour of most Spanish *tintos*; it is more of a *rosé* wine than red. The *tintos* are made from both white and black grapes, in the approximate proportion of 35 kilos of black grapes to 105 kilos of white. It is only in the case of *rosé*, or *rosado*, wines, which are much paler and start life in exactly the same way as the *tintos*, that the wine is siphoned off after only 15 days of fermentation into another *tinaja*, leaving behind in the original pot the black grape-skins that give the wine its colour, before fermentation has finally dissolved the colour pigment in the skins.

The white wines vary in colour considerably, from the very pale colour of the French or German white wines to the more usual richer gold of the true Valdepeñas. The colour does not denote any change in quality; neither is the wine necessarily finer for being pale. In so far as there is a regulator in the making of the wine, the colouring is controlled largely by the amount of grape-skins that are left in the wine for fermentation.

Beyond this, nothing much happens; and, as we have seen, the vinification process is simple indeed. As one bodega-owner said to me, 'We are famous here for not knowing anything about oenology – the wine makes itself'. The whole process can be summed up as follows. The grape-juice is put into the *tinajas*, where it receives its first and secondary fermentations, and it is drawn off through a bung-hole about 18 inches from the bottom of the *tinaja*, leaving the sludge under the bung-hole; the less pure elements are removed from an even lower bung-hole and sent away for distillation into alcohol. Thereafter a man will descend into this vast pot and clean it out ready for the next vintage.

One of the more important virtues of this excellent wine is its lasting property, which is remarkable when you consider how young the wines are at the time of sale. I travelled in Spain extensively in 1950, and it was then that I enjoyed my first Spanish wine; I brought home with me a bottle of Valdepeñas wine, among a few other kinds, and put it in my cellar with various white wines to see if the Valdepeñas did, in fact, travel well. The other wines were all consumed over the years, and they were all good; but the Valdepeñas was overlooked, and I discovered it only in the summer of 1965, when it had been in my cellar for no fewer than 15 years. I produced it at lunch with a Spanish wine-shipper, and it was excellent and had not only kept perfectly but had even improved. Valdepeñas wines have a faint earthy tang, which I personally rather enjoy, but this had gone from the 15-year-old wine, and its excellence had all the dignity of age.

Generally speaking, most of the bodegas keep a few old wines that they refresh under a simple kind of solera system, similar to that used with sherry, but they attach no importance to it and keep the wines merely as interesting exhibits or for their own consumption, and they are not for sale. At the Bodegas Morenito I was given a solera wine of this type, which started as a straight white Valdepeñas 40 years ago, but is now golden brown and has developed strong Madeira characteristics; certainly it is nothing like an ordinary Valdepeñas. The white wine from a 1901 solera that I was given at the Bodegas Bilbainas was a very strong wine indeed and not altogether to my taste. It had a very pleasant 'woody' character, however, and indeed tasted like old sherry. I believe that this is sold in small quantities as an *elaboración especial*. Apparently you have to ask for it to get it, although the solera is quite large.

Bodegas Bilbainas also make other types of wine from varieties of natural Valdepeñas. This is unusual, though, and very few bodegas indulge in this kind of vinous exercise, which is not always successful. Among the types of wine that I saw in this large bodega was a *mistela*, which is luscious and sweet, rather like a muscatel with its grape flavour; it is made by the addition of a small quantity of brandy to stop fermentation after 15 days, before the sugar has been completely broken down. At this bodega they also make altar wine, which is pale and has to be filtered and be of absolute purity in order to satisfy the exacting requirements of the Church authorities. Another by-product is a rather special vermouth, which is not unpleasant and has considerable character, of the Italian rather than the French type. These wines must be and often are made at any bodega; but, as I have said, most of the Valdepeñans stick to making their extremely simple but good wines without bothering about refinements or developments of them.

The wine of La Mancha is made in a completely natural way, and, although there are no official regulations forbidding *chaptalisation*, no sugar is added to assist the wine. The natural wine of Valdepeñas and La Mancha generally has a vinosity of 13°–13½° of alcohol in the white wines, and 13½°–14° in the *tintos*: this, of course, constitutes quite a heady wine and is much stronger than the *ordinaires* of the Midi, which vary between 9° and 11°. It is the *vino tipico* of Madrid, and, even at the best restaurants, if you order a jug of wine with your dinner, say at Botin, you are almost certain to get the best Valdepeñas. And very good it is.

When in Valdepeñas I visited two of the larger bodegas and one of the very smallest. The two larger were Bodegas Morenito owned by Señor Don Gerardo Sánchez and

Bodegas Bilbaines of Señor Don Joaquín Ugarte. In point of fact, Morenito owned two large bodegas with over 400 *tinajas* – indeed an impressive sight. Bilbainas again have a large bodega here, with the air of having been at one time even larger, although it is prosperous today. The distillery there has a tall factory-like chimney with a stork's nest on the top. Upon enquiring what they did about the storks when they lit the fire, I was informed that, since it meant disturbing the storks, they had decided to give up distillation in Valdepeñas, and they no longer made any brandy or liqueurs there. But I don't think they ever made much brandy, and they must have decided in any case to give it up.

The small bodega owned by Señor Don Hilario de la Torre was remarkable. Señor de la Torre is a small farmer, and in one courtyard, which I paced out at 40 feet square (leading off it is his bodega with its *tinajas*), he has his wine-press, and, at the time that I was there, 10 excellent cows, one of which yielded 30 litres of milk a day, and a day-old calf. It was all rather crowded, but the glass of last year's wine I was shown was certainly equal to any Valdepeñas I had drunk. Señor de la Torre has his own vineyard, and he grows enough grapes to make 48,000 litres of this excellent *vino blanco*. There are dozens of other bodegas of this size, and hundreds bigger, all over this quiet town with heavily grilled windows. But the quietude departs for a few days at the time of the vintage, when the tumbrils and *camiones* laden with grapes rumble through the streets on the way to their owner's or some other factor's bodega to be made into wine.

After Valdepeñas a great deal of these good wines are made at El Tomelloso, which is a town of 30,000 people living almost exclusively from wine and its derivatives, including a brandy for which they are particularly noted. Manzanares (which is only 26 kilometres from Valdepeñas), Alcazar de San Juan, Cinco Casas and Daimiel are also noted wine-producing centres. The wine is sometimes marketed under a particular vineyard label, but it is never dated as that of a given year, because there isn't all that much difference between one year and another. There are, of course, a few wines sold with a vineyard label, and some even with the date; but your bodega-owner of Valdepeñas laughs at this, and, as one told me, 'If you see a bottle of Valdepeñas with the date on it, you need not necessarily believe it – nobody in Valdepeñas would'.

CHAPTER SIX

# The Wines of Málaga

MÁLAGA used to be much drunk in England in the days when rich, fruity wines were in favour. It was also sometimes called 'Mountain', because the grapes are grown and some of the wine itself is made in the mountainous country behind Málaga. It is a very large area indeed, ranging as far as Antequera in the north, but most of the vineyards are to be found in the neighbourhood of the Sierra de Almijara.

The wines are without exception sweet, and, while the driest type called *seco* is not quite so sticky as tawny port, it is still on the sweet side, although very agreeable.

There is a considerable recorded history of Málaga grapes that goes back to Roman republican days; Columella, writing in 44 B.C., deals with them very fully and classifies them by cultivation, quality and even soil and specifies whether they were used for eating or for the making of wine. Most of the grapes in the Málaga district are in fact table grapes. Democritus, Pliny, and Virgil in his *Georgics* mention the excellence and diversity of the wine. There are also many records from Moorish sources, which is rather surprising in view of the fact that the drinking of wine was prohibited by Mohammed; the Koran has some extremely nasty things to say about wine-drinking in general, but the Moors sometimes managed to dodge the arm of the law. One writer refers to an old Moslem who, in his last hours, was exhorted by the Imam to ask the forgiveness of Allah for his sins, among which was his liking for wine; the dying man prayed, 'O Creator of all things, I implore you not to leave me in Paradise without Málaga wine'.

The Spanish chroniclers, after the liberation from the Moors, refer constantly to this wine, and Ruiz González de Clavijo, who visited the city of Málaga in May 1403, speaks of the Sierra de Málaga in very glowing terms; not the least of its attractions was the sight of mountains covered with vines and orchards. In the eighteenth century the Andalusian ambassador to Catherine the Great of Russia presented her with 48 cases of assorted Málaga wines, and that famous, or infamous, empress replied with a very enthusiastic letter saying that she was very fond of these wines of Spain, as she called them. In 1792 a priest, who thought it better to write under the *nom de plume* of Cecilio Garcia de la Lena, wrote a book dedicated to the 'Very Illustrious and Ancient Brotherhood of Málaga Vineyard Owners', and this included a complete list of the varieties of grapes grown and the wines made at that time; among the grapes were mentioned the famous Pedro Ximénez, Jaén Blanco, Almunecar, Moscatelon or Moscatel Flamenco (which Pliny called Apianas, because bees liked the fruit), Don Bueno, Cabriel, Casiles Albillas and Teta de Vaca. Of course the famous P.X. is still the favourite grape, and, with Moscatel, Jaén Blanco, Jaén Doradillo and Rome, it is still extensively used.

True Málaga is made from a mixture of these grapes and is rather more than half P.X., only 15% Moscatel, about 20% Lairén (which cuts the sweetness a little) and about 5% of other grapes.

Most of the wine of Málaga is made in the villages, but an ever increasing proportion is made from must that is collected from the presses and brought into Málaga in tankers and transferred into the enormous oak fermenting-vats, where it is kept for about a year before being filtered into oak butts; most of it is sold after a further period of one to three years, or blended for the old soleras that still exist.

In the villages, which are not seen easily from the coast road but lie off in the mountains to the west of the city, the presses are busy from about the end of August onwards; largely because of the mountainous terrain, the vineyards are invariably small, few being of more than 10 acres. My friend Harry Yoxall, to whom I am indebted for a great deal of information on Malaga wines, says in an excellent article in the *Wine and Food Journal* of a few years ago that there are something like 22,000 acres of vines in the *denominación de origen* area of Málaga (a figure unlikely to change greatly), but much of this area is for the cultivation of table grapes rather than for wine.

Under the guidance of Señor Ankersmit I visited the large bodega of Scholtz Hermanos, where the tankers of must had been received from the mountain vineyards and pumped into the enormous oak fermentation-vats, some of which hold as much as 20,000 gallons each, and of which there were perhaps a dozen or more. Over the years, the types of Málaga have become more or less standardized, and most of the big bodegas produce wine of corresponding quality, although some of them have one or two very old soleras, of which they are justly proud. The wine from these soleras is not sold, but is used for blending with the much younger wines to give them true character, which it certainly does. Yoxall mentions having been privileged to taste a 'Lágrima 1787', which runs to 17·4° of alcohol. I was myself given a 'Solera Scholtz 1874', which is really a delicious wine and quite free from the overpowering sweetness of an old P.X. solera. I cannot do better than to quote Yoxall where he describes the wine of these ancient soleras: 'There are interesting, almost surprising undertones beneath its unctuous richness, like the dark fires in the heart of a jewel'.

Málaga 'Lágrima' (*lágrima* in Spanish means a tear) is not to be confused with the Lacrima Cristi of Italy, which is a different wine altogether.

The different types of wine made in Málaga and sold as Málaga are as follows:

| | |
|---|---|
| *Negro* | Made mostly from P.X. grapes, and very dark indeed. |
| *Blanco dulce* | Golden brown to dark amber, and very sweet. |
| *Semidulce* | Rather lighter in colour, not quite so sweet, but sweet nevertheless. |
| *Oscuro* | A rich chestnut colour. |
| *Amontillado* | Made from Lairén grapes, medium dry and usually sold before its tenth year. |
| *'Lágrima'* | Very sweet and dark. |
| *Seco* | Rather similar, as I have said, to tawny port, but slightly drier and better to my taste; as an *apéritif* wine with a dry biscuit at eleven o'clock in the morning, it would equal what bank managers of yore are supposed to have offered their clients. |

There are many other variations on the same theme, but in general these are dessert wines of excellence, I think preferable to the sweet muscatels of France and Italy.

A certain amount of brandy, *anis*, gin and *ponche* (still in its silver bottle) is made in the Málaga district, and I was a little depressed to hear from Señor Ankersmit that the sale of spirits was expanding, although the sale of wine has tended to decline. To this, the tremendous development of the Costa del Sol, with its rash of tourist hotels and fantastic influx of international, spirit-drinking visitors from abroad, may have made some contribution. Be that as it may, I hope to see the situation reversed before I die. Casual visitors to Málaga, should they have time to visit a bodega, might do worse than to visit Garrijo; it has a deservedly busy long bar, in which every kind of Málaga wine and spirits is served straight from the wood at about two pesetas a glass.

The wines of Málaga are quite pure and without added alcohol; for this reason, apart from their other qualities, they have long been popular with the Church authorities as sacramental wines, which must be pure in every respect. This important trade is in the hands of two bodegas that work closely with the Church authorities. I have had my own experience of this, for, several years ago, I bought at an auction a lot of old wines among which were 'eight bottles believed to be altar wine'. None of the wine in the lot was later than 1900 (it included, I remember, some 1870 Château Margaux), and these eight bottles were indeed older; one of them still had a nineteenth-century label stating 'Finest altar wine guaranteed pure by the Most Reverend the Lord Bishop of Málaga' – which is exactly what it was, very old Málaga that, because of its great age, was no longer over-sweet and was absolutely delicious. I fear, however, that it did not reach the altar.

Having examined the bodega system in Málaga and drunk of the wines thereof, I decided to go up into the Sierra de Almijara and taste the wines in the area where most of the grapes are grown and where some of the wine is made. The road runs through El Palo, Cala del Moral and Torre del Mar, all of which towns are suffering from the *urbanización* that is making such an unhappy mark on the Costa del Sol. Turning off the main coastal road at La Caleta for 10 or 12 kilometres up into the mountains, the road runs at first through fields of sugar-cane, beans and similar market-garden crops, but soon the tarred surface gives up, and you are left with a comparatively narrow un-surfaced road, tying itself into knots around and through the foothills of the mountains. Vines now start to be grown abundantly; and everywhere, as far as the eye can reach, the tiny, immaculate white cottages of the small farmers can be seen going right to the top of the lower mountains. As the vineyards climb higher, the terraces get smaller, so that near the top they seem only 2 or 3 feet wide, yet all are perfectly cultivated; they reminded me a great deal of the Inca terrace system of cultivation in the High Andes, though, since the Incas terraced their hills long before the Spanish came, one supposes that this system of utilizing cultivable land is as old as civilization. I passed the village of Algarrobo, white in the sun, with tropical flowers growing abundantly up the sides of the houses, and in 6 kilometres of hair-raising driving came to the village of Sayalonga and drove into the main square, which was all of 50 feet from one side to the other, where the car was soon surrounded by interested and curious inhabitants.

Enquiries were then made as to whether there was a wine-press in the village, and I was courteously escorted to the village wine-shop and presented to Señor Don Rafael Alcoba, who is the owner of the best and largest vineyards in the village, amounting to some 20 hectares. I told him that I should like, if possible, to look at his bodega and see how he made his wine and to taste it. He expressed himself as being delighted to show me his bodega, and while we were talking I was given a glass of excellent 'Mountain', medium gold in colour, dryer than I had tasted in Málaga and delicious. I was assured that this had been made in the village, and the proprietor of the wine-shop said he was very much pleased to be able to demonstrate his excellent wine; he refused all payment. Don Rafael then led the way through this charming village with its up-and-down streets, fortunately unnavigable by motor-cars, the houses freshly painted and with flowers all over them and hanging across the streets everywhere.

The bodega proved to be, as I expected, quite a small one, making 300 *arrobas* (one *arroba* equals about 16 litres) of 'Mountain' in a good year. The grapes are gathered and include a preponderance of P.X.; so far as I could see, however, no effort was made to mix the grapes in any kind of proportion. Mixed they certainly were, but I would hardly call the mixture scientific. Yet the result seemed none the worse for it. The grapes are carried in on muleback and discharged into a treading-bin, where the wine is trampled out of them by foot; I was delighted and surprised to hear this. When there is nothing left but the skins, pips, stalks and so forth these go into a rather primitive press, with a layer of the residue covered first by a grass mat; then by another layer of residue; then by another mat; and then by a few more inches of residue. When the press is full, this gigantic sandwich of mat and residue is pressed and the remaining drops of juice are collected. The juice from the treading and the press flows into a sump, and from there it is taken out in buckets and poured into 300-litre oak *botas*, where it has its first fermentation, taking about 15 days, and then its secondary fermentation, after which it is racked into fresh *botas*. There it is kept for a year; then it is sold, or kept for another year and sold at a higher price. Don Rafael sells his wine to the wine-shops in Málaga, and I think most of the better wines made in the villages probably go the same way; but the bulk of the wine goes to the bodegas in Málaga, as we have seen. I was given to taste of the last year's vintage, and I found it, of its kind, excellent. Later I was privileged to try, at the owner's house, a glass of his older wine, which was even better, still rather sweet to my taste, but undoubtedly excellent 'Mountain'.

Continuing my tour, I passed through a small farmyard that adjoined Don Rafael's bodega; there half a dozen attractive young women were sorting and packing fat raisins. From the stacks of almond shells, I judged that that harvest had already been gathered in and was probably on its way to England. I was then escorted to the house of a neighbour, who owned a few vines and who made possibly one *bota* of wine, part of which he no doubt sold while he kept another part for his own consumption; and there he was, happy as a sandboy, with the must streaming freely from his *alpargatas de esparto*, treading his own grapes on his tiny treading-floor. Outside, on a sunny bank, the grapes were spread to dry in the sun; they alternated in rows, as those that would become raisins and those that were to be brought to the right degree of sweetness for wine. I counted at least five different sorts of grapes in the collection, both black and white; one was a large golden grape called Ojos del Rey (literally translated, this means 'eyes of the king'), which I for one had certainly never heard of before.

This is one of the springs that eventually make up the mighty river of Málaga wine flowing into that city; and the same operation must be going on at this time of writing all over that very wide area. I turned back to continue my travels, leaving Don Rafael with some considerable regret. He was a grave, courteous man who was having difficulty in finding help and was reducing the area of his vines, the trouble being, of course, the attraction to the bright lights and the prosperity that is being created by the tourist trade. Sayalonga was a town of about 1,400 souls, and, if 20 hectares is by far the largest holding, the average must be small indeed.

CHAPTER SEVEN

# The Wines of the Levante

A GREAT deal – in fact, an enormous quantity – of wine is made along the Levantine coast and for some great distance inland, being exported and distributed through the Levantine ports of Alicante, Almería, and Valencia. Nearly all these wines are simply made, honest wines, produced without any attempt at finesse, and they cater for quick and cheap consumption by those who like their wine heavy and, by comparison, sweet. Within this general classification, however, there are degrees, and now and again one comes across some excellent wine that is worthy of comparison with some of the finer wines made in Spain. Levante wines are mostly red, but a good deal of ordinary white wine is made in the Alicante district and is sometimes blended into better quality wines. The alcoholic content ranges from 13° to 16°, and higher if the wine is allowed to age. They are all good table wines, if somewhat coarse by certain standards, but with none of the roughness that is associated with common wines from other Mediterranean countries. A good example is Benicarló, a dark, rich red wine from Castellón de la Plana.

The wines of Murcia are mostly produced in a long valley, where the two wine-making centres are the towns of Jumilla and Yecla, in which most of the bodegas are situated. However, the vines are grown for a long way on both sides of these towns. They are right at the north of the province of Murcia, and, in fact, the vine-belt continues a considerable way into the province of Valencia; but the wines there, although similar, are slightly different in character and somewhat drier. The road to Jumilla from Murcia is rather devious and constitutes a most delightful drive, even if it is hard on the springs, at 800 metres (about 2,500 feet) above sea-level. The wines made here are all *tintos*, from the Morastrell grape, which has some affinity with the Pinot noir of France, in that the grapes are small and are formed in tightly packed bunches, clustered around the main trunk of the vine. Wine-grapes, and indeed all fruits, are grown in profusion in this valley, and a great many table grapes are grown here too, but they are grown on a somewhat different system, the vine being formed into a long trunk rather like that of a standard rose in England; the leaves are suspended on a wire framework so that the grapes hang down from underneath. The wine-grapes are grown in the conventional Spanish style, with roughly 1,500 vines to the hectare, and are pruned to five or six shoots.

The grapes are not made into wine by the growers, but are sold to bodegas in Jumilla or Yecla. One the way to Jumilla I stopped at an *estancia* belonging to Señor Don Jesús García, and was informed that the vintage had begun and he was busy at his bodega in Jumilla. To this I duly presented myself; I was courteously shown over it by Señor García's son, and was given some of these good Jumilla wines to taste. As in Valdepeñas, the grapes, having been cleared of their stalks, are smashed and pumped into very big cement primary-fermentation-vats, after which time the must is pumped into underground vats to complete its tumultuous fermentation, which takes a further seven or eight days. When the first fermentation is complete the resulting wine is pumped into a large number of storage-vats in an adjoining bodega, where it remains for three months, after which it is filtered and is ready for selling, although usually the wines are not sold for some seasons after that. I was given a Murcian wine from the 1964 vintage; it contained about 16° alcohol. I found it good, but obviously strong and rather sweet; a little cloying to the taste, in fact. It appeared to have little tannin in it. These were clearly honest, well-made wines, but, as might be expected, they lacked any kind of delicacy. I was also given a wine that was seven years old; it had 18° alcohol and was somewhat drier with age, having lost none of its essential character.

Most of the Murcian wines are of this sort, but in Alicante a great quantity of rich, sweet wine is made from the Moscatel, Malvasía and Garnacha grapes, mostly the first; and it has the usual character of muscatel wines in that it tastes of the grape and it has a very high alcohol content. There is a further type of wine grown in Alicante called

'Fondillon', which is normally not sold until it is 10 years old; it is limited in quantity and fetches a higher price than the other wines of the region. The best Alicante wines are grown in the valley of Vinalope, which produces excellent table wines, mostly *rosados* but including a few *tintos* and *blancos*. The *rosados* and *tintos* contain 13°–16° of alcohol.

In Valencia, where the coastal plain is extremely fruitful and rich, a much larger variety of vines is cultivated. As well as the Morastrell, which I have already described, the Morenilla, Malvasía, Moscatel, Bobal, Garnacha and our old friend Pedro Ximénez produce between them a great number of wines, but they are all of the same basic character and include red, white and *rosado* wines. The vintage varies somewhat according to the grape grown; it can start as early as late July and can go on until early November. In Requena, one of the towns in this province, are made wines containing as little as 9° of alcohol, whereas some of the wines produced in the region of Liria contain up to 18°. The *tintos* vary in colour from those that are little darker than *rosados* to a wine called 'Carlón', which is almost black and, though a high-grade wine, is very thick and is largely used for blending with lighter wines to give them body.

Valencia wines also include sweet dessert wines made from the Moscatal and Pedro Ximénez grapes, and here again they reach a very high degree of alcohol – as high as 23° in certain cases. Valencia exports more wine than any other province in Spain. Most of it goes to Switzerland and Germany; I do not know what happens to it when it gets there, but the figures speak for themselves. The importance of the export market of Valencia wines can be judged by the fact that even seven years ago, when Spanish wines were not widely known, a total quantity of 864,546 hectolitres was exported, mostly in bulk to Germany, Switzerland, Belgium and Denmark.

## CHAPTER EIGHT

# The Wines of Catalonia

In THE province of Tarragona two kinds of wine are made. One is a sweetish, heavy wine called simply Tarragona; a special variety of this is known as the Priorato. The other consists of a group of excellent clean table wines made throughout the very large Tarragona district. Priorato is a *denominación de origen* in its own right; its district, a small island within the *denominación de origen* area of Tarragona, comprises a series of small foothills to the mountains of volcanic origin, in contrast with the much larger area and better soil of the Tarragona district proper.

Tarragona has had in England what we should call, in today's parlance, a bad press or a bad public image, owing to the fact that, for some decades at the end of the last century and up to the time of the First World War, Tarragona wine was imported in vast quantities and sold in public houses, largely for consumption by the ladies, at a penny or two a glass, on the general principle of 'drunk for a penny and dead drunk for twopence'. It was known as the poor man's port or, more colloquially, as Red Biddy, and it was a ferocious liquid, made from concentrated must and with an alcoholic content of 25° or 30°. Fortunately the taxes imposed on wines with a high alcoholic content successfully put paid to Red Biddy, which had little to commend it either as a wine or a habit, but the present result is that Tarragona wine has an undeservedly bad reputation, and this prejudices the general sale of Tarragona wine in Great Britain, except to the connoisseurs who know that the modern Tarragona has nothing in common with its infamous predecessor. Just how this prejudice can be overcome I do not know, for, although the present generation has probably never heard of its ill reputation, the memory of those in the wine trade is long – and, after all, they are the people who buy the wine in the first place. If anything can be said for public relations, this might well be a job that it could and ought to tackle. The result of it all has been that Tarragona bodegas have more and more been compelled, for the export of their wines, to try to match the popular French types, which they do, but only up to a point. The trouble is that, in matching somebody else's wine, the tendency is to lose the essential character of one's own, and this I find to be happening particularly in Tarragona. The pure Tarragona wines have tremendous character, and, although Priorato is a special district within Tarragona, I propose to start with these wines as having a quite fantastic character that is unique in Spanish viniculture.

The name Priorato comes from the priory of an old Carthusian monastery, now in ruins, that already existed in the fifteenth century, called Scala Dei, situated on the slopes of the Sierra de Montsant ('Holy Mountain'); a good number of villages near by depended on the priory. Lava in the soil here produces wines of very high alcoholic content, as it generally does elsewhere – for instance, on the slopes of Mount Etna in Sicily. Priorato has an extremely pleasant and, indeed, beautiful terrain; as usual, the vines of the Garnacha variety that are grown here produce fruit containing a very high proportion of sugar; it is also of superb quality. The vines are not particularly prolific, with 2 or 3 kilos of grapes per vine, as against some of the vineyards on the coastal plain, where, I am told, some of the vines produce as much as 8–10 kilos, and make correspondingly ordinary wine. Priorato, is, however, quite different, and the vines there make two varieties of wine. The first is a dry wine, which is completely natural when the fermentation has been allowed to take its full course. It is as black as your hat, and of such extreme dryness that it cannot be drunk with any pleasure, but it has an alcoholic content of up to 18° after fermentation; it is the perfect vehicle for giving body in the blending of other wines, and it is used almost exclusively for this purpose. With the sweet wines of Priorato, fermentation is cut at a fairly early stage by the addition of alcohol, which produces superb dessert wines with an alcoholic content of between 14° and 22°, and so 'thick' that the wine sticks to the glass. I must say that they taste a lot better than I have made them sound, as I find upon re-reading what I have just written.

In addition to these two, the dry and sweet wines, Priorato also produces large quantities of *mistela* (must in which the fermentation never starts, because it is stopped at birth); the resulting grape-juice, rightly so-called, is clarified, stored and sold for blending and for cutting down the alcoholic strength of some of the stronger wines elsewhere in Spain and abroad, and to give them some character, which it most certainly does.

Until quite recently, the ageing of the wines was sometimes accelerated by bottling into *bombonas*, which are glass bottles holding about 30 litres and shaped rather like so many pears. This sounds extraordinary and looks extraordinary, but so they are. They were laid out in fields for about a couple of years, exposed to Mediterranean heat in summer and to the mild winter rains. It is necessarily an expensive way of doing things, and it is by now largely discontinued in this region, but I shall describe this method more when we come to the wines of Panadés, where it is still used. So much for the unique wine of Priorato, with its little vineyards and their great big wines.

Vines are grown all over the region of Tarragona; they start somewhere south in the mountainous district of Gandesa and reach to the Panadés region in the north. The wines are made in the village co-operatives, and are brought to the twin towns of Reus and Tarragona (which are of about equal size, having each perhaps 50,000 inhabitants), where lie the bodegas, large and small, in which the wines are stored and blended. I have visited two of these village co-operatives, in Valls and Santas Creus; each makes about 2,500,000 litres of wine in an average year. In the old days the vineyard-owners made their own wine; but this no longer happens. There might be an occasional farmer who gathers his grapes and treads his wine, but this is now a rare practice.

At the time of the vintage, in motoring between the villages of these lovely hills below the Sierra de Montsant, you see the farmers' carts being loaded with *portadores*, which are oval, open barrels into which the basketfuls of grapes from the pickers are tipped and crushed down until they are overflowing; and all along the road stretch vehicles of every size, from the small man's mule, with perhaps two or three *portadores*, to a tractor-drawn wagon full to the brim with grapes from the larger vineyards. They are on their way to their co-operative, and as you leave the villages you mix with further streams of laden vehicles coming in and of empty ones going out. Half-way between villages you begin to pass a similar stream going in to the next co-operative. When such a stream arrives at the co-operative *bodega de elaboración* each whole vehicle, including the mule or tractor, is weighed and a tally-check is given to the driver, together with a little wooden ball that has a number engraved on it. The vehicle is then taken across the yard to the receiving-bin, where the little ball is handed over with the grapes, which are discharged into the crushing-machine; at the same time the ball is put into a pipe, and it arrives simultaneously with a sample of the crushed juice in a miniature laboratory situated just under the crushing-machine. There assistants with saccharo-meter test the juice for sugar content, matching the number on the little ball, and the tally-check is then made out for the weight of the grapes, plus the actual Baumé content, and the owner will be paid at a fixed rate for his grapes, plus or minus so much according to their sugar content. All very simple and ingenious – and, I think, efficient. I found the whole process more than interesting.

These co-operative presses are enormous. In the Santas Creus co-operative the whole process is scientifically and carefully organized on two levels, in an enormous Piranesi-like building, with animated figures at the top shovelling in the grapes, and the monster mechanical presses squeezing out the juice at the rate of hundreds of gallons per hour (which seemed to me more like hundreds of gallons per minute), while at the other end of the press the residue of skins, pips, stalks and what have you is discharged like a continuous sausage of greeny-brown vegetation, which again is ejected into carefully arranged mechanical presses for a second pressing, and trampled down by bare-footed young men, with a further but smaller resulting stream of juice joining the main torrent running into the fermenting-vats from the lower level. In the case of Santas

Creus, the co-operative has a smaller press mainly for a better-quality red wine (most of the wine made in this district is white), but there the stalks are removed before pressing and sacked up and sent to a distillery. This is also what happens to the *orujo*, which is the residue of the pips, stalks and husks from the larger presses of the co-operative. In Spain there seems to be no attempt to make *marc* or *eau-de-vie* as in France. The grape-juice is pumped into underground fermenting-vats (which contain many thousands of litres of must); they are arranged in rows, and you can walk between them. The apertures are the size of manholes, and they are filled to the brim. The wine can be seen bubbling away in its first tumultuous fermentation; the floor of the bodega feels quite hot as you walk on it, and the atmosphere is heavy with the rich smell of fermenting must that pervades the whole building.

The wine goes through both stages of fermentation in these vats, and in the following spring it is usually sold to the owners of the bodegas in Tarragona or Reus, when there is a steady stream of brokers who bring in samples of the wine to the bodegas and arrange the contracts with the blenders. The minimum price, fixed by the Spanish Government, is based on a given figure per degree of alcohol per hectolitre; if trade is bad the co-operative remains assured of a market, for the Government will purchase the wine at that figure. In practice, however, this rarely happens, as the wine is of good quality, and I am told that there is never any difficulty about selling it a peseta or two above the minimum price. The bodega-owner in Tarragona or Reus must pay for half of the wine when he contracts to buy it, and for the remainder at given periods, but he must clear the wine from the co-operative in time for the next vintage.

I was able to visit three bodegas in Tarragona and Reus, of varying sizes. One belongs to Señor José Antonio López Bertrán, who claims that it is the most modern in Tarragona, as it may well be, for it gleams with stainless steel and produces an enormous quantity of wine of an equally gleaming sort, clean and bright and altogether suitable for his expanding export market all over the world.

Another bodega, in Reus and belonging to the well-named Amigó brothers, is rather more old-fashioned; the storage and blending are carried out in huge oak vats in a cob-webby bodega. Señor Don Juan Amigó, who is an anglophile and extremely fluent in English, explained that, so far as he could see, the cobwebs did not affect the wine and the spiders helped to keep down the mosquitos. He makes quite excellent wine, and you can take your choice between stainless steel and cobwebs. I think there is something to be said for the latter.

The third bodega I visited was in Tarragona; it belonged to the President of the local Sindicato de la Vid, Señor Don Manuel Tapias. He produces a smaller quantity of excellent wine, and I gathered that he is not terribly anxious to make more. His well-ordered bodega produces comparatively few wines, of the true Tarragona character, which are all of excellent quality. Most of the bodegas produce true Tarragona wine, which may be dry or sweet, but is largely sweet and is extremely palatable. Moreover, it is altogether honest and unfortified, and it has nothing to do with the ill-reputed Tarragonas of long ago, which were made from must that had been heated almost to boiling point, and produced the vicious liquid I have already discussed. The vinosity, even so, is quite high, and may rise to over 20° in an old wine that may have been blended from a very much older solera. They are all delicious, and I wish they were more popular in England; perhaps they will be one day. Certainly they deserve to be.

For the rest, most of the bodegas make a straightforward dry white wine, which has a characteristic edge to it but is without acidity; it has some affinity with a clean Chablis and yet it is not a Chablis. The *semisecos* are softer and refreshing, while the sweet wines, which contain an element of Moscatel grapes, do not cloy. The white wines all contain 12° to 14° of alcohol; but the red wines, which are mostly dry, are from 14° to 16°, and again they have something of the distinctive flavour I associate with the Priorato wine that is used in the blending of most of them.

The *vino corriente* – the natural white wine, which is produced in great quantities and sold in the wine-shops and bars and forms the common wine in a restaurant – is exceedingly pleasant. It is, in fact, pale golden. The red wine is very red, verging on black. The white wines for export tend to be made very pale, because that seems to be the way the export markets want them. An excellent *rosado* is also made in Tarragona.

It is with some regret that I leave Tarragona, with its Iberian, Roman and medieval walls, its cathedral and its ancient town. I like the wines and I like the people, and I should like, most of all, to see Tarragona wine brought back into a degree of popularity under its own excellent name.

And now for Panadés. The wines made in the district covered by this *denominación de origen* are centred on the town of Villafranca del Panadés, which is roughly half-way between Tarragona and Barcelona, and the town takes a Catalonian pride in the wine it produces. The first thing you see on entering Villafranca on the road from Tarragona is the enormous wine-press at the very beginning of the town, which is a much better beginning than the usual statue to a local dignitary or a war memorial. It is an even bigger press than the ones in the Clos de Vougeot in Burgundy, as I remember them. It was in use in Panadés from the sixteenth century up to the end of the nineteenth century, and another one nearly as big is on show in the town's Museum of Viniculture. The official wine-growing district of Panadés stretches from Vendrell, about 20 kilometres from Tarragona in the south-west, to well beyond Sitges in the north-east, and terminating about 24 kilometres from Barcelona. Villafranca del Panadés is the principal wine-making town, and San Sadurní de Noya has also a great number of bodegas – this is where most of the Spanish sparkling wines are made.

The terrain is mainly hilly from the sea inland, reaching a height of nearly 2,000 feet in the highest parts, where as usual some of the best wines are grown. The temperature changes throughout the area are not great, even between the sea and the mountains, and the rainfall over a long period is considered to be about perfect for vines.

Several sorts of wine are made here, and the *denominación de origen* authorities have classified the standard wines according to their degree of alcohol, from the light white Panadés, which can be as low as 9° (but which may be considerably stronger), to the red Panadés, which can be as high as 16°. The *corriente* wines are made in the upper and central Panadés region; they are white wines of a light greenish-golden colour, and they are all well balanced, mild wines and extremely pleasant to drink.

In Villafranca del Panadés the wine museum, under the directorship of Señor Don Pablo Boada, who was kind enough to show me round, is most impressive; it gives the whole history of viniculture throughout Spain from early times. Here can and should be seen many types of Greek and Roman amphoras, with excellent and accurate models of how wine was made in different ages, and also of types of bodegas generally throughout Spain. Every kind of container is shown here, from the sublimely simple wine-cup to the

ridiculous and elaborate glass bottles much in vogue at the end of the last century, often
in the form of a figure of a man or woman with the neck of the bottle sticking out at the
top of the head; in one silly example a hand holds a pistol, the wine coming out of the
muzzle. There are also great wine-barrels of considerable antiquity, which were in use
until recently, and wine-presses of every size, shape and age, together with a considerable gallery of wine illustrations, cartoons, posters and so on. Here, too, there is,
very wisely, a little bar where the typical wine of Panadés may be drunk and where
pleasant and sensible little souvenirs may be purchased, such as Catalan *porrones* in
various sizes or, if you cannot manage a *porrón* (and I cannot, although I have often
tried), a glass to drink out of in a more Christian manner. The *porrón* is a pear-shaped
flask with a spout and handle; to use it requires some skill, and I am always fascinated
at seeing a virtuoso perform, sometimes holding the *porrón* at arm's length and not
spilling a drop. But to return to the good wines of Panadés.

My escort on this occasion was the President of the Panadés Sindicato de la Vid,
Señor Don Miguel Torres, whose dynamic energy has greatly expanded his bodega,
founded by his grandfather in 1870. The wine, as in Tarragona, is usually made in the
co-operatives throughout the area, and is bought by Señor Torres and his colleagues
and associates in exactly the same way as in Tarragona. But in the Torres bodega,
they make a certain amount of their own wine from their own vineyards, or from
selected grapes that are bought from the farmers. In Panadés the system has always
been to ferment the must in barrels rather than vats, although again this is tending to
die out, especially in the larger bodegas; but I am sentimental enough to regret the
passing of the fermenting-cask for the tile-lined or stainless-steel or cement vat. Nevertheless, even in the most scientific bodegas, the new hogsheads, pipes, *botas* and *bocoyes*
are often filled with sea-water for fourteen days to cut out the 'woody' taste that the
new cask might impart to the wine; this practice is certainly followed where the wine is
made near the coast, as in Tarragona, for example.

There is a great deal of difference in methods throughout Spain, and this is nowhere
more apparent than in Panadés, where, as in the Torres bodega, the methods are
extremely conservative. The process, which I have already mentioned in connection
with the Priorato, of oxidizing the wine by exposure in *bombonas* is one of them. It is
extremely interesting to see quite a large field of pear-shaped glass bottles, looking for all
the world like enormous onions, each of which holds about 30 litres of wine; they have
very porous corks and little metal hats so the rain cannot get in. They are surrounded
by *bocoyes* of wine, all being matured by direct contact with the elements rather than
by the slower process of maturing in the large cool bodegas. The wine stays in its *bombona* for about two years of summer heat and winter rain, when half of it is siphoned off,
and the *bombona* is filled with new wine. In other words, this is a kind of open-air solera
system on a comparatively small and expensive scale. The resulting wine has a character
all its own, and although it is not sold in Spain (but it is sold everywhere else in the
world) as sherry, and cannot be called sherry, it has a strong sherry affinity, though
with its own special character, which I must say I rather liked. I am told that there are
very few of these fields of *bombonas* left, and by modern standards I suppose this method
could hardly be economic or efficient. The old fiddle-shaped *bombona*, which held much
less than its pear-shaped successor, has now, for all practical purposes, gone out.

In the Torres bodega is blended the wine known as 'Sangre de Toro', or bull's blood, which has nothing to do with the Bull's Blood of Hungary and indeed is a finer wine altogether, of a rich, ruby colour, but not as black as in the Hungarian variety. Again, as in Tarragona, the export wines tend to follow popular demand in that there are *seco* and *semiseco* varieties of white and *semiseco* red wines, with a good clean *rosado* as well. I shall, I think, mention two superb wines, typical of Panadés, that I drink here in England, although they are not easy to come by. These are 'Viña Sol', a clean, dry white wine, and 'Coronas', a very delicious, rather heavy red. But Allah in his wisdom has ordained that the juice of the grape can be purveyed much as the vintner wishes, and Panadés is not exempt from the principle that if wines are blended too much they tend to lose their original character, which is a good thing in some of the less agreeable wines, but it is regrettable in others.

Sitges, on the coast south-east of Villafranca, is noted for its dessert wines. These are made in two types, Málvasia (or Malmsey, as we know it in England) and Moscatel, both of high alcoholic strength and with a high sugar content of up to 9° Baumé. The Malvasía or Malmsey is, of course, made in other countries, and whether the Malmsey in which the Duke of Clarence was drowned came from Sitges, Cyprus, the Canaries or somewhere else, we do not know. (Incidentally, how did they drown him in a butt of Malmsey? There is only one entrance, and that is through the bung-hole, so they must have cut the prince up into very small pieces first.) It is generally supposed that the stocks from which the Malvasía grapes are grown were imported from Cyprus by one of the Spanish expeditions to the east in the Middle Ages. Considerable care is needed in the growing of the vines and their grapes, the vintage not taking place until the grape is thoroughly overripe and wrinkled, as in the case of the sweeter sherries. The wine is kept in vat and cask for a long time, and is normally not bottled for seven or eight years in the best qualities, when it reaches a degree of alcohol of about 16°. The Moscatel of Sitges contains about 15° of alcohol and 9° Baumé, and it has the characteristic taste of all muscatels in that the taste of the grape is predominant. Fermentation is normally stopped at an early stage by the addition of a small amount of grape-alcohol to retain the sweetness, and the more commercial wines are ready for selling after one or two years, during which time they are racked from cask to cask three or four times.

The natural white wine of Panadés appears to be very suitable for distillation into brandy, and two of the best of the Spanish brandies, Mascaro and Torres, are equal, in my opinion, to any of those of Jerez.

The red wines of the Torres bodega are made almost entirely on the Bordeaux system; this is exceptional in Spain. After the first fermentation the wine is put straight into hogsheads, and it is racked three times during its first year, twice in the second and once in the third, after which it is clarified with white of egg; it is then ready to be sold, although in practice it may well stay a year or two longer. Here also the best wines are sold as the wine of a given year; this is not necessarily an indication of improvement, because with an equable climate the quality remains firmly constant, but it is an indication of the age of the wine. This bodega has some comparatively old wine, and I was given to drink the Torres 'Coronas' wine of 1941, which was very good, whereas a Bordeaux of that age would certainly not be, and this I think is a good illustration of the difference between the two types of wine.

Probably the most efficient bodega in Panadés is that of the Segura Hermanos, who have one of the most up-to-date plants in Spain – tiles, filters, refrigeration, stainless steel, plastic floors, the lot. Apart from making excellent wine of their own, they specialize in making exactly the right type of basic wine, which is bought by the makers of sparkling wine in the district, to be processed by the *méthode champenoise* and other less reputable ways into sparkling wines.

The delicious wines of Alella must make our next refreshing subject. The *denominación de origen* area of Alella is centred on the small town of the same name about 20 kilometres north of Barcelona just off the coast road, and it is here, if anywhere, that the authentic character of Spanish wine is preserved, to the exclusion of those wines that are blended in the bodegas for marketing to an established pattern laid down by the buying public in other countries. The white wine is made largely from the Garnacha Blanca and Xarello grapes, and the red wine from the Tempranillo and Garnacha Tinta grapes. The vines are grown on a gritty, granite soil that, in itself, is a guarantee that they will not be prolific and that there will be a certain character in the wine. I arrived in the middle of the vintage at the co-operative Alella Vinícola in the town of Alella, and was able to see the whole process from beginning to end, and eventually to taste and appreciate the wines, for which I have formed a good deal of enthusiasm.

While I was there the carts and trailers and *camiones* were coming in laden with grapes. But here the possibly more scientific and less interesting procedure of the tiny wooden balls in Tarragona is not followed; instead, a sample of grapes is pressed at the time of arrival at the weigh-house in a miniature wine-press, in every way a replica of the great wine-presses that have been used for centuries. There are four of these miniature presses in the weigh-house, and, as the loads of grapes arrive, two or three bunches are taken and pressed out on the spot. A sample is whipped upstairs to the laboratory while the grapes are being unloaded into the pressing-chambers opposite, and an analysis is made; the grower is given a tally-check that states the weight of the grapes and their sugar content, according to which he will be paid. I found this operation quite fascinating, particularly in the tiny presses, which are manipulated by hand.

The grapes are shovelled into the press; the stalks are removed, and the grapes are pressed in a series of four pneumatic presses, which ensure that they are not bruised, and that the infusion of excessive tannin from the pips is thus avoided. After this the resulting must is pumped off into fermenting-vats, where it undergoes its first turbulent fermentation. It is then transferred into great oak storage-vats, in which it stays for one or two years, maturing in the wood. No filters are used, nor is alcohol added to fortify the wine, and no wine is ever sold before it is three years old, when it is taken from the enormous oak butts and, normally, bottled for both domestic and export markets, with the exception of England and Switzerland, where it is shipped in bulk because, as the manager of the co-operative said, he can trust his agents there to bottle it and label it in accordance with the specifications. The wine thus made has both character and charm, two qualities that are difficult to combine. It has a most delicious nose, which reminded me distantly of wallflowers of a gone generation. I am sorry to become poetic, but this faint perfume, too light to be called aromatic, needs some description, for I found it in all the wines I tasted at the bodega.

Half a dozen wines are made under the label 'Alella Legítimo', which speaks for itself; the wines are dated according to the year in which they are made, and this is mainly a true indication of the age of the wine. These wines are the true wines of Alella, where red and white wines are made; they do not compare, nor do they attempt to compare, with the great wines of the Médoc or the Côte d'Or, yet they have a special quality of their own that I found not only attractive but quite remarkable. The white wines do not aspire to be Montrachets or Moselles; they are just straight 'Alella Legítimo', and they are quite delicious.

The range of wines is comparatively small. There are two simple white wines. One is dry, the 'Marfil Seco'; the other, not quite so dry (and it is, I think, a little better), is called 'Marfil Blanco'. They both have about 13° of alcohol. There is also an older white wine called 'Super Marfil'; this, with age, has achieved a more golden colour than its younger brethren, but retains the character of dryness and, above all, the fragrance of this distinctive wine. Farther along the line there is a wine called 'Lacre Gualda', which is very old and very dry indeed, of high strength, with a minimum of 17° alcohol, and with a smoothness and fragrance that are altogether exceptional. The red wine, the 'Marfil Tinto', is again strong-bodied, containing 13·5° alcohol, but is smooth and delicate and is typical of that country. A certain amount of sweet wine is made under the name of 'Lacre Violeta'; it is sweet but not cloying, and of a lovely colour, with the characteristic fragrance, but it is essentially a dessert wine. Finally, there is a *rosado*, which is a mixture of the juice from white and red grapes and has an alcoholic content of 13°. The colour is a pale terra-cotta; the wine is quite dry, and again it retains the aroma that I find so interesting and charming in the white and red wines.

Wines have been made in Alella since the Roman days, and there are plenty of records from then on to prove it. This is a comparatively small wine-growing area, confined entirely to its gritty soil; the cultivation both of the grape and of the wine itself is highly regulated according to the tradition peculiar to the area. Above all, and to repeat myself, the wines of Alella have preserved the integrity and character of the Spanish wine to a degree that I did not find anywhere else on the Mediterranean littoral, except perhaps in Priorato, and I hope they will long continue to do so.

These wines are not easily come by, for they are relatively expensive, but they are fine wines in every sense of the word and well worth going to a great deal of trouble to find; in fact, one of the best reasons for visiting the Costa Brava might be to look at the wines of Alella. I am indebted to Señor Don José María Vidal, who, as President of the Consejo Regulador of the Denominación de Origen Alella, believed very firmly in the future of Spanish wines, and who took me to Alella, and also to Señores Rifa and Golderila of the co-operative Alella Vinícola. There are, I believe, only two other co-operatives making the wines of Alella in the whole area, and they also preserve the integrity of the wine and do not try to blend or make it into something else.

North of Alella and towards the French frontier there are wine-growing areas that do not come under any *denominación de origen*. In one such area lies Ampurdán where, under the label of the Barón de Terrades, are made straightforward red and white *vinos de mesa*; they are not particularly distinguished, but they have a character that is essentially Spanish, and they are very good to drink. A sweeter, fortified wine is also made, which is of some character.

At the famous Castillo de Perelada, white, *rosado* and red wines are made. They are sound wines of excellent quality, and have certain lasting properties which I know, because I brought a few bottles back with me from my first tour in Spain in 1950 and drank them only two or three years ago, when they had become rather darker but were not only drinkable but excellent. Perelada also make a sparkling wine by the *cuve close* method; and it is better and rather drier than most of its brethren. These wines are made near the French frontier; all are good examples of their kind.

Inland from Barcelona, in the province of Lérida, the vineyards are comparatively few and far between. An excellent white wine, however, is made in the village of Castell del Remei.

CHAPTER NINE

# Some other Wines of Spain

## Galicia

I MUST confess this province is one of the few areas of Spain to which I have never travelled, and, although I have every intention of going there before very much longer, I cannot claim to be able either to describe the scenery or to give any first-hand information about wines drunk at the bodega. I have, however, drunk of these excellent wines in Madrid and elsewhere, and can commend them as being wines with characters of their own, rather different from those of most Spanish wines, which are inclined to be smooth rather than lively.

Vines are grown generally in this area. The chief wine-growing centre is Ribadavia, not far from Orense and Leiro, although excellent white wines come from Bordones farther west. The wines are not exported much, if at all; but they deserve to be, and I hope the day will come when I shall be able to buy them in London. The main characteristic of the white wines is a slight greyness, which is a little off-putting at first – until you taste them; then you find the difference, for they have a freshness and sharpness that makes them comparable with the famous *vinhos verdes* of Portugal, and this is what mostly distinguishes them from the other Spanish wines. The white wines are often sold with their secondary fermentation incomplete, and with the corks stoutly tied on the bottles with string. The wines don't look very nice, being somewhat cloudy, and the bottles, if you carry them about in a car as I did, are liable to explode, which is not a very good thing for the inside of the car. I had three bottles in all, and one went off as described. The other two never got the chance: they were drunk that night. This wine is very good indeed if taken as what it is – an incomplete wine that should be drunk for excitement or interest, or to quench a thirst, or for any purpose other than criticism. When the wine is completed it is a perfectly well balanced wine with, as I have said, a character all its own, and with an acerbity that makes a very pleasant change. The alcoholic content is low for Spanish wines, never exceeding 11°, and it is sometimes much lower.

There are many different grapes grown in this region, especially the types that are called Caiño, which are considered the best for bottled wines; other types are Brancellao, Pozeo, Souson and the Godello or Treizadura, which give fame to those white Galician wines that are called Tostadillo and are similar to the ones that come from near San-

Plate 51. The sherry grape: the Palomino

tander. Another grape, the Albariño, produces very special white wines, Albariño de Meyra and Albariño de Fefiñanes, which are comparable with the German wines, and are highly valued locally.

Sweet wines are made in Galicia, including the celebrated Tostado, which is somewhat similar to port, and is made by allowing the grapes to dry in the sun and become 'toasted' – hence the name; it contains 14°–16° of alcohol.

As a wine of this sort is produced, you naturally expect that sparkling wine would be made in Galicia, but, as far as I know, it is not made by the *méthode champenoise*. I have not tasted any of the sparkling wines made by the *méthode cuve close*, and I hope none are produced by an injection of carbonic acid gas; the wine would certainly deserve a better fate than that.

## Castile

The wine-producing areas of Castile are centred around Valladolid, and the most important is the village of Rueda (which for a long time has given its name to the wines of that particular district), together with La Seca and Nava del Rey. The wines are very similar to those of the Rioja, but with a slightly higher percentage of alcohol; they are firm to the palate and have an average alcoholic content of between 13° and 14°. They are white, or rather golden, wines, and they have a somewhat sherry-like aroma. They are extremely pleasant to drink.

The impression gained by the traveller across the Castilian plain from (say) Burgos through Valladolid, Zamora and Salamanca is one of dullness. It is a plain about 2,000 feet high, and it stretches for miles and miles with nothing to relieve it except the occasional village, with its statutory three churches and the dovecots, which are a feature of the landscape. The sun in summer is extremely hot here, and in the winter the cold can be intense; not exactly, one would say, the best kind of climate for the making of great wine. Nevertheless, some of the Castilian wines are very good to drink, and are of amazing variety. Most of them are consumed locally, since they do not travel well, and are consequently little known beyond their centres of production. Even in Madrid or Bilbao, they are difficult to come by. They have a good reputation, dating back to the sixteenth and seventeenth centuries, when the wines were fashionable. Most of the wines are white (or *blanco*), but there are a fair number of light *tinto* wines that are equally agreeable. From the province of Valladolid comes one of the greatest Spanish table wines, the 'Vega Sicilia'. The output of this vineyard is very small, and these wines are difficult to find, even in good restaurants; they are also expensive by Spanish standards. To a certain extent, they could be called the Spanish equivalent of the Romanée Conti, although it would be risky to push this comparison too far.

A little to the west, in the Tierra del Vino, are found the wines from Zamora and Toro; the vineyards more or less adjoin those round Tordesillas (which comes under the general Rueda classification), and have some affinity with them. And yet there is a slight distinction that is quite interesting; they reach as far as the upper borders of the Douro before it descends into Portugal. The chief towns of this particular part of Castile, apart from Zamora and Toro, are Corrales, Benavente, Fuentesaúco and Villalpando, and, after reconquest from the Moors, this region was one of the first organized wine-producing regions of the newly formed Christian state, when it made part of the territory belonging to the kings of León. One of these ancient kings once boasted, '*Tengo un toro que da vino y un león que se lo bebe*', which means 'I have a bull that yields wine and a lion that drinks it' – a very pretty pun on the name Toro, which is the wine-producing town, and the name León, which is the neighbouring city where most of the wine was consumed. These wines are quite robust and agreeable to the palate, and have a comparatively high alcoholic content, of 14°–15°. They are a deep rich red; sometimes they are called locally *sangre de toro*, or bull's blood (another pun), but I am told that this is now a trade-name owned by the reputable firm of Torres in Villafranca del Panadés, and may not be used on the label. But the wine is still known as bull's blood locally, and this is not a bad name for it.

Farther north, around Santander in the Liébana region, the Tostadillo wine is produced, which is white, sweetish and suitable for a dessert wine. Very good red wines of a rather startling bright colour are produced that have a somewhat strong character, not at all unpleasant. The wines that come from this area are similar to those in the north of Valladolid. and are either red or dark *rosé*; they have a low alcoholic content but are excellent *vinos corrientes*.

## *Navarre*

Navarre is a large province stretching along the foothills of the Pyrenees from rather north of Logroño and through Puente la Reina to Pamplona. The vines are grown sporadically through this very mountainous region, and the wines vary considerably in style and alcoholic strength, for some are of 16° or 18°, while those of Rebea reach up to 15°; by contrast, various wines produced around Pamplona are of only 9° or 10°, but they look much stronger because they have an intense ruby colour.

The scenery of Navarre is very much more dramatic than that of the Rioja near by, with its gentle charm. Apart from Pamplona, which is very much a tourist city, especially during the fiesta week when the bulls are coursed through the streets, and when much good Navarre wine is drunk, this lovely province is not so much visited by tourists as perhaps it should be. While I have no desire to make it over-popular, I can thoroughly recommend it both for its scenic qualities and for its very pleasant local wines. It is true that several millions of gallons are exported from this province every year; but this is a very small proportion of the whole, most of it being sold for local consumption – and I cannot blame the locals for choosing their own excellent wine rather than buying from elsewhere in Spain.

The best Navarrese wines I tasted bore the *marque* of Señorío de Sarría from Puente la Reina, about 15 miles from Pamplona. In addition to its being a very beautiful town indeed, with one of the most magnificent ancient bridges in Europe (marvellously floodlit by night, incidentally), I found its wines fresh and sparkling; and when I say sparkling I do not mean *pétillant* to taste, but with a vivacity uncommon in Spanish wines. I was delighted with this wine; I thought it very pleasant to drink after the heavy dignity of the Riojan giants. The Riojas are the Spanish grandees, and the wine I tasted of the Señorío de Sarría, a *tinto* three years old, was rather like his beautiful young bride.

The red wine from Las Campanas, Castillo de Tiebas, is quite remarkable and indeed is comparable with the best Riojas. The *rosé* from Las Campanas is also very good. But all these Navarrese wines are extremely drinkable.

## Aragon

Aragon wine is sometimes known by its principal wine-growing town, Cariñena, but wine is made fairly evenly over the region, which comprises the provinces of Zaragoza, Huesca and Teruel. It is what I would call average wine of a pleasant character, most of which is drunk locally. Some very good wines are produced in Aragon, especially those made from the Garnacha grape, which accounts for most of the red wine. Many thousands of litres of this are exported, but I imagine most of the wine would go for *coupage*, and possibly for the improvement of worse wines from other countries. In Aragon the method of wine-making varies a little from that of other districts, for the must is fermented in subterranean wells of a standard size, 3·80 metres (12 feet 5½ inches) deep, 2·80 metres (9 feet 2½ inches) wide, and 2·90 metres (9 feet 6½ inches) long, and a certain amount of treading still goes on, although the modern co-operative has largely made this unnecessary and uneconomical. After the boisterous fermentation the *bagasse* is extracted, pressed and sent to the distillery, and the clear wine is racked off into *bocoyes* for finishing. Eventually a rather sweet wine is produced, 15° before fermentation and finishing up as 9° Baumé, both red and white; but it is unlikely that you will find them outside Aragon, where they are drunk young and fresh. I have before me a copy of the publication *Información Comercial Española*, devoted to wine, in which I read: 'The wine of Cariñena, aside from its own excellent value, has the merit of completing the scale of Spanish wines in all its degrees'. Just exactly what this means I am not at all sure, but even so I shall be inclined to agree with it. The wines of Aragon are, by and large, honest and good.

## Estremadura

The wine-growing district of Estremadura lies between Portugal to the west, Huelva to the south, La Mancha to the east and León to the north; and a great deal of wine is made in this very pleasant province. Its most important one is probably the ill-named Clarete of Guadalcanal. I say ill-named, because it is unnecessary for Spanish wines to bear French names; on the other hand, I have never been quite persuaded that the French have a monopoly of the word 'claret' – certainly they have not of *clarete*. This wine, as its name implies, is a light *rosé*, but with rather more alcoholic content than a true claret. Many typical wines, both red and white, are produced in Almendralejo, the centre of this region, and the red and white wines of Guareña are also considered excellent. They are no better than those of Salvatierra de los Barros, which are prized locally for their intense colour, and those of Albuquerque, which are reputed to have a distinctive aroma.

The red and white wines of this district are usually extremely well made, and they vary in alcoholic strength from 14° to 17°. The red wines are very brilliant; they also throw a crust, which is unusual in Spanish wine. They have a very similar taste, and when they are very young they are sometimes cloudy. This is largely due, I think, to the fact that they are sold before the secondary fermentation is complete, though they don't appear *pétillant*; it may be that they are not clarified, which is more likely, because it seems possible that the yeasts of the fermentation are similar to the 'flower' formed in sherry, and have not been properly cleared, as they are in the great bodegas of Jerez. Moreover, we must remember the very important difference in the price. Certainly they have a very pleasant nose, and a good clean taste, and there are also some strong-bodied *vinos corrientes* of the Trujillo region that have their admirers.

## Huelva

Sometimes known as the *vinos del Condado de Niebla*, the wines of Huelva now have their own *denominación de origen*, deserving special mention and, so far as this study is capable of it, a word of encouragement, because they have had some very hard luck recently.

Huelva lies north-west of the Guadalquivir River, and the district contains the villages of Moguer, Niebla, Almonte, Villalba del Alcor, Manzanilla (which does not make the wine of that name) and Chucena, together with La Palma del Condado, which is the largest, and Bollulos par del Condado. These wines are generally strong, big wines of fairly high alcoholic content, and sometimes sweet. But they are very suitable for blending; they have thus been very much the victims of circumstance. For, chiefly owing to its geographical position just north of the Jerez vineyards, the district has, until recently, been able to sell its wines for blending with sherry at a much higher price than the bodegas would normally be able to get for the *corriente* wine.

Now, however, the winds of change are blowing – and, as far as Huelva is concerned, have blown; for, under the strict limitation of the area in which Jerez wines can be produced and sold as sherry, the excellent wines of Huelva are just too far away, and they can no longer be used for blending with sherry, or command such a high price. This is a considerable misfortune, and many deputations have been sent to Madrid to try to get the *denominación de origen* authorities and the Minister of Agriculture to allow the practice to continue, but with no effect; Huelva will therefore have to work out its own future and establish its own reputation. This may be a good thing in the long run; but it is very hard, and it will be very hard for a year or two yet to come, on those growers who have seen their prices chopped in half by one fell stroke of an administrative pen. Such a state of affairs may well give us pause for a little philosophical reflection on why a wine can command a certain price with a certain name, and only half that price when the name is taken away, although without question it is still the same wine.

The Huelva wines (or Niebla wines, as they were sometimes called) have a considerable history. They are made largely by the local growers, and by the careful but fairly primitive methods still used in Jerez and other parts of Spain, although no doubt some bodegas have been modernized and others will be. Wines have been made here from deepest antiquity, and there are records going back to the Moorish occupation; in fact, the last of the petty sultans of Niebla, Mohammed ben Yahya 'Izz ad-Din (1041–51), considered his cellars his greatest treasure, so one assumes that he did not eventually enter paradise, as promised in the Koran. Personally, I should have said it was worth the gamble.

To sum up, the wines of Huelva are both red and white, but mostly white, and these last have a strong affinity with sherry wine. The demand for Huelva wine is mainly because of its importance for *coupage*, and this is probably the fate of the bulk of the thousands of litres exported; but it is much to be hoped that the local growers, under the reverses they have suffered in not being able to sell their wine for blending with sherry, will do their own blending, and will develop a wine with its own character that will enable them to command a better price.

## The Balearics and the Canaries

So far as the wines of Majorca and the Balearics generally are to be met with, they are available only on their own ground (that is, on the islands), and there is little point in writing about them, except to say that I have tasted them here in England, and that they are very good of their sort (mostly white), but never go higher than the simple *vinos corrientes* that are usually good throughout Spain. I have also looked at the wines of Majorca, both red and *rosado*, from the bodega of Jaime Ripoll Benisalem. They are somewhat heavily flavoured, but have an affinity with Valencian and Murcian wines. But their character is quite distinctive. I am not sure whether they can now be bought outside their island of origin. The chief wine of Minorca is the Alba Flora.

The Canaries, however, are in rather a different category; although the wine has a very considerable history, and has been imported into England for many centuries, its character has somewhat changed from what it was originally. As Canary sack, or just straight Canar, it was always important, and Mistress Quickly in *Henry IV*, Part 2, exclaims, 'That's a marvellous searching wine, and it perfumes the blood ere one can say, "What's this?" ' It sounds as though it didn't taste all that good, either. Nevertheless, Canary wine was drunk by our Elizabethan forefathers in considerable quantities; but just how it compared with the modern Canary we shall never know.

Canary wines are made from several types of grapes, but mostly from the Histan white and black, Lolle black and our dear old friend Pedro Ximénez, without which I think Spain would surely founder. The alcoholic content of these rather dry red and white wines varies between 13° and 15°; in most of the semi-sweet wines, Malvasías and Moscatels, the range is between 15° and 16°, which is normal for Spain. The Malmsey was probably the chief export to Britain in olden days.

Though I have drunk of Canary wines, I have never been to the islands. But I think I should go, if only to find out whether the wines travel well or not. I can think of many worse reasons for going to the Canaries.

CHAPTER TEN

# The Sparkling Wines of Spain

NOWADAYS in England it is illegal to speak of Spanish sparkling wine as champagne, which it most certainly is not, although it is called *champan* throughout Spain and in other parts of the world. Sparkling wine is made mainly in the Panadés area, at Perelada near the French frontier and in the Rioja. These areas have considerably increased their output of sparkling wine during the past few years.

Sparkling wines are made in Spain in three ways: the *méthode champenoise* (at least no one can stop them from using this term for making the wine); the *méthode cuve close*, where the fermentation is carried out in a vat and thereafter the wine is sold and bottled quite quickly, getting its sparkle from the secondary fermentation; and the execrable method by which carbonic acid gas is introduced into a natural still wine – the results are all horrid and give you the sensation of intoxicating, fizzy, sweet lemonade. The Spaniards are not alone in this dubious operation; it is also done in France and Germany.

The Spanish Government proposes to control the manufacture of 'champagne' by stipulating that only the firms who make their sparkling wine by the *méthode champenoise* may describe themselves as *cavas*. Consequently, if when visiting Spain you drop in at a *cava* (as in France you can drop in on any *cave* and be shown around and be given wine to taste), you may be sure that you will see sparkling wine made as it should be; and I strongly advise you, if you have not already seen it, to do so. It is an extremely complicated and interesting process. It is necessarily also very expensive; hence the high price of champagne and other wines in other countries made by the same process.

One of the reasons why the name champagne should not be used in Spain is that the true champagne comes from the tiny Pinot noir and Pinot blanc grapes, grown on the very thin and chalky soil of Champagne, which gives the wine that touch of acerbity and crispness which is not found anywhere else in the world. There is no soil in Spain comparable to that of the Champagne district in France, and no Pinot grapes are grown in Spain. Consequently, Spanish sparkling wine has quite a different character, a softness that is not found in champagne. Finally, it comes down to a matter of taste. If you like your sparkling wine to have an edge to it (or I suppose one might say more appropriately, with champagne, a kiss to it), you will buy your champagne from France; but if you like your wine soft you can hardly do better than to try some of the best qualities of Spanish sparkling wine.

Sparkling wine in Spain, as indeed in France, can be brought to almost any degree of sweetness; this is purely a matter of the amount of *liqueur* that is added at the time of *dégorgement*. I think in this case I have to use the French terms, because they are more readily understood; but perhaps it would be better if I explained the complicated *méthode champenoise* process undergone by sparkling wine before it reaches the end for which it was ordained, whether it be a wedding breakfast or a chorus girl's slipper, or just to make a good wine for you and for me to drink with or before our dinner.

First of all, the grapes are pressed carefully in such a way that the pips will not be bruised and let tannin into the wine, making it bitter. Sparkling wine, which ought to be white or very pale gold, can be made from either white or black grapes, and in Champagne it is made from both. In Spain most of the sparkling wine is made from white grapes; it is what the French would call *blanc de blanc*. If black grapes are used in making the wine the skins are removed from the must before fermentation begins, because it is the pigment from the skins of the grapes that makes the wine red. After pressing, the must can be pumped directly into casks; more often it is pumped into vats for not more than a day to allow the must to settle, and then, before fermentation sets in, the comparatively clear juice is pumped into barrels, where it undergoes its first tumultuous fermentation. While this is going on, if you put your ear to the bung-hole, which is always open, you can hear the wine inside buzzing like a swarm of angry bees. The wine is left in the cask for between six months and a year, but before the secondary fermentation is finished it is clarified and blended in a blending-tank to make the wine of an even quality. This blended wine, called the *cuvée*, is bottled with small amounts of sugar and yeast and corked with temporary corks, and it starts its long ageing in the cellars deep below the earth.

There, lying horizontally in vast bins, these hundreds of thousands of bottles stay with nothing happening at all to them for at least three years, and sometimes longer. After this time they are put in specially made racks, bottom-upward at an angle of 45°, and every day the bottles are given a kind of shake and quarter-turn to send the sediment, the crust that has grown into the wine, to the bottom. This is an extremely expert job, and there are men who do nothing but turn the wine, two bottles at a time, at incredible speed; over the years, they develop enormous muscles in the forearms. This process of turning takes about six months. (At this stage, for the cheaper wine, the bottle can go through its *dégorgement* and be ready to drink; but this is not usual.) The bottles are then placed upside-down, so that the shaken-up sediment will collect at the end of the cork; and there they stay for any period. I know that there is a bin of wine in the upside-down position in Epernay that has been there for 50 years without *dégorgement*; for all I know, there may be some similar in Spain.

The wine is now ready for finishing. When they are required the bottles will be put on specially prepared trolleys with racks, still in the upside-down position, and taken along and put into a machine that freezes the wine solid in the neck of the bottle. Then follows the *dégorgement*, which is the removal of the temporary cork and of the frozen sediment that has accumulated over the years. The *liqueur* is added to the clear wine to give it the necessary degree of sweetness, ranging from 0·05% of *liqueur* for a *brut* or dry wine, to 4 or 5% for our South American friends, who like their sparkling wine sweet as well as good – and 4 or 5% of *liqueur* can make the wine pretty sweet. The *liqueur* is, in fact, grape-sugar. Then the wine is corked with its final cork and wired down; the bottle is washed (and it needs washing after all those years in a cellar), labelled and sent on its way. The wine will not improve in bottle; indeed, it will deteriorate, and only very well made sparkling wine of a very good year will sparkle much after about ten years. In Spain, where the years do not vary, the wine will become flat or still, the sparkle will disappear and the colour will darken. I personally happen to like old champagne, but it is not by any means to everybody's taste. Certainly it is not the kind of thing you expect if you buy a bottle of sparkling wine at a high price.

So, from all this, we can appreciate that champagne is, and must be, a comparatively expensive product. In the whole of Spain there are about 40 firms making wine by the *méthode champenoise*, and more making wine by the *méthode cuve close* and, alas! by injecting carbonic acid gas.

The *cuve close* method is certainly not harmful, but it constitutes an artificial acceleration of a purely natural process, and the wine is sometimes drinkable, as can be seen; but it cannot compare with the long and intricate *méthode champenoise*. It is perhaps unfortunate for the Spanish that, when the famous 'Spanish champagne case' was fought out in the English courts the firm who were the Spanish defendants were making their sparkling wine by the *méthode cuve close*.

I have been taken over the great Codorníu sparkling-wine bodega in San Sadurní de Noya by Señor Don José María Raventós, whose family has been making wine there since 1551, long before Dom Pérignon discovered the art of making champagne. In those days, of course, the Codorníu family made wine as everybody else did, probably a better wine, but just straight wine. In the nineteenth century, however, having tasted the wine of Champagne and made some experiments of their own, they found that the grapes of Panadés were very suitable for the production of sparkling wine, and they tried it out in a small way; this was in 1872, when Don José Raventós produced his first bottles of sparkling wine. Now Codorníu make their wine in several qualities, the best being a very dry wine called 'Non Plus Ultra', which is certainly the best Spanish sparkling wine I have tasted. Moreover, these vast cellars – which, I am informed, are nearly twice as large as any other cellars in the world (and I was surprised to hear this) – are visited every year by some 80,000 tourists, Spanish and foreign, who may be sure of a most interesting visit and a glass of excellent sparkling wine at the end of it.

There are many *cavas* in the Panadés district, and San Sadurní de Noya in particular, that will welcome the casual visitor and refresh him with a glass of very good sparkling wine. Remember that only those firms making their sparkling wine by the *méthode champenoise* can describe themselves as *cavas*. On your way to the Costa Blanca, the Costa del Sol or any point south, do not be afraid to visit – indeed, you should make a point of visiting – a *cava*. You will spend a worthwhile hour or so before you go on your way refreshed.

## CHAPTER ELEVEN

# *Spanish Brandy*

BRANDY is distilled throughout the length and breadth of Spain, and it varies enormously in quality. In Spain it sometimes appears under the label Coñac, which is a pity, because it is nothing like Cognac, and it gives an impression that Spanish brandy is trying to pass itself off as its French elder brother – or rather half-brother, because the two are not really alike except in their method of manufacture. Furthermore, Spanish brandy is comparatively young, whereas the brandies of Cognac are extremely old, and this point is very important in the making of brandy. Brandy is in fact distilled wine, and wine must be defined as the fermented juice of the grape. The word 'brandy' derives from the Dutch *brantewijn*, or burnt wine, and this is really what it is, because the wine from which it is made is burnt or boiled until the alcohol, which becomes a gas at many degrees of heat below that of water, is given off. This is then cooled and liquefied and becomes the clear white spirit that is called brandy. Something like 10 measures of wine are used to make one measure of brandy, so it is comparatively expensive and should command a much higher price. This is one of the things I have rarely understood in my travels in Spain: that a very good Spanish brandy is hardly dearer than wine.

In the making of brandy a great deal depends on the quality of the wine from which it is distilled, which in turn depends on the quality of the grapes from which the wine is made. The Cognac of France is distilled from a grape called the St Emilion; this is not remarkable in itself and does not make a particularly delicious wine, but it has inherent qualities that render the brandy distilled from it quite superb. In Spain the brandy is distilled from the grapes of the country, whatever they may be and wherever they may be bought; and I should not be surprised if the very cheapest odd lots of grapes were used for this purpose, for we must face at once the fact that a great many of the local Spanish brandies are not worth drinking. There are, however, some good brandies up and down the country, and one or two that are truly excellent. But they are rare birds, and the *coñac corriente* is really fit only for what it is mostly served for: to put into coffee on a cold morning.

The main difference between the French and Spanish brandies is that the Spanish ones are sweeter and, by and large, softer. There is nothing against this, and I believe there is a growing market in England for a Spanish brandy that, in its better bottles, I would have no hesitation in drinking myself; indeed, I sometimes do drink it. The factor that is most likely to stop Spanish brandy from rising to the utmost heights is the enormous quantity that is consumed in Spain, which precludes the distiller from building up those soleras (to use the Spanish term) of brandy that are absolutely necessary if it is ever to be great. I believe Spain would have less difficulty in producing the really great brandy than the really great wine, because some of the hundreds of varieties of grapes grown in Spain have an affinity with the St Emilion grape, and, in making brandy, the process is to some extent a mechanical one and is not so subject to the human element. I am perfectly well aware that there are many who would disagree with me, but I repeat that I see no reason why the really great Spanish brandy should not be made in the future, if an enterprising distiller would work for 50 years or so to build up his old casks; the cask plays a great part in the development of fine brandy – as, of course, it does in wine. The casks must be oak of the best quality, and the brandy when it is made must be left for a long, long time.

In the enormous cellars in Cognac, big distillers have what they sometimes call their 'paradise', where are kept the very oldest brandies, which are never sold and are rarely refreshed; the brandy taken from them is used to give a distinctive character to the somewhat younger brandy that is put out under the most famous *marques*. I am aware that most of the brandy-distillers in Spain also have a 'paradise' of this sort, but, since the brandy industry really started in Spain only about 80 years ago and immense quantities have been sold ever since, I doubt very much whether these terribly important stocks have accumulated; I have not found much trace of them in the brandy. After being kept in cask for a hundred years or more, brandy loses strength very rapidly, and the custom in France is to pour it into stone jars and seal it after it gets below about 40° of alcohol. I have tasted such brandy; it is soft and smooth and quite delicious. It is, of course, lifeless; but when mixed with a younger brandy it imparts to it a magnificent character. Brandy once bottled does not improve, so the whole of the maturing process must take place in wood. This is why, when you occasionally see a very dusty bottle with the Napoleonic seal on it and a date such as 1811 you know it must be false. If the brandy were truly of 1811 and had been kept in a bottle it would still be much as it was then, or certainly no better; and if it had been kept in wood and bottled since it would be so weak as hardly to be worth drinking.

My personal favourite among Spanish brandies is called 'Mascaro'; it is made in the Panadés district, which also produces the very good 'Torres' brandy. Of course the big sherry houses put out standard brandies, e.g. 'Veterano' and 'Fundador'. They are very even, and, within their limits, their quality is good.

# CHAPTER TWELVE

# Corks, Porrónes and Glasses

THERE is no lack of excellent cork in Spain, and if you motor from Lisbon to Seville, on both sides of the frontier you will travel long distances through cork-oak forests interspersed with sweet chestnuts, under which brown, lean, long-haired swine graze in enormous herds. These cork-oak forests are extremely picturesque. The bark is stripped from the oak in sections; underneath, the natural wood is a rich browny-red, giving a most extraordinary appearance to the tree. The stripped cork may be seen in vast dumps at occasional clearings in the forest; it is left there for seasoning before being taken away to cork factories.

In Spain, however, the cork is not of tremendous importance to the wine, because this is almost invariably drunk young, and therefore the corks are short, except in some of the great Riojan vineyards, where the corks used are of the French type that is: more than 2 inches long; in those parts wine is sometimes kept to a great age, and the cork is correspondingly more important. The function of the cork is not only to stop the wine from coming out of the bottle but also to stop impurities from going in – because all those microscopic organisms that turn wine into vinegar usually go in through the front door (that is, the cork) from the atmosphere outside; thus, according to the quality of the cork, so the wine will be preserved. In Jerez even the oldest wines are never kept in bottle, and one may expect to find quite a short cork in a bottle containing sherry from an 1819 solera. The reason for this has already been explained, but it is only extremely rarely that the wine is bottled and kept in this way. Most of the Spanish wines you buy in England or abroad will naturally have corks supplied in the country where they were bottled, and they will tend to be rather larger and perhaps better corks than those provided by the Spanish bottlers.

Decanters in Spain follow the form of those found elsewhere, but the typical Spanish wine-container is the *porrón*, which is found throughout the country, but especially in Catalonia, where it is in general use. The object of the *porrón* could be, I suppose, merely to save washing up, for no glass is necessary. Wine is poured from the cask into the pear-shaped glass decanter through a curved funnel that is also the handle; in use, it is tipped, sometimes at arm's length, and the wine emerges in a single stream through the spout, directly into the mouth. Normally (and in Catalonia especially) restaurants and working-class families have a *porrón* of wine standing in the middle of the table; the diners reach for it when they want a drink, then put it back. As the spout never touches the lips, there is no need for glasses. Drinking from a *porrón* is something of a skill, which I have never achieved, although I have tried more than once – disastrously.

Because the *porrón* is in common use everywhere, really ancient ones are comparatively few, by reason of their natural fragility. There are, however, some very old and beautiful *porrones* in the Museum of Viniculture in Villafranca del Panadés.

The traditional glasses of Spain are tulip-shaped and very simple, with the slightest curve outwards at the top. They can be found in good, medium and indifferent qualities throughout the country. There are not, as in France, characteristic glasses for different regional wines, except in Jerez, where the rather beautiful *copita* or tasting-glass is in general use. This is made in two or three sizes. Thus the smaller ones can be used for *finos* and the larger glasses kept for the fine *amontillados* or *olorosos* that have developed a special bouquet through age. In tasting, these are usually held by the foot of the glass rather than by the stem.

There are many variants of glasses and *porrónes*, and sparkling wine is usually, alas! drunk out of what is generally known as a champagne glass, though it is nothing of the kind; I mean the flat-bottomed glass best calculated to disperse the liveliness of the wine in no time at all. The general attitude of the Spanish to their glasses and so on reflects their attitude to wine in general: it is an agreeable necessity of life, but it is not a religion. This, I suppose, accounts for the fact that French glasses are so very much better, generally, than the Spanish ones. There is no doubt that nothing in Spain can compare, for instance, with the beautiful glasses from Baccarat.

## APPENDIX ONE

Approximate acreage of Spanish Vineyards and Quantities of Wine produced.[1]

|  | | *Acres* (approx.) | *Gallons* (average) |
|---|---|---|---|
| **CENTRAL SPAIN** | | | |
| Castile | | 1,440,000 | 168,416,000 |
| Aragon | | 320,000 | 21,972,000 |
| León | | 307,000 | 23,759,000 |
| Estremadura | | 194,000 | 26,962,000 |
| | *Totals* | 2,261,000 | 241,109,000 |
| **MEDITERRANEAN** | | | |
| Levante | | 810,000 | 58,441,000 |
| Catalonia and | | | |
|    Balearic Isles | | 500,000 | 92,922,000 |
| Andalusia | | 282,000 | 31,445,000 |
| | *Totals* | 1,592,000 | 182,808,000 |
| **ATLANTIC** | | | |
| Rioja | | 187,000 | 40,301,000 |
| Galicia | | 94,000 | 43,542,000 |
| Basque Provinces | | 14,000 | 3,663,000 |
| Asturias | | 4,000 | 708,000 |
| Canaries | | 20,000 | 635,000 |
| | *Totals* | 319,000 | 88,849,000 |
| | *Grand Totals* | 4,172,000 | 512,766,000 |

[1] Extracted, with his kind permission, from André L. Simon's *The Commonsense of Wine*.

# APPENDIX TWO

## Capacities of Spanish Wine Containers

As the sizes of wine-containers vary slightly from one bodega to another, the figures given below are approximate.

1 gallon = 4·546 litres

### JEREZ

| | |
|---|---|
| Double butt | 225 gallons |
| Bodega butt | 132–146 gallons |
| Bocoy | 146½ gallons |
| Bota de recibo | 112 gallons |
| Shipping butt | 108 gallons |
| Hogshead | 54 gallons |
| Quarter-cask | 27 gallons |
| Octave | 13½ gallons |
| English bottle | 1⅓ pints |
| Spanish bottle | 1¼ pints |

### RIOJA

| | |
|---|---|
| Cuba | 4,400 gallons |
| Tino | 1,760 or 2,200 gallons |
| Bocoy | 132 gallons |
| Barrica bordelesa | 48 gallons |
| Cuarterola (quarter-cask) | 22 gallons |
| Cántara | 3½ gallons |
| Comporta | 220–220 pounds (grapes) |

### VALDEPENAS

| | |
|---|---|
| Bocoy | 176 gallons |
| Cuba | 54 gallons |
| Barrica | 49½ gallons |
| Arroba | 3½ gallons |

### MALAGA

| | |
|---|---|
| Arroba | 3½ gallons |

### TARRAGONA

| | |
|---|---|
| Drum | 145 gallons |
| Pipe | 115 gallons |
| Half-drum | 88 gallons |

### PANADÉS AND PRIORATO

| | |
|---|---|
| Bombona | 6½ gallons |

# The Wines of
# OTHER VINELANDS OF THE WEST

ANTHONY HOGG

# OTHER VINELANDS

POLAND

*Erz Gebirge* *Riesen Gebirge*

GERMANY

Prague

CZECHOSLOVAKIA

*Danube*

Brno

U.S.S.R.

Basel

Vienna

Zurich

*Carpathians*

SWITZERLAND

Salzburg

AUSTRIA

Tokay

Geneva

Radgona

Budapest

*L. Balaton*

Oradea

FRANCE

Bled

Maribor

Ptuj

*Little Alföld*

HUNGARY

*Gt. Alföld*

Arad

RUMANIA

Ode

Ljublana

Jutomer

Timişoara

ITALY

Zadar

*Dinaric Alps*

DALMATIA

*Transylvanian Alps*

Belgrade

Dragasan

Bucharest

YUGOSLAVIA

Consta

Split

Pleven

Ruse

*Balkan Mts.*

BULGARIA

Varna

Sofia

Stara Zagora

Burgas

Pazardshik

Plovdiv

Perushitsa

Edirne

Tirana

Elbasan

Tekirdag

In stat

ALBANIA

Valona

Salonika

Bursa

GREECE

Troy

MEDITERRANEAN SEA

Smyrna (Izmir)

Athens

Piraeus

CRETE

MEDITERRANE

---

FRANCE

Landeron

St. Blaise

Neuchâtel

•BERNE

SWITZERLAND

MEDITERRANE

Cortaillod

*L. Neuchâtel*

Yverdon

Thun

CÔTE

VAUD

*LAVAUX*

Morgues

LAUSANNE

St. Prex

Rolle

Vévey

Nyon

*Lake Geneva*

Montreux

Commugny

Villeneuve

Sierre

*Rhone*

Bex

GENEVA

Sion

VALAIS

CHABLAIS

Martigny

SCALE

Miles

0          30

0          30

Kilometres

*Val d'Aosta*

ITALY

N

# OF THE WEST

Stalingrad (Volgograd)

*Volga*

Astrakhan

KARA-KALPAK

CASPIAN SEA

Krasnodar
Maikop
Anapa

Sudak
Alushta
Yalta
stopol

BLACK SEA

Caucasus Mts.
GEORGIA
Kutaisi
Poti
*Rion*
Batum

DAGESTAN

Derbent

TURKMENISTAN

Napareuli
Telavi
Tsinandali
Zakataly

Tbilisi
(Tiflis)

L. Sevan
Yerevan
Nor Bayazet

ARMENIA
AZERBAIJAN

Baku

*Kura*

Hasandede

MAZANDERAN
Elburz Mts.
Tehran

Cubuk
Kalecik
nkara

Tabriz

L. Urmia

KHURASAN

TURKEY

Elazig

*Tigris*

CILICIA
Tarsus

Antep
(Gaziantep)
Kilis

KURDISTAN

PERSIA

IRAQ

*Euphrates*

Isfahan

CYPRUS
Limassol
Beirut

SYRIA

LEBANON

Bagdad

A

*Plain of Esdraelon*

ISRAEL

EGYPT

## WESTERN AUSTRIA

CZECHOSLOVAKIA

Retz
Poysdorf

Dürnstein  Krems

*Danube*

Klosterneuberg
VIENNA

Gumpoldskirchen
Voslau
Eisenstadt
*L. Neusiedler*

HUNGARY

Radgona

# Introduction

WITH THE possible exception of Tokay, the wines of the lesser countries make no claim to be classed as 'fine'. Those imported and available in Great Britain are invariably sound wines and often good value for money. Some of the cheapest would be more popular in Britain were it not for our system of duty, which levies a standard charge on table wines irrespective of quality. Such countries, with their lower standard of living and lower production costs, could compete better against Western European wines, which have been popular in England for many centuries, could they be imported under an *ad valorem* system, which, unfortunately for them, is unlikely; the same total revenue would never be raised unless we were to begin to drink far more wine than we do.

My description of these wines is largely limited to their basic nature – red or white, sweet or dry – terms such as 'breed', 'bouquet' or 'finesse' being rarely relevant. I have also attempted to describe where they come from, and if my part of this book becomes a geography lesson with a little history thrown in, I make no apology.

But with wines, words are no substitute for tasting, and readers are recommended to try the 'lesser wines' wherever they can. Forget the existence of Bordeaux, Burgundy and Beaujolais! There are only two questions to be answered, 'Do I like the taste?' and 'Am I prepared to pay the price?'

Wines at present available in Britain are printed in roman capitals throughout.

CHAPTER ONE

# Switzerland

JUST over sixteen million gallons is not a very large wine production. France and Italy each make over a thousand. But for a country the size of Switzerland, where the mountains do not appear to have left any room for vineyards, it is quite an achievement to make as much wine as Austria and nearly as much as Australia. Nearly all the wines are white and dry; none is great, but very few are poor, which is rather what one expects from these efficient people.

Some idea of the variety of Swiss wines is gained from T. G. Shaw in *Wine, The Vine and the Cellar*, 1863. That conscientious wine-merchant lists 'All Known Wines' – French and The Rest'. Among the latter there are at least fifty Swiss wines, two of which he describes as 'fine' and the other forty-eight as 'ordinary' or even 'common'. But the names mean very little today, and it is inconceivable that he really tasted them all – from 'Basel' to 'Bellinzona' – in those early days of steam travel.

Since then many a person in plaster of Paris drowning his or her ski-ing sorrows must have discovered the excellence of Swiss wines. That they have never achieved great popularity in England is certainly not due to bad publicity. Some years ago a booklet described one Swiss wine as 'Crisp, playful, a bit naughty, sometimes even daring'! And another as 'Prince of Love . . . inducing thoughts most wicked'! It sounded (I remarked at the time) more like a passing pinch from an Italian in a crowded tram.

The Swiss, a prosperous people, basically French, German or Italian, are the chief consumers of their own pleasant fresh wines. Their high standard of living tends to make prices a little higher than those of comparable French wines, and as far as Britain is concerned shipping costs are slightly higher.

Viticultural records go back to the tenth century, the Church being the protector from early times; the Bishop of Lausanne, *c.* 1137, playing a similar part to that of Pope Clement in Bordeaux. There are also ancient houses associated with wine, such as the Old Priory of Satigny, which gained possession of the Mandement vineyard by a deed of gift in A.D. 912.

One theory ascribes the variety of vines grown in Switzerland to mercenaries bringing them home from the wars. Certainly martial campaigns usually bring disillusionment and a desire to settle down to peaceful husbandry, so perhaps the Kaspers and the Private Angelos *have* made their contribution. Among these vines – still in cultivation – are the Pinot Gris of Burgundy called Malvoisie, the Marsanne blanche from Tain l'Hermitage called Ermitage and the Traminer of Alsace called Païen. Ermitage must certainly have been brought across from Tain, where the vineyards were a going concern in early years A.D. when Pontius Pilate was Governor of Vienne. The others perhaps followed when the Burgundians invaded Le Valais in A.D. 888. Two other wines met locally in Le Valais – Arvine and Amigue – are certainly of Roman origin.

## Districts and Wines

*VALAIS*. The name is derived from the Roman *Vallis Poenina* (Upper Rhône valley) and the valley is that of the great river associated not only with Côtes du Rhône wines made south of Lyons but with the sparkling Seyssel and the white Vin de Bugey as it sets course from Geneva through French Haute-Savoie.

The Rhône rises in an icy Alpine cave above Gletsch, descending as a rolling torrent through the Gomme to Brigue, where the road and rail from Italy via the Simplon follow it to Lake Leman. There are no vines in the Gomme, only a tough breed of men from which many of the Vatican Guards are recruited. The highest vineyards in Europe begin lower down at Visp, continuing at intervals past Sion and Martigny to the confluence with Lake Leman. Conditions are good here, especially on the sunnier right bank, with irrigation supplied from the river and protection by the mountains.

*White*. The best *known* wine is FENDANT, from the vine of that name, also called Chasselas in France and Gutedal in Germany, which is said to do best in this region. The result is a crisp dry white wine.

JOHANNISBERGER is generally considered to be a finer white Valais wine; cuttings are said to have been planted originally from the Rhineland Schloss Johannisberg. Sparkling wines are also made from the Fendant, and the Valais also makes an estate bottled MALVOISIE, a 'straw-wine type' dessert wine.

Swiss wines are almost always sold by the name of the grape. The only Valais vineyard appearing on labels is Mont d'Or, a 50-acre slope west of Sion rising above the

Lausanne road. The *cépages* here, though mostly Sylvaner and Fendant, include about 15% Riesling.

*Red*. Among the red wine grapes, there are those famous Burgundians – the Pinot noir and the Gamay. Both are used to make the excellent flinty red wine called DOLE. This is not a place nor a vine name; it belongs solely to this wine. By law, the Valais wine laboratory exercises certain controls over the use of the name Dôle, red wines not reaching the required standard being labelled Goron.

*VAUD*. This canton is the major producer of Swiss wine, the vineyards occupying the south-facing slopes along the shores of Lake Leman on either side of Lausanne. On the western side is La Côte; on the eastern, the more picturesque Lavaux. The wines are almost entirely FENDANT, white and dry.

Prominent among village names in La Côte are Féchy, Mont-sur-Rolle, Vinzel and Malessat; and in Lavaux – Lutry, Daley, Villette and Dézaley, where some of the best vineyards are owned by the Lausanne city fathers. These village names are really of no great consequence. Some of their wines appeared at a tasting in London some years ago; they were just as delightful as identical twins, but equally indistinguishable one from another.

*NEUCHÂTEL*. The Swiss wine tour continues in a clockwise arc to the shores of Lake Neuchatel, still part of French-speaking Switzerland, where the vine is still mainly the Fendant. Here the chalky soil favours the making of light sparkling wines. Some village sites are said to be better than others, but since the wines are all sold as NEUCHÂTEL, they are hardly of great interest.

*GENEVA*. Fendant wines are made around the town, which are said to be on the up grade though not as yet exported.

*TICINO*. The southern, Italian-speaking canton is a fairly large producer of red and white wines, known as Nostrano and rather harsh. Recently some Merlot stock has been imported from Bordeaux, and the resultant red wine will be awaited with interest.

*ZURICH*. The northern, German-speaking canton has always been thought too cold for successful viniculture, but a Pinot red wine called Klevener is now being made.

Prominent among Swiss shippers is the firm of Charles Bonvin in Sion, and for a wine-shipper what better name could there be! Alphonse Orsat of Martigny also ships wines to Britain, and there are several Neuchâtel firms represented in London.

CHAPTER TWO

# *Luxembourg*

IT SEEMS very unfair on 'Little Luxembourg' that those 120 miles of Moselle, twisting and turning from Trier to the confluence at Koblenz, receive all the publicity. Little is ever said about the other 180 miles flowing from its source in the Vosges near the Col de Bussang, north to Metz and Thionville and thence along the Luxembourg–German frontier, where 25 miles of Grand Duchy vineyards are to be found.

The wines they make are all white and low in alcohol, broadly similar to the German Moselles, whose name they are certainly entitled to geographically, more so indeed than wines of the Ruwer and the Saar.

In common with other European wine countries, viticulture goes back at least to the Romans. But in the last five hundred years the luckless Luxembourgeois *vignerons* must have received unsought advice from almost every one of these countries as one occupying power succeeded another. In 1443 it was the Burgundians; then came a period of Spanish sovereignty. In 1795 French occupation replaced Austrian hegemony, and after Napoleon, part went to Prussia and part to the Netherlands until they themselves separated. Very properly, Luxembourg loyalty has since been given to her best wine customer – Belgium.

This has been the case since the formation of the Belgian–Luxembourg economic union in 1921, when phylloxera and the post-war spirit brought about extensive re-planting with Riesling, Riesling-Sylvaner, Ruländer, Traminer and Auxerrois to augment the existing Elbling.

In the past few years Benelux production has increased; even though the number of growers has declined from 2,000 to 1,600. Modern methods are bringing higher yields per acre, resulting in a harvest of 5·4 million gallons in 1970, compared to 3·5 million in 1964. Home consumption accounts for two-thirds, while the remainder is exported, principally to Belgium, with Germany and Holland taking small quantities. An average holding of two acres does not encourage individual wine-making, so that there is strong support for co-operatives to bear the expense of up-to-date cellarage, machinery and trained staff.

The industry seems to be admirably controlled by the State, which decrees that only Riesling, Traminer, Ruländer and Auxerrois grapes may be permitted to make quality wines. These are further classified (and labelled accordingly) as *Cru classé*, *Premier Cru*, *Grand Cru*, *Réserve*, and *Grand Réserve*. To use any of these terms, growers, co-operatives and wine-merchants must make application, submitting a sample of the wine concerned for tasting by expert officials. Moreover, in the case of *Réserve* and *Grand Réserve* – the two highest denominations – no applications are permitted before the wine is a year old. When approval is given to any one of the five classes a control number and the number of the cask must be included on each bottle label.

Of greater value to the consumer, is the additional *Marque Nationale* label, which all wines passing this stringent test are required to bear as a mark of authenticity and quality.

No less impressive is the State wine institution and school at Remich, now in its sixtieth year, which enforces the regulations and is responsible for research, trials, etc., such as the Royal Horticultural Society performs in its own field in Britain.

Luxembourg wines should be drunk at 8–10° C (48–50° F) and when one to three years old depending on quality. As in the Ruwer and the Saar, a year with sunshine above the average is needed to show them at their best.

# CHAPTER THREE

# Austria

IN 1815, at the time of the Congress of Vienna, Austria was no mean wine country. The wines we know today as wines of Hungary, Trentino-Alto Adige, and Slovenia (Yugoslavia) were then Austrian. Its dominion stretched over palm and vine south to the Dalmatian coast and east almost to the Black Sea. Moreover, the Austrian Prime Minister, Prince Metternich, had been made a present of Schloss Johannisberg at the Congress.

Wine played no part in the loss of this Empire, though thirst for power certainly did. By 1918 Austria had shrunk to a size not much larger than Scotland, making less wine within the new borders than any other European wine-producing country except Switzerland and the newly formed Czechoslovakia.

Production today is from 45 to 50 million gallons annually, 15% red, 85% white. Of the white wines about one-quarter are of a high standard, comparable to those of Alsace or Trentino-Alto Adige. The vineyards cover some 116,000 acres, involving 90,000 wine families, which shows that the average plot is not much over an acre. With the Alps occupying the west and south, viticulture is confined to the eastern side. Those who go ski-ing in the west – to the Tyrol, for example – are more likely to drink wines from Trentino-Alto Adige (once Austrian South Tyrol) than those of Austrian vineyards.

There are four main wine districts:

> Lower Austria, making 60%, includes those familiar place names Wachau and Weinviertel.
> Burgenland, a flat and warm area round Lake Neusiedl making 33%.
> Styria, in the south-east along the Yugoslav border making 6%.
> Vienna, contributing the remaining 1%, popular in the cheerful taverns of the city.

The white wines are made from a fairly wide variety of grapes. The Riesling, said to be from the Moselle, and more recently the Sauvignon (see Wachau) are cultivated chiefly in the Danube valley. Traminer and Müller-Thurgau (Riesling and Sylvaner named after the inventor) are found in many parts. The Rotgipfler grape makes the full golden wine of Gumpoldkirchner, and the Muscat Ottonel is chiefly associated with the aromatic wine of the Burgenland. A popular wine with the Austrians is that from the Grüner Veltliner.

The St Laurent grape, described as a frost-resistant variety of the Burgundian Pinot noir, makes a red wine, but it does not resemble one of red burgundy.

## Districts and Wines

*WACHAU.* This Danube district running upstream from Krems has become known outside Austria largely owing to wines exported by the firm of Lenz Moser, based at Rohrendorf, near Krems. WACHAUER SCHLUCK, a fresh dry *spritzig* wine from the Sylvaner grape, is now sold by most wine-merchants in Britain, being deservedly popular, though 'Schluck' merely means a drop of wine. A Traminer wine, TRI-FALTER, and the sweet estate-bottled EDELFRÄULEIN from the Muscatel Ottonel grape, both by Moser, are also well known.

The Mosers have been wine people since 1124. Laurenz (Lenz for short) has made a singular contribution to viticulture. At the beginning of this century the width between rows was 3 feet, a space barely sufficient for ox or horse to pass. The plants were cut back, making cultivation an uncomfortable stooping business. These methods, from which he had suffered personally, greatly displeased Lenz Moser. In the teeth of opposition he planted *his* rows three yards apart and allowed the vines to grow up on trellises.

It was a case of 'Viva la libertà' for the vine, with the reactionaries predicting calamity – from pests, frosts and, above all, from loss of quality in the wine. For twenty years Moser was under attack from the whole German-speaking wine world. But he was right.

He was also right as a leading exponent of green manuring, which has slowly replaced the use of dung. Using tractors, the 'high and wide' system now enables one man to work 10 acres in place of ten men before; moreover, fewer plants are needed per acre to reap the same harvest. Lenz Moser's book, *Weinbau Einmal Anders*, has been translated into five languages. When visiting Russia he was astonished to see a vast expanse of vines planted in the Moser manner. He only then realized that Russian had been one of the five!

Recently Lenz Moser has been showing his visitors the first wines made from plantings of the Sauvignon grape in 1951. They are on a par with the best Hocks, and may well have a future if offered for export at the right price.

*WEINVIERTEL.* This name, 'The Vineyard Region', is applied to the main wine-growing district of Lower Austria extending east along the Danube from Krems and north-east across the Kamp valley to the border with Czechoslovakia. The wine towns of Langenois and Dürnstein are worth visiting for their baroque charm. At Dürnstein a statue of Richard Cœur de Lion and Blondin commemorates the troubadour legend, for it was in the castle that the monarch was interned when returning from the Crusade (see Cyprus).

Another Austrian firm of shippers now looking more towards the export trade is Alois Morandell and Son. Quite a wide range of estate-bottled whites, reds and some sparkling wines are available through the firm's London agents. The whites include one full-bodied pleasant dry Riesling called STEINER HUND. The hound, looking like a Boston bull terrier, appears on the label.

*BADEN.* The famous spa with its warm-water springs lies 17 miles south of Vienna at the foot of the *Wienerwald* (the Vienna woods). There is really such a preponderance of warm water from springs in this dry limestone district that a wine is needed to redress the balance, and it is found at Gumpoldskirchen. The vineyards making this well known full golden wine are on the slopes falling to the Vienna basin. Rotgipfler and Riesling are among the varieties grown, the best wine being *Auslese* from the latter. Red wines are made at Bad Vosland farther south.

*BURGENLAND.* Lake Neusiedl, releasing heat acquired throughout the summer, helps to keep the surrounding vineyards frost free during the autumn, making *Spätlese* wines possible in most years. Muller-Thurgau, Gruner Veltliner and Muskat Ottonel predominate, Riesling and Traminer plantings being relatively small. Rust, a pretty town, on the western side and Poltelsdorf to the north-east are the chief centres. Away to the south, the Eisenberg region makes some red wines.

*STYRIA.* These vineyards are on the border south of Graz, where the River Mur flows south into Yugoslavia to become so closely associated with the wines of Lutomer. The distance between the two towns is only 50 miles, soil and climate being so similar that the Austrians would surely benefit by extending their Riesling plantings on the lines of their Slovene neighbours.

CHAPTER FOUR

# Yugoslavia

YUGOSLAVIA, formed in 1918 as 'The Kingdom of the Serbs, Croats and Slovenes', and now 'the Socialist Federal Republic of Yugoslavia' has had a success story, likely to continue, in the export of wine since the war. The first bottle of Ljutomer Riesling reached Britain in 1950; now 4 million bottles of this wine are sold annually.

The making of wine, taught by the Phoenicians, fostered and extended by the Romans, has been among the more stable pastimes in the unstable history of these oppressed peoples, marked by the Venetian hegemony, Turkish raids and occupations, the conquests of Napoleon, inter-religious strife, political intolerance and murder, and finally, subjugation to the Austro-Hungarian Empire, ending in the First World War, with a Nazi occupation to come.

Under the Austrians even the solace of good drinking was largely denied to the Slovenes, for most of their best wines were sent to Austria and Hungary labelled as Austrian products. When independence came in 1918, new names, unknown to the outside world, hardly helped exports, of which their new government had in any event no experience. This was hardly surprising; the inhabitants of Slovenia had never had a government of their own people before. Even by 1938, annual export of wine was estimated at only 160 railway cars, compared to 1,408 in 1956. (For the benefit of train spotters, a railway car holds 2,250 gallons.) This figure has, of course, increased.

Although viticulture is being extended and improved throughout Yugoslavia, it is the Slovene white wines from around Maribor and Ljutomer in the north-east corner which are now esteemed throughout the wine-drinking world for their low-price quality. Looking at a large-scale map showing the vineyards grouped around the Rivers Mura and Drava the pattern recalls the Dordogne and Garonne above Bordeaux till one wonders whether great bottles, too, will eventually come out of Yugoslavia.

## Districts and Wines

*SLOVENIA.* The latitude parallel 45° could well be made into an aerial *Route des Vins.* From above it, as he flies eastwards, the traveller can see Bordeaux, the Rhône Valley, the vineyards of Piedmont, Rumania, Bulgaria, Turkey and, midway, almost immediately below him, those of Slovenia.

The province, by far the most important in Yugoslav wine production, is not only well situated but enjoys a climate tempered by Adriatic warmth and protected from northern cold by the Alps. With the vineyards mostly on slopes from 500 to 1,500 feet high and the occasional cool Bora wind blowing in summer off the mountains, the heat during the time of growth is not excessive, resulting in a good balance between acidity and alcohol in the wines.

*LJUTOMER.* In the north-east corner two rivers, the Mura and the Drava, flow south-east to join each other, eventually meeting the Danube a hundred miles north-west of Belgrade. Medjimurje, the district between them, 40 miles long by 20 wide, would to the French be another *Entre-Deux-Mers.* There are three towns: Maribor, the largest, on the Drava; Ptuj, 15 miles downstream, where those with a good knowledge of eighth-century Slovene will be able to read parchments of that time in the viticultural museum.

The third town is, of course, Ljutomer, whose name is prefixed to Riesling, Sylvaner, Sauvignon, Traminer, Pinot and Muscat, all familiar white-wine grapes planted extensively over this 40- by 20-mile strip.

Some names are less familiar. There are RENSKI RIESLING, medium dry from Riesling vines grown higher up on damper ground, and a sweeter white wine called Muskatni Silvanec. At the south-eastern extremity a locality named Ormož-Jeruzalem makes a white burgundy-style wine called RULANDER. The Crusaders once stopped here (hence the name), describing some local wine as 'Si bon', which has become 'Sipon'; it is sweet and highly regarded locally.

The famous Tiger Milk comes from the estate, Ranina Radgona, Radgona being a town on the right bank of the Mura. Sugar content can be up to 34% in good years, the grapes being *Spätlese* or late picked.

Not all the white wines of the district are made between the two rivers. There are other vineyards to the south of Maribor and Ptuj. Near the former there is the fascinating Ritoznojcan, literally translated as 'the sweat from Rita's back'. It is reassuring perhaps to learn that the wine is a Riesling, not a Rita, slightly sweeter than the Ljutomer.

*THE RIVER SAVA.* Second in importance in Slovenia is this central district, perhaps more Croat than Slovene. This river joins the Danube at Belgrade, after flowing south-east past Ljubljana and on to Zagreb, the vineyards lying midway between these two towns. The climate gives reasonable acidity to white wines such as Laski Riesling, Muskatni Sylvaner and Zeleni Sylvaner. There is also a dark red velvety wine, Zametria Ornina.

On the right bank of the Sava, stretching along its tributary to the Krka, there are vineyards making the *rosé* wine CVICEK, popular in summer and found at its best around the villages of Kostanjevica, Gadovapec and Krsko. Other wines from the Sava are the very sweet CHATEAU FLEUR – both red and white – and a *rosé*, SANS THORN (both trade names of course).

*THE LITTORAL.* This district lies on the Gulf of Trieste protected to the north by the Karavanken ranges and the Triglav massif. This is Gorizia and the northern part of the Istrian peninsula, classic home of Slovene wine, dating back to 283 B.C. Pliny the Elder, in his *Natural History*, Book XIV, Chapter 8, says:

'Julia Augusta, wife of Augustus, attributed her 82 years of age to the Pucian wine, for she drank no other. It grows on the Adriatic Gulf, not far from the source of the Timavus, on rocky hillsides, and the sea breeze allows but a few casks to mature, yet no wine is found more useful medicinally . . .'

CABERNET BRDA, MERLOT and PINOT NOIR are soft red wines. Teran has a good ruby colour and tannin content.

Among the white wines Rebula, Tokajec, Muskatni Sylvaner and Pinot are met locally as well as the sweeter Malvasia and Refshko.

*BOSNIA and HERCEGOVINA*. To members of my generation these two inland provinces in the centre of Yugoslavia will always be associated with stamps not wine. Our boyhood collections of the 'twenties included a most attractive set. One wine, however, is notable; the dry white ZILAVKA is Yugoslavia's nearest approach to a white burgundy, and thoroughly agreeable for those who find the Rieslings too sweet. Originally from the limestone hills near Mostar in Hercegovina, plantings of Zilavka are being extended.

*VOJVODINA*. This autonomous area of Serbia, lying close to the Hungarian border to the north and west of Rumania, is an exercise both in pronunciation and geography. Light white wines are made from Riesling and Furmint grapes.

*DALMATIA*. The coastal strip running roughly from Rab to the Gulf of Kotor needs no introduction to tourists. Its best known wine is DINGAC, a strong, dark, slightly sweet red wine of 14–15° alcohol made on the Peljesac peninsula, just north of Dubrovnik. Plavac is not quite so strong, and Opolo, another red wine, is slightly milder.

Among many Dalmatian local wines, the best known whites are the very sweet Proshak and the mildly pleasant Vugava from the island of Vis, now a naval base forbidden to tourists, off Split.

*MACEDONIA*. In this southernmost province under Turkish rule until 1912 Moslem influence might have precluded the making of much wine. Yet table grapes were always grown, and H. Warner Allen has quoted a reference to 'very tolerable wines' being made in 1824.

Viticulture received encouragement a century later when the League of Nations resettled many Greek refugees from the war in Asia Minor with good results until the Second World War. Then in 1963 nature replaced nationalism as the Balkan troublemaker, devastating the capital, Skopje, by earthquake. Happily the wine region 50 miles south of the town with its extensive cellars was undamaged.

Local wines, as is usual in a hot climate, are strong in alcohol but too low in acidity. Consequently, vineyards are being replanted with Zilavka and Smederevka (dry white), Kavadarka (*rosé*) and Prokupac (rich red).

*SERBIA*. Some 60 miles north-west of Belgrade the River Drava joins the Danube flowing on through the Fruška Gora (fresh hills) to Belgrade. Fruška Gorski Biser is a sparkling wine, a little below the strength of champagne. Both Prokupac – dry red and also *rosé* – and Ruzhica – *rosé* only – are made in many parts of Serbia.

## Liqueurs

MARASCHINO (51°), the world famous liqueur, is made from the sour cherry species, *Ceresca maraska*, which abounds in central and northern Dalmatia. Honey or sugar is added to the distillate for sweetening. The distilleries are mainly in the coastal town of Zadar (Italian 'Zara' from 1918 to 1945), being nationalized after the Second World

War. One well known producer, the Italian firm Drioli, taken over after being at Zara since 1759, reconstructed its factory at Mira, near Venice.

### Fruit Brandies

More famous than any wine of Yugoslavia is that national drink of the Serbs, the plum brandy SLIVOVICA, pronounced 'Shlee-vo-vits', made from the sweet blue plum *Slijiva*. Colourless, like Kirsch or Calvados, and without that additional flavouring which would make it a liqueur, Slivovica is a fruit brandy, with a strength of about 70°, with an almond flavour derived from oil in the stones, some of which are crushed and fermented with the juice of the plum.

To the Serb, and to a lesser extent the Croat and Slovene, Slivovica has been likened to the Highlander's dram – a cure for all ills; but, in a Communist country apparently, a man is permitted to distil his own! It is used as a soporific for young children; to deaden the pain of toothache and on a handkerchief swathed round the temples to cure a headache as if it were eau-de-Cologne.

One variation, among many barely known outside Yugoslavia, is Klekovac, a distillate from one-quarter *Slijiva* and three-quarters juniper berries.

CHAPTER FIVE

# Hungary

OF ALL the lesser wine countries of Europe, Hungary is usually put first by the experts on account of Tokay. 'A truly great wine', declared Raymond Postgate in *The Plain Man's Guide to Wine*. Professor Saintsbury went one stage further: 'No more a wine, but a prince of liqueurs', he said. Nevertheless, it took more than these commendations to spread the name throughout the English-speaking world. It was Noel Coward who did what would now be called a fine P.R. job in his operetta *Bitter Sweet* (1929). 'Tokay, the golden sunshine of a summer's day', sang the stirring chorus of 'café cavaliers' in the Vienna scene inevitable to such works. Today, perhaps, some of the magic associated with 'Imperial Tokay' has gone, for that wine came from one particular vineyard and is no longer made by the state monopoly.

On the production score, Hungary ranks about tenth as a European wine-maker, with about 120 million gallons a year (France and Italy are around 1,300 million each). Wine-making can be traced back to Roman occupation A.D. 276–82, their knowledge passing from Avar to Slav and so on to the Magyars crossing Carpathians in the ninth century to settle in the wide plain which became Hungary. With the Magyars came the Kaliz, a Bulgarian tribe whose name still survives in place names such as Kaloz, Kaliz, Kalic, settling in the Tokay region to the north, where they planted the vine on a large scale.

The history of Middle European countries is punctuated by invasions which descended upon them with great frequency. After the Tartars had ravaged Hungary around 1241, the arrival of Walloon wine-growers came as a relief, for they brought a new grape, the 'froment' (French for wheat), an unprepossessing dull yellow fruit whose name is now familiar to wine-drinkers as 'Furmint'. This is the grape which works the miracle of Tokay.

The discouragement of alcohol under the Moslem rule of the Ottoman Empire constituted a deep depression lasting 160 years from 1526, though after a while even Moslems seem to have deserted Allah for Bacchus. By this time the emergence of hill towns, as in Italy, had brought about more civilized tastes, the demand for red wine being met by Serbian refugees planting their own vines.

By the eighteenth century Hungary had some of the best-equipped cellars in Europe, a development owing much to Count Istvan Szecheny, a statesman who realized the need for scientific methods.

Oenological developments in the past century are marked by replantings on American root-stocks after the phylloxera, and in the last fifty years by the introduction of the Muscatel grape from France, resulting in Muskotaly, with its agreeable bouquet.

Post-war years have seen state reconstruction, state co-operative farms and modern scientific methods resulting in an improvement in quality, a large increase in output and a national export organization known as Monimpex.

State direction may sound rather dull to western ears. But tradition changes little. The toast is still *Egésegeré*; the oldest greeting 'Wine, Wheat, Peace' – with wine always first! Only when you have been put under the table by a twenty-two-year-old blue-eyed blonde cellar-mistress in the state cellars of Balatonfüred do you begin to see that Emmeline Pankhurst must have sown a seed or two when she went to Russia in 1917.

## Districts and Wines

*LAKE BALATON.* Known as 'The Hungarian Sea', Lake Balaton is the largest lake in central and western Europe, 50 miles long by 5 miles wide, with fresh water rarely more than 6 feet deep. The vineyards along the north shore on the slopes of Csopak, Balatonfüred and the extinct volcano Badacsony are steeped in mythology.

The lake's sudden storms are the passions of an angry giant imprisoned by the waters. A pealing of bells is sometimes heard from the Badacsony Bodyguard, a group of basalt columns girding the hill, which reverberate when lightly tapped. The Cain and Abel story (Hans Andersen's Big Claus and Little Claus if you like) is that the vineyards belonged to two brothers – one good, one bad. The bad brother, about to kill the good one by pushing him overboard from a boat (with a rope round his neck plus stone discreetly attached), suddenly hears the bells, forgets his seamanship manual, gets thrown overboard in the coil of rope and is drowned himself. (The lake is in fact more than 6 feet deep in parts, so do not try to spoil the story!)

Since the Balaton climate is not as warm as might be supposed, basalt is helpful to the vine, absorbing heat and passing it to the soil. The lake, too, warming by day and cooling at night, transmits warmth to the vineyards.

According to the researches made by the vinicultural institute on the Badacsony hill, seventeen different varieties of vine are being grown. If the local peasants' conservatism can be overcome, this number will be reduced perhaps to half a dozen. First among these will be the French Pinot gris, which gives BADACSONYI SZURKE BARÁT, an aromatic white wine which matures to a golden yellow. Locally, there is also Szürke Barát, a fragrant slightly sweet dessert wine.

Rarer than this, on account of a less productive species, is Badacsonyi Kéknyelü, known as the Blue Stalk. The Furmint (BALATONI FURMINT) making a fairly dry white table wine will be retained. The Italian Riesling (Olasz Rizling) which fills our glasses with medium dry Hock style wines (Janos, Balatoni are some of the trade names) will certainly continue.

*MOR*. Fifty miles west of Budapest, Mór is 'a young shaver' as Hungarian wine districts go. In the early eighteenth century an influx of Bavarian refugees settled in this wooded area, hacked down the trees and planted vines, not their own varieties but the Magyar Ezerjó, which means 'A Thousand Boons'. They received these; the Ezerjó throve at Mór as never before!

This surprising success is explained partly by the soil and partly by the Bavarians' skilful siting of the vineyards. The soil is sand and locss with a high mica and quartz content, a most distasteful mixture apparently to that root-eating bug the phylloxera which has caused so little trouble that Ezerjó still grows on pure Magyar stock. The siting is on slopes 600 to 800 feet up, protected from severe winter frosts by the hills to the north yet so placed that in June and July there is almost a complete absence of shadow.

The resulting wine MORIEZERJO – after the place and the vine – is dry and golden.

*EGER*. The famous EGRI BIKAVER, known as Bull's Blood, comes from this picturesque baroque town 85 miles north-east of Budapest by road. Though the Bull's Blood association must surely have helped the wine on the road to fame, a Hungarian book gives anxious but emphatic assurances that it has no connection with bulls nor their blood. But it is the right accompaniment for roast ox and, as if to emphasize the point, the book continues with a Hungarian 'Brillat-Savarin's' recipe for roasting an ox whole!

That such a wine has played a part in the town's turbulent history can well be imagined. Pride of place in the annals goes to the repulse of the Turk in 1552, when the women climbed the hill with pitchers of Bull's Blood, fortifying the garrison and fighting to victory beside them. It was too much even for the terrible Turk when the rumour spread through his lines that the enemy was fighting mad on Bull's Blood.

The wine itself is a deep red colour, dry, with a slightly bitter flavour. The grapes – Kadarka 70%, Burgundy 20% and Médoc noir 10%.

Other wines met locally are: The red Kadarka-Siller and Médoc noir, the delicate white Leanyka, which means 'Little Girl'. A little wine is also made from Ezerjó, Mézes Fehér, Kövidinka, Burgundy and Italian Riesling.

*TOKAJ*. Continuing north-east from Eger, Tokay is reached by road in about two hours. The town lies on the Tisza flowing south, eventually to join the Danube near Belgrade. The vineyards are spread over a wide expanse of hill country stretching towards the Hungarian–Czechoslovak border. Bitter controversy has raged in the past over the boundaries of the Tokay sites, but now twenty-five villages are entitled to the coveted label TOKAJI. The soil is crumbled lava on top of volcanic rock and loess, the climate very hot in summer, with a lingering sunny autumn and a hard winter.

Although the Magyars found vineyards of Celtic origin and French and German settlers improved methods, it was not until some seventeenth-century steward of a royal vineyard delayed the vintage because a local war was in the offing that the great sweet wine came about. With the threat over, the *Spätlese* technique, known to the ancients, was discovered.

Wars, too, were also indirectly.responsible for the saying, 'You have to bow before Tokay'. To guard the precious wine against the invader, hidden cellars were built in the hillsides, extensive inside and ideal for maturing the wine. Access through small hidden entrances was impossible without stooping.

Outside Hungary, the Poles were the first to appreciate Tokay. Prince Ferenc Rakoczi II sent consignments to Louis XIV. Peter the Great even bought a vineyard, building a castle from which to survey his domain.

The wine is made from three grapes – the Furmint, the Hárslevelü and the Muskotály, the Furmint providing perhaps 50%. *Tokaji* alone on a label is almost certainly a fraud; it should be followed by *Aszu*, *Szamorodni* or *Essencia*.

*Essencia* (essence, but more romantically known as 'the soul of Tokay') is in truth too scarce to be marketed. This highly sweet concentration is made entirely from shrivelled berries (*Beerenauslese*) for the purpose of sweetening *Aszu* wines. There is no pressing, the juice is allowed to drip from the grapes placed in a tub.

*Aszu* wine is made from normally ripened grapes with the juice of overripe grapes added in measure known as *puttonyos*. The mixing of these grapes is simplified because the vines ripen irregularly, so that normal and overripe grapes can be found at one and the same time. A *puttony* is a hod of 30 lb weight. A wine labelled 'two *puttonyos*' has had two of these hods added to each 35-gallon cask of wine made from normally ripened grapes. The number of *puttonyos* on the label is thus an indication of sugar content, not quality. Wines of three, four and five *puttonyos* are usual, but a very great year is required to achieve six.

*Szamorodni*. This is a table wine made in years not good enough for *Aszu* by pressing all the grapes – ripe and overripe – together. It may be sweet or dry, depending on the year, and one of these words will be printed on the label. Dry *Szamorodni* chilled to 46° F is an excellent *apéritif*. The Hungarians say 'forty drops before the soup'. For the sweet variety, a dessert wine, they recommend 54° F.

Once in cask, Tokay is matured from four to eight years, growing its own variety of 'flor' before being shipped in ½-litre-size bottles, which are traditional. The extent of further development in bottle is debatable, but it need not be opened for 20 years.

*SOMLO*. Somló is an extinct volcano, 26 miles north-west of the lake, whose soil strata resemble those of Vesuvius. From an acreage of only 1,000 a variety of wines are made. They include Furmint, Budai Zöld, Juhfarkú (sheep's tail), Mézes Fehér (white honey) and a red Tramini.

## Other Wines

*SOPRON*. The town, less than 50 miles from Vienna and almost in Austria, has pleasant local white wines from grapes already mentioned.

*SZEKSZARD*. Red Kadarka wines are made in this Danube district, 80 miles south of Budapest.

*PECS*. This large town, 30 miles south-west of Szekszárd, is in the centre of a V between Danube and Drava. There are model vineyards and nurseries. The chief wine is Villany, a strong red with high tannin content.

NEMES KADNAR. A Tokay *rosé*, rather sweet.

## Liqueurs

BARACK PALINKA, 70°, is the national 'short' drink distilled from fermented apricots at Kecskemét in the Hungarian plain.

CHAPTER SIX

# Czechoslovakia

ALTHOUGH Czechoslovakia was part of the wine-growing and drinking Austro-Hungarian empire until 1918, little is heard of her wines today. Only sixteen million gallons are made annually, a small quantity, but which equals Switzerland. The figure represents only twenty bottles per head of the population, and has to be augmented by imports, even though the Czechs are largely beer drinkers. Czech wines are not exported, and those who seek information about them may find their Government officials as responsive as the Pentagon would be if asked for America's latest secrets.

Vineyards are, however, established in all three provinces – Bohemia, Moravia and Slovakia. As with her neighbours Austria and Hungary, Czech white wines are better than red. The best come from Semillon, Sauvignon, Rhine Riesling, Sylvaner and Traminer. In the second class are Italian Riesling, Sylvaner and Furmint. The Pinot noir (known as Burgunder) is the best red grape, but Neuberg, Frankovka and St Laurent are also cultivated. These names, differently spelt in some cases, but easily recognized, appear on labels. The visitor may need guidance in interpreting Vlassky Ryzling, which is the Italian Riesling. Rynsky Ryzling, its superior relative, is comparatively self-evident.

In Czechoslovakia the tourist who hopefully expects cheap wine in its country of origin may be disappointed with the medium-priced wine, but he will at least find consolation in restaurants and hotels, where little profit is taken.

## Districts and Wines

BOHEMIA. The western province is mountainous and as northerly as the Moselle, where success depends greatly on the heat reflected from the rock of the vineyards. The wine centre is at Melnik, some 20 miles north of Prague, where the River Vltava joins the Elbe. From a fine schloss with an imposing bell tower, the terraced vineyards can be surveyed as they slope down to the river, and a local *Weinstube* exists for tasting their creations. Much of the ordinary wine is sold under a trade name, *Ludmilla*, but the better *Crus* retain their grape names, Sylvaner and Traminer being about the best.

Sparkling *Sekt*, popular with the Czechs, is also made in this district.

MORAVIA. The wine-growing centre is the small town of Mikulov on the Austrian border 40 miles due north of Vienna. There are whites and reds, but Moravia is the least productive of the three provinces.

*SLOVAKIA.* On the left bank of the Danube at a point where the frontiers of Austria, Hungary and Czechoslovakia meet is the town of Bratislava, flanked by hills and surrounded by vineyards on the slopes of the Little Carpathians. Bratislava, capital of Slovakia, is a Danube port and centre of the wine-trade, but the main vineyards lie a little to the north around Modca and Trnava and away to the east along the Nitra, a river which flows south to join the Danube. Slovakia makes more wine than all the rest of Czechoslovakia, and is now attempting to emulate her Hungarian neighbour by making Tokay. Lake Balaton is indeed less than a hundred miles from Bratislava, but the Austrian vineyards of the Burgenland are a mere 20 miles across the frontier.

CHAPTER SEVEN

# *Rumania*

LYING between 44° and 47° latitude, with 'the *Route des Vins* parallel' (see Yugoslavia) almost in the centre, Rumania is well placed geographically to make fine wines. Only the climate constitutes a drawback. In summer the shade temperature can exceed 100° F; in winter it can be as cold as in Russia, with bitter winds sweeping over the plains, the Danube icebound and the passes blocked by snow often for half the year.

Yet with the tempering influence of the Black Sea and Mediterranean near at hand it may be – given time and research – that some ideal combination of site, soil and species will produce wines comparable to true burgundy, claret or Hock. The evolution of the Russell lupin and the floribunda rose encourages the belief that such progress is possible in viticulture too. If so, Rumania or Yugoslavia may be the first to make the major breakthrough. Perhaps it has been done already. The Rumanians say that they have far better wines to export than their first bottles available in Britain.

Though the country was under Turkish dominion until 1878 and men and vines have been ravaged respectively by wars and phylloxera for the better part of time since then, Rumania has held tenth place in the international table of wine producers since the middle of the last century. Indeed, it still continues to grow, production having risen from 88 to 137 million gallons in the last few years. This achievement is all the more remarkable since Russia took back Bessarabia in 1947, and with it 40% of Rumania's previous wine production.

As in Bulgaria, a mountain range divides the country. The Carpathians sweep in a sickle-shaped curve from the north-west, meeting the Transylvanian Alps in the centre. To the west, inside the sickle, lies Transylvania, a mountainous afforested province. Outside the sickle, between the mountains and the Black Sea, are the provinces of Wallachia and Moldavia. The two form one enormous plain with some of the richest soil in Europe, excellent for cattle, cereals, vegetables, tobacco and grapes.

Although there now seem to be vineyards all over Rumania, the principal ones are on the east-facing slopes of the hills falling to this plain, and on the southern slopes of the Transylvanian Alps.

The state-run organization appears to provide 220 lb of grapes per head of the population per year, rather more than is good for them, so that wines are now being exported to 32 countries. Many of the vines are familiar to western Europeans, but the richer soil and hotter summers result in fuller and sweeter wines in Rumania.

As in other Communist European countries (and in France too), a plan aims at discarding inferior vine species, increasing production and generally running an expanding industry with modern means. A typical factory is at Foscani, 120 miles north-east of Bucharest. At least a dozen different wines are made, the grapes being brought in from a wide area to be crushed and their juice fermented under carefully controlled conditions before ageing and sterile bottling. Wines of these standards are, of course, improved by blending. Vintage wines are rare in Rumania.

## Districts and Wines

Most Rumanian wines bear the names of their districts and are referred to accordingly. Norton and Langridge, a London firm, ship those wines printed in capitals, whose prices are all very moderate.

*MURFATLER*. This was the name given by the Turks to the small coastal strip better known as Dobruja, enclosed between the Danube and the Black Sea, the greater part of which is in Rumania. On this flat ground under a hot sun, Pinot gris and Pinot Chardonnay yield sweet white dessert wines rich in sugar and alcohol.

*TIRNAVE*. This, the latest arrival, is the favourite child in the Rumanian vineyard family. It lies in the heart of the Carpathians, white-wine grapes such as Traminer, Pinot gris, Italian Riesling and Furmint being grown along the River Tirnave, which flows west to join the Danube beyond the Hungarian border. The various grapes are the instruments in the orchestra, which harmonize to make the wine of Tirnave – so the experts of Fructaexport declare – into a great work! One example is TIRNAVE PERLA, a light medium sweet 'composition'; RULANDER is rather sweeter.

*VALEA CALUGARESCA*. 'The Valley of the Monks', 50 miles north of Bucharest, appears on my large scale map to be in the middle of an oilfield, but in fact the vineyards are on the slopes where the Carpathians meet the plain. MUSCAT OTTONEL, a highly flavoured spicy dessert wine, and SEGARCEA 'CABERNET', an unusual sweet red wine with a dry after-taste, are both made from grapes left on the vine to dry, thereby increasing the sugar content. The lower yield makes them more expensive.

*DRAGASANI*. The vineyards here, in the south-west, are of long standing. In olden times a jug of wine would be left at the gate of each vineyard as a sample for passers-by. The best vineyard was quickly recognized by the first empty jug. SADOVA is a medium sweet *rosé* wine, but many of the grapes have local names, such as Crimposie, Braghina and Gordan, the last named after a General.

*ODOBESTI*. These ancient vineyards of the Putna basin, north-west of Galati, form 'the Midi' of Rumania – the district making the quantity. Galbena de Odobesti is a local grape of ancient repute, but a wide range of European varieties – Italian Riesling, Traminer and Aligoté among the whites and Merlot and Malbec among the reds – are being introduced. NICORESTI is a single vineyard making a full-bodied red wine.

*COTNARI*. This Moldavian district, in the north-east adjoining Odobesti, makes a similar variety. Cotnari 5, a heavy sweet white wine, has gained medals at Montpellier.

*TEREMIA.* Extensive state vineyards are to be found in the Banat, Rumania's south-western region, nearer to Belgrade than to Bucharest. Three local grapes – Majarca, Steinschiller and Creata (a Riesling of Banat) – are used to make a white wine with a greenish tinge. KADARKA is the best of the red wines. Mustoasa of Maderat is a sweet sparkling wine.

## Other Wines

Red and white vermouths are made from some Rumanian wines macerated with indigenous aromatic plants.

## Brandy

*TZUICA*, with a bouquet of plums and almonds, is a fruit brandy. Slibovitza is the Rumanian counterpart of the Yugoslav Slivovitz.

CHAPTER EIGHT

# Bulgaria

IN THE education of the English-speaking world, knowledge of Balkan countries could not be described as a strong point. Faced with one of those examination paper questions, 'state what you know about Bulgaria', the average answer would not exceed a few lines mentioning a small country under Communist rule to be found near the Black Sea. Readers of current travel brochures might recall some bathing resorts; and some of us would remember there was a king called Boris who drove trains.

As a seafaring people, we are little concerned that this country is the junction of two great overland trade routes to Istanbul and the Middle East. From Paris, the Simplon-Orient Express passed through Sofia to link with the north–south line connecting Russia and Rumania with the Mediterranean. Boris drove his trains towards the outlet his country has always wanted, but never achieved.

The word Bulgar (or Bougar) means a cultivator or ploughing peasant, and there are 8 million of these people spread over a land 300 miles wide and 200 deep. To the north, the Danube flowing eastwards forms the frontier with Rumania until it turns north near the Black Sea coast. To the south, the River Maritsa also flows east across the country. Between these two rivers is the high range of Balkan Mountains, also running east and west, splitting Bulgaria transversely in two.

Both rivers are fed by numerous rivers and streams flowing down from the mountains, the fertile valleys being protected from wind and cold by their unusual depth. These valley settlements, growing wheat on the higher table lands and market-garden produce, such as tomatoes and peppers, lower down, have long been typical of Bulgaria. The vine has, of course, been grown since Roman times, but wine as a commercial proposition could hardly be expected in a country under the Moslem rule of the Turkish Empire from 1396 until it gained semi-independence in 1878.

Early viticulture is marked by the legend of Mavrud. Around 800 B.C. Khan Krum, a desperate monarch who devastated Thrace like another Sennacherib, ordered the destruction of all vineyards. The peasants, in fear of their lives, dutifully obeyed, with the exception of the Mavrud family, who were ordered to be executed. But on the day before the execution the King's daughter was attacked by a wolf, and the handsome young son of Mavrud, who was spending his last hours under guard near by, rushed to her rescue, killing the wolf single-handed. Brought before the King, he explained that his source of strength was his daily glass of wine. The King promptly ordered the family's release and repealed the law.

This legend has some basis. Khan Krum did try to have the vineyards replanted with other crops, but clearly some kind of conversion must have taken place, for we also read of his slaying Emperor Nicephorus in battle and turning his skull into a goblet.

When Bulgaria gained a measure of independence in 1878, the phylloxera was destroying vineyards all over Europe, and the time was hardly propitious for organizing a wine industry. Moreover, strained relations with most of her neighbours, culminating in two Balkan wars in 1912 and 1913, followed by the First World War, kept the country unsettled, with a high proportion of the male population in the army.

Under the Communists a transformation is now taking place. Bulgaria is making 46 million gallons of wine a year, which is about twice the production of Australia. Under the energetic organization of Vinprom in Sofia, co-operatives send their wine to be bottled by modern equipment, employing the latest techniques for ageing and fining ordinary wines. Eighty per cent goes for export, medals being won for Bulgarian wines at international wine fairs, such as Budapest and Ljubljana.

In Sofia alone, a factory built in 1961 employs 400 people, working two shifts, and turns out over 30 million bottles a year.

Trade with non-Communist countries is developing fast, wines being shipped chiefly to western Europe, Sweden and Finland. Sales are said to have increased in value from 28 million dollars in 1950 to over 300 million dollars in recent years.

## The Districts

*TRNOVO.* Typical of the steep valleys on the northern side of the central Balkan range is that of the Yantra and its tributaries, which flow north to the Danube. Up this valley, linking north to south, runs the railway over the 4,363-foot Shipka pass. Trnovo, an ancient town, once a Bulgarian capital, gives its name to a province.

It is in this district with its good communications that the main vineyards and wine co-operatives are now established. At Lyaskovits, 4 million bottles of sparkling wines are made annually by both *méthode champenoise* and tank injection. Another town, Sukhindal, is mainly concerned with red wine from the Gamza grape. At Povlikani, 25 million kilos of this grape are pressed each year. Dessert wines and most Bulgarian dry white wines are also made here. In the nearby village of Varbovka a roughly hewn stone etched with wine vessels in the first century A.D. testifies to a long association with viniculture.

*PLOVDIV.* This southern province takes its name from the second town of Bulgaria (Plovdiv was once Philippopolis) on the right bank of the Maritsa. Here the wines enjoyed ancient fame. Mavrud grapes are grown in the valleys around the towns and its neighbour Asennovgrad.

*BLACK SEA.* The third region lies along the Black Sea coast in the hinterland of Bulgaria's two ports Varna and Burgas. Here mostly white grapes are cultivated.

## The Wines

*Red*

GAMZA. Ruby to dark red with a fruity aroma, chiefly made in the Povlikani region. In Bulgaria it may be named after local villages, such as Kramolinska, Suchindolska, Pavlikenska, Videnska and Plevensak.

KADARKA is a sweet red wine.

MELNIK: a claret-type wine.

MAVRUD. A dark red southern Bulgarian wine from the Asennovgrad region in the Maritsa basin. Formerly this district was the best known.

CABERNET. Plantings of the Cabernet Sauvignon grape are being extended. This is a claret-style wine matured in cask for four years before bottling.

*White*

DIMIAT. Dimiat grapes are grown along the Black Sea coast as well as in the Trnovo province. The wine is a yellowish green with a dry Riesling flavour. In Bulgaria it may be met under names such as Warnenski Dimiat, Pomoriiski Dimiat and Prelavski Dimiat.

MISKET. White wine of the Sylvaner type made in various parts. Misket Karlova (Child of the Rose Valley) is a picturesque national name. Songulane and Grozden are similar wines.

SONNENKÜSTE. A dry white wine from the Rehazeteli grape is shipped under this German trade name meaning 'Sunny Coast'.

Other dry white wines are Bulgarische Sonne ('Bulgarian Sun') from the Furmint and Donauperle ('Pearl of the Danube') from Fetiasca grapes.

CHARDONNAY and RIESLING. Small quantities of these wines, living well up to the famous names they bear considering their prices, are now being shipped.

*Sweet Wines.* Small quantities of Sauternes-style wines are made with an alcoholic strength of 11° to 12°. Production of fortified dessert wines, such as Tamianca, Pomori, Bisser and Varna with alcoholic strengths of 16° to 20°, is much larger.

*Rosé.* Principal *rosé* wine is Pamid, light-red to pink, ready to drink in the year after the vintage. Trakia is a blend of Pamid with Mavrud.

*Sparkling.* Iskra, named after the largest river flowing from the mountains to the Danube, is red. Perla is white. Both are natural wines made by secondary fermentation in closed tanks (*méthode cuve close*).

Some vermouths are also made.

## Brandy

Pliska is the wine brandy of Bulgaria. Slivova is a Schnapps; Mastika, a fairly dry anis liqueur and Rosa a pink fruit liqueur.

# CHAPTER NINE

# U.S.S.R.

IN THE 'Socialist Sixth' there is every variety of climate except tropical, and although the agronomist Michurin claimed to have grown vines as far north as Moscow, the wines of any repute are all made in the south not far from that girdle of Bacchus, the latitude parallel 45°. It is reasonable to suppose that their first vineyards were in the Caucasus, planted by peoples spreading northwards from Persia and Asia Minor. The Ancient Greeks took a hand about 700 B.C., penetrating eastward beyond the Black Sea. To them the Caucasus was a land of mystery and romance. They sent the Argonauts to fetch the Golden Fleece from the land of Colchis, which corresponds to the valley of the Rion in Georgia, whose wines now reach our own shores.

In the last decade the U.S.S.R. has extended her vineyards, until she may now become largest grape-growing country in the world. As a wine-producer, however, she may equal Spain, but not France or Italy. Probably no attempt has yet been made towards quality, for such wines as are exported seem inferior to those of her satellites – Rumania and Bulgaria, for example – although similarly priced.

## Districts and Wines

*MOLDAVIA.* This strip, which is really Bessarabia, lying between the Dnieper and the Danube, has long been a bone of contention between Russia and Rumania. After the First World War Russia lost part of it, and its frontier receded to the Dnieper. After the Second World War Russia took it back. Vines are grown almost everywhere; Pinot, Aligoté, Riesling, Fetyeska, Cabernet and Sauvignon being among the species. Probably a quarter of Russia's wine is made here.

In the 1920s the verdict of the *Encyclopaedia Britannica* on Moldavian wines was 'local wine, sour and liable to go bad in transport'. This must have applied at the time to wines in many other more advanced countrics, for poorly made wines, weak in alcohol, just do not stand up to travel. But with present-day scientific methods of vinification, which Communist and capitalist countries are employing alike, sound wines better than *ordinaire* can be made strong enough for export. Whether much of an advance on this standard is possible in Bessarabia seems doubtful on account of the weather. Most of the annual rainfall comes in heavy storms during the summer, washing away the soil down the steep slopes of the terrain.

The Moldavian wine trade mark is a white stork with a bunch of grapes in its beak, the stork being an emblem of happiness and plenty. When Gorodesti was being besieged by the Turks the brave Moldavian defenders ran out of water. The storks – so the story runs – flew in an airlift of grapes in their beaks saving the day – and the defenders.

The principal Moldavian wines exported to Britain are:

NEGRI de PURKAR. A red wine from Cabernet, Saparvi and Rara-Njagra grapes grown on the lower reaches of the Dnieper.

KABERNET. A typical Cabernet red wine.

FETYESKA. A dry white wine.

ALIGOTE. White, less dry than Fetyeska.

*CRIMEA.* The south-eastern coast of the Crimea is a riviera well protected from the rigours of a continental winter by the mountains rising to 5,000 feet which begin only a few miles inland. There are gardens with cypresses, camellias and mimosa; apples, pears and cherries abound. The vine prospers. Romans, Goths, Huns, Greeks, Mongols, Venetians, Genoese and, lastly, British have all invaded the peninsula at various times, contributing in greater or lesser degree to the advance of viticulture or the consumption of wine – usually the latter.

The vineyards continue east across the Straits of Kerch into the Kuban country on the mainland, where Anapa is the chief centre. The best wines come from the limestone slopes behind Yalta, the principal seaside resort, which boasts Russia's largest cellars, holding over a million gallons for ageing in cask or bottle.

Since the Crimean riviera was a favourite haunt of the aristocracy in Czarist times, the wines were well known in Russia as early as the eighteenth century. In 1863 the British wine merchant, T. G. Shaw, in *Wine, the Vine and the Cellar*, was writing:

> On the southern coast of the Crimea, there are three valuable properties belonging to Prince Woronzow. It is well known that his father, the late Prince, devoted much care and money to the finest vines, and the most experienced cultivators and cellarmen, from France, Spain and Germany. The wine produced on his estates of Massandra, Aidanil and Aloupka, both red and white, is of very high quality and bouquet, but so delicate that it requires to be tasted in the open air in order to be fully appreciated.

This point of enhanced appreciation in the open air might well be taken up by our London shippers. It would add enchantment to the City of London scene to see them tasting a range of samples on the pavements of Seething and Mark Lanes or alongside those lunch-hour speakers on Tower Hill, who extol the merits of temperance to audiences mostly employed in the wine-trade.

Shaw, who seems to have been given a tasting of the 1856 and 1857 vintages, uses terms such as 'very fine wine, great flavour', which is high praise from one who otherwise found most wines from the Levant eastwards quite terrible.

In view of past fame, it seems surprising that only one Crimea wine appears to have reached Britain since Russia started to export seriously in 1960. This, still available, is MASSANDRA MUSCATEL, a rich dessert wine.

ANAPA RIESLING is also exported, but it is not strictly from the Crimea.

*GEORGIA.* The wines of this Socialist Republic in the far south above the border with Turkey immediately recall those wartime visits of Churchill to Moscow. At the Kremlin banquet Stalin was always reported as drinking 'a light Georgian wine'. As he was the son of a poor Georgian shoemaker, this was more than likely, but the description 'light' was more politically expedient than vinously accurate.

Georgia is mainly a plateau with the great mountains of the Caucasus, rising to an 18,470-foot peak in Mount Elbruz, giving northern protection to a Black Sea climate. To the south beyond the Turkish border there are the Armenian highlands, and halfway up the coast the River Rion flows into the Black Sea through a wide valley, where a good winter rainfall gives sub-tropical conditions suitable for the vine.

Other vineyards lie farther inland, east beyond Tiflis the capital and around the Alazan River and its many tributaries. This is the Kakhetian region, for the peoples of Georgia are divided into several linguistic groups, of which Kakhetia is one.

The wines tend to be full and the red ones dark. The following are shipped to Britain:

MUKUZANI and SAPERAVI. Two dark, strong dry red wines from eastern Georgia, strength about 14° alcohol.

GOORJUANI and TSINDALI. Two straw-coloured white wines from the western side, strength about 11° alcohol.

Though sparkling wines are made in many parts of Russia, the centre of production is in Tiflis. Some sparkling red and white Georgian wines costing as much as champagne have been exported. A white one, Krasnodar, is charmingly described in a brochure as 'Champanski'.

*ARMENIA.* This republic lying midway between the Black and Caspian Seas is another plateau some 6,000 feet up. With the mountain-tops snow-covered for ten months of the year, it has a slight affinity with Switzerland. In the centre the huge Lake Sevan is in fact larger than all the Swiss lakes put together. Round the lake in volcanic soil are vineyards, which make wine sold as 'Caucasian'. The task of the peasantry, protecting their vines from an average temperature in January of 12° F, is unenviable. Port-, sherry- and champagne-style wines are made, but only two dry white table wines appear to have been exported to date.

CHAPTER TEN

# Greece

WINE IS as old as the hills; quite possibly those same hills to which the Psalmist lifted his eyes from whence came his help. We know, too, of wine jars illustrated in the tombs of the Pharaohs. The dates are obscure, but the evidence shows that wines were being made and drunk in Egypt and Mesopotamia before 5000 B.C. After this the civilizations of Asia Minor fade away and Greece comes into the limelight.

This is not surprising; though the story of great wine is one of the vine struggling for existence in poor soil, the plant does need some rain in winter, which nature provides along the northern shore of the Mediterranean more effectively than along the south. Not only did they plant vines in the heyday of Ancient Greece, which began about 1500 B.C., but this great sea-faring people spread the habit throughout the inland sea. It is to them that we owe the wines of Jerez, Málaga and Sicily. In 600 B.C. they were established at Marseilles, finding in the Rhône valley, one may imagine, the keenest of their oenological pupils. Eastwards they penetrated too, beyond the Crimea to the Caspian.

Whatever their achievements in the export field, the many references to wine by their writers shows that the home market was also in excellent shape. Even Dionysus, who was really the god of fruitfulness and vegetation, came to be regarded solely as the god of wine. Homer, who lived about 800 B.C., it is true, makes no reference to a wine god, but Hesiod, a little later, describes wine as his gift.

Dionysus was born, according to tradition, in Thebes. Semele, his mother, most unwisely as it turned out, asked his father Zeus to appear in his full majesty as god of lightning. Semele was struck dead, but the child was taken care of in the thigh of Zeus.

Once grown up, Dionysus embarked on a world tour to spread the cult of his worship, and to teach the cultivation of the vine. But there was some opposition. The king of Thebes objected to the orgiastic rites introduced among the Theban women. There was (understandably) strong resistance to certain mystic rites, in which the priest representing him was killed. And even though the priest was brought to life again, the king must have had the same suspicions as a man lending his gold watch to the conjuror. But when the god was received hospitably he returned kindness with the gift of the vine, and at Delphi, being a prophet, he was received by Apollo on almost equal terms. His followers included spirits of fertility and the satyrs; his emblems were an ivy leaf and the *kantharos*, a large two-handled goblet. Beyond this the story is obscure. In common with most deities of vegetation, he died and rose again, finally giving way to Bacchus, who first appears in the fifth century B.C.

Athenian addiction to the grape is illustrated by two Symposiums describing wine parties, one by Xenophon, 421 B.C., and the other by Plato, 385 B.C. The word then meant a drinking party.

The Ancient Greeks made one other notable advance on their predecessors. As H. Warner Allen points out in *A History of Wine*, they possessed non-porous jars, which were air-tight, enabling them to mature fine wine to the zenith of its potentialities.

The extent of twentieth-century vineyards is 170,000 acres, of which 62% are planted for wine, 8% for table grapes and 30% for sultanas and currants. The soil is generally chalky rock with a subsoil of chalky marly tuff. It is very dry, the rainfall diminishing towards the east and south. Apart from the plain of Thessaly and a few coastal fringes of flat land, where wheat has priority, Greece is almost entirely mountainous, vines being grown on the lower slopes up to 3,000 feet.

A wide variety of wines are made – red, white and dessert – Retsina and Mavrodaphne being the best known outside Greece.

## Districts and Wines

*PELOPONNESUS.* This southernmost part of Greece, once joined to the mainland by the isthmus of Corinth and now only by the bridge which spans the Corinth canal, is the most important of the wine-makers. On its north-west shore stands the ancient town of Patras, guarding the Straits of Lepanto leading to the canal. Inland among the hills are the vineyards making DEMESTICA, SANTA HELENA and ANTIKA, three dry white table wines, which are to be found in every hotel and restaurant in Athens. Those who do not take kindly to the flavour of Greek vermouth will find them useful also as *apéritifs*.

In 1845 a Bavarian named Gustav Clauss came to Patras and founded the Archaia-Clauss Wine Company in 1861. Judging by the plaques in the company headquarters commemorating visits by various European royalties, Clauss had done pretty well by the time he died in 1908. Nowadays the firm produces over a million bottles a year, one in three being exported to places as far afield as Egypt, the U.S.A. and Málaga, but ownership has been Greek since 1920. The Clauss tradition of recording distinguished visitors has continued, signed letters from such divergent characters as Franz Liszt and Lord Montgomery being among the company's heirlooms.

A second region lies in the centre of the Peloponnesus around the ruins of ancient Mantinea, whose name is given to a well-balanced white wine. The Peloponnesus has one unexpected claim to vinous distinction. The name Malmsey is derived from Napoli di Malvasia, a town of Laconia, the south-eastern part.

*CORINTH.* Red wines from the Agiorgitiko vine planted in the Nemean region called Nemea and High Nemea.

*CONTINENTAL GREECE.* This is the modern term for the mainland of Attica. It includes the long island of Euboea joined to it by the swing bridge at Chalcis and the islands of the Sporades (Skyros, Skiathos, etc.). Sound white wines of 12·5° are made from the Savatiano vine, which stands up to the extreme dryness of the climate better than others. Chalcis gives its name to reds and whites of Euboea made from Savatiano and Roditis. The former is also planted in the famous Archoba vineyard near Delphi.

*MACEDONIA AND THRACE.* Vineyards across the northern provinces between the Adriatic and the Aegean suffered almost total eclipse in the phylloxera plague of the last century. A variety of vines are planted: Popolka alias Black of Naoussa alias Xynomavro of Cosani in western Macedonia; Cinsaut, Chalkidiki and Limnio in the east. But the chief vineyards lie on the slopes of Mount Velia, north of Salonica, the red wine Naoussa being quite well known. Though lower in alcohol than more southern wines, those of Salonica have a general pleasant freshness due to malolactic fermentation.

*CRETE.* Little, if any, Cretan wine finds its way beyond Greece; moreover, the usual visitor imbibing the wonders of the Minoan age on 'the tour' is given little time to sit and drink. But there are strong red wines associated with the Liatica vine and the Romeikon vines from the east and west sides respectively. From Heraklion, Archanes and Peza there are red wines from the Kotsifali, a species cultivated only in Crete.

*THE CYCLADES.* This circular group, cradle of wine in Ancient Greece, includes Naxos, Milos, Mykonos and Santorin. The last named was a great wine-producer a century ago, but the group now concentrates more on tobacco.

*OTHER ISLANDS.* Lemnos, part of the Aegean group guarding the entrance to the Dardanelles, makes a red wine from the Kalamnaki vine and a white Muscat of Alexandria. Rhodes and the other Dodecanese have sound white (Athirit) and red (Amorgiano) wines, of which visitors speak well. Ionian Group. 'Dry, white and pleasing,' wrote one of my correspondents back from holiday, enclosing a simple label which just said 'Corfou'. But the island and its neighbours also makes Mavrodaphne and Muscat of Cephalonia. There are also the red wines Robolo and Ropa.

## Notable Greek Wines

*RETSINA.* Like Beaujolais, RETSINA should be drunk young. That must surely be the only thing the two have in common. To make white wine into Retsina, resin is added from the local pine trees, *Calitris quadrivalvis*, during fermentation. After about a year the wine begins to turn musty, which disproves the theory that resin was originally added as a preservative. The real reason, suggested recently by Cyril Ray in Wine List, (*The Observer*, October 1965), might have been to take away the taste of goatskins. Even so, it does not seem to have been adopted in other countries. Perhaps resin from other species of pine was too unpalatable, or perhaps they just preferred a bouquet of straightforward goat.

Writing in 1863, the wine merchant T. C. Shaw, in *Wine, the Vine and the Cellar*, Chapter XIV, refers to the local habit of mixing 'rosin, chalk and tar'. A century later Cyril Ray discovered a village where they add salt.

Suffice it to say, then, that Retsina is a 'try-anything-once' wine, and plenty of people besides the Greeks find it agreeable. The experiment is not expensive.

*MAVRODAPHNE*. This sweet, sticky Málaga-like dessert wine is well known. Gustav Clauss at Patras began to make it in 1873, naming it – so it is claimed – after a beautiful woman with whom he was in love. Greek scholars, however, may think the name refers to the disappearing Daphne who, pursued by Apollo, prayed for aid just as he was over-taking her and was transformed into a laurel.

*SAMOS MUSCATEL*. Samos, barely a mile from the coast of Asia Minor, was the birthplace of Pythagoras. Those who have wrestled in youth with the square of the hypotenuse may like to think that the theorem could never have emerged without some stimulant at the philosopher's elbow. If so, the glass would have been filled with Samos Muscatel – Byron's Samian wine demanded by Don Juan and dashed down by the bowl.

It is a sweet dessert wine, allegedly made from a grape only to be found on the island, not in my view as good as Mavrodaphne. As with all very sweet wines, a glass or two suffices; dashing down by the bowl is likely to be followed by a bilious attack.

A dry variety is also made.

## Spirits

*Brandy*. Greek brandy compares favourably with other national brandies, apart from Cognac. CAMBUS\*\*\* is a mark which is exported.

*Ouzo*. A favourite Greek *apéritif*, distilled from grapes with aromatic herbs added. Best drunk cold with some water.

*Mastiha*. Distilled from grape alcohol with sap from the Mastiha tree, grown on the island of Chios, added. In the British Mediterranean Fleet before the Second World War Mastiha had a formidable reputation for delayed action. It was said that after a night on Mastiha ashore men would wake up with a great thirst, drink a pint of water and then find themselves incapably drunk. To be in this state when required for duty was a far more serious offence than returning on board drunk.

CHAPTER ELEVEN

# Cyprus

PERSIA is the reputed birthplace of wine. Cyprus, lying only 50 miles from the main-land of Asia, was certainly one of the first European lands to cultivate the grape. The *amphorae* recovered from ancient wrecks give ample proof that the island exported wine to the Egypt of the Pharaohs, to Greece in the Golden Age and later to Rome under the Caesars. St Paul's advice in the Epistle to Timothy, 'Drink no longer water, but use a little wine for thy stomach's sake and thine other infirmities', may well have been

written from personal experience when preaching in Cyprus on his first journey in
A.D. 46.

In the classical world, Cyprus, the traditional birthplace of Aphrodite, was a place of
pilgrimage, bacchanalian rites being performed in her temple near Ktma (old Paphos).
The earliest Aphrodite of Cyprus, to which Aristophanes refers, was a bearded half man,
half woman, whose worship had become debased. But over the centuries she has been
the goddess of fruitfulness (including gardens), evolving eventually as the Latin Venus,
goddess of beauty. Yet her Cypriot birth from the foam (aphros), immortalized by
Botticelli, was a maritime miracle, so that she came to be worshipped by sea-faring
men under other names, such as *Euploia* (giver of prosperous voyages) and *Gatenaina*
(goddess of fair weather).

Little is known about the seven centuries of Byzantine rule. Evidently they were
turbulent times. At one period the governing power found it necessary to deport the
Archbishop and 16,000 citizens.

In May 1191 Cyprus wine flowed liberally for the royal wedding of Richard Cœur de
Lion and Berengaria, daughter of the King of Navarre. Richard, whose fiancée must
have been travelling with the party, had captured Cyprus on his crusading way to the
Holy Land. But rivalries at home soon forced him to return, selling his conquest to the
Knights Templars, who found their Saracen slaves useful in the vineyards. When Philip
II of Spain treacherously destroyed the Templars by means of the Inquisition, the
Knights of St John took over certain areas, known as Commanderies, from which the
oldest wine name still in use – COMMANDARIA – is derived.

The Knights Templars, who were the bankers of Europe, had given the crown of
Cyprus to Guy de Lusignan, a French nobleman whose family ruled until the sixteenth
century. According to one tale a Count Thibaut of Champagne, visiting Cyprus, inter-
ceded for a young nobleman sentenced to death for being found in his fiancée's bedroom. It is difficult to believe such a drastic penalty under *French* rule, but nevertheless
the young couple later visited the kindly Count in Champagne, bringing gifts of vines
which founded the great vineyards of the Marne.

The last Lusignan king, James II, married a Venetian, Catherine Cornaro who,
when widowed, allowed the Serene Republic to take over in 1489. The 82 years of
Venetian rule saw Cypriot wine-merchants established in Southampton and a concession for Commandaria granted by Queen Elizabeth I to Sir Walter Raleigh. Shakespeare's *Othello* is set in the Cyprus of this period, the victorious Moor general being the
Governor with Venetian citizenship. Though the wine-trade flourished, the Cypriots
were oppressed, as may be imagined if their real Venetian masters were as evil as Iago.
Verdi's *Otello* begins with a thunderstorm, a duel and the great wine-drinking scene
with the refrain 'Bevi con me', all in the first act. It is fiery Cyprus at any period. Their
next ruler, Sultan Selim II, was known as 'The Sot', but his particular love of wine was
an isolated case during the next two hundred years under the Turk. On 4 June 1878, as
a wit once said, Britannia dipped her trident into the Mediterranean and came up with
yet another possession. The arrangement was part of an alliance with the Turks against
Russia, and in 1914, with the Turks allied to Germany, Cyprus was declared British.

It is paradoxical that the wine industry, though one of the oldest, is among the last to
be modernized. Improvements in viticulture have been hampered by the difficulty of
importing vine stocks guaranteed free from phylloxera, the pest being at its worst in

Europe in the latter part of the nineteenth century. The report of Mr Fred Rossi, made
at the Government's request in 1956, resulted in the shipping of 3,500 vine cuttings
from Europe under stringent sterile conditions. South Australia, believed phylloxera-
free, has supplied another 2,400, now under observation, planted in sand at the Government quarantine station. A Wine Industry consultant has been appointed, and the
formation of a Wine Institute should follow.

## The Vineyards

Cyprus – a rectangular island with a long thin tail at the eastern end – is 140 miles long
with a width of from 35 to 50 miles – making it about the size of Norfolk. In the centre,
towards the western end, are the Troodos mountains rising to 6,406 feet. The vineyards,
employing one in five of the population, are spread over 140 square miles more or less
on an arc over the slopes. 80 to 85% make red wine; 20 to 15% white. With a consistently hot and dry summer, neither quantity nor quality varies from year to year, so
that a vintage label (if ever used) is solely an indication of age.

## Cyprus Sherry

The natural white wines have a tendency to maderize in the heat, making them
potentially suitable for sherry. Moreover, the latitude is within 2° of that of Jerez.
Experiments are being made in the production of *fino* and *amontillado* types by introducing the 'flor' yeast, upon which these wines depend. They now have developed flor
sherry in Cyprus, and a bodega of 1,000 butts has been formed.

Cyprus has already made considerable progress. The dry sherries now imported at
full strength (28° to 35°), costing the same as the South African, begin to compare with
them. In the medium dry category the gap seems a little wider.

Another type of wine (the term sherry is purposely avoided) is imported at two different strengths, being 'married' by the importers. The lower strength wine qualifies for
a lower rate of duty, so that the final blend can be offered at a lower price. The wine is
sound, the practice legitimate; but the term 'sherry' should surely be confined at least
to those made in the Jerez manner to the same strengths.

A third group is formed of low strength wines nearly always sweet. Abundant sun
gives a sugar content of 4° to 5° Baumé. Since Cyprus is a Commonwealth country, paying a slightly lower rate of duty, these wines can be offered at a little less than any
foreign counterpart.

## Commandaria

The heat in southern Mediterranean latitudes helps the production of sweet dessert
wines, such as Tarragona, Málaga, Mavrodaphne and Sicilian Muscatel. Deserving a
distinguished place in the class is COMMANDARIA (27°). Though hardly likely to
excite the same interest as the place names of Burgundy, there are some twenty villages
recognized as producers, the best known being: Kalokhorio, Zoopiyi, Yerass, Ayias
Mamas, Lania, Sylikou, Dhoros, Monagri and Ayios Georghios.

Commandaria is made from a blend of red and white grapes, the best wines with only
10% of white grapes. Locally they mature Commandaria for many years in Ali Baba-
like earthenware jars.

## Table Wines

*Red.* These form a small but growing part of Cyprus exports. Local taste in red wines is for very full, deep-coloured wines with a high tannin content quite unsuitable for the experienced palates of northern Europe. Lighter wines are, however, being shipped, available in Britain under various trade names.

Local wines are: Opthalma, Matatheftika and Black Mavron, which makes an above-average wine from the slopes of Afames, near the village of Platres.

*White.* Dry white wines are made from *Xynisteri*, grown around Paphos and Larnaca.

*Rosé.* From the Mavron, a *rosé* wine is made both here and in Greece. Called Kokkineli, it is fresh, deep in colour and usually dry. The French troops in Cyprus at the time of the Suez crisis found it the best wine to drink.

CHAPTER TWELVE

# Turkey

To TURKEY belongs the distinction of having planted the first vineyard. How paradoxical, then, that Moslem abstinence should have played such a part in discouraging the most agreeable use of its produce!

Of course this not certain, but Edward Hyams, in *Dionysus: A Social History of the Wine Vine*, makes a strong case for putting the origins of the cultivated wine grape somewhere between the Caspian and the southern shores of the Black Sea between 8000 and 6000 B.C.

Rival claims have been advanced for Transcaucasia, where the wild grape was indigenous and wine must have been made from it, just as members of Women's Institutes make wine from hedgerow blackberries in Britain today. But here the comparison ends; the early neolithic tribes of the Caucasus were primitive barbarians, incapable of planting a parsnip.

The peoples of Mesopotamia, settled on the plains of the Tigris and Euphrates, were, on the other hand, civilized wine-drinkers by 4000 B.C., yet the wild vine was not indigenous there. It seems therefore that the art of viticulture must have been learned from some earlier peoples inhabiting country where the vine did grow wild. Such conditions obtain in the Armenian mountains to the north, where these two rivers have their sources. Here the soil would have been sufficiently fertile for a nomadic tribe to settle. Each year the flood waters in spring would irrigate the land sufficiently for the growing of wheat and other crops of subsistence; the vine, less exacting in its natural needs, would have flourished in the combination of summer heat and winter rain.

Edward Hyams supports his theory with a quotation from the oldest surviving literature, written not on paper but on stone, perhaps as old as the eighteenth century B.C. The translation reads:

> Amethyst it bore as its fruit,
> Grape vine was trellised, good to behold,
> Lapis lazuli it bore as grape clusters,
> Fruit it bore, magnificent to look upon.

It seems too that the Turks were responsible for introducing the vine into north China in the seventh century A.D., though this is not altogether surprising, for the Turinian race includes Manchus and Mongols. Indeed, for every Turk living today within the boundaries of Turkey there is another outside them, chiefly in Iran, Iraq and the Turkish-speaking republics of the U.S.S.R.

Since these earliest times Turkey has become one of the largest grape-growers in the world, picking close to 4 million tons each year. But a further eighteen centuries were needed after Christ before the possibility of making wine on any scale was considered. The development was one of many introduced by Kemal Ataturk, the great man of Turkey between the two world wars, who replaced the Arab script by the Roman alphabet, the Islamic civil code by the Swiss and in general 'westernized' his country. Today Turkish production runs to 52 million litres of wine a year, with red and white in about equal quantities and about one-tenth in dessert wines. Though much is being done to modernize agriculture, methods are still largely primitive. In the ports along the south coast of Turkey they still send ox carts a day's journey into the mountains to collect snow, which is subsequently sold in the shops for cooling drinks. The tourist making a purchase can reflect that he is receiving treatment fit for a Pharaoh, for in ancient times wine was shipped to Egypt in snow-filled holds insulated with straw.

The quality is potentially very good. Though export of wine is a state monopoly, there are three outstanding private vintners: Feltu and Kutman in Istanbul and Metin And in Ankara. Europeans knowledgeable about wine buy from them or from Kavaklidere's under Karakoy Square in Istanbul.

A correspondent who has lived in the country for many years, describes the best white wines available for purchase in Turkey at present as the Feltu 1959 vintage, Kutman's 1948 Dolucas and Metin And's recently marketed Kavaklidere, Cankaya Yildizi, which he believes outclasses any Rieslings made outside Germany.

Dolucas is made from French and German vines planted at Murefte in Thrace sometime between the wars, and some wines made in the 1940s, which are still being drunk privately, were outstanding. The Kavaklidere wines (Cankaya Yildizi is the white; Yakut Damlasi is the red) are sold locally in two qualities. The dearer is recommended.

Of the red wines, my correspondent speaks of the red Feltu 1959 as the best value he has ever met anywhere in the world, and though the Istanbul price was low, he compares the wine favourably with clarets costing over three times as much in London. He is not alone in his opinion. Most of the stock was quickly bought by the Diplomatic Corps, and inspection of the French Embassy cellars would almost certainly reveal the greater part of it!

## Districts and Wines

Turkish wines are usually named from the places where they are made, the grape sometimes being given as well on the label.

*THRACE.* In European Turkey the town Tekirdag, 75 miles west of Istanbul, gives its name to the best known Turkish wine. TEKIRDAG is white and sweeter than the term 'dry' on the label indicates. Trakya can be red or white. Narbag and Kalebag are other wines, but better than these is BUZBAG, red, dry and full-bodied. The best, however, is Papazkarsih, which is fermented for fourteen days. There is also a dessert wine called Misbag.

*BURSA*. This town on the southern side of the Sea of Marmora gives its name to a red wine, which was at one time exported.

*ANKARA*. Sound red and white wines are made in the surrounding hills, place names being Kalecik, Hasandede and Cubnik. The first two improve with bottle age; the last named is best drunk young.

*IZMIR* (Smyrna). A white dessert wine, Bornova Muscat (similar to Samos) is made.

*GAZIANTEP*. The best known wine of this place close to the Syrian border is the red Sergikarasi.

*TOKAT* in the centre of Turkey, 75 miles inland from the Black Sea, makes Narince.

*ELAZIG*. Some say this town in eastern Turkey makes the best of all Turkish wines. Okuzgozu is the formidable name of a formidable red wine with 15° alcohol.

## Brandy

Turkish brandy is surprisingly good. A waiter in an Istanbul café declared it was the best in the world. Without going quite so far as this, it is certainly nearer Cognac than the brandies of many European countries.

Raki, 87° proof with an aniseed flavour, is a spirit *apéritif* drunk with water and ice. The best liqueur is the state monopoly 'Portakal', virtually a Cointreau.

CHAPTER THIRTEEN

# Malta

IN SPITE of spending two pre-war years based on Malta, it was not until I returned, in 1944, that I can remember drinking a bottle of Maltese wine. I was certainly quite unaware that there were vineyards going back to Phoenician times.

This ancient industry has waxed and waned in accordance with the creeds of numerous invaders usually bent on securing the islands for maritime domination. With the Romans in charge, vineyards were encouraged; then in A.D. 396 came a period of Turkish and Arab rule. Roger, the Norman, ousting the Arabs in 1090, brought the feudal system, but with the Turks raiding the islands in the fifteenth century and carrying the inhabitants off to captivity, stability was short-lived. The Knights, coming from Cyprus and Rhodes in 1530, must surely have needed the grape to help them withstand the great siege of 1565. After that, with the Turk finally repulsed and the nobility of Europe flocking to join the gallant Order, the islanders enjoyed comparative peace and a prosperity interrupted for wine-growers only by the American War of Independence. This brought such a phenomenal increase in the price of cotton that vines and olives were uprooted and attempts made to grow cotton instead.

When the French took Malta in 1798 there should have been a future for the wine industry, but Napoleon chose quite the worst place to enforce his anti-clerical laws. Expulsion of foreign monks and no new priests in Malta. No wonder there was a riot. This led to Nelson's taking over the administration after Napoleon's defeat at the Nile, until finally, at the peace treaty in 1814, the Maltese themselves chose to be governed by a nation of beer drinkers.

Under British rule attempts to organize the wine industry seem to have been made in 1870 and again in 1919, an unfortunate moment as it turned out, for the phylloxera arrived the following year. Mr Anthony Cassar had already begun to make and sell wines, his business developing since the last war into Marsovin Ltd with a large up-to-date winery fitted to tackle the export markets.

The need for self-sufficiency emphasized in 1927 led to some measure of planning by the Department of Agriculture. Professor John Borg, an authority on viticulture and horticulture, given the task of increasing wine production, succeeded in halving the quantity of imported wines by 1939. Since the war, with the need more urgent, the Government has raised production and modernized wineries until less than 10,000 hectolitres are imported. Although this is a tremendous drop from the figure of 100,000 in 1927, it does in fact represent four bottles of imported wines per head of the Maltese population. Perhaps they are all being drunk by the tourists, in which case the economists can be satisfied.

The acreage now under vines is officially given as 2,062, which is 2 to 3% of the total area of Malta and its neighbouring island, Gozo. Considering the space taken up by towns, villages and airfields, one would expect to see more evidence of the vine when travelling about. Its elusiveness is partly due to the precaution of planting in hollows – such as disused quarries – as a protection against the Gregale, a north-west wind which can blow with hurricane force. On Gozo vineyards are more apparent; this greener island, hitherto rather inaccessible, can now be reached in twenty minutes by hydrofoil running from Grand Harbour, Valetta.

It is believed that when the Phoenicians first arrived they planted vines as much for shade as for fruit, a possibility that anybody who has spent an August in a Valetta dry dock will readily believe. Their vine was called 'Dielja' – the shade-maker. But the main wine grape is still the Insola, and it was the Knights who decided that this was the best species for the soil and climate. In doing so they were good economists, for this vine is dual purpose. It makes tolerable wine and tolerable eating grapes, so that the growers even today are reluctant to replace it with *cépages* known to make better wine. But recent plantings have included French and Italian cuttings from Pinot, Barbera and Trebbiano.

At each vintage, early in September, the government fixes the prices, and some 9,000 wine farmers in the two islands sell their grapes in bulk, chiefly to the dozen large firms with modern wineries.

There are red, white and *rosés* with an alcoholic content of 12° selling in Malta for around 10p a bottle. The *rosé*, Verdala, is considered among the best. A correspondent living out there, however, declares that Altar wine is far superior to these. It is white from the first pressing, made to high standards required by the Church. Lest the Archbishop should be inundated with enquiries, I hasten to add that it is obtainable in Malta through Marsovin.

With our system of duty levying a standard charge on every bottle of wine irrespective of its basic cost, it is not surprising that attempts to build a market in Britain for Maltese wines have not so far been successful.

Nevertheless, Capital Wine Agencies, an enterprising firm of London shippers specializing in wines of the lesser countries, offer a *rosé*, a 'burgundy', a sweet and a dry white wine. Coleiro Brothers, a Malta firm established in 1888, are also interested in persuading the British to put away their tankards and try the wines of Malta.

CHAPTER FOURTEEN

# *Israel*

ONLY a slender acquaintance with the Bible is necessary to recognize Israel as a wine country. The vineyards of Noah and Naboth come to light in primary education. The Book of Proverbs abounds with references:

> Honour the Lord with thy substance, and with the firstfruits of all thine increase:
> So shall thy barns be filled with plenty, and thy presses shall burst out with new wine.
> > *Proverbs* 3, verses 9 and 10

And again later, Solomon, warning his son against over-indulgence, perhaps exaggerates the symptoms –

> Who hath woe? who hath sorrow? who hath contentions? who hath babbling? who hath wounds without cause? who hath redness of eyes?
> They that tarry long at the wine; they that go to seek mixed wine.
> > *Proverbs* 23, verses 29 and 30[1]

From the dispersion of the Jews in the second century A.D., except for ninety years of Crusaders' rule, right down to 1918, when Allenby defeated the German–Turkish forces, Palestine was under Moslem Arab rule and there was little viticulture. Then in the 1880s came a new development, which was to lay the foundation of the industry as it is today. The Rothschild Barons, James and Nathaniel, were already great proprietors in the Médoc, and now Baron Edmond sent French experts to instruct the New Zionist settlers.

Vineyards arose once again on the plains of Judaea, in the valley of Sharon and along the hills of Samaria. The Baron was a good Samaritan indeed, helping and financing many projects but asking no return for himself. In 1897 he built the cellars at Rishon-le-Zion, giving them nine years later to the growers on condition they formed a Co-operative Society. This was named *Société Co-opérative Vigneronne des Grandes Caves* and is still operating.

Doubtless, too, he was the force behind the Palestine Wine and Trading Company – now The Carmel Wine and Trading Company – which opened its London branch in 1897. Today, for purposes of distinction, London-bottled wines are labelled 'Palwin' and Israel bottlings 'Carmel'.

Since the state of Israel was formed in 1948 the population has almost trebled, presenting the Government with a formidable employment problem. Culture of the vine is part of the mixed agricultural plan. The present 23,000 acres of vineyards represent

---

[1] I first met this quotation waking rather late one morning on board one of H.M. ships. Propped against my early morning cup of tea, long since cold, was a card on which was merely written Proverbs 23, verses 29–30. A messmate had crept into my cabin to leave this fitting epitaph of a 'run ashore' the previous night. The port might well have been Haifa.

one acre of vines to every 465 acres of territory, but only one-third is planted with wine grapes.

## The Vines

*Cépages* are principally as follows:

|  |  |  |
|---|---|---|
| Black: | Alicante Grenache | 40% |
|  | Carignan | 37% |
|  | Alicante Bouschet | 1% |
| White: | Muscat d'Alexandrie | 14% |
|  | Semillon | 4% |
|  | Clairette egreneuse | 1% |
| Others: |  | 3% |

## Vineyards

There are four different types of farm where vineyards are planted.

1. Collective farms, with vines in groups of 30 to 40 acres placed between orchards growing other fruits. The vines are grown on trellises, but many of the grapes will be for the table.
2. Village co-operatives of 100 to 200 acres, in which the average family holding will not be more than 5 acres. While the whole will be machine cultivated, pruning, irrigation and picking are the responsibilities of each family on its respective plot.
3. A few large proprietors with up to 500 acres.
4. Individual farmers not working on a co-operative basis, who are by and large the main source of wine grapes, training their vines *en gobelet* on plots averaging 15 acres.

There are about 700 farmers in group 4, the majority belonging to the *Société Co-Opérative des Vignerons*, which fixes the price of the grapes each year and runs the two big cellars at Richon-Zion and Zicron-Jacob.

## The Wines

A very wide range of Israeli wines, spirits and liqueurs distributed by the Carmel Wine Company can now be obtained through wine merchants in Britain. Some experts consider the dessert wines the most successful.

*Dessert Wines*. Nearly a score of wines are imported in this category. With the exception of some fragrant Muscats, they are red. Carmel Partom is the nearest approach to port, but shows no advantage in price over an average tawny. The remainder are raisin-flavoured after the style of Málaga.

*Red Table Wines*. Adom Atic is a dryish wine something akin to a young Beaujolais suited to everyday drinking. Château Windsor, rather fuller, is nearer to burgundy. The Israeli claret is dryer than either.

*White Table Wines*. These include wines sold as Palwin and Carmel, Graves, Sauternes and Hock, though the last is made from Semillon grapes imported from France at Baron Rothschild's instigation.

*Others*. Vermouth and some sherry-type wines are made and exported, but the prices show little advantage over Spanish sherry or French or Italian vermouth. The same may also be said (with great regret) about an excellent brandy, 777 Richon.

Plate 53. Grape vines in Yugoslavia

# The Wines of

# AUSTRALIA

## and

# NEW ZEALAND

❦

ANDRÉ L. SIMON

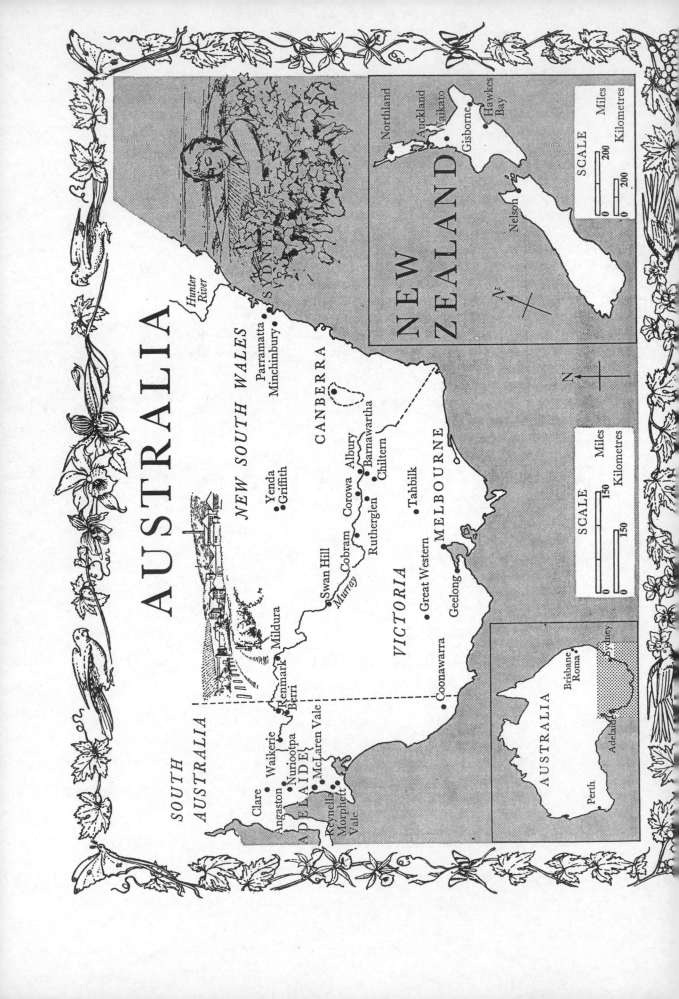

AUSTRALIA

NEW SOUTH WALES

Hunter
River

Parramatta
Minchinbury

SYDNEY

CANBERRA

Yenda
Griffith

Cobram
Swan Hill
Corowa Albury
Rutherglen
Murray

Barnawartha
Chiltern

Tahbilk

VICTORIA

Great Western

MELBOURNE

Geelong

Coonawarra

Mildura

Renmark
Berri

SOUTH
AUSTRALIA

Clare
Angaston
Waikerie
Nuriootpa

ADELAIDE

McLaren Vale

Reynella
Morphett
Vale

NEW
ZEALAND

Northland
Auckland
Waikato
Gisborne
Hawkes
Bay

Nelson

N

SCALE

Miles
Kilometres

200

200

0

0

N

SCALE

Miles
Kilometres

150

150

0

0

AUSTRALIA

Brisbane
Roma

Sydney

Adelaide

Perth

# *Introduction*

THERE are in Australia a great many wines from fair to fine in quality which are characteristically *Australian* wines. They cannot be anything else: they are members of the great family of wines of the world, just as the men who make the wines are members of the great human family. Both the men and the wines of Australia have characteristics of their own which they owe to the soil and sunshine of their native land, and they have good cause to be proud of the name that is theirs.

The first settlers to grow grapes and to make wine in Australia came from England, where they were born either during the second half of the eighteenth century or at the beginning of the nineteenth; that is, at a time when port was rightly known as the Englishman's wine, when much red wine of high alcoholic strength and temptingly low in cost came from the Cape of Good Hope as the poor man's port, when Hamburg brandy, hollands, and rum were incredibly cheap.

They were drunken times such as there had never been before, and such as, happily, have never been known since. Claret, burgundy and champagne also Hocks and Moselles, were the privilege of the rich and the great in the England of the pre-Victorian era; which is why the pioneers of the wine industry in Australia built distilleries as fast as they built wineries, and why there are even today more fortified wines made than tables wines, and a slightly greater tonnage of grapes used in the making of brandy and other spirits than in the making of wine.

None of the early settlers who planted some vines and made some wine during the first half of the nineteenth century in Australia had any background or experience as *vignerons* or vintners. Some were granted great stretches of land, and others purchased large estates, but none other than the first comers had the benefit of cheap convict labour. The shortage of labour, unskilled or semi-skilled, made it quite impossible, in the beginning, to plant and to care for large vineyards. Many of the early settlers, however, liked to have, usually near the homestead, a vineyard large enough to give them every year a little wine for their own drinking, and a good deal more that they could distil into brandy and fortifying spirit.

Grazing and fattening cattle demanded so much less labour than growing grapes, and it also paid better. But money, happily, is not everything, so the love of the grape and the pride of drinking one's own wine may easily become a fascination, unique and almost irresistible. Which is why more vineyards and larger vineyards gradually came into production in many of the valleys of Australia: those of the Parramatta and Hunter Rivers, in New South Wales, first of all; then those of the Murray and Goulburn in Victoria, before reaching South Australia, where there are today more vineyards producing grapes for wine-making than in the other four wine-producing states of Australia put together.

The wine industry of Australia had modest beginnings, and there were a great many obstacles in the way of its progress in a country which had no wine-conscious – let alone wine-loving – population, but a population of spirits- and beer-drinkers. But this is no longer true: wine is now gaining a greater measure of recognition and appreciation than it ever had before in Australia. Today the wine industry is one of the major industries of the country – no less than \$Aust. 200 million (£90·3 million ster.) have been invested in it, and the modern equipment of the Australian wineries and distilleries, not only the larger ones, is equal to the finest of the European countries.

Cold, in this scientific age, works miracles, and refrigeration has done more in Australia than in any other of the world's winelands to raise the standard of quality of wine. The high temperature at the time of the vintage in Australia was for many years a cause of grave anxiety for the Australian *vigneron*, who was unable to check the tempo of fermentation of the new wine and avoid acetic fermentation and other such-like disasters. Today, happily, there is no longer any such danger, as the wine-maker is at all times in complete control of the temperature of the must, or grape-juice, in his vats or tanks as it becomes wine.

From the beginning, in spite of costly mistakes and mishaps, to our own day, in spite of the high cost of modern equipment, Australian wines, the best as the rest, have always been moderately priced by the bottle over the counter, though sometimes (as elsewhere) much too dear in the hotel dining-room. The low basic price was in earlier days a bull point with the masses but a bear point with the classes. No better proof of this do I know than what I was told at the Melbourne Club, Melbourne: during the first one hundred years of the existence of the Club there never was a single bottle of Australian wine in their cellar, where most of the classical growths of European vineyards and most of the great vintages of the past had been given a bin of their own. Now, of course, things are very different, and the wines of Australia occupy pride of place: they are still much cheaper than imported wines, but very much better than they used to be and much better value.

In Australia, as practically everywhere, the small man in any trade or industry has a poor chance of survival. It is certainly regrettable, but it is no less certainly inevitable. The cost of labour, of transport, of raw material and of all else is bound to rise as population grows and demand outstrips supply. Mechanical tractors and all manner of modern agricultural equipment are much too costly for the small *vigneron*: the greater the acreage of the vineyard and the greater the load of grapes to be picked and processed at the time of the vintage, the greater will be the benefit of those mechanical aids. This is why it is the big and very big organizations which are doing more and more of the planting of vineyards, producing the greater proportions of grapes, wines, spirits and their by-products. The small *vigneron* is by no means doomed: he may and he will, we all hope, continue to tend his vineyards as all good vineyards must be tended, with the loving care that is the only truly intelligent care. The big firms will be only too happy to buy his grapes at a rewarding price because his grapes will be better than those of their mammoth vineyards mechanically cultivated. The little man will gradually disappear as a wine-maker, and the big firms will use the grapes they buy from him to make wine which may not be any better than the little man made – when he was lucky – but they will make wine that will be much more consistently safe and sound. It is true, of course, that standardized wines are bound to lose some of their individuality as wines, but the middleman, the wine-dealer who stocks the wine, appreciates above all qualities in a wine its dependability.

Sunshine galore, fertile soil and the best classical varieties of grapes to plant are assets shared alike in Australia by all, however small or big they may be; but the big concerns have financial resources which enable them to keep their wines in cask and bottle longer, thus giving them a better chance to reach the consumers when the wines are at their best. They are also in a much better position to make their wines better known in this age, when too few people still bother to think for themselves, and so many more are content to have their mind made up for them by newsprint, radio or television.

It is unfortunate that Australian wines have been so cheap for so long: it makes it more difficult to market the better wines which necessarily cost a little more – and they are often worth a great deal more. They all share with all the good wines made in the world the two basic qualities of balance and soundness, just as you would expect any good man, woman or child to be sound of body and mind. But that is not enough. Good wines, like all good people, must also have a personality of their own: that is, the characteristics which they owe to the land of their birth, its soil and climate, and also to the care and training of their nursery days.

The world is made of all sorts, and there are all sorts of wines for them all. There is no reason why any of the good wines which are better known than others should be jealous of other good wines not as well known as they are themselves: there can never be too many good wines in the world, any more than there will ever be too many good people.

CHAPTER ONE

# The Vineyards

THE VINEYARDS of Australia may be divided into two main groups, the quality group and the quantity group.

In the vineyards of the quality group an important proportion – if not the whole – of the grapes have been chosen from the better varieties of *Vitis vinifera* grapes, the classic grapes, or aristocrats, as they are sometimes called. They are the varieties of grapes from which all the better wines of the world are made, in Australia, as in California, Chile or South Africa, wherever soil and climatic conditions are suitable, and whenever the aim and ambition of the *vigneron* are to make wines that will be the peers of the more famous of the European wines, all of them made from the same varieties of grapes.

Unfortunately, it happens that the more highly bred any subject may be, the less fertile it will be, and all the aristocrats among vines deserve only too well the name of 'shy-bearers' given to them. Their average production, under favourable conditions, is merely 2 tons of grapes an acre, whereas some vines in irrigated areas bring forth 10 tons an acre; but nobody would expect the quality of their grapes, and of the wine made from them, to be comparable, and it is not. It is only from those 'shy-bearing' vines that wines may be made that will stand the test of time, age with grace, reach a high standard of perfection and possess the so rare and so highly valued distinction which we call, for the lack of a better name, breed.

In the vineyards of the quantity group the majority of the vines belong to the commoner varieties of *vitis vinifera*. They are usually known as 'free-bearers' in opposition to the 'shy-bearers', and they bring forth large quantities of grapes bursting with sugar and water, from which large quantities of wines are made which may have colour and strength, sweetness and a pretty label, but no vinous charm: wines for the thirsty and for the distillery, not for the connoisseur.

The nature of the water and of the sugars in all ripe grapes is exactly the same, just as the nature of the blood in the veins of king and beggar is the same, although by no means identical; but the quantities of water and sugars in all ripe grapes vary from year to year according to the incidence and intensity of rains and sunshine. What is of greater importance as regards the quality of the wine made from all grapes is the nature of the various acids and salts which will be eventually responsible for the distinctive character of different wines. Vegetal acids vary according to the different varieties of vines, and mineral salts according to the geological formation of each vineyard's soil and subsoil.

The more immediately obvious difference, however, between the grapes of 'quality' and 'quantity' vineyards is water. All 'quantity' vineyards are close to a river, and pumps are to them what our heart is to each one of us: these are the vineyards of the 'irrigated areas'. There are also some 'quality' vineyards situated conveniently close to a river, and it gives them the chance of occasional waterings in drought periods, but they are not irrigated, and they retain the right to their title of 'quality' vineyards.

There are vineyards in five of the six states of Australia, but South Australia has a commanding lead in production of wine grapes. New South Wales and Victoria are the next two more important wine-making States; Western Australia has now quite a number of vineyards, but Queensland only very few. It was not always thus: up to about a little more than a hundred years ago New South Wales had more than twice the acreage of vineyards there were in Victoria and South Australia put together, but South Australia took the lead in 1859; Victoria at one stage later shot ahead, but was disastrously affected by phylloxera, and South Australia's lead today in acreage of wine grapes is greater than it has ever been. (Actually, Victoria produces 25% more grapes of all kinds than South Australia, but more than 90% of Victoria's grapes are dried.)

The number of acres planted in vines is of importance 'quantitatively', but the variety of grape selected for planting in each vineyard is of greater importance 'qualitatively'. Today the Australian *vigneron* knows the name, the age and the pedigree of all his vines, the date when planted and their yearly yield. In the beginning, however, and for a long time, there was a great deal of uncertainty and confusion regarding the vines imported from Europe, Madeira and the Cape of Good Hope. We read, for instance, that one of the most enthusiastic amateur *vignerons* among the early settlers in New South Wales, Captain John Macarthur, visited a number of French vineyards, with two of his sons and a French expert guide, in 1815–16, when he bought a large number of cuttings from vines deemed to be the most suitable for growing in New South Wales. He left those cuttings with a London market-gardener, with instructions to ship them to Sydney after they had rooted and were likely to stand the sea voyage. Then he sailed for Australia, and, calling at Madeira *en route*, he followed a similar plan, selecting suitable cuttings to be shipped to him the following year. Unfortunately, when the French cuttings reached him in 1817, and when he got those from Madeira in 1818, they proved to be quite different from those he had selected and most of them had no identifying name of any kind. In 1841, however, one of Captain John Macarthur's sons, William, gave a list of the vines which were in production at the time at Camden Park, the estate near Sydney which his father had named after the then Colonial Secretary, the first Lord Camden. This was the list: Pinot gris, Frontignac, Gouais (La Folle), Verdelho (Madeira), Cabernet Sauvignon, Riesling, Grenache, Mataro.

In 1825 the Australian Agricultural Company ordered from Chiswick, England, a collection of vine cuttings, but there is no record of what happened to them. It was only in 1831, when James Busby brought back from France and Spain no less than 570 different varieties of grapes, that viticulture made a real start in Australia. Busby gave a specimen of every variety to be planted in the Sydney Botanical Gardens, and he planted the rest in his own vineyard, at Kirkton, near the Paterson River, a tributary of the Hunter River, in New South Wales.

In 1840 a group of Adelaide citizens subscribed to a fund for the purchase and importation of an important collection of vine cuttings from the Cape of Good Hope: most of the cuttings were distributed on arrival among the subscribers, but a specimen of each of the different varieties was planted in the Adelaide Botanical Gardens, at the time on the north bank of the Torrens River, opposite the present Zoological Gardens.

Although the Busby collection at Kirkton was the more important, it appears from records still available that the Camden Park nursery supplied most of the vines for the early vineyards of Victoria and South Australia during the second quarter of the nineteenth century.

In his book *The Vine in Australia*, published in Melbourne in 1861, Dr A. C. Kelly remarks that

> at first little attention was paid to the varieties of the vine suited to the soil and climate of this Continent. Vines from all parts of Europe and the most diverse climates were indiscriminately mixed in the same vineyard. A vine from the cold climate of the Rhine or the Neckar was planted alongside of another from the Tagus or the Douro. The first ripened its fruit in February, the other perhaps in April, making it impossible to have both ripe at the vintage. Much time was wasted in introducing varieties altogether unsuited to our climate, and which might have been saved by a preliminary enquiry into the nature of our own climate and a comparison with the climate of Europe. There are many acres in situations as Adelaide planted with vines of northern Europe, which proved so utterly useless that they have been rooted out after ten years trial, to be replaced by the more vigorous vines of the south of Europe.

Nearly one hundred years later, in the *South Australian Journal of Agriculture* of November 1958, the then viticulturist of Roseworthy Agricultural College, Mr C. D. Matthews, wrote of the varieties of vines that were first imported into Australia, as follows: 'Although the Busby and Macarthur vines provided the start for the vine growing industry in South Australia, it is regrettable that they were used, as in many instances the names of the varieties had been lost or altered prior to or during transit from the Continent, and many had been wrongly renamed.'

Today, of course, there is less confusion, but a high degree of specialization, which accounts for the fact that there is but a very small number of varieties of vines cultivated in considerable quantities in the irrigated areas for the making of dried fruit and special wines – Sultanas, Muscat (Gordo), Grenache and Doradillo – whereas there is a greater

variety of vines grown in much smaller quantities for the making of the different
varieties of dry and sweet wines – chiefly Shiraz or Hermitage, Pedro Ximénez,
Semillon, Mataro, Palomino, Riesling or Rhine Riesling, Frontignac, and Ugni Blanc
or white Hermitage; also, but to a much smaller extent, Pinot noir, Cabernet Sauvignon, Verdelho, Chassclas, Malbec and Traminer.

## New South Wales

New South Wales was the cradle of viticulture in Australia. The first thing that the
first Governor, Captain Arthur Phillip, did, as soon as he had a roof over his head, was
to have vines in his garden and grapes on his table. There is no lack of documentary
evidence to show that many early settlers planted a vineyard, built a winery and a
distillery, usually near the homestead. Captain John Macarthur, writing in 1793 from
Sydney to his brother, then in London, mentions that he has 'built a most excellent
brick house' in the centre of his farm, 'with three acres given to grapes and other fruit'.

There were no book-sellers and there were no book-shelves in the early period, and
the pioneers of the pre-Busby days, who had no experience how best to plant vines and
to make wine, must have been very grateful to the editor of *The Sydney Gazette*, who
published on the back page of the first number of his paper, dated Saturday, 5 March
1803, the first of a series of articles to help the amateur *vignerons* of New South Wales
with directions on how to plant a vineyard:

> The ground to be turned up, cleared of weeds, and trenched out to the depth of 18
> inches; or, should it not be encumbered with stumps or roots of trees, underwood or
> brambles, the cuttings of vines may be immediately planted without that precaution . . .
>
> For the purpose of planting the young vines already rooted, holes are to be made with a
> strong hoe, or broad pick-axe, at a discretionary distance of about 2 and a half to 3 feet open
> from each vine, and some mould or old turf must be laid round the foot of each . . .
>
> The method of dressing the vines after the vineyard has been formed, is principally to
> prune them well, and to attend to a minute knowledge of their nature; also what influence
> the change of climate may have operated on them; some will not produce without being
> propped, others best without; and the situation of the land and temperature of the climate
> will determine if the branches have to be carried more or less in height, and consequently
> how to be supported; they may be cut off either in a flat or sloped manner, but care must
> be taken to clear away all dead or defective parts.

The fact that the editor of the first newspaper published in Australia thought fit to
give up space in his journal's first issue to help the *vignerons* of New South Wales proves
beyond any doubt that there must have been at the time a very real and widespread
interest taken in the plaint of new vineyards in New South Wales, and this is confirmed by the records which have survived of early vineyards planted near Sydney – in
the Parramatta Valley, the Rooty Hill area, at Minchinbury and Hawkesbury, before
1825. What is much more remarkable is that those early *vignerons* not only managed to
make wine for their own consumption but wine good enough to be sent to London.

Thus the one-time explorer Gregory Blaxland, who grew grapes at his Brush Farm,
now Ermington, in the Parramatta Valley, sent some of his wine to London in 1822,
and he must have been a proud man when he heard that the Royal Society of Arts had
given his wine a Silver Medal. He sent some more of his wines to London in 1828, and
this time they gave him a Gold Medal.

During the second quarter of the nineteenth century a number of vineyards were planted farther away from Sydney, chiefly in the Hunter River Valley, a hundred miles to the north, where there are still today a few of the original vineyards, and many others which were planted more recently. The most famous among the veterans is Dalwood, in the Pokolbin area, which was first planted in 1828 by George Wyndham. He was a migrant from Wiltshire, and the homestead which he built on the left bank of the Hunter River, from stone quarried by convicts, still stands: it had to be a large house, since he and his wife, Margaret, were blessed with twelve sons and two daughters. The house has been modernized and the vineyard has been enlarged, but there were, up to 1959, some of the original convict-planted vines, noble centenarians, which were then uprooted, as they could no longer pay for their keep. The Dalwood vineyards and estate now belong to Messrs Penfold, who have also given the name 'Dalwood' to a 723-acre estate 40 miles from the parent Dalwood Vineyard and 15 miles west of the diarying centre of Muswellbrook. Three hundred acres of this new Dalwood Estate, which was bought in 1960, were by 1965 planted with the finest table-wine varieties. Here the visitor sees a remarkable sight: vines planted in dead straight rows each nine-tenths of a mile long, giving every facility for the use of tractors, cultivators, mechanical harvesters and so on.

The planting of vineyards and the making of wine were given every encouragement by the early governors of New South Wales, as well as by urban and rural authorities, for their economic value and also partly, if not chiefly, for their 'sobering' appeal. Thus Dr John Lang, whose younger brother Andrew was one of the pioneers of viti-culture in the Hunter River Valley, wrote at the time: 'There is reason to hope that, if the population of New South Wales could by any means be converted into a wine-growing population, they would in due time become a wine-drinking and com-paratively temperate, instead of a rum-drinking and most outrageously intemperate population.'

By far the most famous *vigneron* of New South Wales in the early days was James Busby, who has often been referred to as the father of viticulture in Australia. Before leaving Australia for New Zealand in 1832 he had not only planted a model vineyard of 40 acres, at Kirkton, the estate to which he gave the name of his birthplace, but he had distributed over 20,000 cuttings to about 50 of the Hunter River Valley *vignerons*, and he had also published for the benefit of *vignerons* in all parts of Australia the first book to be published in Australia for their guidance and assistance, a book which was for a long time regarded as the Bible of the Australian *vignerons* in its original and suc-cessive editions. Its full title was *Treatise on the culture of the Vine and the art of making Wine, compiled from the works of Chaptal and other French writers and from the Notes of the Compiler during his residence in the wine Provinces of France.*

Today, there are no longer any vines growing at Kirkton, but there is a dry white wine made from grapes grown in the Hunter area and marketed by the firm of Linde-man under the name of Kirkton Chablis: it so happened that the son of the Dr Linde-man, who founded the firm, married the daughter of James Busby's niece and heir.

Today there are still many vineyards in the Hunter River Valley, and they are re-sponsible for many of the better quality table wines, not merely of New South Wales but of Australia. Most of Hunter vineyards are in the Pokolbin are, a short distance west of Cessnock and Branxton as one comes from Newcastle, where the Hunter flows into the Pacific Ocean. Among the most important of the Hunter vineyards and wineries today, Dalwood (Penfold) is the oldest, Ben Ean (Lindeman) is the largest, Mount Pleasant (McWilliams) is one of the best known. There are a number of long-established Hunter vineyards and wineries, such as Tulloch's, Tyrrell's, Oakvale, Glendore, Bellevue and Sunshine. Of the latest and smallest of Hunter vineyards, the 5-acre vineyard of Cabernet Sauvignon grapes planted in 1963 by an eminent Sydney surgeon, Max Lake, is perhaps the best known.

The vineyards of the Hunter River Valley have had their troubles. Some were washed away by the worst floods of the Hunter, a river which has not too many friends but too many tributaries: when the rains happen to be excessive so many swollen streams rush into the Hunter that the Hunter becomes a menace.

COROWA is a long way to the south-west, upon the right bank of the Murray River, which divides New South Wales from Victoria. The vineyards of Corowa suffered from the phylloxera invasion, but many were replanted, and there are still a number of flourishing vineyards, such as Southern Cross and Felton (Lindeman), two of the largest. Most of the grapes from Corowa vineyards are used for making sweet fortified wines, brandy and fortifying spirit.

GRIFFITH is in the valley of the Murrumbidgee, one of the Murray's main tributaries. It is completely surrounded by vines as far as the eye can see: vines which are irrigated by the water of the Burrinjuck Reservoir. These vines produce very considerable quantities of wine.

ALBURY, on the New South Wales bank of the Murray, and on the road from Sydney to Melbourne, used to have some important vineyards, the last of them at Ettamogah, a few miles from Albury. It was owned by J. T. Fallon, who did not replant the vineyard when it was blighted by the phylloxera in 1906; his manager, John Delappe Lankester, born in 1837, was pensioned off and lived on to 1938.

## *Victoria*

The cult and culture of the grape in Victoria may be traced to the fortunate accident that Charles Joseph Latrobe, who arrived in September 1839 to take charge of affairs at Port Phillip, had lived for some time in his early twenties at Neuchatel, in Switzerland, where he had acquired not only some knowledge but a real appreciation of wine, as well as a bride, Sophie, the daughter of Frederick Auguste de Montmillon, Swiss Counsellor of State. Latrobe first fell in love with Jolimont, the Counsellor's enchanting country estate, which stood among magnificent trees some 2,000 feet above the Lake of Neuchatel, and then he fell in love with the daughter of the house. When they came to Victoria they named their home 'Jolimont' and planted a small vineyard in what was to be the garden of the first Government House in Melbourne. Others followed Latrobe's lead, and he gave them every encouragement: he directed, for instance, the planting of vines at Mayfield, the home of the McCrae family, as appears from an entry in the Georgina McCrae's Journal, dated 9 August 1842:

> Mr. Latrobe came to show Osmond how to plant the vine-cuttings obliquely to the sun, each cutting to have three joints and eyes – one of these to be above ground, the second level with the surface, the third to be rubbed off to make way for the root.

At that time Skene Craig, Commissariat Officer of the Port District, had a vineyard in what is today Collins Street West, one of Melbourne's principal streets, and it is more likely that he had had the advice and blessing of Latrobe, who was his chief.

The greatest service that Latrobe rendered to Australian viticulture, however, was to persuade Clement Deschamps, the son of a head *vigneron* of Neuchatel, and other of his Swiss friends, to come over to Port Phillip and to grow grapes and to make wine as grapes should be grown and wine should be made. This is how Baron de Pury and his cousins the brothers de Castella came to Victoria: they planted vines in the Yarra Valley and made better wine than had ever been made there before. They were not only much better-educated men than the average Australian settler, but they knew much more about viticulture and wine-making; more important still they possessed, as an inheritance from their forebears, that almost mystical love of the tree of life, the vine, which all true wine-lovers regard as one of God's greatest gifts to man.

Another Swiss migrant of more humble station, for whom Latrobe was responsible, was Amiet, the husband of Rose Pelet, Latrobe's Swiss housekeeper: he had a vineyard of his own in what would be called today the centre of Melbourne, and his wine was served at the ball given in Melbourne on 28 November 1850 to celebrate the Port Phillip District's separation from New South Wales to become the Colony of Victoria.

The Melbourne 'municipal' vineyards, as one would expect, soon gave way to bricks and mortar, but old as they were, they were not the first to be planted in the Colony. Edward Henty has always been credited with the planting of the first vineyard in 1834, when he settled at Portland in western Victoria.

In 1838 William Ryrie, who had a cattle station at Yering, some 30 miles east of Melbourne, in the Yarra Valley, planted a vineyard of 30 acres, which was to grow, not many years later, to 3,000 acres and produce some of the finest table wines of Australia. This was chiefly due to the purchase of some of Ryrie's land by the brothers Paul and Hubert de Castella, and Baron de Pury. It was not long before the de Castella wines, marked under the labels of St Hubert and Chateau Yering, as well as the wine of Baron de Pury, marketed under the label Yeringberg, gained and deserved high praise from all wine-lovers and connoisseurs. Unfortunately the number of wine-lovers and connoisseurs was much too small; the great majority of wine-drinkers, then even more than now, did not know and did not ask for the wine that was best: they only knew and only asked for the wine that was the cheapest. The wines of the Swiss colony were given more praises than orders, so that when the phylloxera came and destroyed the vineyards nobody had the heart or the means to replant them.

The same fate befell most of the vineyards which were planted at an early date – that is, before 1850 – at Geelong and Bendigo. The vineyards of the Goulburn River, a southern tributary of the Murray, were planted a little later and fared rather better. The Tabilk run, at Old Crossing Place, where the Goulburn River was first crossed by the explorer Major Mitchell on 9 October 1836, was occupied by Henry Moore from 1842 to 1852, when it was leased to Hugh Glass and John Purcell; Hugh Glass was allowed to purchase the pre-emptive rights of 640 acres, or 1 square mile of the Tabilk lands. He appointed as his manager a Frenchman, Ludovic Marie, who came from Burgundy: he was well known in the Tabilk district, as he had a general store and also ran a punt ferry service across the Goulburn. He planted some table grapes in the garden of his homestead, and they brought forth such beautiful grapes, and such an abundance of them, that Marie could not resist the temptation of experimenting with wine-making grapes. He had no difficulty in persuading Hugh Glass and others that both soil and climate were highly favourable and, on 16 March 1860, the Goulburn Vineyard Proprietary Company was formed, with Ludovic Marie as resident manager, and with Mr R. H. Horne (the poet 'Orion' Horne) as honorary secretary.

The prospectus of the new company was drawn up by Horne, who was once upon a time a friend of Charles Dickens and a regular contributor to *Cornhill*. Would-be subscribers were assured:

> That Victoria is a country eminently adapted by Nature for the culture of Vines is a fact that has long been generally known. The means that we possess here for making wine of the most delicious quality, and better suited to the inhabitants of these colonies as a healthy beverage than most of the light wines which are imported, has also been equally well known to those who are conversant with the subject. The wines of the Rhine and the Moselle can certainly be equalled, but, in some instances, will be surpassed by vintages of the Goulburn, the Loddon, the Campaspe, and, in fact, of the whole Valley of the Murray.
>
> Besides the commercial benefits, the best sanitary and moral results may be anticipated because a wine-drinking population is never a drunken population.

Three months later, on 6 June 1860, at a meeting held at 70 Queen Street, Melbourne, a new company, the Tabilk Vine-yard Proprietary, was formed, with Horne again honorary secretary *pro tem*, and Marie again manager. Mr J. P. Bear, a member of the new board, proposed that an advertisement for the purchase of a million vine cuttings be inserted six times in the leading newspapers of South Australia, Victoria and New South Wales. Later, Horne wrote that those cuttings were planted by a highly qualified *vigneron*, and that 700,000 of them 'took root and produced wine the first year'. (Horne, as we mentioned before, was a poet.) By the end of 1860, 150 acres of the Tabilk run had been cleared under Marie's direction, and 65 acres had been planted with vines. In the *Kilmore Examiner* a correspondent wrote in 1861 that he had visited Tabilk where there were 200 acres of vines 'all of them healthy and free from blight'.

Ludovic Marie left Tabilk in 1862 and there were difficult years ahead, but matters improved soon after the arrival of a Swiss relative of Mrs Latrobe, Leopold Quintin de Soyres, a grandson of Baron de Meuron, and we shall hear more about him when we come to the history of Chateau Tahbilk (as the vineyard came to be named later).

The only considerable township near Tabilk is Magambie, 75 miles north of Melbourne, and, north of Nagambie, on the way to Shepparton, in the Goulburn Valley, there is quite a fair vineyard before Mooroopna; it is known as the Excelsior Vineyard, and it is cared for by George and Trojano Daveniza, great-nephews of the Trojano Daveniza, an Austrian from Dalmatia, who first planted the vineyard in the early 1870s.

Although the vineyards of the Yarra come first in point of seniority, those in a loop of the Murray in the north-east corner of Victoria have been of much greater importance during the past hundred years or so; that is, from 1851, when Lindsay Brown planted a vineyard at Gooramadda, soon after being followed by John Graham, at Netherby, G. F. Morris at Fairfield and, in 1864, by George Sutherland Smith at All Saints, Wahgunyah. The vineyards within a 10-mile radius of Rutherglen added up to 3,000 acres up to 1899, when the phylloxera struck and disaster followed. Since then many vineyards have been replanted, and the Rutherglen or North-East Area is still the largest for the production of quality wines in Victoria. There are still grapes today at Fairfield, the Mia Mia Vineyard, and a winery, and members of the Morris family in charge. There are still grapes growing at All Saints, and the largest assembly of oak casks there is still lodged in the same old winery, and the two grandsons of the original Sutherland Smith are still in charge, with their sons. But there are no longer any grapes growing at Burgoyne's Mount Ophir.

The soil and climate of Victoria's North-East are, of course, the same as before, which is why the dry red wines of the Rutherglen district today are mostly what they have always been: big wines, dark, almost black-red wines, of greater alcoholic strength than the Hunter River table wines, with more power than charm: 'wines for heroes', as they have been called sometimes. However, some Rutherglen wine-makers are now aiming for lighter wines – and with success.

Besides dry table wines, the vineyards of the Rutherglen area also produce good sherries and a large quantity of dessert wines, which must be better than most, since they are always given top prizes at the wine shows.

There is a vine nursery at Wahgunyah and a Government Viticultural Station some 10 miles to the south-east of Rutherglen.

South-west of Rutherglen, but still in Victoria's North-East, is Wangaratta, and there are vineyards within 8 to 15 miles of this prosperous industrial town: they produce grapes from which quality wines are made more akin to the quality wines of the Rutherglen area than any other wines made in Victoria.

Milawa lies between the Ovens and King River valleys a few miles south-west of Wangaratta. Its largest vineyard is that of Brown Brothers, who happen at present to be father and son, John Brown II and John Brown III, son and grandson of John Francis Brown (John Brown I), who planted the first vines there in the 'eighties of the last century. They have now 75 acres in production and another 15 acres newly planted, mostly with Shiraz, Cabernet Sauvignon, Mondeuse, Rhine Riesling and white Hermitage: the old winery has been completely modernized and fitted with all the latest scientific equipment. At Everton, a few miles away nearer the mountains, the John Brown Senior and John Brown Junior of today also own another vineyard of 10 acres, the grapes of which are brought to Milawa at vintage time, to be 'processed'.

About the same distance as Milawa from Wangaratta, but to the south-west, looking towards the Warby Ridge, there are some veteran vineyards at Bundarra, the two most notable being those of the Bailey Brothers and those of Booth's. Alan and Roly Bailey are the fourth generation in charge of the Bundarra vineyard, which was first planted by Alan Bailey I in the 'seventies.

Booth's vineyard is some distance away, nearer the Warby Ridge; it was planted in 1892 by a Mr Opie, and destroyed by the phylloxera 10 years later; it was replanted soon after by Ezra Booth, and today there are some 50 acres in full production: they are in charge of two brothers, Clifford and Geoffrey Booth.

In an altogether different part of Victoria, more than a hundred miles west of Melbourne, the Great Western vineyards are responsible for some of the best-quality wines of Australia, still and sparkling. Their soil is mostly lighter and less fertile than the soil of most other Victorian vineyards: it is richer in lime but poorer in all else, and this is the basic cause of the higher standard of quality of their wines. Unfortunately and inevitably, the average yield of the Great Western vineyards is so much poorer than that of other Victorian vineyards that they have almost ceased to be economic in an age of keen competition, which is one reason why many of the early vineyards of Great Western have now ceased to exist.

There is a township called Great Western: it is by no means Great and it is not particularly Western. It was originally called Weston, from the name of a colourful personality in the gold-digging days; then, in 1860 a great deal of publicity was given to the crossing of the Atlantic by a wonder ship called the *Great Eastern*, and it was then that Weston was dubbed Great Western. This has been its name ever since.

Fifty years ago there were over 2,000 acres of vines in the Great Western area; that is, from Glenorchy, in the north, to about 10 miles below Ararat, in the south, the village of Great Western being half-way between Stawell and Ararat, with the Grampians Mountains 25 miles to the west. Vines were first planted in the area by Messrs Trouettes and Blampied in 1862: their vineyard was just outside the village and they called it St Peter. The following year Joseph and Henry Best each planted a vineyard, the one that was nearest the village being called Great Western and the other Concongella. A little later on there were other vineyards planted a few miles to the west, in the Rhymer area, while in the north, at Doctor's Creek, nearer Stawell, the Stawell Vineyard Company owned the largest of a number of vineyards. In the opposite direction, south of Ararat, there was the Emerald Vineyard Company, owned by Messrs J. and M. Mooney; at Eversley there was the Decameron Vineyard Company and Mr Paul Vautravers' Swiss Vineyard, as well as a number of smaller vineyards.

Mr Hans Irvine, who bought the Great Western vineyard from Joseph Best in 1885, decided to make some sparkling wine in 1887 when he succeeded in bringing out from Champagne a fully qualified expert, Charles Pierlot, and a team of French technicians. It was also Hans Irvine who had underground galleries dug out near his winery in order to give the wine a better chance to have its second fermentation in bottle in the peace of a cool cellar, and also to be binned away under conditions as similar as possible to those existing in France, in Champagne. Incidentally, if those underground galleries are known today, as they have always been, as 'drives', it is because 'drives' is the mining term for underground galleries in mines, and they were made by the miners of the gold diggings.

In 1918 Messrs B. Seppelt and Sons bought Mr Irvine's property – vineyard, winery and 'drives' – and they still own it, but they have greatly improved and modernized the winery, as well as enlarged the vineyards, in recent years. Seppelt's Great Western vineyard has now 650 acres of quality grapes in production, and the 'drives' a run of miles.

Joseph Best's brother, Henry Best, sold his Concongella vineyard of 20 acres to the Stawell Vineyard Company, which eventually sold it to the Thomson family, under whose charge it flourishes today.

Latest in date but greatest in yield, the vineyards of Mildura, in the north-west of Victoria, owe their existence and their fortune to the Chaffey Brothers, George and Ben, two Californians who were the pioneers of large-scale irrigation on the Murray River in the 1880s. Mildura is the name of the town: Mildara is the name of the largest organization responsible for the making and marketing of the Mildura districts wines and spirits.

## South Australia

The vineyards of South Australia have had up to now the rare privilege of being phylloxera-free, which is one of the reasons why there are a great many more wine-producing vineyards in South Australia than in all the other Australian states put together. They may be divided into six main groups as follows:

(1) Adelaide Metropolitan Vineyards;
(2) Barossa Valley, Keyneton, Clare and Watervale vineyards;
(3) Southern Vales vineyards;
(4) Coonawarra vineyards;
(5) Langhorn Creek and Bleasdale vineyards;
(6) Renmark, Berri, Loxton and Waikerie irrigation vineyards.

ADELAIDE METROPOLITAN VINEYARDS. Many vineyards were planted north and south of Adelaide in the early days in areas where dwellings and factory now stand, but there are still today a number of veteran vineyards in what may be called Adelaide suburbs: vineyards the existence of which is gravely threatened by the relentless tide of bricks and mortar. The more important are the vineyards to the east and south of the city (on what was called once upon a time the Adelaide Plain), and on the foothills of the Mount Lofty Range, but there is no trace left of the first vines that were planted at North Adelaide by J. B. Hack in 1837 and George Stevenson in 1838. Actually, the first large commercial planting was that of A. H. Davis, who obtained cuttings from the Busby collection and established them at his farm in the Reedbeds (now Underdale, a western suburb of Adelaide) between 1838 and 1840. That vineyard has also long since disappeared.

There are still vines, however, at Magill, where the first were planted by Dr Penfold in 1844, and at Auldana, where they were planted by Patrick Auld in 1854.

Besides vines and an up-to-date important winery owned by Messrs Penfold at Magill, visitors may still see Dr Penfold's little house, religiously kept by his great-grandchildren as it was 120 years ago, with the original furnishings and a number of souvenirs of the pioneering days. At Auldana, which now belongs to Messrs Penfold, the original vineyard is still being cultivated, and the original winery still stands, but has been modernized.

Near Magill, at Burnside, some of the vines which were originally planted by H. C. Clark in 1858 at Stonyfell have been replaced by other and most likely much more suitable varieties than the first; they are now owned by H. M. Martin and Son, as well as the homestead and winery. There are also other more recently established wineries in the same areas, as well as farther north on the way to Tanunda but still close to the last foothills of the Mount Lofty range: at and near Modbury, where Dr W. T. Angove planted a vineyard at Tea Tree Gully in 1884, and in Hope Valley near by, where Douglas A. Tolley planted a vineyard in 1893; those two vineyards are still in fine fettle (though they have been reduced by urban development), and are cared for by the grandsons of the founder.

No farther from the centre of Adelaide than Magill, but to the south-west of the city, near Glenelg, is Hamilton's Ewell Vineyard. It is still owned by the direct descendants of the first Hamilton who bought the land in 1837, and who is variously credited to have planted his first vineyard in 1838 or 1840.

A little nearer Adelaide, but to the south-west of the city, at Glen Osmond, Woodley Wines now own the winery on the site of the one-time vineyard which was planted in 1856 by Osmond Gilles.

A few miles south of Adelaide, on the slopes of O'Halloran Hill, a Mrs Horne planted a vineyard in 1892; it now belongs to the Robertson family, who have built a modern winery and distillery at Happy Valley. They have retained the original name of the vineyard: Glenloth Wines, John Harper Robertson is the governing director, and his son J. R. W. (Bob) Robertson is manager.

A number of attempts were made in the early days to grow grapes in the open on a commercial scale in the wetter parts of the Adelaide Hills, but all failed, with the exception of the vineyard planted at Clarendon in 1849 by John Edward Peake, who, incidentally, was the first to import direct from Spain the Palomino, Pedro Ximénez, Doradillo, Temprana and Mollar Negro grapes which have been grown in South Australia ever since.

Dr R. M. Schomburgk, who became famous as the Director of the Adelaide Botanical Gardens, planted a small vineyard in 1857, at Buchfelde, now called Loos, west of Gawler, on the Para River; it was he who introduced in South Australia the Sultana grape, little knowing that a hundred years later it would be grown – thanks to irrigation – to a greater extent than any other grape (but for dried fruit rather than wine).

BAROSSA VALLEY. The Barossa Valley is the valley of the Para River; it lies 30 miles to the north-east of Adelaide, and it rises gently during some 20 miles of the Para course; it narrows and expands in turn all the way in a haphazard manner, its width averaging nearly 5 miles.

The Barossa Valley is an enchanting land of orchards, vineyards, olive groves, grassy slopes and clumps of trees, not unlike the Barrosa Valley in Spain, after which (despite the difference in spelling) it is said to have been named; with this difference also, however, that there are many more *vignerons* and market-gardeners, more ease and comfort as well, in the Barossa Valley of South Australia than in the Barrosa Valley of Spain.

There are three principal towns in the Barossa Valley, Tanunda, Nuriootpa and Angaston, each of them with a population of about 2,000 people. There are, however, a number of smaller community centres scattered among the folds of the Valley's rolling downs: flourishing settlements with no sign of poverty anywhere and every token of prosperity nearly everywhere. They bear witness to the foresight and generosity of one of South Australia's early settlers, George Fyfe Angas – Angaston was named after him – who found the money that made it possible for three shiploads of dissenting German Lutherans to leave Germany, and to find liberty of conscience, sunshine, work and happiness in South Australia. This happened in the 'forties of the last century, and those early German migrants were followed by a number of their compatriots during the 'fifties and 'sixties. Many of them came to the Barossa Valley and had no cause to regret it. Some of their descendants have not only made fortunes but they have been, and they still are, among the foremost citizens and most public-minded leaders

Plate 55. Hermitage grapes being harvested in the Hunter Valley, New Sout
Wales, Australia.

of the state: the Gramps of Orlando, and the Seppelts of Seppeltsfield, for instance, have built organizations of major importance and of world-wide repute.

The Barossa Valley is the most important of all the non-irrigated vinelands of Australia, with over 20,000 acres of wine-making grapes, as well as dried-grape vineyards. It produces on an average 38,000 tons of grapes a year, and what is of even greater interest is the fact that the great majority of the grapes grown in the Barossa Valley for wine-making are quality grapes.

As one reaches the Barossa Valley coming from Adelaide there are many small vineyards and orchards before the great stretch of vines at Rowland Flat, the property of Messrs Gramp, whose homestead, winery and distillery of Orlando are one of the outstanding landmarks of the Valley. Farther on, at no great distance, one comes to Tanunda, where a number of firms have their offices, such as Messrs O. Basedow Wines Ltd, Messrs R. H. Binder, Messrs P. T. Falkenberg Ltd.

There are a number of vineyards, mostly small ones, east of Tanunda, but there are many more to the west; that is, on the right bank of the Para River, such as Fromm's, St Hallett, Paradale, Tolley's, Chateau Leonay and North Para (where Erwin and Laurel Hoffman, two of the Barossa Valley's best-known people, are to be found). Farther to the west there is one of the most spectacular estates of the Barossa Valley, at Seppeltsfield, the homestead, winery and distillery of Messrs Seppelt, surrounded by many acres of vineyards.

Leaving Tanunda, road, river and railway lead to Nuriootpa, where Messrs Penfold have, at the edge of the town, a number of well-equipped modern buildings – winery, distillery, laboratory, storage cellars and so on – while Messrs Tolley, Scott and Tolley have their main distillery close by. The South Australian Grape-growers' Co-operative Ltd has its headquarters at Nuriootpa, where also is the establishment of Tarac Barossa Pty Ltd, which processes the marc of the wineries for tartaric acid, grape-seed oil and fortifying spirit. (The tartaric acid goes to Sydney and becomes cream of tartar.)

Proceeding from Nuriootpa to Angaston by road, one passes by a number of vineyards, the oldest of them all being Saltram, a small distance from Angaston; the original vineyard was planted by William Salter in the early 'fifties of the last century, and it now belongs to Messrs H. M. Martin and Son Ltd.

Beyond Angaston, one soon comes to one of the finest homesteads, wineries and vineyards of the Barossa Valley, at Yalumba, where Samuel Smith planted the first 30 acres of vines in 1849. His great-grandchildren still live at Yalumba, but in much greater comfort than their forebear ever knew or dreamt of; it is also quite certain that old Sam would not recognize as his winery the present-day premises replete with the most modern scientific equipment.

The visitor who leaves Yalumba has the choice of two roads. One leads due south to Eden Valley, before reaching Springton, at both of which places Hamilton's have wineries. The other road, at the fork, goes east to Keyneton, once upon a time surrounded by vineyards which produced some very good table wines. The main reason why the Keyneton wines were so good was that the soil of their vineyards was so poor, which is also why there are fewer vineyards now, in an age when quantity pays so much better than quality. Happily, there are exceptions to all rules, and there is still one winery in the area and a large vineyard in fine fettle. There is modern equipment in the winery and none but quality grapes in the vineyard: they are the property of Cyril

Plate 56. The vineyards of Twee Jonge Gezellen in Tulbagh Valley, Cape Province, South Africa.

Henschke, whose father, Paul Alfred Henschke, was the son of Paul Gotthardt Henschke, an Australian-born son of a German migrant who farmed land near Keyneton and eventually planted a small vineyard there about a hundred years ago. Although Keyneton may not claim to be geographically speaking within the Barossa Valley proper, the table wines of the Henschke vineyard can claim to be the peers of the best table wines of the Barossa Valley.

Farther on, some 80 miles from Adelaide, there are a number of vineyards scattered along the hilly and wooded country upon the west side of the road and railway from Clare to Watervale. The best known of the Watervale vineyards is Buring and Sobels' Quelltaler. A little farther on are the winers of the Stanley Wine Company, the Clarevale Co-operative and Roland Birks.

There is but one survivor of the early Clare–Watervale vineyards, the Sevenhill College Vineyard; it was originally planted by the Jesuit Fathers, who came from Austria to South Australian in 1848. They built a college and the Church of St Aloysius, which still stands and is served by their successors. Other vineyards in the same area, such as the one that was planted in 1853 by John Ward, and another planted by Valentine Mayr in 1859, no longer exist.

SOUTHERN VALES. Next to the Barossa Valley, both in acreage and in beauty, the vineyards of the Southern Vales have produced a considerable quantity of quality wine for well over a century. Some of them are nearer Adelaide than any but the Metropolitan vineyards, merely 13 miles to the south-east of the City.

The oldest of the Southern Vales vineyards was planted about 1838 by John Reynell and the small township which has in the course of the years grown around what was once John Reynell's homestead has borne his name ever since: it is called Reynella, which is also the name under which Messrs Walter Reynell and Sons market the wines which they make from the nearby vineyards, which, needless to say, are considerably greater than the original one.

If one leaves Reynella and turns one's back on the St Vincent Gulf, 3 miles to the west, the first of a jumble of vales and gullies – the Southern Vales – one comes to is Morphett Vale. It was there that R. C. H. Walker planted an important vineyard and built a winery, some 60 years ago; both vineyards and winery are now the property of the Emu Wine Company. This important firm has not only increased its vineyards but has built a modern winery and very large storage cellars which are indispensable, since the company 'processes' the grapes and markets the wines of a number of local vinegrowers besides its own.

Next to Morphett Vale, one comes to the very picturesque McLaren Vale, with ironstone in the soil and many vineyards upon slopes facing north, east and west.

The lead given by John Reynell in the early 'forties was soon followed by others, by none with greater enthusiasm and greater faith in wine than Dr A. C. Kelly. He was an Adelaide medical practioner who planted a vineyard near Morphett Vale in 1845 and called it Trinity Vineyard. (Later it was owned by John B. Macmahon, but has now been replaced by houses.) Twenty years later, in 1865, Dr Kelly talked some of his rich Adelaide friends into putting up the necessary money to form a company that would buy the first vineyard that was planted in the McLaren Vale by W. Manning, in 1850: the vineyard was called Tintara, and the company that bought it took the name of Tintara Vineyard Company. It started well, but it did not prosper for very long: in 1873 the Tintara Vineyard Company was in liquidation. There was at the time an acute economic crisis and nobody to bid for the Tintara vineyard and winery. At last, happily, a brave man came forth, Thomas Hardy, was his name, and he bought 'for a song' the bankrupt Tintara Vineyard Company. He already had a little vineyard at Bankside, near Adelaide, with an orchard, and he had made a great success of both; he also made a great success of Tintara, where his grandson and great-grandchildren now own some of the finest vineyards of the McLaren Vale, and make some of the finest wines and brandy of Australia.

Other fine vineyards in the McLaren Vale include Seaview, originally known as Hope Farm, which was first planted by George P. Manning in 1850, and is now owned by Messrs Edwards and Chaffey. These are also in the same area the vineyards of Kay Bros., Osborn's, also Ryecroft (Ingoldby's) and Sparrow farther down. Upon the other side of road and rail the chief vineyard is Johnston's. A new comer is the Southern Vales Co-operative Winery Ltd.

COONAWARRA. A long way to the south-east, on the Mount Gambier road, one comes to Coonawarra, before Penola. There is, at Coonawarra, a large patch – about 10 square miles – of red soil in which grapes and stone-fruit grow exceptionally well, a fact which John Riddoch was the first to realize and to take advantage of when he founded the Coonawarra Fruit Colony in 1890. His lead was soon followed by others, so that by the end of the last century there were 900 acres of vines at Coonawarra.

Unfortunately, the area was off the beaten track and transport was difficult and costly, so that, good as Coonawarra wine was, it proved to be uneconomic to market it. At one stage £3 a ton was all that the wineries offered to the *vignerons* for their grapes. Most of the *vignerons*, naturally enough, gave up growing grapes, but one of them, W. L. Redman, decided that he would no longer sell his grapes but make his own wine and market it himself. He did so with conspicuous success, at first selling his red table wines in bulk, and later in bottle, under his own trade mark 'Rouge Homme'.

In 1965 W. L. Redman and his sons sold the entire enterprise to Lindeman's Wines Pty Ltd, of Sydney, but this transaction takes us a little ahead of our story, for by then interest in the potential of Coonawarra as a vine-growing area had revived.

By 1950 no less than 650 of the original 900 acres of vineyards had been uprooted, but the excellence of the Rouge Homme clarets and their high reputation must have attracted the attention of some of the more important wine-making firms. Messrs S. Wynn and Co. were the first: they bought the bulk of the existing vineyards, 126 acres, in 1951 from Woodley Wines Ltd, together with the big cellar built by John Riddoch; a few years later they had planted new vines to such an extent that they can count upon a thousand tons of grapes from their Coonawarra vineyards. Then came Penfold, who planted some 80 acres of vineyards; also Mildara Wines Ltd, who built a modern cellar with storage for 40,000 gallons of wine. There are also a number of small growers who sell their grapes at vintage time, and at good prices, to one or the other of the local wineries.

By 1963 the total acreage of the Coonawarra vineyards was about 500 acres – double what it was in 1950, and this figure continues to increase.

The vineyards of Coonawarra are the most southerly of all Australian vineyards, which means that their grapes are gathered later than elsewhere; it also means that they are gathered at a time when the heat of the late summer or early autumn is by no means as fierce, and hence much more suitable for the early stages of fermentation. This is all to the good. Unfortunately, it also means that the vines of Coonawarra have more to fear from spring frosts than the vines of more northern location, so that the *vignerons* of Coonawarra are bound to accept greater differences in the quantities of grapes they harvest year by year than happens in most other vineyards of Australia. Thus, Messrs Wynn's vineyards produced 375 tons of grapes in 1960, 98 tons in 1961, 459 tons in 1962, 423 in 1963, etc.

LANGHORNE CREEK. Some twenty-five miles east of Adelaide, at Langhorne Creek, on the Bremer River, at no great distance from the northern shore of Lake Alexandrina, a vineyard was planted by Frank Potts, in 1860: he called it Bleasdale. This vineyard is still thriving and produces a great deal of wine, chiefly dessert wines. There is also an important vineyard at Metala, owned by Mr Dennis Butler: it is planted mostly in Cabernet Sauvignon grapes, which are processed by H. M. Martin and Son at Stonyfell, near Adelaide.

BERRI, RENMARK, WAIKERIE, LOXTON. In the South Australian loop of the Murray River there are considerable quantities of wine made from the produce of irrigated vineyards. The Berri Co-operative Winery and Distillery is an offshoot of the Berri Co-operative Packing Union. It started in a modest way in 1918 with a grape-crusher handling less than a hundred tons of grapes a year, but by 1948 the Berri Distillery had expanded to such an extent that its crushers dealt with 20,000 tons of grapes a season, and its cellars could take in 4 million gallons of wine and spirits. There has been more expansion since then, and there are in the Berri area today some 500 growers, many of them veterans of the two World Wars, whose grapes are processed by the Berri Distillery.

Renmark Growers' Distillery is two years senior to Berri in age, but not its equal in capacity. For 30 years, from 1928 to 1957, Mr D. T. DuRieu, O.B.E., was chairman of the Renmark enterprise; he was also president of the Federal Viticultural Council for seven years and a foundation member of the Wine Board.

Waikerie Co-operative Distillery, formed in 1919, has given splendid service to its grower-members, though in a less spectacular way than the other Murray River co-operatives.

Loxton Co-operative Winery and Distillery, established as a result of a land-settlement scheme after the Second World War, is one of South Australia's biggest brandy-producers.

CHAPTER TWO

# *The Wines of Australia*

GOD GIVETH the grapes; man maketh the wine. There are all kinds of grapes, and there are all sorts of men, in Australia as elsewhere, which is why there is such a variety of different wines in Australia and in other countries in which climatic conditions make it possible and economic to grow in the open wine-making vines that will ripen their grapes every year – or nearly every year.

Wine is the suitably fermented juice of freshly gathered ripe grapes. There is in the juice of all ripe grapes more water than anything else: water which the roots of the vine have found in the soil or sub-soil of the vineyard and sent up to the berries of every bunch of grapes. The quantity of water in grape-juice may and does vary a good deal, but its nature is identically the same in all grapes, whether they be grown at Coona-warra or Clos Vougeot. There is also in the juice of all grapes, when ripe, some grape-sugar, and, again, its quantity may and does vary, but its nature is the same. If there are, as we know, so many wines which are so different it is firstly because there are in the juice of all ripe grapes very small quantities of vegetal substances, mostly acids, which vary with the varieties of grapes; also very small quantities of mineral substances, mostly salts, which vary with the nature of the soil and sub-soil of different vineyards. Although those salts and acids and other substances are there in such very small quantities, their importance is capital: they are responsible for the bouquet and flavour of the wine, and hence for its character, individuality and appeal.

Man maketh the wine, and whatever there may be in the juice of ripe grapes, the raw material from which all wines are made, the quality or the lack of it in any wine depends not only on the acids and mineral substances in the berries but on the know-ledge, the care, the intelligence and probity of the wine-maker from the moment the grapes are picked and brought to him. It will be for him to decide how those grapes are to be crushed or pressed: whether with or without theirs talks; whether in one continuous squeeze that will extract all their juice or in separate pressings, keeping the juice of each pressing separately.

No sooner has the wine-maker secured the juice of his grapes in vat, tank, tub, cask or whatever container of his choice than he must give it his whole attention and make sure that its fermentation will be exactly what he wishes it to be.

Natural as fermentation may be, it is important to keep it under control and make sure that it is not going to be too slow or too quick, as there are a number of accidents that may happen in the course of the molecular regrouping: accidents also are so natural. This control of the fermentation into wine is more necessary in Australia than in Europe because of the relatively high temperature at vintage time in nearly all the vineyards of Australia: high temperature has such a speeding action upon fermentation that the molecular regrouping is rushed in a manner which does not give it a fair chance of doing its work properly.

Today, happily, temperature-control is no longer a problem: it is only an expense. All the great wineries of Australia, and most of the smaller ones as well, have now the necessary equipment for the control of the temperature at all times and practically everywhere.

The control of temperature by air-conditioning methods is an expense which European wine-makers can save, since they never or rarely experience at the time of the vintage temperatures comparable with those of Australia, but the control of fer-mentation by the Australian wine-maker also applies to the years. When wine-making grapes are ripening their skin softens a little, enough for microscopic fungi, blown upon them by the wine, to get a hold and to form, in their thousands, a fine dust-like covering that is known as the 'bloom'. Those strange little fungi stay put until the grapes are crushed; they then get their chance: they get into the juice of the grapes and there they multiply at a very fast rate into very tiny buds which keep on budding – on and on. In Australia, however, the wine-maker calls such natural yeasts 'wild' yeasts, 'wild' because free, and if free a menace or at least a risk. So he kills outright, either by physical or chemical means, the yeasts that come to the crusher or press with the grapes, and he replaces them with scientifically prepared pure yeast: he can thus put in exactly the right kind and quantity, whereas he never could be sure whether the right kind of yeast, or too little or too much of it, had come in with the grapes. Hence his control of fermentation is quite assured.

The modern Australian wine-maker is well informed and well equipped, and an entirely different type of person from his forebears, about whom Dr A. C. Kelly wrote in *The Vine in Australia*, published in Melbourne in 1861: 'It is a notorious fact that modern science has not found its way into the cellar of the *vigneron*, who follows exactly the same routine his fathers have pursued for centuries.'

There can be no doubt whatever today that the great Australian wine firms have the latest and most scientically devised equipment, which represents an investment of many millions; they also have a highly qualified trained staff, and their technicians regularly visit all the more important wine-producing areas of the world to further their knowledge of any progress made in the technological approach to wine-making. The Australia Wine Research Institute at Glen Osmond, South Australia, has been in charge of Mr J. C. M. Fornachon, who is acknowledged by oenologists throughout the world as a master and a leader, particularly in the field of sherries. In addition, there is at Roseworthy Agricultural College, near Adelaide, a wine-making school which has taught students from overseas, as well as from all states of Australia.

All this means that there is much good wine made in Australia. But it does not mean that all wine made in Australia is fine wine: it is not. In Australia, as in all other wine-producing countries, much the greater proportion of all the wines made are *ordinaires*, or plain wines, that will quench the thirst, clear the bowels and rejoice the heart of us all, plain people as most of us are. In Europe, however, considerable quantities of such *ordinaires* or plain wines are drunk by the people who make them, by their families, their friends and practically all men and women in the lower-income group: these people have always been used to drink, as their forebears have done before them, some kind of inexpensive local wine, and it has become a tradition and a daily communion at mealtime.

There is nothing of the sort in Australia. In spite of the fact that many migrants from European wine-drinking lands have settled in Australia, the solid core of people is still made up of two opposite camps: the drinkers and non-drinkers, the hard-liquor camp and strong-tea camp.

Then there is also the climate of most parts of Australia, which absolutely demands cold beer rather than even the best of wines at certain times of the summer. This is why wine is for the majority of Australians the exception rather than the rule, but there are more and more Australians who welcome and provoke occasions that will justify such exceptions. If most of them prefer sweet wine to dry it is because they also like plenty of sugar in their tea and coffee: again the climate may be blamed for this fondness for sugar, or it may be due to the physiological need of people who rarely, if ever, think of saving their physical energy. Whatever the reason may

THE WINES OF AUSTRALIA

be, the fact is that the most popular of the Australian wines, in Australia, is sweet sherry.

Quality wine, in Australia as in all other wine-producing lands, is a small proportion of the total production of the nation's vineyards. It is inevitable. Quality wines are bound to cost more: they are made with greater care, of none but the best grapes, and they are kept longer so that they may have a chance to show how good they can be if given time. In the more famous wine areas of Europe quality wines are getting dearer and dearer all the time, although by no means better and better: most of them bear names which have acquired in the course of time a valuable prestige value, and their world-wide demand is growing faster than their supply.

In Australia the number of wine-lovers, wine connoisseurs and even of wine snobs who would love to be considered connoisseurs may not be very large at present, but it is growing and it is apparently growing faster than the supply of quality table wines, since the 'private reserve' and other high-quality Australian wines command premium prices and are by no means easy to procure. There cannot be any doubt whatever that the appreciation of quality wines is growing in Australia, and at a rapidly increasing tempo. The demand for dry table wines has grown by no less than 30% during the past few years, and the lion's share of the increase has gone to the better-quality 'bin' or 'reserve' wines, which are worth so much more and yet cost so little more.

When the day comes, as surely it will come soon, when there are a great many more educated consumers in Australia – that is, people who will realize that their senses of smell and taste ought to be trained or educated just as their senses of sight and hearing – the demand for quality wines will soar, and so will their supply. Vintners in Australia, more than in many other vinelands, have sunshine, fertile soil, good grapes, modern equipment – all they need to make more of the fine wines which they make now – but they also have shareholders, and they are in duty bound to make wines that they can sell profitably.

If we take a good vintage of recent times, the 1962 vintage, we might well ask what happened to the 42·2 million gallons of wine which official statistics tell us were made in that year.

This is what happened:

> 24,200,000 gallons were distilled;
> 11,000,000 gallons became fortified wines, mostly 'sweet sherry';
> 7,000,000 gallons became dry or sweet table wines and sparkling wines.

## Fortified Wines

Fortified wines are not weak wines which have been bolstered up by an injection of spirit, but either full-strength wines or wines that would have become full strength wines of their own accord if left alone but have been given a still higher alcoholic strength by an addition of brandy or fortifying spirit, either during or after fermentation. The two methods of making fortified wines are known as the port method and the sherry method.

In Australia the withdrawals from bond of fortified wines for home consumption, which may be reasonably considered as the quantities of such wines sold and drunk in

Australia, averaged 3·4 million gallons a year before the last war; but by 1951–52 they had risen in a surprising manner to 13·4 million gallons a year, the highest figure ever recorded.

After that, although production and consumption of fortified wines remained much greater than production and consumption of unfortified or beverage wines, dry and sweet, still and sparkling, excise figures for fortified wines showed, for several years, a slight decline in demand. However, in 1963–64 withdrawals from bond for home consumption showed a rise of half a million gallons. The figures for recent years are:

| | |
|---|---|
| 1959–60 | 9,892,294 gallons |
| 1960–61 | 9,528,111 gallons |
| 1961–62 | 9,397,204 gallons |
| 1962–63 | 9,065,214 gallons |
| 1963–64 | 9,554,676 gallons |

The term 'fortified wines' covers a number of wines, most of them rather sweet, which are marketed in Australia as port (ruby, tawny and white), Madeira, Tokay and, of course, sherry, the best seller of all. There are also a number of such wines which are sold under the registered names or brands of the firms responsible for their making.

Some indication of the relative importance of the demand for the different types of fortified wines is to be found in the statistics supplied by the Federal Wine and Brandy Producers' Council of Australia relating to the varieties and quantities of fortified wines (gallons) sold by wholesalers and *vignerons* of South Australia to retailers and consumers during a four-year period.

| | 1960–1 | 1961–2 | 1962–3 | 1963–4 |
|---|---|---|---|---|
| SHERRY | | | | |
| *Sweet* | 675,500 | 661,200 | 656,500 | 627,500 |
| *Dry* | 106,900 | 101,400 | 119,500 | 133,300 |
| DESSERT WINES | | | | |
| *Sweet white* | 271,900 | 256,700 | 226,500 | 205,600 |
| *Sweet red* | 523,900 | 491,800 | 512,200 | 554,800 |

Sherry is the most popular of all fortified wines in Australia, and the name is used for a great many wines of different standards of quality. The best of them are the dry sherries which have been 'flor'-fermented, and also some of the dry and pale sherries mostly marketed as Flor Fino, Fino Palido, Special Fino, Pale Fino; or else under some registered trade mark such as Dry Friar, Pale Dry Solero, Extra Dry Solero, Del Pedro, Seaview Dry and many more.

There are also a number of sherries which are both sweet and of good quality: some of them are to be found in the 'cream sherry' class. Half-way between the dry and the cream or sweet sherries there are various brands of medium sherries, which vary in quality, sweetness and price.

For practical purposes the dividing line between fortified and unfortified wines in Australia can be considered to be 27% of proof spirit, which is almost equivalent to 15% of ethyl alcohol by volume. In Great Britain and Northern Ireland the Customs accept as 'light' or unfortified wines all Australian wines the alcoholic strength of which is not over 27% of proof spirit, although they will charge the higher rate of duty – that is, the duty on fortified wines – upon any wine from the Continent the alcoholic strength of which is above 25% of proof spirit.

This somewhat curious discrimination in favour of Australian wines is a very small matter, but there is another difference between some of the fortified wines of Australia and the fortified wines of Portugal and Spain that might be considered of more importance, because it could be argued that it might affect not only their cost but their quality.

In Portugal and Spain ports and sherries are always fortified with brandy: that is, distilled wine. In Australia some are fortified with brandy and some with 'fortifying spirit'. However, Australian wine men point out that in Australia fortifying spirit is made only by fermenting grape-sugar and distilling off the alcohol thus formed. This grape-sugar may, in some cases, have been washed from the marc, but one cannot distil alcohol from the pips or skins of grapes unless the sugar is first fermented. By contrast, the fortified wines of Europe, except in certain special areas, including Jerez and the Douro Valley, are often fortified with alcohol derived from sources other than the grape.

## Unfortified Wines

The unfortified wines of Australia may be classed in four groups: one for red and *rosé* wines, one for the sweet white wines, one for the dry white wines and one for the sparkling wines.

None of them are fortified, but none of them are as low in alcoholic strength as the lightest of French and Italian beverage wines. Nevertheless, the old idea that *all* Australian wines are high in alcoholic strength is incorrect: there are many Australian white table wines with strengths between 10 and 11% by volume.

It is true that the lightest European wines are likely to contain even less alcohol than the lightest Australian wines, particularly in poor years; it is also probably true that the *average* strength of wines in Europe is rather less than in Australia; but figures published by reputable authorities suggest that the differences are not tremendous. For instance, Dr Peynaud, of the University of Bordeaux, quoted these figures of alcoholic strength by volume in 1947:

| | | | |
|---|---|---|---|
| 39 Bordeaux whites (including Sauternes) | Min. 10·5 | Max. 15·4 | Mean 13·2 |
| 51 Bordeaux reds | 9 | 12·9 | 11·1 |
| 27 Burgundy whites | 10 | 13·8 | 11·8 |
| 19 Burgundy reds | 12 | 15·7 | 13·5 |

It may be useful to refer back to these figures when, a little later, we discuss in more detail the alcoholic strength of Australian wines.

The demand for table wines in Australia is steadily growing, as appears from the figures (gallons) of their wholesale sales over a five-year period.

| | 1958–9 | 1959–60 | 1960–1 | 1961–2 | 1962–3 | 1963–4 |
|---|---|---|---|---|---|---|
| Dry Red | 1,419,000 | 1,326,000 | 1,439,000 | 1,493,000 | 1,637,000 | 1,892,000 |
| Dry White | 666,000 | 691,000 | 761,000 | 909,000 | 1,034,000 | 1,132,000 |
| Sweet White | 594,000 | 715,000 | 691,000 | 746,000 } | 1,162,000 | 1,368,000 |
| Sparkling Wine | 260,000 | 254,000 | 262,000 | 290,000 } | | |
| Total: | 2,939,000 | 2,986,000 | 3,153,000 | 3,438,000 | 3,833,000 | 4,392,000 |

## Red and Rosé Wines

The two most popular red wines of Australia are marketed under the names of claret and burgundy. They are made in every one of the four main wine-producing states of Australia, irrespective of the nature of the soil of entirely different vineyards.

Most of them are dark in colour and all are fermented with the skins of the grapes. The grapes used are among the varieties known as black in English but called blue in Germany: their outside skin is blue – midnight blue – but they have a crimson lining which will stain the white juice of the grapes pink at first, then ruby and eventually very dark red. Thus the alcoholic strength of all red and *rosé* wines depends upon the ripeness and richness in sugar of the grapes from which they are made, while their colour depends upon the time allowed by the wine-maker for the fermenting grape-juice to extract the colouring matter of the grape-lining.

The majority of Australian dry red wines are wines made from Shiraz or Hermitage grapes, which are good grapes and appear to produce substantial crops in a variety of different soils. The better quality red wines, whether called claret or burgundy, are made from the Cabernet Sauvignon grapes, not only because it is a better grape than Shiraz (though not nearly such a free bearer), but because a Cabernet-made red wine will last longer and improve more markedly than other red wines.

As a rule – a rule with many exceptions – a red wine which is marketed in Australia as claret is likely to be of lower alcoholic strength than its brother marketed as burgundy. In the Hunter River Valley, where many of the lighter and better Australian dry red table wines come from, the average alcoholic strength of the dry red wines is 13% of alcohol by volume, whereas it is 14% in the Rutherglen district. Bordeaux red wines average, as a rule, only about 11% and burgundy red somewhat more than bordeaux though still less than Rutherglen, as indicated by the table quoted earlier.

A number of Australian dry red wines are also marketed under the name of their birthplace and that of the grape or grapes from which they were made, such as Mount Pleasant Hermitage, Coonawarra Cabernet, Dalwood Hermitage, Tahbilk Cabernet or Mildara Cabernet-Shiraz.

The demand for *rosé* wines is not very great, maybe because *rosés* are not generally above 11% or at most 11½% alcohol. Most *rosés* are made from Shiraz or Hermitage grapes, some from Cabernet, some from Merlot and the best from Grenache grapes. They are usually marketed simply as *rosés* with the name of the firm responsible for their bottling and sometimes with the name of the grape from which they were made, such as Angove's *Rosé* or Lindeman's Grenache *Rosé*.

*Rosé* wines are best drunk when young and fresh: unlike red wines, which are more mellow and gracious after from five to ten years at peace in bottle, they have nothing to gain by being kept for a number of years. *Rosé* wines should be served cold – chilled but not frozen.

## White Wines

Most fortified white wines are made from Spanish grapes – Palomino, Pedro Ximénez and Doradillo – but all the unfortified white wines are made from French or German grapes, mostly Semillon – which they call Riesling in the Hunter River Valley – and Riesling, which are often called Rhine Riesling to indicate that they are true Riesling grapes.

White wines are made from white grapes by much the same process as red wines are made from black ones, with this difference, however: that the juice of black grapes is fermented with the red-lined, blue-black skins of the grapes, which give them their colour, whereas the juice of white grapes is fermented without any of the grape-skins, which would give them a golden colour. There was a time when the wines which we call white were golden, often deep-gold verging on orange, and their rich colour was greatly admired, but today fashion has decreed that white wines should be as nearly as possible 'water-white', or colourless, or at least lighter in colour than they used to be. So there are no skins left in the fermentating vat, and some of the white wines of Australia, like almost all other white wines of the world, are practically colourless, although Australia does have some choice examples that match the beautiful golden glow of Yquem, Montrachet or Johannisberg.

The alcoholic strength of the white wines of Australia – usually 11 or 12% of alcohol by volume – is, as a rule, from 1 to 2% less than the strength of the red wines, and the white wines, also as a rule, are not kept back and matured like the reds: they are at their best when young and lively, nine to eighteen months of age – or of youth. This does not mean, however, that those light white wines will not keep: they will, but they have little, if anything, to gain by age.

Most dry white wines are marketed as Riesling, Chablis, Moselle, Hock or white burgundy, and sweet table white wines as Sauternes. There is, however, a generally accepted notion that the names of Chablis and Moselle should be used for the lighter types of white wines, not lighter in colour but of body, and often with a little more acidity: they maybe the wines made from the earlier pickings of the grapes; that is, when the grapes are either barely ripe or still wanting a few days of sunshine to have their full quota of sugar. Obviously, the last grapes to be picked from the same vineyard will have had the benefit of an extra week, maybe two or three, of Australian sunshine, and they will be much more suitable for making bigger wines of the Hock type rather than Moselle, and, more particularly, of the Sauterne type.

The practice is gaining ground to market white wines in the same way as many red table wines are now marketed, either under the names of vineyard and grape or of some registered fancy name, such as Lindeman's Sunshine Riesling, McWilliam's Mt Pleasant Riesling, Penfold's Private Bin Riesling, Gramp's Orlando Barossa Riesling Spatlese, Chateau Reynella Riesling, Seaview Riesling, Lindeman's Coolalta White or Smith's Yalumba Carte d'Or.

## Sparkling Wines

Sparkling wines are made in Australia, as they are made in many other parts of the world, either by the *méthode champenoise* or in *cuve close*. The difference between the two is the difference between anything hand-made and machine-made: the first is better but dearer. The *méthode champenoise* means that the wine will have its second fermentation in its bottle, so that each bottle has to be handled separately to be cleared of all 'rejects' thrown by the wine in the course of its fermentation; then it has to be *dosé* individually, that is, given exactly the right *dose* or quantity of sweetening. In the *cuve close* method the fermentation takes place in a great vat, hermetically closed, from which the wine and just as much of its gas that is good for it will be bottled. It saves a great deal in wages to trained staff, not to mention cellar-space and time.

Sparkling wines are made by both methods in Australia, as elsewhere – mostly white, but also red and *rosé* or pink. White and pink sparkling wines made by the *méthode champenoise* are marketed as Champagne in Australia, and some of the white wines as Sparkling Moselle; the red sparkling wines are marketed as Sparkling Burgundy. There are also, however, considerable quantities of sparkling wines marketed in Australia under the names of registered brands such as Gramp's Barossa Pearl, McWilliam's Chateau Gay.

Of all wines, sparkling wine deserves more than any of the others to be called a fancy wine, and since each one of us is entitled to his or her own fancy, the best sparkling wine, be it white, pink or red, sweet or dry, is the one which you happen to fancy.

## *Nomenclature*

It may be regrettable, but it is quite understandable that the vintners of Australia have given for many years to their wines, and still to many of them, names which belong to very different wines made from grapes grown in European vineyards.

It is obvious that white wines made from Chardonnay grapes grown in the lime-rich and humus-poor vineyards of Chablis, or from Riesling grapes grown on the steep slopes of the Mittel Mosel, cannot possibly have anything in common, save their colour or the lack of it, with white wines made from different grapes grown under entirely different climatic conditions.

It is equally obvious, however, that one cannot be expected to buy a wine with a name that conveys no idea whatever of what it is. There were brave and honest men who did try, and they failed. There was Captain Elder, for instance, who had a vineyard at Glen Osmond, south-east of Adelaide, in 1857: he made a red wine, probably a very nice red wine, which he tried to market as 'Red Osmondea', but he had to call it burgundy to sell it.

It was inevitable then, but conditions are very different now. As distinct from the people who are quite content to explore no farther than sweet sherry, there are now in Australia wine-consumers who are wine-lovers, whose palate is becoming more critical year after year, and who take an intelligent interest in wine. They know perfectly well that Riesling is a quality white grape and Cabernet a quality red grape: give them the name of the grape from which the wine in the bottle was made; give them the name of the grape's native vineyard and the year when the grapes were vintaged, and your modern Australian wine-lover will be much better informed than if he be offered 'Chablis' or 'Hock', which may be any white wine, and 'claret' or 'burgundy', meaning a red wine incognito.

In Australia, as elsewhere, the big firms are growing bigger and the small firms are getting fewer. We live in an age of publicity, and publicity is costly, which is why the big firms with ample financial resources and large stocks of wine have a much better chance than the little man. But why should they spend their money to advertise names like Chablis and Hock for wines which anybody – including the little man – may offer, quite possibly at a lower price? What it pays them to advertise is their own name coupled with the names of grape and vineyard: it is all that the modern Australian wine-consumer asks for.

This is why the more popular table wines today include Penfold's Dalwood Hermitage, McWilliam's Mount Pleasant Hermitage, Lindeman's Coolalta Red Hermitage, Wynn's Coonawarra Cabernet, Emu's Houghton Cabernet, Reynella Cabernet Sauvignon, Seaview Cabernet-Shiraz, Mildara Cabernet-Shiraz or Chateau Tahbilk Cabernet, among the red wines; and among the whites: McWilliam's Mount Pleasant Riesling, Penfold's Private Bin Riesling, Lindeman's Coolalta White, Lindeman's Sunshine Riesling, McWilliam's Lovedale Riesling, Wynn's Modbury Estate Riesling, Chateau Reynella Riesling, Edwards and Chaffey's Seaview Riesling, Hamilton's Springton Riesling, Hardy's Old Castle Riesling, Mildara Golden Bower Riesling, Smith's Yalumba Carte d'Or, Angove's Bookmark Riesling, Lindeman's Cawarra Riesling, Gramp's Orlando Barossa Riesling, Chateau Tahbilk Riesling, Buring and Sobel's Quelltaler, Leo Buring's Leonay Rinegold and so on.

CHAPTER THREE

# The Wine Trade of Australia

CONSIDERING the many difficulties that faced the early vintners of Australia before they could build up a demand for their wines, it is quite remarkable that, in a country where viticulture and wine-making upon a commercial basis are barely 150 years old, there are still a number of vintners who grow grapes where grapes were grown and who make wine where wine was made more than a hundred years ago. There are still vineyards and wineries owned and cared for by the third, fourth and fifth generations of the men who first planted a vineyard and made wine on or near the same spot, and there are a number of others where the original vineyard and winery have changed hands, but are in the good hands of younger owners who carry on the work of the original founder.

The fact that South Australia has had the good fortune to escape the ruinous invasion of phylloxera must be responsible for the much greater number of centenarians among veteran vineyards there than there are in New South Wales and Victoria. Another reason is the fact that vineyards and wineries have survived, near Adelaide, the relentless rise of the bricks-and-mortar tide of suburban development better than they have done near Sydney and Melbourne: it is not easy to visitualize vines growing, as they did, in what is now Collins Street! There are still vineyards that are known as the Adelaide Metropolitan vineyards, although there are now only a few of the many erstwhile Torrens vineyards. There used to be, for instance, in the 'fifties of the last century, an East Torrens Winemaking and Distillation Company, with vineyards at Stepney, a suburb of Adelaide: there was also an Adelaide Winemaking and Distillation Company, with a capital of £10,000, without any vineyards, the function of which was to buy grapes, process them and market wines and brandies.

All the more important firms of today have offices and an efficient staff in the chief cities of Australia and in London; the others have agents in charge of the distribution of their wines who are able to let their principals know which are the types of wines likely to have the greatest appeal.

Up to the outbreak of the First World War the demand for Australian wine in the United Kingdom was for red table wines, 'dry reds': wines that were darker than most, stronger than most and cheaper than most. They did not appeal to wine-connoisseurs, who had a traditional or acquired love of the light, dry wines of France and Germany, but they were gratefully hailed by a great many wine-consumers, who throughly appreciated the dinner comfort which Australian flagon burgundies gave them at a price within their means. The cost of Australian table wines ranged from 13s. to 28s. a dozen bottles, at a time when the duty was merely 1s. a gallon or 2d. a bottle. The demand for the unfortified wines of Australia rose from scratch to nearly a millions gallons a year (963,460 gallons) in 1911.

The declaration of war in 1914 halted the shipping of Australian wine overseas: the allocation of tonnage for war material, foodstuffs, raw materials and the high rates of marine insurance left little hope to the Australian vintners of selling any quantities of wine overseas.

Immediately after the war, however, shipments of wine from Australia began to gather momentum, rising from 176,029 gallons in 1918 to 4,224,504 gallons in 1927, and then became stabilized at an average of 3·5 million gallons a year up to 1940, when the Second World War and submarine terror far worse than during the First War halted all shipments of wine from Australia.

During the 'between-the-wars' period the Australian vintners were faced with the fact that they had too large stocks of fortified wines, in spite of very much greater demand for that type of wine in Australia. This was due to the mass-production of fortified wines in the irrigation areas, where an acre of Doradillo grapes could yield as much as 10 tons of grapes, when an acre (non-irrigated) of Cabernet or Rhine Riesling grapes could not be expected to yield more than 2 tons of grapes.

It was only natural that the Australian vintners would turn to the United Kingdom as the country where they had the best chance of marketing their surplus fortified wines, mostly port and sherry types. At the time the consumption of port and sherry was much greater in the United Kingdom than that of all other wines. It was, however, unfortunate for the Australian vintners that the Anglo-Portuguese Treaty of 1916 had given the protection of the law in England to port and Madeira, restricting the use of those two names to the wines of Portugal and Madeira.

In 1924 Australia's Wine Export Bounty Act became law, because 'the vital need for Australia was to get rid of bulk stocks' (H. E. Laffer, *The Wine Industry of Australia*, 1949, p. 77). Those bulk stocks were all sweet, fortified wines from the irrigated areas, which is why the bounty for which the Act provided applied only to wines of at least 34% proof spirit. The bounty was 2s 9d. a gallon, to which had to be added a refund of 1s. 3d. a gallon paid in excise for the fortifying spirit used in the making of the wine: this meant that the sweet, fortified Australian wines of the port and sherry types had a start of 4s. a gallon F.O.B.

In 1925 the Australian vintners had another present, this time from the British Chancellor of the Exchequer, who announced in the House of Commons, when introducing the year's Budget, that Empire wines not exceeding 27% of proof spirit would pay in future a duty of 2s. a gallon, and that the Empire fortified wines not exceeding

42% of proof spirit would pay 4s. a gallon, whereas the wines of non-Empire countries would pay 3s. a gallon if not exceeding 25% of proof spirit and 8s. a gallon if not exceeding 42%.

In 1927, rather meanly, if we may say so, the Australian Government cut down its bounty by 1s. a gallon.

In 1929 a helping hand was offered to the Australian vintners when the Wine Overseas Marketing Board Act was passed by the Commonwealth Parliament. This Act provided, among other things, for the creation of Board to be known as the Wine Overseas Marketing Board (later to be called, more simply, the Australian Wine Board), and one of the first things that the Board did was to open a London office in 1930, and to appoint Mr H. E. Laffer its first manager, with the title of overseas representative.

In 1930 also the Australian Federal Government imposed steep increases in the rate of excise duty on fortifying spirit, and the wine industry asked that the increase in revenue should go into a fund for payment of the bounty. The Government agreed to establish the Wine Export Encouragement Trust Account, to which part of the excise charges was credited, and from this account the amounts due for the bounty on export were paid.

In the early years of the Trust Account there was no accumulation of funds, but during the Second World War, when wine exports fell sharply, a considerable credit balance was built up, amounting, at the end of 1946, to £1,100,000. Then, however, the Government decided to discontinue the bounty (from 28 February 1947), claiming that increased prices being obtained overseas for wine and a rise in consumption of wine in Australia made it no longer necessary.

Of the £1,100,000 in the Trust Account, £600,000 went into Commonwealth Consolidated Revenue and £500,000 into a new account called this time the Wine Industry Assistance Trust Account. Eight years later, in 1955, it was decided to use this £500,000 to establish and maintain the Australian Wine Institute.

The Institute took over scientific research work which had been begun in a small way as far back as 1934 under the control of a body known as the Oenological Research Committee, which consisted of representatives of the University of Adelaide, the Wine Board and the Federal Viticultural Council.

The research done under the committee's guidance was conducted in the buildings of the Waite Agricultural Research Institute at Glen Osmond, South Australia, with the co-operation and support of the Commonwealth Scientific and Industrial Research Organization.

The new Institute, however, built laboratories of its own, with a pilot winery, across the road from the Waite Institute; its control is vested in a council responsible to the Commonwealth Minister for Primary Industry and the Wine Board.

Mention has already been made of the world-wide recognition that has been given to research on Flor Sherry, for which the Director of the Wine Research Institute, Mr J. C. M. Fornachon, was responsible. But the work of the Institute is, of course by no means confined to studies on Flor: it covers many aspects of vine-growing and wine-making.

One of the most interesting and ambitious projects on which the Institute is currently engaged is being carried out in co-operation with the Soils Division of the

Commonwealth Scientific and Industrial Research Organization, the Commonwealth Bureau of Meteorology and the South Australian Department of Agriculture. It is a long-term project, now in its eighth year, and it has a very important objective: to discover precisely how variations of soil and season influence the major and minor constituents of grapes, which in turn influence the quality of the wine that is made from them.

For this experiment the Institute has established no less than 42 experimental plots of vines scattered over the wine-producing areas of South Australia: in the Barossa Valley, the Springton and Eden Valley area and the Murray Valley. Grapes from the plots are brought to the Institute at vintage time each year and made into wine under standardized conditions in the Institute's pilot winery. Both the grapes and the wines made from them are chemically analysed, and at intervals during maturation the wines are evaluated and compared by tasting. When the experiment is completed it seems certain to provide basic information that will be of first-rate value to vintners and *vignerons* everywhere.

The Australian wine industry is thus quite highly organized on the scientific side; it is no less well organized on the marketing side.

Not only are Australian wines selling in increasing quantity in Australia; they are becoming better known in other countries, and for this much of the credit must go to the Australian Wine Board.

An important decision by the Board was to establish a central supply point in the United Kingdom, with the aim of ensuring that quality Australian wines and brandies would always be available under the makers' labels.

Britain remains the Australian wine trade's best overseas customer: she takes well over a million gallons of wine and brandy a year. Canada comes next, with imports of about 300,000 gallons of wine a year and 50,000 to 60,000 gallons of brandy. Australian wine is now going also to many countries in south-east Asia, the Pacific Islands and the West Indies, and even Japan, not traditionally a wine-drinking country, is today beginning to buy Australian wine.

Australia's total exports of wine and brandy in recent times have ranged between 1·5 and 2 million gallons: a modest figure indeed when compared with the exports of the world's great wine-producing countries, but a figure on which Australian wine men are improving each year.

### ACREAGE OF AUSTRALIAN VINEYARDS

| Financial Year | S.A. | N.S.W. | Victoria | W.A. | Queensland | Total |
|---|---|---|---|---|---|---|
| 1931/32 | 52,498 | 15,360 | 38,215 | 5,139 | 1,749 | 112,961 |
| 1941/42 | 58,416 | 16,478 | 43,238 | 8,841 | 2,903 | 129,879 |
| 1951/52 | 61,214 | 17,047 | 45,267 | 9,358 | 2,819 | 135,705 |
| 1961/62 | 57,836 | 17,607 | 45,105 | 9,017 | 3,203 | 132,768 |

### WINE PRODUCTION (1,000 gallons)

| Financial Year | S.A. | N.S.W. | Victoria | W.A. | Queensland | Total |
|---|---|---|---|---|---|---|
| 1931/32 | 10,665 | 1,590 | 1,530 | 365 | 41 | 14,191 |
| 1941/42 | 11,329 | 3,112 | 1,162 | 410 | 32 | 16,045 |
| 1951/52 | 25,495 | 5,465 | 3,472 | 790 | 33 | 35,255 |
| 1961/62 | 30,831 | 6,442 | 3,605 | 867 | 36 | 41,781 |

CHAPTER FOUR

# New Zealand

GRAPES were grown and wine was made on a commercial scale for the first time in New Zealand about 100 years ago, but there had been some vineyards in both the North and the South Islands some 50 years earlier.

Strange as the coincidence may appear, the first vineyards of New Zealand happened to be planted by men whose morality and purpose were as different as one could expect those of saints and sinners to be.

Among the 'saints' there were men with an almost mystical faith in the grape, the fruit of the 'tree of life'. They believed that there was soil, in New Zealand, just as suitable for viticulture as the soil of many famous European vineyards which had not got the benefit of as sunny and dependable a climate. They fondly hoped that there would be, one day, wine from the vineyards of New Zealand in such plenty and so cheap that it would be the common drink of the common people, instead of beer and spirits, and that it would prove to be a check to both drunkenness and alcoholism.

> The man who could sit under the shade of his own vine, with his wife and children about him, and the ripe clusters hanging within their reach, in such a climate as this, and not feel the highest enjoyment, is incapable of happiness and does not know what the word means.

So wrote, in *Authentic Information relating to New South Wales and New Zealand*, James Busby, the father of Australian viticulture, and the first Resident in New Zealand.

Of course, Busby planted a vineyard as soon as he settled in New Zealand, and he made wine, good wine, indeed, which was praised by one of Busby's more famous guests, Dumont d'Urville, the Commander of *Astrolabe*, who called at the Bay of Islands in 1840. This is what he wrote in his *Journal*, as translated by Olive Wright:

> As I was going over Mr Busby's estate, I noticed a trellis on which several flourishing vines were growing. I asked Mr Flint if the vines produced any grapes in this climate and, contrary to what I had been told in Korora Reka, I heard to my surprise that there had already been attempts to make wine from New Zealand grapes. On reaching his house, Mr Flint offered me a glass of port. I refused it, but with great pleasure I agreed to taste the product of the vineyard I had just seen. I was given a light white wine very sparkling and delicious to taste, which I enjoyed very much. Judging from this sample, I have no doubt that vines will be grown extensively all over the sandy hills of these islands, and very soon New Zealand wine may be exported to English possessions in India.

James Busby was an altruist, an apostle of the grape, and he did his best to encourage settlers to have a little vineyard of their own, in spite of which, or maybe because of this, he was elected the first President of the first temperance society of New Zealand, the Bay of Islands Temperance Society.

He was the most active and the most articulate of the 'Friends of Wine' in New Zealand, but he was not the first.

The Reverend James Marsden was the first to bring the Bible to New Zealand, in

1815, and the grape, three years later. The vines which he planted at Kerikeri, his Mission station, were still flourishing 20 years later, when Darwin called, in 1835, on his round-the-world voyage in *Beagle*: he noted that they were then being tended by Maoris of the Bay of Islands Mission.

On the east or Pacific coast of the North Island vines were first planted by French missionaries, Marist priests from Lyons, in the 1830s. There were 36 of them, and they had with them a number of lay brothers as well as vine-cuttings. Their first vineyard was in Poverty Bay, but it was not long before they had a Mission and a vineyard in Hawke's Bay and elsewhere: in whatever remote area the Fathers gained a foothold the lay brothers' first duty was to clear the ground and plant a vineyard: wine was indispensable for sacramental purposes, as well as highly desirable for the good health of all members of the Mission. The Fathers also found out, as Marsden had done before them, that wine was much liked by the Maoris.

There is still today a Marist Mission with a vineyard in Hawke's Bay; the vineyard is the oldest of New Zealand vineyards, not the oldest in terms of actual seniority of plantation but the oldest with continuity of ownership and management.

Those were some of the 'saints', but who were the 'sinners'? They were the unscupulous land speculators who enticed German and French migrants with baseless promises that they would grow grapes and grow rich, in New Zealand, with ease and speed.

In a booklet which had run to four editions by 1842 the Hon. Henry William Petrie, a propagandist of the New Zealand Company, wrote:

> From the nature of the climate at Port Nicholson, there can be no doubt of the ultimate success of the vine . . . We shall require French and German cultivators to whom the most liberal encouragement should be given. The few French at Akaroa, on Banks Peninsula, have begun to make a business of cultivating the vine, and, I am told, with every prospect of success.

This was not true. The Compagnie Nanto-Bordelaise had brought to Akaroa 30 families of *vignerons*, mostly from the Charente, and one from the Jura, to whom had been promised wonderfully fertile land in which to plant the vine cuttings that were to make their fortune. Bitter, indeed, had been their disappointment when they found that the 5 acres which was the domain of each family, was virgin forest, a tangle of trunks and undergrowth, which they had to clear with hand tools and the tenacity of hard-working French peasants. They did, in time, manage to plant some vines and to make some wine, but the more fortunate among them returned to France and the others found better jobs in New Zealand.

In another book, published in 1845, *Remarks on the Past and Present State of New Zealand*, Walter Brodie wrote: 'In a few years, New Zealand will export much wine. The vine grows luxuriantly, and the few hundreds of Germans who have lately gone out, have turned their attention to the vine only.' Brodie was referring to two ship-loads of German *vignerons* who had come, one in 1843 and the other in 1844, to Nelson, where they had been welcomed in glowing terms by *The Nelson Examiner*: 'No emigrants are more valuable than the German, and we hail the intended cultivation of the vine by them with unfeigned pleasure.'

By the time Brodie's book was published those Germans had been so disgusted at the land offered to them that they had left New Zealand for ever and settled in South Australia.

It is highly probably that, in New Zealand as in Australia, many of the farmers among the early settlers had a vineyard of their own and made some wine either to drink or to distil or for both. The first men, however, to depend entirely for their livelihood upon the sale of the wine which they made from the grapes that they grew and or bought were Charles Levet and Jose Soler.

Charles Levet was a coppersmith of Ely, in Cambridgeshire, who came to New Zealand with a family and with a book from which he could and did learn how to grow grapes in the open and how to make different kinds of wine. He took up land at Wellsford, in the Kaipara harbour, 8 miles by canoe from Port Albert. The country was hilly and thickly timbered, but, by 1863, Levet and his son William, 14 years old at the time, had cleared the stiff soil and carved their vineyard by back-breaking daily labour.

> They planted vines against manuka stakes set two, three, or four feet high, according to the slope of the ground, and from the top of these stakes rough manuka stakes were run towards the face of the hill. The vines were trained along these horizontals, the bunches of fruit hanging almost to the ground at the up-slope end. Seven acres were planted, tied to rude trellis work, and thereafter cultivated by hand. And, to keep off the cold westerlies that sometimes blasted across the harbour, long lines of high paling fences were built across the vineyard (Dick Scott, *Winemakers of New Zealand*, p. 28).

The Levets, father and son, prospered as, indeed, they deserved, after some years of hard work and experimenting with growing different species of grapes and making different types of wine. At first they lived by floating kauri logs downstream for sale to the mills at Port Albert and by splitting kauri shingles that were shipped from Port Albert to Auckland via Onehunga. The time came, however, when the Levets no longer shipped tiles to Auckland but barrels of wine to Israel Wendel, a native of Alsace, who had been granted the first retail wine licence issued in New Zealand: he had opened a wine bar in Karangahape road, Auckland, for the sale of wine – the Levet wines – to be consumed on the premises or taken away from 6 a.m. to 10 p.m. daily. No licensing act was ever more generous as regards opening hours! Much less liberal was an amendment of 1881 providing that no wine-maker could sell any of his own wine for consumption off the premises except in quantities of 2 gallons and more.

The Levets specialized in fortified wines, which they offered to the wine-lovers of the day as port, sherry, Madeira and Constantia, and they claimed that they never sold any wine for consumption before it had been at least five years in oak to mature. Israel Wendel was the best customer of the Levets, and Sir William Jervois, the Governor, was the most illustrious; his successor, Lord Glasgow (1892–97) not only paid a visit to the Levets' vineyard but he gave them permission to use his name and crest on the labels of their wines.

Sad to relate, William Levet died in his fifties, in 1906, his father died two years later, in 1908, aged 85, and their vineyard died with them.

Jose Soler was a Spaniard from Tarragona who planted a vineyard at Wanganui in 1866. At first, to make a living, he sold vegetables and soft fruit from his garden until his vines came to full bearing and until his wine had been given time to mature in oak barrels. He specialized in table wines, chiefly white wines from Riesling grapes, which he sold as Hock, and red wine from Shiraz grapes, which he sold as burgundy: he also made some sparkling wine, being, as far as we know, the first to do so in New Zealand. Most of Soler's wines were made from grapes of his own vines, but he also bought grapes from the Maoris, who had some vineyards up-river; he paid 2d. per lb for the grapes which they brought downstream in canoes at the time of the vintage. The time came, however, when the Marois found more profitable ways of using their land, and they ceased to grow grapes, even when Soler offered them 3d. per lb.

In an interview with Soler, published in *The Farmer* in 1897, it was recorded that his remarkable success in business was due to the fact that he had found out which was the wine 'that the colonial palate prefers, and, as a business man, he makes that wine. He does not theorize about educating the public as to what they ought to drink; he simply manufactures what they want to drink.'

Judges at Wine Exhibitions in those days must have had the 'colonial palate': at the 1906 Christchurch Wine Exhibition Soler sent five of his wines, and he was awarded three Gold Medals; some of the Australian exhibitors complained and demanded a re-judging: it was granted to them, and a judge was chosen who was approved by them: he gave Soler five Gold Medals. When Soler died, in 1906, his wines were in demand practically everywhere in New Zealand, 3,500 gallons of them were consumed annually at the Wanganui Wine Bar, licensed in 1881, but Soler's sons left Wanganui for sheep farming, and Antonio Vidal, one of Soler's nephews who had come from Spain to assist him, also left Wanganui at the old Spaniard's death for Hawke's Bay, where his son and grandsons own one of the more flourishing vineyards and wine businesses.

The success which the Levets and Soler had achieved proved beyond a doubt that there was a nationwide demand for New Zealand wine: it was the best possible incentive for newcomers to try their luck as wine-makers.

The most colourful as well as the most successful of the wine-makers of that period, the pre First World War years, was Assid Abraham Corban, who first came to Auckland from Beirut in 1892. In 1902 he planted his first 4 acres of vines at Henderson, and as early as 1913 the four wines which he sent into an Auckland International Exhibition were awarded two Gold Medals and two Silver Medals. Before his death in 1941 Assid Corban left 30 direct descendants to carry on the good work, and he had the pride to see his Lebanon Vineyard, named after his native land, what it is still today, the premier vineyard and winery of New Zealand, with 350 acres of quality vines in production and a winery capable of handling 750,000 gallons of wine annually.

Also in 1902, a Dalmatian who had come to Auckland in 1890 to try his luck at the gumfields, Stipan Yelich, whose name became anglicized as Stephan Yelas, decided to make wine from half an acre he owned in the Henderson area. This was the modest start of the 25-acre flourishing Pleasant Valley Vineyard, now being ably tended by Stephan's son, Moscow Yelas. Another Dalmatian, Joseph Balich, whose sons now own the well-known Henderson Golden Sunset Vineyard, planted his first vines, in 1912, at night, by candle-light, after a day's work in Assid Corban's vineyard.

In 1914, when a Licensing Amendment Act introduced for the first time wine-makers' licences, 35 such licences were granted.

Besides the professional wine-makers whose business was to make and to sell wine, there were a greater number of amateurs or *hobbyists*, as Dick Scott calls them, many of whom spared neither money nor trouble to make their own wine from grapes of their own. One of the most enthusiastic and wealthy amateurs was William Beetham, who planted a vineyard in 1892, at Masterton, above Wellington, with none but quality grapes, mostly Pinots and Shiraz. In 1897 he mobilized all men, women and children of his large estate at the time of the vintage, and they picked 13½ tons of grapes, which yielded 1,850 gallons of wine when crushed in the ancient and classical way by the bare-legged men of the estate.

Henry Tiffen was another enthusiast, a contemporary of Beetham, but he preferred the more modern and more costly mechanical wine-press to the ancient and classical footwork. His vineyard and his well-equipped winery were in the Hawke's Bay area, where J. N. Williams and Bernard Chambers also had small vineyards of their own, the first near Hastings and the other at Te Mata.

The nation-wide interest in viticulture and in wine during the last decade of the nineteenth century in New Zealand was such that those years were sometimes referred to as the 'grape fever' epoch, and the Administration decided to invite a well-known Italian expert, who had come to Melbourne at the request of the Victoria Government, so that New Zealand *vignerons* might have the benefit of his superior knowledge and his guidance. His name was Romeo Bragato, and he arrived in New Zealand in 1895.

The first thing that Bragato discovered when he started visiting the vineyards of the North Island was that the dreaded pest, the phylloxera, had also arrived recently. He advised the uprooting of the infested vines and the flooding of their vineyard as the only means of getting rid of the bug, but his warning was not heeded, and presently the pest made rapid progress and wiped out most of the vineyards.

Was New Zealand to be wineless after all? God forbid! Bragato came back in 1902 and told the *vignerons* that they would have as good wine again, if they planted phylloxera-resisting briars grafted with any of the quality grapes they grew before the disaster. To help them further, Bragato founded, at the request of the Administration, two Experimental Viticultural Stations, one at Te Kauwhata and the other at Arataki, so that *vignerons* – old or new – could get at all times the guidance they needed as well as suitable cuttings for the kind of soil and sub-soil of their vine-yards.

Hope had only just dawned again for the wine-makers of New Zealand when came the First World War and the economic crisis of its aftermath. Yet, in spite of the most adverse conditions imaginable, there were at all times optimists who had faith in the grape and planted more vines. Thus Friedrich Wohnsiedler, a German who had lived in New Zealand for 40 years, but whose business in Gisborne had been wrecked for no better reason than he had a German name, planted a vineyard at Waihirere, in Poverty Bay, with the help of Peter Guschka. He was no visionary, and the proof is the flourishing Waihirere Vineyards Ltd, which today produce 95,000 gallons a year and is still expanding.

In 1935 the thirty years of official hostility to the wine industry came to an end with the return to power of a Labour Administration and Te Kauwhata was rehabilitated: it was granted funds to expand, to acquire modern equipment and to have the benefit of the experience of a qualified instructor, B. W. Lindeman, from Australia. The *vignerons* and wine-makers of New Zealand were also 'protected' from imports of wine from overseas by a higher import duty of 8s. 6d. instead of 6s. per gallon.

The Second World War, post-war taxation and adverse economic conditions greatly interfered with the progress of viticulture and the sale of wine in New Zealand, as in

Australia. The wine industry of New Zealand never had a fair chance of expansion
before 1950. Since then, however, progress has been highly satisfactory, not spectacular,
but steady and sound, so much so that the total acreage of wine-making vines in bearing
has exceeded a thousand acres since 1960.

|  | 1958/59 | 1959/60 | 1960/61 | 1961/62 | 1968/69 |
|---|---|---|---|---|---|
| Vineyards in bearing | 899 | 958 | 1,004 | 1,079 | 2,964 |
| Newly planted vineyards | 130 | 160 | 175 | 108 | — |
| Total acreage | 1,029 | 1,118 | 1,179 | 1,187 | 2,964 |

Some 98% of the vineyards of New Zealand are located in two areas of the North
Island, the more important of the two being, at present, the Auckland area, which
embraces all vineyards from Hamilton northwards. The second area, smaller now but
developing more rapidly, is the Hawke's Bay stretch of vineyards from Napier to
Hastings, facing the Pacific, but there are also some vineyards about a hundred miles
farther north, in the Gisborne district, which are included for the sake of convenience
in this same 'Pacific' area.

There are vineyards in the southern half of the North Island, here and there, and
there are also a few in the South Island, but they are of no commercial importance,
as the following official figures for an average two-year period show:

|  | Auckland | | Hawke's Bay | | All Others | | Total | |
|---|---|---|---|---|---|---|---|---|
|  | acres | % | acres | % | acres | % | acres | % |
| 1960/61 | 579,246 | 59·6 | 372,373 | 38·3 | 18,950 | 2·1 | 970,569 | 100 |
| 1961/62 | 642,295 | 53·3 | 550,557 | 45·6 | 13,350 | 1·1 | 1,206,202 | 100 |

Official statistics divide the wines of New Zealand into two classes according to their
alcoholic strength: those with an alcoholic strength of over 25% proof spirit are called
dessert wines, and the others table wines. There is no possible doubt that the preference of the New Zealand wine consumers is for the dessert wines, since official figures
show that the demand for dessert wines is over 80% of the total consumption, in spite
of the fact that they cost more, but not a great deal more, than table wines. Very few of
the dessert wines can claim to belong to the quality wines class: they are sweet, spirity,
without any trace of bouquet or breed, or any such nonsense. The standard of quality
of the table wines, however, is distinctly rising, and there are many dry red and dry
white wines which are by no means inferior to the same types of wines sold in Australia
at the same prices. The demand for the better table wines of New Zealand is rising, but
not nearly at the same tempo as the demand for the dessert wines, as the following
representative figures (gallons) show:

|  | 1957/58 | 1958/59 | 1959/60 | 1960/61 | 1961/62 | 1962/63 |
|---|---|---|---|---|---|---|
| Total wines | 110,206 | 151,473 | 137,453 | 133,536 | 172,302 | 234,162 |
| % | 17·6 | 18·2 | 15·6 | 14·5 | 15·0 | 17·7 |
| Dessert wine | 520,200 | 678,349 | 760,695 | 784,603 | 971,670 | 1,086,330 |
| % | 82·4 | 81·8 | 84·4 | 85·5 | 85·0 | 82·3 |
| Total | 630,406 | 829,822 | 878,148 | 918,139 | 1,143,972 | 1,320,492 |

Official statistics indicate that in New Zealand the Administration does not restrict
the use of the name wine to the fermented juice of fresh ripe grapes, but to the fermented juice of other fruits as well. Thus there is a particularly popular white wine sold

in a white bordeaux bottle as *Sauternes* which is made solely from apple juice according to a recipe which 'wine-makers' may get for the asking from the Te Kauwhata Research Station. According to official statistics, the demand for fruit 'wines' fluctuates rapidly, thus their production rose from 1·6% in 1957/58 to 11·1% in 1960/61 and dipped to 2·7% in 1962/63.

|             | 1957/58 | 1958/59 | 1959/60 | 1960/61 | 1961/62   | 1962/63   |
|-------------|---------|---------|---------|---------|-----------|-----------|
| Fruit wines | 10,090  | 24,238  | 40,156  | 59,430  | 62,230    | 35,735    |
| %           | 1·6     | 2·9     | 4·4     | 11·1    | 5·1       | 2·7       |
| Grape wine  | 630·406 | 829·822 | 878,143 | 918,133 | 1,143,972 | 1,132,049 |
| %           | 98·4    | 97·1    | 95·6    | 88·9    | 94·9      | 97·3      |
| Total       | 640·496 | 854,060 | 918,304 | 970,569 | 1,206,202 | 1,167,784 |

A million and a quarter gallons of wine is what the vineyards of New Zealand are expected to bring forth every year: it is not a large quantity by Australian and still less by European standards, and it is somewhat surprising to know that there were in 1964 no less than 155 registered wine-producers in New Zealand. 111 of them were in a small way of business and producing no more than 1,000 gallons, since their aggregate total production was only 117,882 gallons, an average of 1,061 gallons. The total production of the 44 in a larger way of business came to a total of 1,088,320 gallons, an average of 24,735 gallons.

## Auckland-Northland

This is at present the more important of the two main groups of vineyards in the North Island, and although its acreage of vineyards is growing, it is not growing at the same rate as on the east coast of Hawke's Bay area: the increase was 10·9% in 1962 in the Henderson district of the Auckland area, and 47·9% in the Hawke's Bay area.

Henderson, 12 miles from Auckland, is a sprawling, obviously unplanned township, where wineries and residential quarters live happily together. The oldest and best known of the Henderson wineries is Mount Lebanon, the headquarters of Messrs A. A. Corban & Sons. Among the more flourishing vineyards owned and tended by Yugoslavs in the Henderson area mention must be made of the Pleasant Valley Vineyards, one of the oldest, Balich's Golden Sunset, Ivicevich's Panorama and, of course, those Yugoslav *vignerons* G. & F (Mr & Mrs) Mazuran, who have collected in a surprisingly short space of time quite a large number of Diplomas and Medals at different Wine Exhibitions in Australia and in Europe.

The most picturesque, but by no means the largest vineyard of the Henderson district, upon the tree-crested slopes of gentle hills, was planted by one of the few British pioneers, Dudley Russell: his vineyard and winery are known as The Western Vineyard Ltd.

## Hawke's Bay — Gisborne

Most of the vineyards of this area are in the Hawke's Bay Valley, between Napier and Hastings, facing the Pacific Ocean. They may be divided into two groups: (1) those planted in the rich alluvial soil along the course of the Tuki Tuki and other rivers not long before they flow into the ocean at low tide; and (2) those which are planted in the poor sandy soil of the jumble of downs rising between the ocean and the rich grazing grounds of the hinterland. The most important winery of this area is the former Macdonald winery, which has been acquired and greatly enlarged by Messrs. McWilliams of Australia, who also have a large winery at Napier. Among other well-known *vignerons* of the Hawke's Bay area, Messrs Vidal and Toogood Bros, enjoy a high reputation. One of Toogood's vineyards, at Te Awanga, has been in cultivation without a break for the past 72 years and challenges the claim of the Marist Mission's at Greenmeadows to be the oldest of the area. The Mission Fathers manage to make from their 15-acre vineyard every kind of wine for which there is a demand, still and sparkling, sweet and dry, as well as some brandy and liqueurs.

In the Gisborne area, some 150 miles to the north, there are but few vineyards, but they produce some very fair table wines, none better than those of the Wohnsieidler Wine Company Ltd at Ozmond.

In New Zealand, as in Australia, what is mostly lacking is a greater number of wine-conscious consumers ready to pay a little more for much better wines than the standard types at present so much more popular than the better wines.

# *The Wines of*
# SOUTH AFRICA

☙

ANDRÉ L. SIMON

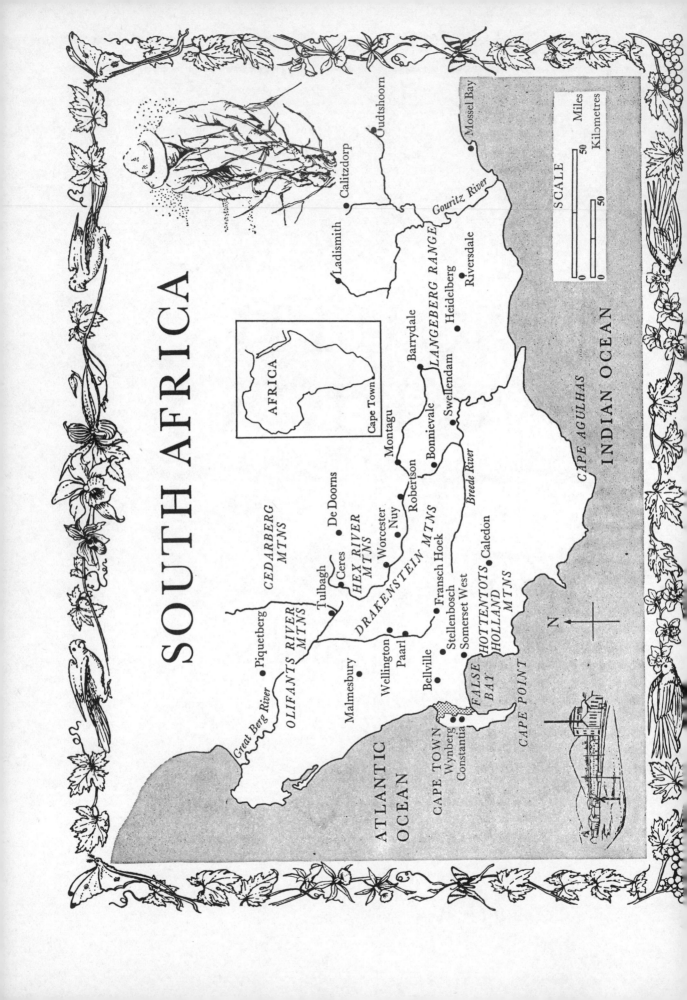

# SOUTH AFRICA

AFRICA

Cape Town

SCALE

Miles

Kilometres

0    50

0    50

ATLANTIC
OCEAN

*Great Berg River*

Piquetberg

*OLIFANT'S RIVER
MTNS*

*CEDARBERG
MTNS*

Tulbagh

Ceres

De Doorns

*HEX RIVER
MTNS*

Worcester

Nuy

Malmesbury

Wellington

Paarl

Bellville

*DRAKENSTEIN MTNS*

Fransch Hoek

Stellenbosch

Somerset West

CAPE TOWN

Wynberg

Constantia

*FALSE
BAY*

*HOTTENTOTS
HOLLAND
MTNS*

Caledon

Robertson

Bonnievale

*Breede River*

Montagu

Barrydale

Swellendam

Heidelberg

*LANGEBERG RANGE*

Riversdale

*Gouritz River*

Ladismith

Calitzdorp

Oudtshoorn

Mossel Bay

*CAPE AGULHAS*

INDIAN OCEAN

*CAPE POINT*

N

# South Africa

THERE are a few vineyards and there is a little wine made in the Transvaal, more as a hobby than a business, and there are grapes, mostly table grapes, grown in the Vaal-Hartz and elsewhere; there are also a number of vineyards along the Orange River, in the Cape, but their grapes never become wine: they are dried into raisins or sultanas. Whoever speaks of the wines of South Africa, or writes about them, means the wines which have been known in England for nearly 300 years as Cape Wines. They are the wines made from the vineyards of the Western Province of the Cape, within latitudes 33° and 34° S. The vineyards of the Cape may be divided into two main sections, the lower ones usually known as the 'Coastal Belt' vineyards; and the upper ones, commonly referred to as the 'Little Karoo' vineyards. Their total acreage, according to official statistics, is 77,284 morgen,[1] with 215,500,000 vines in production.

The Coastal Belt stretches from the Table Bay Peninsula and the Constantia Valley, on the Cape Town side; and from False Bay and Somerset West, on the other side, to Stellenbosch, Paarl, Wellington, Malmesbury, Ceres and the Tulbagh cul-de-sac. The average rainfall in the Coastal Belt vineyards is 25 inches per annum, so that the majority of the vineyards are not irrigated: they are the vineyards responsible for the better sherries and table wines of the Cape, but their productivity is comparatively small, from 3 to 6 tons of grapes per acre.

The Little Karoo area stretches from beyond the Drakenstein Range to the Swatberg Mountains, taking in the districts of Worcester, Robertson, Montagu, Oudtshoorn and Ladysmith. The rainfall in this area varies from 8 to 12 inches per annum, and the heat of the summer is more intense, but, owing to their higher altitudes, the vineyards of the Little Karoo do, occasionally, suffer from late spring frosts. Thanks to the fairly general use of irrigation, the Little Karoo vineyards produce from 6 to 10 tons of grapes per acre, and they are responsible for the sweet Muscats and other dessert wines of the Cape, as well as some of the red table wines of the stouter, darker and fuller types. There is also much of the Little Karoo wines distilled into Cape Brandy, and many of the Little Karoo grapes are dried into currants, raisins and sultanas.

The relative importance of both the irrigated and non-irrigated vineyards of the Coastal Belt and Little Karoo vineyards is shown by these representative figures:

|  | COASTAL BELT | | LITTLE KAROO | |
|  | Morgen | Vines | Morgan | Vines |
|---|---|---|---|---|
| Irrigated | 21,417 | 53,168,238 | 23,251 | 83,287,629 |
| Non-irrigated | 30,996 | 71,841,721 | 1,620 | 7,224,272 |
| Total | 52,413 | 125,009,959 | 24,871 | 90,511,901 |

Geologically, the soil and sub-soil of the vineyards are quite different in the Coastal Belt and Little Karoo. There is a very much greater variety in the Coastal Belt according to the location of the vineyards: in the Cape Peninsula, for instance, Table Mountain sandstone predominates, whereas granite, Malmesbury shales, patches of sandy gravel and heavy loam occur here and there in many parts of the long trail of vinelands from

[1] A morgen equals 2·116 acres; a leaguer is 127 gallons.

647

Somerset West to Tulbagh. In the Little Karoo, however, loose, well-drained soils, light and heavy loams, mostly of great depth, are responsible for the greater fertility of the vineyards and their greater yield of wine every year.

In both the Coastal Belt and Little Karoo vineyards a great deal of attention is paid to the choice of the right kind of grapes to grow, and which are the species best suited to the nature of the soil, a task which is much more difficult in South Africa than in Europe, where they would never think of planting Palomino grapes in Portugal to make sherry, or Cabernets in Burgundy to make claret. In South Africa, as in Australia, all important wineries aim at producing a range of the wines for which there happens to be a good demand, and they grow the same varieties of vines which are grown in Spain and Portugal for the making of sherry and port, as well as Cabernet, Pinot Noir, Cinsault, which is called 'Hermitage' at the Cape, for red table wines with a bordeaux or burgundy character; also Riesling, Clairette Blanche, Green Grape and Steen, a distinctive variety of Cape white grape, for the table white wines, selecting the most suitable site for each variety of grapes. In the Little Karoo Thomson's seedless is mostly grown for sultanas, and Muscat grapes for the making of dessert wines.

At the Cape September, October and November are the spring months of the year, when life returns to the dormant vines, in which the sap rises again: the canes soon begin to swell, and there will then be little buds pushing their woolly heads through the scales; shoots follow, leaves, flowers, pollination and tiny bunches of pin-head berries-to-be. If those infant berries are to grow into fine, full wine-making grapes there must be constant watch over their welfare, warding off enemies from both vegetal and animal menaces – fungoid growths and insect pests, during the summer months, December, January and February: it is during those summer months that the grapes must have rain, or water somehow, to grow up, and sunshine to grow sweet and to be fully ripe at vintage time. Vintage time, when the grapes are picked and pressed, may begin late in February and last until April.

There are now in South Africa a greater number of people than ever before whose chief or sole occupation is either to grow grapes or to make wine; some of them do both, and most of them give to viticulture and wine-making more intelligent care and much better-trained service than their fathers did before them. They drink more of the wines of the country; they know them better, and they also have much better cause to be proud of them. This is what one would expect to find in a land with a 300-years-old tradition of wine-growing and wine-making, a vineland that produced once upon a time the one and only non-European wine ever to challenge the finest dessert wines of the famous classical vineyards of Spain, Portugal, France and Italy – old Constantia! There are still wines made at Constantia, a number of different types of wine, wines which receive bronze, silver and gold medals at wine shows, but none of them would be considered, in Europe, the peer of the finest dessert wines of the famous European vineyards as old Constantia was.

Although the secrets of 'old Constantia' has been lost, the vintners of the Cape of today have benefits and privileges which were totally unknown to their forebears: most valuable of all, and a blessing undreamt of only 50 years ago, they have full control of heat and cold through refrigeration. When the ripe grapes are crushed, at the vintage time, it is of the utmost importance that their sweet juice shall start fermenting as soon as possible and that it shall continue fermenting at a regular, steady rate. This always was a difficult problem for the Cape vintners owing to the usually hot weather they experience at the time of the vintage; it made it very difficult, sometimes impossible, for them to stop the freshly pressed grape-juice fermenting away at much too fast a rate. Modern refrigeration has now settled this important problem: it has made it possible to ensure the correct *tempo* of fermentation, in the course of which sweet unstable grape-juice becomes a dry, dependable wine.

Besides control of temperature, the South African wine industry has now other appreciable benefits, such as a very high standard of technical education, the latest scientific equipment, which not only makes the vintner's task easier but surer and more rewarding, which is why there are now in South Africa tables wines and fortified wines of fine quality, not, of course, challenging the great aristocrats of Bordeaux, the Côte d'Or and the Rhineland, rare and even more costly than rare wines, but the peers of most fine quality wines of all other vinelands.

Obviously, since their wines are made from *Vitis vinifera* grapes, the wines of South Africa are bound to conform to the main types of wines made in Europe, North Africa, Australia and California from the same or similar species of vines, be they dry or sweet white wines, for instance, which the South Africans, unlike the Australians and Californians, do not market as Chablis or Sauternes, nor do they sell their national sparkling wines as champagne.

The Cape vintners also have the unique privilege of having two distinct Ministers of Agriculture to look after them and their interests, one of them having his attention focused on all questions relating to 'production' while the other is chiefly concerned with the marketing of South African wines and brandies.

The Dutch East India Company was granted its first Charter in 1692 for 21 years, and by the end of those 21 years the Company had been both the cause and the beneficiary of the dramatic collapse and eclipse of Portugal as a great maritime power. Portugal was at the time entirely under the domination and misrule of Spain, and her immense colonial empire was defenceless. By the middle of the seventeenth century, when Portugal had regained her independence, the Dutch very wisely took steps to be ready, should a reborn Portuguese Navy attempt to recover the great possessions in the Far East which the Dutch had taken from the Portuguese. It was in 1652 that Jan van Riebeeck, one of the most able members of the Dutch East India Company Directorate, came to the Cape of Good Hope, and Cape Town was born. There had long been a Portuguese port of call at the Cape for ships on their way from and to Europe and the Far East, but it was van Riebeeck who first saw the desirability and the possibility of a settlement where the white man would till the land, raise a family and feel secure from both the hostile natives of the hinterland and seaborne enemies. It was he who planted the first vines in South Africa, and also made the first wine. Jan van Riebeeck probably never dreamt that the small acorn which he planted at the Cape would one day be the source of all the wealth it has brought to the land since then: the vine which he planted, in 1655, at Protea, on the foothills of Table Mountain, in the garden of the Dutch East India Company's Resident Director, was a symbol or token of western civilization – Christendom as it was called at the time – which was to flourish for evermore at the southern end of the black continent!

How happy and legitimately proud Jan van Riebeeck must have been when he wrote in his dairy, on 2 February 1659, that wine had been made that morning for the first time from grapes grown at the Cape!

Jan van Riebeeck's small vineyard of 112 vines made it abundantly clear that grapes could mature in the open and that wine could be made at the Cape, yet it is Simon van der Stel who is known as the father of viticulture in South Africa. He was sent to the Cape from the Netherlands as first governor of the colony in 1679; his ambition was great and his energy was greater still: he had tracks of land cleared of scrub right and left of the Eerste River, east and west of the site where now stands the charming old university town of Stellenbosch, named after him. Simon van der Stel must have had great faith in the vine and a great love for wine, since tradition has made him and his son after him responsible for the planting of vineyards from Somerset West to Draken-stein. It was also Simon van der Stel who welcomed the French Huguenot immigrants: they left France at the time of the Revocation of the Edict de Nantes, in 1685, and, of course, the first thing they did was to plant grapes and to make wine where they were settled between Paarl and Stellenbosch, at Fransch Hoek which means 'French Corner', and Huguenot.

The Dutch Government did not approve all Simon van der Stel's enterprises, some of them, his enemies claimed, brought to the Governor more personal gains than glory to the nation or credit to the administration. The Dutch East India Company, however, had no fault to find with Simon's many activities: on the contrary, they considered that the Company had good cause to be grateful to him, and in order to show their grati-tude for all he had done for the progress of agriculture and viticulture at the Cape they presented him with a grant of land, 900 morgen in all, near Wynberg, about 8½ miles from Cape Town and half-way between Cape Town and False Bay, in the shadow of Table Mountain. It was there that Simon van der Stel built the homestead where he lived during the later years of his life, and where he died in 1712. It was there that he created a model farm and planted a vineyard, naming his estate 'Constantia', after his wife, whose Christian name was Constance.

Whether Simon van der Stel had the advice of some qualified *vigneron* among the French Huguenot immigrants, or whether it was sheer good luck, the site chosen for his vineyard was certainly very good, indeed: it consisted of about 40 acres upon a gentle slope facing south-south-east, and its soil of sandy gravel was ideal for the small Musca-del grapes which were planted there and brought forth, under the sunshine of South Africa, grapes so rich in sugars that, given time to finish fermenting at leisure in oak, their sweet juice became a sweet wine of high alcoholic strength, needing no addition of brandy or any other treatment, fit to last and fit to stand a sea voyage to Europe, the perfect *vin doux naturel.*

When Simon van der Stel died the Constantia Estate was divided into four lots, the first, including the homestead and half the original vineyard, was named Groot Constantia; another lot, with the other half of the original vineyard, was called Klein Constantia. Although Simon van der Stel's original vineyard was divided at his death, the two new proprietors of its two halves were as anxious as Simon had been before them to make the best possible wine, better wine than had ever been made anywhere else in South Africa, so that the reputation of Constantia dessert wine remained very high all through the eighteenth and during the first half of the nineteenth century. We know exactly how wine was made at Groot Constantia at the beginning of the nineteenth century, thanks to the letters which Lady Anne Barnard, the wife of an early Colonial Secretary, wrote from the Cape to her relatives in England. In one of those letters she gives an account of a visit to Groot Constantia under the guidance of 'Mynheer Cloete'.

Lady Anne does not mention whether the wine that she saw being made at Constantia by slaves, who certainly did not know that their fine bronze chests and legs were looked upon with such admiration by the visitors, was red or white. There were both kinds, more of the white than of the red, and there appears to have been an accepted verdict in favour of the red Constantia being superior to the white.

It is both very strange and most unfortunate that, while there was such fine wine made at Constantia in very limited quantities, no other wine proved acceptable overseas when shipped from the Cape, not even the best of the many wines made in large quantities at Drakenstein, Stellenbosch, Fransch Hoek, Paarl, Huguenot and elsewhere. In June 1719, for instance, six small casks of Cape wine were shipped to Amsterdam and six to Batavia, then a few large casks were shipped to Amsterdam and Middelburg; and finally, 1,000 bottles. Sad to relate, none of all these wines proved to be fit for consumption when they reached their destination. Yet, in spite of their failure to find an export market for their wines, the farmers of the Cape must have found viticulture sufficiently rewarding to plant more vineyards and to make more wine. Wine at the Cape, any wine other than Constantia, was ridiculously cheap during the whole of the eighteenth century, that is when all labour was slave labour and inexpensive.

There never was any demand for the wines of the Cape, other than Constantia, either in Holland, Java or England until the nineteenth century, when, in 1805, the English kindly took possession of the Cape. The new regime was anxious to help the farmers of the Western Province sell their wine and brandy and thus gain their support and loyalty, more particularly during the Napoleonic wars, when wine was in very short supply. In 1811 a circular was issued by the admininistration to all wine farmers of the Colony, calling their attention to the importance of improving as much as lay in their power the quality of their wines, that they might be acceptable to a greater number of people in Great Britain. At the same time an official Wine Taster was appointed, whose chief duty was to ascertain that all Cape wines intended for export were of the right quality to stand the long sea voyage, and of a sufficiently high standard of excellence to be a credit to the Colony. No wine could be shipped from the Cape with this official Taster's permit, and to judge from results the men who were chosen to hold this important office must have been knowledgeable and conscientious civil servants: their office lasted from 1811 to 1825, and during those 14 years the quantities of wine exported from the Cape to England rose steadily. Preferential import duties in favour of the Cape wines must have helped the demand but there is no evidence in support of rumours at the time that some of the so-called Cape wines that came to England had been cheap French or Spanish wines shipped to South Africa and blended there with Cape wines.

In 1825 the value of the wine exported from the Cape was greater than the value of any other single commodity exported that year; soon after, however, wool and hides took the first and second place, and wine had dropped to fifth place in 1865 and to eighth place in 1868, when Cape wines no longer enjoyed the benefit of a particularly low import tariff.

Although Gladstone's 'one shilling per gallon' import duty on table wines, whatever their country of origin, practically killed the demand for wines of the Cape during the late 'sixties, the wine farmers of the Cape appear to have accepted their loss with remarkable fortitude, in spite of the fact that they had to cope at about the same time with the scourge of oidium. They checked the inroads of this dreaded disease and planted more vineyards, so that in 1875 there were 68,910,215 vines in production in the Colony, covering an area of 8,588 morgen, 65 roods, and producing 4,485,605 gallons of wine, as well as 1,067,832 gallons of spirits; figures which are all the more surprising considering that the demand for the wines and brandy of the Cape overseas was at its lowest ebb: the total value of all wines and spirits exported from the Cape from 1873 to 1879 was only £107,748. It so happened, by good fortune and not by planning, that the last 25 years of the nineteenth century proved to be a period of unprecedented prosperity: the Diamond Fields were annexed in 1871, when Kimberley and De Beers were also born; full responsible government was conceded in 1872; Basutoland was incorporated in 1869 and a number of other territories were acquired or annexed from year to year. The Colony expanded, as did also the numbers and the means of its population, so much that the supply of wine at times was not equal to the demand. This was also due to a large extent to the fact that it was during this period of prosperity of the Colony that the wine growers of the Cape met with an unparalleled disaster, when their vineyards were practically all destroyed by the accursed American vine louse, the *phylloxera vastatrix*. The bug cannot be seen: it lives underground, settles on the roots of the vine, lives on its sap and kills it. It was noticed for the first time in South Africa on 2 January 1886, at Mowbray, close to Cape Town, and nobody can tell how and why it got there. Nor has anybody ever been able to explain how the pest reached and destroyed within the next few years many of the Coastal Belt vineyards. The administration spent great sums of money, and all to no avail, in attempts to check the invasion; 2 million attacked vines were ordered to be destroyed between 1886 and 1890, but in the end all the old vines had to be uprooted, the soil disinfected and, eventually, planted with American phylloxera-resisting briars, upon which all the old varieties of vines were grafted. From 1891 to 1894, 623,891 plants were imported from France alone, at a cost of £1,476 16s. 5d., and were distributed, free, to the growers: they, in the meantime, propagated the varieties of grapes to be grafted upon the imported stock. Within 13 years there were 19,237,250 grafted vines in production in the Colony.

In 1891, at the time of the phylloxera disaster, there were 73,574,124 vines in production; they produced 6,012,522 gallons of wine, 1,423,043 gallons of spirits and over 2 million pounds of raisins. By 1899 the replanted vineyards already produced 4,826,432 gallons of wine and 1,167,344 gallons of spirits. Five years later the vineyards of the Cape were producing more than during the pre-phylloxera period! The financial crisis which followed the end of the Boer War hit everybody, the wine growers and the wine merchants as much as, if not more than, other members of the community.

Wine had been made and brandy had been distilled in most wineries, year after year without any planned policy or interchange of information, irrespective of the fact that the demand, both at home and overseas, had been steadily decreasing: the inevitable consequences were a piling up of stocks and tumbling prices. The crisis was so grave that the government at the Cape intervened and named a commission, in 1904, to investigate the causes of existing conditions and how best to mend matters. It was on the recommendation of this commission that the government decided, in 1905, to encourage the establishment of co-operative wineries by the grant to them of loans on very favourable terms. As a result of this decision, nine co-operative wineries were established between 1905 and 1909: they were registered under the old Cape of Good Hope Companies Act of 1892, as there was no legislation covering the registration of co-operative societies, an entirely new form of commercial activity until then.

The creation of co-operative wineries had been welcomed by many of the wine-farmers; they hoped that it would help them to enjoy the benefit of co-operative negotiations and marketing; they also wished that it might somehow put a stop to, or at least a brake upon, the evil of price-cutting, a ruinous practice when some particularly hard-pressed wine-makers were prepared to accept any offer for their wine.

Although it was agreed that the creation of co-operative wineries was a step in the right direction, it did nothing whatever to increase the demand which would have been, obviously, the best of all cures for the ill of over-production. Most unfortunately, the all too short boom in the ostrich feathers business collapsed in 1913, and many acres of lucerne no longer wanted for the ostriches became new vineyards, nobody at the time having the right or authority to stop such folly! Then came the First World War.

A surprisingly large proportion of the adult population of South Africa joined the Forces, many of them never to return; all shipments of wine from the Cape were halted for many months; a number of local industries were crippled by the shortage of skilled or semi-skilled labour, and the wholesale price of wine dropped to £2 10s. and £3 per leaguer, that is at less than one penny a bottle. The few existing co-operative wineries could handle but a very small proportion of the total production of wine, and they were, of course, quite unable to create a greater demand for the wines of the Cape.

Strange as it may seem now, when conditions at the Cape are so entirely different from what they were only 50 years ago, the Dutch wine farmers of the Cape, that is about 90% of the total, grew grapes and made wine but did not drink wine: they drank tea and brandy. The rest of the white population at the Cape, a mixed bag of many nationalities besides a large proportion of British drank some of the Cape wines, of course, but not to any really great extent: beer was the drink of all, whisky the tipple of the well-to-do, rum that of seafaring folks, and gin that of most females of uncertain age or doubtful reputation. The more dependable imbibers of Cape wines and brandies were the 'gentlemen of colour', Cape-born, most of them, but not natives, a name which applies in South Africa to the true blacks only, and natives were not permitted to buy or carry 'liquor' in those days; they got all they wanted, however, and more than was good for them, illegally, at fancy prices, from their coloured cousins.

On 16 December 1906 there was a meeting in the Paarl Town Hall, when C. W. M. Kohler was elected chairman and Isaac Perold secretary. Kohler was a fanatic – he said so himself – who was determined to get all the farmers of the Western Province to come together in a solid body who would have the indispensable political power and financial means to get things done, and well done. At this important Paarl meeting Kohler read the draft of the constitution of an organization which he called the Co-operative Viticultural Union of South Africa. This draft was agreed to by all present, with minor alterations, and it was then circulated to all the farmers of the Western Province. It is now in the archives of the K.W.V., at Paarl, and it might well be called their birth certificate, although the original name has been changed to Co-operative Wine Farmers Association or Ko-operative Wijnbouwers Vereniging van Zuid-Afrika – K.W.V. for short.

Although the name of Kohler's association was altered, the aims and objects given in his original draft have been adhered to ever since. His Co-operative Viticultural Union was formed 'for regulating the price and disposing of the wine and brandy produced by the members of the Union, such membership to be confined to *bona fide* producers of wine and brandy'.

How were Kohler's aims and objects to be attained? This is what his draft set out at length to explain, beginning with these words:

> 'All who become members of this Union bind themselves under a penalty of £5 per leaguer, which will be recoverable in any Court of Law, not to sell any must, wine or brandy to any Company or person except by and through the Governing Board of the Union, and at such prices as have been fixed by such Board.'

The unanimous acceptance of his draft constitution at the Paarl meeting was for Kohler a decisive victory.

How to check the over-planting of vineyards and how to dispose of 'surplus' wine have been the two major problems which the K.W.V. had to deal with from its inception, and they were to take 50 years to solve.

Needless to say, a number of the provisions in Kohler's original constitution had to be amended from time to time to meet changing conditions, but its basic aims and objects are exactly the same today as they were at the beginning, some 60 years ago. To implement Kohler's so enthusiastically hailed 'aims and objects', the K.W.V. had to get the whole of the Western Province wine farmers to come together as a solid, politically important body, no easy task, but easier nevertheless than finding means how best to deal with the over-production of wine. The K.W.V. attempted to secure the first condition by prescribing, in terms of its constitution, to its members, every year, the minimum price at which wine had to be sold on the local market. No member was permitted to sell any of his wine below the official price, so that the price could actually be guaranteed each year.

As an attempt to stop, or at least to check, over-production, the K.W.V., by its constitution, was empowered to fix what was to be the proportion of each member's total wine production which would not be saleable on the local market. It was made incumbent upon all members of the K.W.V. to deliver the portion of their crop that was not to be sold on the local market to the K.W.V., without payment having to be made for it. This wine was given the name of 'surplus'. Every member was obliged to contribute to the K.W.V. his share of 'surplus' wine, either in the shape of the wine itself or in the form of its monetary value, in the event of his having been able to dispose of it at a higher price over and above his allotted quantity of wine for sale on the local market. Whatever price a member might be able to get for his wine over and above the official minimum price accrued to him in his private capacity. Thus the K.W.V. efforts to counter over-production's effect was to absorb the surplus itself and to keep it off the local market.

Control over the surplus was from the first one of the most important obligations of the K.W.V., and it has been its greatest pre-occupation ever since. Being assured of stocks, and making sure that wines under its care would be properly handled, was the first and easiest part of the K.W.V.'s duties. More important, and also much more difficult, was the problem of marketing profitably these surplus wines. To create a demand overseas, at prices that will be acceptable and rewarding for its members, is the task which the K.W.V. attempted years ago and one which it has now achieved with conspicuous success. While the local market is of more immediate importance to the members of the K.W.V. every export outlet is the concern of the K.W.V. itself.

The success of the K.W.V. – in due course – was never in doubt: 95% of the wine-farmers became members at the start, and the K.W.V. was able to conclude at an early date agreements with local wine merchants, in terms of which the home market prices were increased considerably and were stabilized for local requirements at £4 16s. and £6 10s. per leaguer, in 1918, and from £5 to £10, in 1919. In those early days, however, the K.W.V. had not had a chance to establish sufficient export outlets, and over 92,000 leaguers of surplus wine had to be destroyed between 1921 and 1923.

It so happened, at about this time, that some of the local wine merchants offered to the wine-farmers higher prices than the K.W.V. official rate, and the few wine farmers who were not members of the K.W.V. could and did accept those prices; this caused a great deal of discontent among members; there were cases of disloyalty among them, and by the end of 1923 matters had reached a parlous state. This was due partly to a sharp rise in production due to the optimism of farmers who planted more vines, but chiefly to the fact that the K.W.V. had found it impossible to ensure the proper application of the various schemes which were being operated in conjunction with the merchants: it lacked the legal powers that were not merely desirable but indispensable.

Between 1918 and 1923 the K.W.V. attempted to stabilize conditions by means of a voluntary co-operative effort. It very nearly succeeded, but it came to realize that the situation could never be effectively controlled unless all, not only 95% of the producers, were obliged by law to market their produce through the K.W.V. on the one hand, and if all the merchants, on the other hand, were also obliged by law to obtain all their supplies through the K.W.V. And these are precisely the powers which the K.W.V. was given when Parliament voted, in 1924, Act 5 'Wine and Spirit Control', an Act which completely changed the character of the South African wine industry.

This Act, which made the transactions of non-members of the K.W.V. subject to the same provisions as those of the members, was later consolidated, with its amendments, into Act No. 38 of 1956.

The 1924 Act recognizes the principle of annual price fixing and surplus declarations by the K.W.V., in terms of its constitution, and it makes these provisions applicable to all producers of wine, whether they be members of the K.W.V. or not. Furthermore, the Act stipulates that all purchases of wine must be made from or through the K.W.V. and that no person may obtain or distil wine without permission. From that time onwards the K.W.V. has had full control of the disposal and distillation of wine.

The obligation which rests upon the K.W.V. to stabilize prices upon the local market, and its object to obtain control over the surplus production, and to keep this surplus off the local market, is therefore, indirectly, confirmed in law, and legally enforceable.

Apart from sales of its products to wholesale liquor merchants, whose purchases must, by law, individually amount to a certain minimum gallonage, the K.W.V. does not sell its products in the Republic of South Africa, nor in certain territories south of the equator. These conditions serve to protect the interests of local merchants, who are also permitted, in certain circumstances, and on request, to purchase supplies from the K.W.V. They also have the right to appeal against any decision by the K.W.V. to a special board of appeal.

As a consequence of all these conditions, the distribution and marketing of liquor on the local market is left entirely in the hands of the local liquor trade.

The admission, in law, that certain powers are vested in the K.W.V., and the bestowal upon the K.W.V. of further powers of control over wines and spirits in 1924, were, however, limited to wines for distilling purposes only. In terms of the 1924 Act, the price fixed by the K.W.V. does not apply to the wine which is intended to be drunk as wine, and which is known as 'good wine'. This does not necessarily mean, however, that distilling wine is an inferior wine. The appellation 'good wine' is solely intended to indicate that there is a difference between the wine which is intended to be consumed as wine and that which is intended for distillation. They are different types of wine, hence not comparable quality for quality.

The result of this was that certain of the provisions of the K.W.V.'s statutes were no longer applicable to 'good wine' – especially provisions which referred to minimum prices for wine and to the delivery of the surplus to the K.W.V. As a consequence, a marked differentiation developed between the 'good wine', on the one hand, and 'distilling wine', on the other.

When the 1924 Act was under discussion in Parliament the producers of 'good wine' brought sound reasons why this wine should not be controlled, and it was exempted. It was also considered unnecessary to control the price of 'good wine', since one could take for granted that, once the price of 'distilling wine' had been controlled, the price of 'good wine' would automatically be stabilized in conformity with the 'distilling wine' price. It soon became evident, however, that this expectation would not be realized: while the 'distilling wine' prices fixed by the K.W.V. remained reasonably stable, the 'good wine' prices were subject to marked fluctuations. The price which the produce received annually for his 'distilling wine' crop was dependent upon the price fixed by the K.W.V. and the portion of the crop declared as surplus. If the price was fixed at £5 per leaguer and the surplus at 50% the grower received £2 10s. per leaguer of 'distilling wine'. Obviously, he was not prepared to sell his 'good wine' at less than £2 10s., since he could have sent his 'good wine' to the K.W.V. as 'distilling wine' had he not expected to sell it at a higher rate than 'distilling wine'. It was this expectation of higher prices which led to the over production of 'good wine' at a time of financial depression at the Cape.

Those farmers who specialized in the production of 'good wine' had to be satisfied with lower quantities per acre if they were to have higher quality wines, which meant that the initial cost of production of 'good wine' would be higher than the initial cost price of 'distilling wine': it could not possibly be sold profitably at the minimum price fixed for 'distilling wine', which only too often at the time producers of 'good wine' had to accept, either from merchants to whom they offered their wine direct or from the K.W.V. when, as a last resource, they sent in their 'good wine' as surplus 'distilling wine'.

This state of affairs was a matter of concern to many, and it was felt that timely steps should be taken to achieve a proper balance between the prices for 'good wine' and 'distilling wine', and also to prevent growers from producing quantity at the expense of quality. After a thorough investigation of the situation control over the the production and marketing of 'good wine' was also vested in the K.W.V. in terms of an amending Act for the Control of Wines and Spirits No. 23 of 1940. This Act stipulated, *inter alia*, that no person may produce wine except under a permit issued to him by the K.W.V., and that such a permit may be not be issued unless the K.W.V. is satisfied that the producer is in possession of the necessary equipment, cellar accommodation and vats or tanks for the making of such wine. The Act empowers the K.W.V. to fix annually, with the approval of the Minister of Agricultural Economics and Marketing, a minimum price, and a quality price for 'good wine', and to fix the percentage of a merchant's purchases, which must be obtained at a price equivalent or superior to the fixed quality price.

It was also ordained that all transactions between merchants and producers must carry the prior approval of the K.W.V., and payments for wine must be made to the K.W.V. In cases where producers wish to sell small quantities of wine to private persons, a permit must first be obtained from the K.W.V., and such wine must also be sold at prices not below the fixed price.

Once the Act which placed 'good wine' under control had become law, the wine industry at the Cape was well and truly organized once and for all, so that the original aims and objects of the K.W.V. could be achieved.

Stabilization within the industry would, however, lead to further expansion of production necessarily, and means had to be found either to limit production or to deal profitably with surplus products. The declaration of a surplus by the K.W.V. had already proved that this was a means of cushioning the temporary shocks of over-production. It could not, however, prevent the injudicious expansion of production, and it was never meant to do so.

In South Africa, as in every other wine-producing country, the export trade has always been, and still is, regarded as of great importance, not only as a source of revenue but also for its prestige value, and this is why the South Africa Wine Farmers Association (London) Ltd, better known as SAWFA, was established, in 1931, 'to effect distribution, maintain continuity of supplies, uniformity of quality, and stability of prices', or, in other words, to create, maintain and stimulate the demand for the wines of South Africa in Great Britain.

Needless to say, while Great Britain was at the time, and still is, its best export market, K.W.V. spared no efforts to create a demand for the wines of South Africa in other parts of the world, and it has agents actively engaged in furthering its interests in more than 30 other overseas markets.

In Great Britain K.W.V. held half the shares of the English company, SAWFA, when it was formed, but it now owns it altogether, and the work of SAWFA has been so good that the stocks of surplus wine in the K.W.V.'s cellars grew less and less until there were none at all left during the immediate post-war years. This led to a new expansion fever, and the old evil of over-production gripped the Western Province again in 1955 and 1956.

By this time, however, and owing to changed circumstances, the regulations of the 1940 Act proved insufficiently effective to achieve the desired curtailing of production. The 1940 Act was therefore amended in 1957 (Act No. 47) to incorporate a detailed scheme for the limitation of the production of wine.

The new scheme provided for a quota to be fixed for each wine farm, which quota constitutes the maximum quantity of wine which may be produced in any year on the farm. Such a quota is fixed in terms of the vines on the property on 21 June 1957, with allowances for vines taken out shortly before with the view to renewing the vineyard, and also allowing for vines purchased before a certain date, or grown and grafted on the farm for planting out in 1957. There is no stipulation as regards the types produced on the farm. It is to be expected, therefore, that each producer will, within the limits set by his quota, devote himself to the production of that type of wine that will yield the highest return; namely, that type of wine for which there is the greater demand.

Contingent upon the approval of the Minister, appeals to a Special Appeal Board may be lodged against important decisions of the K.W.V. concerning quotas or other matters affecting limitation of production.

These control measures, aimed at limiting injudicious expansion, are intended to avert the danger of over-production which has threatened the wine industry at the Cape only too often. A well-regulated production is essential to the stability of any market. Provision is made in the regulations for a controlled increase of quotas at any time, whenever circumstances justify increased production. Thus in 1963, on account of the higher consumption of South African wines, both at home and overseas, the Minister of Agricultural Affairs and Marketing instructed the K.W.V., to request applications for conditional quotas (i.e. in the case of farms which have not had quotas determined) and conditional additional quotas (i.e. in the case of farms where quotas were in operation), and in April 1964 the total quota was increased by 500,000 leaguers.

This increased figure is intended to meet the increased demand, and it may be used either to grant quotas where none had existed or to increase existing quota grants. These grants are made to wine growers who have applied for them within a prescribed period, and they are fixed on a fair basis recommended by the K.W.V., and approved by the Minister.

*The surplus*. The regulations for the limitation of wine production do not affect or influence the annual fixing and declaration of the surplus by the K.W.V. The potential yield is such that the production will continue to be considerably in excess of the total required to satisfy the local demand. The K.W.V. declares this excess as the 'surplus', and it is one of the most important of its functions to receive the surplus, to process it and to sell it on overseas markets.

Surplus wines, of course, never were table or dessert wines of the highest quality, and K.W.V. knew that it would never have a chance to create a market for surplus wines overseas: it never attempted to do so; it distilled them instead, and built up what is probably the largest stock of brandy there is in the world. This has given K.W.V. the chance to offer for sale duly matured brandies, as well as the possibility to process a whole range of fortified wines, either *apéritifs* or 'preprandial' wines, and dessert wines or after-dinner wines.

The successful marketing of the surplus wines overseas by the K.W.V. had a most beneficial stabilizing influence on the wine industry as a whole. Even though it has vast powers and resources, as well as a specialized knowledge of South African wines, the K.W.V. is not sponsored by the South African Government, nor does it receive any subsidy from State funds. It is not a monopoly, since it is an organization created by the wine farmers themselves, and one should realize that the wine farmers can, at any time, if they so wish, dissolve the K.W.V. and distribute its wines and assets among themselves. Clearly, such an eventuality is extremely unlikely, since they recognize that the stability and prosperity which they now enjoy are mainly due to the K.W.V.

*Sherry*. During the past thirty years the K.W.V. has given a great deal of thought and work to the production of sherry, and it is now a wine that is produced and exported

THE WINES OF SOUTH AFRICA

to a far greater extent than all other South African wines. To make wines that would compare as favourably as possible, in colour, strength and flavour with the true sherries of Spain, K.W.V. purchased either grapes or wine made from grapes grown in the more favourable locations of the Coastal Belt, where geographically, topographically and climatically these were conditions similar to those obtaining in Andalucia, and where the grapes grown were mostly the Spanish Palomino grape, curiously enough called 'French' grape in South Africa. 'Flor' fermentation, 'Bodega' lodging and maturing, fortifying with none but grape brandy, all the regular routine of processing sherries at Jerez de la Frontera is faithfully copied and carried out at Paarl, with such skill and success that South African sherries are in much greater repute and demand overseas than all the wines sold under the name of sherry from all countries other than Spain, the wine's original homeland.

South African sherries vary in alcoholic strength from 17 to 20% by volume; in colour from pale amber to brown; in dryness from sharp to sweet; and in age from seven to ten years. Sherry sold by K.W.V. is at least seven but usually eight years in the Paarl Bodegas. The wisdom of the K.W.V. in sparing neither cash nor trouble and time to produce quality wines deserving the name they are given has meant that the demand for South African sherries in Great Britain actually grew faster than the matured stocks at Paarl, so that in 1964 merchants in England had to be satisfied, for a time, with a proportion – it was called a 'quota' – of their orders. This has now been removed.

Besides sherries, the K.W.V. processes at Paarl a number of other fortified dessert wines, of which the three main categories are the port-type wines, the Muscats and blends of port-type and Muscats wines.

The port-grape wines are made mostly from Portuguese varieties of grapes grown in Coastal Belt vineyards, usually irrigated vineyards. The grapes are picked when fully ripe, and none but perfectly sound grapes are used: the grapes are crushed, not by bare-legged men, however, and the fermentation of the must is checked by the addition of brandy when there is still about 25% of the must's original sugars left. Port-type wines are matured at Paarl in pipes of French or Baltic oak for periods of from five to eight years, in great, cool cellars, the temperature of which hardly varies all the year round. To make the different types of wine which the K.W.V. offers to the trade, its expert blenders have a stock of nearly 8 million gallons in oak vats or glass-lined tanks to choose from: it makes it possible for them to maintain a consistency of style and quality for the different 'marks' of these wines. This applies to all styles of port-type wines other than the occasional and experimental vintage type; this is the wine of one single year; it is kept at Paarl for two years only before being shipped to London, where it is bottled in the way vintage port is bottled.

Muscat and Muscadel dessert wines are made in a way similar to that of port-type wines and their alcoholic strength is very much the same, from 17·7 to 20% by volume. They are made, however, mostly by the Little Karoo vineyard chiefly from black Muscat and other Muscats. Practically all Muscat vineyards are irrigated vineyards. The degree of sweetness of all Muscat and Muscadel wines depends upon the proportion of sugar there is still in the must when fermentation is checked by the addition of brandy: none of them are dry wines, of course, and the so-called 'medium sweet' are sweet enough for most people; those that are very 'rich' (meaning the wines, of course, not the people) reach that stage by way of *Jeropigo*.

Obviously, having both the right and the means to choose and buy any of the many wines made in the Western Province every year, the K.W.V. experts can and do produce a whole range of wines from the palest amber to the deepest purple, at high and fairly low alcoholic strength, of stable quality and price, wines which are sold under registered brand names.

With its immense stocks of brandy the K.W.V. can, and does, produce a number of liqueurs (particularly the unique South African liqueur, van der Hum), cordials, vermouths and other products with a close or distant parentage of the grape.

It would be a mistake, however, to imagine that the powers wielded by the K.W.V. have in any way killed private enterprise. It has always been the practice, in South Africa, for the growers to make their own wine in their own way and in their own cellars, and there are still today a number of them who carry on the tradition; what is more, they boast, and rightly so, that their wines are as good as the best and better than most of the wines of South Africa. Unfortunately, the shortage of labour in a number of districts is now such that the wine farmers have had no choice but to set up local co-operative wineries where the pressing of the grapes and the making of the wine from members' grapes is carried out under the supervision of a fully qualified and responsible members' nominee. In 1938 there were but six of such co-operative wineries, and today there are 52 in production, as well as a few more in course of formation.

When the first co-operative wineries were established there were, as there are today, a number of advantages attached to combined action and the sharing of costs, but the individual wine farmer has a right to claim that the wine which he makes from his own grape, in his own way and in his own cellar, will be a better wine: he may be quite right or he may be wrong, it all depends whether he had not only the necessary knowledge, skill and 'know-how' but the no less necessary modern equipment, a refrigeration plant and such like. When any of such important factors happen to be missing the co-operative is safer and altogether more satisfactory.

Although the demand for the wines of South Africa has grown very considerably at the Cape since 1938, when there were 22 wholesale wine-dealers, there are only 46 today, but the volume of their business is much greater. They get the supplies which they need not only from the K.W.V. but from local co-operative wineries and from individual farmers, they are able to buy wines within the first year after the vintage, which they mature, process, blend in any way they think best; thus the wines which they sell to retailers and direct to the consumer through bars and bottle stores of which they have the controlling interests are truly their own wines. All the more important wholesalers belong to their own organized associations, of which the two are the Cape Wholesale Wine Merchants Association and the Cape Distilling Merchants Association.

Three centuries may not be a long period to measure against the history of viticulture in Europe. But in South Africa, where wine-growing is as old as the civilization of the country itself, the time spent in pursuit of the vine, if compared with the results attained, gains in importance and further emphasizes the progress which has been achieved.

# The Wines of
# THE
# AMERICAS

JOHN N. HUTCHISON

# The Americas

## Introduction

THE history of the grape in the New World starts somewhere in the foggy legends of the Vikings, who visited North America at least a thousand years ago, and who reported that grapes grew wild and profusely, what is now the north-eastern United States and south-eastern Canada.

About A.D. 1000 Leif the Lucky was in what is now thought to be Thode Island or Massachusetts. One day a German among his men, named Tyrker, was absent from the camp overlong. Reprimanded by Leif when he finally returned, he is reported to have said, with a broad grin, that he had found grapes, – and grapes, he said, were something that he understood, because of his German origin. Leif sent a part of his command to gather the grapes, filling the 'afterboat' with them. The account suggests that the grapes, or wine made from them, were taken back to Scandinavia.

In 1565 an English captain, John Hawkins, visited Spanish settlements in Florida, and reported that the colonists there had made 20 hogsheads of wine. Two men sent to America by Raleigh wrote that the land 'is so full of grapes as the very beating and surge of the sea overflowed them. . . . I think in all the world the like abundance is not to be found.' That was in 1584. Soon thereafter the first Englishmen to settle in the New World, those whose ill-fated colony was on Roanoke Island, reported that it was lush with grapes, growing to the very beaches. Early New Englanders, too, wrote of grapes 'as big as a musket bullet', so thick over the land as to make travelling difficult. One New England visitor wrote of a single vine bearing 12 bushels in a single season, and described single vines that overwhelmed tall trees.

Those grapes were in all likelihood the *Vitis labrusca* and *Vitis rotundifolia*, which exist today in the virgin woodlands throughout the eastern third of the United States and with others are the parents of many table and wine grapes. Some of these are basic to the wine industries of Ontario, New York and Ohio. It was such grapes which the English colonists found in Virginia, and it was Captain John Smith himself who reported in 1606, 'We made neere twentie gallons of wine.'

But the major line of New World wine history really starts in Mexico, a country which today does not rank high among the wine-making nations. Rafael Heliodoro Valle, a Honduran historian, says that wine was first imported into Mexico in 1518 by Spanish *conquistadores*. At that time the native Mexican Indians drank (as they still do) *pulque*, a sort of beer fermented from the juice of the maguey plant, a desert succulent. But they rapidly learned to drink wine so copiously that the Spaniards attempted, with varying success, to prohibit the sale of wine to them.

European grapes – *Vitis vinifera* – were brought to Mexico in the early sixteenth century, and there is a record of a vineyard growing in 1544. The grape which was de-

*Note:* All gallons referred to in this section are U.S. gallons NOT imperial gallons and tons are short tons; i.e. 2,000 lb.

662

veloped came to be known as the Criolla, which gradually spread as vineyards were established through north-central Mexico. It was acceptable both as a fresh fruit and as a wine grape.

As might be expected, the introduction of wine and wine-making to Mexico produced sociological and moral problems new to the Spanish colonists and to the Indians they dominated. Drunkenness among the Indians was troublesome to a ruling class which regarded hard work, piety and submission as the proper virtues of a *peon*, and yet the liquor and wine traffic was very profitable. Selling wine to the Indians was a major occupation of Spanish merchants, who turned a double profit: they made money on the wine sales and then took every advantage of their helpless customers, who were also their suppliers of many items of trade. The drunken native too readily parted with his produce, his daughters or his wife.

Both Church and State tried, rather weakly, to control such corruption but the bribed magistrates ignored the laws, and the clergy was divided between priests who believed in abstinence and those who either accepted wine as a necessity of communion or were themselves drinkers. Señor Valle illustrates this conflict when he cites an early priest who refused a gift of wine sent him by his bishop. In some monasteries wine could only be taken for the sacrament or as medicine.

There were other conflicts, too. Spanish officials whose positions depended directly on the Crown wanted profits to send back to Spain, and saw the growing native wine industry as a threat to imports. A Spaniard wrote in 1625 that wine-making was forbidden in New Spain, 'so that commerce and the fleet of Spain will conquer'. And yet the monasteries wanted to grow wines for daily beverage, for the sacrament and for a saleable product of their considerable farm properties, worked by Indian *peons*. Slowly, also, there developed commercial vineyards, until they had spread to Baja California and Peru. It was in the latter half of the eighteenth century, then, that the Criolla was taken into what is now the American state of California, probably when Serra, the Franciscan priest, established at San Diego the first of his great chain of missions. Amerine and Singleton, in their *Wine: An Introduction for Americans*, believe that the Mission grape, carried by the monks as they extended the chain, and widely grown in California today for the table and for dessert wines, is the direct descendant of the Criolla. Thus began the first cultivation of the grape in California, now a far more important wine area than the whole of Mexico.

The inevitability that Europeans would take an interest in wine with them to the New World wherever they explored it was borne out on the eastern coast of North America almost as early as the Spanish entry into Mexico. Not long after Captain Smith's cheerful report, the London Company sent experts to the new colony to grow wine grapes; their seventeenth century efforts were a failure. Charles II encouraged other viticultural attempts in America. Philip Wagner, an American oenologist, adds that the Huguenots, Dutch and Swedes all tried; none really succeeded. He believes they failed because phylloxera killed the European root stocks they brought in. Others think that the humid climate, with great extremes of summer heat and winter cold, is equally likely to have caused the failures. In any event, no wine industry of any consequence developed in the East until the nineteenth century, when hybrids were developed from the native grapes, too sour and 'foxy' themselves to make good wines. This was well after the Franciscans had been producing coarse wines in California, but there were modest commercial operations in New York, Ohio and Canada as early as the commercial operations were to rise in California.

It was also in the nineteenth century that wine-making became an important enterprise in South America. The Criolla grape in Peru never produced wine of much quality; most of the wine grapes went into a brandy called Pisco. The climate of Peru is not hospitable to fine grapes.

But the big nineteenth-century emigrations of Italians, Germans and Frenchmen to Latin America, in particular to Argentina and Chile, resulted in the development of modern wines. The same thing occurred in California. Rieslings, Cabernets, Pinots, Merlots, Semillons and Sauvignons were among the fine grapes introduced into these areas – the beginnings of some of the world's good vineyards, and in the case of Argentina the start of a wine industry that today stands, in volume, fourth among the wine countries of the world. Chile and California, as a consequence of this nineteenth-century development, produce some of the best wines made outside Europe.

## Chile

Chile stands thirteenth in output among the wine-making nations of the world, and is generally considered to produce the best wines in South America. They sell throughout the continent and are exported to the U.S.A. and Europe. The land is well suited to wine grapes, as the early Spaniards soon discovered, but it was French and German immigrants in the nineteenth century who influenced the character of the industry. It adopted the French techniques it employs today. With more than a quarter of a million acres in wine grapes, Chile made 88·5 million gallons of wine in 1969, shipping about a million of them out of the country. Disastrous disease reduced the 1965 production by one-third, to about 82 million. The industry employs 60,000 workers. There is little mechanization on the great wine-growing *haciendas*.

The Chilean government has reported that *per capita* wine consumption had fallen from 16 gallons a year in 1938 to 10·7 in 1970, as a result of education against intemperance, restrictions on wine-growing, higher production costs and a production level that has stood about the same while Chile, in 25 years, has doubled her population. In some Chilean districts growers have shifted from wine to table grapes, finding the latter more profitable. In spite of the static level of output, the Chilean wine industry is one of very high quality standards and considerable prosperity.

Three main types of wine are produced in Chile. The hot northern vineyards, and some farther south, produce rich wines, some of them fortified. Dry table wines, both white and red, of high quality, come from the Central Valley, and ordinary wines are produced in south-central Chile. The quality table wines bear great resemblance to those of Bordeaux, although some burgundian types are also grown, and Chilean burgundy is a popular export. Cultivation and wine-making are patterned after bordelaise practices, and the Chilean Ministry of Agriculture declares modestly:

> Chilean wines, in general, may not be equal to a château bordeaux of a good year, but at least they equal, or surpass many bordeaux regional bottlings, and have the advantage of being much less expensive.

The Chilean clarets are made largely of Cabernet grapes; the burgundies of Pinot noir. The Cabernets are considered to be the better. Among the white wines, Riesling is the superior grape, but is a small producer. Popular wines are made from the Sauvignon blanc and Semillon. White *ordinaires* are produced from Côt rouge, Carignane and other heavy-bearing grapes, including one of Spanish origin cultivated in Chile for so long that it is now called the País, or Uva del País – the 'national' grape. It is very probably a descendant of the old Criolla, that sturdy Spanish progenitor whose sap stream still flows so serenely through the Americas.

Chilean vineyards are free of phylloxera, even though it is a problem in Argentina and Peru. Chilean wine-growers believe that the high Andes have prevented the louse from entering from Argentina, and that the terrible searing deserts of the north do not permit it to survive the passage from Peru. The third line of protection, the vast Pacific Ocean, forms Chile's other border. As a consequence, Chilean growers do not graft; their *vinifera* varieties grow on their own roots. The industry has a plan in readiness if phylloxera should come.

In the northern wine zone of Chile, between the Atacama desert and the Choapa River, the principal grape is the Muscat, grown for the table and for heavily alcoholic wines, most of which are distilled into *pisco*, the 'national brandy'. *Pisco* from Chile and Peru became a popular drink among Californians in the days of the Gold Rush, and the 'Pisco punch', a derivative cocktail, remained a well-known drink in San Francisco well after the notorious days of the rowdy Barbary Coast district of the city's gambling hells and dance halls.

The central wine region, between the Aconcagua and Maule Rivers, produces Chile's quality wines. Here the whole industry reflects its Bordeaux parentage, the cultivation techniques, the wine-making processes, the cellar-work and the grape varieties themselves. Only one important difference from Bordeaux culture exists: most of the vines are irrigated, since the rainfall is concentrated in a short season of the winter, and the vines could never survive the long, hot, bone-dry summers. Chileans do not consider the irrigation in any way detrimental to quality.

The best of the quality wines of Chile are probably grown in the Aconcagua and Maipo valleys. The Cabernet is the foundation of these wines, which have true finesse, balance and potential maturity. It is unfortunate that wine-growing in the Aconcagua valley is diminishing because of the profit advantage in growing table grapes and other fruits for export. The Maipo Valley, just south of Santiago, is the principal quality wine-growing centre. Deep-coloured reds of great bouquet grow in the porous sandy soil, which lies over an alluvial subsoil. Cabernet franc and Cabernet Sauvignon grapes produce heavily there, and the growers are perhaps the most progressive and modern in Chile.

Along the coastal mountain range, from Valparaiso Province to Bío-Bío, and even farther south, is a dry area of clay and granitic soils, rich in iron and underlaid in some places with limestone. There are some French varieties – Carignan, Malbec and Semillon – and some Rieslings and Muscatels, but the principal producer is the País, some of which is blended with the other wines. Most of the País, however, is drunk as the Chilean *ordinaire*.

Although the early *conquistadores* grew wine grapes, including the Criolla and the Muscat de Alexandria, in a part of Argentina which is now in Chile, the modern wine industry of Chile came in the middle of the nineteenth century. It was in 1851 that

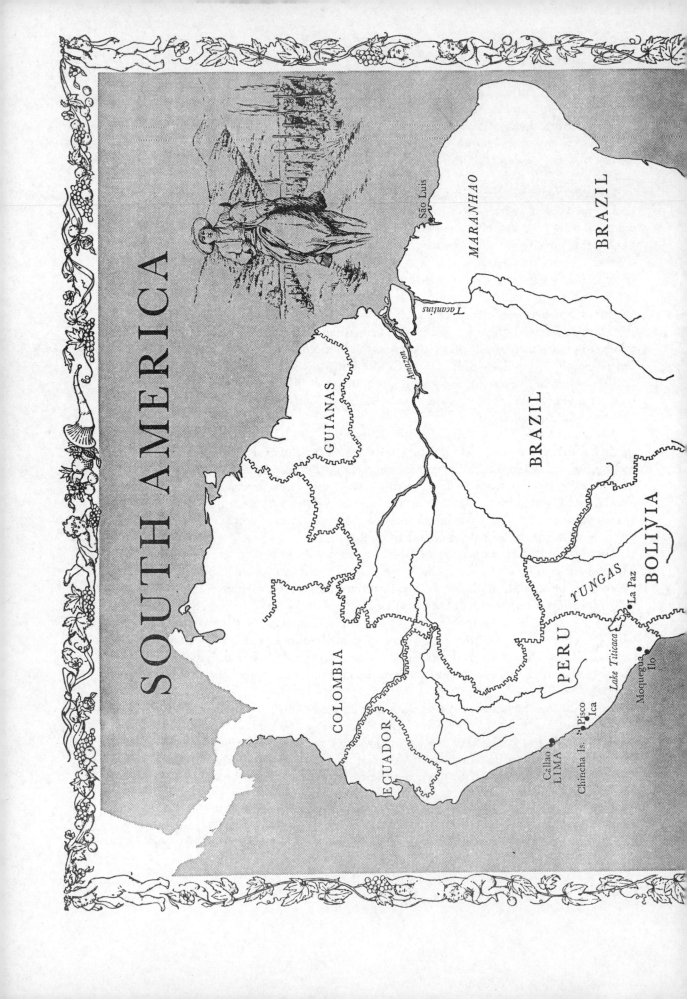

# SOUTH AMERICA

COLOMBIA

GUIANAS

ECUADOR

*Amazon*

*Tocantins*

São Luís

MARANHAO

BRAZIL

BRAZIL

Callao
LIMA

Chincha Is.

Pisco
Ica

PERU

*Lake Titicaca*

*YUNGAS*

La Paz

BOLIVIA

Moquegua
Ilo

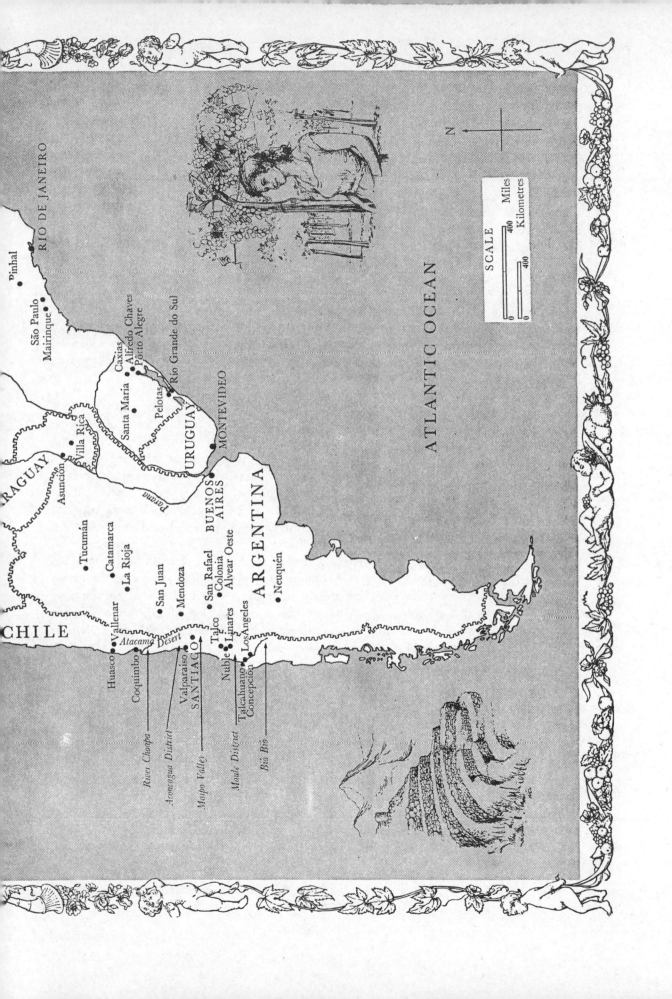

French viticulturists were brought to Chile, along with some of the best French vines. These, planted in the Central Valley, formed the nucleus of the present great table-wine vineyards. They attracted other growers and brought about the importation of additional European varieties. Today there are more than 32,000 vineyards, less than half of them larger than 2½ acres each. The Chilean government has had to assist the growers with loans, the establishment of co-operative wineries and the employment of state technicians who offer advice on modern cultivation. Without these aids, the thousands of small growers could not compete for modern markets. As might be expected in a country so concerned with the welfare of the wine industry, there is also close governmental regulation of wine-growing and production. The law strictly prescribes standards of sanitation, quality and composition of wines, and even controls the amount of acreage which may be planted to grapes. In great part, this governmental solicitude has been influenced by the rather high rate of alcoholism among Chileans. Amerine and Singleton, in *Wine: An Introduction for Americans*, write:

> It is sad that Chile is one of the few countries where wine constitutes a principal source of alcoholism. This is a part of life on the large *haciendas*, where the workers are often allowed as much cheap wine as they can drink on week-ends. The result is that alcoholism from wine is a serious Chilean social problem.

The Chilean government also sternly regulates wine export, with quality controls maintained by the Ministry of Agriculture, the Central Bank and the internal revenue office. White wines for export must contain at least 12% alcohol by volume; reds, 11·5%. The export regulations require the wines to be clear, clean and at least one year old. Minimums and maximums are set for the various components in them. A commission classifies wine in three categories: ordinary new wines, of middle quality; special, older wines of some character and of good quality, and fine, matured wines of superior quality, aroma and taste, called 'reservados' and 'grandes vinos'. These latter hold their own with the better wines of the world.

One of the greatest vineyards of Chile is that of Undurraga, near Santiago, founded in the middle of the last century by a rich, talented gentleman – lawyer, scientist, artist, writer and planter – to whom wine-making was a hobby. But since his death in the early 1950s at the age of 95, Undurraga's six sons have conducted a profitable wine business, and their burgundy and Riesling in Wurzburger-shaped 'boxbeutels' are known in many countries of the world. Other good wines come from San Pedro, Santa Carolina, Carmen, Concho y Toros and Tocornal.

## Argentina

Argentina, which competes with Algeria for fourth place in world wine output, has more than a half million acres in vines, and produces 370 million gallons a year. The wines do not achieve the general standard of those of Chile, but many of them are made with care from good French varieties.

Argentina was first settled in 1502, and wines are thought to have been produced in 1556 from European vines brought there by a priest from Chile. Some wines were shipped commercially in the early seventeenth century. The familiar Criolla, spreading

Plate 57. A typical 'château' in the rural vineyards of New York State.

from Mexico and Peru, also appeared in early Argentina cultivation, and its descendants are still planted there.

The great influence on the Argentine wine industry, however, is that of the large Italian population which came into the country in the 1880s and after the Second World War. Many of them were expert *vignerons*, and although the most of the wine produced in Argentina is drunk by working people more interested in it as a daily beverage than for high considerations of quality, some Argentine producers offer superior wines made with great care. The dry reds, which include some made exclusively with Cabernet Sauvignon grapes, and some in which the Cabernet is blended with Merlot, Malbec and other grapes, are perhaps the best of the country's production. The dry whites have less finesse and character. There is also some high-quality dry red wine made from Sangiovetto Piccolo, to which is added wine from the Trebbiano Florentino grape, sometimes in the proportion of four to one. Blending wines from two or more grapes is common, as is blending wines from two or more years. At a tasting held in London in 1965 a fine red table wine made by Valentin Bianchi in Mendoza contained wines of the Cabernet, gray Pinot, Carignan, Malbec and Lambrusco grapes from the years 1959 to 1962.

Many of these blended wines exceed 13% in alcohol, and are velvety and aromatic, the blenders working with great skill to bring together the ingredients that create a fine vintage. At the London tasting there was also an excellent dry red Mendoza made entirely from the Cabernet, but in equal parts from vintages of 1960, 1961 and 1962. It was made by Gargantini S.A.

The country makes quality white wines from Riesling, Sauvignon blanc and Pinot blanc, although they fail to achieve the standards of the good reds. Common reds, sometimes aged for three years, are produced from Malbec, Barbera Bonarda, Verdot and other high-producer vines, and common whites are often made from Criolla or Pedro Ximénez. They are drunk very young.

Argentina also makes wines similar to sherry and port, but which often fail to achieve the authentic taste and finish of the Spanish and Portuguese originals. Argentine sparkling wines tend to be sweet and unimpressive in comparison with French champagnes. Argentine 'sec' champagnes are made from white Pinot; the Italian-type spumantes are produced from several types of Muscats, sometimes blended with Riesling.

The Mendoza area, an irrigated oasis, is the major wine-producing area of the country, although over-production some years ago caused growers to pull up many vines and replace them with fruits. San Juan province is second in importance, and produces, in addition to some good table wines, large quantities of heavy blending wines and concentrates for vermouth, mistelos and jams. Other areas are the Rio Negro, La Rioja, Salta, Catamarca, Jujuy and small districts near Buenos Aires and Córdoba. The Catamarca wines are distilled for brandies.

Promotion, regulation and improvement of wine in Argentina is the concern of the National Institute of Viticulture, operating under the Economic Ministry. It maintains production standards for the 50,000 vineyards, 2,100 wineries and 1,300 blending plants in the nation, establishes processing requirements and controls alcoholic content and labelling. It promotes legislation concerning wine and other grape products, carries on viticultural, oenological and marketing research, maintains statistics, assists growers with loans and even helps with the construction of co-operative wineries.

Plate 58. An aerial view of a vineyard on Spring Mountain, near St Helena, California.

## *Mexico*

Although Mexico was the cradle of wine-growing in the Americas, it is not a country well suited to fine wine grapes, and its populace has a greater appetite for *pulque* and beer than for wine. The nation has some 42,000 acres in wine grapes, mainly in central Mexico and in Baja California. The hot climate is best adapted to sweet dessert wines. Wine export from Mexico is insignificant.

## *Peru*

Peru is also too hot and arid for good wine production, although the Criolla grape was taken there from Mexico in early times, and a Pisco brandy industry achieved export proportions. Peruvian wines today are unimportant at home and in no demand abroad.

## *Brazil*

While Peru and Mexico are too hot and dry for good wine culture, Brazil is mainly too hot and humid for *Vitis vinifera*, but grows some grapes native to North America. A little Brazilian Riesling has been exported rather experimentally without making a hit abroad. The country produces about 37 million gallons annually from two principal districts, in São Paulo and Rio Grande do Sul provinces, the latter being the largest producer. The wine-makers operate mainly in the Italian tradition, and most of the wines are consumed locally.

Bolivia, Ecuador, Paraguay and Uruguay produce small amounts of wine for local consumption. In Venezuela the large Italian population drinks an alcoholic table beverage made from imported grape concentrates.

## *Canada*

Wine for the sacrament was made by Jesuits in Canada from the same 'fox' grapes that the Vikings found entangled in the trees of the wild land they had discovered some thousand years before. Then in 1811 a German named Schiller opened the first recorded commercial winery. By 1859 wine-making was a recognized Canadian occupation.

There are now a dozen Canadian wineries, turning out about 9 million gallons a year from some 21,000 acres of wines. Almost all the production is in the Niagara Peninsula of southern Ontario, where the climate is tempered by the Great Lakes. The peninsula is at about the latitude of Paris, but the winters are too cold to permit the culture of *Vitis vinifera*, and the wines have the 'foxy' taste that characterizes native American grapes. Hundreds of varieties are grown in Canada, where the province of Ontario has developed many hybrids. About 30 are used for wine. Among these are the Niagara, Dutchess, Elvira and Delaware, to name a few.

Although the 45-mile stretch along the south-western end of Lake Ontario grows nearly all the wine made in Canada, there is a little wine production near Windsor, opposite Detroit, as well as in Saskatchewan and British Columbia.

Canadian vintners produce sweet, heavy ports, sweet and dry sherries, vermouth, red, *rosé* and white table wines, and various sparkling wines. In 1965 the principal producer, Château Gai, began shipping to England, but most of it is consumed in Canada.

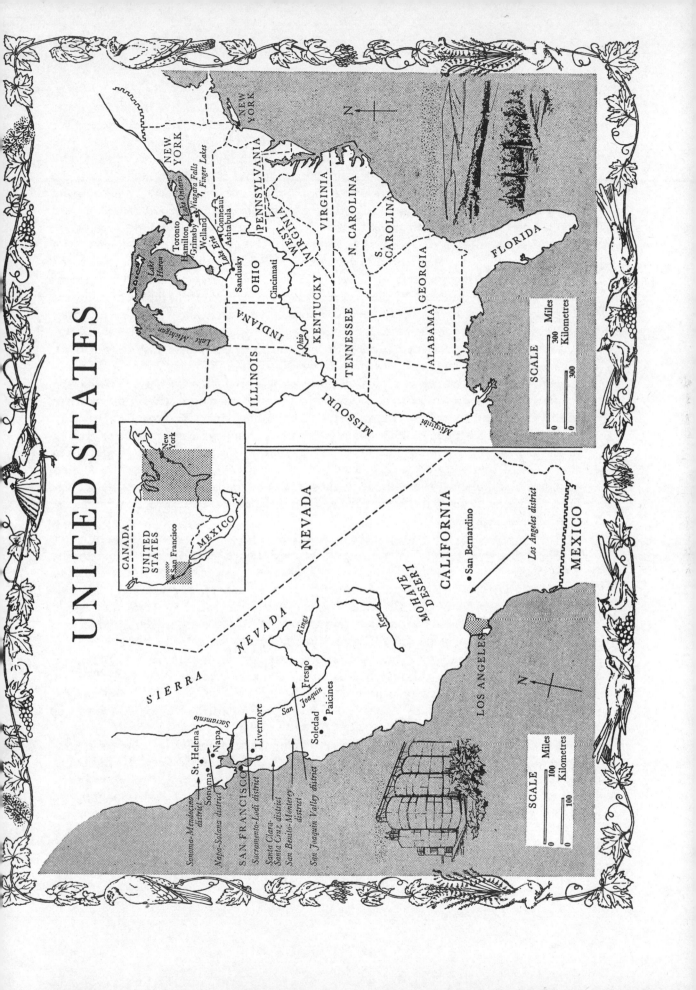

# UNITED STATES

NEW
YORK

NEW
YORK

Toronto
Hamilton
Grimsby
Welland
Lake Ontario
Niagara Falls
Finger Lakes
Conneaut
Ashtabula
Lake Erie

PENNSYLVANIA

W. VIRGINIA

VIRGINIA

Lake Huron

Lake Michigan

Sandusky
OHIO
Cincinnati

INDIANA

Ohio

KENTUCKY

TENNESSEE

N. CAROLINA

S. CAROLINA

GEORGIA

ALABAMA

FLORIDA

ILLINOIS

MISSOURI

Mississippi

SCALE
300 Miles
300 Kilometres
0
0

CANADA

UNITED
STATES

New
York

San Francisco

MEXICO

NEVADA

NEVADA

SIERRA

Sacramento

Kings

San Joaquin

Fresno

Kern

MOHAVE
DESERT

CALIFORNIA

San Bernardino

Los Angeles district

MEXICO

St. Helena
Sonoma
Napa
Livermore
Soledad
Paicines

Sonoma-Mendocino district
Napa-Solana district
SAN FRANCISCO
Sacramento-Lodi district
Santa Clara-Santa Cruz district
San Benito-Monterey district
San Joaquin Valley district

LOS ANGELES

N

SCALE
100 Miles
100 Kilometres
0
0

## New York

Early settlers from Europe failed in numerous efforts to establish *Vitis vinifera* in the colonies of the Eastern sea-board. They were also unsuccessful in making acceptable wines from the wild American *Vitis labrusca*. But cross-breeding and careful selection of the native grapes eventually produced some useful ones. By 1830 vines were planted by wine-makers in the Finger Lakes district of the State of New York. Today this is the second most important wine-producing area of the United States, with one company capable of storing 9 million gallons, and still expanding. The Finger Lakes are long and slender, separated by ridges rising to 1,500 feet above sea-level. The slopes along these ridges have well-drained, stony soil, admirably suited to vineyards. Although some French–American hybrids and a few standard *vinifera* varieties have been introduced experimentally, the vineyards are devoted in the main to the culture of vines almost unknown outside Canada and the U.S.A., and quite different from those of California. The familiar grape names are Concord, Catawba, Delaware, Niagara, Elvira, Dutchess and others exclusive to the east.

Wine-drinkers accustomed to most of the world's wines find themselves surprised, puzzled and not always pleased by the *labrusca* taste, although many New York wine-makers deny that foxiness is typical of most of their product. Many people, too, who drink the New York wines are unaware of the peculiar interconnection in the destinies of this grape and that of the *vinifera* in the history of modern wine-growing.

Phylloxera, the infamous louse plaguing the wine industry, seems to have originated in the U.S.A., with *labrusca*, and other wild grapes unaffected as its host, probably as the result of centuries in which it developed immunity. It was from the U.S.A. that phylloxera is thought to have made its sinister way to France, possibly by way of England, in the middle of the last century, ultimately to spread destruction across the *vinifera* vineyards of Europe.

But it was also the *labrusca*, passive carrier of the plague, that saved its distant European cousins, who rescued by grafting them upon the resistant American root stocks.

Red wines made from the *labrusca* bear about the same degree of taste relationship to real burgundies and clarets that currants bear to raspberries. The wines are thin and delicate, lacking body and bouquet. The whites are somewhat closer to the generic European wines whose names they bear, and the New York sparkling wines are genuinely of high quality. The Taylor Wine Company, which also produces Great Western champagne, is the largest single champagne producer in the U.S.A. and one of the largest in the world, although California as a state out-produces New York. The first New York State champagne was produced in the town of Rheims, on one of the Finger Lakes, in 1863, nearly 20 years after Nicholas Longworth produced his Sparkling Catawba, in Cincinnati, Ohio.

The Taylor Company, and the Pleasant Valley Company it bought in 1962, produce a full range of wines – red, white, sweet, dry and sparkling. They also finish and bottle muscatels bought in California. Their wines are blended and standardized so as not to vary appreciably from one year to another, and, except for the champagnes, are sealed with metal caps; bark corks are not used in the still wines.

A smaller, but important New York winery is Widmer's, which, unlike the mass-production methods of Taylor's, follows many traditional practices. It produces 100%

varietals, unblended as to year, and dated and cork-sealed. It also makes a unique, sun-baked sherry, aged on the winery roof in barrels, fully exposed to the hot summers and bitter New York winters for at least four years – some of it for eight years – before bottling. Widmer's has also succeeded in growing Riesling grapes and producing several *auslese* vintages.

One of the best champagnes in the U.S.A. is made by Gold Seal Vineyards in the Finger Lakes district. Its special pride is its Charles Fournier Brut, named for its creator, now president of the firm, and once manager of Veuve Cliquot in France. There is also a Fournier 'nature', made without dosage. Gold Seal makes a full range of still wines too.

In addition to the Finger Lakes wine district, there are wineries at Batavia, in north-western New York; Lewiston, near the Canadian border, and at scattered other points, including some in and near New York City. All of New York State suffers very severe winters, and the growing season is relatively short. Autumn frosts and occasional droughts are recurring hazards, and the grapes are consistently low in sugar. State law permits 'amelioration', and sugar is customarily used to correct the high acidity characteristic of the *labrusca*, and to raise the percentage of the otherwise deficient alcohol.

The New York wine industry is growing rapidly, with new planting, new production facilities and increasing storage capacity. The U.S.A., in which *per capita* wine consumption is approximately one twenty-fifth that of France is, however, developing its interest, and the wine-makers are striving to meet the rising demand.

New York wine-growers are in some dispute among themselves on the desirability of developing wines from *vinifera*s or from American–French hybrids which can survive the rigorous climate. However, some important vineyards, assisted by a state experiment station, have successfully introduced Johannisberger Riesling, Chardonnay, Traminer, Pinot noir, Cabernet Sauvignon, and various Seibel hybrids. Much of the output is being blended into *labrusca* wines to add grace and character, but some small quantities of named varietals are being made from the *vinifera*s. At a comparative tasting in San Francisco it appeared to some California growers that these wines tasted of *labrusca*. Since the New York growers insisted that the varietals had no *labrusca* in them, it would seem that the so-called 'foxy' taste of the eastern wines must be a '*gout de terroir*' rather than of the grapes themselves.

## Ohio

Nicholas Longworth was a wealthy lawyer and politician who interested himself in wine-growing in the 1820s in what is now an area of the city of Cincinnati, Ohio. He recruited help from the German immigrants who for many years gave Cincinnati most of its cultural character. Longworth turned to a grape reportedly discovered in the forests of South Carolina in 1802, one of a number of wild grapes including the Scup-pernong, Muscadine and 'fox' grape occurring through the eastern half of the U.S.A. Longworth's choice was the Catawba, a *Vitis labrusca* which, unlike the *vinifera*, could survive the extremes of humid heat and deep freezing that characterize the Ohio climate. From it he developed a profitable wine company, which, because of an accidental secondary fermentation he discovered in one bottle in 1847, became the producer of the first American 'champagne'. He later marketed it widely as 'Sparkling Catawba'.

Longworth's vines were long ago swallowed up in the urban complex of Cincinnati, but wine-making remains as a small but thriving industry in Ohio. The Catawba is still its mainstay grape, and it is unfortunate that much of the delicious product of this grape must be labelled 'Sauternes' to get Americans to buy it. The general public of the U.S.A. has a regrettable tendency to look down on wines not made in Europe, even though the same public is widely ignorant about all wine, whatever its origin. Isle St George Sauternes and Haut Sauternes, for those who enjoy sweet wines, are luscious experiences in 'grapey' taste.

The Isle St George vineyards are the property of Meier's Wine Cellars, Ohio's principal producers, operating wineries at Sandusky, on the Lake Erie shore, and at Silverton, near Cincinnati, on the southern border of the state. Isle St George is the former name of 740 acres of flat, rich land, only a mile and a half from the Canadian boundary of Ontario, which bisects the lake. The island was, in fact, once Canadian, and its real present name is Bass Island.

The whole island belong to Meier's, which ferries the grapes to Sandusky, 20 miles away, for crushing and processing. Wine grapes have been grown on Bass Island since 1844. The growing season is six weeks longer than that of the mainland because of the temperature influences of the surrounding lake. Lake Erie freezes solid every winter, sometimes to a depth of 3 feet. The slow return of warm weather because of this ice retards the 'bud break' of the vines in the spring until after any danger of frost. The moderating influence of the summer-warmed water lengthens the autumn growing season to give the fruit maximum maturity. The delayed 'bud break' is also thought to be influenced by the relatively low temperature of the island soil during the spring. The island is nowhere more than 14 feet above the level of the lake, and it is underlaid by limestone formations in which a network of fissures and natural tunnels circulates the ground water. This makes it all the more curious that the centre of the island suffers from occasional summer drought, then requiring some irrigation.

The 350 acres of vines on the island (about half its surface is occupied by resident families and a small airport) are 80% Catawba. The remainder are of Concord – a common American grape – and French–American hybrids, including Baco No. 1 and several Seibels.

During the harvest, pickers from the mainland raise the island's population from 40 to 100. The current annual production of grapes is about 1,000 tons, taken 35 tons at a time to the Sandusky winery, two hours away by ferry.

Like many American wineries, Meier's makes a wide range of wines – sherries, vermouths, ports, burgundy, Rhine, Sauternes and sparkling wines. Meier's also makes apple and blackberry wine, unfermented grape juice and a non-alcoholic sparkling champagne, recommended for 'parsons and teenagers'.

There are about 30 wineries in Ohio. Few of them can store one-tenth as much wine as Meier's, which has a capacity of 1 million gallons. Some have no vines of their own; others have vineyards ranging from 10 to 50 acres. The firm nearest in size to Meier's is Engels and Krudwig of Sandusky, the oldest Ohio winery, founded in 1863. It can store 865,000 gallons. Several small wineries operate in the vicinity of Put-in Bay, and there is one on Catawba Island.

Drinkers accustomed to the taste of *vinifera* wines will be disconcerted by many Ohio wines. But the Catawba is a grape of simple but rich taste, and its vines deserve praise and attention. Champagnes based on Catawba, which have been developed with skill for well over a century, do not have the finesse of genuine champagnes, but they are worthy, charmat-processed wines. It is to be regretted that they must lean on the name of champagne; they could stand on their own quite capably alongside many sekts, spumantes and Vouvrays.

Ohio wines are also made from the native Concord grape and others. The Concord is the familiar garden grape of most of the U.S.A., grown for the table, for unfermented juice which is a popular American breakfast drink, and for jams and jellies. Home-made wine from Concords is in some American families a long tradition. It tends to be strong, astringent and very dark purple. During the nation's unhappy period of Prohibition this harsh wine, often called 'dago red', because of its supposed similarity to Italian Chianti, was sold by bootleggers, often in gallon glass jugs. For many Americans who were young in those days it was the first alcoholic beverage – a discouraging beginning in wine appreciation, albeit a perfectly sound, healthful beverage. No more can be said for many ordinary wines in the world, including Chilean *chica*, or Greek retsina.

## California

Few people are more than vaguely aware that there are two Californias – one in Mexico and one in the U.S.A. South of San Diego, the border between the U.S.A. and Mexico runs straight east to Arizona through a hot, dry country that is barren desert wherever it is not irrigated. Below this line is Baja (Lower) California; the land above this line was, until about 1846, Alta (Upper) California, and since that time has been a part of the U.S.A. The history of European-type wines in the New World is imbedded in both sides of this border.

A Jesuit mission was established in Lower California in 1697, and there Father Juan Ugarte planted grapes. They were probably the common blue-black fruit that came to be known as the Mission. He made wine for his own mission and others later established, and he even shipped some across the narrow gulf to mainland Mexico. North of Ugarte's first mission, that of San Francisco Xavier, a new one, San José de Comundú, was founded in 1708. It, too, had productive vineyards, in spite of soil and climate harshly inhospitable to almost any other crop. In their determination to grow wine for the sacrament and their frugal tables, the priests fought against great obstacles. At Mission Santa Gertrudis a German priest, Father Jorge Retz, cut an irrigation channel for a mile through rock to bring water from a spring, and he carried earth to spread across a rocky area deep enough to root his vines. Having no casks or bottles, he chopped reservoirs in the rocks, filling them with wine and sealing them with pitch.

The shortage of containers for wine was to be a continuous problem, even into the middle of the nineteenth century, when a glass industry was finally developed in San Francisco. The Lower California wine-makers seized eagerly on earthen jugs brought by ships which ran regularly in the 1700s between Manila and the coastal harbours of western Mexico.

Five of the 15 Jesuit missions in Lower California were making wine before the second surge of missions-building began its long drive through Alta California to the north. The new chain of missions was Franciscan, founded by Father Junípero Serra, the visionary and energetic priest who seems to have been the first man to recognize the potential of what has now become the most populous American state. Serra built a mission at San Diego in 1769, and it is probable that he introduced grapes there within the next three or four years – once again undoubtedly the reliable Spanish variety mission which was the standard of the Americas, and which can be assumed to have produced harsh, heavy wines made under conditions which in any event would not have allowed for any finesse.

A case may be made that Junípero Serra was the most important figure in the history of California. For well over 200 years before him the Spaniards had known about Alta California and had sailed along its coast. But the Spaniards were treasure-hunters in the simplest, greediest sense, literally seeking gold, silver and gems, and generally uninterested in the vast potentials of colonial development. Whether Serra's real urge was to convert the small, scattered heathen tribes to the north, or whether he was an imaginative and vigorous pioneer at heart is hard to determine now, but certainly he was the man who opened to the modern world that fabulous, rich coastal empire which lay beyond the fierce mountainous deserts of north-western Mexico.

Having got the San Diego mission under way in the name of God and the King of Spain, he pressed his enterprises northward as he built a great chain of sturdy churches, surrounded by orchards, vineyards, grainfields and barns. Most of the missions remain today. Most of them are along the main route of trade and communications running from California's southern border to the last of the missions to be erected, at Sonoma, north of San Francisco. The twenty-first in the chain, it was built in 1823.

Serra chose his sites with great wisdom, sometimes for their harbours, sometimes for their command of rich valleys and almost always with an eye to viticulture. Most of the important cities of the state – San Diego, San Francisco, Los Angeles, Santa Barbara, Monterey – stand where he put his missions in the wilderness. Where cities have not sprung up, there are towns serving great agricultural districts. The road connecting the missions was – and is – called 'El Camino Real', the King's Highway.

Hard on Serra's heels came small army units to establish 'presidios' for military government, and a few ranchers were given huge tracts of land. The latter promptly planted fruit, including grapes. The earliest viticulture recorded outside the missions was by Governor Pedro Fages, who, in 1783, planted vines near Monterey, the Alta California capital. An Ortega family was making wine and brandy near Santa Ynez (now a Danish settlement called Solvang) at the end of the eighteenth century. Near the Santa Barbara mission, Doña Marcelina Feliz Domínguez planted a grape-vine sometime between 1795 and 1815 which did not die until 1876. Eighteen inches thick at the base, this huge vine bore in a good year 4 tons of grapes. Doña Marcelina, rugged as the vine she owned, lived to be an estimated 105 years old.

Records of the productivity of early California suggest lush returns from the new soil. A French traveller noted in 1827 an abundant production of livestock, fruit and vegetables. There is record of a large vineyard planted in the Los Angeles area in 1805, and the city collected tithes in 1820 on wines presumably produced commercially.

Reports differ on the quality of these early California vintages. An English sea captain who put in at a harbour south of Los Angeles noted, 'Good wine can be procured from the friars, both white and red, the latter being of a peculiarly fine flavour.' A member of an American expedition which spent two months at the San Gabriel mission in 1826–27 wrote of attending a wedding banquet and other meals at which food and wine were varied and generous, and a visitor three years later reported favourably that the same mission produced annually from 400 to 600 barrels of wine and 200 of brandy.

But Richard Henry Dana, the author-sailor, visiting the area in 1835, considered Californians lazy and unenterprising, buying bad European wines when they should have been producing better ones of their own. A Santa Barbara priest, writing in 1833 of the wine at San Luis Rey, called the white wine there 'rather unpleasant' because it has no sweetness whatever, and made the general observation that 'the wines were not the best suited to place before a friend'. He thought the San Gabriel wines the best of those in the missions, mentioning dry and sweet reds, a dry white and a white to which brandy was added during fermentation. All these, apparently, were made of the dark Mission grape. At about the same time William Heath Davis, who credited himself with expertise, wrote that he drank red wine made in San Francisco's Mission Dolores from grapes grown farther south, and that it was as good as any he had ever tasted.

The great missions, built in a burst of expansion, flourished only a few years and then in the early 1830s they began to die. The cause was the independence of Mexico from Spain and the resultant takeover of the mission properties by the state. Vineyards were neglected, abandoned or torn up. Fences fell, to allow cattle to pasture among the trampled vines. Irrigation systems broke down, and winery equipment fell into ruin. But just before the mission chapter began to close, a new era of California wine-making emerged.

Commercial wine-making on a significant scale began in the 1820s with the arrival of Joseph Chapman. Chapman, a wandering American jack-of-all-trades, made friends with various Franciscan wine-makers, and learned a great deal from them. Between 1823 and 1826 he planted 4,000 vines in Los Angeles, and it is speculated that he first produced a wine in about 1827. Other newcomers – French, Dutch and American – entered the field. By 1831, it is estimated, there were 100,000 vines growing in what is now the city of Los Angeles. The wine was given poor marks by a visiting writer, who said the grapes were good but the wine-making methods inferior.

If Chapman was the first to grow wine commercially, a Frenchman, Jean Louis Vignes, presumably destined by his very surname, was the first real founder of professional wine-making in the state. Vignes, born in the Bordeaux region of France, was a cooper and distiller by training. He arrived in Los Angeles in 1831, bought 104 acres, imported French vines and probably turned out his first vintage in 1837. A man with the foresight to be the first to import vine stocks direct from Europe to California, Vignes was also smart enough to make barrels from California oak, and to encourage scores of other Frenchmen, including at least seven relatives, to join him in the new country.

He developed a beautiful domain, El Aliso, on the very land now occupied by the Los Angeles railway station, and like numerous other prosperous ranchers, acquired the title of 'Don', something equivalent to a squire. 'Don Luis' aged some of his wines for ten years, and his brandy as well. He sent many of his wines on ocean voyages for ageing, he carried on a brisk export and California coastal trade, and he came to be a civic leader in Los Angeles. In 1855 he sold his vineyards and winery to his nephews, Jean Louis and Pierre Sansevain, who, as Sansevain Brothers, were to achieve wine-making fame in their own right.

Don Luis had many competitors, though none achieved his success. They were a curious collection – a Belgian named Janssens and a transplanted Southerner named

Benjamin Davis Wilson. (Grandfather to General George S. Patton of the Second World War, Wilson, although a foreigner, was made mayor of Los Angeles under the Mexicans.) And there was also an unusual adventurer, William Wolfskill, who was born on the Kentucky frontier in 1798. His family pushed on west into Missouri when the boy was 11 years old. In 1822 he left, to be a trapper, wandering the great wilderness of the Rocky Mountains and the great south-west. In 1830, as guide to an expedition into California, he gave up his roaming and became an energetic horticulturist. By 1858 only the Sansevain brothers made more wine than he. Wolfskill and his brother, John, had 55,000 vines and a cellar capacity of 100,000 gallons. The Wolfskills were also among the first to open vineyards in northern California.

While the industry thrived in Los Angeles, other southern California areas were also developing wine production. San Diego, Santa Isabel, Santa Monica, Santa Ana and Santa Barbara had vines and wineries. But the supremacy of southern California was shortly to have powerful competition from the San Francisco area to the north. By 1846, when California became part of the U.S.A., the vine had become the one common characteristic of California.

One of the early pioneers of viticulture in the north was General Mariano Guadelupe Vallejo, the Mexican commandant whose headquarters was in Sonoma, 50 miles north of San Francisco. Vallejo, who became a leader in California horticulture, produced 300 gallons of wine and 60 of brandy in 1841. In the decade of the 1840s wine-growing spread rapidly through the area north and north-east of San Francisco. The nationalities concerned were a reflection of the universal interest in wine. John Sutter, the Swiss on whose property the Gold Rush was to start, distilled grape brandy in 1840. Russians who had a fur-trading post on the Sonoma County coast planted 2,000 vines. Irish, French, English and Spanish names abound in the wine history of the 1840s and 1850s. By 1854 a state agricultural society had been formed, and was promoting the virtues of the new state as the greatest wine region of the world. The sentiment was frequently reiterated in the newspapers of the San Francisco area. By 1855 the vineyards of northern California were as important as those in the south. By 1856, 1,500,000 vines were in cultivation in the state; two years later the figure had leaped to 3,900,000. Wine-making had become a major industry in California.

Although the wines were undoubtedly popular, they must certainly have been of indifferent quality by European standards, because most of them were still made from the common Mission grape, and wine-making was in the main not very expert. Cheap foreign wines were sold under California labels; better California wines were sold under foreign labels. The result of each fraud was detrimental to the California product, and it had a widespread poor reputation among connoisseurs.

But the 1850s also brought two great benefactors to the industry. One was Agoston Haraszthy, a Hungarian. The other was a German named Charles Kohler. The decade of the 1850s was one of feverish expansion of the California vineyards, both for wine-making and table grapes, with the latter in as high demand as the wine. The Mission grape served both purposes. Viticulture spread into the foothills of the Sierra, with vines growing on the very slopes among the goldfields. State officials and newspaper editors, interested in attracting more immigrants, beat the drums incessantly to advertise the fortunes to be made in grape-growing. Over-production by the end of the decade, coupled with careless and fraudulent manufacture of low-grade wines, slowed the market and squeezed some inflationary values from the properties, but the depression was temporary. In the 1860s the trend was again climbing sharply upward.

Although the growing population of the new state was consuming most of the wines produced, the period was marked by the development of markets outside California, particularly on the east coast of the U.S.A., to which wine could be sent economically by ship. It was considered to improve significantly by the heat and motion in the ships' holds.

The most successful merchandising of California wines in the 'fifties and 'sixties was probably that of Charles Kohler, another in the examples of new arrivals who turned from other professions to seek their fortunes with the vine. Kohler, born in 1830 in Germany and trained as a musician, arrived in the U.S.A. in 1850, with no assets but his violin and his education. He found work in an orchestra and as an accompanist for Jenny Lind, but like many other restless immigrants, he sought greater opportunity in California. He went there in 1853, by ship to Panama, by trail across the Isthmus and thence again by ship. Many such travellers died in Panama of fever, snakes or accident, but the alternatives were either to sail around the Horn of South America or to face Indians, starvation or freezing while crossing the empty plains and terrible mountains of the American West. The choices were the devil's own.

Kohler was a moderately successful musician and director in San Francisco, but one day, while eating grapes, he was struck with the desire to be a wine-merchant. The outcome was the firm of Kohler and Frohling (the latter a musical colleague), which came to own vineyards, wineries and cellars in the largest wine company in the state. For four years Kohler continued to play his violin every evening to make up the losses in the new venture, but in 1858 he was able to leave music as a profession. By 1860 the firm was storing 120,000 gallons of wine in San Francisco alone. It had a branch office in New York, agents in China, Russia, Japan and several South American countries. In the 'sixties Kohler and Frohling continued to expand, fought off attacks of eastern wine-merchants, built a reputation for good wines and found markets in Denmark, Germany and other European countries. In 1862 the firm assisted in founding California's first glassing works, which blew its first wine-bottle in the next June.

Frohling died in 1862, but Kohler lived until 1887, having become the owner of large manufacturing and agricultural properties and director of a bank, an insurance company and a transportation firm. He was a civic leader of stature, leaving behind him a record of public services and ethical business practice, and a heritage of wisdom to California wine-making. The industry was bedevilled by incompetent manufacture, false labelling, adulteration and every opportunism detrimental to a product demanding the best. Charles Kohler and his nearest competitors, the Sansevain Brothers of Los Angeles, were major elements in the long effort to make it the reputable trade it is today.

While Kohler was pioneering in salesmanship and production for California wines, an older, vastly more experienced man, Agoston Haraszthy de Mokesa, was establishing the basis of modern viniculture in California. Haraszthy, born in 1812 to a noble Hungarian family, had been a colonel in the bodyguard of Francis I Emperor of Austria a lawyer, a civil servant with the title of Count, a country squire and a wine-grower, all before he fled his country as a refugee Hungarian nationalist at the age of 27.

In 1840 he arrived in New York. With American protection he was able to return to Hungary and bring out his mother, father, wife and three sons. He settled in the state of Wisconsin. There he became a contractor and builder, organized a society to encourage German, Swiss and English people to emigrate to the U.S.A., and he collected substantial amounts of money and munitions to support Kossuth's Hungarian revolution of 1848.

Asthma caused him to move from Wisconsin to the drier climate of California. He arrived in San Diego in 1849. The energetic count planted fruit, vegetables and vines the next spring, was elected sheriff of his county in the next year and by 1852 was a member of the state legislature. Then, in the same year, he moved to Crystal Springs Farm, a large holding south of San Francisco, and once more began to create a new career. There he set out vines and trees he imported from Hungary, starting a thriving nursery business which he soon expanded with the purchase of 50 acres in San Francisco. He became assayer and then refiner for the U.S. mint, resigning in 1857 after having been falsely accused of short accounts. Then, to get away from the misty climate of San Francisco, he moved his rooted cuttings to Sonoma County. On his Buena Vista property there he established a vineyard and winery that were to work a permanent influence on the wine industry of California.

It is difficult to write briefly about Haraszthy. This account will pass lightly over his first 40 years, leaving out elaborations on his having operated a sawmill and steam-boat line in Wisconsin, having served as secretary to the viceroy of Hungary, having made himself a masterful rider and hunter, achieved command of several languages, sponsored several California laws and introduced to the state the grape that founded the raisin industry. All these things are in his astonishing record, but the most impressive exercise of his talents and energy was in wine-growing. He is commonly called the single most important influence in the development of the wine industry in California. The principal factor in this influence lay in his untiring effort to improve the vineyards – to persuade the California growers that their soil and climate could produce better wines than they could ever press from the common, coarse Mission grape. Haraszthy bought, in 1857, 560 acres of land in the Sonoma Valley, including an insignificant wine property of some 8,000 vines. By the end of his first year he had planted 80,000 on his own property and that of friends whom he had persuaded to settle near him, he had tunnelled into the hillside to make a 100-foot limestone cellar, and he was making wines and brandy from the old vineyard on the property.

In 1858, while putting in 30,000 more vines, he wrote for the state agricultural society a treatise on wine-growing which, widely distributed, stimulated many new vineyards. And at the end of that year his vineyards were awarded first prize in a state-wide competition. He carried on a friendly competition with his neighbour, General Vallejo, the two vying annually at state and county fairs for first prizes on their wines, fruits and brandies.

Haraszthy urged the state to establish an agricultural college, thus foreseeing the present Department of Viticulture and Enology at the University of California at Davis. He was the first to demonstrate that redwood was a good substitute for oak cooperage. By 1861 he was at the peak of leadership in the industry. Vincent P. Carosso, in *The California Wine Industry, 1830–1895*, says that Sonoma, because of Haraszthy and his friends, became the focus of wine-making information for the state:

It was from here that the Zinfandel, the Flame Tokay, the Black Prince, the Emperor, the Seedless Sultana, the Riesling, the Traminer, the Black Morocco, and numerous other varieties were distributed throughout California. The practical success Haraszthy met with growing all kinds of grapes without irrigation, the superiority of hillside culture for wine grapes, and the use of red-wood casks to alleviate the oak shortage made the Sonoman the most eminent vigneron of the state.

Although Haraszthy had already imported many grape varieties from Europe, and had distributed them widely, he still felt he had hardly begun to experiment with vines. He strove to accelerate the knowledge and testing of European vines. Under his stimulus, the California legislature asked the governor to appoint a commission to further viti-culture. The governor in turn approved Haraszthy's idea that he should visit Europe, study the vineyard and wine-making practices, and bring back a wide selection of vines to be planted experimentally in California. The colonel left for Europe in July 1861. He travelled the vineyards of Europe for five months. He bought 200,000 vines of 1,400 varieties, paying for the trip and the vines personally, on the assumption that such expenses were to be reimbursed by the state of California. Carefully packed and tended *en route*, the vines were received and inspected in New York, repacked and shipped to San Francisco, where they arrived in good order in 1862. They were taken to Haraszthy's Buena Vista vineyards and carefully planted. Then came the anti-climaxes. The great collection, assembled with such meticulous attention from France, Germany, Italy, Spain, Portugal and Hungary, sat at Buena Vista while the governor and the legislature debated for months on how the cuttings should be distributed. Early in 1862 the colonel submitted his bill to the governor – $12,000 to reimburse him for the expense of collecting, shipping and caring for the vines. What followed was the most disgraceful episode in the history of California wine-growing. The legislature, which had authorized the governor to encourage Haraszthy to make the trip, now began an ignominious wrangle in which it was inferred by some that the colonel devised the whole project as an expensive personal junket. Haraszthy never received a cent, and when, a year later, he finally offered the unique collection for sale, few buyers handled the cuttings intelligently. Name tags were smudged or lost, and many vines were improperly planted and pruned. The wonderful collection, worth at least $30,000 at ordinary nursery prices, was dissipated and abused, and before the sorry chapter had ended, Haraszthy, a Republican, even suffered some minor persecution from the predominantly Democratic legislature.

But Haraszthy, who had been in and out of more careers than a townful of average businessmen, went on adding to his reputation as the greatest man in California wine-growing. The state agricultural society chose him for its president in 1862. In the same year he produced his first wine from the Zinfandel grapes. Zinfandel, which some authorities credit him with having brought from Hungary, was to become the most important table-wine grape in California.

Haraszthy, wishing to expand further than his capital would allow, organized the Buena Vista Horticultural Society, capitalized at $600,000. He left the corporation in 1866 and then began to suffer a series of unlucky incidents – a distillery explosion, a winery fire and the failure of some investments. Undaunted as ever, he went to Nicaragua, organized a plantation, built a distillery and erected a sawmill. In 1869 he disappeared, having last been seen attempting to cross a stream on his property.

Speculation, fostered perhaps by those who believed that such a dramatic man should come to a dramatic end, was that he was eaten by an alligator.

The astonishing Hungarian left behind him three sons, all experienced wine-growers, as well as an enormous heritage to the wine, table and raisin industries. He was a power-ful influence in the 50-fold increase in wine production in the state in the 20 years he lived there. His Buena Vista vineyard, which finally fell into virtual ruins, has been restored to production by an owner who also brought back the Buena Vista name and that of Haraszthy to the modern label.

There were other growers in Sonoma who actively sought to improve the wine grapes, some of them pre-dating Haraszthy. There was, of course, his friendly rival, Vallejo, who worked diligently to improve all horticulture, and who saw two of his daughters marry Arpad and Attila, Haraszthy's sons. Captain Nicholas Carriger planted experimental varieties in Sonoma in 1847. William McPherson Hill, a Pennsyl-vanian turned San Francisco broker, established the Hillside Winery in 1852, and at considerable expense introduced grapes from Peru, including Rose of Peru, Italia, Chasselas and Black Hamburg. Two Germans, Emil Dresel and Jacob Gundlach, had early vineyards in Sonoma County, beginning in 1858. Dresel came from a wine-making family. Scores of other growers poured into the country in the 1850s and 1860s, drawn in great part by the success of Haraszthy and Vallejo.

Meanwhile, wine culture moved at a fast pace in other counties in the north. In Santa Clara county the foundations were laid for several vineyards which are still in operation. A retired general, Henry M. Naglee, settled in the same county and intro-duced 150 grape varieties. He became famous for his carefully made brandy.

In Napa, Sonoma's great rival and neighbour county in the production today of California's best red table wines, an explorer, George C. Yount, planted grapes brought from the Sonoma mission. By 1856 he had assembled 13,000 acres in a great ranch, and was growing wine grapes among his various crops. In that year Joseph W. Osborne was growing 9,000 vines on a property thriving today as the wine domain of Beringer Brothers. Charles Krug, who came to California from Prussia, started in Sonoma County as an acquaintance of Haraszthy, and by 1881 was a leader of the industry with his Napa Valley winery, now operated under his name by the Mondavi family.

Alameda county is not a big producer of wines; it is now the most populous of the nine counties touching on the great San Francisco Bay, and the vineyards are faced with the march of suburban sprawl. But the county has long had an outstanding repu-tation for quality wines, particularly its white table varieties. The county contains the Livermore Valley, named for a man who grew wine there in 1848.

In 1849, the time of the Gold Rush, Theophile Vache started vineyards in San Benito County, now belonging to a big company which has recently planted one of the largest table-wine vineyards in America in that county because its Santa Clara county land became too valuable for more than a token vineyard.

Except for segments of the American public comprising European immigrants and Americans strongly oriented towards Europe, wine has always been a luxury beverage in the U.S.A. The huge inflow of immigrants, and the relative prosperity of the 1850s and 1860s, were the economic supports of the wine business in America, both for growers and importers. The California industry went booming into the 'seventies, with big new names, like Padre, Beringer and Inglenook, rising on the scene. But the nation suffered a disastrous economic collapse in 1873, which finally hit the California wine-makers three years later with shattering effect. Over-production, in part a consequence of a new federal law requiring distillers to pay taxes on brandy while it was still being held in storage, drove wine prices down to as little as 10 cents a gallon. Vineyards fell into ruin, while livestock pastured in them and growers went bankrupt. Wines sent by a few un-intelligent makers to a national exposition in Philadelphia were said to have been so poor that they set back by 20 years the already weak reputation of California vint-ages.

The terrible depression had some good effects. It drove a great many bad wine-makers out of the business. It drove most of the over-stocks of bad wine into brandy distillation or the vinegar works. With this catharsis and the return of better times, the industry regained its health by 1880, growing better grape varieties and making better, more matured wines. Then a new disaster struck – the louse, wrecking the world of wine.

Native grapes of the eastern U.S.A., harbouring the 'root louse,' *phylloxera vastatrix*, from time immemorial, were taken to other vineyards of the world for various experi-mentation and hybridization. Opinions differ on just where and when phylloxera entered Europe, but the time was between 1858 and 1863, and it may first have been discovered in England or in south-central France. The louse, living on the sap of the vine, but spending a part of its life cycle on the roots, spread rapidly through France and Germany, destroying thousands of vineyards. By 1875 it had virtually ruined the European wine industry. It was to continue its devastation into Italy, Portugal, South Africa, Spain, Algeria and westward into California before the solution was found, in the very soil from which the pest had come.

Ailments which were undoubtedly caused by phylloxera were noticed in 1860 in Haraszthy's vineyards at Buena Vista. The trouble was first blamed on the soil, whereas, in fact, the louse could have been brought in from France by the colonel himself. The Sonoma Viticultural Club eventually found suspect aphids in a vineyard 2 miles north of Sonoma town, and sent them to the U.S. Department of Agriculture for identifica-tion. The entomologist reported: *Phylloxera vastatrix!* By 1890 the pest had spread to southern California.

In spite of plain evidence and the knowledge of what had happened to the vineyards of Europe, many California growers refused for a long time to believe that the threat was serious. Healthy vines in the rich, new California soil were able to resist the pest for long periods. Professor Eugene W. Hilgard of the University of California College of Agriculture did his best to persuade vineyardists of the danger of the pest, but many of them tried to hide the fact that their vines were infested, ignored his efforts to institute controls and deprecated his whole attitude. By 1880 the louse in California began to spread with greater speed. By that time the French had recognized that planting re-sistant root stocks was the only practical solution; they had tried harsh and expensive insecticides, planting in sterilized sand and heavy flooding, all without real success. Still the stubborn Californians, with a few exceptions, ignored the advice of Hilgard, Professor George Husmann and other experts.

The disease ran into the 1890s before the growers generally adopted the only solution. Today, as in Europe, most *vinifera* varieties in California are grafted on root stocks native to the eastern U.S.A., but several large growers, notably Almadén, Paul Masson and Mirassou, have planted large acreages of *Vitis vinifera* upon their own root stocks under conditions which they believe will not foster phylloxera.

California created in 1880 a State Board of Viticulturists with nine members. After some early confusions and contentions the board became for a time an effective body, acquiring a library of 400 volumes, conducting experiments, developing the control of disease and pests and generally furthering the knowledge and appreciation of grapes and wines. Within 10 years the Board had established itself as an authoritative body, operating usefully in co-operation with the experts of the university. Among other things, it undertook to educate the American public on wine – an enterprise which still offers limitless challenge to the industry.

Real attention was paid to quality from 1885 on. California's wines won 35 gold, silver and bronze metals at the Paris Exposition of 1889. By 1890 California had become a serious competitor with European wines in South America. But California wine-makers were still managing to be their own worst enemies. While some growers were producing better and better wines from better and better varieties of grapes, there were still floods of bad, cheap wine, pouring into the market to give the state a bad name. In a significant letter to a San Francisco newspaper, Professor Hilgard precipitated a bitter argument with wine-growers with his remark that the wine industry had no problem that could not be solved by 'judicious treatment and honorable means'. The shaft struck deep, but the industry's only reaction was resentment, and an effort to form a price-fixing cartel. On into the 'nineties the dissension continued, while the industry fought taxes, tariff wars and the professors. In 1895 the legislature, presumably fed up with it all, abolished the State Board of Viticultural Commissioners and turned its functions, records and properties over to the University. The quarrelling growers were outraged, but time seems to have proved the value of the transfer. The University's great viticulturists and oenologists, along with those of Fresno State College, are today among the world's most eminent, and the industry they serve is among the most skilled and scientific in the wine regions of the earth.

Six million southern Europeans emigrated to the U.S.A. between 1900 and 1915. They were wine-drinkers all, and they raised the nation's consumption sharply. Although the California industry had suffered from extremes of quality, price and production in its days since Joseph Chapman, it had progressed enormously; by 1912 the annual production was 50 million gallons. But a new adversity was to set in. A minority of phenomenally aggressive Americans was starting to turn the nation 'dry'. Bit by bit, under 'local option', the temperance forces and prohibitionists began to win elections in cities, counties and states, forbidding the sale of alcoholic beverages. By 1915 California's wine production had fallen to 12 million gallons as a direct result. Meanwhile, wine-grape shipments went up as millions of citizens who had been too lethargic or too self-conscious to vote against prohibition began 'making their own'. In 1923 Prohibition put its scaly hand on all the nation with a constitutional amendment. It soon corrupted the wine industry. Prohibition brought a sharp upturn in demand and prices for wine grapes. As in earlier vineyard expansion, many profit-seekers and careless growers brought disorder and a bad reputation with them. When Prohibition was repealed in 1934 wine stocks were depleted and the vineyards dominated by high-producing, low-quality varieties. In that year the industry launched a new co-operative effort. It organized the Wine Institute, which has its headquarters in San Francisco and

Plate 59. Oak casks in the tunnels of Buena Vista Vinery, near San Francisco.

has been an important force in the development, improvement and defence of the California industry, as well as a major element in the effort to educate the American public about wine and its use.

Grapes and wine are important products of California today, with its half million acres in vines. Although the state's best wines are the dry table varieties, the largest production is of dessert wines – a term which encompasses all wines above 14% alcohol, including dry sherries and various *apéritifs*. The American taste for wine is clearly improving, however, as is indicated by the shifting balance. The consumption of dry wines is steadily rising, while that of dessert wines is only holding steady. The Californians have reason to be bothered by the fact that, while wine consumption is going up in the U.S.A., and California continues to raise its annual production and sales, the state's wines tend to lag in their share of the national consumption.

California wines today can best be discussed under three main types: the dessert and *apéritif* wines, the flavoured wines and the dry table wines. They also fall into two general categories, which might be typified by the screwtop bottle and the cork, which is to say, the quantity wines and the quality wines.

The warm, irrigated, rich soils of southern California and the great Central Valley produce very heavy yields of grapes for sherries, ports, muscatels and vermouths, few of which have interest for a connoisseur. The best that can be said for most of them is that they are unadulterated, sweet and strong, with many of them containing grape brandy, added to halt fermentation while the grape-sugar content is still high, since in California, still wines may not be artificially sweetened. The unsophisticated American taste has demanded these sweet wines, but the trend is now towards table wines, and the Central Valley and southern California vineyards are accommodating some of their production to the trend.

The flavoured wines are relatively new in the U.S.A. They are commercial successes, made to appeal to those who have not previously been interested in wine. Most of them are based on neutral wines to which natural fruit flavours are added. They belong to that great family of beverages which includes fruit punches, shrubs and cordials. They have as much right in the market as others of the world's *apéritif* wines. Traditionalists abhor these 'wines', but many people in the industry insist that the 13 million gallons sold annually broaden the base of appreciation for better wines.

The pride of most California wine-growers today is in the dry wines, and it is in these types that quality reaches the heights of excellence. It is also fair to say that the low-priced California wines are outright superior to many wines of equal price in the world's markets. Meanwhile, the best standard wines of the state can hold their own with the best standard wines of the world. California wines which can truly compete with the great wines of France and Germany can be found only in small quantities in private cellars or for virtually private sale. The sweeping generalizations, on the one hand, that California can produce no great wines, and, on the other, that its wines 'are as good as any in France' are equally unfair and absurd, and the subjective opinions frequently cited as absolutes are ridiculous. The wine industry in California, as elsewhere, suffers interminably from the wine snob at one end of the scale of opinion and the ignoramus at the other, and often the two are combined in the same individual.

It would be hard to find a dry California wine on a grocer's shelf as poor as French *ordinaire*. It would be even harder to find one which could enter the competition with

Plate 60. Lugs of freshly picked grapes in Napa County, Northern California.

first-growth bordeaux of a good year, or its peer from Burgundy or the Rhine. How many California vintners can lavish the hand labour and attention on their vineyards that are devoted to Château Margaux or La Tâche? And if they could, and the result were as great a wine, how could they develop overnight the world prestige and consequent price advantage of vineyards renowned in the world for 200 years?

The fine wines of California are grown mainly in the region which embraces San Francisco Bay. In what a Londoner visiting San Francisco might think of as its Home Counties, the vineyards occupy small valleys and many slopes where the climate alters little from year to year. There is a great deal of sunshine, the rainfall is usually adequate (although it falls entirely in the winter), frost seldom comes inopportunely and the soil and drainage are well suited to high-quality varieties.

The even conditions from one year to the next produce wines that vary less than the wines of regions with less dependable weather. This has provided the wine-makers with the excuse for labelling most of their wines without dates. There are other reasons: a consumer public little interested in vintages or, occasionally misled through assumptions that because a year was poor in Burgundy it would be a poor one in the Napa Valley. But more and more California wines bear vintage dates, as the customers increase who would at least like to know whether the wine is young or old. Sadly, the dates too often reveal the haste with which California wines are marketed, particularly the better reds. Perhaps the most unsatisfactory aspect of the quality wine trade in California is the same one that grievously afflicts that of France: the eagerness of producers and merchants to satisfy the consumer demand brings much potentially fine wine on the retail market long before it has had time to fulfil its promise. Understandably they are reluctant, or unable, to keep such large capital investment in storage.

Until fairly recent times most California wine was marketed under the generic names familiar in Europe – burgundy, claret, Sauterne (without the final 's') Rhine, Chianti. It had always been felt that the American public needed such appellations for identifying general types. But the makers of premium wines, wishing to sell their product on its own merit, are increasingly labelling their best under the names of the grape varieties from which they are made. A customer buying a California 'burgundy' is assured that it is pure grape, grown and made into wine in California. But if he buys a bottle labelled 'Napa Valley Grey Riesling', the law guarantees that the wine is at least 51% from that grape, that the remainder is from grapes that will blend compatibly, and that the wine is all from the Napa Valley. The label will also reveal whether the grapes were grown in the winery's own vineyards and, sometimes, whether it is 100% of the varietal from which it gets its name.

California has three notably fine red wine grapes, as well as many others which perform creditably. The noblest wine of all the reds comes from an unprepossessing small berry with large seeds, usually borne in scraggly bunches, and too tart and puckery to eat fresh with any pleasure. This is the world-famous Cabernet Sauvignon, grown in the bordelaise region as well as in Italy, the Balkans, Argentina, Chile, Russia and Australia. Maynard Amerine, the great university expert of the state, believes that in California the Cabernet Sauvignon produces a softer and alcoholically stronger wine than it does in Bordeaux, but usually with less tannin. The colour is deep, and in well-matured vintages it takes on the suggestion of brown that characterizes a fine old claret.

Cabernet Sauvignon, which is also occasionally made into *rosé* wines, is a light producer, of 4–6 tons to the acre. It differs from one vineyard to another and from year to year, matures slowly and is all too often put on the market long, long before it is ready to drink. A hybrid relative to the Cabernet Sauvignon is the Ruby Cabernet, sometimes blended with the better grape. The Ruby was developed in an effort to get the combined advantages of Sauvignon flavour and Carignane productivity from a single variety.

Standing below the Cabernet Sauvignon in red-wine quality is the Pinot noir, well known in the Burgundy and Champagne districts of France. It produces even lighter crops than the Cabernet, with 3 or 4 tons per acre the usual expectation. It is lighter in colour, too. It produces beautiful red vintages, smooth, soft and fine, but seldom with the full, 'chewy' character of great burgundies.

The red grape which deserves extra attention in California is the Zinfandel, the mystery grape which Haraszthy may have brought from Hungary, but which has never actually been traced or found there. The Zinfandel is a good producer. It is grown only in California. In good years or bad, it has a brilliant red, sometimes ranging deep into blackberry purple, and often with a taste suggestive of raspberry. There are more Zinfandels grown in California than any other wine-grape variety. Much of the juice from them is blended into other wines to give them life and fruitiness, and to produce medium-priced reds called 'burgundy' or 'mountain red' or 'claret'. Most Zinfandels deserve to be drunk young, like Beaujolais, but now and again, from a cool coastal vineyard, this unique vine produces a big, full, purple, aromatic vintage that goes on improving for many years. Professor Amerine writes of a 1936 Zinfandel that was at its best 20 years later!

Barbera and Charbono are two grapes of Italian origin which made into good varietals – soft but acid, with rich deep colour. The Charbono sometimes produces an outstanding wine capable of some maturity.

Napa and Sonoma counties, north of San Francisco, have the greatest red-wine reputations, but several fine wineries in Santa Cruz, Santa Clara, Alameda and San Benito counties to the south can be expected to add their claims to supremacy. These counties, especially Alameda, also dispute the Napa and Sonoma claims to supremacy in dry white wines.

There is fairly good agreement, however, on which grape is best for white wines. The consensus is for the Pinot Chardonnay, well known in the Chablis and Champagne vineyards of France. It is a meagre yielder. Its best wine is straw to pale gold in colour, fragrant and smooth. Some of the most carefully made Chardonnay develops remarkable body and flavour. Some connoisseurs argue that the Pinot blanc will produce wine as good as that from the Chardonnay. Its characteristic colour is somewhat deeper, its flavour more assertive.

Crowding the Pinot Chardonnay and the Pinot blanc hard in the competition for quality are several other grapes. The white, or Johannisberg, Riesling is among the best of these. It is refreshing, often has more bouquet than is common to California white wines (not very fragrant as a general thing), and although it varies in taste and colour, it sometimes shows a pale green, when the chlorophyl content affects the pressing.

The Sylvaner, or Franken Riesling, is the principal Rhine-type variety in California. It produces a fresh, clean wine, but it is not as stable as the Johannisberg, since it has been known to madeirize while still young. The Emerald Riesling, a hybrid of white

Riesling and Muscadelle, although it is also subject to madeirizing, has been produced with great success by the Paul Masson company. A shipment to London became faintly crackling in 1964, which made it a wine of very special charm. California makers do not go in for 'spritzig' or 'petillant' wines; they make them either still or outright fizzy, but carbon dioxide is sometimes used at low pressure to replace the air between cork and wine.

Two grapes familiar to the Sauternes and Graves districts of France are grown in northern California for first class wines. They are the Semillon and Sauvignon blanc, which perform with distinction, particularly in the Livermore Valley. Each is made in both sweet and dry versions, both of them straw to pale gold in colour, rich and aromatic.

Several northern California wineries make Traminer and Gewürtztraminer. These can be pleasant wines, and occasionally one emerges which has something like the luxurious, spicy character of those in Alsace. Most of them, however, can be said only to be reminiscent of good Alsatian examples, and a great deal of a grape called red Veltliner is reported to be marketed under Traminer labels.

*Rosé* wines do not win great interest among true wine-lovers. They are often compromises drunk on hot summer days, or with certain foods that 'just don't seem to go' with red or white. Within the rather confined range of appreciation of pink wines, however, California probably has examples as good as any in the world, including Tavel, and markedly better than the undistinguished *rosés* that pour from Portugal and Italy into the export markets. The Grenache is the best and most popular of the California grapes going into pink wines, but others quite excellent are pressed from Grignolino, Cabernet Sauvignon, Gamay, Zinfandel and occasionally Pinot noir. As in other countries, the popular taste is catered to by making many of these wines slightly sweet, but some of the dry ones are well worth the attention of the most discriminating wine-lover.

All parts of California produce bubbling wines, ranging from sweet Moscato Spumante, artificially carbonated, to high-quality, bone-dry blancs de blanc produced by the traditional bottle fermentation. Pink and red sparkling wines are also made by the traditional champagne method as well as by the charmat process. California wine laws require that labels reveal whether wines are bottle-fermented or produced by the charmat process (in which the secondary fermentation takes place in glass-lined tanks). Wines in which the bubbles are artificially introduced cannot even be labelled 'sparkling'. But the U.S.A. maintains that 'champagne' has become a generic word not limited to the French product. Consequently, the word is widely used on labels, but always as 'California champagne'.

Some of the best bottle-fermented sparkling wines in California came from the same northern coastal areas which lead in other table wines. The grapes considered best are also those most popular in France – the Pinot noir and the Pinot Chardonnay – but Semillon, Folle Blanche, white Riesling and Sylvaner also go into some of the *cuvées*.

By legal definition, a California wine is dry if it does not exceed 14% of alcohol; few of the state's wines fall below 11·5. But more California wines are in the dessert and *apéritif* classification than in the dry category. Most of these heavy wines – sherry, port, Muscatel, Angelica and Muscat de Frontignan – are grown in the great Central Valley, a vast irrigated empire of fertility. A few of the wines are distinguished, and there are some flor sherries, pressed from Palomino grapes. There are good vermouths, and some muscats which please people who enjoy the unmistakable muscat grape and want a very sweet wine. Some of the ports are well made, from Tinta Madeira and Tinta Cao vines. California also makes a sweet wine called 'Tokay', but bearing no relation in any way to the Hungarian wines of that name.

The new flavoured wines, sold under such advertising names as Bali Hai, Silver Satin and Thunderbird, contain genuine (not artificial) fruit flavours, herbs and other ingredients. These and cheap popular wines of California are often marketed in bottles of unusual shapes, bearing colourful, untraditional labels.

The California wine-growers are a hospitable lot. There are perhaps a hundred wineries in the state which will welcome the passing public to stop in for a taste, and a tour of the facilities. Expert guides lead visitors among the oak cooperage, redwood vats, plastic hoses, glass pipelines, crushing machines and ageing cellars, typified by spotless efficiency and unrelenting scientific control, even in small wineries.

The strict viticulturists divide the state into 'regions' according to a scale of degree days determined by their average temperatures during the growing season. The popular classification, however, is by simpler geographic districts which follow the early pattern of the industry. Haraszthy's old vineyard, Buena Vista, in the Sonoma district, is once again a leading producer there of highest quality vintages. Its owner is Frank Bartholomew, one of the nation's most important news executives, who, with his wife, bought the property in 1943. He takes particular pride in his vintage Cabernet, Zinfandel, Pinot Chardonnay and Johannisberger Riesling, and a bottle-fermented Sparkling Sonoma made from Pinot Chardonnay. In the town of Sonoma itself, a few thousand yards from the old estate of General Vallejo, is the Samuele Sebastiani winery, formerly concerned with the production of bulk wines for other bottlers, but in the field of premium wines under the Sebastiani label since 1954. Among the best of these is a hearty Barbera.

In the Russian River Valley of the same county the three Heck brothers, of Alsatian descent, operate the Korbel winery, specializing in champagnes, mainly from Pinot noir, Pinot blanc and Sauvignon blanc. Farther to the north in Sonoma County, along the Mendocino County border, is the great wine complex of the Italian Swiss Colony, founded in 1881 by an Italian immigrant, Andrea Sbarbaro, who, after achieving great success, died in 1923, some said out of frustration that his beloved winery, stricken by Prohibition, was reduced to bottling grape juice. Italian Swiss today is part of a huge, 1,200-member growers' co-operate claiming to produce one-fourth of all the wine made in the U.S.A. Its wines are mainly in the low- and medium-priced brackets, eminently drinkable. A few, under the 'Asti' label, are made for the premium market.

Across a range of mountains from Sonoma is the Napa district, rivalling Sonoman wines. Here, where Robert Louis Stevenson wrote *The Silverado Squatters* and spent his honeymoon, are many of the most prestigious names in California wine-making. There is Beringer Brothers, founded in 1876, with great limestone tunnels cut into a hill by Chinese coolies. A Beringer speciality is Barenblut (Bear's Blood), blended from Pinot noir. They also make varietal wines from Cabernet Sauvignon, Grignolino, Zinfandel and white Riesling. The Mondavi Brothers operate the Charles Krug winery and still display the old press Krug used in 1858. The Mondavis have put more and more importance on premium varietals bearing vintage dates. Their Cabernet Sauvignon and Pinot noir are fine reds, and they produce a light and fruity Gamay. They make a wide range of fine white wines, led, perhaps, by their Pinot Chardonnay, Johannisberger Riesling and Chenin blanc. The winery stands in a beautifully landscaped area with great shaded lawns, where visitor are sometimes invited to picnic while tasting the vintages. The winery publishes an informative quarterly called *Bottles and Bins*.

One of the greatest individual names in the California industry is that of Louis M. Martini, a vintner for more than 60 years. His wines, from three vineyard areas in the Mayacamas foothills and on the 1,000-foot Mayacamas ridge, are all of high quality, but some are truly extra vintage wines of great fulness and maturity. The vintage reds include Cabernet Sauvignon, Zinfandel and Barbera; the whites, Johannisberger Riesling, Pinot Chardonnay, Gewürztraminer and Chenin blanc. Martini's finest bottles, not seen in ordinary commerce, carry not only the vintage year but the year of bottling, and say which of his three vineyards produced the contents.

Many Californians are willing to argue whether Louis Martini or Beaulieu Vineyards turns out better wines. 'B.V.' was founded by a French immigrant, Georges de La Tour, in 1900, and belongs today to his descendants. It has vineyards at Rutherford and Oakville, produces genuinely great reds and whites and makes some of America's best champagne. Most B.V. varietals are dated, and many of the long-lived reds, if left to age, become big, handsome wines that can compete with great French vintages. They are, unfortunately, rare.

Next door to Beaulieu Vineyards is another fine farm – Inglenook. Its founder added to the curious international character of the early industry, and to the legends of the opportunists who, in the early days, dropped other occupations to become winemakers. Inglenook was founded by a Finnish sea captain named Nybom, who collected a fortune in Alaskan furs and sailed them to San Francisco to sell when he was only 26 years old. That was in 1867. A hobby of wine and a wife who disliked the sea resulted in his purchase of Inglenook in 1879. A great-nephew, John Daniel, Jr., sold the winery in 1964. The winery was a pioneer in varietal labelling and vintage-dating, and specializes in 'estate' bottling – that of wines produced only in its own vineyards.

Stony Hill comprises 30 acres of Chardonnay, Pinot blanc and white Riesling, on which Frederick H. McCrea, a San Francisco businessman, built a small winery in 1951. His output, produced with the greatest care, brings premium prices. Another small winery turning out wines of extra quality is the Heitz Wine Cellars, operated by a young university-trained viticulturist and oenologist, Joseph Heitz. One of his properties was formerly the Brendel winery, which made wine from only one grape – the Grignolino, in both red and pink.

Heitz started the winery in 1961, but has already finished and placed on the market some exceptional vintages from other vineyards, including some Pinot Chardonnay, which would be called a great wine anywhere in the world. Heitz, who once taught oenology at Fresno State College, virtually makes his wines by hand. Some of the Heitz wines were grown in the Hanzell Vineyard, established by the American industrialist and one-time ambassador to Italy, J. D. Zellerbach. Zellerbach, an enthusiast for great red and white burgundies, planted vines on his Sonoma County estate in the 1950s and built a small modern winery, where he conducted a damn-the-expense operation, even bringing oak cooperage from Nuits St Georges. He died while in this pursuit of absolute perfection, and the winery was closed. Its brief candle burned with a high, pure flame, though; the wines it pressed were unquestionably superior. In 1965, revived by Douglas N. Day, the winery crushed a new vintage.

A retired English oil company executive, Jack Taylor, and his wife, Mary, are among the successful come-latelys in Napa wine-growing. They took over an old wine property at 2,400 feet altitude in the Mayacamas Mountains and formed a corporation in which their customers own shares. The whole production, 100% varietals, is sold by mail order or at the winery itself, most of it to the stockholders. Souverain Cellars, which overlooks the Napa Valley from Howell Mountain, is a small operation, with 35 acres of vines and a small, very modern winery which turns out select varietals. It is owned by J. Leland Stewart, who started it as a hobby in 1943, but now spends full time fashioning prize-winning wines with the care a sculptor devotes to his marble.

In the hills 8 miles north-west of the town of Napa are the vineyards and cellars of a Roman Catholic teaching order, the Christian Brothers. They produce 500,000 gallons of good wine annually, as well as a popular brandy. The profits help maintain their Novitiate near the winery and the schools in the San Francisco province of their order.

Christian Brothers wines are not vintage-dated. Many of the finest of them are blended from as many as six or seven vintages of the same varietal, to produce the standards sought. Probably the best of these blended wines is their Cabernet Sauvignon. The winery is also proud of its charmat process champagne, produced under the most exacting controls. Brother Timothy, the renowned cellarmaster who has been in the winery since the repeal of Prohibition, has assembled a staff of oenologists and viticulturists about him which includes several with degrees from the university. The Christian Brothers is a large and prosperous enterprise, still buying land in Napa County for new vineyards, and with a new storage facility covering 45,000 square feet.

Across the Bay, south-east of San Francisco, lies the Livermore Valley of Alameda County, celebrated for white wines. The Wente Brothers vineyards, established in 1883 on gravelly alluvial soils, makes fine table wines from the Semillon, Sauvignon blanc, grey Riesling, Pinot blanc and Pinot Chardonnay. The vineyards are still in the family, and Carl H. Wente's descendants operate today the winery he founded. The Wente's are a wealthy family, well able to make sure that every bottle they sell has been given maximum opportunity to be a fine experience.

An Irishman from the Aran Islands founded Concannon Vineyards in 1883. His grandsons now run it. Its best white wines are vintage-dated dry Semillon, Sauvignon blanc and Riesling. It also produces a vintage red – Cabernet Sauvignon – and a vintage Muscat de Frontignan, which, to lovers of sweet dessert wines, is rich and luscious.

Another great wine-grower attracted by the gravelly alluvium of the valley was Charles Wetmore, the man who organized the State Board of Viticultural Commissioners. He wrote prodigiously about wines, and was a major influence on the industry. He founded the Cresta Blanca winery and won a Grand Prix at the Paris Exposition in 1889. His winery now belongs to a huge distilling corporation, produces large quantities of generics and varietals and is known for its high quality flor sherries, as well as a wide range of other wines. Cresta Blanca makes the only wine in the U.S.A. aided by *botrytis cinerea*, the 'noble rot' which occurs in Europe. South of San Francisco, fine wines are grown abundantly in Santa Clara and San Benito counties, to a lesser extent in the counties of Santa Cruz and San Luis Obispo, and increasingly in Monterey County. The Almadén vineyards were started by Etienne Thée, a Bordeaux farmer, in

1852, who was soon joined by Charles Lefranc, a Parisian tailor. Thée's daughter married Lefranc, who brought the business forward, ageing many of the vintages in French barrels, some of which are still in use. The winery fell into disuse during Prohibition, was bought in 1941 by Louis Benoist, a San Francisco businessman, and is today a very large concern, producing high quality wines.

Paul Masson, a Burgundian by birth, worked at Almaden, and became a son-in-law of Charles Lefranc. In the 1880s he took a property at Saratoga, in the Santa Cruz Mountains, and planted choice grapes. For nearly 60 years he was a great figure in the California wine industry. Now a large firm operating as Paul Masson Vineyards, the winery is a showplace, with ultra-modern buildings designed to attract visitors. A complete range of wines is produced, with a Cabernet Sauvignon leading the reds, an Emerald Riesling one of the best whites and a Grenache rosé which, although slightly sweet, is a fine wine with the traditional onion-skin colour of a good Tavel. Masson makes excellent sparkling wines, some of which are bottled in magnums and jeroboams, and produces special tawny ports and carefully made sherries. Masson wines are sold in London. Like those of other large producers, the wines of Masson are so carefully standardized that they do not vary appreciably from one year to the next.

The vast inland valley of California has many wineries. Most of them produce sweet wines or low-priced table wines – honest, drinkable wines of higher alcoholic content than the low-priced wines of Europe and pleasant taste. A company which stands out among these is that of E. and J. Gallo, whose phenomenal winery is at Modesto, in Stanislaus county. The Gallos are impatient with the wine traditionalists. They are interested only in pleasing more and more consumers – and never mind trying to educate them otherwise. The Gallos make and market some 40 types of wine, including flavoured wines and 'Ripple', slightly and artificially carbonated. They spend large funds in wine research. They invested $6 million in 1958 for their own glass factory. They make bottles in novel shapes. They long ago abandoned wooden cooperage in favour of great glass-lined steel tanks. They drive constantly to use more persuasive labels. They make about 25 million gallons a year; they can store 78·5 million gallons.

The Central Valley has other mammoth producers whose wines are sound, pure, appetizing wines sold at attractive prices. The Roma Wine Company of Fresno has total storage capacity of more than 25 million gallons. Cella Vineyards of Reedley can store 12 million gallons.

As the demand for good wines rises, the lands on which they have been grown tend to shrink. The counties around San Francisco are rapidly being covered over by the spreading cities. Vineyardists cannot afford to grow grapes on land sought for housing or industry. As the metropolitan area widens, the growers must go out of business or look for new areas for vines, and the result is the outward movement of quality planting, particularly to the south of the city, in Monterey and San Benito counties, a hundred miles and more south of San Francisco.

Guided by their own consultant scientists and those of the University and Fresno State College, several important fine-wine producers have purchased land and planted vineyards where fine-wine culture had heretofore been either unknown or incidental. Careful weather observations show that in 'degree days' these areas compare with the cool coastal areas of Sonoma and Napa. They have no frost during the growing season, and although the midday summer temperatures can be high, they fall quickly as the cool winds move in almost every late afternoon from the mountain range above the Pacific coast. The result is an extended ripening season which, coupled with admirably suited soils, provides an environment of enormous opportunity. Largest of the new ventures is that of Almadén. This well-managed company had relinquished to real-estate development all but 50 acres of its grapes at the old winery in Santa Clara county, and has developed what is thought to be the largest fine-wine vineyard in the world in the San Benito area. There, in the rolling floors of small mountain valleys, are more than 4,000 acres of beautiful, vigorous varietals – Pinot noir, Cabernet Sauvignon, Zinfandel, Sauvignon blanc, Grenache, Johannisberger Riesling and others.

Second largest of the new plantings is that of Paul Masson, at Soledad in Monterey County. At the foot of a mountain range bordering the Salinas River Valley, Masson has planted a single tract of 800 acres to fine vines, laid out in precise rectangles. The climate equates with some of the best of the Sonoma–Napa area, and the soil is a deep, gravelly deposit ideal to grape culture. Young, college-trained Jack Farrior is the *vigneron*. Near by, Mirassou Vineyards has a new, 350-acre vineyard on a scenic group of small hills, where 26-year-old Pete Mirassou is the vineyardist. He and his younger brothers, Jim and Dan, are the fifth generation of a California wine family, sharing with their father, a cousin and a brother-in-law the operation of a firm now beginning to concentrate on bottling their own fine wines, hitherto sold mainly in bulk to other wineries.

The Almadén, Mirassou and Masson properties are characterized by their scientific, strictly controlled methods, their very high standards of management and quality, and the boldness with which all three companies have planted them exclusively to ungrafted *vinifera* varieties. With new soil sterilants, constant vigilance and virtual quarantine of the vines the growers expect to keep phylloxera out, or eliminate it instantly if a vine should be attacked. At the Pinnacles vineyard of Masson every grape cutting is sterilized before it enters the property. Tools, equipment and even the boots of the workers are disinfected. Visitors are discouraged from walking into the rows of vines.

The whole vast complex of Almadén vineyards at Paicines in the neighbouring San Benito county, all on *vinifera* roots, is the outstanding illustration of this confidence that phylloxera can at last be challenged, after a century of sinister influence throughout the world. The vines in the new ventures, some of them now eight years old, are producing fine wines. Almadén is now selling vintage-dated 1960s from Paicines. They are clearly competitors to the best from Napa and Sonoma – truly fine wines. The new vineyards are proof that California has ample land on which to expand its quality-wine industry. The new vineyards probably mean that a large new chapter is opening in the history of California wines. Coupled with the strong trend, particularly among young adults, towards wine as an adjunct to dining, the future is quite bright, although there are still some clouds. Although wine production and wine shipping continue to increase in California, they are not doing so at the rate at which consumption of all wines is rising in the U.S.A. Where once California once sold 90% of all wine consumed in the nation, its share is now only 75%. This shrinking share of a booming market means, in part, that the California producers are actually falling behind in their huge effort to convince Americans that they need not look to European wines for quality. The exasperating fact is that a torrent of indifferent foreign wines is accompanying the few fine wines being imported, and many Americans still buy them *because* they are foreign.

The wine industry in the U.S.A. may suffer to some degree from its foreign competition, but its greatest obstacles are made in America. The national government imposes taxes, particularly on sparkling wines, and many of its regulations on wine are a part of the vestigial bigotry that produced Prohibition. Some states put such absurd requirements on which that California makers find it more difficult to ship to them than to export wines to France or England.

Arpad Haraszthy, carrying on where his father left off, once neatly defined the problem:

> The great obstacle to our success . . . is, that the average American is a whiskey-drinking, water-drinking, coffee-drinking, tea-drinking, and consequently dyspepsia-inviting subject, who does not know the use of value of pure light wines taken at the right time and in moderate quantities. The task before us lies in teaching our people how to drink wine, when to drink it, and how much of it to drink.

Long afterwards, in 1964, Robert Mondavi, stepping down from the chairmanship of the Wine Institute, noted regretfully that wine consumption in America still has barely scratched the surface of its potential, 'but,' he added, 'it is beginning to change.'

There is much evidence to support him. Best of it is the immense emphasis placed by the whole industry on very high standards – for whatever grade of wine is being produced. If the California wine-makers restrain their claims while maintaining their progress the world-wide recognition they seek is close at hand.

# *Glossary*

**Abbocato** (I) Sweet, or sweetish (but not luscious)

**Abfullüng** (G) Bottling

**Acerbe** (F) Sharp. Usually due to immature grapes used in the making of the wine

**Agrafe** (F) The metal clip used in Champagne to hold the first cork which is replaced when the wine is *dégorgé*

**Aigre** (F) Sour. A wine on the way to the vinegar tub

**Albariza** (S) White, lime-rich vineyard soil

**Aligoté** (F) The second best white grape of Burgundy; the best being the Chardonnay

**All'annata** (I) 'Of the year' – of a young wine, drunk in the year after the vintage

**Amabile** (I) Sweet, or sweetish (but not luscious)

**Amaro** (I) Bitter, but sometimes used of a dry wine

**Amelioré** (F) Improved. No recommendation; a wine needing improvement was never one of the best

**Amertume** (F) Bitterness. Usually a sign that the wine has been kept too long; also a characteristic of wine that is sick from travel and is not yet ready to drink

**Amontillado** (S) Pale, dry sherry with a mellow flavour

**Amoroso** (S) Golden, rich dessert sherry

**Apfelsäure** (G) Malic acid

**Appellation contrôlée** (F) A description allowed to wines of high quality produced in limited amounts from specific areas and specific types of grape

**Âpre** (F) Harsh. A wine which has lost all trace of its original 'fruit'

**Arenas** (S) Sandy vineyard soil of all best Jerez vineyards

**Arroba** (S) Spanish wine measure

**Astringent** (F) Acid; excessively sharp on the palate; usually the wine of a sunless year

**Atroje** (S) Large, slatted wooden cage in which grapes are pressed by their own weight in Spain

**aus dem Weingute** (G) From the estate or vineyard

**aus der Schatzkammer** (G) From the treasure chamber

**Auslese** (G) *See* page 292

**Barrica** (S) Small keg, barrel

**Barro** (S) Mud, clay

**Beerenauslese** (G) *See* page 293

**Beerwein** (G) Wine made from grapes which have been removed from their stalks before pressing

**Besitz (alleiniger Besitz)** (G) Sole proprietor

**Bestes Fass (Fuder)** (G) Best cask

**Bianco** (I) White

**Blanc de blanc** (F) Made from white grapes only (describing champagne)

**Blanco** (S) White

**Bocoy** (S) Hogshead

**Bodega** (S) Wine-cellar, warehouse, bar

**Bombona** (S) Pear-shaped glass jar for outdoor maturing of wine

**Bonde** (F) Bung

**Bota** (S) Barrel, butt, leather wine-bottle

**Bouche** (F) Mouth. *Vin de Bouche* meant 'top table' or best wine in old French

**Bouché** (F) Corked, in the sense of stoppered with a cork. *Vin bouché* often means the best wine in the house, in France, where *ordinaire* is from the cask

**Bouchonné** (F) Corked, in the sense of corky, a wine from the cask tainted by a defective cork

**Bouquet** (F) The sweet, clean, pleasing and discreet fragrance which none but the better wines have in their gift

**Brennwein** (G) Wine for distillation, i.e. for making brandy

**Brut** (F) Unsweetened (describing champagne); in U.S.A. – naturally fermented in the bottle

**Cabernet Franc** (F) The outstanding black grape of the Médoc; it is grown very extensively in many of the vinelands of the world for the making of fine quality red wines

**Cabinet** (G) *See* page 294

**Capiteux** (F) Heady. A wine usually of high alcoholic strength

**Capataz** (S) Head cellarman

**Capsule** (F) Metal cap protecting the outside face of the cork from damp mould and insects

**Caque** (F) Osier basket used for carrying the picked ripe grapes from vineyard to press at the vintage time

**Cava** (S) Wine-cellar (applies to sparkling wines only)

**Cave** (F) Wine-cellar

**Cellier** (F) Wine-vault or store

**Cementario** (S) 'Cemetery'; private cellar

**Cep** (F) Vine stock

**Cépage** (F) Species of vine; it is to different *cépages* that grapes owe their colour and flavour

**Cerasuolo** (I) Cherry-red, *rosé*

**Chai** (F) An above-ground storage place for wine in casks, as distinct from the cellar which is below ground

**Chambrer** (F) To allow red wine gradually to acquire room temperature

**Chaptaliser** (F) The adding of sugar to the grapes when being crushed at vintage time in order to obtain a higher alcoholic degree than the wine would acquire through the fermentation of its own grape-sugar

**Charnu** (F) Fleshy, in the sense of a red wine with fat body

**Château** (F) Homestead, whether castle or cottage, of a wine-producing Estate. *Mise en bouteille au Château* or *Mise du Château* means that the wine was bottled where it was made. It is a birth certificate but not necessarily a certificate of merit

**Chenin Blanc** (F) A white grape species grown mostly in the Loire valley for making quality white wine

**Climat** (F) The name given in Burgundy to certain vineyards; it means a 'growth' or *cru*

**Coller** (F) To fine, or clarify, a new or young wine in the barrel before racking or bottling it

**Comporta** (S) Upright wooden container in which grapes are carried from the vineyard

**Coñac** (S) Brandy

**Copita** (S) Small glass with short stem and elongated bowl

**Corps** (F) Stout. A wine with full body

**Corriente** (S) Everyday, ordinary

**Corsé** (F) Well-built. A wine with rather bigger body and a greater alcoholic strength than most, but well balanced withal

**Cortado** (S) Sherry classification: rich, nutty type

**Coulant** (F) Easy to drink, in the sense of a simple light, pleasing wine, the first glass of which is not to be the last

**Coupé** (F) Cut, in the sense of a wine blended with another

**Crémant** (F) Creaming, or slightly sparkling; crackling

**Creszenz** (also **Kreszenz**) (G) Growth

**Criadera** (S) 'Nursery' solera

**Crianza** (S) 'Breeding': maturing of wine

**Cru** (F) A named vineyard, or range of vineyards producing wines of the same quality and standard

**Cuve** (F) Vat

**Cuvée** (F) Vatting. The wine made from a blend of wines of the same vintage but of different vineyards; or of different vintages of the same wine; it usually bears a name or a number for the sake of identification until it is all sold or drunk, when another *Cuvée* is offered. In Champagne the wine made from the first pressings of the grapes is the best, and is known as *Vin de Cuvée*

**Dégorger** (F) Removing the sediment from a bottle of champagne by drawing the first cork with very little loss of wine and gas

**Demi-Sec** (F) Rather sweet champagne, not 'half-dry'

**Denominacion de origen** (S) A wine's birth certificate

**Depôt** (F) Sediment

**Dolce** (I) Richly sweet

**Domäne** (G) Domain; as a rule, used for state-owned vineyards

**Doux** (F) Sweet

**Dulce** (S) Sweet

**Dur** (F) Hard. A wine with an excess of tannin

**Durchgegoren** (G) A fully fermented wine; as a rule, without a residue of unfermented sugar; a wine for diabetics

**Eau de vie** (F) Brandy

**Echt** (G) Genuine

**Edelauslese** (G) Selected noble grapes

**Edelbeerenauslese** (G) A Beerenauslese made from noble-rotten grapes that are not dehydrated; i.e. the wine is not quite a Trockenbeerenauslese

**Edelfaule** (G) 'Noble rot'

**Edelgewächs** (G) Noble growth (may be used to describe only a Beeren- or Trockenbeeren-auslese)

**Edelwein** (G) Noble growth

**Egrappées** (F) Grapes which have been freed from their stalks

**Egrappoir** (F) A rotating callender-barrel used for tearing grapes from the stalks

**Eigengewächs, Eigenes Wachstum** (G) Own growth ('from my own vineyard')

**Eiswein** (G) *See* page 295

**Elégant** (F) A delicate, slight but attractive wine

**Entkeimt** (**EK**) (G) Sterilized

**Erben** (G) Heirs, estate of

**Estancia** (S) Residence

**Faible** (F) Weak – of low alcoholic strength

**Fass No.** (G) Cask No.

**Federweisser** (G) *See* page 296

**Feine** (**Feinste**) (G) Fine, Finest (a grower producing more than one cask of the same wine will, in order to distinguish between them, describe them according to quality)

**Ferme** (F) Rather hard but not unpleasantly so

**Feuillette** (F) Half hogshead

**Finit bien** (F) A wine with a particularly pleasing 'farewell' or smooth 'finish'

**Fino** (S) 'Fine'; light, dry, pale Sherry, delicate to taste

**Flaschenschild** (G) Label

**Flor** (S) 'Flower', a peculiar Spanish wine yeast which completely covers the surface of wine in vats or tanks during the last stages of fermentation

**Foudres** (F) Vats of large capacity used for blending wines

**Franc de Goût** (F) Straightforward and intensely 'clean' on the palate

**Frappé** (F) Iced

**Frizzante** (I) Semi-sparkling, prickly; *cf.* the French *pétillant* and the German *spritzig*

**Fruité** (F) Fruity, in the sense of a wine which has retained some of its original grape sugar

**Fuder No.** (G) Cask (of 1,000 *l.*) No.

**Fürst** (G) Prince

**Gamay** (F) One of the most extensively cultivated red wine grapes, which produces more but commoner wine than the Pinot, although in the Maconnais, Chalonnais and Beaujolais it is responsible for quite fair red wines

**Garrafa** (S) Decanter, carafe

**Gazéifié** (F) A sparkling wine with carbonic acid gas pumped into it

**Gebrüder** (G) Brothers

**Gemarkung** (G) Vineyards of a community

**Généreux** (F) A fortified wine, usually sweet and spirity

**Geschwister** (G) Brother(s) and sister(s)

**Gewächs** (G) Growth

**Gezuckert** (G) Sweetened

**Glühwein** (G) Mulled wine; a hot wine (red or white) spiced with cinnamon or clove and sweetened

**Goldbeerenauslese** (G) An Auslese made from fully ripe golden grapes (*Goldbeeren*)

**Goût** (F) Taste

**Goût Américain** (F) A fairly sweet wine, chiefly champagne

**Goût Anglais** (F) A dry wine, chiefly champagne

**Goût de Bois** (F) A wine which tastes of the wood of the cask, a defect due to a faulty stave or too long a stay in the cask

**Goût de Bouchon** (F) A wine tainted by a defective cork

**Goût d'Évent** (F) A wine which tastes flat, usually when left open too long

**Goût Français** (F) A sweet champagne

**Goût de Paille** (F) A wine with an objectionable taste of wet straw

**Goût de Pierre à Fusil** (F) A wine with a not objectionable 'flint' taste

**Goût de Pique** (F) A wine with an objectionable vinegary taste

**Goût de Pourri** (F) A wine with an objectionable mouldy taste

**Goût de Rancio** (F) A wine with a slightly rancio taste due to very old age, when it becomes very sweet and resembles madeira. Some people like it, others do not

**Goût de Terroir** (F) A wine with a distinctively earthy taste peculiar to the soil of its vineyard

**Graf** (G) Count

**Grossier** (F) Common or coarse

**Hauptniederlassung** (G) Head Office

**Hausmarke** (G) Special *cuvée* (q.v.)

**Haustrunk** (G) House drink (the wine the grower makes from the grapecake for his own use and that of his workers)

**Hectare** (F) A land measure equal to 2·47 acres

**Hectolitre** (F) A liquid measure equal to 26·4178 American gallons or 22 English gallons

**Hochgewächs** (G) Superb growth

**Hofkellerei** (G) Royal cellars

**Jahrgang** (G) Vintage, year

**Jungferwein** (G) *See* page 297

**Kabinett** (G) *See* page 294

**Kellerabfüllung, Kellerabzug** (G) Bottled in the cellar of the grower, proprietor who maybe a grower, a merchant or both

**Kellerei** (G) Large, extended cellars

**Kelter** (G) Grape-press

**Kommerzienrat** (G) Commercial Councillor

**Konsumwein** (G) *Vin ordinaire*

**Korkbrand** (G) Branded cork

**Kreis** (G) District

**Kreszenz** also **Creszenz** (G) Growth

**Lagar** (S) Wine-press

**Lage** (G) Site

**Landwein** (G) Local wine *ordinaire*

**Lehr & Versuchsanstalt** (G) Viticultural College and Research Institute

**Liqueur de Tirage** (F) Sugar candy melted in champagne wine and added to champagne at the time of bottling

**Liquoreux** (F) A particularly sweet, fortified wine

**Madérisé** (F) A wine with a slight taste of rancio. It becomes sweeter in ageing and resembles madeira

**Maiwein** (G) *See* page 296

**Manzanilla** (S) Pale, dry sherry with tart flavour; the word means 'small apple'

**Marc** (F) The stalks, pips and skins which are left after the grape-juice has been pressed out of the grapes. If sugar and water and yeast are added to the Marc it ferments and the poor wine made from it is called *Piquette*; when distilled it is called *Eau-de-vie de Marc*. It is distilled usually at a very high strength and needs years of storage to become mellow and acceptable

**Merlot** (F) One of the important species of black grapes responsible for the excellence of the red wines of Bordeaux

**Mesa** (S) Table (thus *vino de mesa* is 'table wine')

**Méthode champenoise** (F) Best method of making sparkling wine: the second fermentation is produced in the bottle, as when making champagne

**Méthode cuve close** (F) Method of making sparkling wine: the second fermentation is produced in bulk in a closed tank

**Millésime** (F) The date of the vintage

**Millésimé** (F) A 'dated' or vintage wine

**Mistela** (S) Very sweet grape-juice, whose fermentation has been stopped at an early stage

**Moëlleux** (F) Soft and smooth

**Mosto** (S) Must; grape-juice before it is fermented

**Mou** (F) Flabby, unattractive wine

**Mouillé** (F) Watered

**Mousseux** (F) Sparkling

**Moût** (F) Unfermented grape-juice or must

**Muffa Nobile** (I) 'Noble rot', permitted to attack grapes from which certain luscious dessert wines are to be made; *cf*. the French *pourriture noble*, in Sauternes, and the German *edelfaule*

**Mûr** (F) Ripe

**Mussante** (I) Sparkling

**Muté** (F) A wine the fermentation of which has been arrested by the addition of spirit to the grape-juice

**Natur, Naturwein** (G) Unblended

**Nature** (F) A still or sparkling champagne which has not been 'sweetened'

**Nero** (I) Black; sometimes used of a red wine

**Nerveux** (F) A wine with every promise of keeping long and improving with age

**Nu** (F) Bare; the price of the wine without the cost of cask or bottling

**Öchsle** (G) This term indicates the number of grammes by which one litre of must is heavier than 1 litre of water, the sugar content representing about 25% of this calibration. Thus, with a reading of 100° Öchsle, 100 litres will contain about 25 kilogrammes of sugar

**Œil de Perdrix** (F) The colour of 'partridge age'. A tawny *Vin Rosé*

**Offener Wein** (G) Wine by the glass

**Oloroso** (S) 'Fragrant'; full-bodied, golden to dark, rather sweet sherry

**Ordinaire** (F) Plain or undistinguished wine

**Original Abfüllung (Orig.-Abfg.)** (G) Bottling at the original Estate

**Originalabzug** (G) Original bottling

**Originalwein** (G) Original wine

**Orijo** (S) Refuse from pressed grapes

**Palma** (S) Sherry classification: fine and dry

**Passe-tous-Grains** (F) A red wine in Burgundy from both Pinot and Gamay grapes

**Passito** (I) Semi-dried – of grapes thus treated to make sweet wine; and the wine thus made

**Pasteurisé** (F) Pasteurized, a wine treated by heat to kill all ferments

**Pays, Vin de** (F) Local wine, usually *ordinaire*

**Paysan, Vin de** (F) Peasant wine, usually *très ordinaire*

**Pellejo** (S) Wine-skin

**Pelure d'Oignon** (F) Onion skin colour, pale tawny. A *Vin Rosé*

**Perlwein** (G) Bubbly wine – a wine containing up to 1½ atmospheres of carbonic acid

**Pétillant** (F) Crackling, slightly sparkling

**Pfarrgut** (G) The parson's vineyard (belonging to the Church and given on lease to the parson as part of his endowment)

**Pièce** (F) Hogshead, holds about 225 litres

**Pinot Blanc** and **Pinot Chardonnay** (F) A white grape grown in Burgundy and Champagne for fine quality wines

**Pinot Noir** or **Noirien** (F) A black grape grown in Burgundy and Champagne for fine quality wines

**Piqué** (F) Pricked. A wine on the way to the vinegar tub

**Piquette** (F) An imitation wine made from the pressed-out husks of grapes, which are flooded with water, sweetened with the cheapest available sugar and fermented with brewer's yeast. A poor, watery and sharp wine

**Pisador** (S) Treader (of grapes)

**Plat** (F) Flat. A dull and flat wine that will never be better and is not worth keeping

**Plâtré** (F) Plastered, that is with gypsum or some sort of lime added to clarify the wine

**Porron** (S) Wine-container with long spout

**Portador** (S) 'Porter'; oval container in which grapes are carried from the vineyard

**Pourriture Noble** (F) A form of mould which settles on Sauvignon, Semillon and Riesling grapes, known as *Botrytis cinerea*; it is responsible for the sweetness of Sauternes and Palatinate wines

**Précoce** (F) Forward. A wine that is maturing uncommonly rapidly

**Pressoir** (F) Apparatus used for pressing the grapes

**Quartaut** (F) A small barrel containing about 56 litres

**Queue** (F) The name given to a couple of hogsheads in Burgundy; many wines are sold by the *queue*, i.e. by two hogsheads

**Race** (F) Breed

**Raya** (S) Sherry classification: usually *oloroso*

**Rein** (G) Pure

**Rentant** (G) Collection Office

**Robe** (F) The wine's colour

**Rosado** (S) *Rosé*

**Rosato** (I) Pink, *rosé*

**Rosé** (F) There are *Vins Rosés*, light red wines made practically everywhere where black grapes grow, chiefly still or table wines in the Gironde and Burgundy, but also sparkling wines in Champagne and the Loire Valley. The majority of still *Vins Rosés* are made of black grapes which are pressed in the champagne fashion, that is with their juice being fermented away from the black skins which hold the red pigment responsible for the colour of all red wines. When the separation of juice and skins is done in a more leisurely manner than is the practice in Champagne it gives the juice a chance to be dyed pink. This easiest of all methods to make *Vins Rosés* is best for all the cheaper types of wine, that is wines which are intended for quick consumption, but it is not so good for wines like Champagne, which may not be drunk until a few years old, as the pink may either fade or become brownish. A much more lasting pink 'dye' is that which is obtained from cochineal: it is absolutely tasteless and has no smell of any sort, so that it may safely be used to colour white wines pink when fashion demands *Vins Rosés*.

**Rosso** (I) Red

**Rotwein** (G) Red wine

**Saint-Emilion** (F) This wine is deeper in colour than most Médoc wines, but it does not last so long and seldom possesses as refined a *bouquet* as the Graves

**Sauvignon Blanc** (F) One of the finest species of white grapes. Used for fine white wines such as Pouilly-Fumé and when mixed with Semillon grapes excellent Sauternes wines are produced

**Schaumwein** (G) Sekt – sparkling wine

**Schillerwein** (G) *See* page 345

**Schloss** (G) Castle

**Schlossabzug** (G) Bottled at the castle

**Schneewein** (G) Snow wine; a term used to describe an ice wine made from grapes gathered when snow covered the vineyards

**Schorle-Morle** (G) A mixture of wine and up to 50% effervescent mineral water

**Sec** (F) Dry, when speaking of table wines. A 'sec' champagne is sweet, but when 'demi-sec' it is sweeter; 'extra-sec' means dry

**Secco** (I) Dry

**Seco** (S) Dry

**Seewein** (G) Wine from the Lake Constance district

**Sekt** (G) Sparkling wine

**Sektkellerei** (G) Sparkling wine manufacturer

**Semillon** (F) A species of white grape which, together with Sauvignon, is responsible for all the best white wines of Bordeaux and many other vineyards

**Sève** (F) As the sap is life to the vine, so is Sève to the wine; it means a well-balanced, well-knit wine with the prospect of a long life

**Solera** (S) Blend, vatting (of strong, old wine)

**Sonderfüllung** (G) Special *cuvée* – special bottling

**Souche** (F) Root stock

**Soutirage** (F) Racking

**Soyeux** (F) Silky, smooth, most attractive wine, free from all traces of tannin or acidity

**Spätlese** (G) *See* page 291

**Spitzengewächs** (G) The very best growth (may be used to describe only a Beeren – or Trockenbeeren-auslese)

**Spitzenwein** (G) The very best wine (may be used to describe only a Beeren – or Trockenbeeren-auslese)

**Spritzig** (G) Effervescent. (Many wines, especially some Moselles, retain some carbonic acid in solution. This prolongs the life of the wine, keeping it fresh, and should not be mistaken for fermentation)

**Spumante** (I) Frothy – hence sparkling

**Staatsweingut** (G) State vineyard/Domain

**Steinwein** (G) 'Stone wine' – wine from the Stein site in Würzburg. The term is frequently used for all Franconian wines, but these may actually be labelled 'Steinwein' only when they come from the Stein vineyard

**Stiftung** (G) A fund established for special purposes

**Sylvaner** (F) One of the white grapes grown on a large scale in Alsace, Germany and Austria for the making of fair-quality white wines

**Syrah** (F) One of the black grapes chiefly grown in the Rhône valley, more particularly at Hermitage, for the making of quality red table wines

**Tendre** (F) Tender, in the sense of light and pleasing but not likely to be a particularly lasting wine

**Tête de Cuvée** (F) First drawing-off of the wine which is made from pickings of chosen, over-ripe grapes, in the Sauternes district. In Burgundy the *Têtes de Cuvée* are the best wines, red or white, from any particular vineyard

**Tinaja** (s) Large earthenware jar

**Tinto** (s) Red

**Tirage** (F) Bottling. Wines, red or white, from any particular vineyard

**Tirage d'Origine** (F) Original bottling, this is used in Burgundy, where some shippers decant wines of any age before sending them to merchants or consumers, free from all lees

**Tonneau** (F) A Bordeaux wine measure equal to 4 hogsheads

**Traube** (G) Grape

**Traubensaft** (G) Grape juice

**Traubensorte** (G) Kind of grape

**Trester** (G) Grape cake

**Trockenbeerenauslese** (G) *See* page 293

**Ungezuckerter Wein** (G) Unsweetened wine

**Usé** (F) Worn. A wine that has been kept too long

**Velours** (F) Velvet. A somewhat full and particularly soft wine

**Vendange** (F) Gathering of the grapes – the grape harvest

**Vendimia** (s) Vintage

**Venencia** (s) A long stick of sprung whalebone with a silver cup at one end and a hook at the other

**Verband Deutscher Naturwein Versteigerer** (G) Association of growers who sell natural wine by auction

**Verbessert** (G) Improved, sweetened

**Verwaltung (Gutsverwaltung)** (G) Administration

**Viejo** (s) Old

**Vigneron** (F) Vine grower

**Vin doux naturel** (F) Unfortified, sweet dessert wine with a minimum alcoholic strength of 14°

**Vino** (s) Wine

**Wachstum** (G) Growth

**Wappen** (G) Crest, coat of arms

**Weinbau** (G) Viticulture

**Weinbaudomäne** (G) Viticultural farm

**Weinbaugebiet** (G) Viticultural district

**Weinberg** (G) Vineyard

**Weingesetz** (G) Wine law

**Weingrosshandlung** (G) Wholesale wine trade

**Weingut** (G) Estate or vineyard

**Weingutsbesitzer** (G) Proprietor of vineyard

**Weinhandlung** (G) Wine trade

**Weinkellerei(n)** (G) Large cellars. Very often used on the label instead of 'wine merchant' or 'wholesale wine merchant'

**Weinstein** (G) Tartaric acid

**Weisswein** (G) White wine

**Winzergenossenschaft** (G) Wine growers' co-operative

**Winzerwein** (G) Wine growers' association

**Wwe (Witwe)** (G) Widow

**Zapato** (s) 'Shoc': a special nail-studded shoe worn for treading grapes

# Bibliography

ADAMS, Leon D., *Commonsense Book of Wine*. New York, 1958

ALLEN, Herbert Warner, *Sherry and Port*. London, 1952; *A Contemplation of Wine*. London, 1951; *A History of Wine*. London, 1961; *Natural Red Wines*. London, 1951; *The Romance of Wine*. 1931; *Through the Wine Glass*. 1954; *White Wines & Cognac*. London, 1952; *Port and the Empire*. 1925; *Vinho do Porto Vinho da Filosofia*. 1940 (translation of *Romance of Wine*. 1931, for Instituto do Vinho do Porto); *Good Wine from Portugal*. 1960

ANDRIEU, Pierre, *Chronologie anecdotique du vignoble français*. Paris, 1944; *Les vins de France et d'ailleurs*. Paris, 1939

Anon, *Colares, O Vinho de*. 1938

AYLETT, Mary, *Country Wines*. Hollywood-by-the-Sea, 1959

BALZER, Robert L., *Pleasures of Wine*. Indianapolis, 1963

BARRY, Sir Edward, *Observations historical, critical, and medical on the wines of the Ancients and the analogy between them and modern wines*. London, 1775

BASSERMANN-JORDAN, F., *Die Geschichte des Weinbaus*. Frankfurt, 1923

BELLOC, Hilaire, *The Praise of Wine. An heroic Poem*. London, 1931

BERGET, Adrien, *Les vins de France. Histoire, géographie et statistique du vignoble français*. Paris, 1900

BERNET, Henri, *Anthologie des poètes du vin*. Lyon, 1944

BERRY, Charles Walter, *Viniana*. London, 1929 and 1934; *A Miscellany of Wine*. London, 1932; *In Search of Wine. A tour of the vineyards of France*. London, 1935

BERTALL, *La Vigne. Voyage autour des vins de France*. Paris, 1878

BILLIARD, Raymond, *La vigne dans l'antiquité*. Lyon, 1913

BODE, Charles, *Wines of Italy*. London, 1956

BOILLOT-DUTHIAU, *Notice sur Meursault, son vignoble et la présentation de ses vins*. Meursault, 1947

BOORDE, A., *The Breviarie of Health*. 1958

BRAZÃO, E., *The Anglo-Portuguese Alliance*. 1957

BRUNET, Raymond, *Les vins de France. Comment les classer, les vinifier, les consommer, les présenter*. 2 vols. Paris, 1925–7; *Le vignoble et les vins d'Alsace*. Paris, 1932

BRUNI, Bruno, *Vini Italiani*. Bologna, 1964

BUCHANAN, Robert, *The Culture of the Grape and Wine-making*. Cincinnati, 1862

BULLIER, Marie, *Visages de la Bourgogne*. Paris, 1942

BUREL, Jacques, *Le vignoble Beaujolais*. Lyon, 1941

BUSBY, J., *Treatise on the Culture of the Vine and the Art of making Wine*. Sydney, 1825

BUTLER, Frank Hedges, *Wine and the Wine-lands of the World*. London, 1926

CAMPBELL, Ian M., *Wayward Tendrils of the vine*. London, 1948; *Reminiscences of a vintner*. London, 1950

CAPONE, Roberto, *Vini Tipici e Pregiati d'Italia*. Florence, 1963

CARLING, T. E., *Wine Aristocracy: a guide to the best wines of the world*. 1957

CASAGNAC, Paul de, *French Wines*. Translated by Guy Knowles. London, 1930

CASTELLACASTELLA, H. de., *John Bull's Vineyard: Australian sketches*. Melbourne, 1886

CAVAZZANA, Giuseppe, *Itinerario Gastronomico ed Enologico d'Italia*. Milan, 1950

CHALONER, Len, *What the Vintners Sell*. London, 1926; *Italian Bouquet*. New York, 1958

CHAMBERLAIN, Samuel, *Bouquet de France. An Epicurean tour of the French Provinces*. New York, 1952

CHAPTAL, *Traité théorique et pratique de la culture de la vigne . . . 2 vols*. Paris, 1801

CÙNSOLO, Felice, *Dizionario del Gourmet*. Milan, 1961

COCKBURN, E., *Port Wine and Oporto*, n.d.

COCKS & FERET, *Bordeaux et ses vins classés par ordre de mérite*. Bordeaux, 12th Edn., 1949 (1st Edn., 1850)

CORREIA DE LOUREIRO, V., *La Region Délimitée des Vins du Dão*. 1949

CROFT, J. A., *Treatise of the Wines of Portugal*. 1788

CROFT-COOKE, R., *Port*. London, 1957; *Madeira*. London, 1962; *Sherry*. London, 1955

DANGUY, M. R. & AUBERTIN, M.Ch., *Les grands vins de Bourgogne*. Dijon, c. 1892

DAVID, Elizabeth, *Italian Food*. London, 1954

DEICHMANN, D. & WOLFF, W., *Weinchronik*. Berlin, 1950

DENMAN, James L., *The Vines and its Fruit*. London, 1875; *A Brief Discourse on Wine*. London, 1861

DES OMBIAUX, Maurice, *Le Gotha des vins de France*. Paris, 1926

DETTORI, Renato G., *Italian Wines and Liqueurs*. Rome, 1953

DEWEY, Suzette, *Wines: for those who have forgotten, and those who want to know*. Chicago, 1934

ELLIS, Charles, *The Origin, Nature, and History of Wine: its use as a beverage lawful and needful to civilized man*. London, 1861

EMERSON, Edward R., *Beverages Past and Present*. 2 vols. New York, 1908

ESCRITT, L. B., *The Small Cellar*. London, 1960

FADIMAN, Clifton, *Dionysus: A Case of Vintage Tales, about Wine*. New York, 1962

FAES, Henri, *Lexique viti-vinicole international: français italien, espagnol, allemand*. Lausanne, 1940

FOILLARD, Léon & DAVIS, Tony., *Le pays et le vin: Beaujolais*. Villefranche-en-Beaujolais, 1929

FORRESTER, J. J. Baron de, *A Word or Two on Port Wine*. 1843

FORTESCUE, Sir John, *Comodytes of England. c.* 1450

FOWLER, J. K., *Recollections of Old Country Life.* 1893

FRANCE, A. P. S., *O Moscatel do Setúbal.* 1938

GALE, Hyman & MARCO, E. Gerald, *The How and When: an authoritative guide to origin, use and classification of the world's choicest vintages and spirits.* Chicago, 1945

GAROGLIO, P. Giovanni, *La Nuova Enologia.* Florence, 3rd Edn., 1965

GAY, Charles, *Vouvray: ses vignes, ses vignerons.* Tours, 1944

GIRARD, L'Abbé André, *La vigne et les vignerons en Sancerrois à travers les siècles.* Sancerre, 1941

GOLDSCHMIDT, E., *Deutschlands Weinbauorte und Weinbergslagen.* Mainz, 1920; *Weingesetz.* Mainz, 1933

GOT, Armand, *Les vins doux naturels.* Perpignan, 1947; *Monbazillac, hosannah de topaze.* Bordeaux, 1949; *La dégustation des vins. Classification des vins.* Beziers 1955

GROSSMANN, Harold, *Grossmann's Guide to Wines, Spirits and Beers.* New York, 1940; Rev. Edns., 1953, 1955

GUYOT, J., *Culture of the Vine and Wine-making.* Trans, from French by L. Marie. Melbourne, 1865

HALLGARTEN, S. F., *Rhineland-Wineland.* London, 1955; *Alsace and Its Wine Gardens.* London, 1957

HARRISON, W., *Description of England.* 1577

HEALY, Maurice, *Claret and the White Wines of Bordeaux.* London, 1934; *Stay me with Flagons.* London, 1940 and 1963 (also published with a running commentary by Ian M. Campbell, and a Memoir by Sir Norman Birkett. London, 1949)

HENDERSON, Alexander, *The History of Ancient and Modern Wines.* London, 1824

HEUSS, R., *Weinbau und Weingärtnerstand in Heilbronn.* Neustadt, 1950

HIERONIMI, H., *Weingesetz.* Munich, 1953

HORNIKEL, E., *The Great Wines of Europe.* London, 1965

HUSENBETH, F. C., *A Guide for the Wine Cellar.* 1834

HYAMS, E., *Dionysus: A Social History of the Wine Vine.* London, 1965

JAMES, W., *A Word Book of Wine.* London, 1962

JEFFS, Julian, *Sherry.* London, 1961

JULLIEN, A., *Topography of All Known Vineyards.* London, 1824

KELLY, A. C., *Wine Growing in Australia.* Adelaide, 1887

KINGSTON, W. H. G., *Lusitanian Sketches.* 1844

KITTEL-BREIDER, H., *Das Buch vom Frankenwein.* Würzburg, 1958

KLENK, E., *Die Weinbeurteilung.* Stuttgart, 1950

LAFORGUE, Germain, *Le vignoble girondin.* Paris, 1947

LAKE, Max, *Hunter Wines.* 1965

LANGENBACH, A., *German Wines and Vines.* London, 1962

LAVALLE, Dr., *Histoire et statistique de la vigne et des grands vins de la Côte d'Or.* Paris, 1855

LAYTON, T. A., *Wine Craft,* 1958; *Modern Wines.* London, 1964

LICHINE, Alexis, *The Wines of France.* New York, 1951; London, 1952; New Edn., 1964

LLOYD, F. C., *The Art and Technique of Wine.* London, 1936

LOUIS, A., *Vignobles et vergers du Midi.* Perpignan, 1946

McMULLEN, Thomas, *A Handbook of wine.* New York, 1852

MAISONNEUVE, Dr P., *Le vigneron angevin.* 2 vols. Angers, 1925-6

MARKHAM, C., *English Housewife,* 1623

MARRISON, L. W., *Wines and Spirits.* London, Rev. Edn., 1963

MAUMENÉ, E., *Traité théorique et pratique du travail des vins.* 2 vols. Paris, n.d.

MENDELSOHN, Oscar, *The Earnest Drinker's Digest: a short and simple account of alcohol, with a glossary, for curious drinkers.* Sydney, 1946; London, 1950

MEW, James & ASHTON, John, *Drinks of the World.* London, 1892

MILLS, Frederick C., *The Wine Guide.* London, 1860

MINISTERIO DELL'AGRICOLTURA, *Principali Vitigni da Vino Coltivati in Italia.* Rome. (In progress, two vols. published.)

MOLEYNS, A., *The Libel of English Policy.* 1436

MONELLI, Paolo, *O. P. ossia Il Vero Bevitore.* Milan, 1963

MOREIRA DA FONSECA, A., *O Vinho do Porto na Epoca dos Almadas.* 1957

MOWAT, Jean, *Anthology of Wine.* London, 1949

MÜLLER, K., *Geschichte des Badischen Weinbaus.* Lahr, 1935; *Rhein-Main.* Frankfurt, 1940

PASTEUR, Louis, *Etudes sur le vin.* Paris, 1924; *Etudes sur le vinaigre et sur le vin.* 1924

PELLEGRINI, Angelo, *The Unprejudiced Palate.* New York, 1948

PENZER, N. M., *The Book of the Wine-label.* London, 1947

PIC, Albert, *Le vignoble de Chablis.* Chablis, c. 1934

POPP, Franz, *Das Moselland und sein Wein.* Bernkastel, 1948

POSTGATE, Raymond, *The Plain Man's Guide to Wine.* London, 1951; New Edn., 1965

POUPON, Pierre & FORGEOT, Pierre, *Les vins de Bourgogne.* Paris, 1952

RAINBIRD, George, *A Pocket Book of Wine.* London, 1963

RAMAIN, Dr Paul, *Les grands vins de France.* Paris, 1931

RAY, Cyril, *The Complete Imbiber,* Nos. 1-7. London, 1956-64

REBOUX, Paul, *L'Algérie et ses vins.* Algiers, 1945

REDDING, Cyrus, *A History and Description of Modern Wines.* London, 1833; Rev. Edns., 1851; 1860; *French Wines and Vineyards.* London, 1860

REIS, A. B., *Roteiro do Vinho Portugues.* 1945

ROBSON, E. I., *A Wayfarer in French Vineyards.* London, 1928

RODIER, Camille, *Le Clos de Vougeot.* Dijon, 1931; *Le vin de Bourgogne: la Côte d'Or.* Dijon, 1937; 1948

ROGER, J. R., *Les vins de Bourdeaux.* Paris, 1954

ROUPNEL, Gaston, *Le Bourgogne.* Paris, 1946

RUDD, Hugh R., *Hocks and Moselles.* London, 1953

SAINTSBURY, G., *Notes on a Cellar-Book.* 1920

SCHEU, G., *Mein Winzerbuch.* Neustadt, 1950

SCHMITT, *Vignes et vins d'Alsace.* Colmar, 1949

SCHOONMAKER, F., *Wines of Germany.* New York, 1956; London, 1957
and MARVEL, Tom, *The Complete Wine Book.* New York, 1934, 1938; London, 1935

SCOTT, Dick, *Winemakers of New Zealand.* Auckland, 1965

SCOTT, J. M., *Vineyards of France.* London, 1950; *The Man who made Wine.* London, 1953

SELLERS, C., *Oporto, New and Old.* 1899

SELTMAN, C., *Wine in the Ancient World,* 1957

SHAND, P. Morton, *A Book of French Wines.* London, 1928; Rev. Edn., 1960; *A Book of other Wines then French.* London, 1929; *A Book of Wine.* London, 1926

SHAW, T. G., *Wine, the Vine and the Cellar.* London, 1936

SHEEN, *Wines and other Fermented Liquors from the Earliest Ages to the Present Time.* London, 1865

SICHEL, Allan, *The Penguin Book of Wines.* London, 1965

SIMON, André L., *The History of the Champagne Trade in England.* London, 1905; *The History of the Wine Trade in England.* London, 1906–9; *In Vino Veritas.* London, 1913; *Wine and Spirits, the Connoisseur's Text-book.* London, 1919; *The Blood of the Grape: the wine trade text-book.* London, 1920; *Wine and the Wine Trade.* London, 1923; *Bottlescrew Days.* London, 1926; *A Dictionary of Wine.* London, 1935; *Vintagewise.* London, 1945; *A Wine Primer.* London, 1946; Rev. Edn., 1956; *Know your Wines.* London, 1956; *The Wine and Food Menu Book.* London, 1956; *Madeira,* 1938; *History of Champagne.* London, 1962; *The Commonsense of Wine.* London and Cleveland, 1966

STREET, Julian, *Wines, their Selection, Care and Service.* New York, 1933; Rev. Edn., 1948

TAIT, G., *Port from the Vine to the Glass,* 1936

TENNENT, Sir James Emerson, *Wine: its use and taxation.* London, 1855

THUDICHUM, Dr J. L. W. & DUPRE, A. A., *A Treatise on the origin, nature and varieties of wine, being a complete Manual of viticulture and oenology.* London, 1872; 2nd. Edn., 1896

TODD, W. J., *Port.* 1926

TOVEY, C., *Wine and Wine Countries.* 1862; 1877

TROOST, Gerhard, *Die Technologie des Weines.* Stuttgart, 1953

VERONELLI, Luigi, *I Vini d'Italia.* Rome, 1961. (The English edition, published in Italy in 1964, is considerably abridged.)

VIZETELLY, Arthur & Ernest, *The Wines of France: with a chapter on cognac and table waters.* London, c. 1908

VIZETELLY, Henry, *The Wines of the World Characterized and Classed.* London, 1875; *Facts about Port.* 1880

VOGT, E., *Weinbau.* Freiburg, 1952; *Der Wein.* Freiburg, 1952

WALL, Bernard, *Italian Life and Landscape.* 2 vols. London, 1950

WARD, E., *The Vineyards and Orchards of South Australia.* Adelaide, 1862

WAUGH, A., *In Praise of Wine.* London, 1959

YOUNGER, William, *Gods, Men and Wine.* London, 1966

ZITZEN, E. G., *Der Wein in der Wort- und Wirtschaft-eschichte.* Bonn, 1952

# Index

N.B. The following abbreviations are used in this index: anc., for ancient; ch. for château; dept. for département; *f* to indicate that the subject occurs also on the following page to that given, *ff* on the following two pages, etc.; *n* refers to a note at the foot of the page; R. stands for river; vd. for vineyard. The conventional abbreviations *q.v.* (*quod vide*, which see) and *et seq.* (*et sequens*, and the following one[s]) are also used. Figures in italics indicate a reference to an illustration.

FEB 0 2 202